MATHEMATICS FOR ECONOMISTS

MATHEMATICS FOR ECONOMISTS

Carl P. Simon
and
Lawrence Blume

W • W • NORTON & COMPANY • NEW YORK • LONDON

The text of this book is composed in Times Roman, with the display set in Optima.
Composition by Integre Technical Publishing Company, Inc. Book design by Jack
Meserole.

Library of Congress Cataloging-in-Publication Data

Blume, Lawrence.
    Mathematics for economists / Lawrence Blume and Carl Simon.
        p.   cm.
    1. Economics, Mathematical.   I. Simon, Carl P., 1945– .
II. Title.
HB135.B59   1994
510'.24339—dc20   93-24962

ISBN 0-393-95733-0

W. W. Norton & Company, Inc., 500 Fifth Avenue, New York, N.Y. 10110
www.wwnorton.com

W. W. Norton & Company Ltd., Castle House, 75/76 Wells Street,
London W1T 3QT

67890

Contents

P A R T   I I   Linear Algebra

P A R T   I I I   Calculus of Several Variables

15   Implicit Functions and Their Derivatives   334

P A R T   I V   Optimization

16   Quadratic Forms and Definite Matrices   375

PART   V   Eigenvalues and Dynamics

P A R T   V I   Advanced Linear Algebra

P A R T   V I I   Advanced Analysis

P A R T   V I I I   Appendices

Preface

For better or worse, mathematics has become the language of modern analytical economics. It quantifies the relationships between economic variables and among economic actors. It formalizes and clarifies properties of these relationships. In the process, it allows economists to identify and analyze those general properties that are critical to the behavior of economic systems.

Elementary economics courses use reasonably simple mathematical techniques to describe and analyze the models they present: high school algebra and geometry, graphs of functions of one variable, and sometimes one-variable calculus. They focus on models with one or two goods in a world of perfect competition, complete information, and no uncertainty. Courses beyond introductory micro- and macroeconomics drop these strong simplifying assumptions. However, the mathematical demands of these more sophisticated models scale up considerably. The goal of this text is to give students of economics and other social sciences a deeper understanding and working knowledge of the mathematics they need to work with these more sophisticated, more realistic, and more interesting models.

WHY THIS BOOK?

We wrote this book because we felt that the available texts on mathematics for economists left unfilled some of the basic needs of teachers and students in this area. In particular, we tried to make the following improvements over other texts.

1. Many texts in this area focus on mathematical *techniques* at the expense of mathematical *ideas* and *intuition*, often presenting a "cookbook approach." Our book develops the student's intuition for how and why the various mathematical techniques work. It contains many more illustrations and figures than competing texts in order to build the reader's geometric intuition. It emphasizes the primary role of calculus in approximating a nonlinear function by a linear function or polynomial in order to build a simple picture of the behavior of the nonlinear function — a principle rich in geometric content.

2. Students learn how to use and apply mathematics by working with concrete examples and exercises. We illustrate every new concept and technique with worked-out examples. We include exercises at the end of every section to give students the necessary experience working with the mathematics presented.

3. This is a book on using mathematics to understand the structure of economics. We believe that this book contains more economics than any other

math-for-economists text. Each chapter begins with a discussion of the economic motivation for the mathematical concepts presented. On the other hand, this is a book on mathematics for economists, not a text of mathematical economics. We do not feel that it is productive to learn advanced mathematics and advanced economics at the same time. Therefore, we have focused on presenting an introduction to the mathematics that students need in order to work with more advanced economic models.

4. Economics is a dynamic field; economic theorists are regularly introducing or using new mathematical ideas and techniques to shed light on economic theory and econometric analysis. As active researchers in economics, we have tried to make many of these new approaches available to students. In this book we present rather complete discussions of topics at the frontier of economic research, topics like quasiconcave functions, concave programing, indirect utility and expenditure functions, envelope theorems, the duality between cost and production, and nonlinear dynamics.

5. It is important that students of economics understand what constitutes a solid proof — a skill that is learned, not innate. Unlike most other texts in the field, we try to present careful proofs of nearly all the mathematical results presented — so that the reader can understand better both the logic behind the math techniques used and the total structure in which each result builds upon previous results. In many of the exercises, students are asked to work out their own proofs, often by adapting proofs presented in the text.

An important motivation for understanding what constitutes a careful proof is the need for students to develop the ability to read an argument and to decide for themselves whether or not the conclusions really do follow from the stated hypotheses. Furthermore, a good proof tells a story; it can be especially valuable by laying bare the underlying structure of a model in such a way that one clearly sees which of the model's component parts are responsible for producing the behavior asserted in the statement of the economic principle. Some readers of this text will go on to draw conclusions from economic models in their own research. We hope that the experience of working with proofs in this text will be a valuable guide to developing one's own ability to read and write proofs.

WHAT'S IN THIS BOOK?

At the core of modern microeconomics is the hypothesis that economic agents consciously choose their most preferred behavior according to the alternatives available to them. The area of mathematics most relevant to such a study is the maximization or minimization of a function of several variables in which the variables are constrained by equalities and inequalities. This mathematical problem in all the necessary generality, sometimes called the Lagrange multiplier problem, is a focal point of this book. (See especially Chapters 16 to 19.) The chapters of this book are arranged so that this material can be reached quickly and efficiently.

This text begins with overviews of one-variable calculus (Chapters 2 to 4) and of exponentials and logarithms (Chapter 5). One can either cover this material during the first weeks of the class or, more commonly we believe, can ask students to read it on their own as a review of the calculus they have taken. The examples and exercises in these earliest chapters should make either process relatively simple.

The analysis of solutions to optimization problems usually involves studying the solutions to the systems of equations given by the first-order conditions. The first half of this book focuses on the study of such systems of equations. We first develop a rather complete theory of the solutions of *linear* systems, focusing on such questions as: Does a solution exist? How many are there? What happens to the solution as the equations change a little? (Chapters 6 to 10.) We then turn to the study of the more realistic and more complex *nonlinear* systems (Chapters 11 to 15). We apply the metaprinciple of calculus to this study of nonlinear systems: the best way to study the behavior of the solutions of a nonlinear system is to examine the behavior of a closely related *linear* system of equations. Finally, we pull all this material together in Chapters 16 to 19 in our discussion of optimization problems — unconstrained and constrained — that is the heart of this text.

Chapters 20 through 25 treat two other basic mathematical issues that arise in the study of economic models. Chapters 20 and 21 give an in-depth presentation of *properties* of economic relationships, such as homogeneity, concavity, and quasiconcavity, while Chapter 22 illustrates how these properties arise naturally in economic models. Furthermore, there are often natural *dynamics* in economic processes: prices adjust, economies grow, policies adapt, economic agents maximize over time. Chapters 23, 24, and 25 introduce the mathematics of dynamic systems, focusing on the eigenvalues of a matrix, linear difference equations, and linear and nonlinear differential equations.

This book is laid out so that one can get to the fundamental results and consequences of constrained optimization problems as quickly as possible. In some cases, for example, in the study of determinants, limits of sequences, and compact sets, there are important topics that are slightly off the beaten path to the study of constrained optimization problems. To keep the presentation as flexible as possible, we have placed the description of these topics in the last five chapters of this book. Chapter 26 presents details about the properties of determinants outlined in Chapter 9. Chapter 27 completes the application of matrix algebra in Chapters 7 and 8 to the determination of the size of the set of solutions of a linear system, ending with a discussion of the Fundamental Theorem of Matrix Algebra. Chapter 28 presents economic applications of the Fundamental Theorem. Chapter 29 does some fine-tuning on the study of sets and sequences introduced in Chapter 12. Chapter 30 collects some of the more complex proofs of the multivariable analysis presented in Chapters 13, 14, and 15. In classroom presentations the material in any of these last five chapters can be presented: 1) right after the corresponding material in the earlier chapter, 2) at the end of the course, or 3) not at all, depending on the amount of time available or the needs of the students.

COORDINATION WITH OTHER COURSES

Often the material in this course is taught concurrently with courses in advanced micro- and macroeconomics. Students are sometimes frustrated with this arrangement because the micro and macro courses usually start working with constrained optimization or dynamics long before these topics can be covered in an orderly mathematical presentation.

We suggest a number of strategies to minimize this frustration. First, we have tried to present the material so that a student can read each introductory chapter in isolation and get a reasonably clear idea of how to work with the material of that chapter, even without a careful reading of earlier chapters. We have done this by including a number of worked exercises with descriptive figures in every introductory chapter.

Often during the first two weeks of our first course on this material, we present a series of short modules that introduces the language and formulation of the more advanced topics so that students can easily read selected parts of later chapters on their own, or at least work out some problems from these chapters.

Finally, we usually ask students who will be taking our course to be familiar with the chapters on one-variable calculus and simple matrix theory before classes begin. We have found that nearly every student has taken a calculus course and nearly two-thirds have had some matrix algebra. So this summer reading requirement — sometimes supplemented by a review session just before classes begin — is helpful in making the mathematical backgrounds of the students in the course more homogeneous.

ACKNOWLEDGMENTS

It is a pleasure to acknowledge the valuable suggestions and comments of our colleagues, students and reviewers: colleagues such as Philippe Artzner, Ted Bergstrom, Ken Binmore, Dee Dechert, David Easley, Leonard Herk, Phil Howrey, John Jacquez, Jan Kmenta, James Koopman, Tapan Mitra, Peter Morgan, John Nachbar, Scott Pierce, Zvi Safra, Hal Varian, and Henry Wan; students such as Kathleen Anderson, Jackie Coolidge, Don Dunbar, Tom George, Kevin Jackson, David Meyer, Ann Simon, David Simon, and John Wooders, and the countless classes at Cornell and Michigan who struggled through early drafts; reviewers such as Richard Anderson, Texas A & M University; James Bergin, Queen's University; Brian Binger, University of Arizona; Mark Feldman, University of Illinois; Roger Folsom, San Jose State University; Femida Handy, York University; John McDonald, University of Illinois; Norman Obst, Michigan State University; John Riley, University of California at Los Angeles; and Myrna Wooders, University of Toronto. We appreciate the assistance of the people at W.W. Norton, especially Drake McFeely, Catherine Wick and Catherine Von Novak. The order of the authors on the cover of this book merely reflects our decision to use different orders for different books that we write.

We dedicate this book to our wives Susan and Maralyn.

PART I

Introduction

Introduction

1.1 MATHEMATICS IN ECONOMIC THEORY

Within the last 30 years, mathematics has emerged as the "language of economics." Today economists view mathematics as an invaluable tool at all levels of study, ranging from the statistical expression of real-world trends to the development of fully abstract economic systems. This text will provide a broad introduction to the close relationship between mathematics and economics.

On the most basic level, mathematics provides the foundations for empirical propositions about economic variables — propositions like "a 10 percent increase in the price of gasoline causes a 5 percent drop in the demand for gasoline." The mathematical expression of this relationship is the *demand function*. In particular, the above observation can be summarized by the statement "the elasticity of demand for gasoline is -0.5." We learn this empirical relationship by using techniques of statistics, which is itself a branch of mathematics. Using statistics, the economist transforms raw data from the real world into numerical generalizations such as the one just mentioned.

Furthermore, once such a statistical relationship has been formulated, it can be combined with others of the same type. Piece by piece, the economist constructs an entire network of interlocking relationships. This network enables the economist to draw conclusions about economic variables that are related to each other only indirectly. Starting with the information that the demand for gasoline (within a certain community) falls half as much as its price rises, the economist might explore how the price of gasoline is related to the price of oil, the cost of living, or the demand for electricity.

At the same time, the role of mathematics in economics extends far beyond the domain of statistical technique. For example, economists construct mathematical representations of markets and communities to understand better how they work. The very process of making a model forces the economist to pick out the most important aspects of a situation and then try to express them mathematically. The finished model provides a structured basis for further study. It is never possible to comprehend all the subtle social, cultural, and economic dimensions of a real-world situation at any one time. However, a mathematical model reduces the complexity of the real world to manageable proportions.

In fact, if we think of a model simply as the reduction and organization of subject matter for study, it is clear that models are not unique to mathematical analysis. Even social sciences such as sociology or anthropology, whose techniques are more "literary" than mathematical, rely heavily on models of some sort, in both the exploration and the presentation of their material. At the same time, there are many reasons why mathematical modeling is particularly helpful in economics.

For one thing, a mathematical model forces the economist to define terms precisely. The economist must state the underlying assumptions clearly before embarking on a complex train of thought. Right from the start, the exact nature of the abstraction the economist is working with is clear not just in the economist's mind, but in the mind of every person who reads the work. As a result, discussion about the real-world relevance of the model is likely to be sharply focused. It may even be possible to translate the theoretical model into statistical formulas, so that its validity can be tested with data from the real world.

Mathematics is used not just to organize facts, but to actively generate and explore new theoretical ideas. Often, economists use mathematical techniques such as logical deduction to derive theorems which apply to a wide variety of economic situations, instead of just to a specific local or national community. Consider, for example, the statement "competitive market allocations of resources are Pareto optimal," a theorem of central importance in most intermediate courses on microeconomic theory. In simplified form, this theorem asserts that in a competitive market system, when markets clear so that supply balances demand, any feasible change in consumption or production that improves the lot of some people will make some others worse off. In marked contrast to statements like "demand for gasoline falls half as much as the price of gasoline rises," this theorem does not originate in direct observation of the day-to-day world. Nor is it expressed statistically. Instead, it is a universal principle logically derived from an idealized, mathematical description of various markets. Because the mathematics used in developing the theorem is so far removed from direct observation, it is impossible to empirically test the theorem's ultimate truth or falsity. Only its applicability to the world economy or to the economy of a particular country or region is ever open to question.

Mathematics is not only a powerful tool for gaining insights from models of the economy; it is also needed to broaden the applicability of a model that is too narrowly constructed to be useful. Exercises in undergraduate economics texts, for instance, usually limit themselves, for the sake of simplicity, to the production or sale of two goods. The advanced student or working economist uses mathematics to extend these textbook models so that they address more information at one time — taking into account inflation, additional goods, additional competitors, or any number of other factors. At this point, let's work through a specific example of this latter use of mathematical modeling in economics. We will see how mathematics is used to increase the scope of a simple geometric model familiar from intermediate microeconomic theory.

1.2   MODELS OF CONSUMER CHOICE

Two-Dimensional Model of Consumer Choice

When we study the neoclassical model of consumer choice in an intermediate microeconomic theory course, we usually assume that the consumer has only two goods to choose from — for the purposes of this discussion, gadgets and widgets. Let x_1 be a variable which represents the amount of gadgets purchased by our consumer, and let x_2 be a variable representing the consumer's purchases of widgets. The pair (x_1, x_2) represents a choice of an amount for both goods and is called a "commodity bundle." If we assume that x_1 and x_2 could be any nonnegative numbers, then the set of all possible commodity bundles can be represented geometrically as the nonnegative quadrant in the plane. We will call this quadrant "commodity space." In Figure 1.1 the number of gadgets in a commodity bundle is measured on the horizontal axis, while the number of widgets is measured on the vertical axis.

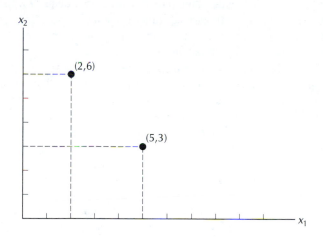

Two commodity bundles in commodity space.

**Figure
1.1**

Consumers have preferences about commodity bundles in commodity space: Given any two commodity bundles, the consumer either prefers one bundle to the other or is indifferent between the two. If the consumer's preferences satisfy some consistency hypotheses, they can be represented by a utility function. A utility function assigns a real number to each commodity bundle. If the consumer prefers commodity bundle (x_1, x_2) to bundle (y_1, y_2), then the utility function assigns a higher number to (x_1, x_2) than to (y_1, y_2). We write $U(x_1, x_2)$ for the number assigned by the utility function to bundle (x_1, x_2). We usually depict this situation by drawing a sampling of the consumer's indifference curves in commodity space, as shown in Figure 1.2. The utility function assigns the same number to all bundles on any given indifference curve. In other words, the consumer is indifferent

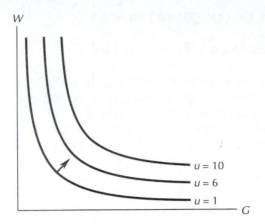

**Figure
1.2**

Indifference curves in commodity space.

between any two bundles on the same indifference curve. The arrow in Figure 1.2 indicates the direction of preference. Commodity bundles on indifference curves far from the origin are preferred to those on indifference curves near the origin to indicate that this consumer prefers "more" to "less."

We use this representation of consumer preferences to describe the consumer's choice. Suppose a consumer is confronted with a set B of commodity bundles and is asked to choose among them. The consumer will choose so as to maximize his or her utility function on the set B. The problem of maximizing a given function on a given set is a mathematical problem.

We have just described a very simple mathematical model of consumer choice. This model has abstracted from — ignored — many aspects of choice that, in some contexts, we would consider very important. For example, how did the consumer "learn" enough about the products to make an informed choice? How does the consumer use this information in making a choice? More generally, where did the consumer's preferences come from, and how are they influenced by the environment in which the decision is being made? Some choice activities are habitual; for example, the decision to light a cigarette. We have said nothing about habit formation in our model. Some choices are regulated by social custom; for example, the decision made by a corporate executive to wear a suit to work. Again, the role of social custom is not explicit in our model. By ignoring these and other aspects of choice, we have constructed a simple, easily understandable model of choice behavior. However, the fact that potentially important factors have been ignored may limit the usefulness of this simple model. For some applications, a more sophisticated model may be required.

Fortunately, we are not interested in using this model to explain all choice behavior. We are interested only in those choices which arise in markets. We describe these choice situations as follows: Associated with each commodity is a price: p_1 for the price of gadgets and p_2 for the price of widgets. Our consumer has M dollars to divide among the two goods. The consumer cannot spend more

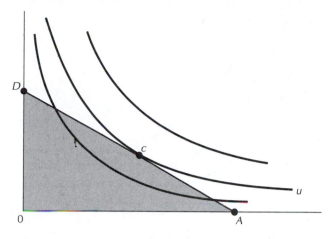

Budget set OAD and indifference curves.

Figure 1.3

money than he or she has. The cost of commodity bundle (x_1, x_2) is $p_1x_1 + p_2x_2$. This cost cannot exceed M. Our theory need only apply to choice sets of the form

$$B = \{(x_1, x_2) : x_1 \geq 0, \ x_2 \geq 0, \ p_1x_1 + p_2x_2 \leq M\}.$$

These are the **budget sets** that the consumer could conceivably face.[1]

Budget sets are easy to visualize. In the commodity space, draw the line segment given by the equation $p_1x_1 + p_2x_2 = M$. Everything on or under this line is affordable. These are the points in the triangle OAD in Figure 1.3.

The maximization problem is also easy to visualize. The consumer will choose from the budget set so as to be on as high an indifference curve as possible. In Figure 1.3 commodity bundle c is the most preferred commodity bundle in OAD. Optimal bundle c — sometimes called the consumer's **bundle demanded** at prices p_1 and p_2 — can be characterized by the fact that the indifference curve u, of which c is a member, lies completely outside the budget set except at the point c, where it is tangent to the budget line. This is usually stated as: At c, the consumer's marginal rate of substitution (the slope of the indifference curve through c) equals the price ratio (the slope of the budget line).

In this two-dimensional setting, various thought experiments can be performed: What happens to the demand for gadgets as the price of gadgets increases? As the price of widgets increases? As income increases? These experiments are sometimes referred to as **comparative statics** problems. The experiments of increasing the consumer's income M and the price p_1 of gadgets are performed in Figures 1.4 and 1.5.

---

[1]This set notation will be used throughout the book. In words, B is the set of all pairs of numbers (x_1, x_2) such that both numbers are nonnegative and the inequality $p_1x_1 + p_2x_2 \leq M$ is satisfied.

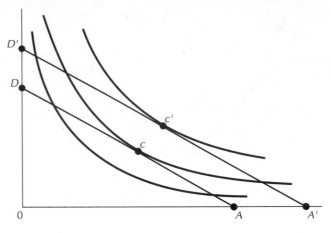

Figure 1.4

Effects of increasing M.

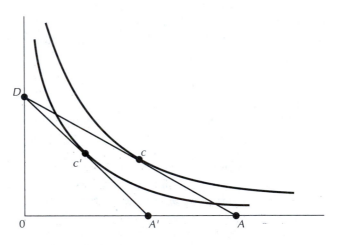

Figure 1.5

Effects of increasing p_1.

In intermediate microeconomics classes, we record the results of these experiments in graphs, such as demand curves and Engel curves. At this point we begin to see some of the limits of this geometric approach. Even in this simplest two-good case, demand for any one good depends on three things: the price of the good, the price of the other good, and income. There is no possible way to represent these relationships simultaneously in a two-dimensional picture. Thus we are left with the rather unsatisfactory method of shifting demand curves around when we want to talk about changes in income or changes in the price of the other good. We also have no convenient way to talk rigorously about how demand is affected by the shape of indifference curves. In intermediate microeconomic theory we typically examine two polar cases — straight line (perfect substitute) indifference curves and right angle (perfect complement) indifference curves. But these are rare special cases. Furthermore, we need to know how results we might discover in this setting are affected by relaxing the hypothesis that there are only two goods.

Multidimensional Model of Consumer Choice

None of these questions can be answered in our geometric framework. We must turn to other mathematical techniques; in particular, multivariate calculus and matrix algebra. To do this, we need to pose the problem analytically. Suppose that our model economy has n goods. Commodity bundles are now lists $(x_1, x_2, \ldots, x_n)$, and a utility function assigns a number $U(x_1, \ldots, x_n)$ to each such list $(x_1, \ldots, x_n)$. The consumer's maximization problem can be stated in the following way

$$\text{maximize } U(x_1, \ldots, x_n)$$

subject to the constraints

$$p_1 x_1 + p_2 x_2 + \cdots + p_n x_n \leq M,$$

$$x_1 \geq 0, \ldots, x_n \geq 0.$$

The system of mathematical equations that one uses to describe the "tangency" conditions when there are n unknowns rather than 2 unknowns is complex. It contains $2n + 1$ different equations and $2n + 1$ unknowns. The study of all the questions of the preceding paragraph reduces to the study of this system of equations. These questions appear in the mathematical analysis as questions about the existence of solutions to the equation system, and questions about how the solutions to the system change with changes in the parameters, such as prices and income. In this text we will discuss ideas and techniques of multivariable calculus and linear algebra that provide sharp answers to these questions.

One-Variable Calculus: Foundations

A central goal of economic theory is to express and understand relationships between economic variables. These relationships are described mathematically by functions. If we are interested in the effect of one economic variable (like government spending) on one other economic variable (like gross national product), we are led to the study of functions of a single variable — a natural place to begin our mathematical analysis.

The key information about these relationships between economic variables concerns how a change in one variable affects the other. How does a change in the money supply affect interest rates? Will a million dollar increase in government spending increase or decrease total production? By how much? When such relationships are expressed in terms of *linear* functions, the effect of a change in one variable on the other is captured by the "slope" of the function. For more general *nonlinear* functions, the effect of this change is captured by the "derivative" of the function. The derivative is simply the generalization of the slope to nonlinear functions. In this chapter, we will define the derivative of a one-variable function and learn how to compute it, all the while keeping aware of its role in quantifying relationships between variables.

2.1 FUNCTIONS ON $\mathbf{R}^1$

Vocabulary of Functions

The basic building blocks of mathematics are numbers and functions. In working with numbers, we will find it convenient to represent them geometrically as points on a number line. The **number line** is a line that extends infinitely far to the right and to the left of a point called the **origin**. The origin is identified with the number 0. Points to the right of the origin represent positive numbers and points to the left represent negative numbers. A basic unit of length is chosen, and successive intervals of this length are marked off from the origin. Those to the right are numbered $+1$, $+2$, $+3$, etc.; those to the left are numbered -1, -2, -3, etc. One can now represent any *positive* real number on the line by finding that point to the *right* of the origin whose distance from the origin in the chosen units is that number. Negative numbers are represented in the same manner, but by moving to the *left*. Consequently, every real number is represented by exactly one point on the line, and each point on the line represents one and only one number. See Figure 2.1. We write **R**¹ for the set of all real numbers.

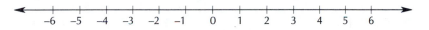

The number line **R**¹.

Figure 2.1

A **function** is simply a rule which assigns a number in **R**¹ to each number in **R**¹. For example, there is the function which assigns to any number the number which is one unit larger. We write this function as $f(x) = x + 1$. To the number 2 it assigns the number 3 and to the number $-3/2$ it assigns the number $-1/2$. We write these assignments as

$$f(2) = 3 \quad \text{and} \quad f(-3/2) = -1/2.$$

The function which assigns to any number its double can be written as $g(x) = 2x$. Write $g(4) = 8$ and $g(-3) = -6$ to indicate that it assigns 8 to 4 and -6 to -3, respectively.

Often, we use one variable, say x, for the input of the function and another variable, say y, for the output of the function. In this notation, we would write the above two functions f and g as

$$y = x + 1 \quad \text{and} \quad y = 2x,$$

respectively. The input variable x is called the **independent variable**, or in economic applications, the **exogenous variable**. The output variable y is called the **dependent variable**, or in economic applications, the **endogenous variable**.

Polynomials

Analytically speaking, the simplest functions are the **monomials**, those functions which can be written as $f(x) = ax^k$ for some number a and some positive integer k; for example,

$$f_1(x) = 3x^4, \quad f_2(x) = -x^7, \quad \text{and} \quad f_3(x) = -10x^2. \tag{1}$$

The positive integer exponent k is called the **degree** of the monomial; the number a is called a **coefficient**. A function which is formed by adding together monomials is called a **polynomial**. For example, if we add the three monomials in (1), we obtain the polynomial

$$h(x) = -x^7 + 3x^4 - 10x^2,$$

where we write the monomial terms of a polynomial in order of decreasing degree. For any polynomial, the highest degree of any monomial that appears in it is called the **degree** of the polynomial. For example, the degree of the above polynomial h is 7.

There are more complex types of·functions: **rational functions**, which are ratios of polynomials, like

$$y = \frac{x^2 + 1}{x - 1}, \quad y = \frac{x^5 + 7x}{5}, \quad y = \frac{x - 1}{x^3 + 3x + 2}, \quad \text{and} \quad y = \frac{x^2 - 1}{x^2 + 1}; \quad (2)$$

exponential functions, in which the variable x appears as an exponent, like $y = 10^x$; **trigonometric functions**, like $y = \sin x$ and $y = \cos x$; and so on.

Graphs

Usually, the essential information about a function is contained in its graph. The **graph** of a function of one variable consists of all points in the Cartesian plane whose coordinates (x, y) satisfy the equation $y = f(x)$. In Figure 2.2 below, the graphs of the five functions mentioned above are drawn.

Increasing and Decreasing Functions

The basic geometric properties of a function are whether it is increasing or decreasing and the location of its local and global minima and maxima. A function is **increasing** if its graph moves upward from left to right. More precisely, a function f is increasing if

$$x_1 > x_2 \quad \text{implies that} \quad f(x_1) > f(x_2).$$

The functions in the first two graphs of Figure 2.2 are increasing functions. A function is **decreasing** if its graph moves downward from left to right, i.e., if

$$x_1 > x_2 \quad \text{implies that} \quad f(x_1) < f(x_2).$$

The fourth function in Figure 2.2, $f_2(x) = -x^7$, is a decreasing function.

The places where a function changes from increasing to decreasing and vice versa are also important. If a function f changes from decreasing to increasing at x_0, the graph of f turns upward around the point $(x_0, f(x_0))$, as in Figure 2.3. This implies that the graph of f lies above the point $(x_0, f(x_0))$ around that point. Such a point $(x_0, f(x_0))$ is called a **local** or **relative minimum** of the function f. If the graph of a function f *never* lies below $(x_0, f(x_0))$, i.e., if $f(x) \geq f(x_0)$ for all x, then $(x_0, f(x_0))$ is called a **global** or **absolute minimum** of f. The point $(0, 0)$ is a global minimum of $f_1(x) = 3x^4$ in Figure 2.2.

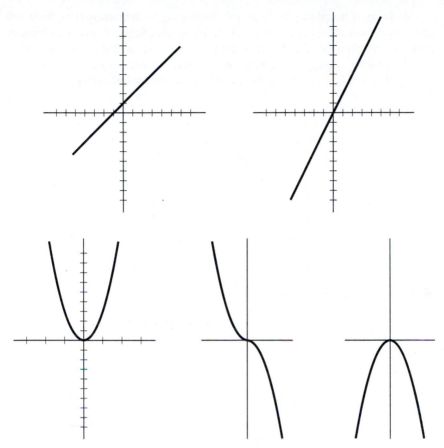

The graphs of $f(x) = x + 1$, $g(x) = 2x$, $f_1(x) = 3x^4$, $f_2(x) - x^7$, and $f_3(x) = -10x^2$.

Figure 2.2

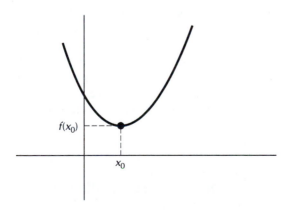

Function f has a minimum at x_0.

Figure 2.3

Similarly, if function g changes from increasing to decreasing at z_0, the graph of g cups downward at $(z_0, g(z_0))$ as in Figure 2.4, and $(z_0, g(z_0))$ is called a **local or relative maximum** of g; analytically, $g(x) \leq g(z_0)$ for all x near z_0. If $g(x) \leq g(z_0)$ for *all* x, then $(z_0, g(z_0))$ is a **global or absolute maximum** of g. The function $f_3 = -10x^2$ in Figure 2.2 has a local and a global maximum at $(0, 0)$.

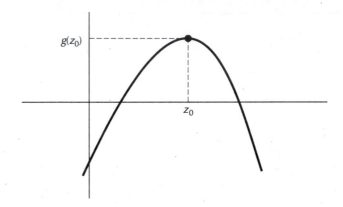

**Figure
2.4**

Function g has a maximum at z_0.

Domain

Some functions are defined only on proper subsets of $\mathbf{R}^1$. Given a function f, the set of numbers x at which $f(x)$ is defined is called the **domain** of f. For each of the five functions in Figure 2.2, the domain is all of $\mathbf{R}^1$. However, since division by zero is undefined, the rational function $f(x) = 1/x$ is not defined at $x = 0$. Since it is defined everywhere else, its domain is $\mathbf{R}^1 - \{0\}$. There are two reasons why the domain of a function might be restricted: mathematics-based and application-based. The most common mathematical reasons for restricting the domain are that one cannot divide by zero and one cannot take the square root (or the logarithm) of a negative number. For example, the domain of the function $h_1(x) = 1/(x^2 - 1)$ is all x except $\{-1, +1\}$, and the domain of the function $h_2(x) = \sqrt{x - 7}$ is all $x \geq 7$.

The domain of a function may also be restricted by the application in which the function arises. For example, if $C(x)$ is the cost of producing x cars, x is naturally a positive integer. The domain of C would be the set of positive integers. If we redefine the cost function so that $F(x)$ is the cost of producing x *tons* of cars, the domain of F is naturally the set of nonnegative real numbers:

$$\mathbf{R}_+ \equiv \{x \in \mathbf{R}^1 : x \geq 0\}.$$

The nonnegative half-line $\mathbf{R}_+$ is a common domain for functions which arise in applications.

Notation   If the domain of the real-valued function $y = f(x)$ is the set $D \subset \mathbf{R}^1$, either for mathematics-based or application-based reasons, we write

$$f: D \to \mathbf{R}^1.$$

Interval Notation

Speaking of subsets of the line, let's review the standard notation for intervals in $\mathbf{R}^1$. Given two real numbers a and b, the set of all numbers between a and b is called an **interval**. If the endpoints a and b are excluded, the interval is called an **open interval** and written as

$$(a, b) \equiv \{x \in \mathbf{R}^1 : a < x < b\}.$$

If both endpoints are included in the interval, the interval is called a **closed interval** and written as

$$[a, b] \equiv \{x \in \mathbf{R}^1 : a \leq x \leq b\}.$$

If only one endpoint is included, the interval is called **half-open** (or **half-closed**) and written as $(a, b]$ or $[a, b)$. There are also five kinds of **infinite intervals**:

$$(a, \infty) = \{x \in \mathbf{R}^1 : x > a\},$$

$$[a, \infty) = \{x \in \mathbf{R}^1 : x \geq a\},$$

$$(-\infty, a) = \{x \in \mathbf{R}^1 : x < a\},$$

$$(-\infty, a] = \{x \in \mathbf{R}^1 : x \leq a\},$$

$$(-\infty, +\infty) = \mathbf{R}^1.$$

EXERCISES

2.1   For each of the following functions, plot enough points to sketch a complete graph. Then answer the following questions:
a) Where is the function increasing and where is it decreasing?
b) Find the local and global maxima and minima of these functions:

i) $y = 3x - 2$;   *ii)* $y = -2x$;   *iii)* $y = x^2 + 1$;
iv) $y = x^3 + x$;   *v)* $y = x^3 - x$;   *vi)* $y = |x|$.

2.2   In economic models, it is natural to assume that total cost functions are increasing functions of output, since more output requires more input, which must be paid for. Name two more types of functions which arise in economics models and are naturally increasing functions. Name two types of such functions that are naturally decreasing functions. Name one type that would probably change from increasing to decreasing.

2.3   The degree of a rational function is the degree of its polynomial numerator minus the degree of its polynomial denominator. Any integer — positive, negative, or zero — can be the degree of a rational function. What is the degree of each of the rational functions in (2)?

2.4   What is the domain of each of the following functions:

$$a) \ y = \frac{1}{x-1}; \qquad b) \ y = \frac{1}{\sqrt{x-1}}; \qquad c) \ y = \frac{1}{\sqrt{x^2+1}};$$

$$d) \ y = \frac{x}{x^2-1}; \qquad e) \ y = \sqrt{1-x^2}; \qquad f) \ y = \frac{1}{\sqrt{1-x^2}-1}.$$

2.5   What is the domain of each of the four rational functions in (2)?

2.6   What is the natural domain of the economics functions mentioned in Exercise 2.2?

2.2   LINEAR FUNCTIONS

The simplest possible functions are the polynomials of degree 0: the constant functions $f(x) = b$. Since such functions assign the same number b to every real number x, they are too simple to be interesting. The simplest *interesting* functions are the polynomials of degree one: functions f of the form

$$f(x) = mx + b.$$

Such functions are called **linear functions** because they are precisely the functions whose graphs are straight lines, as will now be demonstrated.

The Slope of a Line in the Plane

First, let's look at the geometry of lines in the Cartesian plane. The main characteristic which distinguishes one line from another is its steepness, which we call the **slope** of the line. A natural way to measure the slope of a line is to start at any point (x_0, y_0) on the line and move along the line so that the x-coordinate increases by *one unit*. The corresponding change in the y-coordinate is called the slope of the line.

Example 2.1   For example, if we start at the point $(1, 0)$ on the line ℓ_1 in Figure 2.5 and move along the line until we reach the point whose x-coordinate is 2, we will be at the point $(2, 3)$. Since y increases by 3 units in this process, we say that the slope of line ℓ_1 in Figure 2.5 is 3. The diagonal line ℓ_2 in Figure 2.5 makes a 45° angle with the horizontal. Its slope is +1, since when x increases by one unit, so does y as one moves up ℓ_2. The slope of line ℓ_3, which makes an angle of −45° with the horizontal in Figure 2.5, is −1. Lines steeper than

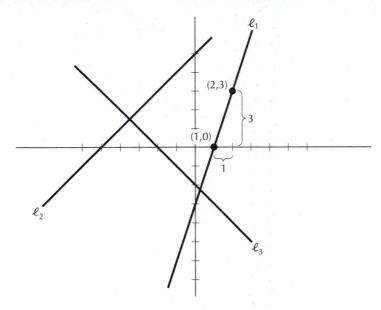

Some slopes in the plane.

**Figure
2.5**

ℓ_2 have slopes between $+1$ and $+\infty$. Lines which slope upward but are flatter than ℓ_2 have slopes between 0 and $+1$. Horizontal lines have slope zero. Lines which slope downward from left to right, like ℓ_3, have negative slope.

We need to convince ourselves that the slope of a line is independent of the starting point in the computation of the slope. To compute the slope of the line in Figure 2.6, we can start at the point (x_1, y_1) and move to the point $(x_1 + 1, y_1')$ in triangle #1. In this case we compute the slope as $y_1' - y_1$, a number which is the ratio of the two legs of right triangle #1. If we start instead at the point (x_2, y_2) and move to $(x_2 + 1, y_2')$, we compute a slope of $y_2' - y_2$, the ratio of the two legs in triangle #2. Note that the corresponding sides of triangles #1 and #2 are parallel to each other. By fundamental results of plane geometry, triangles #1 and #2 are similar to each other and therefore the ratios of corresponding sides are equal:

$$\frac{y_2' - y_2}{1} = \frac{y_1' - y_1}{1}.$$

This proves that one computes the same slope for ℓ no matter where one starts.

Finally, look at right triangle #3 in Figure 2.6, which is formed by moving from (x_3, y_3) to (x_4, y_4) along ℓ. Coordinate x_4 is not necessarily $x_3 + 1$. By the same geometric analysis, triangle #3 is similar to triangles #1 and #2. Therefore, the corresponding ratios are all equal:

$$\frac{y_4 - y_3}{x_4 - x_3} = \frac{y_2' - y_2}{1} = \frac{y_1' - y_1}{1} = \text{slope of } \ell.$$

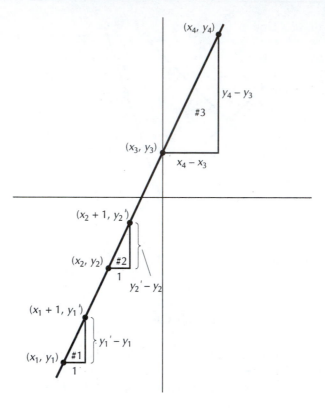

**Figure
2.6**

Computing the slope of line ℓ three ways.

This use of two arbitrary points of a line to compute its slope leads to the following most general definition of the slope of a line.

Definition   Let (x_0, y_0) and (x_1, y_1) be arbitrary points on a line ℓ. The ratio

$$m = \frac{y_1 - y_0}{x_1 - x_0}$$

is called the **slope** of line ℓ. The analysis in Figure 2.6 shows that the slope of ℓ is independent of the two points chosen on ℓ. The same analysis shows that two lines are **parallel** if and only if they have the same slope.

Example 2.2   The slope of the line joining the points (4, 6) and (0, 7) is

$$m = \frac{7 - 6}{0 - 4} = -\frac{1}{4}.$$

This line slopes downward at an angle just less than the horizontal. The slope of the line joining (4, 0) and (0, 1) is also $-1/4$; so these two lines are parallel.

The Equation of a Line

We next find the equation which the points on a given line must satisfy. First, suppose that the line ℓ has slope m and that the line intercepts the y-axis at the point $(0, b)$. This point $(0, b)$ is called the y-**intercept** of ℓ. Let (x, y) denote an arbitrary point on the line. Using (x, y) and $(0, b)$ to compute the slope of the line, we conclude that

$$\frac{y - b}{x - 0} = m,$$

or $\qquad\qquad y - b = mx;\qquad$ that is, $\qquad y = mx + b.$

The following theorem summarizes this simple calculation.

Theorem 2.1   The line whose slope is m and whose y-intercept is the point $(0, b)$ has the equation $y = mx + b$.

Polynomials of Degree One Have Linear Graphs

Now, consider the general polynomial of degree one $f(x) = mx + b$. Its graph is the locus of all points (x, y) which satisfy the equation $y = mx + b$. Given any two points (x_1, y_1) and (x_2, y_2) on this graph, the slope of the line connecting them is

$$\frac{y_2 - y_1}{x_2 - x_1} = \frac{(mx_2 + b) - (mx_1 + b)}{x_2 - x_1}$$

$$= \frac{m(x_2 - x_1)}{x_2 - x_1} = m.$$

Since the slope of this locus is m everywhere, this locus describes a straight line. One checks directly that its y-intercept is b. So, polynomials of degree one do indeed have straight lines as their graphs, and it is natural to call such functions **linear functions**.

In applications, we sometimes need to construct the formula of the linear function from given analytic data. For example, by Theorem 2.1, the line with slope m and y-intercept $(0, b)$ has equation $y = mx + b$. What is the equation of the line with slope m which passes through a more general point, say (x_0, y_0)? As in the proof of Theorem 2.1, use the given point (x_0, y_0) and a generic point on the line (x, y) to compute the slope of the line:

$$\frac{y - y_0}{x - x_0} = m.$$

It follows that the equation of the given line is $y = m(x - x_0) + y_0$, or

$$y = mx + (y_0 - mx_0). \qquad\qquad (3)$$

If, instead, we are given two points on the line, say (x_0, y_0) and (x_1, y_1), we can use these two points to compute the slope m of the line:

$$m = \frac{y_1 - y_0}{x_1 - x_0}.$$

We can then substitute this value for m in (3).

Example 2.3   Let x denote the temperature in degrees Centigrade and let y denote the temperature in degrees Fahrenheit. We know that x and y are linearly related, that 0° Centigrade or 32° Fahrenheit is the freezing temperature of water and that 100° Centigrade or 212° Fahrenheit is the boiling temperature of water. To find the equation which relates degrees Fahrenheit to degrees Centigrade, we find the equation of the line through the points $(0, 32)$ and $(100, 212)$. The slope of this line is

$$\frac{212 - 32}{100 - 0} = \frac{180}{100} = \frac{9}{5}.$$

This means that an increase of 1° Centigrade corresponds to an increase of $9/5^o$ Fahrenheit. Use the slope $9/5$ and the point $(0, 32)$ to express the linear relationship:

$$\frac{y - 32}{x - 0} = \frac{9}{5} \quad \text{or} \quad y = \frac{9}{5}x + 32.$$

Interpreting the Slope of a Linear Function

The slope of the graph of a linear function is a key concept. We will simply call it the **slope of the linear function**. Recall that the slope of a line measures how much y changes as one moves along the line increasing x by one unit. Therefore, the slope of a linear function f measures how much $f(x)$ increases for each unit increase in x. It measures the rate of increase, or better, the **rate of change** of the function f. Linear functions have the same rate of change no matter where one starts.

For example, if x measures time in hours, if $y = f(x)$ is the number of kilometers traveled in x hours, and f is linear, the slope of f measures the number of kilometers traveled *each* hour, that is, the **speed** or **velocity** of the object under study in kilometers per hour.

This view of the slope of a linear function as its rate of change plays a key role in economic analysis. If $C = F(q)$ is a linear cost function which gives the total cost C of manufacturing q units of output, then the slope of F measures the increase in the total manufacturing cost due to the production of one more unit. In effect, it is the cost of making one more unit and is called the **marginal cost**. It plays a central role in the behavior of profit-maximizing firms. If $u = U(x)$ is a linear utility function which measures the utility u or satisfaction of having an income of x dollars, the slope of U measures the added utility from each additional dollar of income. It is called the **marginal utility of income**. If $y = G(z)$ is a linear function which measures the output y achieved by using z units of labor input, then its slope tells how much additional output can be obtained from hiring another unit of labor. It is called the **marginal product of labor**. The rules which characterize the utility-maximizing behavior of consumers and the profit-maximizing behavior of firms all involve these marginal measures, since the decisions about whether or not to consume another unit of some commodity or to produce another unit of output are based not so much on the total amount consumed or produced to date, but rather on how the *next item* consumed will affect total satisfaction or how the *next item* produced will affect revenue, cost, and profit.

EXERCISES

2.7 Estimate the slope of the lines in Figure 2.7.

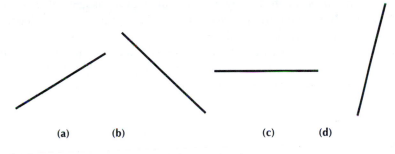

(a)   (b)   (c)   (d)

Four lines in the plane.

Figure 2.7

2.8 Find the formula for the linear function whose graph:
  a) has slope 2 and y-intercept $(0, 3)$,
  b) has slope -3 and y-intercept $(0, 0)$,
  c) has slope 4 and goes through the point $(1, 1)$,
  d) has slope -2 and goes through the point $(2, -2)$,
  e) goes through the points $(2, 3)$ and $(4, 5)$,
  f) goes through the points $(2, -4)$ and $(0, 3)$.
2.9 Assuming that each of the following functions are linear, give an economic interpretation of the slope of the function:
  a) $F(q)$ is the revenue from producing q units of output;
  b) $G(x)$ is the cost of purchasing x units of some commodity;
  c) $H(p)$ is the amount of the commodity consumed when its price is p;
  d) $C(Y)$ is the total national consumption when national income is Y;
  e) $S(Y)$ is the total national savings when national income is Y.

2.3   THE SLOPE OF NONLINEAR FUNCTIONS

We have just seen that the slope of a linear function as a measure of its marginal effect is a key concept for linear functions in economic theory. However, nearly all functions which arise in applications are nonlinear ones. How do we measure the marginal effects of these nonlinear functions?

Suppose that we are studying the nonlinear function $y = f(x)$ and that currently we are at the point $(x_0, f(x_0))$ on the graph of f, as in Figure 2.8. We want to measure the rate of change of f or the steepness of the graph of f when $x = x_0$. A natural solution to this problem is to draw the tangent line to the graph of f at x_0, as pictured in Figure 2.8. Since the tangent line very closely approximates the graph of f around $(x_0, f(x_0))$, it is a good proxy for the graph of f itself. Its slope, which we know how to measure, should really be a good measure for the slope of the nonlinear function at x_0. We note that for nonlinear functions, unlike linear functions, the slope of the tangent line will vary from point to point.

We use the notion of the tangent line approximation to a graph in our daily lives. For example, contractors who plan to build a large mall or power plant and farmers who want to subdivide large plots of land will generally assume that they are working on a *flat plane*, even though they know that they are working on a rather *round planet*. In effect, they are working with the tangent plane to the earth and the computations that they make on it will be exact to 10 or 20 decimal places — easily close enough for their purposes.

So, we define the slope of a nonlinear function f at a point $(x_0, f(x_0))$ on its graph as the slope of the tangent line to the graph of f at that point. We call the slope of the tangent line to the graph of f at $(x_0, f(x_0))$ the **derivative** of f at x_0, and we write it as

$$f'(x_0) \qquad \text{or} \qquad \frac{df}{dx}(x_0).$$

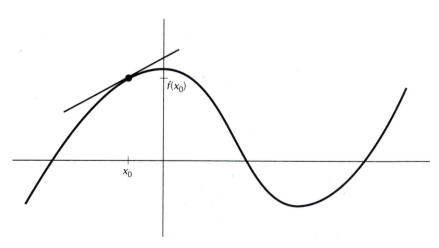

Figure 2.8

The graph of a nonlinear function.

The latter notation comes from the fact that the slope is the change in f divided by the change in x, or $\Delta f / \Delta x$, where we follow the convention of writing a capital Greek delta Δ to denote change.

Since the derivative is such an important concept, we need an analytic definition that we can work with. The first step is to make precise the definition of the tangent line to the graph of f at a point. Try to formulate just such a definition. It is not "the line which meets the graph of f in just one point," because point A in Figure 2.9 shows that we need to add more geometry to this first attempt at a definition. We might expand our first attempt to "the line which meets the graph of f at just one point, but does not cross the graph." However, the x-axis in Figure 2.9 is the true tangent line to the graph of $y = x^3$ at $(0, 0)$, and it does indeed cross the graph of x^3. So, we need to be yet more subtle.

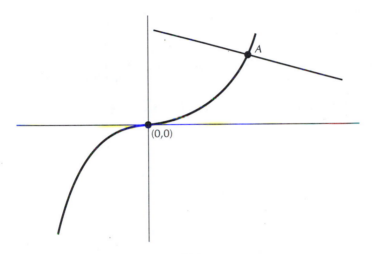

A tangent line (x-axis) and a nontangent line to the graph of x^3.

Figure 2.9

Unfortunately, the only way to handle this problem is to use a limiting process. First, recall that a line segment joining two points on a graph is called a **secant line**. Now, back off a bit from the point $(x_0, f(x_0))$ on the graph of f to the point $(x_0 + h_1, f(x_0 + h_1))$, where h_1 is some small number. Draw the secant line ℓ_1 to the graph joining these two points, as in Figure 2.10. Line ℓ_1 is an approximation to the tangent line. By choosing the second point closer and closer to $(x_0, f(x_0))$, we will be drawing better and better approximations to the desired tangent line. So, choose h_2 closer to zero than h_1 and draw the secant line ℓ_2 of the graph of f joining $(x_0, f(x_0))$ and $(x_0 + h_2, f(x_0 + h_2))$. Continue in this way choosing a sequence $\{h_n\}$ of small numbers which converges monotonically to 0. For each n, draw the secant line ℓ_n through the two *distinct* points on the graph $(x_0, f(x_0))$ and $(x_0 + h_n, f(x_0 + h_n))$. The secant lines $\{\ell_n\}$ geometrically approach the tangent line to the graph of f at $(x_0, f(x_0))$, and their slopes approach the slope of the tangent line. Since ℓ_n passes through the two points $(x_0, f(x_0))$ and $(x_0 + h_n, f(x_0 + h_n))$,

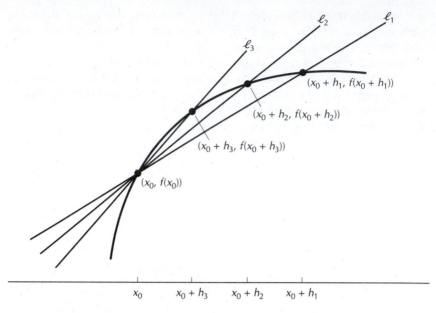

**Figure
2.10**

Approximating the tangent line by a sequence of secant lines.

its slope is

$$\frac{f(x_0 + h_n) - f(x_0)}{(x_0 + h_n) - x_0} = \frac{f(x_0 + h_n) - f(x_0)}{h_n}.$$

Therefore, the slope of the tangent line is the limit of this process as h_n converges to 0.

Definition   Let $(x_0, f(x_0))$ be a point on the graph of $y = f(x)$. The **derivative** of f at x_0, written

$$f'(x_0) \quad \text{or} \quad \frac{df}{dx}(x_0) \quad \text{or} \quad \frac{dy}{dx}(x_0),$$

is the slope of the tangent line to the graph of f at $(x_0, f(x_0))$. Analytically,

$$f'(x_0) = \lim_{h \to 0} \frac{f(x_0 + h) - f(x_0)}{h} \tag{4}$$

if this limit exists. When this limit does exist, we say that the function f is **differentiable** at x_0 with derivative $f'(x_0)$.

2.4   COMPUTING DERIVATIVES

Example 2.4   Let's use formula (4) to compute the derivative of the simplest nonlinear function, $f(x) = x^2$, at the point $x_0 = 3$. Since the graph of x^2 is fairly steep at the point $(3, 9)$ as indicated in Figure 2.11, we expect to find $f'(3)$ considerably larger than 1. For a sequence of h_n's converging to zero, choose the sequence

$$\{h_n\} = 0.1, 0.01, 0.001, \ldots, (0.1)^n, \ldots \tag{5}$$

Table 2.1 summarizes the computations we need to make.

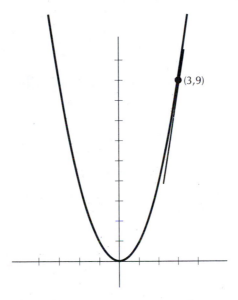

Tangent line to the graph of $f(x) = x^2$ at $x_0 = 3$.

Figure 2.11

As $h_n \to 0$, the quotient in the last column of Table 2.1 approaches 6. Therefore, the slope of the tangent line of the graph of $f(x) = x^2$ at the point $(3, 9)$ is 6; that is, $f'(3) = 6$.

h_n	$x_0 + h_n$	$f(x_0 + h_n)$	$\dfrac{f(x_0 + h_n) - f(x_0)}{h_n}$
0.1	3.1	9.61	6.1
0.01	3.01	9.0601	6.01
0.001	3.001	9.006001	6.001
0.0001	3.0001	9.00060001	6.0001

Table 2.1

Example 2.5   To prove that $f'(3) = 6$, we need to show that

$$\frac{(3 + h_n)^2 - 3^2}{h_n} \to 6, \quad \text{as} \quad h_n \to 0, \tag{6}$$

for *every* sequence $\{h_n\}$ which approaches zero, not just for the sequence (5). We now prove (6) analytically. For any h,

$$\frac{(3 + h)^2 - 3^2}{h} = \frac{9 + 6h + h^2 - 9}{h} = \frac{h(6 + h)}{h} = 6 + h,$$

which clearly converges to 6 as $h \to 0$. Now, we know for sure that $f'(3) = 6$.

Example 2.6   Now, add one more degree of generality and compute the derivative of $f(x) = x^2$ at an arbitrary point x_0. Let $\{h_n\}$ be an arbitrary sequence which converges to 0 as $n \to \infty$. Then,

$$\frac{f(x_0 + h_n) - f(x_0)}{h_n} = \frac{(x_0 + h_n)^2 - x_0^2}{h_n} = \frac{x_0^2 + 2h_n x_0 + h_n^2 - x_0^2}{h_n}$$

$$= \frac{h_n(2x_0 + h_n)}{h_n} = 2x_0 + h_n,$$

which tends to $2x_0$ as $h_n \to 0$. This calculation proves the following theorem.

Theorem 2.2   The derivative of $f(x) = x^2$ at x_0 is $f'(x_0) = 2x_0$.

Theorem 2.2 and Exercise 2.10 can be summarized by the statement that the derivative of x^k is kx^{k-1} for $k = 0, 1, 2, 3, 4$. We next prove that this statement is true for all positive integers k. Later, we'll see that it is true for every real number k, including negative numbers and fractions. In the proof of Theorem 2.2 and in the proofs in part b of Exercise 2.10, we used the explicit formula for $(x + h)^k$ for small integers k. To prove the more general result, we need the general formula for $(x + h)^k$ for any positive integer k, a formula we present in the following lemma. Its proof can be found in any precollege algebra text under "binomial expansion."

Lemma 2.1   For any positive integer k,

$$(x + h)^k = x^k + a_1 x^{k-1} h^1 + \cdots + a_{k-1} x^1 h^{k-1} + a_k h^k, \tag{7}$$

where
$$a_j = \frac{k!}{j! \, (k - j)!}, \quad \text{for} \quad j = 1, \ldots, k.$$

In particular, $a_1 = k$, $a_2 = k(k - 1)/2$, and $a_k = 1$.

Theorem 2.3   For any positive integer k, the derivative of $f(x) = x^k$ at x_0 is $f'(x_0) = kx_0^{k-1}$.

Proof

$$\frac{(x_0 + h)^k - x_0^k}{h} = \frac{x_0^k + kx_0^{k-1}h^1 + \frac{1}{2}k(k-1)x_0^{k-2}h^2 + \cdots + a_k h^k - x_0^k}{h}$$

$$= \frac{h(kx_0^{k-1} + \frac{1}{2}k(k-1)x_0^{k-2}h + \cdots + a_k h^{k-1})}{h}$$

$$= kx_0^{k-1} + \frac{1}{2}k(k-1)x_0^{k-2}h + \cdots + a_k h^{k-1},$$

which approaches kx_0^{k-1} as $h \to 0$. ∎

Rules for Computing Derivatives

The monomials x^k are the basic building blocks for a large class of functions, including all polynomials and rational functions. To compute the derivatives of functions in these larger classes, we need to know how to take the derivative of a sum, difference, product, or quotient of two functions whose derivatives we know how to compute. First, recall that we add, subtract, divide, and multiply functions in the natural way — just by performing these operations on the values of the functions. For example, if $f(x) = x^3$ and $g(x) = 6x^2$, then the sum, product, and quotient functions constructed from these two are, respectively:

$$(f + g)(x) \equiv f(x) + g(x) = x^3 + 6x^2,$$

$$(f \cdot g)(x) \equiv f(x) \cdot g(x) = x^3 \cdot 6x^2 = 6x^5,$$

$$\left(\frac{f}{g}\right)(x) \equiv \frac{f(x)}{g(x)} = \frac{x^3}{6x^2} = \frac{1}{6}x.$$

The following theorem presents the rules for differentiating the sum, difference, product, quotient, and power of functions. These rules, along with Theorem 2.3, will allow us to compute the derivatives of most elementary functions, including all polynomials and rational functions.

Part c of Theorem 2.4 is called the **Product Rule**, part d the **Quotient Rule**, and part e the **Power Rule**. Note that the derivative behaves very nicely with respect to sums and differences of functions, but the rules for differentiating products and quotients are a bit more complicated. The proof of each statement in Theorem 2.4 requires a rather straightforward manipulation of the definition (4) of the derivative. Parts a and b should be proved as an illustrative exercise. The

Theorem 2.4   Suppose that k is an arbitrary constant and that f and g are differentiable functions at $x = x_0$. Then,

a) $(f \pm g)'(x_0) \;=\; f'(x_0) \pm g'(x_0),$

b) $(kf)'(x_0) \quad = k(f'(x_0)),$

c) $(f \cdot g)'(x_0) \;=\; f'(x_0)g(x_0) + f(x_0)g'(x_0),$

d) $\left(\dfrac{f}{g}\right)'(x_0) \quad = \dfrac{f'(x_0)g(x_0) - f(x_0)g'(x_0)}{g(x_0)^2},$

e) $((f(x))^n)' \quad = n(f(x))^{n-1} \cdot f'(x),$

f) $(x^k)' \qquad = kx^{k-1}.$

proofs of parts c, d, and e are a little more subtle. The proof of part f is listed as an exercise below for negative integers k and will be carried out for fractions k in Section 4.2.

Example 2.7   We use Theorems 2.3 and 2.4 to calculate the derivatives of some simple functions.

a) $(x^7 + 3x^6 - 4x^2 + 5)' \quad = 7x^6 + 18x^5 - 8x,$

b) $((x^2 + 3x - 1)(x^4 - 8x))' = (2x + 3)(x^4 - 8x)$

$$+ (x^2 + 3x - 1)(4x^3 - 8)$$

$$= 6x^5 + 15x^4 - 4x^3 - 24x^2 - 48x + 8,$$

c) $\left(\dfrac{x^2 - 1}{x^2 + 1}\right)' \qquad = \dfrac{(2x)(x^2 + 1) - (x^2 - 1)(2x)}{(x^2 + 1)^2}$

$$= \dfrac{4x}{(x^2 + 1)^2},$$

e) $((x^3 - 4x^2 + 1)^5)' \qquad = 5(x^3 - 4x^2 + 1)^4 \cdot (3x^2 - 8x),$

f) $(3x^{2/3} + 3x^{-1})' \qquad = 2x^{-1/3} - 3x^{-2}.$

EXERCISES

2.10   *a)* Use the geometric definition of the derivative to prove that the derivative of a constant function is 0 everywhere and the derivative of $f(x) = mx$ is $f'(x) = m$ for all x.

     b) Use the method of the proof of Theorem 2.2 to prove that the derivative of x^3 is $3x^2$ and the derivative of x^4 is $4x^3$.

2.11   Find the derivative of the following functions at an arbitrary point:

     a) $-7x^3$,   *b)* $12x^{-2}$,

     c) $3x^{-3/2}$,   *d)* $\frac{1}{2}\sqrt{x}$,

     e) $3x^2 - 9x + 7x^{2/5} - 3x^{1/2}$,   *f)* $4x^5 - 3x^{1/2}$,

     g) $(x^2 + 1)(x^2 + 3x + 2)$,   *h)* $(x^{1/2} + x^{-1/2})(4x^5 - 3\sqrt{x})$,

     i) $\dfrac{x-1}{x+1}$,   *j)* $\dfrac{x}{x^2+1}$,

     k) $(x^5 - 3x^2)^7$,   *l)* $5(x^5 - 6x^2 + 3x)^{2/3}$,

     m) $(x^3 + 2x)^3(4x + 5)^2$.

2.12   Find the equation of the tangent line to the graph of the given function for the specified value of x. [Hint: Given a point on a line and the slope of the line, one can construct the equation of the line.]

     a) $f(x) = x^2$, $x_0 = 3$;   *b)* $f(x) = x/(x^2 + 2)$, $x_0 = 1$.

2.13   Prove parts *a* and *b* of Theorem 2.4.

2.14   In Theorem 2.3, we proved that the derivative of $y = x^k$ is $y' = kx^{k-1}$ for all positive integers k. Use the Quotient Rule, Theorem 2.4*d*, to extend this result to negative integers k.

2.5   DIFFERENTIABILITY AND CONTINUITY

As we saw in Section 2.3, a function f is differentiable at x_0 if, geometrically speaking, its graph has a tangent line at $(x_0, f(x_0))$, or analytically speaking, the limit

$$\lim_{h_n \to 0} \frac{f(x_0 + h_n) - f(x_0)}{h_n} \tag{8}$$

exists and is the same for every sequence $\{h_n\}$ which converges to 0. If a function is differentiable at every point x_0 in its domain D, we say that the function is **differentiable**. Only functions whose graphs are "smooth curves" have tangent lines everywhere; in fact, mathematicians commonly use the word "smooth" in place of the word "differentiable."

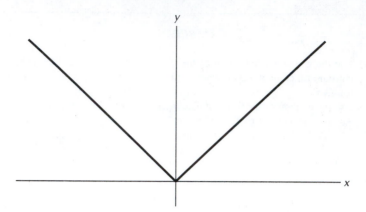

**Figure
2.12**   *The graph of $f(x) = |x|$.*

A Nondifferentiable Function

As an example of a function which is not differentiable everywhere, consider the graph of the absolute value function $f(x) = |x|$ in Figure 2.12. This graph has a sharp corner at the origin. There is no natural tangent line to this graph at $(0, 0)$. Alternatively, as Figure 2.13 indicates, there are infinitely many lines through $(0, 0)$ which lie on one side of the graph and hence would be candidates for the tangent line. Since the graph of $|x|$ has no well-defined tangent line at $x = 0$, the function $|x|$ is not differentiable at $x = 0$.

To see why the *analytic* definition (8) of the derivative does not work for $|x|$, substitute into (8) each of the following two sequences which converge to zero:

$$h_n = \{+.1, +.01, +.001, \ldots, +(.1)^n, \ldots\}$$
$$k_n = \{-.1, -.01, -.001, \ldots, -(.1)^n, \ldots\}.$$

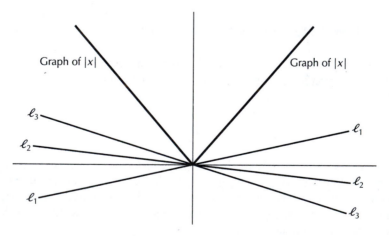

**Figure
2.13**   *Candidates for tangent lines to graph of $|x|$.*

Substituting these sequences into the definition (8) of the derivative, we compute

$$\frac{f(0 + h_n) - f(0)}{h_n} = \frac{h_n - 0}{h_n} = +1 \quad \text{for all} \quad n,$$

$$\frac{f(0 + k_n) - f(0)}{k_n} = \frac{-k_n - 0}{k_n} = -1 \quad \text{for all} \quad n.$$

The first sequence is $\{1, 1, \ldots, 1, \ldots\}$, which clearly converges to $+1$; the second sequence is $\{-1, -1, \ldots, -1, \ldots\}$, which clearly converges to -1. Since different sequences which converge to 0 yield different limits in (8), the function $|x|$ does *not* have a derivative at $x = 0$.

Continuous Functions

A property of functions more fundamental than differentiability is that of continuity. From a geometric point of view, a function is **continuous** if its graph has no breaks. Even though it is not differentiable at $x = 0$, the function $f(x) = |x|$ is still continuous. On the other hand, the function

$$g(x) = \begin{cases} x + 1, & x \geq 0, \\ x^2 - 1, & x < 0, \end{cases} \tag{9}$$

whose graph is pictured in Figure 2.14, is not continuous at $x = 0$. In this case, we call the point $x = 0$ a **discontinuity** of g. It should be clear that the graph of a function cannot have a tangent line at a point of discontinuity. In other words, in order for a function to be differentiable, it must at least be continuous. For functions described by concrete formulas, discontinuities arise when the function is defined by different formulas on different parts of the number line and when the values of these two formulas are different at the point where the formula changes, for example, at the point $x = 0$ in (9).

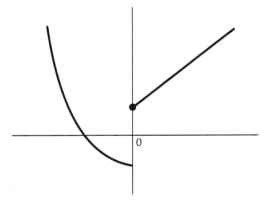

The function g given by (9) is discontinuous at $x = 0$.

Figure 2.14

The break in the graph of g at the origin in Figure 2.14 means that there are points on the x-axis on either side of zero which are arbitrarily close to each other, but whose values under g are not close to each other. Even though $(-.1)^n$ and $(+.1)^n$ are arbitrarily close to each other, $g((-.1)^n)$ is close to -1 while $g((+.1)^n)$ is close to $+1$. As x crosses 0, the value of the function suddenly changes by two units. Small changes in x do not lead to small changes in $g(x)$. This leads to the following more analytic definition of continuity.

Definition   A function $f: D \to \mathbf{R}^1$ is **continuous** at $x_0 \in D$ if for *any* sequence $\{x_n\}$ which converges to x_0 in D, $f(x_n)$ converges to $f(x_0)$. A function is **continuous on a set** $U \subset D$ if it is continuous at every $x \in U$. Finally, we say that a function is continuous if it is continuous at every point in its domain.

The function $g(x)$ defined in (9) does not satisfy this definition at $x = 0$ because

$$\lim_{n \to \infty} f((-.1)^n) = -1, \quad \text{but} \quad f(0) = +1.$$

Most theorems in economic theory require that the function involved be continuous, if not differentiable. Continuity is a reasonable assumption in applications. For example, if $y = f(x)$ is a production function, it is reasonable to assume that a small change in the amount of input x will yield a small change in the corresponding amount y of output produced.

Continuously Differentiable Functions

If f is a differentiable function, its derivative $f'(x)$ is another function of x. It is the function which assigns to each point x the slope of the tangent line to the graph of f at $(x, f(x))$. We can ask whether or not this new function is continuous. Geometrically, the function f' will be continuous if the tangent line to the graph of f at $(x, f(x))$ changes continuously as x changes. If $f'(x)$ is a continuous function of x, we say that the original function f is **continuously differentiable**, or $\mathbf{C}^1$ for short.

Example 2.8   Every polynomial is a continuous function. Since the derivative of a polynomial is a polynomial of one less degree, it is also continuous. Therefore, every polynomial is C^1.

EXERCISES

2.15   Draw a picture of the arguments in the proof that $f(x) = |x|$ does not have a derivative at $x = 0$. Show that f does have a derivative at every point other than 0.

2.16 For each of the following functions, sketch its graph and describe whether it is continuous and/or differentiable at the point of transition of its two formulas:

$$a)\ y = \begin{cases} +x^2, & x \geq 0, \\ -x^2, & x < 0; \end{cases} \qquad b)\ y = \begin{cases} +x^2 + 1, & x \geq 0, \\ -x^2 - 1, & x < 0; \end{cases}$$

$$c)\ y = \begin{cases} x^3, & x \leq 1, \\ x, & x > 1; \end{cases} \qquad d)\ y = \begin{cases} x^3, & x < 1, \\ 3x - 2, & x \geq 1. \end{cases}$$

2.17 Which of the functions in the previous exercise are C^1 everywhere?

2.18 Sketch the graph of the function $f(x) = x^{2/3}$ and describe the continuity and differentiability of this function. [The limit in (8) must be finite for the derivative to exist.]

2.6 HIGHER-ORDER DERIVATIVES

Let f be a C^1 function on $\mathbf{R}^1$. Since its derivative $f'(x)$ is a continuous function on $\mathbf{R}^1$, we can ask whether or not the function f' has a derivative at a point x_0. The derivative of $f'(x)$ at x_0 is called the **second derivative** of f at x_0 and is written

$$f''(x_0) \quad \text{or} \quad \frac{d}{dx}\left(\frac{df}{dx}\right)(x_0) = \frac{d^2 f}{dx^2}(x_0).$$

Example 2.9 The derivative of the function $f(x) = x^3 + 3x^2 + 3x + 1$ is the function $f'(x) = 3x^2 + 6x + 3$. Its derivative, the second derivative of f, is $f''(x) = 6x + 6$.

Example 2.10 Consider the function

$$f(x) = \begin{cases} +\frac{1}{2}x^2, & x \geq 0, \\ -\frac{1}{2}x^2, & x < 0. \end{cases} \tag{10}$$

Since both branches of f equal 0 at the transition point $x = 0$, f is continuous. The same kind of argument shows that f' is continuous, since f' can be written as

$$f'(x) = \begin{cases} +x, & x \geq 0, \\ -x, & x < 0, \end{cases}$$

differentiating both sides of (10). Since f' is continuous, f is C^1. However, because $f'(x) = |x|$, f' is not differentiable at $x = 0$, and therefore $f''(x)$ does not exist at $x = 0$. The second derivative of f does exist at all other points, however.

If f has a second derivative everywhere, then f'' is a well-defined function of x. We will see later that the second derivative has a rich geometric meaning in terms of the shape of the graph of f. If f'' is itself a continuous function of x, then we say that f is **twice continuously differentiable**, or $\mathbf{C^2}$ for short. Every polynomial is a C^2 function.

This process continues. If f is C^2, so that $x \longmapsto f''(x)$ is a continuous function, we can ask whether f'' has a derivative at x_0. If it does, we write this derivative as

$$f'''(x_0) \quad \text{or} \quad f^{[3]}(x_0) \quad \text{or} \quad \frac{d^3 f}{dx^3}(x_0).$$

For example, for the cubic polynomial $f(x)$ in Example 2.9, $f'''(x) = 6$. If $f'''(x)$ exists for all x and if $f'''(x)$ is itself a continuous function of x, then we say that the original function f is $\mathbf{C^3}$.

This process continues for all positive integers. If $f(x)$ has derivatives of order $1, 2, \ldots, k$ and if the kth derivative of f,

$$f^{[k]}(x) = \frac{d^k f}{dx^k}(x);$$

is itself a continuous function, we say that f is $\mathbf{C^k}$. If f has a continuous derivative of every order, that is, if f is C^k for every positive integer k, then we say that f is C^∞ or "infinitely differentiable." All polynomials are C^∞ functions.

EXERCISES

2.19   Sketch the graph of the function in (10).

2.20   Compute the second derivatives of the functions in Exercise 2.11.

2.21   Discuss the continuity and differentiability of the functions: *a*) $f(x) = x^{5/3}$; *b*) $g(x) = [x]$, the largest integer $\leq x$.

2.7   APPROXIMATION BY DIFFERENTIALS

This completes our introduction to the fundamental concepts and calculations of calculus. We turn now to the task of using the derivative to shed light on functions. In the next chapter, the derivative will be used to understand functions more completely, to graph functions more efficiently, to solve optimization problems, and to characterize the maximizer or minimizer of a function, especially in economic settings. We begin our discussion of the uses of calculus by showing how the definition of the derivative leads naturally to the construction of the linear approximation of a function. Since this material is the essence of what calculus is about, it is included in this chapter alongside the fundamental concepts of calculus.

Recall that for a linear function $f(x) = mx + b$, the derivative $f'(x) = m$ gives the slope of the graph of f and measures the rate of change or *marginal change* of f: the increase in the value of f for every unit increase in the value of x.

Let's carry over this marginal analysis to nonlinear functions. After all, this was one of the main reasons for defining the derivative of such an f. In formulating the analytic definition of the derivative of f, we used the fact that the slope of the tangent line to the graph at $(x_0, f(x_0))$ is well approximated by the slope of the secant line through $(x_0, f(x_0))$ and a nearby point $(x_0 + h, f(x_0 + h))$ on the graph. In symbols,

$$\frac{f(x_0 + h) - f(x_0)}{h} \approx f'(x_0) \tag{11}$$

for h small, where $\approx$ means "is well approximated by" or "is close in value to."

If we set $h = 1$ in (11), then (11) becomes

$$f(x_0 + 1) - f(x_0) \approx f'(x_0); \tag{12}$$

in words, the derivative of f at x_0 is a good approximation to the marginal change of f at x_0. Of course, the less curved the graph of f at x_0, the better is the approximation in (12).

Example 2.11   Consider the production function $F(x) = \frac{1}{2}\sqrt{x}$. Suppose that the firm is currently using 100 units of labor input x, so that its output is 5 units. The derivative of the production function F at $x = 100$,

$$F'(100) = \frac{1}{4}100^{-1/2} = \frac{1}{40} = 0.025,$$

is a good measure of the *additional* output that can be achieved by hiring one more unit of labor, the **marginal product of labor**. The actual increase in output is $F(101) - F(100) = 0.02494 \cdots$, pretty close to 0.025.

Even though it is not *exactly* the increase in $y = F(x)$ due to a one unit increase in x, economists still use $F'(x)$ as the marginal change in F because it is easier to work with the single term $F'(x)$ than with the difference $F(x + 1) - F(x)$ and because using the simple term $F'(x)$ avoids the question of what unit to use to measure a one unit increase in x.

What if the change in the amount of input x is not exactly one unit? Return to (11) and substitute Δx, the exact change in x, for h. Multiplying (11) out yields:

$$\Delta y \equiv f(x_0 + \Delta x) - f(x_0) \approx f'(x_0)\Delta x, \tag{13}$$

or
$$f(x_0 + \Delta x) \approx f(x_0) + f'(x_0)\Delta x, \tag{14}$$

where we write Δy for the exact change in $y = f(x)$ when x changes by Δx. Once again, the less curved the graph and/or the smaller the change Δx in x, the better the approximation in (13) and (14).

Example 2.12   Consider again a firm with production function $y = \frac{1}{2}\sqrt{x}$. Suppose it cuts its labor force x from 900 to 896 units. Let's estimate the change in output Δy and the new output y at $x = 896$. We substitute

$$F(x) = \tfrac{1}{2}x^{1/2}, \quad x_0 = 900, \quad \text{and} \quad \Delta x = -4$$

into (13) and (14) and compute that

$$F'(x) = \tfrac{1}{4}x^{-1/2} \quad \text{and} \quad F'(900) = \tfrac{1}{4} \cdot \tfrac{1}{30} = \tfrac{1}{120}.$$

By (13), output will decrease by approximately

$$F'(x_0)\Delta x = \frac{1}{120} \cdot 4 = \frac{1}{30} \text{ units.}$$

By (14), the new output will be approximately

$$F(900) + F'(900)(-4) = 15 - \frac{1}{30} = 14\frac{29}{30} = 14.9666\cdots.$$

The actual new output is $F(896) = 14.9663\cdots$; once again the approximation by derivatives is a good one.

From a mathematical point of view, we can consider (14) as an effective way of approximating $f(x)$ for x close to some x_0 where $f(x_0)$ and $f'(x_0)$ are easily computed. For example, in Example 2.12, we computed $\frac{1}{2}\sqrt{896}$, using our familiarity with $\frac{1}{2}\sqrt{900} = 15$.

Example 2.13   Let's use (14) to estimate the cube root of 1001.5. We know that the cube root of 1000 is 10. Choose $f(x) = x^{1/3}$, $x_0 = 1000$, and $\Delta x = +1.5$. Then,

$$f'(x) = \frac{1}{3}x^{-2/3} \quad \text{and} \quad f'(1000) = \frac{1}{3}(1000)^{-2/3} = \frac{1}{300}.$$

Therefore,

$$f(1001.5) \approx f(1000) + f'(1000) \cdot 1.5 = 10 + \frac{1.5}{300} = 10.005,$$

close to the true value $10.004998\cdots$ of $\sqrt[3]{1001.5}$.

Equations (13) and (14) are merely analytic representations of the geometric fact that the tangent line ℓ to the graph of $y = f(x)$ at $(x_0, f(x_0))$ is a good approximation to the graph itself for x near x_0. As Figure 2.15 indicates, the left-hand sides of (13) and (14) pertain to movement along the graph of f, while the right-hand sides pertain to movement along the tangent line ℓ, because the equation of the tangent line, the line through the point $(x_0, f(x_0))$ with slope $f'(x_0)$, is

$$y = f(x_0) + f'(x_0)(x - x_0) = f(x_0) + f'(x_0)\Delta x.$$

Continue to write Δy for the actual change in f as x changes by Δx, that is, for the change along the graph of f, as in Figure 2.15. Write dy for the change in y along the tangent line ℓ as x changes by Δx. Then, (13) can be written as

$$\Delta y \approx dy = f'(x_0)\Delta x.$$

We usually write dx instead of Δx when we are working with changes along the tangent line, even though Δx is equal to dx. The increments dy and dx along the tangent line ℓ are called **differentials**. We sometimes write the differential df in place of the differential dy. The equation of differentials

$$df = f'(x_0)\,dx \quad \text{or} \quad dy = f'(x_0)\,dx$$

for the variation along the tangent line to the graph of f gives added weight to the notation $\dfrac{df}{dx}$ for the derivative $f'(x)$.

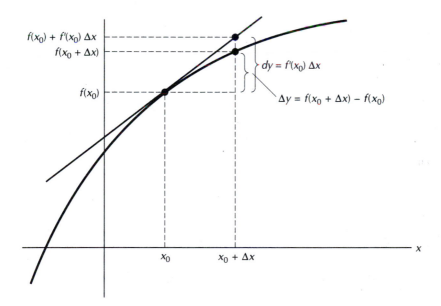

Comparing dy and Δy.

**Figure
2.15**

EXERCISES

2.22 Suppose that the total cost of manufacturing x units of a certain commodity is $C(x) = 2x^2 + 6x + 12$. Use differentials to approximate the cost of producing the 21st unit. Compare this estimate with the cost of actually producing the 21st unit.

2.23 A manufacturer's total cost is $C(x) = 0.1x^3 - 0.25x^2 + 300x + 100$ dollars, where x is the level of production. Estimate the effect on the total cost of an increase in the level of production from 6 to 6.1 units.

2.24 It is estimated that t years from now, the population of a certain town will be $F(t) = 40 - [8/(t + 2)]$. Use differentials to estimate the amount by which the population will increase during the next six months.

2.25 Use differentials to approximate: $a)$ $\sqrt{50}$, $b)$ $\sqrt[4]{9997}$, $c)$ $(10.003)^5$.

One-Variable Calculus: Applications

Now that we have defined the derivative and learned how to compute it in Chapter 2, let's put the derivative to work to shed light on some economic relationships. The first step in studying the relationship between two variables is to draw its graph. For nonlinear functions, this can be a difficult task. Sections 3.1 to 3.4 show how the derivative can help us draw graphs more efficiently and more accurately. Furthermore, many economic problems involve the maximization or minimization of some economic entity, for example, maximization of profits or utility and minimization of costs or risk. Section 3.5 demonstrates how to use the derivative of a function both to solve such optimization problems and to derive the economic principles behind these solutions. This chapter closes with a description in Section 3.6 of the main applications of calculus to microeconomics in the study of production, cost, profit, and demand functions.

3.1 USING THE FIRST DERIVATIVE FOR GRAPHING

The derivative of a function carries much information about the important properties of the function. In this section, we will see that knowing just the signs of a function's first and second derivatives and the location of only a few points on its graph usually enables us to draw an accurate graph of the function.

Positive Derivative Implies Increasing Function

As we discussed at the beginning of the last chapter, the most basic information about a function is whether it is increasing or decreasing and where it changes from one to the other. This is exactly the information we get from the sign of the first derivative of the function.

Theorem 3.1 Suppose that the function f is continuously differentiable at x_0. Then,

(a) if $f'(x_0) > 0$, there is an open interval containing x_0 on which f is increasing, and

(b) if $f'(x_0) < 0$, there is an open interval containing x_0 on which f is decreasing.

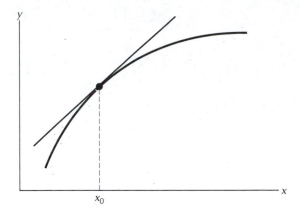

Figure 3.1

If $f'(x_0) > 0$, the graph of f slopes upward.

Proof   We will sketch a geometric and an analytic proof of part *a*. The proof of part *b* is analogous to that of part *a*.

Figure 3.1 illustrates the simple geometric picture behind the statement of Theorem 3.1. Since $f'(x_0)$ is the slope of the tangent line to the graph of f at x_0, $f'(x_0) > 0$ means that the tangent line slopes upward and therefore the graph to which it is tangent slopes upward too.

From an analytic point of view, since f is differentiable at x_0,

$$\lim_{h \to 0} \frac{f(x_0 + h) - f(x_0)}{h} = f'(x_0) > 0.$$

this inequality implies that if h is small and positive, $f(x_0 + h) - f(x_0)$ is positive too. If we write x_1 for $x_0 + h$, this statement becomes: for x_1 near x_0

$$x_1 > x_0 \implies f(x_1) > f(x_0).$$

This means that f is an increasing function near x_0. ■

The following theorem is the *global* version of Theorem 3.1. The proofs of the first two statements follow from the simple observation that if a function is increasing at each point on an interval, it is increasing on the whole interval. The last two statements follow directly from the first two.

Theorem 3.2   Let f be a continuously differentiable function on domain $D \subset \mathbf{R}^1$.

If $f' > 0$ on interval $(a, b) \subset D$, then f is increasing on (a, b).
If $f' < 0$ on interval $(a, b) \subset D$, then f is decreasing on (a, b).
If f is increasing on (a, b), then $f' \geq 0$ on (a, b).
If f is decreasing on (a, b), then $f' \leq 0$ on (a, b).

Theorems 3.1 and 3.2 are useful in applications in which one has some information about the derivatives of f and needs to know whether or not f is increasing. We will present an example of this phenomenon in Section 3.6 when we prove that if marginal cost is greater than average cost, then average cost is increasing.

Using First Derivatives to Sketch Graphs

To use Theorem 3.2 to sketch the graph of a given function f, we need to find the intervals where $f' > 0$ and the intervals where $f' < 0$. To accomplish this:

(1) First find the points at which $f'(x) = 0$ or f' is not defined. Such points are called **critical points** of f. Hopefully, the function under consideration has only finitely many critical points $x_1, x_2, \ldots, x_k$.
(2) Evaluate the function at each of these critical points $x_1, x_2, \ldots, x_k$, and plot the corresponding points on the graph.
(3) Then, check the sign of f' on each of the intervals

$$(-\infty, x_1), (x_1, x_2), \ldots, (x_{k-1}, x_k), (x_k, \infty).$$

On any one of these intervals, f' is defined and nonzero. Since $f'(x) = 0$ only when $x = x_1, \ldots, x_k$ and since f' is continuous, f' cannot change sign on any of these intervals; it must be either *always* negative or *always* positive on each. To see whether f' is positive or negative on any one of these intervals, one need only check the sign of f' at one convenient point in that interval.
(4) If $f' > 0$ on interval I, draw the graph of f increasing over I. If $f' < 0$ on I, draw a decreasing graph over I.

Example 3.1   Consider the cubic function $f(x) = x^3 - 3x$. One easily computes that

$$f'(x) = 3x^2 - 3 = 3(x - 1)(x + 1),$$

which equals zero only at $x = -1, +1$. These are the critical points of f. The corresponding points on the graph of f are $(-1, 2)$ and $(1, -2)$. Next, we check the sign of f' on the three intervals obtained by deleting the critical points from $\mathbf{R}^1$:

$$J_1 = (-\infty, -1), \quad J_2 = (-1, +1), \quad \text{and} \quad J_3 = (+1, +\infty).$$

Choosing a point from each of these three intervals, we note that:

(a) $f'(-2) = 9 > 0$, so $f' > 0$ on J_1 and f is increasing on J_1;
(b) $f'(0) = -3 < 0$, so $f' < 0$ on J_2 and f is decreasing on J_2; and
(c) $f'(+2) = 9 > 0$, so $f' > 0$ on J_3 and f is increasing on J_3.

We have summarized this information on the number line in Figure 3.2, and we have sketched the graph of f in Figure 3.3.

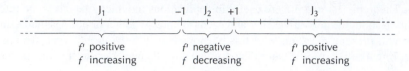

**Figure
3.2**

A summary of first derivative information for $f(x) = x^3 - 3x$.

Since it is easy to compute, you should include the y-intercept $(0, f(0))$ on the graph of f as you sketch it. The y-intercept for the function in Example 3.1 is the origin $(0,0)$. Occasionally, it is straightforward to calculate the x-intercepts of f, the places where $f(x) = 0$. When this calculation is simple, plot these points on the graph too. For the cubic function in Example 3.1, the x-intercepts are the solutions of $f(x) = x(x^2 - 3) = 0$, namely $x = -\sqrt{3}, \ 0, +\sqrt{3}$.

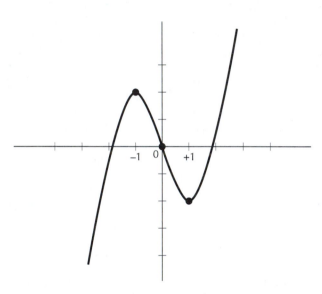

**Figure
3.3**

The graph of $f(x) = x^3 - 3x$.

EXERCISES

3.1 Use the techniques of this section to sketch the graphs of the following functions:

a) $x^3 + 3x$, b) $x^4 - 8x^3 + 18x^2 - 11$, c) $\frac{1}{3}x^3 + 9x + 3$,

d) $x^7 - 7x$, e) $x^{2/3}$, f) $2x^6 - 3x^4 + 2$.

3.2 Write out the corresponding argument for part b of Theorem 3.1.

3.2 SECOND DERIVATIVES AND CONVEXITY

Frequently, we need to know more about the shape of the graph than where it is increasing and where it is decreasing. Consider, for example, a production function $y = f(x)$, a good example of a function which is naturally increasing. The rate of increase for a production function varies with the number x of workers. At first, the additional output that each new worker adds to the production process increases as specialization and cooperation take place. However, after the gains from specialization are achieved, the additional output per new worker slows down and eventually declines as workers compete for limited space and resources. Figure 3.4 shows the graph of such a production function. Note that it is increasing for all x. However, for x between 0 and a, its slope (the marginal product of labor) is increasing too; for x bigger than a, the slope decreases as x increases.

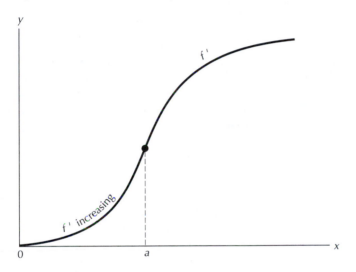

A typical production function.

Figure 3.4

Learning curves, which relate amount learned to time elapsed, often have graphs shaped like that of Figure 3.4. Amount learned per unit time — the slope of the curve — is high at first and increasing. However, as the task becomes learned or as the learner's mind reaches its capacity to hold more data, the rate of learning begins to drop.

For $x \in (0, a)$ in Figure 3.4, the slope of $f'(x)$ is an increasing function. By Theorem 3.2, the derivative of f', $f''(x)$, is nonnegative there: $f''(x) \geq 0$ on $(0, a)$. For $x > a$ in Figure 3.4, f' is a decreasing function of x; so $f''(x) \leq 0$ on (a, ∞). A differentiable function f for which $f''(x) \geq 0$ on an interval I (so that f' is increasing on I) is said to be **concave up** on I. A differentiable function f for which $f''(x) \leq 0$ on an interval I (so that f' is decreasing on I) is said to be **concave down** on I.

An increasing function can be concave up or concave down on its interval of increase. These two cases are illustrated in Figure 3.5. Figure 3.6 shows how a

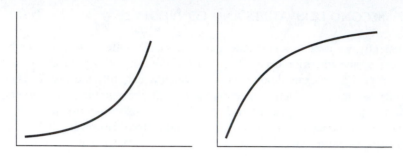

**Figure
3.5**

An increasing function can be concave up or concave down.

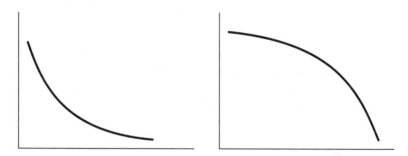

**Figure
3.6**

A decreasing function can be concave up or concave down.

decreasing function can be concave up or concave down on its domain. Note that the slope of f is an increasing function of x for a function which is concave up and is a decreasing function of x for a function which is concave down.

There is also a noncalculus definition of concave up and concave down. This characterization follows from the observation that for a function which is concave up, the secant line joining any two points on the graph lies *above* the graph, as illustrated in Figure 3.7. For any two points a and b, the set of points between a and b is given by the set $I_{ab} = [a, b]$ of all convex combinations of a and b:

$$I_{ab} \equiv \{(1 - t)a + tb : 0 \leq t \leq 1\}.$$

The graph of f above I_{ab} is the set of points

$$\{((1 - t)a + tb, f((1 - t)a + tb)) : 0 \leq t \leq 1\}.$$

On the other hand, the secant line joining the points $(a, f(a))$ and $(b, f(b))$ on the graph of f is given by

$$(1 - t)(a, f(a)) + t(b, f(b)) = ((1 - t)a + tb, \; (1 - t)f(a) + tf(b))$$

for t in $[0, 1]$. Therefore, the statement that the secant line lies above the graph of

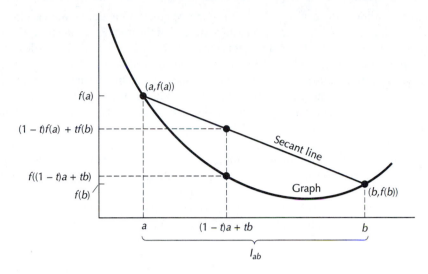

For a function which is concave up, the secant always lies above the graph.

Figure 3.7

f for $x \in I_{ab}$ can be written as

$$(1 - t)f(a) + tf(b) \geq f((1 - t)a + tb) \qquad (1)$$

for $0 \leq t \leq 1$. This characterization of concave up is more general than the $f'' \geq 0$ criterion since it also applies to functions which are not differentiable. Therefore, we'll use it as our definition of concave up. In fact, condition (1) *is equivalent to* the condition $f''(x) \geq 0$ on I_{ab} for a C^2 function.

Definition A function f is called **concave up** or simply **convex** on an interval I if and only if

$$f((1 - t)a + tb) \leq (1 - t)f(a) + tf(b) \qquad (2)$$

for all $a, b \in I$ and all $t \in [0, 1]$. A function f is called **concave down** or simply **concave** on interval I if and only if

$$f((1 - t)a + tb) \geq (1 - t)f(a) + tf(b) \qquad (3)$$

for all $a, b \in I$ and all $t \in [0, 1]$.

Calculus texts prefer the terms "concave up" and "concave down" to the terms "convex" and "concave." However, functions of more than one variable which satisfy condition (2) or (3) play a central role in economic theory, where the terms "convex" and "concave" are standard.

Of course, knowing where a function is convex or concave is valuable information for sketching its graph. For this purpose, one only needs to know where $f'' > 0$ and where $f'' < 0$. The test to see whether a function is convex or concave mimics the test used in determining whether a function is increasing or decreasing, but uses the second derivative instead of the first. First, one finds those points where $f''(x) = 0$ by solving this equation for x. These points are called the **second order critical points** of f or, if the second derivative actually changes sign there, **inflection points** of f. These points divide the domain of f into intervals on each of which f'' is always positive or always negative. On any one such interval, one need only evaluate f'' at a single point in the interval to determine its sign throughout the interval.

Example 3.2   Let's return to Example 3.1, $f(x) = x^3 - 3x$. Using the first derivative, we determined that f is increasing from $-\infty$ to $x = -1$, decreasing from $x = -1$ to $x = +1$, and increasing again from $x = +1$ to $+\infty$. Using only this first derivative test, we find that the graph of f could conceivably be composed of the three straight line segments shown in Figure 3.8.

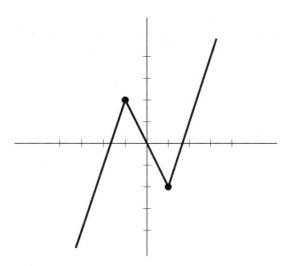

**Figure
3.8**

A candidate for the graph of $f(x) = x^3 - 3x$.

To make this sketch more accurate, we need to compute the regions of concavity and convexity. These regions can be found simply by computing the second derivative of the original function: $f''(x) = 6x$. We note easily that f'' is zero only at 0, that it is negative where x is negative, and that it is positive where x is positive. Therefore, f is concave for x negative and convex for x positive, as shown in Figure 3.3.

EXERCISES

3.3   For the functions in Exercise 3.1, compute the regions of convexity and concavity and include this information on your graphs.

3.4   Sketch the graph of a function which has the following properties:

        a) $f'(x) > 0$ for $x < 1$;   *b)* $f'(x) < 0$ for $x > 1$;
        c) $f''(x) < 0$ for $x < 2$;   *d)* $f''(x) > 0$ for $x > 2$.

3.5   Sketch the graph of a function which has the following properties:
    a) $f'(x) > 0$ for $-4 < x < -2$ and $2 < x < 4$;
    b) $f'(x) < 0$ for $-\infty < x < -4$, $-2 < x < +2$, and $4 < x < \infty$;
    c) $f''(x) > 0$ for $-\infty < x < -3$ and $0 < x < 3$;
    d) $f''(x) < 0$ for $-3 < x < 0$ and for $3 < x < \infty$.

3.3   GRAPHING RATIONAL FUNCTIONS

We complete our discussion of the use of derivatives to sketch the graphs of functions by working with rational functions. Because rational functions have denominators, they are more challenging to graph than polynomials. Furthermore, it is usually easier to visualize the graph of a polynomial than it is the graph of a rational function.

The simplest rational function is $f(x) = 1/x$, whose graph is pictured in Figure 3.9. Since the denominator of a fraction cannot be zero, this function is not defined at $x = 0$. Furthermore, as x approaches 0 from the negative side, the value of $f(x)$ goes to $-\infty$, and as x approaches 0 from the positive side, the value of $f(x)$ goes to $+\infty$. In both cases, the graph of f "cuddles up" to the vertical line through the point $x = 0$, where the function is not defined. Such a vertical line is called a **vertical asymptote** of f.

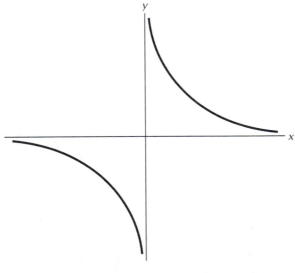

The graph of $f(x) = 1/x$.

**Figure
3.9**

In general, if f is a rational function whose denominator is zero at the point x_0 (and whose numerator is not zero at x_0), then the vertical line $\{x = x_0\}$ is a vertical asymptote of f. On either side of this vertical asymptote, the graph of f goes to $+\infty$ or to $-\infty$; one uses calculus techniques to find out which.

In sketching the graph of a rational function, treat the zeros of the denominator of a rational function like the first and second order critical points that arise in the process of finding the signs of f' and of f'', because f' and f'' can change sign as one crosses a vertical asymptote. In other words, use them to divide the line into intervals on which f' or f'' have constant sign. If f' is negative on the interval just to the left of the vertical asymptote, then f must go to $-\infty$ to the left of the asymptote, since f is decreasing there, just as it is for $1/x$ in Figure 3.9. By similar logic, if f' is positive on that interval, then f goes to $+\infty$ just to the left of the vertical asymptote. A similar analysis works for points on the right-hand side of the vertical asymptote.

Hints for Graphing

(1) Remember that to find the x-intercept of a rational function, you need only set the *numerator* equal to zero. If there is no x-intercept in a given interval between critical points and/or asymptotes, the graph does not cross the x-axis in that interval — an observation which may prove very helpful in sketching an accurate graph.

(2) Since the function, its first derivative, and its second derivative all provide information about each other in the graph of a function, avoid using the word "it" in referring to any of these functions, both in your own mind and in discussing the process of graphing the function with anyone else. If you carefully keep track of which derivative of the function you are working with at any one time, you will save yourself some confusion.

EXERCISES

3.6 Use calculus to sketch the graph of $16(x + 1)/(x - 2)^2$.

3.4 TAILS AND HORIZONTAL ASYMPTOTES

To complete our guide to drawing graphs of polynomials and rational functions, we turn our attention to the "tails" of the graph — the shape of the graph for large positive and large negative values of x.

Tails of Polynomials

For polynomials, the **leading term** — the monomial of highest degree — determines the shape of the tail of the graph. To see why this is true, consider a concrete example: the cubic $x^3 - 4x^2 + 5x - 6$. If x is very big, say $x = 10^{10}$, then x^3 will be 10^{30} — a number with 31 digits. On the other hand, $-4x^2$ will be $-4 \cdot 10^{20}$ — a number with only 21 digits. For $x = 10^{10}$, adding $-4x^2$ to x^3 will not affect the 10 left-most digits of x^3. A calculator which displays only 10 significant digits will not display the effect of this addition at all. The effect of the $5x + 6$ terms is minuscule by comparison. As x gets larger still, the effect of the nonleading terms on the leading term becomes even more insignificant.

In summary, for $|x|$ very large, the graph of a polynomial

$$f(x) = a_0 x^k + a_1 x^{k-1} + \cdots + a_{k-1}x + a_k$$

is determined completely by its leading term $a_0 x^k$. To graph the tail of a general polynomial, we need only know how to graph a general monomial. The graph of the monomial $a_0 x^k$ is determined by the sign of a_0 and the parity of k. If k is even, then both tails go to $+\infty$ as $|x| \to \infty$ if $a_0 > 0$, and both tails go to $-\infty$ as $|x| \to \infty$ if $a_0 < 0$. Think of the graphs of x^2 and of $-x^2$ as examples. If k is odd, one tail of the graph goes to $+\infty$ and the other to $-\infty$ as $|x| \to \infty$, depending once again on the sign of a_0. Think of the graphs of x^3 and $-x^3$ as examples of this phenomenon.

Horizontal Asymptotes of Rational Functions

Next, consider a general rational function:

$$g(x) = \frac{a_0 x^k + a_1 x^{k-1} + \cdots + a_{k-1}x + a_k}{b_0 x^m + b_1 x^{m-1} + \cdots + b_{m-1}x + b_m}, \qquad a_0, b_0 \neq 0.$$

For $|x|$ very large, the behavior of the numerator polynomial is determined by its leading term $a_0 x^k$ and the behavior of the denominator polynomial is determined by its leading term $b_0 x^m$. In other words, for $|x|$ large, the rational function g mirrors the behavior of the monomial

$$\ell(x) = \frac{a_0 x^k}{b_0 x^m} = \frac{a_0}{b_0} x^{k-m}.$$

In particular, if $k > m$, then $\ell(x)$ is a monomial with a positive degree, and the tails of the rational function g go to $\pm\infty$, just like those of a polynomial. On the other hand, if $k < m$, then $\ell(x) \to 0$ as $|x| \to \infty$, just as $1/x$ does in Figure 3.9. In this case, both tails of g are asymptotic to the x-axis as $|x| \to \infty$. We say that the x-axis is a **horizontal asymptote** for the graph of g. This is the situation which arises in Exercise 3.6. Finally, if $k = m$, then the quotient $\ell(x)$ of the leading terms of g is a nonzero constant a_0/b_0. As $|x| \to \infty$, $g(x) \to a_0/b_0$; the graph is asymptotic to the horizontal line $y = a_0/b_0$. This horizontal line is also called a **horizontal asymptote** of the graph of g. Look for both vertical and horizontal asymptotes in the graphs of the rational functions in the exercise below.

EXERCISES

3.7   Sketch the graph of each of the following rational functions:

$$a)\ \frac{x}{x^2-1};\qquad b)\ \frac{x}{x^2+1};\qquad c)\ \frac{x^2}{x+1};$$

$$d)\ \frac{x^2+3x}{x^2-1};\qquad e)\ \frac{x^2+1}{x};\qquad f)\ \frac{1}{x^2+1}.$$

3.8   In each of the four graphs below, the graph of the first derivative f' of a function f is sketched. In each case, determine where the function itself is increasing, decreasing, concave up, and concave down. Put this information on a number line and sketch the graph of the function f, assuming that $f(0) = 0$.

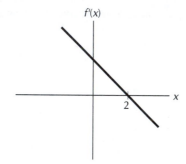

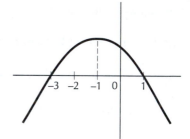

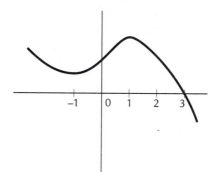

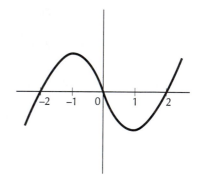

**Figure
3.10**

Graphs of four f'''s.

3.5   MAXIMA AND MINIMA

One of the major uses of calculus in mathematical models is to find and characterize maxima and minima of functions. For example, economists are interested in maximizing utility and profit and in minimizing cost. Recall that a function f has a local or relative maximum at x_0 if $f(x) \leq f(x_0)$ for all x in some open interval containing x_0; f has a global or absolute maximum at x_0 if $f(x) \leq f(x_0)$ for all x in the domain of f. The function f has a local or relative minimum at x_0 if $f(x) \geq f(x_0)$ for all x in some open interval containing x_0; f has a global or absolute minimum at x_0 if $f(x) \geq f(x_0)$ for all x in the domain of f. See the discussion and graphs at the beginning of Chapter 2.

If f has a local maximum (minimum) at x_0, we will simply say that x_0 is a max (min) of f. If we want to emphasize that f has a *global* maximum (minimum) at x_0, we will say that x_0 is a global max (global min) of f.

Local Maxima and Minima on the Boundary and in the Interior

A max or min of a function can occur at an endpoint of the domain of f or at a point which is not an endpoint — in the "interior" of the domain. These two cases are illustrated in Figures 3.11 and 3.12 for functions whose domains are the closed interval $[0, 1]$. In Figure 3.11, f is increasing on $[0, 1]$ and so its max occurs at the endpoint $x = 1$ of $[0, 1]$. In Figure 3.12, the max of f occurs at $x = 1/3$ in the interior of the domain $[0, 1]$. We will call a max (or min) that occurs at a boundary point of the domain of f a **boundary max** or (**boundary min**). We will call a max (or min) which is not an endpoint of the domain of f an **interior max** (or **interior min**). Of course, if the domain of f is all of $\mathbf{R}^1$ or is an open interval, then any max of f will be an interior max.

The calculus criterion for an interior max or min of f is easy to state and to understand.

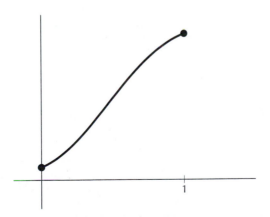

Function with a boundary max at $x = 1$.

**Figure
3.11**

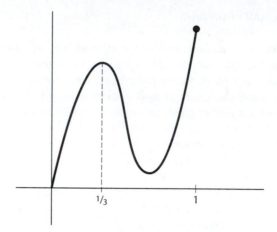

**Figure
3.12**

Function with an interior max at x = 1/3.

Theorem 3.3   If x_0 is an interior max or min of f, then x_0 is a critical point of f.

Proof   From an analytic point of view, a function is neither increasing nor decreasing on an interval about an interior max or min. By Theorem 3.1, its first derivative cannot be positive or negative there; that is, $f'(x_0)$ must be zero or undefined — x_0 is a critical point of f. From a geometric point of view, if the graph of f has a tangent line at a max or a min, that tangent line must be horizontal since the graph turns around there, as in Figure 3.13. In other words, $f'(x_0)$ must be zero. ■

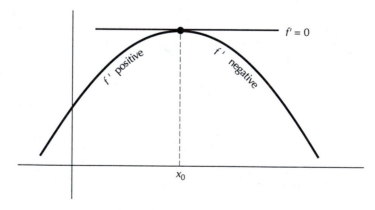

**Figure
3.13**

The graph of f at a max x_0.

Example 3.3   For the function $f(x) = x^3 - 3x$, pictured in Figure 3.3, the local max and local min occur at the critical points $x = -1$ and $x = +1$, respectively.

Example 3.4   As Figure 3.11 illustrates, the derivative of f at a *boundary* max or min need not be zero. The production function pictured in Figure 3.4 has domain $[0, \infty)$. Since it is an increasing function, its (global) min occurs at the boundary point $x = 0$, where the derivative of f is not necessarily zero.

Second Order Conditions

If x_0 is a critical point of a function f, how can we use calculus to decide whether critical point x_0 is a max, a min, or neither? The answer to this question lies in the *second* derivative of f at x_0.

Theorem 3.4

    (*a*) If $f'(x_0) = 0$ and $f''(x_0) < 0$, then x_0 is a max of f;
    (*b*) if $f'(x_0) = 0$ and $f''(x_0) > 0$, then x_0 is a min of f; and
    (*c*) if $f'(x_0) = 0$ and $f''(x_0) = 0$, then x_0 can be a max, a min, or neither.

Proof   We will present a proof of part *a* and leave the proof of part *b* as an exercise. From a geometric point of view, $f'(x_0) = 0$ means that the tangent line to the graph of f is horizontal at x_0, and $f''(x_0) < 0$ means that the graph curves downward, as in Figure 3.13. These two conditions together imply that f has a local max at x_0. From a more analytic point of view, $f''(x_0) < 0$ means that the first derivative f' of f is a decreasing function in an interval about x_0. The facts that f' is decreasing and that $f'(x_0) = 0$ mean that f' is positive to the left of x_0 and negative to the right of x_0. By Theorem 3.1, these two derivative conditions imply that f is increasing to the left of x_0 and decreasing to the right of x_0. In other words, f has a local max at x_0.

    To verify statement c — that anything can happen when $f'(x_0) = 0$ and $f''(x_0) = 0$ — consider the four graphs in Figure 3.14. Each of these four functions satisfies $f'(0) = 0$ and $f''(0) = 0$. However, 0 is a local min for f_1 and a local max for f_2, while f_3 is strictly increasing at 0 and f_4 is strictly decreasing at 0. ∎

Remark   A critical point of f at which the second derivative f'' is zero too is called a **degenerate critical point** of f. As part c of Theorem 3.4 indicates, to determine whether or not any given degenerate critical point is a max, a min, or neither, one needs more information about the function than the sign of its second derivative — information like the sign of f' on a whole interval about the critical point.

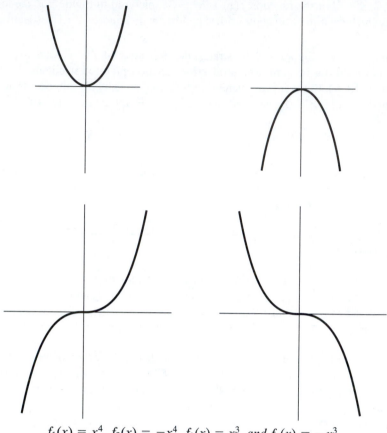

**Figure
3.14**
$f_1(x) = x^4, f_2(x) = -x^4, f_3(x) = x^3,$ *and* $f_4(x) = -x^3.$

Example 3.5   Let's use Theorem 3.4 to find the local max and mins of $f(x) = x^4 - 4x^3 + 4x^2 + 4$. The critical points of f are the solutions of

$$f'(x) = 4x^3 - 12x^2 + 8x = 4x(x - 1)(x - 2) = 0,$$

that is, $x = 0, 1, 2$. These three points are the only candidates for a max or min of f. Let's check the second derivative, $f''(x) = 12x^2 - 24x + 8$, at these three points:

$$f''(0) = 8 > 0, \quad f''(1) = -4 < 0, \quad \text{and} \quad f''(2) = 8 > 0.$$

By Theorem 3.4, $x = 0$ and $x = 2$ are local mins of f and $x = 1$ is a local max. The graph of f is presented in Figure 3.15.

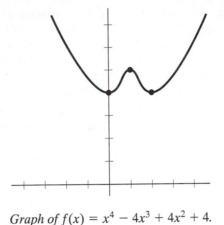

**Figure
3.15**

Graph of $f(x) = x^4 - 4x^3 + 4x^2 + 4$.

Global Maxima and Minima

Note that $x = 0$ and $x = 2$ are global minima of f in Figure 3.15. However, $x = 1$ is definitely not a global max, since f eventually takes on arbitrarily large values as $x \to \infty$. In Figure 3.12, neither critical point is a global max or min of f.

In some problems, we want conditions which will guarantee that a critical point is a *global* max or a *global* min of the function under consideration. For example, if Figure 3.15 represents the profit function of a firm, the firm would be foolish to settle for the local max at $x = 1$, since it can generate arbitrarily large profits by choosing a large value of x. In fact, the function $f(x) = x^4 - 4x^3 + 4x^2 + 4$ has no global max.

In general, it is difficult to find a global max of a function or even to prove that a given local max is a global max. There are, however, three situations in which this problem is somewhat easier:

(1) when f has only one critical point in its domain,
(2) when $f'' > 0$ or $f'' < 0$ throughout the domain of f, and
(3) when the domain of f is a closed finite interval.

We will examine each of these situations.

Functions with Only One Critical Point

Theorem 3.5   Suppose that:

   (a) the domain of f is an interval I (finite or infinite) in $\mathbf{R}^1$,
   (b) x_0 is a local maximum of f, and
   (c) x_0 is the only critical point of f on I.

Then, x_0 is the global maximum of f on I.

Proof   We will show that if x_0 is not the global maximum of f, then f must have another critical point on I. Suppose there is a point y_0 in I with $f(y_0) > f(x_0)$. Suppose further that $y_0 > x_0$. (The case where $y_0 < x_0$ is left as an exercise.) Since f is decreasing just to the right of x_0 and eventually increasing again somewhere to the left of y_0, it must change from decreasing to increasing somewhere between x_0 and y_0, say at z_0. But then z_0 is an interior local minimum of f, and therefore is a critical point other than x_0 — contradicting the hypothesis that x_0 is the only critical point of f. Therefore, x_0 is the global maximum of f on its domain I. ∎

Functions with Nowhere-Zero Second Derivatives

Theorem 3.6   If f is a C^2 function whose domain is an interval I and if f'' is never zero on I, then f has at most one critical point in I. This critical point is a global minimum if $f'' > 0$ and a global maximum if $f'' < 0$.

Proof   Suppose f'' is always positive on domain I. By Theorem 3.2, f' is an increasing function on I. This means that f' can be zero at at most one point. If there *is* a point x_0 where $f'(x_0) = 0$, then x_0 is a local minimum of f since $f''(x_0) > 0$. By Theorem 3.5, x_0 is the *global* minimum of f. ∎

   It follows from Theorem 3.6, and the fact that a function f is convex if and only if $-f$ is concave, that if f is a C^2 convex function, then a critical point of f defined on an interval in $\mathbf{R}^1$ is necessarily a global minimum of f. Any local maximum of f must occur on an endpoint of its domain. Similarly, a critical point of a C^2 concave function f is necessarily a global maximum of x; any local minimum must occur on an endpoint of its domain.

Functions with No Global Max or Min

A function whose domain is an open interval need not have a global maximum or minimum in its domain. For example, the function $f(x) = x^3 - 3x$, whose graph is pictured in Figure 3.3, has neither a global maximum nor a global minimum since its value goes to $+\infty$ as $x \to \infty$ and to $-\infty$ as $x \to -\infty$. Any strictly increasing or strictly decreasing function whose domain is an *open* interval will not have a maximum or a minimum in its domain. At the same time, there exist functions that have a global minimum but no global maximum in their domain. Examples are the function x^4, which is pictured in Figure 3.14, and the function $x^4 - 4x^3 + 4x^2 + 4$, which is pictured in Figure 3.15.

Functions Whose Domains Are Closed Finite Intervals

However, a famous theorem by Weierstrass states that a continuous function whose domain is a *closed and bounded* interval $[a, b]$ must have both a global maximum and a global minimum in this domain (see Theorem 30.1). Furthermore, as we will now see, there is a natural method for calculating these global extrema.

By Theorem 3.3, an interior maximum or minimum of any function must be a critical point of f. The only other candidates for a maximum or minimum are the two endpoints of the domain: $x = a$ and $x = b$. So, if we're looking for the global maximum of a C^1 function f with domain $[a, b]$, we need only:

(1) compute the critical points of f by solving $f'(x) = 0$ for x in (a, b),
(2) evaluate f at these critical points and at the endpoints a and b of its domain, and
(3) choose the point from among these that gives the largest value of f in step 2.

Example 3.6   Suppose that x years after its founding in 1960, the Association of Smart Statisticians had a membership given by the function $f(x) = 2x^3 - 45x^2 + 300x + 500$. In the period between 1960 and 1980, what was its largest and its smallest membership and when were these two extremes realized? Mathematically, this is the problem of maximizing $f(x) = 2x^3 - 45x^2 + 300x + 500$ for x in the closed interval $[0, 20]$. The critical points of f, the solutions of

$$0 = f'(x) = 6x^2 - 90x + 300$$

$$= 6(x^2 - 15x + 50)$$

$$= 6(x - 5)(x - 10),$$

are $x = 5, 10$. To solve the problem, we need only evaluate f at the critical points $x = 5, 10$ and at the boundary points $x = 0, 20$:

$$f(0) = 500, \quad f(5) = 1125, \quad f(10) = 1000, \quad f(20) = 10375.$$

Therefore, the global max occurs at $x = 20$ and the global min occurs at $x = 0$.

EXERCISES

3.9   For each of the following functions f with specified domains D_1 and D_2, find the global maximum and the global minimum of f on each D_i if they exist. Justify your answers.

a) $1/x$ on $D_1 = (1, 2)$ and   on $D_2 = [1, 2]$,

b) $x^3 + 3x$ on $D_1 = (-\infty, +\infty)$ and   on $D_2 = [0, 1]$,

c) $x^3 - 3x$ on $D_1 = [-4, -2]$ and   on $D_2 = [0, \infty)$,

d) $x^2/(x + 1)$ on $D_1 = [0, 10]$ and   on $D_2 = [0, \infty)$,

e) $3x^5 - 5x^3$ on $D_1 = [-2, +2]$ and   on $D_2 = [-\sqrt{2}, +\sqrt{2}]$,

f) $x + (1/x)$ on $D_1 = (0, \infty)$ and   on $D_2 = (-\infty, 0)$,

g) $1/(1 + x^2)$ on $D_1 = (-\infty, +\infty)$ and on $D_2 = [1, 2]$,

h) $3x + 5 + (75/x)$ on $D_1 = [-2, +2]$ and on $D_2 = [1, 10]$.

3.10   A manufacturer produces gizmos at a cost of $5 each. The manufacturer computes that if each gizmo sells for x dollars, $(15 - x)$ gizmos will be sold. What is the manufacturer's profit function? What price should the manufacturer charge to maximize profit?

3.11   A manufacturer can produce economics texts at a cost of $5 apiece. The text currently sells for $10, and at this price 10 texts are sold each day. The manufacturer figures that each dollar decrease in price will sell one additional copy each day. Write out the demand and profit functions. What price x maximizes profit?

3.12   Prove part b of Theorem 3.4.

3.13   Draw the appropriate figure to illustrate the proof of Theorem 3.5, and carry out the proof of Theorem 3.5 for the case in which $y_0 < x_0$.

3.14   Adapt the argument in the proof of Theorem 3.6 to the case where f'' is greater than *or equal to* zero on the domain I.

3.6   APPLICATIONS TO ECONOMICS

In this section we discuss some of the ways in which the concepts and techniques of calculus lead to a better understanding of the principles of economics. So far in this chapter, we have used calculus to study the properties of *specific* functions, like

$$x^3 - 3x \quad \text{and} \quad x^4 - 4x^3 + 4x^2 + 4$$

in Examples 3.1 and 3.5, respectively. We now need to move on to a consideration of *general* types of functions which are distinguished, not by their formulas, but by their properties.

Production Functions

Consider, as an example, a production function $y = f(q)$, which relates the amount of input q, say labor input, to the amount of output y that can be produced with q units of input. Because we want a theory that is broadly applicable when modeling the production process, we assume only that the production function we use has the properties pictured in Figure 3.4 and not that it has a specific functional form, like $f(q) = \sqrt{q}$. When we need to make assumptions about a production function, $y = f(q)$ in an economy, we will only assume that:

(1) it is continuous or maybe C^2,
(2) it is increasing, and
(3) there is a level of input a such that the production function is concave up, for $0 \le q < a$, and concave down for $q > a$.

If f is C^2, these assumptions translate to the following assumptions about the derivative of f:

(2′) $f'(q) > 0$ for all q, and

(3′) for some $a \geq 0$, $f''(q) > 0$ for $q \in [0, a)$ and $f''(q) < 0$ for $q > a$. $\qquad$ (4)

Occasionally, to build our intuition or to construct concrete models of economies, we will work with a general *class* of functional forms. For production functions, we often work with the two-parameter family of functions $y = kq^b$, where k and b are positive constants or **parameters**. Depending on the size of b, these functions are either always concave up or always concave down for $q > 0$. In particular, if $0 < b < 1$, $a = 0$ in (4) and $f(q)$ is always concave down; if $b > 1$, $a = \infty$ in (4) and $f(q)$ is always concave up. The fact that this class of production functions has two parameters which may be adjusted according to the production process under consideration adds some richness and flexibility to its use. Nevertheless, an economist should be uncomfortable with an economic principle that holds only for an economy governed by production functions in this class.

Cost Functions

A **cost function** $C(x)$ assigns to each level of *output x*, the total cost of producing that much output. Like production functions, cost functions are naturally increasing functions of their argument x. However, the independent variable for a cost function is the level of output, while the independent variable for a production function is the level of input.

The derivative $C'(x)$ of a cost function is called the **marginal cost** and is written $MC(x)$. As we discussed in Section 2.7, $MC(x)$ measures the additional cost incurred from the production of one more unit of output when the current output is x.

The **average cost function** also plays an important role in economic theory. It is the function

$$AC(x) = \frac{C(x)}{x},$$

which measures the cost per unit produced. Using calculus, one can derive some useful relationships between the marginal cost and average cost functions.

Theorem 3.7   Suppose the cost function $C(x)$ is a C^1 function. Then,

(a) if $MC > AC$, AC is increasing,
(b) if $MC < AC$, AC is decreasing, and
(c) at an interior minimum of AC, $AC = MC$.

Proof To show whether a function is increasing or decreasing, we need only compute the sign of its first derivative. Using the Quotient Rule, we compute that the first derivative of $AC(x)$ is

$$AC'(x) = \frac{d}{dx}\left(\frac{C(x)}{x}\right) = \frac{C'(x) \cdot x - 1 \cdot C(x)}{x^2}$$

$$= \frac{C'(x) - (C(x)/x)}{x} = \frac{MC - AC}{x}.$$

(a) If $MC > AC$, $AC'(x) > 0$ and $AC(x)$ is increasing.
(b) If $MC < AC$, $AC'(x) < 0$ and $AC(x)$ is decreasing.
(c) If x_0 is an interior minimum of $AC(x)$, then by Theorem 3.3, $AC'(x_0) = 0$ and $MC(x_0) = AC(x_0)$. ∎

Theorem 3.7 has a rich intuitive and geometric content. From an intuitive point of view, the theorem says that if you do better than your average some day, your average goes up that day. On days that you do worse than your average, your average goes down. For baseball fans, a batter who goes hitless in a game will see his batting average drop; a batter who has a "perfect day at the plate" will raise his batting average.

Taking a geometric point of view, consider the graph of cost function $y = C(x)$, as pictured in Figures 3.16 and 3.17. This graph is sometimes called a **cost curve**.

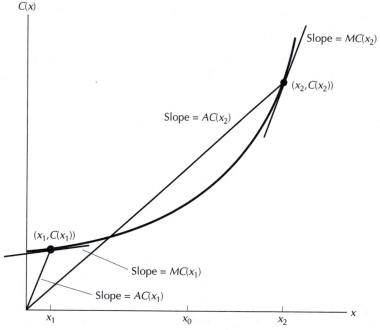

Figure 3.16 *At x_1, $AC > MC$ and AC is decreasing. At x_2, $MC > AC$ and AC is increasing.*

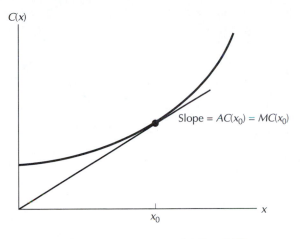

$$\text{Slope} = AC(x_0) = MC(x_0)$$

At x_0, AC is a minimum and AC = MC.

Figure 3.17

The marginal cost at point x, $MC(x)$, can be considered as the slope of the tangent line to this curve at the point $(x, C(x))$. The average cost at x,

$$AC(x) = \frac{C(x) - 0}{x - 0},$$

can be considered as the slope of the line segment from $(x, C(x))$ to the origin $(0, 0)$. The cost curve C in Figures 3.16 and 3.17 is an increasing function, and $C(0) > 0$ implies that there are some **fixed costs** — costs independent of the amount produced. At the points $(x_1, C(x_1))$ and $(x_2, C(x_2))$ on the cost curve in Figure 3.16, we have drawn the tangent line to the graph, whose slope represents $MC(x_i)$, and the line to the origin, whose slope represents $AC(x_i)$. Note that $AC(x_1) > MC(x_1)$ and that $AC(x)$ decreases as x increases from x_1. On the other hand, at the point $(x_2, C(x_2))$, $MC(x_2) > AC(x_2)$ and $AC(x)$ increases as x increases from x_2; this is consistent with Theorem 3.7. In Figure 3.17, we have drawn attention to the point $(x_0, C(x_0))$ on the graph where the slope of the line to the origin is at a minimum. At this minimizing point, $(x_0, C(x_0))$, the line to the origin is actually tangent to the graph: $AC(x_0) = MC(x_0)$, as Theorem 3.7 states.

As x increases from 0 to ∞ in Figures 3.16 and 3.17, the slope of the line from $(x, C(x))$ to the origin starts very large, decreases past x_1, reaches its minimum value at x_0, and then increases again as x passes x_2 and becomes arbitrarily large. If we graph this slope, that is, if we graph the average cost curve $AC(x)$, versus x, we find a U-shaped curve, as pictured in Figure 3.18. We have also drawn the marginal cost curve MC in Figure 3.18. The critical property in this figure is that for $x < x_0$, the MC-curve lies below the AC-curve while AC is decreasing; for $x > x_0$, the MC-curve lies above the AC-curve as AC increases. Figure 3.18 plays a major role in the study of the firm in intermediate microeconomics courses.

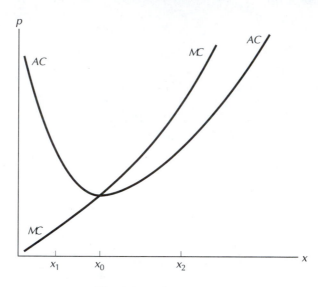

Figure 3.18

The AC- and MC-curves.

Revenue and Profit Functions

Let $C(x)$ continue to denote a firm's cost function relative to its output x. Let $R(x)$ be the firm's **revenue function**, the function which indicates how much money a firm receives for selling x units of its output. Like $C(x)$, $R(x)$ should be an increasing function of x. We write $MR(x)$ for the firm's marginal revenue function $R'(x)$. If $p(x)$ is the unit price when the firm's output is x units, then $R(x)$ is simply $p(x) \cdot x$. In a model of **perfect competition**, that is, a model characterized by the assumptions that there are many firms and that no individual firm can control the output price by its productive activity, the price any firm receives for its output is a constant $p(x) = p$, independent of the amount x it produces. In this case, the firm's revenue function is simply the linear function $R(x) = p \cdot x$, and

$$MR = AR = p; \tag{5}$$

marginal revenue and average revenue are equal.

A firm's **profit function** is simply the difference

$$\Pi(x) = R(x) - C(x)$$

between its revenue and its cost at any level of output x. Economists often use the uppercase Greek letter pi, Π, to denote profit. The domain of Π, R, and C is generally the nonnegative half-line $[0, \infty)$. If we assume that the goal of the firm is to choose the output level x^* that maximizes its profit, then by Theorem 3.3, the optimal output level x^* — if not zero — satisfies

$$\frac{d\Pi}{dx}(x^*) = \frac{dR}{dx}(x^*) - \frac{dC}{dx}(x^*) = MR(x^*) - MC(x^*) = 0,$$

or
$$MR(x^*) = MC(x^*).$$

This principle, that marginal revenue equals marginal cost at the optimal output, is one of the cornerstones of economic theory. It is a rather intuitive guideline. A firm should continue producing output until the cost of producing one more unit (MC) is just offset by the revenue that the additional unit will bring in (MR). If the firm will receive more for the next unit than that unit will add to its cost ($MR > MC$), then producing that next unit will increase the firm's profit and it should carry out the production. If the cost of making one more unit is more than the revenue that the unit will bring in the market ($MC > MR$), then producing that additional unit will cut into the firm's profit; the firm should have stopped production earlier.

Let's look more carefully at the perfectly competitive case where the revenue function is $R(x) = p \cdot x$. In Figure 3.19, we have drawn a typical average cost (AC) and marginal cost (MC) curve, as in Figure 3.18. We have added a horizontal line at $y = p$ to represent a firm's marginal revenue (MR) and average revenue curve (AR), according to (5). The optimal output point x^* — where $MR = MC$ — is darkened in Figure 3.19 at the intersection of the MR- and MC-curves.

If the market price p of the output were to increase, the MR-line $y = p$ in Figure 3.19 would move up and the corresponding optimal output would increase too. At each stage, price p and optimal output x are related by the equation $p = MC(x)$ and the optimal output is represented by a point on the marginal cost

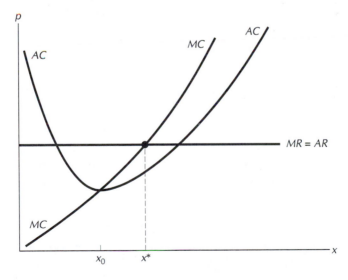

The AC-, MC-, AR-, and MR-curves for a competitive firm.

Figure 3.19

curve. Another way of stating the fact that, for every price, the optimal amount of output a firm will supply lies at the point where the horizontal price line crosses the MC-curve is to say that the MC-curve gives the locus of the price-optimal output combinations. In the language of economics, the MC-curve is the firm's **supply curve**, the curve which relates the market price to the amount produced.

Finally, we bring into the picture the second derivative condition that an interior optimal output x^* must satisfy. Since $\Pi'(x) = p - C'(x)$,

$$\Pi''(x) = 0 - C''(x).$$

At the interior maximizer, $\Pi''(x^*) \le 0$ by Theorem 3.4. This implies that $C''(x) \ge 0$ and leads to the principle that at its optimal output the firm should be experiencing *increasing marginal cost*.

Demand Functions and Elasticity

A firm's revenue function $R(x)$ can be written as the product of the amount sold times the unit selling price. In simple models, we assume that the amount sold equals the amount x produced. In the model of perfect competition analyzed in Figure 3.19, we assumed that the selling price is a scalar p that is independent of the amount produced. However, in models of monopoly (an industry with a single firm) and oligopoly (an industry dominated by a small number of firms), there is usually a relationship between the amount x of the product in the market and the price at which the product sells. If this relationship is represented by a function $x = F(p)$, which expresses the amount x consumed in terms of price level p, then F is called a **demand function**. If the relationship is expressed by a function $p = G(x)$ which expresses the price p in terms of the amount x being consumed, then G is called an **inverse demand function**. In a single-firm industry, it is the inverse demand function that is the natural factor of the revenue function, since the latter can be written as

$$R(x) = p \cdot x = G(x) \cdot x.$$

Since $G(x) = R(x)/x$, the inverse demand function is also the firm's average revenue function.

Economists, of course, are deeply interested in how changes in price affect changes in demand. The natural measure of this sensitivity is the slope of the demand function, $F'(p)$ or $\Delta x/\Delta p$. As we well know, this *marginal demand* describes the effect of a unit increase in price on the purchasing behavior of consumers. However, this sensitivity indicator has one major disadvantage: it is highly dependent on the units used to measure quantity and price. Suppose, for example, that a 10-cent increase in price will lead to a million-gallon decrease in the consumption of gasoline. The marginal demand is

$$\frac{\Delta x}{\Delta p} = \frac{-10^6}{10} = -10^5$$

if we measure x in gallons and p in cents. However, if we measure x in gallons and p in *dollars*, then the marginal demand changes by a factor of 100 to

$$\frac{\Delta x}{\Delta p} = \frac{-10^6}{.10} = -10^7. \tag{6}$$

Finally, if we use a million gallons as our unit of gasoline consumption and the cent as our unit of price, then the marginal demand becomes

$$\frac{\Delta x}{\Delta p} = \frac{-1}{10} = -0.1,$$

100 million times smaller than the measure in (6). Economists would like a measure of the sensitivity of demand to price changes which cannot be manipulated by choice of units and which can be used to compare consumption habits in different countries with different currencies and different measures of weight or volume.

The solution to this problem is to use the percent rate of change instead of the actual change. For any quantity, the **percent rate of change** is the actual change divided by the initial amount:

$$\frac{q_1 - q_0}{q_0} = \frac{\Delta q}{q_0}.$$

Since the numerator and denominator are measured in the same units, the units cancel out in this division process. For example, if the price changes from \$1.25 to \$1.50, the percent rate of change of price is

$$\frac{1.50 - 1.25}{1.25} = \frac{0.25}{1.25} = \frac{1}{5} = 20 \, \text{percent}.$$

It will be 20 percent whether we choose dollars, cents, or French franc equivalents as our unit of currency.

To keep the sensitivity measure completely free of units, we will measure both the change in quantity and the change in price in percentage terms. Our measure of sensitivity now becomes the *percent* change in quantity demanded divided by the *percent* change in price,

$$\frac{\Delta x}{x} \bigg/ \frac{\Delta p}{p}, \tag{7}$$

in other words, the percent change in demand for each 1 percent rise in price. This sensitivity measure is called the **price elasticity of demand** and usually represented by the Greek letter epsilon, ε. Rewrite the double quotient (7) as a single quotient:

$$\varepsilon = \frac{\Delta x}{x} \bigg/ \frac{\Delta p}{p} = \frac{\Delta x}{x} \cdot \frac{p}{\Delta p} = \frac{\Delta x}{\Delta p} \cdot \frac{p}{x} = \frac{\Delta x}{\Delta p} \bigg/ \frac{x}{p}. \tag{8}$$

The factor $\Delta x / \Delta p$ in the last two terms is just the marginal demand, while the quotient x/p in the last term is simply the average demand. So, the elasticity can be thought of as the marginal demand divided by the average demand.

The marginal demand can, of course, be well approximated by the slope $F'(p)$ of the demand function $x = F(p)$. Substituting $F'(p)$ for $\Delta x / \Delta p$ and $F(p)$ for x in (8) yields the calculus form of the **price elasticity**:

$$\varepsilon = \frac{F'(p) \cdot p}{F(p)}. \tag{9}$$

Notation   The discrete version (8) of the price elasticity is called the **arc elasticity** and is usually used to compute ε when we know only a finite number of price-quantity combinations. The differentiable version (9) of the price elasticity is called the **point elasticity** and is used when a continuous demand curve has been estimated or in proving theorems about price elasticity.

We will soon use (9) to prove an illuminating relationship between elasticity and total revenue or expenditure. First, we take a closer look at the elasticity and, in the process, introduce some more vocabulary. A basic assumption about demand functions is that raising the price of a commodity usually lowers the amount consumed. Mathematically speaking, demand is a decreasing function of price. (We are ignoring the empirically rare phenomenon of a Giffen good — a good for which lower prices lead to lower consumption.) This assumption means that $\Delta x / \Delta p$ in (8) and $F'(p)$ in (9) are negative numbers, as we saw in (6), and therefore that the price elasticity of a good is a negative number. (Some intermediate economics texts define the price elasticity as the absolute value of the expression in (8) or (9) to avoid dealing with negative numbers. We won't.)

A good which is rather insensitive to price changes will have a price elasticity close to zero. Necessities, like fuel oil and medical care, are good examples of this phenomenon. On the other hand, a good for which small price increases lead to large drops in consumption — speaking in terms of percentages — will have a price elasticity that is a large negative number. Luxury items, like Lamborghinis and ermine coats, and items with many close substitutes, like Froot Loops or Cap'n Crunch cereals, are examples of this phenomenon. The following definitions add some precision to these concepts.

Definition   A good whose price elasticity lies between 0 and -1 is called **inelastic**. A good whose price elasticity lies between -1 and $-\infty$ is called **elastic**. A good whose price elasticity equals -1 is said to be **unit elastic**.

If the price of a good goes up, the change in total expenditure on that good is, at first glance, indeterminate, since expenditure is price times quantity, and the two move in opposite directions. As the next theorem shows, the elasticity of the good in question resolves this ambiguity.

Theorem 3.8   For an inelastic good, an increase in price leads to an *increase* in total expenditure. For an elastic good, an increase in price leads to a *decrease* in total expenditure.

Proof Let $x = F(p)$ be the demand function for the good under study. The total expenditure at price p is

$$E(p) = p \cdot x = p \cdot F(p).$$

To see whether $E(p)$ is increasing or decreasing, we need only check the sign of its first derivative. By the Product Rule,

$$E'(p) = p \cdot F'(p) + 1 \cdot F(p).$$

Divide both sides by the *positive* quantity $F(p)$:

$$\frac{E'(p)}{F(p)} = \frac{p \cdot F'(p)}{F(p)} + 1 = \varepsilon + 1, \tag{10}$$

by (9). If the good is inelastic, $-1 < \varepsilon < 0$ and $\varepsilon + 1 > 0$. In this case, (10) is positive, $E'(p)$ is positive, and therefore $E(p)$ is an increasing function of p. Similarly, if the good is elastic, $\varepsilon < -1$ and $\varepsilon + 1 < 0$. Now, each expression in (10) is negative, $E'(p)$ is negative, and therefore $E(p)$ is a decreasing function of p. ∎

In working with concrete economic models, economists sometimes use specific functional forms for the economy's demand functions, especially **linear demand**

$$x = F(p) \equiv a - bp, \qquad a, b > 0, \tag{11}$$

and **constant elasticity demand**

$$x = F(p) \equiv kp^{-r}, \qquad k, r > 0. \tag{12}$$

For (11), the demand function is a straight line segment with negative slope $-b$ and x-intercept a, as pictured in Figure 3.20. Since the slope of F differs from

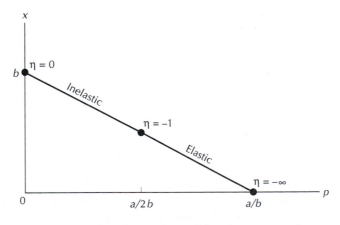

The graph of the linear demand function $x = a - bp$.

Figure 3.20

the elasticity of F, it should not be surprising that the elasticity varies along the demand curve:

$$\varepsilon \equiv \frac{F'(p) \cdot p}{F(p)} = \frac{-bp}{a - bp} = \frac{1}{1 - (a/bp)}$$

from $\varepsilon = 0$ when $p = 0$ and $x = a$ to $\varepsilon = -\infty$ when $p = a/b$ and $x = 0$.

In Figure 3.20, the graph of the demand function $x = F(p)$ is drawn in what appears to be the most natural way — with the independent variable p measured along the horizontal axis and the dependent variable x measured along the vertical axis. However, for all the other quantity-price relationships we have studied so far — cost, revenue, profit, and their marginal and average manifestations — the output x was naturally the independent variable and was represented along the horizontal x-axis while the price variable was naturally the dependent variable and was represented along the vertical y-axis. Because this use of the horizontal and vertical axes is the more common situation for economic functions and because we will want to incorporate the demand relationship into our graphical studies of revenue, cost, and profit curves, as in Figure 3.19, as average revenue curves, we will graph the demand relationship with quantity on the horizontal axis and price on the vertical axis.

This section concludes with the incorporation of the demand, average revenue, and marginal revenue curves into our analyses of the cost curves in Figure 3.18. This was done in Figure 3.19 for the case of perfect competition where the average revenue curve was a horizontal line. Now treat the antipodal case of a pure monopolist facing a linear demand curve $x = a - bp$ for its product. The inverse demand curve is

$$p = \frac{a}{b} - \frac{1}{b}x. \tag{13}$$

If the monopolist wants to sell x units, it will have to charge the price p given by (13). Therefore, the monopolist's revenue function is

$$R(x) = \left(\frac{a}{b} - \frac{1}{b}x \right) \cdot x.$$

The marginal revenue is

$$R'(x) = \frac{a}{b} - \frac{2}{b}x,$$

a curve with the same p-intercept but with twice the slope of the average revenue (= inverse demand) curve. These curves are sketched in Figure 3.21. The optimal output occurs at the point x^* above which the MR- and MC-curves cross. The corresponding selling price p^* can be read off the demand curve above x^* (*not* from

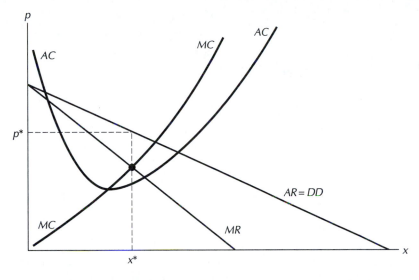

The MC-, AC-, MR- and AR-curves for a pure monopolist.

Figure 3.21

the *MR*-curve). One can use Figure 3.21 to show, for example, that if manufacturing costs increase so that the *MC*-curve rises, then output will decline and price will rise.

EXERCISES

3.15 Show that the function $f(x) = x^3 + x + 1$ has the essential properties of a cost function. Carefully graph its corresponding average cost function and marginal cost function on the same coordinate axes and compare your answer with Figure 3.18.

3.16 What happens to a competitive firm whose cost function exhibits *decreasing* marginal cost everywhere? Construct a concrete cost function of this type and carry out the search for the profit-maximizing output.

3.17 *a*) Which rectangle in Figure 3.19 has an area equal to the firm's optimal revenue at $x = x^*$?

  b) Using the fact that $AC(x) = C(x)/x$ and therefore $C(x) = AC(x) \cdot x$, find the rectangle whose area gives the total cost of output x^*.

  c) Which area in Figure 3.19 represents the firm's optimal profit?

3.18 Prove that the point elasticity is -1 exactly at the midpoint of the linear demand in Figure 3.20.

3.19 Compute the point elasticity for the demand function (12) and conclude why (12) is called the constant elasticity demand.

3.20 What happens to x^* and p^* if the demand curve rises in Figure 3.21?

3.21 Indicate carefully the rectangle in Figure 3.21 whose area gives the monopolist's profit.

3.22 For $F(p) = a - bp$ and $C(x) = kx^2$, calculate explicitly the formula for the optimal output and its price.

One-Variable Calculus: Chain Rule

Many economic situations involve chains of relationships between economic variables: variable A affects variable B which in turn affects variable C. For example, in a model of a firm, the amount of input used determines the amount of output produced, and the amount of output produced determines the firm's revenue. Revenue is a direct function of output and an indirect or composite function of input. This chapter presents the **Chain Rule**, which describes the derivative of a composite function in terms of the derivatives of its component functions, so that if the effect of a change in input on output is known and the effect of a change in output on revenue is known, the effect of a change in input on revenue can be computed.

Section 4.2 focuses on invertible functions. Such functions correspond to relationships between economic variables, say A and B, in which sometimes we want to understand the effect of A on B and other times we are more interested in how B affects A. For example, economists are usually concerned about how a price increase affects demand, but they sometimes focus on how a change in demand affects prices. There is, of course, a close relationship between the derivative of a function and the derivative of its inverse function; if we know one, we can deduce the other. We will use the concept of an inverse function and its derivative in the next chapter when we study the logarithmic function as the inverse of the exponential function.

Finally, at the end of this chapter, these mathematical results are used to compute the derivative of the function $f(x) = x^{m/n}$. This function arises naturally in many economic models, such as Cobb-Douglas utility and production functions.

4.1 COMPOSITE FUNCTIONS AND THE CHAIN RULE

Composite Functions

Section 2.4 described the rules for computing the derivative of a function that is formed by taking the sum, difference, product, or quotient of two other functions. This section presents and then applies the Chain Rule — the formula for differentiating a function which is formed by taking the *composition* of two other functions. If g and h are two functions on $\mathbf{R}^1$, the function formed by first applying function g to any number x and then applying function h to the result $g(x)$ is called the **composition** of functions g and h and is written as

$$f(x) = h(g(x)) \quad \text{or} \quad f(x) = (h \circ g)(x).$$

The function f is called the **composite** of functions h and g; we say that "f is h composed with g" and the "f is g followed by h."

Example 4.1   For example, if $g(x) = x^2$ and $h(x) = x+4$, then $(h \circ g)(x) = x^2+4$. If the order of composition is reversed in this case, then $(g \circ h)(x) = (x + 4)^2$. Note that $h \circ g \neq g \circ h$.

When we compose two functions, we are taking a function of a function. For example, if the second function raises x to the power k, that is, if $h(x) = x^k$, then $h(g(x)) = (g(x))^k$ raises $g(x)$ to the power k. This is the most common composite function one meets in the calculus of polynomials and rational functions. However, when dealing with exponential, logarithmic, and trigonometric functions, one regularly deals with general composite functions.

Example 4.2   The functions which describe a firm's behavior, such as its profit function Π, are usually written as functions of a firm's *output y*. If one wants to study the dependence of a firm's profit on the amount of labor *input L* it uses, one must compose the profit function with the firm's production function $y = f(L)$, the function which tells how much output y the firm can obtain from L units of labor input. The result is a function

$$\mathcal{P}(L) \equiv \Pi\left(f(L)\right) = (\Pi \circ f)(L).$$

For example, if

$$\Pi(y) = -y^4 + 6y^2 - 5 \quad \text{and} \quad f(L) = 5L^{2/3}, \tag{1}$$

then
$$\mathcal{P}(L) = \Pi(f(L)$$
$$= -(5L^{2/3})^4 + 6(5L^{2/3})^2 - 5$$
$$= -625L^{8/3} + 150L^{4/3} - 5. \tag{2}$$

Note that a different letter is used to denote profit as a function of L than to denote profit as a function of y, simply because they are different functions.

Example 4.3   Composite functions arise naturally in **dynamic models** — models in which the variables vary over time. For example, let $x = F(p)$ denote the market demand function for a commodity in terms of its price. Suppose that because of inflation or external events, the commodity's price changes over time according to the function $p = p(t)$. Then, the commodity's demand will also vary over time, in accordance with the composite function

$$\mathcal{F}(t) \equiv F(p(t)).$$

When working with a composite function $f(x) = h(g(x))$, it is natural to call the first function one applies (g in this case) the **inside function** and the second function one applies (h in this case) the **outside function**. For example, in the composition $(x^2 + 3x + 2)^7$, the inside function is $g(x) = x^2 + 3x + 2$ and the outside function is $h(z) = z^7$.

Differentiating Composite Functions: The Chain Rule

In Section 2.4, we introduced the *Power Rule*, which is the rule for taking the derivative of a composite function in which the outside function is $h(z) = z^k$ for some exponent k:

$$\text{Power Rule:} \quad \frac{d}{dx}(g(x))^k = k(g(x))^{k-1} \cdot g'(x). \tag{3}$$

In words, the derivative of a function to the kth power is k times the function to the $(k-1)$th power times the derivative of the function. Since the derivative of $h(z) = z^k$ is $h'(z) = kz^{k-1}$, we can think of (3) as the derivative of the outside function h (evaluated at the inside function g) times the derivative of the inside function g; in symbols,

$$\frac{d}{dx}(h(g(x))) = h'(g(x)) \cdot g'(x). \tag{4}$$

Formula (4) is precisely the formula for differentiating a general composite $h \circ g$ of two functions h and g. In this general form, it is called the **Chain Rule**. It is often quickly summarized as "the derivative of the outside times the derivative of the inside," but one must remember that the derivative of the outside function is evaluated at the inside function.

Example 4.4 Let's apply the Chain Rule (4) to compute the derivative of the composite function $\mathcal{P} = \Pi \circ f$, given by (1) in Example 4.2. The outside function is

$$\Pi(\ ) = -(\ )^4 + 6(\ )^2 - 5;$$

the derivative of the outside function is

$$\Pi'(\ ) = -4(\ )^3 + 12(\ ),$$

and the derivative evaluated at the inside function $f(L) = 5L^{2/3}$ is

$$\Pi'(f(L)) = -4(5L^{2/3})^3 + 12(5L^{2/3}).$$

On the other hand, the derivative of the inside function f is

$$f'(L) = \frac{10}{3}L^{-1/3}.$$

Multiplying these two expressions according to the Chain Rule (3) yields

$$P'(L) = \frac{d}{dL}\left(\Pi(f(L))\right) = \Pi'(f(L)) \cdot f'(L)$$

$$= \left(-4(5L^{2/3})^3 + 12(5L^{2/3})\right) \cdot \left(\frac{10}{3}L^{-1/3}\right),$$

which after simplifying equals

$$(-4 \cdot 125L^2 + 60L^{2/3}) \cdot \left(\frac{10}{3}L^{-1/3}\right) = -\frac{5000}{3}L^{5/3} + 200L^{1/3}.$$

Note that this agrees with what we compute by directly taking the derivative of the expression (2) for the composite function $P(L)$:

$$\left(-625L^{8/3} + 150L^{4/3} - 5\right)' = -\frac{5000}{3}L^{5/3} + 200L^{1/3}.$$

Example 4.5   To see how the Chain Rule works with functions other than generalized polynomials, consider the trigonometric functions sine x and cosine x, which are usually abbreviated as $\sin x$ and $\cos x$. At this point you need only know that the derivative of the function $\sin x$ is the function $\cos x$. To compute the derivative of the composite function

$$f(x) = \sin(x^3 + 4x),$$

note that f is a composite of $(x^3 + 4x)$, the inside function, and $\sin z$, the outside function. The derivative of the outside function is

$$\frac{d}{dz}\sin(\ ) = \cos(\ ).$$

The derivative of the outside function, evaluated at the inside function, is

$$\cos(x^3 + 4x).$$

The derivative of the inside function $(x^3 + 4x)$ is $(3x^2 + 4)$. By the Chain Rule, the derivative of $\sin(x^3 + 4x)$ is

$$\frac{d}{dx}(\sin(x^3 + 4x)) = \cos(x^3 + 4x) \cdot (3x^2 + 4).$$

Notation   In addition to the phrase "derivative of the outside times derivative of the inside," there is one other convenient device for remembering and using the Chain Rule. Continue to write the inside function as $g(x)$ and the outside function as $h(z)$. Then, the Chain Rule can be written as

$$\frac{d(h \circ g)}{dx}(x) = \frac{dh}{dz}(g(x)) \cdot \frac{dg}{dx}(x). \tag{5}$$

To derive a new mnemonic device for the Chain Rule, we will allow ourselves three abuses of notation. First, write the inside function g as $z = g(x)$, since $g(x)$ will be used as the argument of the outside function $h(z)$. Second, temporarily ignoring the above warning about always using different letters for the different functions, write $h(x)$ for $h(g(x))$. Finally, ignoring the fact that $h'(z)$ is evaluated at $z = g(x)$, write (5) as

$$\frac{dh}{dx} = \frac{dh}{dz} \cdot \frac{dz}{dx},$$

which is a deceptively simple-looking formula.

EXERCISES

4.1 For each of the following pairs of functions g and h, write out the composite functions $g \circ h$ and $h \circ g$ in as simple a form as possible. In each case, describe the domain of the composite.

a) $g(x) = x^2 + 4$, $h(z) = 5z - 1$;

b) $g(x) = x^3$, $h(z) = (z - 1)(z + 1)$;

c) $g(x) = (x - 1)/(x + 1)$, $h(z) = (z + 1)/(1 - z)$;

d) $g(x) = 4x + 2$, $h(z) = \frac{1}{4}(z - 2)$;

e) $g(x) = 1/x$, $h(z) = z^2 + 1$.

4.2 For each of the following composite functions, what are the inside and outside functions?   a) $\sqrt{3x^2 + 1}$,   b) $(1/x)^2 + 5(1/x) + 4$,   c) $\cos(2x - 7)$,   d) 3^{4t+1}.

4.3 Use the Chain Rule to compute the derivative of all the composite functions in Exercise 4.1 from the derivatives of the two component functions. Then, compute each derivative directly, using your expression for the composite function, simplify, and compare your answers.

4.4   Repeat the calculations of the previous exercise for the composite functions in Exercise 4.2.

4.5   Given that the derivative of $\sin x$ is $\cos x$, the derivative of $\exp(x)$ is $\exp(x)$ itself, and the derivative of $\log x$ is $1/x$, use the Chain Rule to calculate the derivatives of the following composite functions:

a) $\sin(x^4)$,   b) $\sin(1/x)$,   c) $\sqrt{\sin x}$,   d) $\sin\sqrt{x}$,

e) $\exp(x^2 + 3x)$,   f) $\exp(1/x)$,   g) $\log(x^2 + 4)$,   h) $\sin((x^2 + 4)^2)$.

4.6   A firm computes that at the present moment its output is increasing at a rate of 2 units per hour and that its marginal cost is 12. At what rate is its cost increasing per hour? Explain your answer.

4.2   INVERSE FUNCTIONS AND THEIR DERIVATIVES

The Chain Rule is one of the most useful theorems in calculus, both in analyzing applications and in deriving other principles of calculus. As an illustration, it will be used in this section to derive the formula for the derivative of the inverse of a function when the derivative of the original function is known.

Definition and Examples of the Inverse of a Function

Consider the demand relationship between the market price p and the amount x that consumers are willing to consume at that price. Economists sometimes find it convenient to think of this relationship as defining x as a function of p, for example when computing elasticities, and sometimes as defining p as a function of x, for example when computing marginal revenue in the process of studying the profit-maximizing output. The former function is called a demand function, and the latter an inverse demand function. For example, if the demand function is given by the linear function

$$x = 3 - 2p, \tag{6}$$

then the inverse demand function is obtained by solving (6) for p in terms of x:

$$p = \frac{1}{2}(3 - x). \tag{7}$$

This same inverse relationship exists between the function in Example 2.3, which converts degrees Centigrade to degrees Fahrenheit:

$$F = \frac{9}{5}C + 32, \tag{8}$$

and the function which converts degrees Fahrenheit to degrees Centigrade:

$$C = \frac{5}{9}(F - 32). \tag{9}$$

We say that the function $p \longmapsto 3 - 2p$ in (6) is the *inverse* of the function $x \longmapsto \frac{1}{2}(3 - x)$ in (7), and vice versa. Similarly, the functions $C \longmapsto \frac{9}{5}C + 32$ and $F \longmapsto \frac{5}{9}(F - 32)$ in (8) and (9) are *inverses* of each other. More formally, for any given function $f: E_1 \rightarrow \mathbf{R}^1$, where E_1, the domain of f, is a subset of $\mathbf{R}^1$, we say the function $g: E_2 \rightarrow \mathbf{R}^1$ is an **inverse** of f if

$$g(f(x)) = x \text{ for all } x \text{ in the domain } E_1 \text{ of } f \text{ and}$$
$$f(g(z)) = z \text{ for all } z \text{ in the domain } E_2 \text{ of } g. \tag{10}$$

Example 4.6   To see that the functions described by expressions (6) and (7) are inverses of each other, form their composition by substituting the expression (7) for p into (6):

$$x = 3 - 2\left(\frac{1}{2}(3 - x)\right) = 3 - (3 - x) = x.$$

Example 4.7   Other examples of functions and their inverses are:

$$f(x) = 2x \quad \text{and} \quad g(y) = \tfrac{1}{2}y,$$
$$f(x) = x^2 \quad \text{and} \quad g(y) = \sqrt{y} \quad \text{for } x, y \geq 0,$$
$$f(x) = x^3 \quad \text{and} \quad g(y) = y^{1/3},$$
$$f(x) = \frac{x - 1}{x + 1} \quad \text{and} \quad g(y) = \frac{1 + y}{1 - y},$$
$$f(x) = \frac{1}{x} \quad \text{and} \quad g(y) = \frac{1}{y}.$$

Note that $1/x$ is its own inverse.

Suppose the function f has an inverse g. If f assigns the point y_0 to the point x_0, then g assigns the point x_0 to the point y_0. In symbols,

$$f(x_0) = y_0 \quad \Longleftrightarrow \quad g(y_0) = x_0.$$

If f assigns the same point y_0 to a point $z_0 \neq x_0$, that is, $f(z_0) = y_0$ too, then g would also need to assign z_0 to y_0; that is, $g(y_0) = z_0$. But then g would not be a well-defined function at y_0 since it would assign two different numbers x_0 and z_0

to y_0. In order for f to have an inverse g, f cannot assign the same point to two different points in its domain; in symbols

$$x_1 \neq x_2 \Longrightarrow f(x_1) \neq f(x_2), \tag{11}$$

or equivalently $$f(x_1) = f(x_2) \Longrightarrow x_1 = x_2. \tag{12}$$

A function f that satisfies (11) or (12) on a set E is said to be **one-to-one** or **injective** on E.

To summarize the previous paragraph, in order for a function to be invertible, it must be one-to-one. Conversely, if a function f is one-to-one on a set E, there is a well-defined function $g: f(E) \rightarrow \mathbf{R}^1$ which sends each point y in the image of f back to the (unique) point to which f assigned it. If f is given by a formula which expresses y in terms of x, one finds a formula for its inverse g by rewriting the formula for f to express x in terms of y. If this process determines a unique x for every y, the new formula defines the inverse g of f.

Notation   If f is invertible on its domain, then its inverse is uniquely defined. We often write f^{-1} for the inverse function of f.

It is easy to look at the graph of a function f defined on a interval E of $\mathbf{R}^1$ and determine whether or not f is one-to-one on E. As Figure 4.1 illustrates, the graph of f cannot turn around; that is, it cannot have any local maxima or minima on E. It must be monotonically increasing or monotonically decreasing on E. The function whose graph is pictured in Figure 4.1 is not one-to-one because two points x_1 and x_2 map to the same point y^*.

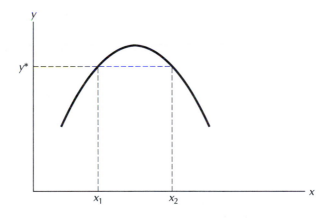

A function is not one-to-one in an interval containing a local max or min.

Figure 4.1

Example 4.8   Consider the function $f(x) = x^2$. As a function defined on all of $\mathbf{R}^1$, f is not one-to-one since it sends both $x = -2$ and $x = +2$ to the point $y = 4$. Its inverse g would have to send $y = 4$ back to one of the two, say to $x = +2$. But then, $g(f(-2)) = g(4) = +2$ and g does not satisfy the definition

(10) of an inverse. However, if we restrict the domain of f to be the nonnegative numbers $[0, \infty)$, as we did in Example 4.7, then the restricted f *is* one-to-one and therefore it has a well-defined inverse $g(y) = \sqrt{y}$. The domain of g is also the interval $[0, \infty)$. See Figure 4.3.

Example 4.9   The function $x^3 - 3x$, whose graph is pictured in Figure 3.2, is not one-to-one on $\mathbf{R}^1$, since $x = -\sqrt{3}, 0, +\sqrt{3}$ all map to $y = 0$. As further evidence, f has two local extrema, so it is not a monotone function. However, since f is monotone for $x > 1$, its restriction to $(1, \infty)$ is invertible.

The following theorem summarizes the discussion thus far.

Theorem 4.1   A function f defined on an interval E in $\mathbf{R}^1$ has a well-defined inverse on the interval $f(E)$ if and only if f is monotonically increasing on all of E or monotonically decreasing on all of E.

For differentiable functions, Theorem 3.2 gives a calculus criterion for a function to be monotonically increasing or decreasing. Combining that result with Theorem 4.1 leads naturally to the following theorem.

Theorem 4.2   A C^1 function f defined on an interval E in $\mathbf{R}^1$ is one-to-one and therefore invertible on E if $f'(x) > 0$ for all $x \in E$ or $f'(x) < 0$ for all $x \in E$.

From a geometric point of view, if f sends x_0 to y_0, so that the point (x_0, y_0) is on the graph of f, then f^{-1} sends y_0 back to x_0 and therefore the point (y_0, x_0) is on its graph. For any point (a, b) on the graph of f, the point (b, a) is on the graph

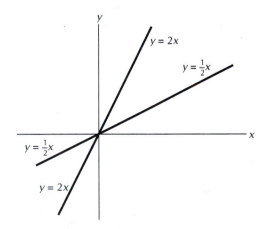

**Figure
4.2**

The graphs of the functions $y = 2x$ and $y = \frac{1}{2}x$.

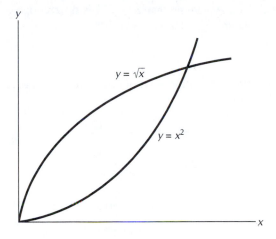

The graphs of the functions $y = x^2$ and $y = \sqrt{x}$ for $x, y \geq 0$.

**Figure
4.3**

of f^{-1}. This means that the graph of f^{-1} is simply the reflection of the graph of f across the diagonal line $\{x = y\}$. Figures 4.2 and 4.3 illustrate this phenomenon for the first two pairs of functions in Example 4.7.

The Derivative of the Inverse Function

Since there is such a close relationship between the graph of an invertible function f and the graph of its inverse f^{-1}, it's not surprising that there is a close relationship between their derivatives. In particular, if f is C^1 so that its graph has a smoothly varying tangent line, the graph of f^{-1} will also have a smoothly varying tangent line; that is, f^{-1} will be C^1 too. The following theorem combines this observation with Theorem 4.2 to give a rather complete picture for the existence and differentiability of the inverse of a C^1 function.

Theorem 4.3   (Inverse Function Theorem)   Let f be a C^1 function defined on the interval I in $\mathbf{R}^1$. If $f'(x) \neq 0$ for all $x \in I$, then:

(a) f is invertible on I,
(b) its inverse g is a C^1 function on the interval $f(I)$, and
(c) for all z in the domain of the inverse function g,

$$g'(z) = \frac{1}{f'(g(z))}.$$ (13)

Proof   The existence of f^{-1} follows from Theorem 4.1. Since the graph of f^{-1} is the reflection of the graph of f across the diagonal line $\{y = x\}$, the graph of f^{-1} will have a well-defined tangent line everywhere, i.e., be differentiable, if the graph of f does. Assuming that $g = f^{-1}$ is differentiable, we compute g' by first writing the inverse relation as in (10):

$$f(g(z)) = z. \tag{14}$$

Now, take the derivative of both sides of (14) with respect to z, using the Chain Rule on the left side:

$$f'(g(z)) \cdot g'(z) = 1,$$

or $$g'(z) = \frac{1}{f'(g(z))}. \quad \blacksquare$$

Example 4.10   The inverse of $y = f(x) \equiv mx$ is $x = g(y) = (1/m)y$. Note that

$$g'(y) = \frac{1}{m} = \frac{1}{f'(x)}.$$

Example 4.11   Let's work with the fourth set of functions in Example 4.7. Start with

$$f(x) = \frac{x-1}{x+1} \quad \text{and} \quad x = 2.$$

Since $f(2) = 1/3$, the inverse g of f sends $1/3$ to 2. Since $f'(x) = 2/(x+1)^2$, $f'(2) = 2/9$. By Theorem 4.3,

$$g'\left(\frac{1}{3}\right) = \frac{1}{f'(2)} = \frac{1}{2/9} = \frac{9}{2}.$$

We can check this answer by computing directly that

$$g(y) = \frac{1+y}{1-y}, \quad g'(y) = \frac{2}{(1-y)^2}, \quad \text{and} \quad g'\left(\frac{1}{3}\right) = \frac{2}{4/9} = \frac{9}{2}.$$

The Derivative of $x^{m/n}$

In Theorem 2.3 and Exercise 2.14, we proved that the derivative of x^k is kx^{k-1} for any integer k. In Theorem 2.4, we stated without proof that this formula holds for any number k. In this section, we will use Theorem 4.3 and the Chain Rule to show that this formula holds for *any rational number* $k = m/n$.

Theorem 4.4   For any positive integer n,

$$\left(x^{1/n}\right)' = \frac{1}{n} x^{(1/n)-1}. \tag{15}$$

Proof   The inverse of $y = x^{1/n}$ is $x = y^n$. By Theorem 4.3,

$$\left(x^{1/n}\right)' = \frac{1}{(y^n)'}, \qquad \text{evaluated at } y = x^{1/n},$$

$$= \frac{1}{ny^{n-1}}, \qquad \text{evaluated at } y = x^{1/n},$$

$$= \frac{1}{nx^{(n-1)/n}} = \frac{1}{n}x^{(1/n)-1}. \qquad \blacksquare$$

Theorem 4.5   For any positive integers m and n,

$$\left(x^{m/n}\right)' = \frac{m}{n}x^{(m/n)-1}. \tag{16}$$

Proof   Since $x^{m/n} = \left(x^{1/n}\right)^m$, we can apply the Chain Rule directly:

$$\left(x^{m/n}\right)' = m\left(x^{1/n}\right)^{m-1} \cdot \left(x^{1/n}\right)', \qquad \text{(by the Chain Rule)}$$

$$= mx^{(m-1)/n} \cdot \frac{1}{n}x^{(1-n)/n}, \qquad \text{(by Theorem 4.4)}$$

$$= \frac{m}{n}x^{(m-n)/n} = \frac{m}{n}x^{(m/n)-1} \qquad \text{(simplifying).} \qquad \blacksquare$$

Having proved that the derivative of x^k is kx^{k-1} for all rational numbers k, we can extend this result to all *real* numbers k by approximating any irrational exponent by a sequence of rational numbers, applying the formula to each rational number in the sequence, and then using a limiting process.

EXERCISES

4.7   Substitute (6) into (7), (8) into (9), and (9) into (8) and verify that the criterion (10) of an inverse function is satisfied.

4.8   Calculate an expression for the inverse of each of the following functions, specifying the domains carefully: *a)* $3x + 6$,   *b)* $1/(x + 1)$,   *c)* $x^{2/3}$,   *d)* $x^2 + x + 2$. [Hint: Use the quadratic formula for *d*.]

4.9   For each of the functions f in the previous exercise, use Theorem 4.3 to compute the derivative of its inverse function at the point $f(1)$. Check your answer by directly taking the derivative of the inverse functions calculated in the previous exercise.

4.10   Apply the Quotient Rule to the results of Theorems 4.4 and 4.5 to derive the corresponding results for *negative* exponents.

Exponents and Logarithms

In the last three chapters, we dealt exclusively with relationships expressed by polynomial functions or by quotients of polynomial functions. However, in many economics models, the function which naturally models the growth of a given economic or financial variable over time has the independent variable t appearing as an *exponent*; for example, $f(t) = 2^t$. These exponential functions occur naturally, for example, as models for the amount of money in an interest-paying savings account or for the amount of debt in a fixed-rate mortgage account after t years.

This chapter focuses on exponential functions and their derivatives. It also describes the inverse of the exponential function — the logarithm, which can turn multiplicative relationships between economic variables into additive relationships that are easier to work with. This chapter closes with applications of exponentials and logarithms to problems of present value, annuities, and optimal holding time.

5.1 EXPONENTIAL FUNCTIONS

When first studying calculus, one works with a rather limited collection of functional forms: polynomials and rational functions and their generalizations to fractional and negative exponents — all functions constructed by applying the usual arithmetic operations to the monomials ax^k. We now enlarge the class of functions under study by including those functions in which the variable x appears as an *exponent*. These functions are naturally called **exponential functions**.

A simple example is $f(x) = 2^x$, a function whose domain is all the real numbers. Recall that:

(1) if x is a positive integer, 2^x means "multiply 2 by itself x times";
(2) if $x = 0$, $2^0 = 1$, by definition;
(3) if $x = 1/n$, $2^{1/n} = \sqrt[n]{2}$, the nth root of 2;
(4) if $x = m/n$, $2^{m/n} = (\sqrt[n]{2})^m$, the mth power of the nth root of 2; and
(5) if x is a negative number, 2^x means $1/2^{|x|}$, the reciprocal of $2^{|x|}$.

In these cases, the number 2 is called the **base** of the exponential function.

To understand this exponential function better, let's draw its graph. Since we do not know how to take the derivative of 2^x yet — $(2^x)'$ is certainly not $x2^{x-1}$ —

x	2^x
-3	$1/8$
-2	$1/4$
-1	$1/2$
0	1
1	2
2	4
3	8

Table 5.1

we will have to plot points. We compute values of 2^x in Table 5.1 and draw the corresponding graph in Figure 5.1.

Note that the graph has the negative x-axis as a horizontal asymptote, but unlike any rational function, the graph approaches this asymptote in only one direction. In the other direction, the graph increases very steeply. In fact, it increases more rapidly than *any* polynomial — "exponentially fast."

In Figure 5.2, the graphs of $f_1(x) = 2^x$, $f_2(x) = 3^x$, and $f_3(x) = 10^x$ are sketched. Note that the graphs are rather similar; the larger the base, the more quickly the graph becomes asymptotic to the x-axis in one direction and steep in the other direction.

The three bases in Figure 5.2 are greater than 1. The graph of $y = b^x$ is a bit different if the base b lies between 0 and 1. Consider $h(x) = (1/2)^x$ as an example. Table 5.2 presents a list of values of (x, y) in the graph of h for small integers x. Note that the entries in the y-column of Table 5.2 are the same as the entries in the y-column of Table 5.1, but in reverse order, because $(1/2)^x = 2^{-x}$. This means that the graph of $h(x) = (1/2)^x$ is simply the reflection of the graph of $f(x) = 2^x$ in the y-axis, as pictured in Figure 5.3. The graphs of $(1/3)^x$ and $(1/10)^x$ look similar to that of $(1/2)^x$.

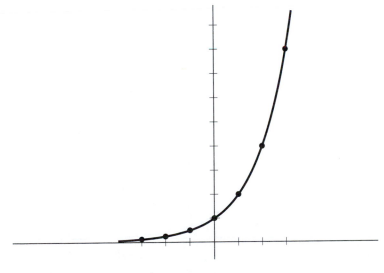

The graph of $y = 2^x$.

Figure 5.1

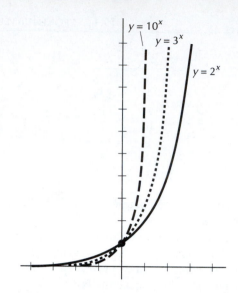

Figure 5.2

The graphs of $f_1(x) = 2^x$, $f_2(x) = 3^x$, and $f_3(x) = 10^x$.

x	$(1/2)^x$
-3	8
-2	4
-1	2
0	1
1	1/2
2	1/4
3	1/8

Table 5.2

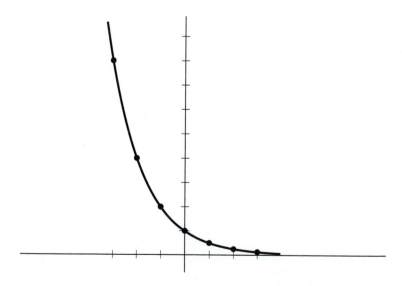

Figure 5.3

The graph of $y = (1/2)^x$.

Negative bases are not allowed for the exponential function. For example, the function $k(x) = (-2)^x$ would take on positive values for x an even integer and negative values for x an odd integer; yet it is never zero in between. Furthermore, since you cannot take the square root of a negative number, the function $(-2)^x$ is not even defined for $x = 1/2$ or, more generally, whenever x is a fraction p/q and q is an even integer. So, we can only work with exponential functions a^x, where a is a number greater than 0.

EXERCISES

5.1   Evaluate each of the following:

$$2^3, \quad 2^{-3}, \quad 8^{1/3}, \quad 8^{2/3}, \quad 8^{-2/3}, \quad \pi^0, \quad 64^{-5/6}, \quad 625^{3/4}, \quad 25^{-5/2}.$$

5.2   Sketch the graph of: *a)* $y = 5^x$;   *b)* $y = .2^x$;   *c)* $y = 3\,(5^x)$;   *d)* $y = 1^x$.

5.2   THE NUMBER *e*

Figure 5.2 presented graphs of exponential functions with bases 2, 3, and 10, respectively. We now introduce a number which is the most important base for an exponential function, the irrational number e. To motivate the definition of e, consider the most basic economic situation — the growth of the investment in a savings account. Suppose that at the beginning of the year, we deposit $\$A$ into a savings account which pays interest at a simple annual interest rate r. If we will let the account grow without deposits or withdrawals, after one year the account will grow to $A + rA = A(1 + r)$ dollars. Similarly, the amount in the account in any one year is $(1 + r)$ times the previous year's amount. After two years, there will be

$$A(1 + r)(1 + r) = A(1 + r)^2$$

dollars in the account. After t years, there will be $A(1 + r)^t$ dollars in the account.

Next, suppose that the bank compounds interest four times a year; at the end of each quarter, it pays interest at $r/4$ times the current principal. After one quarter of a year, the account contains $A + \frac{r}{4}A$ dollars. After one year, that is, after four compoundings, there will be $A\left(1 + \frac{r}{4}\right)^4$ dollars in the account. After t years, the account will grow to $A\left(1 + \frac{r}{4}\right)^{4t}$ dollars.

More generally, if interest is compounded n times a year, there will be $A\left(1 + \frac{r}{n}\right)$ dollars in the account after the first compounding period, $A\left(1 + \frac{r}{n}\right)^n$ dollars in the account after the first year, and $A\left(1 + \frac{r}{n}\right)^{nt}$ dollars in the account after t years.

Many banks compound interest daily; others advertise that they compound interest *continuously*. By what factor does money in the bank grow in one year at interest rate r if interest is compounded so frequently, that is, if n is very large? Mathematically, we are asking, "What is the limit of $(1 + \frac{r}{n})^n$ as $n \to \infty$?" To simplify this calculation, let's begin with a 100 percent annual interest rate; that is, $r = 1$. Some countries, like Israel, Argentina, and Russia, have experienced interest rates of 100 percent and higher in recent years.

We compute $(1 + \frac{1}{n})^n$ with a calculator for various values of n and list the results in Table 5.3.

n	$\left(1 + \dfrac{1}{n}\right)^n$
1	2.0
2	2.25
4	2.4414
10	2.59374
100	2.704814
1,000	2.7169239
10,000	2.7181459
100,000	2.71826824
10,000,000	2.718281693

Table 5.3

One sees in Table 5.3 that the sequence $(1 + \frac{1}{n})^n$ is an increasing sequence in n and converges to a number a little bigger than 2.7. The limit turns out to be an irrational number, in that it cannot be written as a fraction or as a repeating decimal. The letter e is reserved to denote this number; formally,

$$e \equiv \lim_{n \to \infty} \left(1 + \frac{1}{n}\right)^n. \tag{1}$$

To seven decimal places, $e = 2.7182818 \cdots$.

This number e plays the same fundamental role in finance and in economics that the number π plays in geometry. In particular, the function $f(x) = e^x$ is called *the* **exponential function** and is frequently written as $\exp(x)$. Since $2 < e < 3$, the graph of $\exp(x) = e^x$ is shaped like the graphs in Figure 5.2.

Next, we reconsider the general interest rate r and ask: What is the limit of the sequence

$$\left(1 + \frac{r}{n}\right)^n$$

in terms of e? A simple change of variables answers this question. Fix $r > 0$ for the rest of this discussion. Let $m \equiv n/r$; so $n = mr$. As n gets larger and goes to infinity, so does m. (Remember r is fixed.) Since $r/n = 1/m$,

$$\left(1 + \frac{r}{n}\right)^n = \left(1 + \frac{1}{m}\right)^{mr} = \left(\left(1 + \frac{1}{m}\right)^m\right)^r$$

by straightforward substitution. Letting $n \to \infty$, we find

$$\lim_{n \to \infty} \left(1 + \frac{r}{n} \right)^n = \lim_{m \to \infty} \left(\left(1 + \frac{1}{m} \right)^m \right)^r$$

$$= \left(\lim_{m \to \infty} \left(1 + \frac{1}{m} \right)^m \right)^r$$

$$= e^r.$$

In the second step, we used the fact that x^r is a continuous function of x, so that if $\{x_m\}_{m=1}^{\infty}$ is a sequence of numbers which converges to x_0, then the sequence of powers $\{x_m^r\}$ converges to x_0^r; that is

$$\left(\lim_{m \to \infty} x_m \right)^r = \lim_{m \to \infty} (x_m^r).$$

If we let the account grow for t years, then

$$\lim_{n \to \infty} \left(1 + \frac{r}{n} \right)^{nt} = \lim_{n \to \infty} \left(\left(1 + \frac{r}{n} \right)^n \right)^t$$

$$= \left(\lim_{n \to \infty} \left(1 + \frac{r}{n} \right)^n \right)^t$$

$$= (e^r)^t = e^{rt}.$$

The following theorem summarizes these simple limit computations.

Theorem 5.1   As $n \to \infty$, the sequence $\left(1 + \frac{1}{n} \right)^n$ converges to a limit denoted by the symbol e. Furthermore,

$$\lim_{n \to \infty} \left(1 + \frac{k}{n} \right)^n = e^k.$$

If one deposits A dollars in an account which pays annual interest at rate r compounded continuously, then after t years the account will grow to $A e^{rt}$ dollars.

Note the advantages of frequent compounding. At $r = 1$, that is, at a 100 percent interest rate, A dollars will double to $2A$ dollars in a year with no compounding. However, if interest is compounded continuously, then the A dollars will grow to eA dollars with $e > 2.7$; the account nearly triples in size.

5.3   LOGARITHMS

Consider a general exponential function, $y = a^x$, with base $a > 1$. Such an exponential function is a strictly increasing function:

$$x_1 > x_2 \implies a^{x_1} > a^{x_2}.$$

In words, the more times you multiply a by itself, the bigger it gets. As we pointed out in Theorem 4.1, strictly increasing functions have natural inverses. Recall that the inverse of the function $y = f(x)$ is the function obtained by solving $y = f(x)$ for x in terms of y. For example, for $a > 0$, the inverse of the increasing linear function $f(x) = ax + b$ is the linear function $g(y) = (1/a)(y - b)$, which is computed by solving the equation $y = ax + b$ for x in terms of y:

$$y = ax + b \iff x = \frac{1}{a}(y - b). \tag{2}$$

In a sense, the inverse g of f undoes the operation of f, so that

$$g(f(x)) = x.$$

See Section 4.2 for a detailed discussion of the inverse of a function.

We cannot compute the inverse of the increasing exponential function $f(x) = a^x$ explicitly because we can't solve $y = a^x$ for x in terms of y, as we did in (2). However, this inverse function is important enough that we give it a name. We call it the **base** a **logarithm** and write

$$y = \log_a(z) \iff a^y = z.$$

The **logarithm** of z, by definition, is the power to which one must raise a to yield z. It follows immediately from this definition that

$$a^{\log_a(z)} = z \quad \text{and} \quad \log_a(a^z) = z. \tag{3}$$

We often write $\log_a(z)$ without parentheses, as $\log_a z$.

Base 10 Logarithms

Let's first work with base $a = 10$. The logarithmic function for base 10 is such a commonly used logarithm that it is usually written as $y = \text{Log}\, x$ with an uppercase L:

$$y = \text{Log}\, z \iff 10^y = z.$$

Example 5.1   For example, the Log of 1000 is that power of 10 which yields 1000. Since $10^3 = 1000$, Log 1000 = 3. The Log of 0.01 is -2, since $10^{-2} = 0.01$. Here are a few more values of Log z:

$$\text{Log } 10 = 1 \qquad \text{since} \quad 10^1 \qquad = 10,$$

$$\text{Log } 100{,}000 = 5 \qquad \text{since} \quad 10^5 \qquad = 100{,}000,$$

$$\text{Log } 1 = 0 \qquad \text{since} \quad 10^0 \qquad = 1,$$

$$\text{Log } 625 = 2.79588 \cdots \qquad \text{since} \quad 10^{2.79588\cdots} = 625.$$

For most values of z, you'll have to use a calculator or table of logarithms to evaluate Log z.

One forms the graph of the inverse function f^{-1} by reversing the roles of the horizontal and vertical axes in the graph of f. In other words, the graph of the inverse of a function $y = f(x)$ is the reflection of the graph of f across the diagonal $\{x = y\}$, because (y, z) is a point on the graph of f^{-1} if and only if (z, y) is a point on the graph of f. In Figure 5.4, we have drawn the graph of $y = 10^x$ and reflected it across the diagonal $\{x = y\}$ to draw the graph of $y = \text{Log } x$.

Since the negative "x-axis" is a horizontal asymptote for the graph of $y = 10^x$, the negative "y-axis" is a vertical asymptote for the graph of $y = \text{Log } x$. Since 10^x grows very quickly, Log x grows very slowly. At $x = 1000$, Log x is just at $y = 3$; at x equals a million, Log x has just climbed to $y = 6$. Finally, since for *every* x, 10^x is a positive number, Log x is only defined for $x > 0$. Its domain is $\mathbf{R}_{++}$, the set of strictly positive numbers.

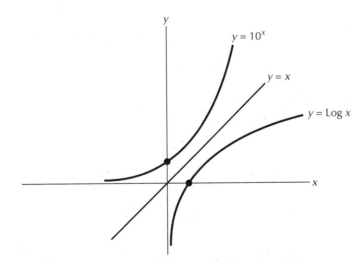

The graph of $y = \text{Log } x$ is the reflection of the graph of $y = 10^x$ across the diagonal $\{y = x\}$.

Figure 5.4

Base e Logarithms

Since *the* exponential function $\exp(x) = e^x$ has all the properties that 10^x has, it also has an inverse. Its inverse works the same way that $\mathrm{Log}\, x$ does. Mirroring the fundamental role that e plays in applications, the inverse of e^x is called the **natural logarithm** function and is written as $\ln x$. Formally,

$$\ln x = y \iff e^y = x;$$

$\ln x$ is the power to which one must raise e to get x. As we saw in general in (3), this definition can also be summarized by the equations

$$e^{\ln x} = x \quad \text{and} \quad \ln e^x = x. \tag{4}$$

The graph of e^x and its reflection across the diagonal, the graph of $\ln x$, are similar to the graphs of 10^x and $\mathrm{Log}\, x$ in Figure 5.4.

Example 5.2   Let's work out some examples. The natural log of 10 is the power of e that gives 10. Since e is a little less than 3 and $3^2 = 9$, e^2 will be a bit less than 9. We have to raise e to a power bigger than 2 to obtain 10. Since $3^3 = 27$, e^3 will be a little less than 27. Thus, we would expect that $\ln 10$ to lie between 2 and 3 and somewhat closer to 2. Using a calculator, we find that the answer to four decimal places is $\ln 10 = 2.3026$.

   We list a few more examples. Cover the right-hand side of this table and try to estimate these natural logarithms.

$\ln e$ = 1	since	e^1	= e;
$\ln 1$ = 0	since	e^0	= 1;
$\ln 0.1 = -2.3025 \cdots$	since	$e^{-2.3025\cdots}$	= 0.1;
$\ln 40 = 3.688 \cdots$	since	$e^{3.688\cdots}$	= 40;
$\ln 2$ = $0.6931 \cdots$	since	$e^{0.6931\cdots}$	= 2.

EXERCISES

5.3   First estimate the following logarithms without a calculator. Then, use your calculator to compute an answer correct to four decimal places:

a) $\mathrm{Log}\, 500$,	*b*) $\mathrm{Log}\, 5$,	*c*) $\mathrm{Log}\, 1234$,	*d*) $\mathrm{Log}\, e$,
e) $\ln 30$,	*f*) $\ln 100$,	*g*) $\ln 3$,	*h*) $\ln \pi$.

5.4   Give the exact values of the following logarithms without using a calculator:

a) Log 10, b) Log 0.001, c) Log(billion),

d) $\log_2 8$, e) $\log_6 36$, f) $\log_5 0.2$,

g) $\ln(e^2)$, h) $\ln\sqrt{e}$, i) $\ln 1$.

5.4   PROPERTIES OF EXP AND LOG

Exponential functions have the following five basic properties:

(1) $a^r \cdot a^s = a^{r+s}$,
(2) $a^{-r} = 1/a^r$,
(3) $a^r/a^s = a^{r-s}$,
(4) $(a^r)^s = a^{rs}$, and
(5) $a^0 = 1$.

Properties 1, 3, and 4 are straightforward when r and s are positive integers. The definitions that $a^{-n} = 1/a^n$, $a^0 = 1$, $a^{1/n}$ is the nth root of a, and $a^{m/n} = (a^{1/n})^m$ are all specifically designed so that the above five rules would hold for *all real* numbers r and s.

These five properties of exponential functions are mirrored by five corresponding properties of the logarithmic functions:

(1) $\log(r \cdot s) = \log r + \log s$,
(2) $\log(1/s) = -\log s$,
(3) $\log(r/s) = \log r - \log s$,
(4) $\log r^s = s \log r$, and
(5) $\log 1 = 0$.

The fifth property of logs follows directly from the fifth property of a^x and the fact that a^x and $\log_a$ are inverses of each other. To prove the other four properties, let $u = \log_a r$ and $v = \log_a s$, so that $r = a^u$ and $s = a^v$. Then, using the fact that $\log_a(a^x) = x$, we find:

(1) $\log(r \cdot s) = \log(a^u \cdot a^v) = \log(a^{u+v}) = u + v = \log r + \log s$,
(2) $\log(1/s) = \log(1/a^v) = \log(a^{-v}) = -v = -\log s$,
(3) $\log(r/s) = \log(a^u/a^v) = \log(a^{u-v}) = u - v = \log r - \log s$,
(4) $\log r^s = \log(a^u)^s = \log a^{us} = us = s \cdot \log r$.

Logarithms are especially useful in bringing a variable x that occurs as an exponent back down to the base line where it can be more easily manipulated.

Example 5.3   To solve the equation $2^{5x} = 10$ for x, we take the Log of both sides:

$$\text{Log } 2^{5x} = \text{Log } 10 \quad \text{or} \quad 5x \cdot \text{Log } 2 = 1.$$

It follows that

$$x = \frac{1}{5 \text{ Log } 2} \approx .6644.$$

We could have used ln instead of Log in this calculation.

Example 5.4   Suppose we want to find out how long it takes A dollars deposited in a saving account to double when the annual interest rate is r compounded continuously. We want to solve the equation

$$2A = Ae^{rt} \tag{5}$$

for the unknown t. We first divide both sides of (5) by A. This eliminates A from the calculation — a fact consistent with our intuition that the doubling time should be independent of the amount of money under consideration. To bring the variable t down to where we can work with it, take the natural log of both sides of the equation $2 = e^{rt}$:

$$\begin{aligned} \ln 2 &= \ln e^{rt} \\ &= rt, \end{aligned} \tag{6}$$

using (4). Solving (6) for t yields the fact that the doubling time is $t = (\ln 2)/r$.

Since $\ln 2 \approx 0.69$, this rule says that to estimate the doubling time for interest rate r, just divide the interest rate into 69. For example, the doubling time at 10 percent interest is $69/10 = 6.9$ years; the doubling time at 8 percent interest is $69/8 = 8.625$ years. This calculation also tells us that it would take 8.625 years for the price level to double if the inflation rate stays constant at 8 percent.

As we discussed in Section 3.6, economists studying the relationship between the price p and the quantity q demanded of some good will often choose to work with the two-parameter family of **constant elasticity demand functions,** $q = kp^{\varepsilon}$, where k and ε are parameters which depend on the good under study. The parameter ε is the most interesting of the two since it equals the elasticity $(p/q)(dq/dp)$. Taking the log of both sides of $q = kp^{\varepsilon}$ yields:

$$\ln q = \ln kp^{\varepsilon} = \ln k + \varepsilon \ln p. \tag{7}$$

In logarithmic coordinates, demand is now a *linear* function whose slope is the elasticity ε.

EXERCISES

5.5 Solve the following equations for x:

a) $2e^{6x} = 18$;   b) $e^{x^2} = 1$;   c) $2^x = e^5$;

d) $2^{x-2} = 5$;   e) $\ln x^2 = 5$;   f) $\ln x^{5/2} - 0.5 \ln x = \ln 25$.

5.6 Derive a formula for the amount of time that it takes money to triple in a bank account that pays interest at rate r compounded continuously.

5.7 How quickly will $500 grow to $600 if the interest rate is 5 percent compounded continuously?

5.5 DERIVATIVES OF EXP AND LOG

To work effectively with exponential and logarithmic functions, we need to compute and use their derivatives. The natural logarithmic and exponential functions have particularly simple derivatives, as the statement of the following theorem indicates.

Theorem 5.2   The functions e^x and $\ln x$ are continuous functions on their domains and have continuous derivatives of every order. Their first derivatives are given by

$$a) \quad (e^x)' = e^x,$$

$$b) \quad (\ln x)' = \frac{1}{x}.$$

If $u(x)$ is a differentiable function, then

$$c) \quad \left(e^{u(x)}\right)' = \left(e^{u(x)}\right) \cdot u'(x),$$

$$d) \quad (\ln u(x))' = \frac{u'(x)}{u(x)} \qquad \text{if } u(x) > 0.$$

We will prove this theorem in stages. That the exponential map is continuous should be intuitively clear from the graph in Figure 5.4; its graph has no jumps or discontinuities. Since the graph of $\ln x$ is just the reflection of the graph of e^x across the diagonal $\{x = y\}$, the graph of $\ln x$ has no discontinuities either, and so the function $\ln x$ is continuous for all x in the set $\mathbf{R}_{++}$ of positive numbers.

It turns out to be easier to compute the derivative of the natural logarithm first.

Lemma 5.1   Given that $y = \ln x$ is a continuous function on $\mathbf{R}_{++}$, it is also differentiable and its derivative is given by

$$(\ln x)' = \frac{1}{x}.$$

Proof   We start, of course, with the difference quotient that defines the derivative, and we then simplify it using the basic properties of the logarithm. Fix $x > 0$.

$$\frac{\ln(x + h) - \ln x}{h} = \frac{1}{h} \ln \left(\frac{x + h}{x} \right) = \ln \left(1 + \frac{h}{x} \right)^{\frac{1}{h}}$$

$$= \ln \left(1 + \frac{1/x}{1/h} \right)^{\frac{1}{h}}.$$

Now, let $m = 1/h$. As $h \to 0$, $m \to \infty$. Continuing our calculation with $m = 1/h$, we find

$$\lim_{h \to 0} \frac{\ln(x + h) - \ln x}{h} = \lim_{m \to \infty} \ln \left(1 + \frac{1/x}{m} \right)^{m}$$

$$= \ln \lim_{m \to \infty} \left(1 + \frac{1/x}{m} \right)^{m}$$

$$= \ln e^{1/x} = \frac{1}{x}.$$

Therefore, $(\ln x)' = 1/x$. The fact that we can interchange ln and lim in the above string of equalities follows from the fact that $y = \ln x$ is a continuous function: $x_m \to x_0$ implies that $\ln x_m \to \ln x_0$; or equivalently,

$$\lim_{m}(\ln x_m) = \ln \left(\lim_{m} x_m \right). \quad \blacksquare$$

The other three conclusions of Theorem 5.2 follow immediately from the Chain Rule, as we now prove.

Lemma 5.2   If $h(x)$ is a differentiable and positive function, then

$$\frac{d}{dx}(\ln h(x)) = \frac{h'(x)}{h(x)}.$$

Proof   We simply apply the Chain Rule to the composite function $f(x) = \ln h(x)$. The derivative of f is the derivative of the *outside* function $\ln y$ — which is $1/y$ — evaluated at the inside function $h(x)$ — so it's $1/h(x)$ — times the derivative $h'(x)$ of the inside function h:

$$(\ln h(x))' = \frac{1}{h(x)} \cdot h'(x) = \frac{h'(x)}{h(x)}. \qquad \blacksquare$$

We can now easily evaluate the derivative of the exponential function $y = e^x$, using the fact that it is the inverse of $\ln x$.

Lemma 5.3 $(e^x)' = e^x$.

Proof   Use the definition of $\ln x$ in (4) to write $\ln e^x = x$. Taking the derivative of both sides of this equation and using the previous lemma, we compute

$$(\ln e^x)' = \frac{1}{e^x} \cdot (e^x)' = 1.$$

It follows that

$$(e^x)' = e^x. \qquad \blacksquare$$

Finally, to prove part c of Theorem 5.2, we simply apply the Chain Rule to the composite function $y = e^{u(x)}$. The outside function is e^z, whose derivative is also e^z. Its derivative evaluated at the inside function is $e^{u(x)}$. Multiplying this by the derivative of the inside function $u(x)$, we conclude that

$$\left(e^{u(x)}\right)' = e^{u(x)} u'(x).$$

Example 5.5   Using Theorem 5.2, we compute the following derivatives:

a) $\left(e^{5x}\right)' = 5e^{5x},$ b) $\left(Ae^{kx}\right)' = Ake^{kx},$

c) $\left(5e^{x^2}\right)' = 10xe^{x^2},$ d) $(e^x \ln x)' = e^x \ln x + \dfrac{e^x}{x},$

e) $\left(\ln x^2\right)' = \dfrac{1}{x^2} \cdot 2x = \dfrac{2}{x},$ f) $\left((\ln x)^2\right)' = \dfrac{2\ln x}{x},$

g) $\left(xe^{3-x}\right)' = e^{3-x} - xe^{3-x}$ h) $\left(\ln(x^2 + 3x + 1)\right)' =$

$\qquad = (1 - x)e^{3-x},$ $\qquad\qquad \dfrac{2x + 3}{x^2 + 3x + 1}.$

Example 5.6   The density function for the standard **normal distribution** is

$$f(x) = \frac{1}{\sqrt{2\pi}} e^{-x^2/2}.$$

Let's use calculus to sketch the graph of its core function

$$g(x) = e^{-x^2/2}.$$

We first note that g is always positive, so its graph lies above the x-axis everywhere. Its first derivative is

$$g'(x) = -xe^{-x^2/2}.$$

Since $e^{-x^2/2}$ is always positive, $g'(x) = 0$ if and only if $x = 0$. Since $g(0) = 1$, the only candidate for max or min of g is the point $(0, 1)$. Furthermore, $g'(x) > 0$ if and only if $x < 0$, and $g'(x) < 0$ if and only if $x > 0$; so g is increasing for $x < 0$ and decreasing for $x > 0$. This tells us that the critical point $(0, 1)$ must be a max, in fact, a global max.

So far, we know that the graph of g stays above the x-axis all the time, increases until it reaches the point $(0, 1)$ on the y-axis, and then decreases to the right of the y-axis. Let's use the second derivative to fine-tune this picture:

$$g''(x) = \left(-xe^{-x^2/2}\right)' = x^2 e^{-x^2/2} - e^{-x^2/2} = \left(x^2 - 1\right)e^{-x^2/2}.$$

Since $e^{-x^2/2} > 0$, $g''(x)$ has the same sign as $(x^2 - 1)$. In particular,

$$g''(0) < 0, \qquad \text{and} \qquad g''(x) = 0 \Longleftrightarrow x = \pm 1. \tag{8}$$

The first inequality in (8) verifies that the critical point $(0, 1)$ is indeed a local max of g. Using the second part of (8), we note that

$$-\infty < x < -1 \quad \Longrightarrow \quad g''(x) > 0,$$
$$-1 < x < +1 \quad \Longrightarrow \quad g''(x) < 0,$$
$$1 < x < +\infty \quad \Longrightarrow \quad g''(x) > 0;$$

this implies that g is concave up on $(-\infty, -1)$ and on $(1, \infty)$ and concave down on $(-1, +1)$. The second order critical points occur at the points $(-1, e^{-1/2})$ and $(1, e^{-1/2})$. Putting all this information together, we sketch the graph of g in Figure 5.5.

The graph of g is the graph of the usual bell-shaped probability distribution. Since f is simply g times $(2\pi)^{-1/2} \approx .39$, the graph of f will be similar to the graph of g but closer to the x-axis.

We now use equation b in Example 5.5 to compute the derivative of the general exponential function $y = b^x$.

Theorem 5.3   For any fixed positive base b,

$$(b^x)' = (\ln b)(b^x). \tag{9}$$

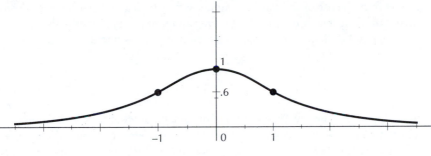

The graph of $e^{-x^2/2}$.

Figure
5.5

Proof Since $b = e^{\ln b}$, then $b^x = (e^{\ln b})^x = e^{(\ln b)x}$. By equation b in Example 5.5,

$$(b^x)' = \left(e^{(\ln b)\cdot x}\right)' = (\ln b)(e^{(\ln b)\cdot x}) = (\ln b)(b^x). \quad \blacksquare$$

Example 5.7 $(10^x)' = (\ln 10)(10^x)$.

Note that $(b^x)' = b^x$ if and only if $\ln b = 1$, that is, if and only if $b = e$. In fact, *the* exponential functions $y = ke^x$ are the only functions which are equal to their derivatives throughout their domains. This fact gives another justification for e being considered the *natural* base for exponential functions.

EXERCISES

5.8 Compute the first and second derivatives of each of the following functions:

a) xe^{3x}, b) e^{x^2+3x-2}, c) $\ln(x^4 + 2)^2$, d) $\dfrac{x}{e^x}$, e) $\dfrac{x}{\ln x}$, f) $\dfrac{\ln x}{x}$.

5.9 Use calculus to sketch the graph of each of the following functions:

a) xe^x, b) xe^{-x}, c) $\cosh(x) \equiv (e^x + e^{-x})/2$.

5.10 Use the equation $10^{\text{Log} x} = x$, Example 5.7, and the method of the proof of Lemma 5.3 to derive a formula for the derivative of $y = \text{Log} x$.

5.6 APPLICATIONS

Present Value

Many economic problems entail comparing amounts of money at different points of time in the same computation. For example, the benefit/cost analysis of the construction of a dam must compare in the same equation this year's cost of construction, future years' costs of maintaining the dam, and future years' monetary benefits from the use of the dam. The simplest way to deal with such comparisons is to use the concept of *present value* to bring all money figures back to the present.

If we put A dollars into an account which compounds interest continuously at rate r, then after t years there will be

$$B = Ae^{rt} \tag{10}$$

dollars in the account, by Theorem 5.1. Conversely, in order to generate B dollars t years from now in an account which compounds interest continuously at rate r, we would have to invest $A = Be^{-rt}$ dollars in the account now, solving (10) for A in terms of B. We call Be^{-rt} the **present value** (PV) of B dollars t years from now (at interest rate r).

Present value can also be defined using *annual* compounding instead of continuous compounding. In an account which compounds interest annually at rate r, a deposit of A dollars now will yield $B = A(1 + r)^t$ dollars t years from now. Conversely, in this framework, the present value of B dollars t years from now is $B/(1 + r)^t = B(1 + r)^{-t}$ dollars. Strictly speaking, this latter framework only makes sense for integer t's. For this reason and because the exponential map e^{rt} is usually easier to work with than $(1 + r)^t$, we will use the continuous compounding version of present value.

Present value can also be defined for *flows* of payments. At interest rate r, the present value of the flow —B_1 dollars t_1 years from now, B_2 dollars t_2 years from now, $\ldots$, B_n dollars t_n years from now — is

$$\text{PV} = B_1 e^{-rt_1} + B_2 e^{-rt_2} + \cdots + B_n e^{-rt_n}. \tag{11}$$

Annuities

An **annuity** is a sequence of equal payments at regular intervals over a specified period of time. The present value of an annuity that pays A dollars at the end of each of the next N years, assuming a constant interest rate r compounded continuously, is

$$\begin{aligned} \text{PV} &= Ae^{-r \cdot 1} + Ae^{-r \cdot 2} + \cdots + Ae^{-r \cdot N} \\ &= A\left(e^{-r} + e^{-r \cdot 2} + \cdots + e^{-r \cdot N}\right). \end{aligned} \tag{12}$$

Since $(a + \cdots + a^n)(1 - a) = a - a^{n+1}$, as one can easily check,

$$a + \cdots + a^n = \frac{a(1 - a^n)}{1 - a}. \tag{13}$$

Substituting $a = e^{-r}$ and $n = N$ from (12) yields a present value for the annuity of

$$\text{PV} = A \cdot \frac{e^{-r}\left(1 - e^{-rN}\right)}{1 - e^{-r}} = \frac{A\left(1 - e^{-rN}\right)}{e^r - 1}. \tag{14}$$

To calculate the present value of an annuity which pays A dollars a year *forever*, we let $N \to \infty$ in (14):

$$PV = \frac{A}{e^r - 1},\tag{15}$$

since $e^{-rN} \to 0$ as $N \to \infty$.

It is sometimes convenient to calculate the present value of an annuity using *annual* compounding instead of continuous compounding. In this case, equation (12) becomes

$$PV = \frac{A}{1 + r} + \cdots + \frac{A}{(1 + r)^N}.$$

Apply equation (13) with $a = 1/(1 + r)$ and $n = N$:

$$PV = A \cdot \frac{1/(1 + r)}{r/(1 + r)}\left(1 - \left(\frac{1}{1 + r}\right)^N\right) = \frac{A}{r}\left(1 - \left(\frac{1}{1 + r}\right)^N\right).\tag{16}$$

To calculate the present value of an annuity which pays A dollars a year forever at interest rate r compounded annually, we let $N \to \infty$ in (16):

$$PV = \frac{A}{r}.\tag{17}$$

The intuition for (17) is straightforward; in order to generate a perpetual flow of A dollars a year from a savings account which pays interest annually at rate r, one must deposit A/r dollars into the account initially.

Optimal Holding Time

Suppose that you own some real estate the market value of which will be $V(t)$ dollars t years from now. If the interest rate remains constant at r over this period, the corresponding time stream of present values is $V(t)e^{-rt}$. Economic theory suggests that the optimal time t_0 to sell this property is at the maximum value of this time stream of present value. The first order conditions for this maximization problem are

$$(V(t)e^{-rt})' = V'(t)e^{-rt} - rV(t)e^{-rt} = 0,$$

or $\qquad\qquad \dfrac{V'(t)}{V(t)} = r$ at t = the optimal selling time t_0. $\qquad$ (18)

Condition (18) is a natural condition for the **optimal holding time**. The left-hand side of (18) gives the rate of change of V divided by the amount of V — a quantity called the **percent rate of change** or simply the **growth rate**. The right-hand side gives the interest rate, which is the percent rate of change of money in the bank. As long as the value of the real estate is growing more rapidly than money in the bank, one should hold on to the real estate. As soon as money in the bank has a higher growth rate, one would do better by selling the property and banking the proceeds at interest rate r. The point at which this switch takes place is given by (18), where the percent rates of change are equal.

This principle of optimal holding time holds in a variety of circumstances, for example, when a wine dealer is trying to decide when to sell a case of wine that is appreciating in value or when a forestry company is trying to decide how long to let the trees grow before cutting them down for sale.

Example 5.8   You own real estate the market value of which t years from now is given by the function $V(t) = 10,000e^{\sqrt{t}}$. Assuming that the interest rate for the foreseeable future will remain at 6 percent, the optimal selling time is given by maximizing the present value

$$F(t) = 10,000e^{\sqrt{t}}e^{-.06t} = 10,000e^{\sqrt{t}-.06t}.$$

The first order condition for this maximization problem is

$$0 = F'(t) = 10,000e^{\sqrt{t}-.06t}\left(\frac{1}{2\sqrt{t}} - .06\right),$$

which holds if and only if

$$\frac{1}{2\sqrt{t_0}} = .06 \quad \text{or} \quad t_0 = \left(\frac{1}{.12}\right)^2 \approx 69.44.$$

Since $F'(t)$ is positive for $0 < t < t_0$ and negative for $t > t_0$, $t_0 \approx 69.44$ is indeed the *global* max of the present value and is the optimal selling time of the real estate.

Logarithmic Derivative

Since the logarithmic operator turns exponentiation into multiplication, multiplication into addition, and division into subtraction, it can often simplify the computation of the derivative of a complex function, because, by Lemma 5.2,

$$(\ln u(x))' = \frac{u'(x)}{u(x)},$$

and therefore
$$u'(x) = (\ln u(x))' \cdot u(x). \tag{19}$$

If $\ln u(x)$ is easier to work with than $u(x)$ itself, one can compute u' more easily using (19) than by computing it directly.

Example 5.9   Let's use this idea to compute the derivative of

$$y = \frac{\sqrt[4]{x^2 - 1}}{x^2 + 1}. \tag{20}$$

The natural log of this function is

$$\ln\left(\frac{\sqrt[4]{x^2 - 1}}{x^2 + 1}\right) = \frac{1}{4}\ln(x^2 - 1) - \ln(x^2 + 1). \tag{21}$$

It is much simpler to compute the derivative of (21) than it is to compute the derivative of the quotient (20):

$$\frac{d}{dx}\ln\left(\frac{\sqrt[4]{x^2 - 1}}{x^2 + 1}\right) = \frac{1}{4}\frac{2x}{x^2 - 1} - \frac{2x}{x^2 + 1}$$

$$= \frac{-3x^3 + 5x}{2(x^2 - 1)(x^2 + 1)}.$$

Now, use (19) to compute y':

$$\left(\frac{\sqrt[4]{x^2 - 1}}{x^2 + 1}\right)' = \frac{-3x^3 + 5x}{2(x^2 - 1)(x^2 + 1)} \cdot \frac{\sqrt[4]{x^2 - 1}}{x^2 + 1}$$

$$= \frac{-3x^3 + 5x}{2(x^2 - 1)^{3/4}(x^2 + 1)^2}.$$

Example 5.10   A favorite calculus problem, which can only be solved by this method, is the computation of the derivative of $g(x) = x^x$. Since

$$(\ln x^x)' = (x \ln x)' = \ln x + 1,$$

the derivative of x^x is $(\ln x + 1) \cdot x^x$, by (19).

Occasionally, scientists prefer to study a given function $y = f(x)$ by comparing $\ln y$ and $\ln x$, that is, by graphing f on log-log graph paper. See, for example, our discussion of constant elasticity demand functions in (7). In this case, they are working with the change of variables

$$Y = \ln y \quad \text{and} \quad X = \ln x.$$

Since $X = \ln x$, $x = e^X$ and $dx/dX = e^X = x$. In XY-coordinates, f becomes

$$Y = \ln f(x) = \ln f(e^X) \equiv F(X).$$

Now, the slope of the graph of $Y = F(X)$, that is, of the graph of f in log-log coordinates, is given by

$$\frac{dF(X)}{dX} = \frac{dF(x(X))}{dx} \cdot \frac{dx}{dX} \qquad \text{(by the Chain Rule)}$$

$$= \frac{d}{dx}(\ln f(x)) \cdot \frac{dx}{dX} = \frac{f'(x)}{f(x)} \cdot x.$$

(22)

The difference approximation of the last term in (22) is

$$\frac{df(x)}{dx} \cdot \frac{x}{f(x)} \approx \frac{\Delta f}{\Delta x} \cdot \frac{x}{f(x)} = \frac{\Delta f}{f(x)} \Big/ \frac{\Delta x}{x},$$

the percent change of f relative to the percent change of x. This is the quotient we have been calling the (point) **elasticity** of f with respect to x, especially if f is a demand function and x represents price or income.

This discussion shows that the slope of the graph of f in log-log coordinates is the (point) elasticity of f:

$$\varepsilon = \frac{f'(x) \cdot x}{f(x)}.$$

In view of this discussion, economists sometimes write this elasticity as

$$\varepsilon = \frac{d(\ln f)}{d(\ln x)}.$$

EXERCISES

5.11   At 10 percent annual interest rate, which of the following has the largest present value:

a) \$215 two years from now,

b) \$100 after each of the next two years, or

c) \$100 now and \$95 two years from now?

5.12   Assuming a 10 percent interest rate compounded continuously, what is the present value of an annuity that pays \$500 a year *a*) for the next five years, *b*) forever?

5.13   Suppose that you own a rare book whose value at time t years from now will be $B(t) = 2^{\sqrt{t}}$ dollars. Assuming a constant interest rate of 5 percent, when is the best time to sell the book and invest the proceeds?

5.14   A wine dealer owns a case of fine wine that can be sold for $Ke^{\sqrt{t}}$ dollars t years from now. If there are no storage costs and the interest rate is r, when should the dealer sell the wine?

5.15   The value of a parcel of land bought for speculation is increasing according to the formula $V = 2000\,e^{t^{1/4}}$. If the interest rate is 10 percent, how long should the parcel be held to maximize present value?

5.16   Use the logarithmic derivative method to compute the derivative of each of the following functions: *a)* $\sqrt{(x^2 + 1)/(x^2 + 4)}$,   *b)* $(x^2)^{x^2}$.

5.17   Use the above discussion to prove that the elasticity of the product of two functions is the sum of the elasticities.

PART II

Linear Algebra

Introduction to Linear Algebra

The analysis of many economic models reduces to the study of systems of equations. Furthermore, some of the most frequently studied economic models are linear models. In the next few chapters, we will study the simplest possible systems of equations — linear systems.

6.1 LINEAR SYSTEMS

Typical linear equations are

$$x_1 + 2x_2 = 3 \quad \text{and} \quad 2x_1 - 3x_2 = 8.$$

They are called linear because their graphs are straight lines. In general, an equation is **linear** if it has the form

$$a_1x_1 + a_2x_2 + \cdots + a_nx_n = b.$$

The letters $a_1, \ldots, a_n$, and b stand for fixed numbers, such as 2, -3, and 8 in the second equation. These are called **parameters**. The letters $x_1, \ldots, x_n$ stand for **variables**. The key feature of the general form of a linear equation is that each term of the equation contains at most one variable, and that variable appears only to the first power rather than to the second, third, or some other power.

There are several reasons why it is natural to begin with systems of linear equations. These are the most elementary equations that can arise. Linear algebra, the study of such systems, is one of the simpler branches of mathematics. It requires no calculus and, at least in the beginning, very little familiarity with functions. It builds on techniques learned in high school, such as the solution of two linear equations in two unknowns via substitution or elimination of variables. It also builds on the simple geometry of the plane and the cube, which is easy to visualize. Linear equations describe geometric objects such as lines and planes. In fact, linear algebra is a simple way to translate the insights of planar and cubical geometry to higher dimensions.

Linear systems have the added advantage that we can often calculate exact solutions to the equations. By contrast, solutions of nonlinear systems often cannot be calculated explicitly, and we can only hope to discover indirectly some of the properties of these solutions. Equally important for linear systems, the precise relationship between the solution of the linear system and various parameters determining the system (the a_i's and b in the equation above) can be easily described.

Of course, linearity is a simplifying assumption. The real world is nonlinear. Calculus exploits the manageability of linear systems to study nonlinear systems. The fundamental idea of calculus is that we can learn much about the behavior of a nonlinear system of equations by studying suitably chosen linear approximations to the system. For example, the best linear approximation to the graph of a nonlinear function at any point on its graph is the tangent line to the graph at that point. We can learn much about the behavior of a function near any point by examining the slope of the tangent line. Whether the function is increasing or decreasing can be determined by seeing whether the tangent line is rising or falling. The first important exercise in the study of the calculus is to learn how to calculate this slope — the *derivative* of the function. For a more prosaic example of the importance of linear approximations, consider that few people disagree with the proposition that the earth is roughly spherical, and yet in constructing homes, skyscrapers, and even cities, we assume that the earth is flat and obtain some rather impressive results using Euclidean planar geometry. Once again we are taking advantage of an effective linear approximation to a nonlinear phenomenon.

Since a primary goal of multivariable calculus is to provide a mechanism for approximating complicated nonlinear systems by simpler linear ones, it makes sense to begin by squeezing out all the information we can about linear systems — the task we take up in the next six chapters.

A final reason for looking at linear systems first is that some of the most frequently studied economic models are linear. We sketch five such models here. As we develop our theory of linear systems, we will often refer back to these models and call attention to the insights which linear theory offers. References for further study of these topics can be found in the notes at the end of the chapter.

6.2   EXAMPLES OF LINEAR MODELS

Example 1: Tax Benefits of Charitable Contributions

A company earns before-tax profits of $100,000. It has agreed to contribute 10 percent of its after-tax profits to the Red Cross Relief Fund. It must pay a state tax of 5 percent of its profits (after the Red Cross donation) and a federal tax of 40 percent of its profits (after the donation and state taxes are paid). How much does the company pay in state taxes, federal taxes, and Red Cross donation?

Without a model to structure our analysis, this problem is rather difficult because each of the three payments must take into consideration the other payments. However, after we write out the (linear) equations which describe the various deductions, we can understand more clearly the relationships between these payments and then solve in a straightforward manner for the payment amounts.

Let C, S, and F represent the amounts of the charitable contribution, state tax, and federal tax, respectively. After-tax profits are $100,000 - (S + F)$; so $C = 0.10 \cdot (100,000 - (S + F))$. We write this as

$$C + 0.1S + 0.1F = 10,000,$$

putting all the variables on one side. The statement that the state tax is 5 percent of the profits net of the donation becomes the equation $S = 0.05 \cdot (100,000 - C)$, or

$$0.05C + S = 5,000.$$

Federal taxes are 40 percent of the profit after deducting C and S; this relation is expressed by the equation $F = 0.40 \cdot [100,000 - (C + S)]$, or

$$0.4C + 0.4S + F = 40,000.$$

We can summarize the payments to be made by the system of linear equations

$$
\begin{aligned}
C + 0.1S + 0.1F &= 10,000 \\
0.05C + S &= 5,000 \qquad (1) \\
0.4C + 0.4S + F &= 40,000.
\end{aligned}
$$

There are a number of ways to solve this system. For example, you can solve the middle equation for S in terms of C, substitute this relation into the first and third equations in (1), and then easily solve the resulting system of two equations in two unknowns to compute

$$C = 5,956, \quad S = 4,702, \quad \text{and} \quad F = 35,737,$$

rounded to the nearest dollar. The next chapter is devoted to the solution of such systems of linear equations. For the moment, note that the firm's after-tax and after-contribution profits are $53,605.

We can use this linear model to compute (Exercise 6.1) that the firm would have had after-tax profits of $57,000, if it had not made the Red Cross donation. So, the $5,956 donation really only cost it $3,395 ($= \$57,000 - \$53,605$). Later, we will develop a formula for C, S, and T in terms of unspecified before-tax profits P and even, in Chapter 26, in terms of the tax rates and contribution percentages.

Example 2: Linear Models of Production

Linear models of production are perhaps the simplest production models to describe. Here we will describe the simplest of the linear models. We will suppose that our economy has $n + 1$ goods. Each of goods 1 through n is produced by one **production process**. There is also one commodity, labor (good 0), which is not produced by any process and which each process uses in production. A production process is simply a list of amounts of goods: so much of good 1, so much of good 2, and so on. These quantities are the amounts of input needed to produce one unit of the process's output. For example, the making of one car requires so much steel, so much plastic, so much labor, so much electricity, and so forth. In fact, some production processes, such as those for steel or automobiles, use some of their own output to aid in subsequent production.

The simplicity of the linear production model is due to two facts. First, in these models, the amounts of inputs needed to produce two automobiles are exactly twice those required for the production of one automobile. Three cars require 3 times as much of the inputs, and so on. In the jargon of microeconomics, each production process exhibits **constant returns to scale**. The production of 2, 3, or k cars requires 2, 3, or k times the amounts of inputs required for the production of 1 car. Second, in these models there is only one way to produce a car. There is no way to substitute electricity for labor in the production of cars. Output cannot be increased by using more of any one factor alone; more of all the factors is needed, and always in the same proportions. This simplifies the analysis of production problems, because the optimal input mix for the production of, say, 1000 cars, does not have to be computed. It is simply 1000 times the optimal input mix required for the production of 1 car.

Before undertaking an abstract analysis, we will work out an example to illustrate the key features of the model. Consider the economy of an organic farm which produces two goods: corn and fertilizer. Corn is produced using corn (to plant) and fertilizer. Fertilizer is made from old corn stalks (and perhaps by feeding the corn to cows, who then produce useful end products). Suppose that the production of 1 ton of corn requires as inputs 0.1 ton of corn and 0.8 ton of fertilizer. The production of 1 ton of fertilizer requires no fertilizer and 0.5 ton of corn.

We can describe each of the two production processes by pairs of numbers (a, b), where a represents the corn input and b represents the fertilizer input. The corn production process is described by the pair of numbers $(0.1, 0.8)$. The fertilizer production process is described by the pair of numbers $(0.5, 0)$.

The most important question to ask of this model is: What can be produced for consumption? Corn is used both in the production of corn and in the production of fertilizer. Fertilizer is used in the production of corn. Is there any way of running both processes so as to leave some corn and some fertilizer for individual consumption? If so, what combinations of corn and fertilizer for consumption are feasible?

Answers to these questions can be found by examining a particular system of linear equations. Suppose the two production processes are run so as to produce x_C tons of corn and x_F tons of fertilizer. The amount of corn actually used in the production of corn is $0.1x_C$ — the amount of corn needed per ton of corn output times the number of tons to be produced. Similarly, the amount of corn used in the production of fertilizer is $0.5x_F$. The amount of corn left over for consumption will be the total amount produced minus the amounts used for production of corn and fertilizer: $x_C - 0.1x_C - 0.5x_F$, or $0.9x_C - 0.5x_F$ tons. The amount of fertilizer needed in production is $0.8x_C$ tons. Thus the amount left over for consumption is $x_F - 0.8x_C$ tons.

Suppose we want our farm to produce for consumption 4 tons of corn and 2 tons of fertilizer. How much total production of corn and fertilizer will be required? Put another way, how much corn and fertilizer will the farm have to produce in order to have 4 tons of corn and 2 tons of fertilizer left over for consumers? We can answer this question by solving the pair of linear equations

$$0.9x_C - 0.5x_F = 4,$$

$$-0.8x_C + \quad x_F = 2.$$

This system is easily solved. Solve the second equation for x_F in terms of x_C:

$$x_F = 0.8x_C + 2. \tag{2}$$

Substitute this expression for x_F into the first equation:

$$0.9x_C - 0.5(0.8x_C + 2) = 4$$

and solve for x_C:

$$0.5x_C = 5, \quad \text{so} \quad x_C = 10.$$

Finally, substitute $x_C = 10$ back into (2) to compute

$$x_F = 0.8 \cdot 10 + 2 = 10.$$

In the general case, the production process for good j can be described by a set of **input-output coefficients** $\{a_{0j}, a_{1j}, \ldots, a_{nj}\}$, where a_{ij} denotes the input of good i needed to output one unit of good j. Keep in mind that the first subscript stands for the input good and the second stands for the output good. The production of x_j units of good j requires $a_{0j}x_j$ units of good 0, $a_{1j}x_j$ units of good 1, and so on.

Total output of good i must be allocated between production activities and consumption. Denote by c_i the consumer demand for good i. This demand is given **exogenously**, which is to say that it is not solved for in the model. Let c_0 be the consumer's supply of labor. Since good 0 (labor) is supplied by consumers rather than demanded by consumers, c_0 will be a negative number. An n-tuple $(c_0, c_1, \ldots, c_n)$ is said to be an **admissible** n-tuple of consumer demands if c_0 is negative, while all the other c_i's are nonnegative. We want each process to produce an output that is sufficient to meet both consumer demand and the input requirements of the n industries. For our simple linear economy, this is the law of supply and demand: output produced must be used in production or in consumption. Let x_j denote the amount of output produced by process j. If process j produces x_j units of output, it will need $a_{ij}x_j$ units of good i. Adding these terms up over all the industries gives the demand for good i: $a_{i1}x_1 + a_{i2}x_2 + \cdots + a_{in}x_n + c_i$. The law of supply and demand then requires

$$x_i = a_{i1}x_1 + a_{i2}x_2 + \cdots + a_{in}x_n + c_i.$$

It is convenient to rearrange this equation to say that consumer demand must equal gross output less the amount of the good needed as an input for the production processes. For good 1, this says

$$(1 - a_{11})x_1 - a_{12}x_2 - \cdots - a_{1n}x_{1n} = c_1.$$

The analogous equation for good i is

$$-a_{i1}x_1 - \cdots - a_{ii-1} + (1 - a_{ii})x_i - a_{ii+1}x_{i+1} - \cdots - a_{in}x_n = c_i.$$

The corresponding law of supply and demand for labor says

$$-a_{01}x_1 - \cdots - a_{0n}x_n = c_0.$$

This leads to the following system of $n + 1$ equations in n unknowns, which summarizes the equilibrium output levels for the entire n-industry economy:

$$
\begin{aligned}
(1 - a_{11})x_1 & - a_{12}x_2 - \cdots & - a_{1n}x_n &= c_1 \\
-a_{21}x_1 + (1 - a_{22})x_2 & - \cdots & - a_{2n}x_n &= c_2 \\
\vdots \qquad\qquad & \vdots & \vdots & \\
-a_{n1}x_1 & - a_{n2}x_2 - \cdots + (1 - a_{nn})x_n &= c_n \\
-a_{01}x_1 & - a_{02}x_2 - \cdots & - a_{0n}x_n &= c_0.
\end{aligned}
\tag{3}
$$

This linear system is called an **open Leontief system** after Wassily Leontief, who first studied this type of system in the 1930s and later won a Nobel Prize in economics for his work. It is said to be **open** because the demand $c_0, \ldots, c_n$ is exogenously given, while the supply of goods is endogenously determined, that is, is determined by the equations under study. In this system of equations, the

a_{ij}'s and the c_i's are given and we must solve for the x_i's, the gross outputs of the industries.

There are a number of algebraic questions associated with these equations whose answers are important for obtaining the economic insights the interindustry model has to offer. For example, what sets of input-output coefficients yield a nonnegative solution of system (3) for some admissible n-tuple of consumer demands? What set of output n-tuples will achieve a specified admissible n-tuple of consumer demands? What set of admissible n-tuples of consumer demands can be obtained from some given set of input-output coefficients?

We have seen how this model sets up in terms of a system of linear equations. But many insights into the workings of the Leontief model can best be understood by studying the geometry of the model. We will study linear systems from the geometric point of view in Chapter 27.

Example 3: Markov Models of Employment

Aggregate unemployment rates do not tell the whole story of unemployment. In order to target appropriate incomes policies it is necessary to see exactly who is unemployed. For example, is most unemployment due to a few people who are unemployed for long periods of time, or is it due to many people, each of whom is only briefly unemployed? Questions like these can be answered by data about the duration of unemployment and the transition between employment and unemployment. Markov models are the probability models commonly used in these studies.

If an individual is not employed in a given week, in the next week he or she may either find a job or remain unemployed. With some chance, say probability p, the individual will find a job, and therefore with probability $1 - p$ that individual will remain unemployed. Similarly, if an individual is employed in a given week, we let q be the probability that he or she will remain employed and therefore $1 - q$ the probability of becoming unemployed. The probabilities $p, q, 1 - p$, and $1 - q$ are called **transition probabilities**. In order to keep this model simple, we will assume that the chances of finding a job are independent of how many weeks the job seeker has been unemployed and that the chances of leaving a job are also independent of the number of weeks worked. Then the random process of leaving jobs and finding new ones is said to be a **Markov process**. The two possibilities, employed and unemployed, are the **states** of the process.

The transition probabilities can lead to a description of the pattern of unemployment over time. For example, suppose that there are x males of working age who are currently employed, and y who are currently unemployed. How will these numbers change next week? Of the x males currently employed, on average qx will remain employed and $(1 - q)x$ will become unemployed. Of the y males currently unemployed, on average py will become employed while $(1 - p)y$ will remain unemployed. Summing up, the average number employed next week will be $qx + py$, and the average number unemployed will be $(1 - q)x + (1 - p)y$. If changes in the size of the labor force are ignored, the week-by-week dynamics of average unemployment are described by the linear equations

$$x_{t+1} = qx_t + py_t$$
$$y_{t+1} = (1 - q)x_t + (1 - p)y_t,$$

(4)

where x_t and y_t are the average numbers of employed and unemployed, respectively, in week t. This system of equations is an example of a linear system of **difference equations**.

Macroeconomist Robert Hall estimated the transition probabilities for various segments of the U.S. population in 1966. For white males the corresponding system (4) of equations is

$$x_{t+1} = .998x_t + .136y_t$$
$$y_{t+1} = .002x_t + .864y_t.$$

(5)

For black males, the system is

$$x_{t+1} = .996x_t + .102y_t$$
$$y_{t+1} = .004x_t + .898y_t.$$

(6)

In the above three systems of equations, note that for any pair of numbers x_t and y_t,

$$x_{t+1} + y_{t+1} = x_t + y_t.$$

In particular, if we start out with data in percentages, so that x_0 and y_0 sum to 1, then x_t and y_t will sum to 1 for all t. To see this, just add the two equations in (4). Furthermore, it is easy to see that if x_t and y_t are nonnegative numbers, then x_{t+1} and y_{t+1} will be also. Thus, if the initial data we plug into the equation at time 0 is a distribution of the population, the data at each time t will also be a distribution.

There are two questions that are typically asked of Markov processes. First, will x_t and y_t ever be constant over time? That is, is there a distribution of the population between the two states that will replicate itself in the dynamics of equation (4)? In other words, is there a nonnegative (x, y) pair with

$$x = qx + py$$
$$y = (1 - q)x + (1 - p)y$$
$$1 = x + y.$$

(7)

Such a pair, if it exists, is called a **stationary distribution**, or a **steady state** of (4). Once such a distribution occurs, it will continue to recur for all time (unless p or q changes).

The second question is contingent on the existence of a stationary distribution. Will the system, starting from any initial distribution of states, converge to a steady state distribution? If so, the system is said to be **globally stable**. Both of these questions can be answered using techniques of linear algebra.

The first two equations of equation system (7) can be rewritten as

$$0 = (q - 1)x + py$$
$$0 = (1 - q)x - py. \tag{8}$$

However, there is really only one distinct equation in (8), since the second equation is just the negative of the first equation and therefore can be discarded. Combining the first equation in system (8) with the remaining equation in (7), we conclude that candidates for steady states will be solutions to the system of equations

$$(q - 1)x + py = 0$$
$$x + y = 1. \tag{9}$$

(We also have the nonnegativity constraint, but this will not be a problem.) To solve system (9), multiply the second equation through by $-p$ and add the result to the first equation. The resulting equation will contain no y's and can easily be solved for x. Then, use either of the equations in (9) to solve for the corresponding y. The resulting solution is

$$x = \frac{p}{1 + p - q} \quad \text{and} \quad y = \frac{1 - q}{1 + p - q}.$$

Applying this formula to Hall's data gives a steady state unemployment rate of 1.4 percent for white males and 3.77 percent for black males. The stability question asks: when is there a tendency to move toward these rates? This analysis is harder than anything else we have done so far, but it still involves linear techniques.

Note that we have seen two different linear systems in the Markov model: system (4) which describes the dynamics of the population distribution, and system (9) which describes the long-run steady state equilibrium.

Example 4: IS-LM Analysis

IS-LM analysis is Sir John Hicks's interpretation of the basic elements of John Maynard Keynes' classic work, the *General Theory of Employment, Interest, and Money*. We examine a simple example of IS-LM analysis: a linear model of a closed economy such as one can find in any undergraduate macroeconomics text.

Consider an economy with no imports, exports, or other leakages. In such an economy, the value of total production equals total spending, which in turn equals total national income, all of which we denote by the variable Y. From the expenditure side, total spending Y can be decomposed into the spending C

by consumers (consumption) plus the spending I by firms (investment) plus the spending G by government:

$$Y = C + I + G.$$

On the consumer side, consumer spending C is proportional to total income Y: $C = bY$, with $0 < b < 1$. The parameter b is called the **marginal propensity to consume**, while $s = 1 - b$ is called the **marginal propensity to save**. On the firms' side, investment I is a decreasing function of the interest rate r. In its simplest linear form, we write this relationship as

$$I = I^o - ar.$$

The parameter a is called the **marginal efficiency of capital**.

Putting these relations together gives the **IS schedule**, the relationship between national income and interest rates consistent with savings and investment behavior

$$Y = bY + (I^o - ar) + G,$$

which we write as

$$sY + ar = I^o + G, \tag{10}$$

where $s = 1-b, a, I^o$, and G are positive parameters. This IS equation is sometimes said to describe the real side of the economy, since it summarizes consumption, investment, and savings decisions.

On the other hand, the **LM equation** is determined by the money market equilibrium condition that money supply M_s equals money demand M_d. The money supply M_s is determined outside the system. Money demand M_d is assumed to have two components: the **transactions** or **precautionary demand** M_{dt} and the **speculative demand** M_{ds}. The transactions demand derives from the fact that most transactions are denominated in money. Thus, as national income rises, so does the demand for funds. We write this relationship as

$$M_{dt} = mY.$$

The speculative demand comes from the portfolio management problem faced by an investor in the economy. The investor must decide whether to hold bonds or money. Money is more liquid but returns no interest, while bonds pay at rate r. It is usually argued that the speculative demand for money varies inversely with the interest rate (directly with the price of bonds). The simplest such relationship is the linear one

$$M_{ds} = M^o - hr.$$

The LM curve is the relationship between national income and interest rates given by the condition that money supply equals total money demand:

$$M_s = mY + M^o - hr,$$

or $$mY - hr = M_s - M^o.$$

The parameters m, h, and M^o are all positive.

Equilibrium in this simple model will occur when both the IS equation (production equilibrium) and the LM equation (monetary equilibrium) are simultaneously satisfied. Equilibrium national income Y and interest rates r are solutions to the system of equations

$$sY + ar = I^o + G$$
$$mY - hr = M_s - M^o. \tag{11}$$

Algebraic questions come into play in examining how solutions (Y, r) depend upon the policy parameters M_s and G and on the behavioral parameters a, h, I^o, m, M^o, and s. The comparative statics of the model — the determination of the relationship between parameters and solutions of the equations — is an algebraic problem on which the tools of linear algebra shed much light.

The importance of studying the linear version of the IS-LM model in addition to the general nonlinear version of the model cannot be underestimated. First, the intuition of the model is most easily seen in its linear form. Second, study of the linear model can suggest what to look for in more general models. Finally, the comparative statics of nonlinear models — the exploration of how solutions to the system change as the parameters describing the system change — is uncovered by approximating the nonlinear model with a linear one, and then studying the linear approximation. These three reasons for focusing on linear models for the study of nonlinear phenomena will recur frequently. The simplicity of linear models commends such models as a first step in the construction of more complex models, and the more complex models are frequently studied by examining carefully chosen linear approximations.

Example 5: Investment and Arbitrage

In the simple neoclassical model of consumer choice, a consumer decides how much of each of the n well-specified goods to consume today. In order to extend this model to the study of investment decisions, we must add two new ingredients — time and uncertainty. Suppose that there are A investment assets, which our investor may buy at the beginning of an investment period and sell at the end of the period. To bring uncertainty into this discussion, assume that S different financial climates are possible during the coming period. We call these conditions **states of nature**. Exactly one of these S states will occur; of course, no one knows which one. An asset will have different returns in different states of nature. Let v_i be the current value of one unit of asset i, and let y_{si} be the value of one unit of asset i at the end of the investment period, including dividends paid, if state s occurs. Then, the **realized return** or **payoff** on the ith asset in state s is

$$R_{si} = \frac{y_{si}}{v_i}.$$

This is the amount the investor will receive per dollar invested in asset i should state s occur. (The realized return can be thought of as 1 plus the *rate of return*.)

Let n_i denote the number of units or **shares** of asset i held. The share amounts n_i can have either sign. A positive n_i indicates a **long position** and thus entitles the investor to *receive* $y_{si}n_i$ if state s occurs. A negative n_i indicates a **short position**; the investor, in effect, borrows n_i shares of asset i and promises to *pay back* $y_{si}n_i$ at the end of the period if state s occurs. In this case, the investment in asset i has a positive rate of return only if $y_{si} < v_i$, that is, if it is cheaper to pay back the borrowed shares that it was to borrow them.

If the investor has wealth w_0 available for investment purposes, the investor's budget constraint is

$$n_1 v_1 + \cdots + n_A v_A = w_0.$$

If state s occurs, the return to the investor of purchasing n_i shares of asset i for $i = 1, \ldots, A$ is

$$R_s = \frac{y_{s1}n_1 + y_{s2}n_2 + \cdots + y_{sA}n_A}{w_0} = \sum_{i=1}^{A} \frac{y_{si}n_i}{w_0}. \tag{12}$$

We usually normalize by letting

$$x_i = \frac{n_i v_i}{w_0}$$

represent the fraction of the investor's wealth held in asset i. Budget constraint (12) becomes simply

$$x_1 + x_2 + \cdots + x_A = 1.$$

The A-tuple $(x_1, x_2, \ldots, x_A)$ is called a **portfolio** and the x_i's are called **portfolio weights**. If state s occurs, the return to the investor of portfolio $(x_1, \ldots, x_A)$ is

$$R_s = \frac{\sum_{i=1}^{A} y_{si}n_i}{w_0} = \sum_{i=1}^{A} \frac{y_{si}}{v_i} \cdot \frac{n_i v_i}{w_0} = \sum_{i=1}^{A} R_{si} x_i$$

by the definitions of R_{si} and x_i.

At this point, we introduce some of the vocabulary of finance theory. A portfolio $(x_1, \ldots, x_A)$ is called **riskless** if it provides the same return in every state of nature:

$$\sum_{i=1}^{A} R_{1i}x_i = \sum_{i=1}^{A} R_{2i}x_i = \cdots = \sum_{i=1}^{A} R_{Si}x_i.$$

A nonzero A-tuple $(x_1, \ldots, x_A)$ is called an **arbitrage portfolio** if

$$x_1 + \cdots + x_A = 0 \qquad \text{(instead of 1)}.$$

In such a "portfolio," the money received from the short sales is used in the purchase of the long positions. Notice that, in an arbitrage portfolio, $n_1v_1 + \cdots + n_Av_A = 0$, so that the portfolio costs nothing.

A portfolio $(x_1, \ldots, x_A)$ is called **duplicable** if there is a different portfolio $(w_1, \ldots, w_A)$ with exactly the same returns in every state:

$$\sum_{i=1}^{A} R_{si}x_i = \sum_{i=1}^{A} R_{si}w_i \qquad \text{for each } s = 1, \ldots, S.$$

A state s^* is called **insurable** if there is a portfolio $(x_1, \ldots, x_A)$ which has a positive return if state s^* occurs and zero return if any other state occurs:

$$\sum_{i=1}^{A} R_{s^*i}x_i > 0$$

$$\sum_{i=1}^{A} R_{si}x_i = 0 \qquad \text{for all } s \neq s^*.$$

The name is appropriate because the given portfolio can provide insurance against the occurrence of state s^*.

It is sometimes convenient to assign a price to each of the s states of nature. An S-tuple $(p_1, \ldots, p_S)$ is called a **state price vector** if

$$
\begin{aligned}
p_1y_{11} + p_2y_{21} + \cdots + p_Sy_{S1} &= v_1 \\
p_1y_{12} + p_2y_{22} + \cdots + p_Sy_{S2} &= v_2 \\
\vdots \qquad\qquad \vdots \qquad\quad \vdots \\
p_1y_{1A} + p_2y_{2A} + \cdots + p_Sy_{SA} &= v_A,
\end{aligned}
\tag{13}
$$

or equivalently,

$$
\begin{aligned}
p_1R_{11} + p_2R_{21} + \cdots + p_SR_{S1} &= 1 \\
p_1R_{12} + p_2R_{22} + \cdots + p_SR_{S2} &= 1 \\
\vdots \qquad\qquad \vdots \qquad\quad \vdots \\
p_1R_{1A} + p_2R_{2A} + \cdots + p_SR_{SA} &= 1.
\end{aligned}
\tag{14}
$$

Systems (13) and (14) state that the current price v_j of asset j is equal to a weighted sum of its returns in each state of nature, with the same weights for each j. The weight p_s for state s is a kind of price for wealth in state s and is often called a **state price**. If we can price states, then the price of each asset is just the value at the state prices of the returns in each state. This is the content of the linear system of equations (13).

Since all the equations in this application are linear, it is not surprising that techniques of linear algebra can answer questions about the existence and characterization of riskless, duplicable, and arbitrage portfolios and of insurable states and state prices.

Example 6.1   Suppose that there are two assets and three possible states. If state 1 occurs, asset 1 returns $R_{11} = 1$ and asset 2 returns $R_{12} = 3$. If state 2 occurs, $R_{21} = 2$ and $R_{22} = 2$. If state 3 occurs, $R_{31} = 3$ and $R_{32} = 1$. If both assets have the same current value and if the investor buys $n_1 = 3$ shares of asset 1 and $n_2 = 1$ share of asset 2, the corresponding portfolio is $(\frac{3}{4}, \frac{1}{4})$ and the returns are

$$R_{11} \cdot \tfrac{3}{4} + R_{12} \cdot \tfrac{1}{4} = \tfrac{3}{2} \qquad \text{in state 1,}$$

$$R_{21} \cdot \tfrac{3}{4} + R_{22} \cdot \tfrac{1}{4} = 2 \qquad \text{in state 2,}$$

$$R_{31} \cdot \tfrac{3}{4} + R_{32} \cdot \tfrac{1}{4} = \tfrac{5}{2} \qquad \text{in state 3.}$$

Portfolio $(\frac{1}{2}, \frac{1}{2})$ is a riskfree portfolio since it yields a return of 2 in all three states (check). The 3-tuple $(\frac{1}{8}, \frac{1}{2}, \frac{1}{8})$ is a pricing system for this economy (check). As we will see in Section 7.4, there are no duplicable portfolios and no insurable states.

These five examples illustrate the important role that linear models play in economics and indeed in all the social sciences. We conclude this chapter by mentioning three other instances where economists use linear algebra. First, many of the elementary techniques of econometrics, such as (generalized) least-squares estimation, rely heavily on linear systems of equations. Second, linear programming, the optimization of a linear function on a set defined by a system of linear equalities and inequalities, is a fundamental economic technique. As such, a number of textbooks are devoted entirely to it and it is the total subject matter of graduate courses in mathematics and engineering, as well as economics. Finally, we will rely on linear algebra techniques when we study the generalization of the second derivative test in calculus to maximization problems which involve (nonlinear) functions of more than one variable.

EXERCISES

6.1   Suppose that the firm in Example 1 did not make any charitable contribution. Write out and solve the system of equations which describe its state and federal taxes. What is the net cost of its $5956 charitable contribution?

6.2   In Missouri, federal income taxes are deducted from state taxes. Write out and solve the system of equations which describes the state and federal taxes and charitable contribution of the firm in Example 1 if it were based in Missouri.

6.3   The economy on the island of Bacchus produces only grapes and wine. The production of 1 pound of grapes requires 1/2 pound of grapes, 1 laborer, and no wine. The production of 1 liter of wine requires 1/2 pound of grapes, 1 laborer, and 1/4 liter of wine. The island has 10 laborers who all together demand 1 pound of grapes and 3 liters of wine for their own consumption. Write out the input-output system for the economy of this island. Can you solve it?

6.4   Suppose that the production of a pound of grapes now requires 7/8 liter of wine. If none of the other input-output coefficients change, write out the new systems for the outputs.

6.5   Suppose that 10 percent of white males of working age and 20 percent of black males of working age are unemployed in 1966. According to Hall's model, what will the corresponding unemployment rates be in 1967?

6.6   For the Markov employment model, Hall gives $p = .106$ and $q = .993$ for black females, and $p = .151$ and $q = .997$ for white females. Write out the Markov systems of difference equations for these two situations. Compute the stationary distributions.

6.7   Consider the IS-LM model of Example 4 with no fiscal policy ($G = 0$). Suppose that $M_s = M^o$; that is, the intercept of the LM curve is 0. Suppose that $I^o = 1000$, $s = 0.2$, $h = 1500$, $a = 2000$, and $m = 0.16$. Write out the explicit IS-LM system of equations. Solve them for the equilibrium GNP Y and the interest rate r.

6.8   Carry out the two checks at the end of Example 5.

NOTES

We present some references for the linear models discussed in this section. For the intellectual origins of input-output models, see F. Quesnay (1694–1774), *Tableau Economique*, and W. Leontief (1906–), *The Structure of the American Economy: 1919–1929* (Cambridge, Mass.: Harvard University Press, 1941). For a good modern treatment, see Chapters 8 and 9 of D. Gale, *The Theory of Linear Economic Models* (New York: McGraw-Hill, 1960). Gale's book is also an excellent reference for the techniques and economic applications of linear programming.

The estimates for the transition probabilities for the employment of various segments in the United States in 1966 are from Robert Hall, "Turnover in the labor force," *Brookings Papers on Economic Activity* 3, 1972, p. 709.

Most undergraduate macroeconomic texts treat IS-LM models. See, for example, Chapter 4 of R. Hall and J. Taylor's *Macroeconomics*, 4th ed. (New York: Norton, 1993.) Keynes's classic in this area is J. M. Keynes (1883–1946), *The General Theory of Employment, Interest, and Money* (New York: Harcourt, Brace, 1936). For Hicks's interpretation of this theory, see J. R. Hicks (1904–1989), "Mr. Keynes and the 'Classics': a Suggested Interpretation," *Econometrica* April 1937, 147–159. Among the good expositions of modern portfolio theory is Jonathan Ingersoll *Theory of Financial Decision Making* (Rowman & Littlefield, 1987).

Systems of Linear Equations

As was discussed in the last chapter, systems of linear equations arise in two ways in economic theory. Some economics models have a natural linear structure, like the five examples in the last chapter. On the other hand, when the relationships among the variables under consideration are described by a system of *nonlinear* equations, one takes the derivative of these equations to convert them to an approximating *linear* system. Theorems of calculus tell us that by studying the properties of this latter linear system, we can learn a lot about the underlying nonlinear system.

In this chapter we begin the study of systems of linear equations by describing techniques for solving such systems. The preferred solution technique — Gaussian elimination — answers the fundamental questions about a given linear system: does a solution exist, and if so, how many solutions are there?

An implicit system is one in which the equations that describe the economic relationships under study have the exogenous and endogenous variables mixed in with each other on the same side of the equal signs. This chapter closes with a discussion of the Linear Implicit Function Theorem, which tells how to use linear algebra techniques to quantify the effect of a change in the exogenous variables on the endogenous ones in a linear implicit system.

7.1   GAUSSIAN AND GAUSS-JORDAN ELIMINATION

We begin our study of linear phenomena by considering the problem of solving linear systems of equations, such as

$$
\begin{array}{ll}
2x_1 + 3x_2 = 7 & \quad x_1 + x_2 + x_3 = 5 \\
\qquad\qquad\qquad \text{or} & \\
x_1 - x_2 = 1 & \quad\qquad x_2 - x_3 = 0.
\end{array}
\tag{1}
$$

The general linear system of m equations in n unknowns can be written

$$
\begin{aligned}
a_{11}x_1 + a_{12}x_2 + \cdots + a_{1n}x_n &= b_1 \\
a_{21}x_1 + a_{22}x_2 + \cdots + a_{2n}x_n &= b_2 \\
\vdots \qquad\quad \vdots \qquad\quad \vdots \\
a_{m1}x_1 + a_{m2}x_2 + \cdots + a_{mn}x_n &= b_m.
\end{aligned}
\tag{2}
$$

In this system, the a_{ij}'s and b_i's are given real numbers; a_{ij} is the **coefficient** of the unknown x_j in the ith equation. A **solution** of system (2) is an n-tuple of real numbers $x_1, x_2, \ldots, x_n$ which satisfies each of the m equations in (2). For example, $x_1 = 2, x_2 = 1$ solves the first system in (1), and $x_1 = 5, x_2 = 0, x_3 = 0$ solves the second.

For a linear system such as (2), we are interested in the following three questions:

(1) Does a solution exist?
(2) How many solutions are there?
(3) Is there an efficient algorithm that computes actual solutions?

There are essentially three ways of solving such systems:

(1) substitution,
(2) elimination of variables, and
(3) matrix methods.

Substitution

Substitution is the method usually taught in beginning algebra classes. To use this method, solve one equation of system (2) for one variable, say x_n, in terms of the other variables in that equation. Substitute this expression for x_n into the other $m - 1$ equations. The result is a new system of $m - 1$ equations in the $n - 1$ unknowns $x_1, \ldots, x_{n-1}$. Continue this process by solving one equation in the new system for x_{n-1} and substituting this expression into the other $m - 2$ equations to obtain a system of $m - 2$ equations in the $n - 2$ variables $x_1, \ldots, x_{n-2}$. Proceed until you reach a system with just a single equation, a situation which is easily solved. Finally, use the earlier expressions of one variable in terms of the others to find all the x_i's.

This sounds complicated but it really is straightforward. We used substitution to solve the input-output system in Section 6.2. Let us see how it works on a *three*-good input-output model.

Example 7.1   The production process for a three-good economy is summarized by the input-output table:

0	0.4	0.3
0.2	0.12	0.14
0.5	0.2	0.05

Table 7.1

Recall from the last chapter that the entries in the second column of Table 7.1 declare that it takes 0.4 unit of good 1, 0.12 unit of good 2, and 0.2 unit of good 3 to produce 1 unit of good 2. We ignore the labor component in this example. Suppose that there is an exogenous demand for 130 units of good 1, 74 units of good 2, and 95 units of good 3. How much will the economy have to produce to meet this demand?

Let x_i denote the amount of good i produced. As we described last chapter, "supply equals demand" leads to the following system of equations:

$$x_1 = 0 \quad x_1 + 0.4 \ x_2 + 0.3 \ x_3 + 130$$
$$x_2 = 0.2x_1 + 0.12x_2 + 0.14x_3 + \ 74$$
$$x_3 = 0.5x_1 + 0.2 \ x_2 + 0.05x_3 + \ 95,$$

which can be rewritten as the system

$$x_1 - 0.4 \ x_2 - 0.3 \ x_3 = 130$$
$$-0.2x_1 + 0.88x_2 - 0.14x_3 = \ 74 \qquad (3)$$
$$-0.5x_1 - 0.2 \ x_2 + 0.95x_3 = \ 95.$$

We write (3a), (3b) and (3c) for the three equations in system (3) in the order given, and similarly for following systems. Solving equation (3a) for x_1 in terms of x_2 and x_3 yields

$$x_1 = 0.4x_2 + 0.3x_3 + 130. \qquad (4)$$

Substitute (4) into equations (3b) and (3c):

$$-0.2(0.4x_2 + 0.3x_3 + 130) + 0.88x_2 - 0.14x_3 = 74$$
$$-0.5(0.4x_2 + 0.3x_3 + 130) - 0.2 \ x_2 + 0.95x_3 = 95,$$

which simplifies to

$$0.8x_2 - 0.2x_3 = 100$$
$$-0.4x_2 + 0.8x_3 = 160. \qquad (5)$$

Now, use substitution to solve subsystem (5) by solving the first equation (5a) for x_2 in terms of x_3:

$$x_2 = 125 + 0.25x_3, \qquad (6)$$

and plugging this expression into the second equation (5b):

$$-0.4(125 + 0.25x_3) + 0.8x_3 = 160,$$

or
$$x_3 = 300.$$

Substitute $x_3 = 300$ into (6) to compute that $x_2 = 200$. (Check.) Finally, substitute $x_2 = 200$ and $x_3 = 300$ into (4) to compute that

$$x_1 = 0.4 \cdot 200 + 0.3 \cdot 300 + 130 = 300.$$

Therefore, this economy needs to produce 300 units of good one, 200 units of good two, and 300 units of good three to meet the exogenous demands.

As this example shows, the substitution method is straightforward, but it can be cumbersome. Furthermore, it does not provide much insight into the nature of the general solution to systems like (3). It is not a method around which one can build a general theory of linear systems. However, it is the most direct method for solving certain systems with a special, very simple form. As such, it will play a role in the general solution technique we now develop.

Elimination of Variables

The method which is most conducive to theoretical analysis is *elimination of variables*, another technique that should be familiar from high school algebra. First, consider the simple system

$$\begin{aligned} x_1 - 2x_2 &= 8 \\ 3x_1 + x_2 &= 3. \end{aligned} \tag{7}$$

We can "eliminate" the variable x_1 from this system by multiplying equation (7a) by -3 to obtain $-3x_1 + 6x_2 = -24$ and adding this new equation to (7b). The result is

$$7x_2 = -21, \quad \text{or} \quad x_2 = -3.$$

To find x_1, we substitute $x_2 = -3$ back into (7b) or (7a) to compute that $x_1 = 2$. We chose to multiply equation (7a) by -3 precisely so that when we added the new equation to equation (7b), we would "eliminate" x_1 from the system.

To solve a general system of m equations by elimination of variables, use the coefficient of x_1 in the first equation to eliminate the x_1 term from all the equations *below* it. To do this, add proper multiples of the first equation to each of the succeeding equations. Now disregard the first equation and eliminate the next variable — usually x_2 — from the last $m - 1$ equations just as before, that is, by adding proper multiples of the second equation to each of the succeeding equations. If the second equation does not contain an x_2 but a lower equation does, you will have to interchange the order of these two equations before proceeding. Continue eliminating variables until you reach the last equation. The resulting simplified system can then easily be solved by substitution.

Let us try this method on the system (3) arising from the three-good input-output Table 7.1:

$$x_1 - 0.4 \ x_2 - 0.3 \ x_3 = 130$$
$$-0.2x_1 + 0.88x_2 - 0.14x_3 = \ \ 74 \qquad\qquad (8)$$
$$-0.5x_1 - 0.2 \ x_2 + 0.95x_3 = \ \ 95$$

We first try to eliminate x_1 from the last two equations by adding to each of these equations a proper multiple of the first equation. To eliminate the $-0.2x_1$-term in (8b), we multiply (8a) by 0.2 and add this new equation to (8b). The result is the following calculation:

$$0.2x_1 - 0.08x_2 - 0.06x_3 = \ \ 26$$
$$+ \ -0.2x_1 + 0.88x_2 - 0.14x_3 = \ \ 74$$
$$\overline{ \ \ 0.8x_2 - \ \ 0.2x_3 = 100.}$$

Similarly, by adding 0.5 times (8a) to (8c), we obtain a new third equation

$$-0.4x_2 + 0.8x_3 = 160.$$

Our system (8) has been transformed to the simpler system

$$1x_1 - 0.4x_2 - 0.3x_3 = 130$$
$$+ \ 0.8x_2 - 0.2x_3 = 100 \qquad\qquad (9)$$
$$- \ 0.4x_2 + 0.8x_3 = 160.$$

In transforming system (8) to system (9), we used only one operation: we added a multiple of one equation to another. This operation is reversible. For example, we can recover (8) from (9) by adding -0.2 times (9a) to (9b) to obtain (8b) and then by adding -0.5 times (9a) to (9c) to obtain (8c). (We continue to write (9a) to denote the first equation in system (9).) There are two other reversible operations one often uses to transform a system of equations: 1) multiplying both sides of an equation by a nonzero scalar and 2) interchanging two equations. These three operations are called the **elementary equation operations**. Since equals are always added to or subtracted from equals or multiplied by the same scalar, the set of x_i's which solve the original system will also solve the transformed system. In fact, since these three operations are reversible, any solution of the transformed system will also be a solution of the original system. Consequently, both systems will have the exact same set of solutions. We call two systems of linear equations **equivalent** if any solution of one system is also a solution of the other.

Fact If one system of linear equations is derived from another by elementary equation operations, then both systems have the same solutions; that is, the systems are equivalent.

Let us return to our elimination procedure and continue working on system (9). Having eliminated x_1 from the last two equations, we now want to eliminate x_2 from the last equation. We apply the elimination process to the system of two equations (9b) and (9c) in two unknowns. Multiply (9b) by 1/2 and add this new equation to (9c) to obtain the new system:

$$1x_1 - 0.4x_2 - 0.3x_3 = 130$$

$$+ 0.8x_2 - 0.2x_3 = 100 \qquad (10)$$

$$+ 0.7x_3 = 210.$$

Since each equation in (10) has one fewer variable than the previous one, this system is particularly amenable to solution by substitution. Thus, $x_3 = 300$ from (10c). Substituting $x_3 = 300$ into (10b) gives $x_2 = 200$. Finally, substituting these two values into (10a) yields $x_1 = 300$. The method used in this paragraph is usually called **back substitution**.

This method of reducing a given system of equations by adding a multiple of one equation to another or by interchanging equations until one reaches a system of the form (10) and then solving (10) via back substitution is called **Gaussian elimination**. The important characteristic of system (10) is that each equation contains fewer variables than the previous equation.

At each stage of the Gaussian elimination process, we want to change some coefficient of our linear system to 0 by adding a multiple of an *earlier* equation to the given one. For example, if you want to use the coefficient a_{3k} in the third equation to eliminate the coefficient a_{5k} in the fifth equation, we add $(-a_{5k}/a_{3k})$ times the third equation to the fifth equation, to get a new fifth equation whose kth coefficient is 0. The coefficient a_{3k} is then called a **pivot**, and we say that we "pivot on a_{3k} to eliminate a_{5k}." At each stage of the elimination procedure, we use a pivot to eliminate all coefficients directly below it. For example, in transforming system (8) to system (9), the coefficient 1 in equation (8a) is the pivot; in transforming system (9) to system (10), the coefficient 0.8 in equation (9b) is the pivot.

Note that 0 can never be a pivot in this process. If you want to eliminate x_k from a subsystem of equations and if the coefficient of x_k is zero in the first equation of this subsystem and nonzero in a subsequent equation, you will have to reverse the order of these two equations before proceeding.

We did not use the operation of transforming an equation by simply multiplying it by a nonzero scalar. There is a variant of Gaussian elimination, called **Gauss-Jordan elimination**, which uses all three elementary equation operations. This method starts like Gaussian elimination, e.g., by transforming (8) to (10). After reaching system (10), multiply each equation in (10) by a scalar so that the first nonzero coefficient is 1:

$$x_1 - 0.4x_2 - 0.3\ x_3 = 130$$
$$x_2 - 0.25x_3 = 125 \tag{11}$$
$$x_3 = 300.$$

Now, instead of using back substitution, use Gaussian elimination methods from the *bottom* equation to the top to eliminate all but the first term on the left-hand side in each equation in (11). For example, add 0.25 times equation (11c) to equation (11b) to eliminate the coefficient of x_3 in (11b) and obtain $x_2 = 200$. Then, add 0.3 times (11c) to (11a) and 0.4 times (11b) to (11a) to obtain the new system:

$$x_1 \qquad = 300$$
$$x_2 \quad = 200 \tag{12}$$
$$x_3 = 300,$$

which needs no further work to see the solution. Gauss-Jordan elimination is particularly useful in developing the theory of linear systems; Gaussian elimination is usually more efficient in solving actual linear systems.

Earlier we mentioned a third method for solving linear systems, namely matrix methods. We will study these methods in the next two chapters, when we discuss matrix inversion and Cramer's rule. For now, it suffices to note that all the intuition behind these more advanced methods derives from Gaussian elimination. The understanding of this technique will provide a solid base on which to build your knowledge of linear algebra.

EXERCISES

7.1   Which of the following equations are linear?

a) $3x_1 - 4x_2 + 5x_3 = 6$;   b) $x_1x_2x_3 = -2$;   c) $x^2 + 6y = 1$;
d) $(x + y)(x - z) = -7$;   e) $x + 3^{1/2}z = 4$;   f) $x + 3z^{1/2} = -4$.

7.2   Solve the following systems by substitution, Gaussian elimination, and Gauss-Jordan elimination:

a)
$$x - 3y + 6z = -1$$
$$2x - 5y + 10z = 0$$
$$3x - 8y + 17z = 1;$$

b)
$$x_1 + x_2 + x_3 = 0$$
$$12x_1 + 2x_2 - 3x_3 = 5$$
$$3x_1 + 4x_2 + x_3 = -4.$$

7.3 Solve the following systems by Gauss-Jordan elimination. Note that the third system requires an equation interchange.

$$
\begin{array}{lll}
a) \;\; 3x + 3y = 4 & b) \;\; 4x + 2y - 3z = 1 & c) \;\; 2x + 2y - z = 2 \\
\quad\;\; x - y = 10; & \quad\;\; 6x + 3y - 5z = 0 & \quad\;\; x + y + z = -2 \\
 & \quad\;\; x + y + 2z = 9; & \quad\;\; 2x - 4y + 3z = 0.
\end{array}
$$

7.4 Formalize the three elementary equation operations using the abstract notation of system (2), and for each operation, write out the operation which reverses its effect.

7.5 Solve the IS-LM system in Exercise 6.7 by substitution.

7.6 Consider the general IS-LM model with no fiscal policy in Chapter 6. Suppose that $M_s = M^o$; that is, the intercept of the LM-curve is 0.

   a) Use substitution to solve this system for Y and r in terms of the other parameters.

   b) How does the equilibrium GNP depend on the marginal propensity to save?

   c) How does the equilibrium interest rate depend on the marginal propensity to save?

7.7 Use Gaussian elimination to solve

$$
\begin{cases}
3x + 3y = 4 \\
-x - y = 10.
\end{cases}
$$

What happens and why?

7.8 Solve the general system

$$
\begin{cases}
a_{11}x_1 + a_{12}x_2 = b_1 \\
a_{21}x_1 + a_{22}x_2 = b_2.
\end{cases}
$$

What assumptions do you have to make about the coefficients a_{ij} in order to find a solution?

7.2 ELEMENTARY ROW OPERATIONS

The focus of our concern in the last section was on the coefficients a_{ij} and b_i of the systems with which we worked. In fact, it was a little inefficient to rewrite the x_i's, the plus signs, and the equal signs each time we transformed a system. It makes sense to simplify the representation of linear system (2) by writing two rectangular arrays of its coefficients, called **matrices**. The first array is

$$
A = \begin{pmatrix}
a_{11} & a_{12} & \cdots & a_{1n} \\
a_{21} & a_{22} & \cdots & a_{2n} \\
\vdots & \vdots & \ddots & \vdots \\
a_{m1} & a_{m2} & \cdots & a_{mn}
\end{pmatrix},
$$

which is called the **coefficient matrix** of (2). When we add on a column corresponding to the right-hand side in system (2), we obtain the matrix

$$\hat{A} = \begin{pmatrix} a_{11} & a_{12} & \cdots & a_{1n} & b_1 \\ a_{21} & a_{22} & \cdots & a_{2n} & b_2 \\ \vdots & \vdots & \ddots & \vdots & \vdots \\ a_{m1} & a_{m2} & \cdots & a_{mn} & b_m \end{pmatrix},$$

which is called the **augmented matrix** of (2). The rows of $\hat{A}$ correspond naturally to the equations of (2). For example,

$$\begin{pmatrix} 1 & -2 \\ 3 & 1 \end{pmatrix} \quad \text{and} \quad \begin{pmatrix} 1 & -2 & 8 \\ 3 & 1 & 3 \end{pmatrix}$$

are the coefficient matrix and the augmented matrix of system (7). For accounting purposes, it is often helpful to draw a vertical line just before the last column of the augmented matrix, where the $=$ signs would naturally appear, e.g.,

$$\begin{pmatrix} 1 & -2 & | & 8 \\ 3 & 1 & | & 3 \end{pmatrix}.$$

Our three elementary equation operations now become **elementary row operations**:

(1) interchange two rows of a matrix,
(2) change a row by adding to it a multiple of another row, and
(3) multiply each element in a row by the same nonzero number.

The new augmented matrix will represent a system of linear equations which is equivalent to the system represented by the old augmented matrix.

To see this equivalence, first observe that each elementary row operation can be reversed. Clearly the interchanging of two rows or the multiplication of a row by a nonzero scalar can be reversed. Suppose we consider the row operation in which k times the second row of the augmented matrix $\hat{A}$ is added to the first row of $\hat{A}$. The new augmented matrix is

$$B = \begin{pmatrix} a_{11} + ka_{21} & \cdots & a_{1n} + ka_{2n} & | & b_1 + kb_2 \\ a_{21} & \cdots & a_{2n} & | & b_2 \\ \vdots & \ddots & \vdots & | & \vdots \\ a_{m1} & \cdots & a_{mn} & | & b_m \end{pmatrix}.$$

However, if we start with B and add $-k$ times the second row to the first row, we will recover $\hat{A}$. Thus the row operation can be reversed. Since elementary row operations correspond to the three operations of adding a multiple of one equation to another equation, multiplying both sides of an equation by the same scalar, and changing the order of the equations, any solution to the original system of equations will be a solution to the transformed system. Since these operations are reversible, any solution to the transformed system of equations will also be a solution to the original system. Consequently the systems represented by matrices $\hat{A}$ and B have *identical solution sets*; they are equivalent.

The goal of performing row operations is to end up with a matrix that looks much like (10). The nice feature about the augmented matrix representing (10)

$$\begin{pmatrix} 1 & -0.4 & -0.3 & | & 130 \\ 0 & 0.8 & -0.2 & | & 100 \\ 0 & 0 & 0.7 & | & 210 \end{pmatrix} \tag{13}$$

is that each row *begins* with more zeros than does the previous row. Such a matrix is said to be in *row echelon form*.

Definition A row of a matrix is said to have k **leading zeros** if the first k elements of the row are all zeros and the $(k + 1)$th element of the row is not zero. With this terminology, a matrix is in **row echelon form** if each row has more leading zeros than the row preceding it.

The first row of the augmented matrix (13) has no leading zeros. The second row has one, and the third row has two. Since each row has more leading zeros than the previous row, matrix (13) is in row echelon form. Let's look at some more concrete examples.

Example 7.2 The matrices

$$\begin{pmatrix} 1 & 2 & 3 \\ 0 & 0 & 4 \\ 0 & 0 & 0 \\ 0 & 0 & 0 \end{pmatrix}, \quad \begin{pmatrix} 1 & 3 & 4 \\ 0 & 1 & 6 \end{pmatrix}, \quad \text{and} \quad \begin{pmatrix} 2 & 3 \\ 0 & 6 \\ 0 & 0 \end{pmatrix}$$

are in row echelon form. If a matrix in row echelon form has a row containing only zeros, then all the subsequent rows must contain only zeros.

Example 7.3 The matrices

$$\begin{pmatrix} 1 & 5 & 2 \\ 2 & 0 & 1 \end{pmatrix} \quad \text{and} \quad \begin{pmatrix} 0 & 7 \\ 9 & 0 \\ 0 & 2 \end{pmatrix}$$

are not in row echelon form.

Example 7.4   The matrix whose diagonal elements (a_{ii}'s) are 1s and whose off-diagonal elements (a_{ij}'s with i not equal to j) are all 0s is in row echelon form. This matrix arises frequently throughout linear algebra, and is called the **identity matrix** when the number of rows is the same as the number of columns:

$$I = \begin{pmatrix} 1 & 0 & \cdots & 0 \\ 0 & 1 & \cdots & 0 \\ \vdots & \vdots & \ddots & \vdots \\ 0 & 0 & \cdots & 1 \end{pmatrix}.$$

Example 7.5   The matrix each of whose elements is 0 is called the **zero matrix** and is in row echelon form:

$$\mathbf{0} = \begin{pmatrix} 0 & 0 & \cdots & 0 \\ 0 & 0 & \cdots & 0 \\ \vdots & \vdots & \ddots & \vdots \\ 0 & 0 & \cdots & 0 \end{pmatrix}.$$

The usefulness of row echelon form can be seen by considering the system of equations (8). The augmented matrix associated with (8) is

$$\begin{pmatrix} 1 & -0.4 & -0.3 & | & 130 \\ -0.2 & 0.88 & -0.14 & | & 74 \\ -0.5 & -0.2 & 0.95 & | & 95 \end{pmatrix},$$

and through various row operations we reduced it to

$$\begin{pmatrix} 1 & -0.4 & -0.3 & | & 130 \\ 0 & 0.8 & -0.2 & | & 100 \\ 0 & 0 & 0.7 & | & 210 \end{pmatrix}. \tag{14}$$

This last matrix is in row echelon form and the corresponding system can be easily solved by substitution. Simply rewrite it in equation form and solve it from bottom to top as we did for system (10).

Because of this connection with Gaussian elimination, it is natural that the first nonzero entry in each row of a matrix in row echelon form be called a **pivot**.

The row echelon form is the goal in the Gaussian elimination process. In Gauss-Jordan elimination, one wants to use row operations to reduce the matrix even further. First, multiply each row of the row echelon form by the reciprocal of the pivot in that row and create a new matrix all of whose pivots are 1s. Then, use these new pivots (starting with the 1 in the last row) to turn each nonzero entry *above* it (in the same column) into a zero.

For example, multiply the second row of (14) by $1/0.8$ and the third row of (14) by $1/0.7$ to achieve the matrix

$$\begin{pmatrix} 1 & -0.4 & -0.3 & | & 130 \\ 0 & 1 & -0.25 & | & 125 \\ 0 & 0 & 1 & | & 300 \end{pmatrix}.$$

Then, use the pivot in row 3 to turn the entries -0.25 and -0.3 above it into zeros — first by adding 0.25 times row 3 to row 2 and then by adding 0.3 times row 3 to row 1. The result is

$$\begin{pmatrix} 1 & -0.4 & 0 & | & 220 \\ 0 & 1 & 0 & | & 200 \\ 0 & 0 & 1 & | & 300 \end{pmatrix}.$$

Finally, use the pivot in row 2 to eliminate the nonzero entry above it by adding 0.4 times row 2 to row 1 to get the matrix

$$\begin{pmatrix} 1 & 0 & 0 & | & 300 \\ 0 & 1 & 0 & | & 200 \\ 0 & 0 & 1 & | & 300 \end{pmatrix}. \tag{15}$$

Notice that this is the augmented matrix for system (12) and that one can read the solution right off the last column of this matrix:

$$x_1 = 300, \qquad x_2 = 200, \qquad x_3 = 300.$$

We say that matrix (15) is in *reduced row echelon form*.

Definition   A row echelon matrix in which each pivot is a 1 and in which each column containing a pivot contains no other nonzero entries is said to be in **reduced row echelon form**.

The matrices in Examples 7.4 and 7.5 above are in reduced row echelon form. Note that in transforming a matrix to row echelon form we work from top left to bottom right. To achieve the reduced row echelon form, we continue in the same way but in the other direction, from bottom right to top left.

EXERCISES

7.9   Describe the row operations involved in going from equations (8) to (10).

7.10   Put the matrices in Examples 7.2 and 7.3 in reduced row echelon form.

7.11 Write the three systems in Exercise 7.3 in matrix form. Then use row operations to find their corresponding row echelon and reduced row echelon forms and to find the solution.

7.12 Use Gauss-Jordan elimination in matrix form to solve the system

$$
\begin{aligned}
w + x + 3y - 2z &= 0 \\
2w + 3x + 7y - 2z &= 9 \\
3w + 5x + 13y - 9z &= 1 \\
-2w + x \quad\quad - z &= 0.
\end{aligned}
$$

7.3 SYSTEMS WITH MANY OR NO SOLUTIONS

As we will study in more detail later, the locus of all points (x_1, x_2) which satisfy the linear equation $a_{11}x_1 + a_{12}x_2 = b_1$ is a straight line in the plane. Therefore, the solution (x_1, x_2) of the two linear equations in two unknowns

$$
\begin{aligned}
a_{11}x_1 + a_{12}x_2 &= b_1 \\
a_{21}x_1 + a_{22}x_2 &= b_2
\end{aligned}
\tag{16}
$$

is a point which lies on both lines of (16) in the Cartesian plane. Solving system (16) is equivalent to finding where the two lines given by (16) cross. In general, two lines in the plane will be nonparallel and will cross in exactly one point. However, the lines given by (16) can be parallel to each other. In this case, they will either coincide or they will never cross. If they coincide, every point on either line is a solution to (16); and (16) has *infinitely* many solutions. An example is the system

$$
\begin{aligned}
x_1 + 2x_2 &= 3 \\
2x_1 + 4x_2 &= 6.
\end{aligned}
$$

In the case where the two parallel lines do not cross, the corresponding system has *no* solution, as the example

$$
\begin{aligned}
x_1 + 2x_2 &= 3 \\
x_1 + 2x_2 &= 4
\end{aligned}
$$

illustrates. Therefore, it follows from geometric considerations that two linear equations in two unknowns can have one solution, no solution, or infinitely many solutions. We will see later in this chapter that this principle holds for every system of *m linear* equations in *n* unknowns.

So far we have worked with examples of systems in which there are exactly as many equations as there are unknowns. As we saw in the input-output model and the Markov model in Chapter 6, systems in which the number of equations differs from the number of unknowns arise naturally.

For example, let us look for a state price system for the investment model in Example 6.1. Substitution of the state returns R_{si} from Example 6.1 into equations (14) in Chapter 6 for the state prices leads to the system

$$
\begin{aligned}
p_1 + 2p_2 + 3p_3 &= 1 \\
3p_1 + 2p_2 + p_3 &= 1,
\end{aligned}
\tag{17}
$$

whose augmented matrix is

$$
\begin{pmatrix}
1 & 2 & 3 & | & 1 \\
3 & 2 & 1 & | & 1
\end{pmatrix}.
$$

Adding -3 times the first row to the second yields the row echelon matrix

$$
\begin{pmatrix}
1 & 2 & 3 & | & 1 \\
0 & -4 & -8 & | & -2
\end{pmatrix}.
$$

To obtain the *reduced* row echelon form, multiply the last equation by $-1/4$:

$$
\begin{pmatrix}
1 & 2 & 3 & | & 1 \\
0 & 1 & 2 & | & 0.5
\end{pmatrix}.
$$

Then, add -2 times the new last row to the first row to eliminate the 2 in the first row above the pivot. The result is

$$
\begin{pmatrix}
1 & 0 & -1 & | & 0 \\
0 & 1 & 2 & | & 0.5
\end{pmatrix},
$$

the reduced row echelon matrix, which corresponds to the system

$$
\begin{aligned}
p_1 \quad - \quad p_3 &= 0 \\
p_2 + 2p_3 &= 0.5.
\end{aligned}
$$

If we write this system as

$$
\begin{aligned}
p_1 &= p_3 \\
p_2 &= 0.5 - 2p_3,
\end{aligned}
\tag{18}
$$

we notice that there is no single solution to (18); for *any* value of p_3, system (18) determines corresponding values of p_1 and p_2. Since system (18) has multiple solutions, so does system (17). For any choice of p_3, (18) determines values of p_1 and p_2 which solve system (17). For example,

$$p_3 = \frac{1}{8}, \quad p_1 = \frac{1}{8}, \quad p_2 = \frac{1}{4};$$

$$p_3 = \frac{1}{6}, \quad p_1 = \frac{1}{6}, \quad p_2 = \frac{1}{6};$$

$$p_3 = \frac{1}{5}, \quad p_1 = \frac{1}{5}, \quad p_2 = \frac{1}{10}.$$

(Check that these three are truly solutions of (17).)

As an example of a system with *no solutions*, consider an investment model with state returns

$$R_{11} = 1 \qquad R_{12} = 3 \qquad R_{13} = 2$$

$$R_{21} = 3 \qquad R_{22} = 1 \qquad R_{23} = 3.$$

Once again by equation (14) in Chapter 6, the corresponding system of equations for a state price vector (p_1, p_2) is

$$1p_1 + 3p_2 = 1$$
$$3p_1 + 1p_2 = 1 \qquad \qquad (19)$$
$$2p_1 + 3p_2 = 1.$$

In system (19), note that the only p_1, p_2 pair that solves the first two equations is $x_1 = 0.25$, $x_2 = 0.25$. Since this pair does not satisfy the third equation, (19) has no solution. When we reduce the augmented matrix of (19) to row echelon form, we obtain

$$\begin{pmatrix} 1 & 3 & | & 1 \\ 0 & -8 & | & -2 \\ 0 & 0 & | & -0.25 \end{pmatrix}.$$

The last row corresponds to the equation

$$0p_1 + 0p_2 = -.25. \qquad \qquad (20)$$

The left-hand side of this equation is always 0 and thus can never equal -0.25. So there is no p_1, p_2 pair which solves this equation. Note that if we replace the last equation in (19) by

$$2p_1 + 2p_2 = 1,$$

then the new system has the unique solution

$$p_1 = 0.25, \qquad p_2 = 0.25,$$

and the row echelon form of the augmented matrix becomes

$$\begin{pmatrix} 1 & 3 & | & 1 \\ 0 & -8 & | & -2 \\ 0 & 0 & | & 0 \end{pmatrix},$$

which contains no contradictions. (Exercise: check all these computations.)

These examples raise the following questions about systems of linear equations.

(1) When does a particular system of linear equations have a solution?
(2) How many solutions does it have? How do we compute them?
(3) What conditions on the coefficient matrix will guarantee the existence of *at least* one solution for any choice of b_i's on the right-hand side of (2)?
(4) What conditions on the coefficient matrix will guarantee the existence of *at most* one solution for any choice of b_i's?
(5) What conditions on the coefficient matrix will guarantee the existence of a *unique* solution for any choice of b_i's?

The answers to these questions can be found by studying augmented matrices in reduced row echelon form. Gauss-Jordan elimination, which achieves the reduced row echelon form, works the same way whether or not the number of equations equals the number of unknowns. Let us recall this procedure one more time. Beginning with an augmented matrix, use row operations to achieve a row echelon matrix B in which the first nonzero entry in each row (that is, the pivot) is a 1. Then use these pivots (starting with the one in the last row) to turn each nonzero entry above it (in the same column) into zero.

For example, if the last pivot is in row h and column k and if a_{jk} is a nonzero entry in row j and (the same) column k with $j < h$, one adds $-a_{jk}$ times row h to row j to achieve a new a'_{jk} equal to zero. One continues until the pivot ($= 1$) is the only nonzero entry in column k. One then moves on to the pivot in row $h - 1$ and uses row operations until it too is the only nonzero entry in its column. These operations will not change the new column k since all the entries above row h in column k are zero. The end result of this process is a row echelon matrix in which each pivot is a 1 and each column which contains a pivot contains no other nonzero entries, that is, a reduced row echelon matrix.

For another example, consider an investment model with three assets and four states. Suppose that shares of the three assets have the following current values:

$$v_1 = 38, \qquad v_2 = 98, \qquad v_3 = 153.$$

As in Section 6.2, we write y_{si} for the value of a share of asset i one year from now if state s occurs. Suppose the y_{si}'s have the following values:

$$y_{11} = 1 \qquad y_{12} = 2 \qquad y_{13} = 3$$

$$y_{21} = 4 \qquad y_{22} = 12 \qquad y_{23} = 18$$

$$y_{31} = 17 \qquad y_{32} = 46 \qquad y_{33} = 69$$

$$y_{41} = 4 \qquad y_{42} = 10 \qquad y_{43} = 17.$$

By (13) in Chapter 6, the state prices p_1, p_2, p_3, p_4 for this model satisfy the system

$$1p_1 + 4p_2 + 17p_3 + 4p_4 = 38$$

$$2p_1 + 12p_2 + 46p_3 + 10p_4 = 98$$

$$3p_1 + 18p_2 + 69p_3 + 17p_4 = 153.$$

Its augmented matrix is

$$\begin{pmatrix} 1 & 4 & 17 & 4 & | & 38 \\ 2 & 12 & 46 & 10 & | & 98 \\ 3 & 18 & 69 & 17 & | & 153 \end{pmatrix},$$

with corresponding row echelon form

$$\begin{pmatrix} 1 & 4 & 17 & 4 & | & 38 \\ 0 & 4 & 12 & 2 & | & 22 \\ 0 & 0 & 0 & 2 & | & 6 \end{pmatrix}.$$

Divide the second row by 4 and the third row by 2 to obtain

$$\begin{pmatrix} 1 & 4 & 17 & 4 & | & 38 \\ 0 & 1 & 3 & 0.5 & | & 5.5 \\ 0 & 0 & 0 & 1 & | & 3 \end{pmatrix}.$$

Work first with the pivot in the third row to change column 4 from

$$\begin{pmatrix} 4 \\ 0.5 \\ 1 \end{pmatrix} \qquad \text{to} \qquad \begin{pmatrix} 0 \\ 0 \\ 1 \end{pmatrix},$$

by adding -0.5 times row 3 to row 2 and then add -4 times row 3 to row 1:

$$\begin{pmatrix} 1 & 4 & 17 & 0 & | & 26 \\ 0 & 1 & 3 & 0 & | & 4 \\ 0 & 0 & 0 & 1 & | & 3 \end{pmatrix}.$$

Now working with the pivot in row 2 and column 2, add -4 times row 2 to row 1 to change the 4 in row 1 to a 0:

$$\begin{pmatrix} 1 & 0 & 5 & 0 & | & 10 \\ 0 & 1 & 3 & 0 & | & 4 \\ 0 & 0 & 0 & 1 & | & 3 \end{pmatrix}.$$

(Note that because the new column 4 contains only 0s in the appropriate places, it was not affected by our work on column 2.) This matrix is now in reduced row echelon form. One can read off the final solution of the linear system from the reduced row echelon form matrix. For example, the linear system corresponding to the previous matrix is

$$
\begin{aligned}
p_1 \quad\quad + 5p_3 \quad\quad &= 10 \\
p_2 + 3p_3 \quad\quad &= 4 \\
p_4 &= 3,
\end{aligned}
$$

which we can rewrite as

$$
\begin{aligned}
p_1 &= 10 - 5p_3 \\
p_2 &= 4 - 3p_3 \\
p_4 &= 3.
\end{aligned}
$$

Observe that p_4 is unambiguously determined, but not the other variables. The variable p_3 is free to take on any value. Once a value for p_3 has been selected, the values of variables p_1 and p_2 are determined by the above equations. This is another system, like system (17), with infinitely many solutions, and all these solutions can be read right off the reduced row echelon matrix.

For example, if we choose $p_3 = 1$, we obtain the price system

$$p_1 = 5, \quad p_2 = 1, \quad p_3 = 1, \quad p_4 = 3.$$

If we choose $p_3 = 0.5$, we obtain the price system

$$p_1 = 7.5, \quad p_2 = 2.5, \quad p_3 = 0.5, \quad p_4 = 3.$$

As a final example, consider the following schematic matrix in which the stars ($*$) represent nonzero pivots and the w's may be either zero or nonzero:

$$\begin{pmatrix} * & w & w & w & w & w & w & | & w \\ 0 & 0 & 0 & * & w & w & w & | & w \\ 0 & 0 & 0 & 0 & * & w & w & | & w \\ 0 & 0 & 0 & 0 & 0 & 0 & * & | & w \end{pmatrix}.$$

This matrix is in row echelon form. The corresponding reduced row echelon form is

$$\begin{pmatrix} 1 & w & w & 0 & 0 & w & 0 & | & w \\ 0 & 0 & 0 & 1 & 0 & w & 0 & | & w \\ 0 & 0 & 0 & 0 & 1 & w & 0 & | & w \\ 0 & 0 & 0 & 0 & 0 & 0 & 1 & | & w \end{pmatrix}.$$

The final solution will have the form

$$x_1 = a_1 - a_2 x_2 - a_3 x_3 - a_4 x_6,$$
$$x_4 = b_1 \qquad\qquad\quad - b_2 x_6,$$
$$x_5 = c_1 \qquad\qquad\qquad - c_2 x_6,$$
$$x_7 = d_1.$$

Here x_7 is the only variable which is unambiguously determined. The variables x_2, x_3, and x_6 are free to take on any values; once values have been selected for these three variables, then values for x_1, x_4, and x_5 are automatically determined.

Some more vocabulary is helpful here. If the jth column of the row echelon matrix $\hat{B}$ contains a pivot, we call x_j a **basic variable**. If the jth column of $\hat{B}$ does not contain a pivot, we call x_j a **free** or **nonbasic variable**. In this terminology, Gauss-Jordan elimination determines a solution of the system in which each basic variable is either unambiguously determined or a linear expression of the free variables. The free variables are free to take on any value. Once one chooses values for the free variables, values for the basic variables are determined.

As in the example above, the free variables are often placed on the right-hand side of the equations to emphasize that their values are not determined by the system; rather, they act as parameters in determining values for the basic variables.

In a given problem which variables are free and which are basic may depend on the order of the operations used in the Gaussian elimination process and on the order in which the variables are indexed.

EXERCISES

7.13   Reduce the following matrices to row echelon and reduced row echelon forms:

$$a) \begin{pmatrix} 1 & 1 \\ -2 & -1 \end{pmatrix}, \qquad b) \begin{pmatrix} 1 & 3 & 4 \\ 2 & 5 & 7 \end{pmatrix}, \qquad c) \begin{pmatrix} -1 & -1 \\ 2 & 1 \\ 1 & 0 \end{pmatrix}.$$

7.14 Solve the system of equations $\begin{cases} -4x + 6y + 4z = 4 \\ 2x - y + z = 1. \end{cases}$

7.15 Use Gauss-Jordan elimination to determine for what values of the parameter k the system

$$x_1 + x_2 = 1$$
$$x_1 - kx_2 = 1$$

has no solutions, one solution, and more than one solution.

7.16 Use Gauss-Jordan elimination to solve the following four systems of linear equations. Which variables are free and which are basic in each solution?

a)
$$w + 2x + y - z = 1$$
$$3w - x - y + 2z = 3$$
$$- x + y - z = 1$$
$$2w + 3x + 3y - 3z = 3;$$

b)
$$w - x + 3y - z = 0$$
$$w + 4x - y + z = 3$$
$$3w + 7x + y + z = 6$$
$$3w + 2x + 5y - z = 3;$$

c)
$$w + 2x + 3y - z = 1$$
$$-w + x + 2y + 3z = 2$$
$$3w - x + y + 2z = 2$$
$$2w + 3x - y + z = 1;$$

d)
$$w + x - y + 2z = 3$$
$$2w + 2x - 2y + 4z = 6$$
$$-3w - 3x + 3y - 6z = -9$$
$$-2w - 2x + 2y - 4z = -6.$$

7.17 a) Use the flexibility of the free variable to find *positive integers* which satisfy the system

$$x + y + z = 13$$
$$x + 5y + 10z = 61.$$

b) Suppose you hand a cashier a dollar bill for a 6-cent piece of candy and receive 16 coins as your change — all pennies, nickels, and dimes. How many coins of each type do you receive? [Hint: See part a.]

7.18 For what values of the parameter a does the following system of equations have a solution?

$$6x + y = 7$$
$$3x + y = 4$$
$$-6x - 2y = a.$$

7.19 From Chapter 6, the stationary distribution in the Markov model of unemployment satisfies the linear system

$$(q - 1)x + py = 0$$
$$(1 - q)x - py = 0$$
$$x + y = 1.$$

a) If p and q lie between 0 and 1, how many solutions does this system have? Why?

b) Ignoring the condition that p and q must be between and 0 and 1, find values of p and q so that this system has no solutions.

7.4   RANK — THE FUNDAMENTAL CRITERION

We now answer the five basic questions about existence and uniqueness of solutions that were posed in Section 7.3. The main criterion involved in the answers to these questions is the rank of a matrix. First, note that we say a row of a matrix is nonzero if and only if it contains at least one nonzero entry.

Definition   The **rank** of a matrix is the number of nonzero rows in its row echelon form.

Since we can reduce any matrix to several different row echelon matrices (if we interchange rows), we need to show that this definition of rank is independent of which row echelon matrix we compute. We will save this for Chapter 27, where we will also discuss the rank of a matrix from a different, more geometric point of view.

Let A and $\hat{A}$ be the coefficient matrix and augmented matrix respectively of a system of linear equations. Let B and $\hat{B}$ be their corresponding row echelon forms. One goes through the same steps in reducing A to B as in reducing $\hat{A}$ to $\hat{B}$ no matter what the last column of $\hat{A}$ is, because the choices of elementary row operations in going from $\hat{A}$ to $\hat{B}$ never involve the last column of the augmented matrix. In other words, $\hat{B}$ is itself an augmented matrix for B.

We first relate the rank of a coefficient matrix A to the rank of a corresponding augmented matrix and to the number of rows and columns of A. Note that the rank of the augmented matrix must be at least as big as the rank of the coefficient matrix because if a row in the augmented matrix contains only zeros, then so does the corresponding row of the coefficient matrix. Furthermore, the definition of rank requires that the rank is less than or equal to the number of rows of the coefficient matrix. Since each nonzero row in the row echelon form contains exactly one pivot, the rank is equal to the number of pivots. Since each column of A can have at most one pivot, the rank is also less than or equal to the number of columns of the coefficient matrix. Fact 7.1 summarizes the observations in this paragraph.

Fact 7.1.   Let A be the coefficient matrix and let $\hat{A}$ be the corresponding augmented matrix. Then,

(*a*) $\operatorname{rank} A \leq \operatorname{rank} \hat{A}$,
(*b*) $\operatorname{rank} A \leq$ number of rows of A, and
(*c*) $\operatorname{rank} A \leq$ number of columns of A.

The following fact relates the ranks of A and of $\hat{A}$ to the existence of a solution of the system in question and gives us our first answer to Question 1 above.

Fact 7.2. A system of linear equations with coefficient matrix A and augmented matrix $\hat{A}$ has a solution if and only if

$$\operatorname{rank}\hat{A} = \operatorname{rank}A.$$

Proof The proof of this statement follows easily from a careful consideration of the row echelon form $\hat{B}$ of $\hat{A}$. If $\operatorname{rank}\hat{A} > \operatorname{rank}A$, then there is a zero row in the row echelon coefficient matrix B which corresponds to a nonzero row in the corresponding row echelon augmented matrix $\hat{B}$. This translates into the equation

$$0x_1 + 0x_2 + \cdots + 0x_n = b' \tag{21}$$

with b' nonzero. Consequently, the row echelon system has no solution and therefore the original system has no solution.

On the other hand, if the row echelon form of the augmented matrix contains no row corresponding to equation (21), that is, if $\operatorname{rank}A = \operatorname{rank}\hat{A}$, then there is nothing to stop Gauss-Jordan elimination from finding a general solution to the original system. As the discussion in the last section indicates, one can easily read off the solution directly from the reduced row echelon form. Some basic variables will be uniquely determined; others will be linear expressions of the free variables. ■

If a system with a solution has free variables, then these variables can take on any value in the general solution of the system. Consequently, the original system has infinitely many solutions. If there are no free variables, then every variable is a basic variable. In this case, Gaussian or Gauss-Jordan elimination determines a unique value for every variable; that is, there is only one solution to the system. We can summarize these observations.

Fact 7.3. A linear system of equations must have either no solution, one solution, or infinitely many solutions. Thus, if a system has more than one solution, it has infinitely many.

Let us look carefully at the case where there are no free variables in the system under study. Since every variable must be a basic variable, each column contains exactly one pivot. Since each nonzero row contains a pivot too, there must be at least as many rows as columns. (There may be some all-zero rows at the bottom of the row echelon matrix.) This proves:

Fact 7.4. If a system has exactly one solution, then the coefficient matrix A has at least as many rows as columns. In other words, a system with a unique solution must have at least as many equations as unknowns.

Fact 7.4 can be expressed another way.

Fact 7.5. If a system of linear equations has more unknowns than equations, it must have either no solution or infinitely many solutions.

Consider a system in which all the b_j's on the right-hand side are 0:

$$a_{11}x_1 + \cdots + a_{1n}x_n = 0$$
$$a_{21}x_1 + \cdots + a_{2n}x_n = 0$$
$$\vdots \qquad \vdots \qquad \vdots$$
$$a_{m1}x_1 + \cdots + a_{mn}x_n = 0.$$

Such a system is called **homogeneous**. As we shall see later, homogeneous systems play an especially important role in the study of linear equations. Any homogeneous system has at least one solution:

$$x_1 = x_2 = \cdots = x_n = 0.$$

The following statement is an immediate consequence of Fact 7.5.

Fact 7.6.   A homogeneous system of linear equations which has more unknowns than equations must have infinitely many distinct solutions.

We now turn to the answers of Questions 3, 4, and 5 of the previous section. In many economic models, the b_i's on the right-hand side of a system of linear equations can be considered as exogenous variables which vary from problem to problem. For each choice of b_i's on the right-hand side, one solves the linear system to find the corresponding values of the endogenous variables $x_1, \ldots, x_n$. For example, in the input-output example in Chapter 6, for each choice of consumption amounts $c_1, \ldots, c_n, c_0$, one wants to compute the required outputs $x_1, \ldots, x_n$. In the linear IS-LM model of Chapter 6, for each choice of policy variables G and M_s and parameters I^* and M^*, one wants to compute the corresponding equilibrium GNP Y and interest rate r. Thus, it becomes especially important to understand what properties of a system will guarantee that it has at least one solution or, better yet, exactly one solution for *any* right-hand side (RHS) $b_1, b_2, \ldots, b_m$. Again the answers flow directly from a careful look at reduced row echelon matrices. First we answer Question 3.

Fact 7.7.   A system of linear equations with coefficient matrix A will have a solution for every choice of RHS $b_1, \ldots, b_m$ if and only if

$$\operatorname{rank} A = \text{number of rows of } A.$$

Proof   (If): If $\operatorname{rank} A$ equals the number of rows of A, then the row echelon matrix B of A has no all-zero rows. Let $b_1, \ldots, b_m$ be a choice of RHS in system (2). Let $\hat{B}$ be the row echelon form of the corresponding augmented matrix. By the remarks at the beginning of this section, $\hat{B}$ is an augmented matrix for B, and hence $\hat{B}$ will have no all-zero rows either. Thus,

$$\operatorname{rank} A = \#\text{ rows of } A = \#\text{ rows of } \hat{A} = \operatorname{rank} \hat{A}.$$

By Fact 7.2, our system has a solution.

(Only If): If $\operatorname{rank} A$ is less than the number of rows of A, then the last row, row m, in the row echelon matrix B of A will contain only zeros. Since B is in row echelon form,

$$B = \begin{pmatrix} * & * & \cdots & * \\ 0 & * & \cdots & * \\ \vdots & \vdots & \ddots & \vdots \\ 0 & 0 & \cdots & 0 \end{pmatrix}$$

Augment B by a column of 1s to make $\hat{B}$:

$$\hat{B} = \left(\begin{array}{cccc|c} * & * & \cdots & * & 1 \\ 0 & * & \cdots & * & 1 \\ \vdots & \vdots & \ddots & \vdots & 1 \\ 0 & 0 & \cdots & 0 & 1 \end{array} \right).$$

The system corresponding to $\hat{B}$ can have no solution because nothing satisfies the equation described by the last row of $\hat{B}$: $0 = 1$. Starting now with $\hat{B}$, reverse in turn each row operation that was applied in transforming A to B. The result is an augmented matrix $\hat{A}$ whose coefficient matrix is our original matrix A. The systems of equations $\hat{A}$ and $\hat{B}$ are equivalent since one was obtained from the other by a sequence of row operations. Since the system corresponding to $\hat{B}$ has no solution, neither does the system corresponding to $\hat{A}$. Since $\hat{A}$ is an augmented matrix for A, we have found a right-hand side for which the system with coefficient matrix A has no solution under the assumption that the rank of A is less than the number of rows of A. This finishes the proof of Fact 7.7. ■

If a system of equations has fewer unknowns than equations, then the corresponding coefficient matrix has fewer columns than rows. Since the rank is less than or equal to the number of columns, which is less than the number of rows, Fact 7.7 ensures that there are RHSs for which the corresponding system has no solutions. We summarize this observation as Fact 7.8.

Fact 7.8.   If a system of linear equations has more equations than unknowns, then there is a right-hand side such that the resulting system has *no* solutions.

Next we turn to Question 4 and state a condition that guarantees that our system will have at most one solution, that is, will never have infinitely many solutions, for *any* choice of RHS $b_1, \ldots, b_m$.

Fact 7.9. Any system of linear equations having A as its coefficient matrix will have at most one solution for every choice of RHS $b_1, \ldots, b_m$ if and only if

$$\operatorname{rank} A = \text{number of columns of } A.$$

Proof (If): If $\operatorname{rank} A$ equals the number of columns of A, then there are as many pivots in the reduced row echelon matrix A'' as there are columns in A''. Since each column can contain at most one pivot, there is a pivot in each column. So, every variable is a basic variable; there are no free variables. The reduced row echelon matrix A'' has the form

$$A'' = \begin{pmatrix} 1 & 0 & 0 & \cdots & 0 \\ 0 & 1 & 0 & \cdots & 0 \\ \vdots & \vdots & \vdots & \ddots & \vdots \\ 0 & 0 & 0 & \cdots & 1 \\ 0 & 0 & 0 & \cdots & 0 \\ \vdots & \vdots & \vdots & \ddots & \vdots \\ 0 & 0 & 0 & \cdots & 0 \end{pmatrix}.$$

If there is a solution for some given RHS $b_1, \ldots, b_m$, it will be unambiguously determined by A''; that is, the solution will be unique.

(Only If): On the other hand, if the rank is less than the number of columns, then there must be some free variables. Choose a RHS so that the system has a solution, for example, $b_1 = \cdots = b_m = 0$. Because the free variables can take on any value in solutions (as shown in the previous section), there are infinitely many solutions to the system. This proves the second half of Fact 7.9. ■

Finally, we combine Facts 7.7 and 7.9 to characterize those coefficient matrices which have the property that for *any* RHS $b_1, \ldots, b_m$, the corresponding system of linear equations has exactly one solution. Such coefficient matrices are called **nonsingular**. They are the ones which will arise most frequently in our study of linear systems and other linear phenomena.

Fact 7.10. A coefficient matrix A is nonsingular, that is, the corresponding linear system has one and only one solution for every choice of right-hand side $b_1, \ldots, b_m$, if and only if

$$\text{number of rows of } A = \text{number of columns of } A = \operatorname{rank} A.$$

Fact 7.10 is a straightforward consequence of Facts 7.7 and 7.9. It tells us that a necessary condition for a system to have a unique solution for every RHS is that there be exactly as many equations as unknowns. The corresponding coefficient matrix must have the same number of rows as columns. Such a matrix is called a **square matrix**.

The problem of determining whether a square matrix has **maximal rank** (that is, rank as in Fact 7.10) is a central one in linear algebra. Fortunately, there is an easily computed number which one can assign to any square matrix which determines whether or not this rank condition holds. This number is called the **determinant** of the matrix; it will be the subject of our discussion in Chapters 9 and 26.

Finally, Fact 7.11 summarizes our findings in this section for a system of m equations in n unknowns — a system whose coefficient matrix has m rows and n columns.

Fact 7.11. Consider the linear system of equations $Ax = b$.

(a) If the number of equations < the number of unknowns, then:
   (i) $Ax = 0$ has infinitely many solutions,
   (ii) for any given b, $Ax = b$ has 0 or infinitely many solutions, and
   (iii) if rank A = number of equations, $Ax = b$ has infinitely many solutions for *every* RHS b.
(b) If the number of equations > the number of unknowns, then:
   (i) $Ax = 0$ has one or infinitely many solutions,
   (ii) for any given b, $Ax = b$ has 0, 1, or infinitely many solutions, and
   (iii) if rank A = number of unknowns, $Ax = b$ has 0 or 1 solution for *every* RHS b.
(c) If the number of equations = the number of unknowns, then:
   (i) $Ax = 0$ has one or infinitely many solutions,
   (ii) for any given b, $Ax = b$ has 0, 1, or infinitely many solutions, and
   (iii) if rank A = number of unknowns = number of equations, $Ax = b$ has exactly 1 solution for *every* RHS b.

Application to Portfolio Theory

We return to our discussion of investment in Example 5 of Section 6.2. There we called an A–tuple $(x_1, \ldots, x_A)$ such that $x_1 + \cdots + x_A = 1$ a **portfolio**, where x_i denotes the fraction of the investor's wealth to be spent on asset i.

Suppose that there are S states of nature and that R_{si} denotes the return at the end of the investment period to a unit of asset i when the period is characterized by state s. The return to portfolio x in state s is $R_s = \sum_{i=1}^{A} R_{si} x_i$. A portfolio is called **riskless** if it provides the same return in every state of nature:

$$\sum_{i=1}^{A} R_{1i} x_i = \sum_{i=1}^{A} R_{2i} x_i = \cdots = \sum_{i=1}^{A} R_{Si} x_i.$$

A portfolio $(x_1, \ldots, x_A)$ is called **duplicable** if there is a different portfolio $(w_1, \ldots, w_A)$ with exactly the same returns in every state:

$$\sum_{i=1}^{A} R_{si} x_i = \sum_{i=1}^{A} R_{si} w_i \qquad \text{for each } s = 1, \ldots, S.$$

A state s^* is called **insurable** if there is a portfolio $(x_1, \ldots, x_A)$ which has a positive return if state s^* occurs and zero return if any other state occurs:

$$\sum_{i=1}^{A} R_{s^* i} x_i > 0$$

$$\sum_{i=1}^{A} R_{si} x_i = 0 \qquad \text{for all } s \neq s^*.$$

For any portfolio **x**, the return to **x** in each state is given by the S–tuple $(R_1, \ldots, R_S)$, where

$$R_{11} x_1 + \cdots + R_{1A} x_A = R_1$$

$$\vdots \qquad \vdots \qquad \qquad \vdots \tag{22}$$

$$R_{S1} x_1 + \cdots + R_{SA} x_A = R_S.$$

Let $\mathcal{R}$ be the $S \times A$ coefficient matrix of the R_{si}'s:

$$\mathcal{R} = \begin{pmatrix} R_{11} & \cdots & R_{1A} \\ \vdots & \ddots & \vdots \\ R_{S1} & \cdots & R_{SA} \end{pmatrix}.$$

Suppose first that the matrix $\mathcal{R}$ has rank $S =$ the number of rows of $\mathcal{R}$. Then, by Fact 7.7, one can solve system (22) for any given S–tuple $(R_1, \ldots, R_S)$ of returns. In particular, if we take $R_1 = \cdots = R_S = b$ for some $b \neq 0$, the solution to (22), when properly normalized so that $x_1 + \cdots + x_A = 1$, will be a riskless asset. If we set $R_k = 1$ and $R_i = 0$ for $i \neq k$, the solution to (22), when properly normalized, will be an insurance portfolio for state k. So, if the rank of $\mathcal{R} = S$, then there is a riskless asset and every state is insurable.

We will argue in Section 28.2 that the converse holds too. If every state is insurable, then $\mathcal{R}$ must have rank S. In particular, if $A < S$, that is, if there are more states of nature than assets, then $\mathcal{R}$ cannot have rank S and there must exist states that are not insurable.

Finally, there are duplicable portfolios if and only if equation (22) has multiple portfolio solutions for some right-hand sides. This situation occurs only if system (22) has free variables, that is, only if the rank of $\mathcal{R}$ is less than A.

Example 7.6 In Example 6.1, we worked with the 3×2 state–return matrix

$$\mathcal{R} = \begin{pmatrix} 1 & 3 \\ 2 & 2 \\ 3 & 1 \end{pmatrix},$$

which has 2 columns and rank 2. We use Gaussian elimination to transform $\mathcal{R}$ to its row echelon form:

$$
\begin{pmatrix} 1 & 3 & | & a \\ 2 & 2 & | & b \\ 3 & 1 & | & c \end{pmatrix} \implies \begin{pmatrix} 1 & 3 & | & a \\ 0 & -4 & | & b - 2a \\ 0 & 0 & | & a + c - 2b \end{pmatrix}.
$$

Since $a + c - 2b = 0$ if $a = b = c = 1$, this market has a riskless asset. Since $a + c - 2b \neq 0$ if (a, b, c) has exactly one nonzero component, there are no insurable states. Since $\mathcal{R}$ has no free variables, there are no duplicable portfolios.

EXERCISES

7.20 Compute the rank of each of the following matrices:

$a)$ $\begin{pmatrix} 2 & -4 \\ -1 & 2 \end{pmatrix},$ $b)$ $\begin{pmatrix} 2 & -4 & 2 \\ -1 & 2 & 1 \end{pmatrix},$ $c)$ $\begin{pmatrix} 1 & 6 & -7 & 3 \\ 1 & 9 & -6 & 4 \\ 1 & 3 & -8 & 4 \end{pmatrix},$

$d)$ $\begin{pmatrix} 1 & 6 & -7 & 3 & 5 \\ 1 & 9 & -6 & 4 & 9 \\ 1 & 3 & -8 & 4 & 2 \\ 2 & 15 & -13 & 11 & 16 \end{pmatrix},$ $e)$ $\begin{pmatrix} 1 & 6 & -7 & 3 & 1 \\ 1 & 9 & -6 & 4 & 2 \\ 1 & 3 & -8 & 4 & 5 \end{pmatrix}.$

7.21 The following five matrices are coefficient matrices of systems of linear equations. For each matrix, what can you say about the number of solutions of the corresponding system: $a)$ when the right-hand side is $b_1 = \cdots = b_m = 0$, and $b)$ for general RHS $b_1, \ldots, b_m$?

$i)$ $\begin{pmatrix} 1 & 4 \\ 2 & 1 \end{pmatrix},$ $ii)$ $\begin{pmatrix} 1 & 4 & 3 \\ 2 & 1 & 0 \end{pmatrix},$ $iii)$ $\begin{pmatrix} 2 & 1 \\ 1 & 4 \\ 0 & 3 \end{pmatrix},$

$iv)$ $\begin{pmatrix} 1 & 4 & 3 \\ 2 & 1 & 0 \\ 1 & 1 & 1 \end{pmatrix},$ $v)$ $\begin{pmatrix} 1 & 4 & 3 \\ 2 & 1 & 0 \\ 0 & 7 & 6 \end{pmatrix}.$

7.22 Repeat Exercise 7.21 for the five matrices in Exercise 7.20.

7.23 Which coefficient matrix in Exercise 7.16 satisfies the conditions of Fact 7.10, that is, is nonsingular?

7.24 Show that a square matrix A is nonsingular if and only if its row echelon forms have no zeros on the diagonal.

7.5 THE LINEAR IMPLICIT FUNCTION THEOREM

The situation described in Fact 7.10 arises frequently in mathematical models, as we discussed last section. The b_i's on the RHS of (2) represent some externally determined parameters, while the linear equations themselves represent some equilibrium condition which determines the internal variables $x_1, \ldots, x_n$. Ideally, there should be a unique equilibrium for each choice of the parameters $b_1, \ldots, b_m$. Fact 7.10 tells us exactly when this ideal situation occurs: the number of equations must equal the number of unknowns and the coefficient matrix must have maximal rank.

In this view, consider once again the IS-LM model described in Chapter 6:

$$sY + ar = I^* + G$$
$$mY - hr = M_s - M^*. \tag{23}$$

Choose numerical values for the parameters s, a, m, h, I^*, G, and M^* in system (23). However, think of M_s, the money supply, as a variable policy parameter which a policymaker can set externally. For each choice of money supply, the economy reaches an equilibrium in Y and r. Since we have two equations in two unknowns, Fact 7.10 tells us that system (23) will indeed determine a unique (Y, r) pair for each choice of M_s provided the coefficient matrix

$$\begin{pmatrix} s & a \\ m & -h \end{pmatrix}$$

has rank two.

In this IS-LM model the variables Y and r are called **endogenous variables** because their values are determined by the system of equations under consideration. On the other hand, M_s is called an **exogenous variable** because its value is determined outside of system (23). If we were to treat s, a, m, h, I^*, G, and M^* as parameters also, then they too would be exogenous variables. Mathematicians would call exogenous variables **independent variables** and endogenous variables **dependent variables**.

A general linear model will have m equations in n unknowns:

$$a_{11}x_1 + a_{12}x_2 + \cdots + a_{1n}x_n = b_1$$
$$\vdots \qquad\qquad \vdots \qquad\qquad \vdots \tag{24}$$
$$a_{m1}x_1 + a_{m2}x_2 + \cdots + a_{mn}x_n = b_m.$$

Usually there will be a natural division of the x_i's into exogenous and endogenous variables given by the model. This division will be successful only if, after choosing values for the exogenous variables and plugging them into system (24), one can then unambiguously solve the system for the rest of the variables, the endogenous ones. Fact 7.10 in the last section tells us the two conditions that must hold in order for this breakdown into exogenous variables and endogenous variables to be successful. There must be exactly as many endogenous variables as there are equations in (24), and the square matrix corresponding to the endogenous variables must have maximal rank m. This statement is a version of the Implicit Function Theorem for linear equations, and is summarized in the following theorem.

Theorem 7.1 Let $x_1, \ldots, x_k$ and $x_{k+1}, \ldots, x_n$ be a partition of the n variables in (24) into endogenous and exogenous variables, respectively. There is, for each choice of values $x_{k+1}^0, \ldots, x_n^0$ for the exogenous variables, a unique set of values $x_1^0, \ldots, x_k^0$ which solves (24) if and only if:

(a) $k = m$ (number of endogenous variables = number of equations) and
(b) the rank of the matrix

$$\begin{pmatrix} a_{11} & a_{12} & \cdots & a_{1k} \\ a_{21} & a_{22} & \cdots & a_{2k} \\ \vdots & \vdots & \ddots & \vdots \\ a_{k1} & a_{k2} & \cdots & a_{kk} \end{pmatrix},$$

corresponding to the endogenous variables, is k.

Under the conditions of Theorem 7.1, we can think of system (24) as implicitly presenting each of the endogenous variables as functions of all the exogenous variables. Later, we will strengthen this result and use it as motivation for the Implicit Function Theorem for nonlinear systems of equations—a result which will be the cornerstone of our treatment of nonlinear equations, especially applied to comparative statics in economic models.

EXERCISES

7.25 For each of the following two systems, we want to separate the variables into exogenous and endogenous ones so that each choice of values for the exogenous variables determines unique values for the endogenous variables. For each system, *a*) determine how many variables can be endogenous at any one time, *b*) determine a successful separation into exogenous and endogenous variables, and *c*) find an explicit formula for the endogenous variables in terms of the exogenous ones:

i)
$$\begin{aligned} x + 2y + z - w &= 1 \\ 3x + 6y - z - 3w &= 2; \end{aligned}$$

ii)
$$\begin{aligned} x + 2y + z - w &= 1 \\ 3x - y - 4z + 2w &= 3 \\ y + z + w &= 0. \end{aligned}$$

7.26 For Example 1 in Chapter 6, write out the linear system which corresponds to equation (1) in Chapter 6 but with the \$100,000 before-tax profit replaced by a general before-tax profit P. Solve the resulting system for C, S, and F in terms of P.

7.27 For the values of the constants in Exercise 6.7, show that each choice of M_s uniquely determines an equilibrium (Y, r).

7.28 *a*) In IS-LM model (23), use Gaussian elimination to find a general formula involving s, a, m, and h which, when satisfied, will guarantee that system (23) determines a unique value of Y and r for each choice of I^*, M^*, G, and M_s.

    b) In this case, find an explicit formula for Y and r in terms of all the other variables.

    c) Note how changes in each of the exogenous variables affect the values of Y and r.

7.29 Consider the system

$$
\begin{aligned}
w - \;\; x + 3y - \;\; z &= 0 \\
w + 4x - \;\; y + 2z &= 3 \\
3w + 7x + \;\; y + \;\; z &= 6.
\end{aligned}
$$

    a) Separate the variables into endogenous and exogenous ones so that each choice of the exogenous variables uniquely determines values for the endogenous ones.

    b) For your answer to *a*, what are the values of the endogenous variables when all the exogenous variables are set equal to 0?

    c) Find a separation into endogenous and exogenous variables (same number of each as in part *a*) that will not work in the sense of *a*. Find a value of the new exogenous variables for which there are infinitely many corresponding values of the endogenous variables.

7.30 Consider the system

$$
\begin{aligned}
w - \;\; x + 3y - z &= 0 \\
w + 4x - \;\; y + z &= 3 \\
3w + 7x + \;\; y + z &= 6.
\end{aligned}
$$

Is there any successful decomposition into endogenous and exogenous variables? Explain.

Matrix Algebra

Matrices were introduced in the previous chapter to organize our calculations for solving systems of linear equations. Matrices play an important role in many other areas of economics and applied mathematics. The *input-output matrix* of Example 2 in Chapter 6, and the *Markov matrix* of Example 3 are but two examples. Other examples include *payoff matrices* from the theory of games, *coefficient matrices* and *correlation matrices* from econometrics, *Slutsky* and *Antonelli matrices* from consumer theory, and the *Hessian* and *bordered Hessian* matrices that embody the second order conditions in multivariable optimization theory.

A **matrix** is simply a rectangular array of numbers. So, any table of data is a matrix. The size of a matrix is indicated by the number of its rows and the number of its columns. A matrix with k rows and n columns is called a $k \times n$ ("k by n") matrix. The number in row i and column j is called the (i, j)th entry, and is often written a_{ij}, as we did in Chapter 7. Two matrices are *equal* if they both have the same size and if the corresponding entries in the two matrices are equal.

Matrices are in a sense generalized numbers. When the sizes are right, two matrices can be added, subtracted, multiplied and even divided. Whenever an economic model uses matrices, we can learn a lot about the underlying model via these algebraic operations. In this chapter, we describe the algebra of matrices. This chapter is a bit more abstract than previous chapters since it focuses on algebraic operations and their properties. But we will use these operations throughout this book. We illustrate this use in Section 8.5 where we derive the basic property of Leontief input-output models.

8.1 MATRIX ALGEBRA

Addition

We begin with addition of matrices. One can add two matrices of the same size, which is to say, with the same number of rows and columns. Their sum is a new matrix of the same size as the two matrices being added. The (i, j)th entry of the sum matrix is simply the sum of the (i, j)th entries of the two matrices being added.

In symbols

$$
\begin{pmatrix} a_{11} & \cdots & a_{1n} \\ \vdots & a_{ij} & \vdots \\ a_{k1} & \cdots & a_{kn} \end{pmatrix} + \begin{pmatrix} b_{11} & \cdots & b_{1n} \\ \vdots & b_{ij} & \vdots \\ b_{k1} & \cdots & b_{kn} \end{pmatrix}
$$

$$
= \begin{pmatrix} a_{11} + b_{11} & \cdots & a_{1n} + b_{1n} \\ \vdots & a_{ij} + b_{ij} & \vdots \\ a_{k1} + b_{k1} & \cdots & a_{kn} + b_{kn} \end{pmatrix}.
$$

For example,

$$
\begin{pmatrix} 3 & 4 & 1 \\ 6 & 7 & 0 \\ -1 & 3 & 8 \end{pmatrix} + \begin{pmatrix} -1 & 0 & 7 \\ 6 & 5 & 1 \\ -1 & 7 & 0 \end{pmatrix} = \begin{pmatrix} 2 & 4 & 8 \\ 12 & 12 & 1 \\ -2 & 10 & 8 \end{pmatrix}
$$

but

$$
\begin{pmatrix} 1 & 2 & 3 \\ 0 & 2 & -2 \end{pmatrix} + \begin{pmatrix} 3 & 6 \\ 1 & 4 \end{pmatrix}
$$

is not defined.

The matrix **0** whose entries are all zero is an *additive identity* since

$$
\begin{pmatrix} a_{11} & \cdots & a_{1n} \\ \vdots & a_{ij} & \vdots \\ a_{k1} & \cdots & a_{kn} \end{pmatrix} + \begin{pmatrix} 0_{11} & \cdots & 0_{1n} \\ \vdots & 0_{ij} & \vdots \\ 0_{k1} & \cdots & 0_{kn} \end{pmatrix} = \begin{pmatrix} a_{11} & \cdots & a_{1n} \\ \vdots & a_{ij} & \vdots \\ a_{k1} & \cdots & a_{kn} \end{pmatrix},
$$

that is, $A + \mathbf{0} = A$ for all matrices A.

Subtraction

Since $-A$ is what one adds to A to obtain **0**,

$$
- \begin{pmatrix} a_{11} & \cdots & a_{1n} \\ \vdots & a_{ij} & \vdots \\ a_{k1} & \cdots & a_{kn} \end{pmatrix} = \begin{pmatrix} -a_{11} & \cdots & -a_{1n} \\ \vdots & -a_{ij} & \vdots \\ -a_{k1} & \cdots & -a_{kn} \end{pmatrix}.
$$

Since $A - B$ is just shorthand for $A + (-B)$, we *subtract* matrices of the same size simply by subtracting their corresponding entries:

$$
\begin{pmatrix} a_{11} & \cdots & a_{1n} \\ \vdots & a_{ij} & \vdots \\ a_{k1} & \cdots & a_{kn} \end{pmatrix} - \begin{pmatrix} b_{11} & \cdots & b_{1n} \\ \vdots & b_{ij} & \vdots \\ b_{k1} & \cdots & b_{kn} \end{pmatrix}
$$

$$
= \begin{pmatrix} a_{11} - b_{11} & \cdots & a_{1n} - b_{1n} \\ \vdots & a_{ij} - b_{ij} & \vdots \\ a_{k1} - b_{kn} & \cdots & a_{kn} - b_{kn} \end{pmatrix}.
$$

Scalar Multiplication

Matrices can be multiplied by ordinary numbers, which we also call **scalars**. This operation is called **scalar multiplication**. Implicitly we have already used this operation in defining $-A$, which is $(-1)A$. More generally, the product of the matrix A and the number r, denoted rA, is the matrix created by multiplying each entry of A by r.

$$r \begin{pmatrix} a_{11} & \cdots & a_{1n} \\ \vdots & a_{ij} & \vdots \\ a_{k1} & \cdots & a_{kn} \end{pmatrix} = \begin{pmatrix} ra_{11} & \cdots & ra_{1n} \\ \vdots & ra_{ij} & \vdots \\ ra_{k1} & \cdots & ra_{kn} \end{pmatrix}.$$

In summary, within the class of $k \times n$ matrices, addition, subtraction, and scalar multiplication are all defined in the obvious way and act just as one would expect.

Matrix Multiplication

Just as two numbers can be multiplied together, so can two matrices. But at this point matrix algebra becomes a little bit more complicated than the algebra for real numbers. There are two differences: Not all pairs of matrices can be multiplied together, and the order in which matrices are multiplied can matter.

We can define the matrix product AB if and only if

number of columns of A = number of rows of B.

For the matrix product to exist, A must be $k \times m$ and B must be $m \times n$. To obtain the (i, j)th entry of AB, multiply the ith row of A and the jth column of B as follows:

$$\begin{pmatrix} a_{i1} & a_{i2} & \cdots & a_{im} \end{pmatrix} \cdot \begin{pmatrix} b_{1j} \\ b_{2j} \\ \vdots \\ b_{mj} \end{pmatrix} = a_{i1}b_{1j} + a_{i2}b_{2j} + \cdots + a_{im}b_{mj}.$$

In other words, the (i, j)th entry of the product AB is defined to be

$$\sum_{h=1}^{m} a_{ih}b_{hj}.$$

For example,

$$\begin{pmatrix} a & b \\ c & d \\ e & f \end{pmatrix} \begin{pmatrix} A & B \\ C & D \end{pmatrix} = \begin{pmatrix} aA + bC & aB + bD \\ cA + dC & cB + dD \\ eA + fC & eB + fD \end{pmatrix}.$$

Note that in this case, the product taken in reverse order,

$$\begin{pmatrix} A & B \\ C & D \end{pmatrix} \begin{pmatrix} a & b \\ c & d \\ e & f \end{pmatrix},$$

is not defined. See Exercise 8.2.

If A is $k \times m$ and B is $m \times n$, then the product AB will be $k \times n$. The product matrix AB inherits the number of its rows from A and the number of its columns from B:

$$\text{number of rows of } AB = \text{number of rows of } A;$$

$$\text{number of columns of } AB = \text{number of columns of } B;$$

$$(k \times m) \cdot (m \times n) = (k \times n).$$

The $n \times n$ matrix

$$I = \begin{pmatrix} 1 & 0 & \cdots & 0 \\ 0 & 1 & \cdots & 0 \\ \vdots & \vdots & \ddots & \vdots \\ 0 & 0 & \cdots & 1 \end{pmatrix},$$

with $a_{ii} = 1$ for all i and $a_{ij} = 0$ for all $i \neq j$, has the property that for any $m \times n$ matrix A,

$$AI = A,$$

and for any $n \times l$ matrix B,

$$IB = B.$$

The matrix I is called the $n \times n$ **identity matrix** because it is a multiplicative identity for matrices just as the number 1 is for real numbers.

Laws of Matrix Algebra

We can think of matrices as generalized numbers because matrix addition, subtraction and multiplication obey most of the same laws that numbers do.

Associative Laws: $(A + B) + C = A + (B + C),$

$$(AB)C = A(BC),$$

Commutative Law for Addition: $A + B = B + A,$

Distributive Laws: $A(B + C) = AB + AC,$

$$(A + B)C = AC + BC.$$

The one important law which numbers satisfy but matrices do not, is the *commutative law for multiplication.* Although $ab = ba$ for all numbers a and b, it is not true that $AB = BA$ for matrices, *even when both products are defined.* We have already seen examples where only one product is defined. But notice that even if both products exist, they need not be the same size. For example, if A is 2×3 and B is 3×2, then AB is 2×2 while BA is 3×3. Even if AB and BA have the same size, AB need not equal BA. For example,

$$\begin{pmatrix} 2 & 1 \\ 1 & 1 \end{pmatrix}\begin{pmatrix} 1 & -1 \\ 0 & 2 \end{pmatrix} = \begin{pmatrix} 2 & 0 \\ 1 & 1 \end{pmatrix},$$

while $$\begin{pmatrix} 1 & -1 \\ 0 & 2 \end{pmatrix}\begin{pmatrix} 2 & 1 \\ 1 & 1 \end{pmatrix} = \begin{pmatrix} 1 & 0 \\ 2 & 2 \end{pmatrix}.$$

Transpose

Finally, there is one other operation on matrices which we shall frequently use. The **transpose** of a $k \times n$ matrix A is the $n \times k$ matrix obtained by interchanging the rows and columns of A. This matrix is often written as A^T. The first row of A becomes the first column of A^T. The second row of A becomes the second column of A^T, and so on. Thus, the (i, j)th entry of A becomes the (j, i)th entry of A^T. For example,

$$\begin{pmatrix} a_{11} & a_{12} & a_{13} \\ a_{21} & a_{22} & a_{23} \end{pmatrix}^T = \begin{pmatrix} a_{11} & a_{21} \\ a_{12} & a_{22} \\ a_{13} & a_{23} \end{pmatrix},$$

$$\begin{pmatrix} a_{11} \\ a_{21} \end{pmatrix}^T = (a_{11} \quad a_{21}).$$

The following rules are fairly straightforward to verify:

$$(A + B)^T = A^T + B^T,$$

$$(A - B)^T = A^T - B^T,$$

$$(A^T)^T = A,$$

$$(rA)^T = rA^T,$$

where A and B are $k \times n$ and r is a scalar. The following rule is not so obvious and takes a little work to prove:

$$(AB)^T = B^T A^T.$$

Note the change in the order of the matrix multiplication.

Theorem 8.1   Let A be a $k \times m$ matrix and B be an $m \times n$ matrix. Then, $(AB)^T = B^T A^T$.

Proof   We will be working with six different matrices: A, B, A^T, B^T, $(AB)^T$, and $B^T A^T$. For notation's sake, if C is any of these matrices, we will write C_{ij} for the (i, j)th element of C. For example, $((AB)^T)_{ij}$ will denote the (i, j)th element of the matrix $(AB)^T$. Now,

$$((AB)^T)_{ij} = (AB)_{ji} \qquad \text{(definition of transpose)}$$

$$= \sum_h A_{jh} \cdot B_{hi} \qquad \text{(definition of matrix multiplication)}$$

$$= \sum_h (A^T)_{hj} \cdot (B^T)_{ih} \qquad \text{(definition of transpose, twice)}$$

$$= \sum_h (B^T)_{ih} \cdot (A^T)_{hj} \qquad (a \cdot b = b \cdot a \text{ for scalars})$$

$$= (B^T A^T)_{ij} \qquad \text{(definition of matrix multiplication.)}$$

Therefore, $(AB)^T = B^T A^T$. ∎

Systems of Equations in Matrix Form

The algebra that we have developed so far is already very powerful. Consider the systems of linear equations from the previous chapter. The typical system looked like

$$a_{11}x_1 + \cdots + a_{1n}x_n = b_1$$
$$a_{21}x_1 + \cdots + a_{2n}x_n = b_2$$
$$\vdots \qquad \vdots \qquad \qquad \vdots$$
$$a_{k1}x_1 + \cdots + a_{kn}x_n = b_k.$$

This system can be expressed much more compactly using the notation suggested by matrix algebra. As before, let A denote the coefficient matrix of the system:

$$A = \begin{pmatrix} a_{11} & \cdots & a_{1n} \\ \vdots & a_{ij} & \vdots \\ a_{k1} & \cdots & a_{kn} \end{pmatrix}.$$

Also, let

$$
\mathbf{x} = \begin{pmatrix} x_1 \\ \vdots \\ x_n \end{pmatrix} \quad \text{and} \quad \mathbf{b} = \begin{pmatrix} b_1 \\ \vdots \\ b_k \end{pmatrix}.
$$

Both $\mathbf{x}$ and $\mathbf{b}$ are matrices, called column matrices. The $n \times 1$ matrix $\mathbf{x}$ contains variables, and the $k \times 1$ matrix $\mathbf{b}$ contains the parameters from the right-hand side of the system. Then, the system of equations can be written as

$$
\begin{pmatrix} a_{11} & \cdots & a_{1n} \\ \vdots & a_{ij} & \vdots \\ a_{k1} & \cdots & a_{kn} \end{pmatrix} \cdot \begin{pmatrix} x_1 \\ \vdots \\ x_n \end{pmatrix} = \begin{pmatrix} b_1 \\ \vdots \\ b_k \end{pmatrix},
$$

or simply as

$$ A\mathbf{x} = \mathbf{b}, $$

where $A\mathbf{x}$ refers to the matrix product of the $k \times n$ matrix A with the $n \times 1$ matrix $\mathbf{x}$. This product is a $k \times 1$ matrix, which must be made equal to the $k \times 1$ matrix $\mathbf{b}$. Check that carrying out the matrix multiplication in $A\mathbf{x} = \mathbf{b}$ and applying the definition of equality of matrices gives back exactly the original system of linear equations. The matrix notation is much more compact than writing out arrays of coefficients, and, as we shall see, it suggests how to find the solution to the system by analogy with the one-variable case.

EXERCISES

8.1 Let

$$
A = \begin{pmatrix} 2 & 3 & 1 \\ 0 & -1 & 2 \end{pmatrix}, \quad B = \begin{pmatrix} 0 & 1 & -1 \\ 4 & -1 & 2 \end{pmatrix}, \quad C = \begin{pmatrix} 1 & 2 \\ 3 & -1 \end{pmatrix},
$$

$$
D = \begin{pmatrix} 2 & 1 \\ 1 & 1 \end{pmatrix}, \quad \text{and} \quad E = \begin{pmatrix} 1 \\ -1 \end{pmatrix}.
$$

a) Compute each of the following matrices if it is defined:

$A + B,$	$A - D,$	$3B,$	$DC,$	$B^T,$	$A^T C^T,$
$C + D,$	$B - A$	$AB,$	$CE,$	$-D,$	$(CE)^T,$
$B + C,$	$D - C,$	$CA,$	$EC,$	$(CA)^T,$	$E^T C^T.$

b) Verify that $(DA)^T = A^T D^T$.
c) Verify that $CD \neq DC$.

8.2   Check that

$$\begin{pmatrix} 2 & 3 & 1 & 4 \\ 0 & -1 & 2 & 1 \\ 5 & 0 & 6 & 0 \end{pmatrix} \begin{pmatrix} 2 & 3 \\ -1 & 0 \\ 0 & 1 \\ 1 & 1 \end{pmatrix} = \begin{pmatrix} 5 & 11 \\ 2 & 3 \\ 10 & 21 \end{pmatrix}.$$

Note that the reverse product is not defined.

8.3   Show that if AB is defined, then $B^T A^T$ is defined but $A^T B^T$ need not be defined.

8.4   If you choose four numbers at random for the entries of a 2×2 matrix A, and four others for another 2×2 matrix B, AB will probably not equal BA. Carry out this procedure a few times.

8.5   It sometimes happens that $AB = BA$.

  a) Check this for $A = \begin{pmatrix} 2 & 1 \\ 1 & 2 \end{pmatrix}$ and $B = \begin{pmatrix} 3 & -4 \\ -4 & 3 \end{pmatrix}$.

  b) Show that if B is a scalar multiple of the 2×2 identity matrix, then $AB = BA$ for *all* 2×2 matrices A.

8.2   SPECIAL KINDS OF MATRICES

Special problems use special kinds of matrices. In this section we describe some of the important classes of $k \times n$ matrices which arise in economic analysis.

Square Matrix. $k = n$, that is, equal number of rows and columns.

Column Matrix. $n = 1$, that is, one column. For example,

$$\begin{pmatrix} a \\ b \\ c \end{pmatrix} \quad \text{and} \quad \begin{pmatrix} 0 \\ 1 \end{pmatrix}.$$

Row Matrix. $k = 1$, that is, one row. For example,

$$(2 \quad 1 \quad 0) \quad \text{and} \quad (2 \quad 3).$$

Diagonal Matrix. $k = n$ and $a_{ij} = 0$ for $i \neq j$, that is, a square matrix in which all nondiagonal entries are 0. For example,

$$\begin{pmatrix} a & 0 \\ 0 & b \end{pmatrix} \quad \text{and} \quad \begin{pmatrix} 1 & 0 & 0 \\ 0 & 2 & 0 \\ 0 & 0 & 3 \end{pmatrix}.$$

Upper-Triangular Matrix. $a_{ij} = 0$ if $i > j$, that is, a matrix (usually square) in which all entries below the diagonal are 0. For example,

$$\begin{pmatrix} a & b \\ 0 & d \end{pmatrix} \quad \text{and} \quad \begin{pmatrix} 1 & 2 & 3 \\ 0 & 4 & 5 \\ 0 & 0 & 6 \end{pmatrix}.$$

Lower-Triangular Matrix. $a_{ij} = 0$ if $i < j$, that is, a matrix (usually square) in which all entries above the diagonal are 0. For example,

$$\begin{pmatrix} a & 0 \\ c & d \end{pmatrix} \quad \text{and} \quad \begin{pmatrix} 1 & 0 & 0 \\ 2 & 3 & 0 \\ 4 & 5 & 6 \end{pmatrix}.$$

Symmetric Matrix. $A^T = A$, that is, $a_{ij} = a_{ji}$ for all i, j. These matrices are necessarily square. For example,

$$\begin{pmatrix} a & b \\ b & d \end{pmatrix} \quad \text{and} \quad \begin{pmatrix} 1 & 2 & 3 \\ 2 & 4 & 5 \\ 3 & 5 & 6 \end{pmatrix}.$$

Idempotent Matrix.   A square matrix B for which $B \cdot B = B$, such as $B = I$ or

$$\begin{pmatrix} 5 & -5 \\ 4 & -4 \end{pmatrix}.$$

Permutation Matrix.   A square matrix of 0s and 1s in which each row and each column contains exactly one 1. For example,

$$\begin{pmatrix} 0 & 1 & 0 \\ 1 & 0 & 0 \\ 0 & 0 & 1 \end{pmatrix}.$$

Nonsingular Matrix.   A square matrix whose rank equals the number of its rows (or columns). When such a matrix arises as a coefficient matrix in a system of linear equations, the system has one and only one solution.

EXERCISES

8.6   Give an example with more than two rows or more than two columns of each of the above types of matrices.

8.7 Show that $\begin{pmatrix} -1 & 2 \\ -1 & 2 \end{pmatrix}$ and $\begin{pmatrix} 3 & 6 \\ -1 & -2 \end{pmatrix}$ are idempotent.

8.8 Let D, U, L, and S denote, respectively, the sets of all diagonal, upper-triangular, lower-triangular, and symmetric matrices.

a) Show that D, U and L are each closed under matrix addition and multiplication, that is, that the sum or product of two matrices in one of the above sets is also a matrix in that set.

b) Show that $D \cap U = D$, $S \cap U = D$, and $D \subset S$.

c) Show that all matrices in D commute with each other. Is this true for matrices in U or S, too?

d) Show that S is closed under addition but not under multiplication.

8.9 How many $n \times n$ permutation matrices are there?

8.10 Is the set of $n \times n$ permutation matrices closed under addition or under matrix multiplication?

8.3   ELEMENTARY MATRICES

Another important class of matrices is the class of **elementary matrices**. Recall that the three elementary row operations that are used to bring a matrix to row echelon form are:

(1) interchanging rows,
(2) adding a multiple of one row to another, and
(3) multiplying a row by a nonzero scalar.

These operations can be performed on a matrix A by premultiplying A by certain special matrices called *elementary matrices*. For example, the following theorem illustrates how to interchange rows i and j of a given matrix A.

Theorem 8.2   Form the permutation matrix E_{ij} by interchanging the ith and jth rows of the identity matrix I. Left-multiplication of a given matrix A by E_{ij} has the effect of interchanging the ith and jth rows of A.

Proof   To see this, let e_{hk} denote a generic element of E_{ij}:

$$
\begin{aligned}
e_{ij} &= e_{ji} = 1, \\
e_{ii} &= e_{jj} = 0, \\
e_{hh} &= 1 \qquad \text{if } h \neq i, j, \\
e_{hk} &= 0 \qquad \text{otherwise.}
\end{aligned}
\tag{1}
$$

The element in row k and column n of $E_{ij}A$ is

$$\sum_m e_{km}a_{mn} = \begin{cases} a_{jn} & k = i, \\ a_{in} & k = j, \\ a_{kn} & k \neq i, j, \end{cases}$$

using (1). Therefore, $E_{ij}A$ is simply A with rows i and j interchanged. ∎

To carry out Row Operation 3, the multiplication of row i by the scalar $r \neq 0$, construct the matrix $E_i(r)$ by multiplying the ith row of the identity matrix I by the scalar r. The effect of premultiplication of A by $E_i(r)$ is to multiply each entry of the ith row of A by r. For example, in the case of the general 3×3 matrix A,

$$E_2(5) \cdot A = \begin{pmatrix} 1 & 0 & 0 \\ 0 & 5 & 0 \\ 0 & 0 & 1 \end{pmatrix} \begin{pmatrix} a_{11} & a_{12} & a_{13} \\ a_{21} & a_{22} & a_{23} \\ a_{31} & a_{32} & a_{33} \end{pmatrix} = \begin{pmatrix} a_{11} & a_{12} & a_{13} \\ 5a_{21} & 5a_{22} & 5a_{23} \\ a_{31} & a_{32} & a_{33} \end{pmatrix}.$$

Finally, to perform Row Operation 2, the addition of r times the ith row of A to the jth row of A, form the matrix $E_{ij}(r)$ by adding r times row i to row j in the identity matrix I. In other words, replace the zero in column i and row j of I with r. Premultiplication of A by $E_{ij}(r)$ will add r times row i to row j in matrix A while leaving the entries in all other rows of A unchanged. For example, in the 3×3 case

$$E_{23}(5) \cdot A = \begin{pmatrix} 1 & 0 & 0 \\ 0 & 1 & 0 \\ 0 & 5 & 1 \end{pmatrix} \begin{pmatrix} a_{11} & a_{12} & a_{13} \\ a_{21} & a_{22} & a_{23} \\ a_{31} & a_{32} & a_{33} \end{pmatrix}$$

$$= \begin{pmatrix} a_{11} & a_{12} & a_{13} \\ a_{21} & a_{22} & a_{23} \\ 5a_{21} + a_{31} & 5a_{22} + a_{32} & 5a_{23} + a_{33} \end{pmatrix}.$$

Definition The matrices E_{ij}, $E_{ij}(r)$ and $E_i(r)$, which are obtained by performing an elementary row operation on the identity matrix, are called **elementary matrices**.

We summarize this discussion in the following theorem, whose proof is left as an exercise.

Theorem 8.3 Let E be an elementary $n \times n$ matrix obtained by performing a particular row operation on the $n \times n$ identity matrix. For any $n \times m$ matrix A, EA is the matrix obtained by performing that same row operation on A.

In Chapter 7, we showed that elementary row operations can be used to reduce any matrix to row echelon form. The matrix version of that fact is stated in the next theorem, whose proof is also left as an exercise.

> **Theorem 8.4** For any $k \times n$ matrix A there exist elementary matrices $E_1, E_2, \ldots, E_m$ such that the matrix product $E_m \cdot E_{m-1} \cdots E_1 \cdot A = U$ where U is in (reduced) row echelon form.

One can represent an elementary equation operation on the linear system $A\mathbf{x} = \mathbf{b}$ by multiplying both sides of the equation by the corresponding elementary matrix E to obtain the new system $EA\mathbf{x} = E\mathbf{b}$. This fact illustrates the convenience of matrix notation for representing systems of equations.

Example 8.1   Consider the matrix

$$
\mathbf{A} = \begin{pmatrix} 1 & 1 & 1 \\ 12 & 2 & -3 \\ 3 & 4 & 1 \end{pmatrix}.
$$

To bring $\mathbf{A}$ to row echelon form, we first add -12 times row 1 to row 2. This operation corresponds to the elementary matrix

$$
E_{12}(-12) = \begin{pmatrix} 1 & 0 & 0 \\ -12 & 1 & 0 \\ 0 & 0 & 1 \end{pmatrix}.
$$

We then add -3 times row 1 to row 3 and finally $1/10$ times row 2 to row 3. These operations correspond to the elementary matrices

$$
E_{13}(-3) = \begin{pmatrix} 1 & 0 & 0 \\ 0 & 1 & 0 \\ -3 & 0 & 1 \end{pmatrix}
$$

and
$$
E_{23}(0.1) = \begin{pmatrix} 1 & 0 & 0 \\ 0 & 1 & 0 \\ 0 & .1 & 1 \end{pmatrix},
$$

respectively. Check that the row echelon form of $\mathbf{A}$ is

$$
\begin{pmatrix} 1 & 1 & 1 \\ 0 & -10 & -15 \\ 0 & 0 & -3.5 \end{pmatrix} = E_{23}(0.1) \cdot E_{13}(-3) \cdot E_{12}(-12) \cdot \mathbf{A}
$$

$$
= \begin{pmatrix} 1 & 0 & 0 \\ -12 & 1 & 0 \\ -4.2 & .1 & 1 \end{pmatrix} \cdot \begin{pmatrix} 1 & 1 & 1 \\ 12 & 2 & -3 \\ 3 & 4 & 1 \end{pmatrix}.
$$

EXERCISES

8.11   Carry out the matrix multiplication in Example 8.1.

8.12   Prove Theorem 8.3.

8.13   Prove Theorem 8.4.

8.14   *a)* Prove the following statement. If P is an $m \times m$ permutation matrix and A is $m \times n$, then PA is the matrix A with its rows permuted according to P. If $p_{ij} = 1$, then the ith row of PA will be the jth row of A.

   b) State and prove a similar statement about the permutation of columns by the multiplication AP.

8.4   ALGEBRA OF SQUARE MATRICES

Within the class $\mathbf{M_n}$ of $n \times n$ (square) matrices, all the arithmetic operations defined so far can be used. The sum, difference and product of two $n \times n$ matrices is $n \times n$. Even transposes of matrices in $\mathbf{M_n}$ are $n \times n$. The $n \times n$ identity matrix I is a true multiplicative identity in $\mathbf{M_n}$ in that $AI = IA = A$ for all A in $\mathbf{M_n}$. The matrix I plays the role in $\mathbf{M_n}$ that the number 1 plays among the real numbers ($\mathbf{M_1}$). Recall, however, that if A and B are in $\mathbf{M_n}$, AB usually will not equal BA.

Since we can add, subtract, and multiply square matrices, it is reasonable to ask if we can divide square matrices too. For numbers, dividing by a is the same as multiplying by $1/a = a^{-1}$, and a^{-1} makes sense as long as $a \neq 0$. To carry out this program for matrices (if we can), we need to make sense of A^{-1} for matrices in $\mathbf{M_n}$. The number a^{-1} is defined to be that number b such that $ab = ba = 1$. The number b is called the inverse of the number a. We do the same for matrices in $\mathbf{M_n}$.

Definition   Let A be a matrix in $\mathbf{M_n}$. The matrix B in $\mathbf{M_n}$ is an **inverse** for A if $AB = BA = I$.

If the matrix B exists, we say that A is **invertible**. Our definition has left open the possibility that a matrix A can have several inverses. This is not true for numbers, and neither is it true for matrices.

Theorem 8.5   An $n \times n$ matrix A can have at most one inverse.

Proof   Suppose that B and C are both inverses of A. Then

$$C = CI = C(AB) = (CA)B = IB = B. \quad \blacksquare$$

If an $n \times n$ matrix A is invertible, we write A^{-1} for its unique inverse matrix. Note that if A is 1×1, then $A^{-1} = 1/A$. So, multiplying by A^{-1} is the analog of dividing by the matrix A.

The only 1×1 matrix which is not invertible is 0. A main goal of this section is to identify exactly which $n \times n$ matrices are not invertible. We will see that a matrix is invertible if and only if it is nonsingular. In fact, the two properties reinforce each other. Recall that a square matrix **A** is called nonsingular if and only if the system $\mathbf{Ax} = \mathbf{b}$ has a unique solution **x** for every right-hand side **b**. Theorem 8.6 below states that if a square matrix has an inverse, then it is nonsingular. The proof of this theorem shows how to use the inverse of **A** to solve a general system $\mathbf{Ax} = \mathbf{b}$. Theorem 8.7 below is the converse statement: if a matrix is nonsingular, then it is invertible. Its proof shows how to use the fact that **A** is nonsingular to compute the inverse of **A**. Before proving these theorems, we need two more definitions and a lemma.

Definition   Let A be an $k \times n$ matrix. The $n \times k$ matrix B is a **right inverse** for A if $AB = I$. The $n \times k$ matrix C is a **left inverse** for A if $CA = I$.

Example 8.2   The matrix $\begin{pmatrix} 0 & 1 \\ 0 & -1 \\ 1 & 2 \end{pmatrix}$ is a right inverse for the matrix $\begin{pmatrix} 1 & 3 & 1 \\ 2 & 1 & 0 \end{pmatrix}$, but not a left inverse. On the other hand, the matrix $\begin{pmatrix} 0 & 0 & 1 \\ 1 & -1 & 2 \end{pmatrix}$ is a left inverse for $\begin{pmatrix} 1 & 2 \\ 3 & 1 \\ 1 & 0 \end{pmatrix}$, but not a right inverse.

Lemma 8.1   If A has a right inverse B and a left inverse C, then A is invertible, and $B = C = A^{-1}$.

Proof   Exactly the same as the proof of Theorem 8.5. ∎

Theorem 8.6   If an $n \times n$ matrix A is invertible, then it is nonsingular, and the unique solution to the system of linear equations $A\mathbf{x} = \mathbf{b}$ is $\mathbf{x} = A^{-1}\mathbf{b}$.

Proof   We want to show that if A is invertible, we can solve any system of equations $A\mathbf{x} = \mathbf{b}$. Multiply each side of this system by A^{-1} to solve for **x**, as follows:

$$A\mathbf{x} = \mathbf{b}$$

$$A^{-1}(A\mathbf{x}) = A^{-1}\mathbf{b},$$

$$(A^{-1}A)\mathbf{x} = A^{-1}\mathbf{b},$$

$$I\mathbf{x} = A^{-1}\mathbf{b},$$

$$\mathbf{x} = A^{-1}\mathbf{b}.$$

Make sure you can justify all the steps in this calculation. ∎

> **Theorem 8.7**   If an $n \times n$ matrix A is nonsingular, then it is invertible.

Proof   Suppose that A is nonsingular. We shall prove that it has an inverse by showing how to compute this inverse. Let $\mathbf{e}_i$ denote the ith column of I. For example, when $n = 3$,

$$\mathbf{e}_1 = \begin{pmatrix} 1 \\ 0 \\ 0 \end{pmatrix}, \quad \mathbf{e}_2 = \begin{pmatrix} 0 \\ 1 \\ 0 \end{pmatrix}, \quad \text{and} \quad \mathbf{e}_3 = \begin{pmatrix} 0 \\ 0 \\ 1 \end{pmatrix}.$$

Write I with a focus on its columns as $[\mathbf{e}_1, \mathbf{e}_2, \mathbf{e}_3]$. Since A is nonsingular, the equation $A\mathbf{x} = \mathbf{e}_i$ has a unique solution $\mathbf{x} = \mathbf{c}_i$. (Of course, $\mathbf{c}_i$ is an $n \times 1$ matrix.) Let C be the matrix whose n columns are the respective solutions $\mathbf{c}_1, \mathbf{c}_2, \ldots, \mathbf{c}_n$. Since one multiplies each row of A by the jth column of C to obtain the jth column of AC, we can write

$$
\begin{aligned}
AC &= A\,[\mathbf{c}_1, \ldots, \mathbf{c}_n] \\
&= [A\mathbf{c}_1, \ldots, A\mathbf{c}_n] \\
&= [\mathbf{e}_1, \ldots, \mathbf{e}_n] \\
&= I.
\end{aligned}
\tag{2}
$$

So C is a right inverse of A.

To see that A has a left inverse too, use Theorem 8.4 to write $EA = U$ where E is a product of elementary matrices and U is the *reduced* row echelon form of A. Since A is nonsingular, U has no zero rows and each column contains exactly one 1. In other words, U is the identity matrix. Therefore, E is a left inverse of A. Since A has a right inverse and a left inverse, it is invertible.   ■

Take time to study the calculation labeled (2) in the proof of Theorem 8.7, since we shall use it often. Once again, it follows from the fact that, to obtain the jth column of AC, one multiplies the rows of A by the jth column of C. No other column of C enters this calculation. In other words, if $\mathbf{c}_j$ is the jth column of C, then $A\mathbf{c}_j$ is the jth column of AC.

The proof of Theorem 8.7 actually shows how to compute the inverse of a nonsingular matrix. To find the ith column $\mathbf{c}_i$ of A^{-1}, we solve the system

$$A\mathbf{x} = \mathbf{e}_i$$

to find the solution $\mathbf{x} = \mathbf{c}_i$. Gauss-Jordan elimination can be used to solve this system for each i. In this case the augmented matrix is $[A \mid \mathbf{e}_i]$. The row operations which will reduce this depend only on the first n columns of the augmented matrix, in other words, only on the matrix A. One never uses the last column of an augmented matrix to determine which row operation to use on a system.

Therefore, the same row operations that reduce $[A \mid \mathbf{e}_i]$ to $[I \mid \mathbf{c}_i]$ will also reduce $[A \mid \mathbf{e}_j]$ to $[I \mid \mathbf{c}_j]$. We can be more efficient and pool all these data into a gigantic augmented matrix $[A \mid \mathbf{e}_1 \cdots \mathbf{e}_n] = [A \mid I]$ and perform Gauss-Jordan elimination only once rather than n times. In this process, the augmented matrix $[A \mid I]$ reduces to $[I \mid A^{-1}]$.

Example 8.3   We can apply this method to find the inverse of matrix A in Example 8.1:

$$A = \begin{pmatrix} 1 & 1 & 1 \\ 12 & 2 & -3 \\ 3 & 4 & 1 \end{pmatrix}. \tag{3}$$

First, augment A with the identity matrix:

$$[A \mid I] = \begin{pmatrix} 1 & 1 & 1 & \mid & 1 & 0 & 0 \\ 12 & 2 & -3 & \mid & 0 & 1 & 0 \\ 3 & 4 & 1 & \mid & 0 & 0 & 1 \end{pmatrix}.$$

Then, perform the row operations on $[A \mid I]$ which reduce A to row echelon form. The first three such operations are described in Example 8.1 and result in the matrix

$$\begin{pmatrix} 1 & 1 & 1 & \mid & 1 & 0 & 0 \\ 0 & -10 & -15 & \mid & -12 & 1 & 0 \\ 0 & 0 & -3.5 & \mid & -4.2 & 0.1 & 1 \end{pmatrix}.$$

Next reduce this matrix to *reduced row echelon form* using the operations described in Section 7.2:

$$\begin{pmatrix} 1 & 0 & 0 & \mid & 0.4 & \frac{3}{35} & -\frac{1}{7} \\ 0 & 1 & 0 & \mid & -0.6 & -\frac{2}{35} & \frac{3}{7} \\ 0 & 0 & 1 & \mid & 1.2 & -\frac{1}{35} & -\frac{2}{7} \end{pmatrix}.$$

As implied by the proof of Theorem 8.7, the right half of this augmented matrix,

$$\begin{pmatrix} 0.4 & \frac{3}{35} & -\frac{1}{7} \\ -0.6 & -\frac{2}{35} & \frac{3}{7} \\ 1.2 & -\frac{1}{35} & -\frac{2}{7} \end{pmatrix}, \tag{4}$$

is the inverse of A.

Example 8.4 We next apply this method to compute the inverse of an arbitrary 2 × 2 matrix

$$A = \begin{pmatrix} a & b \\ c & d \end{pmatrix}. \tag{5}$$

Begin by writing the augmented matrix

$$[A \mid I] = \begin{pmatrix} a & b & \mid & 1 & 0 \\ c & d & \mid & 0 & 1 \end{pmatrix}.$$

If a and c are both 0, A will clearly be singular. Let us assume, then, that $a \neq 0$. First, add $-c/a$ times row 1 to row 2, to obtain the row echelon form

$$\begin{pmatrix} a & b & \mid & 1 & 0 \\ 0 & \dfrac{ad - bc}{a} & \mid & -\dfrac{c}{a} & 1 \end{pmatrix}. \tag{6}$$

This short calculation tells us that when $a \neq 0$, A is nonsingular (and therefore invertible) if and only if $ad - bc \neq 0$. Now we continue with Gauss-Jordan elimination to transform (6) to reduced row echelon form. Multiply the first row of (6) by $1/a$ and the second row of (6) by $a/(ad - bc)$ to obtain the matrix

$$\begin{pmatrix} 1 & \dfrac{b}{a} & \mid & \dfrac{1}{a} & 0 \\ 0 & 1 & \mid & -\dfrac{c}{ad - bc} & \dfrac{a}{ad - bc} \end{pmatrix}$$

whose leading entries are both 1s. To complete the reduction, add $-b/a$ times row 2 to row 1. The final product is

$$\begin{pmatrix} 1 & 0 & \mid & \dfrac{d}{ad - bc} & -\dfrac{b}{ad - bc} \\ 0 & 1 & \mid & -\dfrac{c}{ad - bc} & \dfrac{a}{ad - bc} \end{pmatrix}.$$

Reading off the last half of the augmented matrix, we see that

$$A^{-1} = \frac{1}{ad - bc} \begin{pmatrix} d & -b \\ -c & a \end{pmatrix}. \tag{7}$$

Note that if $ad - bc \neq 0$, a and c cannot both be 0. Thus, by Example 8.3 and Exercise 8.17, we have proven the following theorem on 2 × 2 matrices.

Theorem 8.8   The general 2×2 matrix given by (5) is nonsingular (and therefore invertible) if and only if $ad - bc \neq 0$. Its inverse is matrix (7).

The goal of the next chapter will be to generalize this convenient criterion to the case of arbitrary $n \times n$ matrices.

Putting together the facts about nonsingularity from Chapter 7 with what we have done here, we arrive at the following equivalencies.

Theorem 8.9   For any square matrix A, the following statements are equivalent:

    (a) A is invertible.
    (b) A has a right inverse.
    (c) A has a left inverse.
    (d) Every system $A\mathbf{x} = \mathbf{b}$ has at least one solution for every $\mathbf{b}$.
    (e) Every system $A\mathbf{x} = \mathbf{b}$ has at most one solution for every $\mathbf{b}$.
    (f) A is nonsingular.
    (g) A has maximal rank n.

Proof   We saw the equivalence of statements d) through g) in Section 7.4. The statements and proofs of Theorems 8.6 and 8.7 indicate that statements a) through d) are equivalent. ∎

The following facts about the behavior of the inverse are easy to prove, and are left as an exercise.

Theorem 8.10   Let A and B be square invertible matrices. Then,

    (a) $(A^{-1})^{-1} = A$,
    (b) $(A^T)^{-1} = (A^{-1})^T$,
    (c) AB is invertible, and $(AB)^{-1} = B^{-1}A^{-1}$.

The inverse for matrices works very much like the inverse for numbers. If A and B are invertible, $A + B$ need not be invertible, and even when it is, $(A + B)^{-1}$ is generally not $A^{-1} + B^{-1}$. Even for 1×1 matrices or scalars,

$$(3 + 2)^{-1} = \frac{1}{5}, \quad \text{but} \quad 3^{-1} + 2^{-1} = \frac{5}{6}.$$

If A is a square matrix, we can take integral powers of A. The matrix A^m is defined as the product $A \cdot A \cdots A$ (m times). For example, if

$$A = \begin{pmatrix} 2 & 1 \\ 1 & 1 \end{pmatrix},$$

then
$$A^2 = \begin{pmatrix} 2 & 1 \\ 1 & 1 \end{pmatrix} \cdot \begin{pmatrix} 2 & 1 \\ 1 & 1 \end{pmatrix} = \begin{pmatrix} 5 & 3 \\ 3 & 2 \end{pmatrix}.$$

If A is invertible, we can define negative powers of A as well:

$$A^{-m} = (A^{-1})^m = A^{-1} \cdot A^{-1} \cdots A^{-1} \qquad (m \text{ times}).$$

Taking powers of matrices follows most of the same basic rules as taking powers of scalars. This is summarized in the following theorem.

Theorem 8.11   If A is invertible:

  (a) A^m is invertible for any integer m and $(A^m)^{-1} = (A^{-1})^m = A^{-m}$,
  (b) for any integers r and s, $A^r A^s = A^{r+s}$, and
  (c) for any scalar $r \neq 0$, rA is invertible and $(rA)^{-1} = (1/r)A^{-1}$.

Proof   These easy computations are left as an exercise. ∎

There are some differences between exponentiation of matrices and exponentiation of numbers, all due to the fact that matrix multiplication need not be commutative — that AB need not equal BA. These differences are explored in Exercise 8.27.

Example 8.5   Since each of the elementary row operations is reversible, each of the elementary matrices is invertible and has an elementary matrix for its inverse. For example, the inverse of the permutation matrix E_{ij} is E_{ji} $(= E_{ij})$, the inverse of $E_i(r)$ is $E_i(1/r)$, and the inverse of $E_{ij}(r)$ is $E_{ij}(-r)$.

Since each elementary matrix is invertible, any product of elementary matrices is also invertible by Theorem 8.10c. By inverting the elementary matrices in the statement of Theorem 8.4, we can write any matrix A as a product of elementary matrices times a reduced row echelon matrix U:

$$A = E_1^{-1} \cdot E_2^{-1} \cdots E_m^{-1} \cdot U.$$

Furthermore, if A is nonsingular, its reduced row echelon form is the identity matrix, as we saw in the proof of Theorem 8.7.

The foregoing discussion gives us a decomposition theorem for matrices which we will use in Chapter 26.

Theorem 8.12   Any matrix A can be written as a product

$$A = F_1 \cdots F_m \cdot U$$

where the F_i's are elementary matrices and U is in reduced row echelon form. When A is nonsingular, $U = I$ and $A = F_1 \cdots F_m$.

EXERCISES

8.15   Check that

$$\begin{pmatrix} 2 & 1 \\ 1 & 1 \end{pmatrix}^{-1} = \begin{pmatrix} 1 & -1 \\ -1 & 2 \end{pmatrix} \quad \text{and} \quad \begin{pmatrix} 1 & 1 & 0 \\ 0 & 1 & 1 \\ -1 & 1 & 0 \end{pmatrix}^{-1} = \begin{pmatrix} .5 & 0 & -.5 \\ .5 & 0 & .5 \\ -.5 & 1 & -.5 \end{pmatrix}.$$

8.16   Verify that matrix (4) is the inverse of matrix (3) by direct matrix multiplication.

8.17   Suppose that $a = 0$ but $c \neq 0$ in (5). Show that one obtains the same inverse (7) for A.

8.18   Show by simple matrix multiplication that, if $ad - bc \neq 0$,

$$\frac{1}{ad - bc} \begin{pmatrix} d & -b \\ -c & a \end{pmatrix}$$

is both a left and a right inverse of A.

8.19   Use the technique of Example 8.3 to either invert each of the following matrices or prove that it is singular:

$$a) \begin{pmatrix} 2 & 1 \\ 1 & 1 \end{pmatrix}, \quad b) \begin{pmatrix} 4 & 5 \\ 2 & 4 \end{pmatrix}, \quad c) \begin{pmatrix} 2 & 1 \\ -4 & -2 \end{pmatrix},$$

$$d) \begin{pmatrix} 2 & 4 & 0 \\ 4 & 6 & 3 \\ -6 & -10 & 0 \end{pmatrix}, \quad e) \begin{pmatrix} 2 & 1 & 0 \\ 6 & 2 & 6 \\ -4 & -3 & 9 \end{pmatrix},$$

$$f) \begin{pmatrix} 2 & 6 & 0 & 5 \\ 6 & 21 & 8 & 17 \\ 4 & 12 & -4 & 13 \\ 0 & -3 & -12 & 2 \end{pmatrix}.$$

8.20   Invert the coefficient matrix to solve the following systems of equations:

$$a) \quad \begin{aligned} 2x_1 + x_2 &= 5 \\ x_1 + x_2 &= 3; \end{aligned} \qquad b) \quad \begin{aligned} 2x_1 + x_2 &= 4 \\ 6x_1 + 2x_2 + 6x_3 &= 20 \\ -4x_1 - 3x_2 + 9x_3 &= 3; \end{aligned}$$

$$
\begin{array}{rl}
2x_1 + \ \ 4x_2 \qquad\quad = & 2 \\
c) \qquad 4x_1 + \ \ 6x_2 + 3x_3 = & 1 \\
-6x_1 - 10x_2 \qquad\quad = & -6.
\end{array}
$$

8.21 Show that if A is $n \times n$ and $AB = BA$, then B is also $n \times n$.

8.22 For $A = \begin{pmatrix} 2 & 1 \\ 1 & 1 \end{pmatrix}$, compute $A^3, A^4,$ and A^{-2}.

8.23 Verify the statements about the inverses of elementary matrices in the last sentence of Example 8.5.

8.24 *a)* Use Theorem 8.8 to prove that a 2×2 lower- or upper-triangular matrix is invertible if and only if each diagonal entry is nonzero.
  b) Show that the inverse of a 2×2 lower triangular matrix is lower triangular.
  c) Show that the inverse of a 2×2 upper triangular matrix is upper triangular.

8.25 *a)* Prove Theorem 8.10.
  b) Generalize part *c* to the case of the product of k nonsingular matrices.
  c) Show by example that if A and B are invertible, $A + B$ need not be invertible.
  d) Show that, when it exists, $(A + B)^{-1}$ is generally not $A^{-1} + B^{-1}$.

8.26 Prove Theorem 8.11.

8.27 *a)* Prove that $(AB)^k = A^k B^k$ if $AB = BA$.
  b) Show that $(AB)^k \neq A^k B^k$ in general.
  c) Conclude that $(A + B)^2$ does not equal $A^2 + 2AB + B^2$ unless $AB = BA$.

8.28 What is the inverse of the $n \times n$ diagonal matrix

$$
D = \begin{pmatrix}
d_1 & 0 & 0 & \cdots & 0 \\
0 & d_2 & 0 & \cdots & 0 \\
\vdots & & \vdots & & \vdots \\
0 & 0 & 0 & \cdots & d_n
\end{pmatrix} ?
$$

8.29 Show that the inverse of a 2×2 symmetric matrix S is symmetric.

8.30 Show that the inverse of an $n \times n$ upper-triangular matrix U is upper-triangular. Can you find an easy argument to extend this result to lower-triangular matrices?
[Hint: There are a number of ways to do the first part. You can use the inversion method described in the proof of Theorem 8.7, keeping track of the status of the 0s below the diagonal. Or, you can show by direct calculation that $BU = I$ implies that B has only 0s below the diagonal.]

8.31 Show that for any permutation matrix P, $P^{-1} = P^T$.

8.32 Use Gauss-Jordan elimination to derive a criterion for the invertibility of 3×3 matrices similar to the $ad - bc$ criterion for the 2×2 case. For simplicity, assume that no row interchanges are needed in the elimination process.

8.33 The definitions of left inverse and right inverse apply to nonsquare matrices. Use the ideas in the proof of Theorem 8.7 to prove the following statements for an $m \times n$ matrix A, where $m \neq n$.
  a) A nonsquare matrix cannot have both a left and a right inverse.
  b) If A has one left (right) inverse, it has infinitely many.
  c) If $m < n$, A has a right inverse if and only if rank $A = m$.
  d) If $m > n$, A has a left inverse if and only if rank $A = n$.

8.5   INPUT-OUTPUT MATRICES

The last section showed that solving a system $Ax = \mathbf{b}$ of n equations in n unknowns is closely related to inverting the matrix A since

$$\mathbf{x} = A^{-1}\mathbf{b}. \tag{8}$$

For a single fixed $\mathbf{b}$, it is usually quicker to solve $Ax = \mathbf{b}$ by Gaussian elimination (and back substitution). However, if one is going to work with many different right-hand sides $\mathbf{b}$ and the same A, it may be easier to invert A and use (8).

For example, consider the input-output example of Chapter 6. This is a model of an economy with n industries. Each industry produces a single output, using as inputs the products produced by the other industries. Write x_i for the gross output of product i, and let a_{ij} denote the amount of good i needed to produce one unit of good j. Let c_i denote consumer demand for product i. In Chapter 6, we saw that the market equilibrium condition that supply equal demand is given by the n equations

$$x_i = a_{i1}x_1 + a_{i2}x_2 + \cdots + a_{in}x_n + c_i,$$

for $i = 1, \ldots, n$. In matrix notation this system of equations becomes

$$\mathbf{x} = A\mathbf{x} + \mathbf{c},$$

which is more conveniently written as

$$(I - A)\mathbf{x} = \mathbf{c}. \tag{9}$$

(To keep all n-tuples nonnegative, we will ignore the labor sector described in Chapter 6.)

The matrix A of intermediate factor demands is sometimes called the **technology matrix**. We might expect this to remain relatively constant over long periods of time. The right-hand side of (9), $\mathbf{c}$, can be expected to vary more frequently. Thus it is convenient to study solutions to (9) by working with the inverse:

$$\mathbf{x} = (I - A)^{-1}\mathbf{c}.$$

Notice that in addition to requiring that $I - A$ be invertible, we also require that the solution to (9) be nonnegative whenever $\mathbf{c}$ is nonnegative. This corresponds to the requirement that any solution to our economic system produces nonnegative amounts of each commodity. For this to happen, all entries of the matrix $(I - A)^{-1}$ must be nonnegative. Furthermore, the study of this system is complicated by the fact that all the economic data in the model are contained in the matrix A. It is not enough simply to assume that $I - A$ has a nonnegative inverse. We must find assumptions on A which will imply the desired behavior of $I - A$.

Since the factors of production have different natural units, it is convenient to express them all in monetary terms, say in millions of dollars, in an input-output analysis. In this case, the (i, j)th entry a_{ij} of technology matrix A indicates how many millions of dollars of good i are needed to produce 1 million dollars of good j. The sum of the entries in each column of A gives the total cost of producing 1 million dollars of the product that column represents. Since we expect each industry to make a positive accounting profit, the sum of the entries in each column should be less than 1. This turns out to be one of the conditions on a technology matrix A which will guarantee that $I - A$ has a nonnegative inverse.

Theorem 8.13   Let A be an $n \times n$ matrix with the properties that each entry is nonnegative and the sum of the entries in each column is less than 1. Then, $(I - A)^{-1}$ exists and contains only nonnegative entries.

We will prove Theorem 8.13 at the end of this section. First, to make the preceding discussion concrete, consider a simple three-industry economy, with input-output matrix

$$A = \begin{pmatrix} 0.15 & 0.5 & 0.25 \\ 0.3 & 0.1 & 0.4 \\ 0.15 & 0.3 & 0.2 \end{pmatrix}.$$

Suppose that consumer demand fluctuates between

$$\mathbf{c} = \begin{pmatrix} 20 \\ 20 \\ 10 \end{pmatrix} \quad \text{and} \quad \mathbf{c}' = \begin{pmatrix} 10 \\ 20 \\ 20 \end{pmatrix}.$$

What will be the corresponding industry outputs?

First, compute $I - A$:

$$I - A = \begin{pmatrix} 0.85 & -0.5 & -0.25 \\ -0.3 & 0.9 & -0.4 \\ -0.15 & -0.3 & 0.8 \end{pmatrix}.$$

To invert $I - A$, write the augmented matrix

$$\begin{pmatrix} 0.85 & -0.5 & -0.25 & | & 1 & 0 & 0 \\ -0.3 & 0.9 & -0.4 & | & 0 & 1 & 0 \\ -0.15 & -0.3 & 0.8 & | & 0 & 0 & 1 \end{pmatrix}$$

and use Gauss-Jordan elimination to reduce the first three columns to the identity matrix. The result, rounded to three decimal places, is

$$\begin{pmatrix} 1 & 0 & 0 & | & 1.975 & 1.564 & 1.399 \\ 0 & 1 & 0 & | & 0.988 & 2.115 & 1.366 \\ 0 & 0 & 1 & | & 0.741 & 1.086 & 2.025 \end{pmatrix}.$$

The last three columns are $(I - A)^{-1}$. Note that, as Theorem 8.13 predicts, all entries are positive.

When consumer demand is $\mathbf{c} = \begin{pmatrix} 20 \\ 20 \\ 10 \end{pmatrix}$, the total output should be

$$\mathbf{x} = (I - A)^{-1}\mathbf{c} = \begin{pmatrix} 1.975 & 1.564 & 1.399 \\ 0.988 & 2.115 & 1.366 \\ 0.741 & 1.086 & 2.025 \end{pmatrix} \begin{pmatrix} 20 \\ 20 \\ 10 \end{pmatrix} = \begin{pmatrix} 84.77 \\ 75.72 \\ 56.79 \end{pmatrix}.$$

When consumer demand is $\mathbf{c} = \begin{pmatrix} 10 \\ 20 \\ 20 \end{pmatrix}$, the total output should be

$$\mathbf{x} = (I - A)^{-1}\mathbf{c} = \begin{pmatrix} 1.975 & 1.564 & 1.399 \\ 0.988 & 2.115 & 1.366 \\ 0.741 & 1.086 & 2.025 \end{pmatrix} \begin{pmatrix} 10 \\ 20 \\ 20 \end{pmatrix} = \begin{pmatrix} 79.01 \\ 79.51 \\ 69.63 \end{pmatrix}.$$

Leontief used input-output analysis to study the 1958 U.S. economy. He divided the economy into 81 sectors and aggregated these sectors into six groups of related sectors. We will treat each of the six families as a separate industry in order to simplify our presentation. These six industries are listed in Table 8.1, and their intermediate factor demands are listed in Table 8.2. The units are millions of dollars. So the .173 in row 3 column 2 means that the production of $1 million worth of final metal products requiresthe expenditure of $173,000 on basic metal

	Sector	**Examples**
FN,	Final nonmetal	Leather goods, furniture, foods
FM,	Final metal	Construction mach'ry, household appliances
BM,	Basic metal	Mining, machine shop products
BN,	Basic nonmetal	Glass, wood, textile, and livestock products
E,	Energy	Coal, petroleum, electricity, gas
S,	Services	Govt. services, transportation, real estate

Table 8.1   *The Six Sectors*

	FN	FM	BM	BN	E	S
FN	0.170	0.004	0.000	0.029	0.000	0.008
FM	0.003	0.295	0.018	0.002	0.004	0.016
BM	0.025	0.173	0.460	0.007	0.011	0.007
BN	0.348	0.037	0.021	0.403	0.011	0.048
E	0.007	0.001	0.039	0.025	0.358	0.025
S	0.120	0.074	0.104	0.123	0.173	0.234

Table 8.2   *Internal demands for 1958 U.S. Economy*

FN	$ 99,640
FM	75,548
BM	14,444
BN	33,501
E	23,527
S	263,985

External Demands for 1958 U.S. Economy (in millions of dollars)

Table 8.3

goods. Table 8.3 lists Leontief's estimates of final demands in the 1958 U.S. economy. The problem is to determine how many units had to be produced in each of the six sectors in order to run the U.S. economy in 1958.

To solve the problem, we turn Table 8.2 into the technology matrix A and Table 8.3 into the final demand column matrix $\mathbf{c}$. As before, the goal is to solve $(I - A)\mathbf{x} = \mathbf{c}$ for the output column matrix $\mathbf{x}$:

$$\mathbf{x} = (I - A)^{-1}\mathbf{c}.$$

First, we need to compute the net input-output matrix $I - A$.

$I - A$

$$= \begin{pmatrix} 1 & 0 & 0 & 0 & 0 & 0 \\ 0 & 1 & 0 & 0 & 0 & 0 \\ 0 & 0 & 1 & 0 & 0 & 0 \\ 0 & 0 & 0 & 1 & 0 & 0 \\ 0 & 0 & 0 & 0 & 1 & 0 \\ 0 & 0 & 0 & 0 & 0 & 1 \end{pmatrix} - \begin{pmatrix} 0.170 & 0.004 & 0 & 0.029 & 0 & 0.008 \\ 0.003 & 0.295 & 0.018 & 0.002 & 0.004 & 0.016 \\ 0.025 & 0.173 & 0.460 & 0.007 & 0.011 & 0.007 \\ 0.348 & 0.037 & 0.021 & 0.403 & 0.011 & 0.048 \\ 0.007 & 0.001 & 0.039 & 0.025 & 0.358 & 0.025 \\ 0.120 & 0.074 & 0.104 & 0.123 & 0.173 & 0.234 \end{pmatrix}$$

$$= \begin{pmatrix} 0.830 & -0.004 & 0 & -0.029 & 0 & -0.008 \\ -0.003 & 0.705 & -0.018 & -0.002 & -0.004 & -0.016 \\ -0.025 & -0.173 & 0.540 & -0.007 & -0.011 & -0.007 \\ -0.348 & -0.037 & -0.021 & 0.597 & -0.011 & -0.048 \\ -0.007 & -0.001 & -0.039 & -0.025 & 0.642 & -0.025 \\ -0.120 & -0.074 & -0.104 & -0.123 & -0.173 & 0.766 \end{pmatrix}.$$

The inverse of this net input-output matrix can be computed by the methods of Section 8.4 and then used to compute the gross output column matrix.

$\mathbf{x} = (I - A)^{-1}$

$$= \begin{pmatrix} 1.234 & 0.014 & 0.006 & 0.064 & 0.007 & 0.018 \\ 0.017 & 1.436 & 0.057 & 0.012 & 0.020 & 0.032 \\ 0.071 & 0.465 & 1.877 & 0.019 & 0.045 & 0.031 \\ 0.751 & 0.134 & 0.100 & 1.740 & 0.066 & 0.124 \\ 0.060 & 0.045 & 0.130 & 0.082 & 1.578 & 0.059 \\ 0.339 & 0.236 & 0.307 & 0.312 & 0.376 & 1.349 \end{pmatrix} \begin{pmatrix} 99,640 \\ 75,548 \\ 14,444 \\ 33,501 \\ 23,527 \\ 263,985 \end{pmatrix}$$

$$= \begin{pmatrix} 131,161 \\ 120,324 \\ 79,194 \\ 178,936 \\ 66,703 \\ 426,542 \end{pmatrix}.$$

We conclude, for example, that it requires \$131,161 million worth of final nonmetal products to meet both intermediate and final demands in the 1958 U.S. economy.

Proof of Theorem 8.13

We conclude this section by proving Theorem 8.13. Let A be a technology matrix that satisfies the hypotheses of Theorem 8.13: nonnegative entries and column sums less than 1. Then, $-A$ has all its entries and its column sums between 0 and -1 and $I - A$ satisfies the following three properties:

(a) each off-diagonal entry is ≤ 0,
(b) each diagonal entry is positive, and
(c) the sum of the entries in each column is positive.

Matrices which satisfy these three conditions are a special case of the class of **dominant diagonal matrices**. A more general definition of a dominant diagonal matrix requires that in each column the *absolute value* of the diagonal entry is at least as large as the sum of the absolute values of the other entries in that column. To prove Theorem 8.13, we need only prove the following result.

Theorem 8.14   Let B be a square matrix which satisfies conditions a, b, and c above. Then, all entries of B^{-1} are nonnegative.

Proof   To keep better track of the signs and sizes of the entries of the matrix B, we write it as

$$B = \begin{pmatrix} b_{11} & -b_{12} & \cdots & -b_{1n} \\ -b_{21} & b_{22} & \cdots & -b_{2n} \\ \vdots & \vdots & \ddots & \vdots \\ -b_{n1} & -b_{n2} & \cdots & b_{nn} \end{pmatrix},$$

where $\qquad$ each $b_{ij} \geq 0 \quad$ and $\quad 0 \leq \sum_{h \neq j} b_{hj} < b_{jj}$ $\qquad$ (10)

for all j. Let $\mathbf{c}$ be a vector with all positive entries and consider the system $B\mathbf{x} = \mathbf{c}$. To solve this system, we perform Gaussian elimination on the augmented matrix $[B \mid \mathbf{c}]$. Add b_{j1}/b_{11} times row 1 to row j for all $j > 1$. The result is the new augmented matrix

$$
\begin{pmatrix}
b_{11} & -b_{12} & \cdots & -b_{1n} & \Big| & c_1 \\
0 & b_{22} - \dfrac{b_{21}}{b_{11}}b_{12} & \cdots & -b_{2n} - \dfrac{b_{21}}{b_{11}}b_{1n} & \Big| & c_2 + \dfrac{b_{21}}{b_{11}}c_1 \\
\vdots & \vdots & \ddots & \vdots & \Big| & \vdots \\
0 & -b_{n2} - \dfrac{b_{n1}}{b_{11}}b_{12} & \cdots & b_{nn} - \dfrac{b_{n1}}{b_{11}}b_{1n} & \Big| & c_n + \dfrac{b_{n1}}{b_{11}}c_1
\end{pmatrix}
$$

$$
\equiv \begin{pmatrix} b_{11} & * & \Big| & c_1 \\ \mathbf{0} & \hat{B} & \Big| & \hat{\mathbf{c}} \end{pmatrix}.
$$

The $(n-1) \times (n-1)$ matrix $\hat{B}$ is still dominant diagonal, since its off-diagonal entries are still nonpositive and the sum of the entries in its $(j-1)$th column is

$$
\left(b_{jj} - \frac{b_{j1}}{b_{11}}b_{1j} \right) + \sum_{h \neq 1,j} \left(-b_{hj} - \frac{b_{h1}}{b_{11}}b_{1j} \right)
$$

$$
= b_{jj} - \left(\sum_{h \neq 1,j} b_{hj} \right) - b_{1j}\frac{b_{21} + \cdots + b_{n1}}{b_{11}}
$$

$$
> b_{jj} - \sum_{h \neq 1,j} b_{hj} - b_{1j}
$$

$$
> 0, \qquad\qquad \text{(by (10) twice).}
$$

The new RHS $\hat{\mathbf{c}}$ has all entries positive. Continue applying Gaussian elimination; at each stage, the resulting submatrix still satisfies a, b, and c. We conclude that the row echelon form of $[B \mid \mathbf{c}]$ has the sign pattern

$$
\begin{pmatrix}
+ & - & - & \cdots & - & \Big| & + \\
0 & + & - & \cdots & - & \Big| & + \\
0 & 0 & + & \cdots & - & \Big| & + \\
\vdots & \vdots & \vdots & \ddots & \vdots & \Big| & \vdots \\
0 & 0 & 0 & \cdots & - & \Big| & + \\
0 & 0 & 0 & \cdots & + & \Big| & +
\end{pmatrix}.
$$

Back substitution from such a matrix yields a *positive* solution $\mathbf{x}$ to the system $B\mathbf{x} = \mathbf{c}$. If the nonzero right-hand side $\mathbf{c}$ had some zero entries and if A had some zero off-diagonal terms, the same argument yields a nonnegative solution of $B\mathbf{x} = \mathbf{c}$. Since the columns of B^{-1} are the solution vectors of $B\mathbf{x} = \mathbf{e}_i$ (Theorem 8.7), the entries of B^{-1} are all nonnegative numbers. ∎

EXERCISES

8.34   Let the technology matrix be given by $A = \begin{pmatrix} .7 & .2 & .2 \\ .1 & .6 & .1 \\ .1 & .1 & .6 \end{pmatrix}$. Find the gross output vectors when final demand is:

a) $\begin{pmatrix} 1 \\ 1 \\ 1 \end{pmatrix}$,   b) $\begin{pmatrix} 2 \\ 1 \\ 1 \end{pmatrix}$,   c) $\begin{pmatrix} 2 \\ 1 \\ 2 \end{pmatrix}$.

8.35   Let the general 2×2 technology matrix be given by

$$A = \begin{pmatrix} a & b \\ c & d \end{pmatrix}.$$

Prove Theorem 8.13 directly for such a matrix using Theorem 8.8.

8.6   PARTITIONED MATRICES (optional)

Let A be an $m \times n$ matrix. A **submatrix** of A is a matrix formed by discarding some entire rows and/or columns of A. A **partitioned matrix** is a matrix which has been partitioned into submatrices by horizontal and/or vertical lines which extend along *entire* rows or columns of A. For example,

$$A = \left(\begin{array}{cc|c|ccc} a_{11} & a_{12} & a_{13} & a_{14} & a_{15} & a_{16} \\ \hline a_{21} & a_{22} & a_{23} & a_{24} & a_{25} & a_{26} \\ a_{31} & a_{32} & a_{33} & a_{34} & a_{35} & a_{36} \end{array} \right), \tag{11}$$

which we can write as

$$A = \left(\begin{array}{c|c|c} A_{11} & A_{12} & A_{13} \\ \hline A_{21} & A_{22} & A_{23} \end{array} \right).$$

Each submatrix A_{ij} is called a **block** of A. Augmented matrices are an example of partitioned matrices. They have been partitioned vertically into two blocks.

If A is a square matrix which has been partitioned as

$$A = \begin{pmatrix} A_{11} & 0 & \cdots & 0 \\ 0 & A_{22} & \cdots & 0 \\ \vdots & \vdots & \ddots & \vdots \\ 0 & 0 & \cdots & A_{kk} \end{pmatrix} \tag{12}$$

where each A_{ii} is square and $A_{ij} = 0$ for $i \neq j$, then A is called a **block diagonal** matrix.

Suppose that A and B are two $m \times n$ matrices which are partitioned the same way; that is,

$$A = \begin{pmatrix} A_{11} & A_{12} & A_{13} \\ A_{21} & A_{22} & A_{23} \end{pmatrix} \quad \text{and} \quad B = \begin{pmatrix} B_{11} & B_{12} & B_{13} \\ B_{21} & B_{22} & B_{23} \end{pmatrix}$$

where A_{11} and B_{11} have the same dimensions, A_{12} and B_{12} have the same dimensions, and so on. Then A and B can be added as if the blocks are scalar entries:

$$A + B = \begin{pmatrix} A_{11} + B_{11} & A_{12} + B_{12} & A_{13} + B_{13} \\ A_{21} + B_{21} & A_{22} + B_{22} & A_{23} + B_{23} \end{pmatrix}.$$

Similarly, two partitioned matrices A and C can be multiplied, treating the blocks as scalars, if the blocks are all of a size such that the matrix multiplication of blocks can be done. For example, if

$$A = \begin{pmatrix} A_{11} & A_{12} \\ A_{21} & A_{22} \end{pmatrix} \quad \text{and} \quad C = \begin{pmatrix} C_{11} & C_{12} & C_{13} \\ C_{21} & C_{22} & C_{23} \end{pmatrix}, \tag{13}$$

then

$$AC = \begin{pmatrix} A_{11}C_{11} + A_{12}C_{21} & A_{11}C_{12} + A_{12}C_{22} & A_{11}C_{13} + A_{12}C_{23} \\ A_{21}C_{11} + A_{22}C_{21} & A_{21}C_{12} + A_{22}C_{22} & A_{21}C_{13} + A_{22}C_{23} \end{pmatrix}$$

so long as the various matrix products $A_{ij}C_{jk}$ can be formed. For example, A_{11} must have as many columns as C_{11} has rows, and so on.

We used the block multiplication of partitioned matrices in Section 8.4 when we wrote the matrix product $AA^{-1} = I$ as

$$A(\mathbf{c}_1 \quad \cdots \quad \mathbf{c}_n) = (\mathbf{e}_1 \quad \cdots \quad \mathbf{e}_n),$$

where $\mathbf{c}_i$ is the ith column of A^{-1} and $\mathbf{e}_j$ is the jth column of the identity matrix. In this case, the jth block product yielded the equation $A\mathbf{c}_j = \mathbf{e}_j$ in (2).

One reason for partitioning matrices is that frequently inverses can be computed (or found not to exist) much more easily using the blocks than they can by direct computation. For example, the following result on partitions is useful for deriving propositions about how demand functions depend on the price level.

Theorem 8.15   Let A be a square matrix partitioned as

$$A = \begin{pmatrix} A_{11} & A_{12} \\ A_{21} & A_{22} \end{pmatrix},$$

where A_{11} and A_{22} are square submatrices. If both A_{22} and the matrix

$$D = A_{11} - A_{12}A_{22}^{-1}A_{21}$$

are nonsingular, then A is nonsingular and

$$A^{-1} = \begin{pmatrix} D^{-1} & -D^{-1}A_{12}A_{22}^{-1} \\ -A_{22}^{-1}A_{21}D^{-1} & A_{22}^{-1}(I + A_{21}D^{-1}A_{12}A_{22}^{-1}) \end{pmatrix}. \qquad (14)$$

The proof of this theorem is left as an exercise.

EXERCISES

8.36   What must be true about the sizes of the various blocks A_{11}, A_{12}, C_{11}, and so on, in (13) in order for the block multiplications to make sense?

8.37   Suppose that A is given by (11) and the matrix C is given by

$$C = \begin{pmatrix} c_{11} & | & c_{12} & c_{13} & | & c_{14} \\ c_{21} & | & c_{22} & c_{23} & | & c_{24} \\ \hline c_{31} & | & c_{32} & c_{33} & | & c_{34} \\ \hline c_{41} & | & c_{42} & c_{43} & | & c_{44} \\ c_{51} & | & c_{52} & c_{53} & | & c_{54} \\ c_{61} & | & c_{62} & c_{63} & | & c_{64} \end{pmatrix} = \begin{pmatrix} C_{11} & C_{12} & C_{13} \\ C_{21} & C_{22} & C_{23} \\ C_{31} & C_{32} & C_{33} \end{pmatrix}.$$

a) Check that block multiplication can be carried out for the matrix product AC.

b) Compute the six block products $\Sigma A_{ij}C_{jk}$ for $i = 1, 2$ and $k = 1, 2, 3$.

c) Check that you reach the same answer for the matrix product whether you compute it with the block products or directly.

8.38   Show that the block diagonal matrix A in (12) is invertible if and only if each A_{ii} is invertible. Find A^{-1}.

8.39   Prove Theorem 8.15. First show that the matrix D exists. Then verify by block multiplication that matrix (14) is the inverse of A.

8.40   Replace the hypotheses on the matrix A of Theorem 8.15 by the hypothesis that both A_{11} and $A_{22} - A_{21}A_{11}^{-1}A_{12}$ are invertible. Prove that A is invertible and find its inverse.

8.41   Rewrite the invertibility conditions of Theorem 8.15 for the following cases.

a) $A_{21} = 0$;

b) A_{22} is 1×1 (a scalar);

c) A_{11} is the scalar 0, and $A_{21} = A_{12}^T = \mathbf{p}$ where $\mathbf{p}$ is a column vector.

8.7 DECOMPOSING MATRICES (optional)

This section demonstrates how most matrices can be written as a product of a lower-triangular matrix L and an upper-triangular matrix U. This **LU decomposition** leads to an efficient approach to solving systems of equations (Exercise 8.51 below). It is also the central technique in proving some important theorems about matrices (especially in Chapter 26). This decomposition is a direct consequence of Theorem 8.12 and the following lemma about the product of elementary matrices.

Lemma 8.2   Let L and M be two $n \times n$ lower-triangular matrices. Then, the matrix product LM is lower triangular. If L and M have only 1s on their diagonals, so does LM.

Proof   The (i, j)th entry of the product LM is the product of the ith row of L and the jth column of M. Using the hypothesis that $l_{ik} = 0$ for $k > i$ and $m_{hj} = 0$ for $h < j$, we write this product as:

$$[LM]_{ij} = \begin{pmatrix} l_{i1} & \cdots & l_{i,i-1} & l_{ii} & 0 & \cdots & 0 \end{pmatrix} \cdot \begin{pmatrix} 0 \\ \vdots \\ 0 \\ m_{jj} \\ m_{j+1,j} \\ \vdots \\ m_{nj} \end{pmatrix}. \tag{15}$$

If $i < j$, each of the i nonzero entries at the beginning of the ith row of L will be multiplied by the i zero entries beginning the jth column of M. The result is a zero entry in LM. Therefore, LM is lower triangular.

It follows from (15) that the (i, i)th diagonal entry of LM is $l_{ii}m_{ii}$. If $l_{ii} = m_{ii} = 1$, then $l_{ii}m_{ii} = 1$. ∎

Now we can use our knowledge of elementary matrices to decompose matrices.

Theorem 8.16   Let A be a general $k \times n$ matrix, and suppose that no row interchanges are needed to reduce A to its row echelon form. Then A can be written as a product LU where L is an $k \times k$ lower-triangular matrix with only 1's on the diagonal, and U is an upper-triangular $k \times n$ matrix.

The U in Theorem 8.16 is the row echelon form of A. Although it is not necessarily a square matrix, we will call it upper triangular because its (i, j)th entries are all zero whenever $i > j$.

Proof   Theorem 8.16 is a consequence of Theorems 8.4 and 8.12, which summarize the elementary matrix approach to Gaussian elimination. If no row interchanges are needed to reduce A to its row echelon form U, the only row operation required is the addition of a multiple of one row to a row which is farther down in the matrix. This operation is described by the elementary matrix $E_{ij}(r)$ where $i < j$. These elementary matrices are lower-triangular with 1s on the diagonal. Theorems 8.4 and 8.12 tell us that

$$A = E_1 \cdots E_m \cdot U \tag{16}$$

where E_1 is the inverse of the first elementary matrix used in the row reduction of A, E_2 is the inverse of the second elementary matrix used in the row reduction of A, and so on. In Example 8.5, we noted that the inverse of $E_{ij}(r)$ is $E_{ij}(-r)$. So the matrices $E_1, \ldots, E_m$ are all lower triangular with only 1's on their diagonals. Applying Lemma 8.2, we see that the product $E_1 \cdot E_2$ is lower triangular and has only 1's on the diagonal. Since the matrices E_3 and $E_1 \cdot E_2$ satisfy the hypotheses of the Lemma, $E_1 \cdot E_2 \cdot E_3$ is lower triangular and has 1s on the diagonal. Repeating this argument as many times as is necessary, we can see that the product $L = E_1 \cdots E_m$ is lower triangular and has only 1s on the diagonal. Consequently (16) can be rewritten as $A = LU$ where L is lower triangular with only 1s on the diagonal. ∎

Example 8.6   To illustrate Theorem 8.16, let us return to Example 8.1, where we wrote the row echelon form U of

$$A = \begin{pmatrix} 1 & 1 & 1 \\ 12 & 2 & -3 \\ 3 & 4 & 1 \end{pmatrix}$$

as

$$\begin{pmatrix} 1 & 1 & 1 \\ 0 & -10 & -15 \\ 0 & 0 & -3.5 \end{pmatrix} = E_{23}(.1) \cdot E_{13}(-3) \cdot E_{12}(-12) \cdot A$$

$$= \begin{pmatrix} 1 & 0 & 0 \\ -12 & 1 & 0 \\ -4.2 & .1 & 1 \end{pmatrix} \cdot \begin{pmatrix} 1 & 1 & 1 \\ 12 & 2 & -3 \\ 3 & 4 & 1 \end{pmatrix}.$$

Multiply the right-hand side by the inverses of the elementary matrices:

$$A = E_{12}(-12)^{-1} \cdot E_{13}(-3)^{-1} \cdot E_{23}(.1)^{-1} \cdot U$$

$$= E_{12}(12) \cdot E_{13}(3) \cdot E_{23}(-.1) \cdot U$$

$$= \begin{pmatrix} 1 & 0 & 0 \\ 12 & 1 & 0 \\ 3 & -.1 & 1 \end{pmatrix} \begin{pmatrix} 1 & 1 & 1 \\ 0 & -10 & -15 \\ 0 & 0 & -3.5 \end{pmatrix}$$

$$= LU.$$

Notice that the negatives of the below-diagonal entries of L reflect the elementary row operations used to reduce A to U.

Mathematical Induction

The proof of Theorem 8.16 is not completely rigorous, because the statement "repeating this argument as many times as is necessary" is a bit vague. How do we know that we can really do this? How many times are necessary? There is a formal technique for making this argument, which is called the *principle of mathematical induction*. The principle of mathematical induction is described fully in the first Appendix of this book. Here we will only show how we would apply it in the proof of Theorem 8.16.

In the proof of Theorem 8.16 we want to show that, for all k, the matrix product of k lower-triangular matrices $L_1 \cdot L_2 \cdots L_k$ is lower triangular. This statement is clearly true when $k = 1$. Lemma 8.2 tells us that the statement is true for $k = 2$. For $k = 3$, we write $L_1 \cdot L_2 \cdot L_3$ as $(L_1 \cdot L_2) \cdot L_3$. Since the statement is true for $k = 2$, $(L_1 \cdot L_2)$ is lower triangular. Lemma 8.2 then assures us that the product $L_1 \cdot L_2 \cdot L_3$ is lower triangular, and so on.

To formalize this argument, we divide it into two steps:

(1) the product of two lower-triangular matrices is lower triangular, and
(2) *if* the product of k lower-triangular matrices is lower triangular, *then* the product of $k + 1$ lower-triangular matrices is lower triangular.

Statements 1 and 2 are true by Lemma 8.2. Taken together, statements 1 and 2 allow us to conclude that the product of an arbitrary number k of lower triangular matrices is lower triangular. First, let $k = 2$ in 2, then 1 and 2 imply that the statement is true for $k = 3$. Next, let $k = 3$ in 2 to conclude that the statement is true for $k = 4$, and so on. Statement 2 is called the **inductive hypothesis**. This proof by induction is a bootstrap method that is often used to prove propositions of the form: statement P(k) is true for every positive integer k.

Including Row Interchanges

In the hypothesis of Theorem 8.16 we assumed that no row interchanges were needed to reduce A to its row echelon form. Of course this is not always the case, and so we would like to know what happens to the conclusions of Theorem 8.16 when row interchanges are required. First consider the case of nonsingular A. The answer is very simple (although the proof is sufficiently tricky that we will only sketch it here). Row interchanges are required only because, at some stage in the reduction process, there arises a pivot whose value is 0. So, reduce A to its row echelon form, keeping track of the row interchanges that are required. Suppose now that these row interchanges were to be made *before* we began the reduction. Then all the pivots would be in the right places, and no 0 pivots would be encountered in the row reduction process. How do we swap the rows of A?

The row interchanges can be accomplished by premultiplying A by permutation matrices — E_{ij} matrices. The product of permutation matrices is a permutation matrix (Exercise 8.10), and so, to eliminate the need for row interchanges during the reduction process, we can just premultiply A by the appropriate permutation matrix P. Thus there exists a permutation matrix P, an upper-triangular matrix U, and a lower-triangular matrix L such that $PA = LU$.

When A is singular, the story is not much different. Here, when a 0 pivot is encountered, it may not be possible to replace it with a nonzero pivot using a row interchange. Everything below the pivot may also be 0. This presents no problem; just go on to the next column. Of course some 0 pivots may have nonzero elements below them, so row interchanges may still be required. Nonetheless, our conclusions are not altered. We summarize them in the following theorem:

> **Theorem 8.17**   Let A be a general $k \times n$ matrix. Then one can write $PA = LU$ where P is a $k \times k$ permutation matrix, L is a $k \times k$ lower-triangular matrix with only 1s on the diagonal, and U is a $k \times n$ upper-triangular matrix.

EXERCISES

8.42   For each of the following matrices A, write down the string of elementary matrices which are needed to transform A to its row echelon form.

a) $\begin{pmatrix} 2 & 4 \\ -6 & -13 \end{pmatrix}$,   b) $\begin{pmatrix} 2 & 1 & 0 \\ 6 & 2 & 6 \\ -4 & -3 & 9 \end{pmatrix}$,

c) $\begin{pmatrix} 2 & 4 & 0 & 1 \\ 4 & 6 & 3 & 3 \\ -6 & -10 & 0 & 4 \end{pmatrix}$,   d) $\begin{pmatrix} 2 & 6 & 0 & 5 \\ 6 & 21 & 8 & 17 \\ 0 & -3 & -12 & 2 \\ 4 & 12 & -4 & 13 \end{pmatrix}$.

8.43   Write down the LU decomposition of each matrix in Exercise 8.42.

8.44   Show that the LU decomposition of A is unique if A is square, invertible, and satisfies the hypotheses of Theorem 8.16.

[Hint: Write $A = L_1 U_1 = L_2 U_2$, where the L_i are invertible and lower triangular, with 1s on the diagonal. Show that the U_i are invertible and write $L_2^{-1}L_1 = U_2 U_1^{-1}$. Conclude that both sides are diagonal and that the left side is in fact the identity matrix.]

8.45   Show that the LU decomposition of the $k \times n$ matrix A satisfying the hypothesis of Theorem 8.16 is unique if A has maximal rank.

[Hint: As in the previous exercise, write $L_2^{-1}L_1 U_1 = U_2$. Check that U_1 and U_2 have no 0 rows and then show that the equation $L_2^{-1}L_1 U_1 = U_2$ implies that $L_2^{-1}L_1$ is the identity matrix.]

8.46   Show by example that if A does not have maximal rank, then the LU decomposition of A need not be unique.

8.47 Prove the following proposition: If A is a square, nonsingular matrix and if row reduction of A requires no row interchanges, then A can be written uniquely as $A = LDU$ where L and U are lower- and upper-triangular matrices, respectively, with only 1s on their diagonals and D is a diagonal matrix. The diagonal entries of D are precisely the pivots of A.
[Hint: Start with the LU decomposition of A and decompose U into the product of two matrices, each with the desired properties.]

8.48 Find the LDU decomposition for the matrices in Exercise 8.42a, b, d.

8.49 The following two matrices require row interchanges to achieve their row echelon forms. For each matrix A:
a) Compute the row-echelon form.
b) Construct the permutation matrix P which corresponds to these row interchanges.
c) Compute the row echelon form of PA and compare your answer to that of part a.
d) Find the LU decomposition of PA.

$$i) \begin{pmatrix} 3 & 2 & 0 \\ 6 & 4 & 1 \\ -3 & 4 & 1 \end{pmatrix}, \qquad ii) \begin{pmatrix} 0 & 1 & 1 & 4 \\ 1 & 1 & 2 & 2 \\ -6 & -5 & -11 & -12 \\ 2 & 3 & -2 & 3 \end{pmatrix}.$$

8.50 a) What must be true about the entries of the general 2×2 matrix if row interchanges are required for reduction to row-echelon form?
b) What about the general 3×3 case?

8.51 The LU decomposition provides an efficient way to solve a system of linear equations $A\mathbf{x} = \mathbf{b}$ for different values of $\mathbf{b}$. It requires many fewer arithmetic steps than matrix inversion, and it works when A is not square. Use the LU decomposition to rewrite the system of equations as $LU\mathbf{x} = \mathbf{b}$. Now the system can be solved by first letting $U\mathbf{x} = \mathbf{z}$, solving the system of equations $L\mathbf{z} = \mathbf{b}$ for $\mathbf{z}$, and then solving $U\mathbf{x} = \mathbf{z}$ for $\mathbf{x}$. Since both of these systems are triangular, only back substitution is required to solve them.
a) Verify that the solutions obtained this way are precisely the solutions to $A\mathbf{x} = \mathbf{b}$.
b) Solve the following systems using this technique:

$$\begin{pmatrix} 2 & 4 & 0 \\ 4 & 6 & 3 \\ -6 & -10 & 0 \end{pmatrix} \begin{pmatrix} x_1 \\ x_2 \\ x_3 \end{pmatrix} = \begin{pmatrix} 2 \\ 1 \\ -6 \end{pmatrix}; \quad \begin{pmatrix} 2 & 4 & 0 \\ 4 & 6 & 3 \\ -6 & -10 & 0 \end{pmatrix} \begin{pmatrix} x_1 \\ x_2 \\ x_3 \end{pmatrix} = \begin{pmatrix} 2 \\ 8 \\ -4 \end{pmatrix};$$

$$\begin{pmatrix} 5 & 3 & 1 \\ -5 & -4 & 1 \\ -10 & -9 & 5 \end{pmatrix} \begin{pmatrix} x_1 \\ x_2 \\ x_3 \end{pmatrix} = \begin{pmatrix} 7 \\ -10 \\ -24 \end{pmatrix}; \quad \begin{pmatrix} 5 & 3 & 1 \\ -5 & -4 & 1 \\ -10 & -9 & 5 \end{pmatrix} \begin{pmatrix} x_1 \\ x_2 \\ x_3 \end{pmatrix} = \begin{pmatrix} 2 \\ -5 \\ -14 \end{pmatrix}.$$

NOTES

For an excellent summary of Leontief's study, see W. Leontief, "The structure of the U.S. economy," *Scientific American* 212 (April 1965). Our discussion of Leontief's 1958 model is adapted from the presentation in Stanley Grossman, *Applied Mathematics for the Management, Life, and Social Sciences* (Belmont, Calif.: Wadsworth, 1983). Our proof of Theorem 8.14 is adapted from Carl Simon, "Some Fine-Tuning for Dominant Diagonal Matrices," *Economic Letters* 30 (1989), 217–221.

Determinants:
An Overview

The most important matrices in economic models are square matrices, in which the number of unknowns equals the number of equations. For example, all the matrices for economic analysis listed in the first paragraph of Chapter 8 are square matrices. The most important square matrices are the nonsingular ones. These are precisely the coefficient matrices A such that the system of n equations in n unknowns

$$a_{11}x_1 + a_{12}x_2 + \cdots + a_{1n}x_n = b_1$$
$$a_{21}x_1 + a_{22}x_2 + \cdots + a_{2n}x_n = b_2$$

$$\vdots \qquad\qquad \vdots \qquad\quad \vdots \tag{1}$$

$$a_{n1}x_1 + a_{n2}x_2 + \cdots + a_{nn}x_n = b_n$$

or in matrix notation $A\mathbf{x} = \mathbf{b}$, has one and only one solution for each right-hand side $\mathbf{b}$. As we saw in the last chapter, these are also the matrices which are invertible. Since not all square matrices are nonsingular, we will describe in this chapter a straightforward test to *determine* whether or not a given matrix is nonsingular. In particular, for any square matrix we will define a number called the *determinant*, with the property that the square matrix is nonsingular if and only if its determinant is not zero. Later we will use the determinant for other tasks, for example, for developing an *explicit formula* for the solution of (1) in terms of the a_{ij}'s and b_i's, for deriving a formula for the inverse of a matrix, and for classifying the behavior of quadratic functions.

Many mathematical models in economics center around constrained maximization or minimization problems. Determinants play a role here too, because the second order condition for such problems requires that one check the signs of determinants of certain matrices of second derivatives.

The determinant can be a fairly complex expression. For a general $n \times n$ matrix there are $n!$ terms, each the product of n different entries of the matrix. Some of the proofs of its properties are also fairly complex. Consequently, this chapter presents a comprehensive *overview* of the determinant: how to compute it and how to use it, with relatively little motivation and no complex proofs. Chapter 26 contains a complete analysis of the determinant, including proofs of its important properties and major uses. Depending on the amount of detail with which one wants to cover determinants, one can: 1) read this chapter and skip Chapter 26, at least for the time being; 2) read Chapter 26 now and skip this chapter; or 3) read this chapter as an overview on determinants, follow it with a careful reading of Chapter 26, and then return to Chapter 10.

9.1   THE DETERMINANT OF A MATRIX

Defining the Determinant

The determinant of a matrix is defined inductively. There is a natural definition for 1×1 matrices. Then, we use this definition to define the determinant of 2×2 matrices. Once we have defined the determinant for 2×2 matrices, we use this definition to define the determinant for 3×3 matrices, and so on.

A 1×1 matrix is just a scalar (a). Since the inverse of a, $1/a$, exists if and only if a is nonzero, it is natural to define the determinant of such a matrix to be just that scalar a:

$$\det(a) = a.$$

For a 2×2 matrix

$$A = \begin{pmatrix} a_{11} & a_{12} \\ a_{21} & a_{22} \end{pmatrix},$$

Theorem 8.8 states that A is nonsingular if and only if $a_{11}a_{22} - a_{12}a_{21} \neq 0$. Therefore, we define the determinant of a 2×2 matrix A:

$$\det \begin{pmatrix} a_{11} & a_{12} \\ a_{21} & a_{22} \end{pmatrix} = a_{11}a_{22} - a_{12}a_{21}. \tag{2}$$

Notice that (2) is just the product of the two diagonal entries minus the product of the two off-diagonal entries. In order to motivate the general definition of a determinant, we write (2) as follows:

$$\det \begin{pmatrix} a_{11} & a_{12} \\ a_{21} & a_{22} \end{pmatrix} = a_{11} \det(a_{22}) - a_{12} \det(a_{21}). \tag{3}$$

The first term on the right-hand side of (3) is the $(1, 1)$th entry of A times the determinant of the submatrix obtained by deleting from A the row and column which contain that entry; the second term is the $(1, 2)$th entry times the determinant of the submatrix obtained by deleting from A the row and column which contain that entry. The terms alternate in sign; the term containing a_{11} receives a plus sign and the term containing a_{12} receives a minus sign.

The following definitions will simplify the task of defining the determinant of an $n \times n$ matrix.

Definition   Let A be an $n \times n$ matrix. Let A_{ij} be the $(n-1) \times (n-1)$ submatrix obtained by deleting row i and column j from A. Then, the scalar

$$M_{ij} \equiv \det A_{ij}$$

is called the (i, j)th **minor** of A and the scalar

$$C_{ij} \equiv (-1)^{i+j} M_{ij}$$

is called the (i, j)th **cofactor** of A. A cofactor is a signed minor. Note that $M_{ij} = C_{ij}$ if $(i + j)$ is even and $M_{ij} = -C_{ij}$ if $(i + j)$ is odd.
Formula (3) can be written as

$$\det A = a_{11} M_{11} - a_{12} M_{12} = a_{11} C_{11} + a_{12} C_{12}.$$

We use this expression as motivation for the definition of the determinant of a 3×3 matrix.

Definition   The **determinant** of a 3×3 matrix is given by

$$\det \begin{pmatrix} a_{11} & a_{12} & a_{13} \\ a_{21} & a_{22} & a_{23} \\ a_{31} & a_{32} & a_{33} \end{pmatrix} = a_{11} C_{11} + a_{12} C_{12} + a_{13} C_{13}$$

$$= a_{11} M_{11} - a_{12} M_{12} + a_{13} M_{13}$$

$$= a_{11} \cdot \det \begin{pmatrix} a_{22} & a_{23} \\ a_{32} & a_{33} \end{pmatrix} - a_{12} \cdot \det \begin{pmatrix} a_{21} & a_{23} \\ a_{31} & a_{33} \end{pmatrix}$$

$$+ a_{13} \cdot \det \begin{pmatrix} a_{21} & a_{22} \\ a_{31} & a_{32} \end{pmatrix}.$$

The jth term on the right-hand side of the definition is a_{1j} times the determinant of the submatrix obtained by deleting row 1 and column j from A. The term is preceeded by a plus sign if $1 + j$ is even and by a minus sign if $1 + j$ is odd.

Definition   The **determinant** of an $n \times n$ matrix A is given by

$$\det A = a_{11} C_{11} + a_{12} C_{12} + \cdots + a_{1n} C_{1n}$$

$$= a_{11} M_{11} - a_{12} M_{12} + \cdots + (-1)^{n+1} a_{1n} M_{1n}. \tag{4}$$

Notation   In referring to the determinant of a $n \times n$ matrix A, one sometimes writes

$$\begin{vmatrix} a_{11} & a_{12} & \cdots & a_{1n} \\ \vdots & \vdots & \vdots & \vdots \\ a_{n1} & a_{n2} & \cdots & a_{nn} \end{vmatrix} \qquad \text{for} \qquad \det \begin{pmatrix} a_{11} & a_{12} & \cdots & a_{1n} \\ \vdots & \vdots & \vdots & \vdots \\ a_{n1} & a_{n2} & \cdots & a_{nn} \end{pmatrix},$$

and $|A|$ for $\det A$.

Computing the Determinant

Our definition of the determinant of a matrix involves expanding along its first row. There is nothing special about the first row. It turns out that one can use any row or column to compute the determinant of a matrix. For example, if one uses, say, the *second column* to compute the determinant of a 3×3 matrix, one computes

$$\det A = -a_{12} \cdot \det \begin{pmatrix} a_{21} & a_{23} \\ a_{31} & a_{33} \end{pmatrix} + a_{22} \cdot \det \begin{pmatrix} a_{11} & a_{13} \\ a_{31} & a_{33} \end{pmatrix} - a_{32} \cdot \det \begin{pmatrix} a_{11} & a_{13} \\ a_{21} & a_{23} \end{pmatrix},$$

or equivalently,

$$\det A = a_{12}C_{12} + a_{22}C_{22} + a_{32}C_{32}. \tag{5}$$

The jth term on the right-hand side of (5) is a_{j2} times the determinant of the submatrix obtained by deleting the row and column of A which contains a_{j2}; it is preceded by a plus sign if $(j + 2)$ is even and by a minus sign if $(j + 2)$ is odd.

In general, the determinant of an $n \times n$ matrix involves $n!$ terms, each a product of n entries. This can be a time-consuming computation. There are certain classes of matrices whose determinants are easy to compute, as the following theorem illustrates.

Theorem 9.1   The determinant of a lower-triangular, upper-triangular, or diagonal matrix is simply the product of its diagonal entries.

Example 9.1   For a lower- or upper-triangular 2×2 matrix A, $a_{12} = 0$ or $a_{21} = 0$. Therefore, by (2)

$$\det A = a_{11}a_{22} - 0 = a_{11}a_{22}.$$

For a lower-triangular 3×3 matrix, use the definition to compute

$$\det \begin{pmatrix} a_{11} & 0 & 0 \\ a_{21} & a_{22} & 0 \\ a_{31} & a_{32} & a_{33} \end{pmatrix} = a_{11}C_{11} + 0 \cdot C_{12} + 0 \cdot C_{13}$$

$$= a_{11} \det \begin{pmatrix} a_{22} & 0 \\ a_{32} & a_{33} \end{pmatrix} = a_{11}a_{22}a_{33}.$$

Theorem 9.1 along with the following theorem often leads to simpler calculations of $\det A$.

Theorem 9.2 Let A be an $n \times n$ matrix and let R be its row echelon form. Then

$$\det A = \pm \det R.$$

If no row interchanges are used to compute R from A, then $\det A = \det R$.

One can frequently combine the previous two theorems to compute $\det A$ more efficiently. First, convert A to its row echelon form R. Since R is an upper-triangular matrix, its determinant is simply the product of its diagonal entries.

Remark There is an easy-to-remember mnemonic device for computing the determinant of a 3×3 matrix A, that **works only for** 3×3 **matrices**. Form the partitioned matrix $\hat{A}$ by recopying the first and second rows of A right below A, as in Figure 9.1. Starting from a_{11} at the top left corner of $\hat{A}$, add together the three products along the three "diagonals" indicated by the solid lines in Figure 9.1:

$$a_{11}a_{22}a_{33} + a_{21}a_{32}a_{13} + a_{31}a_{12}a_{23}. \tag{6}$$

Then, starting from a_{21} at the bottom left corner of $\hat{A}$, subtract from (6) the three products along the three "counterdiagonals" indicated by the dotted lines in Figure 9.1:

$$-a_{21}a_{12}a_{33} - a_{11}a_{32}a_{23} - a_{31}a_{22}a_{13}. \tag{7}$$

The result (6) + (7) is the determinant of A.

Example 9.2 Using this method, it is easy to see that

$$\det \begin{pmatrix} 0 & 1 & 2 \\ 3 & 4 & 5 \\ 6 & 7 & 8 \end{pmatrix} = 0 \cdot 4 \cdot 8 + 3 \cdot 7 \cdot 2 + 6 \cdot 1 \cdot 5$$
$$- 3 \cdot 1 \cdot 8 - 0 \cdot 7 \cdot 5 - 6 \cdot 4 \cdot 2$$
$$= 0 + 42 + 30 - 24 - 48$$
$$= 0.$$

Main Property of the Determinant

Finally, we put the above facts about determinants together to derive the main property of the determinant — the determinant *determines* whether or not a square matrix is nonsingular.

$$\hat{A} = \begin{pmatrix} a_{11} & a_{12} & a_{13} \\ a_{21} & a_{22} & a_{23} \\ a_{31} & a_{32} & a_{33} \\ a_{11} & a_{12} & a_{13} \\ a_{21} & a_{22} & a_{23} \end{pmatrix}$$

Computing the determinant of a 3 × 3 matrix.

**Figure
9.1**

Theorem 9.3   A square matrix is nonsingular if and only if its determinant is nonzero.

Proof Sketch   Recall that a square matrix A is nonsingular if and only if its row echelon form R has no all-zero rows. Since each row of the square matrix R has more leading zeros than the previous row, R has no all-zero rows if and only if the jth row of R has exactly $(j-1)$ leading zeros. This occurs if and only if R has no zeros on its diagonal. Since $\det R$ is the product of its diagonal entries, A is nonsingular if and only if $\det R$ is nonzero. Since $\det R = \pm \det A$, A is nonsingular if and only if $\det A$ is nonzero. ∎

Theorem 9.3 is obvious for 1×1 matrices, because the equation $ax = b$ has a unique solution, $x = b/a$, for every b if and only if $a \neq 0$. Theorem 8.8 demonstrates Theorem 9.3 for 2×2 matrices.

EXERCISES

9.1   Write out the complete expression for the determinant of a 3×3 matrix — six terms, each a product of three entries.

9.2   Write out the definition of the determinant of a 4×4 matrix in terms of the determinants of certain of its 3×3 submatrices. How many terms are there in the complete expansion of the determinant of a 4×4 matrix?

9.3   Compute out the expression on the right-hand side of (5). Show that it equals the expression calculated in Exercise 9.1.

9.4   Show that one obtains the same formula for the determinant of a 2×2 matrix, no matter which row or column one uses for the expansion.

9.5   Use a formula for the determinant to verify Theorem 9.1 for upper-triangular 3×3 matrices.

9.6   Verify the conclusion of Theorem 9.2 for 2×2 matrices by showing that the determinant of a general 2×2 matrix is not changed if one adds r times row 1 to row 2.

9.7   For each of the following matrices, compute the row echelon form and verify the conclusion of Theorem 9.2:

$$a) \begin{pmatrix} 1 & 1 \\ 2 & 1 \end{pmatrix}, \qquad b) \begin{pmatrix} 2 & 4 & 0 \\ 4 & 6 & 3 \\ -6 & -10 & 0 \end{pmatrix}, \qquad c) \begin{pmatrix} 0 & 1 & 2 \\ 3 & 4 & 5 \\ 0 & 7 & 8 \end{pmatrix}.$$

9.8   Use the observation following Theorem 9.2 to carry out a quick calculation of the determinant of each of the following matrices:

$$a) \begin{pmatrix} 1 & 1 & 1 \\ 1 & 4 & 2 \\ 1 & 4 & 3 \end{pmatrix}, \qquad b) \begin{pmatrix} 1 & 1 & 1 \\ 0 & 4 & 5 \\ 1 & 9 & 6 \end{pmatrix}.$$

9.9   Use Theorem 9.3 to determine which of the matrices in Exercises 9.7 and 9.8 are nonsingular.

9.2   USES OF THE DETERMINANT

Since the determinant tells whether or not A^{-1} exists and whether or not $Ax = b$ has a unique solution, it is not surprising that one can use the determinant to derive a formula for A^{-1} and a formula for the solution x of $Ax = b$. First, we define the adjoint matrix of A as the transpose of the matrix of cofactors of A.

Definition   For any $n \times n$ matrix A, let C_{ij} denote the (i, j)th cofactor of A, that is, $(-1)^{i+j}$ times the determinant of the submatrix obtained by deleting row i and column j from A. The $n \times n$ matrix whose (i, j)th entry is C_{ji}, the (j, i)th cofactor of A (note the switch in indices), is called the **adjoint** of A and is written **adj** A.

Theorem 9.4   Let A be a nonsingular matrix. Then,

(a) $A^{-1} = \dfrac{1}{\det A} \cdot \text{adj} A$, and

(b) (**Cramer's rule**) the unique solution $x = (x_1, \cdots, x_n)$ of the $n \times n$ system $Ax = b$ is

$$x_i = \frac{\det B_i}{\det A}, \qquad \text{for } i = 1, \ldots, n,$$

where B_i is the matrix A with the right-hand side b replacing the ith column of A.

For 3×3 systems,

$$a_{11}x_1 + a_{12}x_2 + a_{13}x_3 = b_1$$
$$a_{21}x_1 + a_{22}x_2 + a_{23}x_3 = b_2$$
$$a_{31}x_1 + a_{32}x_2 + a_{33}x_3 = b_3.$$

Cramer's rule states that

$$x_1 = \frac{\begin{vmatrix} b_1 & a_{12} & a_{13} \\ b_2 & a_{22} & a_{23} \\ b_3 & a_{32} & a_{33} \\ a_{11} & a_{12} & a_{13} \\ a_{21} & a_{22} & a_{23} \\ a_{31} & a_{32} & a_{33} \end{vmatrix}}{}, \quad x_2 = \frac{\begin{vmatrix} a_{11} & b_1 & a_{13} \\ a_{21} & b_2 & a_{23} \\ a_{31} & b_3 & a_{33} \\ a_{11} & a_{12} & a_{13} \\ a_{21} & a_{22} & a_{23} \\ a_{31} & a_{32} & a_{33} \end{vmatrix}}{}, \quad x_3 = \frac{\begin{vmatrix} a_{11} & a_{12} & b_1 \\ a_{21} & a_{22} & b_2 \\ a_{31} & a_{32} & b_3 \\ a_{11} & a_{12} & a_{13} \\ a_{21} & a_{22} & a_{23} \\ a_{31} & a_{32} & a_{33} \end{vmatrix}}{}.$$

Example 9.3   Use Theorem 9.4 to invert the matrix

$$A = \begin{pmatrix} 2 & 4 & 5 \\ 0 & 3 & 0 \\ 1 & 0 & 1 \end{pmatrix}. \tag{8}$$

$$C_{11} = + \begin{vmatrix} 3 & 0 \\ 0 & 1 \end{vmatrix} = 3, \quad C_{12} = - \begin{vmatrix} 0 & 0 \\ 1 & 1 \end{vmatrix} = 0, \quad C_{13} = + \begin{vmatrix} 0 & 3 \\ 1 & 0 \end{vmatrix} = -3,$$

$$C_{21} = - \begin{vmatrix} 4 & 5 \\ 0 & 1 \end{vmatrix} = -4, \quad C_{22} = + \begin{vmatrix} 2 & 5 \\ 1 & 1 \end{vmatrix} = -3, \quad C_{23} = - \begin{vmatrix} 2 & 4 \\ 1 & 0 \end{vmatrix} = 4,$$

$$C_{31} = + \begin{vmatrix} 4 & 5 \\ 3 & 0 \end{vmatrix} = -15, \quad C_{32} = - \begin{vmatrix} 2 & 5 \\ 0 & 0 \end{vmatrix} = 0, \quad C_{33} = + \begin{vmatrix} 2 & 4 \\ 0 & 3 \end{vmatrix} = 6,$$

$$\det A = -9,$$

$$\text{adj} A = \begin{pmatrix} C_{11} & C_{21} & C_{31} \\ C_{12} & C_{22} & C_{32} \\ C_{13} & C_{23} & C_{33} \end{pmatrix} = \begin{pmatrix} 3 & -4 & -15 \\ 0 & -3 & 0 \\ -3 & 4 & 6 \end{pmatrix}.$$

So,
$$A^{-1} = -\frac{1}{9} \begin{pmatrix} 3 & -4 & -15 \\ 0 & -3 & 0 \\ -3 & 4 & 6 \end{pmatrix}. \tag{9}$$

Example 9.4   We can use Cramer's rule to calculate x_3 for the system in Example 7.1, which we write in matrix form as

$$\begin{pmatrix} 1 & 1 & 1 \\ 12 & 2 & -3 \\ 3 & 4 & 1 \end{pmatrix} \begin{pmatrix} x_1 \\ x_2 \\ x_3 \end{pmatrix} = \begin{pmatrix} 0 \\ 5 \\ -4 \end{pmatrix}.$$

The determinant of the coefficient matrix A is 35. The determinant of

$$B_3 = \begin{pmatrix} 1 & 1 & 0 \\ 12 & 2 & 5 \\ 3 & 4 & -4 \end{pmatrix}$$

is also 35. Thus, $x_3 = |B_3|/|A| = 1$.

Finally, we note three algebraic properties of the determinant function which we will find important in our use of determinants.

Theorem 9.5   Let A be a square matrix. Then,

(a) $\det A^T = \det A$,
(b) $\det(A \cdot B) = (\det A)(\det B)$, and
(c) $\det(A + B) \neq \det A + \det B$,   in general.

Gaussian elimination is a much more efficient method of solving a system of n equations in n unknowns than is Cramer's rule. Cramer's rule requires the evaluation of $(n + 1)$ determinants. Each determinant is a sum of $n!$ terms and each term is a product of n entries. So, Cramer's rule requires $(n+1)!$ operations. On the other hand, the number of arithmetic operations required by Gaussian elimination for such a system is on the order of n^3. If $n = 6$ as in the Leontief model in Section 8.5, then $(n + 1)!$ is 5040, while n^3 is only 216; the difference grows exponentially as n increases.

Nevertheless, Cramer's rule is particularly useful for small linear systems in which the coefficients a_{ij} are parameters and for which one wants to obtain a general formula for the endogenous variables (the x_i's) in terms of the parameters and the exogenous variables (the b_j's). One can then see more clearly how changes in the parameters affect the values of the endogenous variables.

EXERCISES

9.10   Verify directly that matrix (9) really is the inverse of matrix (8) in Example 9.3.

9.11   Use Theorem 9.4 to invert the following matrices:

$$a) \begin{pmatrix} 4 & 3 \\ 1 & 1 \end{pmatrix}, \qquad b) \begin{pmatrix} 1 & 2 & 3 \\ 0 & 5 & 6 \\ 1 & 0 & 8 \end{pmatrix}, \qquad c) \begin{pmatrix} a & b \\ c & d \end{pmatrix}.$$

9.12   Use Cramer's rule to compute x_1 and x_2 in Example 9.4.

9.13   Use Cramer's rule to solve the following systems of equations:

$$a) \begin{array}{l} 5x_1 + x_2 = 3 \\ 2x_1 - x_2 = 4; \end{array} \qquad b) \begin{array}{l} 2x_1 - 3x_2 = 2 \\ 4x_1 - 6x_2 + x_3 = 7 \\ x_1 + 10x_2 = 1. \end{array}$$

9.14   Verify the conclusions of Theorem 9.5 for the following pairs of matrices:

$$a) \ A = \begin{pmatrix} 4 & 5 \\ 1 & 1 \end{pmatrix}, \qquad B = \begin{pmatrix} 3 & 4 \\ 1 & 1 \end{pmatrix};$$

b) $A = \begin{pmatrix} 1 & 2 & 3 \\ 0 & 4 & 5 \\ 0 & 0 & 6 \end{pmatrix}$, $B = \begin{pmatrix} 1 & 0 & 0 \\ 2 & 3 & 0 \\ 4 & 5 & 6 \end{pmatrix}$;

c) $A = \begin{pmatrix} a & b \\ c & d \end{pmatrix}$, $B = \begin{pmatrix} e & f \\ g & h \end{pmatrix}$.

9.3 IS-LM ANALYSIS VIA CRAMER'S RULE

As an illustrative example, consider the linear IS-LM national income model described in Chapter 6:

$$sY + ar = I^o + G$$
$$mY - hr = M_s - M^o \tag{10}$$

where Y = net national product

r = interest rate

s = marginal propensity to save,

a = marginal efficiency of capital,

I = investment $(= I^o - ar)$,

m = money balances needed per dollar of transactions,

G = government spending,

M_s = money supply.

All the parameters are positive. Because the coefficients in this system are parameters instead of numbers, it is easiest to solve (10) using Cramer's rule:

$$Y = \frac{\begin{vmatrix} I^o + G & a \\ M_s - M^o & -h \end{vmatrix}}{\begin{vmatrix} s & a \\ m & -h \end{vmatrix}} = \frac{(I^o + G)h + a(M_s - M^o)}{sh + am}$$

$$r = \frac{\begin{vmatrix} s & I^o + G \\ m & M_s - M^o \end{vmatrix}}{\begin{vmatrix} s & a \\ m & -h \end{vmatrix}} = \frac{(I^o + G)m - s(M_s - M^o)}{sh + am}.$$

One can now use these expressions to see that, in this model, an increase in I^o, G, or M_s or a decrease in M^o or m will lead to an increase in the equilibrium net product Y. An increase in I^o or M^o or a decrease in M_s, h, or m will lead to an increase in equilibrium interest rate r.

EXERCISES

9.15 Verify the assertions in the last two sentences before these exercises.

9.16 If you are familiar with partial derivatives, compute

$$\frac{\partial Y}{\partial a} = \frac{-rh}{(sh + am)} \le 0.$$

So an increase in the marginal efficiency of capital a will bring down the equilibrium Y and r. How will the equilibrium Y change if h increases? How will the equilibrium r change if m or s increases?

9.17 If we introduce tax rate t and let the consumption function depend on after-tax income, $C = b(Y - tY)$, then system (10) becomes

$$(1 - t)sY + ar = I^o + G$$
$$mY - hr = M_s - M^o.$$

Use Cramer's rule to see how the equilibrium Y and r are affected by the tax rate t.

9.18 Consider the following more elaborate linear IS-LM.

$a)\ Y\ = C + I + G$ $b)\ C = c_0 + c_1(Y - T) - c_2 r$

$c)\ T\ = t_0 + t_1 Y$ $d)\ I\ = I^o + a_0 Y - ar$

$e)\ M_s = mY + M^o - hr.$

Substitute c into b to obtain b'; then substitute b' and d into a to get the new IS-curve. Combine this with e and use Cramer's rule to solve this system for Y and r in terms of the exogenous variables. Show that an increase in G or a reduction of t_0 or t_1 will increase Y; in macroeconomic terms, Keynesian fiscal policy "works" in this model. Show that these changes also increase r. Regarding monetary policy, show that an increase in M_s increases Y and lowers r.

9.19 What is the effect of an increase in I^o, c_0, or m?

9.20 For Example 1 in Chapter 6, write out the linear system which corresponds to equation (1) in Chapter 6, but with a general before-tax profit P, a general contribution percentage c, and general state and federal tax rates r and f. Use Cramer's rule to compute C, S, and F in terms of P, c, s, and f.

Euclidean Spaces

As we discussed at the end of Chapter 1, one of the main uses of mathematical analysis in economic theory is to help construct the appropriate geometric and analytic generalizations of the two-dimensional geometric models that are the mainstay of undergraduate economics courses. In this chapter, we begin these constructions by studying how to generalize notions of points, lines, planes, distances, and angles to n-dimensional Euclidean spaces. Later, our analyses of n-commodity economies will make heavy use of these concepts.

The first three sections of this chapter present the basic geometry of coordinates, points and displacements in n-space. If this material is familiar to most students, it can be left as a background reading assignment.

10.1   POINTS AND VECTORS IN EUCLIDEAN SPACE

The Real Line

The simplest geometric object is the number line — the geometric realization of the set of all real numbers. The number line was defined carefully at the beginning of Chapter 2. Every real number is represented by exactly one point on the line, and each point on the line represents one and only one number. Figure 10.1 shows part of a number line.

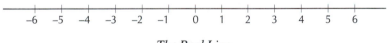

Figure 10.1

The Real Line.

The Plane

In some of our economic examples, we have used pairs of numbers to represent economic objects, for example, consumption bundles in Chapter 1. Pairs of numbers also have a geometric representation, called the **Cartesian plane** or **Euclidean 2-space**, and written as $\mathbf{R}^2$. To depict $\mathbf{R}^2$, first draw two perpendicular number lines: one horizontal to represent the first **component** x_1 of the pair (x_1, x_2) and the other vertical to represent the second component x_2 of (x_1, x_2). The unit length is usually the same along each line (although it need not be). These two

199

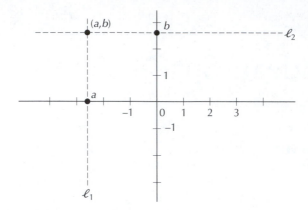

**Figure
10.2**   *Identifying a point in the plane with an ordered pair.*

number lines are called **coordinate axes**. They intersect at their origins. Figure
10.2 shows how each point in the plane is identified with a unique pair of numbers.
We have used the Cartesian plane in Chapter 2 to draw graphs of functions of one
variable.

A point **p** in the Cartesian plane represents a pair of numbers (a, b) as follows:
draw a vertical line ℓ_1 and a horizontal line ℓ_2 through the point **p**. The vertical
line crosses the x_1-axis at a, and the horizontal line crosses the x_2-axis at b. We
associate the pair (a, b) with the point **p**. To go the other way — to find the point
p which represents the pair (a, b) — find a on the x_1-axis, and through it draw
the vertical line ℓ_1. Find b on the x_2-axis, and through it draw the horizontal line
ℓ_2. The intersection of the two lines ℓ_1 and ℓ_2 is the point **p**, which we will
sometimes write as **p**(a, b). The number a is called the x_1-**coordinate** of **p**, and b
is called the x_2-**coordinate** of **p**. In Figure 10.3 we show a number of points and
their coordinates.

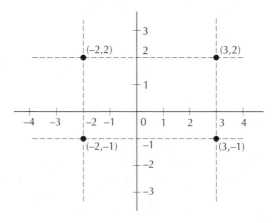

**Figure
10.3**   *Coordinates of points in* **R**^{2}.

The point of intersection of the horizontal and vertical number lines is our reference point for measuring the location of **p**. It is called the **origin**, and we denote it by the symbol **0**, since it is represented by the pair (0, 0).

Three Dimensions and More

Similarly, one can visualize 3-dimensional Euclidean space $\mathbf{R}^3$ by drawing three mutually perpendicular number lines. As before, each one of these number lines is called a **coordinate axis**: the x_1-axis, the x_2-axis, and the x_3-axis, respectively. One usually draws the x_2-axis as the horizontal axis and the x_3-axis as the vertical axis on the plane of the page and then pictures the x_1-axis as coming out of the page toward one, as in Figure 10.4.

The process of identifying a point with a particular triple of numbers uses the techniques that we used in $\mathbf{R}^2$. The process is illustrated in Figure 10.5. To

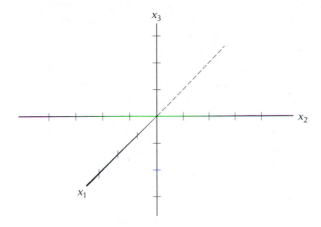

The coordinate axes in $\mathbf{R}^3$.

Figure 10.4

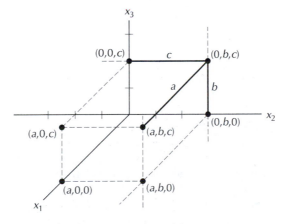

The point **p** *with coordinates* (a, b, c).

Figure 10.5

find the point represented by the triple (a, b, c); forget about a for a moment, and locate the point representing (b, c) in the x_2x_3-plane — the plane of the page. This is a 2-space exercise that we already know how to do. From the point (b, c) in the plane of the page, move a units in the direction parallel to the x_1-axis. March out of the page if a is positive, and march behind the page if a is negative. If a is 0, remain where you are. The point $\mathbf{p}$ at which you finish represents (a, b, c) and is sometimes denoted by $\mathbf{p}(a, b, c)$. We could have just as easily started in the x_1x_3-plane and then moved b units to the right (for positive b), or in the x_1x_2-plane and then moved c units up (for positive c). Check to see that you end up at the same point no matter which method you use.

Finding the coordinates that describe a particular point $\mathbf{p}$ is just as easy. Starting from $\mathbf{p}$, move parallel to the x_1-axis until you reach x_2x_3-plane. The distance moved is a; it is positive if the move was into the page and negative if the move was out toward you. The coordinates b and c are now found using the 2-space technique. Again, the answer is independent of which plane you head for first. This description and the accompanying diagram (Figure 10.5) is an example of a situation where a picture is worth a thousand words.

Of course, we cannot draw geometric pictures of higher-dimensional Euclidean spaces, but we can use our pictures of $\mathbf{R}^1$, $\mathbf{R}^2$, and $\mathbf{R}^3$ to guide our intuition. We will see that the formulas describing geometric objects and their properties in $\mathbf{R}^2$ and $\mathbf{R}^3$ generalize readily to higher dimensions. The real line $\mathbf{R}^1$ consists of single numbers. The plane $\mathbf{R}^2$ consists of **ordered pairs** of numbers. We say *ordered* pairs because the order of the numbers matters; $(1, 0)$ is not the same as $(0, 1)$. Euclidean n-space consists of ordered n-tuples of numbers — ordered lists of n numbers. For example, Euclidean 3-space contains ordered triples (a, b, c) of numbers. Euclidean 5-space contains ordered 5-tuples (a, b, c, d, e). Euclidean n-space is usually referred to as $\mathbf{R}^n$. The number n in $\mathbf{R}^n$ refers to how many numbers are needed to describe each location. It is called the **dimension** of $\mathbf{R}^n$. Thus $\mathbf{R}^5$ has 5 dimensions, while $\mathbf{R}^2$ has only two dimensions. Each space will have its origin, the point with respect to which we make our coordinate measurements. As we did in $\mathbf{R}^2$, we will always refer to the origin by the symbol $\mathbf{0}$.

10.2   VECTORS

Euclidean spaces are useful for modeling a wide variety of economic phenomena because n-tuples of numbers have many useful interpretations. Thus far we have emphasized their interpretation as locations, or points in n-space. For example, the point $(3, 2)$ represents a particular location in the plane, found by going 3 units to the right and 2 units up from the origin. This is just the way we use coordinates on a map of a country to find the location of a particular city. We use coordinates to describe locations in exactly the same way in higher dimensions. Many economic applications require us to think of n-tuples of numbers as locations. For example, we think of consumption bundles as locations in commodity space.

We can also interpret n-tuples as **displacements**. This is a useful way of thinking about vectors for doing calculus. We picture these displacements as arrows in $\mathbf{R}^n$. The displacement $(3, 2)$ means: *move* 3 units to the right and 2 units up from your current location. The tail of the arrow marks the initial location; the head marks the location after the displacement is made. In Figure 10.6, each arrow represents the displacement $(3, 2)$, but in each case the displacement is applied to a different initial location.

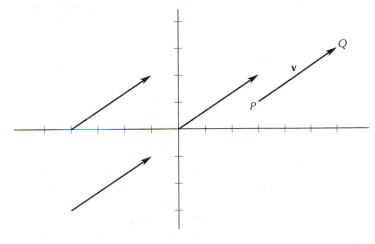

The displacement $(3, 2)$.

Figure 10.6

For example, the tail of the displacement labeled $\mathbf{v}$ in Figure 10.6 is at the location $(3, 1)$, and the head is at $(6, 3)$. We will sometimes write $\overrightarrow{PQ}$ for the displacement whose tail is at the point P and head at the point Q. Two arrows represent the same displacement if they are parallel and have the same length and direction. For our purposes, two such arrows are equivalent; regardless of their different initial and terminal locations, they both represent the same displacement. The essential ingredients of a displacement are its magnitude and direction.

How do we assign an n-tuple to a particular arrow? We measure how far we have to move in each direction to get from the tail to the head of the arrow. For example, consider the arrow $\mathbf{v}$ in Figure 10.6. To get from the tail to the head we have to move 3 units in the x_1-direction and 2 units in the x_2-direction. Thus $\mathbf{v}$ must represent the displacement $(3, 2)$. More formally, if a displacement goes from the initial location (a, b) to the terminal location (c, d), then the move in the x_1-direction is $c - a$, since $a + (c - a) = c$; and the move in the x_2-direction is $d - b$, since $b + (d - b) = d$. Thus the displacement is $(c - a, d - b)$. This method of subtracting corresponding coordinates applies to higher dimensions as well. The displacement from the point $\mathbf{p}(a_1, a_2, \ldots, a_n)$ to the point $\mathbf{q}(b_1, b_2, \ldots, b_n)$ in $\mathbf{R}^n$ is written

$$\overrightarrow{\mathbf{pq}} = (b_1 - a_1, b_2 - a_2, \ldots, b_n - a_n).$$

Figure 10.6 illustrates that there are many $(3, 2)$ displacements. In any given discussion, all the displacements will usually have the same initial location (tail). Often, this initial location will naturally be $\mathbf{0}$, the origin. From this initial location,

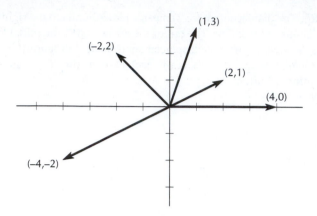

**Figure
10.7**   *Some displacements in the plane.*

the *displacement* (3, 2) takes us to the *location* (3, 2). With this "canonical repre-sentation" of displacements, we can think of locations as displacements from the origin. Several different displacements are shown in Figure 10.7.

We have just seen that the very different concepts of location and displace-ment have a common mathematical representation as *n*-tuples of numbers. These concepts act alike mathematically, and so we give them a common name: **vectors**.

Some books distinguish between locations and displacements by writing a location as a row vector (a, b) and a displacement as a column vector $\begin{pmatrix} a \\ b \end{pmatrix}$. This approach is unwieldy and unnecessary. From now on we will use the word "vector" to refer to both locations and displacements. It will either be explicitly mentioned, or clear from the context, whether locations or displacements are meant in any particular discussion.

EXERCISES

10.1   Draw a number line and locate (approximately) the points 1, 3/2, −2, $\sqrt{2}$, π, and $-\pi/2$.

10.2   Draw a Cartesian plane and locate on it the following points: (1, 1), (−1/2, 3/2), (0, 0), (0, −4), (π, −$\sqrt{2}$).

10.3   Draw a plane, and show the path you would traverse were you to start at (−1, 3), displace yourself first by the vector (1, −3), and then by the vector (−1, −3).

10.4   For the points P and Q listed below, draw the corresponding displacement vector $\overrightarrow{PQ}$ and compute the corresponding *n*-tuple for $\overrightarrow{PQ}$:

a) $P(0, 0)$ and $Q(2, −1)$,   *b)* $P(3, 2)$ and $Q(1, 1)$,

c) $P(3, 2)$ and $Q(5, 3)$,   *d)* $P(0, 1)$ and $Q(3, 1)$,

e) $P(0, 0, 0)$ and $Q(1, 2, 4)$,   *f)* $P(0, 1, 0)$ and $Q(2, −1, 3)$.

10.3   THE ALGEBRA OF VECTORS

There are four basic algebraic operations for the real numbers, $\mathbf{R}^1$: addition, subtraction, multiplication and division. This section introduces the three basic algebraic operations on higher-dimensional Euclidean spaces: vector addition and subtraction and scalar multiplication.

Addition and Subtraction

We add two vectors just as we add two numbers. We simply add separately the corresponding coordinates of the two vectors. Thus

$$(3, 2) + (4, 1) = (7, 3),$$

and

$$(x_1, x_2, x_3) + (y_1, y_2, y_3) = (x_1 + y_1, \ x_2 + y_2, \ x_3 + y_3).$$

Notice that we can only add together two vectors from the same vector space. The sum $(2, 1) + (3, 4, 1)$ is not defined, since the first vector lives in $\mathbf{R}^2$ while the second vector lives in $\mathbf{R}^3$. Furthermore, the sum of two vectors from $\mathbf{R}^n$ is a vector, and it lives in $\mathbf{R}^n$. When we add $(3, 5, 1, 0) + (0, 0, 0, 1)$ from $\mathbf{R}^4$, we get the vector $(3, 5, 1, 1)$ which is also in $\mathbf{R}^4$.

To develop a geometric intuition for vector addition, it is most natural to think of vectors as displacement arrows. If $\mathbf{u} = (a, b)$ and $\mathbf{v} = (c, d)$ in $\mathbf{R}^2$, then we want $\mathbf{u} + \mathbf{v}$ to represent a displacement of $a + c$ units to the right and $b + d$ units up. Intuitively, we can think of this displacement as follows: Start at some initial location. Apply displacement $\mathbf{u}$. Now apply displacement $\mathbf{v}$ to the terminal location of the displacement $\mathbf{u}$. In other words, move $\mathbf{v}$ until its tail is at the head of $\mathbf{u}$. Then, $\mathbf{u} + \mathbf{v}$ is the displacement from the tail of $\mathbf{u}$ to the head of $\mathbf{v}$, as in Figure 10.8. Verify that $\mathbf{u} + \mathbf{v}$, as drawn, has coordinates $(a + c, b + d)$.

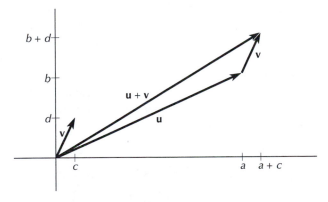

The sum of two vectors in the plane.

Figure 10.8

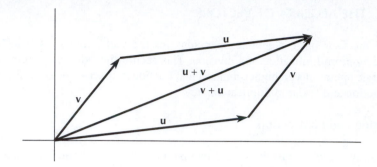

**Figure
10.9**

$$\mathbf{u} + \mathbf{v} = \mathbf{v} + \mathbf{u}.$$

Figure 10.9 shows that it makes no difference whether we think of $\mathbf{u} + \mathbf{v}$ as displacing first by $\mathbf{u}$ and then by $\mathbf{v}$ or first by $\mathbf{v}$ and then by $\mathbf{u}$. Since the two arrows representing $\mathbf{u}$ in Figure 10.9 are parallel and have the same length and similarly for the two representations of $\mathbf{v}$, the quadrilateral in Figure 10.9 is a parallelogram. Its diagonal represents both $\mathbf{u} + \mathbf{v}$ and $\mathbf{v} + \mathbf{u}$. Formally, Figure 10.9 shows that $\mathbf{u} + \mathbf{v} = \mathbf{v} + \mathbf{u}$; vector addition, like addition of real numbers, is **commutative**.

One can use the parallelogram in Figure 10.9 to draw $\mathbf{u} + \mathbf{v}$ while keeping the tails of $\mathbf{u}$ and $\mathbf{v}$ at the same point. First, draw the complete parallelogram which has $\mathbf{u}$ and $\mathbf{v}$ as adjacent sides, as in Figure 10.9. Then, take $\mathbf{u} + \mathbf{v}$ as the diagonal of this parallelogram with its tail at the common tail of $\mathbf{u}$ and $\mathbf{v}$. Physicists use displacements vectors to represent forces acting at a given point. If vectors $\mathbf{u}$ and $\mathbf{v}$ represent two forces at point P, then the vector $\mathbf{u} + \mathbf{v}$ represents the force which results when both forces are applied at P at the same time.

Vector addition obeys the other rules which the addition of real numbers obeys. These are: the associative rule, the existence of a zero (an additive identity), and the existence of an additive inverse. The zero vector is the vector which represents no displacement at all. Analytically we write

$$\mathbf{0} = (0, 0, \ldots, 0).$$

Geometrically, it is a displacement $\overrightarrow{PP}$ having the same terminal point as initial point. Check both algebraically and geometrically that $\mathbf{u} + \mathbf{0} = \mathbf{u}$.

If $\mathbf{u} = (a_1, a_2, \ldots, a_n)$, then the negative of $\mathbf{u}$, written $-\mathbf{u}$ and called "minus $\mathbf{u}$", is the vector $(-a_1, -a_2, \ldots, -a_n)$. Geometrically, one interchanges the head and tail of $\mathbf{u}$ to obtain the head and tail of $-\mathbf{u}$. Symbolically, $-\overrightarrow{PQ} = \overrightarrow{QP}$. Check that the algebraic and geometric points of view are consistent and that $\mathbf{u} + (-\mathbf{u}) = \mathbf{0}$.

In the real numbers, subtraction is defined by the equation $a - b = a + (-b)$. We can use the same rule to define subtraction for vectors. Thus

$$(4, 3, 5) - (1, 3, 2) = (4, 3, 5) + (-1, -3, -2)$$
$$= (4 - 1, 3 - 3, 5 - 2)$$
$$= (3, 0, 3).$$

More generally, for vectors in **R^n**,

$$(a_1, a_2, \ldots, a_n) - (b_1, b_2, \ldots, b_n) = (a_1 - b_1, a_2 - b_2, \ldots, a_n - b_n).$$

Geometrically we think of subtraction as completing the triangle in Figure 10.8. Given **u** and **u** + **v**, find **v** to make the diagram work. Put another way, **x** − **y** is that vector which, when added to **y**, gives **x**. Subtraction finds the missing leg of the triangle in Figure 10.10.

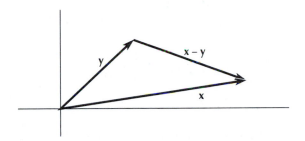

Geometric representation of **x** − **y**.

Figure 10.10

Scalar Multiplication

It is generally not possible to multiply two vectors in a nice way so as to generalize the multiplication of real numbers. For example, coordinatewise multiplication does not satisfy the basic properties that the multiplication of real numbers satisfies. For one thing, the coordinatewise product of two nonzero vectors, such as $(1, 0)$ and $(0, 1)$, could be the zero vector. When this happens, division, the inverse operation to multiplication, cannot be defined. However, there is a vector space operation which corresponds to statements like, "go twice as far" or "you are halfway there." This operation is called **scalar multiplication**. In it we multiply a vector, coordinatewise, by a real number, or **scalar**. If r is a scalar and $\mathbf{x} = (x_1, \ldots, x_n)$ is a vector, then their product is

$$r \cdot \mathbf{x} = (rx_1, \ldots, rx_n).$$

For example, $2 \cdot (1, 1) = (2, 2)$, and $\frac{1}{2} \cdot (-4, 2) = (-2, 1)$.

Geometrically, scalar multiplication of a displacement vector **x** by a nonnegative scalar r corresponds to stretching or shrinking **x** by the factor r without changing its direction, as in Figure 10.11. Scalar multiplication by a negative scalar causes not only a change in the length of a vector but also a reverse in direction.

In the algebra of the real numbers, addition and multiplication are linked by the **distributive laws**:

$$a \cdot (b + c) = ab + ac \quad \text{and} \quad (a + b) \cdot c = ac + bc.$$

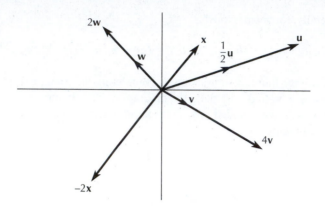

**Figure
10.11**

Scalar multiplication in the plane.

There are distributive laws in Euclidean spaces as well. It is easy to see that vector addition distributes over scalar multiplication and that scalar multiplication distributes over vector addition:

(a) $(r + s)\mathbf{u} = r\mathbf{u} + s\mathbf{u}$ for all scalars r, s and vectors $\mathbf{u}$.

(b) $r(\mathbf{u} + \mathbf{v}) = r\mathbf{u} + r\mathbf{v}$ for all scalars r and vectors $\mathbf{u}$, $\mathbf{v}$.

Any set of objects with a vector addition and scalar multiplication which satisfies the rules we have outlined in this section is called a **vector space**. The elements of the set are called **vectors**. (The operations of vector addition and scalar multiplication are the operations of matrix addition and scalar multiplication of matrices, respectively, applied to $1 \times n$ or $n \times 1$ matrices, as defined in Section 1 of Chapter 8. The scalar product of the next section will also correspond to a matrix operation.)

EXERCISES

10.5   Let $\mathbf{u} = (1, 2)$, $\mathbf{v} = (0, 1)$, $\mathbf{w} = (1, -3)$, $\mathbf{x} = (1, 2, 0)$, and $\mathbf{z} = (0, 1, 1)$. Compute the following vectors, whenever they are defined: $\mathbf{u} + \mathbf{v}$, $-4\mathbf{w}$, $\mathbf{u} + \mathbf{z}$, $3\mathbf{z}$, $2\mathbf{v}$, $\mathbf{u} + 2\mathbf{v}$, $\mathbf{u} - \mathbf{v}$, $3\mathbf{x} + \mathbf{z}$, $-2\mathbf{x}$, $\mathbf{w} + 2\mathbf{x}$.

10.6   Carry out all of the possible operations in Exercise 10.5 *geometrically*.

10.7   Show that $-\mathbf{u} = (-1)\mathbf{u}$.

10.8   Prove the distributive laws for vectors in $\mathbf{R}^n$.

10.9   Use Figure 10.12 to give a geometric proof of the **associative law** for vector addition: $\mathbf{u} + (\mathbf{v} + \mathbf{w}) = (\mathbf{u} + \mathbf{v}) + \mathbf{w}$.

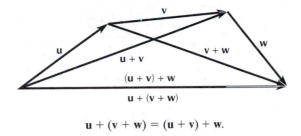

$$\mathbf{u} + (\mathbf{v} + \mathbf{w}) = (\mathbf{u} + \mathbf{v}) + \mathbf{w}.$$

**Figure
10.12**

10.4 LENGTH AND INNER PRODUCT IN R^n

Among the key geometric concepts that guide our analysis of two-dimensional economic models are length, distance and angle. In this section, we describe the *n*-dimensional analogues of these concepts which we will use for more complex, higher dimensional economic models.

When we build mathematical models of economic phenomena in Euclidean spaces, we will often be interested in the geometric properties of these spaces, for example, the distance between two points or the angle between two vectors. In this section we develop the analytical tools needed to study these properties. In fact, all the geometrical results of planar (that is, two-dimensional) Euclidean geometry can be derived using purely analytical techniques. Furthermore, these analytic techniques are all we have for generalizing the results of plane geometry to higher-dimensional Euclidean spaces.

Length and Distance

The most basic geometric property is distance or length. If P and Q are two points in $\mathbf{R}^n$, we write $\overline{PQ}$ for the line segment joining P to Q and $\overrightarrow{PQ}$ for the vector from P to Q.

Notation   The **length** of line segment $\overline{PQ}$ is denoted by the symbol $\|\overline{PQ}\|$. The vertical lines draw attention to the analogy of length in the plane with absolute value in the line.

We now develop a formula for $\|\overline{PQ}\|$, or equivalently, for the **distance** between points P and Q. First, consider the case where P and Q lie in the plane $\mathbf{R}^2$ and have the same x_2-coordinate. We have pictured this situation in Figure 10.13, where P has coordinates (a_1, b) and Q has coordinates (a_2, b). The length of this line is clearly the length of the line segment connecting a_1 and a_2 on the x_1-axis. Since length is always a positive number, the length of this segment on the x_1-axis is simply $|a_2 - a_1|$. We conclude that $\|\overline{PQ}\| = |a_2 - a_1|$, as in Figure 10.13.

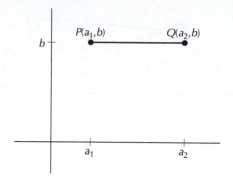

**Figure
10.13**

$$\|\overline{PQ}\| = |a_2 - a_1|.$$

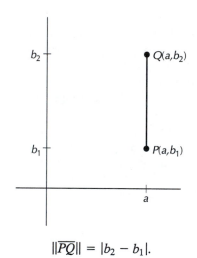

**Figure
10.14**

$$\|\overline{PQ}\| = |b_2 - b_1|.$$

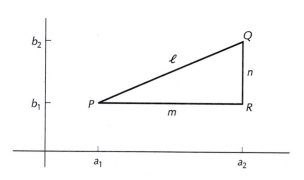

**Figure
10.15**

Computing $\|\overline{PQ}\|$ in the plane.

Next, consider the case where P and Q have the same x_1-component. Say P is (a, b_1) and Q is (a, b_2), as in Figure 10.14. Here, the distance is naturally $|b_2 - b_1|$.

Finally, we consider the general case, as pictured in Figure 10.15. To compute the length of line ℓ joining points $P(a_1, b_1)$ and $Q(a_2, b_2)$, mark the intermediate point $R(a_2, b_1)$. Let m be the (horizontal) line segment from $P(a_1, b_1)$ to $R(a_2, b_1)$ and let n be the (vertical) line segment from $Q(a_2, b_2)$ to $R(a_2, b_1)$. The corresponding triangle PRQ is a right triangle whose hypotenuse is the line segment ℓ.

Apply the Pythagorean Theorem to deduce the length of ℓ:

$$(\text{length } \ell)^2 = (\text{length } m)^2 + (\text{length } n)^2$$
$$= |a_1 - a_2|^2 + |b_1 - b_2|^2.$$

Taking the square root of both sides of this equation gives

$$\|\overline{PQ}\| = \text{length } \ell = \sqrt{(a_1 - a_2)^2 + (b_1 - b_2)^2}. \tag{1}$$

We can apply this argument to higher dimensions, as pictured in Figure 10.16. To find the distance from $P(a_1, b_1, c_1)$ to $Q(a_2, b_2, c_2)$ in $\mathbf{R}^3$, we use the point $R(a_2, b_2, c_1)$, which has the same x_3-coordinate as P and the same x_1- and x_2-coordinates as Q. Since P and R have the same x_3-coordinate, the segment PR lies on the $x_3 = c_1$ plane, which is parallel to the x_1x_2-plane ($x_3 = 0$). Since Q and R have the same x_1- and x_2-coordinates, segment QR is parallel to the x_3-axis and therefore perpendicular to the segment PR. Therefore, $\triangle PRQ$ is a right triangle with hypotenuse PQ. By the Pythagorean Theorem,

$$\|PQ\|^2 = \|PR\|^2 + \|RQ\|^2. \tag{2}$$

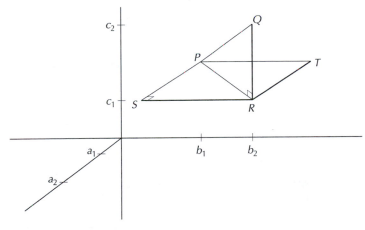

Computing the length of line PQ in $\mathbf{R}^3$.

**Figure
10.16**

Since RQ is parallel to the x_3-axis, its length is simply $|c_2 - c_1|$. To find the length of PR, we work in the two-dimensional plane through PR parallel to the x_1x_2-plane. Note that if $S = (a_2, b_1, c_1)$, PS is parallel to the x_1-axis and therefore has length $|a_2 - a_1|$, and SR is parallel to the x_2-axis with length $|b_2 - b_1|$. Applying the Pythagorean Theorem to right triangle PSR yields:

$$\|PR\|^2 = \|PS\|^2 + \|SR\|^2$$
$$= |a_2 - a_1|^2 + |b_2 - b_1|^2.$$

Substituting this into Equation (2) yields:

$$\|PQ\|^2 = |a_2 - a_1|^2 + |b_2 - b_1|^2 + |c_2 - c_1|^2.$$

Therefore, the distance from P to Q is

$$\|PQ\| = \sqrt{(a_2 - a_1)^2 + (b_2 - b_1)^2 + (c_2 - c_1)^2}. \tag{3}$$

Formulas (1) and (3) generalize readily to points in higher dimensional Euclidean spaces. If $(x_1, x_2, \ldots, x_n)$ and $(y_1, y_2, \ldots, y_n)$ are the coordinates of $\mathbf{x}$ and $\mathbf{y}$, respectively, in Euclidean n-space, then the **distance** between $\mathbf{x}$ and $\mathbf{y}$ is

$$\sqrt{(x_1 - y_1)^2 + (x_2 - y_2)^2 + \cdots + (x_n - y_n)^2}.$$

We will use this same formula whether we think of $\mathbf{x}$ and $\mathbf{y}$ as points or as displacement vectors. Recall that $\mathbf{x} - \mathbf{y}$ is the vector joining points $\mathbf{x}$ and $\mathbf{y}$ and its length $\|\mathbf{x} - \mathbf{y}\|$ is the same as the distance between these two points. Thus, it is natural to write

$$\|\mathbf{x} - \mathbf{y}\| = \sqrt{(x_1 - y_1)^2 + (x_2 - y_2)^2 + \cdots + (x_n - y_n)^2}$$

In particular, if we take $\mathbf{y}$ to be $\mathbf{0}$, then the distance from the point $\mathbf{x} = (x_1, \ldots, x_n)$ to the origin or the **length** of the vector $\mathbf{x}$ is

$$\|\mathbf{x}\| = \sqrt{x_1^2 + \cdots + x_n^2}.$$

We can now make more precise the effect of scalar multiplication on the length of a vector $\mathbf{v}$. If r is a positive scalar, the length of $r\mathbf{v}$ is r times the length of $\mathbf{v}$. If r is a negative scalar, the length of $r\mathbf{v}$ is $|r|$ times the length of $\mathbf{v}$. This can be summarized as follows.

Theorem 10.1 $\|r\mathbf{v}\| = |r| \cdot \|\mathbf{v}\|$ for all r in $\mathbf{R}^1$ and $\mathbf{v}$ in $\mathbf{R}^n$.

Proof

$$\|r(v_1, \ldots, v_n)\| = \|(rv_1, rv_2, \ldots, rv_n)\|$$

$$= \sqrt{(rv_1)^2 + \cdots + (rv_n)^2}$$

$$= \sqrt{r^2(v_1^2 + \cdots + v_n^2)}$$

$$= |r|\sqrt{v_1^2 + \cdots + v_n^2}, \quad \text{since} \quad \sqrt{r^2} = |r|. \qquad \blacksquare$$

Given a non-zero displacement vector **v**, we will occasionally need to find a vector **w** which points in the same direction as **v**, but has length 1. Such a vector **w** is called the **unit vector** in the direction of **v**, or sometimes simply the **direction** of **v**. To achieve such a vector **w**, simply premultiply **v** by the scalar $r = \frac{1}{\|v\|}$, because

$$\left\| \frac{1}{\|v\|} \cdot v \right\| = \left| \frac{1}{\|v\|} \right| \cdot \|v\| = \frac{1}{\|v\|} \cdot \|v\| = 1.$$

Example 10.1 For example, the length of $(1, -2, 3)$ in **R^3** is

$$\|(1, -2, 3)\| = \sqrt{1^2 + (-2)^2 + 3^2} = \sqrt{14}.$$

It follows that

$$\frac{1}{\sqrt{14}}(1, -2, 3) = \left(\frac{1}{\sqrt{14}}, \frac{-2}{\sqrt{14}}, \frac{3}{\sqrt{14}} \right)$$

is a vector which points in the same direction as $(1, -2, 3)$ but has length 1.

The Inner Product

We have learned how to add and subtract two vectors and how to compute the distance between them. In this section we introduce another operation on pairs of vectors, the Euclidean inner product. This operation assigns a number to each pair of vectors. We will see that it is connected to the notion of "angle between two vectors," and therefore is useful for discussing geometric problems.

Definition Let $\mathbf{u} = (u_1, \ldots, u_n)$ and $\mathbf{v} = (v_1, \ldots, v_n)$ be two vectors in **R^n**. The **Euclidean inner product** of **u** and **v**, written as $\mathbf{u} \cdot \mathbf{v}$, is the *number*

$$\mathbf{u} \cdot \mathbf{v} = u_1 v_1 + u_2 v_2 + \cdots + u_n v_n.$$

Because of the dot in the notation, the Euclidean inner product is often called the **dot product**. To emphasize that the result of the operation is a scalar, the Euclidean inner product is also called the **scalar product**. In the exercises to this section, we introduce the outer product or cross product as a way of multiplying two vectors in $\mathbf{R}^3$ to obtain another vector in $\mathbf{R}^3$.

Example 10.2   If $\mathbf{u} = (4, -1, 2)$ and $\mathbf{v} = (6, 3, -4)$, then

$$\mathbf{u} \cdot \mathbf{v} = 4 \cdot 6 + (-1) \cdot 3 + 2 \cdot (-4) = 13.$$

The following theorem summarizes the basic analytical properties of the inner product — properties that we will use often in this text. Its proof is straightforward and is left as an exercise. Work out the relationships in this theorem to build up a working knowledge of inner product.

Theorem 10.2   Let $\mathbf{u}, \mathbf{v}, \mathbf{w}$ be arbitrary vectors in $\mathbf{R}^n$ and let r be an arbitrary scalar. Then,

(a) $\mathbf{u} \cdot \mathbf{v} = \mathbf{v} \cdot \mathbf{u}$,

(b) $\mathbf{u} \cdot (\mathbf{v} + \mathbf{w}) = \mathbf{u} \cdot \mathbf{v} + \mathbf{u} \cdot \mathbf{w}$,

(c) $\mathbf{u} \cdot (r\mathbf{v}) = r(\mathbf{u} \cdot \mathbf{v}) = (r\mathbf{u}) \cdot \mathbf{v}$,

(d) $\mathbf{u} \cdot \mathbf{u} \geq 0$,

(e) $\mathbf{u} \cdot \mathbf{u} = 0$ implies $\mathbf{u} = \mathbf{0}$, and

(f) $(\mathbf{u} + \mathbf{v}) \cdot (\mathbf{u} + \mathbf{v}) = \mathbf{u} \cdot \mathbf{u} + 2(\mathbf{u} \cdot \mathbf{v}) + \mathbf{v} \cdot \mathbf{v}$.

The Euclidean inner product is closely connected to the Euclidean length of a vector. Since

$$\mathbf{u} \cdot \mathbf{u} = u_1^2 + u_2^2 + \cdots + u_n^2 \quad \text{and} \quad \|\mathbf{u}\| = \sqrt{u_1^2 + u_2^2 + \cdots + u_n^2},$$

$$\|\mathbf{u}\| = \sqrt{\mathbf{u} \cdot \mathbf{u}}.$$

Consequently, the distance between two vectors $\mathbf{u}$ and $\mathbf{v}$ can be written in terms of the inner product as

$$\|\mathbf{u} - \mathbf{v}\| = \sqrt{(\mathbf{u} - \mathbf{v}) \cdot (\mathbf{u} - \mathbf{v})}.$$

Any two vectors $\mathbf{u}$ and $\mathbf{v}$ in $\mathbf{R}^n$ determine a plane, as illustrated in Figure 10.17. In that plane we can measure the angle θ between $\mathbf{u}$ and $\mathbf{v}$. The inner product yields an important connection between the lengths of $\mathbf{u}$ and $\mathbf{v}$ and the angle θ between $\mathbf{u}$ and $\mathbf{v}$.

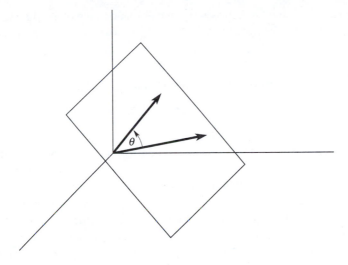

The angle between two vectors in $\mathbf{R^n}$.

Figure
10.17

Theorem 10.3   Let $\mathbf{u}$ and $\mathbf{v}$ be two vectors in $\mathbf{R^n}$. Let θ be the angle between them. Then,

$$\mathbf{u} \cdot \mathbf{v} = \|\mathbf{u}\| \, \|\mathbf{v}\| \cos \theta.$$

Remark   Recall that to measure the cosine of an angle $\theta = \angle BAC$ as in Figure 10.18, draw the perpendicular from B to a point D on the line containing A and C. Then, in the right triangle BAD, the cosine of θ is the length of adjacent side AD divided by the length of hypotenuse AB. See the Appendix of this book for more details. If θ is an *obtuse* angle (between 90 degrees and 270 degrees), then Figure 10.19 is the relevant diagram and the cosine of θ is the *negative* of $\|AD\|/\|AB\|$.

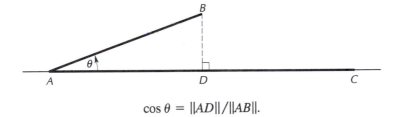

$\cos \theta = \|AD\|/\|AB\|$.

Figure
10.18

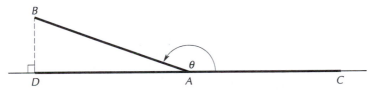

Computing the cosine of an obtuse angle: $\cos \theta = -\|AD\|/\|AB\|$.

Figure
10.19

In either case, cosine θ lies between -1 and $+1$ since a leg of a right triangle can never be longer than the hypotenuse. For us, the important properties of $\cos \theta$ are:

$$\cos \theta > 0 \qquad \text{if } \theta \text{ is acute,}$$

$$\cos \theta < 0 \qquad \text{if } \theta \text{ is obtuse,}$$

$$\cos \theta = 0 \qquad \text{if } \theta \text{ is a right angle.}$$

Proof of Theorem 10.3   The following proof is a bit more complex than the other proofs we have seen. It uses the Pythagorean Theorem again. Without loss of generality, we can work with $\mathbf{u}$ and $\mathbf{v}$ as vectors with tails at the origin $\mathbf{0}$; say $\mathbf{u} = \overrightarrow{OP}$ and $\mathbf{v} = \overrightarrow{OQ}$. Let ℓ be the line through the vector $\mathbf{v}$, that is, the line through the points $\mathbf{0}$ and Q. Draw the perpendicular line segment m from the point P (the head of $\mathbf{u}$) to the line ℓ, as in Figure 10.20. Let R be the point where m meets ℓ. Since R lies on ℓ, $\overrightarrow{OR}$ is a scalar multiple of $\mathbf{v} = \overrightarrow{OQ}$. Write $\overrightarrow{OR} = t\mathbf{v}$. Since $\mathbf{u}$, $t\mathbf{v}$, and the segment m are the three sides of the right triangle OPR, we can write m as the vector $\mathbf{u} - t\mathbf{v}$. Since $\mathbf{u}$ is the hypotenuse of this right triangle,

$$\cos \theta = \frac{\|t\mathbf{v}\|}{\|\mathbf{u}\|} = \frac{t\|\mathbf{v}\|}{\|\mathbf{u}\|}. \tag{4}$$

On the other hand, by the Pythagorean Theorem and Theorem 10.2, the square of the length of the hypotenuse is:

$$\|\mathbf{u}\|^2 = \|t\mathbf{v}\|^2 + \|\mathbf{u} - t\mathbf{v}\|^2$$

$$= t^2\|\mathbf{v}\|^2 + (\mathbf{u} - t\mathbf{v}) \cdot (\mathbf{u} - t\mathbf{v})$$

$$= t^2\|\mathbf{v}\|^2 + \mathbf{u} \cdot \mathbf{u} - 2\mathbf{u} \cdot (t\mathbf{v}) + (t\mathbf{v}) \cdot (t\mathbf{v})$$

$$= t^2\|\mathbf{v}\|^2 + \|\mathbf{u}\|^2 - 2t(\mathbf{u} \cdot \mathbf{v}) + t^2\|\mathbf{v}\|^2,$$

or

$$2t(\mathbf{u} \cdot \mathbf{v}) = 2t^2\|\mathbf{v}\|^2.$$

It follows that

$$t = \frac{\mathbf{u} \cdot \mathbf{v}}{\|\mathbf{v}\|^2}. \tag{5}$$

Plugging equation (5) into equation (4) yields

$$\cos \theta = \frac{\mathbf{u} \cdot \mathbf{v}}{\|\mathbf{u}\| \, \|\mathbf{v}\|}. \qquad \blacksquare$$

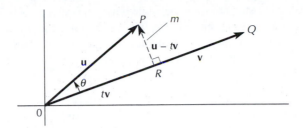

Choose t so that **v** *and* **u** $-$ t**v** *are perpendicular.*

**Figure
10.20**

   The following example illustrates how one can use the inner product to compute angles explicitly.

Example 10.3   We will use the inner product to compute the angle between the diagonal of a cube and one of its sides. Consider a cube in $\mathbf{R^3}$ with each side of length c. Position this cube in $\mathbf{R^3}$ in the most natural manner, i.e., with vertices at $O(0,0,0)$, $P_1(c,0,0)$, $P_2(0,c,0)$, and $P_3(0,0,c)$, as in Figure 10.21. Write $\mathbf{u_i}$ for the vector $\overrightarrow{OP_i}$ for $i = 1, 2, 3$. Then, the diagonal $\mathbf{d}$ is $\mathbf{u_1} + \mathbf{u_2} + \mathbf{u_3}$, which is the vector (c, c, c).
   The angle θ between $\mathbf{u_1}$ and $\mathbf{d}$ satisfies

$$\cos \theta = \frac{\mathbf{u_1} \cdot \mathbf{d}}{\|\mathbf{u_1}\| \, \|\mathbf{d}\|} = \frac{(c,0,0) \cdot (c,c,c)}{c \cdot \sqrt{c^2 + c^2 + c^2}}$$

$$= \frac{c^2}{c\sqrt{3c^2}} = \frac{1}{\sqrt{3}}.$$

Using a trig table or calculator, one finds that $\cos \theta = 1/\sqrt{3}$ implies that $\theta \approx 54°44'$.

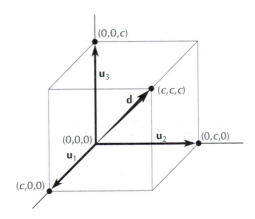

Cube of side c.

**Figure
10.21**

Rarely do we care to know that the angle between two vectors is 71° or $3\pi/7$ radians. More often, we are interested in whether the angle is acute, obtuse, or a right angle. Since $\cos\theta$ is positive when θ is acute, negative when θ is obtuse, and zero when θ is a right angle, the dot product tells us the information we want by Theorem 10.3.

Theorem 10.4   The angle between vectors **u** and **v** in $\mathbf{R}^n$ is

(a) acute, if $\mathbf{u} \cdot \mathbf{v} > 0$,
(b) obtuse, if $\mathbf{u} \cdot \mathbf{v} < 0$,
(c) right, if $\mathbf{u} \cdot \mathbf{v} = 0$.

When this angle is a right angle, we say that **u** and **v** are **orthogonal**. So, vectors **u** and **v** are orthogonal if and only if $\mathbf{u} \cdot \mathbf{v} = u_1 v_1 + \cdots + u_n v_n = 0$, a simple check indeed.

We have taken some liberties with the case where one of the vectors is zero. When this occurs, θ is not defined. However, we will run into no difficulties with the concept of orthogonality if we simply watch for zero vectors.

Finally, we use Theorem 10.3 to derive a basic property of length or norm — the **triangle inequality**. This rule states that any side of a triangle is shorter than the sum of the lengths of the other two sides. Intuitively, it follows from the fact that the straight line segment gives the shortest path between any two points in $\mathbf{R}^n$. In vector notation, we want to prove that

$$\|\mathbf{u} + \mathbf{v}\| \leq \|\mathbf{u}\| + \|\mathbf{v}\| \quad \text{for all } \mathbf{u}, \mathbf{v} \text{ in } \mathbf{R}^n.$$

Figure 10.22 illustrates the equivalence of this analytic formulation with the above statement about triangles.

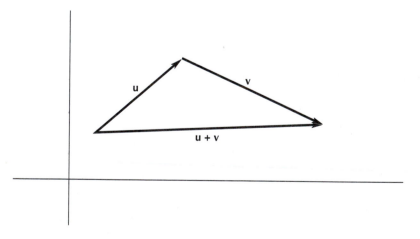

Figure 10.22

u, **v**, *and* **u** + **v** *are three sides of a triangle.*

Theorem 10.5 For any two vectors $\mathbf{u}$, $\mathbf{v}$ in $\mathbf{R}^n$,

$$\|\mathbf{u} + \mathbf{v}\| \leq \|\mathbf{u}\| + \|\mathbf{v}\|. \qquad (6)$$

Proof Recall that

$$\frac{\mathbf{u} \cdot \mathbf{v}}{\|\mathbf{u}\| \cdot \|\mathbf{v}\|} = \cos \theta \leq 1$$

by Theorem 10.3. Therefore,

$$\mathbf{u} \cdot \mathbf{v} \leq \|\mathbf{u}\| \cdot \|\mathbf{v}\|,$$

$$\|\mathbf{u}\|^2 + 2(\mathbf{u} \cdot \mathbf{v}) + \|\mathbf{v}\|^2 \leq \|\mathbf{u}\|^2 + 2\|\mathbf{u}\|\|\mathbf{v}\| + \|\mathbf{v}\|^2,$$

$$\mathbf{u} \cdot \mathbf{u} + \mathbf{u} \cdot \mathbf{v} + \mathbf{v} \cdot \mathbf{u} + \mathbf{v} \cdot \mathbf{v} \leq (\|\mathbf{u}\| + \|\mathbf{v}\|)^2,$$

$$(\mathbf{u} + \mathbf{v}) \cdot (\mathbf{u} + \mathbf{v}) \leq (\|\mathbf{u}\| + \|\mathbf{v}\|)^2,$$

$$\|\mathbf{u} + \mathbf{v}\|^2 \leq (\|\mathbf{u}\| + \|\mathbf{v}\|)^2,$$

$$\|\mathbf{u} + \mathbf{v}\| \leq \|\mathbf{u}\| + \|\mathbf{v}\|. \qquad \blacksquare$$

We will use the triangle inequality (6) over and over again in our study of Euclidean spaces. Just about every mathematical statement involving an inequality requires the triangle inequality in its proof. The next theorem presents a variant of the triangle inequality which we will also use frequently in our analysis, especially when we want to derive a lower bound for some expression. To understand this result more fully, you should test it on pairs of real numbers, especially pairs with opposite signs.

Theorem 10.6 For any two vectors $\mathbf{x}$ and $\mathbf{y}$ in $\mathbf{R}^n$,

$$\big| \|\mathbf{x}\| - \|\mathbf{y}\| \big| \leq \|\mathbf{x} - \mathbf{y}\|.$$

Proof Apply Theorem 10.5 with $\mathbf{u} = \mathbf{x} - \mathbf{y}$ and $\mathbf{v} = \mathbf{y}$ in (6), to obtain the inequality $\|\mathbf{x}\| \leq \|\mathbf{x} - \mathbf{y}\| + \|\mathbf{y}\|$, or

$$\|\mathbf{x}\| - \|\mathbf{y}\| \leq \|\mathbf{x} - \mathbf{y}\|. \qquad (7)$$

Now apply Theorem 10.5 with $\mathbf{u} = \mathbf{y} - \mathbf{x}$ and $\mathbf{v} = \mathbf{x}$ in (6) to obtain the inequality $\|\mathbf{y}\| \leq \|\mathbf{y} - \mathbf{x}\| + \|\mathbf{x}\|$, or

$$\|\mathbf{y}\| - \|\mathbf{x}\| \leq \|\mathbf{y} - \mathbf{x}\| = \|\mathbf{x} - \mathbf{y}\|. \qquad (8)$$

Inequalities (7) and (8) imply that

$$| \, \|x\| - \|y\| \, | \leq \|x - y\|. \qquad \blacksquare$$

The three basic properties of Euclidean length are:

(1) $\|u\| \geq 0$ and $\|u\| = 0$ only when $u = 0$.
(2) $\|ru\| = |r| \|u\|$
(3) $\|u + v\| \leq \|u\| + \|v\|$.

Any assignment of a real number to a vector that satisfies these three properties is called a **norm**. Exercise 10.16 lists other norms that arise naturally in applications. We will say more about norms in the last section of Chapter 29.

EXERCISES

10.10   Find the length of the following vectors. Draw the vectors for a through g:

a) $(3, 4)$,   b) $(0, -3)$,   c) $(1, 1, 1)$,   d) $(3, 3)$,   e) $(-1, -1)$,
f) $(1, 2, 3)$,   g) $(2, 0)$,   h) $(1, 2, 3, 4)$,   i) $(3, 0, 0, 0, 0)$.

10.11   Find the distance from P to Q, drawing the picture wherever possible:

a) $P(0, 0)$, $Q(3, -4)$;   b) $P(1, -1)$, $Q(7, 7)$;
c) $P(5, 2)$, $Q(1, 2)$;   d) $P(1, 1, -1)$, $Q(2, -1, 5)$;
e) $P(1, 2, 3, 4)$, $Q(1, 0, -1, 0)$.

10.12   For each of the following pairs of vectors, first determine whether the angle between them is acute, obtuse, or right and then calculate this angle:

a) $u = (1, 0)$, $v = (2, 2)$;   b) $u = (4, 1)$, $v = (2, -8)$;
c) $u = (1, 1, 0)$, $v = (1, 2, 1)$;   d) $u = (1, -1, 0)$, $v = (1, 2, 1)$;
e) $u = (1, 0, 0, 0, 0)$, $v = (1, 1, 1, 1, 1)$.

10.13   For each of the following vectors, find a vector of length 1 which points in the same direction. a) $(3, 4)$, b) $(6, 0)$, c) $(1, 1, 1)$, d) $(-1, 2, -3)$.

10.14   For each of the vectors in the last exercise, find a vector of length five which points in the opposite direction.

10.15   Prove that $\|u - v\|^2 = \|u\|^2 - 2u \cdot v + \|v\|^2$.

10.16   a) In view of the last paragraph in this section, prove that each of the following is a norm in $\mathbf{R}^2$:

$$\||(u_1, u_2)\|| = |u_1| + |u_2|,$$

$$\||(u_1, u_2)\|| = \max\{|u_1|, |u_2|\}.$$

b) What are the analogous norms in $\mathbf{R}^n$?

10.17   Provide a complete and careful proof of Theorem 10.2.

10.18 Fill in all the details in the proof of Theorem 10.3.

10.19 For a rectangular $2' \times 3' \times 4'$ box, find the angle that the longest diagonal makes with the $4'$-side.

10.20 Use vector notation to prove that the diagonals of a rhombus are orthogonal to each other. See Figure 10.23.

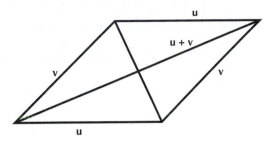

If $\|\mathbf{u}\| = \|\mathbf{v}\|$, this quadrilateral is a rhombus.

**Figure
10.23**

10.21 Prove the following identities.

a) $\|\mathbf{u} + \mathbf{v}\|^2 + \|\mathbf{u} - \mathbf{v}\|^2 = 2\|\mathbf{u}\|^2 + 2\|\mathbf{v}\|^2$,

b) $\mathbf{u} \cdot \mathbf{v} = \frac{1}{4}\|\mathbf{u} + \mathbf{v}\|^2 - \frac{1}{4}\|\mathbf{u} - \mathbf{v}\|^2$.

10.22 Prove that if $\mathbf{u}$ and $\mathbf{v}$ are orthogonal vectors, then $\|\mathbf{u} + \mathbf{v}\|^2 = \|\mathbf{u}\|^2 + \|\mathbf{v}\|^2$. Explain why this statement is called the general version of the Pythagorean Theorem.

10.23 The **cross product** is a commonly-used multiplication of vectors in $\mathbf{R}^3$, for which the product of two vectors in $\mathbf{R}^3$ is another *vector* in $\mathbf{R}^3$. It is defined as follows, using the determinant notation introduced in Chapter 9:

$$(u_1, u_2, u_3) \times (v_1, v_2, v_3) = (u_2 v_3 - u_3 v_2, u_3 v_1 - u_1 v_3, u_1 v_2 - u_2 v_1)$$

$$= \left(\begin{vmatrix} u_2 & u_3 \\ v_2 & v_3 \end{vmatrix}, -\begin{vmatrix} u_1 & u_3 \\ v_1 & v_3 \end{vmatrix}, \begin{vmatrix} u_1 & u_2 \\ v_1 & v_2 \end{vmatrix} \right).$$

Prove the following properties of the cross-product:

a) $\mathbf{u} \times \mathbf{v} = -\mathbf{v} \times \mathbf{u}$,

b) $\mathbf{u} \times \mathbf{v}$ is perpendicular to $\mathbf{u}$,

c) $\mathbf{u} \times \mathbf{v}$ is perpendicular to $\mathbf{v}$,

d) $(r\mathbf{u}) \times \mathbf{v} = r(\mathbf{u} \times \mathbf{v}) = \mathbf{u} \times (r\mathbf{v})$,

e) $(\mathbf{u}_1 + \mathbf{u}_2) \times \mathbf{v} = (\mathbf{u}_1 \times \mathbf{v}) + (\mathbf{u}_2 \times \mathbf{v})$,

f) $\|\mathbf{u} \times \mathbf{v}\|^2 = \|\mathbf{u}\|^2\|\mathbf{v}\|^2 - (\mathbf{u} \cdot \mathbf{v})^2$,

g) $\|\mathbf{u} \times \mathbf{v}\| = \|\mathbf{u}\|\|\mathbf{v}\| \sin \theta$ (use item *f* and Theorem 10.3),

h) $\mathbf{u} \times \mathbf{u} = \mathbf{0}$,

i) $\mathbf{u} \cdot (\mathbf{v} \times \mathbf{w}) = \begin{vmatrix} u_1 & u_2 & u_3 \\ v_1 & v_2 & v_3 \\ w_1 & w_2 & w_3 \end{vmatrix}$.

10.24 Show that the cross-product can be represented **symbolically** as

$$\mathbf{u} \times \mathbf{v} = \begin{vmatrix} \mathbf{e}_1 & \mathbf{e}_2 & \mathbf{e}_3 \\ u_1 & u_2 & u_3 \\ v_1 & v_2 & v_3 \end{vmatrix},$$

where $\mathbf{e}_1 = (1, 0, 0)$, $\mathbf{e}_2 = (0, 1, 0)$, and $e_3 = (0, 0, 1)$. Treat the $\mathbf{e}_i$'s as points or symbols in the expansion of the determinant.

10.25 Use the cross product to find a vector perpendicular to both $\mathbf{u}$ and $\mathbf{v}$:

$$a)\ \mathbf{u} = (1, 0, 1) \quad \mathbf{v} = (1, 1, 1),$$
$$b)\ \mathbf{u} = (1, -1, 2) \quad \mathbf{v} = (0, 5, -3).$$

10.26 Consider the parallelogram determined by the vectors $\mathbf{u}$ and $\mathbf{v}$ in $\mathbf{R}^3$, as in Figure 10.24.

  a) Show that the area of this parallelogram is $\|\mathbf{u} \times \mathbf{v}\|$. [Hint: Express height h in terms of $\mathbf{u}$, $\mathbf{v}$, and θ.]

  b) Find the area of the triangle in $\mathbf{R}^3$ whose vertices are $(1, -1, 2)$, $(0, 1, 3)$, and $(2, 1, 0)$.

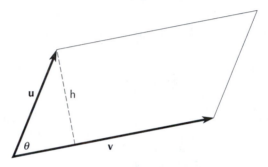

Figure 10.24

The parallelogram spanned by $\mathbf{u}$ *and* $\mathbf{v}$.

10.5   LINES

The fundamental objects of Euclidean geometry are points, lines, and planes. These next two sections show how to describe lines and planes and their higher-dimensional analogues.

First, we will work with lines in $\mathbf{R}^2$. In high school algebra, we learn that straight lines have an equation of the form

$$x_2 = mx_1 + b. \tag{9}$$

The coefficient m is the slope of the line and the coefficient b is the y-intercept. This algebraic representation of the line is convenient for solving equations. However, it is not the most useful equation for representing geometric objects. What is the equation of line v in Figure 10.25? We cannot solve for x_2 in terms of x_1. More important than the awkwardness of this special case is the need for an algebraic representation which clearly expresses the geometry of the line. We will often find a *parametric representation* of the line more useful.

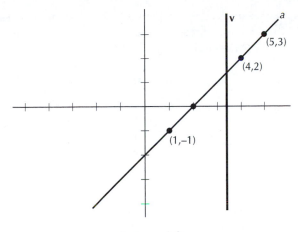

Lines in $\mathbf{R}^2$.

Figure 10.25

A parametric representation of a point on a line uses a parameter t in the coordinate expression of the point; more formally, a **parametric representation** is an expression $(x_1(t), x_2(t))$ with parameter t in $\mathbf{R}^1$. The point $\mathbf{x} = (x_1, x_2)$ is on the line if and only if $\mathbf{x} = (x_1(t^*), x_2(t^*))$ for some value t^* of the parameter t. To make matters concrete, you might think of t as representing time, and the parameterization as describing the transversal of a path. The coordinates $(x_1(t), x_2(t))$ describe the particular location which is reached at time t.

A line is completely determined by two things: a point $\mathbf{x}_0$ on the line and a direction $\mathbf{v}$ in which to move from $\mathbf{x}_0$. Geometrically, to describe motion in the direction $\mathbf{v}$ from the point $\mathbf{x}_0$, we simply add scalar multiples of $\mathbf{v}$ to $\mathbf{x}_0$ as in Figure 10.26. The result is the parametric representation

$$\mathbf{x}(t) = \mathbf{x}_0 + t\mathbf{v}. \qquad (10)$$

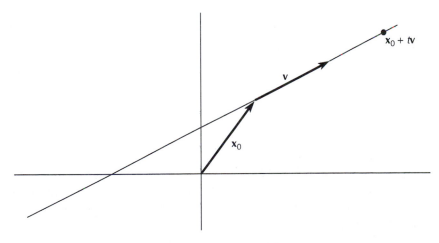

Parametric line in $\mathbf{R}^2$.

Figure 10.26

Example 10.4   For example, line *a* in Figure 10.25 is the line which goes through the point (4, 2) and moves directly to the northeast — in the direction (1, 1). It is described by the parameterization

$$\mathbf{x}(t) = (x_1(t), x_2(t))$$
$$= (4, 2) + t(1, 1)$$
$$= (4 + t \cdot 1, \ 2 + t \cdot 1),$$

or

$$x_1 = 4 + t \cdot 1 \tag{11}$$

$$x_2 = 2 + t \cdot 1. \tag{12}$$

Figure 10.25 shows that (5, 3) and (1, −1) are on line *a*. The first point is reached when $t = 1$, and the second when $t = -3$.

Note that the same line can be described by different parametric equations. For example, we can also view line *a* in Figure 10.25 as the line through the point (1, −1) in the direction (2, 2). This yields the parameterization

$$(x_1(t), x_2(t)) = (1, -1) + t(2, 2) = (1 + 2t, -1 + 2t).$$

With this parameterization, the line passes through (4, 2) when $t = 1.5$ and through (5, 3) when $t = 2$.

Of course, the parameterization (10) works in all dimensions. For example, the line in $\mathbf{R}^3$ through the point $\mathbf{x}_0 = (2, 1, 3)$ in the direction $\mathbf{v} = (4, -2, 5)$ has the parameterization

$$\mathbf{x}(t) = (x_1(t), x_2(t), x_3(t))$$
$$= (2, 1, 3) + t(4, -2, 5)$$
$$= (2 + 4t, \ 1 - 2t, \ 3 + 5t).$$

Another way to determine a line is to identify two points on the line. Suppose that $\mathbf{x}$ and $\mathbf{y}$ lie on a line ℓ. Then, ℓ can be viewed as the line which goes through $\mathbf{x}$ and points in the direction $\mathbf{y} - \mathbf{x}$. Thus, a parameterization for the line is

$$\mathbf{x}(t) = \mathbf{x} + t(\mathbf{y} - \mathbf{x})$$
$$= \mathbf{x} + t\mathbf{y} - t\mathbf{x} \tag{13}$$
$$= (1 - t)\mathbf{x} + t\mathbf{y}.$$

When $t = 0$, we are at point $\mathbf{x}$; and when $t = 1$, we are at point $\mathbf{y}$. When t lies between 0 and 1, we are at points between $\mathbf{x}$ and $\mathbf{y}$. Consequently, we parameterize the **line segment joining x to y** as

$$\ell(\mathbf{x}, \mathbf{y}) = \{(1 - t)\mathbf{x} + t\mathbf{y} : 0 \le t \le 1\}.$$

Given two points $\mathbf{x} = (a, b)$ and $\mathbf{y} = (c, d)$ on a line ℓ in the plane, one can write the parameterized equation of ℓ as (13) or the nonparameterized equation of ℓ as

$$x_2 - b = \frac{d - b}{c - a}(x_1 - a).$$

One can use these two expressions to pass from the parameterized equation of a line in the plane to the nonparameterized equation, and vice versa, by first finding two points on the line from the given equation and using these points to find the new equation. One can also pass *directly* from form (10) to form (9) by solving the equations in (10) for t and then setting the new equations equal to each other. For example, in equations (11, 12)

$$t = \frac{x_1 - 4}{1} \quad \text{and} \quad t = \frac{x_2 - 2}{1}.$$

So, $\qquad \dfrac{x_1 - 4}{1} = \dfrac{x_2 - 2}{1}, \quad \text{or} \quad x_2 = x_1 - 2.$

To go the other way, just note that equation (9) is the equation of the line through the point $(0, b)$ in the direction $(1, m)$.

EXERCISES

10.27 Show that the midpoint of $\ell(\mathbf{x}, \mathbf{y})$ occurs where $t = \frac{1}{2}$. In other words, if $\mathbf{z} = \frac{1}{2}\mathbf{x} + \frac{1}{2}\mathbf{y}$, show that $\|\mathbf{x} - \mathbf{z}\| = \|\mathbf{y} - \mathbf{z}\|$.

10.28 For each of the following pairs of points $\mathbf{p}_1$, $\mathbf{p}_2$, write the parametric equation of the line through $\mathbf{p}_1$ and $\mathbf{p}_2$, find the midpoint of $\ell(\mathbf{p}_1, \mathbf{p}_2)$, and sketch the line.

a) $\mathbf{p}_1 = (3, 0)$, $\qquad \mathbf{p}_2 = (5, 0)$;

b) $\mathbf{p}_1 = (1, 0)$, $\qquad \mathbf{p}_2 = (0, 1)$;

c) $\mathbf{p}_1 = (1, 0, 1)$, $\qquad \mathbf{p}_2 = (2, 1, 0)$.

10.29 Is the point $\begin{pmatrix} 11 \\ 14 \\ 17 \\ 18 \end{pmatrix}$ on the line $\begin{pmatrix} 1 \\ 2 \\ 3 \\ 4 \end{pmatrix} + t \begin{pmatrix} 5 \\ 6 \\ 7 \\ 8 \end{pmatrix}$?

10.30 Transform each of the following parameterized equations into the form (9):

a) $\begin{matrix} x_1 = 4 - 2t \\ x_2 = 3 + 6t; \end{matrix}$ b) $\begin{matrix} x_1 = 3 + t \\ x_2 = 5 - t; \end{matrix}$ c) $\begin{matrix} x_1 = 3 + t \\ x_2 = 5. \end{matrix}$

10.31 Transform each of the following nonparameterized equations into the form (10):

a) $2x_2 = 3x_1 + 5$; b) $x_2 = -x_1 + 7$; c) $x_1 = 6$.

10.6   PLANES

Parametric Equations

A line is one-dimensional. Intuitively, the dimension of the line is reflected in the fact that it can be described using only one parameter. Planes are two-dimensional, and so it stands to reason that they are described by expressions with two parameters.

To be more concrete, let $\mathcal{P}$ be a plane in $\mathbf{R}^3$ through the origin. Let $\mathbf{v}$ and $\mathbf{w}$ be two vectors in $\mathcal{P}$, as shown in Figure 10.27. Choose $\mathbf{v}$ and $\mathbf{w}$ so that they point in different directions, in other words, so that neither is a scalar multiple of the other. In this case, we say that $\mathbf{v}$ and $\mathbf{w}$ are **linearly independent**, a topic to be discussed in more detail in the next chapter. For any scalars s and t, the vector $s\mathbf{v} + t\mathbf{w}$ is called a **linear combination** of $\mathbf{v}$ and $\mathbf{w}$. By our geometric interpretation of scalar multiplication and vector addition, it should be clear that all linear combinations of $\mathbf{v}$ and $\mathbf{w}$ lie on the plane $\mathcal{P}$. In fact, if we take every linear combination of $\mathbf{v}$ and $\mathbf{w}$, we recover the entire plane $\mathcal{P}$. The equation

$$\mathbf{x} = s\mathbf{v} + t\mathbf{w}$$

or

$$x_1 = sv_1 + tw_1$$
$$x_2 = sv_2 + tw_2$$
$$x_3 = sv_3 + tw_3,$$

provides a parameterization of the plane $\mathcal{P}$.

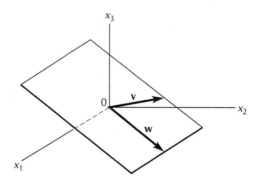

Figure 10.27

A plane $\mathcal{P}$ through the origin.

If the plane does not pass through the origin but through the point $\mathbf{p} \neq \mathbf{0}$ and if $\mathbf{v}$ and $\mathbf{w}$ are linearly independent direction vectors from $\mathbf{p}$ which still lie in the plane, then as indicated in Figure 10.28, we can use the above method to parameterize the plane as

$$\mathbf{x} = \mathbf{p} + s\mathbf{v} + t\mathbf{w}, \qquad s, t \text{ in } \mathbf{R}^1. \tag{14}$$

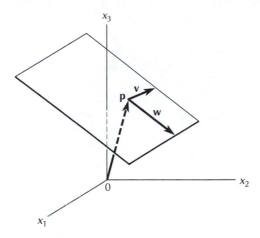

**Figure
10.28**

A plane not through the origin.

Just as two points determine a line, three (non-collinear) points determine a plane. To find the parametric equation of the plane containing the points **p**, **q**, and **r**, note that we can picture **q** − **p** and **r** − **p** as displacement vectors from **p** which lie on the plane. So, one parameterization of the plane is

$$\mathbf{x}(s, t) = \mathbf{p} + s(\mathbf{q} - \mathbf{p}) + t(\mathbf{r} - \mathbf{p})$$
$$= (1 - s - t)\mathbf{p} + s\mathbf{q} + t\mathbf{r}. \tag{15}$$

Compare (15) with the corresponding parameterized equation (13) of a line. From equation (15), we see that a plane is the set of those linear combinations of three fixed vectors whose coefficients sum to 1:

$$\mathbf{x} = t_1\mathbf{p} + t_2\mathbf{q} + t_3\mathbf{r}, \qquad t_1 + t_2 + t_3 = 1. \tag{16}$$

If we further restrict the scalars t_i in (16) so that they are nonnegative, we obtain the (filled-in) triangle in $\mathbf{R}^3$ whose vertices are **p**, **q**, and **r** — the darkened region in Figure 10.29. The numbers (t_1, t_2, t_3) are called the **barycentric coordinates** of a point in this triangle. For example, the barycentric coordinates of the vertex **p** are $(1, 0, 0)$ since $t_1 = 1$, $t_2 = 0$, and $t_3 = 0$ in expression (16) yield the point **p**. Similarly, the barycentric coordinates of the vertices **q** and **r** are $(0, 1, 0)$ and $(0, 0, 1)$, respectively. The center of mass or centroid of this triangle is the point

$$\mathbf{x} = \frac{1}{3}\mathbf{p} + \frac{1}{3}\mathbf{q} + \frac{1}{3}\mathbf{r},$$

whose barycentric coordinates are $(1/3, 1/3, 1/3)$.

Equations such as (14) and (15) give a parameterization of a two-dimensional plane in any Euclidean space, not just $\mathbf{R}^3$. For example, the two-dimensional plane

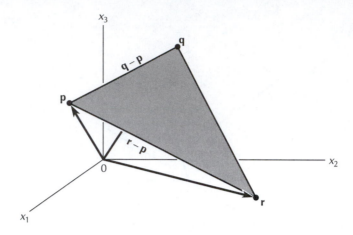

Figure 10.29

Triangle with vertices **p, q,** *and* **r.**

through the points $(1, 2, 3, 4)$, $(5, 6, 7, 8)$, and $(9, 0, 1, 2)$ in $\mathbf{R}^4$ has the parametric equations

$$x_1 = 1r + 5s + 9t$$

$$x_2 = 2r + 6s + 0t$$

$$x_3 = 3r + 7s + 1t$$

$$x_4 = 4r + 8s + 2t, \qquad \text{where } r + s + t = 1.$$

Nonparametric Equations

We turn now to the *nonparametric equations of a plane* in $\mathbf{R}^3$. Just as with a line in $\mathbf{R}^2$, a plane in $\mathbf{R}^3$ is completely described by giving its inclination and a point on it. We usually express its inclination by specifying a vector **n**, called a **normal vector**, which is perpendicular to the plane. Suppose we want to write the equation for the plane through the point $\mathbf{p} = (x_0, y_0, z_0)$ and having the normal vector $\mathbf{n} = (a, b, c)$. If $\mathbf{x} = (x, y, z)$ is an arbitrary point on the plane, then $\mathbf{x} - \mathbf{p}$ will be a vector in the plane and consequently will be perpendicular to **n**, as in Figure 10.30.

Recalling that two vectors are perpendicular if and only if their dot product is zero, we write

$$0 = \mathbf{n} \cdot (\mathbf{x} - \mathbf{p}) = (a, b, c) \cdot (x - x_0, y - y_0, z - z_0),$$

or
$$a(x - x_0) + b(y - y_0) + c(z - z_0) = 0. \tag{17}$$

Form (17) is called the **point-normal equation** of the plane. It is sometimes written as

$$ax + by + cz = d, \tag{18}$$

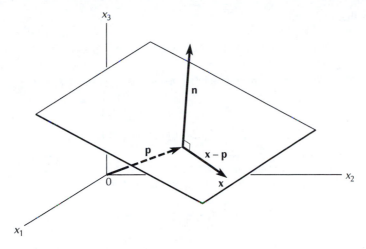

*Plane through **p** with normal **n**.*

**Figure
10.30**

where, in this case, $d = ax_0 + by_0 + cz_0$. Conversely, one can see that equation (18) is the equation of the plane which has normal vector (a, b, c) and which contains each of the points $(0, 0, d/c)$, $(0, d/b, 0)$, and $(d/a, 0, 0)$.

Example 10.5 The equation of the plane through the point $(1, 2, 3)$ with normal vector $(4, 5, 6)$ is

$$4(x - 1) + 5(y - 2) + 6(z - 3) = 0$$

or

$$4x + 5y + 6z = 32.$$

Example 10.6 The equation $3x - y + 4z = 12$ is a nonparametric equation of the plane through the point $(4, 0, 0)$ (or $(0, 0, 3)$ or $(0, -12, 0)$ or $(5, 7, 1)$) with normal vector $\mathbf{n} = (3, -1, 4)$.

To go from a nonparametric equation (18) of a plane to a parametric one, just use (18) to find three points on the plane and then use equation (15). It is more difficult to go from a parametric representation to a nonparametric one, because we need to find a normal $\mathbf{n}$ to the plane given vectors $\mathbf{v}$ and $\mathbf{w}$ parallel to the plane. There are two ways to compute such an $\mathbf{n}$. First, one may use the exercises in the last section and take $\mathbf{n}$ to be the cross product $\mathbf{v} \times \mathbf{w}$. Alternatively, given $\mathbf{v}$ and $\mathbf{w}$, one can solve the system of equations $\mathbf{n} \cdot \mathbf{v} = 0$ and $\mathbf{n} \cdot \mathbf{w} = 0$ explicitly for $\mathbf{n}$.

Example 10.7 To find the point-normal equation of the plane $\mathcal{P}$ which contains the points

$$\mathbf{p} = (2, 1, 1), \quad \mathbf{q} = (1, 0, -3), \quad \text{and} \quad \mathbf{r} = (0, 1, 7),$$

note that vectors

$$\mathbf{v} \equiv \mathbf{q} - \mathbf{p} = (-1, -1, -4) \quad \text{and} \quad \mathbf{u} \equiv \mathbf{r} - \mathbf{p} = (-2, 0, 6)$$

both lie on $\mathcal{P}$. To find a normal $\mathbf{n} = (n_1, n_2, n_3)$ to $\mathcal{P}$, solve the system

$$\mathbf{n} \cdot \mathbf{v} = \quad -n_1 - \quad n_2 - 4n_3 = 0$$
$$\mathbf{n} \cdot \mathbf{u} = -2n_1 + 0n_2 + 6n_3 = 0,$$

say by Gaussian elimination, to compute that $\mathbf{n}$ is any multiple of $(3, -7, 1)$. Finally, use $\mathbf{n}$ and $\mathbf{p}$ to write out the point-normal form

$$3(x - 2) - 7(y - 1) + 1(z - 1) = 0$$

or
$$3x - 7y + z = 0.$$

Hyperplanes

A line in $\mathbf{R}^2$ and a plane in $\mathbf{R}^3$ are examples of sets described by a single linear equation in $\mathbf{R}^n$. Such spaces are often called **hyperplanes**. A line in $\mathbf{R}^2$ can be written as

$$a_1 x_1 + a_2 x_2 = d,$$

and a plane in $\mathbf{R}^3$ can be written in point-normal form as

$$a_1 x_1 + a_2 x_2 + a_3 x_3 = d.$$

Similarly, a hyperplane in $\mathbf{R}^n$ can be written in point-normal form as

$$a_1 x_1 + a_2 x_2 + \cdots + a_n x_n = d. \tag{19}$$

The hyperplane described by equation (19) can be thought of as the set of all vectors with tail at $(0, \ldots, 0, d/a_n)$ which are perpendicular to the vector $\mathbf{n} = (a_1, \ldots, a_n)$. We continue to call $\mathbf{n}$ a normal vector to the hyperplane.

EXERCISES

10.32 Does the point $\begin{pmatrix} 4 \\ 3 \\ 2 \end{pmatrix}$ lie on the plane $\begin{pmatrix} 1 \\ 2 \\ 3 \end{pmatrix} + t \begin{pmatrix} 1 \\ 1 \\ 0 \end{pmatrix} + s \begin{pmatrix} 0 \\ 1 \\ 1 \end{pmatrix}$?

10.33 Derive parametric and nonparametric equations for the lines which pass through each of the following pairs of points in $\mathbf{R}^2$:

   a) $(1, 2)$ and $(3, 6)$;   b) $(1, 1)$ and $(4, 10)$;   c) $(3, 0)$ and $(0, 4)$.

10.34 Write the parametric equations for each of the following lines and planes:

$$a) \; x_2 = 3x_1 - 7; \qquad\qquad b) \; 3x_1 + 4x_2 = 12;$$
$$c) \; x_1 + x_2 + x_3 = 3; \qquad d) \; x_1 - 2x_2 + 3x_3 = 6.$$

10.35 Write nonparametric equations for each of the following lines and planes:
a) $x = 3 - 4t, \quad y = 1 + 2t$;
b) $x = 2t, \quad y = 1 + t$;
c) $x = 1 + s + t, \quad y = 2 + 3s + 4t, \quad z = s - t$;
d) $x = 2 - 3s + t, \quad y = 4, \quad z = 1 + s + t$.

10.36 Derive parametric and nonparametric equations for the planes through each of the following triplets of points in $\mathbf{R}^3$:
a) $(6, 0, 0), \; (0, -6, 0), \; (0, 0, 3)$;
b) $(0, 3, 2), \; (3, 3, 1), \; (2, 5, 0)$.

10.37 Nonparametric equations of a line in $\mathbf{R}^3$ are equations of the form

$$\frac{x - x_0}{a} = \frac{y - y_0}{b} = \frac{z - z_0}{c}. \tag{20}$$

These are called **symmetric equations** of the line. They can be derived from the parametric equations by eliminating t, just as one does in the plane.
a) What are the parametric equations which correspond to the symmetric equations (20)?
b) In form (20), one can view the line as the intersection of which two planes?
c) Find the symmetric equations of the following two lines in $\mathbf{R}^3$:

$$i) \; x_1 = 2 - t \qquad\qquad ii) \; x_1 = 1 + 4t$$
$$x_2 = 3 + 4t \qquad\qquad\quad x_2 = 2 + 5t$$
$$x_3 = 1 + 5t; \qquad\qquad\quad x_3 = 3 + 6t.$$

d) For each line in part c, find the equations of two planes whose intersection is that line.

10.38 Determine whether the following pairs of planes intersect;

$$a) \; x + 2y - 3z = 6 \quad \text{and} \qquad x + 3y - 2z = \; 6;$$
$$b) \; x + 2y - 3z = 6 \quad \text{and} \quad -2x - 4y + 6z = 10.$$

10.39 Find a nonparametric equation of the plane:
a) through the point $(1, 2, 3)$ and normal to the vector $(1, -1, 0)$,
b) through the point $(1, 1, -1)$ and perpendicular to the line $(x_1, x_2, x_3) = (4 - 3t, 2 + t, 6 + 5t)$,
c) whose intercepts are $(a, 0, 0), (0, b, 0)$, and $(0, 0, c)$ with a, b, and c all nonzero.

10.40 Find the intersection of the plane $x + y + z = 1$ and the line $x = 3 + t, y = 1 - 7t, z = 3 - 3t$.

10.41 Use Gaussian elimination to find the equation of the line which is the intersection of the planes $x + y - z = 4$ and $x + 2y + z = 3$.

10.7   ECONOMIC APPLICATIONS

Budget Sets in Commodity Space

An important application of Euclidean spaces in economic theory is the notion of a commodity space. In an economy with n commodities, let x_i denote the amount of commodity i. Assume that each commodity is completely divisible so that x_i can be any nonnegative number. The vector

$$\mathbf{x} = (x_1, x_2, \ldots, x_n)$$

which assigns a nonnegative quantity to each of the n commodities is called a **commodity bundle**. Since we are dealing only with nonnegative quantities, the set of all commodity bundles is the **positive orthant** of $\mathbf{R}^n$

$$\{(x_1, \ldots, x_n) : x_1 \geq 0, \ldots, x_n \geq 0\}$$

and is called a **commodity space**.

Let $p_i > 0$ denote the price of commodity i. Then, the cost of purchasing commodity bundle $\mathbf{x} = (x_1, \ldots, x_n)$ is

$$p_1 x_1 + p_2 x_2 + \cdots + p_n x_n = \mathbf{p} \cdot \mathbf{x}.$$

A consumer with income I can purchase only bundles $\mathbf{x}$ such that $\mathbf{p} \cdot \mathbf{x} \leq I$. This subset of commodity space is called the consumer's **budget set**. It is bounded above by the hyperplane $\mathbf{p} \cdot \mathbf{x} = I$, whose normal vector is just the price vector $\mathbf{p}$. We have drawn the usual two-dimensional picture for this situation in Figure 10.31.

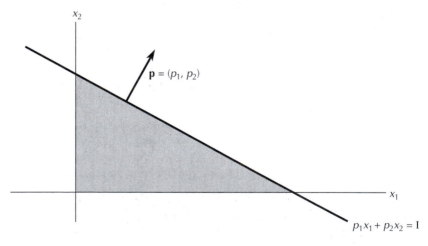

Figure 10.31

A consumer's budget set, $\mathbf{p} \cdot \mathbf{x} \leq I$, in commodity space.

Input Space

A similar situation exists for a production process which uses n inputs. If x_i denotes an amount of input i, then $\mathbf{x} = (x_1, \ldots, x_n)$ is an **input vector** in **input space**, which is also the positive orthant in $\mathbf{R}^n$. If w_i denotes the cost per unit of input i and $\mathbf{w} = (w_1, \ldots, w_n)$, then the cost of purchasing input bundle $\mathbf{x}$ is $\mathbf{w} \cdot \mathbf{x}$. The set of all input bundles which have a total cost C, an isocost set, is that part of the hyperplane $\mathbf{w} \cdot \mathbf{x} = C$ which lies in the positive orthant. The price vector $\mathbf{w}$ is normal to this hyperplane. If we fix $\mathbf{w}$ and let C vary, we obtain isocost hyperplanes which are parallel to each other.

Depending on the situation under study, we sometimes write inputs as *negative* numbers. In this case, input space would be the negative orthant in $\mathbf{R}^n$.

Probability Simplex

A hyperplane that arises frequently in applications is the space of **probability vectors**

$$P_n = \{(p_1, \ldots, p_n) : p_i \geq 0 \text{ and } p_1 + p_2 + \cdots + p_n = 1\},$$

which we call a **probability simplex**. In these applications there are n mutually exclusive states of the world and p_i is the probability that state i occurs. Since one of these n states must occur, the p_i's sum to 1. The probability simplex P_n is part of a hyperplane in $\mathbf{R}^n$ whose normal vector is $\mathbf{1} = (1, 1, \ldots, 1)$; P_3 is pictured in Figure 10.32.

One can also consider P_n as the set of barycentric coordinates with respect to the points

$$\mathbf{e}_1 = (1, 0, \ldots, 0), \ldots, \mathbf{e}_n = (0, 0, \ldots, 0, 1).$$

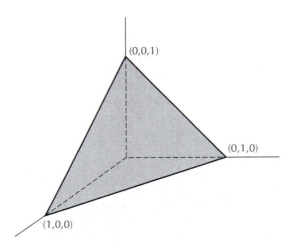

The probability simplex for $n = 3$.

Figure 10.32

The Investment Model

The portfolio analysis introduced in Example 5 of Chapter 6 fits naturally into the geometric framework of this chapter.

Suppose that an investor is choosing the fraction x_i of his or her wealth to invest in asset i. If there are A different investment opportunities, a **portfolio** is an A-tuple $\mathbf{x} = (x_1, \ldots, x_A)$. Since the x_i's represent fractions of total wealth, they must sum to 1. Therefore the budget constraint is

$$x_1 + x_2 + \cdots + x_A = 1.$$

However, since we allow short positions, x_i may be negative. In this case, the budget set is the entire hyperplane

$$\mathbf{x} \cdot \mathbf{1} = 1$$

normal to the vector $\mathbf{1} = (1, 1, \ldots, 1)$. Figure 10.32 shows the intersection of this hyperplane with the positive orthant of $\mathbf{R^n}$ (for $n = 3$).

Suppose that there are S possible financial climates or "states of nature" in the coming investment period. Let r_{si} denote the return on asset i if state s occurs. Form the **state s return vector**

$$\mathbf{r}_s = (r_{s1}, r_{s2}, \ldots, r_{sA}).$$

Then, the return to the investor of portfolio $\mathbf{x} = (x_1, \ldots, x_A)$ is $\mathbf{r}_s \cdot \mathbf{x}$. A portfolio $\mathbf{x}$ is riskless if it returns the same return in every state of nature:

$$\mathbf{r}_1 \cdot \mathbf{x} = \mathbf{r}_2 \cdot \mathbf{x} = \cdots = \mathbf{r}_S \cdot \mathbf{x}.$$

IS-LM Analysis

We have discussed a linear Keynesian macroeconomic model and Hicks' **IS-LM** interpretation of it in Chapter 6 and again in Chapter 9. In Exercise 9.18, we examined a more or less complete version of this model in five linear equations which could be combined into two equations as

$$[1 - c_1(1 - t_1) - a_0]Y + (a + c_2)r = c_0 - c_1 t_0 + I^* + G$$
$$mY - hr = M_s - M^*.$$

The first equation represents the production equilibrium and is called the IS (investment-savings) equation. The second represents the money market equilibrium and is called the LM (liquidity-money) equation. In intermediate macroeconomics courses, one studies this system graphically by drawing the IS-line and the LM-line in the plane, as in Figure 10.33. The normal vector to the IS-line is

$$(1 - c_1(1 - t_1) - a_0, \ a + c_2).$$

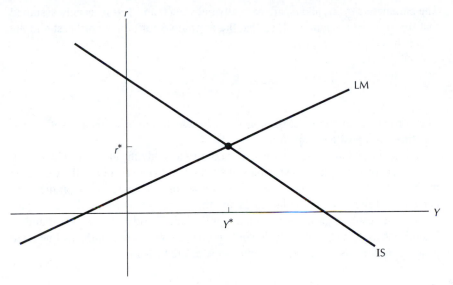

The graphs of the IS- and LM-lines.

**Figure
10.33**

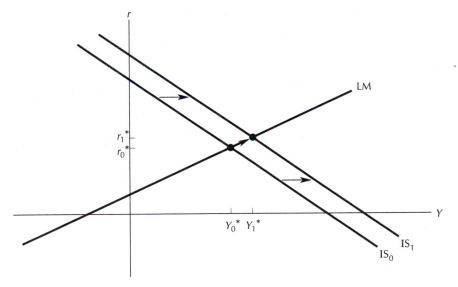

The effect of an increase in G or I.*

**Figure
10.34**

The parameters c_1, t_1, and a_0 are naturally between 0 and 1. It is usually assumed that $0 < c_1(1 - t_1) + a_0 < 1$, so that the normal vector points northeast and the IS-line has negative slope

$$-\frac{a + c_2}{1 - c_1(1 - t_1) - a_0}.$$

The normal vector to the LM-line is $(m, -h)$ which points southeast, and so the LM-line has a positive slope h/m.

Using these diagrams, one can use geometry to study the effects of changes in parameters or in exogenous variables, just as we did analytically in the exercises in Section 9.3. For example, if G or I^* increases or if t_0 decreases, then the right hand side of the IS-equation increases and the IS-line shifts outward as in Figure 10.34. The result is an increase in the equilibrium Y and r, just as we found in Exercise 9.15. Note that this result would hold even if the slope of the IS-line were positive, as long as it was less than the slope of the LM-line.

EXERCISES

10.42   Use the diagram in Figure 10.33 to find the effect on Y and r of an increase in each of the variables I^*, M_s, m, h, a_0, a, c_0, and t_1.

Linear Independence

Many economic problems deal with number or size. How many equilibria does a model of an economy or a game have? How large is the production possibility set? Since these sets are often described as solutions of a system of equations, questions of size often reduce to questions about the size of the set of solutions to a particular system of equations. If there are *finitely* many solutions, the exact number of solutions gives a satisfactory answer. But if there are *infinitely* many solutions, the size of the solution set is best captured by its *dimension*. We have a good intuition about the difference between a one-dimensional line and a two-dimensional plane. In this chapter, we will give a precise definition of "dimension" for linear spaces. The key underlying concept is that of linear independence.

The most direct relevant mathematical question is the size, that is, the dimension, of the set of solutions of a system of linear equations $Ax = b$. Chapter 27 presents a sharp answer to this question via the *Fundamental Theorem of Linear Algebra*: the dimension of the solution set of $Ax = b$ is the number of variables minus the rank of A. Chapter 27 also investigates the size of the set of right-hand sides b for which a given system $Ax = b$ has a solution; and we present an in-depth description of the dimension of an abstract vector space. Chapter 28 presents applications of these concepts to portfolio analysis, voting paradoxes, and activity analysis. Those who have the time are encouraged to read Chapters 27 and 28 between Chapters 11 and 12.

Linear independence is defined and characterized in Section 11.1. The complementary notion of span is the focus of Section 11.2. The concept of a basis for Euclidean space is introduced in Section 11.3.

11.1   LINEAR INDEPENDENCE

In Section 10.5, we noted that the set of all scalar multiples of a nonzero vector v is a straight line through the origin. In this chapter, we denote this set by $\mathcal{L}[v]$:

$$\mathcal{L}[v] \equiv \{rv : r \in \mathbf{R}\},$$

and call it the line *generated* or *spanned* by v. See Figure 11.1. For example, if $v = (1, 0, \ldots, 0)$, then $\mathcal{L}[v]$ is the x_1-axis in $\mathbf{R}^n$. If $v = (1, 1)$ in $\mathbf{R}^2$, then $\mathcal{L}[v]$ is the diagonal line pictured in Figure 11.1.

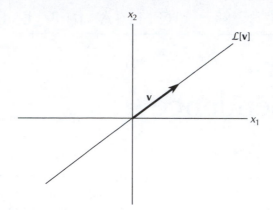

**Figure
11.1**

The line $\mathcal{L}[\mathbf{v}]$ spanned by vector $\mathbf{v}$.

Definition

If we start with two nonzero vectors $\mathbf{v}_1$ and $\mathbf{v}_2$ (considered as vectors with their tails at the origin), we can take all possible *linear combinations* of $\mathbf{v}_1$ and $\mathbf{v}_2$ to obtain the set *spanned* by $\mathbf{v}_1$ and $\mathbf{v}_2$:

$$\mathcal{L}[\mathbf{v}_1, \mathbf{v}_2] \equiv \{r_1\mathbf{v}_1 + r_2\mathbf{v}_2 : r_1 \in \mathbf{R} \text{ and } r_2 \in \mathbf{R}\}.$$

If $\mathbf{v}_1$ is a multiple of $\mathbf{v}_2$, then $\mathcal{L}[\mathbf{v}_1, \mathbf{v}_2] = \mathcal{L}[\mathbf{v}_2]$ is simply the line spanned by $\mathbf{v}_2$, as in Figure 11.2. However, if $\mathbf{v}_1$ is not a multiple of $\mathbf{v}_2$, then together they generate a two-dimensional plane $\mathcal{L}[\mathbf{v}_1, \mathbf{v}_2]$, which contains the lines $\mathcal{L}[\mathbf{v}_1]$ and $\mathcal{L}[\mathbf{v}_2]$, as in Figure 11.3.

If $\mathbf{v}_1$ is a multiple of $\mathbf{v}_2$, or vice versa, we say that $\mathbf{v}_1$ and $\mathbf{v}_2$ are **linearly dependent**. Otherwise, we say that $\mathbf{v}_1$ and $\mathbf{v}_2$ are **linearly independent**. We now develop a precise way of expressing these two concepts. If $\mathbf{v}_1$ is a multiple of $\mathbf{v}_2$,

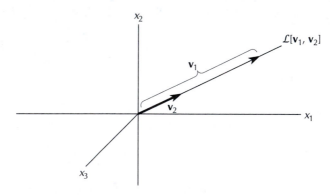

**Figure
11.2**

If $\mathbf{v}_1$ is a multiple of $\mathbf{v}_2$, $\mathcal{L}[\mathbf{v}_1, \mathbf{v}_2] = \mathcal{L}[\mathbf{v}_2]$, a line.

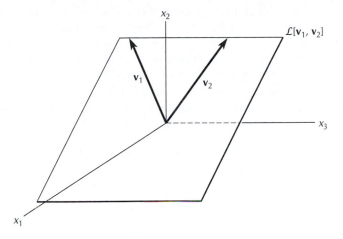

If $\mathbf{v}_1$ is not a multiple of $\mathbf{v}_2$, then the set $\mathcal{L}[\mathbf{v}_1, \mathbf{v}_2]$ is a plane.

Figure 11.3

we write

$$\mathbf{v}_1 = r_2\mathbf{v}_2 \quad \text{or} \quad \mathbf{v}_1 - r_2\mathbf{v}_2 = \mathbf{0} \tag{1}$$

for some scalar r_2. If $\mathbf{v}_2$ is a multiple of $\mathbf{v}_1$, we write

$$\mathbf{v}_2 = r_1\mathbf{v}_1 \quad \text{or} \quad r_1\mathbf{v}_1 - \mathbf{v}_2 = \mathbf{0} \tag{2}$$

for some scalar r_1. We can combine statements (1) and (2) by defining $\mathbf{v}_1$ and $\mathbf{v}_2$ to be **linearly dependent** if there exist scalars c_1 and c_2, *not both zero*, so that

$$c_1\mathbf{v}_1 + c_2\mathbf{v}_2 = \mathbf{0}, \qquad c_1 \text{ or } c_2 \text{ nonzero.} \tag{3}$$

In Exercise 11.1 below, you are asked to show that (3) is an equivalent definition to (1) and (2).

From this point of view, we say that $\mathbf{v}_1$ and $\mathbf{v}_2$ are **linearly independent** if there are no scalars c_1 and c_2, at least one nonzero, so that (3) holds. A working version of this definition is the following:

vectors $\mathbf{v}_1$ and $\mathbf{v}_2$ are **linearly independent** if

$$c_1\mathbf{v}_1 + c_2\mathbf{v}_2 = \mathbf{0} \quad \Longrightarrow \quad c_1 = c_2 = 0. \tag{4}$$

This process extends to larger collections of vectors. The set of all **linear combinations** of three vectors $\mathbf{v}_1$, $\mathbf{v}_2$, and $\mathbf{v}_3$,

$$\mathcal{L}[\mathbf{v}_1, \mathbf{v}_2, \mathbf{v}_3] \equiv \{r_1\mathbf{v}_1 + r_2\mathbf{v}_2 + r_3\mathbf{v}_3 : r_1, r_2, r_3 \in \mathbf{R}\},$$

yields a three-dimensional space, provided that no one of $\mathbf{v}_1$, $\mathbf{v}_2$, and $\mathbf{v}_3$ is a linear combination of the other two. If, say, $\mathbf{v}_3$ is a linear combination of $\mathbf{v}_1$ and $\mathbf{v}_2$, that is, $\mathbf{v}_3 = r_1\mathbf{v}_1 + r_2\mathbf{v}_2$, while $\mathbf{v}_1$ and $\mathbf{v}_2$ are linearly independent, then $\mathcal{L}[\mathbf{v}_1, \mathbf{v}_2]$ is a plane and $\mathbf{v}_3$ lies on this plane; so all combinations of $\mathbf{v}_1$, $\mathbf{v}_2$, and $\mathbf{v}_3$, $\mathcal{L}[\mathbf{v}_1, \mathbf{v}_2, \mathbf{v}_3]$, yield just the plane $\mathcal{L}[\mathbf{v}_1, \mathbf{v}_2]$, as pictured in Figure 11.4. As before, we say that $\mathbf{v}_1$, $\mathbf{v}_2$, and $\mathbf{v}_3$ are linearly dependent if one of them can be written as a linear combination of the other two. The working version of this definition is that some *nonzero* combination of $\mathbf{v}_1$, $\mathbf{v}_2$, and $\mathbf{v}_3$ yields the **0**-vector:

$\mathbf{v}_1$, $\mathbf{v}_2$, $\mathbf{v}_3$ are **linearly dependent** if and only if there exist scalars

c_1, c_2, c_3, not all zero, such that $c_1\mathbf{v}_1 + c_2\mathbf{v}_2 + c_3\mathbf{v}_3 = \mathbf{0}$. (5)

Conversely, we say:

$\mathbf{v}_1$, $\mathbf{v}_2$, $\mathbf{v}_3$ are **linearly independent** if and only if

$c_1\mathbf{v}_1 + c_2\mathbf{v}_2 + c_3\mathbf{v}_3 = \mathbf{0} \implies c_1 = c_2 = c_3 = 0.$ (6)

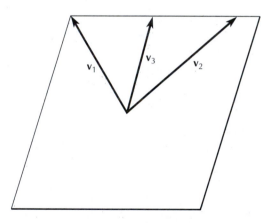

Figure 11.4 $\mathcal{L}[\mathbf{v}_1, \mathbf{v}_2, \mathbf{v}_3]$ *is a plane if* $\mathbf{v}_3$ *is a linear combination of* $\mathbf{v}_1$ *and* $\mathbf{v}_2$.

It is straightforward now to generalize the concepts of linear dependence and linear independence to arbitrary finite collections of vectors in $\mathbf{R}^n$ by extending definitions (5) and (6) in the natural way.

Definition   Vectors $\mathbf{v}_1$, $\mathbf{v}_2, \ldots, \mathbf{v}_k$ in $\mathbf{R}^n$ are **linearly dependent** if and only if there exist scalars $c_1, c_2, \ldots, c_k$, *not all zero*, such that

$$c_1\mathbf{v}_1 + c_2\mathbf{v}_2 + \cdots + c_k\mathbf{v}_k = \mathbf{0}.$$

Vectors $\mathbf{v}_1$, $\mathbf{v}_2, \ldots, \mathbf{v}_k$ in $\mathbf{R}^n$ are **linearly independent** if and only if $c_1\mathbf{v}_1 + \cdots + c_k\mathbf{v}_k = \mathbf{0}$ for scalars $c_1, \ldots, c_k$ implies that $c_1 = \cdots = c_k = 0.$

Example 11.1   The vectors

$$\mathbf{e}_1 = \begin{pmatrix} 1 \\ 0 \\ \vdots \\ 0 \end{pmatrix}, \ldots, \mathbf{e}_n = \begin{pmatrix} 0 \\ 0 \\ \vdots \\ 1 \end{pmatrix}$$

in $\mathbf{R}^n$ are linearly independent, because if $c_1, \ldots, c_n$ are scalars such that $c_1\mathbf{e}_1 + c_2\mathbf{e}_2 + \cdots + c_n\mathbf{e}_n = \mathbf{0}$,

$$c_1\begin{pmatrix} 1 \\ 0 \\ \vdots \\ 0 \end{pmatrix} + c_2\begin{pmatrix} 0 \\ 1 \\ \vdots \\ 0 \end{pmatrix} + \cdots + c_n\begin{pmatrix} 0 \\ 0 \\ \vdots \\ 1 \end{pmatrix} = \begin{pmatrix} c_1 \\ c_2 \\ \vdots \\ c_n \end{pmatrix} = \begin{pmatrix} 0 \\ 0 \\ \vdots \\ 0 \end{pmatrix}.$$

The last vector equation implies that $c_1 = c_2 = \cdots = c_n = 0$.

Example 11.2   The vectors

$$\mathbf{w}_1 = \begin{pmatrix} 1 \\ 2 \\ 3 \end{pmatrix}, \quad \mathbf{w}_2 = \begin{pmatrix} 4 \\ 5 \\ 6 \end{pmatrix}, \quad \text{and} \quad \mathbf{w}_3 = \begin{pmatrix} 7 \\ 8 \\ 9 \end{pmatrix}$$

are linearly dependent in $\mathbf{R}^3$, since

$$1 \cdot \begin{pmatrix} 1 \\ 2 \\ 3 \end{pmatrix} - 2 \cdot \begin{pmatrix} 4 \\ 5 \\ 6 \end{pmatrix} + 1 \cdot \begin{pmatrix} 7 \\ 8 \\ 9 \end{pmatrix} = \begin{pmatrix} 0 \\ 0 \\ 0 \end{pmatrix},$$

as can easily be verified.

Checking Linear Independence

How would one decide whether or not $\mathbf{w}_1$, $\mathbf{w}_2$, and $\mathbf{w}_3$ in Example 11.2 are linearly independent starting from scratch? To use definition (5), start with the equation

$$c_1\begin{pmatrix} 1 \\ 2 \\ 3 \end{pmatrix} + c_2\begin{pmatrix} 4 \\ 5 \\ 6 \end{pmatrix} + c_3\begin{pmatrix} 7 \\ 8 \\ 9 \end{pmatrix} = \begin{pmatrix} 0 \\ 0 \\ 0 \end{pmatrix}, \tag{7}$$

and solve this system for all possible values of c_1, c_2, and c_3. Multiplying system (7) out yields

$$\begin{aligned} 1c_1 + 4c_2 + 7c_3 &= 0 \\ 2c_1 + 5c_2 + 8c_3 &= 0 \\ 3c_1 + 6c_2 + 9c_3 &= 0, \end{aligned} \tag{8}$$

a system of linear equations in the variables c_1, c_2, and c_3. The matrix formulation of system (8) is

$$\begin{pmatrix} 1 & 4 & 7 \\ 2 & 5 & 8 \\ 3 & 6 & 9 \end{pmatrix} \begin{pmatrix} c_1 \\ c_2 \\ c_3 \end{pmatrix} = \begin{pmatrix} 0 \\ 0 \\ 0 \end{pmatrix}. \tag{9}$$

Note that the coefficient matrix in (9) is simply the matrix whose columns are the original three vectors $\mathbf{w}_1$, $\mathbf{w}_2$, and $\mathbf{w}_3$. So, the question of the linear independence of $\mathbf{w}_1$, $\mathbf{w}_2$, and $\mathbf{w}_3$ reduces to a consideration of the coefficient matrix whose columns are $\mathbf{w}_1$, $\mathbf{w}_2$, and $\mathbf{w}_3$. In that case, we reduce the coefficient matrix to its row echelon form:

$$\begin{pmatrix} 1 & 4 & 7 \\ 2 & 5 & 8 \\ 3 & 6 & 9 \end{pmatrix} \Longrightarrow \begin{pmatrix} 1 & 4 & 7 \\ 0 & -3 & -6 \\ 0 & 0 & 0 \end{pmatrix},$$

and conclude that, because its row echelon form has a row of zeros, the coefficient matrix in (9) is singular and therefore that system (9) has a nonzero solution (in fact, infinitely many). One such solution is easily seen to be

$$c_1 = 1, \quad c_2 = -2, \quad \text{and} \quad c_3 = 1,$$

the coefficients we used in Example 11.2. We conclude that $\mathbf{w}_1$, $\mathbf{w}_2$, and $\mathbf{w}_3$ are linearly dependent.

The analysis with $\mathbf{w}_1$, $\mathbf{w}_2$, and $\mathbf{w}_3$ in the previous example can easily be generalized to prove the following theorem by substituting general $\mathbf{v}_1, \ldots, \mathbf{v}_k$ in steps (7) to (9) for $\mathbf{w}_1$, $\mathbf{w}_2$, and $\mathbf{w}_3$ in Example 11.2.

Theorem 11.1 Vectors $\mathbf{v}_1, \ldots, \mathbf{v}_k$ in $\mathbf{R}^n$ are linearly dependent if and only if the linear system

$$A \begin{pmatrix} c_1 \\ \vdots \\ c_k \end{pmatrix} = \mathbf{0}$$

has a nonzero solution $(c_1, \ldots, c_k)$, where A is the $n \times k$ matrix whose columns are the vectors $\mathbf{v}_1, \ldots, \mathbf{v}_k$ under study:

$$A = (\mathbf{v}_1 \quad \mathbf{v}_2 \quad \cdots \quad \mathbf{v}_k).$$

The following is a restatement of Theorem 11.1 for the case $k = n$, using the fact that a square matrix is nonsingular if and only if its determinant is not zero.

Theorem 11.2   A set of n vectors $\mathbf{v}_1, \ldots, \mathbf{v}_n$ in $\mathbf{R}^n$ is linearly independent if and only if

$$\det(\mathbf{v}_1 \quad \mathbf{v}_2 \quad \cdots \quad \mathbf{v}_n) \neq 0.$$

For example, the matrix whose columns are the vectors $\mathbf{e}_1, \ldots, \mathbf{e}_n$ in $\mathbf{R}^n$ in Example 11.1 is the identity matrix, whose determinant is one. We conclude from Theorem 11.2 that $\mathbf{e}_1, \ldots, \mathbf{e}_n$ form a linearly independent set of n-vectors.

We can use Theorem 11.1 to derive a basic result about linear independence. It generalizes the fact that any two vectors on a line are linearly dependent and any three vectors in a plane are linearly dependent.

Theorem 11.3   If $k > n$, any set of k vectors in $\mathbf{R}^n$ is linearly dependent.

Proof   Let $\mathbf{v}_1, \ldots, \mathbf{v}_k$ be k vectors in $\mathbf{R}^n$ with $k > n$. By Theorem 11.1, the $\mathbf{v}_i$'s are linearly dependent if and only if the system

$$A\mathbf{c} = (\mathbf{v}_1 \quad \mathbf{v}_2 \quad \cdots \quad \mathbf{v}_k) \begin{pmatrix} c_1 \\ \vdots \\ c_k \end{pmatrix} = \mathbf{0}$$

has a nonzero solution $\mathbf{c}$. But by Fact 7.6 in Section 7.4, any matrix A with more columns than rows will have a free variable and therefore $A\mathbf{c} = \mathbf{0}$ will have infinitely many solutions, all but one of which are nonzero. ■

EXERCISES

11.1   Show that if (1) or (2) holds, then (3) holds and, if (3) holds, then (1) or (2) holds.

11.2   Which of the following pairs or triplets of vectors are linearly independent?

   a) $(2, 1)$, $(1, 2)$;   b) $(2, 1)$, $(-4, -2)$;
   c) $(1, 1, 0)$, $(0, 1, 1)$;   d) $(1, 1, 0)$, $(0, 1, 1)$, $(1, 0, 1)$.

11.3   Determine whether or not each of the following collections of vectors in $\mathbf{R}^4$ are linearly independent:

$$a) \quad \begin{pmatrix} 1 \\ 0 \\ 1 \\ 0 \end{pmatrix}, \begin{pmatrix} 1 \\ 0 \\ 0 \\ 1 \end{pmatrix}, \begin{pmatrix} 0 \\ 0 \\ 1 \\ 1 \end{pmatrix}; \qquad b) \quad \begin{pmatrix} 1 \\ 0 \\ 1 \\ 0 \end{pmatrix}, \begin{pmatrix} 1 \\ 0 \\ -1 \\ 0 \end{pmatrix}, \begin{pmatrix} 1 \\ 0 \\ 0 \\ 0 \end{pmatrix}.$$

11.4   Prove that if (4) holds, then $\mathbf{v}_1$ is not a multiple of $\mathbf{v}_2$ and $\mathbf{v}_2$ is not a multiple of $\mathbf{v}_1$.

11.5 *a)* Show that if $\mathbf{v}_1$, $\mathbf{v}_2$, and $\mathbf{v}_3$ do not satisfy (5), they satisfy (6), and vice versa.

   b) Show that (5) is equivalent to the statement that one of $\mathbf{v}_1$, $\mathbf{v}_2$, and $\mathbf{v}_3$ is a linear combination of the other two.

11.6 Prove that any collection of vectors that includes the zero-vector cannot be linearly independent.

11.7 Prove Theorem 11.1.

11.8 Prove Theorem 11.2.

11.2 SPANNING SETS

Let $\mathbf{v}_1, \ldots, \mathbf{v}_k$ be a fixed set of k vectors in $\mathbf{R}^n$. In the last section, we spoke of the set of all **linear combinations** of $\mathbf{v}_1, \ldots, \mathbf{v}_k$,

$$\mathcal{L}[\mathbf{v}_1, \ldots, \mathbf{v}_k] \equiv \{c_1\mathbf{v}_1 + \cdots + c_k\mathbf{v}_k : c_1, \ldots, c_k \in \mathbf{R}\},$$

and called it the set **generated** or **spanned** by $\mathbf{v}_1, \ldots, \mathbf{v}_k$.

Suppose that we are given a subset V of $\mathbf{R}^n$. It is reasonable to ask whether or not there exists $\mathbf{v}_1, \ldots, \mathbf{v}_k$ in $\mathbf{R}^n$ such that every vector in V can be written as a linear combination of $\mathbf{v}_1, \ldots, \mathbf{v}_k$:

$$V = \mathcal{L}[\mathbf{v}_1, \ldots, \mathbf{v}_k]. \tag{10}$$

When (10) occurs, we say that $\mathbf{v}_1, \ldots, \mathbf{v}_k$ **span** V.

Example 11.3 Every line through the origin is the span of a nonzero vector on the line. For example, the x_1-axis is the span of $\mathbf{e}_1 = (1, 0, \ldots, 0)$, and the diagonal line

$$\Delta \equiv \{(a, a, \ldots, a) \in \mathbf{R}^n : a \in \mathbf{R}\}$$

is the span of the vector $(1, 1, \ldots, 1)$.

Example 11.4 The x_1x_2-plane in $\mathbf{R}^3$ is the span of the unit vectors $\mathbf{e}_1 = (1, 0, 0)$ and $\mathbf{e}_2 = (0, 1, 0)$, because any vector $(a, b, 0)$ in this plane can be written as

$$\begin{pmatrix} a \\ b \\ 0 \end{pmatrix} = a\begin{pmatrix} 1 \\ 0 \\ 0 \end{pmatrix} + b\begin{pmatrix} 0 \\ 1 \\ 0 \end{pmatrix}.$$

Example 11.5 The n-dimensional Euclidean space itself is spanned by the vectors $\mathbf{e}_1, \ldots, \mathbf{e}_n$ of Example 11.1. For, if $(a_1, \ldots, a_n)$ is an arbitrary vector in $\mathbf{R}^n$, then we can write

$$
\begin{pmatrix} a_1 \\ a_2 \\ \vdots \\ a_n \end{pmatrix} = a_1 \begin{pmatrix} 1 \\ 0 \\ \vdots \\ 0 \end{pmatrix} + a_2 \begin{pmatrix} 0 \\ 1 \\ \vdots \\ 0 \end{pmatrix} + \cdots + a_n \begin{pmatrix} 0 \\ 0 \\ \vdots \\ 1 \end{pmatrix}.
$$

Example 11.6   Different sets of vectors can span the same space. For example, each of the following sets of vectors spans $\mathbf{R}^2$:

a) $\begin{pmatrix} 1 \\ 0 \end{pmatrix}$, $\begin{pmatrix} 0 \\ 1 \end{pmatrix}$;

b) $\begin{pmatrix} -1 \\ 0 \end{pmatrix}$, $\begin{pmatrix} 0 \\ 1 \end{pmatrix}$;

c) $\begin{pmatrix} 1 \\ 0 \end{pmatrix}$, $\begin{pmatrix} 0 \\ 1 \end{pmatrix}$, $\begin{pmatrix} 1 \\ 1 \end{pmatrix}$;

d) $\begin{pmatrix} 1 \\ -1 \end{pmatrix}$, $\begin{pmatrix} 1 \\ 1 \end{pmatrix}$;

e) $\begin{pmatrix} 1 \\ -1 \end{pmatrix}$, $\begin{pmatrix} 1 \\ 1 \end{pmatrix}$, $\begin{pmatrix} 3 \\ 4 \end{pmatrix}$.

Theorem 11.1 presented a matrix criterion for checking whether a given set of vectors is linearly independent. The following theorem carries out the analogous task for checking whether a set of vectors spans.

Theorem 11.4   Let $\mathbf{v}_1, \ldots, \mathbf{v}_k$ be a set of k vectors in $\mathbf{R}^n$. Form the $n \times k$ matrix whose columns are these $\mathbf{v}_j$'s:

$$
A = (\mathbf{v}_1 \quad \mathbf{v}_2 \quad \cdots \quad \mathbf{v}_k). \tag{11}
$$

Let $\mathbf{b}$ be a vector in $\mathbf{R}^n$. Then, $\mathbf{b}$ lies in the space $\mathcal{L}[\mathbf{v}_1, \ldots, \mathbf{v}_k]$ spanned by $\mathbf{v}_1, \ldots, \mathbf{v}_k$ if and only if the system $A\mathbf{c} = \mathbf{b}$ has a solution $\mathbf{c}$.

Proof   Write $\mathbf{v}_1, \ldots, \mathbf{v}_k$ in coordinates as

$$
\mathbf{v}_1 = \begin{pmatrix} v_{11} \\ \vdots \\ v_{1n} \end{pmatrix}, \ldots, \mathbf{v}_k = \begin{pmatrix} v_{k1} \\ \vdots \\ v_{kn} \end{pmatrix}.
$$

Then, $\mathbf{b}$ is in $\mathcal{L}[\mathbf{v}_1, \ldots, \mathbf{v}_k]$ if and only if we can find $c_1, \ldots, c_k$ such that

$$c_1 \mathbf{v}_1 + \cdots + c_k \mathbf{v}_k = \mathbf{b},$$

or

$$c_1 \begin{pmatrix} v_{11} \\ \vdots \\ v_{1n} \end{pmatrix} + \cdots + c_k \begin{pmatrix} v_{k1} \\ \vdots \\ v_{kn} \end{pmatrix} = \begin{pmatrix} b_1 \\ \vdots \\ b_n \end{pmatrix},$$

or

$$c_1 v_{11} + \cdots + c_k v_{k1} = b_1$$
$$\vdots \qquad \vdots \qquad \vdots$$
$$c_1 v_{1n} + \cdots + c_k v_{kn} = b_n,$$

or

$$\begin{pmatrix} v_{11} & \cdots & v_{k1} \\ \vdots & \ddots & \vdots \\ v_{1n} & \cdots & v_{kn} \end{pmatrix} \begin{pmatrix} c_1 \\ \vdots \\ c_k \end{pmatrix} = \begin{pmatrix} b_1 \\ \vdots \\ b_n \end{pmatrix}. \tag{12}$$

So, $\mathbf{b} \in \mathcal{L}[\mathbf{v}_1, \ldots, \mathbf{v}_k]$ if and only if system (12) has a solution $\mathbf{c}$. ∎

The following corollary of Theorem 11.4 provides a simple criterion for whether or not a given set of vectors spans all of $\mathbf{R}^n$. Its proof is left as a simple exercise.

Theorem 11.5   Let $\mathbf{v}_1, \ldots, \mathbf{v}_k$ be a collection of vectors in $\mathbf{R}^n$. Form the $n \times k$ matrix A whose columns are these $\mathbf{v}_j$'s, as in (11). Then, $\mathbf{v}_1, \ldots, \mathbf{v}_k$ span $\mathbf{R}^n$ if and only if the system of equations $A\mathbf{x} = \mathbf{b}$ has a solution $\mathbf{x}$ for every right-hand side $\mathbf{b}$.

In Example 11.5, we found n vectors that span $\mathbf{R}^n$. In Example 11.6, we listed various collections of two or three vectors that span $\mathbf{R}^2$. Clearly, it takes at least two vectors to span $\mathbf{R}^2$. The next theorem, which follows easily from Theorem 11.5, states that one needs at least n vectors to span $\mathbf{R}^n$.

Theorem 11.6   A set of vectors that spans $\mathbf{R}^n$ must contain at least n vectors.

Proof   By Theorem 11.5, $\mathbf{v}_1, \ldots, \mathbf{v}_k$ span $\mathbf{R}^n$ if and only if system (12) has a solution $\mathbf{c}$ for every right-hand side $\mathbf{b} \in \mathbf{R}^n$. Fact 7.7 tells us that if system (12) has a solution for each right-hand side, then the rank of the coefficient matrix equals the number of rows, n. Fact 7.1 states that the rank of the coefficient matrix is always less than or equal to the number of columns, k. Therefore, if k vectors span $\mathbf{R}^n$, then $n \leq k$. ∎

EXERCISES

11.9   *a*) Write $(2, 2)$ as a linear combination of $(1, 2)$ and $(1, 4)$.

  b) Write $(1, 2, 3)$ as a linear combination of $(1, 1, 0)$, $(1, 0, 1)$, and $(0, 1, 1)$.

11.10   Do $\begin{pmatrix} 1 \\ 2 \\ 3 \end{pmatrix}$, $\begin{pmatrix} 4 \\ 5 \\ 12 \end{pmatrix}$, and $\begin{pmatrix} 0 \\ 8 \\ 0 \end{pmatrix}$ span $\mathbf{R}^3$? Explain.

11.11   Prove Theorem 11.5.

11.3   BASIS AND DIMENSION IN $\mathbf{R}^n$

If we have a spanning set of vectors, we can always throw in $\mathbf{0}$ or any linear combination of the vectors in the spanning set to create a larger spanning set. But what we would really like to do is to go the other way and find an efficient spanning set.

Example 11.7   Let W be the set of all linear combinations of $\mathbf{v}_1 = (1, 1, 1)$, $\mathbf{v}_2 = (1, -1, -1)$, and $\mathbf{v}_3 = (2, 0, 0)$ in $\mathbf{R}^3$: $W = \mathcal{L}[\mathbf{v}_1, \mathbf{v}_2, \mathbf{v}_3]$. Note that $\mathbf{v}_3 = \mathbf{v}_1 + \mathbf{v}_2$. Thus, any vector which is a linear combination of $\mathbf{v}_1$, $\mathbf{v}_2$, and $\mathbf{v}_3$ can be written as a linear combination of just $\mathbf{v}_1$ and $\mathbf{v}_2$, because if $\mathbf{w} \in W$, then there are scalars a, b, and c such that

$$\mathbf{w} = a\mathbf{v}_1 + b\mathbf{v}_2 + c\mathbf{v}_3$$
$$= a\mathbf{v}_1 + b\mathbf{v}_2 + c(\mathbf{v}_1 + \mathbf{v}_2)$$
$$= (a + c)\mathbf{v}_1 + (b + c)\mathbf{v}_2.$$

The set $\{\mathbf{v}_1, \mathbf{v}_2\}$ is a more "efficient" spanning set than is the set $\{\mathbf{v}_1, \mathbf{v}_2, \mathbf{v}_3\}$.

For the sake of efficiency, if $\mathbf{v}_1, \ldots, \mathbf{v}_k$ span V, we would like to find the *smallest* possible subset of $\mathbf{v}_1, \ldots, \mathbf{v}_k$ that spans V. However, this is precisely the role of the concept of linear independence that we considered in Section 11.1. If $\mathbf{v}_1, \ldots, \mathbf{v}_k$ are linearly independent, no one of these vectors is a linear combination of the others and therefore no proper subset of $\mathbf{v}_1, \ldots, \mathbf{v}_k$ spans $\mathcal{L}[\mathbf{v}_1, \ldots, \mathbf{v}_k]$. The set $\mathbf{v}_1, \ldots, \mathbf{v}_k$ spans $\mathcal{L}[\mathbf{v}_1, \ldots, \mathbf{v}_k]$ most efficiently. In this case, we call $\mathbf{v}_1, \ldots, \mathbf{v}_k$ a *basis* of $\mathcal{L}[\mathbf{v}_1, \ldots, \mathbf{v}_k]$. Since $\mathcal{L}[\mathbf{v}_1, \ldots, \mathbf{v}_k]$ can be spanned by different sets of vectors, as illustrated in Example 11.6, we define a basis more generally as any set of *linearly independent* vectors that *span* $\mathcal{L}[\mathbf{v}_1, \ldots, \mathbf{v}_k]$.

Definition   Let $\mathbf{v}_1, \ldots, \mathbf{v}_k$ be a fixed set of k vectors in $\mathbf{R}^n$. Let V be the set $\mathcal{L}[\mathbf{v}_1, \ldots, \mathbf{v}_k]$ spanned by $\mathbf{v}_1, \ldots, \mathbf{v}_k$. Then, if $\mathbf{v}_1, \ldots, \mathbf{v}_k$ are linearly independent, $\mathbf{v}_1, \ldots, \mathbf{v}_k$ is called a **basis** of V. More generally, let $\mathbf{w}_1, \ldots, \mathbf{w}_m$ be a collection of vectors in V. Then, $\mathbf{w}_1, \ldots, \mathbf{w}_m$ forms a **basis** of V if:

(*a*) $\mathbf{w}_1, \ldots, \mathbf{w}_m$ span V, and
(*b*) $\mathbf{w}_1, \ldots, \mathbf{w}_m$ are linearly independent.

Example 11.8   We conclude from Examples 11.1 and 11.5 that the unit vectors

$$\mathbf{e}_1 = \begin{pmatrix} 1 \\ 0 \\ \vdots \\ 0 \end{pmatrix}, \ldots, \mathbf{e}_n = \begin{pmatrix} 0 \\ 0 \\ \vdots \\ 1 \end{pmatrix}$$

form a basis of $\mathbf{R}^n$. Since this is such a natural basis, it is called the **canonical basis** of $\mathbf{R}^n$.

Example 11.9   Example 11.6 presents five collections of vectors that span $\mathbf{R}^2$. By Theorem 11.3, collections c and e are not linearly independent since each contains more than two vectors. However, the collections in a, b and d are linearly independent (exercise), and therefore, each forms a basis of $\mathbf{R}^2$.

Notice that each basis in $\mathbf{R}^2$ singled out in Example 11.9 is composed of *two* vectors. This is natural since $\mathbf{R}^2$ is a plane and two linearly independent vectors span a plane. The following theorem generalizes this result to $\mathbf{R}^n$.

Theorem 11.7   Every basis of $\mathbf{R}^n$ contains n vectors.

Proof   By Theorem 11.3, a basis of $\mathbf{R}^n$ cannot contain more than n elements; otherwise, the set under consideration would not be linearly independent. By Theorem 11.6, a basis of $\mathbf{R}^n$ cannot contain fewer than n elements; otherwise, the set under consideration would not span $\mathbf{R}^n$. It follows that a basis of $\mathbf{R}^n$ must have exactly n elements.   ■

We can combine Theorems 11.1, 11.2, and 11.5 and the fact that a square matrix is nonsingular if and only if its determinant is nonzero to achieve the following equivalence of the notions of linear independence, spanning, and basis for n vectors in $\mathbf{R}^n$.

Theorem 11.8   Let $\mathbf{v}_1, \ldots, \mathbf{v}_n$ be a collection of n vectors in $\mathbf{R}^n$. Form the $n \times n$ matrix A whose columns are these $\mathbf{v}_j$'s: $A = (\, \mathbf{v}_1 \quad \mathbf{v}_2 \quad \cdots \quad \mathbf{v}_n \,)$. Then, the following statements are equivalent:

(a) $\mathbf{v}_1, \ldots, \mathbf{v}_n$ are linearly independent,
(b) $\mathbf{v}_1, \ldots, \mathbf{v}_n$ span $\mathbf{R}^n$,
(c) $\mathbf{v}_1, \ldots, \mathbf{v}_n$ form a basis of $\mathbf{R}^n$, and
(d) the determinant of A is nonzero.

Dimension

The fact that every basis of $\mathbf{R^n}$ contains exactly n vectors tells us that there are n independent directions in $\mathbf{R^n}$. We express this when we say that $\mathbf{R^n}$ is n-dimensional. We can use the idea of basis to extend the concept of dimension to other subsets of $\mathbf{R^n}$. In particular, let V be the set $\mathcal{L}[\mathbf{v}_1, \ldots, \mathbf{v}_k]$ generated by the set of vectors $\mathbf{v}_1, \ldots, \mathbf{v}_k$. If $\mathbf{v}_1, \ldots, \mathbf{v}_k$ are linearly independent, they form a basis of V. In Chapter 27, we prove that *every* basis of V has exactly k vectors — the analogue of Theorem 11.7 for proper subsets of $\mathbf{R^n}$. This number k of vectors in every basis of V is called the dimension of V.

EXERCISES

11.12   Which of the following are bases of $\mathbf{R}^2$?

$a)\ \begin{pmatrix} 1 \\ 1 \end{pmatrix}, \begin{pmatrix} -2 \\ -2 \end{pmatrix}$ $b)\ \begin{pmatrix} 1 \\ 1 \end{pmatrix}, \begin{pmatrix} 2 \\ -2 \end{pmatrix}$ $c)\ \begin{pmatrix} 1 \\ -1 \end{pmatrix}, \begin{pmatrix} -2 \\ 2 \end{pmatrix}$ $d)\ \begin{pmatrix} 1 \\ -1 \end{pmatrix}, \begin{pmatrix} 1 \\ 0 \end{pmatrix}.$

11.13   Show that the collections in a, b and d in Example 11.6 form a basis of $\mathbf{R}^2$.

11.14   Which of the following are bases in $\mathbf{R}^3$?

$a)\ \begin{pmatrix} 1 \\ 1 \\ 1 \end{pmatrix}, \begin{pmatrix} 1 \\ 2 \\ 1 \end{pmatrix};$ $b)\ \begin{pmatrix} 1 \\ 1 \\ 1 \end{pmatrix}, \begin{pmatrix} 1 \\ 2 \\ 1 \end{pmatrix}, \begin{pmatrix} 1 \\ 0 \\ 1 \end{pmatrix};$ $c)\ \begin{pmatrix} 6 \\ 3 \\ 9 \end{pmatrix}, \begin{pmatrix} 5 \\ 2 \\ 8 \end{pmatrix}, \begin{pmatrix} 4 \\ 1 \\ 7 \end{pmatrix};$

$d)\ \begin{pmatrix} 1 \\ 1 \\ 1 \end{pmatrix}, \begin{pmatrix} 1 \\ 2 \\ 1 \end{pmatrix}, \begin{pmatrix} 1 \\ 0 \\ 0 \end{pmatrix};$ $e)\ \begin{pmatrix} 1 \\ 1 \\ 1 \end{pmatrix}, \begin{pmatrix} 1 \\ 2 \\ 1 \end{pmatrix}, \begin{pmatrix} 1 \\ 0 \\ 0 \end{pmatrix}, \begin{pmatrix} 0 \\ 1 \\ 0 \end{pmatrix}.$

11.15   Prove Theorem 11.8.

11.4   EPILOGUE

This completes our introduction to linear independence, spanning, and dimension. You may want to delve more deeply into these topics before going on to the study of nonlinear functions in Part 3. If so, the following chapters of more advanced material would fit in naturally here:

Chapter 27: Subspaces Attached to a Matrix   As the continuation of Chapter 11, this chapter defines an abstract vector space and its subspaces and carries the notion of dimension to such spaces. As important examples, it studies three subspaces attached to any matrix: the row space, the column space, and the nullspace.

It concludes with a complete characterization of the size, that is, dimension, of the set of solutions to a system of linear equation $A\mathbf{x} = \mathbf{b}$.

Chapter 28: Applications of Linear Independence   This chapter presents applications of the material in Chapters 11 and 27 to portfolio analysis, activity analysis, and voting paradoxes.

PART III

Calculus of Several Variables

CHAPTER 12

Limits and Open Sets

A central concern in economic theory is the effect of a small change in one economic variable x on some other economic variable y. How will a change in x to a nearby x' affect y? Before we can make this effect precise, we need to have a working knowledge of the concepts of *small change* and *nearby*. What does it mean to say that one commodity bundle or input bundle is close to another? What does a small change in prices mean? How can we quantify trends in prices or consumption?

This chapter focuses on these questions by studying in some detail the notions of sequence, limit, neighborhood, open set and closed set. From a mathematical point of view, the *limit of a sequence* is the concept that separates high school mathematics from college mathematics. Limits play a key role, for example, in the definitions of a continuous function, the derivative of a function, and even the number e.

Our study of nearness begins with a careful look at sequences and their limits: first in $\mathbf{R}^1$ in Section 12.2, and then in $\mathbf{R}^n$ in Section 12.3. Sections 12.4 and 12.5 define open and closed sets and describe the complementarity between these two topics. Open and closed sets play an important role in clarifying the hypotheses behind most economic principles. For example, theorems which characterize economic equilibria often require that the underlying space of commodities be a *closed and bounded set* since the existence of an equilibrium is guaranteed for such sets. Section 12.6 discusses the properties of closed and bounded sets.

The exposition of this chapter follows a careful logical development as one principle is deduced from previous ones. As a result, this chapter has more proofs in it than earlier chapters. Most of these proofs are short and straightforward. Work at understanding these proofs since the ability to follow a logical argument and occasionally even to produce one is a valuable asset for working effectively in economics.

12.1 SEQUENCES OF REAL NUMBERS

Definition

The **natural numbers** — also called the **positive integers** — are just the usual counting numbers: $1, 2, 3, 4, \ldots$. A **sequence** of real numbers is an assignment of a real number to each natural number. A sequence is usually written as

$\{x_1, x_2, x_3, \ldots, x_n, \ldots\}$, where x_1 is the real number assigned to the natural number 1, the *first* number in the sequence; x_2 is the real number assigned to 2, the *second* number in the sequence; and so on.

Example 12.1   Some examples of a sequence of real numbers are:

a) $\{1, 2, 3, 4, \ldots\}$,

b) $\left\{1, \dfrac{1}{2}, \dfrac{1}{3}, \dfrac{1}{4}, \ldots\right\}$,

c) $\left\{1, \dfrac{1}{2}, 4, \dfrac{1}{8}, 16, \ldots\right\}$,

d) $\left\{0, -\dfrac{1}{2}, \dfrac{2}{3}, -\dfrac{3}{4}, \dfrac{4}{5}, \ldots\right\}$,

e) $\{-1, 1, -1, 1, -1, \ldots\}$,

f) $\left\{\dfrac{2}{1}, \dfrac{3}{2}, \dfrac{4}{3}, \dfrac{5}{4}, \ldots\right\}$,

g) $\{3.1, 3.14, 3.141, 3.1415, \ldots\}$,

h) $\{1, 4, 1, 5, 9, \ldots\}$.

For each natural number n, each sequence has a well-defined nth number x_n. For example, the nth number in sequence b is $1/n$, the nth number in sequence e is $(-1)^n$, the nth number in sequence f is $(n+1)/n$, and the nth number in sequence g is the truncation of the decimal expansion of the number π to n decimal places. We sometimes write a typical sequence $\{x_1, x_2, x_3, \ldots\}$ as $\{x_n\}_{n=1}^{\infty}$.

Limit of a Sequence

There are basically three kinds of sequences:

(1) sequences like b, f, and g, in which the entries get closer and closer and stay close to some limiting value;
(2) sequences like a in which the entries increase without bound; and
(3) sequences like c, d, e, and h in which neither behavior occurs so that the entries jump back and forth on the number line.

We are most interested in the first type of sequence — the one in which the entries *approach* arbitrarily close and *stay* arbitrarily close to some real number, called the *limit* of the sequence. Notice that we need both parts of this statement. The entries of sequence c get arbitrarily close to 0 but they do not stay there; the entries of sequence d get arbitrarily close to both $+1$ and -1, but the sequence does not stay close to either. Neither sequence c nor sequence d has a definite limit.

In order to define the concept of a limit carefully, we need to formalize the notion that number s is close to number r if s lies in some small interval about r. More precisely, let ε (epsilon) denote a small, positive real number, as is the custom in mathematics. Then, the ε-interval about the number r is defined to be the interval

$$I_\varepsilon(r) \equiv \{s \in \mathbf{R} : |s - r| < \varepsilon\}. \tag{1}$$

In interval notation, $I_\varepsilon(r) = (r - \varepsilon, r + \varepsilon)$. Intuitively speaking, if s is in $I_\varepsilon(r)$ and if ε is small, then s is "close" to r. The smaller ε is, the closer s is to r.

Definition   Let $\{x_1, x_2, x_3, \ldots\}$ be a sequence of real numbers and let r be a real number. We say that r is the **limit** of this sequence if for *any* (small) positive number ε, there is a positive integer N such that for all $n \geq N$, x_n is in the ε-interval about r; that is,

$$|x_n - r| < \varepsilon.$$

In this case, we say that the sequence **converges to** r and we write

$$\lim x_n = r \quad \text{or} \quad \lim_{n \to \infty} x_n = r \quad \text{or simply} \quad x_n \to r.$$

This definition states that x_n converges to r if no matter how small an interval one chooses about r, from some point on ($n \geq N$ in the above definition) the entries of the sequence get into and stay in that interval. Of course, how soon the sequence gets into the interval will, in general, depend on the size of the interval; in other words, N depends on the size of ε. In the above examples, sequence b converges to 0, sequence f converges to 1, and sequence g converges to π.

Example 12.2   Here are three more sequences which converge to 0:

$$1, 0, \frac{1}{2}, 0, \frac{1}{3}, 0, \ldots,$$

$$1, -\frac{1}{2}, \frac{1}{3}, -\frac{1}{4}, \ldots,$$

$$\frac{1}{1}, \frac{3}{1}, \frac{1}{2}, \frac{3}{2}, \frac{1}{3}, \frac{3}{3}, \frac{1}{4}, \ldots.$$

Notice that the elements of the converging sequence need not be distinct from each other or distinct from the limit, as the first sequence in Example 12.2 illustrates. The convergence need not be all from one side, down to the limit, or up to the limit, as the second sequence illustrates. Finally, the convergence need not be monotonic: each element need not be closer to the limit than all previous elements. This is illustrated by the third sequence in Example 12.2. All that convergence requires is that ultimately the elements remain within any prespecified distance of the limit.

As mentioned above, sequences c, d, and e in Example 12.1 do not converge to a limit. Although their entries get arbitrarily close to some number — 0 in c; and +1 and −1 in d and e — they don't stay close. If the entries of a sequence get arbitrarily close to some number, that number is called an accumulation point of the sequence. More formally, r is an **accumulation point** or **cluster point** of the sequence $\{x_n\}$ if for *any* positive ε there are *infinitely* many elements of the sequence in the interval $I_\varepsilon(r)$, as defined in (1). A limit is a special case of an accumulation point. A sequence can have a number of different accumulation points, as illustrated by sequences d and e in Example 12.1. However, a sequence can have only one limit.

Theorem 12.1   A sequence can have at most one limit.

Proof   We want to formalize the intuitive notion that a sequence cannot get arbitrarily close and *stay* arbitrarily close to two different points. Suppose that a sequence $\{x_n\}_{n=1}^\infty$ has two limits: r_1 and r_2. Take ε to be some number less than half the distance between r_1 and r_2, say $\varepsilon = \frac{1}{4}|r_1 - r_2|$, so that $I_\varepsilon(r_1)$ and $I_\varepsilon(r_2)$ are disjoint intervals, as in Figure 12.1. Since $x_n \to r_1$, there is an N_1 such that for $n \geq N_1$ all the x_n are in $I_\varepsilon(r_1)$; and since $x_n \to r_2$, there is an N_2 such that for all $n \geq N_2$ all the x_n are in $I_\varepsilon(r_2)$. Therefore, for *all* $n \geq \max\{N_1, N_2\}$, x_n are in both $I_\varepsilon(r_1)$ and $I_\varepsilon(r_2)$. But no point can be in both $I_\varepsilon(r_1)$ and $I_\varepsilon(r_2)$ — a contradiction which proves the theorem. ∎

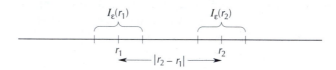

Figure 12.1   *The intervals $I_\varepsilon(r_1)$ and $I_\varepsilon(r_2)$ are disjoint for $\varepsilon = \frac{1}{4}|r_1 - r_2|$.*

In studying sequences, one often must consider the subsequences of a given sequence. To define the concept of a subsequence carefully, think of a sequence as the image of a function F from the natural numbers to the real numbers, where we write $F(n)$ as x_n. Now, let M be any *infinite* subset of the natural numbers. Write M as $\{n_1, n_2, n_3, \ldots\}$, where

$$n_1 < n_2 < n_3 < \cdots.$$

Create a new sequence $\{y_n\}$, where

$$y_j = x_{n_j}, \quad \text{for } j = 1, 2, 3, \ldots.$$

This new sequence $\{y_j\}_{j=1}^\infty$ is called a **subsequence** of the original sequence $\{x_n\}$. In short, we construct a subsequence of a sequence by choosing an *infinite* collection of the entries of the original sequence in the order that these elements appear in the original sequence. (See Exercise 12.2.)

Algebraic Properties of Limits

It should be intuitively clear that limits of sequences are preserved by algebraic operations. For example, if $\{x_n\}_{n=1}^\infty$ gets arbitrarily close to x and if $\{y_n\}_{n=1}^\infty$ gets arbitrarily close to y, then the sequence of the sums $\{x_n + y_n\}_{n=1}^{\infty}$ gets arbitrarily close to $x + y$, and similarly for differences, products, and quotients. Work at understanding the next two proofs as completely as possible in order to develop a good working knowledge of the notion of limits, and of the notion of a careful proof. The proofs of most theorems about sequences and their limits require the triangle inequality, often more than once:

$$|x + y| \le |x| + |y| \qquad \text{for all } x, y. \tag{2}$$

Some proofs also call for the subtraction variant of the triangle inequality:

$$\big|\,|x| - |y|\,\big| \le |x - y| \qquad \text{for all } x, y. \tag{3}$$

For real numbers, one can prove inequalities (2) and (3) directly, for example, by looking at cases based on the signs of x and y. (Exercise.) For vectors in $\mathbf{R^n}$, one replaces the absolute values in inequality (2) by norms. In this case, the corresponding statement is the Triangle Inequality. See Theorems 10.5 and 10.6.

Theorem 12.2 Let $\{x_n\}_{n=1}^{\infty}$ and $\{y_n\}_{n=1}^{\infty}$ be sequences with limits x and y, respectively. Then the sequence $\{x_n + y_n\}_{n=1}^{\infty}$ converges to the limit $x + y$.

Proof Choose and fix a small positive number ε. [Just about all proofs about limits begin this way.] Since we know that $x_n \to x$ and $y_n \to y$, there exists an integer N_1 such that

$$|x_n - x| < \frac{\varepsilon}{2} \qquad \text{for } n \ge N_1$$

and an integer N_2 such that

$$|y_n - y| < \frac{\varepsilon}{2} \qquad \text{for } n \ge N_2.$$

Let $N = \max\{N_1, N_2\}$. Then for all $n \ge N$,

$$|(x_n + y_n) - (x + y)| = |(x_n - x) + (y_n - y)|$$
$$\le |x_n - x| + |y_n - y| \qquad \text{by (2)}$$
$$\le \frac{\varepsilon}{2} + \frac{\varepsilon}{2}$$
$$= \varepsilon. \qquad \blacksquare$$

We next prove that if $x_n \to x$ and $y_n \to y$, then $x_n y_n \to xy$. This proof is a bit more tedious than that of Theorem 12.2, and can be skipped at first reading. We will begin by writing the critical difference $|xy - x_n y_n|$ as a sum of three terms, each of which involves the distances $|x_n - x|$ and $|y_n - y|$ which we know something about. We will then choose a positive ε. To show that the sum of the three terms in less than ε for large N, we show that each is less than $\varepsilon/3$ for large enough N.

Theorem 12.3   Let $\{x_n\}_{n=1}^{\infty}$ and $\{y_n\}_{n=1}^{\infty}$ be sequences with limits x and y, respectively. Then the sequence of products $\{x_n y_n\}_{n=1}^{\infty}$ converges to the limit xy.

Proof   To show that $|xy - x_n y_n|$ is small when $|x - x_n|$ and $|y - y_n|$ are small, try to write the former in terms of the latter two. We will accomplish this by using the mathematician's trick of adding and subtracting the same element to a given expression; in fact, we'll do this twice.

$$|x \cdot y - x_n \cdot y_n| = |x \cdot y - x \cdot y_n + x \cdot y_n - x_n \cdot y_n| \qquad \text{(once)}$$

$$= |x \cdot (y - y_n) + (x - x_n) \cdot y_n|$$

$$= |x \cdot (y - y_n) + (x - x_n) \cdot (y_n - y + y)| \qquad \text{(twice)}$$

$$= |x \cdot (y - y_n) + (x - x_n) \cdot (y_n - y) + (x - x_n) \cdot y|$$

$$\leq |x \cdot (y - y_n)| + |(x - x_n) \cdot (y_n - y)| + |(x - x_n) \cdot y|$$

$$\text{(using the triple triangle inequality)}$$

$$\leq |x||y - y_n| + |x - x_n||y_n - y| + |x - x_n||y|.$$

We know that each term in the last expression goes to zero. To make this process precise, proceed just as in the proof of Theorem 12.2. Choose and fix a small positive number ε, with $\varepsilon < 1$. Since $x_n \to x$, there is an integer N_1 such that

$$n \geq N_1 \quad \Longrightarrow \quad |x - x_n| < \frac{\varepsilon}{3(|y| + 1)}.$$

Since $y_n \to y$, there is an integer N_2 such that

$$n \geq N_2 \quad \Longrightarrow \quad |y - y_n| < \frac{\varepsilon}{3(|x| + 1)}.$$

Don't lose sight of the fact that since ε and $|x|$ are fixed real numbers, so is $\varepsilon/[3(|x|+1)]$. The 3s in these expressions come from the fact that there are three terms in the each of the expressions above. In order to make this expression less than ε, we will make each of the three terms less than $\varepsilon/3$. To make the first term, $|x||y - y_n|$, less than $\varepsilon/3$, we want $|y - y_n| < \varepsilon/(3|x|)$. We add an extra 1 to the denominator on the right to handle the case where x might be 0. Take $N = \max\{N_1, N_2\}$. Then, if $n \geq N$,

$$|x \cdot y - x_n \cdot y_n| \le |x||y - y_n| + |x - x_n||y_n - y| + |x - x_n||y|$$

$$\le |x| \frac{\varepsilon}{3(|x| + 1)} + \frac{\varepsilon}{3(|y| + 1)} \frac{\varepsilon}{3(|x| + 1)} + \frac{\varepsilon}{3(|y| + 1)}|y|$$

$$= \frac{|x|}{(|x| + 1)} \frac{\varepsilon}{3} + \frac{\varepsilon^2}{3^2} \frac{1}{(|y| + 1)} \frac{1}{(|x| + 1)} + \frac{|y|}{(|y| + 1)} \frac{\varepsilon}{3}$$

$$\le \frac{\varepsilon}{3} + \left(\frac{\varepsilon}{3}\right)^2 + \frac{\varepsilon}{3}$$

$$\le \varepsilon.$$

Here, we have used the facts that

$$\frac{|x|}{|x| + 1} < 1, \qquad \frac{|y|}{|y| + 1} < 1, \qquad \frac{1}{|x| + 1} < 1, \qquad \frac{1}{|y| + 1} < 1,$$

and $\varepsilon < 1 \implies \left(\dfrac{\varepsilon}{3}\right) < 1 \implies \left(\dfrac{\varepsilon}{3}\right)^2 < \dfrac{\varepsilon}{3}.$ ∎

Another important property of sequences is that they preserve weak order relations, as the following theorem shows.

Theorem 12.4 Let $\{x_n\}_{n=1}^{\infty}$ be a convergent sequence with limit x, and let b be a number such that $x_n \le b$ for all n. Then, $x \le b$. If $x_n \ge b$ for all n, then $x \ge b$.

Proof We will prove only the first statement. The proof of the second statement is almost identical. Suppose, then, that $x_n \le b$ for all n, and suppose that $x > b$. Choose ε so that $0 < \varepsilon < x - b$; then, $b < x - \varepsilon$ and $I_\varepsilon(x) = (x - \varepsilon, x + \varepsilon)$ lies to the right of b on the number line. There is an integer N such that for all $n \ge N$, $x_n \in I_\varepsilon(x)$. For these x_n's, $b < x_n$; this is a contradiction to the hypothesis that all the x_n's were $\le b$. ∎

EXERCISES

12.1 Write out the nth term for the rest of the sequences in Example 12.1.

12.2 Explain why each of the following sets is not a subsequence of the last sequence in Example 12.2:

a) $\left\{\dfrac{1}{1}, \dfrac{3}{2}, \dfrac{1}{2}, \dfrac{1}{3}, \dfrac{1}{4}, \dfrac{1}{5}, \ldots\right\},$ b) $\left\{\dfrac{3}{1}, \dfrac{3}{2}, \dfrac{3}{3}\right\},$ c) $\left\{\dfrac{1}{1}, \dfrac{2}{1}, \dfrac{1}{2}, \dfrac{1}{3}, \dfrac{1}{4}, \dfrac{1}{5}, \ldots\right\}.$

12.3 Give a direct proof of inequalities (2) and (3) for real numbers.

12.4   Prove that $|xy| = |x| \cdot |y|$ for all x, y.

12.5   Prove that $|x + y + z| \le |x| + |y| + |z|$ for all numbers x, y, z.

12.6   Prove that if $\{x_n\}_{n=1}^{\infty}$ and $\{y_n\}_{n=1}^{\infty}$ are sequences with limits x and y, respectively, then the sequence $\{x_n - y_n\}_{n=1}^{\infty}$ converges to the limit $x - y$.

12.7   Suppose that $\{x_n\}_{n=1}^{\infty}$ is a sequence of real numbers that converges to x_0 and that all x_n and x_0 are nonzero.
 a) Prove that there is a positive number B such that $|x_n| \ge B$ for all n.
 b) Using *a*, prove that $\{1/x_n\}$ converges to $\{1/x_0\}$.

12.8   Let $\{x_n\}_{n=1}^{\infty}$ and $\{y_n\}_{n=1}^{\infty}$ be convergent sequences with limits x and y, respectively. Suppose that all the y_n's and y are nonzero. Show that the sequence $\{x_n/y_n\}_{n=1}^{\infty}$ converges to x/y.

12.9   A sequence is said to be **bounded** if there is a number B such that $|x_n| \le B$ for all n. Show that if $\{x_n\}_{n=1}^{\infty}$ converges to 0 and if $\{y_n\}_{n=1}^{\infty}$ is bounded, then the product sequence converges to 0.

12.10   Write out the proof of the last sentence in the statement of Theorem 12.4.

12.2 SEQUENCES IN $\mathbf{R}^m$

A sequence in $\mathbf{R}^m$ is just what we would expect it to be: an assignment of a *vector* in $\mathbf{R}^m$ to each natural number n: $\{x_1, x_2, x_3, \ldots\}$. For such sequences we need to keep track of two different indices: one for the m coordinates of each m-vector, and the other to indicate which element in the sequence is under consideration.

Before we can carefully define convergence, we need to make precise our notion of closeness in $\mathbf{R}^m$, as we did at the beginning of the previous section for sequences in $\mathbf{R}^1$. Recall from Chapter 10 that the distance between any two vectors $\mathbf{x}$ and $\mathbf{y}$ in $\mathbf{R}^m$ is the norm of their difference:

$$d(\mathbf{x}, \mathbf{y}) = \|\mathbf{x} - \mathbf{y}\| = \sqrt{(x_1 - y_1)^2 + \cdots + (x_m - y_m)^2}.$$

By this definition, the distance between two numbers is the length of the line segment between them, as indicated in Figure 12.2. The distance measure or

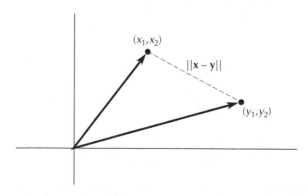

Figure 12.2   *The distance between two vectors in the plane.*

"metric" defined by the Euclidean norm of the difference is frequently referred to as the **Euclidean metric**.

The triangle inequality (Theorem 10.5) implies that for any three vectors $\mathbf{x}$, $\mathbf{y}$, and $\mathbf{z}$,

$$\|\mathbf{x} - \mathbf{z}\| = \|(\mathbf{x} - \mathbf{y}) + (\mathbf{y} - \mathbf{z})\|$$
$$\leq \|\mathbf{x} - \mathbf{y}\| + \|\mathbf{y} - \mathbf{z}\|,$$

or

$$d(\mathbf{x}, \mathbf{z}) \leq d(\mathbf{x}, \mathbf{y}) + d(\mathbf{y}, \mathbf{z}). \tag{4}$$

The generalization of the ε-interval $I_\varepsilon(r)$ about a point r on $\mathbf{R^1}$ is the ε-ball in $\mathbf{R^m}$.

Definition   Let $\mathbf{r}$ be a vector in $\mathbf{R^m}$ and let ε be a positive number. The ε-**ball about r** is

$$B_\varepsilon(\mathbf{r}) \equiv \{\mathbf{x} \in \mathbf{R^m} : \|\mathbf{x} - \mathbf{r}\| < \varepsilon\}.$$

Intuitively, a vector $\mathbf{x}$ in $\mathbf{R^m}$ is close to $\mathbf{r}$ if $\mathbf{x}$ is in some $B_\varepsilon(\mathbf{r})$ for a small but positive ε. The smaller ε is, the closer $\mathbf{x}$ is to $\mathbf{r}$.

Definition   A sequence of vectors $\{\mathbf{x}_1, \mathbf{x}_2, \mathbf{x}_3, \ldots\}$ is said to **converge** to the vector $\mathbf{x}$ if for any choice of a positive real number ε, there is an integer N such that, for all $n \geq N$, $\mathbf{x}_n \in B_\varepsilon(\mathbf{x})$; that is,

$$d(\mathbf{x}_n, \mathbf{x}) = \|\mathbf{x}_n - \mathbf{x}\| < \varepsilon.$$

The vector $\mathbf{x}$ is called the **limit** of the sequence.

In other words, a sequence of vectors $\{\mathbf{x}_n\}_{n=1}^\infty$ converges to a limit vector $\mathbf{x}$ if and only if the sequence of distances from the vector $\mathbf{x}_n$ to $\mathbf{x}$, $\{\|\mathbf{x}_n - \mathbf{x}\|\}_{n=1}^\infty$, converges to 0 in $\mathbf{R^1}$.

Example 12.3   Because of the extra dimensions to move around in, a convergent sequence can move in all kinds of spirals in $\mathbf{R^m}$ as it converges to its limit. For example, let $\{a_n\}$ be the sequence of $+1$s and -1s which changes sign *every other term*:

$$\{a_n\}_{n=1}^\infty = \{1, 1, -1, -1, 1, 1, -1, -1, 1, 1, -1, -1, 1, \ldots\}.$$

Now, construct the sequence $\{\mathbf{x}_n\}_{n=1}^\infty$ in which $\mathbf{x}_n = \left(\dfrac{a_n}{n}, \dfrac{a_{n+1}}{(n+1)}\right)$:

$$\left\{\left(1, \frac{1}{2}\right), \left(\frac{1}{2}, -\frac{1}{3}\right), \left(-\frac{1}{3}, -\frac{1}{4}\right), \left(-\frac{1}{4}, \frac{1}{5}\right), \left(\frac{1}{5}, \frac{1}{6}\right), \ldots\right\}. \tag{5}$$

Note that the $\mathbf{x}_n$'s move clockwise in $\mathbf{R^2}$ from quadrant to quadrant, as they converge to the origin, as illustrated in Figure 12.3.

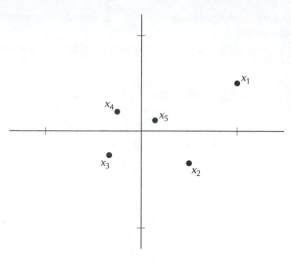

**Figure
12.3**

The convergent sequence (5) in $\mathbf{R}^2$.

However, if the sequence $\{\mathbf{x}_n\}$ is converging to $\mathbf{x}$, then each component of the $\mathbf{x}_n$'s must be converging to the corresponding component of the limit vector $\mathbf{x}$, and conversely. This equivalence between the convergence of a sequence of vectors and the convergence of each of its components reduces the problem of verifying the convergence of a sequence of vectors in $\mathbf{R}^m$ to the problem of verifying the convergence of m sequences in $\mathbf{R}^1$.

Theorem 12.5   A sequence of vectors in $\mathbf{R}^m$ converges if and only if all m sequences of its components converge in $\mathbf{R}^1$.

Proof   (If) Let $\{\mathbf{x}_n\}_{n=1}^{\infty}$ be a sequence of vectors in $\mathbf{R}^m$. Write $\mathbf{x}_n = (x_{1n}, \ldots, x_{mn})$. Suppose each of the m sequences of numbers $\{x_{in}\}_{n=1}^{\infty}$, $i = 1, \ldots, m$, converges to a limit x_i^*. Let $\mathbf{x}^* = (x_1^*, \ldots, x_m^*)$. Choose and fix a small positive number ε. For each i between 1 and m, there exists an integer N_i such that, if $n \geq N_i$, then $|x_{in} - x_i^*| < \varepsilon/\sqrt{m}$. Let $N = \max\{N_1, \ldots, N_m\}$. Suppose $n \geq N$. Then,

$$\|\mathbf{x}_n - \mathbf{x}^*\| = \sqrt{(x_{1n} - x_1^*)^2 + \cdots + (x_{mn} - x_m^*)^2}$$

$$< \sqrt{\frac{\varepsilon^2}{m} + \cdots + \frac{\varepsilon^2}{m}}$$

$$= \varepsilon.$$

Thus, $\{\mathbf{x}_n\}_{n=1}^{\infty}$ converges to $\mathbf{x}^*$.

(Only if) To prove the converse, suppose $\{\mathbf{x}_n\}_{n=1}^{\infty}$ converges to $\mathbf{x}^*$. Choose $\varepsilon > 0$, as usual. Then, there exists an integer N such that for all $n \geq N$,

$\|\mathbf{x}_n - \mathbf{x}^*\| < \varepsilon$. But then for $n \geq N$ and for each component i,

$$|x_{in} - x_i^*| \leq \sqrt{(x_{1n} - x_1^*)^2 + \cdots + (x_{mn} - x_m^*)^2}$$

$$= \|\mathbf{x}_n - \mathbf{x}^*\| < \varepsilon. \quad \blacksquare$$

Theorem 12.5 enables us to apply the results about sequences in $\mathbf{R}^1$ to sequences in $\mathbf{R}^m$. For example, the next theorem is the generalization of Theorems 12.2 and 12.3 in that it states that all the vector operations we have defined in previous chapters are preserved under limits.

Theorem 12.6 Let $\{\mathbf{x}_n\}_{n=1}^\infty$ and $\{\mathbf{y}_n\}_{n=1}^\infty$ be convergent sequences of vectors in $\mathbf{R}^m$ with limits $\mathbf{x}$ and $\mathbf{y}$, respectively; and let $\{c_n\}_{n=1}^\infty$ be a convergent sequence of real numbers with limit c. Then the sequence $\{c_n \mathbf{x}_n + \mathbf{y}_n\}_{n=1}^\infty$ converges to limit $c\mathbf{x} + \mathbf{y}$.

Proof As usual, begin by choosing a positive number ε. Note that

$$\|(c_n \mathbf{x}_n + \mathbf{y}_n) - (c\mathbf{x} + \mathbf{y})\| \leq \|c_n \mathbf{x}_n - c\mathbf{x}\| + \|\mathbf{y}_n - \mathbf{y}\|. \tag{6}$$

Since the sequence of $\mathbf{y}_n$'s converges to $\mathbf{y}$, we know there exists an integer N_1 such that for all $n \geq N_1$, $\|\mathbf{y}_n - \mathbf{y}\| < \varepsilon/2$. On the other hand, for each component i, the sequence $\{c_n x_{in}\}$ converges to cx_i by Theorem 12.3. By Theorem 12.5 this implies that the sequence $\{c_n \mathbf{x}_n\}_{n=1}^\infty$ converges to $c\mathbf{x}$. Thus there exists an N_2 such that for all $n \geq N_2$, $\|c_n \mathbf{x}_n - c\mathbf{x}\| < \varepsilon/2$. It follows that for all $n \geq N = \max\{N_1, N_2\}$, $\|c_n \mathbf{x}_n - c\mathbf{x}\| + \|\mathbf{y}_n - \mathbf{y}\| < \varepsilon$ and therefore by (6)

$$\|(c_n \mathbf{x}_n + \mathbf{y}_n) - (c\mathbf{x} + \mathbf{y})\| < \varepsilon. \quad \blacksquare$$

A similar argument can be used to show that the sequence of inner products of two convergent sequences of vectors converges to the inner product of the limits. This is left as an exercise.

The definitions of accumulation point and subsequence extend naturally into $\mathbf{R}^m$.

Definition The vector $\mathbf{x}$ is an **accumulation point** of the sequence $\{\mathbf{x}_n\}_{n=1}^\infty$ if for any given $\varepsilon > 0$ there are infinitely many integers n such that $\|\mathbf{x}_n - \mathbf{x}\| < \varepsilon$.

A point that is a limit also satisfies the definition of an accumulation point — an infinite number of terms in the sequence are within any given distance of the limit point. But the definition of limit requires something more. *All* terms sufficiently far out in a convergent sequence are required to be within a given distance of the limit, not just an infinite number of them. As we saw in $\mathbf{R}^1$, a consequence of this distinction is that although a sequence can have several accumulation points, a convergent sequence can have only one limit. The uniqueness of limits in $\mathbf{R}^m$ follows directly from Theorems 12.1 and 12.5.

Definition A sequence $\{\mathbf{y}_j\}_{j=1}^{\infty}$ of vectors in $\mathbf{R}^m$ is a **subsequence** of sequence $\{\mathbf{x}_i\}_{i=1}^{\infty}$ in $\mathbf{R}^m$ if there exists an *infinite* increasing set of natural numbers $\{n_j\}$ with

$$n_1 < n_2 < n_3 < n_4 < \cdots,$$

such that $\mathbf{y}_1 = \mathbf{x}_{n_1}, \mathbf{y}_2 = \mathbf{x}_{n_2}, \mathbf{y}_3 = \mathbf{x}_{n_3}$, and so on.

If a sequence has an accumulation point, it may nonetheless have no limit, as sequences c and d in Example 12.1 illustrate. However, each sequence with an accumulation point has a subsequence that converges to one of its accumulation points. For example, in sequence c the even-numbered terms form a convergent subsequence with limit 0. In sequence d, the even-numbered terms are a convergent subsequence with limit -1 while the odd-numbered terms are a convergent subsequence with limit 1.

EXERCISES

12.11 Show that if $\{\mathbf{x}_n\}_{n=1}^{\infty}$ and $\{\mathbf{y}_n\}_{n=1}^{\infty}$ are two sequences of vectors in $\mathbf{R}^k$ convergent to $\mathbf{x}$ and $\mathbf{y}$, respectively, then $\{\mathbf{x}_n \cdot \mathbf{y}_n\}_{n=1}^{\infty}$ converges to $\mathbf{x} \cdot \mathbf{y}$.

12.12 Show that a *convergent* sequence in $\mathbf{R}^m$ can have only one accumulation point, and therefore only one limit.

12.3 OPEN SETS

Our discussion of sequences leads naturally to the study of open and closed sets in $\mathbf{R}^m$. The definition of a closed set directly requires the concept of a convergent sequence. The definition of an open set requires the use of ε-balls. Although these two definitions seem unrelated, we will see that the concepts are truly complementary.

We start with open sets since they are the most basic topological construction. For a vector $\mathbf{z}$ in $\mathbf{R}^m$ and a positive number ε, the ε-ball about $\mathbf{z}$ is $B_\varepsilon(\mathbf{z}) = \{\mathbf{x} \in \mathbf{R}^m : \|\mathbf{x} - \mathbf{z}\| < \varepsilon\}$. Sometimes $B_\varepsilon(\mathbf{z})$ is called the open ε-ball to distinguish it from the closed ball $\{\mathbf{x} \in \mathbf{R}^m : \|\mathbf{x} - \mathbf{z}\| \le \varepsilon\}$, which includes the boundary. Open balls are important examples of a more general class of sets called open sets.

Definition A set S in $\mathbf{R}^m$ is **open** if for each $\mathbf{x} \in S$, there exists an open ε-ball around $\mathbf{x}$ completely contained in S:

$$\mathbf{x} \in S \quad \Longrightarrow \quad \text{there is an } \varepsilon > 0 \text{ such that } B_\varepsilon(\mathbf{x}) \subset S.$$

An open set S containing the point $\mathbf{x}$ is called an **open neighborhood** of $\mathbf{x}$.

The word "open" has a connotation of "no boundary": from any point one can always move a little distance in *any* direction and still be in the set. The definition of an open set makes this idea precise: each element in an open set contains a whole ball around it that lies in the set. Consequently, open sets cannot contain their "boundary points."

Example 12.4 The interval

$$(0, 1) \equiv \{x \in \mathbf{R} : 0 < x < 1\}$$

is an open set. If b is a point in $(0, 1)$, then $b \neq 0$ or 1. The number $b/2$ is closer to 0 than b is and is still in $(0, 1)$, while the number $b + (1 - b)/2$ is closer to 1 than b is and is still in $(0, 1)$. If $\varepsilon = \min\{b/2, (1 - b)/2\}$, the interval $(b - \varepsilon, b + \varepsilon)$ is an open interval about b in $(0, 1)$. (Check.)

The definition of an open set also implies that such sets are "thick" or "full-dimensional," since an open set in $\mathbf{R}^m$ contains an m-dimensional ball around each of its points. Consequently, a line in $\mathbf{R}^2$ is not an open set. As indicated in Figure 12.4, because a line is a one-dimensional subset of $\mathbf{R}^2$, the ball around any point on the line contains points which are not on the line. Similarly, a line or plane in $\mathbf{R}^3$ cannot be open and one-point sets are never open.

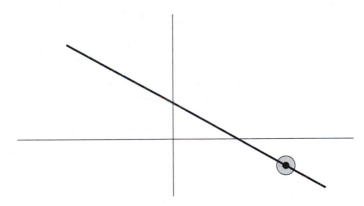

A ball about any point on a line in $\mathbf{R}^2$ contains points not on the line.

Figure 12.4

It should be intuitively clear that open ε-balls are open sets. The next theorem and Figure 12.5 make this idea precise.

Theorem 12.7 Open balls are open sets.

Proof Let B be the open ball $B_\varepsilon(\mathbf{x})$ about $\mathbf{x}$, and let $\mathbf{y}$ be an arbitrary point in B. We want to show that there is some ball about $\mathbf{y}$ that lies completely in B. Let $\delta \equiv \|\mathbf{x} - \mathbf{y}\| < \varepsilon$. We will show that the open ball V of radius $\varepsilon - \delta$ around $\mathbf{y}$ is contained in B, as suggested by Figure 12.5. Let $\mathbf{z}$ be an arbitrary point in V.

Then, by the triangle inequality,

$$\|z - x\| \le \|z - y\| + \|y - x\| < (\varepsilon - \delta) + \delta = \varepsilon.$$

Thus, $V \subset B$. ■

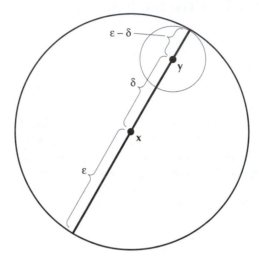

**Figure
12.5**

If $y \in B_\varepsilon(x)$ *and* $\delta = \|x - y\|$, *then* $B_{\varepsilon-\delta}(y) \subset B_\varepsilon(x)$.

The next theorem describes the behavior of open sets under the set operations of union and intersection and allows us to construct interesting examples of open sets.

Theorem 12.8

(*a*) Any union of open sets is open.
(*b*) The *finite* intersection of open sets is open.

Proof   *a*): Let S be any union of open sets S_i, and let $x \in S$. The point x is in S by virtue of its being a member of some set S_j. Since S_j is open, there is an open ball B around x contained in S_j. Then B is contained in the union S of the S_i.
b): Let $S_1, \ldots, S_n$ be open sets, and let $S = \cap_{i=1}^n S_i$. If x is in S, then x is in each S_i. Since each S_i is open, for each i there is an ε_i such that $B_{\varepsilon_i}(x) \subset S_i$. Let $\varepsilon = \min \varepsilon_i$. The ball $B_\varepsilon(x)$ is contained in each $B_{\varepsilon_i}(x)$, and therefore is contained in each S_i. Thus, it is contained in the intersection S of the S_i's. ■

Note that any union of open sets is open; however, the intersection of an *infinite* number of open sets need not be open. For example, consider the open intervals $S_n = (-1/n, +1/n)$ in $\mathbf{R}^1$. The set S_n is the interval of radius $1/n$ around 0. It is easy to see that $\cap_{n=1}^{\infty} S_n$ is just the point $\{0\}$; if y is any point different from 0, $y \notin S_n$ for all $n > 1/y$, and so $y \notin S$. But $\{0\}$ is not an open set.

Interior of a Set

The fact that arbitrary unions of open sets are open allows us to construct a set-theoretic operation on all sets, which produces open sets.

Definition Suppose that S is a subset of $\mathbf{R}^n$. Let int S denote the union of all open sets contained in S. The open set int S is called the **interior** of S.

By its definition, the interior of a set can be considered as the largest open set which is contained in the given set. For example, the interior of the closed ε-ball about $\mathbf{x}$ is the open ε-ball about $\mathbf{x}$. The interior of the half-open interval $[\mathbf{a}, \mathbf{b})$ is the open interval $(\mathbf{a}, \mathbf{b})$. The interior of a line in the plane is the empty set, since no subset of the line in $\mathbf{R}^2$ is open in $\mathbf{R}^2$. As Exercise 12.16 below shows, the interior of an open set S is the set S itself.

EXERCISES

12.13 Use Theorem 12.8 to draw some open sets in the plane which are not balls.

12.14 Prove that the positive orthant

$$\mathbf{R}_+^m = \{(x_1, \ldots, x_m) : x_i > 0 \text{ for } i = 1, \ldots, m\}$$

is an open subset of $\mathbf{R}^m$ by finding a formula for ε in terms of the x_i's.

12.15 Show that open balls on the real line are exactly the open intervals: sets of the form $(\mathbf{a}, \mathbf{b}) = \{\mathbf{x} : \mathbf{a} < \mathbf{x} < \mathbf{b}\}$, defined for two given numbers $\mathbf{a}$ and $\mathbf{b}$.

12.16 Show that any open set is the union of open balls. Conclude that any open set is its own interior.

12.17 Show that if $\mathbf{x} \in$ int S and $\{\mathbf{x}_n\}_{n=1}^{\infty}$ is a sequence converging to $\mathbf{x}$, then $\mathbf{x}_n \in S$ for all sufficiently large n. This statement about sequences is sometimes used as the definition of an open set or of the interior of a set.

12.4 CLOSED SETS

The concept of a closed set also plays a fundamental role in the geometry and analysis of Euclidean spaces.

Definition A set S in $\mathbf{R}^m$ is **closed** if, whenever $\{\mathbf{x}_n\}_{n=1}^{\infty}$ is a *convergent* sequence completely contained in S, its limit is also contained in S.

The definition of a closed set states that if $\mathbf{x}$ is a given point and if there are points in a closed set F which are arbitrarily close to $\mathbf{x}$, then $\mathbf{x}$ must be in F too.

Consequently, a closed set must contain all its "boundary points," just the opposite of the situation with open sets. In fact, closedness and openness are complementary properties in that the complement of an open set is closed and the complement of a closed set is open. Recall that the **complement** of a set S is the set of all points that are not in S.

Theorem 12.9   A set S in $\mathbf{R}^m$ is closed if and only if its complement, $S^c = \mathbf{R}^m - S$, is open.

Proof   (Only if) Let S be closed. We need to show that its complement, T is open. In other words, we need to show that for any $\mathbf{x} \in T$, there is an $\varepsilon > 0$ such that $B_\varepsilon(\mathbf{x}) \subset T$. Choose $\mathbf{x} \in T$ and suppose that this is not the case, that is, that no $B_\varepsilon(\mathbf{x})$ lies completely in T. Then for all $\varepsilon > 0$, $B_\varepsilon(\mathbf{x}) \cap S \neq \varnothing$. In particular, for each positive integer n, there is an element $\mathbf{x}_n$ of S in $B_{1/n}(\mathbf{x})$. The sequence $\{\mathbf{x}_n\}_{n=1}^\infty$ lies in S and converges to $\mathbf{x}$ since $\|\mathbf{x}_n - \mathbf{x}\| < 1/n$. Since S is closed, $\mathbf{x}$ is in S — a contradiction to our choice of $\mathbf{x}$ in T.

   (If) Let S be the complement of an open set T. Let $\{\mathbf{x}_n\}_{n=1}^\infty$ be a convergent sequence in S with limit $\mathbf{x}$. To show that S is closed, we need to show that $\mathbf{x} \in S$. Suppose not. Then $\mathbf{x} \in T$. Since T is open, there exists an open neighborhood $B_\varepsilon(\mathbf{x})$ of $\mathbf{x}$ contained in T. Since the sequence converges to $\mathbf{x}$, for n large enough, $\mathbf{x}_n \in B_\varepsilon(\mathbf{x})$, so $\mathbf{x}_n \in T$ — again a contradiction, since the $\mathbf{x}_n$'s are in S, the complement of T. ∎

   Using Theorem 12.9 together with Theorem 12.8, we obtain the next theorem simply by set-theoretic complementation, since

$$\text{complement of } \cup S_i = \cap\{\text{complement of } S_i\}.$$

The proof is left as an exercise.

Theorem 12.10

   (*a*) Any intersection of closed sets is closed.
   (*b*) The finite union of closed sets is closed.

   Just as arbitrary intersections of open sets need not be open, so too arbitrary unions of closed sets need not be closed. For example, consider the closed sets $S_n = [-n/(n+1), n/(n+1)]$ for $n \geq 1$. The reader should check that $\cup_{n\geq 1} S_n = (-1, 1)$, is an open interval.

Closure of a Set

Complementing the operation that produces the interior of a set is the closure-operation.

Definition   Suppose that S is a subset of $\mathbf{R}^m$. Let $\mathrm{cl}\, S$ (or sometimes $\bar{S}$) denote the intersection of all closed sets containing S. The closed set $\mathrm{cl}\, S$ is called the **closure** of S.

By its definition, the closure of S is the smallest closed set which contains S. The following theorem is a sequential characterization of the closure of a set.

> **Theorem 12.11**   Let S be a set in $\mathbf{R}^1$. Then $\mathbf{x}$ is in cl S if and only if there is a sequence of points in S converging to $\mathbf{x}$.

Proof (If) Let $\{\mathbf{x}_n\}_{n=1}^{\infty}$ be a convergent sequence of points in a set S, with limit $\mathbf{x}$. Then $\{\mathbf{x}_n\}_{n=1}^{\infty} \subset T$ for any closed set $T \supset S$; so $\mathbf{x} \in T$. Since this is true for any closed subset T containing S, $\mathbf{x} \in$ cl S.

(Only If) Suppose $\mathbf{x} \in$ cl S. Then we claim that for all $\varepsilon > 0, B_\varepsilon(\mathbf{x}) \cap S \neq \varnothing$, because if for some $\varepsilon > 0$, $B_\varepsilon(\mathbf{x}) \cap S = \varnothing$, then the complement of $B_\varepsilon(\mathbf{x})$ is a closed set containing S and not containing $\mathbf{x}$ — a contradiction to $\mathbf{x} \in$ cl S. Now construct a sequence $\{\mathbf{x}_n\}_{n=1}^{\infty}$ by choosing $\mathbf{x}_n \in B_{1/n}(\mathbf{x}) \cap S$. This is a sequence in S with limit $\mathbf{x}$. ∎

Boundary of a Set

At this point, we can make precise the notion of the boundary of a set, a concept which guided our intuition in our discussion of open and closed sets. Roughly speaking, a point $\mathbf{x}$ is on the boundary of a set S if there are points inside S arbitrarily close to $\mathbf{x}$ and points outside S arbitrarily close to $\mathbf{x}$.

Definition   A point $\mathbf{x}$ is in the **boundary** of a set S if every open ball about $\mathbf{x}$ contains both points in S and points in the complement of S.

The following theorem follows essentially for the definition of a boundary point.

> **Theorem 12.12**   The set of boundary points of a set S equals cl $S \cap$ cl S^c.

There are plenty of sets which are neither open nor closed; for example, the half-open interval $(a, b]$ in $\mathbf{R}^1$, the sequence $\{1/n : n = 1, 2, \ldots\}$ without its limit 0 in $\mathbf{R}^1$, and a line minus a point in the plane. There are only two sets which are both open and closed in $\mathbf{R}^m$: $\mathbf{R}^m$ itself and, by default, the empty set. See Exercises 12.27 and 12.28.

EXERCISES

12.18   Show that *closed intervals* in $\mathbf{R}^1$ — sets of the form $\{x : \mathbf{a} \leq x \leq \mathbf{b}\}$ for fixed numbers $\mathbf{a}$ and $\mathbf{b}$ — are closed sets.

12.19   Show that *closed balls* in $\mathbf{R}^n$ — sets of the form $\{\mathbf{x} : \|\mathbf{x} - \mathbf{z}\| \leq \varepsilon\}$ for fixed $\mathbf{z}$ and ε — are closed sets.

12.20   Prove that any finite set is a closed set. Prove that the set of integers is a closed set.

12.21   For each of the following subsets of the plane, draw the set, state whether it is open, closed, or neither, and justify your answer in a word or two:

a) $\{(x, y) : -1 < x < +1, y = 0\}$,   *b)* $\{(x, y) : x \text{ and } y \text{ are integers}\}$,

c) $\{(x, y) : x + y = 1\}$,   *d)* $\{(x, y) : x + y < 1\}$,

e) $\{(x, y) : x = 0 \text{ or } y = 0\}$.

12.22 Prove Theorem 12.10 using what you know about complements of sets. Also prove the theorem directly from the definition of a closed set.

12.23 Suppose that S is a subset of $\mathbf{R}^n$ with complement T. Show that cl S is the complement of int T.

12.24 We generalize the definition of an accumulation point of a sequence to arbitrary sets by defining $\mathbf{x}$ to be an **accumulation point** of a set S if every ball about $\mathbf{x}$ contains points of S other than $\mathbf{x}$. Note that $\mathbf{x}$ need not lie in S. If S is closed, show that it contains all its accumulation points. For general S, prove that cl S is the union of S and its accumulation points.

12.25 Show that the three examples in the last paragraph are neither open nor closed.

12.26 Prove Theorem 12.12.

12.27 Show that $\mathbf{R}^m$ and the empty set satisfy the definitions of an open set and of a closed set in $\mathbf{R}^m$.

12.28 Prove that no nonempty, proper subset of $\mathbf{R}^m$ can be both open and closed. [Hint: Suppose that such a set S exists. First find a line segment ℓ in $\mathbf{R}^m$ with one end at a point $\mathbf{a}$ in S and the other end at a point $\mathbf{b}$ not in S. Find the point $\mathbf{c}$ on ℓ with the properties that all the points on ℓ between $\mathbf{a}$ and $\mathbf{c}$ are in the open set S and $\mathbf{c}$ is the furthest point on ℓ from $\mathbf{a}$ with this property. Since S is closed and open, $\mathbf{c} \in S$ and all points close enough to $\mathbf{c}$ on ℓ are in S — a contradiction to the choice of $\mathbf{c}$.]

12.5   COMPACT SETS

The next most important sets after open sets and closed sets are the compact sets, basically because they have many of the desirable properties that finite sets have. Economic theory, especially microeconomics, is concerned with the consequences of optimization — the search for a point in some set at which a given function takes on the maximum or minimum value it can achieve on the set. Compact sets play an important role in questions about the *existence* of optima. We saw in Chapter 3 that a continuous function defined on an open interval (a, b) or on an infinite interval $(-\infty, +\infty)$ need not achieve a maximum value on that interval; take for example, the linear function $f(x) = 2x$. However, on any *bounded closed* interval $[a, b]$, a continuous function does achieve its maximum, possibly at one of the endpoints. Compact sets are the appropriate generalizations of bounded closed intervals to higher dimensions. We will prove in Chapter 30 that a continuous function defined on a compact set always achieves its maximum value on that set.

Recall that a set S in $\mathbf{R}^n$ is **bounded** if there exists a number B such that $\|\mathbf{x}\| \leq B$ for all $\mathbf{x} \in S$, that is, if S is contained in some ball in $\mathbf{R}^n$. Examples of bounded sets include any interval or finite union of intervals in $\mathbf{R}^1$ except for those which have $+\infty$ or $-\infty$ as an endpoint. Any disk in the plane with finite radius is bounded. Examples of sets which are not bounded include the integers in $\mathbf{R}^1$, any hyperplane, or any ray.

Definition A set S in $\mathbf{R}^n$ is **compact** if and only if it is both closed and bounded.

Thus, any closed interval in $\mathbf{R}^1$ with finite endpoints is compact, but open intervals are not compact. Any closed disk of finite radius in the plane is compact, but other disks are not.

An important feature of compact sets is that *any* sequence defined on a compact set must contain a subsequence that actually converges, a result known as the **Bolzano-Weierstrass Theorem**. This feature of compact sets will be used a dozen times in this book. In this section we prove this result for the compact interval $[0, 1]$ on $\mathbf{R}^1$ and sketch the general proof. Chapter 29 presents a careful proof for a general compact set in $\mathbf{R}^n$.

Theorem 12.13 Any sequence contained in the closed and bounded interval $[0, 1]$ has a convergent subsequence.

Proof Let $\{x_n\}_{n=1}^{\infty}$ be an arbitrary sequence in $[0, 1]$. One of the two subintervals $[0, 1/2]$ or $[1/2, 1]$ of $[0, 1]$ must contain an (*infinite*) subsequence of $\{x_n\}_{n=1}^{\infty}$, since the union of two finite sets is a finite set. Say, for simplicity of argument, that $[0, 1/2]$ contains an infinite subsequence and let $y_1 = x_{n_1}$ be an entry of that subsequence. Now, divide $[0, 1/2]$ into two subintervals $[0, 1/4]$ and $[1/4, 1/2]$. One of these two contains an infinite subsequence of $\{x_n\}_{n=1}^{\infty}$, say $[1/4, 1/2]$. Let $y_2 = x_{n_2}$ be an element of such a subsequence with $n_2 > n_1$. Now, divide this subinterval $[1/4, 1/2]$ into two compact subintervals $[1/4, 3/8]$ and $[3/8, 1/2]$. One of these two intervals contains an infinite subsequence of $\{x_n\}_{n=1}^{\infty}$. Let $y_3 = x_{n_3}$ be an element of such a subsequence, with $n_3 > n_2$. Keep dividing into smaller and smaller subintervals and choosing a subinterval that contains an (*infinite*) subsequence of the original sequence $\{x_n\}_{n=1}^{\infty}$ and an element of the sequence in that subinterval further down the sequence than previously chosen elements. Finally, one proves that the sequence of y_j's so constructed is a convergent subsequence of $\{x_n\}_{n=1}^{\infty}$. ∎

This same argument works for any compact interval $[a, b]$ in $\mathbf{R}^1$ and, in fact, for any rectangle $[a_1, b_1] \times [a_2, b_2]$ in $\mathbf{R}^2$ and any generalized box

$$B \equiv \{(x_1, \ldots, x_n) \in \mathbf{R}^n : a_1 \le x_1 \le b_1, \ldots, a_n \le x_n \le b_n\}$$

in $\mathbf{R}^n$. Find a collapsing sequence of boxes $B_1 \supset B_2 \supset B_3 \supset \cdots$, each of which contains an infinite subsequence of $\{x_n\}_{n=1}^{\infty}$. Choose a subsequence $\{y_n\}_{n=1}^{\infty}$ such that $y_k = x_{n_k}$ for some k and $n_1 < n_2 < n_3 < \cdots$. For a general compact subset C of $\mathbf{R}^n$, we can find a generalized box B that contains C, since C is bounded. Then, perform the above bisection argument in $C \cap B$. The bottom line is the *Bolzano-Weierstrass Theorem*, whose complete proof is presented in Chapter 29.

Theorem 12.14 Let C be a compact subset in $\mathbf{R}^n$ and let $\{x_n\}_{n=1}^{\infty}$ be any sequence in C. Then, $\{x_n\}_{n=1}^{\infty}$ has a *convergent* subsequence whose limit lies in C.

EXERCISES

12.29 Prove that a closed subset of a compact set is compact.

12.30 Prove that every finite set is compact.

12.31 Which of the five sets in Exercise 12.21 are compact sets?

12.32 Prove that the intersection of compact sets is compact and that the finite union of compact sets is compact. Show that the infinite union of compact sets need not be compact.

12.6 EPILOGUE

This chapter has covered the basic notions of limits and of open and closed sets needed for a careful exposition of multivariable calculus. The discussion in this chapter is continued in Chapter 29, where more advanced topics are discussed. Time permitting, Chapter 29 can be read at this point while these ideas are still fresh. The first section of Chapter 29 continues our description of the important properties of sequences. So far, the only way we can tell whether or not a sequence converges is to actually identify a limit for it; but we sometimes want to prove that abstract sequences with certain special properties converge to a limit without specifying any concrete limit. Section 29.1 introduces the concept of a **Cauchy convergence**, which allows us to capture the concept of convergence without actually finding a limit. Section 29.2 continues our discussion of compact sets, including a careful proof of the Bolzano-Weierstrass Theorem. The rest of Chapter 29 deals with connected sets and with different norms on $\mathbf{R}^n$.

C H A P T E R 1 3

Functions of Several Variables

Production functions, cost functions, profit functions, utility functions, demand functions — functions permeate economic analysis. These functions are the mathematical representations of the relationships among a collection of economic variables. This chapter begins the study of *nonlinear* functions of several variables. It develops some vocabulary for working with multivariable functions and indicates how to visualize these underlying relationships geometrically, at least, when there are only three or four variables involved.

13.1 FUNCTIONS BETWEEN EUCLIDEAN SPACES

Definition   A **function** from a set A to a set B is a rule that assigns to each object in A, one and only one object in B. In this case, we write $f\colon A \to B$.

As we discussed in Chapter 2 for functions defined on $\mathbf{R}^1$, if $f\colon A \to B$, the set A of elements on which f is defined is called the **domain** of the function f; the set B in which f takes its values is called the **target** or **target space** of f. We write $f(\mathbf{x})$ for the element of B which f assigns to the element $\mathbf{x}$ of A. In this case, we say that $\mathbf{y} = f(\mathbf{x})$ is the **image** of $\mathbf{x}$ under f. The set of all $f(\mathbf{x})$'s for $\mathbf{x}$ in the domain of f, that is, the set of all those elements in B that are images under f of elements in the domain A, is called the **image** of f.

Example 13.1   Consider the function $f\colon \mathbf{R}^2 \to \mathbf{R}^1$ defined by $f(x, y) = x^2 + y^2$. The domain of f is all of $\mathbf{R}^2$, the target space of f is $\mathbf{R}^1$, and the image of f is the set of all nonnegative real numbers.

Example 13.2   The domain of the function $g(x) = 1/x$ is $\mathbf{R}^1 - \{0\}$, all real numbers except 0. Its image is $\mathbf{R}^1 - \{0\}$, too.

Remark   If $\mathbf{x}$ is a point in the domain of a function f, then $f(\mathbf{x})$ is a point in the target space. It is inappropriate to write "$f(\mathbf{x})$" to denote the *function* itself. To denote a specific function f, one should write just the symbol f, or use the mapping notation $\mathbf{x} \longmapsto f(\mathbf{x})$.

273

Functions from $\mathbf{R}^n$ to $\mathbf{R}$

In elementary calculus and economics, one deals almost exclusively with functions of a single variable, as we did in Chapters 2 to 5. However, most real-world phenomena involve more than one parameter. For example, in elementary microeconomics courses, one uses demand functions $q = f(p)$ in which the quantity demanded is simply a function of its own price. A more realistic approach also considers the dependence of quantity demanded on the prices of other goods in the market and on income y: $q = f(p_1, p_2, y)$. A concrete example is the constant elasticity demand function

$$q_1 = f(p_1, p_2, y) = k_1 p_1^{a_{11}} p_2^{a_{12}} y^{b_1}, \tag{1}$$

where a_{11}, a_{12}, and b_1 are elasticities.

As another simple example, the amount of money (z) currently in a savings account depends on how much was originally invested (A), what the annual interest rate (r) is, how many times (n) a year interest is compounded, and how many years (t) since the original deposit. As we noted in Chapter 5, the functional relationship between these variables is

$$z = A\left(1 + \frac{r}{n}\right)^{nt}.$$

We would like to understand how changes in any of these variables affect the amount currently on deposit.

Two multivariable functions which play a central role in economic theory are production functions and utility functions. Consider a firm which uses n inputs to produce a single output. For $i = 1, \ldots, n$, let x_i denote the amount of input i. The vector $(x_1, \ldots, x_n)$ is called an **input bundle**. The firm's **production function** assigns to each input bundle $(x_1, \ldots, x_n)$ the maximal output $y = f(x_1, \ldots, x_n)$ that it can achieve from that input bundle. If we allow only one input to vary and fix the amounts of the other $(n - 1)$ inputs, say at $x_2^*, \ldots, x_n^*$, then the production function becomes a single-variable function

$$x_1 \longmapsto f(x_1, x_2^*, \ldots, x_n^*).$$

This sometimes occurs in the study of the firm's **short-run** decisions. In general, we will want to know the effect of changes in the amounts of more than one input. If we are allowed to vary the amounts of all n inputs, then we are studying the firm's **long-run** decision process.

The production function is the cornerstone of the theory of the firm. Among the explicit production functions which applied economists regularly use are the following:

$$q = a_1 x_1 + a_2 x_2 \qquad\qquad \text{linear,}$$

$$q = k x_1^{b_1} x_2^{b_2} \qquad\qquad \text{Cobb-Douglas,}$$

$$q = \min\left\{\frac{x_1}{c_1}, \frac{x_2}{c_2}\right\} \qquad\qquad \text{input-output,}$$

$$q = k(c_1 x_1^{-a} + c_2 x_2^{-a})^{-b/a} \qquad \text{constant elasticity of substitution.}$$

The generalization of these production functions to more than two inputs is straightforward.

In studying the behavior of individual consumers in an economy with k commodities, let x_i denote the amount of commodity i. As indicated in Chapter 1, the vector $(x_1, \ldots, x_k)$ which designates an amount for each of the k commodities is called a **commodity bundle**. A **utility function** is a function which assigns a number $u(x_1, \ldots, x_k)$ to each commodity bundle — a number which measures the consumer's degree of satisfaction or utility with the given commodity bundle. In this context, an economist is interested in which trades of commodity bundles will increase the consumer's utility. Applied microeconomists often use the same functional forms for utility functions that are on the above list of production functions.

Functions from $\mathbf{R}^k$ to $\mathbf{R}^m$

Most real-world firms produce more than one product. To model their production, we need a production function for each product. For example, if the firm uses three inputs to produce two outputs, we need two separate production functions $q_1 = f_1(x_1, x_2, x_3)$ and $q_2 = f_2(x_1, x_2, x_3)$. In this case, we can write $\mathbf{q} = (q_1, q_2)$ as an **output bundle** for this firm and summarize the firm's activities by a function $F = (f_1, f_2)$ whose domain lies in $\mathbf{R}^3$ and whose target space is $\mathbf{R}^2$:

$$\mathbf{q} = (q_1, q_1) = (f_1(x_1, x_2, x_3), f_2(x_1, x_2, x_3)) \equiv F(x_1, x_2, x_3).$$

We write $F: \mathbf{R}^3 \rightarrow \mathbf{R}^2$. A firm which uses k inputs to produce m products would have a production function $F: \mathbf{R}^k \rightarrow \mathbf{R}^m$.

Similarly, in an economy with m consumers and k commodities, each consumer has a utility function, say $u^i(x_1, \ldots, x_k)$ for the ith consumer. A consumption bundle for the whole economy would be a choice of a commodity vector for each of the m consumers:

$$\mathbf{x} = (x_1^1, \ldots, x_k^1; x_1^2, \ldots, x_k^2; \ldots; x_1^m, \ldots, x_k^m) \in \mathbf{R}^{km}.$$

The **utility mapping** $\mathbf{u}: \mathbf{R}^{km} \rightarrow \mathbf{R}^m$ defined by

$$\mathbf{u}(x_1^1, \ldots, x_k^1; \ldots; x_1^m, \ldots, x_k^m) = \left(u^1(x_1^1, \ldots, x_k^1), \ldots, u^m(x_1^m, \ldots, x_k^m)\right)$$

gives the utility level of each consumer with that consumer's commodity bundle. It is a measure of the state of the economy as a whole.

Equation (1) is the constant elasticity demand function, which expresses the demand for one good in terms of its own price and that of the other good and income. If the second good has a similar demand function, the demand side of the economy would be summarized by the demand mapping $Q: \mathbf{R}^3 \to \mathbf{R}^2$:

$$Q(p_1, p_2, y) = (k_1 p_1^{a_{11}} p_2^{a_{12}} y^{b_1}, \; k_2 p_1^{a_{21}} p_2^{a_{22}} y^{b_2}).$$

As a final example of a function whose target space is $\mathbf{R}^m$, $m > 1$, consider a vector of the key macroeconomic variables which present a reasonably complete picture of the economy at each instant of time:

$$\mathbf{x} = (Y, C, I, G, T, M, P, R, \pi, N) \in \mathbf{R}^{10},$$

where Y is GNP, C is consumption, I is investment spending, G is government spending, T is tax collection, M is money supply, P is a price index, R is the interest rate, π is the inflation rate, and N measures employment. A macroeconomist's dream would be to find a function $f: \mathbf{R}^{10} \to \mathbf{R}^{10}$ which would accurately assign to each 10-tuple of today's economic variables the value of all these variables one month from now. In effect, this function would be 10 separate functions from $\mathbf{R}^{10}$ into $\mathbf{R}^1$; for example next month's GNP would be written as

$$Y_1 = f_1(Y_0, C_0, I_0, G_0, T_0, M_0, P_0, R_0, \pi_0, N_0),$$

and similarly for $C_1, \ldots, N_1$.

A simpler function in this context is the function

$$g: t \longmapsto (Y(t), C(t), I(t), G(t), T(t), M(t), P(t), R(t), \pi(t), N(t)),$$

which assigns to each moment in time from 1900 to the present the value of each of the macroeconomic variables at that time. The function g is a function from a subset of $\mathbf{R}^1$ into $\mathbf{R}^{10}$. In essence, it is ten separate real-valued functions, combined into one.

Just as we can take m related functions from $\mathbf{R}^k$ to $\mathbf{R}^1$ to form a single function from $\mathbf{R}^k$ to $\mathbf{R}^m$, we can just as easily go the other way. If f is a function from $\mathbf{R}^k$ to $\mathbf{R}^m$, then to each $\mathbf{x}$ in its domain, f assigns a vector $\mathbf{y} = f(\mathbf{x})$ in its target space. Write the ith component of $f(\mathbf{x})$ as $f_i(\mathbf{x})$. Then, we can think of f_i as a function from the domain of f into $\mathbf{R}^1$ and we can write $f = (f_1, \ldots, f_m)$. The real-valued function f_i is called the ith **component** function of f. So, in a very real sense, each function into $\mathbf{R}^m$ can be considered as m functions into $\mathbf{R}^1$. For example, the function

$$f(x_1, x_2, x_3) = (x_1^2 x_2 x_3, \; x_1 + x_2 + x_3)$$

is a function from $\mathbf{R}^3$ to $\mathbf{R}^2$; its two component functions are

$$f_1(x_1, x_2, x_3) = x_1^2 x_2 x_3 \quad \text{and} \quad f_2(x_1, x_2, x_3) = x_1 + x_2 + x_3.$$

13.2 GEOMETRIC REPRESENTATION OF FUNCTIONS

Graphs of Functions of Two Variables

In studying functions from $\mathbf{R}^1$ to $\mathbf{R}^1$, we often find that the graph of a function provides more useful information than the analytic formula. It is usually difficult simply to look at the defining formula and understand where the function is increasing, where it is decreasing, and where it reaches its maximum value — critical information for a function like a profit function. Furthermore, most functions that arise in economics are characterized by the *shapes of their graphs*: demand functions usually slope downward, supply functions usually slope upward, production functions usually slope upward but at a decreasing rate, and so on. In short, the picture is not just "worth a thousand words"; sometimes, it's all that counts.

We want to extend this valuable geometric technique to functions of several variables. Just as we need two dimensions to draw the graph of a function from $\mathbf{R}^1$ to $\mathbf{R}^1$, we need three dimensions to draw the graph of a function from $\mathbf{R}^2$ to $\mathbf{R}^1$. For ease of notation in this section, we will use (x, y, z) notation instead of (x_1, x_2, x_3) notation to describe the construction of these graphs. For each value (x, y) in the domain, we evaluate f at (x, y) and mark the point $(x, y, f(x, y))$ in $\mathbf{R}^3$. Doing this for all (x, y), we sweep out the complete two-dimensional graph. For example, in Figure 13.1, we have drawn the graph of $f(x, y) = x^2 + y^2$ and have labeled a number of points on the graph. In Figure 13.2, we have done the same for $f(x, y) = y^2 - x^2$. Try to generate enough points so that the graphs in these two figures become plausible.

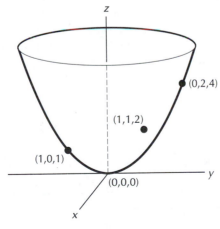

The graph of $f(x, y) = x^2 + y^2$.

Figure 13.1

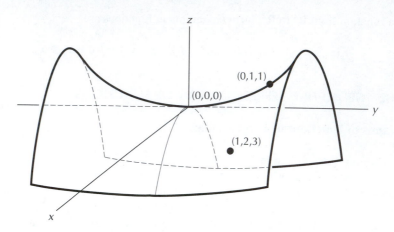

**Figure
13.2**

The graph of $f(x, y) = y^2 - x^2$.

A more systematic way to generate such graphs is to draw the usual one-dimensional graphs on various two-dimensional slices $\{y = a\}$ or $\{x = b\}$ for different values of a and b and then put these slices together. For example, consider the function $z = x^2 + y^2$ again. Its restriction to the $\{y = 0\}$-plane, that is, the xz-plane, is $z = x^2 + 0$, the standard parabola whose graph is pictured in the middle slice in Figure 13.3. Its restriction to the $\{y = 1\}$- and $\{y = -1\}$-planes is $z = x^2 + 1$, which is the usual parabola pushed up one unit. Its restriction to the $\{y = 2\}$ and $\{y = -2\}$ planes is $z = x^2 + 4$, the usual parabola pushed up four units. On the other hand, the restriction to the yz-plane $\{x = 0\}$ is the usual parabola, $z = 0 + y^2$. Put all the slices in Figure 13.3 together, using the parabola in the $\{x = 0\}$-plane as a guide. This process is pictured in Figure 13.4; from there, one can easily recover the complete graph pictured in Figure 13.1.

Let's do the same for $z = y^2 - x^2$. The restriction to each slice $\{y = b\}$ is the upside-down parabola $z = b^2 - x^2$, which is pushed up b^2 units. These are pictured in Figure 13.5. The restriction to the perpendicular plane $\{x = 0\}$ is the standard parabola $z = y^2$. To put all these slices together, picture the parabola $z = y^2$ on the slice $\{x = 0\}$ and then "hang" each of the upside-down parabolas in Figure 13.5 onto this rightside-up parabola, as sketched in Figure 13.6. You should be able to interpolate the rest of the graph and see it as the saddle-shaped graph of Figure 13.2.

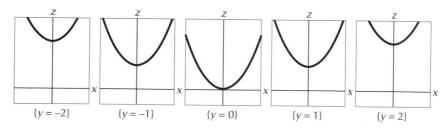

$\{y = -2\}$ $\{y = -1\}$ $\{y = 0\}$ $\{y = 1\}$ $\{y = 2\}$

**Figure
13.3**

Slices of $z = x^2 + y^2$ in the $\{y = b\}$-planes.

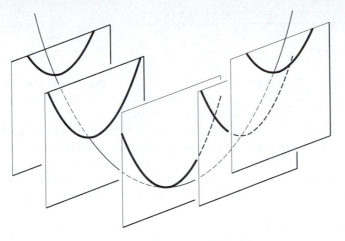

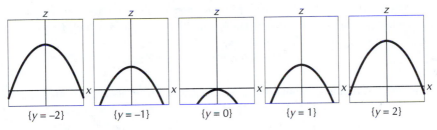

Putting the slices together.

Figure
13.4

$\{y = -2\}$ $\{y = -1\}$ $\{y = 0\}$ $\{y = 1\}$ $\{y = 2\}$

Restrictions of $z = y^2 - x^2$ to the planes $\{y = b\}$.

Figure
13.5

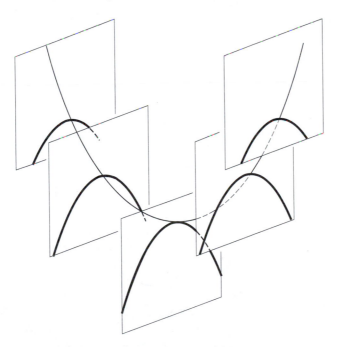

Putting the slices in Figure 13.5 together.

Figure
13.6

Level Curves

These graphs are tricky to draw. Not many of us have a good enough sense of three-dimensional perspective to sketch these graphs so that we can squeeze out all the information that we can obtain from graphs of functions of *one* variable. Fortunately, there is another way to visualize a function from $\mathbf{R}^2$ to $\mathbf{R}^1$ which requires only two-dimensional sketching — the study of level curves in the plane. For each (x, y) we once again evaluate $f(x, y)$ to obtain, say, z_0. Then, we sketch the locus *in the xy-plane* of all other (x, y) pairs for which f has the same value z_0. This locus, which will usually be a curve, is called a **level curve** of f.

Example 13.3   Let's work again with $f(x, y) = x^2 + y^2$. Start with the point $(0, 1)$ at which f equals 1. Now find *all* the points where f takes on the value 1. This is the set $\{(x, y) : x^2 + y^2 = 1\}$, a circle of radius 1 about the origin in the plane. We also write this level curve as $f^{-1}(1)$. Then, choose another point, say $(2, 1)$ at which f takes on the value 5. The set of all points (x, y) at which f equals 5 is

$$f^{-1}(5) = \{(x, y) : x^2 + y^2 = 5\},$$

a circle of radius $\sqrt{5}$ about the origin. Compute level sets for two more points and draw these curves; for example, we have drawn in Figure 13.7 the level curves $f^{-1}(1)$, $f^{-1}(5)$, $f^{-1}(4)$, and $f^{-1}(9)$, all circles about the origin.

Every point on the plane lies on one and only one level curve of f. For $z = x^2 + y^2$, all the level curves are circles about the origin, except that $f^{-1}(0)$ is just the origin itself.

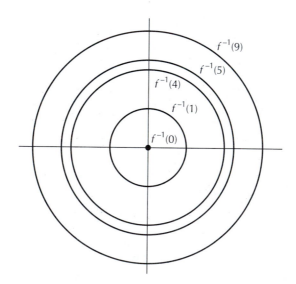

Figure 13.7

Level curves of $z = x^2 + y^2$.

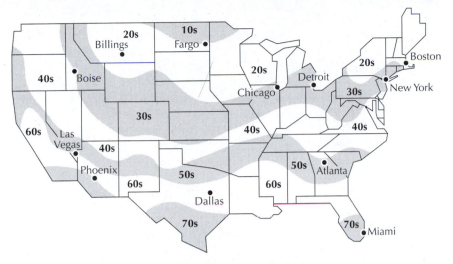

A weather map for the United States.

Figure 13.8

Level curves arise naturally in real-world situations. For example, let $T(x, y)$ be the function which gives the temperature at the point whose latitude is x and whose longitude is y. A weather forecaster, who wants to describe the function T to television viewers, usually does this most effectively by displaying various level curves of T — **isotherms** — at which $T = 50°, 60°, 70°$, and so on. The viewer can usually interpret this map rather easily. The $20°, 30°, 40°, 50°, 60°$, and $70°$ isotherms in the weather map in Figure 13.8 are represented as the boundary curves between the shaded and unshaded regions. For example, the $40°$ isotherm is the curve through Boise between the shaded 30s region and the unshaded 40s region.

Another natural use of level sets occurs in hiking or mountain climbing maps. Each curve on a typical hiking map, such as the one in Figure 13.9, runs through points which are the exact same height above sea level. For example, points A and B on the map are at 700 meters, and points C and D are at 680 meters. Point E is roughly at 695 meters. A person who wanted to keep at the same height (for example, a person mowing the lawn on this terrain) would try to walk along one of these level curves. On the other hand, a person looking for the steepest climb would move in the direction where different level curves are closest together, for example, in the direction of the arrow at point F. A person looking for a reasonably flat place to walk (or to tee up a golf ball) would look for a region where the level curves are spaced far from each other, for example, at point G. The level curves in Figure 13.9 provide a rather complete picture of the possibilities of walking in a given region.

Drawing Graphs from Level Sets

After one draws a complete set of level curves in the plane, it becomes much easier to visualize the two-dimensional graph in three-dimensional space. Starting with

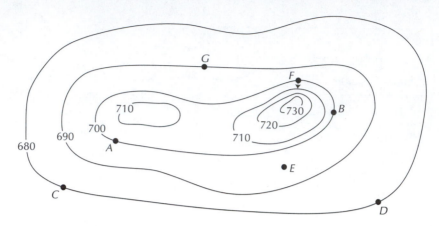

**Figure
13.9**

A hiking map with its level curves.

a sketch of the level curves of $f(x, y)$ in the xy-plane, picture the coordinate axes in $\mathbf{R}^3$ so that the x- and y-axes are on the plane of the page and the z-axis comes out from the page toward you. Consider, for example, the level curve $f^{-1}(10)$, the set of all points at which f takes on the value 10. Picture pulling this level curve up so that it rests in a plane $\{z = 10\}$, 10 units above the plane of the page. Similarly, for each $b > 0$, "pull" $f^{-1}(b)$ up to the plane $\{z = b\}$, b units above the plane of the page. If the circles in Figure 13.7 were pulled up to the indicated height, the result would be the bowl-shaped graph in Figure 13.1. What would we obtain if we pulled the level curves of the hiking map in Figure 13.9 up their indicated heights? We would obtain an exact three-dimensional replica of the terrain under study. We would recover the hills!

Planar Level Sets in Economics

Economists use level sets to study the two fundamental functions of micro-economics — production functions and utility functions. For example, one of the simplest production functions is the Cobb-Douglas function: $Q = x \cdot y$, where x and y measure amounts of two inputs, say capital and labor, and Q is the amount of output that can be produced using x units of capital and y units of labor. Level sets for production functions are called **isoquants**. The isoquant for $Q = 5$ passes through all input vectors (x, y) which yield five units of output. A convenient way to sketch the level curve $\{xy = 5\}$ is to solve the equation $\{xy = 5\}$ for y in terms of x and then to graph this new equation $y = g(x)$ as one does in elementary calculus:

$$xy = 5 \quad \text{implies} \quad y = \frac{5}{x},$$

whose graph is labeled I_5 in Figure 13.10. Similarly, to find the isoquant for $Q = 10$, we change $xy = 10$ to $y = 10/x$ and draw the graph of the latter

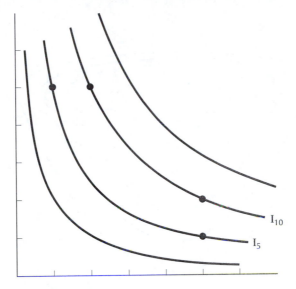

Isoquants of the production function $Q = xy$.

**Figure
13.10**

in xy-space, obtaining the curve I_{10} in Figure 13.10. Continue in this way until you have drawn sufficiently many isoquants to obtain a complete picture of the production function. In fact, all Cobb-Douglas production functions $Q = kx^{\alpha}y^{\beta}$, $k, \alpha, \beta > 0$, have level curves similar to those in Figure 13.10.

Economists' treatment of utility functions is similar to their work with production functions. In fact, the level sets of a typical utility function have the same shapes as the isoquants in Figure 13.10, as you will recognize from your intermediate microeconomics course. The level curves of a utility function are called **indifference curves**, because the consumer is indifferent between any two commodity bundles (x_1, y_1) and (x_2, y_2) on the same level curve; both (x_1, y_1) and (x_2, y_2) provide the same amount of satisfaction. In fact, in consumer theory, the utility levels which are assigned to any level curves are not of consequence, as they are in production theory. Only the shapes and locations of the indifference curves matter.

Representing Functions from $\mathbf{R}^k$ to $\mathbf{R}^1$ for $k > 2$

How do we represent geometrically functions from $\mathbf{R}^k$ to $\mathbf{R}^1$ for $k \geq 3$? The graph of a function from $\mathbf{R}^3$ to $\mathbf{R}^1$ sits naturally in $\mathbf{R}^4$, where we can't picture it. We can do a couple of things to help us better understand such a function f. First, we can draw the three-dimensional graphs of the restrictions of f to various two-dimensional slices $\{x_i = b\}$ and then try to imagine how these slices would fit together. Alternatively, we can try to picture the sets in $\mathbf{R}^3$ on which f takes on constant values. These sets, now called **level sets** instead of level curves, will be surfaces in $\mathbf{R}^3$. For example, we have drawn some level sets of $z = x_3 - x_1^2 - x_2^2$ in Figure 13.11 and some level sets of $z = x_1 + x_2 + x_3$ in Figure 13.12. One might

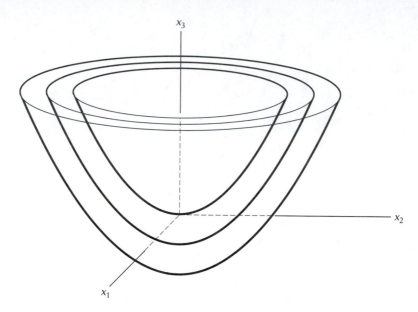

Figure 13.11

Some level sets of $z = x_3 - x_1^2 - x_2^2$.

sketch these level sets using the same approach used in sketching level curves. For each fixed value of z, solve the equation $z = f(x_1, x_2, x_3)$ for x_3 in terms of the other variables: $x_3 = g(x_1, x_2)$, and then graph g using the techniques described above for graphing functions of two variables.

For higher dimensions, one can only try to build illuminating analogies with lower-dimensional graphs.

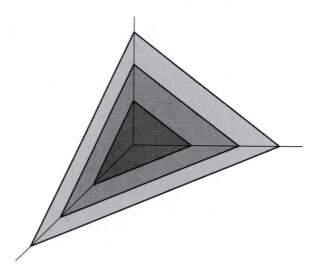

Figure 13.12

Some level sets of $z = x_1 + x_2 + x_3$.

Images of Functions from R^1 to R^m

We have discussed drawing graphs for functions from R^1 to R^1 or from R^2 to R^1 and drawing level sets for functions from R^2 to R^1 or from R^3 to R^1. There is one more situation in which one can draw illuminating geometric representations, namely, functions from R^1 to R^2 or from R^1 to R^3. A typical function from R^1 to R^2 would be written as $\mathbf{f}(t) = (f_1(t), f_2(t))$, where f_1 and f_2 are the component functions of $\mathbf{f}$, as discussed at the end of the previous section. For each t, $\mathbf{f}(t)$ is a point in R^2. If we mark each such point $\mathbf{f}(t)$ in the x_1x_2-plane, we will trace out a path or curve in the plane. In the vocabulary of Section 13.1, this curve is the **image** of the function $\mathbf{f}$. We have already worked with such curves when we wrote the parameterized equation of a line in R^m through the point $\mathbf{x}_0$ in the direction $\mathbf{v}$ as $\mathbf{f}(t) = \mathbf{x}_0 + t\mathbf{v}$ in Chapter 10. The line itself is the image of $\mathbf{f}$. In Figures 13.13 to 13.15, we have drawn three parameterized curves which are the images

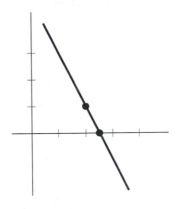

Parameterized curve $(1 + t, 3 - 2t)$.

Figure 13.13

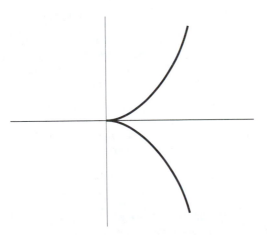

The parameterized curve (t^2, t^3).

Figure 13.14

**Figure
13.15**

Parameterized curve $(\cos t, \sin t, t)$.

of functions whose domain is $\mathbf{R}^1$. Try to reproduce these curves and to understand the differences between graphs, level sets, and parameterized curves.

EXERCISES

13.1   Use the slice method to sketch the graphs of the following functions:

a) $z = -x^2 - y^2$;   b) $z = y - x^2$;   c) $z = ye^{-x}$;
d) $z = y - x$;   e) $z = x^2 - y^2$;   f) $z = y/x$.

13.2   For each of the functions in the previous exercise, draw a significant number of level curves. Then, use these level curves to redraw the graphs.

13.3   If you had the graph of $z = f(x, y)$, how would you use it to draw level curves of f?

13.4   Describe another example where a map with level curves occurs naturally in real life. What are the implications of curves being close together in this situation?

13.5   Verify that the level sets in Figures 13.11 and 13.12 are correct.

13.6   Sketch level sets for each of the following functions from $\mathbf{R}^3$ to $\mathbf{R}^1$:

a) $f(x_1, x_2, x_3) = x_1^2 + x_2^2 + x_3^2$;   b) $f(x_1, x_2, x_3) = x_1^2 + x_2^2$;
c) $f(x_1, x_2, x_3) = x_1^2 - x_2 - x_3$;   d) $f(x_1, x_2, x_3) = x_1 + 2x_2 + 3x_3$.

13.7   Using the same scale on separate sheets of tracing paper, carefully draw a significant number of level curves of each of the following Cobb-Douglas functions. Then, discuss how the relative sizes of the exponents of these functions affect the relative shapes and locations of the level curves of Q.

a) $Q = L^{1/4}K^{3/4}$;   b) $Q = L^{1/2}K^{1/2}$;   c) $Q = L^{7/8}K^{1/8}$;   d) $Q = LK$.

13.8   Verify the parameterized curves in Figures 13.13, 13.14, and 13.15.

13.9   Sketch each of the following parameterized curves:

a) $\mathbf{f}(t) = (4 - 2t, 1 + t)$;   b) $\mathbf{f}(t) = (t^2, t^2 + 2)$;
c) $\mathbf{f}(t) = (\cos t, \sin t)$;   d) $\mathbf{f}(t) = (t, t^2, t^3)$.

13.10   Consider general function $f: \mathbf{R}^1 \to \mathbf{R}^1$. Show that the graph of f in the plane is exactly the parameterized curve $F(t) = (t, f(t))$.

13.3   SPECIAL KINDS OF FUNCTIONS

In this section, we develop our vocabulary about functions by discussing several kinds of functions that arise frequently. Terms such as "linear", "quadratic", "monomial", and "polynomial" should be familiar from your work with functions of one variable. In this section, we describe their natural generalizations to functions of several variables.

Linear Functions on $\mathbf{R}^k$

Most of the first half of this book has focused on linear equations and spaces. Linear functions have played at least an implicit role in much of this discussion.

Definition   A **linear function** from $\mathbf{R}^k$ to $\mathbf{R}^m$ is a function f that preserves the vector space structure:

$$f(\mathbf{x} + \mathbf{y}) = f(\mathbf{x}) + f(\mathbf{y}) \quad \text{and} \quad f(r\mathbf{x}) = rf(\mathbf{x}) \tag{2}$$

for all $\mathbf{x}$ and $\mathbf{y}$ in $\mathbf{R}^k$ and all scalars r. Linear functions are sometimes called **linear transformations**.

An example of a linear function is the function $f: \mathbf{R}^k \to \mathbf{R}^1$ defined by

$$f(\mathbf{x}) = \mathbf{a} \cdot \mathbf{x} = a_1 x_1 + a_2 x_2 + \cdots + a_k x_k, \tag{3}$$

for some vector $\mathbf{a} = (a_1, \ldots, a_k)$ in $\mathbf{R}^k$. (Check that this function satisfies definition (2)).

The following theorem states that every linear real-valued function is of the form $f(\mathbf{x}) = \mathbf{a} \cdot \mathbf{x}$.

> **Theorem 13.1**   Let $f: \mathbf{R}^k \to \mathbf{R}^1$ be a linear function. Then, there exists a vector $\mathbf{a} \in \mathbf{R}^k$ such that $f(\mathbf{x}) = \mathbf{a} \cdot \mathbf{x}$ for all $\mathbf{x} \in \mathbf{R}^k$.

Proof   For simplicity of notation, we will write a careful proof for $k = 3$. The same method works for general $\mathbf{R}^k$. (Exercise.) Let

$$\mathbf{e}_1 = \begin{pmatrix} 1 \\ 0 \\ 0 \end{pmatrix}, \quad \mathbf{e}_2 = \begin{pmatrix} 0 \\ 1 \\ 0 \end{pmatrix}, \quad \mathbf{e}_3 = \begin{pmatrix} 0 \\ 0 \\ 1 \end{pmatrix} \tag{4}$$

be the **canonical basis** of $\mathbf{R}^3$. Let $a_i = f(\mathbf{e}_i)$ for $i = 1, 2, 3$; and let $\mathbf{a} = (a_1, a_2, a_3)$. Then, for any vector $\mathbf{x} \in \mathbf{R}^3$,

$$\mathbf{x} = \begin{pmatrix} x_1 \\ x_2 \\ x_3 \end{pmatrix} = x_1 \begin{pmatrix} 1 \\ 0 \\ 0 \end{pmatrix} + x_2 \begin{pmatrix} 0 \\ 1 \\ 0 \end{pmatrix} + x_3 \begin{pmatrix} 0 \\ 0 \\ 1 \end{pmatrix} = x_1 \mathbf{e}_1 + x_2 \mathbf{e}_2 + x_3 \mathbf{e}_3,$$

and
$$f(\mathbf{x}) = f(x_1\mathbf{e}_1 + x_2\mathbf{e}_2 + x_3\mathbf{e}_3)$$
$$= x_1 f(\mathbf{e}_1) + x_2 f(\mathbf{e}_2) + x_3 f(\mathbf{e}_3)$$
$$= x_1 a_1 + x_2 a_2 + x_3 a_3$$
$$= \mathbf{a} \cdot \mathbf{x}. \quad \blacksquare$$

Theorem 13.1 implies that every real-valued linear function on $\mathbf{R}^k$ can be associated with a unique vector $\mathbf{a} \in \mathbf{R}^k$ or with a unique $1 \times k$ matrix $(a_1 \quad a_2 \quad \cdots \quad a_k)$ so that

$$f(\mathbf{x}) = \mathbf{a} \cdot \mathbf{x} = (a_1 \quad \cdots \quad a_k) \begin{pmatrix} x_1 \\ \vdots \\ x_k \end{pmatrix}. \tag{5}$$

Conversely, every such $\mathbf{a}$ induces a linear map, as (3) shows.

The same correspondence between linear functions and matrices carries over to functions from $\mathbf{R}^k$ to $\mathbf{R}^m$. If A is an $m \times k$ matrix, then the function $f_A(\mathbf{x}) = A\mathbf{x}$ is a linear function. The following theorem proves the converse.

Theorem 13.2   Let $f: \mathbf{R}^k \rightarrow \mathbf{R}^m$ be a linear function. Then, there exists an $m \times k$ matrix A such that $f(\mathbf{x}) = A\mathbf{x}$ for all $\mathbf{x} \in \mathbf{R}^k$.

Proof   The proof is basically the same as that of Theorem 13.1. Let $\mathbf{e}_1, \ldots, \mathbf{e}_k$ be the canonical basis of $\mathbf{R}^k$, as in (4). For each $j = 1, \ldots, k$, let $\mathbf{a}_j = f(\mathbf{e}_j) \in \mathbf{R}^m$. Let A be the $m \times k$ matrix whose jth column is the column vector $\mathbf{a}_j$. For any $\mathbf{x} = (x_1, \ldots, x_k)$ in $\mathbf{R}^k$,

$$f(\mathbf{x}) = f(x_1\mathbf{e}_1 + \cdots + x_k\mathbf{e}_k)$$
$$= x_1 f(\mathbf{e}_1) + \cdots + x_k \mathbf{f}(\mathbf{e}_k)$$
$$= x_1 \mathbf{a}_1 + \cdots + x_k \mathbf{a}_k$$
$$= (\mathbf{a}_1 \quad \mathbf{a}_2 \quad \cdots \quad \mathbf{a}_k) \begin{pmatrix} x_1 \\ x_2 \\ \vdots \\ x_k \end{pmatrix}$$
$$= A \begin{pmatrix} x_1 \\ x_2 \\ \vdots \\ x_k \end{pmatrix} = A\mathbf{x}. \quad \blacksquare$$

Theorem 13.2 underlines the one-to-one correspondence between linear functions from $\mathbf{R}^k$ to $\mathbf{R}^m$ and $m \times k$ matrices. Each linear f is an f_A for a unique $m \times k$

matrix A. This fact will play an important role in the rest of this book. Matrices are not simply rectangular arrays of numbers or convenient ways of tabulating data or of codifying linear systems of equations. Matrices are representations of linear functions. When we use calculus to do its main task, namely to approximate a nonlinear function f at a given point by a linear one, the derivative of f, we will write that linear function as a matrix. In other words, derivatives of functions from $\mathbf{R}^k$ to $\mathbf{R}^m$ are $m \times k$ matrices.

The level sets of a linear function (5) are the sets $\mathbf{a} \cdot \mathbf{x} = b$ that we called *hyperplanes* in Section 10.6: for example, one-dimensional lines in $\mathbf{R}^2$ and two-dimensional planes in $\mathbf{R}^3$, as Figure 13.12 illustrates.

Quadratic Forms

A linear monomial from $\mathbf{R}^1$ to $\mathbf{R}^1$ is simply a function of the form $f(x) = ax$. The next level of complexity is the quadratic $f(x) = bx^2$. The natural generalization of a quadratic to two variables is the quadratic form

$$Q(x_1, x_2) = a_{11}x_1^2 + a_{12}x_1x_2 + a_{22}x_2^2, \tag{6}$$

in which the exponents in each term sum to 2. The general quadratic form in three variables is

$$Q(x_1, x_2, x_3) = a_{11}x_1^2 + a_{12}x_1x_2 + a_{13}x_1x_3 \\ + a_{22}x_2^2 + a_{23}x_2x_3 + a_{33}x_3^2. \tag{7}$$

Definition   A **quadratic form** on $\mathbf{R}^k$ is a real-valued function of the form

$$Q(x_1, \ldots, x_k) = \sum_{i,j=1}^{k} a_{ij}x_ix_j.$$

Quadratic forms are so important in multivariable analysis that we will devote all of Chapter 16 to describing their main properties.

The level curve of a general quadratic form (6) on $\mathbf{R}^2$,

$$a_{11}x_1^2 + a_{12}x_1x_2 + a_{22}x_2^2 = b, \tag{8}$$

is an ellipse, a hyperbola, a pair of lines, or possibly, the empty set. Since all these curves can be realized by slicing a standard cone by a plane, as in Figure 13.16, they are called **conic sections**. Which of these conic sections occurs depends on the values of the coefficients a_{11}, a_{12}, and a_{22} and b. In Chapter 16, we will find an algorithm, involving a_{11}, a_{12}, and a_{22}, which will allow us to distinguish among these possibilities.

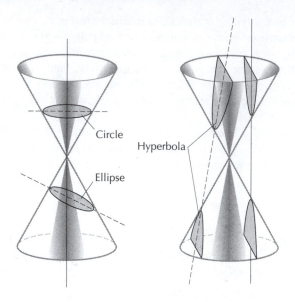

Figure 13.16

An ellipse and a hyperbola as the intersection of a cone and a plane.

Example 13.4 Equation (8) is much easier to analyze when the coefficient a_{12} of the x_1x_2-term is zero. Then, (8) becomes

$$a_{11} x_1^2 + a_{22} x_2^2 = b. \tag{9}$$

If a_{11} and b have the same sign and $a_{11} = a_{22}$ in (9), then (9) is the equation of a circle. More generally, if a_{11}, a_{22}, and b have the same sign, then (9) is the equation of an ellipse with axes of length $\sqrt{b/a_{11}}$ and $\sqrt{b/a_{22}}$. If a_{11} and a_{22} have the same sign and b has the opposite sign, then equation (9) has no solutions. If a_{11} and a_{22} have opposite signs, then (9) is the equation of a hyperbola.

Example 13.5 On the other hand, when $a_{11} = a_{22} = 0$ in (8), then (8) becomes $a_{12}x_1x_2 = b$. This family of hyperbolas is the set of isoquants of the Cobb-Douglas production function $f(x_1, x_2) = a_{12}x_1x_2$, as Figure 13.10 illustrates.

Matrix Representation of Quadratic Forms

Just as a linear function $f(x_1, \ldots, x_n) = a_1x_1 + a_2x_2 + \cdots + a_nx_n$ has a matrix representation as in (5), a quadratic form has a matrix representation, too. For example, we can write the general quadratic form (8) on $\mathbf{R}^2$ as

$$a_{11} x_1^2 + a_{12} x_1x_2 + a_{22} x_2^2 = (x_1 \quad x_2) \begin{pmatrix} a_{11} & a_{12} \\ 0 & a_{22} \end{pmatrix} \begin{pmatrix} x_1 \\ x_2 \end{pmatrix}.$$

(Check this!) In fact, many different matrices will work for each Q, depending on how we apportion the coefficient a_{12} of the cross term in (8) between the (1, 2) and (2, 1) entries of the matrix. As we will see, the ideal way to apportion a_{12} is to divide it equally so that the resulting matrix is a symmetric one:

$$a_{11}\,x_1^2 + a_{12}\,x_1x_2 + a_{22}\,x_2^2 = (x_1 \quad x_2)\begin{pmatrix} a_{11} & \frac{1}{2}a_{12} \\ \frac{1}{2}a_{12} & a_{22} \end{pmatrix}\begin{pmatrix} x_1 \\ x_2 \end{pmatrix}.$$

(Check this, too.) Similarly, we can use a symmetric 3×3 matrix to represent the general quadratic form (7) on $\mathbf{R}^3$:

$$Q(x_1, x_2, x_3) = (x_1 \quad x_2 \quad x_3)\begin{pmatrix} a_{11} & \frac{1}{2}a_{12} & \frac{1}{2}a_{13} \\ \frac{1}{2}a_{12} & a_{22} & \frac{1}{2}a_{23} \\ \frac{1}{2}a_{13} & \frac{1}{2}a_{23} & a_{33} \end{pmatrix}\begin{pmatrix} x_1 \\ x_2 \\ x_3 \end{pmatrix}.$$

This constructive procedure yields a proof for the basic theorem about representing quadratic forms on $\mathbf{R}^n$.

Theorem 13.3   The general quadratic form

$$Q(x_1, \ldots, x_n) = \sum_{i \le j} a_{ij}x_ix_j$$

can be written as

$$(x_1 \quad x_2 \quad \cdots \quad x_n)\begin{pmatrix} a_{11} & \frac{1}{2}a_{12} & \cdots & \frac{1}{2}a_{1n} \\ \frac{1}{2}a_{12} & a_{22} & \cdots & \frac{1}{2}a_{2n} \\ \vdots & \vdots & \ddots & \vdots \\ \frac{1}{2}a_{1n} & \frac{1}{2}a_{2n} & \cdots & a_{nn} \end{pmatrix}\begin{pmatrix} x_1 \\ x_2 \\ \vdots \\ x_n \end{pmatrix},$$

that is, as $\mathbf{x}^T A\mathbf{x}$,

where A is a (unique) symmetric matrix. Conversely, if A is a symmetric matrix, then the real-valued function $Q(\mathbf{x}) = \mathbf{x}^T A\mathbf{x}$, as above, is a quadratic form.

The proof of Theorem 13.3 is a straightforward calculation which we leave as an exercise.

Polynomials

Linear functions and quadratic forms are special cases of the general class of functions, called polynomials, which in turn are simply finite sums of monomials.

Definition A function $f: \mathbf{R}^k \to \mathbf{R}^1$ is a **monomial** if it can be written as

$$f(x_1, \ldots, x_k) = c x_1^{a_1} x_2^{a_2} \cdots x_k^{a_k},$$

where c is a scalar and the exponents $a_1, \ldots, a_k$ are nonnegative integers. The sum of the exponents $a_1 + \cdots + a_k$ is called the **degree** of the monomial.

Example 13.6

    (a) $f(x_1, x_2) = -4x_1^2 x_2$ is a monomial of degree three;

    (b) $f(x_1, x_2, x_3) = 3x_1^2 x_2^3 x_3$ is a monomial of degree six;

    (c) a constant function is a monomial of degree zero;

    (d) each term of a linear function is a monomial of degree one, as Theorems 13.1 and 13.2 assert; and

    (e) each term of a quadratic form is a monomial of degree two, as expressions (6) and (7) illustrate.

Definition A function $f: \mathbf{R}^k \to \mathbf{R}^1$ is called a **polynomial** if f is the finite sum of monomials on $\mathbf{R}^k$. The highest degree which occurs among these monomials is called the **degree** of the polynomial. A function $f: \mathbf{R}^k \to \mathbf{R}^m$ is called a **polynomial** if each of its component functions is a real-valued polynomial.

Example 13.7 If $f: \mathbf{R}^k \to \mathbf{R}^m$ is a polynomial of *degree one*, then each component of f has the form

$$f_i(\mathbf{x}) = \mathbf{a}_i \cdot \mathbf{x} + b_i.$$

Therefore, f itself has the form: $f(\mathbf{x}) = A\mathbf{x} + \mathbf{b}$, for some $m \times k$ matrix A and some m-vector $\mathbf{b}$. Such a function is called an **affine function**.

EXERCISES

13.11 Write the following linear functions in matrix form:

    a) $f(x_1, x_2, x_3) = 2x_1 - 3x_2 + 5x_3$;

    b) $f(x_1, x_2) = (2x_1 - 3x_2, x_1 - 4x_2, x_1)$;

    c) $f(x_1, x_2, x_3) = (x_1 - x_3, 2x_1 + 3x_2 - 6x_3, x_3 + 2x_2)$.

13.12 Write the following quadratic forms in matrix form:

    a) $x_1^2 - 2x_1x_2 + x_2^2$,

    b) $5x_1^2 - 10x_1x_2 - x_2^2$,

    c) $x_1^2 + 2x_2^2 + 3x_3^2 + 4x_1x_2 - 6x_1x_3 + 8x_2x_3$.

13.13 Write three functions from $\mathbf{R}^1$ to $\mathbf{R}^1$ that are not polynomials.

13.14 Prove Theorem 13.1 on $\mathbf{R}^k$.

13.15 Prove that a linear function from $\mathbf{R}^k$ to $\mathbf{R}^m$ sends a line in $\mathbf{R}^k$ to a point or a line in $\mathbf{R}^m$.

13.4 CONTINUOUS FUNCTIONS

Functions that map nearby points into nearby points are called continuous functions, just as they are for functions on $\mathbf{R}^1$. Nearly all the basic functions which arise in mathematical models in the sciences are assumed to be continuous. For example, a production function is continuous if a small change in the input vector yields a small change in the corresponding output vector — a very reasonable assumption. This section formally defines continuity and discusses some of its properties.

Some introductory calculus texts describe a function of one variable as continuous if you can draw its graph without lifting your pencil from the paper. This idea captures the essence of continuity. To transform it into a working definition, we use the concepts of sequences and their limits. Let x_0 be a point in the domain of a function $f: \mathbf{R}^1 \to \mathbf{R}^1$. Let $\{x_n\}$ be any sequence of real numbers that converges to x_0. Form the sequence $\{(x_n, f(x_n))\}_{n=1}^{\infty}$ of points in $\mathbf{R}^2$ on the graph of f above each x_n. The statement that the graph of f is a connected curve means that the point $(x_0, f(x_0))$ on the graph of f above x_0 is the limit of the points $\{(x_n, f(x_n))\}$. In other words, as $x_n \to x_0$, $f(x_n) \to f(x_0)$. See Figure 13.17. This observation leads to the following definition of continuity.

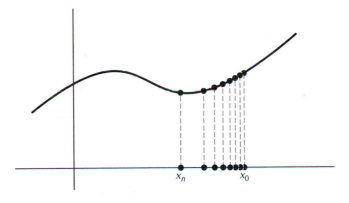

A continuous function.

Figure 13.17

Definition   Let f be a function from $\mathbf{R}^k$ to $\mathbf{R}^m$. Let $\mathbf{x}_0$ be a vector in $\mathbf{R}^k$, and $\mathbf{y} = f(\mathbf{x}_0)$ its image. The function f is **continuous** at $\mathbf{x}_0$ if whenever $\{\mathbf{x}_n\}_{n=1}^{\infty}$ is a sequence in $\mathbf{R}^k$ which converges to $\mathbf{x}_0$, then the sequence $\{f(\mathbf{x}_n)\}_{n=1}^{\infty}$ in $\mathbf{R}^m$ converges to $f(\mathbf{x}_0)$. The function f is said to be **continuous** if it is continuous at every point in its domain.

Intuitively speaking, this definition says that f is continuous at $\mathbf{x}_0$ if one can accurately predict the image of f at $\mathbf{x}_0$ knowing the images of all $\mathbf{x}$ near to (but not equal to) $\mathbf{x}_0$, that is, if $f(\mathbf{x}_0)$ is what you would expect to find when you know all $f(\mathbf{x})$ for $\mathbf{x} \neq \mathbf{x}_0$.

Example 13.8 Perhaps, continuous functions are best understood by seeing what a discontinuous function looks like. If f is not continuous at $\mathbf{x}$, there is a sequence $\{\mathbf{x}_n\}_{n=1}^{\infty}$ which converges to $\mathbf{x}$ and for which $f(\mathbf{x}_n)$ does not converge to $f(\mathbf{x})$. For example, consider the function

$$f(\mathbf{x}) = \begin{cases} 1, & \text{if } \mathbf{x} > 0, \\ 0, & \text{if } \mathbf{x} \leq 0, \end{cases}$$

whose graph is pictured in Figure 13.18. Note that $f(0) = 0$, but $f(\mathbf{x}) = 1$ for $\mathbf{x}$ arbitrarily close to 0 on the right side of 0. The sequence $1/n$ converges to 0, but $f(1/n) = 1$ converges to 1, which is not $f(0)$. This function is not continuous at the point where its graph has a gap.

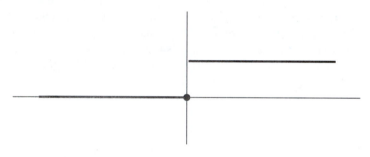

Figure 13.18 *A gap in the graph of a discontinuous function.*

This sequential characterization of continuity is very useful in proving that algebraic combinations of continuous functions are still continuous. Recall that if f and g are two functions from $\mathbf{R}^k$ to $\mathbf{R}^m$, one can define a new function $(f + g)$ from $\mathbf{R}^k$ to $\mathbf{R}^m$ by $(f + g)(\mathbf{x}) = f(\mathbf{x}) + g(\mathbf{x})$ for all $\mathbf{x}$, and similarly for $f - g$ and $f \cdot g$.

Theorem 13.4 Let f and g be functions from $\mathbf{R}^k$ to $\mathbf{R}^m$. Suppose f and g are continuous at $\mathbf{x}$. Then, $f + g$, $f - g$, and $f \cdot g$ are all continuous at $\mathbf{x}$.

Proof Let $\{\mathbf{x}_n\}_{n=1}^{\infty}$ be a sequence converging to $\mathbf{x}$. By continuity, $f(\mathbf{x}_n)$ converges to $f(\mathbf{x})$ and $g(\mathbf{x}_n)$ converges to $g(\mathbf{x})$. By Theorem 12.6, $f(\mathbf{x}_n) + g(\mathbf{x}_n) = (f + g)(\mathbf{x}_n)$ converges to $f(\mathbf{x}) + g(\mathbf{x}) = (f + g)(\mathbf{x})$. Therefore, $f + g$ is continuous at $\mathbf{x}$, too. The same argument works for $f - g$ and $f \cdot g$. ∎

The following theorem uses our sequential characterization of continuity and the fact that a sequence in $\mathbf{R}^m$ converges if and only if each of the m sequences of its components converges in $\mathbf{R}^1$ to assert that a function into $\mathbf{R}^m$ is continuous if and only if each of its component functions into $\mathbf{R}^1$ is continuous. Its proof is left as an exercise.

> **Theorem 13.5**   Let $f = (f_1, \ldots, f_m)$ be a function from $\mathbf{R}^k$ to $\mathbf{R}^m$. Then, f is continuous at $\mathbf{x}$ if and only if each of its component functions $f_i : \mathbf{R}^k \to \mathbf{R}^1$ is continuous at $\mathbf{x}$.

EXERCISES

13.16   Suppose that f and g are both functions from $\mathbf{R}^k$ to $\mathbf{R}^1$, which are continuous at $\mathbf{x} \in \mathbf{R}^k$. Suppose that $g(\mathbf{x}) \neq 0$. Prove that the quotient function f/g is defined and continuous at $\mathbf{x}$.

13.17   Suppose that $f : \mathbf{R}^k \to \mathbf{R}^1$ is a continuous function and that $f(\mathbf{x}^*) > 0$. Show that there is a ball $B = B_\delta(\mathbf{x}^*)$ such that $f(\mathbf{x}) > 0$ for all $\mathbf{x} \in B$.

13.18   Complete the proof of Theorem 13.4.

13.19   Prove Theorem 13.5.

13.20   Prove carefully that $h : \mathbf{R}^k \to \mathbf{R}^1$ defined by $h(x_1, x_2, \ldots, x_k) = x_i$ is continuous on $\mathbf{R}^k$. Conclude that any monomial $g(x_1, x_2, \ldots, x_k) = cx_1^{n_1} x_2^{n_2} \cdots x_k^{n_k}$ is continuous on $\mathbf{R}^k$ and that any polynomial from $\mathbf{R}^k$ to $\mathbf{R}^m$ is continuous on $\mathbf{R}^k$.

13.21   Let $f : \mathbf{R}^k \to \mathbf{R}^1$ be continuous at the point $\mathbf{a} = (a_1, \ldots, a_k)$. Consider the function $g : \mathbf{R}^1 \to \mathbf{R}^1$ defined by $g(t) = f(t, a_2, \ldots, a_k)$. Show that g is continuous at a_1. This result implies that if f is continuous, its restriction to any line parallel to a coordinate axis is also continuous. However, the converse is not true. Consider the function $f(x, y) = xy^2/(x^2 + y^4)$. Show that $f_1(t) = f(t, a)$ and $f_2(t) = f(a, t)$ are continuous functions of t for each fixed a. Show that f itself is not continuous at $(0, 0)$. [Hint: Take a sequence on the diagonal.]

13.5   VOCABULARY OF FUNCTIONS

In this section, we recall some of the vocabulary of functions. Remember from Section 13.1 that if $f : A \to B$, then A is the **domain** of f and B is the **target space** of f. The set of $\mathbf{y}$'s in B which are images $\mathbf{y} = f(\mathbf{x})$ of points $\mathbf{x}$ in A is called the image, or sometimes the **range**, of f and is written $f(A)$.

If C is any subset of A, then the **image** of C under f is

$$f(C) \equiv \{\mathbf{b} \in B : \mathbf{b} = f(\mathbf{a}) \text{ for some } \mathbf{a} \in C\}.$$

On the other hand, if V is a subset of the target space B, then the **preimage** of V under f is the set of all points in the domain whose image lies in V. We usually write the preimage of V as

$$f^{-1}(V) \equiv \{\mathbf{a} \in A : f(\mathbf{a}) \text{ lies in } V\}.$$

The image and preimage are operations on sets which are more or less inverse to each other. For example, to find $f(f^{-1}(V))$, we ask ourselves where does f send all the points that map into V. The answer, of course, is that these points map into V: $V \supset f(f^{-1}(V))$. On the other hand, to understand $f^{-1}(f(U))$, we ask what is the set of all the points that have the same image as U? Certainly, the points in U are in this set, but there may be other points outside U which have the same image as points in U. Therefore, we write $U \subset f^{-1}(f(U))$. The following theorem collects the important facts about the image and the preimage operations. Its proof is a simple exercise in set theory.

Theorem 13.6   Consider the function $f: A \rightarrow B$. Let U_1 and U_2 be arbitrary subsets of the domain A, and let V_1 and V_2 be arbitrary subsets of the target space B. Then,

(a) if $U_1 \subset U_2$, $f(U_1) \subset f(U_2)$;
(b) if $V_1 \subset V_2$, $f^{-1}(V_1) \subset f^{-1}(V_2)$;
(c) for all sets U, $U \subset f^{-1}(f(U))$;
(d) for all sets V, $f(f^{-1}(V)) \subset V$; and
(e) for all sets V, $f^{-1}(V^c) = (f^{-1}(V))^c$.

Figure 13.19 illustrates some of the statements in Theorem 13.6.

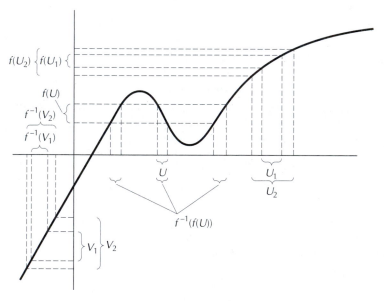

**Figure
13.19**

An illustration of the statements in Theorem 13.6.

Onto Functions and One-to-One Functions

If for each element $\mathbf{b} \in B$ there is an element $\mathbf{a} \in A$ such that $\mathbf{b} = f(\mathbf{a})$, in other words, if the whole target space of f is the image of f, we say that f maps A **onto** B or that f is **surjective**.

A complementary notion is that of a one-to-one function, a concept that first arose in our discussion in Section 4.2 of the inverse of a function. In general, a function $f:A \rightarrow B$ is **one-to-one** or **injective** on a subset C of A if and only if for every $\mathbf{x}$, $\mathbf{y}$ in C

$$f(\mathbf{x}) = f(\mathbf{y}) \quad \Rightarrow \quad \mathbf{x} = \mathbf{y}.$$

In other words, f is one-to-one on $C \subset A$ if each $\mathbf{b} \in f(C)$ is the image of precisely one element of C.

The concepts of onto and one-to-one are especially important when one is working with equations in $\mathbf{x}$ of the form $f(\mathbf{x}) = \mathbf{b}$. The function f is onto if the equation $f(\mathbf{x}) = \mathbf{b}$ has *at least* one solution for every right-hand side $\mathbf{b}$. It is one-to-one if the equation $f(\mathbf{x}) = \mathbf{b}$ has *at most* one solution for each right-hand side $\mathbf{b}$.

Inverse Functions

When $f:A \rightarrow B$ is one-to-one on a set $C \subset A$, there is a natural function from $f(C)$ back to C which assigns to each $\mathbf{b} \in f(C)$ the unique point in C which mapped to it. This map is called the **inverse** of f on C and is written as

$$f^{-1}: f(C) \rightarrow C.$$

For example, the inverse of the function which converts degrees Fahrenheit to degrees Centigrade is the function which converts degrees Centigrade to degrees Fahrenheit. The logarithm is the inverse of the exponential map; multiplication by one-half is the inverse of multiplication by two.

An inverse function that arises naturally in economics is the **inverse demand function**. The demand function assigns to any price p of a commodity the amount $q = D(p)$ that will be consumed at that price. If one makes the usual assumption that q decreases as p increases, then the demand function will be one-to-one on its domain. Its inverse, the inverse demand function, assigns to each quantity q of the good under study the price $p = D^{-1}(q)$ at which consumers will purchase q units of the commodity. Both the demand and the inverse demand functions are important in economic analysis. When computing the price elasticity of demand, economists need to work with q as a function of p. When computing the profit-maximizing output of a monopolist firm, economists need to work with p as a function of q.

Example 13.9   Consider again the function $f: \mathbf{R}^2 \to \mathbf{R}^1$ defined by $f(x_1, x_2) = x_1^2 + x_2^2$. Its target space is $\mathbf{R}^1$; its image is the set of all nonnegative real numbers. Since these two are not the same, f is not onto. Neither is f one-to-one since $f(1, 0) = f(0, 1) = 1$.

Example 13.10   The target space of the function $g(x) = 1/x$ is $\mathbf{R}^1$, but its image is $\mathbf{R}^1 - \{0\}$, all real numbers except 0. This function is not onto. However, it is one-to-one since no two numbers map to the same number under g. In terms of the graph of g, g is one-to-one because each horizontal line $\{y = b\}$ which intersects the graph of g intersects it at only one point.

Example 13.11   Consider the functions f and g from $\mathbf{R}^1$ to $\mathbf{R}^1$ defined by $f(x) = 2x$ and $g(x) = 2x - 1$. For both of these, the domain and image are all of $\mathbf{R}^1$. Both are one-to-one maps of $\mathbf{R}^1$ onto $\mathbf{R}^1$. Their inverses are given by

$$f^{-1}(y) = \frac{1}{2}y \quad \text{and} \quad g^{-1}(y) = \frac{1}{2}(y + 1).$$

To find the formula for g^{-1}, just solve $y = 2x - 1$ for x in terms of y.

Composition of Functions

In Section 4.1, we introduced the composition operator for pairs of functions of one variable. In general, this operation is only defined for functions f and g if the domain of one contains the image of the other.

Definition   Let $f: A \to B$ and $g: C \to D$ be two functions. Suppose that B, the image of f, is a subset of C, the domain of g. Then, the **composition** of f with g, $g \circ f: A \to D$, is defined as the function

$$(g \circ f)(\mathbf{x}) = g(f(\mathbf{x})) \quad \text{for all } \mathbf{x} \in A.$$

The composition of f with g is illustrated in Figure 13.20.

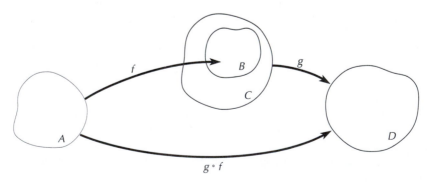

Figure 13.20

The composition of f with g.

Example 13.12 The function $h(x) = \sin x^2$ is the composition of $f(x) = x^2$ with $g(x) = \sin x$. The function $h(x) = (x + 4)^3$ is the composition of $f(x) = x + 4$ with $g(x) = x^3$. The function $h(x, y) = \sqrt{x^2 + y}$ is the composition of $f(x, y) = x^2 + y$ with $g(z) = \sqrt{z}$.

We use the method of proof of Theorem 13.4 to prove that the composition of two continuous functions defined on Euclidean spaces is a continuous function.

Theorem 13.7   Let $f : \mathbf{R}^k \to \mathbf{R}^m$ be a continuous function at $\mathbf{x} \in \mathbf{R}^k$. Let $g : \mathbf{R}^m \to \mathbf{R}^n$ be a continuous function at $f(\mathbf{x}) \in \mathbf{R}^m$. Then, the composition $g \circ f : \mathbf{R}^k \to \mathbf{R}^n$ is a continuous function at $\mathbf{x}$.

Proof   Let $\{\mathbf{x}_n\}_{n=1}^{\infty}$ be a sequence in $\mathbf{R}^k$ converging to $\mathbf{x}$. By the continuity of f at $\mathbf{x}$, $\{f(\mathbf{x}_n)\}_{n=1}^{\infty}$ converges to $f(\mathbf{x})$. By the continuity of g at $f(\mathbf{x})$, the sequence $\{g(f(\mathbf{x}_n))\}_{n=1}^{\infty}$ converges to $g(f(\mathbf{x}))$. Therefore, $g \circ f$ is continuous at $\mathbf{x}$. ∎

The language of functions and their compositions yields a good working definition of the concepts of sequence and subsequence. A **sequence** in $\mathbf{R}^m$ is simply a function f from the set $\mathbf{Z}^+$ of positive integers into $\mathbf{R}^m$. We usually write $f(n)$ as $\mathbf{x}_n$. To construct a subsequence of this sequence, let $g: \mathbf{Z}^+ \to \mathbf{Z}^+$ be a function which preserves the usual order on $\mathbf{Z}$: $k < \ell \Rightarrow g(k) < g(\ell)$. Then, the composition $g \circ f: \mathbf{Z}^+ \to \mathbf{R}^m$ is a typical subsequence of f.

EXERCISES

13.22   Prove Theorem 13.6.

13.23   For each of the following functions, what is the domain and the image of f? Which ones are one-to-one? For those which are one-to-one, write the expression for the inverse. Which ones are onto?

a) $f(x) = 3x - 7$; b) $f(x) = x^2 - 1$; c) $f(x) = e^x$;
d) $f(x) = x^3 - x$; e) $f(x) = x/(x^2 + 1)$; f) $f(x) = x^3$;
g) $f(x) = 1/x$; h) $f(x) = \sqrt{x - 1}$; i) $f(x) = xe^{-x}$.

13.24   For each of the following functions, write h as a composition of two functions f and g:

a) $h(x) = \log(x^2 + 1)$; b) $h(x) = (\sin x)^2$;
c) $h(x) = (\cos x^3, \sin x^3)$; d) $h(x, y) = (x^2 y)^3 + x^2 y$.

Calculus of Several Variables

A primary goal in economic analysis is to understand how a change in one economic variable affects another. Chapter 3 demonstrated that one-variable calculus is the primary tool for understanding the effects of such changes in economic relationships that are defined by functions of a single variable: $y = f(x)$. This chapter introduces multivariable calculus as the primary tool for understanding how variables affect others in economic relationships described by functions of *several* variables: $y = f(x_1, \ldots, x_n)$.

14.1   DEFINITIONS AND EXAMPLES

To apply calculus to the study of functions of several variables, we take the simplest approach. We change one variable at a time, keeping all the other variables constant. Since in this case we are not looking at the total variation of f but just the partial variation — the variation brought about by the change in only one variable, say x_i — the corresponding derivative is called the **partial derivative** of f with respect to x_i. It is written $\dfrac{\partial f}{\partial x_i}$ with Greek ∂'s (deltas) instead of the Roman d's. Other common ways of referring to $\partial f / \partial x_i$ include f_i, f_{x_i}, and $D_i f$.

Recall that the derivative of a function f of one variable at x_0 is

$$\frac{df}{dx}(x_0) = \lim_{h \to 0} \frac{f(x_0 + h) - f(x_0)}{h}.$$

The partial derivative with respect to x_i of a function $f(x_1, \ldots, x_n)$ of several variables at $\mathbf{x}^0 = (x_1^0, \ldots, x_n^0)$ is defined in a similar manner.

Definition   Let $f: \mathbf{R}^n \to \mathbf{R}$. Then for each variable x_i at each point $\mathbf{x}^0 = (x_1^0, \ldots, x_n^0)$ in the domain of f,

$$\frac{\partial f}{\partial x_i}(x_1^0, \ldots, x_n^0) = \lim_{h \to 0} \frac{f(x_1^0, \ldots, x_i^0 + h, \ldots, x_n^0) - f(x_1^0, \ldots, x_i^0, \ldots, x_n^0)}{h},$$

if this limit exists. Only the ith variable changes; the others are treated as constants.

Example 14.1   Consider the function $f(x, y) = 3x^2y^2 + 4xy^3 + 7y$. We compute $\partial f / \partial x$ by treating y as a constant. The first term is x^2 times a "constant" $(3y^2)$; so its derivative is $2x$ times the constant; that is,

$$\frac{\partial}{\partial x}(3x^2y^2) = 2x \cdot 3y^2 = 6xy^2.$$

The second term is a "constant" times x; its derivative is just the constant

$$\frac{\partial}{\partial x}(4xy^3) = 4y^3.$$

Finally, since we treat $7y$ as a constant in computing $\dfrac{\partial}{\partial x}$, its derivative is 0:

$$\frac{\partial}{\partial x}(7y) = 0.$$

Put this all together using the fact that the derivative of the sum is the sum of the derivatives:

$$\frac{\partial}{\partial x}(3x^2y^2 + 4xy^3 + 7y) = 6xy^2 + 4y^3.$$

To compute the partial derivative with respect to y, treat x as a constant. The first term of f is y^2 times a constant; its y-derivative is $2y$ times the constant:

$$\frac{\partial}{\partial y}(3x^2y^2) = (2y)(3x^2) = 6x^2y.$$

The second term is y^3 times a constant; its y-derivative is $3y^2$ times the constant:

$$\frac{\partial}{\partial y}(4xy^3) = (3y^2)(4x) = 12xy^2.$$

Finally, the y-derivative of $7y$ is, of course, 7. Putting these calculations together, we find

$$\frac{\partial}{\partial y}(3x^2y^2 + 4xy^3 + 7y) = 6x^2y + 12xy^2 + 7.$$

EXERCISES

14.1 Compute all the partial derivatives of the following functions:

a) $4x^2y - 3xy^3 + 6x$;   b) xy;   c) xy^2;

d) e^{2x+3y};   e) $\dfrac{x+y}{x-y}$;   f) $3x^2y - 7x\sqrt{y}$.

14.2 Compute the partial derivatives of the Cobb-Douglas production function $q = kx_1^{a_1}x_2^{a_2}$ and of the Constant Elasticity of Substitution (CES) production function $q = k(c_1x_1^{-a} + c_2x_2^{-a})^{-h/a}$, assuming all the parameters are positive.

14.2   ECONOMIC INTERPRETATION

Marginal Products

For a function $y = f(x)$ of one variable, the derivative $f'(x)$ measures (infinitesimally) how a Δx-change in x affects y:

$$\Delta y \approx f'(x)\Delta x.$$

The same interpretation applies to functions of several variables. For example, let $Q = F(K, L)$ be a **production function**, which relates the output Q to amounts of capital input K and labor input L. If the firm is presently using K^* units of capital and L^* units of labor to produce $Q^* = F(K^*, L^*)$ units of output, then the partial derivative

$$\frac{\partial F}{\partial K}(K^*, L^*)$$

is the rate at which output changes with respect to capital K, keeping L fixed at L^*. If capital increases by ΔK, then output will increase by

$$\Delta Q \approx \frac{\partial F}{\partial K}(K^*, L^*) \cdot \Delta K.$$

Setting $\Delta K = 1$, we see that $(\partial F/\partial K)(K^*, L^*)$ estimates the change in output due to a one unit increase in capital (with L fixed). Hence, $(\partial F/\partial K)(K^*, L^*)$ is called the **marginal product of capital** or MPK. Similarly, $(\partial F/\partial L)(K^*, L^*)$ is the rate at which output changes with respect to labor, with capital held fixed at K^*. Since it is a good estimate of the change in output for a one unit increase in labor input,

$(\partial F/\partial L)(K^*, L^*)$ is called the **marginal product of labor** (often abbreviated as MPL).

Example 14.2   Consider the Cobb-Douglas production function

$$Q = 4K^{3/4}L^{1/4}.$$

When $K = 10,000$ and $L = 625$, output Q is

$$Q = 4 \cdot 10,000^{3/4} \cdot 625^{1/4} = 4 \cdot 10^3 \cdot 5 = 20,000.$$

Computing partial derivatives,

$$\frac{\partial Q}{\partial K} = (4L^{1/4})\left(\frac{3}{4}K^{-1/4}\right) = 3L^{1/4}K^{-1/4}$$

(remember to treat L as constant) and

$$\frac{\partial Q}{\partial L} = (4K^{3/4})\left(\frac{1}{4}L^{-3/4}\right) = K^{3/4}L^{-3/4}$$

(treating K as constant). Furthermore,

$$\frac{\partial Q}{\partial K}(10,000,625) = \frac{3 \cdot 625^{1/4}}{10,000^{1/4}} = \frac{3 \cdot 5}{10} = 1.5, \qquad (1)$$

$$\frac{\partial Q}{\partial L}(10,000,625) = \frac{10,000^{3/4}}{625^{3/4}} = \frac{10^3}{5^3} = 8. \qquad (2)$$

If L is held constant and K increased by ΔK, Q will increase by approximately $1.5 \cdot \Delta K$. For an increase in K of 10 units, we use (1) to estimate $Q(10,010,625)$ to be

$$20,000 + 1.5 \cdot 10 = 20,015,$$

which is a good approximation to $Q(10,010,625) = 20,014.998\ldots$, the actual output to three decimal places. Similarly, because of (2), a 2-unit *decrease* in L should induce a $2 \cdot 8 = 16$-unit decrease in Q. Consequently, we estimate $Q(10,000,623)$ to be

$$20,000 + 8 \cdot (-2) = 19,984,$$

a good approximation to $Q(10,000,623) = 19,983.981\ldots$, the actual value to three decimal places.

By a similar analysis, if $U(x_1, \ldots, x_n)$ is a utility function, then the partial derivative $(\partial U / \partial x_i)(x_1^*, \ldots, x_n^*)$ estimates the added utility from an additional unit of good i and is called the **marginal utility of good** i at $\mathbf{x}^*$.

Elasticity

If $Q_1 = Q_1(P_1, P_2, I)$ represents the demand for good 1 in terms of the prices of goods 1 and 2 and income, then $\partial Q_1 / \partial P_1$ is the rate of change of demand with respect to own price. If the price of good 1 rises by a small amount ΔP_1, the demand for good 1 will change roughly by

$$\Delta Q_1 \approx \frac{\partial Q_1}{\partial P_1} \cdot \Delta P_1. \tag{3}$$

In general, we would expect $\partial Q_1 / \partial P_1$ to be negative. As we discussed in our presentation of elasticity in Chapter 3, the quantity $\partial Q_1 / \partial P_1$ is unsatisfactory as a measure of price sensitivity because it depends too heavily on the units used. To remove this dependency on units, economists measure the sensitivity of demand in percentage terms. More precisely, they define the **own price elasticity of demand** as

$$\varepsilon_1 = \frac{\% \text{ change in demand}}{\% \text{ change in own price}} = \frac{\Delta Q_1 / Q_1}{\Delta P_1 / P_1} = \frac{P_1}{Q_1} \cdot \frac{\Delta Q_1}{\Delta P_1}.$$

Since
$$\frac{\Delta Q_1}{\Delta P_1} = \frac{Q_1(P_1 + \Delta P_1) - Q_1(P_1)}{\Delta P_1} \approx \frac{\partial Q_1}{\partial P_1}$$

for small ΔP_1 by (3), this elasticity in calculus terms is

$$\varepsilon_1 = \frac{P_1^* \cdot \dfrac{\partial Q_1}{\partial P_1}(P_1^*, P_2^*, I^*)}{Q_1(P_1^*, P_2^*, I^*)}.$$

It is usually negative. If it lies between -1 and 0, good 1 is called **inelastic**. If this elasticity lies between $-\infty$ and -1, good 1 is called **elastic** — a small percentage change in price results in a large percentage change in quantity demanded.

To study the sensitivity in demand of one good to price changes in *other goods*, economists use the **cross price elasticity of demand**

$$\varepsilon_{Q_1, P_2} = \frac{\% \text{ change in demand for good 1}}{\% \text{ change in price of good 2}} = \frac{\Delta Q_1 / Q_1}{\Delta P_2 / P_2},$$

or in calculus terms

$$\varepsilon_{Q_1, P_2} = \frac{P_2^* \cdot \frac{\partial Q_1}{\partial P_2}(P_1^*, P_2^*, I^*)}{Q_1(P_1^*, P_2^*, I^*)}.$$

These cross elasticities can take on either sign. If ε_{Q_1, P_2} and ε_{Q_2, P_1} are both positive, goods 1 and 2 are called **substitutes**. A price increase in good 1 leads consumers to demand more of good 2 as a substitute for good 1. If ε_{Q_1, P_2} and ε_{Q_2, P_1} are both negative, goods 1 and 2 are called **complements**. In this case, if the price of one good goes up, demand for both goods decreases (assuming own price elasticities are negative). In other words, the demands for complements move together.

Finally, when economists want to measure the sensitivity of demand to changes in income, say at a given set of prices and incomes (P_1^*, P_2^*, I^*), they study the **income elasticity of demand**

$$\varepsilon_{Q_1, I} = \frac{\% \text{ change in demand}}{\% \text{ change in income}} = \frac{\Delta Q_1 / Q_1}{\Delta I / I},$$

or in calculus terms

$$\varepsilon_{Q_1, I} = \frac{I}{Q_1} \frac{\partial Q_1}{\partial I},$$

all evaluated at (P_1^*, P_2^*, I^*).

14.3 GEOMETRIC INTERPRETATION

Recall that we can represent a function $z = f(x, y)$ geometrically either by drawing its graph in $\mathbf{R}^3$ or its level curves in $\mathbf{R}^2$. When we study $(\partial f / \partial x)(a, b)$, we are holding y constant at b and looking at variations in x around $x = a$. In terms of the graph, we are looking at f only on the two-dimensional slice $\{y = b\}$ in $\mathbf{R}^3$, as in Figure 14.1.

On this slice, the graph of f is a curve — the graph of the function of *one* variable $x \longmapsto f(x, b)$. The partial derivative $(\partial f / \partial x)(a, b)$ is the slope of the tangent line to this graph on this slice, line ℓ in Figure 14.1. Similarly, $(\partial f / \partial y)(a, b)$ is the slope of the tangent line to the curve which is the intersection of the graph of f with the slice $\{x = a\}$, as illustrated in Figure 14.2.

If we are studying the level curves of $z = f(x, y)$, then $(\partial f / \partial y)(a, b)$ is the (infinitesimal) variation of f restricted to the vertical line $\{x = a\}$ as in

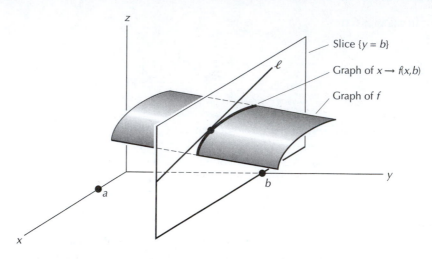

Figure 14.1

The graph of $x \longmapsto f(x, b)$ on the slice $\{y = b\}$.

Figure 14.3. We keep x fixed and vary only y. In other words, $(\partial f / \partial y)(a, b)$ measures the rate of change of f in the vertical direction. If the level curves just above (a, b) represent higher values of f than $f(a, b)$, $(\partial f / \partial y)(a, b)$ will be positive. The magnitude of $(\partial f / \partial y)(a, b)$ will depend on just how "close" the representative level curves above (a, b) are to each other. If Figure 14.3 represents a hiker's map indicating meters above sea level, then $(\partial f / \partial y)(a, b)$ represents the change in height above sea level as a result of a step 1 meter to the north. The closer the level curves are to each other, the more f changes as y increases by one unit, the larger is $(\partial f / \partial y)$. In Figure 14.3, $(\partial f / \partial y)(a, b)$ is larger than $(\partial f / \partial y)(a', b')$.

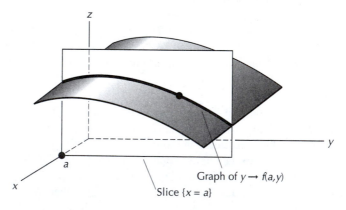

Figure 14.2

The graph of $y \longmapsto f(a, y)$ on the slice $\{x = a\}$.

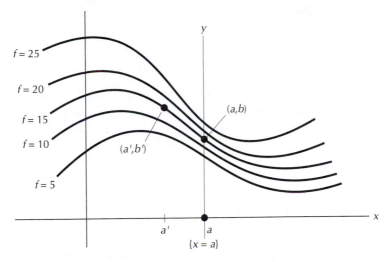

$(\partial f / \partial y)(a, b)$ *measures the change in f on* $\{x = a\}$.

Figure 14.3

EXERCISES

14.3 If $T(x, y)$ is the temperature function, interpret $(\partial T / \partial x)(x^*, y^*)$.

14.4 Consider the production function $Q = 9L^{2/3}K^{1/3}$.

  a) What is the output when $L = 1000$ and $K = 216$?

  b) Use marginal analysis to estimate $Q(998, 216)$ and $Q(1000, 217.5)$.

  c) Use a calculator to compute these two values of Q to three decimal places and compare these values with your estimates in *b*.

  d) How big must ΔL be in order for the difference between $Q(1000 + \Delta L, 216)$ and its linear approximation, $Q(1000, 216) + (\partial Q/\partial L)(1000, 216)\Delta L$, to differ by more than two units? (Plug increasing values of ΔL into these two expressions.)

14.5 The demand function $Q_1 = K_1 P_1^{a_{11}} P_2^{a_{12}} I^{b_1}$ is called a **constant elasticity demand function**.

  a) Compute the three elasticities (own price, cross price, and income) and show that they are all constants.

  b) What are reasonable ranges for the four parameters in Q_1?

14.4 THE TOTAL DERIVATIVE

Suppose we are interested in the behavior of a function $F(x, y)$ of two variables in the neighborhood of a given point (x^*, y^*). As we noted in Section 14.2, calculus of one variable tells us that if we hold y fixed at y^* and change x^* to $x^* + \Delta x$, then

$$F(x^* + \Delta x, y^*) - F(x^*, y^*) \approx \frac{\partial F}{\partial x}(x^*, y^*)\Delta x; \qquad (4)$$

if we hold x^* fixed and change y^* to $y^* + \Delta y$, then

$$F(x^*, y^* + \Delta y) - F(x^*, y^*) \approx \frac{\partial F}{\partial y}(x^*, y^*)\Delta y. \tag{5}$$

What if we allow both x and y to vary simultaneously? Since we are working in the realm of linear approximations, it is natural that the effect of the combined change is roughly the *sum* of the effects of the one-variable changes:

$$F(x^* + \Delta x, y^* + \Delta y) - F(x^*, y^*) \approx \frac{\partial F}{\partial x}(x^*, y^*)\Delta x + \frac{\partial F}{\partial y}(x^*, y^*)\Delta y. \tag{6}$$

We sometimes use (6) in the form

$$F(x^* + \Delta x, y^* + \Delta y) \approx F(x^*, y^*) + \frac{\partial F}{\partial x}(x^*, y^*)\Delta x + \frac{\partial F}{\partial y}(x^*, y^*)\Delta y. \tag{7}$$

Example 14.3   In Section 14.2, we worked with the production function $Q = F(K, L) = 4K^{3/4}L^{1/4}$ around the point $(K^*, L^*) = (10{,}000, 625)$. We used (4) to estimate that $F(10{,}010, 625)$ is 20,015 and (5) to estimate that $F(10{,}000, 623)$ is 19,984. If we want to consider the effect of *both* changes, we would use (7) to estimate

$$F(10{,}010, 623)$$

$$\approx F(10{,}000, 625) + \frac{\partial F}{\partial K}(10{,}000, 625) \cdot 10 + \frac{\partial F}{\partial L}(10{,}000, 625) \cdot (-2)$$

$$= 20{,}000 + 1.5 \cdot 10 + 8 \cdot -2$$

$$= 19{,}999,$$

which compares well with the exact value of $19{,}998.967\ldots$.

Geometric Interpretation

What is the geometric significance of the approximation (7)? For a function of one variable, the corresponding approximation is

$$f(x^* + h) \approx f(x^*) + f'(x^*)h. \tag{8}$$

As we discussed in Section 2.7, the right-hand side of (8) is the parameterized equation of the tangent line to the graph of f at x^*. So, (8) simply states that the tangent line to the graph of f at x^* is a good approximation to the graph itself in the vicinity of $(x^*, f(x^*))$, as illustrated in Figure 14.4.

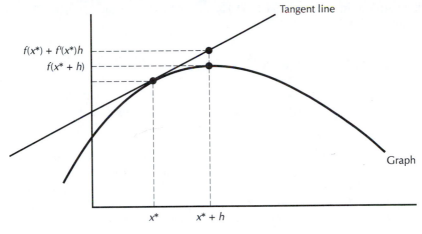

Tangent line

$f(x^*) + f'(x^*)h$

$f(x^* + h)$

Graph

x^* $x^* + h$

The geometry of expression (8).

Figure 14.4

For a function $z = F(x, y)$ of two variables, the graph is a two-dimensional surface in $\mathbf{R}^3$ and the analogue of the tangent line in Figure 14.4 is the tangent plane to the graph, as illustrated in Figure 14.5. We show next that (7) states that the tangent *plane* to the graph of F at $(x^*, y^*, F(x^*, y^*))$ is a good approximation to the graph itself in the vicinity of $(x^*, y^*, F(x^*, y^*))$. Recall from Chapter 10 that to compute the parameterized equation of the tangent plane $\mathcal{P}$ through the point $\mathbf{p}$, we need two independent vectors $\mathbf{u}$ and $\mathbf{v}$ in the plane with base at $\mathbf{p}$. In this case, we parameterize the plane as

$$\{\mathbf{x} = \mathbf{p} + s\mathbf{u} + t\mathbf{v} : s, t \in \mathbf{R}^1\}. \tag{9}$$

By the discussion in the previous section, the vectors $(1, 0, (\partial F/\partial x)(x^*, y^*))$ and $(0, 1, (\partial F/\partial y)(x^*, y^*))$ are two independent vectors in the tangent plane $\mathcal{P}$, as

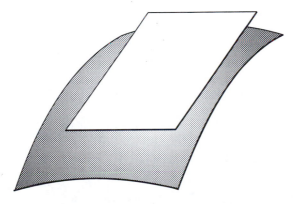

The tangent plane to the graph of F.

Figure 14.5

illustrated in Figures 14.1 and 14.2. Therefore, by (9) the tangent plane $\mathcal{P}$ can be parameterized as

$$((x^*, y^*, F(x^*, y^*)) + s(1, 0, \frac{\partial F}{\partial x}(x^*, y^*)) + t(0, 1, \frac{\partial F}{\partial y}(x^*, y^*))$$

$$= (x^* + s, \ y^* + t, \ F(x^*, y^*) + \frac{\partial F}{\partial x}(x^*, y^*) \cdot s + \frac{\partial F}{\partial y}(x^*, y^*) \cdot t).$$

Writing Δx for s and Δy for t, we see that the right-hand side of (7) is exactly the parameterized equation of the tangent plane and therefore that (7) is an analytical expression of the geometric fact that the tangent plane is a good approximation to the graph. As we mentioned in Chapter 6, we use this approximation all the time when we use *linear* mathematics for major construction projects on our *round* earth.

Notation   We use dx, dy, and dF when we are working on the tangent plane to the graph of F at (x^*, y^*):

$$dx = \Delta x, \quad dy = \Delta y, \quad \text{and} \quad dF = \frac{\partial F}{\partial x}(x^*, y^*)dx + \frac{\partial F}{\partial y}(x^*, y^*)dy,$$

just as we do for functions of one variable. These variations on the tangent plane are called **differentials**. Expression (6) states that the change ΔF on the graph of F is approximately the change dF on the tangent plane. The above expression for dF in terms of dx and dy is called the **total differential** of F at (x^*, y^*).

Linear Approximation

We have seen that the tangent plane $\mathcal{P}$ can be considered the graph of the affine mapping

$$(s, t) \longmapsto F(x^*, y^*) + \frac{\partial F}{\partial x}(x^*, y^*)s + \frac{\partial F}{\partial y}(x^*, y^*)t.$$

We can interpret (6) as saying that the change

$$F(x^* + s, y^* + t) - F(x^*, y^*)$$

can be approximated by the *linear* mapping

$$(s, t) \longmapsto \frac{\partial F}{\partial x}(x^*, y^*)s + \frac{\partial F}{\partial y}(x^*, y^*)t,$$

which can be written in matrix form as

$$\left(\frac{\partial F}{\partial x}(x^*, y^*) \quad \frac{\partial F}{\partial y}(x^*, y^*) \right) \binom{s}{t}.$$

Thus, we consider the matrix

$$\left(\frac{\partial F}{\partial x}(x^*, y^*) \quad \frac{\partial F}{\partial y}(x^*, y^*) \right)$$

as representing the linear approximation of F around (x^*, y^*). In this sense, we call this linear map and the matrix which represents it **the derivative** of F at (x^*, y^*) and write it as

$$DF(x^*, y^*) = DF_{(x^*, y^*)} = \left(\frac{\partial F}{\partial x}(x^*, y^*) \quad \frac{\partial F}{\partial y}(x^*, y^*) \right).$$

It is rather natural to form a matrix whose entries are all the partial derivatives of F and call it *the* derivative of F. But, it is important to realize that more is happening here since the linear mapping which this matrix represents is the appropriate **linear approximation** of F at (x^*, y^*).

Functions of More than Two Variables

The observations and analytical expressions for functions on $\mathbf{R}^2$ carry over in a natural way to functions on $\mathbf{R}^n$. If we are studying a function $F(x_1, \ldots, x_n)$ of n variables in a neighborhood of some selected point $\mathbf{x}^* = (x_1^*, \ldots, x_n^*)$, then

$$F(x_1^* + \Delta x_1, \ldots, x_n^* + \Delta x_n)$$
$$\approx F(x_1^*, \ldots, x_n^*) + \frac{\partial F}{\partial x_1}(\mathbf{x}^*)\Delta x_1 + \cdots + \frac{\partial F}{\partial x_n}(\mathbf{x}^*)\Delta x_n. \qquad (10)$$

The right-hand side of (10) is the parametric representation of the (n-dimensional) tangent hyperplane $\mathcal{H}$ to the n-dimensional graph of F in $\mathbf{R}^{n+1}$. We frequently use the **differentials** $dF, dx_1, \ldots, dx_n$ to denote changes on the hyperplane $\mathcal{H}$. Expression (10) states that in the vicinity of $\mathbf{x}^*$, the tangent hyperplane to the graph of F is a good approximation to the graph itself in that the actual change $\Delta F = F(\mathbf{x}^* + \Delta \mathbf{x}) - F(\mathbf{x}^*)$ is well approximated by the **total differential**

$$dF = \frac{\partial F}{\partial x_1}(\mathbf{x}^*)dx_1 + \cdots + \frac{\partial F}{\partial x_n}(\mathbf{x}^*)dx_n \qquad (11)$$

on the tangent hyperplane with $dx_i = \Delta x_i$ for all i. Since the tangent hyperplane is the graph of the affine function

$$(h_1, \ldots, h_n) \longmapsto F(\mathbf{x}^*) + \frac{\partial F}{\partial x_1}(\mathbf{x}^*)h_1 + \cdots + \frac{\partial F}{\partial x_n}(\mathbf{x}^*)h_n,$$

(10) states that the linear mapping

$$(h_1, \ldots, h_n) \longmapsto \frac{\partial F}{\partial x_1}(\mathbf{x}^*)h_1 + \cdots + \frac{\partial F}{\partial x_n}(\mathbf{x}^*)h_n \tag{12}$$

is a good approximation to the actual change in F. We call the linear map (12) and the matrix

$$DF_{\mathbf{x}^*} = \left(\frac{\partial F}{\partial x_1}(\mathbf{x}^*) \quad \cdots \quad \frac{\partial F}{\partial x_n}(\mathbf{x}^*) \right) \tag{13}$$

which represents it the **derivative** of F at $\mathbf{x}^*$, or sometimes the **Jacobian derivative** of F at $\mathbf{x}^*$.

EXERCISES

14.6   Consider the constant elasticity demand function $Q = 6p_1^{-2}p_2^{3/2}$, where Q is the demand for good 1 and p_i is the price of good i for $i = 1, 2$. Suppose current prices are $p_1 = 6$ and $p_2 = 9$.
   a) What is the current demand for Q?
   b) Use differentials to estimate the change in demand as p_1 increases by 0.25 and p_2 decreases by 0.5.
   c) Similarly, estimate the change in demand when both prices increase by 0.2.
   d) Estimate the total demands for situations b and c and compare your estimates with the actual demands.

14.7   A firm has the Cobb-Douglas production function $y = 10x_1^{1/3}x_2^{1/2}x_3^{1/6}$. Currently, it is using the input bundle $(27, 16, 64)$.
   a) How much is it producing?
   b) Use differentials to approximate its new output when x_1 increases to 27.1, x_2 decreases to 15.7, and x_3 remains the same.
   c) Use a calculator to compare you answer in part b with the actual output.
   d) Do b and c for $\Delta x_1 = \Delta x_2 = 0.2$ and $\Delta x_3 = -0.4$.

14.8   Use differentials to approximate each of the following:
   a) $f(x, y) = x^4 + 2x^2y^2 + xy^4 + 10y$ at $x = 10.36$ and $y = 1.04$;
   b) $f(x, y) = 6x^{2/3}y^{1/2}$ at $x = 998$ and $y = 101.5$;
   c) $f(x, y, z) = \sqrt{x^{1/2} + y^{1/3} + 5z^2}$ at $x = 4.2$, $y = 7.95$, and $z = 1.02$.

14.9 Use calculus and no calculator to estimate the output given by the production function $Q = 3K^{2/3}L^{1/3}$ when: a) $K = 1000$ and $L = 125$, b) $K = 998$ and $L = 128$.

14.10 Estimate $\sqrt{(4.1)^3 - (2.95)^3 - (1.02)^3}$ via differentials.

14.5 THE CHAIN RULE

Section 14.3 showed that partial derivatives describe how a function changes in directions parallel to the coordinate axes. This section will demonstrate how the partial derivatives can be used to describe how a function changes in any direction. More generally, we are often interested in how a function changes as we move along a curve in its domain. For example, if inputs are changing with time, we may want to know how the corresponding outputs are changing with time. We begin our answer to this question by reviewing parameterized curves in $\mathbf{R}^n$, a discussion begun in Section 13.2.

Curves

Definition A **curve** in $\mathbf{R}^n$ is an n-tuple of continuous functions

$$\mathbf{x}(t) = (x_1(t), \ldots, x_n(t)),$$

where each x_i maps $\mathbf{R}$ to $\mathbf{R}$. The functions $x_i(t)$ are called **coordinate functions** and t is the **parameter** describing the curve. The n-tuple $(x_1(t), \ldots, x_n(t))$ describes the coordinates of the curve at the point where the parameter value is t. If one thinks of t as denoting elapsed time, then $\mathbf{x}(t) = (x_1(t), \ldots, x_n(t))$ gives the position of a point on its trajectory in $\mathbf{R}^n$ at time t.

Example 14.4 For a very concrete example, consider a trip by car from New York to Los Angeles. The path of the trip can be drawn on a map; it is a curve. There are many different ways of parameterizing this curve. One might describe the curve by reporting the map coordinates that identify the location of the car when the car has been underway for t hours. In this case, the curve is parameterized by the time of the trip. Alternatively, one might use the total distance traveled to parameterize the path which describes the trip.

Example 14.5 The line segment connecting $(0, 0)$ and $(1, 1)$ is a curve. One possible parameterization is

$$x(t) = t, \qquad y(t) = t, \qquad 0 \le t \le 1.$$

Another parameterization is $x(t) = t^2$, $y(t) = t^2$, for $0 \le t \le 1$.

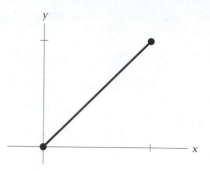

The line connecting $(0, 0)$ *and* $(1, 1)$.

Tangent Vector to a Curve

Let $\mathbf{x}(t) = (x_1(t), \ldots, x_n(t))$ be a parameterized curve in $\mathbf{R}^n$. If the parameter t represents time, then $x_j'(t)$ is the instantaneous velocity of the jth coordinate along the curve at time t. Thus, it is reasonable to call the *vector* of the component velocities

$$\mathbf{x}'(t) = (x_1'(t), \ldots, x_n'(t))$$

the **velocity vector** of the curve at t.

   If one considers $\mathbf{x}'(t_0)$ as a vector in $\mathbf{R}^n$ with tail at the point $\mathbf{x}_0 = \mathbf{x}(t_0)$, then $\mathbf{x}'(t_0)$ will be tangent to the curve at $\mathbf{x}(t_0)$. To see this, let $\{h_j\}$ be a sequence of numbers tending to 0. Then, $\mathbf{x}(t_0 + h_j)$ is a sequence of points on the curve tending to $\mathbf{x}(t_0)$, as in Figure 14.7. The vector from $\mathbf{x}(t_0)$ to $\mathbf{x}(t_0 + h_j)$ in $\mathbf{R}^n$ can be

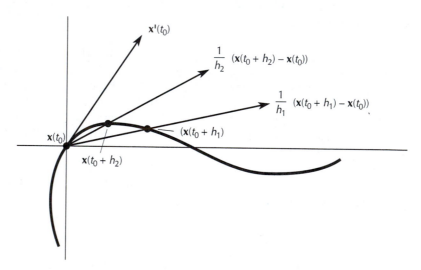

The tangent vector of a curve as a limit of secant vectors.

written as

$$\mathbf{x}(t_0 + h_j) - \mathbf{x}(t_0). \tag{14}$$

For h_j close to 0,

$$\frac{1}{h_j} \left(\mathbf{x}(t_0 + h_j) - \mathbf{x}(t_0) \right) = \frac{\mathbf{x}(t_0 + h_j) - \mathbf{x}(t_0)}{h_j} \tag{15}$$

just lengthens the vectors in (14), as in Figure 14.7. As $h_j \to 0$, the limiting vector will be tangent to the curve at $\mathbf{x}(t_0)$. But, this limiting vector is

$$\lim_{h_j \to 0} \frac{\mathbf{x}(t_0 + h_j) - \mathbf{x}(t_0)}{h_j}$$

$$= \left(\lim_{h_j \to 0} \frac{x_1(t_0 + h_j) - x_1(t_0)}{h_j}, \dots, \lim_{h_j \to 0} \frac{x_n(t_0 + h_j) - x_n(t_0)}{h_j} \right)$$

$$= (x_1'(t_0), \dots, x_n'(t_0)) = \mathbf{x}'(t_0).$$

Thus, $\mathbf{x}'(t_0)$ is also called the **tangent vector** to the curve at $\mathbf{x}(t_0)$.

Example 14.6   Consider the curve

$$x(t) = t^3, \qquad y(t) = t^2.$$

The image of this curve is shown in Figure 14.8. When $t = 1$, we are at the point $P(1, 1)$. Its tangent vector there is

$$(3t^2, 2t)_{t=1} = (3, 2),$$

which is drawn in Figure 14.8 as a vector with tail at $P(1, 1)$ and its head at $(4, 3) = (3 + 1, 2 + 1)$.

Note that this curve is not smooth at $(0, 0)$ where $t = 0$ and hence does not have a well-defined tangent vector there. This fact is mirrored by the observation that its tangent vector there is

$$(x'(0), y'(0)) = \left(3t^2, 2t \right)_{t=0} = (0, 0),$$

the zero-vector. This "pointed" curve is said to have a **cusp** at the origin.

Irregular behavior such as the cusp of Example 14.6 can be ruled out by imposing more regularity conditions on the behavior of curves. Sufficient for our purposes is the following.

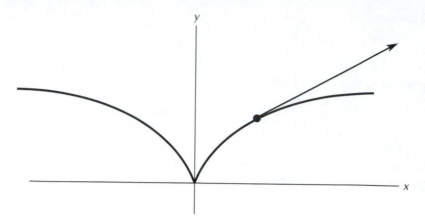

**Figure
14.8**

Tangent vector to a parameterized curve.

Definition A curve $(x_1(t), \ldots, x_n(t))$ is **regular** if and only if each $x_i'(t)$ is continuous in t and $(x_1'(t), \ldots, x_n'(t)) \neq (0, \ldots, 0)$ for all t.

We can also define what it means for a curve to be regular at a given point $\mathbf{x}_0$.

Differentiating along a Curve: The Chain Rule

Let $(x_1(t), \ldots, x_n(t))$, $a \le t \le b$, be a regular curve. Frequently, we will want to know how a function f defined on $\mathbf{R}^n$ behaves along the curve. In evaluating f along the curve, we are led to study the function of one variable

$$g(t) = f(x_1(t), \ldots, x_n(t)), \quad a \le t \le b. \tag{16}$$

Since $g : \mathbf{R}^1 \to \mathbf{R}^1$, its one-variable derivative $g'(t)$ gives the rate of change of f along the curve $\mathbf{x}(t)$. If $\mathbf{x}(t)$ had only one component, that is, if $\mathbf{x}(t)$ were a curve in $\mathbf{R}^1$, then $g(t) = f(\mathbf{x}(t))$ and we would use the Calculus I Chain Rule (of Section 4.1) to compute

$$g'(t) = f'(x(t)) \cdot x'(t). \tag{17}$$

In words, the derivative of the composite function $f(x(t))$ is the derivative of the outside function $f(x)$ (evaluated at the inside function) times the derivative of the inside function $x(t)$.

When there is more than one inside function as in the case (16) under consideration, we compute the derivative using the analogue of (17). We take the derivative with respect to each inside function one at a time:

$$\frac{dg}{dt} = \frac{\partial f}{\partial x_1}(\mathbf{x}(t))x_1'(t) + \frac{\partial f}{\partial x_2}(\mathbf{x}(t))x_2'(t) + \cdots + \frac{\partial f}{\partial x_n}(\mathbf{x}(t))x_n'(t). \tag{18}$$

The derivative of the composite is the derivative $\partial f / \partial x_1$ of f with respect to the first inside slot times the derivative of the function $x_1(t)$ in the first slot plus the derivative $\partial f / \partial x_2$ of f with respect to the second slot times the derivative of the function $x_2(t)$ in that slot, and so on.

For later reference, we state the Chain Rule as a formal theorem. First, we need the following definition.

Definition   A function $f: \mathbf{R}^n \to \mathbf{R}^1$ is **continuously differentiable** (or C^1) on an open set $U \subset \mathbf{R}^n$ if and only if for each i, $(\partial f / \partial x_i)(\mathbf{x})$ exists for all $\mathbf{x}$ in U and is continuous in $\mathbf{x}$. Similarly, a curve $\mathbf{x}: (a, b) \to \mathbf{R}^n$ is continuously differentiable (or C^1) if each component function $x_i(t)$ is itself continuously differentiable.

Theorem 14.1   (Chain Rule I) If $\mathbf{x}(t) = (x_1(t), \ldots, x_n(t))$ is a C^1 curve on an interval about t_0 and f is a C^1 function on a ball about $\mathbf{x}(t_0)$, then $g(t) \equiv f(x_1(t), \ldots, x_n(t))$ is a C^1 function at t_0 and

$$\frac{dg}{dt}(t_0) = \frac{\partial f}{\partial x_1}(\mathbf{x}(t_0))\, x_1'(t_0)$$

$$+ \frac{\partial f}{\partial x_2}(\mathbf{x}(t_0))\, x_2'(t_0) + \cdots + \frac{\partial f}{\partial x_n}(\mathbf{x}(t_0))\, x_n'(t_0). \tag{19}$$

Example 14.7   Let $f(x, y) = x^2 + y^2$, and let $x(t) = t$ and $y(t) = t$. The curve $(x(t), y(t))$ is a straight line ℓ through the origin, with velocity vector $(1, 1)$ at each t. The function $g(t) = f(x(t), y(t))$ measures the (square of) the distance from the origin as one moves out along ℓ. We will compute the derivative of $g(t)$ when $t = 1$. This is simple to do directly. Since $g(t) = 2t^2$, $g'(t) = 4t$ and $g'(1) = 4$.

If we use the Chain Rule, we first compute $\partial f / \partial x = 2x$ and $\partial f / \partial y = 2y$, and $x'(t) = y'(t) = 1$. When $t = 1$, $x = y = 1$. Therefore,

$$g'(1) = \frac{\partial f}{\partial x}(1, 1) \cdot 1 + \frac{\partial f}{\partial y}(1, 1) \cdot 1 = 2 \cdot 1 + 2 \cdot 1 = 4.$$

Sometimes the Chain Rule (19) is written as

$$\frac{df}{dt} = \frac{\partial f}{\partial x_1} \cdot \frac{dx_1}{dt} + \frac{\partial f}{\partial x_2} \cdot \frac{dx_2}{dt} + \cdots + \frac{\partial f}{\partial x_n} \cdot \frac{dx_n}{dt}, \tag{20}$$

where the left-hand side of (20) stands for $(d/dt)f(\mathbf{x}(t))$. Notice that if one ignores all the dt's in the denominators in (20), one recaptures rule (11) on total differentials.

Equation (20) also suggests a natural generalization of the Chain Rule to the case where the inside function is a function of several variables. Consider a function $\mathbf{u}: \mathbf{R}^s \to \mathbf{R}^n$,

$$\mathbf{u}(t) = \big(u_1(t_1, \ldots, t_s), u_2(t_1, \ldots, t_s), \ldots, u_n(t_1, \ldots, t_s)\big).$$

Then, for any function $f: \mathbf{R}^n \to \mathbf{R}^1$, the composite function

$$g(t_1, \ldots, t_s) \equiv f\big(u_1(\mathbf{t}), u_2(\mathbf{t}), \ldots, u_n(\mathbf{t})\big)$$

is a function from $\mathbf{R}^s$ to $\mathbf{R}^1$. We differentiate such a function by varying one t_i at a time, holding the others fixed. As a result, Theorem 14.1 leads to the more general Chain Rule — Chain Rule II:

$$\frac{\partial g}{\partial t_i}(\mathbf{t}) = \frac{\partial f}{\partial x_1}(\mathbf{u}(\mathbf{t})) \cdot \frac{\partial u_1}{\partial t_i}(\mathbf{t}) + \frac{\partial f}{\partial x_2}(\mathbf{u}(\mathbf{t})) \cdot \frac{\partial u_2}{\partial t_i}(\mathbf{t})$$
$$+ \cdots + \frac{\partial f}{\partial x_n}(\mathbf{u}(\mathbf{t})) \cdot \frac{\partial u_n}{\partial t_i}(\mathbf{t}). \tag{21}$$

Example 14.8 Consider the Cobb-Douglas production function $Q = 4K^{3/4}L^{1/4}$. Suppose that the inputs K and L vary with time t and the interest rate r, via the expressions

$$K(t, r) = \frac{10t^2}{r} \quad \text{and} \quad L(t, r) = 6t^2 + 250r.$$

We calculate the rate of change of output Q with respect to t when $t = 10$ and $r = 0.1$.
First, note that

$$\frac{\partial Q}{\partial t} = \frac{\partial Q}{\partial K} \cdot \frac{\partial K}{\partial t} + \frac{\partial Q}{\partial L} \cdot \frac{\partial L}{\partial t}$$
$$= \big(3K^{-1/4}L^{1/4}\big) \cdot (20tr^{-1}) + \big(K^{3/4}L^{-3/4}\big) \cdot (12t).$$

Since $K(10, 0.1) = 10{,}000$ and $L(10, 0.1) = 625$, at $t = 10$ and $r = 0.1$, the above expression equals

$$\big(3 \cdot 10{,}000^{-1/4}625^{1/4}\big) \cdot (20 \cdot 10 \cdot 10) + \big(10{,}000^{3/4} \cdot 625^{-3/4}\big) \cdot (12 \cdot 10)$$
$$= 3{,}960.$$

EXERCISES

14.11 Let $f(x, y) = 3xy^2 + 2x$ where $x(t) = -3t^2$ and $y(t) = 4t^3 + t$.
  a) Use the Chain Rule to find a general expression for the rate of change of the composite $f(x(t), y(t))$ with respect to t.

b) Use substitution and direct differentiation to compute the rate of change of the composite $f(x(t), y(t))$ with respect to t. Compare this answer with your answer to part *a*.

14.12 At a given moment in time, the marginal product of labor is 2.5 and the marginal product of capital is 3, the amount of capital is increasing by 2 each unit of time and the rate of change of labor is $+0.5$. What is the rate of change of output?

14.13 Calculate dz/dt at $t = 0$ if

$$z = \frac{5t^2 + 3xy}{2w^2 y}, \qquad x = t^2 + 1, \quad y = \sqrt{t^2 + 1}, \quad \text{and} \quad w = e^t + 1.$$

(This is a little tricky since there is a t in the original function. If it helps, add the equation $t = t$ to the expressions for x, y, and w in terms of t.)

14.14 Calculate the rate of change of output with respect to changes in r in Example 14.8 when $t = 10$ and $r = 0.1$.

14.15 A bat named Bob moves along a path such that his position at time t is $(2t, t^2, 1 + t^2)$ from $t = 0$ until time $t = 1$. At time $t = 1$, he leaves this path and flies off along the tangent line to his path, maintaining the speed he had at time $t = 1$. What will Bob's position be at time $t = 3$?

14.16 The university's solar car is racing on Australia's roads on the path $(x, y) = (e^t + 5t^2, t^4 - 4t)$. What are the coordinates of the car when its velocity vector is pointing parallel to the *x*-axis?

14.17 Let $w(r, s)$ be a function from $\mathbf{R}^2$ to $\mathbf{R}^1$. Let $r = y - x$ and $s = y + x$. Let $F(x, y) = w(r(x, y), s(x, y))$. Compute $\partial F / \partial x$ and $\partial F / \partial y$ in terms of $\partial w / \partial r$ and $\partial w / \partial s$.

14.6 DIRECTIONAL DERIVATIVES AND GRADIENTS

Directional Derivatives

In this section, we will see how the Chain Rule enables us to compute the rate of change of a function $F(x_1, \ldots, x_n)$ at a given point $\mathbf{x}^*$ in any given direction $\mathbf{v} = (v_1, \ldots, v_n)$. To parameterize the direction $\mathbf{v}$ from the point $\mathbf{x}^*$, write the parameterized equation of the line through $\mathbf{x}^*$ in the direction $\mathbf{v}$:

$$\mathbf{x} = \mathbf{x}^* + t\mathbf{v}.$$

To see how F changes along that line, first evaluate F along this line:

$$g(t) \equiv F(\mathbf{x}^* + t\mathbf{v}) = F(x_1^* + tv_1, \ldots, x_n^* + tv_n)$$

and then use the Chain Rule to take the derivative of g at $t = 0$:

$$g'(0) = \frac{\partial F}{\partial x_1}(\mathbf{x}^*)v_1 + \frac{\partial F}{\partial x_2}(\mathbf{x}^*)v_2 + \cdots + \frac{\partial F}{\partial x_n}(\mathbf{x}^*)\, v_n,$$

or in matrix notation,

$$\left(\frac{\partial F}{\partial x_1}(\mathbf{x}^*) \quad \cdots \quad \frac{\partial F}{\partial x_n}(\mathbf{x}^*) \right) \begin{pmatrix} v_1 \\ v_2 \\ \vdots \\ v_n \end{pmatrix} = DF_{\mathbf{x}^*} \cdot \mathbf{v}. \tag{22}$$

The expression in (22) is called the **derivative of F at $\mathbf{x}^*$ in the direction v**. Other notations for this directional derivative are

$$\frac{\partial F}{\partial \mathbf{v}}(\mathbf{x}^*) \quad \text{and} \quad D_{\mathbf{v}}F(\mathbf{x}^*).$$

In this context, if we want to know how a given function F changes at $\mathbf{x}^*$ in the direction $\mathbf{e}_1 = (1, 0, \dots, 0)$ parallel to the x_1-axis, we compute

$$DF_{\mathbf{x}^*}(\mathbf{e}_1) = \left(\frac{\partial F}{\partial x_1}(\mathbf{x}^*) \quad \cdots \quad \frac{\partial F}{\partial x_n}(\mathbf{x}^*) \right) \begin{pmatrix} 1 \\ 0 \\ \vdots \\ 0 \end{pmatrix} = \frac{\partial F}{\partial x_1}(\mathbf{x}^*),$$

just what we would expect for the derivative of F in the x_1-direction.

Example 14.9   Consider again the production function

$$Q = F(K, L) = 4K^{3/4}L^{1/4}$$

at $(K, L) = (10{,}000, 625)$. The derivative of F at $(10{,}000, 625)$ in the direction $(1, 1)$ is simply

$$\frac{\partial F}{\partial K}(10{,}000, 625) \cdot 1 + \frac{\partial F}{\partial L}(10{,}000, 625) \cdot 1 = 1.5 \cdot 1 + 8 \cdot 1 = 9.5.$$

The Gradient Vector

We have been writing the derivative of $y = F(x_1, \dots, x_n)$ at a point $\mathbf{x}^*$ as the row matrix

$$DF_{\mathbf{x}^*} = \left(\frac{\partial F}{\partial x_1}(\mathbf{x}^*) \quad \cdots \quad \frac{\partial F}{\partial x_n}(\mathbf{x}^*) \right),$$

regarding it as a linear function which approximates F around $\mathbf{x}^*$. Sometimes, we write the derivative of F at $\mathbf{x}^*$ as a *column* matrix:

$$\begin{pmatrix} \dfrac{\partial F}{\partial x_1}(x^*) \\ \vdots \\ \dfrac{\partial F}{\partial x_n}(\mathbf{x}^*) \end{pmatrix}.$$

We think of this column matrix as a *vector* in $\mathbf{R}^n$ with tail at $\mathbf{x}^*$. We write it as $\nabla F(\mathbf{x}^*)$, or sometimes as grad $F(\mathbf{x}^*)$, and call it the **gradient** or **gradient vector** of F at $\mathbf{x}^*$.

The important characteristics of a vector are its length and direction. The length and direction of the gradient vector $\nabla F(\mathbf{x})$ have significance. First, notice that the directional derivative of F at $\mathbf{x}$ in the direction $\mathbf{v}$, $DF_{\mathbf{x}}(\mathbf{v})$, can be represented by the dot product of the vectors $\nabla F(\mathbf{x})$ and $\mathbf{v}$:

$$\nabla F(\mathbf{x}^*) \cdot \mathbf{v} = \begin{pmatrix} \dfrac{\partial F}{\partial x_1}(x^*) \\ \vdots \\ \dfrac{\partial F}{\partial x_n}(\mathbf{x}^*) \end{pmatrix} \cdot \begin{pmatrix} v_1 \\ v_2 \\ \vdots \\ v_n \end{pmatrix} = \sum_{i=1}^{n} \dfrac{\partial F}{\partial x_i}(\mathbf{x}^*)v_i.$$

We concentrate for a while solely on the direction of $\mathbf{v}$, ignoring its length $\|\mathbf{v}\|$. To operationalize this emphasis on the direction, we will work only with vectors $\mathbf{v}$ of length 1: $\|\mathbf{v}\| = 1$. Some texts even make the condition $\|\mathbf{v}\| = 1$ part of the definition of the directional derivative $DF_{\mathbf{x}}(\mathbf{v})$ of F at $\mathbf{x}$ in the *direction* $\mathbf{v}$.

Example 14.10   Again considering the production function of the previous example, we ask at what rate would production increase if we increased K and L at the same rate? Since we are not told the magnitude of the change, only its direction, we use the *unit* vector $(1/\sqrt{2}, 1/\sqrt{2})$ in the direction $(1, 1)$. The rate of change of F in the *direction* $(1/\sqrt{2}, 1/\sqrt{2})$ is

$$1.5 \cdot \frac{1}{\sqrt{2}} + 8 \cdot \frac{1}{\sqrt{2}} = \frac{9.5}{\sqrt{2}} \approx 6.7175.$$

Since it is equivalent to the directional derivative, $\nabla F(\mathbf{x}^*) \cdot \mathbf{v}$ measures the rate at which F rises or falls as one moves out from $\mathbf{x}^*$ in the direction $\mathbf{v}$. By the usual property of dot products (Theorem 10.3), the derivative of F in the direction $\mathbf{v}$ equals

$$\nabla F(\mathbf{x}^*) \cdot \mathbf{v} = \|\nabla F(\mathbf{x}^*)\|\|\mathbf{v}\| \cos \theta = \|\nabla F(\mathbf{x}^*)\| \cos \theta, \qquad (23)$$

since $\|\mathbf{v}\| = 1$, where θ is the angle between the vectors $\nabla F(\mathbf{x}^*)$ and $\mathbf{v}$ at the base point $\mathbf{x}^*$, as in Figure 14.9.

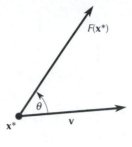

**Figure
14.9**

$$\nabla F(\mathbf{x}^*) \cdot \mathbf{v}.$$

At this point, it is natural to ask: in what *direction* does F increase most rapidly? Since $\cos \theta$ varies between -1 and $+1$, (23) implies that $\nabla F(\mathbf{x}^*) \cdot \mathbf{v}$ will be largest among vectors $\mathbf{v}$ of unit length when $\cos \theta = 1$, that is, when $\theta = 0°$. Therefore, $\nabla F(\mathbf{x}^*) \cdot \mathbf{v}$ is largest as $\mathbf{v}$ varies among vectors of unit length, when $\mathbf{v}$ points in the same direction as $\nabla F(\mathbf{x}^*)$. The following theorem formalizes this result.

Theorem 14.2   Let $F: \mathbf{R}^n \rightarrow \mathbf{R}^1$ be a C^1 function. At any point $\mathbf{x}$ in the domain of F at which $\nabla F(\mathbf{x}) \neq \mathbf{0}$, the gradient vector $\nabla F(\mathbf{x})$ points at $\mathbf{x}$ into the direction in which F increases most rapidly.

Example 14.11   We consider once again the production function $Q = 4K^{3/4}L^{1/4}$. Suppose again that the current input bundle is $(10,000,625)$. If we want to know in what proportions we should add K and L to $(10,000,625)$ to increase production most rapidly, we compute the gradient vector

$$\nabla F(10,000,625) = \begin{pmatrix} 1.5 \\ 8 \end{pmatrix}$$

and deduce that we should add K and L at a ratio of 1.5 to 8. This change is pictured in Figure 14.10.

Example 14.12   If $z = F(x, y)$ represents the height above sea level on a mountain climber's map, then $\nabla F(x^*, y^*)$ points in the direction of the steepest climb from the point (x^*, y^*). If $F(x, y)$ represents the temperature at the point (x^*, y^*) on a weather map, then $\nabla F(x^*, y^*)$ points into the direction one would move from (x^*, y^*) to increase temperature most rapidly.

EXERCISES

14.18   In what direction should one move from the point $(2, 3)$ to increase $4x^2y$ most rapidly? Present your answer as a vector of length 1.

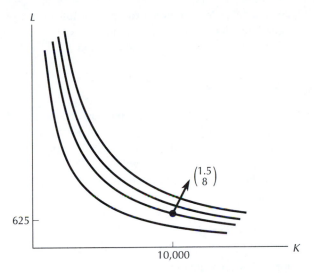

The gradient points in the direction at which output increases most rapidly.

Figure 14.10

14.19 Consider the function $y^2 e^{3x}$. In what direction should one move from the point $(0, 3)$ to increase the value of this function most rapidly? Express your answer as a vector of length 1.

14.20 Compute the directional derivative of $f(x, y) = xy^2 + x^3 y$ at the point $(4, -2)$ in the direction $(1/\sqrt{10}, 3/\sqrt{10})$.

14.7 EXPLICIT FUNCTIONS FROM $\mathbf{R^n}$ TO $\mathbf{R^m}$

Up to now we have been studying functions with only one endogenous variable. As we remarked in Chapter 13, functions with several endogenous variables arise naturally in economic models. In these cases, when there are m endogenous variables in the system, there should be m separate functions to determine their values. For example, a multiproduct firm which transforms n inputs into m outputs has a production function for each output:

$$
\begin{aligned}
q_1 &= f_1(x_1, \ldots, x_n) \\
q_2 &= f_2(x_1, \ldots, x_n) \\
&\;\;\vdots \qquad\quad \vdots \\
q_m &= f_m(x_1, \ldots, x_n).
\end{aligned}
\tag{24}
$$

Instead of viewing (24) as m functions of n variables, we can view (24) as a single function from $\mathbf{R^n}$ to $\mathbf{R^m}$:

$$
F(\mathbf{x}) = \big(f_1(x_1, \ldots, x_n), f_2(x_1, \ldots, x_n), \ldots, f_m(x_1, \ldots, x_n)\big).
\tag{25}
$$

Section 13.2 listed a number of economic examples of functions from $\mathbf{R}^n$ to $\mathbf{R}^m$, for example, demand functions and utility mappings.

On the other hand, if we start with a single function

$$F: \mathbf{R}^n \to \mathbf{R}^m \tag{26}$$

from $\mathbf{R}^n$ to $\mathbf{R}^m$ as in (25), we see that each component of F is a function from $\mathbf{R}^n$ to $\mathbf{R}^1$, and we can work with F as m functions from $\mathbf{R}^n$ to $\mathbf{R}^1$, as in (24). This method is especially useful when we develop and use the theorems of calculus for a function as in (25) or (26). We simply apply the usual theory to each component $f_i: \mathbf{R}^n \to \mathbf{R}^1$ separately and then combine all the information learned back into one big vector or matrix.

Approximation by Differentials

For example, suppose we are studying

$$F = (f_1, \ldots, f_m): \mathbf{R}^n \to \mathbf{R}^m$$

at a specific point $\mathbf{x}^* = (x_1^*, \ldots, x_n^*)$ in $\mathbf{R}^n$ and we want to use approximation by differentials to estimate the effect of a change at $\mathbf{x}^*$ by $\Delta \mathbf{x} = (\Delta x_1, \ldots, \Delta x_n)$. We first apply the discussion in Section 14.4 to each component f_i of F:

$$f_1(\mathbf{x}^* + \Delta \mathbf{x}) - f_1(\mathbf{x}^*) \approx \frac{\partial f_1}{\partial x_1}(\mathbf{x}^*)\Delta x_1 + \cdots + \frac{\partial f_1}{\partial x_n}(\mathbf{x}^*)\Delta x_n$$

$$f_2(\mathbf{x}^* + \Delta \mathbf{x}) - f_2(\mathbf{x}^*) \approx \frac{\partial f_2}{\partial x_1}(\mathbf{x}^*)\Delta x_1 + \cdots + \frac{\partial f_2}{\partial x_n}(\mathbf{x}^*)\Delta x_n$$

$$\vdots \qquad\qquad \vdots \qquad\qquad \vdots$$

$$f_m(\mathbf{x}^* + \Delta \mathbf{x}) - f_m(\mathbf{x}^*) \approx \frac{\partial f_m}{\partial x_1}(\mathbf{x}^*)\Delta x_1 + \cdots + \frac{\partial f_m}{\partial x_n}(\mathbf{x}^*)\Delta x_n.$$

Then, we use vector and matrix notation to combine these results and get

$$F(\mathbf{x}^* + \Delta \mathbf{x}) - F(\mathbf{x}^*) \approx \begin{pmatrix} \frac{\partial f_1}{\partial x_1}(\mathbf{x}^*) & \cdots & \frac{\partial f_1}{\partial x_n}(\mathbf{x}^*) \\ \vdots & \ddots & \vdots \\ \frac{\partial f_m}{\partial x_1}(\mathbf{x}^*) & \cdots & \frac{\partial f_m}{\partial x_n}(\mathbf{x}^*) \end{pmatrix} \begin{pmatrix} \Delta x_1 \\ \Delta x_2 \\ \vdots \\ \Delta x_n \end{pmatrix}. \tag{27}$$

Expression (27) describes the linear approximation of F at $\mathbf{x}^*$. We write the matrix on the right-hand side in (27) as

$$DF(\mathbf{x}^*) = DF_{\mathbf{x}^*} = \begin{pmatrix} \dfrac{\partial f_1}{\partial x_1}(\mathbf{x}^*) & \dfrac{\partial f_1}{\partial x_2}(\mathbf{x}^*) & \cdots & \dfrac{\partial f_1}{\partial x_n}(\mathbf{x}^*) \\ \vdots & \vdots & \ddots & \vdots \\ \dfrac{\partial f_m}{\partial x_1}(\mathbf{x}^*) & \dfrac{\partial f_m}{\partial x_2}(\mathbf{x}^*) & \cdots & \dfrac{\partial f_m}{\partial x_n}(\mathbf{x}^*) \end{pmatrix} \tag{28}$$

and call it **the derivative** or the **Jacobian derivative** of F at $\mathbf{x}^*$. Of course, (27) is the natural generalization of (13) to m endogenous variables.

As we emphasized in Section 14.4, it is natural to form a matrix composed of all the first order partial derivatives of the f_i's and call it *the* derivative of F. But more is happening here! Expression (27) states that the linear map which this matrix represents is the effective linear approximation of F around $\mathbf{x}^*$. This is the essence of what calculus is all about. In studying the behavior of a nonlinear function $F \colon \mathbf{R^n} \to \mathbf{R^m}$ in the vicinity of some special point $\mathbf{x}^*$:

(1) we use derivatives to form the linear approximation $DF(\mathbf{x}^*)$,
(2) we use linear theory to study the behavior of the linear mapping $DF(\mathbf{x}^*)$, and
(3) we use calculus theory to translate information about the linear function $DF(\mathbf{x}^*)$ to the corresponding information about the nonlinear function F in a neighborhood of $\mathbf{x}^*$.

Example 14.13 In a two-commodity world, consider the pair of constant-elasticity demand functions

$$q_1 = 6p_1^{-2}p_2^{3/2}y \quad \text{and} \quad q_2 = 4p_1p_2^{-1}y^2$$

in the vicinity of the current prices and income

$$p_1^* = 6, \quad p_2^* = 9, \quad \text{and} \quad y^* = 2.$$

If we handle each of these as separate functions q_i, we compute

$$\begin{aligned} dq_1 &= \frac{\partial q_1}{\partial p_1}dp_1 + \frac{\partial q_1}{\partial p_2}dp_2 + \frac{\partial q_1}{\partial y}dy \\ &= \left(-12p_1^{-3}p_2^{3/2}y\right)dp_1 + \left(9p_1^{-2}p_2^{1/2}y\right)dp_2 + \left(6p_1^{-2}p_2^{3/2}\right)dy \\ &= -3dp_1 + 1.5dp_2 + 4.5dy \qquad \text{at } (6,9,2), \end{aligned}$$

$$\begin{aligned} dq_2 &= \frac{\partial q_2}{\partial p_1}dp_1 + \frac{\partial q_2}{\partial p_2}dp_2 + \frac{\partial q_2}{\partial y}dy \\ &= \left(4p_2^{-1}y^2\right)dp_1 + \left(-4p_1p_2^{-2}y^2\right)dp_2 + \left(8p_1p_2^{-1}y\right)dy \\ &= \frac{16}{9}dp_1 - \frac{32}{27}dp_2 + \frac{32}{3}dy \qquad \text{at } (6,9,2). \end{aligned}$$

For example, if both prices rise by 0.1 ($dp_1 = dp_2 = 0.1$) and income falls by 0.1 ($dy = -0.1$), then $dq_1 = 6$ and $dq_2 \approx -1$. In matrix notation, this calculation becomes

$$
\begin{pmatrix} dq_1 \\ dq_2 \end{pmatrix} = \begin{pmatrix} \dfrac{\partial q_1}{\partial p_1} & \dfrac{\partial q_1}{\partial p_2} & \dfrac{\partial q_1}{\partial y} \\[2mm] \dfrac{\partial q_2}{\partial p_1} & \dfrac{\partial q_2}{\partial p_2} & \dfrac{\partial q_2}{\partial y} \end{pmatrix} \begin{pmatrix} dp_1 \\ dp_2 \\ dy \end{pmatrix}
$$

$$
= \begin{pmatrix} -3 & 1.5 & 4.5 \\ 16/9 & -32/27 & 32/3 \end{pmatrix} \begin{pmatrix} 0.1 \\ 0.1 \\ -0.1 \end{pmatrix} = \begin{pmatrix} 6 \\ -1.0074 \end{pmatrix}.
$$

The Chain Rule

The **Chain Rule** has a particularly natural extension to functions from $\mathbf{R}^n$ to $\mathbf{R}^m$, as the following theorem indicates.

Theorem 14.3   (Chain Rule III) Let $F: \mathbf{R}^n \to \mathbf{R}^m$ and let $\mathbf{a}: \mathbf{R}^1 \to \mathbf{R}^n$ be C^1 functions. Then, the composite function $g(t) = F(\mathbf{a}(t))$ is a C^1 function from $\mathbf{R}^1$ to $\mathbf{R}^m$ and

$$
g_i'(t) = \sum_j \frac{\partial f_i}{\partial x_j}(a_1(t), \ldots, a_n(t)) a_j'(t) = Df_i(\mathbf{a}(t)) \cdot \mathbf{a}'(t). \tag{29}
$$

Putting all these component conditions together, we obtain the vector equation

$$
g'(t) = D(F \circ \mathbf{a})(t) = DF(\mathbf{a}(t)) \cdot \mathbf{a}'(t).
$$

Example 14.14   In Example 14.13, suppose that p_1, p_2, and y are varying over time according to the equations

$$
p_1(t) = \sqrt{12t}, \quad p_2(t) = t^2, \quad \text{and} \quad y(t) = t - 1.
$$

How is demand changing with respect to time at $t = 3$?
   Notice that $(p_1(3), p_2(3), y(3)) = (6, 9, 2)$. Therefore,

$$
\begin{pmatrix} \dfrac{dq_1}{dt} \\[3mm] \dfrac{dq_2}{dt} \end{pmatrix} = \begin{pmatrix} \dfrac{\partial q_1}{\partial p_1} & \dfrac{\partial q_1}{\partial p_2} & \dfrac{\partial q_1}{\partial y} \\[2mm] \dfrac{\partial q_2}{\partial p_1} & \dfrac{\partial q_2}{\partial p_2} & \dfrac{\partial q_2}{\partial y} \end{pmatrix} \begin{pmatrix} p_1'(3) \\ p_2'(3) \\ y'(3) \end{pmatrix}
$$

$$
= \begin{pmatrix} -3 & 1.5 & 4.5 \\ 16/9 & -32/27 & 32/3 \end{pmatrix} \begin{pmatrix} 1 \\ 6 \\ 1 \end{pmatrix} = \begin{pmatrix} 10.5 \\ 5.333 \end{pmatrix}.
$$

We can push the Chain Rule one step further by replacing the curve $\mathbf{a}: \mathbf{R^1} \to \mathbf{R^n}$ by a function $\mathbf{a}: \mathbf{R^s} \to \mathbf{R^n}$, as we did in (21). Then, the composition $g(\mathbf{t}) = F(\mathbf{a(t)})$ is a function from $\mathbf{R^s}$ to $\mathbf{R^m}$. If we hold $s - 1$ coordinates of $\mathbf{t}$ fixed and differentiate g with respect to t_h, then (29) becomes

$$\frac{\partial g_i}{\partial t_h} = \sum_j \frac{\partial f_i}{\partial x_j}(\mathbf{a(t)}) \cdot \frac{\partial \mathbf{a}_j}{\partial t_h}(\mathbf{t}) = Df_i(\mathbf{a(t)}) \cdot \begin{pmatrix} \dfrac{\partial \mathbf{a}_1}{\partial t_h} \\ \dfrac{\partial \mathbf{a}_2}{\partial t_h} \\ \vdots \\ \dfrac{\partial \mathbf{a}_n}{\partial t_h} \end{pmatrix}.$$

Putting these equations together for $i = 1, \ldots, m$ to form the matrix $Dg(\mathbf{t})$ of all the $\partial g_i / \partial t_h$, we find

$$Dg(\mathbf{t}) = \begin{pmatrix} \dfrac{\partial f_1}{\partial x_1} & \cdots & \dfrac{\partial f_1}{\partial x_n} \\ \vdots & \ddots & \vdots \\ \dfrac{\partial f_m}{\partial x_1} & \cdots & \dfrac{\partial f_m}{\partial x_n} \end{pmatrix} \begin{pmatrix} \dfrac{\partial \mathbf{a}_1}{\partial t_1} & \cdots & \dfrac{\partial \mathbf{a}_1}{\partial t_s} \\ \vdots & \ddots & \vdots \\ \dfrac{\partial \mathbf{a}_n}{\partial t_1} & \cdots & \dfrac{\partial \mathbf{a}_n}{\partial t_s} \end{pmatrix}$$

$$= DF(\mathbf{a(t)}) \cdot D\mathbf{a(t)}.$$

Theorem 14.4   (Chain Rule IV) Let $F: \mathbf{R^n} \to \mathbf{R^m}$ and $A: \mathbf{R^s} \to \mathbf{R^n}$ be C^1 functions. Let $\mathbf{s}^* \in \mathbf{R^s}$ and $\mathbf{x}^* = A(\mathbf{s}^*) \in \mathbf{R^n}$. Consider the composite function

$$H = F \circ A : \mathbf{R^s} \to \mathbf{R^n}.$$

Let $DF(\mathbf{x}^*)$ be the $m \times n$ Jacobian matrix of the partial derivatives of F at $\mathbf{x}^*$ and let $DA(\mathbf{s}^*)$ be the $n \times s$ Jacobian matrix of partial derivatives of A at $\mathbf{s}^*$. Then, the Jacobian matrix $DH(\mathbf{s}^*)$ is given by the matrix product of the Jacobians:

$$DH(\mathbf{s}^*) = D(F \circ A)(\mathbf{s}^*) = DF(\mathbf{x}^*) \cdot DA(\mathbf{s}^*).$$

Since matrix multiplication can be viewed as the composition of the corresponding linear mappings, the Chain Rule says that the *derivative of the composite mapping is the composition of the derivatives of the component maps*, evaluated at the proper points.

EXERCISES

14.21   Suppose that in Example 14.13, prices and income are functions of the independent variables time t and interest rate r, via the equations $p_1 = \sqrt{12t}$, $p_2 = 10rt^2$, and

$y = 20r$. Find the rate of change of quantity demanded, q_1 and q_2, with respect to both time and interest rate when $t = 3$ and $r = 0.1$.

14.22   Given that $G(x, y) = (x^2 + 1, y^2)$ and $F(u, v) = (u + v, v^2)$, compute the Jacobian derivative matrix of $F(G(x, y))$ at the point $(x, y) = (1, 1)$.

14.8   HIGHER-ORDER DERIVATIVES

The partial derivative $\partial f / \partial x_i$ of a function $y = f(x_1, \ldots, x_n)$ is itself a function of n variables, as the examples and exercises in this chapter illustrate. Just as with a function of a single variable, we can continue taking partial derivatives of these partial derivatives and these higher-order derivatives are frequently significant.

Continuously Differentiable Functions

Not every function has a derivative at every point. In Section 2.5, we saw that $f(x) = |x|$ does not have a derivative at $x = 0$. Geometrically, its graph has a corner at $x = 0$ and therefore no unambiguous tangent line there, as Figure 2.13 illustrates. We say that $|x|$ is *not differentiable* at $x = 0$. As we discussed in Section 2.5, if $y = f(x)$ has a derivative $f'(x)$ for every x in some interval J, we say that f is **differentiable** on J. If $f'(x)$ is also continuous at every x in J, we say that f is **continuously differentiable** or C^1 on J. If f is C^1, we can continue trying to calculate its higher-order derivatives. If $f'(x)$ has a derivative $(f')'(x) = f''(x)$ at every point of J, we say that f is **twice differentiable** on J. If this second derivative f'' is continuous, we say that f is **twice continuously differentiable**, or in short, C^2 on J. Similarly, if all the derivatives of f of order $\leq k$ exist and are continuous on J — we say f is k-**times continuously differentiable** or C^k on J. If f is C^k for every k — every derivative of every order of f exists and is continuous, we say that f is C^∞ (read "C-infinity").

The same terminology holds for functions of several variables. If

$$\frac{\partial f}{\partial x_i}(\mathbf{x}^*) = \lim_{h \to 0} \frac{f(x_1^*, \ldots, x_i^* + h, x_{i+1}^*, \ldots, x_n^*) - f(x_1^*, \ldots, x_i^*, \ldots, x_n^*)}{h}$$

exists for each i, we say f is **differentiable** at $\mathbf{x}^*$. If these n partial derivative functions are continuous functions at a point $\mathbf{x}^*$ in $\mathbf{R}^n$, we say that f is **continuously differentiable** or C^1 at $\mathbf{x}^*$. If all n ($\partial f / \partial x_i$)'s are themselves differentiable on an open region J of $\mathbf{R}^n$, we can compute their partial derivatives. For example,

$$\frac{\partial}{\partial x_j} \left(\frac{\partial f}{\partial x_i} \right)$$

is called the $x_i x_j$-second order partial derivative of f. It is usually written without the parentheses, abbreviating $\partial \partial$ as ∂^2 :

$$\frac{\partial^2 f}{\partial x_j \partial x_i}.$$

The $x_i x_i$-derivative is usually written as $\dfrac{\partial^2 f}{\partial x_i^2}$ instead of as $\dfrac{\partial^2 f}{\partial x_i \partial x_i}$. Terms of the form $\dfrac{\partial^2 f}{\partial x_i \partial x_j}$ with $i \neq j$ are called **cross partial derivatives** or **mixed partial derivatives**.

Second Order Derivatives and Hessians

Example 14.15   Let's take second derivatives of the production function $Q = 4K^{3/4}L^{1/4}$. In Example 14.2, we found

$$\frac{\partial Q}{\partial K} = 3K^{-1/4}L^{1/4} \quad \text{and} \quad \frac{\partial Q}{\partial L} = K^{3/4}L^{-3/4}.$$

So

$$\frac{\partial^2 Q}{\partial L \partial K} = \frac{\partial}{\partial L}\left(\frac{\partial Q}{\partial K}\right) = \frac{\partial}{\partial L}\left(3K^{-1/4}L^{1/4}\right) = \frac{3}{4}K^{-1/4}L^{-3/4}.$$

The other cross partial is

$$\frac{\partial^2 Q}{\partial K \partial L} = \frac{\partial}{\partial K}\left(\frac{\partial Q}{\partial L}\right) = \frac{\partial}{\partial K}\left(K^{3/4}L^{-3/4}\right) = \frac{3}{4}K^{-1/4}L^{-3/4}.$$

The two remaining own partial derivatives are

$$\frac{\partial^2 Q}{\partial L^2} = \frac{\partial}{\partial L}\left(\frac{\partial Q}{\partial L}\right) = \frac{\partial}{\partial L}(K^{3/4}L^{-3/4}) = -\frac{3}{4}K^{3/4}L^{-7/4}$$

and

$$\frac{\partial^2 Q}{\partial K^2} = \frac{\partial}{\partial K}\left(\frac{\partial Q}{\partial K}\right) = \frac{\partial}{\partial K}(3K^{-1/4}L^{1/4}) = -\frac{3}{4}K^{-5/4}L^{1/4}.$$

Notice that a function of 2 variables has 4 second order partial derivatives. A function of n variables will have n^2 second order partial derivatives. It is natural to arrange these n^2 partial derivatives into an $n \times n$ matrix whose (i, j)th entry is $(\partial^2 f / \partial x_j \partial x_i)(\mathbf{x}^*)$. This matrix is called the **Hessian** or **Hessian matrix** of f and written as $D^2 f(\mathbf{x})$ or $D^2 f_{\mathbf{x}}$:

$$D^2 f_{\mathbf{x}} \equiv \begin{pmatrix} \dfrac{\partial^2 f}{\partial x_1{}^2} & \dfrac{\partial^2 f}{\partial x_2 \partial x_1} & \cdots & \dfrac{\partial^2 f}{\partial x_n \partial x_1} \\[2ex] \dfrac{\partial^2 f}{\partial x_1 \partial x_2} & \dfrac{\partial^2 f}{\partial x_2{}^2} & \cdots & \dfrac{\partial^2 f}{\partial x_n \partial x_2} \\[2ex] \vdots & \vdots & \ddots & \vdots \\[2ex] \dfrac{\partial^2 f}{\partial x_1 \partial x_n} & \dfrac{\partial^2 f}{\partial x_2 \partial x_n} & \cdots & \dfrac{\partial^2 f}{\partial x_n{}^2} \end{pmatrix}.$$

If all these n^2 second order derivatives of f exist and are themselves continuous functions of $(x_1, \cdots, x_n)$, we say that f is **twice continuously differentiable** or C^2.

Young's Theorem

A priori, there is no reason for $\dfrac{\partial^2 f}{\partial x_2 \partial x_1}$ to be related to $\dfrac{\partial^2 f}{\partial x_1 \partial x_2}$. They are different derivatives of different functions. Notice, however, in Example 14.15 that

$$\frac{\partial^2 Q}{\partial L \, \partial K} = \frac{3}{4} K^{-1/4} L^{-3/4} = \frac{\partial^2 Q}{\partial K \, \partial L}.$$

It turns out that these mixed partials are equal in general — an important result known as **Young's theorem**.

Theorem 14.5   Suppose that $y = f(x_1, \cdots, x_n)$ is C^2 on an open region J in R^n. Then, for all $\mathbf{x}$ in J and for each pair of indices i, j,

$$\frac{\partial^2 f}{\partial x_i \partial x_j}(\mathbf{x}) = \frac{\partial^2 f}{\partial x_j \partial x_i}(\mathbf{x}).$$

Example 14.16   Consider the general Cobb-Douglas production function $Q = kx^a y^b$. Then,

$$\frac{\partial Q}{\partial x} = akx^{a-1} y^b, \qquad\qquad \frac{\partial Q}{\partial y} = bkx^a y^{b-1},$$

$$\frac{\partial^2 Q}{\partial x \partial y} = abkx^{a-1} y^{b-1}, \quad \text{and} \quad \frac{\partial^2 Q}{\partial y \partial x} = abkx^{a-1} y^{b-1},$$

with the latter two expressions equal as Young's theorem mandates.

Theorem 14.5 states that the order of differentiation does *not* matter for a general C^2 function. Even though the hypotheses can be weakened slightly (both second order partials must exist, of course, but only one need be continuous), there are examples of weird functions which are twice differentiable but not *continuously* twice differentiable and whose mixed partials are not equal. See Exercise 14.28 below.

Fortunately, just about every function we will meet in applications will be C^2 and therefore its mixed partials will be equal. It is important to note that Young's theorem implies that the Hessian is a *symmetric matrix*.

Higher-Order Derivatives

We can continue taking higher order derivatives, and Young's theorem holds for these cases. For example, if we take an $x_1x_2x_4$-derivative of order three, then the order of differentiation does not matter for a C^3-function:

$$\frac{\partial^3 f}{\partial x_1 \partial x_2 \partial x_4} = \frac{\partial^3 f}{\partial x_1 \partial x_4 \partial x_2} = \frac{\partial^3 f}{\partial x_2 \partial x_1 \partial x_4}$$

$$= \frac{\partial^3 f}{\partial x_2 \partial x_4 \partial x_1} = \frac{\partial^3 f}{\partial x_4 \partial x_1 \partial x_2} = \frac{\partial^3 f}{\partial x_4 \partial x_2 \partial x_1}.$$

A function on $\mathbf{R}^n$ is C^3 (or 3 times continuously differentiable) if all of its n^3 third order partial derivatives exist and are continuous. We can keep going and define kth order partial derivatives and C^k functions. For C^k functions, the order with which one takes the k partial derivatives does not matter.

An Economic Application

For a production function $Q = F(K, L)$, $(\partial Q/\partial L)(K^*, L^*)$ measures the marginal product of labor (MPL) — intuitively the additional output as a result of hiring another worker while keeping the amount of capital equipment K^* fixed. It is reasonable to assume that eventually the benefits from adding another worker will decrease as more workers are added to the same assembly line or plot of farm land. For example, crowding may cause some inefficiencies. Economists typically assume that, at least from some point on, the rate of growth of MPL diminishes. In terms of the production function, these assumptions mean that $\partial Q/\partial L$ is positive but eventually decreasing in L, so that $\partial^2 Q/\partial L^2$ is eventually negative. Similarly, they assume that $\partial Q/\partial K$ is positive and $\partial^2 Q/\partial K^2$ is eventually negative. The negativity of these second order partials is sometimes called the *law of diminishing marginal productivity*.

Notation Other frequently used notation for second order partial derivatives includes

$$\frac{\partial^2 f}{\partial x \partial y} = f_{xy} = D_{xy}f \qquad \text{and} \qquad \frac{\partial^2 f}{\partial x_i \partial x_j} = f_{x_i x_j} = f_{ij} = D_{ij}f.$$

Sometimes, a prime or two is added for emphasis: f'_x, f''_{xy}, and so on. These same notational tricks are also used to indicate partial derivatives of higher order, such as f_{ijk} and so forth.

EXERCISES

14.23   Compute the Hessian matrix for each of the six functions in Exercise 14.1. Verify that each is a symmetric matrix.

14.24   Compute all the third order partial derivatives of the production function $Q = 4K^{3/4}L^{1/4}$. Use Young's theorem to speed up this process.

14.25   Use Young's theorem for second order partial derivatives to prove Young's theorem for C^3 third order partial derivatives.

14.26   For what values of their parameters do Cobb-Douglas and CES production functions obey the law of diminishing marginal returns?

14.27   Consider the production function $Q = K^{3/4}L^{3/4}$. Show that marginal productivity of each factor is diminishing. Show, however, that for any strictly positive input combination, if the input combination is doubled, then output more than doubles.

14.28   The goal of this exercise is to examine a C^1 function for which the conclusion of Theorem 14.5 fails — the cross partials are not equal. Let

$$f(x, y) = \begin{cases} 0 & \text{if } (x, y) = (0, 0), \\ \dfrac{x^3 y - xy^3}{x^2 + y^2} & \text{otherwise.} \end{cases}$$

a) Prove that f is zero along the x-axis and the y-axis. Conclude that $(\partial f/\partial x)(0, 0)$ and $(\partial f/\partial y)(0, 0)$ are both 0.

b) Compute $\partial f/\partial x$ and $\partial f/\partial y$ for $(x, y) \neq (0, 0)$.

c) Conclude that $(\partial f/\partial x)(0, y) = -y$ and $(\partial f/\partial y)(x, 0) = x$.

d) Show that

$$\frac{\partial^2 f}{\partial y \partial x}(0, 0) = \frac{\partial}{\partial y}\left(\frac{\partial f}{\partial x}\right)(0, 0) = \lim_{y \to 0} \frac{\dfrac{\partial f}{\partial x}(0, y) - \dfrac{\partial f}{\partial x}(0, 0)}{y} = -1.$$

e) Show that

$$\frac{\partial^2 f}{\partial x \partial y}(0, 0) = \frac{\partial}{\partial x}\left(\frac{\partial f}{\partial y}\right)(0, 0) = \lim_{x \to 0} \frac{\dfrac{\partial f}{\partial y}(x, 0) - \dfrac{\partial f}{\partial y}(0, 0)}{x} = +1.$$

and conclude that the mixed partials are not equal at $(0, 0)$.

f) Compute $(\partial^2 f/\partial x \partial y)(x, y)$ for all (x, y) other than $(0, 0)$.

g) Use f to show that $(\partial^2 f/\partial x \partial y)(x, x) = 0$ for $x > 0$.

h) Compare e and g to show that $(\partial^2 f/\partial x \partial y)(x, y)$ is discontinuous at the origin. Therefore, f is not C^2 and the hypotheses of Theorem 14.5 do not hold.

14.9   Epilogue

Our discussion of the concepts and techniques of advanced calculus continues in Chapter 30, where we construct Taylor polynomial approximations of differentiable functions. In the process we will prove two important theorems of economic analysis: 1) Weierstrass's theorem that a continuous function whose domain is a compact set achieves its maximum value and its minimum value on its domain and 2) the second order sufficient condition for the optimization problems that lie at the core of economic theory.

Implicit Functions and Their Derivatives

So far, we have been working only with functions in which the endogenous or dependent variables are explicit functions of the exogenous or independent variables. In other words, all the functions we have studied have had the x_i's on the right side and the y on the left side:

$$y = F(x_1, \ldots, x_n). \tag{1}$$

When the variables are separated as in (1), we say that the endogenous variable is an **explicit function** of the exogenous variables.

This ideal situation does not always occur in economic models. Frequently, the equations which arise naturally, for example, as first order conditions in a maximization problem, have the exogenous variables mixed in with the endogenous variables, as in

$$G(x_1, x_2, \ldots, x_n, y) = 0. \tag{2}$$

If for each $(x_1, \ldots, x_n)$ equation (2) determines a corresponding value y, we say that the equation (2) defines the endogenous variable y as an **implicit function** of the exogenous variables $x_1, \ldots, x_n$. An expression like (2) is often so complicated that one cannot solve it to separate the exogenous variables on one side and the endogenous on the other, as in (1). However, we still want to answer the basic question: how does a small change in one of the exogenous variables affect the value of the endogenous variable? This chapter will demonstrate how to answer this question for implicit functions.

15.1 IMPLICIT FUNCTIONS

Examples

Let's start with some simple examples.

Example 15.1 The equations

$$4x + 2y = 5 \quad \text{or} \quad 4x + 2y - 5 = 0 \tag{3}$$

express y as an implicit function of x. Of course, in this case, we can easily solve (3) and write y as an explicit function of x:

$$y = 2.5 - 2x.$$

Example 15.2 A more complex example of an implicit function is the equation

$$y^2 - 5xy + 4x^2 = 0. \tag{4}$$

We substitute any specified value of x into (4) and then solve the resulting quadratic equation for y. For example, when $x = 0$, (4) becomes $y^2 = 0$, whose solution is $y = 0$. When $x = 1$, (4) becomes $y^2 - 5y + 4 = 0$, whose solutions are $y = 1$ and $y = 4$. (When there are more than one choice of y for a given value of x, there is often some additional information which leads to a choice of a single y value.) Even though (4) is more complex than (3), we can still convert (4) into an explicit function (actually, a correspondence) by applying the quadratic formula to it:

$$y = \frac{5x \pm \sqrt{25x^2 - 16x^2}}{2} = \frac{1}{2}(5x \pm 3x) = \begin{cases} 4x \\ x. \end{cases}$$

Example 15.3 Applying the quadratic formula to the *implicit* function: $xy^2 - 3y - e^x = 0$ yields an *explicit* function

$$y = \frac{1}{2x}(3 \pm \sqrt{9 + 4xe^x}).$$

However, this explicit function may very well be more difficult to work with than the original implicit function.

Example 15.4 Changing one exponent in (4) to construct the implicit function

$$y^5 - 5xy + 4x^2 = 0 \tag{5}$$

yields an expression which cannot be solved into an explicit function because there is no general formula for solving quintic equations. However, (5) still defines y as a function of x. For example, when $x = 0$, (5) becomes $y^5 = 0$, whose solution is $y = 0$. When $x = 1$, (5) becomes $y^5 - 5y + 4 = 0$, with solution $y = 1$.

Example 15.5   Consider a profit-maximizing firm that uses a single input x at a cost of w dollars per unit to produce a single output via a production function $y = f(x)$. If output sells for p dollars a unit, the firm's profit function for any fixed p and w is

$$\Pi(x) = p \cdot f(x) - w \cdot x.$$

One takes the x-derivative of this profit function to derive the equation for the profit-maximizing choice of x:

$$pf'(x) - w = 0. \tag{6}$$

Think of p and w as exogenous variables. For each choice of p and w, the firm will want to choose x that satisfies (6). There is no reason to limit the models to production functions for which (6) can be solved explicitly for x in terms of p and w. To study the profit-maximizing behavior of a general firm, we need to work with (6) as defining x as an *implicit* function of p and w. We will want to know, for example, how the optimal choice of input x changes as p or w increases. If there are multiple solutions x of (6) for a given p and w, we can usually choose among the solution candidates by using second order conditions for a maximum or by looking for the *global* maximizer.

The fact that we can write down an implicit function $G(x, y) = c$ does not mean that this equation automatically defines y as a function of x. For example, consider the simple implicit function

$$x^2 + y^2 = 1. \tag{7}$$

When $x > 1$, there is no y which satisfies (7). However, usually we start with a specific solution (x_0, y_0) of the implicit equation $G(x, y) = c$ and ask if we vary x a little from x_0, can we find a y near the original y_0 that satisfies the equation. For example, if we start with the solution $x = 0, y = 1$ of (7) and vary x a little, we can find a unique $y = \sqrt{1 - x^2}$ near $y = 1$ that corresponds to the new x. We can even draw the graph of this explicit relationship around the point $(0, 1)$, as we do in Figure 15.1.

However, if we start at the solution $x = 1, y = 0$ of (7), then no such functional relationship exists. As Figure 15.2 indicates, if we increase x a little to $x = 1 + \varepsilon$, then there is no corresponding y so that $(1 + \varepsilon, y)$ solves (7). If we decrease x a little to $1 - \varepsilon$, then there are two equally good candidates for y *near* $y = 0$, namely

$$y = +\sqrt{2\varepsilon - \varepsilon^2} \quad \text{and} \quad y = -\sqrt{2\varepsilon - \varepsilon^2}.$$

As Figure 15.2 illustrates, because the curve $x^2 + y^2 = 1$ is vertical around $(1, 0)$, it does *not* define y as a function of x there.

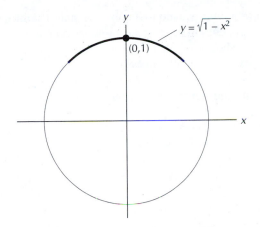

The graph of $x^2 + y^2 = 1$ near the point $(0, 1)$.

**Figure
15.1**

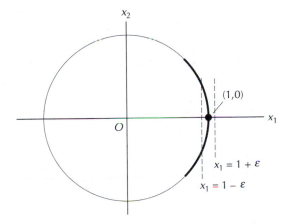

The graph of $x^2 + y^2 = 1$ near the point $(1, 0)$.

**Figure
15.2**

The Implicit Function Theorem for R^2

For a given implicit function $G(x, y) = c$ and a specified solution point (x_0, y_0), we want to know the answers to the following two questions:

(1) Does $G(x, y) = c$ determine y as a continuous function of x for x near x_0 and y near y_0?
(2) If so, how do changes in x affect the corresponding y's?

Let's phrase these two questions more analytically.

(1) Given the implicit equation $G(x, y) = c$ and a point (x_0, y_0) such that $G(x_0, y_0) = c$, does there exist a continuous function $y = y(x)$ defined on an interval I about x_0 so that:

(a) $G(x, y(x)) = c$ for all x in I and

(b) $y(x_0) = y_0$?

(2) If $y(x)$ exists and is differentiable, what is $y'(x_0)$?

Notice that the statement "$y(x)$ exists" is much more general than the statement "an explicit function $y(x)$ can be written down."

It turns out that the answers of these two questions are closely related to each other in that if the first question has a positive answer, one can easily use the Chain Rule to compute a formula for $y'(x)$ in terms of $\partial G/\partial x$ and $\partial G/\partial y$. On the other hand, this formula for $y'(x)$ in terms of $\partial G/\partial x$ and $\partial G/\partial y$ leads to the natural criterion for an affirmative answer to the existence question.

Example 15.6   Let's look at a specific example first. Consider the cubic implicit function

$$x^2 - 3xy + y^3 - 7 = 0 \qquad (8)$$

around the point $x = 4$, $y = 3$. (Check that this point satisfies (8).) Suppose that we could find a function $y = y(x)$ which solves (8). Plugging this function into (8) yields

$$x^2 - 3xy(x) + y(x)^3 - 7 = 0.$$

Differentiate this expression with respect to x, using the product rule to differentiate the second term and the Chain Rule to differentiate the third term:

$$2x - 3y(x) - 3xy'(x) + 3y(x)^2 \cdot y'(x) = 0,$$

or

$$y'(x) = -\frac{2x - 3y}{3y^2 - 3x}. \qquad (9)$$

At $x = 4, y = 3$, we find

$$y'(4) = -\frac{2 \cdot 4 - 3 \cdot 3}{3 \cdot 3^2 - 3 \cdot 4} = \frac{1}{15}.$$

We conclude that if there is a function $y(x)$ which solves (8) and if it is differentiable, then as x changes by Δx, the corresponding y will change by $\Delta x/15$.

Now, let's carry this computation out more generally for the implicit function $G(x, y) = c$ around the specific point $x = x_0, y = y_0$. We suppose that there is a

C^1 solution $y = y(x)$ to the equation $G(x, y) = c$, that is, that

$$G(x, y(x)) = c. \tag{10}$$

We will use the Chain Rule (Theorem 14.1) to differentiate (10) with respect to x at x_0:

$$\frac{\partial G}{\partial x}(x_0, y(x_0)) \cdot \frac{dx}{dx} + \frac{\partial G}{\partial y}(x_0, y(x_0)) \cdot \frac{dy}{dx}(x_0) = 0,$$

or

$$\frac{\partial G}{\partial x}(x_0, y_0) + \frac{\partial G}{\partial y}(x_0, y_0) \cdot y'(x_0) = 0.$$

Solving for $y'(x_0)$ yields

$$y'(x_0) = -\frac{\dfrac{\partial G}{\partial x}(x_0, y_0)}{\dfrac{\partial G}{\partial y}(x_0, y_0)}. \tag{11}$$

We see from (11) that if the solution $y(x)$ of $G(x, y) = c$ exists and is differentiable, it is necessary that $(\partial G/\partial y)(x_0, y_0)$ be nonzero. As the following fundamental result of mathematical analysis indicates, this necessary condition is also a sufficient condition.

Theorem 15.1   (Implicit Function Theorem) Let $G(x, y)$ be a C^1 function on a ball about (x_0, y_0) in $\mathbf{R}^2$. Suppose that $G(x_0, y_0) = c$ and consider the expression

$$G(x, y) = c.$$

If $(\partial G/\partial y)(x_0, y_0) \neq 0$, then there exists a C^1 function $y = y(x)$ defined on an interval I about the point x_0 such that:

(a) $G(x, y(x)) \equiv c$ for all x in I,
(b) $y(x_0) = y_0$, and

(c) $y'(x_0) = -\dfrac{\dfrac{\partial G}{\partial x}(x_0, y_0)}{\dfrac{\partial G}{\partial y}(x_0, y_0)}.$

Example 15.7   Consider the equation

$$G(x, y) \equiv x^2 - 3xy + y^3 - 7 = 0 \qquad (12)$$

about the point $(x_0, y_0) = (4, 3)$ in Example 15.6. One computes that

$$\frac{\partial G}{\partial x} = 2x - 3y = -1 \qquad \text{at } (4, 3)$$

$$\frac{\partial G}{\partial y} = -3x + 3y^2 = 15 \qquad \text{at } (4, 3).$$

Since $(\partial G/\partial y)(4, 3) = 15 \neq 0$, Theorem 15.1 tells us that (12) does indeed define y as a C^1 function of x around $x_0 = 4$, $y_0 = 3$. Furthermore,

$$y'(x_0) = -\frac{\dfrac{\partial G}{\partial x}(x_0, y_0)}{\dfrac{\partial G}{\partial y}(x_0, y_0)} = \frac{1}{15},$$

just as we discovered in Example 15.6. We can now conclude that the solution corresponding to $x_1 = 4.3$ is roughly

$$y_1 \approx y_0 + y'(x_0)\Delta x = 3 + \left(\frac{1}{15}\right) \cdot .3 = 3.02,$$

which compares well with the actual $y_1 = 3.01475\ldots$, which had to be computed numerically.

Example 15.8   Return to the equation $x^2 + y^2 = 1$. We saw that this equation does determine y as a function of x around the point $x = 0$ and $y = 1$. We can easily compute that $\partial G/\partial y = 2y = 2 \neq 0$ at $(0, 1)$. So, Theorem 15.1 assures us that $y(x)$ exists. Furthermore, it tells us that

$$y'(x)\Big|_{x=0} = -\frac{\partial G/\partial x}{\partial G/\partial y} = -\frac{2x}{2y} = -\frac{0}{2} = 0,$$

when $x = 0$ and $y = 1$. In this case, we have an explicit formula

$$y(x) = \sqrt{1 - x^2} \qquad (13)$$

for $y(x)$. We can compute directly from (13) that

$$y'(x) = \frac{-x}{\sqrt{1 - x^2}}$$

which does indeed equal zero when $x = 0$. Of course, we can see in Figure 15.1 that the graph of $y(x)$ is horizontal at $(0, 1)$, so its derivative should be zero.

On the other hand, we noted in Figure 15.2 that no nice function $y(x)$ exists for $x^2 + y^2 = 1$ around $x = 1$, $y = 0$. This is consistent with Theorem 15.1, since $\partial G/\partial y = 2y = 0$ at $(1, 0)$.

Several Exogenous Variables in an Implicit Function

Theorem 15.1 and the discussion around it carry over in a straightforward way to the situation where there are many exogenous variables, but still one equation and therefore one endogenous variable:

$$G(x_1, \ldots, x_k, y) = c. \tag{14}$$

Around a given point $(x_1^*, \ldots, x_k^*, y^*)$, we want to vary $\mathbf{x} = (x_1, \ldots, x_k)$ and then find a y-value which corresponds to each such $(x_1, \ldots, x_k)$. In this case, we say that equation (14) defines y as an **implicit function** of $(x_1, \ldots, x_k)$. Once again, given G and $(\mathbf{x}^*, y^*)$, we want to know whether this functional relationship exists and, if it does, how does y change if any of the x_i's change from x_i^*. Since we are working with a function of several variables $(x_1, \ldots, x_k)$, we will hold all but one of the x_i's constant and vary one exogenous variable at a time. But this puts us right back in the two-variable situation that we have been discussing.

The natural extension of Theorem 15.1 to this setting is the following.

Theorem 15.2 **(Implicit Function Theorem)** Let $G(x_1, \ldots, x_k, y)$ be a C^1 function around the point $(x_1^*, \ldots, x_k^*, y^*)$. Suppose further that $(x_1^*, \ldots, x_k^*, y^*)$ satisfies

$$G(x_1^*, \ldots, x_k^*, y^*) = c$$

and that

$$\frac{\partial G}{\partial y}(x_1^*, \ldots, x_k^*, y^*) \neq 0.$$

Then, there is a C^1 function $y = y(x_1, \ldots, x_n)$ defined on an open ball B about $(x_1^*, \ldots, x_k^*)$ so that:

(a) $G(x_1, \ldots, x_k, y(x_1, \ldots, x_k)) = c$ for all $(x_1, \ldots, x_k) \in B$,
(b) $y^* = y(x_1^*, \ldots, x_k^*)$, and
(c) for each index i,

$$\frac{\partial y}{\partial x_i}(x_1^*, \ldots, x_k^*) = - \frac{\dfrac{\partial G}{\partial x_i}(x_1^*, \ldots, x_k^*, y^*)}{\dfrac{\partial G}{\partial y}(x_1^*, \ldots, x_k^*, y^*)}. \tag{15}$$

EXERCISES

15.1 *a*) Prove that the expression $x^2 - xy^3 + y^5 = 17$ is an implicit function of y in terms of x in a neighborhood of $(x, y) = (5, 2)$.

b) Then, estimate the y value which corresponds to $x = 4.8$.

15.2 Suppose that we want to solve $G(x, y) = c$ for x as a function of y around some point (x_0, y_0). Write out a careful statement of the Implicit Function Theorem to handle this case.

15.3 For equation (8), estimate y when $x = 3.7$.

15.4 Can you solve (8) for y as a function of x when $x = 0$. If so, estimate the y's that correspond to $x = -.1$ and to $x = .15$ respectively.

15.5 Use the implicit form and the explicit form to compute $y'(x)$ for $(x, y) = (1, 1)$ in Example 15.2.

15.6 Consider the function $F(x_1, x_2, y) = x_1^2 - x_2^2 + y^3$.

a) If $x_1 = 6$ and $x_2 = 3$, find a y which satisfies $F(x_1, x_2, y) = 0$.

b) Does this equation define y as an implicit function of x_1 and x_2 near $x_1 = 6$, $x_2 = 3$?

c) If so, compute $(\partial y / \partial x_1)(6, 3)$ and $(\partial y / \partial x_2)(6, 3)$.

d) If x_1 increases to 6.2 and x_2 decreases to 2.9, estimate the corresponding change in y.

15.7 Consider the profit-maximizing firm in Example 15.5. If p increases by Δp and w increases by Δw, what will be the corresponding effect on the optimal input amount x?

15.8 Consider the equation $x^3 + 3y^2 + 4xz^2 - 3z^2y = 1$. Does this equation define z as a function of x and y:

a) In a neighborhood of $x = 1, y = 1$?

b) In a neighborhood of $x = 1, y = 0$?

c) In a neighborhood of $x = 0.5, y = 0$? If so, compute $\partial z / \partial x$ and $\partial z / \partial y$ at this point.

15.9 Consider $3x^2yz + xyz^2 = 30$ as defining x as an implicit function of y and z around the point $x = 1, y = 3, z = 2$.

a) If y increases to 3.2 and z remains at 2, use the Implicit Function Theorem to estimate the corresponding x.

b) Use the quadratic formula to solve $3x^2yz + xyz^2 = 30$ for x as an explicit function of y and z. Use approximation by differentials on this explicit formula to estimate x when y is 3.2 and $z = 2$.

c) Which way was easier?

15.2 LEVEL CURVES AND THEIR TANGENTS

Geometric Interpretation of the Implicit Function Theorem

In this section, we look at the Implicit Function Theorem from a more geometric point of view. In general, we would expect that the equation $G(x, y) = c$ of two variables defines a curve in the plane. For example, the equation $Ax + By = C$

defines a line in the plane and the equation $x^2 + y^2 = 1$ defines a circle in the plane. We can view the Implicit Function Theorem as telling us the following geometric information:

> When the set of points in the plane which satisfy the equation $G(x, y) = c$ can be considered as the graph of a function $y = f(x)$ of one variable, especially in the neighborhood of some fixed solution (x_0, y_0).

Example 15.9   Consider again the equation $x^2 + y^2 = 1$, which describes a circle of radius 1. Figure 15.1 indicates that we can think of the arc of the circle about the point $(0, 1)$ as the graph of a function $y = f(x)(= \sqrt{1 - x^2})$. However, as Figure 15.2 indicates, the arc of the circle about $(1, 0)$ cannot be considered as the graph of a function $y = f(x)$. Such an f would be double-valued for x to the left of $x = 1$ and empty-valued for x to the right of $x = 1$.

In addition to telling us whether the locus $G(x, y) = c$ can be described as the graph of a function $y = f(x)$, the Implicit Function Theorem also tells us the slope $f'(x)$ of the tangent line to the graph at (x, y). Consequently, it tells us the slope of the curve at $G(x, y) = c$. We summarize this geometric interpretation of the Implicit Function Theorem as follows.

Theorem 15.3   Let (x_0, y_0) be a point on the locus of points $G(x, y) = c$ in the plane, where G is a C^1 function of two variables. If $(\partial G/\partial y)(x_0, y_0) \neq 0$, then $G(x, y) = c$ defines a smooth curve around (x_0, y_0) which can be thought of as the graph of a C^1 function $y = f(x)$. Furthermore, the slope of this curve is:

$$-\frac{\dfrac{\partial G}{\partial x}(x_0, y_0)}{\dfrac{\partial G}{\partial y}(x_0, y_0)}.$$

If $(\partial G/\partial y)(x_0, y_0) = 0$, but $(\partial G/\partial x)(x_0, y_0) \neq 0$, then the Implicit Function Theorem tells us that the locus of points $G(x, y) = c$ is a smooth curve about (x_0, y_0), which we can consider as defining x as a function of y. It also tells us that the tangent line to the curve at (x_0, y_0) is parallel to the y-axis, i.e., vertical.

Definition   A point (x_0, y_0) is called a **regular point** of the C^1 function $G(x, y)$ if

$$\frac{\partial G}{\partial x}(x_0, y_0) \neq 0 \quad \text{or} \quad \frac{\partial G}{\partial y}(x_0, y_0) \neq 0.$$

If every point (x, y) on the locus $G(x, y) = c$ is a regular point of G, then we call the level set $\{(x, y) : G(x, y) = c\}$ a **regular curve** or sometimes a one-dimensional **manifold**.

If $G(x, y) = c$ is a regular curve in the plane, then Theorem 15.3 states that at each point on the curve, the curve can be considered as defining y as a function of x or x as a function of y. Furthermore, there is a well-defined tangent line at each point on this curve.

Proof Sketch

The Implicit Function Theorem is so important that we would be remiss to avoid a discussion of its proof. So, we now sketch a proof of the above geometric version of the Implicit Function Theorem — Theorem 15.3.

Let G be a C^1 function on $\mathbf{R}^2$, as in the statement of Theorem 15.3. We suppose that $G(x_0, y_0) = 0$ and that $(\partial G/\partial y)(x_0, y_0) \neq 0$; without loss of generality, we assume that $(\partial G/\partial y)(x_0, y_0) > 0$. Since G is C^1, $(\partial G/\partial y)$ is continuous and we can find an $\varepsilon > 0$ and a small square

$$S \equiv \{(x, y) : x_0 - \varepsilon \leq x \leq x_0 + \varepsilon, \ y_0 - \varepsilon \leq y \leq y_0 + \varepsilon\}$$

for which $(\partial G/\partial y)(x, y) > 0$ for all $(x, y) \in S$. For $x_1 \in (x_0 - \varepsilon, x_0 + \varepsilon)$, let ℓ_{x_1} denote the vertical line segment in S through (x_1, y_0), as in Figure 15.3:

$$\ell_{x_1} \equiv \{(x, y) : x = x_1, \ y_0 - \varepsilon \leq y \leq y_0 + \varepsilon\} \subset S.$$

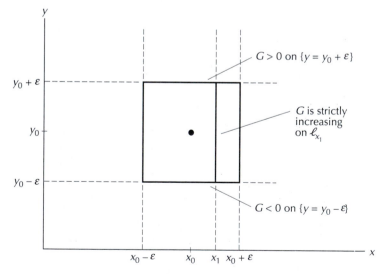

Figure 15.3

The square S in $\mathbf{R}^2$.

Since $(\partial G/\partial y)$ is positive on each ℓ_x, G is strictly increasing on each ℓ_x. Since $G(x_0, y_0) = 0$ and G is strictly increasing on ℓ_{x_0}, $G(x_0, y_0 - \varepsilon) < 0$ and $G(x_0, y_0 + \varepsilon) > 0$. By the continuity of $\partial G/\partial y$, we can choose the ε in the definition of S small enough so that

$$G(x, y_0 - \varepsilon) < 0 \quad \text{and} \quad G(x, y_0 + \varepsilon) > 0 \quad \text{for all } x \in (x_0 - \varepsilon, x_0 + \varepsilon).$$

In other words, G is negative on the bottom side of the square S and positive on the top side of S. On each vertical segment ℓ_x:

(1) G is negative at the bottommost point $(x, y_0 - \varepsilon)$,
(2) G is positive at the topmost point $(x, y_0 + \varepsilon)$, and
(3) G is strictly increasing.

It follows that for each x in $(x_0 - \varepsilon, x_0 + \varepsilon)$, there is a unique $y = y(x)$, depending on x, for which $G(x, y) = 0$. A little more work shows that the continuity of G implies that the dependency of $y(x)$ on x is continuous and that the differentiability of G implies that the dependency of $y(x)$ on x is differentiable. This $y(x)$ is the smooth function in the conclusion of Theorem 15.3.

Relationship to the Gradient

In Section 14.6, we learned that the gradient vector $\nabla G(x, y)$ of a C^1 function G points into the direction of greatest increase. Now, we will prove a complementary result: that the gradient is always perpendicular to the level curve; that is, it is perpendicular to the tangent line to the level curve at (x, y). Of course, in order to make this assertion, we need to guarantee that the level curve of G through (x_0, y_0) really does have a tangent line. By the Implicit Function Theorem, we need only require that (x_0, y_0) be a regular point of G.

Theorem 15.4   Let G be a C^1 function on a neighborhood of (x_0, y_0). Suppose that (x_0, y_0) is a regular point of G. Then, the gradient vector $\nabla G(x_0, y_0)$ is perpendicular to the level set of G at (x_0, y_0).

Proof   Let (x_0, y_0) be a regular point of G:

$$\nabla G(x_0, y_0) = \left(\frac{\partial G}{\partial x}(x_0, y_0), \frac{\partial G}{\partial y}(x_0, y_0) \right) \neq (0, 0).$$

If $(\partial G/\partial y)(x_0, y_0) = 0$, then the gradient is a horizontal vector and the tangent to the level set is a vertical line, as we saw above. In this case, the two are perpendicular to each other. In general, the slope of the level set of G through

(x_0, y_0) is

$$-\frac{\dfrac{\partial G}{\partial x}(x_0, y_0)}{\dfrac{\partial G}{\partial y}(x_0, y_0)}.$$

The vector which realizes this slope is

$$\mathbf{v} = \left(1, -\frac{\dfrac{\partial G}{\partial x}(x_0, y_0)}{\dfrac{\partial G}{\partial y}(x_0, y_0)}\right).$$

Since

$$\mathbf{v} \cdot \nabla G(x_0, y_0) = \left(1, -\frac{\dfrac{\partial G}{\partial x}(x_0, y_0)}{\dfrac{\partial G}{\partial y}(x_0, y_0)}\right) \cdot \left(\frac{\partial G}{\partial x}, \frac{\partial G}{\partial y}\right) = 0,$$

$\mathbf{v}$ and $\nabla G(x_0, y_0)$ point in perpendicular directions. ∎

Example 15.10   The gradient of $G(x, y) = x^2 + y^2$ is the vertical vector $(0, 2)$ at the point $(0, 1)$, where the circle is horizontal; and it is the horizontal vector $(2, 0)$ at the point $(1, 0)$ where the circle is vertical. See Figure 15.4.

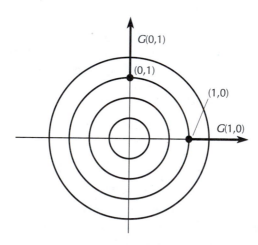

Figure 15.4

Gradients of $G(x, y) = x^2 + y^2$.

The geometry behind the statement of Theorem 15.4 gives a geometric justification of the hypotheses of the Implicit Function Theorem. If $G(x, y) = c$ defines a regular curve around the point (x_0, y_0), this curve will be the graph of a function $y = f(x)$ if and only if the curve is not vertical at (x_0, y_0), that is, if and only if the gradient is not horizontal at (x_0, y_0), that is, if and only if the y-component $\partial G / \partial y$, of $\nabla G(x_0, y_0)$ is not zero.

Tangent to the Level Set Using Differentials

We present one more piece of evidence for the conclusion of the Implicit Function Theorem that the slope of the level set $G(x, y) = c$ at (x_0, y_0) is $-(\partial G / \partial x)(x_0, y_0)/(\partial G / \partial y)(x_0, y_0)$. In Section 14.4, we used differentials to approximate the change in G in the vicinity of (x_0, y_0):

$$G(x_0 + \Delta x, y_0 + \Delta y) - G(x_0, y_0) \approx \frac{\partial G}{\partial x}(x_0, y_0)\Delta x + \frac{\partial G}{\partial y}(x_0, y_0)\Delta y. \qquad (16)$$

We can use (16) to ask what combinations of linear movements Δx and Δy from (x_0, y_0) lead to *no change* in G. This should be the direction of the tangent line to the level set $\{G(x, y) = G(x_0, y_0)\}$ at (x_0, y_0). To find this direction, just set ΔG, the left hand side of (16), equal to zero:

$$0 = \frac{\partial G}{\partial x}(x_0, y_0)\Delta x + \frac{\partial G}{\partial y}(x_0, y_0)\Delta y. \qquad (17)$$

The direction of no change in G at (x_0, y_0) is given by solving (17) for $\Delta y/\Delta x$:

$$\frac{\Delta y}{\Delta x} = -\frac{\dfrac{\partial G}{\partial x}(x_0, y_0)}{\dfrac{\partial G}{\partial y}(x_0, y_0)}. \qquad (18)$$

We can use expressions (17) and (18) to restate Theorems 15.3 and 15.4 in terms of the tangent directions to the level set of G at (x_0, y_0).

Theorem 15.5   Let G be a C^1 function on a neighborhood of (x_0, y_0). Suppose that (x_0, y_0) is a regular point of G. Then, the vector $\mathbf{v} = (v_1, v_2)$ points in the direction parallel to the tangent line to the level set of G at (x_0, y_0) if and only if

$$DG(x_0, y_0)\,\mathbf{v} = \frac{\partial G}{\partial x}(x_0, y_0)\,v_1 + \frac{\partial G}{\partial y}(x_0, y_0)\,v_2 = 0$$

that is, $\mathbf{v}$ is in the nullspace of $DG(x_0, y_0)$.

This use of the Implicit Function Theorem is the natural approach when studying the slope of an indifference curve of a utility function and the slope of an isoquant of a production function, since in these situations we really are interested in which directions to move to keep the function constant. Recall that the level curve of a utility function $U(x, y)$ is called an **indifference curve** of U. Its slope at (x_0, y_0) is called the **marginal rate of substitution (MRS)** of U at (x_0, y_0) since it measures, in a marginal sense, how much more of good y the consumer would require to compensate for the loss of one unit of good x to keep the same level of satisfaction. By the Implicit Function Theorem, the MRS at (x_0, y_0) is:

$$-\frac{\frac{\partial U}{\partial x}(x_0, y_0)}{\frac{\partial U}{\partial y}(x_0, y_0)}.$$

Similarly, if $Q = F(K, L)$ is a production function, its level curves are called **isoquants** and the slope $-F_K/F_L$ of an isoquant at (K_0, L_0) is called the **marginal rate of technical substitution (MRTS)**. It measures how much of one input would be needed to compensate for a one-unit loss of the other unit while keeping production at the same level.

Level Sets of Functions of Several Variables

For a function $F(x_1, \ldots, x_n)$ of more than two variables, the level sets will in general be $(n - 1)$-dimensional objects. For example, the level set $Ax + By + Cz = D$ is a two-dimensional plane in $\mathbf{R}^3$, and the level set $x^2 + y^2 + z^2 = 1$ is a two-dimensional sphere of radius 1, as pictured in Figure 15.5. On both of these sets, at each point there are two independent directions in which one can move. If some $(\partial F/\partial x_i)(\mathbf{x}^*) \neq 0$, then the Implicit Function Theorem tells us that the level set of F through $\mathbf{x}^*$ can be considered as the graph of a function of x_i in terms of $x_1, \ldots, x_{i-1}, x_{i+1}, \ldots, x_n$ around $\mathbf{x}^*$ in $\mathbf{R}^n$:

$$x_i = f(x_1, \ldots, x_{i-1}, x_{i+1}, \ldots, x_n).$$

In this case, the tangent hyperplane to the level set of F is the tangent hyperplane to the graph of f. As in two dimensions, the gradient vector

$$\nabla F(\mathbf{x}^*) = \left(\frac{\partial F}{\partial x_1}(\mathbf{x}^*), \ldots, \frac{\partial F}{\partial x_n}(\mathbf{x}^*)\right)$$

is perpendicular to the tangent hyperplane of the level set.

Example 15.11   The point $(0, 0, 1)$ is the "north pole" on the sphere $x^2 + y^2 + z^2 = 1$. The gradient vector there is $(0, 0, 2)$ which points due north, perpendicular to the sphere at $(0, 0, 1)$, as illustrated in Figure 15.5.

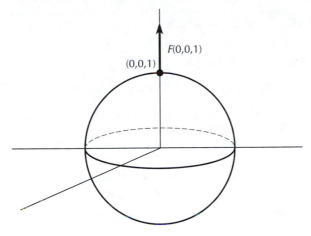

The sphere $x^2 + y^2 + z^2 = 1$ in $\mathbf{R}^3$.

**Figure
15.5**

Example 15.12   By the discussion in Section 10.6, the vector

$$\mathbf{n} = (A, B, C)$$

is perpendicular (or normal) to the plane

$$Ax + By + Cy = D$$

at every point on the plane. Since $\mathbf{n}$ is also the gradient vector ∇F of $F(x, y, z) = Ax + By + Cz$, we see that ∇F is perpendicular to the level set $F(x, y, z) = D$, as we computed above.

For future reference, we summarize the analogue of Theorem 15.4 for implicit functions of several variables. First, we extend the definition of a regular curve to define a regular surface.

Definition   A point $\mathbf{x}^*$ is called a **regular point** of the C^1 function $F(x_1, \ldots, x_n)$ if $\nabla F(\mathbf{x}^*) \neq 0$, that is, if some $(\partial F / \partial x_i)(\mathbf{x}^*)$ is not zero. If every point on the level set

$$\mathcal{F}_c \equiv \{(x_1, \ldots, x_n) : F(x_1, \ldots, x_n) = c\}$$

is a regular point of F, then we call $\mathcal{F}_c$ a **regular surface** or $(n - 1)$-dimensional **manifold** in $\mathbf{R^n}$.

Theorem 15.6   If $F: \mathbf{R}^n \to \mathbf{R}^1$ is a C^1 function, if $\mathbf{x}^*$ is a point in $\mathbf{R}^n$, and if some $(\partial F / \partial x_i)(\mathbf{x}^*) \neq 0$, then:

(a) the level set of F through $\mathbf{x}^*$,

$$\mathcal{F}_{F(\mathbf{x}^*)} \equiv \{(x_1, \ldots, x_n) : F(x_1, \ldots, x_n) = F(\mathbf{x}^*)\}, \tag{19}$$

can be viewed as the graph of a real-valued C^1 function of $(n-1)$ variables in a neighborhood of $\mathbf{x}^*$;

(b) the gradient vector $\nabla F(\mathbf{x}^*)$, considered as a vector at $\mathbf{x}^*$, is perpendicular to the tangent hyperplane of $\mathcal{F}_{F(\mathbf{x}^*)}$ at $\mathbf{x}^*$; and

(c) the vector $\mathbf{v}$, as a vector with its tail at $\mathbf{x}^*$, is a tangent vector to the level set (19) at $\mathbf{x}^*$ if and only if $\mathbf{v}$ is in the nullspace of $DF(\mathbf{x}^*)$; that is, $DF(\mathbf{x}^*)\mathbf{v} = \mathbf{0}$.

EXERCISES

15.10 a) For $(x, y) = (1, 1), (1, 0),$ and $(-2, 1)$, draw the level sets of $f(x, y) = x^2 + y^2$ through (x, y) and the gradient vector of f at (x, y).

b) Repeat this process for $f(x, y) = x^2 - y^2$.

15.11 a) Write an equation involving the partial derivatives of $f(x, y)$ and $g(x, y)$ that is equivalent to the condition that the level curves of f and g intersect only at right angles.

b) Show that the level curves intersect orthogonally if $f_x = g_y$ and $f_y = -g_x$.

15.12 Consider the function $f(x, y) = x^2 e^y$.

a) What is the slope of the level set at $x = 2, y = 0$?

b) In what direction should one move from the point $(2, 0)$ in order to increase f most quickly? Express your answer as a vector of length 1.

15.13 A firm uses x hours of unskilled labor and y hours of skilled labor each day to produce $Q(x, y) = 60x^{2/3}y^{1/3}$ units of output per day. It currently employs 64 hours of unskilled labor and 27 hours of skilled labor.

a) What is its current output?

b) In what direction (expressed as a unit vector) should it change (x, y) if it wants to increase output most rapidly?

c) The firm is planning to hire an additional hour and a half of skilled labor. Use calculus to estimate the corresponding change in unskilled labor that would keep its output at its current level.

15.3   SYSTEMS OF IMPLICIT FUNCTIONS

Definition   A set of m equations in $m + n$ unknowns

$$G_1(x_1, \ldots, x_{m+n}) = c_1$$

$$\vdots \qquad \vdots \qquad \qquad \vdots \tag{20}$$

$$G_m(x_1, \ldots, x_{m+n}) = c_m$$

is called a system of **implicit functions** if there is a partition of the variables into exogenous variables and endogenous variables, so that if one substitutes into (20) numerical values for the exogenous variables, the resulting system can be solved uniquely (in some sense) for corresponding values of the endogenous variables. This is the natural generalization of the single-equation implicit function that we considered in Section 15.1.

Linear Systems

The last section of Chapter 7 discussed *linear* implicit systems and concluded that, for such systems, in order for each choice of values of the exogenous variables to determine a unique set of values of the endogenous equations, it is necessary and sufficient that:

(1) the number of endogenous variables equal the number of equations, and
(2) the (square) matrix of coefficients corresponding to the endogenous variables be nonsingular.

Example 15.13   Consider the linear system of implicit functions

$$
\begin{aligned}
4x + 2y + 2z - r + 3s &= 5 \\
2x \quad\quad + 2z + 8r - 5s &= 7 \\
2x + 2y \quad\quad + r - s &= 0.
\end{aligned}
\tag{21}
$$

Since there are three equations, we need three endogenous variables and therefore two exogenous variables. Let's try to work with y, z and r as endogenous and x and s as exogenous. Putting the exogenous variables on the right side and the endogenous variables on the left, we rewrite (21) as

$$
\begin{pmatrix} 2 & 2 & -1 \\ 0 & 2 & 8 \\ 2 & 0 & 1 \end{pmatrix}
\begin{pmatrix} y \\ z \\ r \end{pmatrix}
=
\begin{pmatrix} 5 - 4x - 3s \\ 7 - 2x + 5s \\ -2x + s \end{pmatrix}.
\tag{22}
$$

Since the determinant of the coefficient matrix in (22) is 40, we can invert (22) and solve for (y, z, r) *explicitly* in terms of x and s:

$$
\begin{pmatrix} y \\ z \\ r \end{pmatrix}
=
\begin{pmatrix} 2 & 2 & -1 \\ 0 & 2 & 8 \\ 2 & 0 & 1 \end{pmatrix}^{-1}
\begin{pmatrix} 5 - 4x - 3s \\ 7 - 2x + 5s \\ -2x + s \end{pmatrix},
$$

or

$$
\begin{pmatrix} y \\ z \\ r \end{pmatrix}
=
\frac{1}{40}
\begin{pmatrix} 2 & -2 & 18 \\ 16 & 4 & -16 \\ -4 & 4 & 4 \end{pmatrix}
\begin{pmatrix} 5 - 4x - 3s \\ 7 - 2x + 5s \\ -2x + s \end{pmatrix}.
$$

On the other hand, if we want x, y, and z to be endogenous, we have to solve the system

$$\begin{pmatrix} 4 & 2 & 2 \\ 2 & 0 & 2 \\ 2 & 2 & 0 \end{pmatrix} \begin{pmatrix} x \\ y \\ z \end{pmatrix} = \begin{pmatrix} 5 + r - 3s \\ 7 - 8r + 5s \\ 0 - r + s \end{pmatrix}. \tag{23}$$

Since the determinant of the coefficient matrix in (23) is zero, we know that there are right-hand sides for which (23) cannot be solved for (x, y, z). For example, take $r = -5$ and $s = 0$. Then, (23) becomes

$$4x + 2y + 2z = 0$$

$$2x \quad\ \ + 2z = 47$$

$$2x + 2y \quad\ \ = 5.$$

Adding the last two equations yields the inconsistent system:

$$4x + 2y + 2z = 0$$

$$4x + 2y + 2z = 52.$$

Since there is no solution in (x, y, z) for $(r, s) = (-5, 0)$, this partition into exogenous and endogenous variables does not work.

Example 15.14   A classical system of implicit functions in economics is the Keynesian linear IS-LM model:

$$Y = C + I + G \qquad \text{(GNP accounting identity)}$$

$$C = a + b(Y - T) \quad \text{(consumption function)}$$

$$I = i_0 - i_1 r \qquad\quad \text{(investment function)}$$

$$M^s = c_1 Y - c_2 r \qquad \text{(money market equilibrium)},$$

where Y is GNP or national income, C is consumer consumption, I is investment, G is government spending, T is tax collection, M^s is money supply, r is the interest rate, and the other six lowercase letters stand for *positive* behavioral parameters, with $0 < b < 1$. We follow the standard method of substituting the second two equations into the first equation and simplifying to obtain the system

$$(1 - b)Y + i_1 r = a + i_0 + G - bT$$

$$c_1 Y - c_2 r = M^s. \tag{24}$$

The natural endogenous variables in this model are Y and r, the variables on the left-hand side of (24). The (Y, r) coefficient matrix in (24),

$$\begin{pmatrix} 1 - b & i_1 \\ c_1 & -c_2 \end{pmatrix}, \tag{25}$$

has determinant $-c_2(1-b) - i_1c_1$, which is nonzero since $0 < b < 1$. Therefore, we can solve system (24) for Y and r; in this case, we can invert the matrix (25) to obtain the explicit solution

$$\begin{pmatrix} Y \\ r \end{pmatrix} = \frac{1}{c_2(1-b) + i_1c_1} \begin{pmatrix} c_2 & i_1 \\ c_1 & -(1-b) \end{pmatrix} \begin{pmatrix} a + i_0 + G - bT \\ M^s \end{pmatrix}.$$

Nonlinear Systems

The corresponding result for nonlinear systems follows from the usual calculus paradigm: linearize by taking the derivative, apply the linear theorem to this linearized system, and transfer these results back to the original nonlinear system. We write the basic nonlinear system of m equations in $m + n$ unknowns as

$$F_1(y_1, \ldots, y_m, x_1, \ldots, x_n) = c_1$$

$$F_2(y_1, \ldots, y_m, x_1, \ldots, x_n) = c_2$$

$$\vdots \qquad\qquad \vdots \tag{26}$$

$$F_m(y_1, \ldots, y_m, x_1, \ldots, x_n) = c_m,$$

where we want $y_1, \ldots, y_m$ to be endogenous and $x_1, \ldots, x_n$ to be exogenous. From the linear theory, we know that there should be as many endogenous variables as there are independent equations, in this case m. The linearization of system (26) about the point $(\mathbf{y}^*, \mathbf{x}^*)$ is

$$\frac{\partial F_1}{\partial y_1}dy_1 + \cdots + \frac{\partial F_1}{\partial y_m}dy_m + \frac{\partial F_1}{\partial x_1}dx_1 + \cdots + \frac{\partial F_1}{\partial x_n}dx_n = 0$$

$$\vdots \qquad\qquad\qquad \vdots \qquad\qquad \vdots \tag{27}$$

$$\frac{\partial F_m}{\partial y_1}dy_1 + \cdots + \frac{\partial F_m}{\partial y_m}dy_m + \frac{\partial F_m}{\partial x_1}dx_1 + \cdots + \frac{\partial F_m}{\partial x_n}dx_n = 0,$$

where all the partial derivatives are evaluated at the point $(\mathbf{y}^*, \mathbf{x}^*)$. By the Linear Implicit Function Theorem, the linear system (27) can be solved for $dy_1, \ldots, dy_m$

in terms of $dx_1, \ldots, dx_n$ if and only if the coefficient matrix of the dy_i's,

$$\frac{\partial(F_1, \ldots, F_m)}{\partial(y_1, \ldots, y_m)} \equiv \begin{pmatrix} \dfrac{\partial F_1}{\partial y_1} & \cdots & \dfrac{\partial F_1}{\partial y_m} \\ \vdots & \ddots & \vdots \\ \dfrac{\partial F_m}{\partial y_1} & \cdots & \dfrac{\partial F_m}{\partial y_m} \end{pmatrix} \tag{28}$$

is nonsingular at $(\mathbf{y}^*, \mathbf{x}^*)$. Because this system is linear, when the coefficient matrix (28) is nonsingular, we can use the inverse of (28) to solve the system (27) for the dy_i's in terms of the dx_j's and everything else

$$\begin{pmatrix} dy_1 \\ \vdots \\ dy_m \end{pmatrix} = - \begin{pmatrix} \dfrac{\partial F_1}{\partial y_1} & \cdots & \dfrac{\partial F_1}{\partial y_m} \\ \vdots & \ddots & \vdots \\ \dfrac{\partial F_m}{\partial y_1} & \cdots & \dfrac{\partial F_m}{\partial y_m} \end{pmatrix}^{-1} \begin{pmatrix} \sum_{i=1}^{n} \dfrac{\partial F_1}{\partial x_i} dx_i \\ \vdots \\ \sum_{i=1}^{n} \dfrac{\partial F_m}{\partial x_i} dx_i \end{pmatrix}. \tag{29}$$

Since the linear approximation (27) of the original system (26) is a true implicit function of the dy_i's in terms of the dx_j's, the basic principle of calculus leads us to the conclusion that the nonlinear system (26) defines the y_i's as implicit functions of the x_j's, at least in a neighborhood of $(\mathbf{y}^*, \mathbf{x}^*)$.

Furthermore, one can actually use the linear solution (29) of the dy_i's in terms of the dx_j's to find the derivatives of the y_i's with respect to the x_j's at $(\mathbf{x}^*, \mathbf{y}^*)$. To compute $\partial y_k / \partial x_h$ for some fixed indices h and k, recall that this derivative estimates the effect on y_k of a one unit increase in x_h $(dx_h = 1)$. So, we set all the dx_j's equal to zero in (27) or (29) except dx_h and then we solve (27) or (29) for the corresponding dy_i's. If we use (29), we find

$$\begin{pmatrix} \dfrac{\partial y_1}{\partial x_h} \\ \vdots \\ \dfrac{\partial y_m}{\partial x_h} \end{pmatrix} = - \begin{pmatrix} \dfrac{\partial F_1}{\partial y_1} & \cdots & \dfrac{\partial F_1}{\partial y_m} \\ \vdots & \ddots & \vdots \\ \dfrac{\partial F_m}{\partial y_1} & \cdots & \dfrac{\partial F_m}{\partial y_m} \end{pmatrix}^{-1} \begin{pmatrix} \dfrac{\partial F_1}{\partial x_h} \\ \vdots \\ \dfrac{\partial F_m}{\partial x_h} \end{pmatrix}. \tag{30}$$

Alternatively, we can apply Cramer's rule to (27) and compute

$$\frac{\partial y_k}{\partial x_h} = -\frac{\det \begin{pmatrix} \dfrac{\partial F_1}{\partial y_1} & \cdots & \dfrac{\partial F_1}{\partial x_h} & \cdots & \dfrac{\partial F_1}{\partial y_m} \\ \vdots & \ddots & \vdots & \ddots & \vdots \\ \dfrac{\partial F_m}{\partial y_1} & \cdots & \dfrac{\partial F_m}{\partial x_h} & \cdots & \dfrac{\partial F_m}{\partial y_m} \end{pmatrix}}{\det \begin{pmatrix} \dfrac{\partial F_1}{\partial y_1} & \cdots & \dfrac{\partial F_1}{\partial y_k} & \cdots & \dfrac{\partial F_1}{\partial y_m} \\ \vdots & \ddots & \vdots & \ddots & \vdots \\ \dfrac{\partial F_m}{\partial y_1} & \cdots & \dfrac{\partial F_m}{\partial y_k} & \cdots & \dfrac{\partial F_m}{\partial y_m} \end{pmatrix}}$$

(31)

$$\equiv -\frac{\det \dfrac{\partial(F_1, \ldots, F_k, \ldots, F_m)}{\partial(y_1, \ldots, x_h, \ldots, y_m)}}{\det \dfrac{\partial(F_1, \ldots, F_k, \ldots, F_m)}{\partial(y_1, \ldots, y_k, \ldots, y_m)}}.$$

The following theorem — the most general form of the Implicit Function Theorem — summarizes these conclusions.

Theorem 15.7 Let $F_1, \ldots, F_m \colon \mathbf{R}^{m+n} \to \mathbf{R}^1$ be C^1 functions. Consider the system of equations

$$F_1(y_1, \ldots, y_m, x_1, \ldots, x_n) = c_1$$
$$\vdots \qquad\qquad\qquad \vdots$$
$$F_m(y_1, \ldots, y_m, x_1, \ldots, x_n) = c_m$$

(32)

as possibly defining $y_1, \ldots, y_m$ as implicit functions of $x_1, \ldots, x_n$. Suppose that $(\mathbf{y}^*, \mathbf{x}^*)$ is a solution of (32). If the determinant of the $m \times m$ matrix

$$\begin{pmatrix} \dfrac{\partial F_1}{\partial y_1} & \cdots & \dfrac{\partial F_1}{\partial y_m} \\ \vdots & \ddots & \vdots \\ \dfrac{\partial F_m}{\partial y_1} & \cdots & \dfrac{\partial F_m}{\partial y_m} \end{pmatrix} \equiv \frac{\partial(F_1, \ldots, F_h, \ldots, F_m)}{\partial(y_1, \ldots, y_h \ldots, y_m)}$$

evaluated at $(\mathbf{y}^*, \mathbf{x}^*)$ is nonzero, then there exist C^1 functions

$$y_1 = f_1(x_1, \ldots, x_n)$$
$$\vdots \qquad \vdots$$
$$y_m = f_m(x_1, \ldots, x_n)$$

(33)

defined on a ball B about $\mathbf{x}^*$ such that

$$F_1(f_1(\mathbf{x}), \ldots, f_m(\mathbf{x}), x_1, \ldots, x_n) = c_1$$

$$\vdots \qquad\qquad\qquad \vdots$$

$$F_m(f_1(\mathbf{x}), \ldots, f_m(\mathbf{x}), x_1, \ldots, x_n) = c_m$$

for all $\mathbf{x} = (x_1, \ldots, x_n)$ in B and

$$y_1^* = f_1(x_1^*, \ldots, x_n^*)$$

$$\vdots \qquad \vdots$$

$$y_m^* = f_m(x_1^*, \ldots, x_n^*).$$

Furthermore, one can compute $(\partial f_k / \partial x_h)(\mathbf{y}^*, \mathbf{x}^*) = (\partial y_k / \partial x_h)(\mathbf{y}^*, \mathbf{x}^*)$ by setting $dx_h = 1$ and $dx_j = 0$ for $j \neq h$ in (27) and solving the resulting system for dy_k. This can be accomplished:

(a) by inverting the nonsingular matrix (28) to obtain the solution (30) or
(b) by applying Cramer's rule to (27) to obtain the solution (31).

Example 15.15   Consider the system of equations

$$F_1(x, y, a) \equiv x^2 + axy + y^2 - 1 = 0$$
$$F_2(x, y, a) \equiv x^2 + y^2 \ - a^2 + 3 = 0 \tag{34}$$

around the point $x = 0, y = 1, a = 2$. If we change a a little to a' near $a = 2$, can we find (x', y') near $(0, 1)$ so that (x', y', a') satisfies these two equations? To answer this question, we need the Jacobian of (F_1, F_2) with respect to the endogenous variables x and y at the point $x = 0, y = 1, a = 2$:

$$\det \begin{pmatrix} \dfrac{\partial F_1}{\partial x} & \dfrac{\partial F_1}{\partial y} \\[2mm] \dfrac{\partial F_2}{\partial x} & \dfrac{\partial F_2}{\partial y} \end{pmatrix} (0, 1, 2) = \det \begin{pmatrix} 2 & 2 \\ 0 & 2 \end{pmatrix} = 4 \neq 0.$$

So, we can solve system (34) for x and y as functions of a near $(0, 1, 2)$.
   Furthermore, at $x = 0, y = 1, a = 2$,

$$\frac{dy}{da} = -\frac{\det \dfrac{\partial(F_1, F_2)}{\partial(x, a)}}{\det \dfrac{\partial(F_1, F_2)}{\partial(x, y)}} = -\frac{\det \begin{pmatrix} 2x + ay & xy \\ 2x & -2a \end{pmatrix}}{\det \begin{pmatrix} 2x + ay & ax + 2y \\ 2x & 2y \end{pmatrix}},$$

and, plugging in $(0, 1, 2)$,

$$\frac{dy}{da}(2) = -\frac{\det\begin{pmatrix} 2 & 0 \\ 0 & -4 \end{pmatrix}}{\det\begin{pmatrix} 2 & 2 \\ 0 & 2 \end{pmatrix}} = \frac{8}{4} = 2 > 0.$$

Therefore, if a increases to 2.1, the corresponding y will increase to about 1.2.

Let's use the other method to compute the effect on x. Take differentials of the nonlinear system

$$(2x + ay)\, dx + (ax + 2y)\, dy + xy\, da = 0$$
$$2x\, dx + 2y\, dy - 2a\, da = 0.$$

Plug in $x = 0$, $y = 1$, $a = 2$:

$$2\, dx + 2\, dy = 0\, da$$
$$0\, dx + 2\, dy = 4\, da.$$

Clearly, $dy = 2\, da$ (as we just computed above) and $dx = -dy = -2\, da$. So, if a increases to 2.1, the corresponding x will decrease roughly to $-.2$.

Example 15.16 A natural nonlinear generalization of the linear IS-LM model in Example 15.14 is the system

$$Y = C + I + G$$
$$C = C(Y - T)$$
$$I = I(r)$$
$$M^s = M(Y, r),$$

where the nonlinear functions $x \longmapsto C(x)$, $r \longmapsto I(r)$, and $(Y, r) \longmapsto M(Y, r)$ satisfy

$$0 < C'(x) < 1, \quad I'(r) < 0, \quad \frac{\partial M}{\partial Y} > 0, \quad \text{and} \quad \frac{\partial M}{\partial r} < 0. \qquad (35)$$

The analogue to system (24) is

$$Y - C(Y - T) - I(r) = G$$
$$M(Y, r) = M^s, \qquad (36)$$

which we want to define Y and r as implicit functions of G, M^s, and T. Suppose that the current (G, M^s, T) is (G^*, M^{s*}, T^*) and that the corresponding (Y, r)-

equilibrium is (Y^*, r^*). If we vary (G, M^s, T) a little, is there a corresponding equilibrium (Y, r) and how does it change? The linearization of system (36) is

$$\left(1 - C'(Y^* - T^*)\right) dY - I'(r^*) \, dr = dG - C'(Y^* - T^*) \, dT$$

$$\frac{\partial M}{\partial Y} \, dY + \frac{\partial M}{\partial r} \, dr = dM^s$$

or

$$\begin{pmatrix} 1 - C'(Y^* - T^*) & -I'(r^*) \\ \dfrac{\partial M}{\partial Y} & \dfrac{\partial M}{\partial r} \end{pmatrix} \begin{pmatrix} dY \\ dr \end{pmatrix} \qquad (37)$$

$$= \begin{pmatrix} dG - C'(Y^* - T^*) \, dT \\ dM^s \end{pmatrix},$$

all evaluated at $(Y^*, r^*, G^*, M^{s*}, T^*)$. The determinant of the coefficient matrix in (37),

$$D \equiv \left(1 - C'(Y^* - T^*)\right) \frac{\partial M}{\partial r} + I'(r^*) \frac{\partial M}{\partial Y},$$

is negative by (35), and therefore is nonzero. By Theorem 15.7, the system (36) really does define Y and r as implicit functions of G, M^s, and T around $(Y^*, r^*, G^*, M^{s*}, T^*)$. Inverting (37), we compute

$$\begin{pmatrix} dY \\ dr \end{pmatrix} = \frac{1}{D} \begin{pmatrix} \dfrac{\partial M}{\partial r} & I'(r) \\ -\dfrac{\partial M}{\partial Y} & 1 - C'(Y^* - T^*) \end{pmatrix} \begin{pmatrix} dG - C'(Y^* - T^*) dT \\ dM^s \end{pmatrix}.$$

If we increase government spending G, keeping M^s and T fixed, we find

$$dY = \frac{1}{D} \frac{\partial M}{\partial r} \, dG \quad \text{and} \quad dr = -\frac{1}{D} \frac{\partial M}{\partial Y} \, dG,$$

so that both Y and r increase.

EXERCISES

15.14 Carry out the calculations in Example 15.14.

15.15 For the linear and the nonlinear IS-LM models (24) and (36), how are the equilibrium Y and r affected by an increase in M^s? by an increase in T?

15.16 One solution of the system $x^3 y - z = 1$, $x + y^2 + z^3 = 6$ is $x = 1, y = 2, z = 1$. Use calculus to estimate the corresponding x and y when $z = 1.1$.

15.17   Consider the system of equations

$$y^2 + 2u^2 + v^2 - xy = 15, \quad 2y^2 + u^2 + v^2 + xy = 38,$$

at the solution $x = 1, y = 4, u = 1, v = -1$. Think of u and v as exogenous and x and y as endogenous. Use calculus to estimate the values of x and y that correspond to $u = .9$ and $v = -1.1$.

15.18   One solution of the system

$$2x^2 + 3xyz - 4uv = 16, \quad x + y + 3z + u - v = 10$$

is $x = 1, y = 2, z = 3, u = 0, v = 1$. If one varies u and v near their original values and plugs these new values into this system, can one find unique values of x, y and z that still satisfy this system? Explain.

15.19   Does the system $xz^3 + y^2v^4 = 2$, $xz + yvz^2 = 2$ define v and z as C^1 functions of x and y around the point $(1, 1, 1, 1)$? If so, find $\partial z/\partial x$, $\partial z/\partial y$, $\partial v/\partial x$, and $\partial v/\partial y$ there.

15.20   Check that $x = 1, y = 4, u = 1, v = -1$ is a solution of the system

$$y^2 + 2u^2 + v^2 - xy = 15, \quad 2y^2 + u^2 + v^2 + xy = 38.$$

If y increases to 4.02 and x stays fixed, does there exist a (u, v) near $(1, -1)$ which solves this system? If not, why not? If yes, estimate the new u and v.

15.21   The economy of Northern Saskatchewan is in equilibrium when the system of equations

$$2xz + xy + z - 2\sqrt{z} = 11 \quad xyz = 6$$

is satisfied. One solution of this set of equations is $x = 3, y = 2, z = 1$, and Northern Saskatchewan is in equilibrium at this point. Suppose that the prime minister discovers that the variable z (output of beaver pelts) can be conrolled by simple decree.

a) If the prime minister raises z to 1.1, use calculus to estimate the change in x and y.

b) If x were in the control of the prime minister and not y or z, explain why you cannot use this method to estimate the effect of reducing x from 3 to 2.95.

15.22   Consider the system of equations

$$x + 2y + z = 5, \quad 3x^2yz = 12,$$

as defining some endogenous variables in terms of some exogenous variables.

a) Divide the three variables into exogenous ones and endogenous ones in a neighborhood of $x = 2, y = 1, z = 1$ so that the Implicit Function Theorem applies.

b) If each of the exogenous variables in your answer to *a)* increases by 0.25, use calculus to estimate how each of the endogenous variables will change.

15.23   Consider the system of two equations in three unknowns: $x + 2y + z = 5, 3x^2yz = 12$.

a) At the point $x = 2, y = 1, z = 1$, why can we treat z as an exogenous variable and x and y are the dependent variables?

b) If z rises to 1.2, use calculus to estimate the corresponding x and y.

15.24   A firm uses two inputs to produce its output via the Cobb-Douglas production function $z = x^a y^b$, where $a = b = .5$. Its current level of inputs is $x = 25$, $y = 100$. The firm will introduce a new technology that will change the b-exponent on its production function to $b = .504$, with no change to a. Use calculus to estimate the input combination which will keep the total output the same and the sum of the inputs the same. [Hint: Work with the system $x^a y^b = c$ (or better $a \ln x + b \ln y = \ln c$) and $x + y = 125$.]

15.25   Treat the linear IS-LM model at the beginning of Example 15.14 as four equations. What is the natural choice of endogenous variables? Can this four-equation system be solved for these endogenous variables in terms of the other variables?

15.4   APPLICATION: COMPARATIVE STATICS

Let's put the Implicit Function Theorem to work in the most basic microeconomic example of general equilibrium: a pure exchange economy with two consumers — numbered 1 and 2 — and two consumption goods — parameterized by x and y. We suppose that consumer 1 has initial endowment $(e_1, 0)$ and that consumer 2 has initial endowment $(0, e_2)$. To describe the consumers' preferences, let u_1 and u_2 be C^2, strictly concave ($u_i'' < 0$) functions of a single variable and let α be a scalar between 0 and 1. For $i = 1, 2$, we assume that consumer i's preferences over consumption bundles (x, y) are described by the utility function

$$U_i(x_i, y_i) \equiv \alpha u_i(x_i) + (1 - \alpha) u_i(y_i). \tag{38}$$

These U_i's include Cobb-Douglas utility functions. (Exercise.) Let p and q denote the price of a unit of good 1 and good 2, respectively. In this example, we will write the equations for the equilibrium prices and consumption bundles for this model and then study how these bundles are affected by changes in the consumers' initial endowments.

Consumer i wants to consume the bundle (x_i, y_i) that maximizes U_i subject to the affordability constraint

$$px_i + qy_i = \text{value of initial endowment}. \tag{39}$$

As one learns in intermediate microeconomics, and as we will discuss more fully in Chapter 18, at the bundle of choice, the consumer's marginal rate of substitution between the two goods, that is, the consumer's *internal* relative valuation of the goods

$$\frac{\dfrac{\partial U_i}{\partial x_i}(x_i, y_i)}{\dfrac{\partial U_i}{\partial y_i}(x_i, y_i)} = \frac{\alpha u_i'(x_i)}{(1 - \alpha) u_i'(y_i)}, \tag{40}$$

must equal the price ratio p/q, the market's *external* relative valuation of the two goods. By (38), (39) and (40), the equations that describe the optimal choice for consumer 1 are

$$\frac{\alpha u_1'(x_1)}{(1-\alpha)u_1'(y_1)} = \frac{p}{q}, \tag{41}$$

$$px_1 + qy_1 = pe_1, \tag{42}$$

and the corresponding equations for consumer 2

$$\frac{\alpha u_2'(x_2)}{(1-\alpha)u_2'(y_2)} = \frac{p}{q}, \tag{43}$$

$$px_2 + qy_2 = qe_2. \tag{44}$$

Since we are dealing with a pure exchange economy, the total amounts of both commodities are fixed:

$$x_1 + x_2 = e_1, \tag{45}$$

$$y_1 + y_2 = e_2. \tag{46}$$

Equations (41) through (46) form a system of six equations in the six unknowns x_1, y_1, x_2, y_2, p, and q. As usual, all prices are relative: multiplying both prices by the same scalar does not change equations (41) through (46). To remove this ambiguity, we will set $q = 1$. In the language of economics, we are treating good 2 as the *numeraire*.

We can ignore equation (44) because it is implied by equations (42), (45) and (46). (Exercise.) The remaining five equations can be written as

$$\frac{\alpha}{1-\alpha}u_1'(x_1) - pu_1'(y_1) = 0$$

$$px_1 + y_1 - pe_1 = 0$$

$$\frac{\alpha}{1-\alpha}u_2'(x_2) - pu_2'(y_2) = 0 \tag{47}$$

$$x_1 + x_2 - e_1 = 0$$

$$y_1 + y_2 - e_2 = 0.$$

We begin by setting both endowments equal to $1 : e_1 = e_2 = 1$. In this case, the unique solution of system (47) is

$$x_1 = y_1 = \alpha$$

$$x_2 = y_2 = 1 - \alpha \tag{48}$$

$$p = \frac{\alpha}{1-\alpha}.$$

(Exercise.) We ask how a change in the initial endowment e_2 affects the equilibrium consumption bundles and prices (48), keeping e_1 fixed.

The linearization of system (48) is

$$\frac{\alpha}{1-\alpha}u_1''(x_1)\,dx_1 - pu_1''(y_1)\,dy_1 - u_1'(y_1)\,dp = 0$$

$$p\,dx_1 + 1\,dy_1 + (x_1-1)\,dp = 0$$

$$\frac{\alpha}{1-\alpha}u_2''(x_2)\,dx_2 - pu_2''(y_2)\,dy_2 - u_2'(y_2)\,dp = 0 \qquad (49)$$

$$1\,dx_1 + 1\,dx_2 = 0$$

$$1\,dy_1 + 1\,dy_2 = de_2.$$

The Implicit Function Theorem tells us that, if we can solve linear system (49) for dx_1, dx_2, dy_1, dy_2, dp, then we can compute $\partial x_1/\partial e_2$, $\partial x_2/\partial e_2$, $\partial y_1/\partial e_2$, $\partial y_2/\partial e_2$, and $\partial p/\partial e_2$.

The easiest way to solve system (49) is to solve the last two equations for dx_2 and dy_2:

$$dx_2 = -dx_1 \qquad dy_2 = de_2 - dy_1,$$

and substitute (48) and these expressions for dx_2 and dy_2 into the first three equations of (49):

$$\frac{\alpha}{1-\alpha}u_1''(\alpha)\,dx_1 - \frac{\alpha}{1-\alpha}u_1''(\alpha)\,dy_1 - u_1'(\alpha)\,dp = 0$$

$$\frac{\alpha}{1-\alpha}\,dx_1 + dy_1 + (\alpha-1)\,dp = 0$$

$$-\frac{\alpha}{1-\alpha}u_2''(1-\alpha)\,dx_1 + \frac{\alpha}{1-\alpha}u_2''(1-\alpha)\,dy_1 - u_2'(1-\alpha)\,dp$$

$$= \frac{\alpha}{1-\alpha}u_2''(1-\alpha)\,de_2.$$

Multiply the first equation through by $(1-\alpha)/u_1'(\alpha)$, the second equation through by $(1-\alpha)$, and the third equation through by $(1-\alpha)^2/\alpha u_2'(1-\alpha)$:

$$\begin{pmatrix} \dfrac{\alpha u_1''(\alpha)}{u_1'(\alpha)} & -\dfrac{\alpha u_1''(\alpha)}{u_1'(\alpha)} & -(1-\alpha) \\[2ex] \alpha & 1-\alpha & -(1-\alpha)^2 \\[2ex] -\dfrac{(1-\alpha)u_2''(1-\alpha)}{u_2'(1-\alpha)} & \dfrac{(1-\alpha)u_2''(1-\alpha)}{u_2'(1-\alpha)} & -\dfrac{(1-\alpha)^2}{\alpha} \end{pmatrix} \begin{pmatrix} dx_1 \\[2ex] dy_1 \\[2ex] dp \end{pmatrix}$$

$$= \begin{pmatrix} 0 \\[1ex] 0 \\[1ex] \dfrac{(1-\alpha)u_2''(1-\alpha)}{u_2'(1-\alpha)} \end{pmatrix} de_2 \qquad (50)$$

Let
$$r_i(z) \equiv -\frac{z\, u_i''(z)}{u_i'(z)}. \tag{51}$$

Expression (51) is a measure of the concavity of u_i; in studies of portfolio choice, it is called the **Arrow-Pratt measure of relative risk aversion**. For our purposes, it suffices to know that $r_1(z)$ and $r_2(z)$ are strictly positive. Rewrite system (50) as

$$\begin{pmatrix} -r_1(\alpha) & r_1(\alpha) & -(1-\alpha) \\ \alpha & 1-\alpha & -(1-\alpha)^2 \\ r_2(1-\alpha) & -r_2(1-\alpha) & -\dfrac{(1-\alpha)^2}{\alpha} \end{pmatrix} \begin{pmatrix} dx_1 \\ dy_1 \\ dp \end{pmatrix} = \begin{pmatrix} 0 \\ 0 \\ -r_2(1-\alpha)de_2 \end{pmatrix}.$$

This system can be solved using Cramer's rule to get

$$dx_1 = \frac{-R_2(1-R_1)(1-\alpha)^2}{D}\, de_2$$

$$dy_1 = \frac{(1-\alpha)R_2[R_1(1-\alpha)+\alpha]}{D}\, de_2 \tag{52}$$

$$dp = \frac{R_1 R_2}{D}\, de_2,$$

where
$$R_1 \equiv r_1(\alpha) > 0, \qquad R_2 \equiv r_2(1-\alpha) > 0$$

and
$$D \equiv \frac{R_1(1-\alpha)^2}{\alpha} + R_2(1-\alpha)$$

$$= -(1-\alpha)^2 \left(\frac{u_1''(\alpha)}{u_1'(\alpha)} + \frac{u_2''(1-\alpha)}{u_2'(1-\alpha)} \right) > 0.$$

By the Implicit Function Theorem,

$$\frac{\partial x_1}{\partial e_2} = \frac{-R_2(1-R_1)(1-\alpha)^2}{D}$$

$$\frac{\partial x_2}{\partial e_2} = \frac{R_2(1-R_1)(1-\alpha)^2}{D}$$

$$\frac{\partial y_1}{\partial e_2} = \frac{(1-\alpha)R_2[R_1(1-\alpha)+\alpha]}{D} \tag{53}$$

$$\frac{\partial y_2}{\partial e_2} = 1 - \frac{(1-\alpha)R_2[R_1(1-\alpha)+\alpha]}{D}$$

$$\frac{\partial p}{\partial e_2} = \frac{R_1 R_2}{D}.$$

We conclude that when the initial endowments are $e_1 = e_2 = 1$, an increase of e_2, the endowment of good 2, leads to a rise in the price of good 1 relative to good 2 ($\partial p/\partial e_2 > 0$), and a rise in the consumption of good 2 by consumer 1 ($\partial y_1/\partial e_2 > 0$). What happens to good 1 depends upon the utility functions.

EXERCISES

15.26   Show that the utility functions (38) include Cobb-Douglas preferences.
15.27   Show that equation (44) is implied by equations (42), (45) and (46).
15.28   Show that when $e_1 = e_2 = 1$, (48) is the unique solution of system (47).
15.29   Verify the expressions in (52) and (53).
15.30   Compute the exact partial derivatives in (53) for $u_1(z) = u_2(z) = \ln z$ and $\alpha = 1/2$.
15.31   Compute the comparative statics that results from a change in e_1, holding e_2 fixed.
15.32   Compute and interpret the comparative statics that results from an increase in α.

15.5   THE INVERSE FUNCTION THEOREM (optional)

In this section, we present one more approach to the Implicit Function Theorem. This approach presents another illustration of the basic paradigm of calculus, namely, that one can learn a lot about a nonlinear function from its linear approximation. In this context, to solve a problem about the behavior of a nonlinear function F in the vicinity of a given point $\mathbf{x}^*$, take the derivative $DF_{\mathbf{x}^*}$ of F at $\mathbf{x}^*$, use the tools of linear algebra to glean the appropriate information about the linear function $DF_{\mathbf{x}^*}$, and use the techniques of calculus to transfer this information back to the original F.

For example, suppose that F is a C^1 function from $\mathbf{R}^n$ to $\mathbf{R}^m$, that $\mathbf{b}_0$ is a given point in the target space $\mathbf{R}^m$, and that $\mathbf{x}_0$ is a solution of the system of equations

$$F(\mathbf{x}) = \mathbf{b}_0. \tag{54}$$

A basic question of equilibrium analysis is: what happens if we vary $\mathbf{b}_0$ a little to $\mathbf{b}_1$? Does the corresponding equation $F(\mathbf{x}) = \mathbf{b}_1$ still have a solution? If it does, how many solutions does it have?

The main purpose of Chapter 7 was to answer these questions for a *linear* system of equations

$$A\mathbf{x} = \mathbf{b}_0. \tag{55}$$

The answers depended on the size and rank of A.

If A is $m \times n$, then (55) has a solution for every right-hand side $\mathbf{b}_0$ if and only if $m \le n$ and the rank of A is m; (55) has *at most one* solution for every right hand side $\mathbf{b}_0$ if and only if $m \ge n$ and the rank of A is n.

Before going further, we recall some appropriate vocabulary, introduced in Chapter 13.

Definition   A function $F: \mathbf{R}^n \to \mathbf{R}^m$ is **onto** or **surjective** if for *every* $\mathbf{b}$ in $\mathbf{R}^m$, there is *at least one* $\mathbf{x}$ in $\mathbf{R}^n$ such that $F(\mathbf{x}) = \mathbf{b}$. A function F is **one-to-one** or **injective** if for any $\mathbf{b}$ in $\mathbf{R}^m$, there is *at most one* $\mathbf{x}$ in $\mathbf{R}^n$ such that $F(\mathbf{x}) = \mathbf{b}$.

The function F is surjective if and only if the system $F(\mathbf{x}) = \mathbf{b}$ has at least one solution $\mathbf{x}^*$ for every $\mathbf{b}$; F is injective if and only if the system $F(\mathbf{x}) = \mathbf{b}$ never has more than one solution $\mathbf{x}^*$ for any $\mathbf{b}$.

The local versions of surjectivity and injectivity are also important. In these cases we are interested in solutions of $F(\mathbf{x}) = \mathbf{b}$ only for values of $\mathbf{b}$ near a specified $\mathbf{b}_0$.

Definition   Let $\mathbf{x}_0$ be a point in the domain of $F: \mathbf{R}^n \to \mathbf{R}^m$ with $F(\mathbf{x}_0) = \mathbf{b}_0$. Then, F is **locally onto** (or **locally surjective**) at $\mathbf{x}_0$ if, given any open ball $B_r(\mathbf{x}_0)$ about $\mathbf{x}_0$ in $\mathbf{R}^n$, there is a ball $B_s(\mathbf{b}_0)$ about $\mathbf{b}_0$ in $\mathbf{R}^m$ such that for every $\mathbf{b}$ in $B_s(\mathbf{b}_0)$ there is at least one $\mathbf{x}$ in $B_r(\mathbf{x}_0)$ such that $F(\mathbf{x}) = \mathbf{b}$. Similarly, F is **locally one-to-one** (or **locally injective**) at $\mathbf{x}_0$ if there is a ball $B_r(\mathbf{x}_0)$ about $\mathbf{x}_0$ in $\mathbf{R}^n$ and a ball $B_s(\mathbf{b}_0)$ about $\mathbf{b}_0$ in $\mathbf{R}^m$ such that for every $\mathbf{b}$ in $B_s(\mathbf{b}_0)$ there is at most one $\mathbf{x}$ in $B_r(\mathbf{x}_0)$ such that $F(\mathbf{x}) = \mathbf{b}$.

In words, F is locally onto at $\mathbf{x}_0$ if when $\mathbf{b}_0$ is perturbed a little to $\mathbf{b}_1$ there is still an $\mathbf{x}_1$ near $\mathbf{x}_0$ such that $F(\mathbf{x}_1) = \mathbf{b}_1$; F is locally one-to-one if when $\mathbf{b}_0$ is perturbed a little to $\mathbf{b}_1$ there is at most one $\mathbf{x}_1$ near $\mathbf{x}_0$ such that $F(\mathbf{x}_1) = \mathbf{b}_1$. In this terminology, we can write the Implicit Function Theorem as follows.

Theorem 15.8   Let $F: \mathbf{R}^n \to \mathbf{R}^m$ be a C^1 function with $F(\mathbf{x}^*) = \mathbf{b}^*$. Let $DF_{\mathbf{x}^*}$ denote the $m \times n$ Jacobian matrix of F at $\mathbf{x}^*$.

(a) If $DF_{\mathbf{x}^*}$ is onto ($n \geq m = \operatorname{rank} DF_{\mathbf{x}^*}$), then F is locally onto at $\mathbf{x}^*$.

(b) If $DF_{\mathbf{x}^*}$ is one-to-one ($m \geq n = \operatorname{rank} DF_{\mathbf{x}^*}$), then F is locally one-to-one at $\mathbf{x}^*$.

Proof   First, suppose that $DF_{\mathbf{x}^*}$ is onto, that is, that $(DF_{\mathbf{x}^*})\mathbf{y} = \mathbf{b}$ has a solution $\mathbf{y}$ for every right-hand side $\mathbf{b}$. By the results of Chapter 7, $n \geq m = \operatorname{rank} DF_{\mathbf{x}^*}$. The fact that $DF_{\mathbf{x}^*}$ has maximal rank m means that it has a nonsingular $m \times m$ submatrix. For ease of notation, we assume that it is the leftmost $m \times m$ submatrix

$$
\begin{pmatrix}
\dfrac{\partial F_1}{\partial x_1}(\mathbf{x}^*) & \cdots & \dfrac{\partial F_1}{\partial x_m}(\mathbf{x}^*) \\
\vdots & \ddots & \vdots \\
\dfrac{\partial F_m}{\partial x_1}(\mathbf{x}^*) & \cdots & \dfrac{\partial F_m}{\partial x_m}(\mathbf{x}^*)
\end{pmatrix}
\tag{56}
$$

that is nonsingular. Apply the Implicit function Theorem to the system

$$F_1(x_1, \ldots, x_m, x_{m+1}, \ldots, x_n) - b_1 = 0$$

$$\vdots \qquad \qquad \vdots \qquad \qquad (57)$$

$$F_m(x_1, \ldots, x_m, x_{m+1}, \ldots, x_n) - b_m = 0.$$

Since (56) is nonsingular, we can consider $x_1, \ldots, x_m$ as endogenous variables and the rest of the variables, namely $x_{m+1}, \ldots, x_n, b_1, \ldots, b_m$ as exogenous. So that for each choice of $(x_{m+1}, \ldots, x_n, b_1, \ldots, b_m)$ near $(x_{m+1}^*, \ldots, x_n^*, b_1^*, \ldots, b_m^*)$, there exists a point $(x_1, \ldots, x_m)$ near $(x_1^*, \ldots, x_m^*)$ such that the system (57) is satisfied. In particular, there is a ball $B_s(\mathbf{b}^*)$ about $\mathbf{b}^*$ so that if we choose $\mathbf{b}' = (b_1', \ldots, b_m')$ in $B_s(\mathbf{b}^*)$ and keep $x_{m+1}, \ldots, x_n$ fixed, we can find $\mathbf{x}' = (x_1', \ldots, x_m', x_{m+1}^*, \ldots, x_n^*)$ near $\mathbf{x}^*$ so that $F(\mathbf{x}') = \mathbf{b}'$. This proves that F is locally onto at $\mathbf{x}^*$.

Now suppose that $DF_{\mathbf{x}^*}$ is one-to-one. This means that $n \leq m$ and the matrix $DF_{\mathbf{x}^*}$ has rank n; this in turn implies that $DF_{\mathbf{x}^*}$ has a nonsingular $n \times n$ submatrix. For notation's sake, we will assume that it's the topmost $n \times n$ submatrix

$$\begin{pmatrix} \dfrac{\partial F_1}{\partial x_1}(\mathbf{x}^*) & \cdots & \dfrac{\partial F_1}{\partial x_n}(\mathbf{x}^*) \\ \vdots & \ddots & \vdots \\ \dfrac{\partial F_n}{\partial x_1}(\mathbf{x}^*) & \cdots & \dfrac{\partial F_n}{\partial x_n}(\mathbf{x}^*) \end{pmatrix} \qquad (58)$$

that is nonsingular. Consider the first n equations of system (57):

$$F_1(x_1, \ldots, x_n) - b_1 = 0$$

$$\vdots \qquad \qquad \vdots \qquad \qquad (59)$$

$$F_n(x_1, \ldots, x_n) - b_n = 0.$$

Since (58) is nonsingular, the Implicit Function Theorem tells us that system (59) can be solved for $x_1, \ldots, x_n$ in terms of $b_1, \ldots, b_n$ near $\mathbf{x}^*$ and $(b_1^*, \ldots, b_n^*)$:

$$x_1 = \phi_1(b_1, \ldots, b_n)$$

$$\vdots \qquad \qquad \vdots \qquad \qquad (60)$$

$$x_n = \phi_n(b_1, \ldots, b_n).$$

To prove that F is locally one-to-one at $\mathbf{x}^*$, suppose $F(\mathbf{x}') = F(\mathbf{y}') = \mathbf{b}'$ for $\mathbf{x}', \mathbf{y}'$ near $\mathbf{x}^*$ and $\mathbf{b}'$ near $\mathbf{b}^*$. By (60),

$$\mathbf{x}' = \phi(b_1', \ldots, b_n') \quad \text{and} \quad \mathbf{y}' = \phi(b_1', \ldots, b_n').$$

Therefore, $\mathbf{x}' = \mathbf{y}'$ and F is locally one-to-one near $\mathbf{x}^*$. ■

Finally, let us put the two parts of Theorem 15.8 together. A continuous function F that is one-to-one and onto from a set U to a set V has a natural inverse function $F^{-1}: V \rightarrow U$. The following version of Theorem 15.8 is called the **Inverse Function Theorem**.

Theorem 15.9   (Inverse Function Theorem) Let $F: \mathbf{R}^n \rightarrow \mathbf{R}^n$ be a C^1 function with $F(\mathbf{x}^*) = \mathbf{y}^*$. If $DF_{\mathbf{x}^*}$ is nonsingular, then there exists an open ball $B_r(\mathbf{x}^*)$ about $\mathbf{x}^*$ and an open set V about $\mathbf{y}^*$ such that F is a one-to-one and onto map from $B_r(\mathbf{x}^*)$ to V. The natural inverse map $F^{-1}: V \rightarrow B_r(\mathbf{x}^*)$ is also C^1 and

$$(DF^{-1})_{F(\mathbf{x}^*)} = (DF_{\mathbf{x}^*})^{-1}.$$

Proof   The first part of Theorem 15.9 follows immediately from the two parts of Theorem 15.8. The local inverse of F is just the map ϕ in (60), which is C^1 by the Implicit Function Theorem. To compute the derivative of ϕ, just apply the Chain Rule (Theorem 14.4) to the equation $\phi(F(\mathbf{x})) = \mathbf{x}$ to obtain

$$D\phi_{F(\mathbf{x}^*)} \cdot DF_{\mathbf{x}^*} = I,$$

or
$$DF^{-1}_{F(\mathbf{x}^*)} = D\phi_{F(\mathbf{x}^*)} = (DF_{\mathbf{x}^*})^{-1}. \quad \blacksquare$$

The Inverse Function Theorem is a powerful result. In general, it is nearly impossible to check directly that a given map is one-to-one and onto. By Theorem 15.9, we need only show that its derivative is a nonsingular matrix — a much easier task.

Note that in order for a smooth map from $\mathbf{R}^n$ to $\mathbf{R}^m$ to be invertible, we need $m = n$. A continuous one-to-one map F from a set U *onto* a set V which has a continuous inverse $F^{-1}: V \rightarrow U$ is called a **homeomorphism** between U and V. If F and F^{-1} are C^1, F is called a **diffeomorphism** between U and V. Analytically, a diffeomorphism can be considered as a reparameterization or a change of coordinates on U.

Example 15.17   Consider the function $F(x, y) = (x^2 - y^2, 2xy)$. Its Jacobian derivative has determinant $4(x^2 + y^2)$ at the point (x, y). By the Inverse Function Theorem, F is locally invertible at every point except $(0, 0)$. It turns out that F is not *globally* one-to-one. In the first exercise below, you are asked to show that $(0, 0)$ is the only point in the target space that has only one preimage.

EXERCISES

15.33   Solve the system $x^2 - y^2 = a$, $2xy = b$ for (x, y) in terms of (a, b). Show that every nonzero (a, b) has exactly two preimages.

15.34   Prove that F is one-to-one if and only if for all $\mathbf{x}, \mathbf{y} \in \mathbf{R}^n$, $F(\mathbf{x}) = F(\mathbf{y})$ implies that $\mathbf{x} = \mathbf{y}$.

15.35 State a simple $\mathbf{R}^1$ version of the Inverse Function Theorem.

15.36 Show that the map $F(x, y) = (x + e^y, y + e^{-x})$ is everywhere locally invertible.

15.37 Show that $f(t) = (\cos t, \sin t)$ is locally one-to-one but not globally one-to-one.

15.38 Show that $F(x, y) = (e^y \cos x, e^y \sin x)$ is locally one-to-one and onto, but not globally one-to-one.

15.39 Show that $f(x) = e^x$ is locally onto but not globally onto.

15.6 APPLICATION: SIMPSON'S PARADOX

Suppose that a pharmaceutical firm tests its new cough medicine in Chicago (C) and in Detroit (C'). In each city a test group (T) of coughers receives the new medicine and a control group (T') receives the old standard treatment. Some people in the test groups become healthy (H), while others keep coughing (H'). Suppose that in each city, the new cough medicine is judged to be successful because a higher percentage of people who took the new medicine stopped coughing than people who took the old standard. In symbols,

$$P(H : CT) > P(H : CT') \tag{61}$$

and
$$P(H : C'T) > P(H : C'T'), \tag{62}$$

where we write $P(A : B)$ for the *conditional probability* that a person is in group A, given that the person is in group B. Is it possible that for the *aggregated* results, the group with the old medicine does better than the group with the new medicine:

$$P(H : T') > P(H : T)? \tag{63}$$

Indeed, it is! This surprising possibility is known as **Simpson's Paradox**. In fact, any or all of the three inequalities (61), (62), (63) can be reversed.

One simple way to see this is to use the Implicit Function Theorem. Write

$$S_1 = CT, \quad S_2 = C'T, \quad S_3 = CT', \quad S_4 = C'T'$$

as mutually disjoint sets. For example, S_1 is the set of the test members in Chicago that received the new medicine. Let x_j denote $P(H : S_j)$. For example, x_2 is the fraction of those participants who live in Detroit and who received the medicine that recovered.

Let d_j denote the fraction of the total test group that is in subgroup S_j, so that

$$d_1 + d_2 + d_3 + d_4 = 1. \tag{64}$$

By the standard rules of conditional probabilities,

$$P(H : T) = P(H : TC) \cdot P(TC : T) + P(H : TC') \cdot P(TC' : T)$$

$$= x_1 \cdot \frac{d_1}{d_1 + d_2} + x_2 \cdot \frac{d_2}{d_1 + d_2}$$

and $P(H : T') = P(H : T'C) \cdot P(T'C : T') + P(H : T'C') \cdot P(T'C' : T')$

$$= x_3 \cdot \frac{d_3}{d_3 + d_4} + x_4 \cdot \frac{d_4}{d_3 + d_4}.$$

Form the map

$F(x_1, x_2, x_3, x_4, d_1, d_2, d_3, d_4)$

$$\equiv \left(x_1 - x_3, \ x_2 - x_4, \ \frac{x_1 d_1}{d_1 + d_2} + \frac{x_2 d_2}{d_1 + d_2} - \frac{x_3 d_3}{d_3 + d_4} - \frac{x_4 d_4}{d_3 + d_4} \right).$$

Since each x_i is in $[0, 1]$ and each (d_1, d_2, d_3, d_4) is in the three-dimensional affine set

$$\Sigma(4) \equiv \left\{ (d_1, d_2, d_3, d_4) : d_i \geq 0, \ \sum_i d_i = 1 \right\},$$

$F: [0, 1]^4 \times \Sigma(4) \longrightarrow \mathbf{R}^3$. The domain of F is seven-dimensional; we can use $d_4 = 1 - d_1 - d_2 - d_3$ to eliminate d_4 in the expression for F:

$$F(x_1, x_2, x_3, x_4, d_1, d_2, d_3) = \left(x_1 - x_3, \ x_2 - x_4, \right.$$

$$\left. \frac{x_1 d_1}{d_1 + d_2} + \frac{x_2 d_2}{d_1 + d_2} - \frac{x_3 d_3}{1 - d_1 - d_2} - \frac{x_4(1 - d_1 - d_2 - d_3)}{1 - d_1 - d_2} \right).$$

The Jacobian DF of F has the form:

$$\begin{pmatrix} 1 & 0 & -1 & * & * & * & 0 \\ 0 & 1 & 0 & * & * & * & 0 \\ \dfrac{d_1}{d_1 + d_2} & \dfrac{d_2}{d_1 + d_2} & -\dfrac{d_3}{1 - d_1 - d_2} & * & * & * & \dfrac{x_4 - x_3}{1 - d_1 - d_2} \end{pmatrix}.$$

If we take $x_3 \neq x_4$, columns 1, 2, and 7 of DF are linearly independent and DF has rank three. Let $(\mathbf{x}^*, \mathbf{d}^*)$ be a point with the properties

$$x_1^* = x_3^* \neq x_2^* = x_4^*, \quad \text{and} \quad d_1^* = d_2^* = d_3^* = d_4^* = \frac{1}{4}.$$

Then, $F(\mathbf{x}^*, \mathbf{d}^*) = \mathbf{0}$ and $DF(\mathbf{x}^*, \mathbf{d}^*)$ has maximal rank. By the Implicit Function Theorem, F is onto a neighborhood of $(0, 0, 0)$. In other words, if we choose any sign pattern $(\varepsilon_1, \varepsilon_2, \varepsilon_3)$, where each $\varepsilon_i = \pm 1$, in the target space $\mathbf{R}^3$ and a point $\mathbf{z} = (z_1, z_2, z_3)$ near $(0, 0, 0)$ that realizes this sign pattern, then there exists a point $(\mathbf{x}', \mathbf{d}')$ in $[0, 1]^4 \times \Sigma(4)$, such that $F(\mathbf{x}', \mathbf{d}') = \mathbf{z}$. The point $(\mathbf{x}', \mathbf{d}')$ corresponds to a partitioning of the test population into $S_1, \ldots, S_4$ so that the 3-tuple

$$(P(H:CT) - P(H:CT'), \; P(H:C'T) - P(H:C'T'),$$
$$P(H:T') - P(H:T))$$

has the preassigned sign pattern $(\varepsilon_1, \varepsilon_2, \varepsilon_3)$.

Example 15.18   Suppose that in each city 300 persons participate in the test. Suppose that in Chicago 240 receive the new medicine and 60 the old, of which 90 of the former (37.5%) and 20 of the latter (33.3%) recover. Suppose that in Detroit 60 receive the new medicine and 240 the old, of which 30 of the former (50%) and 110 of the latter (45.8%) recover. The new medicine does better than the old in each city. However, in the aggregate sample of 600, 120 of the 300 that took the new medicine recover (40%), while 130 of the 300 that took the old medicine recover (43.3%).

We can complicate the test arrangements even more so that almost any combination of results can occur. Suppose that in each city the tests are conducted in a university facility (U) and in a private lab (U'). There exist samples in which the new cough medicine is more successful than the old at each of the four labs and in the aggregate in each city, but less successful when aggregated over the whole test population. In other samples, the conclusions oscillate with the level: the new medicine is less successful than the old at each of the four facilities, is more successful in each city, but is less successful in the aggregate sample, and so on.

    We sketch the extension of the above argument to this situation. Now, there are eight mutually exclusive groups:

$$S_1 = TCU, \quad S_2 = TCU', \quad S_3 = TC'U, \quad S_4 = TC'U',$$
$$S_5 = T'CU, \quad S_6 = T'CU', \quad S_7 = T'C'U, \quad S_8 = T'C'U'.$$

Once again, let $x_i = P(H:S_i)$ and $d_i = P(S_i)$ for $i = 1, \ldots, 8$. Let

$$y_1 = P(H:TC), \quad y_2 = P(H:TC'), \quad y_3 = P(H:T'C), \quad y_4 = P(H:T'C'),$$

aggregating over the type of test lab. Let

$$z_1 = P(H:T) \quad \text{and} \quad z_2 = P(H:T'),$$

the overall aggregate variables. We write the y_j's and z_j's in terms of the x_i's and d_i's as follows: Each

$$y_j = \frac{x_{2j-1}d_{2j-1} + x_{2j}d_{2j}}{d_{2j-1} + d_{2j}}, \quad z_1 = \frac{\sum_{j=1}^{4} x_j d_j}{\sum_{j=1}^{4} d_j}, \quad z_2 = \frac{\sum_{j=5}^{8} x_j d_j}{\sum_{j=5}^{8} d_j}. \quad (65)$$

As usual, write the probability simplex $\{\mathbf{d} \in \mathbf{R}^8 : \mathbf{d} \geq \mathbf{0}, \sum_i d_i = 1\}$ as $\Sigma(8)$. The comparison map is now

$$F: [0, 1]^8 \times \Sigma(8) \to \mathbf{R}^7,$$

defined by

$$F(x_1, \ldots, x_8, d_1, \ldots, d_8) = (x_1 - x_5, \ldots, x_4 - x_8, y_1 - y_3, y_2 - y_4, z_1 - z_2),$$

but we must substitute for the y_j's and z_j's using (65) and then write $d_8 = 1 - d_1 - \cdots - d_7$. As we did earlier, we choose a point $(\mathbf{x}^*, \mathbf{d}^*)$ with the properties:

1) $F(\mathbf{x}^*, \mathbf{d}^*) = \mathbf{0}$,

2) $DF(\mathbf{x}^*, \mathbf{d}^*)$ has maximal rank 7.

(66)

(Exercise.) Finally, apply the Implicit Function Theorem to show that any sign pattern in the 7-dimensional target space can be realized as the image under F of points near $(\mathbf{x}^*, \mathbf{d}^*)$. ·

The behavior described in this section in which the conclusion of aggregated data differs from a common conclusion of the subpopulations turns out to be a characteristic of models built on conditional probabilities or on the nonlinear combination of random variables. This kind of inconsistent behavior occurs with many, if not most, statistical decision processes, including the Kruskal-Wallis test.

EXERCISES

15.40 Find a point $(\mathbf{x}^*, \mathbf{d}^*)$ that satisfies condition (66) and finish the Implicit Function Theorem argument.

NOTES

D. G. Saari pioneered the approach in the last section. See: D. G. Saari, "The sources of some paradoxes from social choice and probability." *Journal of Economic Theory* 41 (1987) 1–22. The material in this section can naturally be considered as the nonlinear analogue of the material on voting paradoxes in Chapter 28. See D. Haunsberger and D. G. Saari, "The lack of consistency for statistical decision procedures." *American Statistician* 45 (1991), 252–255, for an exposition of how the inconsistent behavior in Simpson's Paradox occurs with a host of other statistical decision processes, including the Kruskal-Wallis test.

Optimization

Quadratic Forms and Definite Matrices

The natural starting point for the study of optimization problems is the simplest such problem: the optimization of a *quadratic form*. There are a number of good reasons for studying *quadratic* optimization problems first. Quadratic forms are the simplest functions after linear ones. Like linear functions, they have matrix representations, so that studying the properties of a quadratic form reduces to studying properties of a symmetric matrix. Quadratic forms provide an excellent introduction to the vocabulary and techniques of optimization problems. Furthermore, the second order conditions that distinguish maxima from minima in economic optimization problems are stated in terms of quadratic forms. Finally, a number of economic optimization problems have a quadratic objective function, for example, risk minimization problems in finance, where riskiness is measured by the (quadratic) variance of the returns from investments.

Example 16.1   Among the functions of one variable, the simplest functions with a unique global extremum are the pure quadratics: $y = x^2$ and $y = -x^2$. The former has a global minimum at $x = 0$; the latter has a global maximum at $x = 0$, as illustrated in Figure 16.1.

16.1   QUADRATIC FORMS

Recall the definition of a quadratic form on $\mathbf{R}^n$ from Section 13.3.

Definition   A **quadratic form** on $\mathbf{R}^n$ is a real-valued function of the form

$$Q(x_1, \ldots, x_n) = \sum_{i \leq j} a_{ij} x_i x_j, \tag{1}$$

in which each term is a monomial of degree two.

The presentation in Section 13.3 showed that each quadratic form Q can be represented by a *symmetric* matrix A so that

$$Q(\mathbf{x}) = \mathbf{x}^T \cdot A \cdot \mathbf{x}. \tag{2}$$

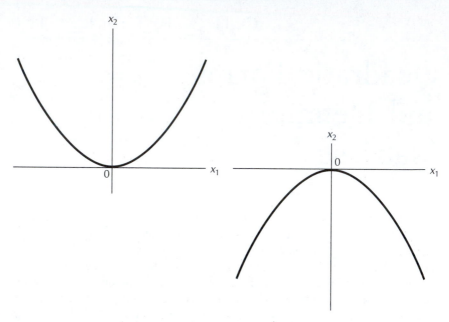

**Figure
16.1**   *The functions of $f(x) = x^2$ and $f(x) = -x^2$.*

For example, the general two-dimensional quadratic form

$$a_{11}x_1^2 + a_{12}x_1x_2 + a_{22}x_2^2 \tag{3}$$

can be written as

$$(x_1 \quad x_2)\begin{pmatrix} a_{11} & \frac{1}{2}a_{12} \\ \frac{1}{2}a_{12} & a_{22} \end{pmatrix}\begin{pmatrix} x_1 \\ x_2 \end{pmatrix}.$$

And the general three dimensional quadratic form

$$a_{11}x_1^2 + a_{22}x_2^2 + a_{33}x_3^2 + a_{12}x_1x_2 + a_{13}x_1x_3 + a_{23}x_2x_3 \tag{4}$$

can be written as:

$$(x_1 \quad x_2 \quad x_3)\begin{pmatrix} a_{11} & \frac{1}{2}a_{12} & \frac{1}{2}a_{13} \\ \frac{1}{2}a_{12} & a_{22} & \frac{1}{2}a_{23} \\ \frac{1}{2}a_{13} & \frac{1}{2}a_{23} & a_{33} \end{pmatrix}\begin{pmatrix} x_1 \\ x_2 \\ x_3 \end{pmatrix}.$$

16.2   DEFINITENESS OF QUADRATIC FORMS

A quadratic form always takes on the value zero at the point $\mathbf{x} = \mathbf{0}$. Its distinguishing characteristic is the set of values it takes when $\mathbf{x} \neq \mathbf{0}$. In this chapter, we focus on the question of whether $\mathbf{x} = \mathbf{0}$ is a max, a min or neither of the quadratic forms under consideration.

The general quadratic form of one variable is $y = ax^2$. If $a > 0$, then ax^2 is always ≥ 0 and equals 0 only when $x = 0$. Such a form is called **positive definite**; $x = 0$ is its global *minimizer*. If $a < 0$, then ax^2 is always ≤ 0 and equals 0 only when $x = 0$. Such a quadratic form is called **negative definite**; $x = 0$ is its global *maximizer*. Figure 16.1 illustrates these two situations.

In two dimensions, the quadratic form $Q_1(x_1, x_2) = x_1^2 + x_2^2$ is always greater than zero at $(x_1, x_2) \neq (0, 0)$. So, we call Q_1 **positive definite**. Quadratic forms like $Q_2(x_1, x_2) = -x_1^2 - x_2^2$, which are strictly negative except at the origin, are called **negative definite**. Quadratic forms like $Q_3(x_1, x_2) = x_1^2 - x_2^2$, which take on both positive and negative values ($Q_3(1, 0) = +1$ and $Q_3(0, 1) = -1$) are called **indefinite**.

There are two intermediate cases: a quadratic form which is always ≥ 0 but may equal zero at some nonzero $\mathbf{x}$'s is called **positive semidefinite**. This property is illustrated by the quadratic form

$$Q_4(x_1, x_2) = (x_1 + x_2)^2 = x_1^2 + 2x_1x_2 + x_2^2,$$

which is never negative but which equals zero at nonzero points such as $(x_1, x_2) = (1, -1)$ or $(-2, 2)$. A quadratic form like $Q_5(x_1, x_2) = -(x_1 + x_2)^2$, which is never positive but can be zero at points other than the origin, is called **negative semidefinite**.

Figures 16.2 through 16.6 present the graphs of the above five quadratic forms $Q_1, \ldots, Q_5$. Every quadratic form on $\mathbf{R}^2$ has a graph similar to one of these five. For example, every positive definite quadratic on $\mathbf{R}^2$ has a bowl shaped graph as in Figure 16.2, and every indefinite quadratic on $\mathbf{R}^2$ has a saddle-shaped graph as in Figure 16.4.

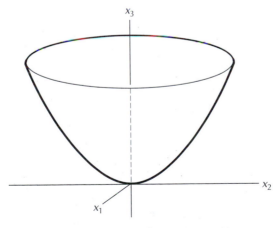

Graph of the positive definite form $Q_1(x_1, x_2) = x_1^2 + x_2^2$.

Figure 16.2

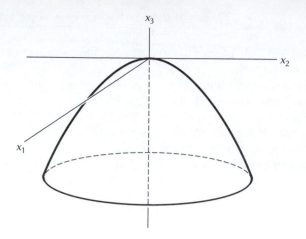

Figure 16.3

Graph of the negative definite form $Q_2(x_1, x_2) = -x_1^2 - x_2^2$.

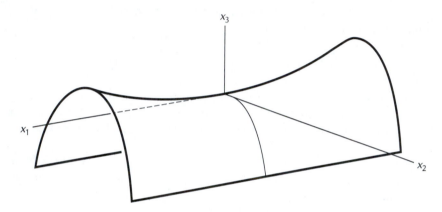

Figure 16.4

The graph of the indefinite form $Q_3(x_1, x_2) = x_1^2 - x_2^2$.

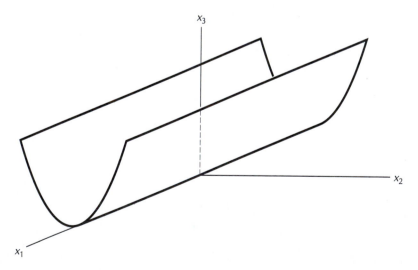

Figure 16.5

The graph of the positive semidefinite form $Q_4(x_1, x_2) = (x_1 + x_2)^2$.

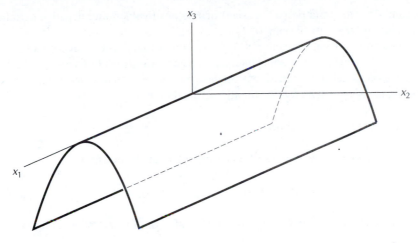

The graph of the negative semidefinite form $Q_5(x_1, x_2) = -(x_1 + x_2)^2$.

**Figure
16.6**

Definite Symmetric Matrices

A symmetric matrix is called positive definite, positive semidefinite, negative definite, etc., according to the definiteness of the corresponding quadratic form $Q(\mathbf{x}) = \mathbf{x}^T A \mathbf{x}$. Since we will usually be applying this terminology to symmetric matrices directly, we focus on such matrices for our formal definitions of definiteness.

Definition   Let A be an $n \times n$ symmetric matrix, then A is:

(*a*) **positive definite** if $\mathbf{x}^T A \mathbf{x} > 0$ for all $\mathbf{x} \neq \mathbf{0}$ in $\mathbf{R}^n$,
(*b*) **positive semidefinite** if $\mathbf{x}^T A \mathbf{x} \geq 0$ for all $\mathbf{x} \neq \mathbf{0}$ in $\mathbf{R}^n$,
(*c*) **negative definite** if $\mathbf{x}^T A \mathbf{x} < 0$ for all $\mathbf{x} \neq \mathbf{0}$ in $\mathbf{R}^n$,
(*d*) **negative semidefinite** if $\mathbf{x}^T A \mathbf{x} \leq 0$ for all $\mathbf{x} \neq \mathbf{0}$ in $\mathbf{R}^n$, and
(*e*) **indefinite** if $\mathbf{x}^T A \mathbf{x} > 0$ for some $\mathbf{x}$ in $\mathbf{R}^n$ and < 0 for some other $\mathbf{x}$ in $\mathbf{R}^n$.

Remark   A matrix that is positive (negative) definite is automatically positive (negative) semidefinite. Otherwise, every symmetric matrix falls into one of the above five categories.

Application: Second Order Conditions and Convexity

The definiteness of a symmetric matrix plays an important role in economic theory and in applied mathematics in general. For example, for a function $y = f(x)$ of one variable, the sign of the second derivative $f''(x_0)$ at a critical point x_0 of f gives a necessary condition and a sufficient condition for determining whether x_0 is a maximum of f, a minimum of f, or neither. The generalization of this second derivative test to higher dimensions involves checking whether the second derivative matrix (or Hessian) of f is positive definite, negative definite, or indefinite at a critical point of f.

In a similar vein, a function $y = f(x)$ of one variable is concave if its second derivative $f''(x)$ is ≤ 0 on some interval. The generalization of this result to higher dimensions states that a function is concave on some region if its second derivative matrix is *negative semidefinite* for all $\mathbf{x}$ in the region.

Application: Conic Sections

In plane geometry, the conic section described by the level curve

$$Q(x_1, x_2) \equiv a_{11}x_1^2 + a_{12}x_1x_2 + a_{22}x_2^2 = 1 \qquad (5)$$

is completely determined by the definiteness of Q or of its associated matrix

$$A = \begin{pmatrix} a_{11} & \frac{1}{2}a_{12} \\ \frac{1}{2}a_{12} & a_{22} \end{pmatrix}.$$

Figure 16.7 illustrates the connection. The horizontal plane $\{x_3 = 1\}$ cuts the graph in Figure 16.2 in an ellipse or circle. Therefore, if A is positive definite, the set (5) is an ellipse or circle. Since $\{x_3 = 1\}$ cuts the graph in Figure 16.4 in an hyperbola, as also illustrated in Figure 16.7, equation (5) describes an hyperbola if A is

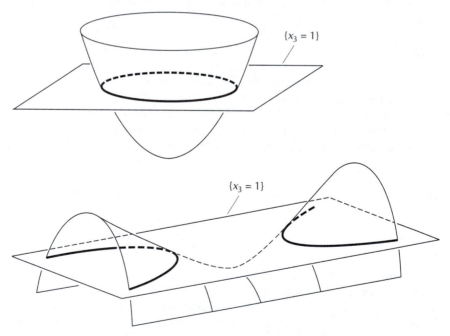

Figure 16.7

Levels sets of graphs of quadratic forms.

indefinite. Since $\{x_3 = 1\}$ cuts the graph of Figure 16.5 in a pair of parallel lines, equation (5) defines two lines if A is positive semidefinite but not positive definite. Finally, since the plane $\{x_3 = 1\}$ lies strictly above the graphs in Figures 16.3 and 16.6, the set (5) is empty if A is negative definite or even negative semidefinite.

Principal Minors of a Matrix

In this section we will describe a simple test for the definiteness of a quadratic form or of a symmetric matrix. To describe this algorithm, we need some more vocabulary.

Definition   Let A be an $n \times n$ matrix. A $k \times k$ submatrix of A formed by deleting $n - k$ columns, say columns $i_1, i_2, \ldots, i_{n-k}$ *and the same $n - k$ rows*, rows $i_1, i_2, \ldots, i_{n-k}$, from A is called a kth order **principal submatrix** of A. The determinant of a $k \times k$ principal submatrix is called a kth order **principal minor** of A.

Example 16.2   For a general 3×3 matrix

$$A = \begin{pmatrix} a_{11} & a_{12} & a_{13} \\ a_{21} & a_{22} & a_{23} \\ a_{31} & a_{32} & a_{33} \end{pmatrix},$$

there is one third order principal minor: $\det(A)$. There are three second order principal minors:

(1) $\begin{vmatrix} a_{11} & a_{12} \\ a_{21} & a_{22} \end{vmatrix}$, formed by deleting column 3 and row 3 from A;

(2) $\begin{vmatrix} a_{11} & a_{13} \\ a_{31} & a_{33} \end{vmatrix}$, formed by deleting column 2 and row 2 from A;

(3) $\begin{vmatrix} a_{22} & a_{23} \\ a_{32} & a_{33} \end{vmatrix}$, formed by deleting column 1 and row 1 from A.

There are three first order principal minors:

(1) $|a_{11}|$, formed by deleting the last 2 rows and columns,
(2) $|a_{22}|$, formed by deleting the first and third rows and the first and third columns, and
(3) $|a_{33}|$, formed by deleting the first 2 rows and columns.

It is important to understand why no other submatrix of A is a principal submatrix. For practice, list all the principal minors of a general 4×4 matrix.

Among the kth order principal minors of a given matrix, there is one special one that we want to highlight.

Definition Let A be an $n \times n$ matrix. The kth order principal submatrix of A obtained by deleting the *last $n - k$* rows and the *last $n - k$* columns from A is called the kth order **leading principal submatrix** of A. Its determinant is called the kth order **leading principal minor** of A. We will denote the kth order leading principal submatrix by A_k and the corresponding leading principal minor by $|A_k|$.

An $n \times n$ matrix has n leading principal submatrices — the top-leftmost 1×1 submatrix, the top-leftmost 2×2 submatrix, etc. For the general 3×3 matrix of Example 16.2, the three leading principal minors are

$$
|a_{11}|, \quad
\begin{vmatrix} a_{11} & a_{12} \\ a_{21} & a_{22} \end{vmatrix}, \quad
\begin{vmatrix} a_{11} & a_{12} & a_{13} \\ a_{21} & a_{22} & a_{23} \\ a_{31} & a_{32} & a_{33} \end{vmatrix}.
$$

The following theorem provides a straightforward algorithm which uses the leading principal minors to determine the definiteness of a given matrix. We present its proof in the Appendix of this chapter. We will present other criteria for the definiteness of a symmetric matrix in Section 23.7.

Theorem 16.1 Let A be an $n \times n$ symmetric matrix. Then,

(a) A is positive definite if and only if all its n leading principal minors are (strictly) positive.

(b) A is negative definite if and only if its n leading principal minors alternate in sign as follows:

$$
|A_1| < 0, \quad |A_2| > 0, \quad |A_3| < 0, \quad \text{etc.}
$$

The kth order leading principal minor should have the same sign as $(-1)^k$.

(c) If some kth order leading principal minor of A (or some pair of them) is nonzero but does not fit either of the above two sign patterns, then A is indefinite. This case occurs when A has a *negative* kth order leading principal minor for an *even* integer k or when A has a negative kth order leading principal minor and a positive ℓth order leading principal minor for two distinct *odd* integers k and ℓ.

One way that the leading principal minor test of Theorem 16.1 can fail for a given symmetric matrix A is that some leading principal minor of A is *zero* while the nonzero ones fit the sign pattern in either a) or b) of Theorem 16.1. When this occurs, the matrix A is *not* definite and it may or it may not be semidefinite. In this case, to check for semidefiniteness, one no longer has the luxury of checking only the n *leading* principal minors of A, but must check the sign of *every* principal minor of A, using the test described by the following theorem.

Theorem 16.2 Let A be an $n \times n$ symmetric matrix. Then, A is positive semidefinite if and only if every principal minor of A is ≥ 0; A is negative semidefinite if and only if every principal minor of odd order is ≤ 0 and every principal minor of even order is ≥ 0.

Example 16.3 Suppose A is a 4×4 symmetric matrix and, as usual, write $|A_i|$ for its ith order *leading* principal minor.

(a) If $|A_1| > 0$, $|A_2| > 0$, $|A_3| > 0$, $|A_4| > 0$, then A is positive definite (and conversely).

(b) If $|A_1| < 0$, $|A_2| > 0$, $|A_3| < 0$, $|A_4| > 0$, then A is negative definite (and conversely).

(c) If $|A_1| > 0$, $|A_2| > 0$, $|A_3| = 0$, $|A_4| < 0$, then A is indefinite because of A_4.

(d) If $|A_1| < 0$, $|A_2| < 0$, $|A_3| < 0$, $|A_4| < 0$, then A is indefinite because of A_2 (and A_4).

(e) If $|A_1| = 0$, $|A_2| < 0$, $|A_3| > 0$, $|A_4| = 0$, then A is indefinite because of A_2.

(f) If $|A_1| > 0$, $|A_2| = 0$, $|A_3| > 0$, $|A_4| > 0$, then A is not definite. It is not negative semidefinite, but it may be positive semidefinite. To check for positive semidefiniteness, one must check all 15 principal minors of A, not just the four leading principal ones. If none of the principal minors are negative, then A is positive semidefinite. If at least one of them is negative, A is indefinite.

(g) If $|A_1| = 0$, $|A_2| > 0$, $|A_3| = 0$, $|A_4| > 0$, then A is not definite, but it may be positive semidefinite or negative semidefinite. To decide, one must again check all 15 of its principal minors.

To motivate these two theorems and to understand their algorithms better, we will examine them in some detail for the simplest symmetric matrices — diagonal matrices and then 2×2 matrices.

The Definiteness of Diagonal Matrices

The simplest $n \times n$ symmetric matrices are the diagonal matrices. They also correspond to the simplest quadratic forms since

$$(x_1 \quad x_2 \quad \cdots \quad x_n) \begin{pmatrix} a_1 & 0 & \cdots & 0 \\ 0 & a_2 & \cdots & 0 \\ \vdots & \vdots & \ddots & \vdots \\ 0 & 0 & \cdots & a_n \end{pmatrix} \begin{pmatrix} x_1 \\ x_2 \\ \vdots \\ x_n \end{pmatrix} \qquad (6)$$

$$= a_1 x_1^2 + a_2 x_2^2 + \cdots + a_n x_n^2,$$

a sum of squares. Clearly, this quadratic form will be positive definite if and only if all the a_i's are positive and negative definite if and only if all the a_i's are negative. It will be positive semidefinite if and only if all the a_i's are ≥ 0 and negative semidefinite if and only if all the a_i's are ≤ 0. If there are two a_i's of opposite signs, this form will be indefinite.

Since all the principal submatrices are diagonal matrices, their determinants — the principal minors — are just products of the a_i's. If all the a_i's are positive, then all their products are positive and so all the leading principal minors are positive. If all the a_i's are negative (so the form is negative definite), then products of odd numbers of the a_i's will be negative and products of even numbers of the a_i's will be positive. This corresponds to the alternating signs condition in b) of Theorem 16.1 and indicates why we should expect such an alternating sign condition instead of an all negative condition in the test for negative definiteness.

If a_1 is zero in (6), the form cannot be definite since it will be zero when evaluated at $(1, 0, \ldots, 0)$. Notice that in this diagonal case, all the *leading* principal minors of (6) will also be zero, independent of the signs of the other a_i's. In order to check that all the a_i's have the proper sign when some of them are zero, one must check much more than just the leading principal minors.

The Definiteness of 2 × 2 Matrices

One can verify Theorems 16.1 and 16.2 directly for 2×2 symmetric matrices by completing the square in the corresponding quadratic form. Consider the general quadratic form on $\mathbf{R}^2$:

$$
Q(x_1, x_2) = (x_1 \quad x_2) \begin{pmatrix} a & b \\ b & c \end{pmatrix} \begin{pmatrix} x_1 \\ x_2 \end{pmatrix}
$$

$$
= ax_1^2 + 2bx_1x_2 + cx_2^2. \tag{7}
$$

For ease of notation, we are using a, b, and c in this example in place of a_{11}, a_{12}, and a_{22}, respectively. If $a = 0$, then Q cannot be positive or negative definite because $Q(1, 0) = 0$. So, assume now that $a \neq 0$ and complete the square in (7) by adding and subtracting $b^2x_2^2/a$ in expression (7):

$$
Q(x_1, x_2) = ax_1^2 + 2bx_1x_2 + cx_2^2 + \frac{b^2}{a}x_2^2 - \frac{b^2}{a}x_2^2
$$

$$
= a \left(x_1^2 + \frac{2b}{a}x_1x_2 + \frac{b^2}{a^2}x_2^2 \right) - \frac{b^2}{a}x_2^2 + cx_2^2
$$

$$
= a \left(x_1 + \frac{b}{a}x_2 \right)^2 + \frac{(ac - b^2)}{a}x_2^2. \tag{8}
$$

If both coefficients, a and $(ac - b^2)/a$ in (8) are positive, then Q will never be negative. It will equal zero only when

$$x_1 + \frac{b}{a}x_2 = 0 \quad \text{and} \quad x_2 = 0,$$

that is, when $x_1 = 0$ and $x_2 = 0$. In other words, if

$$|a| > 0 \quad \text{and} \quad \det A = \begin{vmatrix} a & b \\ b & c \end{vmatrix} > 0,$$

then Q is positive definite. Conversely, in order for Q to be positive definite, we need both a and $\det A = ac - b^2$ to be positive.

Similarly, Q will be negative definite if and only if both coefficients in expression (8), a and $(ac - b^2)/a$, are negative. This situation occurs if and only if $a < 0$ and $ac - b^2 > 0$, that is, when the leading principal minors alternate in sign.

If $(ac - b^2)$, the second order principal minor, is negative, then the two coefficients in (8) have opposite signs. In particular,

$$Q\left(\frac{b}{a}, -1\right) = \frac{ac - b^2}{a} \quad \text{and} \quad Q(1, 0) = a$$

will have opposite signs; so Q is *indefinite*.

Example 16.4   Consider

$$A = \begin{pmatrix} 2 & 3 \\ 3 & 7 \end{pmatrix} \quad \text{and} \quad B = \begin{pmatrix} 2 & 4 \\ 4 & 7 \end{pmatrix}.$$

Since $|A_1| = 2$ and $|A_2| = 5$, A is positive definite. Since $|B_1| = 2$ and $|B_2| = -2$, B is indefinite.

Example 16.5   Consider

$$C = \begin{pmatrix} 0 & 0 \\ 0 & c \end{pmatrix}.$$

Note that $|C_1| = 0$ and $|C_2| = 0$. The definiteness of C depends completely on c; C is positive semidefinite if $c \geq 0$ and negative semidefinite if $c \leq 0$. This is especially obvious if one looks at the corresponding quadratic form $Q_C(x_1, x_2) = cx_2^2$.

EXERCISES

16.1 Determine the definiteness of the following symmetric matrices:

a) $\begin{pmatrix} 2 & -1 \\ -1 & 1 \end{pmatrix}$ b) $\begin{pmatrix} -3 & 4 \\ 4 & -5 \end{pmatrix}$ c) $\begin{pmatrix} -3 & 4 \\ 4 & -6 \end{pmatrix}$ d) $\begin{pmatrix} 2 & 4 \\ 4 & 8 \end{pmatrix}$

e) $\begin{pmatrix} 1 & 2 & 0 \\ 2 & 4 & 5 \\ 0 & 5 & 6 \end{pmatrix}$ f) $\begin{pmatrix} -1 & 1 & 0 \\ 1 & -1 & 0 \\ 0 & 0 & -2 \end{pmatrix}$ g) $\begin{pmatrix} 1 & 0 & 3 & 0 \\ 0 & 2 & 0 & 5 \\ 3 & 0 & 4 & 0 \\ 0 & 5 & 0 & 6 \end{pmatrix}$.

16.2 Let $Q(\mathbf{x}) = \mathbf{x}^T A \mathbf{x}$ be a quadratic form on $\mathbf{R}^n$. By evaluating Q on each of the coordinate axes in $\mathbf{R}^n$, prove that a necessary condition for a symmetric matrix to be positive definite (positive semidefinite) is that all the diagonal entries be positive (nonnegative). State and prove the corresponding result for negative and negative semidefinite matrices. Give an example to show that this necessary condition is not sufficient.

16.3 Using the method of the previous exercise, sketch a proof that if A is positive (or negative) definite, then every principal submatrix of A is also positive (or negative) definite.

16.4 How many kth order principal minors will an $n \times n$ matrix have for each $k \le n$?

16.5 Mimic the computation in (8) to prove Theorem 16.1 for a general symmetric 3×3 matrix. [Hint: After "completing the square" twice, you should find that

$$(x_1 \quad x_2 \quad x_3) \begin{pmatrix} a_{11} & a_{12} & a_{13} \\ a_{12} & a_{22} & a_{23} \\ a_{13} & a_{23} & a_{33} \end{pmatrix} \begin{pmatrix} x_1 \\ x_2 \\ x_3 \end{pmatrix} =$$

$$|A_1| \left(x_1 + \frac{a_{12}}{a_{11}} x_2 + \frac{a_{13}}{a_{11}} x_3 \right)^2 + \frac{|A_2|}{|A_1|} \left(x_2 + \frac{a_{11}a_{23} - a_{12}a_{13}}{|A_2|} x_3 \right)^2 + \frac{|A_3|}{|A_2|}(x_3)^2.]$$

16.3 LINEAR CONSTRAINTS AND BORDERED MATRICES

Definiteness and Optimality

Keep in mind the fact that determining the definiteness of a quadratic form Q is equivalent to determining whether $\mathbf{x} = \mathbf{0}$ is a max, a min, or neither for the real-valued function Q. For example, $\mathbf{x} = \mathbf{0}$ is the unique *global minimum* of quadratic form Q if and only if Q is positive definite, by the very definition of positive definiteness. Similarly, $\mathbf{x} = \mathbf{0}$ is the unique *global maximum* of Q if and only if Q is negative definite.

The characterization of definiteness in Theorem 16.1 works only if there are no constraints in the problem under consideration, that is, if $\mathbf{x}$ can take on any value in $\mathbf{R}^n$. If there are constraints, the analysis becomes more delicate.

Example 16.6   The quadratic form $Q(x_1, x_2) = x_1^2 - x_2^2$ on $\mathbf{R}^2$ is indefinite; the origin is neither a max nor a min. But, if we restrict our attention to the x_1-axis, that is, if we impose the constraint $x_2 = 0$, then $Q(x_1, 0) = x_1^2$ has a strict global minimum at $x_1 = 0$, and therefore Q is positive definite on the constraint set $\{x_2 = 0\}$. Alternatively, if we impose the constraint $x_1 = 0$ and consider Q only on the x_2-axis, then $x_2 = 0$ is a global max of $Q(0, x_2) = -x_2^2$ and Q is negative definite on the subspace $\{x_1 = 0\}$. On the line $x_1 - 2x_2 = 0$, $Q(2x_2, x_2) = (2x_2)^2 - x_2^2 = 3x_2^2$ is positive definite.

As will be shown in Chapter 19, the second order condition which distinguishes maxima from minima in a *constrained* optimization problem is a condition on the definiteness of a quadratic form which is restricted to a linear subspace. Since most optimization problems in economics involve constraints on the variables under study, the rest of this chapter will discuss the definiteness of quadratic forms which are restricted to linear subspaces of $\mathbf{R}^n$.

Let us look in detail at the simplest such problem: the problem of determining the definiteness of, or of optimizing, a general quadratic form of two variables:

$$Q(x_1, x_2) = ax_1^2 + 2bx_1x_2 + cx_2^2 = (x_1 \quad x_2) \begin{pmatrix} a & b \\ b & c \end{pmatrix} \begin{pmatrix} x_1 \\ x_2 \end{pmatrix}, \qquad (9)$$

on the general linear subspace

$$Ax_1 + Bx_2 = 0. \qquad (10)$$

In Example 16.6, we worked with $A = 0$, then with $B = 0$, and finally with $A = 1$ and $B = -2$.

Since our focus is on the matrix and not on the quadratic form itself, we have multiplied the coefficient of x_1x_2 in (9) by 2 so that we do not have to deal with $1/2$s in the corresponding matrix. The simplest approach to this problem is to solve (10) for x_1 in terms of x_2; obtain $x_1 = -Bx_2/A$, and then substitute this expression for x_1 in the objective function (9):

$$Q\left(-\frac{Bx_2}{A}, x_2\right) = a\left(-\frac{Bx_2}{A}\right)^2 + 2b\left(-\frac{Bx_2}{A}\right)x_2 + cx_2^2$$

$$= \frac{aB^2}{A^2}x_2^2 - \frac{2bB}{A}x_2^2 + cx_2^2 \qquad (11)$$

$$= \frac{aB^2 - 2bAB + cA^2}{A^2}x_2^2.$$

We conclude from (11) that Q is positive definite on the constraint set (10) if and only if $aB^2 - 2bAB + cA^2 > 0$ and negative definite on (10) if and only if $aB^2 - 2bAB + cA^2 < 0$. There is a convenient way of writing this expression:

$$aB^2 - 2bAB + cA^2 = -\det \begin{pmatrix} 0 & A & B \\ A & a & b \\ B & b & c \end{pmatrix}. \tag{12}$$

The matrix in (12) is obtained by "bordering" the 2×2 matrix (9) of the quadratic Q on the top and left by the coefficients of the linear constraint (10). The following theorem summarizes these calculations.

Theorem 16.3   The quadratic form $Q(x_1, x_2) = ax_1^2 + 2bx_1x_2 + cx_2^2$ is positive (respectively, negative) definite on the constraint set $Ax_1 + Bx_2 = 0$ if and only if

$$\det \begin{pmatrix} 0 & A & B \\ A & a & b \\ B & b & c \end{pmatrix}$$

is negative (respectively, positive).

This same result holds for the general problem of determining the definiteness of

$$Q(\mathbf{x}) = \mathbf{x}^T A \mathbf{x} = (x_1 \quad \cdots \quad x_n) \begin{pmatrix} a_{11} & a_{12} & \cdots & a_{1n} \\ a_{12} & a_{22} & \cdots & a_{2n} \\ \vdots & \vdots & \ddots & \vdots \\ a_{1n} & a_{2n} & \cdots & a_{nn} \end{pmatrix} \begin{pmatrix} x_1 \\ x_2 \\ \vdots \\ x_n \end{pmatrix} \tag{13}$$

on the linear constraint set

$$\begin{pmatrix} B_{11} & B_{12} & \cdots & B_{1n} \\ \vdots & \vdots & \ddots & \vdots \\ B_{m1} & B_{m2} & \cdots & B_{mn} \end{pmatrix} \begin{pmatrix} x_1 \\ x_2 \\ \vdots \\ x_n \end{pmatrix} = \begin{pmatrix} 0 \\ 0 \\ \vdots \\ 0 \end{pmatrix}. \tag{14}$$

Border the matrix (13) of the quadratic form on the top and on the left by the matrix (14) of the linear constraints:

$$H = \left(\begin{array}{ccc|ccc} 0 & \cdots & 0 & B_{11} & \cdots & B_{1n} \\ \vdots & \ddots & \vdots & \vdots & \ddots & \vdots \\ 0 & \cdots & 0 & B_{m1} & \cdots & B_{mn} \\ \hline B_{11} & \cdots & B_{m1} & a_{11} & \cdots & a_{1n} \\ \vdots & \ddots & \vdots & \vdots & \ddots & \vdots \\ B_{1n} & \cdots & B_{mn} & a_{1n} & \cdots & a_{nn} \end{array} \right). \tag{15}$$

We first need to figure out which submatrices of H to consider. In studying the quadratic (9) on the constraint set (10), we had only one condition to check in Theorem 16.3 because our single constraint in $\mathbf{R}^2$ resulted in a *one*-dimensional problem. The above problem (13, 14) has m linear equations of n variables. We therefore expect that this problem is really $n - m$ dimensional and therefore that we will have $n - m$ conditions to check for the matrix H in (15). Furthermore, from our experience in Section 16.2, we expect that we will look for leading principal minors of the *same* sign to check for positive definiteness and for leading principal minors of *alternating* signs to check for negative definiteness. The following theorem indicates that these expectations are correct, and it makes precise the exact sign patterns that we need to verify.

Theorem 16.4   To determine the definiteness of a quadratic form (13) of n variables, $Q(\mathbf{x}) = \mathbf{x}^T A \mathbf{x}$, when restricted to a constraint set (14) given by m linear equations $B\mathbf{x} = \mathbf{0}$, construct the $(n + m) \times (n + m)$ symmetric matrix H by bordering the matrix A above and to the left by the coefficients B of the linear constraints:

$$H = \begin{pmatrix} \mathbf{0} & B \\ B^T & A \end{pmatrix}.$$

Check the signs of the *last* $n - m$ leading principal minors of H, starting with the determinant of H itself.

(a) If det H has the same sign as $(-1)^n$ and if these last $n - m$ leading principal minors *alternate* in sign, then Q is *negative definite* on the constraint set $B\mathbf{x} = \mathbf{0}$, and $\mathbf{x} = \mathbf{0}$ is a strict global max of Q on this constraint set.

(b) If det H and these last $n - m$ leading principal minors all have the *same* sign as $(-1)^m$, then Q is *positive definite* on the constraint set $B\mathbf{x} = \mathbf{0}$, and $\mathbf{x} = \mathbf{0}$ is a strict global min of Q on this constraint set.

(c) If both of these conditions a) and b) are violated by *nonzero* leading principal minors, then Q is *indefinite* on the constraint set $B\mathbf{x} = \mathbf{0}$, and $\mathbf{x} = \mathbf{0}$ is neither a max nor a min of Q on this constraint set.

We will not present the rather intricate proof of this theorem here. Notice that its conclusions are consistent with the conclusions of Theorem 16.3 for $n = 2$ and $m = 1$, where for the case of two variables and one constraint, we only needed to compute $n - m = 2 - 1 = 1$ determinant. Exercise 16.9 looks at some important special cases of Theorem 16.4.

Example 16.7   To check the definiteness of

$$Q(x_1, x_2, x_3, x_4) = x_1^2 - x_2^2 + x_3^2 + x_4^2 + 4x_2x_3 - 2x_1x_4$$

on the constraint set

$$x_2 + x_3 + x_4 = 0, \qquad x_1 - 9x_2 + x_4 = 0,$$

form the bordered matrix

$$
H_6 = \begin{pmatrix}
0 & 0 & | & 0 & 1 & 1 & 1 \\
0 & 0 & | & 1 & -9 & 0 & 1 \\
\hline
0 & 1 & | & 1 & 0 & 0 & -1 \\
1 & -9 & | & 0 & -1 & 2 & 0 \\
1 & 0 & | & 0 & 2 & 1 & 0 \\
1 & 1 & | & -1 & 0 & 0 & 1
\end{pmatrix}.
$$

Since this problem has $n = 4$ variables and $m = 2$ constraints, we need to check the largest $n - m = 2$ leading principal submatrices of H_6: H_6 itself and

$$
H_5 = \begin{pmatrix}
0 & 0 & | & 0 & 1 & 1 \\
0 & 0 & | & 1 & -9 & 0 \\
\hline
0 & 1 & | & 1 & 0 & 0 \\
1 & -9 & | & 0 & -1 & 2 \\
1 & 0 & | & 0 & 2 & 1
\end{pmatrix}.
$$

Since $m = 2$ and $(-1)^2 = +1$, we need $\det H_6 > 0$ and $\det H_5 > 0$ to verify positive definiteness. Since $n = 4$ and $(-1)^n = +1$, we need $\det H_6 > 0$ and $\det H_5 < 0$ to verify negative definiteness. In fact, $\det H_6 = 24$ and $\det H_5 = 77$; so Q is positive definite on the constraint set, and $\mathbf{x} = \mathbf{0}$ is a min of Q restricted to the constraint set.

Remark   If the test for constrained definiteness of Theorem 16.4 fails only because one or more of the last $n - m$ leading principal minors is zero, then we would like a test for semidefiniteness, analogous to the statement of Theorem 16.2 for the unconstrained problem. Unfortunately, tests for constrained semidefiniteness are much more tedious to state than the criteria described in Theorem 16.2. Fortunately, such tests are rarely required in applications.

One Constraint

Constrained maximization problems with just one effective constraint are common in economic theory. For the problem of checking the definiteness of a quadratic Q subject to a single constraint $A_1x_1 + \ldots + A_nx_n = 0$, Theorem 16.4 states that one needs to check the last $n - 1$ leading principal minors of

$$
H_{n+1} = \begin{pmatrix}
0 & A_1 & \cdots & A_n \\
A_1 & a_{11} & \cdots & a_{1n} \\
\vdots & \vdots & \ddots & \vdots \\
A_n & a_{1n} & \cdots & a_{nn}
\end{pmatrix}. \tag{16}
$$

The only omitted leading principal submatrices are:

$$H_1 = (0) \quad \text{and} \quad H_2 = \begin{pmatrix} 0 & A_1 \\ A_1 & a_{11} \end{pmatrix}.$$

Let's suppose that $A_1 \neq 0$. (One of the A_i's must be nonzero.) Then, $\det H_2 = -A_1^2 < 0$. Since $m = 1$ and $(-1)^1 = -1$, the criterion for constrained positive definiteness is that the last $n - 1$ leading principal minors of (16) are negative. Since $\det H_2 < 0$, this criterion is equivalent to the statement that the last n leading principal minors have the same sign. The criterion for constrained negative definiteness is that $\det H_{n+1}$ have the sign of $(-1)^n$ and that $\det H_3, \ldots, \det H_{n+1}$ alternate in sign. This means, in this case, that $\det H_3$ must be positive. It follows that the condition for constrained negative definiteness is equivalent to the condition that the last n leading principal minors of H_{n+1} alternate in sign. The following theorem summarizes this discussion for $m = 1$ and yields an easier-to-remember approach for the problem of determining definiteness when there is only one linear constraint.

Theorem 16.5   To determine the definiteness of a quadratic $Q(x_1, \ldots, x_n)$ subject to *one* linear constraint, form the usual $(n + 1) \times (n + 1)$ bordered matrix H, as in (16). Suppose that $A_1 \neq 0$. If the last n leading principal minors of H_{n+1} have the same sign, Q is positive definite on the constraint set (and $\mathbf{x} = \mathbf{0}$ is a constrained min of Q). If the last n leading principal minors of H_{n+1} alternate in sign, Q is negative definite on the constraint set (and $\mathbf{x} = \mathbf{0}$ is a constrained max of Q).

Other Approaches

For the sake of completeness, we mention two alternative approaches to the problem of determining the definiteness of a quadratic form of n variables subject to m linear equations. The statement of Theorem 16.4 focuses on the sign of the largest submatrix H_{m+n} as the cornerstone of the algorithm. Some presentations focus instead on the smallest of the last $n - m$ leading principal submatrices: H_{2m+1}, the $(2m + 1)$th order leading principal submatrix. Theorem 16.4 implies the following alternative checks:

(A) To verify positive definiteness, check that $\det H_{2m+1}$ has the same sign as $(-1)^m$ and that all the larger leading principal minors have this sign too.

(B) To verify negative definiteness, check that $\det H_{2m+1}$ has the sign of $(-1)^{m+1}$ and that the leading principal minors of larger order alternate in sign.

Some texts prefer to construct the bordered matrix H by bordering the matrix A of the quadratic form $Q(\mathbf{x}) = \mathbf{x}^T A \mathbf{x}$ *below* and to the *right* by the matrix B for the linear equations $B\mathbf{x} = \mathbf{0}$:

$$H_{m+n} = \begin{pmatrix} A & B^T \\ B & \mathbf{0} \end{pmatrix}.$$

In this situation, one must still check $n - m$ principal minors. However, the corresponding principal submatrices are no longer leading ones, but "border-preserving" ones. One removes from H_{m+n}, one at a time, the $n - m - 1$ rows and columns which contain the last $n - m - 1$ rows and columns of the matrix A, that is, rows and columns $n, n - 1, \ldots, m + 2$ of H_{m+n}.

Example 16.8 To use this approach for the problem in Example 16.7, form the bordered matrix

$$\hat{H} = \left(\begin{array}{cccc|cc} 1 & 0 & 0 & -1 & 0 & 1 \\ 0 & -1 & 2 & 0 & 1 & -9 \\ 0 & 2 & 1 & 0 & 1 & 0 \\ -1 & 0 & 0 & 1 & 1 & 1 \\ \hline 0 & 1 & 1 & 1 & 0 & 0 \\ 1 & -9 & 0 & 1 & 0 & 0 \end{array}\right)$$

and then form the submatrix $\hat{H}_5$ by removing row 4 and column 4 from $\hat{H}$, the row and column just before the border of $\hat{H}$:

$$\hat{H}_5 = \left(\begin{array}{ccc|cc} 1 & 0 & 0 & 0 & 1 \\ 0 & -1 & 2 & 1 & -9 \\ 0 & 2 & 1 & 1 & 0 \\ \hline 0 & 1 & 1 & 0 & 0 \\ 1 & -9 & 0 & 0 & 0 \end{array}\right).$$

Note that $\det \hat{H} = 24$ and $\det \hat{H}_5 = 77$, just as we found for the corresponding minors in Example 16.7.

EXERCISES

16.6 Determine the definiteness of the following constrained quadratics:
   a) $Q(x_1, x_2) = x_1^2 + 2x_1x_2 - x_2^2$, subject to $x_1 + x_2 = 0$.
   b) $Q(x_1, x_2) = 4x_1^2 + 2x_1x_2 - x_2^2$, subject to $x_1 + x_2 = 0$.
   c) $Q(x_1, x_2, x_3) = x_1^2 + x_2^2 - x_3^2 + 4x_1x_3 - 2x_1x_2$, subject to $x_1 + x_2 + x_3 = 0$ and $x_1 + x_2 - x_3 = 0$.
   d) $Q(x_1, x_2, x_3) = x_1^2 + x_2^2 + x_3^2 + 4x_1x_3 - 2x_1x_2$, subject to $x_1 + x_2 + x_3 = 0$ and $x_1 + x_2 - x_3 = 0$.
   e) $Q(x_1, x_2, x_3) = x_1^2 - x_3^2 + 4x_1x_2 - 6x_2x_3$, subject to $x_1 + x_2 - x_3 = 0$.

16.7 Prove that statements A and B above are equivalent to the statement of Theorem 16.4.

16.8 Use the theory of determinants to show why the corresponding minors in Examples 16.7 and 16.8 have the same values.

16.9 Use the techniques of Theorem 16.3 to verify Theorem 16.4 for the general problem with: a) three variables and one constraint, b) three variables and two constraints.

16.4 APPENDIX

This section presents the proof of Theorem 16.1. This proof has two major ingredients: the principle of induction and the theory of partitioned matrices as developed in Section 8.7. We will prove Theorem 16.1 for positive definite matrices and leave the proof for negative definite matrices as an exercise. First, we need two simple lemmas.

Lemma 16.1 If A is a positive or negative definite matrix, then A is nonsingular.

Proof Suppose that such an A is singular. Then, there exists a nonzero vector $\mathbf{x}$ such that $A\mathbf{x} = \mathbf{0}$. But then,

$$\mathbf{x}^T \cdot A\mathbf{x} = \mathbf{x}^T \cdot \mathbf{0} = 0,$$

a contradiction to the definiteness of A. ∎

Lemma 16.2 Suppose that A is a symmetric matrix and that Q is a nonsingular matrix. Then, $Q^T A Q$ is a symmetric matrix, and A is positive (negative) definite if and only if $Q^T A Q$ is positive (negative) definite.

Proof To see that $Q^T A Q$ is symmetric, one checks directly that it equals its own transpose:

$$(Q^T A Q)^T = Q^T A^T (Q^T)^T = Q^T A^T Q = Q^T A Q.$$

Suppose that $Q^T A Q$ is positive definite. Let $\mathbf{x} \neq \mathbf{0}$ be an arbitrary nonzero vector in $\mathbf{R}^n$. Since Q is nonsingular, there exists a nonzero vector $\mathbf{y}$ such that $\mathbf{x} = Q\mathbf{y}$. Then

$$\mathbf{x}^T A \mathbf{x} = (Q\mathbf{y})^T A (Q\mathbf{y}) = \mathbf{y}^T Q^T A Q \mathbf{y} = \mathbf{y}^T (Q^T A Q) \mathbf{y},$$

which is positive, since $Q^T A Q$ is positive definite. Therefore, A is positive definite.

On the other hand, if A is positive definite and $\mathbf{z}$ is an arbitrary nonzero vector, then $Q\mathbf{z}$ will be nonzero too, since Q is nonsingular. Therefore,

$$0 < (Q\mathbf{z})^T A (Q\mathbf{z}) = \mathbf{z}^T Q^T A Q \mathbf{z} = \mathbf{z}^T (Q^T A Q)\mathbf{z},$$

and $Q^T A Q$ is positive definite. ∎

Theorem 16.1   Let A be a symmetric matrix. Then, A is positive definite if and only if all its leading principal minors are positive.

Proof   We will prove this result by using induction on the size n of A. The result is trivially true for 1×1 matrices. We proved it for 2×2 matrices in Section 16.2. We suppose that the theorem is true for $n \times n$ matrices and prove it true for $(n + 1) \times (n + 1)$ matrices.

Let A be an $(n + 1) \times (n + 1)$ symmetric matrix. Write A_j for the $j \times j$ leading principal submatrix of A for $j = 1, \ldots, n + 1$.

We first prove that if all the A_j's have positive determinants, then A is positive definite. The leading principal submatrices of A_n are $A_1, \ldots, A_n$, which are positive definite by hypothesis, since they are the first n leading principal submatrices of A. By the inductive hypothesis that the theorem is true for $n \times n$ matrices, the $n \times n$ symmetric matrix A_n is positive definite. By Lemma 16.1 above, A_n is invertible. Partition A as

$$A = \left(\begin{array}{c|c} A_n & \mathbf{a} \\ \hline \mathbf{a}^T & a_{n+1,n+1} \end{array} \right), \tag{17}$$

where $\mathbf{a}$ denotes the $n \times 1$ column matrix

$$\mathbf{a} = \left(\begin{array}{c} a_{1,n+1} \\ \vdots \\ a_{n,n+1} \end{array} \right).$$

Let $d = a_{n+1,n+1} - \mathbf{a}^T (A_n)^{-1} \mathbf{a}$, let I_n denote the $n \times n$ identity matrix, and let $\mathbf{0}_n$ denote the $n \times 1$ column matrix of all 0s. Then, the matrix A in (17) can be written as

$$A = \left(\begin{array}{c|c} I_n & \mathbf{0}_n \\ \hline (A_n^{-1}\mathbf{a})^T & 1 \end{array} \right) \left(\begin{array}{c|c} A_n & \mathbf{0}_n \\ \hline \mathbf{0}_n^T & d \end{array} \right) \left(\begin{array}{c|c} I_n & A_n^{-1}\mathbf{a} \\ \hline \mathbf{0}_n^T & 1 \end{array} \right) \tag{18}$$

$$\equiv Q^T B Q.$$

(Exercise.) By properties of the determinant,

$$\det Q = \det Q^T = 1 \qquad \text{and} \qquad \det B = d \cdot \det A_n.$$

Therefore, $$\det A = d \cdot \det A_n. \tag{19}$$

Since $\det A > 0$ and $\det A_n > 0$, then $d > 0$.

Let $\mathbf{X}$ be an arbitrary $(n + 1)$-vector. Write $\mathbf{X}$ as

$$\mathbf{X} = \left(\begin{array}{c} \mathbf{x} \\ x_{n+1} \end{array} \right),$$

where $\mathbf{x}$ is an n-vector. Then,

$$\mathbf{X}^T B \mathbf{X} = (\mathbf{x}^T \quad x_{n+1}) \left(\begin{array}{c|c} A_n & \mathbf{0}_n \\ \hline \mathbf{0}_n^T & d \end{array} \right) \left(\begin{array}{c} \mathbf{x} \\ x_{n+1} \end{array} \right) \tag{20}$$

$$= \mathbf{x}^T A_n \mathbf{x} + d x_{n+1}^2.$$

Since A_n is positive definite by inductive hypothesis and $d > 0$, this last expression is strictly positive. Therefore, $B = Q^T A Q$ is positive definite. By Lemma 16.2, A is positive definite.

To prove the converse — A positive definite implies that all the $|A_j|$'s are positive — we use induction once more. We have seen that this result is true for 1×1 and 2×2 matrices. Assume that it is true for $n \times n$ symmetric matrices, and let A be an $(n + 1) \times (n + 1)$ positive definite symmetric matrix. We first show that all the A_j's are positive definite. Let $\mathbf{x}_j$ be a nonzero j-vector, and let $\mathbf{0}^*$ be the zero $(n + 1) - j$ vector. Then

$$0 < (\mathbf{x}_j^T \quad \mathbf{0}^*) A \left(\begin{array}{c} \mathbf{x}_j \\ \mathbf{0}^* \end{array} \right) = \mathbf{x}_j^T A_j \mathbf{x}_j;$$

and A_j is positive definite.

In particular, since A_n is positive definite, the inductive hypothesis tells us that $A_1, \ldots, A_n$ all have positive determinants. We need only prove that the determinant of A itself is positive. Since A_n is invertible, we can once again write A as $Q^T B Q$ as in (18) and conclude that (19) still holds. Since A is positive definite, B is positive definite by Lemma 16.2. Choose $\mathbf{X}$ in (20) so that $\mathbf{x} = \mathbf{0}$ and $x_{n+1} = 1$. Then,

$$0 < \mathbf{X}^T B \mathbf{X} = d.$$

Since $\det A_n > 0$ and $d > 0$, $\det A > 0$. ∎

EXERCISES

16.10 Show that the block decomposition (18) is correct.

16.11 Prove the corresponding theorem for negative definite matrices.

Unconstrained Optimization

Since optimization plays such a major role in economic theory, this chapter on unconstrained optimization and the next three chapters on constrained optimization can be considered the core of this book. This chapter turns from the matrix criteria that specify the conditions for optimizing a quadratic form to the first and second order derivative conditions that characterize the optima of a general differentiable function. Just as techniques of calculus play a major role in optimization problems for functions of one variable, they play an equally important role for functions of several variables. The main results for multivariable functions are analogous to the one-dimensional results:

(1) a necessary condition for $\mathbf{x}_0$ to be an interior max of $z = F(\mathbf{x})$ is that the first derivatives of F at $\mathbf{x}_0$ be zero, and

(2) if we include an appropriate condition on the second derivatives of F, this necessary condition becomes a sufficient condition.

17.1 DEFINITIONS

The definitions of a maximum and minimum for a function of several variables are the same as the corresponding definitions for a function of one variable. Let $F: U \rightarrow \mathbf{R}^1$ be a real-valued function of n variables, whose domain U is a subset of $\mathbf{R}^n$.

(1) A point $\mathbf{x}^* \in U$ is a **max** of F on U if $F(\mathbf{x}^*) \geq F(\mathbf{x})$ for all $\mathbf{x} \in U$.

(2) $\mathbf{x}^* \in U$ is a **strict max** if $\mathbf{x}^*$ is a max and $F(\mathbf{x}^*) > F(\mathbf{x})$ for all $\mathbf{x} \neq \mathbf{x}^*$ in U.

(3) $\mathbf{x}^* \in U$ is a **local (or relative) max** of F if there is a ball $B_r(\mathbf{x}^*)$ about $\mathbf{x}^*$ such that $F(\mathbf{x}^*) \geq F(\mathbf{x})$ for all $\mathbf{x} \in B_r(\mathbf{x}^*) \cap U$.

(4) $\mathbf{x}^* \in U$ is a **strict local max** of F if there is a ball $B_r(\mathbf{x}^*)$ about $\mathbf{x}^*$ such that $F(\mathbf{x}^*) > F(\mathbf{x})$ for all $\mathbf{x} \neq \mathbf{x}^*$ in $B_r(\mathbf{x}^*) \cap U$.

In other words, a point $\mathbf{x}^*$ is a local max if there are no *nearby* points at which F takes on a larger value. Of course, a max is always a local max. If we want to

396

emphasize that a point $\mathbf{x}^*$ is a max of F on the whole domain U, not just a local max, we call $\mathbf{x}^*$ a **global max** or **absolute max** of F on U.

To be precise, we should say, for example in (1), that $\mathbf{x}^*$ is a **maximizer** or **maximum point** of F, or that F has its **maximum value** at $\mathbf{x}^*$. The word "max" is a convenient shortcut.

Reversing the inequalities in the above four definitions leads to the definitions of a global min, a strict global min, a local min, and a strict local min, respectively.

17.2   FIRST ORDER CONDITIONS

The first order condition for a point x^* to be a max or min of a function f of one variable is that $f'(x^*) = 0$, that is, that x^* be a **critical point** of f. This condition requires that x^* not be an endpoint of the interval under consideration, in other words, that x^* lie in the interior of the domain of f. The same first order condition works for a function F of n variables. However, a function of n variables has n first derivatives: the partials $\partial F / \partial x_i$. The n-dimensional analogue of $f'(x^*) = 0$ is that each $\partial F / \partial x_i = 0$ at $\mathbf{x}^*$. In this case, $\mathbf{x}^*$ is an **interior point** of the domain of F if there is a whole ball $B_r(\mathbf{x}^*)$ about $\mathbf{x}^*$ in the domain of F.

Theorem 17.1   Let $F: U \to \mathbf{R}^1$ be a C^1 function defined on a subset U of $\mathbf{R}^n$. If $\mathbf{x}^*$ is a local max or min of F in U and if $\mathbf{x}^*$ is an interior point of U, then

$$\frac{\partial F}{\partial x_i}(\mathbf{x}^*) = 0 \quad \text{for } i = 1, \ldots, n. \tag{1}$$

Proof   We will work with the local max case; the same proof works for the min case. Let $B = B_r(\mathbf{x}^*)$ be a ball about $\mathbf{x}^*$ in U with the property that $F(\mathbf{x}^*) \geq F(\mathbf{x})$ for all $\mathbf{x} \in B$. Since $\mathbf{x}^*$ maximizes F on B, along each *line segment* through $\mathbf{x}^*$ that lies in B and that is parallel to one of the axes, F takes on its maximum value at $\mathbf{x}^*$. In other words, x_i^* maximizes the function of *one* variable:

$$x_i \longmapsto F(x_1^*, \ldots, x_{i-1}^*, x_i, x_{i+1}^*, \ldots, x_n^*)$$

for $x_i \in (x_i^* - r, x_i^* + r)$. Apply the one-variable maximization criterion of Theorem 3.3 to each of these n one-dimensional problems to conclude that

$$\frac{\partial F}{\partial x_1}(\mathbf{x}^*) = 0, \ldots, \frac{\partial F}{\partial x_n}(\mathbf{x}^*) = 0. \quad \blacksquare$$

Example 17.1   To find the local maxs and mins of $F(x, y) = x^3 - y^3 + 9xy$, one computes the first order partial derivatives and sets them equal to zero:

$$\frac{\partial F}{\partial x} = 3x^2 + 9y = 0 \quad \text{and} \quad \frac{\partial F}{\partial y} = -3y^2 + 9x = 0. \tag{2}$$

The first equation yields: $y = -\frac{1}{3}x^2$. Substitute this into the second equation:

$$0 = -3y^2 + 9x = -3\left(-\frac{1}{3}x^2\right)^2 + 9x = -\frac{1}{3}x^4 + 9x.$$

This equation can be written as: $27x - x^4 = x(27 - x^3) = 0$, whose solutions are $x = 0$ and $x = 3$. Substitute these solutions into $y = -\frac{1}{3}x^2$ to conclude that the solutions to (2) are the two points $(0, 0)$ and $(3, -3)$. At this stage, we can conclude that the only candidates for a local max or min of F are these two points: $(0, 0)$ and $(3, -3)$. We are unable to say whether either of these two is a max or a min.

17.3   SECOND ORDER CONDITIONS

Definition   As we did for functions of one variable, we say that the n-vector $\mathbf{x}^*$ is a **critical point** of a function $F(x_1, \ldots, x_n)$ if $\mathbf{x}^*$ satisfies

$$\frac{\partial F}{\partial x_i}(\mathbf{x}^*) = 0 \quad \text{for } i = 1, \ldots, n. \tag{3}$$

The critical points of $F(x, y) = x^3 - y^3 + 9xy$ in Example 17.1 are $(0, 0)$ and $(3, -3)$. To determine whether either of these critical points is a max or a min, we need to use a condition on the second derivatives of F, as we did for functions of one variable. As noted in Chapter 14, a C^2 function of n variables has n^2 second order partial derivatives at each point in its domain and it is natural to combine them into an $n \times n$ matrix, called the **Hessian** of F:

$$D^2F(\mathbf{x}^*) = \begin{pmatrix} \dfrac{\partial^2 F}{\partial x_1^2}(\mathbf{x}^*) & \cdots & \dfrac{\partial^2 F}{\partial x_n \partial x_1}(\mathbf{x}^*) \\ \vdots & \ddots & \vdots \\ \dfrac{\partial^2 F}{\partial x_1 \partial x_n}(\mathbf{x}^*) & \cdots & \dfrac{\partial^2 F}{\partial x_n^2}(\mathbf{x}^*) \end{pmatrix}. \tag{4}$$

Since cross-partials are equal for a C^2 function (Theorem 14.5), $D^2F(\mathbf{x}^*)$ is a symmetric matrix.

Sufficient Conditions

The second order condition for a critical point x^* of a function f on $\mathbf{R}^1$ to be a max is that the second derivative $f''(x^*)$ be negative. The corresponding condition for a function F of n variables is that the second derivative $D^2F(\mathbf{x}^*)$ be *negative definite* as a symmetric matrix at the critical point $\mathbf{x}^*$. Similarly, the second order sufficient condition for a critical point of a function f of one variable to be a local min is that $f''(x^*)$ be positive; the analogous second order condition for an n-dimensional critical point $\mathbf{x}^*$ to be a local min is that the Hessian of F at $\mathbf{x}^*$, $D^2F(\mathbf{x}^*)$, be *positive definite*.

Theorem 17.2 Let $F: U \to \mathbf{R}^1$ be a C^2 function whose domain is an open set U in $\mathbf{R}^n$. Suppose that $\mathbf{x}^*$ is a critical point of F in that it satisfies (3).

(1) If the Hessian $D^2F(\mathbf{x}^*)$ is a negative definite symmetric matrix, then $\mathbf{x}^*$ is a strict local max of F ;

(2) If the Hessian $D^2F(\mathbf{x}^*)$ is a positive definite symmetric matrix, then $\mathbf{x}^*$ is a strict local min of F.

(3) If $D^2F(\mathbf{x}^*)$ is indefinite, then $\mathbf{x}^*$ is neither a local max nor a local min of F.

Definition A critical point $\mathbf{x}^*$ of F for which the Hessian $D^2F(\mathbf{x}^*)$ is indefinite is called a **saddle point** of F. A saddle point $\mathbf{x}^*$ is a min of F in some directions and a max of F in other directions. Therefore, its graph, like that of $F(x_1, x_2) = x_1^2 - x_2^2$ in Figure 16.4, is saddle-shaped.

We will present a careful proof of Theorem 17.2 in Chapter 30 after we develop the theory of Taylor polynomial approximation. The idea behind the proof is a simple one. Let $\mathbf{x}^*$ be a critical point of F, as in the statement of Theorem 17.2. The presentation in Chapter 30 shows how to approximate a C^2 function by its Taylor polynomial of order two about $\mathbf{x}^*$:

$$F(\mathbf{x}^* + \mathbf{h}) = F(\mathbf{x}^*) + DF(\mathbf{x}^*)\mathbf{h} + \frac{1}{2}\mathbf{h}^T D^2F(\mathbf{x}^*)\mathbf{h} + R(\mathbf{h}), \qquad (5)$$

where $DF(\mathbf{x}^*)$ is the Jacobian matrix of F at $\mathbf{x}^*$, $D^2F(\mathbf{x})$ is the Hessian matrix (4) of second order partial derivatives of F at $\mathbf{x}^*$, and $R(\mathbf{h})$ is the remainder term that goes to 0 very quickly as $\mathbf{h} \to \mathbf{0}$. In this proof sketch, we will ignore the negligbly small remainder term $R(\mathbf{h})$ and, as in the hypothesis of Theorem 17.2, set $DF(\mathbf{x}^*)$ equal to zero. We can then write equation (5) as

$$F(\mathbf{x}^* + \mathbf{h}) - F(\mathbf{x}^*) \approx \frac{1}{2}\mathbf{h}^T D^2F(\mathbf{x}^*)\mathbf{h}. \qquad (6)$$

If $D^2F(\mathbf{x}^*)$ is negative definite, then for all (small enough) $\mathbf{h} \neq \mathbf{0}$, the right-hand side of (6) is negative. Then, the left hand-side is negative too:

$$F(\mathbf{x}^* + \mathbf{h}) - F(\mathbf{x}^*) < 0 \quad \text{or} \quad F(\mathbf{x}^* + \mathbf{h}) < F(\mathbf{x}^*),$$

for all small enough $\mathbf{h} \neq \mathbf{0}$. In other words, $\mathbf{x}^*$ is a strict local max of F. The complete proof in Chapter 30 works out the details of the Taylor polynomial representation (5) and shows how to handle the remainder term R in the above argument.

The presentation in Chapter 16 developed an analytic characterization of positive definite and negative definite matrices. In terms of that formulation, Theorem 17.2 can be restated as the following theorems.

Theorem 17.3   Let $F: U \to \mathbf{R}^1$ be a C^2 function whose domain is an open set U in $\mathbf{R}^1$. Suppose that

$$\frac{\partial F}{\partial x_i}(\mathbf{x}^*) = 0 \quad \text{for } i = 1, \ldots, n$$

and that the n leading principal minors of $D^2 F(\mathbf{x}^*)$ alternate in sign

$$|F_{x_1 x_1}| < 0, \quad \begin{vmatrix} F_{x_1 x_1} & F_{x_2 x_1} \\ F_{x_1 x_2} & F_{x_2 x_2} \end{vmatrix} > 0, \quad \begin{vmatrix} F_{x_1 x_1} & F_{x_2 x_1} & F_{x_3 x_1} \\ F_{x_1 x_2} & F_{x_2 x_2} & F_{x_3 x_2} \\ F_{x_1 x_3} & F_{x_2 x_3} & F_{x_3 x_3} \end{vmatrix} < 0, \ldots$$

at $\mathbf{x}^*$. Then, $\mathbf{x}^*$ is a strict local max of F.

Theorem 17.4   Let $F: U \to \mathbf{R}^1$ be a C^2 function whose domain is an open set U in $\mathbf{R}^n$. Suppose that

$$\frac{\partial F}{\partial x_i}(\mathbf{x}^*) = 0 \quad \text{for } i = 1, \ldots, n$$

and that the n leading principal minors of $D^2 F(\mathbf{x}^*)$ are all positive:

$$|F_{x_1 x_1}| > 0, \quad \begin{vmatrix} F_{x_1 x_1} & F_{x_2 x_1} \\ F_{x_1 x_2} & F_{x_2 x_2} \end{vmatrix} > 0, \quad \begin{vmatrix} F_{x_1 x_1} & F_{x_2 x_1} & F_{x_3 x_1} \\ F_{x_1 x_2} & F_{x_2 x_2} & F_{x_3 x_2} \\ F_{x_1 x_3} & F_{x_2 x_3} & F_{x_3 x_3} \end{vmatrix} > 0, \ldots$$

at $\mathbf{x}^*$. Then, $\mathbf{x}^*$ is a strict local min of F.

Theorem 17.5   Let $F: U \to \mathbf{R}^1$ be a C^2 function whose domain is an open set U in $\mathbf{R}^n$. Suppose that

$$\frac{\partial F}{\partial x_i}(\mathbf{x}^*) = 0 \quad \text{for } i = 1, \ldots, n$$

and that some nonzero leading principal minors of $D^2 F(\mathbf{x}^*)$ violate the sign patterns in the hypotheses of Theorems 17.3 and 17.4. Then, $\mathbf{x}^*$ is a saddle point of F; it is neither a local max nor a local min.

Necessary Conditions

The second order *necessary* condition for a max or min of a function of one variable is weaker than the second order *sufficient* condition. The weak inequality of the necessary condition, namely, that $f''(x^*) \leq 0$ at a local max and that $f''(x^*) \geq 0$ at a local min, replaces the strict inequality of the sufficient condition. The functions $f_1(x) = x^4$ and $f_2(x) = -x^4$ provide the simplest illustrations of the difference between the necessary and sufficient conditions on $\mathbf{R}^1$. For both functions, $f_i'(0) = 0$ and $f_i''(0) = 0$; yet f_1 has a strict global *min* at $x = 0$ and f_2 has a strict global *max* at $x = 0$.

A similar weakening occurs for functions of several variables. In this case, one replaces the negative definite and positive definite conditions on the Hessian of F in the sufficient conditions of Theorems 17.3 and 17.4 by requirements that the Hessian must be negative *semidefinite* at a local max and positive *semidefinite* at a local min.

Theorem 17.6   Let $F: U \to \mathbf{R}^1$ be a C^2 function whose domain U is in $\mathbf{R}^n$. Suppose that $\mathbf{x}^*$ is an interior point of U and that $\mathbf{x}^*$ is a local max (respectively, min) of F. Then, $DF(\mathbf{x}^*) = \mathbf{0}$ and $D^2F(\mathbf{x}^*)$ is negative semidefinite (respectively, positive semidefinite).

The discussion in Chapter 16 showed that a symmetric function is positive semidefinite if and only if all of its $2^n - 1$ principal minors are ≥ 0 and that a symmetric matrix is negative semidefinite if and only if all of its principal minors of odd order are ≤ 0 and all of its principal minors of even order are ≥ 0. With this analytical test for semidefiniteness in mind, we rewrite Theorem 17.6 as follows.

Theorem 17.7   Let $F: U \to \mathbf{R}^1$ be a C^2 function of n variables. Suppose that $\mathbf{x}^*$ is an interior point of U.

(a) If $\mathbf{x}^*$ is a local min of F, then $(\partial F/\partial x_i)(\mathbf{x}^*) = 0$ for $i = 1, \ldots, n$ and all the principal minors of the Hessian $D^2F(\mathbf{x}^*)$ are ≥ 0.

(b) If $\mathbf{x}^*$ is a local max of F, then $(\partial F/\partial x_i)(\mathbf{x}^*) = 0$ for $i = 1, \ldots, n$ and all the principal minors of the Hessian $D^2F(\mathbf{x}^*)$ of odd order are ≤ 0 and all the principal minors of the Hessian $D^2F(\mathbf{x}^*)$ of even order are ≥ 0.

The proof of Theorem 17.6 is in Chapter 30. Now, let's apply all our second order conditions to the cubic function in Example 17.1.

Example 17.2   In Example 17.1, we computed that the critical points of $F(x, y) = x^3 - y^3 + 9xy$ are $(0, 0)$ and $(3, -3)$. By differentiating the first derivatives in expression (2), we compute that the Hessian of F is

$$\begin{pmatrix} F_{xx} & F_{yx} \\ F_{yx} & F_{yy} \end{pmatrix} = \begin{pmatrix} 6x & 9 \\ 9 & -6y \end{pmatrix}.$$

The first order leading principal minor is $F_{xx} = 6x$ and the second order leading principal minor is $\det D^2 F(\mathbf{x}) = -36xy - 81$. At $(0,0)$, these two minors are 0 and -81, respectively. Since the second order leading principal minor is negative, $(0,0)$ is a saddle of F — neither a max nor a min. At $(3, -3)$, these two minors are 18 and 243. Since these two numbers are positive, $D^2 F(3, -3)$ is positive definite and $(3, -3)$ is a strict local min of F.

Notice that $(3, -3)$ is not a *global* min, because at the point $(0, n)$, $F(0, n) = -n^3$, which goes to $-\infty$ as $n \to \infty$.

EXERCISES

17.1 For each of the following functions defined on $\mathbf{R}^2$, find the critical points and classify these as local max, local min, saddle point, or "can't tell":

a) $x^4 + x^2 - 6xy + 3y^2$,   *b)* $x^2 - 6xy + 2y^2 + 10x + 2y - 5$,

c) $xy^2 + x^3 y - xy$,   *d)* $3x^4 + 3x^2 y - y^3$.

17.2 For each of the following functions defined on $\mathbf{R}^3$, find the critical points and classify them as local max, local min, saddle point, or "can't tell":
a) $x^2 + 6xy + y^2 - 3yz + 4z^2 - 10x - 5y - 21z$,
b) $(x^2 + 2y^2 + 3z^2)e^{-(x^2 + y^2 + z^2)}$.

17.4   GLOBAL MAXIMA AND MINIMA

The first and second order sufficient conditions of the last section will find all the local maxima and minima of a differentiable function whose domain is an open set in $\mathbf{R}^n$. As Example 17.2 illustrates, these conditions say nothing about whether or not any of these local extrema is a *global* max or min. In this section, we will discuss sufficient conditions for global maxima and minima of a real-valued function on $\mathbf{R}^n$.

The study of one-dimensional optimization problems in Section 3.5 put forth two conditions for a critical point x^* of f to be a global max (or min), when f is a C^2 function defined on a connected interval I of $\mathbf{R}^1$:

(1) x^* is a local max (or min) and it's the only critical point of f in I; or
(2) $f'' \leq 0$ on all of I (or $f'' \geq 0$ on I for a min), that is, f is a concave function on I (or f is a convex function for a min).

Condition 1 does not work in higher dimensions, as the function F whose level sets are pictured in Figure 17.1 illustrates. The point A in Figure 17.1 is a local max of F in the open set U. Even though A is the only critical point of F in U, the function F takes on a higher value at point B.

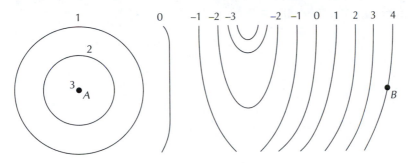

Level sets of a function whose unique local max is not a global max.

Figure 17.1

Global Maxima of Concave Functions

Condition 2 *does* work in higher dimensions. As we have seen, the n-dimensional version of $f''(x) \leq 0$ states that the Hessian $D^2F(\mathbf{x})$ is negative semidefinite. We will see in Chapter 20 that this condition is exactly the second derivative criterion for F to be a concave function. The following theorem summarizes the first and second order criteria for a function on $\mathbf{R^n}$ to be a concave or convex function and relates these properties to global extrema.

Theorem 17.8 Let $F: U \to \mathbf{R}^1$ be a C^2 function whose domain is a convex open subset U of $\mathbf{R^n}$.

  (*a*) The following three conditions are equivalent:
    (*i*) F is a concave function on U; and
    (*ii*) $F(\mathbf{y}) - F(\mathbf{x}) \leq DF(\mathbf{x})(\mathbf{y} - \mathbf{x})$ for all $\mathbf{x}, \mathbf{y} \in U$; and
    (*iii*) $D^2F(\mathbf{x})$ is negative semidefinite for all $\mathbf{x} \in U$.
  (*b*) The following three conditions are equivalent:
    (*i*) F is a convex function on U; and
    (*ii*) $F(\mathbf{y}) - F(\mathbf{x}) \geq DF(\mathbf{x})(\mathbf{y} - \mathbf{x})$ for all $\mathbf{x}, \mathbf{y} \in U$; and
    (*iii*) $D^2F(\mathbf{x})$ is positive semidefinite for all $\mathbf{x} \in U$.
  (*c*) If F is a concave function on U and $DF(\mathbf{x}^*) = \mathbf{0}$ for some $\mathbf{x}^* \in U$, then $\mathbf{x}^*$ is a *global max* of F on U.
  (*d*) If F is a convex function on U and $DF(\mathbf{x}^*) = \mathbf{0}$ for some $\mathbf{x}^* \in U$, then $\mathbf{x}^*$ is a *global min* of F on U.

We will present a careful proof of these results in Chapter 20, where we give a complete introduction to the study of smooth concave and convex functions. To get a flavor of that proof, we sketch the proof that $ai \Longrightarrow aii \Longrightarrow c$ for functions of one variable here.

Proof Sketch on $\mathbf{R}^1$:   By definition, a function F is concave on U if and only if

$$tF(y) + (1 - t)F(x) \leq F(ty + (1 - t)x) \qquad (7)$$

for all $x, y \in U$ and all $t \in [0, 1]$. Write (7) as

$$F(y) - F(x) \le \frac{F(x + t(y - x)) - F(x)}{t},$$

or, letting $h = t(y - x)$, as

$$F(y) - F(x) \le \frac{F(x + h) - F(x)}{h} (y - x). \tag{8}$$

Taking limits as $h \to 0$, (8) becomes

$$F(y) - F(x) \le F'(x)(y - x). \tag{9}$$

This shows that *ai* implies *aii*.

To prove *c*, suppose that F is concave and that $F'(x^*) = 0$. Then, by inequality (9) above, for all $y \in U$,

$$F(y) - F(x^*) \le 0 \cdot (y - x^*) = 0;$$

that is, $F(y) \le F(x^*)$ for all $y \in U$. Therefore, x^* is a global max of F in U. ■

There is an interesting comparison between Theorem 17.8 and Theorem 17.2. In order to guarantee that a critical point $\mathbf{x}^*$ of a C^2 function F is a local max, we need to show that $D^2F(\mathbf{x}^*)$ is negative definite; showing $D^2F(\mathbf{x}^*)$ negative semidefinite is not strong enough. However, if we can show that $D^2F(\mathbf{y})$ is negative semidefinite not just at $\mathbf{x}^*$ but for all $\mathbf{y}$ in a whole ball about $\mathbf{x}^*$, then by Theorem 17.8, we can conclude that $\mathbf{x}^*$ is a max of F. For example, evaluating $f_i''(0)$ cannot distinguish the critical point 0 as a min of $f_1(x) = x^4$ from 0 as a max of $f_2(x) = -x^4$. However, since $f_2''(x) = -12x^2 \le 0$ for all $x \in \mathbf{R}^1$, we know by Theorem 17.8 that 0 is a max of f_2 on $\mathbf{R}^1$.

EXERCISES

17.3   Which of the maxima and minima in Exercise 17.1 are global maxima or global minima?

17.5   ECONOMIC APPLICATIONS

Most of the principles of economic theory are derived from the first order conditions — and sometimes the second order conditions — of an underlying optimization problem. We have seen some examples of this phenomenon in our discussion of the economic applications of functions of *one* variable in Section 3.6.

Profit-Maximizing Firm

The simplest multivariable example occurs in the study of the profit-maximizing firm. Suppose a firm uses n inputs to produce a single product. If $\mathbf{x} \in \mathbf{R}^n_+$ represents an input bundle, if $y = G(\mathbf{x})$ is the firm's C^1 production function, and if p is the selling price of its product, then the firm's revenue $R(\mathbf{x}) = pG(\mathbf{x})$. If $C(\mathbf{x})$ represents the cost of input bundle $\mathbf{x}$, the firm's profit $F(\mathbf{x})$ from optimal use of input bundle $\mathbf{x}$ is

$$F(\mathbf{x}) = R(\mathbf{x}) - C(\mathbf{x}).$$

Assume that R and C are such that the profit-maximizing firm uses a positive amount of each input so that the profit-maximizing $\mathbf{x}$ occurs in the interior of the positive orthant $\mathbf{R}^n_+$. Then, by Theorem 17.1, the partial derivatives of F must be zero at the profit-maximizing $\mathbf{x}^*$:

$$0 = \frac{\partial F}{\partial x_i}(\mathbf{x}^*) = \frac{\partial R}{\partial x_i}(\mathbf{x}^*) - \frac{\partial C}{\partial x_i}(\mathbf{x}^*). \tag{10}$$

In particular, the *marginal revenue product* from using one more unit of input i must just balance the marginal cost of purchasing another unit of input i.

Suppose that each input i has constant unit cost w_i, so that

$$C(\mathbf{x}) = w_1 x_1 + \ldots + w_n x_n = \mathbf{w} \cdot \mathbf{x}.$$

The first order conditions (10) now become

$$\frac{\partial R}{\partial x_i}(\mathbf{x}^*) = p \frac{\partial G}{\partial x_i}(\mathbf{x}^*) = w_i \quad \text{or} \quad \frac{\partial G}{\partial x_i}(\mathbf{x}^*) = \frac{w_i}{p}.$$

for $i = 1, \ldots, n$. The second order necessary condition in Theorem 17.7 requires that $D^2 F(\mathbf{x}^*)$ be negative semidefinite. In the case of constant marginal cost, this second order condition implies that the Hessian of the production function $D^2 G(\mathbf{x}^*)$ must be negative semidefinite at the optimal input bundle. In particular, this implies that each $\partial^2 G / \partial x_i^2$ must be ≤ 0 at $\mathbf{x}^*$. Another way of saying this is that the profit-maximizing input vectors occur only in those regions of the input space where all the $\partial^2 G / \partial x_i^2$'s are ≤ 0. If for each $\mathbf{x} \in \mathbf{R}^n_+$, there is an index i such that $(\partial^2 G / \partial x_i^2)(\mathbf{x}) > 0$, then the firm under study cannot have a profit-maximizing output in the interior of $\mathbf{R}^n_+$.

Discriminating Monopolist

The model of a discriminating monopolist is another example of a maximization problem to which the results of this chapter apply. Suppose that a monopolist faces two distinct and separated markets, for example, a domestic market and a foreign market, each with its own demand function. Let Q_i be the amount supplied to market i and let $P_i = G_i(Q_i)$ be the inverse demand function for market i, so that the revenue from supplying Q_i units of output to market i is $Q_iG_i(Q_i)$. Suppose that production costs C depend only on the total produced $Q = Q_1 + Q_2$; that is, the firm's cost function can be written as $C(Q_1 + Q_2)$. Its profit is then

$$F(Q_1, Q_2) = Q_1 \cdot G_1(Q_1) + Q_2 \cdot G_2(Q_2) - C(Q_1 + Q_2).$$

If we know that the firm will produce a positive amount for each market, then our problem is to compute the maxima of the profit function F in the interior of the positive quadrant. These maximizers satisfy

$$0 = \frac{\partial F}{\partial Q_1} = \frac{d(Q_1G_1(Q_1))}{dQ_1} - C'(Q_1 + Q_2)$$

$$0 = \frac{\partial F}{\partial Q_2} = \frac{d(Q_2G_2(Q_2))}{dQ_2} - C'(Q_1 + Q_2)$$

or

$$\frac{d(Q_1G_1(Q_1))}{dQ_1} = \frac{d(Q_2G_2(Q_2))}{dQ_2} = C'(Q_1 + Q_2).$$

The marginal revenue in *each* market should just equal the marginal cost of the total output.

Example 17.3 A monopolist producing a single output has two types of customers. If it produces Q_1 units for customers of type 1, then these customers are willing to pay a price of $50 - 5Q_1$ dollars per unit. If it produces Q_2 units for customers of type 2, then these customers are willing to pay a price of $100 - 10Q_2$ dollars per unit. The monopolist's cost of manufacturing Q units of output is $90 + 20Q$ dollars. In order to maximize profits, how much should the monopolist produce for each market?

This discriminating monopolist's profit function is

$$F(Q_1, Q_2) = Q_1(50 - 5Q_1) + Q_2(100 - 10Q_2) - (90 + 20(Q_1 + Q_2)).$$

The critical points of F satisfy

$$\frac{\partial F}{\partial Q_1} = 50 - 10Q_1 - 20 = 0, \quad \text{or} \quad Q_1 = 3,$$

$$\frac{\partial F}{\partial Q_2} = 100 - 20Q_2 - 20 = 0, \quad \text{or} \quad Q_2 = 4.$$

Now check the second order conditions. Since

$$F_{Q_1Q_1} = -10, \quad F_{Q_2Q_2} = -20, \quad F_{Q_1Q_2} = F_{Q_2Q_1} = 0,$$

the first order leading principal minor of $D^2F(3, 4)$ is -10 and the second order leading principal minor is 200. Therefore, F is a concave function and the point $(3, 4)$ is the profit-maximizing supply plan over all plans in the positive orthant.

Least Squares Analysis

Scientists studying the data from some observations or experiments are often interested in discovering whether the variables under study may be linearly related, or at least in finding the linear graph which best fits the data points. Suppose that we are studying the relationship between two variables, so that each observation can be represented by a point (x_i, y_i) in the plane. If we have only two points, then by the method of Section 2.2, we can find the equation of the unique straight line that passes through these two points. However, if there are three or more data points, it is unlikely that they will line up on a single line. In this case, we'd like to find the line that best fits these data points, both to shed light on any underlying patterns and possibly to predict other points.

Suppose that the data points are: $(x_1, y_1), \dots, (x_n, y_n)$, $n \geq 3$, as pictured in Figure 17.2. For any given line $y = mx + b$, we can measure the vertical distance from each of these n points to the line. These distances are represented by the lengths of the dotted vertical line segments $d_1, \dots, d_n$ in Figure 17.2. The x-coordinate of the point on the line corresponding to (x_i, y_i) is x_i itself, since we are taking vertical distances. Since the equation of the line is $y = mx + b$, the corresponding y-value of this point on the line is $y_i = mx_i + b$, as we have noted in Figure 17.2. The vertical distance from the data point (x_i, y_i) to the point on the line $(x_i, mx_i + b)$ is $|mx_i + b - y_i|$. Since we are working with calculus and the absolute value function is not differentiable, we replace $|mx_i + b - y_i|$ by $(mx_i + b - y_i)^2$. We use the square since we want the distance to be a positive number; otherwise, a point which is, say, 100 units above the line and a point which is 100 units below

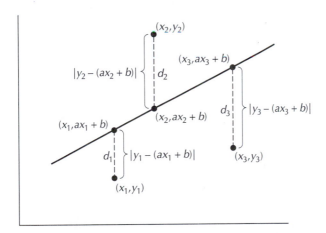

The aggregate distance from three data points to a line.

Figure 17.2

the line will cancel each other out in this process. In summary, if we are given n data points in the plane: $(x_1, y_1), \ldots, (x_n, y_n)$, and a straight line whose equation is $y = mx + b$, then we can write the *aggregate distance* from the n points to the line as

$$S = (mx_1 + b - y_1)^2 + (mx_2 + b - y_2)^2 + \cdots + (mx_n + b - y_n)^2. \qquad (11)$$

Consider calculating S for a number of different lines, so that S becomes a function of m and b:

$$S(m, b) = \sum_{i=1}^{n} (mx_i + b - y_i)^2.$$

The line which best fits the n data points should be the line whose parameters m^* and b^* minimize the total discrepancy S. Since m and b can be any real numbers, to find the minima of S, we first find its critical points by solving

$$\frac{\partial S}{\partial m} = \sum_{i=1}^{n} 2(mx_i + b - y_i) \cdot x_i = 0,$$

$$\frac{\partial S}{\partial b} = \sum_{i=1}^{n} 2(mx_i + b - y_i) \cdot 1 = 0, \qquad (12)$$

using the Chain Rule on each summand in (11). [Remember: the x_i's and y_i's are knowns here; the m's and the b's are the variables.] Divide the equations in (12) through by 2 and redistribute the summation signs to obtain the system of two equations in two unknowns:

$$\sum_i mx_i^2 + \sum_i bx_i - \sum_i x_i y_i = 0$$

$$\sum_i mx_i + \sum_i b - \sum_i y_i = 0,$$

or

$$\left(\sum_i x_i^2 \right) m + \left(\sum_i x_i \right) b = \sum_i x_i y_i$$

$$\left(\sum_i x_i \right) m + n \cdot b = \sum_i y_i \qquad (13)$$

We can solve (13) using Cramer's rule:

$$m^* = \frac{\begin{vmatrix} \sum x_i y_i & \sum x_i \\ \sum y_i & n \end{vmatrix}}{\begin{vmatrix} \sum x_i^2 & \sum x_i \\ \sum x_i & n \end{vmatrix}} = \frac{n \sum_i x_i y_i - \left(\sum_i x_i \right) \left(\sum_i y_i \right)}{n \sum_i x_i^2 - \left(\sum_i x_i \right)^2} \qquad (14)$$

$$b^* = \frac{\begin{vmatrix} \sum x_i^2 & \sum x_i y_i \\ \sum x_i & \sum y_i \end{vmatrix}}{\begin{vmatrix} \sum x_i^2 & \sum x_i \\ \sum x_i & n \end{vmatrix}} = \frac{(\sum_i x_i^2)(\sum_i y_i) - (\sum_i x_i)(\sum_i x_i y_i)}{n \sum_i x_i^2 - (\sum_i x_i)^2}. \tag{15}$$

Example 17.4 To find the straight line which best fits the points $(0, 4)$, $(3, 3)$, $(4, 2)$, $(3, 1)$, and $(5, 0)$, construct a table:

i	x_i	y_i	$x_i y_i$	x_i^2
1	0	4	0	0
2	3	3	9	9
3	4	2	8	16
4	3	1	3	9
5	5	0	0	25
$\sum$	15	10	20	59

Then, by (14) and (15),

$$m^* = \frac{5 \cdot 20 - 15 \cdot 10}{5 \cdot 59 - 15 \cdot 15} = -\frac{5}{7}$$

$$b^* = \frac{59 \cdot 10 - 15 \cdot 20}{5 \cdot 59 - 15 \cdot 15} = \frac{29}{7}.$$

The line which best fits these five points has the equation

$$y = -\frac{5}{7}x + \frac{29}{7} \qquad \text{or} \qquad 5x + 7y = 29.$$

Vocabulary The technique we have been discussing is called the **method of least squares** or **regression analysis**. In this case, the line $y = m^*x + b^*$ which best fits the data points is called the **regression line**.

EXERCISES

17.4 A firm uses two inputs to produce a single product. If its production function is $Q = x^{1/4} y^{1/4}$ and if it sells its output for a dollar a unit and buys each input for $4 dollars a unit, find its profit-maximizing input bundle. (Check the second order conditions.)

17.5 More generally, suppose that a firm has a Cobb-Douglas production function $Q = x^a y^b$ and that it faces output price p and input prices w and r, respectively. Solve the first order conditions for a profit-maximizing input bundle. Use the second order conditions to determine the values of the parameters a, b, p, w, and r for which this solution is a global max.

17.6 Dingbat Airlines has regular flights between Ypsilanti and Kalamazoo. It can treat business and pleasure travelers as separate markets by demanding advance purchase and Saturday night stay-over for pleasure travelers. Suppose that it notes a demand function of $Q = 16 - p$ for business travelers and a demand function $Q = 10 - p$ for pleasure travelers and that it has a cost function for all travelers of $C(Q) = 10 + Q^2$. How much should it charge in each market to maximize its profit?

17.7 For the discriminating monopolist in Example 17.3, compute the demand function for the market as a whole, without price discrimination. Compute the firm's profit-maximizing output for this situation and compare the profit to the computation in Example 17.3.

17.8 Find the equation of the line which best fits the data points: $(1, 2)$, $(3, 4)$, $(5, 3)$, and $(6, 6)$.

17.9 *a*) Prove that $2ab \leq a^2 + b^2$ for all numbers a, b.
   b) Use this result to show that

$$(x_1 + \cdots + x_n)^2 = x_1^2 + \cdots + x_n^2 + \sum_{i<j} 2x_i x_j$$

$$\leq x_1^2 + \cdots + x_n^2 + (n-1)(x_1^2 + \cdots + x_n^2)$$

$$= n(x_1^2 + \cdots + x_n^2).$$

   c) Conclude that the point (m^*, b^*) in (14) and (15) is a global minimizer of the function S in (11).

17.10 Use parts *a* and *b* of the previous exercise to determine the geometric interpretation of a zero determinant in the numerators of (14) and (15).

17.11 Given a collection of points $\{(x_i, y_i, z_i)\}_{i=1}^n$ in $\mathbf{R}^3$, find an equation for the coefficients A, B, and C of the plane $z = Ax + By + C$ whose graph best fits these points.

17.12 Divide the equations (14) and (15) through by n^3 to express the least-squares coefficients m^* and b^* in terms of *average values* of the x_i's, y_i's, and so on.

Constrained Optimization I: First Order Conditions

Economics is often defined as the study of the optimal allocation of scarce resources. The word "optimal" implies that we are dealing with some sort of an optimization problem. The word "scarce" implies that the objects in this optimization problem are not free to take on any value but are constrained. A household's consumption is constrained by its available income; a firm's production is constrained by the cost and availability of its inputs. Thus, constrained optimization problems lie at the heart of economic theory. The central mathematical problem here is that of maximizing (or in the case of cost, expenditure, or risk, minimizing) a function of several variables, where these variables are bound by some constraining equations. The prototype problem is

$$\text{maximize} \quad f(x_1, \ldots, x_n)$$

where $(x_1, \ldots, x_n) \in \mathbf{R^n}$ must satisfy

$$g_1(x_1, \ldots, x_n) \leq b_1, \ldots, g_k(x_1, \ldots, x_n) \leq b_k,$$

$$h_1(x_1, \ldots, x_n) = c_1, \ldots, h_m(x_1, \ldots, x_n) = c_m. \tag{1}$$

The function f is called the **objective function**, while $g_1, \ldots, g_k$ and $h_1, \ldots, h_m$ are called **constraint functions**. The g_j's define **inequality constraints**, and the h_i's define **equality constraints**. In applications, the most common inequality constraints are **nonnegativity constraints**: $x_1 \geq 0, \ldots, x_n \geq 0$. Equality constraints often arise as definitions of one variable in terms of others. This chapter begins the treatment of constrained maximization problems. We bring all the mathematical background of the previous chapters to bear on this central topic of economic theory.

411

18.1   EXAMPLES

We begin by discussing some important economic examples of constrained optimization problems.

Example 18.1   (**Utility Maximization Problem**) In this most basic problem, x_i represents the amount of commodity i and $f(x_1, \ldots, x_n)$, usually written as $U(x_1, \ldots, x_n)$, measures the individual's level of utility or satisfaction with consuming x_1 units of good 1, x_2 units of good 2, and so on. Let $p_1, \ldots, p_n$ denote the prices of the commodities and let I denote the individual's income. The consumer wants to

$$\text{maximize} \quad U(x_1, \ldots, x_n)$$
$$\text{subject to} \quad p_1 x_1 + p_2 x_2 + \cdots + p_n x_n \leq I,$$
$$x_1 \geq 0, x_2 \geq 0, \ldots, x_n \geq 0.$$

To be consistent with the general format in (1), the nonnegativity constraints $x_i \geq 0$ should be written as $-x_i \leq 0$ so that all inequality constraints are written with $\leq$ signs. However, when we first formulate a problem mathematically, we will write the constraints in their most natural form. Later, when we begin working with the constrained problem, we will worry about the proper mathematical conventions.

Example 18.2   (**Utility Maximization with Labor/Leisure Choice**) Let U, $x_1, \ldots, x_n, p_1, \ldots, p_n$ be as in the preceding example. In addition, let w denote the wage rate, I' the consumer's nonwage income, ℓ_0 hours of labor, and ℓ_1 hours of leisure. The consumer has $I' + w\ell_0$ dollars to spend and wants to

$$\text{maximize} \quad U(x_1, \ldots, x_n, \ell_1)$$
$$\text{subject to} \quad p_1 x_1 + \cdots + p_n x_n \leq I' + w\ell_0,$$
$$\ell_0 + \ell_1 = 24,$$
$$x_1 \geq 0, \ldots, x_n \geq 0, \ell_0 \geq 0, \ell_1 \geq 0.$$

Example 18.3   (**Profit Maximization of a Competitive Firm**) Suppose that a firm in a competitive industry uses n inputs to manufacture its product. Let y denote the amount of its output, and let $x_1, \ldots, x_n$ denote the amounts of its inputs — all flow concepts. Let $y = f(x_1, \ldots, x_n)$ denote the firm's production function, describing the maximal amount of output that can be produced from the input bundle $(x_1, \ldots, x_n)$. Let p be the unit price of the output and let w_i denote the cost of input i. The firm's goal is to choose $(x_1, \ldots, x_n)$ to maximize its **profit**

$$\Pi(x_1, \ldots, x_n) = pf(x_1, \ldots, x_n) - \sum_1^n w_i x_i$$

under the constraints

$$pf(x_1, \ldots, x_n) - \sum_1^n w_i x_i \geq 0,$$

$$g_1(\mathbf{x}) \leq b_1, \ldots, g_k(\mathbf{x}) \leq b_k,$$

$$x_1 \geq 0, \ldots, x_n \geq 0.$$

The first inequality constraint reflects the requirement that the firm make a nonnegative profit. The g_j-constraints represent constraints on the availability of the inputs.

18.2   EQUALITY CONSTRAINTS

Two Variables and One Equality Constraint

We begin with the simplest constrained maximization problem, that of maximizing a function $f(x_1, x_2)$ of two variables subject to a single equality constraint: $h(x_1, x_2) = c$. The student of economics first encounters such a problem in the utility maximization problem in an intermediate microeconomics course:

$$\text{maximize} \quad f(x_1, x_2)$$

$$\text{subject to} \quad p_1 x_1 + p_2 x_2 = I.$$

We ignore for a moment the requirement that x_1 and x_2 should be nonnegative and the possibility that not all income I may be spent.

With this model of consumer choice in mind, let us examine the usual geometric solution to such a problem. First, draw the constraint set C in the $x_1 x_2$-plane — the thick line in Figure 18.1. Then, draw a representative sample of the level curves of the objective function f. Geometrically, our goal is to find the highest-valued level curve of f which meets the constraint set. The highest level curve of f cannot cross the constraint curve C; if it did, nearby *higher* level sets would cross too, as occurs at point **b** in Figure 18.1. This highest level set of f must touch C (so that the constraint is satisfied) but must otherwise lie on one side of C (since it cannot cross over C). Another way of saying this is that the highest level curve of f to touch the constraint set C must be *tangent* to C at the constrained max. This situation occurs at point $\mathbf{x}^*$ in Figure 18.1.

The fact that the level curve of f is tangent to the constraint set C at the constrained maximizer $\mathbf{x}^*$ means that the slope of the level set of f equals the slope of the constraint curve C at $\mathbf{x}^*$. Recall from Section 15.2 that the slope of the level set of f at $\mathbf{x}^*$ is

$$-\frac{\partial f}{\partial x_1}(\mathbf{x}^*) \bigg/ \frac{\partial f}{\partial x_2}(\mathbf{x}^*)$$

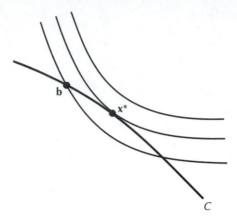

Figure 18.1 *At the constrained max* $\mathbf{x}^*$, *the highest level curve of f is tangent to the constraint set C.*

and the slope of the constraint set $\{h(x_1, x_2) = c\}$ at $\mathbf{x}^*$ is

$$-\frac{\partial h}{\partial x_1}(\mathbf{x}^*)\Big/ \frac{\partial h}{\partial x_2}(\mathbf{x}^*).$$

The fact that these two slopes are equal at $\mathbf{x}^*$ means

$$\frac{\dfrac{\partial f}{\partial x_1}(\mathbf{x}^*)}{\dfrac{\partial f}{\partial x_2}(\mathbf{x}^*)} = \frac{\dfrac{\partial h}{\partial x_1}(\mathbf{x}^*)}{\dfrac{\partial h}{\partial x_2}(\mathbf{x}^*)}. \tag{2}$$

As we will see shortly, it is handy to rewrite this equation as

$$\frac{\dfrac{\partial f}{\partial x_1}(\mathbf{x}^*)}{\dfrac{\partial h}{\partial x_1}(\mathbf{x}^*)} = \frac{\dfrac{\partial f}{\partial x_2}(\mathbf{x}^*)}{\dfrac{\partial h}{\partial x_2}(\mathbf{x}^*)}. \tag{3}$$

To avoid working with (possibly) zero denominators, let μ denote the common value of the two quotients in (3):

$$\frac{\dfrac{\partial f}{\partial x_1}(\mathbf{x}^*)}{\dfrac{\partial h}{\partial x_1}(\mathbf{x}^*)} = \frac{\dfrac{\partial f}{\partial x_2}(\mathbf{x}^*)}{\dfrac{\partial h}{\partial x_2}(\mathbf{x}^*)} = \mu. \tag{4}$$

Rewrite (4) as the two equations

$$\frac{\partial f}{\partial x_1}(\mathbf{x}^*) - \mu \frac{\partial h}{\partial x_1}(\mathbf{x}^*) = 0,$$

$$\frac{\partial f}{\partial x_2}(\mathbf{x}^*) - \mu \frac{\partial h}{\partial x_2}(\mathbf{x}^*) = 0. \tag{5}$$

Since we have to solve for the three unknowns (x_1, x_2, μ), we need three equations — one more than is listed in (5). But we do have a third equation: the constraint equation $h(x_1, x_2) = c$. Including the constraint equation with the two equations in (5) yields a system of three equations in three unknowns:

$$\frac{\partial f}{\partial x_1}(\mathbf{x}) - \mu \frac{\partial h}{\partial x_1}(\mathbf{x}) = 0$$

$$\frac{\partial f}{\partial x_2}(\mathbf{x}) - \mu \frac{\partial h}{\partial x_2}(\mathbf{x}) = 0 \tag{6}$$

$$h(x_1, x_2) - c = 0.$$

There is a convenient way of writing this system (6). Form the **Lagrangian function**

$$L(x_1, x_2, \mu) \equiv f(x_1, x_2) - \mu \left(h(x_1, x_2) - c \right).$$

Find the critical points of the Lagrangian L by computing $\partial L / \partial x_1$, $\partial L / \partial x_2$, and $\partial L / \partial \mu$ and setting each equal to zero. As can easily be checked, the result of this process is precisely system (6). Note that since μ just multiplies the constraint in the definition of L, the equation $\partial L / \partial \mu = 0$ is equivalent to the constraint equation $c - h(x_1, x_2) = 0$. This new variable μ which multiplies the constraint is called a **Lagrange multiplier**.

This process is truly magical. When we want to maximize a function in an unconstrained problem, we simply solve for its critical points by setting its first order partial derivatives equal to zero. However, by the introduction of the Lagrange multiplier μ into the constrained problem, we have transformed a two-variable constrained problem to the problem of finding the *critical points* of a function $L(x_1, x_2, \mu)$ of one more variable. In a sense, we have reduced a *constrained* optimization problem in two variables to an *unconstrained* problem in three variables. The penalty for this reduction is the inclusion of a new and somewhat artificial variable μ. As we will see in Chapter 19, this new variable μ is loaded with economic meaning; it will give us a new measure of value of the scarce resources in the problem under consideration.

A word of caution is in order here. This reduction would not have worked if both $\partial h / \partial x_1$ and $\partial h / \partial x_2$ were zero at the maximizer $\mathbf{x}^*$ in equation (3). For this reason, we will need to make the assumption that $\partial h / \partial x_1$ or $\partial h / \partial x_2$ (or both) is not zero at the constrained maximizer. Since this is a (slight) restriction on the constraint set, it is called a **constraint qualification**. If the constraint is linear, as it is in the utility maximization problems of Examples 18.1 and 18.2, this constraint qualification will automatically be satisfied.

We can now summarize our geometric analysis of the problem of maximizing (or minimizing) a function of two variables restricted by a single equality constraint.

Theorem 18.1 Let f and h be C^1 functions of two variables. Suppose that $\mathbf{x}^* = (x_1^*, x_2^*)$ is a solution of the problem

$$\text{maximize} \quad f(x_1, x_2)$$

$$\text{subject to} \quad h(x_1, x_2) = c$$

Suppose further that (x_1^*, x_2^*) is not a critical point of h. Then, there is a real number μ^* such that (x_1^*, x_2^*, μ^*) is a critical point of the Lagrangian function

$$L(x_1, x_2, \mu) \equiv f(x_1, x_2) - \mu[h(x_1, x_2) - c].$$

In other words, at (x_1^*, x_2^*, μ^*)

$$\frac{\partial L}{\partial x_1} = 0, \quad \frac{\partial L}{\partial x_2} = 0, \quad \text{and} \quad \frac{\partial L}{\partial \mu} = 0.$$

Remark Our geometric proof of Theorem 18.1 was based on the fact that the level curves of f and of h are tangent at (x_1^*, x_2^*) and therefore have equal slope. We now present another version of this proof based on the fact that the gradient vectors

$$\nabla f(\mathbf{x}) = \begin{pmatrix} \dfrac{\partial f}{\partial x_1} \\ \dfrac{\partial f}{\partial x_2} \end{pmatrix} \quad \text{and} \quad \nabla h(\mathbf{x}) = \begin{pmatrix} \dfrac{\partial h}{\partial x_1} \\ \dfrac{\partial h}{\partial x_2} \end{pmatrix},$$

considered as displacement vectors or arrows at the point $\mathbf{x}$, are perpendicular to the level sets of f and h respectively. Since the level sets of f and h have the same slope at $\mathbf{x}^*$, the gradient vectors $\nabla f(\mathbf{x}^*)$ and $\nabla h(\mathbf{x}^*)$ must line up at $\mathbf{x}^*$; they point in the same direction as in the left side of Figure 18.2 or in opposite directions as in the right side of Figure 18.2. In either case, the gradients are scalar multiples of each other. If we write this *multiplier* as μ^*, then we find $\nabla f(\mathbf{x}^*) = \mu^* \nabla h(\mathbf{x}^*)$;

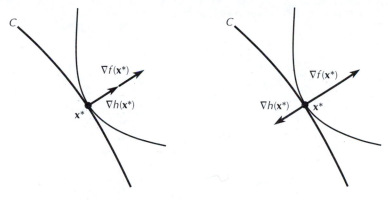

$\nabla f(\mathbf{x}^*)$ *and* $\nabla h(\mathbf{x}^*)$ *line up at the constrained max or min* $\mathbf{x}^*$.

**Figure
18.2**

that is,

$$\begin{pmatrix} \dfrac{\partial f}{\partial x_1} \\[2mm] \dfrac{\partial f}{\partial x_2} \end{pmatrix} = \mu^* \begin{pmatrix} \dfrac{\partial h}{\partial x_1} \\[2mm] \dfrac{\partial h}{\partial x_2} \end{pmatrix}.$$

This immediately translates into system (5).

We present an analytic proof of Theorem 18.1 in the last section of Chapter 19.

Remark If we were minimizing f instead of maximizing f on the constraint set C_h, we would have used the same arguments that we used in the geometric proof of Theorem 18.1. In other words, the conclusion of Theorem 18.1 holds whether we are maximizing f or minimizing f on C_h. In Section 19.3, we will describe a second order condition that distinguishes maxima from minima.

Example 18.4 Let's use Theorem 18.1 to solve a simple utility maximization problem:

$$\begin{aligned} \text{maximize} \quad & f(x_1, x_2) = x_1 x_2 \\ \text{subject to} \quad & h(x_1, x_2) \equiv x_1 + 4x_2 = 16. \end{aligned} \qquad (7)$$

Since the gradient of h is $(1, 4)$, h has no critical points and the constraint qualification is satisfied. Form the Lagrangian

$$L(x_1, x_2, \mu) = x_1 x_2 - \mu(x_1 + 4x_2 - 16),$$

and set its partial derivatives equal to zero:

$$\frac{\partial L}{\partial x_1} = x_2 - \mu = 0$$

$$\frac{\partial L}{\partial x_2} = x_1 - 4\mu = 0 \tag{8}$$

$$\frac{\partial L}{\partial \mu} = -(x_1 + 4x_2 - 16) = 0.$$

Note that, as expected, the equation $\partial L/\partial \mu = 0$ just repeats the equality constraint. We want to solve this system (8) of three equations in three unknowns. In this simple example, system (8) is linear and we can use the methods of Chapter 7. Since (8) is simple, we will use substitution.

From the first two equations in (8),

$$\mu = x_2 = \frac{1}{4}x_1, \tag{9}$$

and therefore

$$x_1 = 4x_2 \tag{10}$$

Substitute (10) into the third equation in (8):

$$(4x_2) + 4x_2 = 16, \quad \text{or} \quad x_2 = 2.$$

From (9) and (10), we conclude the solution of system (8) is

$$x_1 = 8, \quad x_2 = 2, \quad \mu = 2.$$

Theorem 18.1 states that the only candidate for a solution to problem (7) is $x_1 = 8, x_2 = 2$.

Example 18.5   Let's work out a more complex example:

$$\text{maximize} \quad f(x_1, x_2) = x_1^2 x_2$$

$$\text{subject to} \quad (x_1, x_2) \quad \text{in the constraint set}$$

$$C_h = \{(x_1, x_2) : 2x_1^2 + x_2^2 = 3\}.$$

To check the constraint qualification, we compute the critical points of $h(x_1, x_2) = 2x_1^2 + x_2^2$. The only such critical point occurs at $(x_1, x_2) = (0, 0)$ — a point which is *not* in the constraint set C_h. Therefore, the constraint qualification for this problem is satisfied. Now, form the Lagrangian

$$L(x_1, x_2, \mu) = x_1^2 x_2 - \mu(2x_1^2 + x_2^2 - 3),$$

compute its partial derivatives, and set them equal to 0:

$$\frac{\partial L}{\partial x_1} = 2x_1x_2 - 4\mu x_1 = 2x_1(x_2 - 2\mu) = 0$$

$$\frac{\partial L}{\partial x_2} = x_1^2 - 2\mu x_2 = 0 \tag{11}$$

$$\frac{\partial L}{\partial \mu} = -2x_1^2 - x_2^2 + 3 = 0.$$

Once again, the equation $\partial L/\partial \mu = 0$ just repeats the equality constraint. We want to solve this *nonlinear* system (11) of three equations in three unknowns. The usual method is to solve one of the first two equations for μ and plug this expression into the other to eliminate μ as a variable in the computation.

The first equation in (11) yields $x_1 = 0$ or $x_2 = 2\mu$. We work with each of these two cases separately. If $x_1 = 0$, then $x_2 = \pm\sqrt{3}$ from the third equation and $\mu = 0$ from the second. Therefore,

$$(0, \sqrt{3}, 0) \quad \text{and} \quad (0, -\sqrt{3}, 0)$$

are two solutions of system (11).

If $x_1 \neq 0$ in (11), then $x_2 = 2\mu$ or $\mu = x_2/2$ by the first equation in (11). Plug $\mu = x_2/2$ into the second equation of (11) to find $x_1^2 = x_2^2$. Plug this expression into the third equation to obtain $3x_1^2 = 3$ or $x_1 = \pm1$. Since $x_1^2 = x_2^2$, $x_1 = \pm1$ implies that $x_2 = \pm1$ and, via the first equation, that $\mu = 0.5$ when $x_2 = +1$, and $\mu = -0.5$ when $x_2 = -1$. Consequently, we obtain four more solutions of system (11) of first order conditions:

$$(1, 1, 0.5), \quad (-1, -1, -0.5), \quad (1, -1, -0.5), \quad \text{and} \quad (-1, 1, 0.5).$$

As we will see in Chapter 30, the fact the constraint set C_h is a compact set means that a constrained max exists for this problem. (Theorem 30.1.) Since we don't have a second order test and we know by Theorem 18.1 that the constrained max is one of these six candidates, we can plug each of the six candidates into $f(x_1, x_2)$ and see which gives the highest value. Since

$$f(1, 1) = f(-1, 1) \quad = 1,$$
$$f(1, -1) = f(-1, -1) = -1,$$
$$f(0, \sqrt{3}) = f(0, -\sqrt{3}) = 0,$$

the max occurs at $(1, 1)$ and $(-1, 1)$. Note that $(1, -1)$ and $(-1, -1)$ *minimize* f on C_h. See Exercise 18.1.

The computations in Examples 18.4 and 18.5 illustrate how one applies Theorem 18.1. First, check the constraint qualification by calculating the critical points of the constraint function h, that is, the solutions of $\partial h / \partial x_1 = 0$ and $\partial h / \partial x_2 = 0$. If none of these lie in the constraint set, we can write out the Lagrangian, set its partial derivatives equal to zero, and solve the resulting system of equations. If the constraint set does contain a critical point of the constraint function, then we include this point among our candidates for a solution to the original constrained maximization problem, along with the critical points of the Lagrangian. We will say more about constraint qualifications next chapter.

Several Equality Constraints

We consider next the problem of maximizing a function $f(x_1, \ldots, x_n)$ of n variables constrained by more than one, say m, *equality* constraints. Let the functions $h_1(\mathbf{x}), \ldots, h_m(\mathbf{x})$ define the constraint set. In other words, we want to

maximize or minimize $\quad f(x_1, \ldots, x_n)$

subject to $\quad C_h = \{\mathbf{x} = (x_1, \ldots, x_n) \mid h_1(\mathbf{x}) = a_1, \ldots, h_m(\mathbf{x}) = a_m\}.$

We will need to generalize to m functions the constraint qualification that we used for one function of two variables:

$$\left(\frac{\partial h}{\partial x_1}(\mathbf{x}^*), \frac{\partial h}{\partial x_2}(\mathbf{x}^*) \right) \neq (0, 0). \tag{12}$$

If we have just one constraint, $h(x_1, \ldots, x_n) = a$, then the natural generalization of (12) is that some first order partial derivative of h is not zero at the optimal $\mathbf{x}^*$:

$$\left(\frac{\partial h}{\partial x_1}(\mathbf{x}^*), \frac{\partial h}{\partial x_2}(\mathbf{x}^*), \ldots, \frac{\partial h}{\partial x_n}(\mathbf{x}^*) \right) \neq (0, 0, \ldots, 0). \tag{13}$$

If we are dealing with m constraint functions, $m > 1$, the natural generalization of (12) and (13) involves the Jacobian derivative

$$Dh(\mathbf{x}^*) = \begin{pmatrix} \frac{\partial h_1}{\partial x_1}(\mathbf{x}^*) & \cdots & \frac{\partial h_1}{\partial x_n}(\mathbf{x}^*) \\ \frac{\partial h_2}{\partial x_1}(\mathbf{x}^*) & \cdots & \frac{\partial h_2}{\partial x_n}(\mathbf{x}^*) \\ \vdots & \ddots & \vdots \\ \frac{\partial h_m}{\partial x_1}(\mathbf{x}^*) & \cdots & \frac{\partial h_m}{\partial x_n}(\mathbf{x}^*) \end{pmatrix}$$

of the constraint functions. In general, a point $\mathbf{x}^*$ is called a **critical point** of $\mathbf{h} = (h_1, \ldots, h_m)$ if the rank of the matrix $Dh(\mathbf{x}^*)$ is $< m$. Therefore, the natural generalization of the constraint qualification (13) is that the rank of $D\mathbf{h}(\mathbf{x})$ be m — as large as it can be. More formally, we say that $(h_1, \ldots, h_m)$ satisfies the **nondegenerate constraint qualification (NDCQ)** at $\mathbf{x}^*$ if the rank of the Jacobian matrix $D\mathbf{h}(\mathbf{x}^*)$ at $\mathbf{x}^*$ is m. The NDCQ is a regularity condition, like the definition of a regular curve in Section 14.5. It implies that the constraint set has a well-defined $n - m$-dimensional tangent plane everywhere.

The statement of the general theorem for maximizing a function of n variables constrained by m equality constraints is a straightforward generalization of Theorem 18.1. However, we can't use our two-dimensional geometric proof. We will present a complete proof in Section 19.6.

Theorem 18.2   Let $f, h_1, \ldots, h_m$ be C^1 functions of n variables. Consider the problem of maximizing (or minimizing) $f(\mathbf{x})$ on the constraint set

$$C_\mathbf{h} \equiv \{\mathbf{x} = (x_1, \cdots, x_n) : h_1(\mathbf{x}) = a_1, \ldots, h_m(\mathbf{x}) = a_m\}.$$

Suppose that $\mathbf{x}^* \in C_\mathbf{h}$ and that $\mathbf{x}^*$ is a (local) max or min of f on $C_\mathbf{h}$. Suppose further that $\mathbf{x}^*$ satisfies condition NDCQ above. Then, there exist $\mu_1^*, \ldots, \mu_m^*$ such that $(x_1^*, \ldots, x_n^*, \mu_1^*, \ldots, \mu_m^*) \equiv (\mathbf{x}^*, \mu^*)$ is a critical point of the Lagrangian

$$L(\mathbf{x}, \mu) \equiv f(\mathbf{x}) - \mu_1[h_1(\mathbf{x}) - a_1] - \mu_2[h_2(\mathbf{x}) - a_2] - \cdots - \mu_m[h_m(\mathbf{x}) - a_m].$$

In other words,

$$\frac{\partial L}{\partial x_1}(\mathbf{x}^*, \mu^*) = 0, \ldots, \frac{\partial L}{\partial x_n}(\mathbf{x}^*, \mu^*) = 0,$$

$$\frac{\partial L}{\partial \mu_1}(\mathbf{x}^*, \mu^*) = 0, \ldots, \frac{\partial L}{\partial \mu_m}(\mathbf{x}^*, \mu^*) = 0. \tag{14}$$

Example 18.6   Consider the problem of maximizing $f(x, y, z) = xyz$ on the constraint set defined by

$$h_1(x, y, z) \equiv x^2 + y^2 = 1 \qquad \text{and} \qquad h_2(x, y, z) \equiv x + z = 1.$$

Looking at this problem geometrically first, we see that the set defined by h_1 is the cylinder C_1 parallel to the z-axis, as drawn in Figure 18.3. The set defined by h_2 is the plane C_2 parallel to the y-axis, as drawn in Figure 18.3. The actual constraint set $C_\mathbf{h}$ is the intersection of C_1 and C_2.

Now let's tackle this problem analytically. First, compute the Jacobian matrix of the constraint functions

$$D\mathbf{h}(x, y, z) = \begin{pmatrix} 2x & 2y & 0 \\ 1 & 0 & 1 \end{pmatrix}.$$

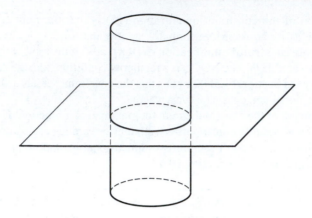

**Figure
18.3**

The constraint set in Example 18.6.

Its rank is less than 2 if and only if $x = y = 0$. Since any point with $x = y = 0$ would violate the first constraint, all points in the constraint set satisfy NDCQ. Next, form the Lagrangian

$$L(x, y, z, \mu_1, \mu_2) = xyz - \mu_1(x^2 + y^2 - 1) - \mu_2(x + z - 1),$$

and set its first partial derivatives equal to 0:

$$\frac{\partial L}{\partial x} = yz - 2\mu_1 x - \mu_2 = 0$$

$$\frac{\partial L}{\partial y} = xz - 2\mu_1 y \qquad = 0$$

$$\frac{\partial L}{\partial z} = xy - \mu_2 \qquad = 0$$

$$\frac{\partial L}{\partial \mu_1} = 1 - x^2 - y^2 \qquad = 0$$

$$\frac{\partial L}{\partial \mu_2} = 1 - x - z \qquad = 0.$$

Solve the second and third equations for μ_1 and μ_2 in terms of x, y, and z and plug these into the first equation to obtain

$$yz - 2\left(\frac{xz}{2y}\right)x - xy = 0,$$

or

$$y^2z - x^2z - xy^2 = 0. \qquad (15)$$

Then, solve the fourth equation for y^2 in terms of x^2 and the last equation for z in terms of x and plug these into (15) to obtain

$$(1 - x^2)(1 - x) - x^2(1 - x) - x(1 - x^2) = 0.$$

The result is a cubic equation with $x = 1$ as one root. One can divide the cubic through by $x - 1$ and solve the resulting quadratic to obtain $x = \frac{1}{6}(-1 \pm \sqrt{13})$, approximately -0.7676 and 0.4343. Plugging these numbers into the constraints, we obtain the four solution candidates

$$x \simeq \quad 0.4343, \qquad y \simeq \pm 0.9008, \qquad z \simeq 0.5657;$$

$$x \simeq -0.7676, \qquad y \simeq \pm 0.6409, \qquad z \simeq 1.7676.$$

Evaluating the objective function at these four points, we find that the maximizer is

$$x \simeq -0.7676, \quad y \simeq -0.6409, \quad z \simeq 1.7676.$$

As Example 18.6 illustrates, we use Theorem 18.2 just as we used Theorem 18.1. The candidates for the constrained maximizer are the critical points of the constraint functions *and* the critical points of the Lagrangian.

EXERCISES

18.1 For the problem of Example 18.5, draw C_h and some level sets of f, as in Figure 18.1, to get a geometric interpretation of the solutions. Use this picture to determine whether the points $(0, \pm\sqrt{3})$ are local max, local min, or neither.

18.2 Find the maximum and minimum distance from the origin to the ellipse $x^2 + xy + y^2 = 3$. [Hint: Use $x^2 + y^2$ as your objective function.]

18.3 Find the point on the parabola $y = x^2$ that is closest to the point $(2, 1)$. (Estimate the solution of the cubic equation which results.)

18.4 Find the general expression (in terms of all the parameters) for the commodity bundle (x_1, x_2) which maximizes the Cobb-Douglas utility function $U(x_1, x_2) = kx_1^a x_2^{1-a}$ on the budget set $p_1 x_1 + p_2 x_2 = I$.

18.5 Find the point closest to the origin in $\mathbf{R}^3$ that is on both the planes $3x + y + z = 5$ and $x + y + z = 1$.

18.6 Find the max and min of $f(x, y, z) = x + y + z^2$ subject to $x^2 + y^2 + z^2 = 1$ and $y = 0$.

18.7 Maximize $f(x, y, z) = yz + xz$ subject to $y^2 + z^2 = 1$ and $xz = 3$.

18.8 Show that the NDCQ implies that $m \leq n$.

18.9 Maximize $x^2 y^2 z^2$ subject to $x^2 + y^2 + z^2 = c^2$, where c is some fixed positive constant. What is the maximum value of the objective function on the constraint set? Show that for all x, y, z,

$$x^2 y^2 z^2 \leq \left(\frac{1}{3}(x^2 + y^2 + z^2)\right)^3, \quad \text{or} \quad (x^2 y^2 z^2)^{1/3} \leq \frac{x^2 + y^2 + z^2}{3}.$$

This equality states that the **geometric mean** of three positive numbers is always $\leq$ the **arithmetic mean** or **average** of these three numbers. Furthermore, these means are equal only when the three numbers are equal. Of course, the same proof works for all sets of n positive numbers:

$$(x_1^2 \cdot x_2^2 \cdots x_n^2)^{\frac{1}{n}} \leq \frac{x_1^2 + x_2^2 + \cdots + x_n^2}{n}$$

with equality if and only if $x_1^2 = x_2^2 = \cdots = x_n^2$.

18.3   INEQUALITY CONSTRAINTS

In the previous section, we worked solely with constraint sets defined by *equality* constraints:

$$h_1(x_1, \ldots, x_n) = c_1, \ldots, h_m(x_1, \ldots, x_n) = c_m.$$

To find the maximum or minimum of a function on such a constraint set, we simply constructed the Lagrangian, set its $(m + n)$ first partial derivatives equal to zero, and then solved these $(m + n)$ equations in $(m + n)$ unknowns — worrying a little about constraint qualifications along the way. However, the vast majority of constrained optimization problems that arise in economics have their constraints defined by *inequalities*:

$$g_1(x_1, \ldots, x_n) \leq b_1, \ldots, g_k(x_1, \ldots, x_n) \leq b_k.$$

Unfortunately, the method for finding the constrained maxima in problems with inequality constraints is a bit more complex than the method we used for equality constraints. The first order conditions involve both equalities and inequalities and their solution entails the investigation of a number of cases.

As a matter of bookkeeping, for the rest of this chapter we will continue to use h's to denote functions which define equality constraints and we will use g's to denote functions which define inequality constraints. We will use μ's for the multipliers of the h's and λ's for the multipliers of the g's. This convention will be especially helpful when we work with the general case which includes both equality and inequality constraints.

One Inequality Constraint

Let's begin again by looking at the simplest case — two variables and one *inequality* constraint:

$$\text{maximize} \quad f(x, y)$$

$$\text{subject to} \quad g(x, y) \leq b.$$

In Figure 18.4, the thicker curve is the curve $g(x, y) = b$; the region to the left and below this curve is the constraint set $g(x, y) \leq b$. The thinner lines are the level sets of the objective function f. By studying Figure 18.4, one notes that the highest level curve of f which meets the constraint set meets it at the point **p**. Since **p** lies on the boundary of the constraint set where $g(x, y) = b$, we say that the constraint is **binding** (or is active, effective, or tight) at **p**. As we noted in Figure 18.1, the level set of f and the level set of g are tangent to each other at **p**. As in Figure 18.2, this means that $\nabla f(\mathbf{p})$ and $\nabla g(\mathbf{p})$ line up — point in the same direction or in opposite directions — and therefore that $\nabla f(\mathbf{p})$ is a multiple of $\nabla g(\mathbf{p})$. If we let λ denote the multiplier, then $\nabla f(\mathbf{p}) = \lambda \nabla g(\mathbf{p})$, or

$$\nabla f(\mathbf{p}) - \lambda \nabla g(\mathbf{p}) = \mathbf{0}. \tag{16}$$

This time, however, the sign of the multiplier is important! Recall from Section 14.6 that $\nabla f(\mathbf{p})$ points in the direction in which f *increases* most rapidly at **p**. In particular, $\nabla g(\mathbf{p})$ points to the set $g(x, y) \geq b$, and not to the set $g(x, y) \leq b$. Since **p** maximizes f on the set $g(x, y) \leq b$, the gradient of f cannot point to the constraint set. If it did, we could increase f and still keep $g(x, y) \leq b$. So, $\nabla f(\mathbf{p})$ must point to the region where $g(x, y) \geq b$. This means that $\nabla f(\mathbf{p})$ and $\nabla g(\mathbf{p})$ *point in the same direction*. Thus, if $\nabla f(\mathbf{p}) = \lambda \nabla g(\mathbf{p})$, the multiplier λ must be ≥ 0. It is worthwhile to take the time to understand clearly this difference between equality and inequality constraints.

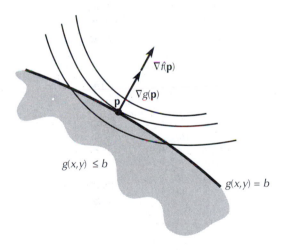

∇f *and* ∇g *point in the same direction at the maximizer* **p**.

Figure 18.4

Consequently, for the situation depicted in Figure 18.4, we still form the Lagrangian function

$$L(x, y, \lambda) = f(x, y) - \lambda[g(x, y) - b]$$

and, as shown in (16), set

$$\frac{\partial L}{\partial x} = \frac{\partial f}{\partial x} - \lambda \frac{\partial g}{\partial x} \quad \text{and} \quad \frac{\partial L}{\partial y} = \frac{\partial f}{\partial y} - \lambda \frac{\partial g}{\partial y}$$

both equal to zero. We require, as we did in the previous section, the constraint qualification that the maximizer not be a critical point of the constraint function g.

Before we consider $\partial L / \partial \lambda$, there is one more situation we need to examine. Suppose that the maximum of f on the constraint set $g(x, y) \leq b$ occurs not where $g(x, y) = b$ but at a point where $g(x, y) < b$. Figure 18.5 depicts this scenario, where we still use a thicker line to represent the boundary $g(x, y) = b$ of the constraint set. The full constraint set $g(x, y) \leq b$ lies to the left and below this curve. However, this time the maximum of f occurs at the point $\mathbf{q}$ in the interior of the constraint set. There is a point $\mathbf{r}$ on the level set $g(x, y) = b$ where this level set is tangent to a level set of f, but ∇f and ∇g point in opposite directions at $\mathbf{r}$. In fact, one can increase the value of f by moving further *into* the constraint set from $\mathbf{r}$ until one reaches $\mathbf{q}$. Since $g(x, y)$ is strictly less than b at $\mathbf{q}$, in other words $\mathbf{q}$ is in the interior of the constraint set, we say that the constraint is **not binding** (inactive, ineffective, loose) at $\mathbf{q}$. Note that the point $\mathbf{q}$ must be a local max of f, that is, a local *unconstrained* max. By Theorem 17.1, this means that

$$\frac{\partial f}{\partial x}(\mathbf{q}) = 0 \quad \text{and} \quad \frac{\partial f}{\partial y}(\mathbf{q}) = 0.$$

The derivatives of g do not enter the criterion or the calculations at $\mathbf{q}$. We can still use our Lagrangian

$$L(x, y, \lambda) = f(x, y) - \lambda[g(x, y) - b]$$

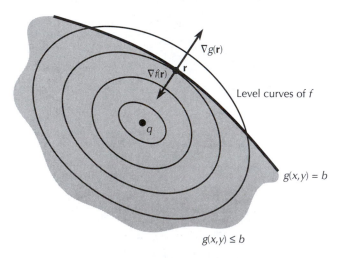

Figure 18.5   *The situation in which the constraint is not binding.*

and set $\partial L/\partial x$ and $\partial L/\partial y$ equal to zero, *provided* that we set λ equal to zero. Setting $\lambda = 0$ causes the constraint function to drop out of the analysis; this is just what we want when the constraint is not binding at the max.

In summary, either the constraint is binding, that is, $g(x, y) - b = 0$ as in Figure 18.4, in which case the multiplier λ must be ≥ 0, or the constraint is not binding as in Figure 18.5, in which case the multiplier λ must be zero. Such a condition in which one of two inequalities must be binding is called a **complementary slackness condition**. A convenient way to summarize such a condition that one of two numbers be zero is to say that their *product* must be zero. Therefore, we will summarize our criterion that either $g(x, y) - b = 0$ or $\lambda = 0$ by requiring that

$$\lambda \cdot [g(x, y) - b] = 0. \tag{17}$$

Since we do not know *a priori* whether or not the constraint will be binding at the maximizer, we cannot use the condition $\partial L/\partial \mu = 0$ that we used with equality constraints since this condition is equivalent to $g(x, y) - b = 0$. We will replace this statement by condition (17), which says that *either* the constraint is binding or its multiplier is zero (or, in rare circumstances, both). Putting these two cases together, we can summarize our observations in this section by the following theorem.

Theorem 18.3 Suppose that f and g are C^1 functions on $\mathbf{R}^2$ and that (x^*, y^*) maximizes f on the constraint set $g(x, y) \leq b$. If $g(x^*, y^*) = b$, suppose that

$$\frac{\partial g}{\partial x}(x^*, y^*) \neq 0 \quad \text{or} \quad \frac{\partial g}{\partial y}(x^*, y^*) \neq 0.$$

In any case, form the Lagrangian function

$$L(x, y, \lambda) = f(x, y) - \lambda \cdot [g(x, y) - b].$$

Then, there is a multiplier λ^* such that:

(a) $\dfrac{\partial L}{\partial x}(x^*, y^*, \lambda^*) = 0,$

(b) $\dfrac{\partial L}{\partial y}(x^*, y^*, \lambda^*) = 0,$

(c) $\lambda^* \cdot [g(x^*, y^*) - b] = 0,$

(d) $\lambda^* \geq 0,$

(e) $g(x^*, y^*) \leq b.$

Remark In some texts, the constraint is written as $g(x, y) \geq b$ instead of as $g(x, y) \leq b$ and the Lagrangian is then written as $L(x, y, \lambda) = f(x, y) + \lambda \cdot [g(x, y) - b]$. These two changes cancel each other so that the conclusion of Theorem 18.3 still holds at a constrained max.

Notice the similarities and differences between the statement of Theorem 18.2 which treats equality constraints and the statement of Theorem 18.3 which covers inequality constraints:

(1) Both use the same Lagrangian L and both require that the derivatives of L with respect to the x_i's be zero.
(2) The condition that $\partial L / \partial \mu = h(x, y) - c = 0$ for equality constraints may no longer hold for inequality constraints since the constraint need not be binding at the maximizer in the inequality constraint case. It is replaced by two conditions:

$$\lambda \cdot [g(x, y) - b] = 0 \quad \text{and} \quad \frac{\partial L}{\partial \lambda} = g(x, y) - b \leq 0.$$

The second of these two conditions is simply a repetition of the inequality constraint itself.
(3) Both situations require that we check a constraint qualification. However, we need only check the constraint qualification for an inequality constraint if that constraint is binding at the solution candidate.
(4) There were no restrictions on the sign of the multiplier in the equality constraint situation; however, the multiplier for inequality constraints must be nonnegative.
(5) For equality constraints (and for problems with no constraints), the same first order conditions that work for maximization problems also hold for minimization problems. However, the argument, summarized in Figure 18.4, that $\nabla f(\mathbf{p})$ and $\nabla g(\mathbf{p})$ point in the *same* direction for inequality constraints holds only for the maximization problem. The same line of reasoning concludes that $\nabla f(\mathbf{p})$ and $\nabla g(\mathbf{p})$ must point in *opposite* directions in a constrained minimization problem. We will say more about the distinction between minimization problems and maximization problems in Section 18.5.

Example 18.7 Consider the problem of maximizing $f(x, y) = xy$ on the constraint set $g(x, y) = x^2 + y^2 \leq 1$. The only critical point of g occurs at the origin — far away from the boundary of the constraint set $x^2 + y^2 = 1$. So, the constraint qualification will be satisfied at any candidate for a solution. Form the Lagrangian

$$L(x, y, \lambda) = xy - \lambda(x^2 + y^2 - 1),$$

and write out the first order conditions described in Theorem 18.3:

$$\frac{\partial L}{\partial x} = y - 2\lambda x = 0, \qquad \frac{\partial L}{\partial y} = x - 2\lambda y = 0,$$

$$\lambda(x^2 + y^2 - 1) = 0, \quad x^2 + y^2 \leq 1, \qquad \lambda \geq 0.$$

The first two equations yield

$$\lambda = \frac{y}{2x} = \frac{x}{2y}, \quad \text{or} \quad x^2 = y^2. \tag{18}$$

If $\lambda = 0$, then $x = y = 0$. This combination satisfies all the first order conditions, so it is a candidate for a solution. If $\lambda \neq 0$, then the third equation becomes $x^2 + y^2 - 1 = 0$. Combining this with (18), we find that $x^2 = y^2 = 1/2$, or $x = \pm 1/\sqrt{2}$, $y = \pm 1/\sqrt{2}$. Combining these with the equation for λ in (18), we find the following four candidates:

$$x = +\frac{1}{\sqrt{2}}, \quad y = +\frac{1}{\sqrt{2}}, \quad \lambda = +\frac{1}{2};$$

$$x = -\frac{1}{\sqrt{2}}, \quad y = -\frac{1}{\sqrt{2}}, \quad \lambda = +\frac{1}{2};$$

$$x = +\frac{1}{\sqrt{2}}, \quad y = -\frac{1}{\sqrt{2}}, \quad \lambda = -\frac{1}{2};$$

$$x = -\frac{1}{\sqrt{2}}, \quad y = +\frac{1}{\sqrt{2}}, \quad \lambda = -\frac{1}{2}.$$

We disregard the last two candidates since they involve a negative multiplier. So, including $(0, 0, 0)$, there are three candidates which satisfy all five first order conditions. Plugging these three into the objective function, we find that

$$x = \frac{1}{\sqrt{2}}, \; y = \frac{1}{\sqrt{2}} \quad \text{and} \quad x = -\frac{1}{\sqrt{2}}, \; y = -\frac{1}{\sqrt{2}}$$

are the solutions of our original problem.

The two points with the negative multipliers are the solutions of the problem of *minimizing xy* on the constraint set $x^2 + y^2 \leq 1$.

One way to think of condition c in Theorem 18.3 is that if $\lambda > 0$, we know the constraint will be binding and we can treat it as an equality constraint instead of as an inequality constraint — a much simpler criterion to work with. In some economics problems this type of analysis can give us useful information about the phenomenon under study, as the following example illustrates.

Example 18.8   Consider once again the standard utility maximization problem of Example 18.1. We continue to ignore the nonnegativity constraints but now do not force the budget constraint to be binding in the statement of the problem. We will see that the tightness of the budget constraint — the conclusion that the consumer spends all the available income — is a consequence of a natural monotonicity assumption on the utility function.

Our goal is to maximize a C^1 utility function $U(x_1, x_2)$ subject to the budget constraint $p_1 x_1 + p_2 x_2 \leq I$, where p_1 and p_2 represent positive unit prices. We assume that for each commodity bundle (x_1, x_2),

$$\frac{\partial U}{\partial x_1}(x_1, x_2) > 0 \quad \text{or} \quad \frac{\partial U}{\partial x_2}(x_1, x_2) > 0.$$

This is a version of the usual monotonicity or nonsatiation assumption. It states that the commodities under study are *goods* in that increasing consumption increases utility. Since the usual constraint qualification is satisfied, we can form the Lagrangian

$$L(x_1, x_2, \lambda) = U(x_1, x_2) - \lambda(p_1 x_1 + p_2 x_2 - I)$$

and compute its x_1- and x_2-critical points:

$$\frac{\partial L}{\partial x_1}(x_1, x_2) = \frac{\partial U}{\partial x_1}(x_1, x_2) - \lambda p_1 = 0,$$

$$\frac{\partial L}{\partial x_2}(x_1, x_2) = \frac{\partial U}{\partial x_2}(x_1, x_2) - \lambda p_2 = 0. \tag{19}$$

At the maximizer, the multiplier λ cannot be zero; otherwise both $\partial U/\partial x_1$ and $\partial U/\partial x_2$ would be zero in (19) — a contradiction to our monotonicity assumption. Since

$$\lambda > 0 \quad \text{and} \quad \lambda(p_1 x_1 + p_2 x_2 - I) = 0,$$

it follows that $p_1 x_1 + p_2 x_2 = I$; the consumer will spend all available income and we can treat the budget constraint as an equality constraint.

Several Inequality Constraints

The generalization of Theorem 18.3 to more variables and more constraints is straightforward. We will present its statement here and then work through some concrete problems using it, but delay its proof until Section 19.6. Recall that a constraint $g(\mathbf{x}) \leq b$ is **binding** (active, effective) at a solution candidate $\mathbf{x}^*$ if $g(\mathbf{x}^*) = b$. If $g(\mathbf{x}^*) < b$, we say that the constraint is **not binding** (inactive, ineffective) at $\mathbf{x}^*$.

Theorem 18.4   Suppose that $f, g_1, \ldots, g_k$ are C^1 functions of n variables. Suppose that $\mathbf{x}^* \in \mathbf{R}^n$ is a local maximizer of f on the constraint set defined by the k inequalities

$$g_1(x_1, \ldots, x_n) \leq b_1, \ldots, g_k(x_1, \ldots, x_n) \leq b_k.$$

For ease of notation, assume that the first k_0 constraints are binding at $\mathbf{x}^*$ and that the last $k - k_0$ constraints are not binding. Suppose that the following nondegenerate constraint qualification is satisfied at $\mathbf{x}^*$.

The rank at $\mathbf{x}^*$ of the Jacobian matrix of the *binding* constraints

$$
\begin{pmatrix}
\dfrac{\partial g_1}{\partial x_1}(\mathbf{x}^*) & \cdots & \dfrac{\partial g_1}{\partial x_n}(\mathbf{x}^*) \\
\vdots & \ddots & \vdots \\
\dfrac{\partial g_{k_0}}{\partial x_1}(\mathbf{x}^*) & \cdots & \dfrac{\partial g_{k_0}}{\partial x_n}(\mathbf{x}^*)
\end{pmatrix}
$$

is k_0 — as large as it can be.

Form the Lagrangian

$$
L(x_1, \ldots, x_n, \lambda_1, \ldots, \lambda_k) \equiv f(\mathbf{x}) - \lambda_1[g_1(\mathbf{x}) - b_1] - \cdots - \lambda_k[g_k(\mathbf{x}) - b_k].
$$

Then, there exist multipliers $\lambda_1^*, \ldots, \lambda_k^*$ such that:

(a) $\dfrac{\partial L}{\partial x_1}(\mathbf{x}^*, \lambda^*) = 0, \ldots, \dfrac{\partial L}{\partial x_n}(\mathbf{x}^*, \lambda^*) = 0,$

(b) $\lambda_1^*[g_1(\mathbf{x}^*) - b_1] = 0, \ldots, \lambda_k^*[g_k(\mathbf{x}^*) - b_k] = 0,$

(c) $\lambda_1^* \geq 0, \ldots, \lambda_k^* \geq 0,$

(d) $g_1(\mathbf{x}^*) \leq b_1, \ldots, g_k(\mathbf{x}^*) \leq b_k.$

Remark The constraint qualification in the statement of Theorem 18.4 is the natural generalization of the constraint qualifications in Theorems 18.2 and 18.3. This condition involves only the *binding* constraints since the nonbinding constraints should play no role in the first order conditions. Then, we treat the binding constraints just as we did the equality constraints in Theorem 18.2, by assuming that their Jacobian has maximal rank. We will still abbreviate this version of the nondegenerate constraint qualifications as NDCQ.

Example 18.9 Consider the problem of maximizing $f(x, y, z) = xyz$ on the constraint set defined by the inequalities

$$
x + y + z \leq 1, \quad x \geq 0, \quad y \geq 0, \quad \text{and} \quad z \geq 0.
$$

This is the typical example of a utility maximization problem in a three-dimensional commodity space. Since we need to write all our inequality constraints consistently — with a $\leq$ — we write the three nonnegativity constraints as

$$
-x \leq 0, \quad -y \leq 0, \quad \text{and} \quad -z \leq 0.
$$

The Jacobian of the constraint functions is

$$\begin{pmatrix} 1 & 1 & 1 \\ -1 & 0 & 0 \\ 0 & -1 & 0 \\ 0 & 0 & -1 \end{pmatrix}.$$

Since its columns are linearly independent, it has rank three. Since at most three of the four constraints can be binding at any one time, the NDCQ holds at any solution candidate. Form the Lagrangian

$$L(x, y, z, \lambda_1, \lambda_2, \lambda_3, \lambda_4) = xyz - \lambda_1(x + y + z - 1)$$
$$- \lambda_2(-x) - \lambda_3(-y) - \lambda_4(-z).$$

Because of the double minus signs in the last three terms of this Lagrangian, we can rewrite it more aesthetically as

$$L(x, y, z, \lambda_1, \lambda_2, \lambda_3, \lambda_4) = xyz - \lambda_1(x + y + z - 1) + \lambda_2 x + \lambda_3 y + \lambda_4 z.$$

From now on, we will treat nonnegativity constraints this way, by including them in the Lagrangian as $+\lambda_i x_i$ rather than as $-\lambda_i(-x_i)$. We now write out the complete set of first order conditions, according to Theorem 18.4:

$$(1) \quad \frac{\partial L}{\partial x} = yz - \lambda_1 + \lambda_2 = 0,$$

$$(2) \quad \frac{\partial L}{\partial y} = xz - \lambda_1 + \lambda_3 = 0,$$

$$(3) \quad \frac{\partial L}{\partial z} = xy - \lambda_1 + \lambda_4 = 0,$$

(4) $\lambda_1(x + y + z - 1) = 0,$ (5) $\lambda_2 x = 0,$

(6) $\lambda_3 y = 0,$ (7) $\lambda_4 z = 0,$

(8) $\lambda_1 \geq 0,$ (9) $\lambda_2 \geq 0,$

(10) $\lambda_3 \geq 0,$ (11) $\lambda_4 \geq 0,$

(12) $x + y + z \leq 1,$ (13) $x \geq 0,$

(14) $y \geq 0,$ (15) $z \geq 0.$

Rewrite conditions 1, 2, and 3, without minus signs, as

$$\lambda_1 = yz + \lambda_2 = xz + \lambda_3 = xy + \lambda_4. \tag{20}$$

We will look at two cases: $\lambda_1 = 0$ and $\lambda_1 > 0$.

If $\lambda_1 = 0$ in equation (20), then because every variable in equation (20) is nonnegative,

$$yz = xz = xy = 0 \quad \text{and} \quad \lambda_1 = \lambda_2 = \lambda_3 = \lambda_4 = 0. \tag{21}$$

Equations (21) lead to the (infinite) set of solution candidates in which two of the variables equal zero and the third is any number in the interval $[0, 1]$. In particular, the objective function equals zero for all (x, y, z) which satisfy equations (21).

Next, look at the case $\lambda_1 > 0$. By condition 4, $x + y + z = 1$; at least one of x, y, z must be nonzero. Suppose for a moment that $x = 0$. Then, using equations (20) and the assumption that $\lambda_1 > 0$, we see that $\lambda_3 = \lambda_4 = \lambda_1 > 0$. But then, conditions 6 and 7 imply that $y = z = 0$ — a contradiction to $x + y + z = 1$. Since the assumption that $x = 0$ leads to a contradiction, we conclude that $x > 0$. Similar arguments show that y and z are positive too. Then, conditions 5, 6, and 7 imply that $\lambda_2 = \lambda_3 = \lambda_4 = 0$ and equations (20) become simply

$$yz = xz = xy.$$

It follows now that

$$x = y = z = \frac{1}{3} \tag{22}$$

and, by using equation (20) once more, that $\lambda_1 = 1/9$. Since

$$f\left(\frac{1}{3}, \frac{1}{3}, \frac{1}{3}\right) = \frac{1}{27} > 0,$$

(22) is the solution of the constrained maximization problem.

As this example shows, the solution of a constrained maximization problem usually involves breaking the first order conditions into a number of cases. It is often easiest to start with the nonnegativity constraints or the signs of the multipliers. In Example 18.9, we first worked with the case $\lambda_1 = 0$. Each case needs to be carried out until either a complete candidate for a solution is computed, including values for the multipliers, or a contradiction to one of the first order conditions is reached. While working with any given case, one might have to break that case into two subcases depending on whether or not a second inequality constraint is binding or not. In Example 18.9, while studying the case $\lambda_1 > 0$, we had to examine two subcases depending on the sign of x.

In economic theory, however, one rarely needs to compute the maxima or minima of a specific problem. One is usually more interested in studying the first order conditions which arise in a specific *type* of problem, since these can lead to interesting relationships between the variables of the problem or even to a general economic principle. We have provided a number of concrete examples and exercises in this chapter to make it easier to understand and work with the first order conditions of Theorem 18.4. In this vein, one more concrete example with inequality constraints is presented in the last section of this chapter.

EXERCISES

18.10   Find the maximizer of $f(x, y) = x^2 + y^2$, subject to the constraints $2x + y \leq 2$, $x \geq 0, y \geq 0$.

18.11   Find the maximizer of $f(x, y) = 2y^2 - x$, subject to the constraints $x^2 + y^2 \leq 1$, $x \geq 0, y \geq 0$.

18.12   Consider the problem of maximizing $f(x, y, z) = xyz + z$, subject to the constraints $x^2 + y^2 + z \leq 6, x \geq 0, y \geq 0, z \geq 0$.

  a) Write out a complete set of first order conditions for this problem.
  b) Determine whether or not the constraint $x^2 + y^2 + z \leq 6$ is binding at any solution.
  c) Find a solution of the first order conditions that includes $x = 0$.
  d) Find three equations in the three unknowns x, y, z that must be satisfied if $x \neq 0$ at the solution.
  e) Show that $x = 1, y = 1, z = 4$ satisfies these equations.

18.13   Show that the budget inequality constraint is binding in Example 18.8 even in the presence of the nonnegativity constraints $x_1 \geq 0$, $x_2 \geq 0$. In the process, check the NDCQ for this more general problem.

18.14   Allow more general prices and income in Example 18.9; in other words, change the constraint $x + y + z \leq 1$ to the constraint $p_1 x + p_2 y + p_3 z \leq I$.

18.4   MIXED CONSTRAINTS

As we noted in Example 18.8, some maximization problems involve both equality and inequality constraints. It is straightforward to combine the statements of Theorems 18.2 and 18.4 into one result which handles the general case.

Theorem 18.5   Suppose that $f, g_1, \ldots, g_k, h_1, \ldots, h_m$ are C^1 functions of n variables. Suppose that $\mathbf{x}^* \in \mathbf{R}^n$ is a local maximizer of f on the constraint set defined by the k inequalities and m equalities:

$$g_1(x_1, \ldots, x_n) \leq b_1, \ldots, \quad g_k(x_1, \ldots, x_n) \leq b_k,$$

$$h_1(x_1, \ldots, x_n) = c_1, \ldots, \quad h_m(x_1, \ldots, x_n) = c_m.$$

Without loss of generality, we can assume that the first k_0 inequality constraints are binding at $\mathbf{x}^*$ and that the other $k - k_0$ inequality constraints are not binding. Suppose that the following nondegenerate constraint qualification is satisfied at $\mathbf{x}^*$:

The rank at $\mathbf{x}^*$ of the Jacobian matrix of the equality constraints and the *binding* inequality constraints

$$\begin{pmatrix} \dfrac{\partial g_1}{\partial x_1}(\mathbf{x}^*) & \cdots & \dfrac{\partial g_1}{\partial x_n}(\mathbf{x}^*) \\ \vdots & \ddots & \vdots \\ \dfrac{\partial g_{k_0}}{\partial x_1}(\mathbf{x}^*) & \cdots & \dfrac{\partial g_{k_0}}{\partial x_n}(\mathbf{x}^*) \\ \dfrac{\partial h_1}{\partial x_1}(\mathbf{x}^*) & \cdots & \dfrac{\partial h_1}{\partial x_n}(\mathbf{x}^*) \\ \vdots & \ddots & \vdots \\ \dfrac{\partial h_m}{\partial x_1}(\mathbf{x}^*) & \cdots & \dfrac{\partial h_m}{\partial x_n}(\mathbf{x}^*) \end{pmatrix}$$

is $k_0 + m$ — as large as it can be.

Form the Lagrangian

$$L(x_1, \ldots, x_n, \lambda_1, \ldots, \lambda_k, \mu_1, \ldots, \mu_m)$$
$$\equiv f(\mathbf{x}) - \lambda_1[g_1(\mathbf{x}) - b_1] - \cdots - \lambda_k[g_k(\mathbf{x}) - b_k]$$
$$- \mu_1[h_1(\mathbf{x}) - c_1] - \cdots - \mu_m[h_m(\mathbf{x}) - c_m].$$

Then, there exist multipliers $\lambda_1^*, \ldots, \lambda_k^*, \mu_1^*, \ldots, \mu_m^*$ such that:

(a) $\dfrac{\partial L}{\partial x_1}(\mathbf{x}^*, \lambda^*) = 0, \ldots, \dfrac{\partial L}{\partial x_n}(\mathbf{x}^*, \lambda^*) = 0,$

(b) $\lambda_1^*[g_1(\mathbf{x}^*) - b_1] = 0, \ldots, \lambda_k^*[g_k(\mathbf{x}^*) - b_k] = 0,$

(c) $h_1(\mathbf{x}^*) = c_1, \ldots, h_m(\mathbf{x}^*) = c_m,$

(d) $\lambda_1^* \geq 0, \ldots, \lambda_k^* \geq 0,$

(e) $g_1(\mathbf{x}^*) \leq b_1, \ldots, g_k(\mathbf{x}^*) \leq b_k.$

Example 18.10   Consider the problem of maximizing $x - y^2$ on the constraint set $x^2 + y^2 = 4$, $x \geq 0$, $y \geq 0$. Checking the NDCQ, first note that the gradient of $x^2 + y^2$ is zero only at the origin, a point which is not in the constraint set. If either nonnegativity constraint is binding, then the solution candidate is $(2, 0)$ or $(0, 2)$. In both cases, the corresponding 2×2 Jacobian matrix of constraints has rank two. Therefore, the NDCQ will automatically be satisfied. Form the Lagrangian

$$L = x - y^2 - \mu(x^2 + y^2 - 4) + \lambda_1 x + \lambda_2 y.$$

The first order conditions become:

$$(1) \quad \frac{\partial L}{\partial x} = 1 - 2\mu x + \lambda_1 \quad = 0,$$

$$(2) \quad \frac{\partial L}{\partial y} = -2y - 2\mu y + \lambda_2 = 0,$$

$$(3) \quad x^2 + y^2 - 4 = 0,$$

$(4) \quad \lambda_1 x = 0,$ $\qquad\qquad (5) \quad \lambda_2 y = 0,$

$(6) \quad \lambda_1 \geq 0,$ $\qquad\qquad (7) \quad \lambda_2 \geq 0,$

$(8) \quad x \geq 0,$ $\qquad\qquad (9) \quad y \geq 0.$

Write 1 without minus signs as $1 + \lambda_1 = 2\mu x$. Since $\lambda_1 \geq 0$, $1 + \lambda_1 > 0$. Therefore, $\mu > 0$ and $x > 0$ (and $\lambda_1 = 0$). Write 2 as $2y(1 + \mu) = \lambda_2$. Since $1 + \mu > 0$, either both y and λ_2 are zero or both are positive. By 5, both cannot be positive. Therefore, $\lambda_2 = y = 0$. Now, $x = 2$ by 3 and 8, $\lambda_1 = 0$ by 4, and $\mu = 1/4$ by 1. This leads to the solution

$$(x, y, \mu, \lambda_1, \lambda_2) = (2, 0, 1/4, 0, 0).$$

EXERCISES

18.15   Maximize $3xy - x^3$ subject to the constraints $2x - y = -5, 5x + 2y \geq 37, x \geq 0,$ $y \geq 0$.

18.5   CONSTRAINED MINIMIZATION PROBLEMS

For the equality constrained problems that we considered in Section 18.2, the first order conditions for a minimization problem are the same as the first order conditions for a maximization problem. However, in Section 18.3 on *inequality* constrained problems, our discussion about the sign of the multiplier applied only to maximization problems. The same argument would show that if we wanted to minimize f instead of maximize it over the same constraint set, we would write the Lagrangian the same way but would require that the multipliers be ≤ 0. This fact is illustrated in Example 18.7 in which the minimizing points correspond to negative multipliers.

However, there is a more common way of treating constrained minimization problems. The inequality constraints in a minimization problem are usually presented as $g(\mathbf{x}) \geq b$, instead of as $g(\mathbf{x}) \leq b$ as they are in maximization problems. Therefore, we will use a formulation for minimization problems which takes advantage of this situation and which is a more natural analogue to our approach for maximization problems, especially for studying duality. We present this formulation as a theorem — the analogue of Theorem 18.5 for maximization problems.

Theorem 18.6 Suppose that $f, g_1, \ldots, g_k, h_1, \ldots, h_m$ are C^1 functions of n variables. Suppose that $\mathbf{x}^* \in \mathbf{R}^n$ is a local **minimizer** of f on the constraint set defined by the k inequalities and m equalities:

$$g_1(x_1, \ldots, x_n) \geq b_1, \ldots, g_k(x_1, \ldots, x_n) \geq b_k,$$

$$h_1(x_1, \ldots, x_n) = c_1, \ldots, h_m(x_1, \ldots, x_n) = c_m.$$

Without loss of generality, we can assume that the first k_0 inequality constraints are binding at $\mathbf{x}^*$ and that the other $k - k_0$ inequality constraints are not binding. Suppose that the following nondegenerate constraint qualification is satisfied at $\mathbf{x}^*$:

The rank at $\mathbf{x}^*$ of the Jacobian matrix of the equality constraints and the *binding* inequality constraints

$$\begin{pmatrix} \frac{\partial g_1}{\partial x_1}(\mathbf{x}^*) & \cdots & \frac{\partial g_1}{\partial x_n}(\mathbf{x}^*) \\ \vdots & \ddots & \vdots \\ \frac{\partial g_{k_0}}{\partial x_1}(\mathbf{x}^*) & \cdots & \frac{\partial g_{k_0}}{\partial x_n}(\mathbf{x}^*) \\ \frac{\partial h_1}{\partial x_1}(\mathbf{x}^*) & \cdots & \frac{\partial h_1}{\partial x_n}(\mathbf{x}^*) \\ \vdots & \ddots & \vdots \\ \frac{\partial h_m}{\partial x_1}(\mathbf{x}^*) & \cdots & \frac{\partial h_m}{\partial x_n}(\mathbf{x}^*) \end{pmatrix}$$

is $k_0 + m$ — as large as it can be.

Form the Lagrangian

$$L(x_1, \ldots, x_n, \lambda_1, \ldots, \lambda_k, \mu_1, \ldots, \mu_m)$$
$$\equiv f(\mathbf{x}) - \lambda_1[g_1(\mathbf{x}) - b_1] - \cdots - \lambda_k[g_k(\mathbf{x}) - b_k]$$
$$- \mu_1[h_1(\mathbf{x}) - c_1] - \cdots - \mu_m[h_m(\mathbf{x}) - c_m].$$

Then, there exist multipliers $\lambda_1^*, \ldots, \lambda_k^*, \mu_1^*, \ldots, \mu_m^*$ such that:

(a) $\frac{\partial L}{\partial x_1}(\mathbf{x}^*, \lambda^*) = 0, \ldots, \frac{\partial L}{\partial x_n}(\mathbf{x}^*, \lambda^*) = 0,$

(b) $\lambda_1^*[g_1(\mathbf{x}^*) - b_1] = 0, \ldots, \lambda_k^*[g_k(\mathbf{x}^*) - b_k] = 0,$

(c) $h_1(\mathbf{x}^*) = c_1, \ldots, h_m(\mathbf{x}^*) = c_m,$

(d) $\lambda_1^* \geq 0, \ldots, \lambda_k^* \geq 0,$ and

(e) $g_1(\mathbf{x}^*) \geq b_1, \ldots, g_k(\mathbf{x}^*) \geq b_k.$

To use this formulation, we need to write all the inequality constraints in the form $g(\mathbf{x}) \geq b$. For example, we would write the constraint $x^2 + y^2 \leq 5$ as the constraint $-(x^2 + y^2) \geq -5$. Note that in this case, the nonnegativity constraints are already in the right form; now, they enter the Lagrangian as $-\lambda_i x_i$.

Other texts may take other approaches to constrained min problems (and even to constrained max problems). Other possible formulations for constrained minimization problems are:

(1) Replace f by $-f$, because minimizing f is equivalent to maximizing $-f$. Otherwise, keep everything else the same as in the constrained max formulation, including the form of the inequality constraints.
(2) Put the multipliers in the Lagrangian with plus signs instead of with minus signs, keeping the constraints as they had been for the constrained maximization problem.

Example 18.11   Consider the problem

$$\text{minimize} \quad f(x, y) = 2y - x^2$$
$$\text{subject to} \quad x^2 + y^2 \leq 1, \quad x \geq 0, \quad y \geq 0. \tag{23}$$

Before writing the Lagrangian, we write the first constraint as $-x^2 - y^2 \geq -1$. Then, the Lagrangian is

$$L(x, y, \lambda_1, \lambda_2, \lambda_3,) = 2y - x^2 - \lambda_1(-x^2 - y^2 + 1) - \lambda_2 x - \lambda_3 y.$$

The first order conditions are

$$\frac{\partial L}{\partial x} = -2x + 2\lambda_1 x - \lambda_2 = 0, \tag{24}$$

$$\frac{\partial L}{\partial y} = 2 + 2\lambda_1 y - \lambda_3 = 0, \tag{25}$$

$$\lambda_1(-x^2 - y^2 + 1) = 0, \tag{26}$$

$$\lambda_2 x = 0, \quad \lambda_3 y = 0, \tag{27}$$

$$\lambda_1, \lambda_2, \lambda_3, \geq 0, \tag{28}$$

along with the original constraints (23).

An effective way to start the solution of such a system of equations and inequalities is to rewrite the $\partial L/\partial x_i = 0$ equations without minus signs. In this case, equations (24) and (25) become

$$2x + \lambda_2 = 2\lambda_1 x, \tag{29}$$

$$2 + 2\lambda_1 y = \lambda_3. \tag{30}$$

Since every variable in (29) and (30) is nonnegative, we can read immediately from (30) that $\lambda_3 \geq 2 > 0$. We conclude from (27) that $y = 0$ and from (30) that $\lambda_3 = 2$.

Next, we examine two cases, depending on the sign of x. If $x = 0$, then $\lambda_1 = 0$ by (26) and the fact that $y = 0$, and $\lambda_2 = 0$ by (24). Thus, $(x, y) = (0, 0)$ satisfies the first order conditions (24) to (28), and $f(0, 0) = 0$.

If $x > 0$, then $\lambda_2 = 0$ by (27), $\lambda_1 = 1$ by (29), and $x^2 + y^2 = 1$ by (26). Since $y = 0$, $x^2 = 1$; since $x \geq 0$, $x = 1$. The solution $(x, y) = (1, 0)$ of the first order conditions leads to the value $f(1, 0) = -1$ of the objective function. We conclude that $(x, y) = (1, 0)$ minimizes $f(x, y) = 2y - x^2$ on the constraint set (23).

EXERCISES

18.16 Check that the NDCQ are satisfied in Example 18.11.

18.17 Minimize $x^2 - 2y$ subject to the constraints $x^2 + y^2 \leq 1$, $x \geq 0$, $y \geq 0$.

18.18 Minimize $2x^2 + 2y^2 - 2xy - 9y$ on the constraint set

$$4x + 3y \leq 10, \quad y - 4x^2 \geq -2, \quad x \geq 0, \quad y \geq 0.$$

This is a rather complex problem, so we provide a few hints for its solutions. 1) As usual, first write out the Lagrangian and the complete set of first order conditions. 2) Rewrite the first two equations of the first order conditions without minus signs. 3) Examine each of the following three cases: $x = 0, y = 0$; $x > 0, y = 0$; and $x = 0, y > 0$, separately and show that each leads to a violation of the first order conditions. 4) Conclude that $x > 0$ and $y > 0$ and that each of their multipliers λ_3 and λ_4 are zero. 5) Look at four cases according to the positivity of λ_1 and λ_2. Show that each of the three cases: $\lambda_1 = 0, \lambda_2 = 0$; $\lambda_1 = 0, \lambda_2 > 0$; and $\lambda_1 > 0, \lambda_2 > 0$ leads to a contradiction of the first order conditions. 6) Compute the solution that corresponds to $\lambda_1 > 0$ and $\lambda_2 = 0$.

18.19 Present a geometric proof that in the problem of minimizing $f(x, y)$ on the constraint set $g(x, y) \geq b$, the gradient of f and the gradient of g point in the *same* direction at a minimizer for which the constraint is binding.

18.6 KUHN-TUCKER FORMULATION

The most common constrained maximization problems in economics involve only inequality constraints and a complete set of nonnegativity constraints:

$$\text{maximize} \quad f(x_1, \ldots, x_n)$$

$$\text{subject to} \quad g_1(x_1, \ldots, x_n) \leq b_1, \ldots, g_k(x_1, \ldots, x_n) \leq b_k, \tag{31}$$

$$x_1 \geq 0, \ldots, x_n \geq 0.$$

Notice that we have separated the nonnegativity constraints from the rest of the inequality constraints. This situation is so common that a special Lagrangian has been devised to handle it. Since the approach we are about to describe goes back to the pioneering work of Harold Kuhn and A. W. Tucker on inequality constrained maximization problems, it is known as the **Kuhn-Tucker formulation.**

We will assume throughout this section that the usual NDCQ holds at the solution $\mathbf{x}^*$ of problem (31). If we use the techniques of Section 18.3 to solve problem (31), we would write the Lagrangian as

$$L(\mathbf{x}, \lambda_1, \dots, \lambda_k, \nu_1, \dots, \nu_n)$$
$$= f(\mathbf{x}) - \lambda_1 \cdot [g_1(\mathbf{x}) - b_1] - \dots - \lambda_k \cdot [g_k(\mathbf{x}) - b_k] + \nu_1 x_1 + \dots + \nu_n x_n.$$

The corresponding first order conditions are

$$\frac{\partial L}{\partial x_1} = \frac{\partial f}{\partial x_1} - \lambda_1 \frac{\partial g_1}{\partial x_1} - \dots - \lambda_k \frac{\partial g_k}{\partial x_1} + \nu_1 = 0,$$
$$\vdots \qquad\qquad \vdots \qquad\qquad \vdots \qquad\qquad (32)$$
$$\frac{\partial L}{\partial x_n} = \frac{\partial f}{\partial x_n} - \lambda_n \frac{\partial g_1}{\partial x_n} - \dots - \lambda_k \frac{\partial g_k}{\partial x_n} + \nu_n = 0,$$

$$\lambda_1 (g_1(\mathbf{x}) - b_1) = -\lambda_1 \frac{\partial L}{\partial \lambda_1} = 0$$
$$\vdots \qquad \vdots \qquad \vdots \qquad\qquad (33)$$
$$\lambda_k (g_k(\mathbf{x}) - b_k) = -\lambda_k \frac{\partial L}{\partial \lambda_k} = 0,$$

$$\nu_1 x_1 = 0$$
$$\vdots \quad \vdots \qquad\qquad (34)$$
$$\nu_n x_n = 0,$$

$$\lambda_1, \dots, \lambda_k, \nu_1, \dots, \nu_n \geq 0,$$

plus the inequalities in (31).

Kuhn and Tucker worked with a Lagrangian $\tilde{L}$ which did *not* include the nonnegativity constraints:

$$\tilde{L}(\mathbf{x}, \lambda_1, \dots, \lambda_k) \equiv f(\mathbf{x}) - \lambda_1 \cdot [g_1(\mathbf{x}) - b_1] - \dots - \lambda_k \cdot [g_k(\mathbf{x}) - b_k]. \quad (35)$$

We will call $\tilde{L}$ the **Kuhn-Tucker Lagrangian.** Note that

$$L(\mathbf{x}, \lambda_1, \dots, \lambda_k, \nu_1, \dots, \nu_n) = \tilde{L}(\mathbf{x}, \lambda_1, \dots, \lambda_k) + \nu_1 x_1 + \dots + \nu_n x_n.$$

For $j = 1, \dots, n$, rewrite (32) as

$$\frac{\partial L}{\partial x_j} = \frac{\partial \tilde{L}}{\partial x_j} + \nu_j = 0, \tag{36}$$

or

$$\frac{\partial \tilde{L}}{\partial x_j} = -\nu_j \tag{37}$$

at the solution for each j. By (34), (37), and the equations $\nu_j \geq 0$,

$$\frac{\partial \tilde{L}}{\partial x_j} \leq 0 \quad \text{and} \quad x_j \frac{\partial \tilde{L}}{\partial x_j} = 0. \tag{38}$$

On the other hand, for any $\mathbf{x}$,

$$\frac{\partial \tilde{L}}{\partial \lambda_j} = \frac{\partial L}{\partial \lambda_j} = b_j - g_j(\mathbf{x}) \geq 0. \tag{39}$$

Combining (34), (38), and (39), we find that the first order conditions in terms of the Kuhn-Tucker Lagrangian are

$$\frac{\partial \tilde{L}}{\partial x_1} \leq 0, \dots, \quad \frac{\partial \tilde{L}}{\partial x_n} \leq 0, \quad \frac{\partial \tilde{L}}{\partial \lambda_1} \geq 0, \dots, \quad \frac{\partial \tilde{L}}{\partial \lambda_k} \geq 0,$$

$$\tag{40}$$

$$x_1 \frac{\partial \tilde{L}}{\partial x_1} = 0, \dots, x_n \frac{\partial \tilde{L}}{\partial x_n} = 0, \quad \lambda_1 \frac{\partial \tilde{L}}{\partial \lambda_1} = 0, \dots, \lambda_k \frac{\partial \tilde{L}}{\partial \lambda_k} = 0.$$

This formulation has some advantages over the formulation of Section 18.3. First, it involves $n + k$ equations in $n + k$ unknowns, compared with the $2n + k$ equations in $2n + k$ unknowns in system (32) to (34). However, in solving a specific numerical problem, as in the exercises at the end of Section 18.3, it is often easier to work with the ν_j's in the original formulation. A more important advantage of (40) is the symmetric way that the x_i's and λ_j's enter the first order conditions. This approach leads naturally to considerations of the dual problem to (31) — the minimization problem in which the λ_j's become the primary variables. The following theorem summarizes the observations of this section.

Theorem 18.7 Consider the constrained maximization problem (31) with no equality constraints and with a complete set of nonnegativity constraints. Form the Kuhn-Tucker Lagrangian $\tilde{L}$ as in (35). Suppose that $\mathbf{x}^*$ is a solution of (31) and that the matrix $(\partial g_i/\partial x_j)$ has maximal rank at $\mathbf{x}^*$, where the i's vary over the indices of the g_i-constraints that are binding at $\mathbf{x}^*$ and the j's range over the indices j for which $x_j^* > 0$. Then, there exist nonnegative multipliers $\lambda_1^*, \dots, \lambda_k^*$ such that $x_1^*, \dots, x_n^*, \lambda_1^*, \dots, \lambda_k^*$ satisfies the system of equalities and inequalities (40).

Example 18.12   In this framework, the Kuhn-Tucker Lagrangian for the usual utility maximization problem of Example 18.1 would be

$$\tilde{L}(x_1, x_2, \lambda) = U(x_1, x_2) - \lambda(p_1 x_1 + p_2 x_2 - I),$$

and the first order conditions are:

$$\frac{\partial U}{\partial x_1} - \lambda p_1 \leq 0, \qquad \frac{\partial U}{\partial x_2} - \lambda p_2 \leq 0,$$

$$x_1 \cdot \left(\frac{\partial U}{\partial x_1} - \lambda p_1\right) = 0, \qquad x_2 \cdot \left(\frac{\partial U}{\partial x_2} - \lambda p_1\right) = 0,$$

$$\frac{\partial \tilde{L}}{\partial \lambda} = I - p_1 x_1 - p_2 x_2 \geq 0, \qquad \lambda \frac{\partial \tilde{L}}{\partial \lambda} = \lambda(I - p_1 x_1 - p_2 x_2) = 0.$$

EXERCISES

18.20 Show that the usual NDCQ as applied to problem (31) leads to the constraint qualification in the statement of Theorem 18.7.

18.21 Write out the Kuhn-Tucker formulation for a constrained *minimization* problem.

18.7 EXAMPLES AND APPLICATIONS

Application: A Sales-Maximizing Firm with Advertising

Programming principles are used to determine the effect of such items as advertising, sales maximization, taxes, and government constraints on the optimal behavior of a firm. We close this chapter with two examples of such studies.

Suppose that a firm has its policies determined by a manager whose objective function is to maximize sales, i.e., revenue, without letting profit drop below some fixed level. To spice up the problem, let's add an advertising cost $a \in \mathbf{R}_+$. Let $R(y, a)$ denote the firm's revenue when the level of production is $y \in \mathbf{R}_+$ and the advertising cost is $a \in \mathbf{R}_+$. Let $C(y)$ denote the cost of manufacturing y units of output. We assume that C and R are C^1 functions, $C' > 0$, and $\partial R/\partial a > 0$. Our programming problem is to maximize $R(y, a)$ subject to the constraints

$$\Pi \equiv R(y, a) - C(y) - a \geq m, \quad y \geq 0, \quad a \geq 0.$$

Assume that (y^*, a^*) is an optimal solution with $y^* > 0$. Form the Lagrangian

$$L(y, a; \lambda_1, \lambda_2) \equiv R(y, a) + \lambda_1 a - \lambda_2(m - R(y, a) + C(y) + a).$$

Under the assumption that the NDCQ holds at (y^*, a^*), the first order conditions are

$$\frac{\partial L}{\partial y} = (1 + \lambda_2)\frac{\partial R}{\partial y} - \lambda_2 C'(y) = 0, \tag{41}$$

$$\frac{\partial L}{\partial a} = (1 + \lambda_2)\frac{\partial R}{\partial a} + \lambda_1 - \lambda_2 = 0, \tag{42}$$

$$\lambda_1 a = 0, \quad \text{and} \quad \lambda_2\big(m - R(y, a) + C(y) + a\big) = 0. \tag{43}$$

Since $\partial R/\partial a > 0$ and $\lambda_2 \geq 0$ in (42), $\lambda_1 - \lambda_2 < 0$. Since $\lambda_1 \geq 0$, λ_2 must be strictly positive. Therefore, $\Pi(y^*, a^*) = m$; *the profit realized is the minimal profit allowed.*

Since $\lambda_2 > 0$ and $C'(y^*) > 0$ in (41), $\partial R/\partial y > 0$, and the marginal revenue is positive at the optimal level. On the other hand, the marginal profit $\partial \Pi/\partial y$ is negative at (y^*, a^*), since by (41),

$$(1 + \lambda_2)\frac{\partial \Pi}{\partial y}(y^*, a^*) = (1 + \lambda_2)\left(\frac{\partial R^*}{\partial y} - C'(y)\right)$$

$$= \frac{\partial L}{\partial y}(y^*, a^*) - C'(y^*)$$

$$= 0 - C'(y^*)$$

$$< 0.$$

Consequently, *output y^* is greater than the output in the profit-maximizing situation.*

Application: The Averch-Johnson Effect

Consider the effect of a fair-rate-of-return regulatory constraint on the behavior of a monopolist firm that uses capital and labor to produce a single commodity. In this case, the price charged by the firm is subject to public control in that a regulatory agency ensures that, after the firm subtracts its operating expenses from its revenues, the remaining net revenue should just suffice to compensate the firm for its investment in plant and equipment. This example is due to H. Averch and L. Johnson (see chapter Notes), who applied their analysis to the Federal Communications Commission regulation of the telephone and telegraph industry.

Let $y = f(x_1, x_2)$ denote the amount of output produced from x_1 units of capital and x_2 units of labor. Suppose that production requires positive amounts of both capital and labor in that $y = 0$ if $x_1 = 0$ or $x_2 = 0$. Let $p(y)$ denote the inverse demand function and $R(y) = p(y)y$ the revenue from the sales of y units of output. Let r_1 denote the interest cost involved in holding one unit of plant and equipment, and let c_1 denote the acquisition cost per unit of plant and material. Let r_2 denote the wages paid per unit of labor. For simplicity, choose units so that $c_1 = 1$.

Now $c_1 x_1$ is the value of capital used in production, $r_2 x_2$ is the total cost of labor, and $(R(y) - r_2 x_2)/c_1 x_1$ is the rate of return on plant and equipment. The regulatory constraint is expressed by the fact that there is a constant $s_1 > 0$ such that

$$\frac{R(y) - r_2 x_2}{c_1 x_1} \leq s_1. \tag{44}$$

Assuming that the firm's objective is to maximize profit, the firm faces the following optimization problem:

$$\begin{aligned}
\text{maximize} \quad & \pi = R(f(x_1, x_2)) - r_1 x_1 - r_2 x_2 \\
\text{subject to} \quad & R(f(x_1, x_2)) - r_2 x_2 - s_1 x_1 \leq 0. \\
& x_1 \geq 0, \quad x_2 \geq 0
\end{aligned} \tag{45}$$

We write $R^*(x_1, x_2)$ for $R(f(x_1, x_2))$, the firm's revenue as a function of its inputs. We will assume that R^* has sufficient regularity so that the NDCQ is satsfied at solutions of (45). The Lagrangian for problem (45) is

$$L = R^*(x_1, x_2) - r_1 x_1 - r_2 x_2 - \lambda(R^*(x_1, x_2) - r_2 x_2 - s_1 x_1) + \nu_1 x_1 + \nu_2 x_2.$$

Necessary conditions for optimization are that there exist λ, ν_1, ν_2 all nonnegative such that

$$\frac{\partial L}{\partial x_1} = (1 - \lambda)\frac{\partial R^*}{\partial x_1} - r_1 + \lambda s_1 + \nu_1 = 0, \tag{46}$$

$$\frac{\partial L}{\partial x_2} = (1 - \lambda)\frac{\partial R^*}{\partial x_2} - (1 - \lambda)r_2 + \nu_2 = 0, \tag{47}$$

$$\lambda(R^*(x_1, x_2) - r_2 x_2 - s_1 x_1) = 0, \quad \nu_1 x_1 = 0, \quad \text{and} \quad \nu_2 x_2 = 0. \tag{48}$$

We first claim that the allowable rate of return s_1 must be greater than the cost of capital r_1 in order for the firm to realize any profit. Suppose $s_1 \leq r_1$. Then,

$$\begin{aligned}
\pi &= R^*(x_1, x_2) - r_1 x_1 - r_2 x_2 \\
&= (R^*(x_1, x_2) - s_1 x_1 - r_2 x_2) + (s_1 - r_1)x_1 \\
&\leq 0 + (s_1 - r_1)x_1 \quad \text{(by (44))} \\
&\leq 0.
\end{aligned}$$

Thus, we can assume that $s_1 > r_1$ and that x_1 and x_2 are positive, in which case, $\nu_1 = \nu_2 = 0$. This also means that $\lambda \neq 1$ in (46). We claim that λ must be less than 1. To see this, choose s_1 so large that the regulatory constraint is ineffective, that is, $\lambda = 0$. As s_1 tends back toward r_1, λ varies continuously, but it can never reach 1. Consequently, $0 \leq \lambda < 1$.

Since $\nu_2 = 0$ and $1 - \lambda \neq 0$ in (47),

$$\frac{\partial(p(y)y)}{\partial x_2} = r_2,$$

as in the unregulated situation. By (46),

$$\frac{\partial(p(y)y)}{\partial x_1} \leq \frac{r_1 - \lambda s_1}{1 - \lambda}$$

$$= r_1 - \frac{(1 - \lambda)}{(1 - \lambda)}r_1 + \frac{r_1 - \lambda s_1}{1 - \lambda}$$

$$= r_1 - \frac{\lambda(s_1 - r_1)}{1 - \lambda}.$$

If $\lambda > 0$ so that the regulatory constraint is binding, $\lambda/(1 - \lambda) > 0$. Since $s_1 - r_1 > 0$ too,

$$r_1 > \frac{\partial(p(y)y)}{\partial x_1}$$

at the maximizer. Therefore, input of capital is such that its marginal cost is greater than its marginal revenue product. The firm substitutes capital for labor and operates at a level of output where cost is not minimized. Thus, the regulatory constraint distorts the efficient relative proportions of capital and labor that would be used in the absence of the regulatory constraint.

One More Worked Example

We close this chapter on first order conditions by working out the solution of a rather complex constrained maximization problem with one inequality constraint and two nonnegativity constraints.

Example 18.13   Consider the problem of maximizing $f(x, y) = x^2 + x + 4y^2$ subject to the inequality constraints

$$2x + 2y \leq 1, \quad x \geq 0, \quad \text{and} \quad y \geq 0.$$

The Jacobian of the constraint functions is

$$\begin{pmatrix} 2 & 2 \\ -1 & 0 \\ 0 & -1 \end{pmatrix}.$$

At most two constraints can be binding at the same time, and any 2×2 submatrix of this Jacobian has rank two. Therefore, the NDCQ will hold at any solution candidate. Form the Lagrangian

$$L(x, y, \lambda_1, \lambda_2, \lambda_3) = x^2 + x + 4y^2 - \lambda_1(2x + 2y - 1) + \lambda_2 x + \lambda_3 y,$$

where we treat the nonnegativity constraints as in the previous example. Next, write the first order conditions:

$$1) \quad \frac{\partial L}{\partial x} = 2x + 1 - 2\lambda_1 + \lambda_2 = 0,$$

$$2) \quad \frac{\partial L}{\partial y} = 8y - 2\lambda_1 + \lambda_3 \quad = 0,$$

3) $\lambda_1(2x + 2y - 1) = 0,$ 4) $\lambda_2 x = 0,$ 5) $\lambda_3 y = 0,$

6) $\lambda_1 \geq 0,$ 7) $\lambda_2 \geq 0,$ 8) $\lambda_3 \geq 0,$

9) $2x + 2y \leq 1,$ 10) $x \geq 0,$ 11) $y \geq 0.$

Rewrite condition 1 without minus signs as $2x + 1 + \lambda_2 = 2\lambda_1$. Along with conditions 7 and 10, this equation implies that $2\lambda_1 \geq 1 > 0$, and this, by condition 3, implies that the first constraint is binding:

$$2x + 2y = 1. \tag{49}$$

Now we need to examine a few cases. Let's first look at the case $\lambda_2 > 0$. In this case, it follows from condition 4 that $x = 0$, from equation (49) that $y = 0.5$, and from condition 5 that $\lambda_3 = 0$. Plugging $y = 0.5$ and $\lambda_3 = 0$ into condition 2 yields $\lambda_1 = 2$. Plugging $x = 0$ and $\lambda_1 = 2$ into condition 1 yields $\lambda_2 = 3$. So, the assumption that $\lambda_2 > 0$ leads to the candidate

$$(x, y, \lambda_1, \lambda_2, \lambda_3) = (0, 0.5, 2, 3, 0).$$

Now, let's try the opposite case: $\lambda_2 = 0$. Combining conditions 1 and 2, we find

$$2x + 1 + \lambda_2 = 8y + \lambda_3 = 2\lambda_1. \tag{50}$$

Substituting $\lambda_2 = 0$ and $2x = 1 - 2y$ from equation (49), we find

$$1 - 2y + 1 = 8y + \lambda_3, \quad \text{or} \quad 2 = 10y + \lambda_3.$$

Combining the latter equation with condition 5 leads to the conclusion that either $y = 0$ or $\lambda_3 = 0$, but not both. If $y = 0$, then $\lambda_3 = 2$; by equation (49), $x = 0.5$; and by equation (50), $\lambda_1 = 1$. If, instead, $\lambda_3 = 0$, then $y = 0.2$, $x = 0.3$, and $\lambda_1 = 0.8$. Consequently, the case $\lambda_2 = 0$ leads to the two candidates

$$(x, y, \lambda_1, \lambda_2, \lambda_3) = \begin{cases} (0.5, 0, 1, 0, 2) & \text{or} \\ (0.3, 0.2, 0.8, 0, 0). \end{cases}$$

By evaluating the objective function at each of these three candidates, we find that the constrained maximum occurs at the point $x = 0$, $y = 0.5$, where $\lambda_1 = 2$, $\lambda_2 = 3$, and $\lambda_3 = 0$.

NOTES

See C. Simon, "Scalar and Vector Maximization: Calculus Techniques with Economic Applications," in (S. Reiter, ed.) *Studies in Mathematical Economics*, (Washington, D.C.: Mathematical Association of America, 1986), pp. 62–159, for an earlier version of the material in this chapter and Chapters 19, 21, and 22. For further discussion on the sales maximization application in Section 18.7, see W. J. Baumol, *Economic Theory and Operations Research* (Englewood Cliffs, N.J.: Prentice Hall, 1961); and H. Kuhn, "Lectures on mathematical economics," in G. Dantzig and A. Veinott (eds.), *Mathematics of the Decision Sciences,* American Math. Soc. Lectures in Applied Math., vol. 12, Providence, RI, 1968, pp. 49–84. The Averch-Johnson analysis is presented in H. Averch and L. Johnson, "Behavior of the firm under regulatory constraint," *American Economic Review* 52 (1962), 1052–1069. See E. E. Zajac, "Lagrange Multiplier Values at Constrained Optima," *Journal of Economic Theory* 4 (1972), 125–131, for a more careful and detailed argument that $0 \le \lambda < 1$ in the Averch-Johnson example.

Constrained Optimization II

This chapter continues our presentation of the central mathematical technique in economic theory: the solution of constrained optimization problems. The last chapter introduced the Lagrangian formulation of that solution and focused on its most important aspect: the first order conditions that form the basis of a large number of economic principles. This chapter looks at three other aspects of the Lagrangian approach:

(1) the sensitivity of the optimal value of the objective function to changes in the parameters of the problem,
(2) the second order conditions that distinguish maxima from minima, and
(3) the constraint qualifications that are a subtle but necessary hypothesis in the Lagrangian approach.

The last section of this chapter contains careful proofs of the basic first order conditions of the last chapter.

19.1 THE MEANING OF THE MULTIPLIER

In solving constrained optimization problems, we seem to be deriving extraneous information in the values of the multipliers $(\lambda_1^*, \ldots, \lambda_m^*)$. However, the multipliers play an important role in economic analysis — in some problems, a role at least as important as that of the maximizer itself. We will see in this section that the multipliers measure the sensitivity of the optimal value of the objective function to changes in the right-hand sides of the constraints and, as a result, they provide a natural measure of value for scarce resources in economics maximization problems.

One Equality Constraint

We return to the simplest problem — two variables and one equality constraint:

$$\text{maximize} \quad f(x, y)$$
$$\text{subject to} \quad h(x, y) = a \tag{1}$$

We will consider a as a parameter which varies from problem to problem. For any fixed value of a, write $(x^*(a), y^*(a))$ for the solution to problem (1), and write $\mu^*(a)$ for the multiplier which corresponds to this solution. Let $f(x^*(a), y^*(a))$ be the corresponding *optimal value* of the objective function. We prove that under reasonable conditions which hold for nearly all constrained maximization problems, $\mu^*(a)$ measures the rate of change of the optimal value of f with respect to the parameter a, or roughly speaking, the (infinitesimal) effect of a unit increase in a on $f(x^*(a), y^*(a))$.

Theorem 19.1 Let f and h be C^1 functions of two variables. For any fixed value of the parameter a, let $(x^*(a), y^*(a))$ be the solution of problem (1) with corresponding multiplier $\mu^*(a)$. Suppose that x^*, y^*, and μ^* are C^1 functions of a and that NDCQ holds at $(x^*(a), y^*(a), \mu^*(a))$. Then,

$$\mu^*(a) = \frac{d}{da} f(x^*(a), y^*(a)). \tag{2}$$

Proof The Lagrangian for problem (1) is

$$L(x, y, \mu; a) \equiv f(x, y) - \mu(h(x, y) - a), \tag{3}$$

with a entering as a parameter. By Theorem 18.1, the solution $(x^*(a), y^*(a), \mu^*(a))$ of (1) satisfies

$$0 = \frac{\partial L}{\partial x}(x^*(a), y^*(a), \mu^*(a); a)$$
$$= \frac{\partial f}{\partial x}(x^*(a), y^*(a), \mu^*(a)) - \mu^*(a)\frac{\partial h}{\partial x}(x^*(a), y^*(a), \mu^*(a)),$$
$$0 = \frac{\partial L}{\partial y}(x^*(a), y^*(a), \mu^*(a); a) \tag{4}$$
$$= \frac{\partial f}{\partial y}(x^*(a), y^*(a), \mu^*(a)) - \mu^*(a)\frac{\partial h}{\partial y}(x^*(a), y^*(a), \mu^*(a)),$$

for all a. Furthermore, since $h(x^*(a), y^*(a)) = a$ for all a,

$$\frac{\partial h}{\partial x}(x^*, y^*)\frac{dx^*}{da}(a) + \frac{\partial h}{\partial y}(x^*, y^*)\frac{dy^*}{da}(a) = 1 \tag{5}$$

for every a. Therefore, using the Chain Rule and equations (4) and (5),

$$\frac{d}{da} f(x^*(a), y^*(a)) = \frac{\partial f}{\partial x}(x^*(a), y^*(a)) \frac{dx^*}{da}(a) + \frac{\partial f}{\partial y}(x^*(a), y^*(a)) \frac{dy^*}{da}(a)$$

$$= \mu^* \frac{\partial h}{\partial x}(x^*(a), y^*(a)) \frac{dx^*}{da}(a) + \mu^* \frac{\partial h}{\partial y}(x^*(a), y^*(a)) \frac{dy^*}{da}(a)$$

$$= \mu^* \left[\frac{\partial h}{\partial x}(x^*(a), y^*(a)) \frac{dx^*}{da}(a) + \frac{\partial h}{\partial y}(x^*(a), y^*(a)) \frac{dy^*}{da}(a) \right]$$

$$= \mu^* \cdot 1. \quad \blacksquare$$

Example 19.1   In Example 18.5, we found that a maximizer of $f(x_1, x_2) = x_1^2 x_2$ on the constraint set $2x_1^2 + x_2^2 = 3$ is $x_1 = 1, x_2 = 1$, with multiplier $\mu = 0.5$. The maximum value of f is $f^* = f(1, 1) = 1$. Redo the problem, this time using the constraint $2x_1^2 + x_2^2 = 3.3$. The same computation as in Example 18.5 yields the solution $x_1 = x_2 = \sqrt{1.1}$, with maximum value $f^* = (1.1)^{3/2} \approx 1.1537$, an increase of 0.1537 over the original f^*.

On the other hand, Theorem 19.1 predicts that changing the right-hand side of the constraint by 0.3 unit would change the maximum value of the objective function by roughly

$$0.3 \cdot \mu = 0.3 \cdot 0.5 = 0.15 \text{ unit,}$$

an approximation correct to two decimal places.

Several Equality Constraints

The statement and proof of the natural generalization of Theorem 19.1 to several variables and several equality constraints is straightforward.

Theorem 19.2   Let $f, h_1, \ldots, h_m$ be C^1 functions on $\mathbf{R}^n$. Let $\mathbf{a} = (a_1, \ldots, a_m)$ be an m-tuple of exogenous parameters, and consider the problem $(P_\mathbf{a})$ of maximizing $f(x_1, \ldots, x_n)$ subject to the constraints

$$h_1(x_1, \ldots, x_n) = a_1, \ldots, h_m(x_1, \ldots, x_n) = a_m.$$

Let $x_1^*(\mathbf{a}), \ldots, x_n^*(\mathbf{a})$ denote the solution of problem $(P_\mathbf{a})$, with corresponding Lagrange multipliers $\mu_1^*(\mathbf{a}), \ldots, \mu_m^*(\mathbf{a})$. Suppose further that the x_i^*'s and μ_j^*'s are differentiable functions of $(a_1, \ldots, a_m)$ and that NDCQ holds. Then, for each $j = 1, \ldots, m$,

$$\mu_j^*(a_1, \ldots, a_m) = \frac{\partial}{\partial a_j} f(x_1^*(a_1, \ldots, a_m), \ldots, x_n^*(a_1, \ldots, a_m)). \qquad (6)$$

Inequality Constraints

Theorems 19.1 and 19.2 hold equally well for inequality constraints, as the following theorem indicates. For ease of exposition, we will assume that all the constraints under consideration are inequality constraints. The statement of the corresponding result for mixed constraints is straightforward.

Theorem 19.3   Let $\mathbf{a}^* = (a_1^*, \ldots, a_k^*)$ be a k-tuple. Consider the problem $(Q_{\mathbf{a}^*})$ of maximizing $f(x_1, \ldots, x_n)$ subject to the k inequality constraints

$$g_1(x_1, \ldots, x_n) \leq a_1^*, \ldots, g_k(x_1, \ldots, x_n) \leq a_k^*. \tag{7}$$

Let $x_1^*(\mathbf{a}^*), \ldots, x_n^*(\mathbf{a}^*)$ denote the solution of problem $(Q_{\mathbf{a}^*})$, and let $\lambda_1^*(\mathbf{a}^*)$, $\ldots, \lambda_k^*(\mathbf{a}^*)$ be the corresponding Lagrange multipliers. Suppose that as $\mathbf{a}$ varies near $\mathbf{a}^*$, $x_1^*, \ldots, x_n^*$, and $\lambda_1^*, \ldots, \lambda_k^*$ are differentiable functions of $(a_1, \ldots, a_k)$ and that the NDCQ holds at $\mathbf{a}^*$. Then, for each $j = 1, \ldots, k$,

$$\lambda_j^*(a_1^*, \ldots, a_k^*) = \frac{\partial}{\partial a_j} f(x_1^*(a_1^*, \ldots, a_k^*), \ldots, x_n^*(a_1^*, \ldots, a_k^*)). \tag{8}$$

Proof   (Sketch) For ease of notation, we write $\mathbf{a}^*$ simply as $\mathbf{a}$. As usual, we break the inequality constraints into two groups: the binding ones and the nonbinding ones. The binding constraints can be treated as equality constraints, and so we apply Theorem 19.2 to them. Let g_j be the constraint function for one of the *nonbinding* constraints: $g_j(\mathbf{x}^*(\mathbf{a})) < a_j$. Let C be the constraint set described by the inequalities (7). Let a_j' be any number such that

$$g_j(\mathbf{x}^*(\mathbf{a})) < a_j' < a_j;$$

and let C' be the constraint set described by inequalities (7) with $g_j(\mathbf{x}) \leq a_j'$ replacing $g_j(\mathbf{x}) \leq a_j$.

Since $\mathbf{x}^*(\mathbf{a})$ maximizes f on C, since $C' \subset C$, and since $\mathbf{x}^*(\mathbf{a}) \in C'$, it follows that $\mathbf{x}^*(\mathbf{a})$ maximizes f on C'. In other words, if

$$\mathbf{a}' = (a_1, \ldots, a_{j-1}, a_j', a_{j+1}, \ldots, a_k),$$

then $\mathbf{x}^*(\mathbf{a}') = \mathbf{x}^*(\mathbf{a})$ and therefore $f(\mathbf{x}^*(\mathbf{a}')) = f(\mathbf{x}^*(\mathbf{a}))$; that is, varying a_j a bit does not affect the maximum value of f. This implies that

$$\frac{\partial}{\partial a_j} f(x_1^*(a_1, \ldots, a_m), \ldots, x_n^*(a_1, \ldots, a_m)) = 0.$$

Since $\lambda_j^*(\mathbf{a})$ is zero too by Theorem 18.4, equation (8) still holds for nonbinding inequality constraints. ∎

Example 19.2   In Example 18.9, we computed that the max of xyz on the set

$$x + y + z \leq 1, \quad x \geq 0, \quad y \geq 0, \quad z \geq 0$$

occurs at $x = y = z = 1/3$, where $xyz = 1/27$. The four multipliers are 1/9, 0, 0, and 0, respectively.

   (*a*) If we change the first constraint to $x + y + z \leq 0.9$, we compute that
        the solution occurs at $x = y = z = 0.3$, where $xyz = 0.027$. Theorem
        19.3 predicts that the new optimal value would be

$$\frac{1}{27} + \frac{1}{9} \cdot \left(-\frac{1}{10} \right) \approx 0.0259,$$

        an estimate that is off by only .0011 or four percent.
   (*b*) If, instead, we change the second constraint from $x \geq 0$ to $x \geq 0.1$,
        we do not change the solution or the optimum value because the new
        region is a subset of the old region and it still contains the optimal point
        for the old region. This result is consistent with Theorem 19.3 since the
        multiplier for the (nonbinding) constraint $x \geq 0$ was zero.

Interpreting the Multiplier

Finally, we consider the central role that equation (8) plays in economic theory. Think of the objective function $f(\mathbf{x})$ in problem (Q_a) of Theorem 19.3 as the profit function of a firm and think of the a_j's on the right-hand sides of the constraints as representing the amounts available for inputs in the firm's production process. For example, in an activity analysis problem, we suppose that the firm's production process consists of n different productive activities and that x_i represents the level of intensity of activity i. Let $g_j(x_1, \ldots, x_n)$ denote the amount of input j that the firm requires to run activity one at level x_1, activity two at level x_2, and so forth. Let a_j denote the amount of input j available to the firm, leading to the inequality constraints $g_j(x_1, \ldots, x_n) \leq a_j$. Let $f(x_1, \ldots, x_n)$ denote the profits that the firm realizes from its products when it runs the activities at levels $x_1, \ldots, x_n$, respectively. In this situation,

$$\frac{\partial}{\partial a_j} f(x_1^*(\mathbf{a}), \ldots, x_n^*(\mathbf{a}))$$

represents the change in the optimal profit resulting from the availability of one more unit of input j. By (8), the jth multiplier $\lambda_j^*(\mathbf{a})$ represents this infinitesimal change. It tells how valuable another unit of input j would be to the firm's profits. Alternatively, it tells the maximum amount the firm would be willing to pay to acquire another unit of input j. For this reason, $\lambda_j^*(\mathbf{a})$ is often called the **internal value** or **imputed value**, or more frequently, the **shadow price** of input j. It may be a more important index to the firm than the external market price of input j.

EXERCISES

19.1 *a*) Find the maximum and minimum distance from the origin to the ellipse $x^2 + xy + y^2 = 3.3$.

  b) Use Theorem 19.1 and your answer to Exercise 18.2 to estimate the answers to part *a*.

19.2 Find the maximum of $x + y + z^2$ subject to the constraints $x^2 + y^2 + z^2 = 0.8$, $y = 0$:

  a) by using Theorem 19.1 and Exercise 18.6,

  b) by doing the calculation from scratch.

19.3 If x thousand dollars is spent on labor and y thousand dollars is spent on equipment, a certain factory produces $Q(x, y) = 50x^{1/2}y^2$ units of output.

  a) How should \$80,000 be allocated between labor and equipment to yield the largest possible output?

  b) Use Theorem 19.1 to estimate the change in maximum output if this allocation decreased by \$1000.

  c) Compute the exact change in b).

19.4 Use Theorem 19.3 and Exercise 18.11 to estimate the maximum value of $f(x, y) = 2y^2 - x$ on the constraint set $x^2 + y^2 \leq 0.9$, $x \geq 0$, and $y \geq 0$.

19.5 Use Theorem 19.3 and Exercise 18.12 to estimate the maximum value of $f(x, y, z) = xyz + z$ on the constraint set $x^2 + y^2 + z \leq 6.2$, $x \geq 0$, $y \geq 0$, and $z \geq 0$.

19.6 Use the Implicit Function Theorem to write out a specific inequality which would guarantee the validity of the assumption in Theorem 19.1 that the solution $(x(a), y(a))$ of Problem (1) depends smoothly on a.

19.7 Prove Theorem 19.2.

19.8 Write out the statement of the theorem which corresponds to Theorems 19.2 and 19.3, but for both equality and inequality constraints.

19.9 Write out the statement of the theorem which corresponds to Theorems 19.2 and 19.3 for a constrained minimization problem.

19.2 ENVELOPE THEOREMS

Theorems 19.1, 19.2, and 19.3 are special cases of a class of theorems which describe how the optimal value of the objective function in a parameterized optimization problem changes as one of the parameters change. Such theorems are called **Envelope Theorems**. We begin with the Envelope Theorem for unconstrained problems.

Unconstrained Problems

Theorem 19.4 Let $f(\mathbf{x}; a)$ be a C^1 function of $\mathbf{x} \in \mathbf{R}^n$ and the scalar a. For each choice of the parameter a, consider the unconstrained maximization problem

$$\text{maximize} \quad f(\mathbf{x}; a) \quad \text{with respect to} \quad \mathbf{x}. \tag{9}$$

Let $\mathbf{x}^*(a)$ be a solution of this problem. Suppose that $\mathbf{x}^*(a)$ is a C^1 function of a. Then,

$$\frac{d}{da} f(\mathbf{x}^*(a); a) = \frac{\partial}{\partial a} f(\mathbf{x}^*(a); a). \tag{10}$$

Proof   We compute via the Chain Rule that

$$\frac{d}{da} f(\mathbf{x}^*(a); a) = \sum_i \frac{\partial f}{\partial x_i} (\mathbf{x}^*(a); a) \cdot \frac{dx_i^*}{da}(a) + \frac{\partial f}{\partial a}(\mathbf{x}^*(a); a) \cdot 1$$

$$= \frac{\partial f}{\partial a}(\mathbf{x}^*(a); a),$$

since $\dfrac{\partial f}{\partial x_i}(\mathbf{x}^*(a); a) = 0$ for $i = 1, \dots, n$, by the usual first order conditions from Chapter 17. ∎

Notice the similarities between the proofs of Theorem 19.1 and Theorem 19.4. At first glance, conclusion (10) of Theorem 19.4 looks uninteresting because both sides of (10) seem so similar. But the *partial* derivative on the right-hand side of (10) is a lot easier to deal with than the *total* derivative on the left-hand side, as the following examples illustrate.

Example 19.3   Consider the problem of maximizing

$$f(x; a) = -a^3 x^4 + 15x^3 - e^a x^2 + 17$$

around $a = 1$. Since f is a quartic polynomial in x with a negative leading coefficient when $a = 1$, $f(x) \to -\infty$ as $x \to \pm\infty$. Therefore, f does have a finite global maximizer $x^*(a)$ for each value of a near 1. By (10),

$$\frac{d}{da} f(\mathbf{x}^*(a); a) = \frac{\partial}{\partial a} f(\mathbf{x}^*(a); a) = -3a^2 x^{*4} - e^a x^{*2},$$

which is negative at all a and all $x \neq 0$. So, even without solving for the optimal $x^*(a)$, we can tell that as a increases beyond 0, $f(x^*(a); a)$ is a decreasing function of a. The peak of the graph of the function $x \mapsto f(x; a)$ decreases as a increases.

Example 19.4   What will be the effect of a unit increase in a on the maximum value of $f(x; a) = -x^2 + 2ax + 4a^2$, where we maximize f with respect to x for each a? First, let's compute the answer directly. The equation for the maximizer of f is

$$f'(x) = -2x + 2a = 0;$$

so, $x^*(a) = a$. Plugging this into $f(x; a)$ leads to

$$f(x^*(a); a) = f(a, a) = -a^2 + 2a \cdot a + 4a^2 = 5a^2, \qquad (11)$$

which will increase at a rate of $10a$ as a increases.

If, instead, we had applied the envelope theorem, we could have skipped step (11) and found directly that

$$\frac{df^*}{da} = \frac{\partial f}{\partial a}(x^*(a); a)) = 2x + 8a = 10a,$$

since $x^*(a) = a$.

Example 19.5 A Silicon Valley firm produces an output of microchips denoted by y and has a cost function $c(y)$, with $c'(y) > 0$ and $c''(y) > 0$. Of the chips it produces, a fraction $1 - \alpha$ are unavoidably defective and cannot be sold. Working chips can be sold at a price p, and the microchip market is highly competitive. How will an increase in production quality affect the firm's profit?

The firm's profit function is

$$\pi(p, \alpha) = \max_{y}[p\alpha y - c(y)],$$

where "$\max_y$" means the maximum value as y varies. The conditions on the cost function guarantee that there is a nonzero profit-maximizing output $y^*(\alpha)$ which depends smoothly on α. The derivative of optimal profit π with respect to α is:

$$\frac{d\pi}{d\alpha} = \frac{\partial}{\partial \alpha}(p\alpha y - c(y)) = py > 0.$$

As one would suspect, increasing the fraction of nondefective chips will increase the firm's profit. Once again, we were able to determine this without actually solving for the optimal output.

Of course, Theorem 19.4 generalizes easily to the case where there is more than one parameter. One works with one parameter at a time and finds that

$$\frac{d}{da_i}f(x_1^*(\mathbf{a}), \ldots, x_n^*(\mathbf{a}); a_1, \ldots, a_k) = \frac{\partial}{\partial a_i}f(x_1^*(\mathbf{a}), \ldots, x_n^*(\mathbf{a}); a_1, \ldots, a_k).$$

Constrained Problems

The most general envelope theorem deals with *constrained* problems in which there are parameters in both the objective function and in the constraints. For example, consider the problem of maximizing $f(\mathbf{x}; a)$ subject to the constraints

$h_1(\mathbf{x}; a) = 0, \ldots, h_k(\mathbf{x}; a) = 0$. If f does not depend on a and if each $h_i(\mathbf{x}; a)$ can be written as $h_i(\mathbf{x}) - a$, then we are back to the situation in Theorem 19.2. So the case under consideration is more general than the other two cases we have looked at. However, the answer is nearly as straightforward. As the next theorem indicates, the rate of change of $f(\mathbf{x}^*(a); a)$ with respect to a equals the *partial* derivative with respect to a, not of f, but of the corresponding Lagrangian function.

Theorem 19.5   Let $f, h_1, \ldots h_k : \mathbf{R}^n \times \mathbf{R}^1 \to \mathbf{R}^1$ be C^1 functions. Let $\mathbf{x}^*(a) = (x_1^*(a), \ldots, x_n^*(a))$ denote the solution of the problem of maximizing $\mathbf{x} \longmapsto f(\mathbf{x}; a)$ on the constraint set

$$h_1(\mathbf{x}; a) = 0, \ldots, h_k(\mathbf{x}; a) = 0,$$

for any fixed choice of the parameter a. Suppose that $\mathbf{x}^*(a)$ and the Lagrange multipliers $\mu_1(a), \ldots, \mu_k(a)$ are C^1 functions of a and that the NDCQ holds. Then,

$$\frac{d}{da} f(\mathbf{x}^*(a); a) = \frac{\partial L}{\partial a}(\mathbf{x}^*(a), \mu(a); a), \tag{12}$$

where L is the natural Lagrangian for this problem.

Note, as in expression (10), that the left hand side of (12) is a total derivative while the right hand side is a partial derivative. The proof of Theorem 19.5 is similar to the proofs of Theorems 19.1 and Theorem 19.4 and will be left as an exercise.

Example 19.6   Change the constraint in Example 18.7 from $x^2 + y^2 \leq 1$ to $x^2 + 1.1\, y^2 \leq 1$, keeping the objective function $f(x, y) = xy$. If we write both constraints as $x^2 + ay^2 \leq 1$, the Lagrangian for the parameterized problem is

$$L(x, y, \lambda; a) = xy - \lambda(x^2 + ay^2 - 1).$$

The solution for the original $(a = 1)$ problem was $x = y = 1/\sqrt{2}$, $\lambda = 1/2$. The Envelope Theorem tells us that as a changes from 1 to 1.1, the optimal value of f changes by approximately

$$\frac{\partial L}{\partial a}\left(\frac{1}{\sqrt{2}}, \frac{1}{\sqrt{2}}, \frac{1}{2}; 1\right) \cdot (0.1).$$

Since

$$\frac{\partial L}{\partial a} = -\lambda y^2 = -\frac{1}{2} \cdot \left(\frac{1}{\sqrt{2}}\right)^2 = -\frac{1}{4},$$

the optimal value will decrease by approximately $.1/4 = .025$ to $.475$. One can calculate directly that the solution to the new problem is $x = 1/\sqrt{2}$, $y = 1/\sqrt{2.2}$, with maximum objective value of f approximately equal to 0.4767.

All the theorems in the last two sections had two basic hypotheses: the smooth dependence of the maximizers and multipliers on the parameters and the nondegenerate constraint qualification (NDCQ). In Section 19.4, we will look at these hypotheses more carefully and restate them in terms of properties of the objective and constraint functions of the problem.

EXERCISES

19.10 Write out a careful proof of Theorem 19.5.

19.11 Recover the statement of the Lagrange Multiplier Theorem (Theorem 19.1) from the statement of Theorem 19.5.

19.12 Use Exercise 18.2 and the Envelope Theorem to estimate the maximum and minimum distance from the origin to the ellipse $x^2 + xy + 0.9y^2 = 3$.

19.13 Use Example 18.13 and the Envelope Theorem to estimate the maximum value of $x^2 + x + 4.1y^2$ on the constraint set: $2x + 2y \le 1$, $x \ge 0$, $y \ge 0$.

19.3 SECOND ORDER CONDITIONS

In the analysis of an economic model, the *first order* conditions for a maximization problem often yield an economic principle. The corresponding *second order* conditions provide some fine tuning on these principles. For example, as we noted in Section 3.6, for a firm in a competitive industry, the first order condition for profit maximization implies that marginal revenue equals marginal cost at the profit-maximizing output. The second order condition for profit maximization requires that at the profit-maximizing output, the firm must be experiencing *increasing marginal cost*, as illustrated in Figure 19.1. From a computational point of view, the second order condition can often help choose a maximizer from the set of candidates which satisfy the first order conditions. For example, second order conditions would rule out $q = q_1$ as a profit-maximizing output in Figure 19.1.

Furthermore, the second order conditions in a maximization problem play a role in the comparative statics analysis of the solution of that problem. As just mentioned, the first order conditions describe the relationship that must occur between the exogenous variables and the endogenous variables at the optimizing solution. In comparative statics or sensitivity analysis, we ask how changes in the exogenous variables affect the optimal values of the endogenous variables. To answer this question, we call on the Implicit Function Theorem and compute total differentials of the first order conditions. We are then led naturally to working with

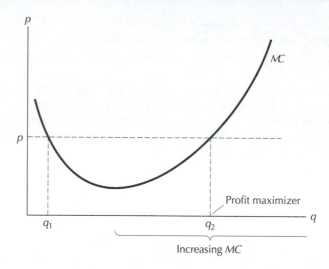

Figure 19.1

MC vs. price for a competitive industry.

a linear system of equations whose coefficient matrix is the matrix of the *second order* conditions of the original maximization problem. The sign of the determinant of that matrix becomes important, for example, when one uses Cramer's rule to solve the resulting system for the differentials of the endogenous variables. The next section illustrates this use of the second order conditions and relates this approach to the theorems of the first two sections.

In Section 17.3, we saw that the second order condition for maximizing an *unconstrained* function $f(x_1, \ldots, x_n)$ of n variables is that the Hessian of f at the maximizer $\mathbf{x}^*$

$$D^2 f(\mathbf{x}^*) = \begin{pmatrix} \dfrac{\partial^2 f}{\partial x_1^2} & \cdots & \dfrac{\partial f^2}{\partial x_n x_1} \\ \vdots & \ddots & \vdots \\ \dfrac{\partial f^2}{\partial x_1 x_n} & \cdots & \dfrac{\partial f^2}{\partial x_n^2} \end{pmatrix}$$

be negative definite. More precisely, at a maximum $f(\mathbf{x}^*)$, $Df(\mathbf{x}^*)$ must be zero and $D^2 f(\mathbf{x}^*)$ must be *negative semidefinite* (necessary conditions):

$$\mathbf{v}^T \left(D^2 f(\mathbf{x}^*) \right) \mathbf{v} \leq 0 \quad \text{for all nonzero vectors } \mathbf{v}.$$

To *guarantee* that a point $\mathbf{x}^*$ is a local maximizer, we need $Df(\mathbf{x}^*) = \mathbf{0}$ and $D^2 f(\mathbf{x}^*)$ *negative definite* (sufficient conditions):

$$\mathbf{v}^T \left(D^2 f(\mathbf{x}^*) \right) \mathbf{v} < 0 \quad \text{for all nonzero vectors } \mathbf{v}.$$

In this section we will focus on the sufficient second order conditions for *constrained* maximization and minimization problems. Just as the second order conditions for unconstrained problems lead to consideration of the definiteness of certain quadratic forms, the second order conditions for constrained problems are closely related to the definiteness of a quadratic form *restricted to a linear subspace* — material covered in Section 16.3.

Constrained Maximization Problems

Intuitively, the second order condition for a constrained maximization problem:

(1) should involve the negative definiteness of some Hessian matrix, but
(2) should only be concerned with directions along the constraint set.

For example, suppose that the objective function is a *quadratic* function $Q(\mathbf{x}) = \mathbf{x}^T H \mathbf{x} = \sum h_{ij} x_i x_j$ for some symmetric matrix $H = ((h_{ij}))$ and that the constraint set is defined by the system of *linear* equations $A\mathbf{x} = \mathbf{0}$. Since $\mathbf{0}$ is in the constraint set and since it is a critical point of Q, it is natural to ask whether $\mathbf{0}$ is the constrained max. Analytically, we want to know whether

$$0 \geq \mathbf{x}^T H \mathbf{x} \quad \text{for all} \quad \mathbf{x} \quad \text{such that} \quad A\mathbf{x} = \mathbf{0}.$$

As we saw in Chapter 16, we are asking whether Q is negative definite on the constraint set $A\mathbf{x} = \mathbf{0}$. The algebraic condition for determining whether or not $\mathbf{x}^T H \mathbf{x}$ is negative on the linear constraint set $A\mathbf{x} = \mathbf{0}$ involves the signs of certain leading principal minors of the *bordered matrix*:

$$\begin{pmatrix} 0 & A \\ A^T & H \end{pmatrix}.$$

For the problem of maximizing a general $f(\mathbf{x})$ subject to the possibly nonlinear equality constraints $h_1(\mathbf{x}) = c_1, \ldots, h_k(\mathbf{x}) = c_k$, the first order conditions entail finding the critical points of the Lagrangian function

$$L(x_1, \ldots, x_n, \mu_1, \ldots, \mu_k)$$
$$= f(\mathbf{x}) - \mu_1(h_1(\mathbf{x}) - c_1) - \cdots - \mu_k(h_k(\mathbf{x}) - c_k). \tag{13}$$

Let $(\mathbf{x}^*, \mu^*)$ be a critical point of L. We expect that the second order condition involves the negative definiteness of a quadratic form along a linear constraint set. A natural candidate for the quadratic form is the Hessian of the Lagrangian function with respect to $x_1, \ldots, x_n$. The natural linear constraint set for this problem is the hyperplane which is tangent to the constraint set $\{\mathbf{x} \in \mathbf{R}^n : \mathbf{h}(\mathbf{x}) = \mathbf{c}\}$ at the point $\mathbf{x}^*$.

The following theorem states that these natural candidates do indeed yield the proper second order sufficient conditions for a constrained max. First, recall (Theorem 15.6) that the tangent space to $\{\mathbf{h}(\mathbf{x}) = \mathbf{c}\}$ at the point $\mathbf{x}^*$ is the set of vectors $\mathbf{v}$ such that $D\mathbf{h}(\mathbf{x}^*)\mathbf{v} = \mathbf{0}$ (considered as vectors with their tails at $\mathbf{x}^*$). To see this, let $\mathbf{x}(t)$ be a curve at $\mathbf{x}^*$ on this constraint set with tangent vector $\mathbf{v}$, so that $\mathbf{x}(0) = \mathbf{x}^*$, $\mathbf{x}'(0) = \mathbf{v}$, and $\mathbf{h}(\mathbf{x}(t)) = \mathbf{c}$. Then, by the Chain Rule,

$$0 = \frac{d}{dt}\mathbf{h}(\mathbf{x}(t))\bigg|_{t=0} = D\mathbf{h}(\mathbf{x}(0)) \cdot \mathbf{x}'(0) = D\mathbf{h}(\mathbf{x}^*)\mathbf{v};$$

in words, the tangent vector $\mathbf{v}$ to any curve in the constraint set $\{h(\mathbf{x}) = c\}$ satisfies $D\mathbf{h}(\mathbf{x}^*)\mathbf{v} = \mathbf{0}$.

Theorem 19.6   Let $f, h_1, \ldots, h_k$ be C^2 functions on $\mathbf{R}^n$. Consider the problem of maximizing f on the constraint set

$$C_h \equiv \{\mathbf{x} : h_1(\mathbf{x}) = c_1, \ldots, h_k(\mathbf{x}) = c_k\}.$$

Form the Lagrangian (13), and suppose that:

(a) $\mathbf{x}^*$ lies in the constraint set C_h,
(b) there exist $\mu_1^*, \ldots, \mu_k^*$ such that

$$\frac{\partial L}{\partial x_1} = 0, \ldots, \frac{\partial L}{\partial x_n} = 0, \frac{\partial L}{\partial \mu_1} = 0, \ldots, \frac{\partial L}{\partial \mu_k} = 0$$

at $(x_1^*, \ldots, x_n^*, \mu_1^*, \ldots, \mu_k^*)$.
(c) the Hessian of L with respect to $\mathbf{x}$ at $(\mathbf{x}^*, \mu^*)$, $D_\mathbf{x}^2 L(\mathbf{x}^*, \mu^*)$, is negative definite on the linear constraint set $\{\mathbf{v} : D\mathbf{h}(\mathbf{x}^*)\mathbf{v} = \mathbf{0}\}$; that is,

$$\mathbf{v} \neq \mathbf{0} \quad \text{and} \quad D\mathbf{h}(\mathbf{x}^*)\mathbf{v} = \mathbf{0} \Longrightarrow \mathbf{v}^T(D_\mathbf{x}^2 L(\mathbf{x}^*, \mu^*))\mathbf{v} < 0. \quad (14)$$

Then, $\mathbf{x}^*$ is a strict local constrained max of f on C_h.

In Section 16.3 we learned the condition on bordered matrices for verifying second order condition (14). Border the $n \times n$ Hessian $D_\mathbf{x}^2 L(\mathbf{x}^*, \mu^*)$ with the $k \times n$ constraint matrix $D\mathbf{h}(\mathbf{x}^*)$:

$$H \equiv \begin{pmatrix} \mathbf{0} & D\mathbf{h}(\mathbf{x}^*) \\ D\mathbf{h}(\mathbf{x}^*)^T & D_\mathbf{x}^2 L(\mathbf{x}^*, \mu^*) \end{pmatrix}$$

$$= \begin{pmatrix} 0 & \cdots & 0 & | & \frac{\partial h_1}{\partial x_1} & \cdots & \frac{\partial h_1}{\partial x_n} \\ \vdots & \ddots & \vdots & | & \vdots & \ddots & \vdots \\ 0 & \cdots & 0 & | & \frac{\partial h_k}{\partial x_1} & \cdots & \frac{\partial h_k}{\partial x_n} \\ - & - & - & - & - & - & - \\ \frac{\partial h_1}{\partial x_1} & \cdots & \frac{\partial h_k}{\partial x_1} & | & \frac{\partial^2 L}{\partial x_1^2} & \cdots & \frac{\partial^2 L}{\partial x_n x_1} \\ \vdots & \ddots & \vdots & | & \vdots & \ddots & \vdots \\ \frac{\partial h_1}{\partial x_n} & \cdots & \frac{\partial h_k}{\partial x_n} & | & \frac{\partial^2 L}{\partial x_1 x_n} & \cdots & \frac{\partial^2 L}{\partial x_n^2} \end{pmatrix}. \quad (15)$$

If the last $(n - k)$ *leading principal minors* of matrix (15) alternate in sign, with the sign of the determinant of the $(k + n) \times (k + n)$ matrix H in (15) the same as the sign of $(-1)^n$, then condition c of Theorem 19.6 holds.

As one more indication of the naturalness of the statement of Theorem 19.6, note that the Hessian of the Lagrangian (13) with respect to *all* $(n + k)$ variables $\mu_1, \ldots, \mu_k, x_1, \ldots, x_n$ is

$$
D^2_{(\mu, x)}L = \begin{pmatrix}
0 & \cdots & 0 & | & -\dfrac{\partial h_1}{\partial x_1} & \cdots & -\dfrac{\partial h_1}{\partial x_n} \\
\vdots & \ddots & \vdots & | & \vdots & \ddots & \vdots \\
0 & \cdots & 0 & | & -\dfrac{\partial h_k}{\partial x_1} & \cdots & -\dfrac{\partial h_k}{\partial x_n} \\
\overline{} & \overline{} & \overline{} & & \overline{} & & \overline{} \\
-\dfrac{\partial h_1}{\partial x_1} & \cdots & -\dfrac{\partial h_k}{\partial x_1} & | & \dfrac{\partial^2 L}{\partial x_1^2} & \cdots & \dfrac{\partial^2 L}{\partial x_n x_1} \\
\vdots & \ddots & \vdots & | & \vdots & \ddots & \vdots \\
-\dfrac{\partial h_1}{\partial x_n} & \cdots & -\dfrac{\partial h_k}{\partial x_n} & | & \dfrac{\partial^2 L}{\partial x_1 x_n} & \cdots & \dfrac{\partial^2 L}{\partial x_n^2}
\end{pmatrix}, \tag{16}
$$

since $\dfrac{\partial^2 L}{\partial x_i \partial \mu_j} = -\dfrac{\partial h_j}{\partial x_i}$. If we multiply each of the last n rows and each of the last n columns in (16) by -1, we will not change the sign of $\det D^2L$ or of any of its principal minors since this process involves an even number of multiplications by -1 in every case. The result is the bordered Hessian (15). So, the bordered Hessian H in (15) has the same principal minors as the full Hessian (16) of the Lagrangian L. Recall, however, that the second order condition for the constrained maximization problem involves checking only the last $n - k$ of the $n + k$ leading principal minors of $D^2_{(x, \mu)}L$.

Let's work out the proof of Theorem 19.6 for the simplest constrained maximization problem: two variables and one equality constraint. The proof for the general case is presented in Chapter 30.

Theorem 19.7   Let f and h be C^2 functions on $\mathbf{R}^2$. Consider the problem of maximizing f on the constraint set $C_h = \{ (x, y) : h(x, y) = c\}$. Form the Lagrangian

$$L(x, y, \mu) = f(x, y) - \mu(h(x, y) - c).$$

Suppose that (x^*, y^*, μ^*) satisfies:

(a) $\dfrac{\partial L}{\partial x} = 0, \quad \dfrac{\partial L}{\partial y} = 0, \quad \dfrac{\partial L}{\partial \mu} = 0 \quad$ at $(x^*, y^*, \mu^*), \quad$ and

(b) $\det \begin{vmatrix} 0 & \dfrac{\partial h}{\partial x} & \dfrac{\partial h}{\partial y} \\[2mm] \dfrac{\partial h}{\partial x} & \dfrac{\partial^2 L}{\partial x^2} & \dfrac{\partial^2 L}{\partial x \partial y} \\[2mm] \dfrac{\partial h}{\partial y} & \dfrac{\partial^2 L}{\partial y \partial x} & \dfrac{\partial^2 L}{\partial y^2} \end{vmatrix} > 0$ at (x^*, y^*, μ^*).

Then, (x^*, y^*) is a local *max* of f on C_h.

Proof Condition b implies that

$$\frac{\partial h}{\partial x}(x^*, y^*) \neq 0 \quad \text{or} \quad \frac{\partial h}{\partial y}(x^*, y^*) \neq 0.$$

We assume that $(\partial h / \partial y)(x^*, y^*) \neq 0$, without loss of generality. Then, by the Implicit Function Theorem (Theorem 15.1), the constraint set C_h can be considered as the graph of a C^1 function $y = \phi(x)$ around (x^*, y^*); in other words,

$$h(x, \phi(x)) = C \quad \text{for all } x \text{ near } x^*. \tag{17}$$

Differentiating (17) yields

$$\frac{\partial h}{\partial x}(x, \phi(x)) + \frac{\partial h}{\partial y}(x, \phi(x)) \, \phi'(x) = 0 \tag{18}$$

or

$$\phi'(x) = -\frac{\dfrac{\partial h}{\partial x}(x, \phi(x))}{\dfrac{\partial h}{\partial y}(x, \phi(x))}. \tag{19}$$

Let

$$F(x) \equiv f(x, \phi(x)) \tag{20}$$

be f evaluated on C_h, a function of *one* unconstrained variable. By the usual first and second order conditions for such functions, if $F'(x^*) = 0$ and $F''(x^*) < 0$, then x^* will be a strict local max of F and $(x^*, y^*) = (x^*, \phi(x^*))$ will be a local constrained max of f.

So, we compute $F'(x^*)$ and $F''(x^*)$. Now,

$$F'(x) = \frac{\partial f}{\partial x}(x, \phi(x)) + \frac{\partial f}{\partial y}(x, \phi(x))\phi'(x). \tag{21}$$

Multiply equation (18) by $-\mu^*$ and add it to (21), evaluating both at $x = x^*$:

$$F'(x^*) = \left(\frac{\partial f}{\partial x}(x^*, y^*) - \mu^* \frac{\partial h}{\partial x}(x^*, y^*)\right)$$

$$+ \phi'(x^*)\left(\frac{\partial f}{\partial y}(x^*, y^*) - \mu^* \frac{\partial h}{\partial y}(x^*, y^*)\right) \qquad (22)$$

$$= \frac{\partial L}{\partial x}(x^*, y^*) + \phi'(x^*)\frac{\partial L}{\partial y}(x^*, y^*).$$

By hypothesis a of the theorem, $F'(x^*) = 0$.

Now, take another derivative of $F(x)$ at x^*, setting $y^* = \phi(x^*)$ in (22):

$$F''(x^*) = \frac{\partial^2 L}{\partial x^2} + 2\frac{\partial^2 L}{\partial x \partial y}\, \phi'(x^*) + \frac{\partial^2 L}{\partial y^2}\, \phi'(x^*)^2$$

$$= \frac{\partial^2 L}{\partial x^2} + 2\frac{\partial^2 L}{\partial x \partial y}\left(-\frac{\partial h/\partial x}{\partial h/\partial y}\right) + \frac{\partial^2 L}{\partial y^2}\left(-\frac{\partial h/\partial x}{\partial h/\partial y}\right)^2 \qquad \text{by (19)}$$

$$= \frac{1}{\left(\frac{\partial h}{\partial y}\right)^2}\left[\frac{\partial^2 L}{\partial x^2}\left(\frac{\partial h}{\partial y}\right)^2 - 2\frac{\partial^2 L}{\partial x \partial y}\frac{\partial h}{\partial x}\frac{\partial h}{\partial y} + \frac{\partial^2 L}{\partial y^2}\left(\frac{\partial h}{\partial x}\right)^2\right]$$

which is negative, by hypothesis b of the theorem.

Since $F'(x^*) = 0$ and $F''(x^*) < 0$,

$$x \longmapsto F(x) = f(x, \phi(x))$$

has a local max at x^*, and therefore, f restricted to C_h has a local max at (x^*, y^*).
∎

Minimization Problems

Remark   We have been concentrating on constrained *maximization* problems, up to this point. The second order conditions for a constrained *minimization* problem involve the *positive* definiteness of $D_x^2 L(x^*, \mu^*)$ on the nullspace of $Dh(x^*)$ — replacing (14) by

$$\mathbf{v} \neq \mathbf{0} \quad \text{and} \quad Dh(x^*)\mathbf{v} = \mathbf{0} \Longrightarrow \mathbf{v}^T(D_x^2 L(x^*, \mu^*))\mathbf{v} > 0 \qquad (23)$$

in the statement of Theorem 19.6. By our discussion in Section 16.3, the bordered Hessian conditions for (23) are that the last $(n - k)$ leading principal minors of (15) all have the *same* sign as $(-1)^k$, where k is the number of constraints. For the case $n = 2$ and $k = 1$ in Theorem 19.7, this positive definiteness condition requires that the determinant in Condition b of Theorem 19.7 be negative.

Example 19.7   In Example 18.5, we considered the problem of maximizing $f(x_1, x_2) = x_1^2 x_2$ on the constraint set $h(x_1, x_2) = 2x_1^2 + x_2^2 = 3$. There, we found six solutions to the first order conditions (18.11):

$$(x_1, x_2, \mu) = \begin{cases} (0, \pm\sqrt{3}, 0) \\ (\pm 1, +1, +.5) \\ (\pm 1, -1, -.5). \end{cases}$$

Let us use second order conditions to decide which of these points are local maxima and which are local minima.

Differentiate the first order conditions (18.11) once again to obtain the general bordered Hessian

$$H = \begin{pmatrix} 0 & h_{x_1} & h_{x_2} \\ h_{x_1} & L_{x_1 x_1} & L_{x_1 x_2} \\ h_{x_2} & L_{x_2 x_1} & L_{x_2 x_2} \end{pmatrix} = \begin{pmatrix} 0 & 4x_1 & 2x_2 \\ 4x_1 & 2x_2 - 4\mu & 2x_1 \\ 2x_2 & 2x_1 & -2\mu \end{pmatrix}.$$

This problem has $n = 2$ variables and $k = 1$ equality constraint. As Theorem 19.7 indicates, we need only check the sign of $n - k = 1$ determinant — the determinant of H itself. If $\det H$ has the same sign as $(-1)^n = +1$, that is, if $\det H > 0$, at a candidate point, that point is a local max. If $\det H$ has the same sign as $(-1)^k = -1$, that is, if $\det H < 0$, at the candidate point, that point is a local min.

At the points $(\pm 1, -1, -0.5)$,

$$H = \begin{pmatrix} 0 & \pm 4 & 2 \\ \pm 4 & 0 & \pm 2 \\ -2 & \pm 2 & 1 \end{pmatrix}.$$

In either case, $\det H = -16$; so these two points are local minima.

At the points $(\pm 1, 1, 0.5)$,

$$H = \begin{pmatrix} 0 & \pm 4 & 2 \\ \pm 4 & 0 & \pm 2 \\ 2 & \pm 2 & -1 \end{pmatrix}.$$

In either case, $\det H = +48$; so these two points are local maxima.

These computations support the observations we made at the end of Example 18.5. However, we were not able to determine the character of $(x_1, x_2) = (0, \pm\sqrt{3})$ by simply plugging these points into the objective function in Example 18.5. Since $\mu = 0$ for these points, the corresponding bordered Hessian is

$$H = \begin{pmatrix} 0 & 0 & \pm 2\sqrt{3} \\ 0 & \pm 2\sqrt{3} & 0 \\ \pm 2\sqrt{3} & 0 & 0 \end{pmatrix}.$$

For $(x_1, x_2) = (0, +\sqrt{3})$, $\det H = -24\sqrt{3} < 0$; this point is a local min. For $(x_1, x_2) = (0, -\sqrt{3})$, $\det H = +24\sqrt{3} > 0$; this point is a local max. These calculations, which should agree with the conclusions of the geometric approach in Exercise 18.1, illustrate that extrema computed via first and second order conditions of Theorem 19.6 need not be *global* extrema.

Example 19.8   Consider the problem of maximizing $x^2y^2z^2$ subject to the constraint $x^2 + y^2 + z^2 = 3$, a special case of Exercise 18.9. The first order conditions are

$$\frac{\partial L}{\partial x} = 2xy^2z^2 - 2\mu x \quad = 0$$

$$\frac{\partial L}{\partial y} = 2x^2yz^2 - 2\mu y \quad = 0$$

$$\frac{\partial L}{\partial z} = 2x^2y^2z - 2\mu z \quad = 0$$

$$-\frac{\partial L}{\partial \mu} = x^2 + y^2 + z^2 - 3 = 0$$

with solution $x^2 = y^2 = z^2 = \mu = 1$. The bordered Hessian for this problem is

$$\begin{pmatrix} 0 & 2x & 2y & 2z \\ 2x & 2y^2z^2 - 2\mu & 4xyz^2 & 4xy^2z \\ 2y & 4xyz^2 & 2x^2z^2 - 2\mu & 4x^2yz \\ 2z & 4xy^2z & 4x^2yz & 2x^2y^2 - 2\mu \end{pmatrix}.$$

At $x = y = z = \mu = 1$, the bordered Hessian becomes

$$\begin{pmatrix} 0 & 2 & 2 & | & 2 \\ 2 & 0 & 4 & | & 4 \\ 2 & 4 & 0 & | & 4 \\ \hline 2 & 4 & 4 & & 0 \end{pmatrix} \tag{24}$$

Since $n = 3$ and $k = 1$, we have to check the signs of two leading principal minors: the 3×3 submatrix H_3 above the dashed lines in (24) and the complete 4×4 matrix H_4 in (24). One computes that $\det H_3 = 32$ and $\det H_4 = -192$. Since these determinants alternate in sign and since the sign of $\det H_4$ is the sign of $(-1)^3 = -1$, the candidate $x = y = z = 1$ is indeed local constrained max by Theorem 19.6.

Inequality Constraints

To include inequality constraints in the statement of Theorem 19.6, we call on the natural techniques that we used at this stage of our discussion of first order conditions, in Section 18.3. Given a solution $(\mathbf{x}^*, \lambda^*)$ of the first order conditions, divide the inequality constraints into binding constraints and nonbinding constraints at $\mathbf{x}^*$. On the one hand, we treat the binding inequality constraints like equality constraints; on the other hand, the multipliers for the nonbinding constraints must be zero and these constraints drop out of the Lagrangian. The following theorem summarizes these considerations for a constrained maximization problem.

Theorem 19.8   Let $f, g_1, \ldots, g_m, h_1, \ldots, h_k$ be C^2 functions on $\mathbf{R}^n$. Consider the problem of maximizing f on the constraint set

$$C_{g,h} \equiv \{\, \mathbf{x} : g_1(\mathbf{x}) \leq b_1, \ldots, g_m(\mathbf{x}) \leq b_m, \ h_1(\mathbf{x}) = c_1, \ldots, h_k(\mathbf{x}) = c_k \}.$$

Form the Lagrangian

$$L(x_1, \ldots, x_n, \lambda_1, \ldots, \lambda_m, \mu_1, \ldots, \mu_k)$$
$$= f(\mathbf{x}) - \lambda_1\big(g_1(\mathbf{x}) - b_1\big) - \cdots - \lambda_m\big(g_m(\mathbf{x}) - b_m\big)$$
$$- \mu_1\big(h_1(\mathbf{x}) - c_1\big) - \cdots - \mu_k\big(h_k(\mathbf{x}) - c_k\big).$$

(a) Suppose that there exist $\lambda_1^*, \ldots, \lambda_m^*, \mu_1^*, \ldots, \mu_k^*$ such that the first order conditions of Theorem 18.5 are satisfied; that is,

$$\frac{\partial L}{\partial x_1} = 0, \ldots, \frac{\partial L}{\partial x_n} = 0, \quad \text{at } (\mathbf{x}^*, \lambda^*, \mu^*),$$

$$\lambda_1^* \geq 0, \ldots, \lambda_m^* \geq 0,$$

$$\lambda_1^*\big(g_1(\mathbf{x}^*) - b_1\big) = 0, \ldots, \lambda_m^*\big(g_m(\mathbf{x}^*) - b_m\big) = 0,$$

$$h_1(\mathbf{x}^*) = c_1, \ldots, h_k(\mathbf{x}^*) = c_k.$$

(b) For notation's sake, suppose that $g_1, \ldots, g_e$ are binding at $\mathbf{x}^*$ and $g_{e+1}, \ldots, g_m$ are not binding. Write $(g_1, \ldots, g_e)$ as $\mathbf{g}_E$. Suppose that the Hessian of L with respect to $\mathbf{x}$ at $(\mathbf{x}^*, \lambda^*, \mu^*)$ is negative definite on the linear constraint set

$$\{\, \mathbf{v} : D\mathbf{g}_E(\mathbf{x}^*)\mathbf{v} = \mathbf{0} \quad \text{and} \quad D\mathbf{h}(\mathbf{x}^*)\mathbf{v} = \mathbf{0} \}$$

that is, $\mathbf{v} \neq \mathbf{0}, \quad D\mathbf{g}_E(\mathbf{x}^*)\mathbf{v} = \mathbf{0}, \quad D\mathbf{h}(\mathbf{x}^*)\mathbf{v} = \mathbf{0}$

$$\Longrightarrow \mathbf{v}^T \cdot \big(D_{\mathbf{x}}^2 L(\mathbf{x}^*, \lambda^*, \mu^*)\big) \cdot \mathbf{v} < 0.$$

Then $\mathbf{x}^*$ is a strict local constrained max of f on $C_{g,h}$.

To check condition (b), form the **bordered Hessian**

$$
\begin{pmatrix}
0 & \cdots & 0 & 0 & \cdots & 0 & \bigg| & \dfrac{\partial g_1}{\partial x_1} & \cdots & \dfrac{\partial g_1}{\partial x_n} \\
\vdots & \ddots & \vdots & \vdots & \ddots & \vdots & \bigg| & \vdots & \ddots & \vdots \\
0 & \cdots & 0 & 0 & \cdots & 0 & \bigg| & \dfrac{\partial g_e}{\partial x_1} & \cdots & \dfrac{\partial g_e}{\partial x_n} \\
0 & \cdots & 0 & 0 & \cdots & 0 & \bigg| & \dfrac{\partial h_1}{\partial x_1} & \cdots & \dfrac{\partial h_1}{\partial x_n} \\
\vdots & \ddots & \vdots & \vdots & \ddots & \vdots & \bigg| & \vdots & \ddots & \vdots \\
0 & \cdots & 0 & 0 & \cdots & 0 & \bigg| & \dfrac{\partial h_k}{\partial x_1} & \cdots & \dfrac{\partial h_k}{\partial x_n} \\
\hline
\dfrac{\partial g_1}{\partial x_1} & \cdots & \dfrac{\partial g_e}{\partial x_1} & \dfrac{\partial h_1}{\partial x_1} & \cdots & \dfrac{\partial h_k}{\partial x_1} & \bigg| & \dfrac{\partial^2 L}{\partial x_1^2} & \cdots & \dfrac{\partial^2 L}{\partial x_n x_1} \\
\vdots & \ddots & \vdots & \vdots & \ddots & \vdots & \bigg| & \vdots & \ddots & \vdots \\
\dfrac{\partial g_1}{\partial x_n} & \cdots & \dfrac{\partial g_e}{\partial x_n} & \dfrac{\partial h_1}{\partial x_n} & \cdots & \dfrac{\partial h_k}{\partial x_n} & \bigg| & \dfrac{\partial^2 L}{\partial x_1 x_n} & \cdots & \dfrac{\partial^2 L}{\partial x_n^2}
\end{pmatrix}.
$$

If the last $n - (e + k)$ leading principal minors alternate in sign with the sign of the determinant of the largest matrix the same as the sign of $(-1)^n$, then condition c holds.

A little care has to be taken in writing the minimization version of Theorem 19.8. In particular, the minimization problem should be presented in standard form, as in Theorem 18.6. One makes the following changes in the wording of Theorem 19.8 for an inequality-constrained minimization problem:

(1) change the word "maximizing" to "minimizing" on line two,
(2) write the inequality constraints as $g_i(\mathbf{x}) \geq b_i$ in the presentation of the constraint set C_{gh},
(3) change "negative definite" and "< 0" in condition (b) to "positive definite" and > 0,
(4) change "max" to "min" in the concluding sentence.

The bordered Hessian check requires that the last $n - (e + k)$ leading principal minors all have the same sign as $(-1)^{e+k}$.

Alternative Approaches to the Bordered Hessian Condition

The bordered Hessian condition for a constrained max or min can be presented in different ways. The two most common alternatives to our presentation involve the position of the border in the bordered Hessian and the rules for the signs of the leading principal minors to distinguish a max from a min. Many texts place the Jacobian $D\mathbf{h}(\mathbf{x}^*)$ of the constraint functions to the right and below the Hessian $D_{\mathbf{x}}^2 L(\mathbf{x}^*, \lambda^*)$ of the Lagrangian with respect to the x_i's:

$$
H = \left(
\begin{array}{ccc|ccc}
\dfrac{\partial^2 L}{\partial x_1^2} & \cdots & \dfrac{\partial^2 L}{\partial x_1 \partial x_n} & \dfrac{\partial h_1}{\partial x_1} & \cdots & \dfrac{\partial h_k}{\partial x_1} \\
\vdots & \ddots & \vdots & \vdots & \ddots & \vdots \\
\dfrac{\partial^2 L}{\partial x_n \partial x_1} & \cdots & \dfrac{\partial^2 L}{\partial x_n^2} & \dfrac{\partial h_1}{\partial x_n} & \cdots & \dfrac{\partial h_k}{\partial x_n} \\
\hline
\dfrac{\partial h_1}{\partial x_1} & \cdots & \dfrac{\partial h_1}{\partial x_n} & 0 & \cdots & 0 \\
\vdots & \ddots & \vdots & \vdots & \ddots & \vdots \\
\dfrac{\partial h_k}{\partial x_1} & \cdots & \dfrac{\partial h_k}{\partial x_n} & 0 & \cdots & 0
\end{array}
\right).
\tag{25}
$$

Instead of examining the *last* $n - k$ leading principal minors, this point of view looks at the $n - k$ largest principal minors which "respect the borders"; after computing the determinant of all of H, one first throws away row n and column n of H, then row $n - 1$ and column $n - 1$ of H, and so on.

Furthermore, some texts state the sign conditions by emphasizing the sign of the *smallest* principal minor checked instead of the sign of the whole bordered Hessian H. For a constrained minimization problem, the $n - k$ principal minors all have the same sign; for a constrained maximization problem, they alternate in sign. For a constrained minimization problem, the sign of the smallest principal minor checked is the same as the sign of $(-1)^k$; for a constrained maximization problem, the sign of the smallest principal minor checked is the same as the sign of $(-1)^{k+1}$.

Necessary Second Order Conditions

Theorems 19.6, 19.7, and 19.8 state *sufficient* second order conditions for a candidate point to be a solution of a constrained maximization problem, namely, that the Hessian $D_{\mathbf{x}}^2 L(\mathbf{x}^*, \lambda^*)$ of the Lagrangian with respect to the x_i's be negative definite on the nullspace of the Jacobian $D\mathbf{h}(\mathbf{x}^*)$ of the constraint functions — condition (14) in Theorem 19.6. The corresponding *necessary* condition that a constrained maximizer must satisfy is, of course, that $D_{\mathbf{x}}^2 L(\mathbf{x}^*, \lambda^*)$ be negative *semidefinite* on the nullspace of $D\mathbf{h}(\mathbf{x}^*)$. The complete characterization of constrained negative semidefiniteness in terms of principal submatrices of the bordered Hessian is a bit too complex to state here in all its generality. It certainly requires that each of the largest $n - k$ leading principal minors must be zero or have the same sign as $(-1)^k$. If $DL(\mathbf{x}^*) = \mathbf{0}$ but one of the last $n - k$ leading principal minors of the bordered Hessian is nonzero and has the wrong sign for negative definiteness, then the candidate cannot be a local constrained max.

EXERCISES

19.14 Check the second order conditions for the solutions of the first order conditions in Exercises 18.2, 18.3, 18.5, 18.6, and 18.7.

19.15 Redo the proof of Theorem 19.7 for the case $(\partial h/\partial y)(x^*, y^*) = 0$.

19.16 Rewrite the proof of Theorem 19.7 for the constrained minimization problem.

19.17 Write out a complete proof of Theorem 19.8 for the case of two variables and one *inequality* constraint.

19.4 SMOOTH DEPENDENCE ON THE PARAMETERS

All the results in the first two sections of this chapter had two basic hypotheses: the smooth dependence of the maximizers on the parameters of the problem and the nondegenerate constraint qualification (NDCQ). In this section, we will look at these hypotheses a little more carefully and show how to phrase them in terms of the problem's objective and constraint functions.

Consider first the parameterized unconstrained problem (9) of Theorem 19.5:

$$F(a) = \max_{\mathbf{x}} f(\mathbf{x}; a). \qquad (26)$$

Since there are no nonnegativity constraints and we are assuming that a maximizer $\mathbf{x}^*(a)$ exists, then $\mathbf{x}^*(a)$ is a solution of the usual first order conditions

$$\frac{\partial f}{\partial x_1}(x_1, \ldots, x_n; a) = 0$$

$$\vdots \qquad \vdots \qquad\qquad (27)$$

$$\frac{\partial f}{\partial x_n}(x_1, \ldots, x_n; a) = 0.$$

By the Implicit Function Theorem (Theorem 15.7), we can solve these n equations (27) for the n unknowns $x_1, \ldots, x_n$ as C^1 functions of the exogenous variable a provided that the Jacobian of the functions in (27), with respect to the endogenous variables $x_1, \ldots, x_n$, is nonsingular at $(\mathbf{x}^*(a); a)$. But the Jacobian of the first order partial derivatives $\partial f/\partial x_i$ is simply the Hessian of f at $(\mathbf{x}^*(a); a)$:

$$D^2 f_{(\mathbf{x}^*(a);a)} = \begin{pmatrix} \dfrac{\partial^2 f}{\partial x_1{}^2} & \dfrac{\partial^2 f}{\partial x_2 \partial x_1} & \cdots & \dfrac{\partial^2 f}{\partial x_n \partial x_1} \\[2ex] \dfrac{\partial^2 f}{\partial x_1 \partial x_2} & \dfrac{\partial^2 f}{\partial x_2{}^2} & \cdots & \dfrac{\partial^2 f}{\partial x_n \partial x_2} \\[2ex] \vdots & \vdots & \ddots & \vdots \\[2ex] \dfrac{\partial^2 f}{\partial x_1 \partial x_n} & \dfrac{\partial^2 f}{\partial x_2 \partial x_n} & \cdots & \dfrac{\partial^2 f}{\partial x_n{}^2} \end{pmatrix}. \qquad (28)$$

By our work with critical points of real-valued functions in Chapter 17, the Hessian matrix $D^2 f$ is generally nonsingular. In fact, since (26) is a maximization problem, the determinant of the Hessian should have the same sign as $(-1)^n$ by the usual second order necessary conditions, as described at the end of Section 17.3.

To summarize, we can replace the hypothesis that $\mathbf{x}^*(a)$ is a C^1 function of a in Theorem 19.4 by the hypothesis that $\mathbf{x}^*(a)$ is a *nondegenerate* critical point of f in that the Hessian matrix (28) of f is nonsingular at $(\mathbf{x}^*(a); a)$.

A similar analysis works for constrained problems. Consider the parameterized constrained maximization problem (S_a):

$$\text{maximize} \quad f(\mathbf{x}; a)$$

$$\text{subject to} \quad h_1(\mathbf{x}; a) = 0, \ldots, h_k(\mathbf{x}; a) = 0, \tag{S_a}$$

as discussed in Theorem 19.5. Assuming that NDCQ

$$\text{rank} \begin{pmatrix} \dfrac{\partial h_1}{\partial x_1}(\mathbf{x}^*(a); a) & \cdots & \dfrac{\partial h_1}{\partial x_n}(\mathbf{x}^*(a); a) \\ \vdots & \ddots & \vdots \\ \dfrac{\partial h_k}{\partial x_1}(\mathbf{x}^*(a); a) & \cdots & \dfrac{\partial h_k}{\partial x_n}(\mathbf{x}^*(a); a) \end{pmatrix} = k \tag{29}$$

holds at $\mathbf{x}^*(a)$, we write the Lagrangian for Problem (S_a) as

$$L(x_1, \ldots, x_n, \mu_1, \ldots, \mu_k; a) = f(\mathbf{x}; a) - \mu_1 h_1(\mathbf{x}; a)$$

$$- \cdots - \mu_k h_k(\mathbf{x}; a).$$

The constrained maximizer $\mathbf{x}^*(a)$ must satisfy the first order conditions

$$\frac{\partial L}{\partial x_1}(\mathbf{x}, \mu; a) = 0, \ldots, \frac{\partial L}{\partial x_n}(\mathbf{x}, \mu; a) = 0,$$

$$\frac{\partial L}{\partial \mu_1}(\mathbf{x}, \mu; a) = 0, \ldots, \frac{\partial L}{\partial \mu_k}(\mathbf{x}, \mu; a) = 0, \tag{30}$$

a system of $n + k$ equations in $n + k$ unknowns $x_1, \ldots, x_n, \mu_1, \ldots, \mu_k$. Once again, we call on the Implicit Function Theorem for conditions that will guarantee that $\mathbf{x}^*(a)$ and $\mu^*(a)$ depend smoothly on the exogenous variable a; the Jacobian of the defining equations (30) with respect to the endogenous variables must be an $(n + k) \times (n + k)$ nonsingular matrix at $(\mathbf{x}^*(a), \mu^*(a); a)$. This Jacobian is simply the *Hessian* of the Lagrangian

$$D^2L_{\mathbf{x},\mu} = \begin{pmatrix} \dfrac{\partial^2 L}{\partial x_1{}^2} & \cdots & \dfrac{\partial^2 L}{\partial x_n \partial x_1} & \dfrac{\partial^2 L}{\partial \mu_1 \partial x_1} & \cdots & \dfrac{\partial^2 L}{\partial \mu_k \partial x_1} \\[2ex] \vdots & \ddots & \vdots & \vdots & \ddots & \vdots \\[2ex] \dfrac{\partial^2 L}{\partial x_1 \partial x_n} & \cdots & \dfrac{\partial^2 L}{\partial x_n{}^2} & \dfrac{\partial^2 L}{\partial \mu_1 \partial x_n} & \cdots & \dfrac{\partial^2 L}{\partial \mu_k \partial x_n} \\[2ex] \dfrac{\partial^2 L}{\partial x_1 \partial \mu_1} & \cdots & \dfrac{\partial^2 L}{\partial x_n \partial \mu_1} & \dfrac{\partial^2 L}{\partial \mu_1{}^2} & \cdots & \dfrac{\partial^2 L}{\partial \mu_k \partial \mu_1} \\[2ex] \vdots & \ddots & \vdots & \vdots & \ddots & \vdots \\[2ex] \dfrac{\partial^2 L}{\partial x_1 \partial \mu_k} & \cdots & \dfrac{\partial^2 L}{\partial x_n \partial \mu_k} & \dfrac{\partial^2 L}{\partial \mu_1 \partial \mu_k} & \cdots & \dfrac{\partial^2 L}{\partial \mu_k{}^2} \end{pmatrix}$$

$$= \begin{pmatrix} \dfrac{\partial^2 L}{\partial x_1{}^2} & \cdots & \dfrac{\partial^2 L}{\partial x_n \partial x_1} & -\dfrac{\partial h_1}{\partial x_1} & \cdots & -\dfrac{\partial h_k}{\partial x_1} \\[2ex] \vdots & \ddots & \vdots & \vdots & \ddots & \vdots \\[2ex] \dfrac{\partial^2 L}{\partial x_1 \partial x_n} & \cdots & \dfrac{\partial^2 L}{\partial x_n{}^2} & -\dfrac{\partial h_1}{\partial x_n} & \cdots & -\dfrac{\partial h_k}{\partial x_n} \\[2ex] -\dfrac{\partial h_1}{\partial x_1} & \cdots & -\dfrac{\partial h_1}{\partial x_n} & 0 & \cdots & 0 \\[2ex] \vdots & \ddots & \vdots & \vdots & \ddots & \vdots \\[2ex] -\dfrac{\partial h_k}{\partial x_1} & \cdots & -\dfrac{\partial h_k}{\partial x_n} & 0 & \cdots & 0 \end{pmatrix}.$$

$$(31)$$

evaluated at $(\mathbf{x}^*(a), \mu^*(a); a)$.

As we learned in Section 19.3, for example, in expression (25), this is one form of the matrix one uses to check the second order conditions for a constrained max. As in the unconstrained problem, this Hessian usually has nonzero determinant. In fact, for a *nondegenerate* constrained maximization problem (S_a), its determinant has the same sign as $(-1)^n$.

Note that the Jacobian (29) of the constraint functions Dh plays a major role in this Hessian. In fact, as you are asked to verify in Exercise 19.9, the determinant of D^2L will be zero if Dh does not have maximal rank k. So, the natural condition that guarantees that $\mathbf{x}^*(a)$ and the $\mu_j^*(a)$'s depend smoothly on the parameter a includes the nondegenerate constraint qualification NDCQ.

In summary, we can replace the condition in Theorem 19.5 that $\mathbf{x}^*(a)$ and the $\mu_i(a)$'s be C^1 functions of the parameter a and the requirement of the non-degenerate constraint qualification by the nondegenerate second order condition for constrained problems, namely that the Hessian of the Lagrangian has nonzero determinant at $(\mathbf{x}^*(a), \mu^*(a); a)$.

Theorem 19.9 Let $\mathbf{x}^*(a)$ be the solution of the parameterized constrained maximization problem (S_a), and let $\mu^*(a)$ be the corresponding Lagrange multiplier. Fix the value of the parameter at $a = a_o$. If the Hessian matrix (31) is nonsingular at the point $(\mathbf{x}^*(a_o), \mu^*(a_o); a_o)$, then:

(a) $\mathbf{x}^*(a)$ and $\mu^*(a)$ are C^1 functions of a at $a = a_o$; and
(b) the NDCQ holds at $(\mathbf{x}^*(a_o), \mu^*(a_o); a_o)$.

Finally, we remark that the envelope theorems and their variations are true even without such nondegeneracy conditions, in fact, even without smoothness assumptions on f and the h_j's. In this case, we need to assume that all the functions involved are concave or convex functions.

EXERCISES

19.18 Consider the problem of maximizing $x_1^2 x_2$ on the constraint set $2x_1^2 + x_2^2 = a$, as in Example 18.5. Use the Implicit Function Theorem directly on the first order conditions of this problem to prove that the solutions $x_1(a), x_2(a), \lambda(a)$ depend smoothly on the parameter a near $a = 3$.

19.19 Prove that if Dh in (29) does not have maximal rank, then D^2L in (31) has zero determinant.

19.5 CONSTRAINT QUALIFICATIONS

In applying the theorems of Chapter 18 to find the solutions of a constrained optimization problem, we have been checking the constraint qualification by calculating the critical points of the constraint functions. If none of these critical points lie in the constraint set, we write out the Lagrangian, use its partial derivatives to write out the system of first order conditions, and solve this system of equations. If the constraint set *does* contain critical points of the constraint functions, then we include these points among our candidates for a solution to the original constrained maximization problem, along with the solutions of the first order conditions.

When working with economic applications or studying general economic theory, one usually does not know the exact functional form of the constraint functions of the problem under study. Therefore, it is helpful to have versions of the theorems of Chapter 18 which do not impose hypotheses on the constraint functions and which incorporate both types of candidates for constrained maxima — critical points of the Lagrangian and critical points of the constraint function — into a single criterion. Such a criterion does exist. However, it requires one more multiplier — a multiplier for the objective function itself.

To describe this variation, we begin, as usual, with the simplest case — the problem with two variables and one equality constraint. The following theorem summarizes this alternative approach.

Theorem 19.10   Let f and h be C^1 functions of two variables. Suppose that $\mathbf{x}^* = (x_1^*, x_2^*)$ is a solution of the problem

$$\text{maximize} \qquad f(x_1, x_2)$$

$$\text{on the constraint set} \quad \{(x_1, x_2) : h(x_1, x_2) = c\}.$$

Construct the Lagrangian

$$L(x_1, x_2, \mu_0, \mu_1) \equiv \mu_0 f(x_1, x_2) - \mu_1[h(x_1, x_2) - c],$$

including a multiplier μ_0 for the objective function. Then, there exist multipliers μ_0^* and μ_1^* such that:

(a) μ_0^* and μ_1^* are not both zero,
(b) μ_0^* is either 0 or 1,
(c) the quadruple $(x_1^*, x_2^*, \mu_0^*, \mu_1^*)$ satisfies the equations

$$\frac{\partial L}{\partial x_1} = \mu_0 \frac{\partial f}{\partial x_1}(x_1, x_2) - \mu_1 \frac{\partial h}{\partial x_1}(x_1, x_2) = 0$$

$$\frac{\partial L}{\partial x_2} = \mu_0 \frac{\partial f}{\partial x_2}(x_1, x_2) - \mu_1 \frac{\partial h}{\partial x_2}(x_1, x_2) = 0 \tag{32}$$

$$\frac{\partial L}{\partial \mu_1} = c - h(x_1, x_2) = 0.$$

Proof   Suppose that (x_1^*, x_2^*) is a solution of the constrained maximization problem. If (x_1^*, x_2^*) is not a critical point of h, we can set $\mu_0 = 1$ and use Theorem 18.1 to deduce that (x_1^*, x_2^*, μ_1^*) satisfies system (32). On the other hand, if (x_1^*, x_2^*) is a critical point of h so that $\partial h/\partial x_1$ and $\partial h/\partial x_2$ in (32) are zero at (x_1^*, x_2^*), we can take μ_1^* to be any *nonzero* number and set μ_0^* equal to zero. The resulting $(x_1^*, x_2^*, \mu_0^*, \mu_1^*)$ will be a solution of system (32). ∎

In concrete calculations with specified functional forms, it is easier to apply the method of Theorem 18.1 and of Example 18.5: first check for the critical points of h that lie in the constraint set, then calculate the critical points of the usual Lagrangian with $\mu_0 = 1$. The following example illustrates both methods.

Example 19.9   Consider the problem of maximizing $f(x, y) = x$ on the constraint set C_h defined by $h(x, y) \equiv x^3 + y^2 = 0$. The constraint set is the cusp drawn in Figure 19.2. (Check.) Since we are trying to maximize x, we want to find the point on C_h furthest to the right in Figure 19.2. The only solution is clearly the cusp point at the origin.

Now, let's try this analytically. If we use Theorem 18.1, we look first for the critical points of h by solving

$$\frac{\partial h}{\partial x} = 3x^2 = 0 \quad \text{and} \quad \frac{\partial h}{\partial y} = 2y = 0.$$

The only solution is $(0, 0)$, which does indeed lie on the constraint set. Now, find the critical points of the Lagrangian

$$L(x, y, \mu) = f(x, y) - \mu[h(x, y) - c] = x - \mu(x^3 + y^2),$$

by solving the system

$$\frac{\partial L}{\partial x} = 1 - 3\mu x^2 \quad = 0$$

$$\frac{\partial L}{\partial y} = -2\mu y \quad = 0$$

$$\frac{\partial L}{\partial \mu} = -(x^3 + y^2) = 0.$$

This system has *no* solution. (Verify!) Consequently, the only candidate for a solution of the maximization problem is the critical point of h, $(0, 0)$, which is indeed the solution of the problem.

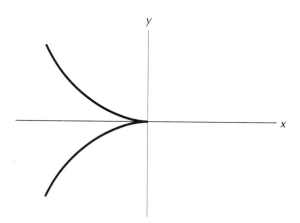

Figure 19.2

The constraint set $x^3 + y^2 = 0$.

Finally, we could have used Theorem 19.10 and worked with

$$L(x, y, \mu_0, \mu_1) = \mu_0 x - \mu_1(x^3 + y^2).$$

In this case, we are looking for solutions of

$$\frac{\partial L}{\partial x} = \mu_0 - 3\mu_1 x^2 = 0$$

$$\frac{\partial L}{\partial y} = -2\mu_1 y \qquad = 0$$

$$\frac{\partial L}{\partial \mu_1} = -(x^3 + y^2) = 0,$$

where $(\mu_0, \mu_1) \neq (0,0)$. The only solution with $(\mu_0, \mu_1) \neq (0,0)$ is $x = y = \mu_0 = 0$ and $\mu_1 = $ anything nonzero. (Check.) This does indeed give the constrained maximizer.

This example shows that we really do require a constraint qualification in the statement of Theorem 18.1. Of course, Theorem 19.10 holds for the general constrained optimization problem with equality and/or inequality constraints on $\mathbf{R}^n$. We state the version for inequality constraints here. This theorem is sometimes called the **Fritz John Theorem**.

Theorem 19.11   Suppose that $f, g_1, \ldots, g_k$ are C^1 functions of n variables. Suppose that $\mathbf{x}^*$ is a local maximizer of f on the constraint set defined by the k inequalities

$$g_1(x_1, \ldots, x_n) \leq b_1, \ldots, g_k(x_1, \ldots, x_n) \leq b_k.$$

Form the Lagrangian

$$L(x_1, \ldots, x_n, \lambda_0, \lambda_1, \ldots, \lambda_k) \equiv \lambda_0 f(\mathbf{x}) - \lambda_1[g_1(\mathbf{x}) - b_1] - \cdots - \lambda_k[g_k(\mathbf{x}) - b_k],$$

with a multiplier λ_0 for the objective function. Then, there exist multipliers $\boldsymbol{\lambda}^* = (\lambda_0^*, \lambda_1^*, \ldots, \lambda_k^*)$ such that:

(a) $\dfrac{\partial L}{\partial x_1}(\mathbf{x}^*, \boldsymbol{\lambda}^*) = 0, \ldots, \dfrac{\partial L}{\partial x_n}(\mathbf{x}^*, \boldsymbol{\lambda}^*) = 0,$

(b) $\lambda_1^*[g_1(\mathbf{x}^*) - b_1] = 0, \ldots, \lambda_k^*[g_k(\mathbf{x}^*) - b_k] = 0,$

(c) $\lambda_1^* \geq 0, \ldots \lambda_k^* \geq 0,$

(d) $g_1(\mathbf{x}^*) \leq b_1, \ldots, g_k(\mathbf{x}^*) \leq b_k,$

(e) $\lambda_0^* = 0$ or 1, and

(f) $(\lambda_0^*, \lambda_1^*, \ldots, \lambda_k^*) \neq (0, 0, \ldots, 0).$

Example 19.10   Let us solve the problem in Example 18.9 using Theorem 19.11. Without checking any constraint qualification, we would write the Lagrangian

$$L(x, y, \lambda_0, \lambda_1, \lambda_2, \lambda_3, \lambda_4) = \lambda_0 xyz - \lambda_1(x + y + z - 1) + \lambda_2 x + \lambda_3 y + \lambda_4 z.$$

The fifteen first order conditions in Example 18.9 would remain the same, except that the first three would each begin with a λ_0. We would also add conditions e and f from Theorem 19.11. If $\lambda_0^* = 0$, then equation 20 in Chapter 18 becomes

$$\lambda_1 = \lambda_2 = \lambda_3 = \lambda_4,$$

none of which can be zero by Condition f in Theorem 19.11. But if $\lambda_1, \lambda_2, \lambda_3$, and λ_4 are positive, all the constraints would have to be binding: $x = 0, y = 0, z = 0, x + y + z = 1$ — an impossibility. We conclude that $\lambda_0^* = 1$ and proceed as in Example 18.9.

We would clearly prefer that $\lambda_0^* \neq 0$; otherwise, the objective function — the very function we are maximizing — drops completely out of the first order conditions. For this reason, we prefer to have some qualification on the constraint functions which guarantees that we can take $\lambda_0^* = 1$, hence the name "constraint qualification."

The first order conditions of the last chapter emphasized the nondegenerate constraint qualification (NDCQ). However, there are other constraint qualifications which guarantee that λ_0^* can be set equal to 1. The following theorem lists some of the more commonly used constraint qualifications for the inequality constrained maximization problem.

Theorem 19.12   Let $f, g_1, \ldots, g_k$ be as in Theorem 19.11, and suppose that $\mathbf{x}^* \in \mathbf{R}^n$ is a local maximizer of f on the constraint set defined by

$$g_1(\mathbf{x}) \leq b_1, \ldots, g_k(\mathbf{x}) \leq b_k.$$

For ease of notation, suppose that $g_1, \ldots, g_h$ yield binding constraints at $\mathbf{x}^*$ and that $g_{h+1}, \ldots, g_k$ are not binding at $\mathbf{x}^*$. Suppose that the *binding* constraint functions satisfy one of the following properties:

(a) (**NDCQ**) the $h \times n$ Jacobian matrix $(\partial g_i / \partial x_j (\mathbf{x}^*))$, $i = 1, \ldots, h, j = 1, \ldots, n$, has maximal rank h,

(b) (**Karush–Kuhn–Tucker CQ**) For any vector $\mathbf{v}$ in $\mathbf{R}^n$ with the property that $Dg_i(\mathbf{x}^*)(\mathbf{v}) \leq 0$ for $i = 1, \ldots, h$, there exists $\epsilon > 0$ and a C^1 curve $\alpha: [0, \epsilon) \to \mathbf{R}^n$ such that:
   (i) $\alpha(0) = \mathbf{x}^*$,
   (ii) $\alpha'(0) = \mathbf{v}$, and
   (iii) $g_i(\alpha(t)) \leq b_i$ for all $i = 1, 2, \ldots, k$ and all $t \in [0, \epsilon)$.

(c) (**Slater CQ**) There is a ball U about $\mathbf{x}^*$ in $\mathbf{R}^n$ such that $g_1, \ldots, g_h$ are convex functions on U and there exists $\mathbf{z} \in U$ so that each $g_i(\mathbf{z}) < b_i$.

(d) $g_1, \ldots, g_h$ are concave functions.

(e) $g_1, \ldots, g_h$ are linear functions.

Then, we can take $\lambda_0^* = 1$ in the conclusion of Theorem 19.11.

The first constraint qualification in the statement of Theorem 19.12 is the NDCQ which we used throughout Chapter 18. The second constraint qualification is the condition which Kuhn and Tucker used in their pioneering work on inequality constrained problems. It is designed to rule out cusps in the constraint set, like the one in Example 19.9. (See Exercise 19.23.) The third constraint qualification requires that the constraint set have a nonempty interior and that the binding constraint functions be convex functions.

The last three constraint qualifications in Theorem 19.12 are particularly helpful in economics applications because they are assumptions on the general character of the constraint functions — assumptions which are common in economic theory. Condition e in Theorem 19.12 is especially important because linear constraints are common in economics models. For example, we can automatically take $\lambda_0^* = 1$ in the utility maximization problem of Example 18.1 because all of its constraint functions are linear. The same statement can be made for the problems in Examples 18.9 and 18.13. Entire books are devoted to linear programming problems — constrained optimization problems in which the objective function and all the constraint functions are linear. By Theorem 19.12, we can take $\lambda_0 = 1$ in all these problems. We can take $\lambda_0^* = 1$ in Example 18.7 because its constraint function is a convex function. The proof of Theorem 19.12 is an application of Farkas' lemma, which we omit at this point.

For minimization problems with inequality constraints of the form $g_i(x) \geq b_i$, Theorem 19.12 still holds provided that we reverse the two $\leq$'s in Condition b, and interchange the words "concave" and "convex" in Conditions c and d.

EXERCISES

19.20 Following the guidelines of Example 19.10, carry out the analogous application of Theorem 19.11 for Example 18.13.

19.21 Which of the last three constraint qualifications in Theorem 19.12 hold for the constraint functions in Exercises 18.10, 18.11, 18.12, 18.17 and 18.18?

19.22 Consider the problem of maximizing x subject to $y - x^4 \leq 0$, $x^3 - y \leq 0$, and $x \leq 1/2$. Try solving this problem with and without using a multiplier λ_0 for the objective function.

19.23 Verify that constraint qualification b in Theorem 19.12 is not satisfied in Example 19.9.

19.6   PROOFS OF FIRST ORDER CONDITIONS

In this concluding section, we present complete proofs of the major theorems of Chapter 18. For some of these theorems, we have already presented geometric arguments for lower dimensional versions. However, the results of Chapter 18 are important enough to warrant complete, careful proofs.

Furthermore, the proofs we present here are good examples of the mathematical proofs one encounters in advanced economic theory. They use much of the mathematical theory developed in the earlier chapters of this book. In particular, they rely heavily on:

(1) the Implicit Function Theorem (Section 15.3),
(2) the Chain Rule for functions of several variables (Section 14.5), and
(3) the fact that the rows of an $m \times n$ matrix ($m \le n$) are linearly independent n-vectors if and only if the matrix has rank m.

Let's say a little more about this last statement. In Section 7.4, we defined the *rank* of an $m \times n$ matrix A as the number of nonzero rows in its row echelon form A_R. In particular, if A has rank m, the m rows of A_R are all nonzero. Since each row in A_R starts with more zeros than does the row above it, it is easy to see that the rows of A_R are linearly independent (Lemma 27.1). However, one can go back and forth between the rows of A and the rows of A_R just by adding multiples of one row to another. It follows that all the rows of A_R are linearly independent if and only if all the rows of A are linearly independent. Statement 3 above now follows. See Section 27.3 for a complete discussion.

Proof of Theorems 18.1 and 18.2: Equality Constraints

We are assuming that:

(1) $\mathbf{x}^*$ maximizes f on the constraint set

$$h_1(\mathbf{x}^*) = c_1, \ldots, \mathbf{h}_m(\mathbf{x}^*) = c_m; \tag{33}$$

(2) the $m \times n$ Jacobian $D\mathbf{h}(\mathbf{x}^*)$ of the constraint functions $\mathbf{h}$ has maximal rank m at $\mathbf{x}^*$:

$$m = \operatorname{rank} D\mathbf{h}(\mathbf{x}^*) = \operatorname{rank} \begin{pmatrix} \dfrac{\partial h_1}{\partial x_1}(\mathbf{x}^*) & \cdots & \dfrac{\partial h_1}{\partial x_n}(\mathbf{x}^*) \\ \vdots & \ddots & \vdots \\ \dfrac{\partial h_m}{\partial x_1}(\mathbf{x}^*) & \cdots & \dfrac{\partial h_m}{\partial x_n}(\mathbf{x}^*) \end{pmatrix}. \tag{34}$$

We first claim that the $(m + 1) \times n$ Jacobian matrix

$$\begin{pmatrix} \dfrac{\partial f}{\partial x_1}(\mathbf{x}^*) & \cdots & \dfrac{\partial f}{\partial x_n}(\mathbf{x}^*) \\ \dfrac{\partial h_1}{\partial x_1}(\mathbf{x}^*) & \cdots & \dfrac{\partial h_1}{\partial x_n}(\mathbf{x}^*) \\ \vdots & \ddots & \vdots \\ \dfrac{\partial h_m}{\partial x_1}(\mathbf{x}^*) & \cdots & \dfrac{\partial h_m}{\partial x_n}(\mathbf{x}^*) \end{pmatrix}. \tag{35}$$

does *not* have maximal rank. Let $c_0 = f(\mathbf{x}^*)$. Consider the system of equations

$$\begin{aligned} f(x_1, \ldots, x_n) &= c_0 \\ h_1(x_1, \ldots, x_n) &= c_1 \\ \vdots \quad &\quad \vdots \\ h_m(x_1, \ldots, x_n) &= c_m. \end{aligned} \tag{36}$$

We know that $(x_1^*, \ldots, x_n^*)$ is a solution of system (36). Think of the right-hand sides $c_0, c_1, \ldots, c_m$ as exogenous variables. Then, the matrix (35) is simply the Jacobian of the system (36) with respect to the endogenous variables $x_1, \ldots, x_n$.

Suppose that matrix (35) *does* have maximal rank $m + 1$. Then, by the Implicit Function Theorem, we can vary the c_i's to c_i''s a little bit and still find a solution $x', \ldots, x_n'$ to the revised system (36) with the c_i''s on the right-hand side. In particular, we could find a solution $x_1^{**}, \ldots, x_n^{**}$ to the perturbed system

$$\begin{aligned} f(x_1, \ldots, x_n) &= c_0 + \varepsilon \\ h_1(x_1, \ldots, x_n) &= c_1 \\ \vdots \quad &\quad \vdots \\ h_m(x_1, \ldots, x_n) &= c_m, \end{aligned} \tag{37}$$

where ε is a small *positive* number. Looking at the last m equations in (37), we see that $(x_1^{**}, \ldots, x_n^{**})$ still satisfies the constraints (33). However, comparing the first equation of (36) to the first equation of (37), we see that

$$f(\mathbf{x}^{**}) > f(\mathbf{x}^*)$$

since $c_0 + \varepsilon > c_0$. This contradicts our assumption that $\mathbf{x}^*$ maximizes f on constraint set (33). We conclude that matrix (35) does not have rank $m + 1$. This means that its $m + 1$ rows are linearly dependent; that is, there exist scalars

$\alpha_0, \alpha_1, \ldots, \alpha_n$, not all zero, so that

$$\alpha_0 \begin{pmatrix} \dfrac{\partial f}{\partial x_1}(\mathbf{x}^*) \\ \vdots \\ \dfrac{\partial f}{\partial x_n}(\mathbf{x}^*) \end{pmatrix} + \alpha_1 \begin{pmatrix} \dfrac{\partial h_1}{\partial x_1}(\mathbf{x}^*) \\ \vdots \\ \dfrac{\partial h_1}{\partial x_n}(\mathbf{x}^*) \end{pmatrix} + \cdots + \alpha_m \begin{pmatrix} \dfrac{\partial h_m}{\partial x_1}(\mathbf{x}^*) \\ \vdots \\ \dfrac{\partial h_m}{\partial x_n}(\mathbf{x}^*) \end{pmatrix} = \begin{pmatrix} 0 \\ 0 \\ \vdots \\ 0 \end{pmatrix}. \tag{38}$$

We next show that NDCQ (34) implies that $\alpha_0 \neq 0$. For, if $\alpha_0 = 0$ in (38), then $\nabla h_1(\mathbf{x}^*), \ldots, \nabla h_m(\mathbf{x}^*)$ are linearly dependent by (38). This means that matrix (34) which has the $\nabla h_i(\mathbf{x}^*)$'s as its m rows does *not* have maximal rank — a contradiction to hypothesis b. We conclude that $\alpha_0 \neq 0$.

Finally, divide (38) through by the nonzero number α_0 and let $\mu_i = -\alpha_i/\alpha_0$ for $i = 0, \ldots, m$. Then, (38) becomes

$$\nabla f(\mathbf{x}^*) - \mu_1 \nabla h_1(\mathbf{x}^*) - \cdots - \mu_m \nabla h_m(\mathbf{x}^*) = \mathbf{0};$$

this is precisely the conclusion of Theorem 18.2.

Note that if we do not assume the NDCQ (34), then we obtain the conclusion of the Fritz John Theorem, Theorem 19.11, for equality constraints.

Proof of Theorems 18.3 and 18.4: Inequality Constraints

We turn to the proofs of the corresponding theorems for *inequality* constraints. Now, we are assuming that:

(1) $\mathbf{x}^* \in \mathbf{R}^n$ maximizes f on the constraint set

$$g_1(\mathbf{x}) \leq b_1, \ldots, g_k(\mathbf{x}) \leq b_k; \tag{39}$$

(2) only $g_1, \ldots, g_e$ are binding at $\mathbf{x}^*$:

$$g_1(\mathbf{x}^*) = b_1, \ldots, g_e(\mathbf{x}^*) = b_e, \tag{40}$$

$$g_{e+1}(\mathbf{x}^*) < b_{e+1}, \ldots, g_k(\mathbf{x}^*) < b_k; \tag{41}$$

(3) the $e \times n$ Jacobian matrix $D\mathbf{g}_E(\mathbf{x}^*)$ has maximal rank e; that is,

$$m = \operatorname{rank} D\mathbf{g}_E(\mathbf{x}^*) = \operatorname{rank} \begin{pmatrix} \dfrac{\partial g_1}{\partial x_1}(\mathbf{x}^*) & \cdots & \dfrac{\partial g_1}{\partial x_n}(\mathbf{x}^*) \\ \vdots & \ddots & \vdots \\ \dfrac{\partial g_e}{\partial x_1}(\mathbf{x}^*) & \cdots & \dfrac{\partial g_e}{\partial x_n}(\mathbf{x}^*) \end{pmatrix}. \tag{42}$$

Since the g_i's are continuous functions, there is a open ball $B = B_r(\mathbf{x}^*)$ of radius $r > 0$ about $\mathbf{x}^*$ such that $g_j(\mathbf{x}) < b_j$ for all $\mathbf{x} \in B$ and for $j = e + 1, \ldots, n$. We will work in the open set B for the rest of this proof.

Note that $\mathbf{x}^*$ maximizes f in B over the constraint set

$$g_1(\mathbf{x}) = b_1, \ldots, g_e(\mathbf{x}) = b_e, \tag{43}$$

because if there were another point $\mathbf{x}^{**}$ in B that satisfied (43) and gave a higher value of f, then this point would yield a higher value of f on the original constraint set (39) and contradict the definition of $\mathbf{x}^*$. Furthermore, by (42), $\mathbf{x}^*$ satisfies the NDCQ for the problem of maximizing f on the constraint set (43). Therefore, by Theorem 18.2, there exist $\mu_1^*, \ldots, \mu_e^*$ such that

$$\frac{\partial \hat{L}}{\partial x_1}(\mathbf{x}^*, \mu^*) = 0, \ldots, \frac{\partial \hat{L}}{\partial x_n}(\mathbf{x}^*, \mu^*) = 0,$$

$$g_1(\mathbf{x}^*) - b_1 = 0, \ldots, g_e(\mathbf{x}^*) - b_e = 0, \tag{44}$$

where $\hat{L}(\mathbf{x}, \mu) \equiv f(\mathbf{x}) - \mu_1[g_1(\mathbf{x}) - b_1] - \cdots - \mu_e[g_e(\mathbf{x}) - b_e].$

Now, consider the usual Lagrangian

$$L(\mathbf{x}, \lambda_1, \ldots, \lambda_k) \equiv f(\mathbf{x}) - \lambda_1 \cdot [g-1(\mathbf{x}) - b_1] - \cdots - \lambda_k \cdot [g_k(\mathbf{x}) - b_k]. \tag{45}$$

Let $\lambda_i^* = \mu_i^*$ for $i = 1, \ldots, e$ and set $\lambda_j^* = 0$ for $j = e + 1, \ldots, m$. Using this choice of the λ_j^*'s and noting equation (44), we see that $(\mathbf{x}^*, \lambda^*)$ is a solution of the $n + k$ equations in $n + k$ unknowns:

$$\frac{\partial L}{\partial x_1}(\mathbf{x}^*, \lambda^*) = 0, \ldots, \frac{\partial L}{\partial x_n}(\mathbf{x}^*, \lambda^*) = 0, \tag{46}$$

$$\lambda_1^* \cdot [g_1(\mathbf{x}^*) - b_1] = 0, \ldots, \lambda_e^* \cdot [g_e(\mathbf{x}^*) - b_e] = 0,$$

$$\lambda_{e+1}^* \cdot [g_{e+1}(\mathbf{x}^*) - b_{e+1}] = 0, \ldots, \lambda_k^* \cdot [g(\mathbf{x}^*) - b_k] = 0.$$

Except for the condition that all the λ_i's must be ≥ 0, we have completed the proof of the first order conditions of Theorem 18.4. We turn now to the proof that the λ_i's must be ≥ 0.

Consider the system of e equations in $n + e$ variables:

$$g_1(x_1, \ldots, x_n) = b_1$$

$$\vdots \qquad \vdots \tag{47}$$

$$g_e(x_1, \ldots, x_n) = b_e.$$

By the rank condition (42) and the Implicit Function Theorem (Theorem 15.7), there exist e coordinates $x_{j_1}, \ldots, x_{j_e}$ such that we can consider system (47) as implicitly defining $x_{j_1}, \ldots, x_{j_e}$ in terms of the rest of the x_i's and all the b_j's. In this latter set of exogenous variables, hold $b_2, \ldots, b_e$ constant, hold the exogenous x_j's constant, and let b_1 decrease linearly: $t \longmapsto b_1 - t$ for $t \geq 0$. By the Implicit Function Theorem, as the exogenous variable b_1 varies, we can still solve system (47) for $x_{j_1}, \ldots, x_{j_e}$. This means, in particular, that there is a C^1 curve $\mathbf{x}(t)$ defined for $t \in [0, \varepsilon)$, such that $\mathbf{x}(0) = \mathbf{x}^*$ and, for all $t \in [0, \varepsilon)$,

$$g_1(\mathbf{x}(t)) = b_1 - t \quad \text{and} \quad g_j(\mathbf{x}(t)) = b_j \quad \text{for} \quad j = 2, \ldots, e. \tag{48}$$

Let $\mathbf{v} = \mathbf{x}'(0)$. Applying the Chain Rule to (48), we conclude that

$$Dg_1(\mathbf{x}^*)\mathbf{v} = -1, \quad Dg_j(\mathbf{x}^*)\mathbf{v} = 0 \quad \text{for} \quad j = 2, \ldots, e. \tag{49}$$

Since $\mathbf{x}(t)$ lies in the constraint set for all t and $\mathbf{x}^*$ maximizes f in the constraint set, f must be nonincreasing along $\mathbf{x}(t)$. Therefore,

$$\frac{d}{dt} f(\mathbf{x}(t)) \bigg|_{t=0} = Df(\mathbf{x}^*)\mathbf{v} \leq 0.$$

Let $D_{\mathbf{x}}L(\mathbf{x}^*)$ denote the derivative of the Lagrangian (45) with respect to $\mathbf{x}$. By our first order conditions (46) and by (49),

$$\begin{aligned}
\mathbf{0} &= D_{\mathbf{x}}L(\mathbf{x}^*)\mathbf{v} \\
&= Df(\mathbf{x}^*)\mathbf{v} - \sum_i \lambda_i Dg_i(\mathbf{x}^*)\mathbf{v} \\
&= Df(\mathbf{x}^*)\mathbf{v} - \lambda_1 Dg_1(\mathbf{x}^*)\mathbf{v} \\
&= Df(\mathbf{x}^*)\mathbf{v} + \lambda_1.
\end{aligned}$$

Since $Df(\mathbf{x}^*)\mathbf{v} \leq 0$, we conclude that $\lambda_1 \geq 0$. A similar argument shows that $\lambda_j \geq 0$ for $j = 1, \ldots, e$. This finishes the proof of Theorem 18.4.

The argument just presented works equally well when the problem contains both inequality constraints and equality constraints, provided that NDCQ is valid at $\mathbf{x}^*$ for the combined equality and *binding* inequality constraints.

EXERCISES

19.24   Write out the proof that $\lambda_2 \geq 0$ in the proof of Theorem 18.4.
19.25   Write out a careful proof of Theorem 18.5 for mixed constraints.

Homogeneous and Homothetic Functions

Chapters 14 and 15 examined the basic properties of differentiable functions. They showed that a lot of information can be gleaned from the fact that a differentiable function is well approximated at each point by a linear function. Economists often work with functions which have other strong properties, such as homogeneity or convexity. Sometimes, these properties arise naturally for specific functions; for example, demand functions are naturally homogeneous in prices and income. Other times, economists make these assumptions in order to prove theorems about economic models; for example, we can say a lot more about models with homothetic utility functions or concave profit functions than we can without such assumptions.

The next two chapters will examine the important properties of special kinds of functions which arise in economic models. There are two basic categories of such functions: homogeneous functions and concave/convex functions. Each of these categories has a cardinal and an ordinal component — concepts that we will develop in Section 20.4. As we will see, homogeneity and concavity are cardinal properties; *homotheticity* is the ordinal analogue of homogeneity and *quasiconcavity* is the ordinal analogue of concavity.

Each of these classes are defined without regard to the differentiability of the function. However, we can and will develop especially strong results for differentiable functions in each of these categories. In particular, we will prove simple calculus-based criteria for determining whether or not a given differentiable function is in any of these classes.

20.1 HOMOGENEOUS FUNCTIONS

Definition and Examples

Homogeneous functions arise naturally throughout economics. Profit functions and cost functions that are derived from production functions, and demand functions that are derived from utility functions are automatically homogeneous in the standard economic models.

Students should be familiar with homogeneous functions from their elementary algebra courses. For example, a monomial of one variable, $y = ax^k$, is homogeneous of degree k. A mixture, such as $y = x^3 + 3x^2$, is not homogeneous at all.

For functions of several variables, a monomial $z = ax_1^{k_1}x_2^{k_2}x_3^{k_3}$ is homogeneous of degree $k_1 + k_2 + k_3$. Its degree is the sum of the exponents. For example, $z = 8x_1^3x_2$ is homogeneous of degree four and $z = 3x_1^2x_2x_3^4$ is homogeneous of degree seven. The sum of monomials of degree k is a homogeneous function of degree k. The sum of monomials of *different* degrees is *not* homogeneous.

Example 20.1

(a) $x_1^2x_2 + 3x_1x_2^2 + x_2^3$ is homogeneous of degree three, since each term is homogeneous of degree three.

(b) $x_1^7x_2x_3^2 + 5x_1^6x_2^4 - x_2^5x_3^5$ is homogeneous of degree ten, since each term is homogeneous of degree ten.

(c) $4x_1^2x_2^3 - 5x_1x_2^2$ is not homogeneous since the first term has degree five and the second has degree three.

(d) A linear function, $z = a_1x_1 + a_2x_2 + \cdots + a_nx_n$, is homogeneous of degree one.

(e) A quadratic form, $z = \sum a_{ij}x_ix_j$, is homogeneous of degree two.

Thus, one can usually tell whether a specific function is homogeneous just by looking at its formula. This intuition provides an analytical definition which will be important in deriving results about homogeneous functions.

Definition For any scalar k, a real-valued function $f(x_1, \ldots, x_n)$ is **homogeneous of degree** k if

$$f(tx_1, \ldots, tx_n) = t^k f(x_1, \ldots, x_n) \quad \text{for all } x_1, \ldots, x_n \text{ and all } t > 0. \quad (1)$$

We will usually be working with homogeneous functions defined on the positive orthant $\mathbf{R}_+^n$. In any case, the domain of a homogeneous function must be a **cone**, a set with the property that whenever $\mathbf{x}$ is in the set, every positive scalar multiple $t\mathbf{x}$ of $\mathbf{x}$ is in the set.

Example 20.2 Replacing x_1, x_2, and x_3 by tx_1, tx_2, and tx_3 respectively in Examples 20.1a and 20.1b yields

$$(tx_1)^2(tx_2) + 3(tx_1)(tx_2)^2 + (tx_2)^3 = t^2x_1^2tx_2 + 3tx_1t^2x_2^2 + t^3x_2^3$$
$$= t^3(x_1^2x_2 + 3x_1x_2^2 + x_2^3)$$

and $\quad (tx_1)^7(tx_2)(tx_3)^2 + (tx_1)^6(tx_2)^4 + (tx_2)^5(tx_3)^5$
$$= t^{10}(x_1^7x_2x_3^2 + x_1^6x_2^4 + x_2^5x_3^5).$$

However, no such relationship exists for Example 20.1c. (Try it!)

With the above formal definition, we can extend the candidates for homogeneous functions beyond the class of polynomials. In particular, we can allow fractional or negative exponents and quotients of functions.

Example 20.3   The function

$$f_1(x_1, x_2) = 30x_1^{1/2}x_2^{3/2} - 2x_1^3x_2^{-1}$$

is homogeneous of degree two. The function

$$f_2(x_1, x_2) = x_1^{1/2}x_2^{1/4} + x_1^2x_2^{-5/4}$$

is homogeneous of degree three-quarters. The fractional exponents in these two examples give one reason for making the restriction $t > 0$ in the definition of homogeneous. The function

$$f_3(x_1, x_2) = \frac{x_1^7 - 3x_1^2x_2^5}{x_1^4 + 2x_1^2x_2^2 + x_2^4}$$

is homogeneous of degree three ($= 7 - 4$).

Example 20.4   However, the only homogeneous functions of one variable are the functions of the form $z = ax^k$, where k is any real number. To prove this statement, let $z = f(x)$ be an arbitrary homogeneous function of one variable. Let $a \equiv f(1)$ and let x be arbitrary. Then,

$$f(x) = f(x \cdot 1) = x^k f(1) = ax^k.$$

Homogeneous Functions in Economics

Economists often find it convenient to work with homogeneous functions as production functions. For example, if $q = f(x_1, \ldots, x_n)$ is a production function which is homogeneous of degree one, then

$$f(tx_1, \ldots, tx_n) = tf(x_1, \ldots, x_n), \tag{2}$$

for all input bundles $(x_1, \ldots, x_n)$ and all $t > 0$. Taking $t = 2$, equation (2) says that if the firm doubles all inputs, it doubles its output too. For $t = 3$, if it triples each input, it triples the corresponding output. Such a firm is said to exhibit **constant returns to scale**. Suppose, on the other hand, the production function is homogeneous of degree $k > 1$. If such a firm were to double the amount of each input, its output would rise by a factor of 2^k. Since $k > 1$, its output would more than double. Such a firm is said to exhibit **increasing returns to scale**. Finally, a firm which has a production function that is homogeneous of degree $k < 1$, will have its output increase by a factor less than two when it doubles all its inputs. Such a firm exhibits **decreasing returns to scale**.

A specific homogeneous functional form which economists frequently use as a production or utility function is the **Cobb-Douglas function**

$$q = Ax_1^{a_1}x_2^{a_2}\cdots x_n^{a_n}, \tag{3}$$

a monomial with exponents $a_1, \ldots, a_n$ that are usually positive fractions. Since the pioneering work of mathematician C. W. Cobb and economist (and later U.S. Senator) Paul Douglas in the 1920s, economists interested in estimating the production function of a specific firm or industry will often try to find the Cobb-Douglas production function which best fits the firm's input-output data. They can often use linear ordinary least squares techniques since by taking the logarithm of both sides of function (3), they can work with the log of the output as a *linear* function of the logs of the inputs:

$$\log q = \log A + a_1 \log x_1 + \cdots + a_n \log x_n.$$

Notice that a Cobb-Douglas production function exhibits decreasing, constant, or increasing returns to scale according to whether the sum of its exponents is less than, equal to, or greater than 1. Economists have usually found in their empirical studies that this sum is very close to 1.

While production functions are often homogeneous *by assumption*, demand functions are homogeneous *by nature* (at least if we ignore the "money illusion"). Recall that a demand function $\mathbf{x} = D(p_1, \ldots, p_n, I)$ associates to each price vector $\mathbf{p} = (p_1, \ldots, p_n)$ and income level I, an individual's most-preferred consumption bundle $\mathbf{x}$ at those prices and income. It is the solution of the basic consumer maximization problem: $\mathbf{x} = D(\mathbf{p}, I)$ maximizes $U(\mathbf{x})$ subject to the constraints $x_i \geq 0$ for all i and

$$p_1 x_1 + \cdots + p_n x_n \leq I. \tag{4}$$

Notice that if all the prices and the consumer's income tripled, constraint (4) would not change. We could just divide the new inequality (4) through by 3 to return to the original inequality. In particular, the optimal consumption bundle $\mathbf{x}$ would not be affected. In terms of the demand function,

$$D(tp_1, \ldots, tp_n, tI) = D(p_1, \ldots, p_n, I) \quad \text{for all } p_1, \ldots, p_n, I. \tag{5}$$

Since $t^0 = 1$, equation (5) states that demand is homogeneous of degree zero in $\mathbf{p}$ and I. Since each individual demand function is homogeneous of degree zero, the sum of these individual demands, aggregate demand, is also homogeneous of degree zero. Theorems 22.3 and 22.4 present some specific economic principles that are consequences of the homogeneity of demand functions.

Finally, a similar, straightforward calculation shows that for a firm in a competitive market, the (minimal) cost function is a homogeneous function of input prices and the optimal profit function is a homogeneous function of output price.

Properties of Homogeneous Functions

Homogeneity is a rather strong assumption for a production function and especially for a utility function. We next look at the consequences of choosing a homogeneous function by answering the following questions:

(1) What can one say about the level sets of a homogeneous function?
(2) What useful analytical properties do homogeneous functions have?

First, we prove a rather intuitive property of differentiable homogeneous functions — that the partial derivatives of a function homogeneous of degree k are themselves homogeneous of degree $k - 1$. This property is rather obvious for homogeneous *polynomials*. The following theorem proves it for general homogeneous functions.

Theorem 20.1   Let $z = f(\mathbf{x})$ be a C^1 function on an open cone in $\mathbf{R^n}$. If f is homogeneous of degree k, its first order partial derivatives are homogeneous of degree $k - 1$.

Proof   For simplicity of notation, we prove this theorem for $\partial f / \partial x_1$. By hypothesis,

$$f(tx_1, tx_2, \ldots, tx_n) = t^k f(x_1, x_2, \ldots, x_n). \tag{6}$$

Think of (6) as an expression in the $n+1$ variables $t, x_1, \ldots, x_n$. Hold $t, x_2, \ldots, x_n$ fixed in expression (6) and take the partial derivative of both sides of (6) with respect to x_1. By the Chain Rule, the result is

$$\frac{\partial f}{\partial x_1}(tx_1, \ldots, tx_n) \cdot t = t^k \frac{\partial f}{\partial x_1}(x_1, \ldots, x_n),$$

or, dividing both sides by t,

$$\frac{\partial f}{\partial x_1}(t\mathbf{x}) = t^{k-1} \frac{\partial f}{\partial x_1}(\mathbf{x}). \quad \blacksquare$$

The basic geometric property of homogeneous functions is a direct consequence of the definition of homogeneous. Let $q = f(\mathbf{x})$ be a production function that is homogeneous of degree one. In Figure 20.1, we have labeled as $\mathbf{x}_i$ four points on the isoquant for $\{q = 1\}$. Let $\mathbf{w}_i = 2\mathbf{x}_i$ for $i = 1, 2, 3, 4$. Since f is homogeneous of degree one,

$$f(\mathbf{w}_i) = f(2\mathbf{x}_i) = 2f(\mathbf{x}_i) = 2.$$

The $\mathbf{w}_i$'s are all on the isoquant $\{q = 2\}$. More generally, if we translate each point $\mathbf{x}$ on the isoquant $\{q = 1\}$ by a factor r along rays from the origin, we generate the isoquant $\{q = r\}$. If f is homogeneous of degree k, then if we translate points on the isoquant $\{q = 1\}$ by a factor r along rays from the origin, we generate the isoquant $\{q = r^k\}$, since $f(r\mathbf{x}) = r^k f(\mathbf{x}) = r^k$ if $f(\mathbf{x}) = 1$. In summary, the level sets of a homogeneous function are *radial expansions and contractions* of each other.

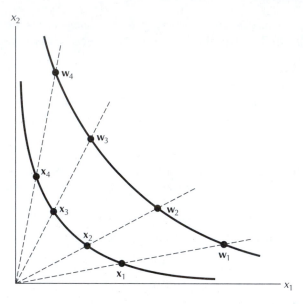

Figure 20.1

$f(2\mathbf{x}_i) = 2f(\mathbf{x}_i) = 2$ *if f is homogeneous of degree one and $f(\mathbf{x}_i) = 1$.*

One consequence of this observation is expressed in the following theorem.

Theorem 20.2   Let $q = f(\mathbf{x})$ be a C^1 homogeneous function on the positive orthant. The tangent planes to the level sets of f have constant slope along each ray from the origin.

Proof   For simplicity, we will prove this theorem for a homogeneous production function on $\mathbf{R}^2_+$. Basically we want to show that the marginal rate of technical substitution (MRTS) is constant along rays from the origin. Let (L_0, K_0) and $(L_1, K_1) = t(L_0, K_0)$ be two input bundles on the same ray from the origin, as illustrated in Figure 20.2. We write f'_L for $\partial f / \partial L$. The MRTS at (L_1, K_1) equals

$$\frac{f'_L(L_1, K_1)}{f'_K(L_1, K_1)} = \frac{f'_L(tL_0, tK_0)}{f'_K(tL_0, tK_0)} \qquad \text{(by definition of } (L_1, K_1)\text{)},$$

$$= \frac{t^{k-1} f'_L(L_0, K_0)}{t^{k-1} f'_K(L_0, K_0)} \qquad \text{(by Theorem 20.1)},$$

$$= \frac{f'_L(L_0, K_0)}{f'_K(L_0, K_0)} \qquad \text{(the MRTS at } (L_0, K_0)\text{)}. \qquad \blacksquare$$

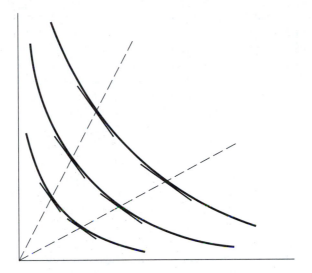

*The MRTS of a homogeneous function is constant along rays from **0**.*

Figure 20.2

Theorem 20.2 has important consequences for utility and production functions. For example, suppose that $U(\mathbf{x})$ is a homogeneous utility function. Fix prices at $\mathbf{p} = (p_1, \ldots, p_n)$ and fix income at I_0. Consider once again the problem of maximizing $U(\mathbf{x})$ subject to the budget constraint $p_1 x_1 + \cdots + p_n x_n \leq I_0$. The usual geometric solution to this problem is presented in Figure 20.3. At the maximizer $\mathbf{x}(I_0)$, the level curve of U is tangent to the budget line. Analytically, at $\mathbf{x}(I_0)$ the slope of the level curve (or the marginal rate of substitution), $-U'_{x_1}/U'_{x_2}$, equals the slope of the budget line, $-p_1/p_2$.

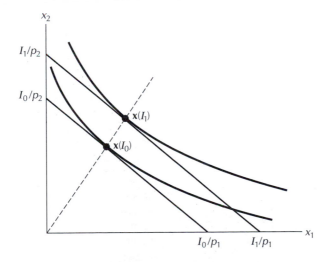

Bundle $\mathbf{x}(I_0)$ maximizes utility on the budget set for income I_0.

Figure 20.3

Now increase income by a factor of r to I_1, while holding prices constant. The corresponding budget line will move out *parallel* to itself, as in Figure 20.3. Its slope remains $-p_1/p_2$. The solution to the new utility maximization problem occurs at the point on the new budget line where the marginal rate of substitution equals $-p_1/p_2$. Since the utility function is homogeneous, this point will lie at the intersection of the new budget line and the ray from the origin through $\mathbf{x}(I_0)$, as in Figure 20.3, by Theorem 20.2. The parameterized curve $I \longmapsto \mathbf{x}(I)$ in Figure 20.3 that indicates the bundle demanded for different income levels is called the **income expansion path**. We have just shown that the income expansion path for a *homogeneous* utility function is a ray from the origin.

Since the budget line in Figure 20.3 moved out by a factor r, the new bundle of choice $\mathbf{x}(I_1)$ is a multiple of the former one by a factor r. Analytically, $\mathbf{x}(I_1) = \mathbf{x}(rI_0) = r\mathbf{x}(I_0)$. In other words, for a homogeneous utility function of degree k, the corresponding demand function is a homogeneous function of degree one in income; doubling income doubles consumption of every good.

The fact that demand as a function of the single variable income is homogeneous of degree one in this model means that every component $x_i(I)$ of $\mathbf{x}(I)$ is a linear function of income: $x_i(I) = a_i I$, by Example 20.4. It follows that each *income elasticity of demand* is identically 1, since $x_i = a_i I$ implies

$$\frac{dx_i}{dI} \cdot \frac{I}{x_i} = a_i \cdot \frac{I}{a_i I} = 1.$$

Given a production function $q = f(\mathbf{x})$ and a cost C of inputs, the firm wants to choose the input bundle $\mathbf{x}$ that maximizes revenue $pf(\mathbf{x})$, subject to $\mathbf{w} \cdot \mathbf{x} \leq C$. If the production function is homogeneous, the above analysis shows that the optimal choice of each input is a linear function of cost: $x_i(C) = a_i C$. Plugging these expressions into the homogeneous production function yields

$$\begin{aligned} q = q(C) &= f(x_1(C), \ldots, x_n(C)) \\ &= f(a_1 C, \ldots, a_n C) = C^k f(a_1, \ldots, a_n) \\ &= C^k a^*. \end{aligned}$$

Therefore, the cost function — the function that relates input cost and optimal output — is $C(q) = bq^{1/k}$, where $b = (a^*)^{-1/k}$. We summarize the results of this discussion in the following theorem.

Theorem 20.3 Let $U(\mathbf{x})$ be a utility function on $\mathbf{R}^n_+$ that is homogeneous of degree k. Then,

    (*i*) the MRS is constant along rays from the origin,
    (*ii*) income expansion paths are rays from the origin,
    (*iii*) the corresponding demand depends linearly on income, and
    (*iv*) the income elasticity of demand is identically 1.

Let $q = f(\mathbf{x})$ be a production function on $\mathbf{R}_+^n$ that is homogeneous of degree k. Then,

(*i*) the marginal rate of technical substitution (MRTS) is constant along rays from the origin, and

(*ii*) the corresponding cost function is homogeneous of degree $1/k$: $C(q) = bq^{1/k}$.

A Calculus Criterion for Homogeneity

We complete our discussion of homogeneous functions by presenting a calculus criterion which is a necessary and sufficient condition for a C^1 function to be homogeneous. The necessary condition, commonly known as Euler's theorem, is a useful analytic tool in working with homogeneous functions. This condition is related to the fact that when you take the derivative of a monomial, you multiply its coefficient by the original exponent and then lower the exponent by 1: $(ax^k)' = kax^{k-1}$. Therefore,

$$x(ax^k)' = k(ax^k); \quad \text{that is,} \quad xf'(x) = kf(x).$$

The following theorem is the n-dimensional version of this result.

Theorem 20.4 (**Euler's theorem**) Let $f(\mathbf{x})$ be a C^1 homogeneous function of degree k on $\mathbf{R}_+^n$. Then, for all $\mathbf{x}$,

$$x_1 \frac{\partial f}{\partial x_1}(\mathbf{x}) + x_2 \frac{\partial f}{\partial x_2}(\mathbf{x}) + \cdots + x_n \frac{\partial f}{\partial x_n}(\mathbf{x}) = kf(\mathbf{x}), \tag{7}$$

or, in gradient notation,

$$\mathbf{x} \cdot \nabla f(\mathbf{x}) = kf(\mathbf{x}).$$

Proof Simply differentiate each side of the definition (1) of homogeneous function with respect to t and then set $t = 1$:

$$\frac{d}{dt} f(tx_1, \ldots, tx_n) = \frac{\partial f}{\partial x_1}(t\mathbf{x})x_1 + \cdots + \frac{\partial f}{\partial x_n}(t\mathbf{x})x_n$$

$$\frac{d}{dt}[t^k f(x_1, \ldots, x_n)] = kt^{k-1} f(x_1, \ldots, x_n).$$

The two left-hand sides are equal by the definition of homogeneous. Set $t = 1$ in the two right-hand sides to get the desired result (7). ∎

Though it is less frequently used, we present the converse of Euler's theorem for the sake of completeness. Its proof involves the use of differential equations and will be presented in the Appendix of Chapter 24.

Theorem 20.5 Suppose that $f(x_1, \ldots, x_n)$ is a C^1 function on the positive orthant $\mathbf{R}^n_+$. Suppose that

$$x_1 \frac{\partial f}{\partial x_1}(\mathbf{x}) + \cdots + x_n \frac{\partial f}{\partial x_n}(\mathbf{x}) = k f(x_1, \ldots, x_n)$$

for all $\mathbf{x}$ in $\mathbf{R}^n_+$. Then, f is homogeneous of degree k.

Economic Applications of Euler's Theorem

A standard application of Euler's Theorem in economics is the story of "product exhaustion" for firms with homogeneous production functions. If a firm has a production function $q = f(x_1, \ldots, x_n)$ that is homogeneous of degree one, then (7) becomes

$$x_1 \frac{\partial f}{\partial x_1}(\mathbf{x}) + \cdots + x_n \frac{\partial f}{\partial x_n}(\mathbf{x}) = f(\mathbf{x}) = q. \tag{8}$$

For each input, multiply the amount used, x_i, by its marginal product $\partial f / \partial x_i$, and sum over all the inputs. The result, according to (8), is the amount of output q. To understand the implication of (8), suppose the usual profit-maximizing criterion, namely that the firm pays each factor x_i its marginal revenue product $p \cdot (\partial f / \partial x_i)$, so that it hires each factor until the contribution of that factor to the output of the firm just equals the cost of acquiring additional units of that factor. (See Section 17.5.) Then, the firm's total payment will be

$$x_1 p \frac{\partial f}{\partial x_1}(\mathbf{x}) + \cdots + x_n p \frac{\partial f}{\partial x_n}(\mathbf{x}).$$

But by equation (8), this is just $p \cdot q$, the value of the firm's output. So the revenue of the firm with a constant-returns-to-scale production function is exactly exhausted in making payments to all the factors. Such firms make zero economic profit. If the degree of homogeneity were greater than one, total payments would exceed the value of output; if the degree were less than one, total payments would be less than the value of output and the firm would make a positive profit.

As another application of Euler's theorem, let $q = f(x_1, x_2)$ be a production function which satisfies:

(1) constant returns to scale: $f(t\mathbf{x}) = t f(\mathbf{x})$, and
(2) decreasing marginal product of x_1: $\partial^2 f / \partial x_1^2 < 0$.

Since f is homogeneous of degree one, its partial derivative $\partial f/\partial x_1$ is homogeneous of degree zero. Apply Euler's theorem to $\partial f/\partial x_1$:

$$0 \cdot \frac{\partial f}{\partial x_1} = x_1 \cdot \frac{\partial}{\partial x_1}\left(\frac{\partial f}{\partial x_1}\right) + x_2 \cdot \frac{\partial}{\partial x_2}\left(\frac{\partial f}{\partial x_1}\right),$$

or

$$\frac{\partial^2 f}{\partial x_2 \partial x_1} = -\frac{x_1}{x_2}\frac{\partial^2 f}{\partial x_1^2},$$

which is positive since $f''_{x_1 x_1} < 0$. This positive cross partial derivative means that the marginal product of one factor increases when the other factor is increased. This result is sometimes called **Wicksell's law**.

EXERCISES

20.1 Which of the following functions are homogeneous? What are the degrees of homogeneity of the homogeneous ones?

a) $3x^5 y + 2x^2 y^4 - 3x^3 y^3$,   b) $3x^5 y + 2x^2 y^4 - 3x^3 y^4$,

c) $x^{1/2} y^{-1/2} + 3xy^{-1} + 7$,   d) $x^{3/4} y^{1/4} + 6x$,

e) $x^{3/4} y^{1/4} + 6x + 4$,   f) $\dfrac{(x^2 - y^2)}{(x^2 + y^2)} + 3$.

20.2 Verify Euler's theorem for the functions in Examples 20.1 and 20.3.

20.3 Prove that the product of homogeneous functions is homogeneous.

20.4 Consider the constant elasticity of substitution (CES) production function $F(x_1, x_2) = A\left(a_0 + a_1 x_1^p + a_2 x_2^p\right)^{1/p}$. Show that F has constant returns to scale when $a_0 = 0$.

20.5 If $y = f(x_1, x_2)$ is C^2 and homogeneous of degree r, show that

$$x_1^2 f''_{x_1 x_1} + 2x_1 x_2 f''_{x_1 x_2} + x_2^2 f''_{x_2 x_2} = r(r-1)f.$$

20.6 Prove that if f and g are functions on $\mathbf{R}^n$ that are homogeneous of *different* degrees, then $f + g$ is not homogeneous.

20.7 Is the zero function $f(\mathbf{x}) \equiv 0$ homogeneous? If so, of what degree? How does your answer relate to the previous exercise?

20.2 HOMOGENIZING A FUNCTION

Homogeneous functions have so many nice properties and arise so naturally in applications that it is natural to ask whether any arbitrary function can be considered as the restriction of a homogeneous function that is defined on a higher-dimensional space. The answer to this question is a definite yes, and the construction is fairly straightforward.

Theorem 20.6   Let $(x_1, \ldots, x_n) \longmapsto f(x_1, \ldots, x_n)$ be a real-valued function defined on a cone C in $\mathbf{R}^n$. Let k be an integer. Define a new function F of $n+1$ variables by

$$F(x_1, \ldots, x_n, z) = z^k \cdot f\left(\frac{x_1}{z}, \ldots, \frac{x_n}{z}\right). \tag{9}$$

Then, F is a homogeneous function of degree k on the cone $C \times \mathbf{R}_+$ in $\mathbf{R}^{n+1}$. Since $f(\mathbf{x}) = F(\mathbf{x}, 1)$ for all $\mathbf{x} \in C$, we can consider f as the restriction of F to an n-dimensional subset of $\mathbf{R}^{n+1}$.

Proof   For any $t \in \mathbf{R}_+$ and $(\mathbf{x}, z) \in C \times \mathbf{R}_+$,

$$F(t\mathbf{x}, tz) = (tz)^k f\left(\frac{1}{tz} t\mathbf{x}\right) \qquad \text{(by the definition (9) of } F\text{)}$$

$$= t^k \cdot z^k f\left(\frac{1}{z}\mathbf{x}\right)$$

$$= t^k F(\mathbf{x}, z) \qquad \text{(by the definition (9) of } F\text{).} \qquad \blacksquare$$

The converse of Theorem 20.6 is also true. If F is a homogeneous extension of f, then F and f must be related by (9).

Theorem 20.7   Suppose that $(\mathbf{x}, z) \longmapsto F(\mathbf{x}, z)$ is a function that is homogeneous of degree k on a set $C \times \mathbf{R}_+$ for some cone C in $\mathbf{R}^n$ and that

$$F(\mathbf{x}, 1) = f(\mathbf{x}) \quad \text{for all } \mathbf{x} \in C. \tag{10}$$

Then, $F(\mathbf{x}, z) = z^k f\left(\frac{1}{z}\mathbf{x}\right)$ for all $(\mathbf{x}, z) \in C \times \mathbf{R}_+$.

Proof   Since F is homogeneous of degree k,

$$F(\mathbf{x}, z) = F\left(z \cdot \left(\frac{1}{z}\mathbf{x}, 1\right)\right)$$

$$= z^k \cdot F\left(\frac{1}{z}\mathbf{x}, 1\right)$$

$$= z^k \cdot f\left(\frac{1}{z}\mathbf{x}\right) \qquad \text{(by (10)).} \qquad \blacksquare$$

Example 20.5   If $f(x) = x^a$ on $\mathbf{R}_+$, then its homogenization of degree one is

$$F(x, y) = y \cdot \left(\frac{x}{y}\right)^a = x^a y^{1-a}.$$

Example 20.6   If f is the nonhomogeneous function $x \longmapsto x - ax^2$, then its degree-one homogenization is

$$F(x, y) = y \cdot f\left(\frac{x}{y}\right)$$

$$= y\left[\left(\frac{x}{y}\right) - a\left(\frac{x}{y}\right)^2\right]$$

$$= x - a\frac{x^2}{y}.$$

Economic Applications of Homogenization

If we are given a function f of $n - 1$ variables and we know that it is the restriction of some homogeneous function F of n variables, we can use Theorems 20.6 and 20.7 to construct F from f. For example, f might be a production function that has been estimated using an incomplete list of factors $x_1, \ldots, x_{n-1}$. Suppose that there is one unestimated factor and that the complete production function of all n factors is known to have constant returns to scale. By Theorem 20.7, $F(x_1, \ldots, x_n) = x_n \cdot f\left(\frac{x_1}{x_n}, \ldots, \frac{x_{n-1}}{x_n}\right)$. With this explicit formula for F, one can compute such things as the marginal product of the hidden factor.

Example 20.7   In a two-factor constant-returns-to-scale production process, an econometrician estimates that when the second factor is held constant, the production function for the first factor is $f_1(x_1) = x_1^a$ for some $a \in (0, 1)$. Then, the complete production function would be the Cobb-Douglas production function $F(x_1, x_2) = x_1^a x_2^{1-a}$, as we computed in Example 20.5. If units are chosen so that $x_2 = 1$ during the estimation of f_1, then the estimated function is the restriction $f_1(x_1) = F(x_1, 1)$. The marginal product of the hidden factor x_2 when $x_2 = 1$ is

$$\frac{\partial F}{\partial x_2}(x_1, 1) = (1 - a)x_1^a \cdot x_2^{-a}\Big|_{x_2=1}$$

$$= (1 - a)f(x_1)$$

in the specially chosen units of x_2 for which $f(x_1) = F(x_1, 1)$.

In consumer theory, we know that demand functions must be homogeneous of degree zero in all commodities. Suppose, for example, that we are studying a two-good market, say cookies and milk. Suppose that we calculate the demand $D_1(p_1)$ for milk in a situation where the price of cookies is held constant. To obtain the demand function for milk as a function of both prices, we simply homogenize the milk demand function, using (9) with $k = 0$:

$$D(p_1, p_2) = D_1\left(\frac{p_1}{p_2}\right)$$

in units such that $p_2 = 1$ in the estimation of D_1.

Example 20.8   For example, if the demand function for milk with p_2 held constant at $p_2 = 1$ is the constant elasticity function $Q_1 = bp_1^{-a}$, then the complete demand function for milk is $Q_1 = bp_1^{-a}p_2^a$, a homogeneous function of degree zero, as it should be.

EXERCISES

20.8   Write the degree-one homogenization of each of the following functions:

$a)\ e^x,$ $b)\ \ln x,$ $c)\ 5,$ $d)\ x_1^2 + x_2^3,$ $e)\ x_1^2 + x_2^2.$

20.3   CARDINAL VERSUS ORDINAL UTILITY

As Theorem 20.3 indicates, homogeneous functions have some properties that make them useful functional forms for utility or production functions. But modern utility is an *ordinal* theory, not *cardinal*. And homogeneity is a *cardinal* property, not *ordinal*. This section will clarify the meaning of the concepts *cardinal* and *ordinal*, and will look at the ordinal content of homogeneity. The next section will look at the larger class of all functions which have these same ordinal properties. They are called *homothetic functions*.

A utility function could be said to measure the level of satisfaction associated with each commodity bundle. However, no economist really believes that a real number can be assigned to each commodity bundle which expresses (in utils?) the consumer's level of satisfaction with that bundle. Economists do believe that consumers have well-behaved preferences over bundles and that, given any two bundles, a consumer can indicate a preference of one over the other or indifference between the two. Although economists usually work with utility functions, they are really only concerned with the level sets of such functions, not with the number which the utility function assigns to any given level set. In utility theory, these level sets are called indifference sets, or indifference curves when the level sets are curves. A property of utility functions is called **ordinal** if it depends only on the shape and location of a consumer's indifference sets. On the other hand, a property is called **cardinal** if it also depends on the actual amount of utility that the utility function assigns to each indifference set.

In this context, we say two functions are **equivalent** if they have the exact same indifference sets, although they may assign different numbers to any given indifference set. For example, let $u(x, y)$ be a utility function on $\mathbf{R}_+^2$. Let $v(x, y)$ be the utility function $u(x, y) + 1$. These two functions have the exact same set of indifference curves. The function v assigns a number one unit larger than the number that the function u assigns to each indifference curve. For example, the indifference curve $\{u = 13\}$ coincides with the indifference curve $\{v = 14\}$. The functions u and v represent the same preferences and are therefore equivalent. As a second example, the utility function $w(x, y) = [u(x, y)]^2$ is also equivalent to u. If

$$w(x_1, y_1) = w(x_2, y_2) = a, \quad \text{then} \quad u(x_1, y_1) = u(x_2, y_2) = \sqrt{a}.$$

To all bundles which w assigns utility 9, u assigns utility 3, and vice versa. The utility functions u and w have the same indifference curves; they just attach different numbers to them. If $g_1(z) = z + 1$ and $g_2(z) = z^2$, then we can write $v = g_1 \circ u$ and $w = g_2 \circ u$. We say that v and w are monotonic transformations of u.

Definition   Let I be an interval on the real line. Then, $g : I \to \mathbf{R}$ is a **monotonic transformation** of I if g is a strictly increasing function on I. Furthermore, if g is a monotonic transformation and u is a real-valued function of n variables, then we say that

$$g \circ u : \mathbf{x} \mapsto g(u(\mathbf{x}))$$

is a **monotonic transformation of u**.

Of course, if g is differentiable, then g is a monotonic transformation if $g'(x) > 0$ for all x in I. (We could allow such a g to have a zero derivative at isolated points. For example, z^3 is strictly increasing, even though its derivative is zero at $z = 0$ and positive everywhere else.)

Example 20.9   The functions

$$3z + 2, \quad z^2, \quad e^z, \quad \text{and} \quad \ln z$$

are all monotonic transformations of $\mathbf{R}_{++}$, the set of all positive scalars. Consequently, the utility functions

$$3xy + 2, \quad (xy)^2, \quad (xy)^3 + xy, \quad e^{(xy)}, \quad \text{and} \quad \ln xy = \ln x + \ln y \quad (11)$$

are monotonic transformations of the utility function $u(x, y) = xy$.

We can now give a precise definition of an ordinal property.

Definition   A characteristic of functions is called **ordinal** if every monotonic transformation of a function with this characteristic still has this characteristic.
   Cardinal properties are not preserved by monotonic transformations.

Example 20.10   Consider the class of utility functions on $\mathbf{R}_+^2$ that are mono-
mials — polynomials with only one term; for example, the polynomial $u(x, y) = x^2 y$. The utility function $v(x, y) = x^2 y + 1$ is a monotonic transformation of
u. As we discussed above, both u and v have the same indifference curves.
However, v is not a monomial. So, being monomial is a cardinal property. We
should be uncomfortable with any theorem which only holds for *monomial*
utility functions.

Example 20.11   A utility function $u(x_1, x_2)$ is **monotone in** x_1 if for each fixed
x_2, u is an increasing function of x_1. If u is differentiable, we could write this
property as $\partial u/\partial x_1 > 0$. Intuitively, monotonicity in x_1 means that increasing
consumption of commodity one increases utility; in other words, commodity
one is a *good*. This property depends only on the shape and location of the
level sets of u and on the direction of higher utility. Therefore, it is an ordinal
property. Analytically, if $g(z)$ is a monotonic transformation with $g' > 0$, then
by the Chain Rule

$$\frac{\partial}{\partial x_1} \left[g(u(x_1, x_2)) \right] = g'(u(x_1, x_2)) \cdot \frac{\partial u}{\partial x_1}(x_1, x_2) > 0.$$

Example 20.12   Because of their preference for ordinal concepts over cardinal
concepts, economists would much rather work with the marginal rate of substitution (MRS) than with the marginal utility (MU) of any given utility function,
because MU is a cardinal concept. For example, if $v = 2u$,

$$\frac{\partial v}{\partial x_1}(x_1^*, x_2^*) = 2\frac{\partial u}{\partial x_1}(x_1^*, x_2^*).$$

Thus, equivalent utility functions have different marginal utilities at the same
bundle. On the other hand, MRS is an ordinal concept. Let v be a general
monotonic transformation of u: $v(x, y) = g(u(x, y))$. The MRS for v at

$$\frac{\dfrac{\partial v}{\partial x}(x^*, y^*)}{\dfrac{\partial v}{\partial y}(x^*, y^*)} = \frac{\dfrac{\partial}{\partial x} g(u(x^*, y^*))}{\dfrac{\partial}{\partial y} g(u(x^*, y^*))}$$

$$= \frac{g'(u(x^*, y^*)) \cdot \frac{\partial u}{\partial x}(x^*, y^*)}{g'(u(x^*, y^*)) \cdot \frac{\partial u}{\partial y}(x^*, y^*)}$$

$$= \frac{\frac{\partial u}{\partial x}(x^*, y^*)}{\frac{\partial u}{\partial y}(x^*, y^*)},$$

the MRS for u at (x^*, y^*).

Remark   In dealing with production functions, we care a lot about the number that a production function assigns to any isoquant. The level of output for each input has full meaning here. In other words, the distinction between cardinal and ordinal is of no concern when we are speaking about production functions.

EXERCISES

20.9   For each of the five utility functions in (11) in Example 20.9, identify the level sets which correspond to the level sets $\{xy = 1\}$ and $\{xy = 4\}$ of u. For example, the level set $\{xy = 1\}$ corresponds to the level set $\{3xy + 2 = 5\}$. In each case, convince yourself that these level curves are indeed identical by finding four bundles on the level set of xy and showing that these bundles are on the corresponding level sets of the other five utility functions.

20.10   Show directly that each of the five equivalent utility functions in Example 20.9 have the same marginal rates of substitution at the bundle (2, 1). Show that they have different marginal utilities (of good one) at (2, 1).

20.11   Which of the following are monotonic transformations of $\mathbf{R}_+$?

   a) $z^4 + z^2$,   *b)* $z^4 - z^2$,   *c)* $z/(z + 1)$,   *d)* $\sqrt{z}$,   *e)* $\sqrt{z^2 + 4}$.

20.12   Which of the following functions are equivalent to xy? For those which are, what monotonic transformation provides this equivalence?

   a) $7x^2y^2 + 2$,   *b)* $\ln x + \ln y + 1$,   *c)* $x^2 y$,   *d)* $x^{1/3}y^{1/3}$.

20.13   Use the monotonic transformation z^k to prove that every homogeneous function is equivalent to a homogeneous function of degree one.

20.14   Is having decreasing marginal utility, $(\partial^2 U/\partial x_i^2) < 0$ for all i, an ordinal property? Why?

20.15   Prove that any function $f: \mathbf{R}^1 \to \mathbf{R}^1$ with $f' > 0$ everywhere is equivalent to a homogeneous function of degree one.

20.4   HOMOTHETIC FUNCTIONS

Motivation and Definition

As we stated at the beginning of the previous section, homogeneity is a cardinal property, not an ordinal one. We need only one example to verify this, but we will present two. The functions $g_1(z) = z^3 + z$ and $g_2(z) = z + 1$ are both monotonic transformations. However, if we apply these transformations to the homogeneous function $u(x, y) = xy$, we obtain the *nonhomogeneous functions* $v(x, y) = x^3 y^3 + xy$ and $w(x, y) = xy + 1$.

Nevertheless, as Theorem 20.3 indicates, many of the important properties that make homogeneous functions so useful in utility theory are ordinal properties:

(1) Level sets are radial expansions and contractions of each other.
(2) The slope of level sets is constant along rays from the origin.

These two properties are clearly ordinal; they pertain only to the shape and slopes of level curves with no concern at all about the numbers attached to these level sets. Their consequences for demand theory are described in Theorem 20.3: Income expansion paths are rays coming out of the origin, and the income elasticity of demand is everywhere 1.

We now define a class of ordinal functions — a class that has all the ordinal properties that homogeneous functions have.

Definition   A function $v: \mathbf{R}^n_+ \rightarrow \mathbf{R}$ is called **homothetic** if it is a monotone transformation of a homogeneous function, that is, if there is a monotonic transformation $z \mapsto g(z)$ of $\mathbf{R}_+$ and a homogeneous function $u : \mathbf{R}^n_+ \rightarrow \mathbf{R}_+$ such that $v(\mathbf{x}) = g(u(\mathbf{x}))$ for all $\mathbf{x}$ in the domain.

Example 20.13   The two functions at the beginning of this section,

$$v(x, y) = x^3 y^3 + xy \quad \text{and} \quad w(x, y) = xy + 1,$$

are homothetic functions with $u(x, y) = xy$ and with $g_1(z) = z^3 + z$ and $g_2(z) = z + 1$, respectively. The five examples in Example 20.1 are homothetic functions.

It should be clear by its definition that homotheticity is an ordinal property. To prove this analytically, we need to prove that a monotonic transformation of a homothetic function is still homothetic. Let $z \mapsto h(z)$ be a monotonic transformation and let $\mathbf{x} \mapsto v(\mathbf{x})$ be a homothetic transformation. We need to check that $h \circ v$ is homothetic. By the definition of homothetic, $v(\mathbf{x})$ can be written as $v(\mathbf{x}) = g(u(\mathbf{x}))$, where g is a monotonic transformation and $z = u(\mathbf{x})$ is a homogeneous function. Now

$$h(v(\mathbf{x})) = h(g(u(\mathbf{x}))) = (h \circ g)(u(\mathbf{x})).$$

Since u is homogeneous, we need only show that $h \circ g$ is a monotonic transformation, in other words, that a monotonic transformation of a monotonic transformation is still a monotonic transformation.

Let $z_2 > z_1$. Since g is strictly increasing, $g(z_2) > g(z_1)$. Since h is strictly increasing, $h(g(z_2)) > h(g(z_1))$; that is, $(h \circ g)(z_2) > (h \circ g)(z_1)$. This implies that $h \circ g$ is a monotonic transformation, and therefore that $h \circ v = (h \circ g) \circ u$ is a monotonic transformation of the homogeneous function u; that is, $h \circ v$ is homothetic.

Characterizing Homothetic Functions

This section began with a discussion of the two primary ordinal properties of homogeneous functions. As we will now see, these properties characterize homothetic utility functions. The key property is the first: level sets are radial expansions and contractions of one another. Before proving that this property characterizes homothetic utility functions, we need some definitions that extend the notion of a monotone function to higher dimensions.

Definition   If $\mathbf{x}, \mathbf{y} \in \mathbf{R}^n$, write

$$\mathbf{x} \geq \mathbf{y} \quad \text{if} \quad x_i \geq y_i \text{ for } i = 1, \ldots, n,$$

$$\mathbf{x} > \mathbf{y} \quad \text{if} \quad x_i > y_i \text{ for } i = 1, \ldots, n,$$

A function $u: \mathbf{R}^n_+ \to \mathbf{R}$ is **monotone** if for all $\mathbf{x}, \mathbf{y} \in \mathbf{R}^n_+$,

$$\mathbf{x} \geq \mathbf{y} \quad \Longrightarrow \quad u(\mathbf{x}) \geq u(\mathbf{y}).$$

The function u is **strictly monotone** if for all $\mathbf{x}, \mathbf{y} \in \mathbf{R}^n_+$,

$$\mathbf{x} > \mathbf{y} \quad \Longrightarrow \quad u(\mathbf{x}) > u(\mathbf{y}).$$

Monotonicity and strict monotonicity are natural properties of utility functions in that they capture the essence of the "more is better" aspect of preferences. The following theorem gives us the promised characterization of homothetic functions.

Theorem 20.8   Let $u : \mathbf{R}^n_+ \to \mathbf{R}$ be a strictly monotonic function. Then, u is homothetic if and only if for all $\mathbf{x}$ and $\mathbf{y}$ in $\mathbf{R}^n_+$,

$$u(\mathbf{x}) \geq u(\mathbf{y}) \quad \Longleftrightarrow \quad u(\alpha\mathbf{x}) \geq u(\alpha\mathbf{y}) \quad \text{for all } \alpha > 0. \qquad (12)$$

Proof We first show that if u satisfies (12), it is homothetic. Let $\mathbf{e}$ denote the vector $(1, 1, \ldots, 1)$, that spans the diagonal Δ in $\mathbf{R}^n$. Define function $f: \mathbf{R}_+ \to \mathbf{R}$ by

$$f(t) = u(t\mathbf{e}).$$

Since u is strictly increasing, so is f; and therefore, f has a strictly increasing inverse g. Let $v = g \circ u$. Then,

$$f \circ v = f \circ (g \circ u) = (f \circ g) \circ u = u.$$

To prove that $u = f \circ v$ is homothetic, we need only show that v is homogeneous.

For any scalar a, the function $a \mapsto g(a)$ tells how far up the diagonal Δ the level set $u^{-1}(a)$ meets Δ. Consequently, $v(\mathbf{x}) = g(u(\mathbf{x}))$ tells how far up Δ the u-level set through $\mathbf{x}$ crosses Δ. Analytically, $t = v(\mathbf{x})$ is the solution of

$$u(\mathbf{x}) = u(t\mathbf{e}). \tag{13}$$

Let $\alpha > 0$ be a scalar. By (12) and Exercise 20.20,

$$u(\mathbf{x}) = u(t\mathbf{e}) \quad \Longrightarrow \quad u(\alpha\mathbf{x}) = u(\alpha t\mathbf{e}). \tag{14}$$

But, (14) indicates that αt is the solution of (13) with $\alpha\mathbf{x}$ replacing $\mathbf{x}$. In other words, $v(\alpha\mathbf{x}) = \alpha v(\mathbf{x})$; v is homogeneous of degree one. Since v is homogeneous and f is increasing, $u = f \circ v$ is homothetic.

To prove the converse, suppose first that u is *linear homogeneous*, that is, homogeneous of degree 1, and that $u(\mathbf{x}) \geq u(\mathbf{y})$ and $\alpha > 0$. These two properties yield

$$u(\alpha\mathbf{x}) = \alpha u(\mathbf{x})$$

$$\geq \alpha u(\mathbf{y})$$

$$= u(\alpha\mathbf{y});$$

so, property (12) holds.

More generally, suppose that u is homothetic, so that $u = g_1 \circ v$, with g_1 increasing and v homogeneous of degree k. Write v as $g_2 \circ h$, where $g_2(z) = z^k$ and $h(\mathbf{x}) = v(\mathbf{x})^{1/k}$. One checks easily that v is homogeneous of degree one and that g_2 is increasing, so that we can write u as $u = f \circ h$ with $f \equiv g_1 \circ g_2$ increasing and h linear homogeneous.

Once again, suppose $u(\mathbf{x}) \geq u(\mathbf{y})$ and $\alpha > 0$. Since f is strictly increasing, it has a strictly increasing inverse f^{-1}:

$$f^{-1}(u(\mathbf{x})) \geq f^{-1}(u(\mathbf{y})),$$

$$v(\mathbf{x}) \geq v(\mathbf{y}),$$

$$v(\alpha\mathbf{x}) = \alpha v(\mathbf{x}) \geq \alpha v(\mathbf{y}) = v(\alpha\mathbf{y}),$$

$$f(v(\alpha\mathbf{x})) \geq f(v(\alpha\mathbf{y})),$$

$$u(\alpha\mathbf{x}) \geq u(\alpha\mathbf{y});$$

and so u satisfies property (12). ■

The second ordinal property of homogencity is that the slope of level sets is constant along rays from the origin. This property provides a calculus-based necessary condition for homotheticity, just as Euler's theorem does for homogeneity.

Theorem 20.9   Let u be a C^1 function on $\mathbf{R}^n_+$. If u is homothetic, then the slopes of the tangent planes to the level sets of u are constant along rays from the origin; in other words, for *every* i, j and for every $\mathbf{x}$ in $\mathbf{R}^n_+$,

$$\frac{\dfrac{\partial u}{\partial x_i}(t\mathbf{x})}{\dfrac{\partial u}{\partial x_j}(t\mathbf{x})} = \frac{\dfrac{\partial u}{\partial x_i}(\mathbf{x})}{\dfrac{\partial u}{\partial x_j}(\mathbf{x})} \qquad \text{for all } t > 0. \tag{15}$$

Theorem 20.9 states that if u is homothetic, then its marginal rate of substitution is a homogeneous function of degree zero.

Proof   The proof is a straightforward combination of the proofs of Theorem 20.2 and Example 20.12, and will be left as an exercise.

In fact, the converse of Theorem 20.9 is also true. It provides us with a calculus-based *sufficient* condition for showing that a given function is homothetic. Some texts *define* a function to be homothetic if its marginal rate of substitution is homogeneous of degree zero. As in the case of the converse to Euler's theorem, the proof of the converse to Theorem 20.9, which we omit, involves differential equations.

Theorem 20.10   Let u be a C^1 function on $\mathbf{R}^n_+$. If condition (15) holds for all $\mathbf{x}$ in $\mathbf{R}^n_+$, all $t > 0$, and all i, j, then u is homothetic.

EXERCISES

20.16 Using the arguments in Example 20.13 and in Exercise 20.13, show that we can replace "homogeneous" by "homogeneous of degree one" in the definition of homothetic.

20.17 Which of the following functions are homothetic? Give a reason for each answer.

a) $e^{x^2 y} e^{xy^2}$,   b) $2 \log x + 3 \log y$,   c) $x^3 y^6 + 3x^2 y^4 + 6xy^2 + 9$,

d) $x^2 y + xy$,   e) $x^2 y^2 / (xy + 1)$.

20.18 Use Theorems 20.9 and 20.10 to check the homotheticity of the functions in Exercise 20.17 and to determine whether or not $f(x, y) = x^4 + x^2 y^2 + y^4 - 3x - 8y$ is homothetic.

20.19 Write out a complete, careful proof of Theorem 20.9.

20.20 Show that for a strictly monotone function u, the two inequalities in condition (12) can be replaced without loss of generality by equalities.

Concave and Quasiconcave Functions

Concave functions play a role in economic theory similar to the role that homogeneous functions play. Both classes arise naturally in economic models — homogeneous functions as demand functions, concave functions as expenditure functions. Profit functions and cost functions are naturally both homogeneous and concave. Both classes have desirable properties for utility and production functions. Both classes have straightforward calculus-based characterizations — homogeneous functions via Euler's theorem, concave functions via a second derivative test. Finally, both classes are cardinal and need to be modified for full use in utility theory.

On the other hand, concavity is a concept that is very different from homogeneity. As we will see, there are functions which are homogeneous but not concave or convex, and there are functions which are concave or convex but not homogeneous. In a sense, these two properties are complementary; economists often prefer to work with production functions that have both properties.

21.1   CONCAVE AND CONVEX FUNCTIONS

Students first meet concave and convex functions in their study of functions of one variable in Calculus I, as we did in Section 3.2. The definitions of concavity and convexity are the same for functions of n variables as they are for functions of one variable.

Definition   A real-valued function f defined on a convex subset U of $\mathbf{R}^n$ is **concave** if for all $\mathbf{x}, \mathbf{y}$ in U and for all t between 0 and 1,

$$f(t\mathbf{x} + (1 - t)\mathbf{y}) \geq tf(\mathbf{x}) + (1 - t)f(\mathbf{y}). \qquad (1)$$

A real-valued function g defined on a convex subset U of $\mathbf{R}^n$ is **convex** if for all $\mathbf{x}, \mathbf{y}$ in U and for all t between 0 and 1,

$$g(t\mathbf{x} + (1 - t)\mathbf{y}) \leq tg(\mathbf{x}) + (1 - t)g(\mathbf{y}). \qquad (2)$$

Remark   Notice that f is concave if and only if $-f$ is convex. To every property of concave functions, there is a naturally corresponding property of convex functions.

Remark   Many introductory calculus texts call convex functions "concave up" and concave functions "concave down," as we did in Section 3.2. From now on, we will stick with the more classical terms: "convex" and "concave."

Remark   Do not confuse the notion of a convex *function* with that of a convex *set*. A set U is a **convex set** if whenever $\mathbf{x}$ and $\mathbf{y}$ are points in U, the line segment joining $\mathbf{x}$ to $\mathbf{y}$,

$$\ell(\mathbf{x}, \mathbf{y}) \equiv \{(t\mathbf{x} + (1 - t)\mathbf{y} : 0 \leq t \leq 1\},$$

is also in U. In Figure 21.1, the ball in (a) and the interior of the triangle in (b) are convex sets, while the *annulus* (region between two concentric circles) in (c) and the star in (d) are not convex sets, as the line segments in these last two shapes indicate. The definition of a concave or convex function f requires that whenever f is defined at $\mathbf{x}$ and at $\mathbf{y}$, it is defined on the segment $\ell(\mathbf{x}, \mathbf{y})$. Thus convex and concave functions are required to have convex domains. In this section, all functions will be defined on convex sets, whether the function is concave, convex, or neither. This is not the only connections between convex sets and convex and concave functions. Check that f is concave if and only if $\{(x, y) : y \leq f(x)\}$ is a convex set, and work out the corresponding statement for convex functions. Almost all functions in economics, especially utility and production functions, have convex sets as their natural domains

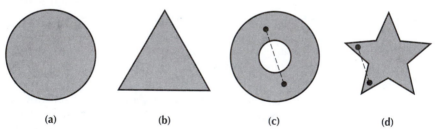

(a)   (b)   (c)   (d)

**Figure
21.1**   *Parts (a) and (b) represent convex sets; (c) and (d) illustrate nonconvex sets.*

Students usually develop a geometric intuition for concave and convex functions of one variable in Calculus I. They can recognize a concave function by its graph because, as Figure 21.2 illustrates, the inequality (1) in the definition of a concave function has the following geometric interpretation:

A function f of n variables is concave if and only if any secant line connecting two points on the graph of f lies *below* the graph. A function is convex if and only if any secant line connecting two points on its graph lies *above* its graph.

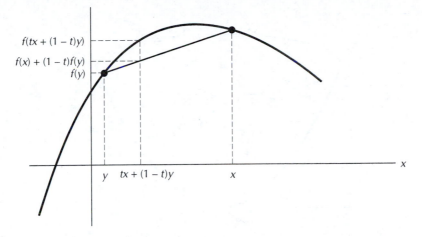

$f(tx + (1 - t)y)$

$f(x) + (1 - t)f(y)$

$f(y)$

x

$y \quad tx + (1 - t)y \qquad x$

The geometric interpretation of the definition of a concave function.

**Figure
21.2**

This property is illustrated in Figures 21.3 and 21.4, which present the graphs of two prototypical convex functions: $y = x^2$ and $z = x_1^2 + x_2^2$.

In developing an intuition for concave functions of several variables and in proving theorems about their properties, it is useful to notice that a function of n variables defined on a convex set U is concave if and only if its restriction to any line segment in U is a concave function of *one* variable. This should be intuitively clear since the definition (1) of a concave function is a statement about its behavior on line segments. Because it is such a useful fact, we provide a careful analytical proof. In the remainder of this section, we will use this result to reduce the proofs of theorems about concave functions on $\mathbf{R}^n$ to statements about concave functions of a single variable.

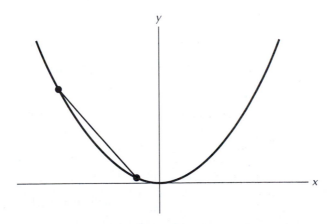

y

x

The graph of the convex function $y = x^2$.

**Figure
21.3**

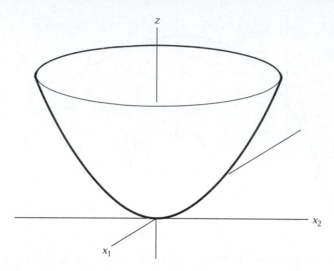

**Figure
21.4**

The graph of the convex function $z = x_1^2 + x_2^2$.

Theorem 21.1 Let f be a function defined on a convex subset U of $\mathbf{R}^n$. Then, f is concave (convex) if and only if its restriction to every line segment in U is a concave (convex) function of one variable.

Proof Suppose that the restriction of f to every line segment in U is a concave function. To prove that f is a concave function on U, let $\mathbf{x}$ and $\mathbf{y}$ be arbitrary points in U. Let $g(t) \equiv f(t\mathbf{x} + (1-t)\mathbf{y})$. By hypothesis, g is concave. So, for t between 0 and 1,

$$
\begin{aligned}
f(t\mathbf{x} + (1-t)\mathbf{y}) &= g(t) && \text{(definition of } g) \\
&= g(t \cdot 1 + (1-t) \cdot 0) && \\
&\geq tg(1) + (1-t)g(0) && \text{(since } g \text{ is concave)} \\
&= tf(\mathbf{x}) + (1-t)f(\mathbf{y}). && \text{(definition of } g)
\end{aligned}
$$

Consequently, f is concave.

Conversely, suppose that f is concave. We want to show that $g(t) \equiv f(t\mathbf{x} + (1-t)\mathbf{y})$, the restriction of f to the line containing $\mathbf{x}$ and $\mathbf{y}$ is concave. To do this, fix s_1 and s_2 and let t be between 0 and 1. Then,

$$
g(ts_1 + (1-t)s_2) = f\big((ts_1 + (1-t)s_2)\mathbf{x} + (1 - (ts_1 + (1-t)s_2))\mathbf{y}\big)
$$

$$
\text{(definition of } g)
$$

$$
= f\big(t(s_1\mathbf{x} + (1-s_1)\mathbf{y}) + (1-t)(s_2\mathbf{x} + (1-s_2)\mathbf{y})\big)
$$

$$
\text{(rearranging)}
$$

$$\geq tf(s_1\mathbf{x} + (1 - s_1)\mathbf{y}) + (1 - t)f(s_2\mathbf{x} + (1 - s_2)\mathbf{y})$$

$$\text{(concavity of } f)$$

$$= tg(s_1) + (1 - t)g(s_2) \quad \text{(definition of } g).$$

Therefore, g is concave. The proof for convex functions is nearly identical. ∎

The goal of the remainder of this section is to understand concave and convex functions more deeply by working toward three concrete goals:

(1) to develop simple calculus-based tests for concavity or convexity,
(2) to discover the desirable properties that concave and convex functions have; and
(3) to see how concave and convex functions arise in economic models.

In our discussions, we will usually work with concave functions rather than convex functions, since any statement about one type can easily be translated into a statement about the other. When we summarize our results in the statements of theorems, we will state the results for both types of functions.

Calculus Criteria for Concavity

As the discussion thus far illustrates, one can tell whether or not a function on $\mathbf{R}^n$ is concave by looking at its graph in $\mathbf{R}^{n+1}$. In fact, a more geometric way of phrasing the definition of concavity is to say: a function of n variables is concave if and only if the set **below** its graph in $\mathbf{R}^{n+1}$ is a convex set, as in Figure 21.2; a function is convex if and only if the set **above** its graph in $\mathbf{R}^{n+1}$ is a convex set, as in Figures 21.3 and 21.4. (See Exercise 21.5.)

Of course, it is usually not practical or even possible to draw the graph of a function to test for concavity. We need a more analytic criterion. Students studying functions of one variable in Calculus I learn two simple analytic tests for concavity:

(1) A C^1 function on an interval I is concave if and only if its first derivative $f'(x)$ is a decreasing function of x for x on I.
(2) A C^2 function f is concave on an interval I if and only if its second derivative $f''(x)$ is ≤ 0 for all x in I.

(See Section 3.2.) As one might guess from Theorem 21.1, the generalizations of these criteria work in all dimensions. We must first figure out what these generalizations are.

The natural generalization of the first derivative $f'(x)$ to functions of several variables is the (Jacobian) matrix of the first order partial derivatives of f:

$$Df(\mathbf{x}) = \left(\frac{\partial f}{\partial x_1}(\mathbf{x}) \quad \frac{\partial f}{\partial x_2}(\mathbf{x}) \quad \cdots \quad \frac{\partial f}{\partial x_n}(\mathbf{x}) \right).$$

Since this first derivative $Df(\mathbf{x})$ can be thought of as n functions of n variables, that is, as a function from $\mathbf{R}^n$ to $\mathbf{R}^n$, we need to work a little to interpret the statement "$Df(\mathbf{x})$ is a decreasing function." The following theorem provides a closely related first order condition for concavity on $\mathbf{R}^1$ that has an obvious generalization to functions of several variables.

Theorem 21.2   Let f be a C^1 function on an interval I in $\mathbf{R}$. Then, f is concave on I if and only if

$$f(y) - f(x) \leq f'(x)(y - x) \quad \text{for all } x, y \in I. \tag{3}$$

The function f is convex on I if and only if

$$f(y) - f(x) \geq f'(x)(y - x) \quad \text{for all } x, y \in I.$$

Remark   First we show that condition (3) means that f' is a decreasing function. Divide both sides of (3) by $(y - x)$; remember to reverse the inequality when $y - x < 0$. The results are

$$\frac{f(y) - f(x)}{y - x} \leq f'(x) \quad \text{for all } y > x \in I \tag{4}$$

and

$$\frac{f(y) - f(x)}{y - x} \geq f'(x) \quad \text{for all } y < x \in I. \tag{5}$$

To see that (4) and (5) imply that f' is decreasing, suppose $z_1 < z_2$ in I. Then,

$$
\begin{aligned}
f'(z_1) &\geq \frac{f(z_2) - f(z_1)}{z_2 - z_1} &&\text{(by (4) with } x = z_1 \text{ and } y = z_2) \\[2mm]
&= \frac{f(z_1) - f(z_2)}{z_1 - z_2} &&\text{(multiplying top and bottom by } -1) \\[2mm]
&\geq f'(z_2) &&\text{(by (5) with } x = z_2 \text{ and } y = z_1)
\end{aligned}
$$

Proof of Theorem 21.2.   Suppose that f is a concave function on I. Let $x, y \in I$ and let $t \in (0, 1]$. Then,

$$tf(y) + (1 - t)f(x) \leq f(ty + (1 - t)x)$$

or

$$f(y) - f(x) \leq \frac{f(x + t(y - x)) - f(x)}{t}$$

$$= \frac{f(x + t(y - x)) - f(x)}{t(y - x)}(y - x).$$

Condition (3) follows by letting $t \to 0$ in the last expression.

On the other hand, suppose (3) holds for all x, y in I. Then,

$$f(x) - f((1 - t)x + ty) \leq f'((1 - t)x + ty)(x - ((1 - t)x + ty))$$
$$= -tf'((1 - t)x + ty)(y - x).$$

Similarly,

$$f(y) - f((1 - t)x + ty) \leq (1 - t)f'((1 - t)x + ty)(y - x).$$

Multiply the first inequality through by $(1 - t)$ and the second by t; then add the two to obtain

$$(1 - t)f(x) + tf(y) \leq f((1 - t)x + ty). \qquad \blacksquare$$

The natural generalization of condition (3) to functions of several variables is now straightforward.

Theorem 21.3 Let f be a C^1 function on a convex subset U of $\mathbf{R}^n$. Then, f is concave on U if and only if for all $\mathbf{x}$, $\mathbf{y}$ in U:

$$f(\mathbf{y}) - f(\mathbf{x}) \leq Df(\mathbf{x})(\mathbf{y} - \mathbf{x});$$

that is,

$$f(\mathbf{y}) - f(\mathbf{x}) \leq \frac{\partial f}{\partial x_1}(\mathbf{x})(y_1 - x_1) + \cdots + \frac{\partial f}{\partial x_n}(\mathbf{x})(y_n - x_n). \qquad (6)$$

Similarly, f is convex on U if and only if $f(\mathbf{y}) - f(\mathbf{x}) \geq Df(\mathbf{x})(\mathbf{y} - \mathbf{x})$ for all $\mathbf{x}$, $\mathbf{y}$ in U.

Proof Let $\mathbf{x}$ and $\mathbf{y}$ be arbitrary points in U. Let

$$g_{\mathbf{x},\mathbf{y}}(t) \equiv f(t\mathbf{y} + (1 - t)\mathbf{x})$$
$$= f(x_1 + t(y_1 - x_1), \ldots, x_n + t(y_n - x_n)).$$

Then, by the Chain Rule,

$$g'_{\mathbf{x},\mathbf{y}}(t) = \sum_{i=1}^{n} \frac{\partial f}{\partial x_i}(\mathbf{x} + t(\mathbf{y} - \mathbf{x}))(y_i - x_i) \qquad (7)$$

and

$$g'_{\mathbf{x},\mathbf{y}}(0) = \sum_{i=1}^{n} \frac{\partial f}{\partial x_i}(\mathbf{x})(y_i - x_i) = Df(\mathbf{x})(\mathbf{y} - \mathbf{x}).$$

By Theorems 21.1 and 21.2, f is concave if and only if every such $g_{x,y}$ is concave if and only if for every $x, y \in U$,

$$g_{x,y}(1) - g_{x,y}(0) \leq g'_{x,y}(0)(1 - 0) = g'_{x,y}(0)$$

if and only if for every $x, y \in U$,

$$f(y) - f(x) \leq Df(x)(y - x). \quad \blacksquare$$

Corollary 21.4   If f is a C^1 concave function on a convex set U and if $x_0 \in U$, then

$$Df(x_0)(y - x_0) \leq 0 \quad \text{implies} \quad f(y) \leq f(x_0). \tag{8}$$

In particular, if $Df(x_0)(y - x_0) \leq 0$ for all $y \in U$, then x_0 is a global max of f.

Let's stop to consider the geometry of this situation. To this end, we'll use the more geometric concept of the gradient vector $\nabla f(x_0)$ instead of the derivative matrix $Df(x_0)$. Recall from Section 15.2 that $\nabla f(x_0)$ is a vector perpendicular to the level set of f through x_0. Inequality (8) says that if the vector from x_0 to y makes an obtuse angle with $\nabla f(x_0)$ at x_0, that is, if $\nabla f(x_0) \cdot (y - x_0) \leq 0$, then $f(y) \leq f(x_0)$. Alternatively, since $\nabla f(x_0)$ is perpendicular to the tangent hyperplane of the level set of f at x_0, condition (8) says that for a concave function the set $\{z : f(z) \geq f(x_0)\}$, including the level set $\{z : f(z) = f(x_0)\}$, lies above the hyperplane tangent to the level set of f at x_0. In short, if f is concave, then every level set of f lies above any of its tangent planes, where "above" means in the direction of increasing values of f. See Figure 21.5.

Example 21.1   Let us apply the test of Theorem 21.3 to show that $f(x_1, x_2) = x_1^2 + x_2^2$ is convex on $\mathbf{R}^n$. The function f is convex if and only if

$$(y_1^2 + y_2^2) - (x_1^2 + x_2^2) \geq (2x_1 \quad 2x_2) \begin{pmatrix} y_1 - x_1 \\ y_2 - x_2 \end{pmatrix}$$

$$= 2x_1 y_1 - 2x_1^2 + 2x_2 y_2 - 2x_2^2$$

if and only if

$$y_1^2 + y_2^2 + x_1^2 + x_2^2 - 2x_1 y_1 - 2x_2 y_2 \geq 0$$

if and only if

$$(y_1 - x_1)^2 + (y_2 - x_2)^2 \geq 0,$$

which is true for all (x_1, x_2) and (y_1, y_2) in $\mathbf{R}^2$.

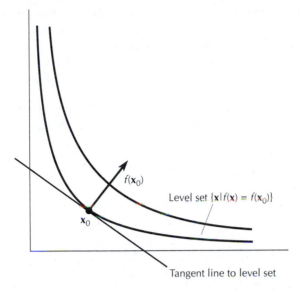

Relationship between grad $f(\mathbf{x}_0)$ and the level set through $\mathbf{x}_0$ for a concave f.

**Figure
21.5**

Theorem 21.3 is a very useful technique for proving properties about concave and convex functions. However, since it involves checking an *inequality* for all $\mathbf{x}$ and $\mathbf{y}$ in the domain, it is usually not a practical test for checking whether any given function is concave or convex. For the latter purpose, we will find it more practical to use the generalization of the second derivative test: f is concave on an interval I if and only if $f''(x) \leq 0$ for all x in I. (See Section 3.2.) The natural generalization of the second derivative $f''(x)$ to functions of several variables is the Hessian matrix of all the second order partial derivatives of f on $\mathbf{R}^1$:

$$D^2 f(\mathbf{x}) = \begin{pmatrix} f_{x_1 x_1} & f_{x_1 x_2} & \cdots & f_{x_1 x_n} \\ f_{x_2 x_1} & f_{x_2 x_2} & \cdots & f_{x_2 x_n} \\ \vdots & \vdots & \ddots & \vdots \\ f_{x_n x_1} & f_{x_n x_2} & \cdots & f_{x_n x_n} \end{pmatrix},$$

where we write $f_{x_i x_j}$ for $\partial^2 f / \partial x_i \partial x_j$ and each entry is evaluated at the point $\mathbf{x}$. The natural generalization of $f''(x) \leq 0$ is the statement that the Hessian matrix $D^2 f(\mathbf{x})$ is negative semidefinite at every $\mathbf{x}$ in the domain of f. The following theorem summarizes the second order test for concave and convex functions on $\mathbf{R}^n$.

Theorem 21.5   Let f be a C^2 function on an open convex subset U of $\mathbf{R}^n$. Then, f is a concave function on U if and only if the Hessian $D^2 f(\mathbf{x})$ is negative semidefinite for all $\mathbf{x}$ in U. The function f is a convex function on U if and only if $D^2 f(\mathbf{x})$ is positive semidefinite for all $\mathbf{x}$ in U.

Remark   Recall from Section 16.2 that a matrix H is positive definite if and only if $\mathbf{v}^T H \mathbf{v} > 0$ for all $\mathbf{v} \neq \mathbf{0}$ in $\mathbf{R}^n$; H is negative definite if and only if $\mathbf{v}^T H \mathbf{v} < 0$ for all $\mathbf{v} \neq \mathbf{0}$ in $\mathbf{R}^n$. Replacing the strict inequalities above by weak ones yields the definitions of positive semidefinite and negative semidefinite. Theorem 16.1 from Chapter 16 provides analytic necessary and sufficient conditions for a matrix to be definite or semidefinite:

(1) A matrix H is positive definite if and only if its n leading principal minors are all > 0.
(2) A matrix H is negative definite if and only if its n leading principal minors alternate in sign with the odd order ones being negative and the even order ones being positive.
(3) A matrix H is positive semidefinite if and only if its $2^n - 1$ principal minors are all ≥ 0.
(4) A matrix H is negative semidefinite if and only if its $2^n - 1$ principal minors are alternate in sign so that the odd order ones are ≤ 0 and the even order ones are ≥ 0.

Proof of Theorem 21.5.   As in the previous proof, let $\mathbf{x}$ and $\mathbf{y}$ be arbitrary points in U and let $g_{\mathbf{x},\mathbf{y}}(t) \equiv f(t\mathbf{y} + (1 - t)\mathbf{x})$. Then, f is concave on U if and only if each $g_{\mathbf{x},\mathbf{y}}(t)$ is concave, which is equivalent to each $g_{\mathbf{x},\mathbf{y}}''(t) \leq 0$. Now, by equation (7) and the Chain Rule,

$$g_{\mathbf{x},\mathbf{y}}''(t) = \frac{d}{dt}\left(\sum_{i=1}^{n} \frac{\partial f}{\partial x_i}(\mathbf{x} + t(\mathbf{y} - \mathbf{x}))(y_i - x_i)\right)$$

$$= \sum_{j=1}^{n}\sum_{i=1}^{n} \frac{\partial^2 f}{\partial x_i \partial x_j}(\mathbf{x} + t(\mathbf{y} - \mathbf{x}))(y_j - x_j)(y_i - x_i)$$

$$= \sum_{i,j=1}^{n} (y_j - x_j)\frac{\partial^2 f}{\partial x_i \partial x_j}(\mathbf{x} + t(\mathbf{y} - \mathbf{x}))(y_i - x_i)$$

$$= (\mathbf{y} - \mathbf{x})^T \cdot D^2 f(\mathbf{x} + t(\mathbf{y} - \mathbf{x})) \cdot (\mathbf{y} - \mathbf{x}).$$

If every $D^2 f(\mathbf{z})$ is negative semidefinite, then it follows that:

(a) every $g_{\mathbf{x},\mathbf{y}}''(t) \leq 0$,
(b) every $g_{\mathbf{x},\mathbf{y}}$ is concave, and
(c) f itself is concave.

Conversely, suppose that f is concave on U. Let $\mathbf{z}$ be an arbitrary point in U and let $\mathbf{v}$ be an arbitrary displacement vector in $\mathbf{R}^n$. We want to show that $\mathbf{v}^T D^2 f(\mathbf{z})\mathbf{v} \leq 0$. Since U is open, there is a $t_0 > 0$ such that $\mathbf{y} = \mathbf{z} + t_0\mathbf{v}$ is in U. Since f is concave, $g_{\mathbf{z},\mathbf{y}}$ is concave and $g_{\mathbf{z},\mathbf{y}}''(0) \leq 0$. By the previous paragraph,

$$0 \geq g''_{z,y}(0) = (\mathbf{y} - \mathbf{z})^T \cdot D^2 f(\mathbf{z}) \cdot (\mathbf{y} - \mathbf{z})$$
$$= (t_0 \mathbf{v})^T \cdot D^2 f(\mathbf{z}) \cdot (t_0 \mathbf{v})$$
$$= (t_0^2)[\mathbf{v}^T \cdot D^2 f(\mathbf{z}) \cdot \mathbf{v}].$$

Therefore, $\mathbf{v}^T \cdot D^2 f(\mathbf{z}) \cdot \mathbf{v} \leq 0$, and $D^2 f(\mathbf{z})$ is negative semidefinite for all $\mathbf{z}$ in U. ∎

Example 21.2 The Hessian of the function $f(x, y) = x^4 + x^2 y^2 + y^4 - 3x - 8y$ is

$$D^2 f(x, y) = \begin{pmatrix} 12x^2 + 2y^2 & 4xy \\ 4xy & 2x^2 + 12y^2 \end{pmatrix}.$$

For $(x, y) \neq (0, 0)$, the two leading principal minors, $12x^2 + 2y^2$ and $24x^4 + 132x^2 y^2 + 24y^4$, are both positive, so f is a convex function on all $\mathbf{R}^n$.

Example 21.3 A commonly used simple utility or production function is $F(x, y) = xy$. Its Hessian is

$$D^2 F(x, y) = \begin{pmatrix} 0 & 1 \\ 1 & 0 \end{pmatrix},$$

whose second order principal minor is $\det D^2 F(x, y) = -1$. Since this second order principal minor is negative, $D^2 F$ is indefinite and F is neither concave nor convex.

Example 21.4 Consider the monotonic transformation of the function F in the previous example by the function $g(z) = z^{1/4}$: $G(x, y) = x^{1/4} y^{1/4}$, defined only on the positive quadrant $\mathbf{R}^2_+$. The Hessian of G is

$$D^2 G(x, y) = \begin{pmatrix} -\frac{3}{16} x^{-7/4} y^{1/4} & \frac{1}{16} x^{-3/4} y^{-3/4} \\ \frac{1}{16} x^{-3/4} y^{-3/4} & -\frac{3}{16} x^{1/4} y^{-7/4} \end{pmatrix}.$$

For $x > 0, y > 0$, the first order leading principal minor is negative and the second order leading principal minor, $x^{-3/2} y^{-3/2}/128$, is positive. Therefore, $D^2 G(x, y)$ is negative definite on $\mathbf{R}^2_+$ and G is a concave function on $\mathbf{R}^2_+$.

Example 21.5 Now, consider the general Cobb-Douglas function on $\mathbf{R}^2_+$: $U(x, y) = x^a y^b$. Its Hessian is

$$D^2 U(x, y) = \begin{pmatrix} a(a-1)x^{a-2} y^b & abx^{a-1} y^{b-1} \\ abx^{a-1} y^{b-1} & b(b-1)x^a y^{b-2} \end{pmatrix},$$

whose determinant is

$$\det D^2 U(x, y) = ab(1 - a - b)x^{2a-2}y^{2b-2}.$$

In order for U to be concave on $\mathbf{R}^2_+$, we need $a(a-1) < 0$ and $ab(1-a-b) > 0$; that is, we need $0 < a < 1$, $0 < b < 1$, and $a + b \le 1$. In summary, a Cobb-Douglas production function on $\mathbf{R}^2_+$ is concave if and only if it exhibits constant or decreasing returns to scale.

Remark These four examples illustrate some relationships among the various classes of functions we have been studying. Examples 21.3 and 21.5 show that a function can be homogeneous or homothetic and not be concave or convex. Example 21.2, along with Exercise 20.13, shows that a function can be convex or concave and not be homogeneous or homothetic. Examples 21.4 and 21.5 show that a function can be both concave (or convex) *and* homogeneous (or homothetic). Finally, the last three examples clearly show that concavity is a *cardinal property*; a monotonic transformation of a concave function need not be concave.

EXERCISES

21.1 Prove that every linear function is homogeneous, concave, *and* convex.

21.2 Which of the following functions on $\mathbf{R}^n$ are concave or convex? At least *attempt* the first order test of Theorem 21.3, before settling down with the second order test of Theorem 21.5.

a) $f(x) = 3e^x + 5x^4 - \ln x$; b) $f(x, y) = -3x^2 + 2xy - y^2 + 3x - 4y + 1$;

c) $f(x, y, z) = 3e^x + 5y^4 - \ln z$; d) $f(x, y, z) = Ax^a y^b z^c$, $a, b, c > 0$.

21.3 Prove that a quadratic form on $\mathbf{R}^n$ is concave if and only if it is negative semidefinite. Prove that it is convex if and only if it is positive semidefinite. What can be said about the more general "quadratic function" $f(\mathbf{x}) = \mathbf{x}^T A\mathbf{x} + \mathbf{b} \cdot \mathbf{x} + c$?

21.4 Prove that every homogeneous function on $\mathbf{R}^1_+$ is either concave or convex.

21.5 Prove that a function of n variables is concave if and only if the set **below** its graph in $\mathbf{R}^{n+1}$ is a convex set. By Theorem 21.1, one need only prove this statement for functions of one variable.

21.6 Interpret inequalities (4) and (5) geometrically.

21.7 Suppose that f is concave and that g is the affine function $x \longmapsto ax + b$, with $a \ge 0$. Prove that $g \circ f$ is concave.

21.8 Let f and g be functions on $\mathbf{R}^1$. What assumptions on f and g guarantee that the composite $f \circ g$ is a concave function?

21.9 For what concave functions f is $1/f$ a convex function?

21.10 The product of two homogeneous functions is always homogeneous. Give conditions under which the product of two concave functions is concave.

21.2   PROPERTIES OF CONCAVE FUNCTIONS

The three properties that make concave functions so valuable in economics are that their critical points are automatically global maxima, that the weighted sum of concave functions is a concave function, and that the level sets of a concave function have just the right shapes for consumption and production theory.

  As shown in Chapter 17, in using calculus to find the interior maximum of a function f, one first finds the critical points of f by setting its first derivatives equal to zero and solving the corresponding equations. Then, one uses a second derivative test to separate the maxima from the minima and saddles, and one evaluates the function at all the local maxima to decide which of these local maxima is the global maximum. However, one never needs these extra steps for a *concave* function. A critical point of a concave function is automatically a maximum, and in fact a global maximum.

Theorem 21.6   Let f be a concave (convex) function on an open, convex subset U of $\mathbf{R}^n$. If $\mathbf{x}_0$ is a critical point of f, that is, $Df(\mathbf{x}_0) = \mathbf{0}$, then $\mathbf{x}_0 \in U$ is a *global maximizer (minimizer)* of f on U.

Proof   To prove that a critical point of a concave function is automatically a global maximizer, we simply refer to Theorem 21.3 and Corollary 21.4. If f is concave and $Df(\mathbf{x}_0) = \mathbf{0}$, then by inequalities (6) and (8), $f(\mathbf{y}) - f(\mathbf{x}_0) \leq 0$ for all $\mathbf{y}$ in U. In other words, for all $\mathbf{y} \in U$, $f(\mathbf{y}) \leq f(\mathbf{x}_0)$, or $\mathbf{x}_0$ is a global maximizer of f on U. ∎

  In fact, an even stronger result than Theorem 21.6 holds for concave functions. In the discussion above the statement of Theorem 21.6, we were speaking only of interior maxima. But frequently, the global maximum occurs on the *boundary* on the convex domain U. Corollary 21.4 immediately gives the following condition for a global maximum of a concave function, even if the maximizer is on the boundary of the domain. We leave its proof as an exercise. Note that this theorem includes Theorem 21.6 as a special case.

Theorem 21.7   Let f be a C^1 function defined on a convex subset U of $\mathbf{R}^n$. If f is a concave function and if $\mathbf{x}_0$ is a point in U which satisfies $Df(\mathbf{x}_0)(\mathbf{y}-\mathbf{x}_0) \leq 0$ for all $\mathbf{y} \in U$, then $\mathbf{x}_0$ is *global maximizer* of f on U. If f is a convex function and if $\mathbf{x}_0$ is a point in U which satisfies $Df(\mathbf{x}_0)(\mathbf{y} - \mathbf{x}_0) \geq 0$ for all $\mathbf{y} \in U$, then $\mathbf{x}_0$ is a *global minimizer* of f on U.

Example 21.6   If f is a C^1 *increasing*, concave function of one variable on the interval $[a,b]$, then $f'(b)(x - b) \leq 0$ for all $x \in [a,b]$. (Why?) By Theorem 21.7, b is the global maximizer of f on $[a,b]$.

Example 21.7 Consider the concave function $U(x, y) = x^{1/4}y^{1/4}$ on the (convex) triangle

$$B = \{(x, y) : x \geq 0, y \geq 0, x + y \leq 2\}.$$

By symmetry, we would expect that $(x_0, y_0) = (1,1)$ is the maximizer of U on B. To prove this, use Theorem 21.7. Let (x, y) be an arbitrary point in B. Then,

$$\frac{\partial U}{\partial x}(1, 1)(x - 1) + \frac{\partial U}{\partial y}(1, 1)(y - 1) = \frac{1}{4}(x - 1) + \frac{1}{4}(y - 1)$$

$$= \frac{1}{4}(x + y - 2)$$

$$\leq 0$$

since $x + y - 2 \leq 0$ for (x, y) in the constraint set B. By Theorem 21.7, $(1,1)$ is the global maximizer of U on B.

The property that critical points of concave functions are global maximizers is an important one in economic theory. For example, many economic principles, such as marginal rate of substitution equals the price ratio, or marginal revenue equals marginal cost are simply the first order *necessary* conditions of the corresponding maximization problem. Ideally, an economist would like such a rule to also be a *sufficient* condition guaranteeing that utility or profit is being maximized so that it can provide a guideline for economic behavior. This situation does occur when the objective function is concave. Furthermore, an economist, who wants to analyze how the maximizer in a parameterized problem depends on the parameters involved, will usually apply the implicit function theorem to the equations of the first order necessary conditions for maximization. The only situation in which it can be guaranteed that the solution to these perturbed equations is indeed a maximum for all values of the parameters occurs when the objective function is concave.

Example 21.8 Consider the problem of maximizing profit for a firm whose production function is $y = g(\mathbf{x})$, where y denotes output and $\mathbf{x}$ denotes the input bundle. If p denotes the price of the output and w_i is the cost per unit of input i, then the firm's profit function is

$$\Pi(\mathbf{x}) = pg(\mathbf{x}) - (w_1 x_1 + \cdots + w_n x_n). \tag{9}$$

As can easily be checked, Π will be a concave function provided that the production function is a concave function. (Exercise.) In this case, the first order condition

$$p\frac{\partial g}{\partial x_i} = w_i \quad \text{for } i = 1, 2, \ldots, n, \tag{10}$$

which says marginal revenue product equals the factor price for each input, is both necessary and sufficient for an interior profit maximizer. If one wants to study the effect of changes in w_i or p on the optimal input bundle, one would apply the comparative statics analysis to system (10). Since profit is concave for all p and $\mathbf{w}$, the solution to system (10) will automatically be the *optimal* input for all choices of p and $\mathbf{w}$.

A second valuable property of concave functions is that they behave well under addition and scalar multiplication by positive numbers, as the following theorem indicates. Its proof follows directly from the definition (1) of a concave function and is left as an exercise.

Theorem 21.8 Let $f_1, \ldots, f_k$ be concave (convex) functions, each defined on the same convex subset U of $\mathbf{R}^n$. Let $a_1, \ldots, a_k$ be positive numbers. Then, $a_1 f_1 + \cdots + a_k f_k$ is a concave (convex) function on U.

One can use Theorem 21.8 and the fact that linear functions are concave to deduce immediately that, if the production function g in Example 21.8 is concave, so is the corresponding profit function Π. One can sometimes use Theorem 21.8 to prove that a sum of functions is concave by showing that each summand is itself concave. For example, $f(x_1, \ldots, x_n) = a_1 x_1^{k_1} + \cdots + a_n x_n^{k_n}$ is concave on $\mathbf{R}^n_+$ provided each $a_i \geq 0$ and each k_i lies between 0 and 1. (See Exercise 21.4.)

Such a summation occurs in social welfare theory. In an economy with m consumers with utility functions $u_1, \ldots, u_m$ respectively, one measure of the social welfare of any allocation of resources is the sum $a_1 u_1 + \cdots + a_m u_m$, where the a_i's are any set of positive weights. If the u_i's are all concave, the corresponding social welfare function will be concave. In this case, the set of maximizers of the various social welfare functions will be the set of Pareto optimal allocations.

A third advantage of concave functions is that their level sets have just the right shapes: they bound convex subsets "from below."

Theorem 21.9 Let f be a function defined on a convex set U in $\mathbf{R}^n$. If f is concave, then for every $\mathbf{x}_0$ in U, the set

$$C_{x_0}^+ \equiv \{\mathbf{x} \in U : f(\mathbf{x}) \geq f(\mathbf{x}_0)\}$$

is a *convex* set. If f is convex, then for every $\mathbf{x}_0$ in U, the set

$$C_{x_0}^- \equiv \{\mathbf{x} \in U : f(\mathbf{x}) \leq f(\mathbf{x}_0)\}$$

is a *convex* set.

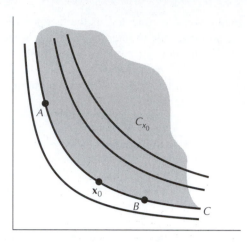

**Figure
21.6**   *The set "above" the level curve C is a convex set for a concave utility function.*

Proof   Let $\mathbf{x}$ and $\mathbf{y}$ be two points in $C_{x_0}^+$ so that $f(\mathbf{x}) \geq f(\mathbf{x}_0)$ and $f(\mathbf{y}) \geq f(\mathbf{x}_0)$. Then,

$$f(t\mathbf{x} + (1 - t)\mathbf{y}) \geq tf(\mathbf{x}) + (1 - t)f(\mathbf{y})$$
$$\geq tf(\mathbf{x}_0) + (1 - t)f(\mathbf{x}_0)$$
$$= f(\mathbf{x}_0).$$

So, $t\mathbf{x} + (1 - t)\mathbf{y}$ is in $C_{x_0}^+$ and $C_{x_0}^+$ is a convex set. ∎

The property that the set above any level set of a concave function is a convex set is a natural requirement for utility and production functions. For example, consider an indifference curve C of the concave utility function U pictured in Figure 21.6. Two bundles A and B have been labeled on curve C. By Theorem 21.9, the shaded region in Figure 21.6, which represents all bundles which are preferred to bundles A and B, is a convex set. In particular, the set of convex combinations of A and B — the bundles that can be formed by mixing the contents of bundles A and B — all lie on the line segment joining A to B and therefore lie in the shaded area. Thus, concave utility functions have the desirable property that given any two bundles A and B of "goods", a consumer with a concave utility function, will always prefer a mixture of bundles A and B to either A or B. An elementary microeconomics text might phrase this property as: a consumer would prefer a bundle containing a mixture of soda and chips to a bundle of all soda and no chips and to a bundle of no soda and all chips.

A more important advantage of the shape of the indifference curve in Figure 21.6 is that it displays a *diminishing marginal rate of substitution*. As one moves left to right along the indifference curve C increasing consumption of good one, the consumer is willing to give up more and more units of good one to gain an additional unit of good two. This property — a central axiom of consumer theory — is a property of concave utility functions because each level set forms the boundary of a convex region.

Concave Functions in Economics

We have just described three properties of concave functions that make them especially useful in economic models. In addition, there are some functions which arise in economic models that are naturally concave. For example, consider the **expenditure function** $e(\mathbf{p}, u)$, which describes the minimal amount of income necessary to achieve utility u at the prices $\mathbf{p}$. It can be described analytically as

$$e(\mathbf{p}, u) = \min\{p_1 x_1 + \ldots + p_n x_n : u(\mathbf{x}) \geq u\},$$

and will be studied in more detail in Section 22.1.

Theorem 21.10   The expenditure function is concave and homogeneous of degree one in $\mathbf{p}$.

Proof   Let $(\mathbf{p}, \mathbf{x})$ and $(\mathbf{p}', \mathbf{x}')$ be two price-consumption combinations that minimize expenditure at utility level u. Let $\mathbf{p}'' = t\mathbf{p} + (1 - t)\mathbf{p}'$ for any t between 0 and 1; and let $\mathbf{x}''$ be the corresponding expenditure minimizing bundle. Then,

$$e(\mathbf{p}'', u) = \mathbf{p}'' \cdot \mathbf{x}'' = t\mathbf{p} \cdot \mathbf{x}'' + (1 - t)\mathbf{p}' \cdot \mathbf{x}''. \tag{11}$$

But $\mathbf{x}''$ is not necessarily the cheapest way to achieve utility u at prices $\mathbf{p}$ or $\mathbf{p}'$. Therefore,

$$\mathbf{p} \cdot \mathbf{x}'' \geq e(\mathbf{p}, u) \quad \text{and} \quad \mathbf{p}' \cdot \mathbf{x}'' \geq e(\mathbf{p}', u) \tag{12}$$

Combining (11) and (12) yields the concavity of $e(\mathbf{p}, u)$ in $\mathbf{p}$:

$$e(\mathbf{p}'', u) \geq te(\mathbf{p}, u) + (1 - t)e(\mathbf{p}', u).$$

To see that $e(t\mathbf{p}, u) = te(\mathbf{p}, u)$, notice that from the above definition of the expenditure function, the $\mathbf{x}$ which minimizes $\mathbf{p} \cdot \mathbf{x}$ subject to $u(\mathbf{x}) \geq u$ will also minimize $t\mathbf{p} \cdot \mathbf{x}$ with the same constraint.   ∎

In fact, all that the above proof requires is that we were minimizing a *linear* objective function on a constraint set and that the function under consideration is just the minimum value. A number of other economic functions arise this way. For example, the cost function $c(\mathbf{w}, y)$ corresponding to a given production function g can be considered the minimum cost needed to produce output y, when input prices are given by $\mathbf{w}$:

$$c(\mathbf{w}, y) = \min\{w_1 x_1 + \cdots + w_n x_n : g(\mathbf{x}) = y\}.$$

The same argument as in the proof of Theorem 21.10 shows that $c(\mathbf{w}, y)$ is concave and homogeneous in factor prices $\mathbf{w}$. Finally, consider the optimal profit function $\pi(p, \mathbf{w})$ which is the maximum profit that can be achieved when the price of the output is p and the cost of the inputs is $\mathbf{w}$. Write π as

$$\pi(p, \mathbf{w}) = \max_{y, \mathbf{x}}\{py - \mathbf{w} \cdot \mathbf{x} : y \leq g(\mathbf{x})\}. \tag{13}$$

Then, $\pi(p, \mathbf{w})$ is *convex* and homogeneous of degree one in $(p, \mathbf{w})$. (Exercise.)

These three functions illustrate a general phenomenon about optimizing linear objective functions, which we state in the following theorem. The proof we leave as an exercise.

Theorem 21.11   Consider the problem of maximizing the linear objective function $\mathbf{a} \cdot \mathbf{x}$ with respect to $\mathbf{x}$ on a given constraint set. The value of the optimal objective function will be a convex and homogeneous of degree one function of the parameter $\mathbf{a}$. For a minimization problem with a linear objective function, the optimal value of the objective function will be a concave and homogeneous of degree one function of $\mathbf{a}$.

Finally, concave utility functions play a major role in expected utility theory because, as K. Arrow first observed, in such models the level of risk aversion of a consumer is measured by the concavity of the consumer's utility function.

EXERCISES

21.11   Prove that the profit function (9) in Example 21.8 is concave if the production function $y = g(\mathbf{x})$ is concave.

21.12   Suppose that a one-product monopolist faces an inverse demand function $p = F(q)$ and a cost function $q \longmapsto C(q)$.
  a) Write out the expression for its profit as a function of q.
  b) What assumptions on F and C yield a concave profit function?

21.13   Prove Theorem 21.7. Show that it implies Theorem 21.6.

21.14   Write out the proof of Theorem 21.2 for convex functions.

21.15   Prove Theorem 21.8 directly from the definition (1) of a concave function.

21.16   Prove that $\pi(p, \mathbf{w})$ in (13) is *convex* and homogeneous of degree one in $(p, \mathbf{w})$.

21.17   Prove Theorem 21.11.

21.3   QUASICONCAVE AND QUASICONVEX FUNCTIONS

Concave functions pose the same dilemma that homogeneous functions did in Section 20.2. They have many desirable properties for production and utility functions. However, as Examples 21.3, 21.4, and 21.5 clearly indicate, concavity is a *cardinal* property. It depends on the numbers which the function assigns to the level sets, not just on the shape of the level sets. In other words, a monotonic transformation of a concave function need *not* be concave.

However, concave functions have one fundamental ordinal property, as Theorem 21.9 indicates. Their level sets bound convex sets from below. This property leads to the highly desirable condition of diminishing marginal rate of substitution for indifference curves.

Just as we did for homogeneous functions, we give a name to the class of functions which have the desired ordinal property that concave functions have. A somewhat natural name for a function that is the ordinal version of a concave function is a quasiconcave function.

Definition   A function f defined on a convex subset U of $\mathbf{R}^n$ is **quasiconcave** if for every real number a,

$$C_a^+ \equiv \{\mathbf{x} \in U : f(\mathbf{x}) \geq a\}$$

is a convex set. Similarly, f is **quasiconvex** if for every real number a,

$$C_a^- \equiv \{\mathbf{x} \in U : f(\mathbf{x}) \leq a\}$$

is a convex set.

We present some alternative definitions of quasiconcave and quasiconvex in the following theorem, whose proof is left as an exercise.

Theorem 21.12   Let f be a function defined on a convex set U in $\mathbf{R}^n$. Then, the following statements are equivalent to each other:

(*a*) f is a quasiconcave function on U.
(*b*) For all $\mathbf{x}, \mathbf{y} \in U$ and all $t \in [0, 1]$,

$$f(\mathbf{x}) \geq f(\mathbf{y}) \quad \text{implies} \quad f(t\mathbf{x} + (1-t)\mathbf{y}) \geq f(\mathbf{y}).$$

(*c*) For all $\mathbf{x}, \mathbf{y} \in U$ and all $t \in [0, 1]$,

$$f(t\mathbf{x} + (1-t)\mathbf{y}) \geq \min\{f(\mathbf{x}), f(\mathbf{y})\}.$$

By Theorem 21.9, every concave function is quasiconcave and every convex function is quasiconvex. Furthermore, any monotonic transformation of a concave function is a quasiconcave function. In particular, since every Cobb-Douglas function is a monotonic transformation of a Cobb-Douglas function with decreasing returns to scale, every Cobb-Douglas function of two variables is quasiconcave.

Theorem 21.13   Every Cobb-Douglas function $F(x, y) = Ax^a y^b$ with A, a, and b all positive is quasiconcave.

Example 21.9   Consider the Leontief or fixed-coefficient production function $Q(x, y) = \min\{ax, by\}$ with $a, b > 0$. The level sets of Q are drawn in Figure 21.7. Certainly, the region above and to the right of any of this function's L-shaped level sets is a convex set. Therefore, Q is quasiconcave.

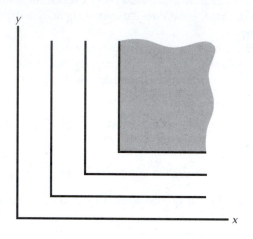

Figure 21.7

Fixed-coefficient production function.

Example 21.10   Consider the constant elasticity of substitution (CES) production function

$$Q(x, y) = (a_1 x_1^r + a_2 x_2^r)^{1/r}, \quad \text{where } 0 < r < 1.$$

By Theorem 21.8 and Exercise 21.4, $(a_1 x_1^r + a_2 x_2^r)$ is concave. Since $g(z) = z^{1/r}$ is a monotonic transformation, Q is a monotonic transformation of a concave function and therefore is quasiconcave.

Example 21.11   Let $y = f(x)$ be any increasing function on $\mathbf{R}^1$, as in Figure 21.8. For any x^*, $\{x : f(x) \geq f(x^*)\}$ is just the interval $[x^*, \infty)$, a convex subset of $\mathbf{R}^1$. So, f is quasiconcave. On the other hand, $\{x : f(x) \leq f(x^*)\}$ is the convex set $(-\infty, x^*]$. Therefore, an increasing function on $\mathbf{R}^1$ is both quasiconcave and quasiconvex. The same argument applies to a decreasing function.

Example 21.12   Any function on $\mathbf{R}^1$ which rises monotonically until it reaches a global maximum and then monotonically falls, such as $y = -x^2$ or the bell-shaped probability density function $y = ke^{-x^2}$, is a quasiconcave function, as Figure 21.9 indicates. For any x_1 as in Figure 21.9, there is a x_2 such that $f(x_1) = f(x_2)$. Then, $\{x : f(x) \geq f(x_1)\}$ is the convex interval $[x_1, x_2]$.

Remark   Notice that we take a slightly different tack in going from concave to quasiconcave than we did in going from homogeneous to homothetic. In the latter case, we simply defined a homothetic function as any function which has

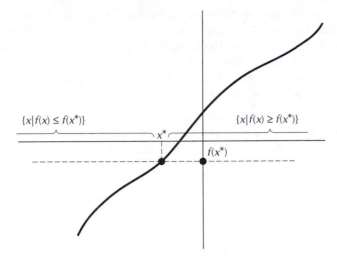

$\{x|f(x) \leq f(x^*)\}$ $\{x|f(x) \geq f(x^*)\}$

x^*

$f(x^*)$

An increasing function on $\mathbf{R}^1$ is both quasiconcave and quasiconvex.

**Figure
21.8**

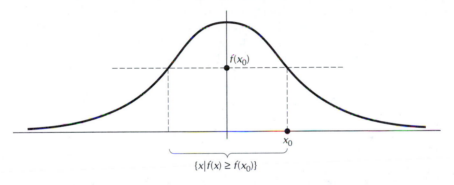

$f(x_0)$

x_0

$\{x|f(x) \geq f(x_0)\}$

These bell-shaped functions are quasiconcave.

**Figure
21.9**

the same level sets as a homogeneous function. In the former case, we defined a quasiconcave function as any function which has the desired ordinal property of concave functions. It is natural to ask if indeed any quasiconcave function is equivalent to some concave function by a monotonic transformation. K. Arrow and A. Enthoven considered this question in their path-breaking treatise on quasiconcave functions and provided a concrete example of a quasiconcave function which is *not* a monotonic transformation of any concave function. (See the Notes at the end of this chapter.)

Calculus Criteria

We now work toward developing calculus criteria for quasiconcavity. Analogous to Theorem 21.3 for concave functions, there is a necessary and sufficient first derivative test for quasiconcavity, that provides a useful technique for proving theorems about quasiconcave functions. Like Theorem 21.3, it is too unwieldy to use for checking whether or not any specific function is quasiconcave, so we will develop a simpler *second* order test in the next section. Since we have first order conditions for the other special classes of functions, we present this first order condition for quasiconcave functions.

Theorem 21.14   Suppose that F is a C^1 function on an open convex subset U of $\mathbf{R}^n$. Then, F is quasiconcave on U if and only if

$$F(\mathbf{y}) \geq F(\mathbf{x}) \text{ implies that } DF(\mathbf{x})(\mathbf{y} - \mathbf{x}) \geq 0; \tag{14}$$

F is quasiconvex on U if and only if

$$F(\mathbf{y}) \leq F(\mathbf{x}) \text{ implies that } DF(\mathbf{x})(\mathbf{y} - \mathbf{x}) \leq 0.$$

Proof   Suppose that F is quasiconcave on U and that $F(\mathbf{y}) \geq F(\mathbf{x})$ for some $\mathbf{x}, \mathbf{y} \in U$. Then, for all $t \in [0, 1]$,

$$F(\mathbf{x} + t(\mathbf{y} - \mathbf{x})) \geq F(\mathbf{x}).$$

Since

$$\frac{F(\mathbf{x} + t(\mathbf{y} - \mathbf{x})) - F(\mathbf{x})}{t} \geq 0$$

for all $t \in (0, 1)$, we let $t \to 0$ to obtain

$$DF(\mathbf{x})(\mathbf{y} - \mathbf{x}) \geq 0.$$

The proof of the converse follows the same type of argument, but is a bit more intricate and can be found in the Appendix to this chapter. ∎

Remark   By Theorem 21.9, all concave functions are quasiconcave. This fact can also be seen by comparing the corresponding first order conditions (6) and (14). As Examples 21.8 and 21.9 illustrate, not every quasiconcave function is concave. In fact, quasiconcave functions fail to have two of the three important properties of concave functions that we highlighted earlier. First of all, a critical point of a quasiconcave function need not be a maximum, let alone a global maximum. For example, the function $y = x^3$ in $\mathbf{R}^1$ is quasiconcave by Example 21.8; its critical point $x = 0$ is certainly not any kind of a maximum. Secondly, the sum of quasiconcave functions need not be quasiconcave. For example, $f_1(x) = x^3$ and $f_2(x) = -x$ are both monotone functions on $\mathbf{R}^1$ (and therefore quasiconcave). However, $f_3 = x^3 - x$ is neither quasiconcave nor quasiconvex. (Check.)

However, a quasiconcave function that is also homogeneous of degree one *is* concave, as the following Theorem indicates.

> **Theorem 21.15**   Suppose that F is a real-valued, positive function defined on a convex cone C in $\mathbf{R}^n$. If F is homogeneous of degree one and quasiconcave on C, it is concave on C.

The proof of Theorem 21.15 is straightforward, but a bit long, and is presented in the Appendix of this chapter.

EXERCISES

21.18   For each of the following functions on $\mathbf{R}^1$, determine whether it is quasiconcave, quasiconvex, both, or neither:

a) e^x,   b) $\ln x$,   c) $x^3 + x$,   d) $x^3 - x$,

e) $x^4 - x^2$,   f) $x^4 + x^2$,   g) $3x^3 - 5x^2 + 7x$,   h) $\sin x$.

21.19   Write out a careful proof of Theorem 21.12. The proof is straightforward but should help one's understanding of quasiconcave functions and reinforce one's ability to prove theorems.

21.20   Write out the corresponding theorem for quasiconvex functions.

21.21   Prove that a quasiconcave function cannot have a strict interior minimum.

21.22   Let $f_1, \ldots, f_k$ be concave functions of one variable. Let $g(z)$ be a monotonic transformation. Prove that $F(x_1, \ldots, x_k) = g(f_1(x_1) + \cdots + f_k(x_k))$ is a quasiconcave function.

21.4 PSEUDOCONCAVE FUNCTIONS

In order to develop the most useful calculus criterion for quasiconcavity and quasiconvexity, namely the appropriate second order condition, we introduce one more class of functions, a class that forms a link between concave functions and quasiconcave functions. This class of functions was specifically defined by O. Mangasarian (see Chapter Notes) so that it is very close to the class of quasiconcave functions, yet it retains the important property of concave functions that critical points are automatically global maxima.

Definition   Let U be an open convex subset of $\mathbf{R}^n$. A C^1 function $F: U \rightarrow \mathbf{R}$ is **pseudoconcave** at $\mathbf{x}^* \in U$ if

$$DF(\mathbf{x}^*)(\mathbf{y} - \mathbf{x}^*) \leq 0 \quad \text{implies} \quad F(\mathbf{y}) \leq F(\mathbf{x}^*) \tag{15}$$

for all $\mathbf{y} \in U$. The function F is pseudoconcave on U if (15) holds for all $\mathbf{x}^* \in U$. To define a **pseudoconvex function** on U, one simply reverses the first inequality in (15).

As Corollary 21.4 points out, the first order criterion (21.3) for concavity clearly implies the defining condition (15) for pseudoconcavity; thus a C^1 concave function is always pseudoconcave. Furthermore, condition (15) is exactly the condition one uses to prove that a critical point of a concave function is automatically a *global max*. Since we will refer to it in later chapters, we state this observation as a theorem.

Theorem 21.16   Let U be a convex subset of $\mathbf{R}^n$, and let $F: U \to \mathbf{R}$ be a C^1 pseudoconcave function. If $\mathbf{x}^* \in U$ has the property $DF(\mathbf{x}^*)(\mathbf{y} - \mathbf{x}^*) \leq 0$ for all $\mathbf{y} \in U$, for example, $DF(\mathbf{x}^*) = \mathbf{0}$, then $\mathbf{x}^*$ is a global max of F on U. An analogous result holds for pseudoconvex functions.

To see how pseudoconcavity relates to quasiconcavity at the other end of the link, note that the contrapositive of the first order criterion (14) for quasiconcavity,

$$DF(\mathbf{x})(\mathbf{y} - \mathbf{x}) < 0 \quad \text{implies} \quad F(\mathbf{y}) < F(\mathbf{x}), \tag{16}$$

is very nearly the definition (15) of a pseudoconcave function; one merely has to change the $<$ signs in (16) to $\leq$ signs to obtain (15). The following theorem makes precise the close relationship between pseudoconcave and quasiconcave functions. Its proof is straightforward. However, we delay the proof until the Appendix of this chapter so as not to break the flow of our presentation at this point. Try to write out the proof before reading the Appendix.

Theorem 21.17   Let U be a convex subset of $\mathbf{R}^n$. Let $F: U \to \mathbf{R}$ be a C^1 function. Then,

(a) if F is pseudoconcave on U, F is quasiconcave on U, and
(b) if U is open and if $\nabla F(\mathbf{x}) \neq \mathbf{0}$ for all $\mathbf{x} \in U$, then F is pseudoconcave on U if and only if F is quasiconcave on U.

The primary reason for introducing pseudoconcave functions is the fact that there is a straightforward second derivative test for such functions, a test that is also the most efficient check that a given function is *quasiconcave*. This second order condition arises from a constrained maximization approach to pseudoconcave functions, which is summarized in the following theorem.

Theorem 21.18   Let U be an open convex subset of $\mathbf{R}^n$. Let $F: U \to \mathbf{R}$ be a C^1 function on U. Then, F is pseudoconcave on U if and only if for each $\mathbf{x}^*$ in U, $\mathbf{x}^*$ itself is the solution to the constrained maximization problem

$$\text{maximize} \quad F(\mathbf{x})$$
$$\text{subject to} \quad C_{\mathbf{x}^*} \equiv \{\mathbf{y} \in U : DF(\mathbf{x}^*)(\mathbf{y} - \mathbf{x}^*) \leq 0\}. \tag{17}$$

The proof of Theorem 21.18 follows immediately from noticing that the defining condition (15) of pseudoconcavity is equivalent to the maximization statement of Theorem 21.18. Details are left as an exercise.

Chapters 18 and 19 developed first and second order necessary and sufficient conditions for constrained maximization problems like (17). For any given $\mathbf{x}^*$, the Lagrangian function for Problem (17) is

$$L(\mathbf{x}, \lambda) = F(\mathbf{x}) - \lambda\, DF(\mathbf{x}^*) \cdot (\mathbf{x} - \mathbf{x}^*)$$

$$= F(\mathbf{x}) - \lambda \sum_i \frac{\partial F}{\partial x_i}(\mathbf{x}^*)(x_i - x_i^*).$$

Since the constraint in (17) is a linear one, we do not need a multiplier for the objective function by Theorem 19.12. Since

$$\frac{\partial L}{\partial x_i}(\mathbf{x}^*, 1) = \frac{\partial F}{\partial x_i}(\mathbf{x}^*) - 1 \cdot \frac{\partial F}{\partial x_i}(\mathbf{x}^*) = 0,$$

$\mathbf{x} = \mathbf{x}^*, \lambda = 1$ is a solution of the first order condition for Problem (17). The corresponding second order sufficient condition that $\mathbf{x}^*$ must satisfy to be a solution of (17) involves the bordered Hessian H of F. This matrix H is formed by bordering the usual Hessian $D^2F(\mathbf{x})$ above and to the left by the first order partial derivatives $DF(\mathbf{x})$ of F:

$$H = \begin{pmatrix} 0 & F'_{x_1} & F'_{x_2} & \cdots & F'_{x_n} \\ F'_{x_1} & F''_{x_1 x_1} & F''_{x_1 x_2} & \cdots & F''_{x_1 x_n} \\ F'_{x_2} & F''_{x_2 x_1} & F''_{x_2 x_2} & \cdots & F''_{x_2 x_n} \\ \vdots & \vdots & \vdots & \ddots & \vdots \\ F'_{x_n} & F''_{x_n x_1} & F''_{x_n x_2} & \cdots & F''_{x_n x_n} \end{pmatrix}. \tag{18}$$

To carry out the second order test, one calculates the $(n - 1)$ largest *leading principal minors* of H, beginning with the top leftmost 3×3 submatrix and continuing to the full $(n + 1) \times (n + 1)$ matrix H, as described in Section 16.3. We want these last $(n - 1)$ leading principal minors of H to alternate in sign with the smallest one, the leading 3×3 minor, which is positive. The corresponding sufficient condition for pseudoconvexity requires that the last $(n - 1)$ leading principal minors of H all be negative. In both cases, these sign patterns must hold for all $\mathbf{x}$ in the domain of F. The following theorem summarizes this test for pseudoconcavity.

Theorem 21.19 Let F be a C^2 function on an open convex subset W in $\mathbf{R}^n$. Consider the bordered Hessian H in (18).

(a) If the largest $(n - 1)$ leading principal minors of H alternate in sign, *for all* $\mathbf{x} \in$ W, with the smallest of these — the third order leading principal minor — positive, then F is pseudoconcave, and therefore quasiconcave, on W.

(b) If these largest $(n - 1)$ leading principal minors are all negative for all $\mathbf{x} \in$ W, then F is pseudoconvex, and therefore quasiconvex, on W.

Remark The condition of Theorem 21.19 is a sufficient condition but not a necessary one. There are a number of necessary conditions in the literature. One such necessary condition is that we replace all the strong inequalities regarding the leading principal minors of H in Theorem 21.19 by weak inequalities and apply this test to *all* of the principal minors of H which include the first row and column and which are at least 3×3 in size, not just the *leading* principal minors. See the Notes at the end of this chapter for references.

To better understand Theorem 21.19, we write out its two-dimensional version — a version which requires computing the sign of only one determinant, since the corresponding bordered Hessian is itself 3×3. We present a special proof for this two-dimensional version in the Appendix of this chapter, a proof which does not use the constrained optimization approach (17) to pseudoconcavity. To simplify matters, we focus directly on quasiconcave monotone functions.

Theorem 21.20 Let F be a C^2 function on a convex set W in $\mathbf{R}^2$. Suppose that F is monotone in that $F'_x > 0$ and $F'_y > 0$ on W. If the determinant

$$\begin{vmatrix} 0 & F'_x & F'_y \\ F'_x & F''_{xx} & F''_{xy} \\ F'_y & F''_{xy} & F''_{yy} \end{vmatrix} \tag{19}$$

is > 0 for all $(x, y) \in W$, then F is quasiconcave on W. If the determinant (19) is negative for all $(x, y) \in W$, then F is quasiconvex on W.

Conversely, if F is quasiconcave on W, then the determinant (19) is ≥ 0; if F is quasiconvex on W, then the determinant (19) is ≤ 0 for all $(x, y) \in W$.

Remark As mentioned in our discussion on bordered matrices in Chapter 16, some texts "border the Hessian" on the right and below by $DF(\mathbf{x})$ rather than on the left and above as we did in (18):

$$\begin{pmatrix} F''_{x_1 x_1} & F''_{x_1 x_2} & \cdots & F''_{x_1 x_n} & F'_{x_1} \\ F''_{x_2 x_1} & F''_{x_2 x_2} & \cdots & F''_{x_2 x_n} & F'_{x_2} \\ \vdots & \vdots & \ddots & \vdots & \vdots \\ F''_{x_n x_1} & F''_{x_n x_2} & \cdots & F''_{x_n x_n} & F'_{x_n} \\ F'_{x_1} & F'_{x_2} & \cdots & F'_{x_n} & 0 \end{pmatrix}.$$

In this case, one applies the test of Theorem 21.19 to the last $(n-1)$ *trailing* principal minors, which are formed by deleting the *first k* rows and columns from the bordered Hessian. As in Theorem 21.19, we need the bottom-right hand 3×3 principal minor to be positive and all the larger trailing principal minors to alternate in sign in order to guarantee that F is quasiconcave.

Example 21.13 Theorem 21.13 implies that the Cobb-Douglas function $U(x, y) = x^a y^b$ is quasiconcave on $\mathbf{R}^2_+$ for $a, b > 0$ since it is a monotone transformation of a concave function. Let's use Theorem 21.20 to prove the quasiconcavity of U. The bordered Hessian (19) is

$$\begin{pmatrix} 0 & ax^{a-1}y^b & bx^a y^{b-1} \\ ax^{a-1}y^b & a(a-1)x^{a-2}y^b & abx^{a-1}y^{b-1} \\ bx^a y^{b-1} & abx^{a-1}y^{b-1} & b(b-1)x^a y^{b-2} \end{pmatrix},$$

whose determinant is

$$(ab + ab^2 + a^2 b)x^{3a-2}y^{3b-2},$$

which is always positive for $x > 0$, $y > 0$, $a > 0$, and $b > 0$. By Theorem 21.20, U is pseudoconcave, and therefore quasiconcave.

EXERCISES

21.23 We have three practical ways of checking for the quasiconcavity of a given function. We can show that it has the same level sets as a concave function. We can use the method of the proof of Theorem 21.20 in the Appendix to show that its level sets are graphs of convex functions on $\mathbf{R}^{n-1}$. We can use the bordered Hessian test of Theorem 21.19. For each of the following functions, determine whether it is quasiconcave, quasiconvex, neither, or both:

a) $f(x, y) = ye^{-x}$ on $\mathbf{R}^2$;

b) $f(x, y) = ye^{-x}$ on $\mathbf{R}^2_+$;

c) $f(x, y) = (2x + 3y)^3$ on $\mathbf{R}^2$;

d) $f(x, y, z) = (e^x + 5y^4 + |z|)^{1/2}$;

e) $f(x, y) = (y - x^4)^{1/3}$;

f) $f(x, y) = \dfrac{y}{x^2 + 1}$ on $\mathbf{R}^2_+$;

g) $f(x, y) = \dfrac{y}{x^2 + 1}$ on $\mathbf{R}^2$;

h) $f(x, y) = yx^{-2}$ on $\mathbf{R}^2_+$;

i) $ke^{x^T Ax}$, where A is a positive definite matrix and k is a positive constant.

21.24 Prove Theorem 21.18.

21.25 Let $L: \mathbf{R}^m \to \mathbf{R}^n$ be a linear function. Let $f: \mathbf{R}^n \to \mathbf{R}$. Show that if f is quasiconcave, so is $f \circ L$ and that if f is pseudoconcave, so is $f \circ L$.

21.5   CONCAVE PROGRAMMING

As we have seen throughout this chapter, not only do concave and quasiconcave functions arise naturally in economics, but such functions also provide much more structure in the analysis of the optimization problems that lie at the heart of economic theory. In particular, the first order necessary conditions that characterize the solution of the general differentiable optimization problem are also sufficient conditions when the functions involved are concave.

Unconstrained Problems

We begin by repeating the statement of Theorem 21.6 for the *unconstrained* concave programming problem. Recall by Theorem 21.16 that Theorem 21.6 holds even if f is pseudoconcave, but not necessarily if f is quasiconcave.

Theorem 21.21   Let U be a convex subset of $\mathbf{R}^n$. Let $f : U \to \mathbf{R}$ be a C^1 concave (convex) function on U. Then, $\mathbf{x}^*$ is a global max of f on U *if and only if* $Df(\mathbf{x}^*)(\mathbf{x} - \mathbf{x}^*) \leq 0$ for all $\mathbf{x} \in U$. In particular, if U is open, or if $\mathbf{x}^*$ is an interior point of U, then $\mathbf{x}^*$ is a global max (min) of f on U *if and only if* $Df(\mathbf{x}^*) = \mathbf{0}$.

Constrained Problems

For constrained problems, we need some concavity or convexity hypotheses on the constraint functions too.

Theorem 21.22   Let U be a convex open subset of $\mathbf{R}^n$. Let $f : U \to \mathbf{R}$ be a C^1 pseudoconcave function on U, for example, f quasiconcave with nonvanishing gradient. Let $g_1, \ldots, g_k : U \to \mathbf{R}$ be C^1 quasiconvex functions. Consider the programming problem

$$\text{maximize} \quad f(x)$$
$$\text{subject to} \quad \mathbf{x} \in C_\mathbf{b} \equiv \{\mathbf{x} \in U : g_i(\mathbf{x}) \leq b_i, \ i = 1, \ldots, k\}. \tag{20}$$

Suppose that one of the constraint qualifications in Theorem 19.12 holds. Form the Lagrangian

$$L(\mathbf{x}, \lambda_1, \ldots, \lambda_k) \equiv f(\mathbf{x}) - \sum_{i=1}^{k} \lambda_i [g_i(\mathbf{x}) - b_i]. \tag{21}$$

If there exist $\mathbf{x}^*$ and λ^* such that

$$\frac{\partial L}{\partial x_j}(\mathbf{x}^*, \lambda^*) = 0, \qquad \text{for } j = 1, \ldots, n, \tag{22}$$

and $\quad \lambda_i^* \geq 0, \quad g_i(\mathbf{x}^*) \leq b_i, \quad \lambda_i^* \cdot (g_i(\mathbf{x}^*) - b_i) = 0, \quad \text{for } i = 1, \ldots, k.$ (23)

Then, $\mathbf{x}^*$ is a *global* max of f on the constraint set $C_\mathbf{b}$.

Proof   Write condition (22) as

$$Df(\mathbf{x}^*) - \sum_{i=1}^{k} \lambda_i^* Dg_i(\mathbf{x}^*) = \mathbf{0}. \tag{24}$$

Let $\mathbf{x}$ be an arbitrary point in the constraint set. For each binding constraint g_i, $g_i(\mathbf{x}) \leq g_i(\mathbf{x}^*)$. Since g_i is quasiconvex,

$$Dg_i(\mathbf{x}^*)(\mathbf{x} - \mathbf{x}^*) \leq 0, \tag{25}$$

by Theorem 21.14. Since $\lambda_i^* = 0$ for the nonbinding constraints g_i by (23),

$$\lambda_i^* Dg_i(\mathbf{x}^*)(\mathbf{x} - \mathbf{x}^*) \leq 0,$$

for all i and all $\mathbf{x} \in C_\mathbf{b}$. By (24),

$$Df(\mathbf{x}^*)(\mathbf{x} - \mathbf{x}^*) \leq 0, \tag{26}$$

for all $\mathbf{x} \in C_\mathbf{b}$. Since f is pseudoconcave, (26) implies that $f(\mathbf{x}) \leq f(\mathbf{x}^*)$ and, therefore, that $\mathbf{x}^*$ is a global max of f on $C_\mathbf{b}$.   ∎

Remark
  (1) We really only needed the *binding* inequality constraints to be quasiconvex in the proof of Theorem 21.21.
  (2) The most natural constraint qualifications for problem (20) are either that the g_i's are linear or that the g_i's are convex functions with $g_i(\mathbf{z}^*) < b_i$ for some $\mathbf{z}^* \in U$ and all i. See Theorem 19.12.
  (3) As in the statement of Theorem 21.7, the sufficient condition (22) for a global max of Problem (20) can be weakened to

$$D_\mathbf{x} L(\mathbf{x}^*, \lambda^*)(\mathbf{x} - \mathbf{x}^*) \leq \mathbf{0} \quad \text{for all } \mathbf{x} \in C_\mathbf{b}. \tag{27}$$

As the following theorem indicates, both the set of maximizers and the maximal value function for problem (20) have nice properties in concave programming problems.

Theorem 21.23   Let $f, g_1, \ldots, g_k$ be as in the hypothesis of Theorem 21.22.

  (*a*) For any fixed $\mathbf{b} = (b_1, \ldots, b_k) \in \mathbf{R}^k$, let $Z(\mathbf{b})$ denote the set of $\mathbf{x} \in C_\mathbf{b}$ that are global maximizers of f on $C_\mathbf{b}$. Then, $Z(\mathbf{b})$ is a convex set.
  (*b*) For any $\mathbf{b} \in \mathbf{R}^k$, let $V(\mathbf{b})$ denote the maximal value of the objective function f in problem (20). If f is concave and the g_i's are convex, then $\mathbf{b} \mapsto V(\mathbf{b})$ is a *concave function* of $\mathbf{b}$.

Proof

(a) Suppose that $\mathbf{x}^1$ and $\mathbf{x}^2$ are in $Z(\mathbf{b})$, and let

$$\mathbf{x}^3 = t\mathbf{x}^1 + (1 - t)\mathbf{x}^2 \in \ell(\mathbf{x}^1, \mathbf{x}^2).$$

Since the g_i's are quasiconvex functions, $C_{\mathbf{b}}$ is a convex set and $\mathbf{x}^3 \in C_{\mathbf{b}}$. Since f is quasiconcave,

$$f(\mathbf{x}^3) \geq \min\{f(\mathbf{x}^1), f(\mathbf{x}^2)\}.$$

Since $f(\mathbf{x}^1) = f(\mathbf{x}^2) = \max \{f(\mathbf{x}) : \mathbf{x} \in C_{\mathbf{b}}\}$, $f(\mathbf{x}^3) = f(\mathbf{x}^2)$ and $\mathbf{x}^3$ is in $Z(\mathbf{b})$, also. Therefore, $Z(\mathbf{b})$ is a convex set.

(b) Let $\mathbf{b}^3 = t\,\mathbf{b}^1 + (1 - t)\,\mathbf{b}^2$, and let $\mathbf{x}^i \in Z(\mathbf{b}^i)$ for $i = 1, 2, 3$. Then, for $j = 1, \ldots, k$,

$$g_j(t\mathbf{x}^1 + (1 - t)\mathbf{x}^2) \leq tg_j(\mathbf{x}^1) + (1 - t)\,g_j(\mathbf{x}^2) \quad \text{(convexity of } g_j)$$

$$\leq t\,b_j^1 + (1 - t)\,b_j^2 \quad \text{since} \quad (g_j(\mathbf{x}^i) \leq b_j^i, i = 1, 2)$$

$$= b_j^3,$$

and so $t\mathbf{x}^1 + (1 - t)\mathbf{x}^2$ is in $C_{\mathbf{b}^3}$. Therefore,

$$V(\mathbf{b}^3) = f(\mathbf{x}^3)$$

$$\geq f(t\mathbf{x}^1 + (1 - t)\mathbf{x}^2) \quad \text{(since } \mathbf{x}^3 \in Z(\mathbf{b}^3))$$

$$\geq tf(\mathbf{x}^1) + (1 - t)f(\mathbf{x}^2) \quad \text{(concavity of } f)$$

$$= tV(\mathbf{b}_1) + (1 - t)V(\mathbf{b}^2). \quad \blacksquare$$

Saddle Point Approach

In order to *compute* maxima of a constrained optimization problem like (20), one often considers the corresponding *saddle point problem*, especially when the functions involved are concave.

Definition   Let U be a convex subset of $\mathbf{R}^n$. Consider the Lagrangian function (21) for the programming problem (20), as a function of $\mathbf{x}$ and λ. Then, $(\mathbf{x}^*, \lambda^*)$ is **saddle point** of L if

$$L(\mathbf{x}, \lambda^*) \leq L(\mathbf{x}^*, \lambda^*) \leq L(\mathbf{x}^*, \lambda) \qquad (28)$$

for all $\lambda \geq \mathbf{0}$ and all $\mathbf{x} \in U$. Usually, $U = \mathbf{R}^n$ or $U = \mathbf{R}^n_+$, the positive orthant of $\mathbf{R}^n$. In the latter case, we say that $(\mathbf{x}^*, \lambda^*)$ is a **nonnegative saddle point** of L.

> **Theorem 21.24** If $(\mathbf{x}^*, \lambda^*)$ is a (nonnegative) saddle point for L in Problem (20), then $\mathbf{x}^*$ maximizes f on $C_\mathbf{b}$ ($C_\mathbf{b} \cap \mathbf{R}_+^n$).

Proof   We first show that $\mathbf{x}^*$ is in $C_\mathbf{b}$. The right side of (28) implies that

$$\sum_{i=1}^{k}(\lambda_i - \lambda_i^*)(g_i(\mathbf{x}^*) - b_i) \le 0, \tag{29}$$

for all $\lambda_i \ge 0$. For any fixed h, plug $\lambda_h = \lambda_h^* + 1$ and $\lambda_i = \lambda_i^*$ for all $i \ne h$ into (29). Then, (29) becomes $g_h(\mathbf{x}^*) - b_h \le 0$. Therefore, $\mathbf{x}^* \in C_\mathbf{b}$.

It follows that $\sum_i \lambda_i^*(g_i(\mathbf{x}^*) - b_i) \le 0$. On the other hand, setting each $\lambda_h = 0$ in (29) yields $\sum_i \lambda_i^*(g_i(\mathbf{x}^*) - b_i) \ge 0$, and thus

$$\sum_i \lambda_i^*(g_i(\mathbf{x}^*) - b_i) = 0 \quad \text{and each} \quad \lambda_i^*(g_i(\mathbf{x}^*) - b_i) = 0. \tag{30}$$

If $\mathbf{x} \in C_\mathbf{b}$, then, since each $\lambda_i^*(g_i(\mathbf{x}) - b_i) \le 0$,

$$\begin{aligned}
f(\mathbf{x}) &\le f(\mathbf{x}) - \sum_i \lambda_i^*(g_i(\mathbf{x}) - b_i) \\
&\le f(\mathbf{x}^*) - \sum_i \lambda_i^*(g_i(\mathbf{x}^*) - b_i) \qquad \text{by (28)} \\
&= f(\mathbf{x}^*) \qquad\qquad\qquad\qquad\quad \text{by (30).} \quad\blacksquare
\end{aligned}$$

Notice that there were no concavity hypotheses in the statement of Theorem 21.24. In concave programming, solutions of saddle point problems are more or less equivalent to solutions of programming problems, as the following theorem, due to Kuhn and Tucker, points out.

> **Theorem 21.25** Suppose that $U = \mathbf{R}_+^n$ or that U is an open convex subset of $\mathbf{R}^n$. Suppose that f is a C^1 concave function and that $g_1, \ldots, g_k$ are C^1 convex functions on U. Suppose that $\mathbf{x}^*$ maximizes f on the constraint set $C_\mathbf{b}$ as defined in (20). Suppose further that one of the constraint qualifications in Theorem 19.12 holds. Then, there exists $\lambda^* \ge \mathbf{0}$ such that $(\mathbf{x}^*, \lambda^*)$ is a saddle point of the Lagrangian (21).

Proof   First, work with the case where U is an *open* subset of $\mathbf{R}^n$, for example, $\mathbf{R}^n$ itself. By the usual first order condition, there exists $\lambda^* \ge \mathbf{0}$ such that $\lambda_i^* \cdot (g_i(\mathbf{x}^*) - b_i) = 0$ for $i = 1, \ldots, k$ and

$$D_\mathbf{x} L(\mathbf{x}^*, \lambda^*) = Df(\mathbf{x}^*) - \sum_i \lambda_i^* Dg_i(\mathbf{x}^*) = \mathbf{0}. \tag{31}$$

By Theorem 21.8, the function $\mathbf{x} \mapsto L(\mathbf{x}, \lambda^*)$ is a concave function of $\mathbf{x}$. By the first derivative criterion for concavity in Theorem 21.3 and by (31), for any $\mathbf{x} \in C_\mathbf{b}$,

$$L(\mathbf{x}, \lambda^*) - L(\mathbf{x}^*, \lambda^*) \le D_\mathbf{x} L(\mathbf{x}^*, \lambda^*)(\mathbf{x} - \mathbf{x}^*) = \mathbf{0}. \tag{32}$$

On the other hand, for any $\lambda \ge \mathbf{0}$ in $\mathbf{R}^k$,

$$L(\mathbf{x}^*, \lambda^*) = f(\mathbf{x}^*) - \sum_i \lambda_i^* (g_i(\mathbf{x}^*) - b_i)$$

$$= f(\mathbf{x}^*) \quad \text{(since each } \lambda_i^* (g_i(\mathbf{x}^*) - b_i) = 0)$$

$$\le f(\mathbf{x}^*) - \sum_i \lambda_i (g_i(\mathbf{x}^*) - b_i)$$

$$= L(\mathbf{x}^*, \lambda).$$

Now, suppose that $U = \mathbf{R}_+^n$, so that we are looking for a *nonnegative* saddle point. The function (21) is now the Kuhn-Tucker Lagrangian of problem (20), as discussed in Section 18.6. By the first order conditions for a constrained max at $\mathbf{x}^*$ in Section 18.6, there is a $\lambda^* \ge \mathbf{0}$ such that

$$\frac{\partial L}{\partial x_i}(\mathbf{x}^*, \lambda^*) \le 0, \quad x_i^* \ge 0, \quad \text{and} \quad x_i^* \frac{\partial L}{\partial x_i}(\mathbf{x}^*, \lambda^*) = 0. \tag{33}$$

Conditions (33) replace the above equation (31). Now,

$$D_\mathbf{x} L(\mathbf{x}^*, \lambda^*)(\mathbf{x} - \mathbf{x}^*) = \sum_i \frac{\partial L}{\partial x_i}(\mathbf{x}^*, \lambda^*)x_i - \frac{\partial L}{\partial x_i}(\mathbf{x}^*, \lambda^*)x_i^* \le 0$$

for $x_i \ge 0$, by (33). The rest of the above proof goes through after one replaces "$= \mathbf{0}$" at the end of (32) by "$\le \mathbf{0}$." ∎

To give some indication of the interest in the saddle point approach in economics, we return to the *activity analysis* models of a firm's behavior. In these models, a firm has n production processes; $x_i \ge 0$ represents the level of activity of process i, for $i = 1, \dots, n$. For each *activity vector* $\mathbf{x} = (x_1, \dots, x_n)$, $f(\mathbf{x})$ denotes the firm's profit when it runs process i at level x_i and $g_j(\mathbf{x})$ denotes the amount of resource j required at activity level $\mathbf{x}$. Let b_j denote the amount of resource currently available. The firm's optimization problem is to choose $\mathbf{x}$ to maximize $f(\mathbf{x})$ subject to $g_j(\mathbf{x}) \le b_j$ for $j = 1, \dots, k$ and $\mathbf{x} \ge \mathbf{0}$.

If we let U be the positive orthant of $\mathbf{R}^n$, the (Kuhn-Tucker) Lagrangian for this problem is

$$L(\mathbf{x}, \lambda) = f(\mathbf{x}) + \sum_{j=1}^k \lambda_j (b_j - g_j(\mathbf{x})). \tag{34}$$

By the discussion in Section 19.1, the multiplier λ_j can be considered as the shadow price or internal valuation of factor j. Thus, the Lagrangian function (34) can be considered the combined value of the firm's output $f(\mathbf{x})$ and the unused balance of its resources $\sum_j \lambda_j(b_j - g_j(\mathbf{x}))$. The existence of a saddle point $(\mathbf{x}^*, \lambda^*)$ expresses an equilibrium between the value of the output and the value of these unused resources. It is a basic step in the equilibrium theory for production economies. It is especially important in studying firms that deal with activities like investment, fisheries, or timber, in which decisions must be made about whether to use resources or to let them continue to grow at their natural rate.

EXERCISES

21.26 Use the problem of maximizing Cobb-Douglas utility $U(x, y) = xy$ on the budget set $2x + 2y \le 8$ to show that one cannot replace the hypothesis of the concavity of f in Theorem 21.25 by the weaker hypothesis that f is quasiconcave or pseudoconcave.

21.27 Suppose that $(\mathbf{x}, \mathbf{a}) \mapsto f(\mathbf{x}, \mathbf{a})$ is a concave function of $\mathbf{x} \in \mathbf{R}^n$ and of the parameter $\mathbf{a} \in \mathbf{R}^m$, and that $(\mathbf{x}, \mathbf{a}) \mapsto g_i(\mathbf{x}, \mathbf{a})$ are convex functions of $\mathbf{x} \in \mathbf{R}^n$ and $\mathbf{a} \in \mathbf{R}^m$ for $i = 1, \ldots, k$. Let $C_\mathbf{a} = \{\mathbf{x} \in \mathbf{R}^n : g_i(\mathbf{x}, \mathbf{a}) \le 0,\ i = 1, \ldots, k\}$. Let $Z(\mathbf{a})$ denote the set of maximizers of $f(\cdot, \mathbf{a})$ on $C_\mathbf{a}$; and let $V(\mathbf{a}) = f(Z(\mathbf{a}), \mathbf{a})$. Show that V is a concave function of $\mathbf{a}$.

21.28 In the previous exercise, drop the dependence of g_i on $\mathbf{a}$ and the convexity hypothesis on the g_i's. Suppose only that each $\mathbf{a} \mapsto f(\mathbf{x}, \mathbf{a})$ is a *convex* function of $\mathbf{a}$. Show that the maximum value function $\mathbf{a} \mapsto V(\mathbf{a})$ is a convex function of $\mathbf{a}$.

21.6 APPENDIX

This section presents proofs that were omitted in the earlier sections.

Proof of the Sufficiency Test of Theorem 21.14

> **Theorem 21.14** Suppose that F is a C^1 function on an open convex subset U of $\mathbf{R}^n$. If for all $\mathbf{x}, \mathbf{y} \in U$,
>
> $$F(\mathbf{y}) \ge F(\mathbf{x}) \quad \text{implies that} \quad DF(\mathbf{x})(\mathbf{y} - \mathbf{x}) \ge 0, \qquad (35)$$
>
> then F is quasiconcave on U.

Proof Choose $\mathbf{x}_0$ and $\mathbf{x}_1$ in U with $\mathbf{x}_0 \ne \mathbf{x}_1$ and $F(\mathbf{x}_1) \ge F(\mathbf{x}_0)$. Let $\mathbf{x}_t = \mathbf{x}_0 + t(\mathbf{x}_1 - \mathbf{x}_0)$ parameterize the line from $\mathbf{x}_0$ to $\mathbf{x}_1$. We want to prove that $F(\mathbf{x}_t) \ge F(\mathbf{x}_0)$ for all $t \in [0, 1]$.

To reach a contradiction, suppose that there is a $t^* \in (0, 1)$ such that $F(\mathbf{x}_1) \ge F(\mathbf{x}_0) > F(\mathbf{x}_{t^*})$. Let $J = [t_1, t_2]$ be a (connected) interval in $(0, 1)$ with

$t^* \in J$, with $F(\mathbf{x}_0) \geq F(\mathbf{x}_t)$ for all $t \in J$, and $F(\mathbf{x}_{t_1}) = F(\mathbf{x}_{t_2}) = F(\mathbf{x}_0)$. We first claim that

$$DF(\mathbf{x}_t)(\mathbf{x}_1 - \mathbf{x}_0) = 0 \quad \text{for all} \quad t \in J, \tag{36}$$

because if $t \in J$, $F(\mathbf{x}_1) \geq F(\mathbf{x}_0) \geq F(\mathbf{x}_t)$. By (35),

$$DF(\mathbf{x}_t)(\mathbf{x}_0 - \mathbf{x}_t) \geq 0 \quad \text{and} \quad DF(\mathbf{x}_t)(\mathbf{x}_1 - \mathbf{x}_t) \geq 0. \tag{37}$$

By definition,

$$\mathbf{x}_0 - \mathbf{x}_t = -t(\mathbf{x}_1 - \mathbf{x}_0) \quad \text{and} \quad \mathbf{x}_1 - \mathbf{x}_t = (1 - t)(\mathbf{x}_1 - \mathbf{x}_0).$$

Plugging these equalities into (37) yields

$$-tDF(\mathbf{x}_t)(\mathbf{x}_1 - \mathbf{x}_0) \geq 0 \quad \text{and} \quad (1 - t)DF(\mathbf{x}_t)(\mathbf{x}_1 - \mathbf{x}_0) \geq 0.$$

Since t and $1 - t$ are positive, $DF(\mathbf{x}_t)(\mathbf{x}_1 - \mathbf{x}_0) = 0$; this proves claim (36). On the other hand,

$$
\begin{aligned}
0 < F(\mathbf{x}_0) &- F(\mathbf{x}_{t^*}) \\
&= F(\mathbf{x}_{t_1}) - F(\mathbf{x}_{t^*}) \\
&= DF(\mathbf{x}_{t_3})(\mathbf{x}_{t_1} - \mathbf{x}_{t^*}) \quad \text{for some } t_3 \in (t_1, t^*) \\
&\qquad\qquad\qquad\qquad \text{(by the Mean Value Theorem of Section 30.1} \\
&\qquad\qquad\qquad\qquad \text{and the Chain Rule)} \\
&= (t^* - t_1)DF(\mathbf{x}_{t_3})(\mathbf{x}_1 - \mathbf{x}_0),
\end{aligned}
$$

since $\mathbf{x}_{t_1} - \mathbf{x}_{t^*} = (t_1 - t^*)(\mathbf{x}_1 - \mathbf{x}_0)$. This contradiction to claim (36) implies that there is no t^* with $F(\mathbf{x}_{t^*}) < F(\mathbf{x}_0)$. Since $F(\mathbf{x}_t) \geq F(\mathbf{x}_0)$ for all $t \in [0, 1]$, F is quasiconcave by Theorem 21.12. ∎

Proof of Theorem 21.15

Theorem 21.15   Suppose that F is a real-valued, positive function defined on a convex cone C in $\mathbf{R}^n$. If F is homogeneous of degree one and quasiconcave on C, it is concave on C.

Proof   We will show that the subgraph of F, that is, the set below the graph of F in $\mathbf{R}^{n+1}$,

$$G_F \equiv \{(\mathbf{x}, y) \in C \times \mathbf{R}_+ : y \leq F(\mathbf{x})\},$$

is a convex set. (See Exercise 21.5.) We first show that

$$G_F^+ \equiv \{(\mathbf{x}, y) \in G_F : 0 < y \leq F(\mathbf{x})\}$$

is a convex set. Let $(\mathbf{x}, y)$ and $(\mathbf{x}', y')$ be points in G_F^+, so that $0 < y \le F(\mathbf{x})$ and $0 < y' \le F(\mathbf{x}')$. Since F is homogeneous of degree one, $y > 0$, and $(\mathbf{x}, y) \in G_F^+$,

$$F\left(\frac{\mathbf{x}}{y}\right) = \frac{1}{y} \cdot F(\mathbf{x}) \ge \frac{1}{y} \cdot y = 1.$$

Similarly, $F\left(\dfrac{\mathbf{x}'}{y'}\right) \ge 1$. Therefore,

$$\left(\frac{\mathbf{x}}{y}, 1\right) \quad \text{and} \quad \left(\frac{\mathbf{x}'}{y'}, 1\right) \quad \text{are in} \quad G_F^+.$$

Let $\lambda \in [0, 1]$, and define

$$\theta \equiv \frac{\lambda y}{\lambda y + (1 - \lambda)y'}.$$

Then, θ is also in $[0, 1]$. Since F is quasiconcave,

$$F\left(\theta\left(\frac{\mathbf{x}}{y}\right) + (1 - \theta)\left(\frac{\mathbf{x}'}{y'}\right)\right) \ge 1,$$

that is,

$$\left(\theta\left(\frac{\mathbf{x}}{y}\right) + (1 - \theta)\left(\frac{\mathbf{x}'}{y'}\right), 1\right) \quad \text{is in} \quad G_F^+.$$

By the definition of θ,

$$\left(\theta\left(\frac{\mathbf{x}}{y}\right) + (1 - \theta)\left(\frac{\mathbf{x}'}{y'}\right), 1\right) = \left(\frac{\lambda \mathbf{x} + (1 - \lambda)\mathbf{x}'}{\lambda y + (1 - \lambda)y'}, 1\right).$$

Once again by the homogeneity of F,

$$(\lambda \mathbf{x} + (1 - \lambda)\mathbf{x}', \lambda y + (1 - \lambda)y') \quad \text{is in} \quad G_F^+;$$

that is, $\lambda(\mathbf{x}, y) + (1 - \lambda)(\mathbf{x}', y')$ is in G_F^+, and G_F^+ is a convex set.

To see that G_F is convex, let $\gamma = \{(\mathbf{x}_t, y_t) : 0 \le t \le 1\}$ be a line segment with its endpoints in G_F. If the endpoints of γ lie in G_F^+, then γ lies in G_F^+ by the argument of the preceding paragraph. If both endpoints of γ lie below $y = 0$, then so does the segment; in this case, the segment γ lies below the graph of F because the graph of the positive function F lies above the $\{y = 0\}$-hyperplane. If one endpoint of γ lies above $\{y = 0\}$ and one below, break γ into two segments, one below $\{y = 0\}$ and one above $\{y = 0\}$, and apply the above arguments to each piece separately. ∎

Proof of Theorem 21.17

Theorem 21.17   Let U be a convex subset of $\mathbf{R}^n$. Let $F: U \to \mathbf{R}$ be a C^1 function. Then,

(a) if F is pseudoconcave on U, F is quasiconcave on U, and
(b) if U is open and if $\nabla F(\mathbf{x}) \neq \mathbf{0}$ for all $\mathbf{x} \in U$, then F is pseudoconcave on U if and only if F is quasiconcave on U.

Proof

(a) Suppose that F is pseudoconcave on U. Let $\mathbf{y}_0$ and $\mathbf{y}_1$ be two points in U with $F(\mathbf{y}_1) \geq F(\mathbf{y}_0)$. Let $\mathbf{y}_t \equiv \mathbf{y}_0 + t(\mathbf{y}_1 - \mathbf{y}_0)$ for $0 \leq t \leq 1$, so that the line segment is parameterized from $\mathbf{y}_0$ to $\mathbf{y}_1$. Let $g(t) = F(\mathbf{y}_t)$.

We claim that $F(\mathbf{y}_t) \geq F(\mathbf{y}_0)$ for all $t \in [0, 1]$. This claim holds automatically if the minimum value of g on $[0, 1]$ occurs at $t = 0$ or $t = 1$. We can assume then that the minimum value of g on $[0, 1]$ occurs at some t^* in the open interval $(0, 1)$. In this case,

$$0 = g'(t^*) = DF(\mathbf{y}_0 + t^*(\mathbf{y}_1 - \mathbf{y}_0)) \cdot (\mathbf{y}_1 - \mathbf{y}_0)$$

by the usual first order condition for a minimum and the Chain Rule; then,

$$0 = DF(\mathbf{y}_0 + t^*(\mathbf{y}_1 - \mathbf{y}_0)) \cdot (-t^*(\mathbf{y}_1 - \mathbf{y}_0)).$$

Applying the definition (15) of pseudoconcavity with $\mathbf{x}^* = \mathbf{y}_0 + t^*(\mathbf{y}_1 - \mathbf{y}_0)$ and $\mathbf{y} = \mathbf{y}_0$, we conclude that

$$F(\mathbf{y}_0 + t^*(\mathbf{y}_1 - \mathbf{y}_0)) \geq F(\mathbf{y}_0);$$

this proves the claim at the beginning of this paragraph. By Theorem 21.12, F is quasiconcave on U.

(b) Suppose, now, that F is quasiconcave on U, that U is open, and $\nabla F(\mathbf{x})$ is never zero for $\mathbf{x} \in U$. To prove that F is pseudoconcave, we assume that $DF(\mathbf{x}^*)(\mathbf{y} - \mathbf{x}^*) \leq 0$, as in the hypothesis of (15), and prove that $F(\mathbf{y}) \leq F(\mathbf{x}^*)$. If $DF(\mathbf{x}^*)(\mathbf{y} - \mathbf{x}^*) < 0$, then $F(\mathbf{y}) < F(\mathbf{x}^*)$ by (16). We need only rule out the case

$$DF(\mathbf{x}^*)(\mathbf{y} - \mathbf{x}^*) = 0 \quad \text{and} \quad F(\mathbf{y}) > F(\mathbf{x}^*). \tag{38}$$

We will show that, under the hypotheses of this theorem and under assumption (38), we can perturb $\mathbf{y}$ to $\mathbf{y}'$ so that

$$DF(\mathbf{x}^*)(\mathbf{y}' - \mathbf{x}^*) < 0 \quad \text{and} \quad F(\mathbf{y}') > F(\mathbf{x}^*); \tag{39}$$

this contradicts our assumption that F is quasiconcave. Let $\mathbf{v}$ be the nonzero vector $-\nabla F(\mathbf{x}^*)$. For all $t > 0$,

$$DF(\mathbf{x}^*)(\mathbf{y} + t\mathbf{v} - \mathbf{x}^*) = DF(\mathbf{x}^*)(t\mathbf{v} + \mathbf{y} - \mathbf{x}^*)$$
$$= tDF(\mathbf{x}^*)(\mathbf{v}) + DF(\mathbf{x}^*)(\mathbf{y} - \mathbf{x}^*)$$
$$= -t\|\nabla F(\mathbf{x}^*)\|^2 + 0$$
$$< 0.$$

Since F is continuous at $\mathbf{y}$, we can choose nonzero t small enough so that

$$F(\mathbf{y} + t\mathbf{v}) > F(\mathbf{x}^*) \quad \text{and} \quad DF(\mathbf{x}^*)(\mathbf{y} + t\mathbf{v} - \mathbf{x}^*) < 0;$$

that is, $\mathbf{y}' = \mathbf{y} + t\mathbf{v}$ satisfies (39) — a contradiction to the characterization (16) of quasiconcavity. This contradiction proves that (38) cannot hold and therefore that F is pseudoconcave. ∎

Proof of Theorem 21.20

We now prove the bordered Hessian test for pseudoconcavity and quasiconcavity for functions of two variables, a special case of Theorem 21.19. For simplicity, we will work with C^2 utility functions U in the plane which are quasiconcave and monotone. The former means that indifference curves bound convex sets from below; the latter means that utility is strictly increasing as the amount of either good increases. In fact, we will write this monotonicity assumption as $U_x' > 0$ and $U_y' > 0$. Quasiconcavity and monotonicity imply that the level sets of U are as in Figure 21.10.

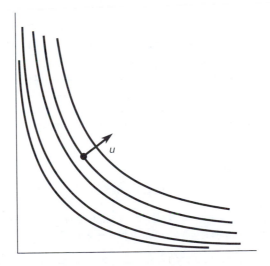

Indifference curves of a monotone, quasiconcave utility function.

Figure 21.10

Theorem 21.20 Let U be a C^2 function on a convex set W in $\mathbf{R}^2$. Suppose that U is monotone in that $U'_x > 0$ and $U'_y > 0$ on W. If the determinant

$$\begin{vmatrix} 0 & U'_x & U'_y \\ U'_x & U''_{xx} & U''_{xy} \\ U'_y & U''_{xy} & U''_{yy} \end{vmatrix}. \tag{40}$$

is > 0 on W, then U is quasiconcave on W. Conversely, if U is quasiconcave on W, then the determinant (40) is ≥ 0.

Proof Think of each level curve as a graph of a function $y = g(x)$. (We can do this by the monotonicity assumption $U'_y > 0$. See Exercise 21.29.) Since U is quasiconcave, the set above the graph of g (i.e., above the level set of U) is a convex set. Therefore, the quasiconcavity of U implies the convexity of g as a function of one variable (Exercise 21.5), which in turn implies that $g''(x) \geq 0$. Now, by Theorem 15.1, $g'(x)$ is the marginal rate of substitution $-U'_x(x, g(x))/U'_y(x, g(x))$. Therefore,

$$0 \leq g''(x) = \frac{d}{dx}\left(-\frac{U'_x(x, g(x))}{U'_y(x, g(x))} \right)$$

$$= -\frac{(U''_{xx} + U''_{xy}g'(x))U'_y - (U''_{yx} + U''_{yy}g'(x))U'_x}{(U'_y)^2}$$

$$= \frac{-(U'_y)^2 U''_{xx} - (U'_x)^2 U''_{yy} + 2U'_x U'_y U''_{xy}}{(U'_y)^3} \tag{41}$$

using $g'(x) = -U'_x/U'_y$. The numerator in expression (41) is simply the determinant (40).

Conversely, one can follow the above steps in reverse order to conclude that if the determinant (40) is positive, then $g''(x) > 0$, g is a convex function, the set above the graph of g is a convex set, and finally that the set above each level curve of U is a convex set. So, U is quasiconcave. ∎

EXERCISES

21.29 Why does the assumption $\partial U/\partial y > 0$ imply that we can work with each level curve of $U(x, y)$ as a graph of a function $y = g(x)$?

NOTES

(*a*) One of the earliest papers on quasiconcave functions is K. Arrow and A. Enthoven, "Quasiconcave programming," *Econometrica* 29 (1961) 779–800. It includes a concrete example of a quasiconcave function which is *not* a monotonic transformation of any concave function.

(*b*) One of the earliest papers on pseudoconcave functions is O. Mangasarian, "Pseudoconvex functions," *Society for Industrial and Applied Mathematics Journal on Control* 3 (1965), 281–290. Mangasarian defined pseudoconcave functions as a class that retains some of the more interesting properties of quasiconcave functions and of concave functions.

(*c*) Papers on the relationship between concave, pseudoconcave and quasiconcave functions include Arrow and Enthoven, "Quasiconcave programming," J. Ferland, "Mathematical programming problems with quasiconvex objective functions," *Mathematical Programming* 3 (1972) 296–301; and J-P. Crouzeix and J. Ferland, "Criteria for quasiconvexity and pseudoconvexity: relationships and comparisons," *Mathematical Programming* 23 (1982) 193–205. These papers also give necessary conditions for a function to be pseudoconcave.

Economic Applications

22.1 UTILITY AND DEMAND

As we stated at the beginning of Chapter 18, the characterization of economics as the study of the optimal allocation of scarce resources leads to a central role in economic theory for the mathematics of constrained optimization. In this chapter we will apply the theory we have developed in the last four chapters to the two principal optimization problems in economics: the consumer's utility maximization problem and the firm's profit maximization problem.

The main purpose of this chapter is to illustrate how one applies the Lagrange multiplier theorems of Chapters 18 and 19. Consequently, the proofs of the economic principles described in this chapter are worked out with more attention to detail than proofs of other results in this book. These are situations where the methods used are as interesting as the results achieved.

Utility Maximization

We focus first on the utility maximization problem that we have discussed a number of times already. In an economy with n divisible commodities, let x_i denote the amount of commodity i. Let $U(x_1, \ldots, x_n)$ be the consumer's **utility function**, which measures the consumer's level of satisfaction with **commodity bundle x** $= (x_1, \ldots, x_n)$. Let $p_j > 0$ denote the price of a unit of commodity j and let $I > 0$ denote the income which the consumer has available to spend on these n commodities. The consumer's goal is to

$$\text{maximize} \quad U(x_1, \ldots, x_n)$$

subject to the budget constraint

$$p_1 x_1 + \cdots + p_n x_n \leq I \tag{1}$$

$$x_1 \geq 0, \ldots, x_n \geq 0.$$

In this section we will concentrate on properties which can be derived using calculus. So we assume that U is a C^1 function. We further assume that the commodities are "goods" in that increasing consumption increases utility. We formalize this *monotonicity* assumption by requiring:

for each $\mathbf{x}$ satisfying (1), there exists an i such that $\dfrac{\partial U}{\partial x_i}(\mathbf{x}) > 0.$ (2)

As we saw in Example 18.8, this assumption implies that all income is spent; the budget constraint is binding at a utility maximizer. The following theorem summarizes the application of our first and second order conditions for a constrained max to this problem.

Theorem 22.1 Let $U: \mathbf{R}^n_+ \to \mathbf{R}^1$ be a C^1 function that satisfies monotonicity assumption (2). Let $\mathbf{p}$ be a positive price vector. Suppose $\mathbf{x}^* \neq \mathbf{0}$ maximizes U on the constraint set (1). Then, there is a scalar $\lambda^* > 0$ such that:

(a)
$$\frac{1}{p_i}\frac{\partial U}{\partial x_i}(\mathbf{x}^*) \le \lambda^* \quad \text{for} \quad i = 1, \ldots, n \tag{3}$$

with equality for those i for which $x_i^* > 0$.

(b) If each $x_i^* > 0$, then

$$\frac{\partial U}{\partial x_j}(\mathbf{x}^*) > 0 \quad \text{and} \quad \frac{\partial U}{\partial x_j}(\mathbf{x}^*) = \lambda^* p_j \quad \text{for all} \quad j, \tag{4}$$

and

$$\frac{1}{p_i}\frac{\partial U}{\partial x_i}(\mathbf{x}^*) = \frac{1}{p_j}\frac{\partial U}{\partial x_j}(\mathbf{x}^*), \quad \text{or} \quad \frac{\dfrac{\partial U}{\partial x_i}(\mathbf{x}^*)}{\dfrac{\partial U}{\partial x_j}(\mathbf{x}^*)} = \frac{p_i}{p_j}. \tag{5}$$

(c) The budget constraint is binding:

$$\mathbf{p} \cdot \mathbf{x}^* = I. \tag{6}$$

Conversely, suppose that U is a C^1 function which satisfies the monotonicity assumption (2) and that $\mathbf{x}^*$ is a point in the budget set (1) that satisfies $x_i^* > 0$ for all i and the first order conditions (5) for all i, j.

(d) If U is C^2 and if

$$(-1)^k \cdot \det \begin{pmatrix} 0 & \dfrac{\partial U}{\partial x_1}(\mathbf{x}^*) & \cdots & \dfrac{\partial U}{\partial x_k}(\mathbf{x}^*) \\[2ex] \dfrac{\partial U}{\partial x_1}(\mathbf{x}^*) & \dfrac{\partial^2 U}{\partial x_1^2}(\mathbf{x}^*) & \cdots & \dfrac{\partial^2 U}{\partial x_k \partial x_1}(\mathbf{x}^*) \\[2ex] \vdots & \vdots & \ddots & \vdots \\[2ex] \dfrac{\partial U}{\partial x_k}(\mathbf{x}^*) & \dfrac{\partial^2 U}{\partial x_1 \partial x_k}(\mathbf{x}^*) & \cdots & \dfrac{\partial^2 U}{\partial x_k^2}(\mathbf{x}^*) \end{pmatrix} > 0 \tag{7}$$

for $k = 2, \ldots, n$, then $\mathbf{x}^*$ is a strict local solution to the utility maximization problem (1).

(e) If U is quasiconcave and $\nabla U(\mathbf{x}) \neq \mathbf{0}$ for all $\mathbf{x} \neq \mathbf{0}$, then $\mathbf{x}^*$ is a global solution to problem (1).

Proof The first part of this proof is a straightforward application of Theorems 18.4 and 19.8. The Lagrangian for this problem is

$$L(x_1, \ldots, x_n; \lambda, \nu_1, \ldots, \nu_n) = U(\mathbf{x}) - \lambda \left(\sum_i p_i x_i - I \right) + \sum_i \nu_i x_i,$$

where we use λ to denote the multiplier for the budget constraint. Since the constraints in (1) are linear, the linear constraint qualification of Theorem 19.12 is satisfied at all $\mathbf{x}$. The first order conditions are (1) along with

$$\frac{\partial L}{\partial x_i} = \frac{\partial U}{\partial x_i}(\mathbf{x}) - \lambda p_i + \nu_i = 0, \quad i = 1, \ldots, n; \tag{8}$$

$$\lambda \left(\sum_i p_i x_i - I \right) = 0; \tag{9}$$

$$\nu_i x_i = 0, \quad i = 1, \ldots, n; \tag{10}$$

$$\lambda \geq 0; \quad \text{and} \quad \nu_1 \geq 0, \ldots, \nu_n \geq 0. \tag{11}$$

Rewrite (8) and (11) as

$$\frac{1}{p_i} \frac{\partial U}{\partial x_i}(\mathbf{x}^*) - \lambda = -\frac{\nu_i}{p_i} \leq 0. \tag{12}$$

Conclusion (3) follows immediately. By applying (12) to the commodity h for which $(\partial U / \partial x_h)(\mathbf{x}^*) > 0$, one concludes that $\lambda > 0$. If x_i^* and x_j^* are > 0, then $\nu_i = \nu_j = 0$ by (10), and (12) becomes

$$\frac{1}{p_i} \frac{\partial U}{\partial x_i}(\mathbf{x}^*) = \lambda = \frac{1}{p_j} \frac{\partial U}{\partial x_j}(\mathbf{x}^*).$$

Statement b) follows immediately. As we have seen in Example 18.8, statement c) follows from (9) and the conclusion $\lambda > 0$.

To prove part d — the second order sufficient condition — recall from Section 19.3 that the bordered Hessian for this problem is

$$\begin{pmatrix} 0 & p_1 & \cdots & p_n \\ p_1 & \dfrac{\partial^2 U}{\partial x_1^2} & \cdots & \dfrac{\partial^2 U}{\partial x_n \partial x_1} \\ \vdots & \vdots & \ddots & \vdots \\ p_n & \dfrac{\partial^2 U}{\partial x_1 \partial x_n} & \cdots & \dfrac{\partial^2 U}{\partial x_n^2} \end{pmatrix} \tag{13}$$

and that, if the determinants of its last $n - 1$ leading principal minors alternate in sign, with the largest having the sign of $(-1)^n$, then the second order sufficient conditions for a constrained maximizer are satisfied. Replace each p_j in the first row and first column of (13) by $(1/\lambda)(\partial U/\partial x_j)(\mathbf{x}^*)$, according to condition (4). It follows that at the point $\mathbf{x}^*$,

$$
\det \begin{pmatrix}
0 & p_1 & \cdots & p_k \\
p_1 & \dfrac{\partial^2 U}{\partial x_1^2} & \cdots & \dfrac{\partial^2 U}{\partial x_k \partial x_1} \\
\vdots & \vdots & \ddots & \vdots \\
p_k & \dfrac{\partial^2 U}{\partial x_1 \partial x_k} & \cdots & \dfrac{\partial^2 U}{\partial x_k^2}
\end{pmatrix}
$$

$$
= \det \begin{pmatrix}
0 & \dfrac{1}{\lambda}\dfrac{\partial U}{\partial x_1} & \cdots & \dfrac{1}{\lambda}\dfrac{\partial U}{\partial x_k} \\
\dfrac{1}{\lambda}\dfrac{\partial U}{\partial x_1} & \dfrac{\partial^2 U}{\partial x_1^2} & \cdots & \dfrac{\partial^2 U}{\partial x_k \partial x_1} \\
\vdots & \vdots & \ddots & \vdots \\
\dfrac{1}{\lambda}\dfrac{\partial U}{\partial x_k} & \dfrac{\partial^2 U}{\partial x_1 \partial x_k} & \cdots & \dfrac{\partial^2 U}{\partial x_k^2}
\end{pmatrix}
$$

$$
= \frac{1}{\lambda^2} \det \begin{pmatrix}
0 & \dfrac{\partial U}{\partial x_1} & \cdots & \dfrac{\partial U}{\partial x_k} \\
\dfrac{\partial U}{\partial x_1} & \dfrac{\partial^2 U}{\partial x_1^2} & \cdots & \dfrac{\partial^2 U}{\partial x_k \partial x_1} \\
\vdots & \vdots & \ddots & \vdots \\
\dfrac{\partial U}{\partial x_k} & \dfrac{\partial^2 U}{\partial x_1 \partial x_k} & \cdots & \dfrac{\partial^2 U}{\partial x_k^2}
\end{pmatrix} .
$$

Therefore, the signs of the principal minors of the matrices in (7) and (13) will be the same.

To prove part *e*, apply Theorems 21.17 and 21.22 to this problem. ∎

The Demand Function

For any price vector $\mathbf{p}$ and income I, write $\mathbf{x} = \xi(\mathbf{p}, I)$ for the commodity bundle which maximizes $\mathbf{x} \longmapsto U(\mathbf{x})$ on the constraint set (1). As we have seen, the function ξ is called the consumer's **demand function**, or sometimes **Marshallian demand function**. This demand function need not be continuous or even single-valued. To ensure that it is locally single-valued and differentiable, we make the assumption discussed in Section 19.4, namely, that the Jacobian of the first order conditions (8) and (9) which determine $\mathbf{x}^* = \xi(\mathbf{p}, I)$ is nonsingular.

Theorem 22.2   Suppose that U is a C^2 pseudoconcave utility function and that $\xi(\mathbf{p}, I)$ is the solution of utility maximization problem (1). Let $\mathbf{p}^* > \mathbf{0}$ and $I^* > 0$ be a positive price vector and income respectively. Suppose that $\xi(\mathbf{p}^*, I^*)$ is a strictly positive vector and that (7) holds for $k = n$ at $\mathbf{x} = \xi(\mathbf{p}^*, I^*)$. Then, $\xi(\mathbf{p}, I)$ and the Lagrange multiplier $\lambda(\mathbf{p}, I)$ in condition a of Theorem 22.1 are single-valued C^1 functions of $(\mathbf{p}, I)$ in an open neighborhood about $(\mathbf{p}^*, I^*)$. Furthermore,

$$\lambda(\mathbf{p}, I) = \frac{\partial U(\xi(\mathbf{p}, I))}{\partial I}, \tag{14}$$

and the multiplier $\lambda(\mathbf{p}, I)$ measures the sensitivity of the optimal utility to changes in the initial wealth I.

Proof   The $n + 1$ equations (8) and (9) determine $(\mathbf{x}, \lambda)$ as functions of $(\mathbf{p}, I)$. The matrix in (13) is the matrix of the derivatives of these equations with respect to the endogenous variables $(\mathbf{x}, \lambda)$. By the determinant calculations at the end of the proof of Theorem 22.1, this matrix will have nonzero determinant if and only if (7) holds for $k = n$. In this case, the Implicit Function Theorem tells us that we can solve (8) and (9) for $\mathbf{x}$ and λ as C^1 functions of $(\mathbf{p}, I)$ for $\mathbf{p}$ near $\mathbf{p}^*$ and I near I^*. By the last statement of Theorem 22.1, these $\mathbf{x}$'s which satisfy (8) and (9) will be constrained utility maximizers; that is, each such $\mathbf{x}$ will equal $\xi(\mathbf{p}, I)$. Equation (14) is a direct application of the Envelope Theorem (19.3) to this utility maximization problem.   ∎

Remark   Because of equality (14), the Lagrange multiplier λ for the utility maximization problem is often called the **marginal utility of income**.

Example 22.1   We use Theorems 22.1 and 22.2 to compute the demand function and the marginal utility of money for the Cobb-Douglas utility function $U(x_1, x_2) = x_1^a x_2^b$, where $a > 0$, $b > 0$, and $a + b = 1$. By (5), the maximizer must satisfy

$$\frac{ax_1^{a-1}x_2^b}{bx_1^a x_2^{b-1}} = \frac{p_1}{p_2},$$

which simplifies to

$$ap_2x_2 = bp_1x_1. \tag{15}$$

Combine (15) with the budget constraint

$$p_1x_1 + p_2x_2 = I$$

to compute

$$x_1 = \frac{aI}{p_1} \quad \text{and} \quad x_2 = \frac{bI}{p_2}. \tag{16}$$

So, the demand function for the Cobb-Douglas utility function is

$$\xi(p_1, p_2, I) = \left(\frac{aI}{p_1}, \frac{bI}{p_2} \right). \tag{17}$$

One uses (3), (4), and (16) to solve for the multiplier $\lambda(\mathbf{p}, I)$:

$$\lambda = \frac{a x_1^{a-1} x_2^b}{p_1} = \frac{a}{p_1} \left(\frac{aI}{p_1} \right)^{a-1} \cdot \left(\frac{bI}{p_2} \right)^b = \frac{a^a b^b}{p_1^a p_2^b}.$$

Next, we derive a number of characteristics of the demand function $\xi(\mathbf{p}, I)$ from its two most basic properties:

$$\sum_{i=1}^n p_i \xi_i(\mathbf{p}, I) = I, \tag{18}$$

$$\xi(r\mathbf{p}, rI) = \xi(\mathbf{p}, I) \quad \text{for all } r > 0. \tag{19}$$

The first property is just a restatement of (6), the fact that all income is spent at the utility maximizer. The second property follows directly from the fact that multiplying all the p_i's by a scalar r and multiplying I by r does not change the budget constraint (1). The same $\mathbf{x}^*$ which maximizes U on budget set (1) also maximizes U subject to the constraints

$$\sum_i (rp_i)x_i \le rI, \qquad rp_1 \ge 0, \ldots, rp_n \ge 0.$$

Recall from Chapter 21 that (19) is the statement that ξ is *homogeneous of degree zero*. If we differentiate (18) with respect to p_j and I and (19) with respect to r, the following theorem results.

Theorem 22.3 Let $(\mathbf{p}, I) \longmapsto \xi(\mathbf{p}, I)$ be the demand function for utility function U. Suppose that $\mathbf{p}^* > \mathbf{0}, I^* > 0$, and $\xi(\mathbf{p}^*, I^*) > 0$ and that U satisfies (7) at $\xi(\mathbf{p}^*, I^*)$. Then, for $j = 1, \ldots, n$ and all $(\mathbf{p}, I)$ near $(\mathbf{p}^*, I^*)$,

$$\xi_j(\mathbf{p}, I) + \sum_{i=1}^n p_i \frac{\partial \xi_i}{\partial p_j}(\mathbf{p}, I) = 0 \tag{20}$$

$$\sum_{i=1}^n p_i \frac{\partial \xi_i}{\partial I}(\mathbf{p}, I) = 1 \tag{21}$$

$$\sum_{i=1}^n p_i \frac{\partial \xi_j}{\partial p_i}(\mathbf{p}, I) + I \frac{\partial \xi_j}{\partial I}(\mathbf{p}, I) = 0. \tag{22}$$

Proof The hypotheses and Theorem 22.2 are just what are needed to ensure that ξ is a differentiable function in a neighborhood of $(\mathbf{p}^*, I^*)$. Differentiate (18) with respect to p_j to obtain (20); differentiate (18) with respect to I to obtain (21); differentiate (19) with respect to r and then set $r = 1$ to obtain (22). Note that (22) is just Euler's theorem (Theorem 20.4) for homogeneous functions applied to ξ. ∎

The results of Theorem 22.3 are often written in terms of elasticities. Recall the following definitions of demand elasticities from Section 14.2:

$$\text{own price elasticity} \quad \equiv \quad \frac{\Delta \xi_i}{\xi_i} \Big/ \frac{\Delta p_i}{p_i} \approx \frac{p_i}{\xi_i} \frac{\partial \xi_i}{\partial p_i} = \varepsilon_{ii}, \tag{23}$$

$$\text{cross price elasticity} \quad \equiv \quad \frac{\Delta \xi_i}{\xi_i} \Big/ \frac{\Delta p_j}{p_j} \approx \frac{p_j}{\xi_i} \frac{\partial \xi_i}{\partial p_j} = \varepsilon_{ij}, \tag{24}$$

$$\text{income elasticity} \quad \equiv \quad \frac{\Delta \xi_i}{\xi_i} \Big/ \frac{\Delta I}{I} \approx \frac{I}{\xi_i} \frac{\partial \xi_i}{\partial I} = \eta_i. \tag{25}$$

Finally, let s_i denote the proportion of income that is spent on commodity i:

$$s_i \equiv \frac{p_i \xi_i}{I}. \tag{26}$$

Theorem 22.4 Let $\mathbf{p}^* > 0, I^* > 0$, and $\xi(\mathbf{p}, I)$ be as in Theorem 22.3. Let ε_{ii}, ε_{ij}, and η_i be the elasticities as defined in (23), (24), and (25), and let s_i be the expenditure share as defined in (26). Then, for each j,

$$s_1 \varepsilon_{1j} + \cdots + s_n \varepsilon_{nj} = -s_j, \tag{27}$$

$$s_1 \eta_1 + \cdots + s_n \eta_n = 1, \tag{28}$$

$$\varepsilon_{j1} + \cdots + \varepsilon_{jn} + \eta_j = 0. \tag{29}$$

Proof We'll prove the first equality (27) and leave the proofs of the other two as exercises. Multiply each term in (20) by p_j/I and put the first term on the right-hand side:

$$\sum_i \frac{p_i}{I} \frac{\partial \xi_i}{\partial p_j} p_j = -\frac{p_j \xi_j}{I}.$$

Now, multiply the ith term in the summation on the left by ξ_i/ξ_i:

$$\sum_i \frac{p_i \xi_i}{I} \frac{\partial \xi_i}{\partial p_j} \frac{p_j}{\xi_i} = -\frac{\xi_j p_j}{I}. \tag{30}$$

Apply the definitions of the elasticities in (23) and (24) to translate (30) to (27). ∎

Each of the conclusions of Theorem 22.4 says something about the response of demand to changes in prices or income. Equation (27) implies that the average response in the demand for all goods to a price increase in one good is negative, where the weights for the average are given by the expenditure shares. Equation (28) states that the average income elasticity is 1; if income increases by 5 percent, then the share-weighted average increase in demand will be 5 percent. Equation (29) provides further fine-tuning for the elasticities. For example, in a two-good economy, (29) implies that if one good has income elasticity 1, then the other good must be a substitute if the first good is price elastic and a complement if the first good is price inelastic.

The Indirect Utility Function

We next define and study some functions which shed light on utility and demand functions. First, let

$$V(\mathbf{p}, I) \equiv U(\xi(\mathbf{p}, I)) \tag{31}$$

be the maximal utility obtainable with income I when the price system is $\mathbf{p}$. The function V is called the consumer's **indirect utility function**. If U is C^2 and satisfies (2) and (7), then ξ is C^1 by Theorem 22.2 and V is C^1 too, by the Chain Rule. Equation (14) gives us the partial derivative of V with respect to I: $\partial V/\partial I = \lambda$.

The following Theorem, usually known as **Roy's identity** relates the derivatives of $V(\mathbf{p}, I)$ to the Marshallian demand function ξ.

Theorem 22.5   (**Roy's identity**) Let $U(\mathbf{x})$ be a C^2 utility function that satisfies monotonicity assumption (2) and nondegeneracy assumption (7). Let $\xi(\mathbf{p}, I)$ be the demand function for U and $V(\mathbf{p}, I)$ the corresponding indirect utility function. Then, if $\mathbf{p}, I$, and $\xi(\mathbf{p}, I)$ are all strictly positive,

$$\xi_i(\mathbf{p}, I) = -\frac{\dfrac{\partial V(\mathbf{p}, I)}{\partial p_i}}{\dfrac{\partial V(\mathbf{p}, I)}{\partial I}}, \quad \text{for } i = 1, \ldots, n.$$

Proof   By Theorem 22.2, ξ and V are C^1 functions of $\mathbf{p}$ and I. Take the derivative of the identity (31) with respect to p_i:

$$\frac{\partial V}{\partial p_i} = \sum_j \frac{\partial U}{\partial x_j} \cdot \frac{\partial \xi_j}{\partial p_i}$$

$$= \sum_j \lambda p_j \cdot \frac{\partial \xi_j}{\partial p_i} \qquad \text{(by (4) of Theorem 22.1)}$$

$$= \frac{\partial V}{\partial I} \sum_j p_j \frac{\partial \xi_j}{\partial p_i} \qquad \text{(by (14) of Theorem 22.2)}$$

$$= \frac{\partial V}{\partial I} \cdot (-\xi_i(\mathbf{p}, I)) \qquad \text{(by (20) of Theorem 22.3).} \qquad \blacksquare$$

Example 22.2   Continuing our calculations with the Cobb-Douglas utility function from Example 22.1, we compute that the indirect utility function is

$$V(\mathbf{p}, I) = U\left(\frac{aI}{p_1}, \frac{bI}{p_2}\right) = \left(\frac{aI}{p_1}\right)^a \left(\frac{bI}{p_2}\right)^b = \frac{a^a b^b I}{p_1^a p_2^b}.$$

To test Roy's identity, we compute that

$$\frac{\partial V}{\partial p_1} = -\frac{a^{a+1} b^b I}{p_1^{a-1} p_2^b}$$

and

$$\frac{\partial V}{\partial I} = \lambda = \frac{a^a b^b}{p_1^a p_2^b}.$$

The quotient of these two equals

$$-\frac{aI}{p_1} = -\xi_1,$$

as Theorem 22.5 predicts.

The Expenditure and Compensated Demand Functions

To delve more deeply into properties of the demand function and indirect utility function, it is handy to consider the related (or dual) problem of choosing the commodity bundle that achieves a fixed level of utility at minimum expenditure:

$$\text{minimize} \quad \mathbf{p} \cdot \mathbf{x}$$
$$\text{subject to} \quad U(\mathbf{x}) \geq u \qquad (32)$$
$$\mathbf{x} \geq \mathbf{0}.$$

For any choice of $\mathbf{p}$ and u, let $\mathbf{Z}(\mathbf{p}, u)$ denote the commodity bundle which solves problem (32); $\mathbf{Z}(\mathbf{p}, u)$ is called the **compensated demand function** (or **Hicksian demand function**) since, in its construction, income changes compensate for price changes to keep the consumer at a fixed level of utility. Analogous to the indirect utility function, we define the consumer's **expenditure function** $E(\mathbf{p}, u)$ as the optimal value of the objective function for problem (32):

$$E(\mathbf{p}, u) \equiv \mathbf{p} \cdot \mathbf{Z}(\mathbf{p}, u).$$

The expenditure function $E(\mathbf{p}, u)$ is the (minimal) cost to the consumer for achieving utility level u when the price system is $\mathbf{p}$. We proved in Theorem 21.10 that the expenditure function, as a function of $\mathbf{p}$ for each fixed u, is concave and homogeneous of degree one. We'll see shortly that E acts very much like a utility function itself.

Since the constraint function of the utility maximization problem is the objective function of the expenditure minimization problem and the objective function of the utility maximization problem is the constraint function of the expenditure minimization problem, we say that these two problems are **dual** to each other. As the following theorems indicate, these two problems have the same first order conditions and therefore the same solutions. This theorem also computes the first order partial derivatives of the expenditure function E.

Theorem 22.6 Suppose that U is a C^1 function that satisfies the following version of monotonicity condition (2):

$$\text{for all}\quad \mathbf{x} \neq \mathbf{0}, \quad \text{there exist } i \text{ such that}\quad \frac{\partial U}{\partial x_i}(\mathbf{x}) \cdot x_i > 0. \qquad (33)$$

For fixed positive price system $\mathbf{p}^*$ and utility level u^*, let $\mathbf{z}^* = \mathbf{Z}(\mathbf{p}^*, u^*)$ denote the solution of the problem (32). Then,

(a) the first and second order conditions of problem (32) are the same as those (3), (4), (5), and (7) for the utility maximization problem;

(b) $U(\mathbf{Z}(\mathbf{p}^*, u^*)) = u^*$;

(c) if U is C^2 and satisfies (7) for $k = 2, \ldots, n$ and if each component of $\mathbf{Z}(\mathbf{p}^*, u^*)$ is positive, then $\mathbf{Z}(\mathbf{p}, u)$ and $E(\mathbf{p}, u)$ are C^1 functions for all $(\mathbf{p}, u)$ in a neighborhood of $(\mathbf{p}^*, u^*)$;

(d) if U is C^2 and satisfies (7) for $k = 2, \ldots, n$, $\partial E / \partial u$ equals the positive Lagrange multiplier for problem (32), and therefore, E is an increasing function of u for each fixed $\mathbf{p}$; and

(e) If U is C^2 and satisfies (7) for $k = 2, \ldots, n$,

$$\frac{\partial E}{\partial p_i}(\mathbf{p}, I) = z_i^*(\mathbf{p}, I). \qquad (34)$$

Proof We will just sketch the proof here since it is similar to the proofs of Theorems 22.1 and 22.2. The Lagrangian for this constrained minimization problem is

$$\tilde{L}(\mathbf{x}, \nu, \nu_1, \ldots, \nu_n) = \sum_i p_i x_i - \nu\big(U(\mathbf{x}) - u\big) - \sum_i \nu_i x_i.$$

Condition (33) is just what one needs to guarantee the NDCQ. The first order conditions turn out to be the same as (8), (10), and (11) in the proof of

Theorem 22.1, with λ in (8) corresponding to $1/\nu$ in this problem. Once again, the first order conditions and monotonicity condition (33) imply that the multiplier is positive and therefore the constraint $U(\mathbf{x}) \geq u$ in (32) is binding; this proves b. Conclusion c follows from the argument of Theorem 22.2. Conclusion d is the analogue of equation (14) in Theorem 22.2. Conclusion e is a direct consequence of the Envelope Theorem (19.4) applied to (32). ∎

Next, we show that the utility maximization problem and its dual (32) have the same solution, when the proper adjustments are made to make the problems comparable. The proof requires only the continuous analogue of the monotonicity assumptions (2) and (33) that we have been making.

Theorem 22.7   Suppose that $U(\mathbf{x})$ is a continuous function such that for each $\mathbf{x} \neq \mathbf{0}$, there exists an index i such that U is strictly increasing in x_i at $\mathbf{x}$. Then, for any $\mathbf{p} > \mathbf{0}, I > 0$, and u,

(a) $\mathbf{Z}(\mathbf{p}, u) = \xi(\mathbf{p}, E(\mathbf{p}, u))$,
(b) $\xi(\mathbf{p}, I) = \mathbf{Z}(\mathbf{p}, V(\mathbf{p}, I))$,
(c) $u = V(\mathbf{p}, E(\mathbf{p}, u))$, and
(d) $I = E(\mathbf{p}, V(\mathbf{p}, I))$.

Proof   We will prove a by contradiction. Let $\mathbf{z}^* = \mathbf{Z}(\mathbf{p}, u)$; in other words, $\mathbf{z}^*$ minimizes $\mathbf{p} \cdot \mathbf{x}$ subject to $U(\mathbf{x}) \geq u$ and $\mathbf{x} \geq \mathbf{0}$. Let $I^* = E(\mathbf{p}, u) = \mathbf{p} \cdot \mathbf{z}^*$. By conclusion b of Theorem 22.6, $U(\mathbf{z}^*) = u$. We want to show that $\mathbf{z}^*$ maximizes $U(\mathbf{x})$ subject to the constraints $\mathbf{p} \cdot \mathbf{x} \leq I^*$ and $\mathbf{x} \geq \mathbf{0}$. Suppose that it doesn't; that is, suppose that there exists

$$\mathbf{z}' \geq \mathbf{0} \quad \text{such that} \quad \mathbf{p} \cdot \mathbf{z}' \leq I^*, \quad \text{but} \quad U(\mathbf{z}') > U(\mathbf{z}^*). \tag{35}$$

Since U is continuous and monotone and each p_i is > 0, we can perturb $\mathbf{z}'$ just a little to $\mathbf{z}'' \geq \mathbf{0}$ so that

$$\mathbf{p} \cdot \mathbf{z}'' < \mathbf{p} \cdot \mathbf{z}' \leq I^*, \quad \text{while} \quad U(\mathbf{z}'') > U(\mathbf{z}^*) = u.$$

But the existence of such a $\mathbf{z}''$ contradicts the fact that $\mathbf{z}^*$ *minimizes* $\mathbf{p} \cdot \mathbf{x}$ subject to $U(\mathbf{x}) \geq u$. This contradiction implies that the assumption in (35) is false, that is, that $\mathbf{z}^*$ is the utility maximizer on the budget set

$$\mathbf{z}^* = \xi(\mathbf{p}, I^*) = \xi(\mathbf{p}, E(\mathbf{p}, u));$$

this proves a.
    To prove c, note that

$$V(\mathbf{p}, E(\mathbf{p}, u)) = U(\xi(\mathbf{p}, E(\mathbf{p}, u))) = U(\mathbf{Z}(\mathbf{p}, u)) = U(\mathbf{z}^*) = u,$$

by the definition of V, part a of this theorem, and conclusion b of Theorem 22.6.

The proofs of b and d are analogous to the proofs of a and c and are left as an exercise. ∎

Remark The function $M(\mathbf{p}, \mathbf{x}) \equiv E(\mathbf{p}, U(\mathbf{x}))$ arises frequently in welfare economics, where it is known as the **compensation function**. Given a price system $\mathbf{p}$ and a consumption bundle $\mathbf{x}$, $M(\mathbf{p}, \mathbf{x})$ tells how much money a consumer would need at those prices to be as well-off as when consuming the bundle $\mathbf{x}$. By conclusion d of Theorem 22.6, $E(\mathbf{p}, u)$ is an increasing function of u. Therefore, for fixed price system $\mathbf{p}$, $M(\mathbf{p}, \mathbf{x})$ is a monotonic transformation of the utility function U and is itself a utility function. In this vein, M is sometimes called the **money metric utility function**.

The Slutsky Equation

The expenditure function leads to a simple proof of the Slutsky Equation, the equation which describes the relationship between Marshallian and Hicksian demand and which yields the important decomposition of the effect of a price change into the substitution effect and the income effect.

Theorem 22.8 **(Slutsky Equation)** Let U be a C^2 utility function that satisfies monotonicity assumption (2) and nondegeneracy assumption (7). Let $\xi(\mathbf{p}, I)$ be the (Marshallian) demand for U and $\mathbf{Z}(\mathbf{p}, u)$ the corresponding Hicksian demand. Then, if $\mathbf{p}$, I, and $\xi(\mathbf{p}, I)$ are all strictly positive,

$$\frac{\partial \xi_j(\mathbf{p}, I)}{\partial p_i} = \frac{\partial Z_j(\mathbf{p}, V(\mathbf{p}, I))}{\partial p_i} - \frac{\partial \xi_j(\mathbf{p}, I)}{\partial I} \cdot \xi_i, \tag{36}$$

for all $i, j = 1, \ldots, n$.

Proof The hypotheses and Theorems 22.2 and 22.6 ensure that $\mathbf{Z}$, ξ, and V are differentiable functions. Differentiate statement a of Theorem 22.7,

$$Z_j(\mathbf{p}, u) = \xi_j(\mathbf{p}, E(\mathbf{p}, u)),$$

with respect to p_i, using the Chain Rule:

$$\frac{\partial Z_j}{\partial p_i}(\mathbf{p}, u) = \frac{\partial \xi_j}{\partial p_i}(\mathbf{p}, I) + \frac{\partial \xi_j}{\partial I}(\mathbf{p}, E(\mathbf{p}, u)) \cdot \frac{\partial E}{\partial p_i}(\mathbf{p}, u). \tag{37}$$

But by (34) in Theorem 22.6, $\partial E / \partial p_i$ is simply ξ_i. Finally, rearrange the terms in (37) to obtain (36). ∎

The Slutsky Equation (36) decomposes the change in demand Δx_j due to a change in price Δp_i into two separate effects: the substitution effect and the income effect. Write the Slutsky Equation as

$$\Delta x_j \approx \frac{\partial \xi_j}{\partial p_i}(\mathbf{p}, I) \cdot \Delta p_i = \frac{\partial Z_j}{\partial p_i}(\mathbf{p}, u) \cdot \Delta p_i - \frac{\partial \xi_j}{\partial I}(\mathbf{p}, I) \cdot \xi_i \Delta p_i.$$

The term

$$\frac{\partial Z_j}{\partial p_i}(\mathbf{p}, u) \cdot \Delta p_i$$

represents the **substitution effect** of the price change during which utility is held constant. The term

$$\frac{\partial \xi_j}{\partial I}(\mathbf{p}, I) \cdot \xi_i \Delta p_i$$

represents the **income effect**, the change in "purchasing power," $\xi_i \Delta p_i$, due to the price change, times the impact, $\partial \xi_j / \partial I$, of this change on demand, holding prices constant.

Remark   This proof, based on the papers by L. McKenzie and P. Cook, is quite an improvement over the proofs found in many older texts, which directly use the first order conditions for utility maximization.

We close our treatment of demand theory with some final observations about Marshallian and Hicksian demand functions.

Theorem 22.9   Let U be a utility function with differentiable Marshallian and Hicksian demand functions, $\xi(\mathbf{p}, I)$ and $\mathbf{Z}(\mathbf{p}, u)$ respectively. Then, the matrix of "substitution terms" is a symmetric matrix:

$$\frac{\partial Z_j(\mathbf{p}, u)}{\partial p_i} = \frac{\partial Z_i(\mathbf{p}, u)}{\partial p_j},$$

or equivalently

$$\frac{\partial \xi_j}{\partial p_i}(\mathbf{p}, I) + \xi_i \frac{\partial \xi_j}{\partial I}(\mathbf{p}, I) = \frac{\partial \xi_i}{\partial p_j}(\mathbf{p}, I) + \xi_j \frac{\partial \xi_i}{\partial I}(\mathbf{p}, I). \qquad (38)$$

Proof   By equation (34) in Theorem 22.6,

$$Z_j(\mathbf{p}, u) = \frac{\partial E}{\partial p_j}(\mathbf{p}, u).$$

Take the p_i derivative of this identity and use Young's theorem (14.5):

$$\frac{\partial Z_j}{\partial p_i} = \frac{\partial^2 E}{\partial p_i \partial p_j} = \frac{\partial^2 E}{\partial p_j \partial p_i} = \frac{\partial Z_i}{\partial p_j}.$$

To obtain (38), apply (37) from the proof of the Slutsky Equation. ∎

We saw in Theorem 21.10 that the expenditure is a concave function of $\mathbf{p}$ and therefore has a negative semidefinite Hessian. By the proof of Theorem 22.9, this implies that the matrix of substitution effects is negative semidefinite and, in particular, that the diagonal terms $\partial Z_i / \partial p_i$ are all ≤ 0. While Marshallian demand need not decrease as own price increases, *Hicksian demand always decreases as own price increases.*

An important problem in demand theory is to find conditions which determine whether or not a given candidate $(\mathbf{p}, I) \longmapsto \xi(\mathbf{p}, I)$ for a demand function actually arises from utility maximization. It turns out that if $\xi(\mathbf{p}, I)$ is homogeneous of degree zero and if the derivatives of ξ satisfy the symmetry condition (38) of Theorem 22.9, then there is a well-behaved utility function whose demand function is ξ.

EXERCISES

22.1 Redo Examples 22.1 and 22.2 without assuming $a + b = 1$.

22.2 Expand on Example 22.1 by computing the demand function and the marginal utility of money for a (degree one) Cobb-Douglas utility function of n commodities.

22.3 Derive equations (28) and (29) in Theorem 22.4.

22.4 Carry out the details of the proof of Theorem 22.6.

22.5 Prove parts b and d of Theorem 22.7.

22.6 Give another proof of Roy's identity by differentiating statement c of Theorem 22.7 with respect to p_i.

22.7 Check the Slutsky Equations for Cobb-Douglas utility functions.

22.8 Use the Implicit Function Theorem on the first and second order conditions for the expenditure minimization problem (32) and the utility maximization problem to give the "classical" proof of Theorem 22.9, even for an economy with two goods.

22.9 Compute the Marshallian demand functions, indirect utility function, and expenditure function (a little tricky) for the **constant elasticity of substitution (CES)** utility function $U(x_1, x_2) = \left(x_1^r + x_2^r \right)^{1/r}$.

22.2 ECONOMIC APPLICATION: PROFIT AND COST

The Profit-Maximizing Firm

We turn to applications of our theorems on constrained optimization to the economic behavior of a firm. Given the price and supply of each input, the price and demand of each output, and the technological relations between input and output, the firm must decide how much to produce and how much input to use in this production in order to meet its economic objectives. For the sake of simplicity, we will work with a firm that produces a single commodity from n inputs. Let x_i denote the quantity of input i, $\mathbf{x} = (x_1, \ldots, x_n)$ the resulting **input vector**, and $y \in \mathbf{R}$ the amount of output produced. We assume that the firm has a **production function** $f: \mathbf{R}^n_+ \to \mathbf{R}$, where $f(\mathbf{x})$ denotes the maximum output obtainable from input vector $\mathbf{x}$.

In the most general situation, we would let $p(y)$ and $\mathbf{w}(\mathbf{x})$ denote the **inverse demand functions** for output and input, respectively; that is, $p(y)$ is the unit price a firm can charge for its output if its level of output is y and $\mathbf{w}(\mathbf{x}) \in \mathbf{R}^n_+$ is the input price vector which the firm will pay when it purchases input vector $\mathbf{x}$. For a firm in *perfect competition*, p and $\mathbf{w}$ are constants. For a *monopolist* firm, $\mathbf{w}$ is constant but p is not, and the firm can control the price of its product by varying production amounts. For a *monopsonist* firm, p is constant but $\mathbf{w}$ is not, and the firm can influence the price of an input by varying its purchases of the input.

The simplest case to consider is that of a firm in a perfectly competitive market, whose goal is to maximize its profit. Let p be the price of a unit of its output; let $\mathbf{w}$ denote its constant cost vector. The firm's *profit* Π is its *revenue* $py = pf(\mathbf{x})$ minus its *cost* $\mathbf{w} \cdot \mathbf{x}$. Its goal is to

$$\text{maximize} \quad \Pi(\mathbf{x}) = pf(\mathbf{x}) - \mathbf{w} \cdot \mathbf{x}, \quad \mathbf{x} \geq \mathbf{0}. \tag{39}$$

The following theorem, the analogue of Theorems 22.1 and 22.2 for utility maximization, gives the necessary and sufficient conditions for an input vector $\mathbf{x}^*$ to be a profit-maximizing choice.

Theorem 22.10   Suppose that f is a C^2 production function and that $\mathbf{x}^*$ is the maximizer of problem (39). Then, for each $i = 1, \ldots, n$,

$$p \frac{\partial f}{\partial x_i}(\mathbf{x}^*) \leq w_i \tag{40}$$

with
$$p \frac{\partial f}{\partial x_i}(\mathbf{x}^*) = w_i \quad \text{for all } i \text{ such that} \quad x_i^* > 0. \tag{41}$$

If each $x_i^* > 0$, then the Hessian of f is negative semidefinite at $\mathbf{x}^*$.
   Conversely, if $\mathbf{x}^*$ is a vector such that:

(a) $x_i^* > 0$ for all i,
(b) condition (41) holds, and
(c) the Hessian $D^2 f(\mathbf{x}^*)$ is negative definite; that is,

$$(-1)^k \det \begin{pmatrix} \dfrac{\partial^2 f}{\partial x_1{}^2} & \cdots & \dfrac{\partial^2 f}{\partial x_k \partial x_1} \\ \vdots & \ddots & \vdots \\ \dfrac{\partial^2 f}{\partial x_1 \partial x_k} & \cdots & \dfrac{\partial^2 f}{\partial x_k{}^2} \end{pmatrix} > 0 \qquad (42)$$

for $k = 1, \ldots, n$,

then $\mathbf{x}^*$ is a strict local profit-maximizer. In this case $\mathbf{x}^*$ is a C^1 function of p and $\mathbf{w}$.

The proof of Theorem 22.10 is similar to the proofs of Theorems 22.1 and 22.2, and is left as an exercise.

The first order condition (41) for profit-maximization states that when a firm is operating at the optimal input level, an additional unit of output will bring in as much revenue as it costs to produce that unit. By analogy with what we did for the utility maximization problem, we define $\chi(p, \mathbf{w}) = \mathbf{x}^*$ to be the solution of problem (39) for a fixed p and $\mathbf{w}$. The mapping χ is called the **factor demand correspondence**. The function $F(p, \mathbf{w}) = f(\chi(p, \mathbf{w}))$ is called the firm's **output supply function**. It tells how much output the profit-maximizing firm will supply when prices are p for output and $\mathbf{w}$ for inputs. It is a component of the demand-supply analysis that is the focal point of elementary economics courses. By the converse part of Theorem 22.10, χ and F will be (single-valued, at least locally) C^1 functions of p and $\mathbf{w}$ provided (42) holds.

One can derive properties of these functions by using techniques similar to those in Theorems 22.5 and 22.6 of the previous section.

Theorem 22.11   Suppose that the production function $\mathbf{x} \mapsto f(\mathbf{x})$ of a profit-maximizing firm satisfies (41) and (42) at the *positive* profit-maximizing input vector $\mathbf{x}^* = \chi(p, \mathbf{w})$. Let

$$\Pi^*(p, \mathbf{w}) = \Pi(\chi(p, \mathbf{w}))$$

be the optimal profit function. Then,

$$\frac{\partial \Pi^*(p, \mathbf{w})}{\partial p} = y = F(p, \mathbf{w}), \qquad (43)$$

$$\frac{\partial \Pi^*(p, \mathbf{w})}{\partial w_i} = -x_i^* = -\chi_i(p, \mathbf{w}), \qquad (44)$$

$$\frac{\partial \chi_i}{\partial w_j}(p, \mathbf{w}) = \frac{\partial \chi_j}{\partial w_i}(p, \mathbf{w}), \qquad (45)$$

$$\frac{\partial \chi_i}{\partial p}(p, \mathbf{w}) = -\frac{\partial F}{\partial w_i}(p, \mathbf{w}). \qquad (46)$$

Proof   Hypotheses (42) and Theorem 22.1 imply that ξ and χ are differentiable functions. Equations (43) and (44) are direct applications of the Envelope Theorem (19.4) to the maximal profit function Π^*. To derive (45), take the derivative of (44) with respect to w_j, and use Young's theorem, (14.5) and (44) again:

$$\frac{\partial \chi_i}{\partial w_j}(p, \mathbf{w}) = -\frac{\partial^2 \Pi^*}{\partial w_j \partial w_i} = -\frac{\partial^2 \Pi^*}{\partial w_i \partial w_j} = \frac{\partial \chi_j}{\partial w_i}(p, \mathbf{w}).$$

To derive (46), take the derivative of (44) with respect to p, use Young's theorem, and then apply (43):

$$\frac{\partial \chi_i}{\partial p}(p, \mathbf{w}) = -\frac{\partial^2 \Pi^*}{\partial p \partial w_i} = -\frac{\partial^2 \Pi^*}{\partial w_i \partial p} = -\frac{\partial F}{\partial w_i}(p, \mathbf{w}). \quad \blacksquare$$

Equations (43) and (44) together are known as **Hotelling's lemma**. Equation (44) is simply the statement that if the price of input i rises by 1 cent and the firm uses x_i units of this input, then its profit will decrease by x_i cents, even taking into consideration possible changes in production. Symmetry condition (45) is called the **reciprocity condition**. It states that the effect of a change in the wage of the ith input on the demand of the jth input is the same as the effect of a change in the wage of the jth input on the demand for the ith input. Equation (46) implies that an increase in the output price raises the demand for input i if and only if an increase in the wage of input i reduces the optimal output. We saw (Theorem 21.11) that the optimal objective function $\Pi^*(p, \mathbf{w})$ is a convex function and so its Hessian is positive semidefinite. Among other things, this implies that the diagonal terms of the Hessian are nonnegative; and that

$$\frac{\partial \chi_i}{\partial w_i} = -\frac{\partial^2 \Pi^*}{\partial w_i^2} \leq 0, \quad \text{for all } i. \tag{47}$$

An increase in the price of input i leads to a decrease in its usage.

The exercises develop homogeneity properties of χ and Π^*: χ is homogeneous of degree zero and Π^* is homogeneous of degree one in $(p, \mathbf{w})$.

The Cost Function

The optimal profit function $\Pi^*(p, \mathbf{w})$ of a firm plays the role that the indirect utility function $V(\mathbf{p}, I)$ does for the consumer. We will see now that the firm's *cost function* plays a role in the theory of the firm's behavior analogous to the role of the *expenditure function* in the theory of a consumer's behavior.

A firm would always like to produce its output in the cheapest possible manner. This fact is especially important in those cases in which the firm cannot view the price p of its output as fixed, for example, when it is the only supplier of that output. We are thus led to consider the problem of finding a *cost minimizing* way to produce a given level of output:

$$\text{minimize} \quad \mathbf{w} \cdot \mathbf{x}$$

$$\text{subject to} \quad f(\mathbf{x}) = y, \tag{48}$$

$$\mathbf{x} \geq \mathbf{0}.$$

The following theorem summarizes the first and second order conditions for a firm's cost minimization problem (48).

Theorem 22.12   Suppose that $\mathbf{z}^*(\mathbf{w}, y)$ is the solution of the cost-minimization problem (48). Suppose that f is a C^1 production function that satisfies the monotonicity assumption:

$$\text{for each} \quad \mathbf{x} \neq \mathbf{0}, \quad \text{there is an index } i \text{ such that} \quad x_i \frac{\partial f(\mathbf{x})}{\partial x_i} > 0.$$

Then,

(a) there is a positive scalar λ such that $\mathbf{z}^*$ satisfies

$$w_i \geq \lambda \frac{\partial f}{\partial x_i}(\mathbf{z}^*) \tag{49}$$

with $\quad w_i = \lambda \dfrac{\partial f}{\partial x_i}(\mathbf{z}^*) \quad$ for all i such that $\quad z_i^* > 0$;

(b) if z_i^* and z_j^* are positive, then

$$\frac{w_i}{w_j} = \frac{\dfrac{\partial f}{\partial x_i}(\mathbf{z}^*)}{\dfrac{\partial f}{\partial x_j}(\mathbf{z}^*)}; \tag{50}$$

(c) if f is C^2 and if $\mathbf{z}^* > \mathbf{0}$, then

$$(-1)^k \det \begin{pmatrix} 0 & \dfrac{\partial f}{\partial x_1} & \cdots & \dfrac{\partial f}{\partial x_k} \\ \dfrac{\partial f}{\partial x_1} & \dfrac{\partial^2 f}{\partial x_1^2} & \cdots & \dfrac{\partial^2 f}{\partial x_1 \partial x_k} \\ \vdots & \vdots & \ddots & \vdots \\ \dfrac{\partial f}{\partial x_k} & \dfrac{\partial^2 f}{\partial x_k \partial x_1} & \cdots & \dfrac{\partial^2 f}{\partial x_k^2} \end{pmatrix} \geq 0 \tag{51}$$

for $k = 2, \ldots, n$

> Conversely, if f is C^2, if $\mathbf{z}^*$ is a positive vector which satisfies (50) for all i, j, and if (51) holds with strict inequality for $k = 2, \ldots, n$, then $\mathbf{z}^*$ is a strict local cost-minimizing solution of problem (48). In this case, the minimizer $\mathbf{z}^*(\mathbf{w}, p)$ is a C^1 function of $\mathbf{w}$ and p.

The proof of Theorem 22.12 is similar to that of Theorems 22.1 and 22.10 and will be left as an exercise. The primary first order condition (50) is the same as the first order condition for the profit-maximization in Theorem 22.10 (and analogous to the first order condition (5) for utility maximization). So, we treat the profit-maximization problem and the cost-minimization problem (48) as dual to each other. Write $C(y, \mathbf{w})$ for the minimal cost of producing output bundle y when input prices are given by $\mathbf{w}$:

$$C(y, \mathbf{w}) \equiv \mathbf{z}^*(y, \mathbf{w}) \cdot \mathbf{w}, \tag{52}$$

the optimal value of the objective function of problem (48). This is the usual cost function $y \longmapsto C(y)$ in elementary and intermediate microeconomics texts. By Theorem 21.11, C is concave and homogeneous as a function of $\mathbf{w}$. The cost function C is the analogue of the expenditure function in consumer theory, and the solution $\mathbf{z}^*(y, \mathbf{w})$ plays the role of Hicksian demand in consumer theory. The function $\mathbf{z}^*(y, \mathbf{w})$ is sometimes called the firm's **conditional factor demand** — "conditional" because it depends on the level of output as well as on the input prices. By applying the Envelope Theorem (19.4) to problem (48), one proves the analogue of equation (34) in consumer theory. (Exercise.) In producer theory, this equation is known as **Shephard's lemma**.

> **Theorem 22.13   (Shephard's lemma.)** Suppose that the firm's production function is C^2, satisfies the monotonicity condition in the statement of Theorem 22.12, and satisfies the second order condition (51) with strict inequalities for $k = 2, \ldots, n$. Let $\mathbf{z}^*(y, \mathbf{w})$ denote the firm's conditional demand function for input i. Suppose that $\mathbf{w} > \mathbf{0}$ and $\mathbf{z}^* > \mathbf{0}$. Then,
>
> $$z_i^*(y, \mathbf{w}) = \frac{\partial C(y, \mathbf{w})}{\partial w_i}, \quad i = 1, \ldots, n, \tag{53}$$
>
> and $$\frac{\partial z_i^*}{\partial w_j} = \frac{\partial z_j^*}{\partial w_i}, \qquad \text{for all } i \text{ and } j. \tag{54}$$

Example 22.3   Let's derive the cost function for a Cobb-Douglas production function,

$$y = k x_1^a x_2^b, \tag{55}$$

for a two-input firm. From (50) the first order conditions are

$$\frac{w_1}{w_2} = \frac{a x_1^{a-1} x_2^b}{b x_1^a x_2^{b-1}} = \frac{a\, x_2}{b\, x_1},$$

or

$$b w_1 x_1 = a w_2 x_2. \tag{56}$$

Combining (56) with (55) yields

$$x_1 = \frac{a w_2 x_2}{b w_1} = \frac{a w_2}{b w_1} \left(\frac{y}{k x_1^a}\right)^{1/b},$$

which solves to

$$x_1 = \left(\frac{a w_2}{b w_1 k^{1/b}}\right)^{b/(a+b)} y^{1/(a+b)}. \tag{57}$$

Similarly, one computes

$$x_2 = \left(\frac{a w_2 k^{1/a}}{b w_1}\right)^{-a/(a+b)} y^{1/(a+b)}. \tag{58}$$

Now, substitute (57) and (58) into the cost function to obtain

$$C = w_1 x_1 + w_2 x_2$$

$$= \left[w_1 \left(\frac{a w_2}{b w_1 k^{1/b}}\right)^{b/(a+b)} + w_2 \left(\frac{a w_2 k^{1/a}}{b w_1}\right)^{-a/(a+b)} \right] y^{1/(a+b)}$$

$$= K w_1^{a/(a+b)} w_2^{b/(a+b)} y^{1/(a+b)},$$

where $K \equiv k^{-1/(a+b)} \left[\left(\frac{a}{b}\right)^{b/(a+b)} + \left(\frac{a}{b}\right)^{-a/(a+b)} \right].$

Shephard's lemma is particularly useful in going in the other direction, that is, in deriving the production function which corresponds to a given cost function. An economist studying the behavior of a firm would conceivably find it easier to estimate its cost function than its production function. Duality theory, in particular Shephard's lemma, tells us what functional forms are acceptable candidates for cost functions and how to recover information from them about the firm's production and input demand functions. The following example illustrates the derivation of a production function from a cost function.

Example 22.4   Let's start with the cost function we derived in the previous
example,

$$C(w_1, w_2, y) = K w_1^a w_2^{1-a} y^b,$$

and use Shephard's lemma to derive the corresponding production function.
According to Shephard's lemma,

$$x_1(\mathbf{w}, y) = \frac{\partial C}{\partial w_1} = K a w_1^{a-1} w_2^{1-a} y^b = K a y^b \left(\frac{w_2}{w_1}\right)^{1-a},$$

$$x_2(\mathbf{w}, y) = \frac{\partial C}{\partial w_2} = K(1-a) w_1^a w_2^{-a} y^b = K(1-a) y^b \left(\frac{w_2}{w_1}\right)^{-a}.$$

Solve these two equations for w_2/w_1 and equate the results:

$$\frac{w_2}{w_1} = \left(\frac{x_1}{K a y^b}\right)^{1/(1-a)} = \left(\frac{x_2}{K(1-a)y^b}\right)^{-1/a}.$$

Raise these last two expressions to the $-a(1-a)$ power:

$$K^a a^a y^{ab} x_1^{-a} = K^{a-1}(1-a)^{a-1} y^{b(a-1)} x_2^{1-a},$$

or
$$y = \kappa x_1^{a/b} x_2^{(1-a)/b},$$

where $\kappa = [K a^a (1-a)^{1-a}]^{-1/b}$. We have recovered the Cobb-Douglas production function.

EXERCISES

22.10 Prove that the factor demand correspondence χ is homogeneous of degree zero:
$\chi(rp, r\mathbf{w}) = \chi(p, \mathbf{w})$ for all $r > 0$.

22.11 Prove that optimal profit Π^* is homogeneous of degree one:
$\Pi^*(rp, r\mathbf{w}) = r\Pi^*(p, \mathbf{w})$ for all $r > 0$.

22.12 Write out a careful proof of Theorem 22.10.

22.13 Prove Theorem 22.12.

22.14 Prove Theorem 22.13.

22.15 Use the Implicit Function Theorem on the first and second order conditions of the
cost minimization problem to prove (54) for $n = 2$.

22.16 Derive the production function which corresponds to the cost function $C(y, \mathbf{w}) =
y(w_1 + \sqrt{w_1 w_2} + w_2)$.

22.3   PARETO OPTIMA

In Sections 22.1 and 22.2, we studied an individual consumer maximizing utility under budgetary constraints and a single firm maximizing profits while producing a single output from a stock of available resources. The next step is to examine economies in which a number of consumers and firms compete among themselves for goods and services. To treat such problems as *independent* maximization problems would be to ignore the constraints on the stock of available goods and resources and the interactions between the various components of the economy. Furthermore, such a treatment will usually lead to a mathematical problem with an empty solution set. In this section, we introduce the notion of a vector maximum or Pareto optimum for situations where a number of agents are trying to meet their independent objectives.

Definition   Let C be a subset of $\mathbf{R}^n$. Let $u_1, \ldots, u_A$ be real-valued functions on C. Then, $\mathbf{u} = (u_1, \ldots, u_A)$ has a **vector maximum** or **Pareto optimum** at $\mathbf{x}^* \in C$ if there is no $\mathbf{x} \in C$ such that

$$u_i(\mathbf{x}) \geq u_i(\mathbf{x}^*) \quad \text{for all } i \quad \text{and} \quad u_j(\mathbf{x}) > u_j(\mathbf{x}^*) \quad \text{for some } j,$$

that is, such that

$$\mathbf{u}(\mathbf{x}) \geq \mathbf{u}(\mathbf{x}^*) \quad \text{and} \quad \mathbf{u}(\mathbf{x}) \neq \mathbf{u}(\mathbf{x}^*)$$

in the usual partial ordering on $\mathbf{R}^a$.

A Pareto optimum is a natural equilibrium for an economy. Mathematically speaking, it is a maximal element in the ordering on $\mathbf{R}^n$ generated by the u_i's. In economic terms, it is an allocation in which no one can be made better-off without someone else becoming worse-off. In this section we will show how one can derive necessary and sufficient conditions for a Pareto optimum from the constrained *scalar* maximization theorems of Chapters 18 and 19. In the next section, we will apply these results to the theory of the consumer. The following theorem is the key step in this process.

Theorem 22.14   Let C be a subset of $\mathbf{R}^n$; let $u_i : C \to \mathbf{R}$ for $i = 1, \ldots, A$. A necessary and sufficient condition that $\mathbf{x}^* \in C$ be a Pareto optimum for $\mathbf{u} = (u_1, \ldots, u_A)$ is that for each $i = 1, \ldots, A$, $\mathbf{x}^*$ maximizes u_i on the constraint set

$$C_i \equiv \{\mathbf{x} \in C : u_j(\mathbf{x}) \geq u_j(\mathbf{x}^*), j = 1, \ldots, A; j \neq i\}. \tag{59}$$

Proof   Suppose that $\mathbf{x}^*$ is a Pareto optimizer of $\mathbf{u}$. If $\mathbf{x}^*$ does not satisfy (59) for some k, then there is an $\mathbf{x} \in C$ such that $u_j(\mathbf{x}) \geq u_j(\mathbf{x}^*)$ for all j and $u_k(\mathbf{x}) > u_k(\mathbf{x}^*)$; this contradicts the Pareto optimality of $\mathbf{x}^*$.

Conversely, suppose that $\mathbf{x}^*$ maximizes each u_k on C_k. If $\mathbf{x}^*$ is not a Pareto optimum of $\mathbf{u}$ on C, there is an $\mathbf{x} \in C$ and an index k such that $u_i(\mathbf{x}) \geq u_i(\mathbf{x}^*)$ for all i and $u_k(\mathbf{x}) > u_k(\mathbf{x}^*)$; this contradicts the maximality of $\mathbf{x}^*$ for u_k on C_k. ∎

Necessary Conditions for a Pareto Optimum

We use Theorem 22.14 to derive the basic necessary condition for a Pareto optimum. For real-valued functions $g_1, \ldots, g_M, h_1, \ldots, h_N$ on $\mathbf{R}^n$ and scalars $b_1, \ldots, b_M, a_1, \ldots, a_N$, we will use the notation of Chapter 18 and work on the constraint set

$$C_{g,h} \equiv \{\mathbf{x} \in \mathbf{R}^n : g_i(\mathbf{x}) \leq b_i, \ i = 1, \ldots, M; \ h_j(\mathbf{x}) = a_j, \ j = 1, \ldots, N\}.$$

Theorem 22.15 Suppose that $u_1, \ldots, u_A, g_1, \ldots, g_M, h_1, \ldots, h_N$ are C^1 functions on $\mathbf{R}^n$. Suppose that $\mathbf{x}^* \in \mathbf{R}^n$ is a *Pareto optimum* for $\mathbf{u} = (u_1, \ldots, u_A)$ on $C_{g,h}$. Then, there exist scalars $\alpha_1, \ldots, \alpha_A, \lambda_1, \ldots, \lambda_M, \mu_1, \ldots, \mu_N$, *not all zero*, such that

$$\alpha_i \geq 0, \quad i = 1, \ldots, A;$$

$$\lambda_j \geq 0 \quad \text{and} \quad \lambda_j(g_j(\mathbf{x}^*) - b_j) = 0, \quad j = 1, \ldots, M; \quad (60)$$

$$\sum_{i=1}^A \alpha_i Du_i(\mathbf{x}^*) - \sum_{j=1}^M \lambda_j Dg_j(\mathbf{x}^*) - \sum_{k=1}^N \mu_k Dh_k(\mathbf{x}^*) = \mathbf{0}. \quad (61)$$

Proof Since $\mathbf{x}^*$ is a Pareto optimum of $\mathbf{u}$ on $C_{g,h}$, $\mathbf{x}^*$ maximizes u_1 on the set

$$\{\mathbf{x} \in C_{g,h} : u_j(\mathbf{x}) \geq u_j(\mathbf{x}^*), \ j = 2, \ldots, A\}.$$

The Lagrangian for this scalar maximization problem is

$$L = \alpha_1 u_1(\mathbf{x}) - \sum_{i=2}^A \alpha_i(u_i(\mathbf{x}^*) - u_i(\mathbf{x})) - \sum_{j=1}^M \lambda_j(g_j(\mathbf{x}) - b_j) - \sum_{k=1}^N \mu_k(h_k(\mathbf{x}) - a_k).$$

$$(62)$$

We include a multiplier α_1 for the objective function because we have not assumed any constraint qualifications. By Theorem 19.11, there exist $\alpha_1 \geq 0$, $\alpha_2, \ldots, \alpha_A, \lambda_1, \ldots, \lambda_M$ and $\mu_1, \ldots, \mu_N$ *not all zero* such that (60) holds and $D_{\mathbf{x}} L(\mathbf{x}^*; \alpha, \lambda, \mu) = \mathbf{0}$. But this latter equation is precisely equation (61). ∎

As in our scalar maximization problems, we would like to have *strictly positive* multipliers α_i for the objective functions u_i for $i = 1, \ldots, A$. To achieve this goal, we need to bring into this discussion the constraint qualifications for the scalar maximization problems.

Theorem 22.16   Let the u_i's, g_j's, and h_k's be as in the hypothesis of Theorem 22.15. For $i = 1, \ldots, A$, let $u^{(i)}$ denote the mapping

$$u^{(i)} \equiv (u_1, \ldots, u_{i-1}, u_{i+1}, \ldots, u_A).$$

For $\mathbf{x}^*$ a Pareto optimum as in Theorem 22.15, suppose that $g_1, \ldots, g_e$ are binding inequality constraints at $\mathbf{x}^*$ and that $g_{e+1}, \ldots, g_M$ are not binding at $\mathbf{x}^*$. Write g_E for the map $(g_1, \ldots, g_e)$ of the binding constraint functions. Suppose that one of the following vector maximization constraint qualifications are satisfied at $\mathbf{x}^*$:

   (a) The matrix $D(u^{(i)}, g_E, h)(\mathbf{x}^*)$ has maximal rank for each $i = 1, \ldots, A$.
   (b) The u_i's are concave, the g_j's are convex, the h_k's are linear, and for each $i = 1, \ldots, A$, there is a $\mathbf{z}^i \in C_{g,h}$ such that $u^{(i)}(\mathbf{z}^i) > u^{(i)}(\mathbf{x}^*)$ and $g_E(\mathbf{z}^i) < b_E$.

Then, conclusions (60) and (61) of Theorem 22.15 hold with $\alpha_1, \ldots, \alpha_A$ all *strictly positive*.

Proof   Apply Theorem 19.12 to problem (59) for each fixed $i \in \{1, \ldots, A\}$. There exist

$$\alpha_1^i, \ldots, \alpha_A^i, \lambda_1^i, \ldots, \lambda_M^i, \mu_1^i, \ldots, \mu_N^i$$

such that the α_j^i's and the λ_j^i's are all nonnegative, $\alpha_i^i = 1$, all the $\lambda_j^i(g_j(\mathbf{x}^*) - b_j) = 0$, and first order condition (61) holds with superscript i's on the multipliers in (61). Finally, add up these A systems of first order conditions. The multipliers for the sum will be

$$\alpha_j = \sum_{i=1}^a \alpha_j^i \geq 1, \quad \lambda_j = \sum_{i=1}^a \lambda_j^i \geq 0, \quad \text{and} \quad \mu_k = \sum_{i=1}^a \mu_k^i. \quad \blacksquare$$

Sufficient Conditions for a Pareto Optimum

Finally, we can use the sufficient conditions of Sections 19.3 and 21.5 for scalar maximization problems to derive sufficient conditions for a vector $\mathbf{x}^*$ to be a Pareto optimum.

Theorem 22.17   Let the u_i's, g_j's, and h_k's be C^2 functions as in the hypothesis of Theorem 22.15. Suppose that:

(a) $\mathbf{x}^*$ is in $C_{g,h}$;
(b) there exists scalars $\alpha_1, \cdots, \alpha_A, \lambda_1, \ldots, \lambda_M, \mu_1, \ldots, \mu_N$ such that (60) and (61) hold at $\mathbf{x}^*$; and
(c) $\mathbf{v}^T D_{\mathbf{x}}^2 \hat{L}(\mathbf{x}^*)\mathbf{v} < 0$ for all $\mathbf{v} \neq \mathbf{0}$ such that:
  (i) $\alpha_i Du_i(\mathbf{x}^*)\mathbf{v} = 0$, for $i = 1, \ldots A$,
  (ii) $\lambda_j Dg_j(\mathbf{x}^*)\mathbf{v} = 0$, for $j = 1, \ldots, M$, and
  (iii) $Dh_k(\mathbf{x}^*)\mathbf{v} = 0$, for $k = 1, \ldots, N$,
  where $\hat{L}$ denotes the Lagrangian function

$$\hat{L}(\mathbf{x}) = \sum_{i=1}^{A} \alpha_i u_i(\mathbf{x}) - \sum_{j=1}^{M} \lambda_j \big(g_j(\mathbf{x}) - b_j\big) - \sum_{k=1}^{N} \mu_k \big(h_k(\mathbf{x}) - a_k\big). \tag{63}$$

Then, there is an open ball B about $\mathbf{x}^*$ such that $\mathbf{x}^*$ is a Pareto optimum for $\mathbf{u}$ restricted B.

Proof   One shows that for $i = 1, \ldots, A$, $\mathbf{x}^*$ is a local solution of problem (59) with $C = C_{g,h}$. We work with $i = 1$, as an illustration. The Lagrangian for this problem is precisely the function in (62). Of course, we choose the multipliers in b to be the multipliers for this scalar maximization problem.

We want to apply the second order sufficient condition of Theorem 19.8 to show that $\mathbf{x}^*$ maximizes u_1 on its constraint set. Accordingly, choose $\mathbf{v} \neq \mathbf{0}$ to satisfy conditions *i* (except for index $i = 1$), *ii*, and *iii*. Since $D_{\mathbf{x}}L(\mathbf{x}^*)\mathbf{v} = D_{\mathbf{x}}\hat{L}(\mathbf{x}^*)\mathbf{v} = 0$,

$$-\alpha_1 Du_1(\mathbf{x}^*)\mathbf{v} = \sum_{i=2}^{A} \alpha_i Du_i(\mathbf{x}^*)\mathbf{v} - \sum_{j=1}^{M} \lambda_j Dg_j(\mathbf{x}^*)\mathbf{v} - \sum_{k=1}^{N} \mu_k Dh(\mathbf{x}^*)\mathbf{v} = 0.$$

Therefore, $-\alpha_1 Du_1(\mathbf{x}^*)\mathbf{v} = 0$, too. By hypothesis,

$$\mathbf{v}^T D^2 L(\mathbf{x}^*)\mathbf{v} = \mathbf{v}^T D^2 \hat{L}(\mathbf{x}^*)\mathbf{v} < 0.$$

By Theorem 19.8, $\mathbf{x}^*$ is a strict local max of u_1 restricted to

$$\{\mathbf{x} \in \mathbf{R}^n : u^{(1)}(\mathbf{x}) \geq u^{(1)}(\mathbf{x}^*),\ \mathbf{g}(\mathbf{x}) \leq \mathbf{b},\ \mathbf{h}(\mathbf{x}) = \mathbf{a}\}.$$

By Theorem 22.14, $\mathbf{x}^*$ is a local Pareto optimum of $\mathbf{u}$. ∎

In the next section, we will need the following first order sufficient condition for a Pareto optimum. Its proof is a straightforward application of Theorems 22.14 and 21.22, and is left as an exercise.

Theorem 22.18   Let the u_i's, g_j's, and h_k's be C^1 functions as in the hypothesis of Theorem 22.15. Suppose that:

(a) $\mathbf{x}^*$ is in $C_{g,h}$;
(b) there exists scalars $\alpha_1, \ldots, \alpha_A, \lambda_1, \ldots, \lambda_M, \mu_1, \ldots, \mu_N$ such that (60) and (61) hold at $\mathbf{x}^*$;
(c) the α_i's are all strictly positive; and
(d) the u_i's are pseudoconcave, the g_j's are quasiconvex, and the h_k's are linear.

Then, $\mathbf{x}^*$ is a global Pareto optimum for $\mathbf{u}$ on $C_{g,h}$.

EXERCISES

22.17   Give careful definitions of a local Pareto optimum, a strict Pareto optimum, and a strict local Pareto optimum.

22.18   Show that the $\mathbf{x}^*$ in Theorem 22.17 is a strict local Pareto optimum.

22.19   Prove Theorem 22.18.

22.4   THE FUNDAMENTAL WELFARE THEOREMS

In this section we apply the last section's theorems on Pareto optima to study the interactions of consumers. In the process, we will discuss and prove the two Fundamental Theorems of Welfare Economics. We suppose that there are A consumers in an economy with n goods. We use superscripts to keep track of consumers and subscripts to designate the goods; for example, x_j^k denotes the amount of good j consumed by consumer k. We assume that the kth consumer has a C^1 utility function $u^k \colon \mathbf{R}_+^n \to \mathbf{R}$ and an initial **endowment** bundle y^k in $\mathbf{R}_+^n$.

We work with a closed economy in that the total amount of each commodity remains fixed during the consumers' interactions. So, if $\mathbf{b} = \sum_1^A y^k$, the *state space* of this problem is:

$$\Omega \equiv \{\mathbf{Z} = (\mathbf{z}^1, \ldots, \mathbf{z}^A) \in (\mathbf{R}_+^n)^A : \sum_{k=1}^A \mathbf{z}^k = \mathbf{b}\}.$$

An element of Ω is called a **commodity allocation**. Each utility function u^k can be considered as a function U^k on Ω by writing:

$$U^k(\mathbf{z}^1, \ldots, \mathbf{z}^A) = u^k(\mathbf{z}^k), \quad \text{for } k = 1, \ldots, A, \tag{64}$$

so that Ω is the common domain of the A utility functions — the set we called C in the last section. Finally, we combine these A utility functions to form the **utility mapping**

$$U = (U^1, \ldots, U^A): \Omega \rightarrow \mathbf{R}^A.$$

In this setting, an **economy** is a utility mapping U, an initial commodity allocation $(\mathbf{y}^1, \ldots, \mathbf{y}^A)$, and a price system $\mathbf{p}$.

In this section we characterize those allocations that the market *should achieve,* Pareto optima, and those which the market *does achieve,* competitive equilibria. The important question, "How well does the market allocate resources?" can then be stated as, "What is the relationship between competitive equilibrium and pareto optimal allocations?" We will address this question here, but first we characterize the Pareto optimal bundles.

Theorem 22.19   Consider an economy in which agent k has a C^1 utility function u^k and nonzero allocation $\mathbf{y}^k \in \mathbf{R}_+^n$ for $k = 1, \ldots, A$. Let $U = (U^1, \ldots, U^A): \Omega \rightarrow \mathbf{R}^A$ be as defined in (64). Let $\mathbf{b} = \sum_1^A \mathbf{y}^k$ denote the supply vector of the economy. Suppose that each $b_i > 0$ and that the following monotonicity assumption is satisfied:

$$\frac{\partial u^k}{\partial x_j^k}(\mathbf{y}^k) > 0 \quad \text{for } k = 1, \ldots, A; j = 1, \ldots, n. \tag{65}$$

(a) If $\mathbf{Y} = (\mathbf{y}^1, \ldots, \mathbf{y}^A)$ is a Pareto optimum, then there exist strictly positive multipliers $\alpha_1, \ldots, \alpha_A$ and a vector $\mathbf{c} = (c_1, \ldots, c_n)$ with each $c_i > 0$ such that

$$\alpha^k \nabla u^k(\mathbf{y}^k) \leq \mathbf{c}, \quad \text{for} \quad k = 1, \ldots, A \tag{66}$$

$$\alpha^k \frac{\partial u^k}{\partial x_j^k}(\mathbf{y}^k) = c_j, \quad \text{whenever} \quad y_j^k \neq 0. \tag{67}$$

(b) If, in addition, the Pareto optimal $\mathbf{Y}$ has each $y_j^k > 0$, then
   (i) $\alpha^k \nabla u^k(\mathbf{y}^k) = \mathbf{c}$, for $k = 1, \ldots, A$;
   (ii) $\sum_k \alpha^k DU^k(\mathbf{Y})\mathbf{V} = \mathbf{0}$ for all $\mathbf{V} = (\mathbf{v}^1, \ldots, \mathbf{v}^A) \in (\mathbf{R}^n)^A$ such that $\sum_k \mathbf{v}^k = \mathbf{0}$.
   (iii) at $\mathbf{Y}$, the marginal rate of substitution of good i for good j is the same for all consumers, that is,

$$\frac{\partial u^k}{\partial x_i^k}(\mathbf{y}^k) \bigg/ \frac{\partial u^k}{\partial x_j^k}(\mathbf{y}^k) = \frac{\partial u^m}{\partial x_i^m}(\mathbf{y}^m) \bigg/ \frac{\partial u^m}{\partial x_j^m}(\mathbf{y}^m) \tag{68}$$

for all $k, m \in \{1, \ldots, A\}$ and all $i, j \in \{1, \ldots, n\}$.

(c) If, in addition, the u^ks are quasiconcave, these conditions are also sufficient. In particular, suppose that the u^ks are quasiconcave as well as monotonic (65) and that $\mathbf{Y} \in \Omega$ is an allocation such that each consumer's consumption bundle is nonzero. If there exist strictly positive multipliers $\alpha_1, \ldots, \alpha_A$ and a vector $\mathbf{c} = (c_1, \ldots, c_n)$ with each $c_i > 0$ such that equations (66) and (67) are satisfied, then $\mathbf{Y}$ is a Pareto optimal allocation.

Proof This theorem is a fairly straightforward application of Theorems 22.15 and 22.18. The Lagrangian for this optimization problem is

$$L(\mathbf{x}^1, \ldots, \mathbf{x}^A, \alpha^1, \ldots, \alpha^A, \mu^1, \ldots, \mu^A, \mathbf{c})$$

$$= \sum_1^A \alpha^k u^k(\mathbf{x}^k) - \mathbf{c} \cdot \left(\sum_1^A \mathbf{x}^k - \mathbf{b} \right) + \sum_1^A \mu^k \cdot \mathbf{x}^k. \tag{69}$$

Setting the derivatives of L with respect to $\mathbf{x}^k$ equal to 0 yields:

$$\alpha^k \nabla u^k(\mathbf{x}^k) - \mathbf{c} + \mu^k = \mathbf{0}. \tag{70}$$

In addition,

$$\mu^k \cdot \mathbf{x}^k = \mathbf{0}. \tag{71}$$

By Theorem 22.15, since $\mathbf{Y}$ is a Pareto optimum, there exists a set of multipliers $\alpha^1, \ldots, \alpha^A, \mu^1, \ldots, \mu^A, \mathbf{c}$, that solves (70) at $\mathbf{x}^k = \mathbf{y}^k$ with each α^k and μ_i^k nonnegative. Conditions (66, 67) follow from (70) and the fact, by (71), that each $\mu_i^k \geq 0$ and $= 0$ when $y_i^k > 0$.

We next show that *some* $\alpha^k > 0$. Let $i \in \{1, \ldots, n\}$. Since $b_i > 0$, there exists k such that $y_i^k > 0$. Then, $\mu_i^k = 0$ and

$$\alpha^k \frac{\partial u^k}{\partial x_i^k}(\mathbf{y}^k) = c_i. \tag{72}$$

If $\alpha^1 = \cdots = \alpha^k = 0$, every $c_i = 0$ by (72); and then by (70), every $\mu_i^k = 0$, too. This contradicts the conclusion of Theorem 22.15 that some multiplier is nonzero. We conclude that some $\alpha^k > 0$, say α^1. Then,

$$\alpha^1 \frac{\partial u^1}{\partial x_j^1}(\mathbf{y}^1) \leq c_j \quad \text{and} \quad \frac{\partial u^1}{\partial x_j^1}(\mathbf{y}^1) > 0 \quad \text{for all } j.$$

Therefore, $c_j > 0$ for $j = 1, \ldots, n$.

Now, let $k \in \{1, \ldots, A\}$ be arbitrary. Since $\mathbf{y}^k \neq \mathbf{0}$, there exists i such that $y_i^k > 0$ and (72) holds for k and i. Since $c_i > 0$ and $(\partial u^k / \partial x_i^k)(\mathbf{y}^k) > 0$, $\alpha_k > 0$, too.

Proof of *b*: Since each $y_i^k > 0$, each $\mu_i^k = 0$; and (67) becomes conclusion *i*. To prove part *ii*, let $\mathbf{V} = (\mathbf{v}^1, \ldots, \mathbf{v}^A)$ with $\sum_k \mathbf{v}^A = \mathbf{0}$. Then,

$$\sum_{k=1}^{A} \alpha^k DU^k(\mathbf{Y})\mathbf{V} = \sum_k \alpha^k Du^k(\mathbf{y}^k)\mathbf{v}^k$$

$$= \sum_{k=1}^{A} \mathbf{c} \cdot \mathbf{v}^k = \mathbf{c} \cdot \sum_{k=1}^{A} \mathbf{v}^k \qquad (73)$$

$$= \mathbf{0}.$$

Conclusion *iii* about the marginal rate of substitution follows immediately from (72), since each side of (68) equals c_i/c_j.

Proof of *c*: Let $\alpha_1, \ldots, \alpha_A, c_1, \ldots, c_n$ be positive scalars such that (66) and (67) hold. We want to show that the conclusion of Theorem 22.18 holds, so we will verify its hypotheses. Since the u^ks are quasiconcave and (65) holds, the u^ks are pseudoconcave by Theorem 21.17; everything else is linear. Define vectors μ^k by $\mu^k = \mathbf{c} - \alpha^k \nabla u^k(\mathbf{y}^k)$. The μ_j^ks will be the multipliers for the nonnegativity constraints in condition 2 of Theorem 22.18. By equation (66), the μ_j^ks are all nonnegative; by (67), if $y_j^k \neq 0$, $\mu_j^k = 0$. Therefore, equation (60) is satisfied. The remaining hypothesis, equation (61), is satisfied, since the derivative of the Lagrangian (69) with respect to $\mathbf{x}^k$, evaluated at $\mathbf{Y}, \mathbf{c}, \mu$ is

$$\alpha^k \nabla u^k(\mathbf{y}^k) - \mathbf{c} + \mu^k = \mathbf{0}. \qquad \blacksquare$$

Competitive Equilibrium

A Pareto optimum is an ideal of what an economy should achieve. Whether or not an economy actually reaches a Pareto optimal allocation is an important question. In order to answer it, we first characterize those allocations that the market will achieve — the *competitive equilibria*.

Let $\mathbf{Y} = (\mathbf{y}^1, \ldots, \mathbf{y}^A)$ be an initial commodity bundle in Ω. We continue to write $\mathbf{p}$ for the economy's price vector. At price system $\mathbf{p}$, the agent holding bundle $\mathbf{y}^k$ has wealth $w^k = \mathbf{p} \cdot \mathbf{y}^k$. In this case, agent k's budget set is:

$$B(\mathbf{p}, \mathbf{y}^k) \equiv \{\mathbf{x} \in \mathbf{R}_+^n : \mathbf{p} \cdot \mathbf{x} \leq \mathbf{p} \cdot \mathbf{y}^k\}.$$

Agent k wants to maximize u^k on the budget set $B(\mathbf{p}, \mathbf{y}^k)$. Let $\xi^k(\mathbf{p}, \mathbf{y}^k)$ denote the solution of this problem, agent k's "bundle demanded". For simplicity of notation, we will assume that each ξ^k is a single-valued function. However, much of the theory developed in this section holds for demand *correspondences* as well as for demand functions.

The *aggregate demand* of the A consumers is the vector $\sum_{k=1}^{A} \xi(\mathbf{p}, \mathbf{y}^k)$, and the *commodity allocation demanded* is

$$\mathbf{Z}(\mathbf{p}, \mathbf{Y}) = (\xi^1(\mathbf{p}, \mathbf{y}^1), \ldots, \xi^A(\mathbf{p}, \mathbf{y}^A)) \in (\mathbf{R}_+^n)^A.$$

Definition   If the bundle demanded $\mathbf{Z}(\mathbf{p}, \mathbf{Y})$ is in Ω, that is, if the total demand vector equals the total supply vector,

$$\sum_{k=1}^{A} \xi^k(\mathbf{p}, \mathbf{y}^k) = \sum_{k=1}^{A} \mathbf{y}^k = \mathbf{b},$$

then we say that

    (1) $\mathbf{p}$ is the **equilibrium price** for $\mathbf{Y}$,
    (2) $\mathbf{Z}(\mathbf{p}, \mathbf{Y})$ is a **competitive equilibrium allocation**, and
    (3) $(\mathbf{p}, \mathbf{Z}(\mathbf{p}, \mathbf{Y}))$ is a **competitive equilibrium** (relative to initial allocation $\mathbf{Y}$).

At a competitive equilibrium $(\mathbf{p}, \mathbf{Z})$, each consumer is maximizing utility on his or her budget set for price system $\mathbf{p}$, and the total commodity bundle demanded $\sum \mathbf{z}^k$ just balances with the total available $\sum \mathbf{y}^k$.

Fundamental Theorems of Welfare Economics

Now we can ask, "How well does the market allocate resources?" The next two theorems — often called the **Fundamental Theorems of Welfare Economics** — answer this question: a competitive equilibrium allocation is always a Pareto optimum, and a Pareto optimal allocation can always be realized as a competitive equilibrium allocation for some price vector $\mathbf{p}$.

We will prove the First Fundamental Theorem, the statement that competitive equilibria are Pareto optimal, in an old-fashioned manner. Many texts present a short and simple proof of this proposition which involves no calculus at all. But the calculus approach we develop here, although less general, establishes the following important interpretation of competitive equilibrium prices. The competitive equilibrium prices are Lagrange multipliers for the resource constraints. They measure the relative scarcity of commodities and therefore can be viewed as measuring the social benefits of relaxing the resource constraints.

Theorem 22.20   Let $U = (U^1, \ldots, U^A): \Omega \to \mathbf{R}^A$ be as defined in (64). Suppose that each u^k is quasiconcave and satsifies the monotonicity assumption (65) of Theorem 22.19. Let $\mathbf{Y} = (\mathbf{y}^1, \ldots, \mathbf{y}^A)$ be an initial endowment for each consumer. Suppose that $(\hat{\mathbf{Y}}, \mathbf{p})$ is a competitive equilibrium for $\mathbf{Y}$ and that each $\hat{\mathbf{y}}^k \neq 0$. Then $\hat{\mathbf{Y}}$ is a *Pareto optimum* for $(u^1, \ldots, u^A)$ that is Pareto superior to $\mathbf{Y}$.

Proof   Let $(\mathbf{p}, \hat{\mathbf{Y}})$ be the competitive equilibrium of the hypothesis. By definition, $\hat{\mathbf{Y}}$ is in Ω. By assumption, the u^ks are monotonic and quasiconcave, and are therefore pseudoconcave. To apply Theorem 22.19, it remains only to find multipliers λ^k and $\mathbf{c}$ which satisfy the first order conditions (66) and (67).

Since each consumer is maximizing utility on his or her budget set, it follows from Theorem 22.1 that there are positive scalars λ^k such that

$$\frac{1}{\lambda^k}\frac{\partial U^k}{\partial \mathbf{x}^k}(\hat{\mathbf{y}}^k) \leq \mathbf{p}$$

with equality whenever $\hat{y}_i^k > 0$. Letting $\alpha^k = 1/\lambda^k$ and $\mathbf{c} = \mathbf{p}$ in the statement of Theorem 22.19, we see that these are just the conditions of equations (66) and (67), respectively. By Theorem 22.19, $\hat{\mathbf{Y}}$ is Pareto optimal. ∎

The Second Fundamental Theorem of Welfare Economics is the converse of Theorem 22.20. It says that every Pareto optimum can be realized as a competitive equilibrium.

Theorem 22.21 Let Ω, $\mathbf{b}$, and $u^1,\ldots,u^A$ be as in the hypothesis of Theorem 22.19. Suppose further that each u^k is a quasiconcave function, and that $\mathbf{Y} = (\mathbf{y}^1,\ldots,\mathbf{y}^A)$ is a Pareto optimum for U, with each $y_i^k > 0$. Then, there is a positive price system $\mathbf{p}$ in $\mathbf{R^n}$ such that $(\mathbf{p}, \mathbf{Y})$ is a competitive equilibrium on Ω.

Proof By Theorem 22.19, there is a positive vector $\mathbf{c} \in \mathbf{R^n}$ and positive multipliers $\alpha^1,\ldots,\alpha^A$ such that

$$\alpha^k \nabla u^k(\mathbf{y}^k) = \mathbf{c}, \quad \text{for } k = 1,\ldots,A. \tag{74}$$

Let $\mathbf{p} = \mathbf{c}$ and let $\lambda = 1/\alpha^k$. By Theorem 22.1, (74) is precisely the first order condition for maximizing u^k on $B(\mathbf{p}, \mathbf{y}^k)$. Since $\nabla u^k(\mathbf{y}^k) \neq \mathbf{0}$ by (65) and since u^k is quasiconcave by hypothesis, u^k is pseudoconcave by Theorem 21.17. By Theorem 21.22, the first order necessary conditions (74) for a maximizer are also sufficient conditions when the objective function is pseudoconcave.

We conclude that $\mathbf{y}^k$ maximizes u^k on $B(\mathbf{p}, \mathbf{y}^k)$. Since this is true for $k = 1,\ldots,A$, $\mathbf{Y}$ is a competitive equilibrium for U. ∎

By the proofs of the two preceding theorems the competitive equilibrium prices are Lagrange multipliers for the resource constraints in the Pareto optimization problem. This relationship can be pushed even further. Suppose that consumers' utility functions are quasiconcave and monotonic, and that $\hat{\mathbf{Y}}$ is a consumption allocation in which no consumer receives 0 of every good. Suppose there exist positive scalars $\lambda^1,\ldots,\lambda^A$ such that $\hat{\mathbf{Y}}$ maximizes the function

$$W(\mathbf{Y}) = \sum_{k=0}^{A}\frac{1}{\lambda^k}u^k(\mathbf{y}^k) \tag{75}$$

on commodity space Ω. The first-order necessary conditions for this optimization problem give multipliers $\mathbf{p} = (p_1,\ldots,p_n)$ for the resource constraints such that, taking $\mathbf{c} = \mathbf{p}$ and $\alpha^k = 1/\lambda^k$, equations (66) and (67) are satisfied. (Exercise.) Thus, $\hat{\mathbf{Y}}$ is Pareto optimal and can be realized as a competitive equilibrium allocation with equilibrium prices $\mathbf{p}$. We see that competitive equilibrium allocations maximize the weighted sum of utilities, where the weight for each consumer is one over the consumer's marginal utility of income and where income is computed as the value of the initial endowment at the equilibrium prices. The multipliers for the resource constraints can be interpreted along the lines suggested by the discussion in Section 19.1. In particular, the equilibrium price p_i measures the rate at which the value of the objective function $W(\mathbf{Y})$ at the maximum would increase as the aggregate endowment of commodity i was increased. It is in this sense that prices reflect the scarcity of resources.

EXERCISES

22.20 Verify the first equality in (73).

22.21 Show that the first order necessary condition for the problem of maximizing the function W (75) on Ω gives multipliers as described in the last paragraph.

22.22 Consider an economy with two consumers and two commodities. Consumer i has an endowment of one unit of good i and none of any other good. Consumer i has utility function $u^i(x_1, x_2) = \beta_i \log x_1 + (1 - \beta_i) \log x_2$, where each β_i lies strictly between 0 and 1.

a) Find the competitive equilibrium allocation (in this example there is only one).

b) Find *all* of the Pareto optimal allocations for this economy.

22.23 Again consider an economy with two consumers and two commodities. Suppose the aggregate endowment of both commodities is 2. Consumer 1 has the utility function $u^1(x_1, x_2) = \log(x_1 + 1) + \log(x_2 + 1)$. Consumer 2 has utility function $u(x_1, x_2) = x_2 - (x_1 - 1)^2$.

a) Find all the Pareto optima.

b) Can the Pareto optimal allocation which gives consumer 2 the consumption bundle $(1, 2)$ be realized as a competitive equilibrium? Discuss your answer in light of the hypotheses and conclusions of Theorem 22.21.

NOTES

The proof of the Slutsky Equation in Theorem 22.8 is based on the papers by L. McKenzie ("Demand Theory without a Utility Index," *Review of Economic Studies* 24 (1957) 185–189) and P. Cook ("A One-Line Proof of the Slutsky Equation," *American Economic Review* 42 (1972) 139). It is quite an improvement over the proofs found in many older texts, which directly use the first order conditions for utility maximization.

The material in Sections 3 and 4 is adapted from: C. Simon, "Scalar and Vector Maximization: Calculus Techniques with Economic Applications," *Studies in Mathematical Economics*. (S. Reiter, editor). Washington, D.C.: Mathematical Association of America (1986), 62–159.

The calculus approach to Pareto optimality was pioneered in 1942 (*Econometrica* 10, pp 215–28) by Oscar Lange, later Poland's Ambassador to the United States and the United Nations, and the Chairman of the Polish State Economic Council. The example of the last problem is due to Kenneth Arrow and appears in another fundamental paper on the Welfare theorems, "An Extension of the Basic Theorems of Classical Welfare Economics," *Proceedings of the Second Berkeley Symposium on Mathematical Statistics and Probability* (J. Neyman, ed.) Berkeley, CA: The University of California Press (1951).

PART V

Eigenvalues and Dynamics

Eigenvalues and Eigenvectors

Chapters 6 through 11 described the use of matrices in the study of linear equations, an area that is one of the cornerstones of applied mathematics. We switch now to another aspect of matrices that is an invaluable tool in the study of linear and *nonlinear* systems of equations — the eigenvalues and eigenvectors of a square matrix. As we will see in the next three chapters, eigenvalues and eigenvectors play a central role in many aspects of economic theory. They are the components of the explicit solutions of *linear* dynamic models. Furthermore, the signs of eigenvalues determine the stability of equilibria in *nonlinear* dynamic models. These signs are also the key ingredient in determining the definiteness of a symmetric matrix. Consequently, they play a central role in the second order conditions that distinguish maxima from minima in economic optimization problems.

The eigenvalues of a given $n \times n$ matrix are the n numbers which summarize the essential properties of that matrix. Since these n numbers really characterize the matrix under study, they are often called the "characteristic values" of the matrix. We'll use the more common German term: "eigenvalues."

There are two aspects to the study of eigenvalues: learning what they are and learning how they are used. Both tasks are rather straightforward, especially if learned one at a time. The next section describes what eigenvalues and eigenvectors are and how to compute them for a number of matrices. The following two sections give a glimpse of how they arise and what they are used for, in a discussion of the role of eigenvalues in solving systems of linear difference equations and in taking powers and roots of a given matrix. Sections 4 and 5 discuss some of the subtleties that arise in the study and use of eigenvalues. Section 6 gives an overview of the use of eigenvalues and eigenvectors in solving Markov processes. Section 7 describes the important properties of eigenvalues and eigenvectors of *symmetric* matrices, while Section 8 relates these properties to the definiteness of quadratic forms.

23.1   DEFINITIONS AND EXAMPLES

Definition   Let A be a square matrix. An **eigenvalue** of A is a number r which when subtracted from each of the diagonal entries of A converts A into a singular matrix. Subtracting a scalar r from each diagonal entry of A is the same as

579

subtracting r times the identity matrix I from A. Therefore, r is an eigenvalue of A if and only if $A - rI$ is a singular matrix.

Example 23.1   Sometimes, one can eyeball a matrix to discover one or more of its eigenvalues. Consider, for example, the matrix

$$A = \begin{pmatrix} 3 & 1 & 1 \\ 1 & 3 & 1 \\ 1 & 1 & 3 \end{pmatrix}.$$

Subtracting 2 from each diagonal entry transforms A into the *singular* matrix

$$\begin{pmatrix} 1 & 1 & 1 \\ 1 & 1 & 1 \\ 1 & 1 & 1 \end{pmatrix}.$$

Therefore, 2 is an eigenvalue of A.

Example 23.2   Let's look for the eigenvalues of the *diagonal matrix* $\begin{pmatrix} 2 & 0 \\ 0 & 3 \end{pmatrix}$. Subtracting a 2 from each of the diagonal entries yields the singular matrix $\begin{pmatrix} 0 & 0 \\ 0 & 1 \end{pmatrix}$. Subtracting a 3 from each of the diagonal entries yields the singular matrix $\begin{pmatrix} -1 & 0 \\ 0 & 0 \end{pmatrix}$. Therefore, 2 and 3 are eigenvalues of $\begin{pmatrix} 2 & 0 \\ 0 & 3 \end{pmatrix}$.

In fact, Example 23.2 illustrates a general principle about the eigenvalues of a diagonal matrix.

Theorem 23.1   The diagonal entries of a diagonal matrix D are eigenvalues of D.

The following theorem is another direct consequence of the definition of an eigenvalue.

Theorem 23.2   A square matrix A is singular if and only if 0 is an eigenvalue of A.

Example 23.3   Consider the matrix $B = \begin{pmatrix} 1 & -1 \\ -1 & 1 \end{pmatrix}$. Since the first row is the negative of the second, B is a singular matrix and, therefore, 0 is an eigenvalue of B. We can use the observation in Example 23.1 to find a second eigenvalue, because subtracting 2 from each diagonal entry of B yields the singular matrix $\begin{pmatrix} -1 & -1 \\ -1 & -1 \end{pmatrix}$. We conclude that 0 and 2 are eigenvalues of B.

Example 23.4 A matrix M whose entries are nonnegative and whose columns (or rows) each add to 1, such as

$$\begin{pmatrix} 1/4 & 2/3 \\ 3/4 & 1/3 \end{pmatrix}, \tag{1}$$

is called a **Markov matrix**. As we will see in Section 23.6, Markov matrices play a major role in the dynamics of economic systems. If we subtract a 1 from each diagonal entry of the Markov matrix (1), then each column of the transformed matrix

$$M - 1I = \begin{pmatrix} -3/4 & 2/3 \\ 3/4 & -2/3 \end{pmatrix}$$

adds up to 0. But if the columns of a square matrix add up to $(0,\ldots,0)$, the rows are linearly dependent and the matrix must be singular. It follows that $r = 1$ is an eigenvalue of matrix (1). The same argument shows that $r = 1$ is an eigenvalue of every Markov matrix.

For most matrices, one can't just look at the matrix to find out what number to subtract from its diagonal entries to make the matrix singular. A more systematic way of finding eigenvalues is needed. Let's formalize the process under discussion. The principal technique for determining whether or not a given matrix is singular is the determinant; a matrix is singular if and only if its determinant is zero. Therefore, r is an eigenvalue of A; that is, $A - rI$ is a singular matrix, if and only if

$$\det(A - rI) = 0. \tag{2}$$

For an $n \times n$ matrix A, the left-hand side of equation (2) is an nth order polynomial in the variable r, called the **characteristic polynomial** of A. The number r is an eigenvalue of A if and only if r is a zero of the characteristic polynomial of A. For example, for a general 2×2 matrix, the characteristic polynomial is

$$\det(A - rI) = \det \begin{pmatrix} a_{11} - r & a_{12} \\ a_{21} & a_{22} - r \end{pmatrix}$$
$$= r^2 - (a_{11} + a_{22})r + (a_{11}a_{22} - a_{12}a_{21}), \tag{3}$$

a second order polynomial. An nth order polynomial has at most n roots — exactly n if one counts roots with their multiplicity and counts complex roots. Therefore, a 2×2 matrix has at most two eigenvalues; an $n \times n$ matrix has at most n eigenvalues.

Recall from Chapter 8 that a square matrix B is nonsingular if and only if the only solution of $B\mathbf{x} = \mathbf{0}$ is $\mathbf{x} = \mathbf{0}$. Conversely, B is singular if and only if the system $B\mathbf{x} = \mathbf{0}$ has a nonzero solution. The fact that the square matrix $A - rI$ is a singular matrix when r is an eigenvalue of A means that the system of equations

$(A - rI)\mathbf{v} = \mathbf{0}$ has a solution other than $\mathbf{v} = \mathbf{0}$. When r is an eigenvalue of A, a *nonzero* vector $\mathbf{v}$ such that

$$(A - rI)\mathbf{v} = \mathbf{0} \tag{4}$$

is called an **eigenvector** of A corresponding to eigenvalue r. We demand that $\mathbf{v}$ be nonzero because the zero-vector, $\mathbf{v} = \mathbf{0}$, is a solution of (4) for any r. Multiplying out equation (4) yields

$$A\mathbf{v} - rI\mathbf{v} = \mathbf{0}$$

$$A\mathbf{v} - r\mathbf{v} = \mathbf{0}$$

$$A\mathbf{v} = r\mathbf{v}.$$

If r is an eigenvalue and $\mathbf{v}$ is a corresponding eigenvector, then $A\mathbf{v} = r\mathbf{v}$. This process works both ways. If $A\mathbf{v} = r\mathbf{v}$ for some nonzero vector $\mathbf{v}$, then

$$A\mathbf{v} - r\mathbf{v} = \mathbf{0}$$

$$A\mathbf{v} - rI\mathbf{v} = \mathbf{0}$$

$$(A - rI)\mathbf{v} = \mathbf{0}.$$

Since $\mathbf{v}$ is nonzero, this last equation can only hold when $A - rI$ is singular. The following theorem summarizes the observations of the last two paragraphs.

Theorem 23.3   Let A be an $n \times n$ matrix and let r be a scalar. Then, the following statements are equivalent:

(a) Subtracting r from each diagonal entry of A transforms A into a singular matrix.
(b) $A - rI$ is a singular matrix.
(c) $\det(A - rI) = 0$.
(d) $(A - rI)\mathbf{v} = \mathbf{0}$ for some nonzero vector $\mathbf{v}$.
(e) $A\mathbf{v} = r\mathbf{v}$ for some nonzero vector $\mathbf{v}$.

Each of these five statements could be used as the definition of an eigenvalue. In fact, most texts use statement e of Theorem 23.3 as the definition of an eigenvalue. A number of texts use other names for eigenvalues and eigenvectors: characteristic values and characteristic vectors, proper values and proper vectors, and latent values and latent vectors. We will stick with the terms "eigenvalues" and "eigenvectors." Let's calculate the eigenvalues and eigenvectors of some sample matrices.

Example 23.5   Find the eigenvalues and eigenvectors of the 2×2 matrix

$$A = \begin{pmatrix} -1 & 3 \\ +2 & 0 \end{pmatrix}.$$

Its characteristic polynomial is

$$\det(A - rI) = \det \begin{pmatrix} -1 - r & 3 \\ 2 & 0 - r \end{pmatrix}$$

$$= r(r + 1) - 6 = r^2 + r - 6 = (r + 3)(r - 2).$$

The eigenvalues of A are the roots of the characteristic polynomial: -3 and 2. To find the corresponding eigenvectors, use statement d of Theorem 23.3. First, subtract eigenvalue -3 from the diagonal entries of A and solve

$$\left(A - (-3)I\right)\mathbf{v} = \begin{pmatrix} 2 & 3 \\ 2 & 3 \end{pmatrix} \begin{pmatrix} v_1 \\ v_2 \end{pmatrix} = \begin{pmatrix} 0 \\ 0 \end{pmatrix} \tag{5}$$

for v_1 and v_2. For a 2×2 matrix, these equations are easily solved just by looking carefully at the equation. For example, we can take $v_1 = 3$ and $v_2 = -2$ and conclude that one eigenvector is $\begin{pmatrix} 3 \\ -2 \end{pmatrix}$. There are other eigenvectors, such as

$$\begin{pmatrix} 1 \\ -2/3 \end{pmatrix}, \quad \begin{pmatrix} -3 \\ 2 \end{pmatrix}, \quad \text{and} \quad \begin{pmatrix} -3/2 \\ 1 \end{pmatrix}.$$

In general, one chooses the "simplest" of the nonzero candidates. The (one-dimensional) set of all solutions of linear equation (5) — including $\mathbf{v} = \mathbf{0}$ — is called the **eigenspace** of A with respect to -3.

To find the eigenvector for eigenvalue $r = 2$, subtract 2 from the diagonal entries of A:

$$(A - 2I)\mathbf{v} = \begin{pmatrix} -3 & 3 \\ 2 & -2 \end{pmatrix} \begin{pmatrix} v_1 \\ v_2 \end{pmatrix} = \begin{pmatrix} 0 \\ 0 \end{pmatrix}.$$

The simplest solution is $\begin{pmatrix} 1 \\ 1 \end{pmatrix}$; but any multiple of $\begin{pmatrix} 1 \\ 1 \end{pmatrix}$ is also an eigenvector for 2. The eigenspace for eigenvalue 2 is the diagonal line in $\mathbf{R}^2$.

Example 23.6   Let's compute the eigenvalues and eigenvectors of the 3×3 matrix

$$B = \begin{pmatrix} 1 & 0 & 2 \\ 0 & 5 & 0 \\ 3 & 0 & 2 \end{pmatrix}.$$

Its characteristic equation is

$$
\det \begin{pmatrix} 1-r & 0 & 2 \\ 0 & 5-r & 0 \\ 3 & 0 & 2-r \end{pmatrix} = (5-r)(r-4)(r+1).
$$

Therefore, the eigenvalues of B are $r = 5, 4, -1$. To compute an eigenvector corresponding to $r = 5$, we compute the **nullspace** of $(B - 5I)$; that is, we solve the system

$$
(B - 5I)\mathbf{v} = \begin{pmatrix} -4 & 0 & 2 \\ 0 & 0 & 0 \\ 3 & 0 & -3 \end{pmatrix} \begin{pmatrix} v_1 \\ v_2 \\ v_3 \end{pmatrix} = \begin{pmatrix} -4v_1 + 2v_3 \\ 0 \\ 3v_1 - 3v_3 \end{pmatrix} = \begin{pmatrix} 0 \\ 0 \\ 0 \end{pmatrix},
$$

whose solution is $v_1 = v_3 = 0$, $v_2 =$ anything. So, we'll take $\mathbf{v}_1 = \begin{pmatrix} 0 \\ 1 \\ 0 \end{pmatrix}$ as an eigenvector for $r = 5$.

To find an eigenvector for $r = 4$, solve

$$
(B - 4I)\mathbf{v} = \begin{pmatrix} -3 & 0 & 2 \\ 0 & 1 & 0 \\ 3 & 0 & -2 \end{pmatrix} \begin{pmatrix} v_1 \\ v_2 \\ v_3 \end{pmatrix} = \begin{pmatrix} 0 \\ 0 \\ 0 \end{pmatrix}.
$$

This system reduces to the two equations

$$
-3v_1 + 2v_3 = 0
$$

$$
v_2 = 0.
$$

A simple eigenvector for $r = 4$ is $\begin{pmatrix} 2 \\ 0 \\ 3 \end{pmatrix}$. This same method yields the eigen-

vector $\begin{pmatrix} 1 \\ 0 \\ -1 \end{pmatrix}$ for eigenvalue $r = -1$.

In some problems, one will need to use Gaussian elimination to solve the linear system $(A - rI)\mathbf{v} = \mathbf{0}$ for an eigenvector $\mathbf{v}$.

EXERCISES

23.1   Check that $\begin{pmatrix} 1 \\ 0 \\ -1 \end{pmatrix}$ is an eigenvector for $r = -1$ in Example 23.6.

23.2   For each of the following $n \times n$ matrices, find n eigenvalues and their eigenvectors. Try to find at least one eigenvalue by inspection:

a) $\begin{pmatrix} 3 & 0 \\ 4 & 5 \end{pmatrix}$,   b) $\begin{pmatrix} -1 & 3 \\ -2 & 4 \end{pmatrix}$,   c) $\begin{pmatrix} 0 & -2 \\ 1 & -3 \end{pmatrix}$,   d) $\begin{pmatrix} 0 & 0 & -2 \\ 0 & 7 & 0 \\ 1 & 0 & -3 \end{pmatrix}$.

23.3 Write out a careful proof of Theorem 23.1.

23.4 Prove that the eigenvalues of an upper- or lower-triangular matrix are precisely its diagonal entries.

23.5 Suppose that A is an invertible matrix. Show that $(A - rI)\mathbf{v} = \mathbf{0}$ implies that $(A^{-1} - \frac{1}{r}I)\mathbf{v} = \mathbf{0}$. Conclude that for an invertible matrix A, r is an eigenvalue of A if and only if $1/r$ is an eigenvalue of A^{-1}.

23.2 SOLVING LINEAR DIFFERENCE EQUATIONS

One-Dimensional Equations

In this section we will see how eigenvalues and eigenvectors are used to solve k-dimensional dynamical problems modeled with linear difference equations. Linear difference equations in *one* dimension are very easy to solve. A typical such equation is

$$y_{n+1} = ay_n, \tag{6}$$

for some constant a. This difference equation states that the amount of y in any period will be proportional to the amount that existed in the previous period, with proportionality constant a. This equation arises, for example, as the equation for the amount of money in a savings account whose principal is left untouched and whose interest in compounded once a year, because if there are y_n dollars in the bank in any period, say period n, then there will be $y_n + \rho y_n = (1 + \rho)y_n$ dollars in the bank in the next period (period $n + 1$), where ρ is the annual interest rate: $y_{n+1} = (1 + \rho)y_n$.

A solution of difference equation (6) is an expression for y_n in terms of the initial amount y_0, a, and n. Such a solution is easily found. By assumption,

$$y_1 = ay_0.$$

Therefore,
$$y_2 = ay_1 = a(ay_0) = a^2 y_0$$
$$y_3 = ay_2 = a(a^2 y_0) = a^3 y_0 \tag{7}$$

and so on. The solution of (6) is

$$y_n = a^n y_0.$$

For the bank account problem,

$$y_n = (1 + \rho)^n y_0. \tag{8}$$

If we know the initial deposit y_0, this expression tells us the size of the account after n years for any n, provided there are no additions to or withdrawals from the account. For example, if $\rho = 0.05$, $y_0 = 100$, and $n = 4$, then by (8) $y_4 = (1.05)^4 \cdot 100 = 121.55$. After four years, there will be \$121.55 in the account.

Two-Dimensional Systems: An Example

Now, consider a system of *two* linear difference equations, in which the size of each variable depends linearly on the sizes of *both* variables in the previous period:

$$x_{n+1} = ax_n + by_n$$
$$y_{n+1} = cx_n + dy_n. \tag{9}$$

For example, in Chapter 6, we introduced a dynamic model of employment:

$$x_{n+1} = qx_n + py_n$$
$$y_{n+1} = (1 - q)x_n + (1 - p)y_n, \tag{10}$$

where x_n represents the number of persons employed during period n and y_n represents the number unemployed in period n, p is the probability that an unemployed person will find a job in any given period and q is the probability that an employed person will remain employed from one period to the next.

In matrix form, the system of difference equations (9) becomes

$$\mathbf{z}_{n+1} = \begin{pmatrix} x_{n+1} \\ y_{n+1} \end{pmatrix} = \begin{pmatrix} a & b \\ c & d \end{pmatrix} \begin{pmatrix} x_n \\ y_n \end{pmatrix} \equiv A\mathbf{z}_n.$$

If $b = c = 0$ in these equations, they are uncoupled:

$$x_{n+1} = ax_n$$
$$y_{n+1} = dy_n.$$

Then, they are easily solved as two separate one-dimensional problems:

$$x_n = a^n x_0 \quad \text{and} \quad y_n = d^n y_0.$$

When the equations in (9) are coupled ($b \neq 0$ or $c \neq 0$), the technique for solving the system is to find a change of variables that *uncouples* these equations. This technique of finding a change of variables which uncouples the equations in a multidimensional problem is a common and important one.

Conic Sections

The technique of changing variables to uncouple the equations in a multidimensional problem is used by precalculus students to determine which conic section is described by a given quadratic equation of two variables. When there are no cross terms in the quadratic,

$$Ax^2 + Cy^2 = D,$$

it is easy to determine which conic section this equation describes:

(1) a circle if $A = C$ and A, C and D have the same sign,
(2) an ellipse if $A \neq C$ and A, C and D have the same sign,
(3) a hyperbola if A and C have opposite signs and $D \neq 0$, or
(4) two lines if A and C have opposite signs and $D = 0$.

However, if the quadratic has cross terms,

$$Ax^2 + Bxy + Cy^2 = D, \tag{11}$$

then the question is more difficult to answer. The trick for resolving the question is to find a change of coordinates

$$x = \alpha X + \beta Y$$
$$y = \gamma X + \delta Y,$$

so that when written in the new coordinates the quadratic (11) has no XY-term. Geometrically, we are looking for a coordinate system whose axes line up with the axes of the conic section, as in Figure 23.1.

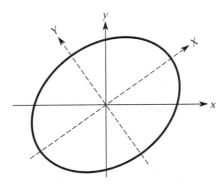

A conic section in a coordinate system adapted for it.

Figure 23.1

The Leslie Population Model

Let's work out a concrete example of using a change of coordinates to solve a particular linear system of difference equations. We will see that the eigenvalues and eigenvectors of the underlying matrix play a major role in this process.

We will work with a system of equations that arises naturally in population dynamics. Consider an organism that lives for two years. Let b_1 be the birth rate of individuals in their first year and b_2 the birth rate for individuals in their second year. Let d_1 denote the death rate of first-year individuals, so that $(1 - d_1)$ of the first-year individuals survive to year two. Let x_n and y_n denote the number of first-year individuals and second-year individuals, respectively, in year n. The dynamics over time of this population are described by the system of difference equations

$$x_{n+1} = b_1 x_n + b_2 y_n$$
$$y_{n+1} = (1 - d_1)x_n \tag{12}$$

System (12) is called a **Leslie model** after the mathematical demographer P. H. Leslie, who introduced it in 1945.

Example 23.7   Consider the coupled system of difference equations generated by a Leslie model with $b_1 = 1$, $b_2 = 4$, and $d_1 = 0.5$

$$x_{n+1} = 1x_n + 4y_n$$
$$y_{n+1} = 0.5x_n + 0y_n. \tag{13}$$

The right change of coordinates for solving this system is

$$X = \frac{1}{6}x + \frac{1}{3}y$$
$$Y = -\frac{1}{6}x + \frac{2}{3}y, \tag{14}$$

whose inverse transformation is

$$x = 4X - 2Y$$
$$y = X + Y. \tag{15}$$

We'll see later that these transformations arise directly from a consideration of the eigenvalues and eigenvectors of the matrix representation of the original problem (13). In matrix form, these transformations are

$$\begin{pmatrix} X \\ Y \end{pmatrix} = \begin{pmatrix} \frac{1}{6} & \frac{1}{3} \\ -\frac{1}{6} & \frac{2}{3} \end{pmatrix} \begin{pmatrix} x \\ y \end{pmatrix} \tag{16}$$

and

$$\begin{pmatrix} x \\ y \end{pmatrix} = \begin{pmatrix} 4 & -2 \\ 1 & 1 \end{pmatrix} \begin{pmatrix} X \\ Y \end{pmatrix}. \tag{17}$$

These two matrices are necessarily inverse to each other. (Check.)

Now, use these transformations to change system (13) from x, y-variables to X, Y-variables:

$$X_{n+1} = \frac{1}{6}x_{n+1} + \frac{1}{3}y_{n+1} = \frac{1}{6}(x_n + 4y_n) + \frac{1}{3}\left(\frac{1}{2}x_n\right)$$

$$Y_{n+1} = -\frac{1}{6}x_{n+1} + \frac{2}{3}y_{n+1} = -\frac{1}{6}(x_n + 4y_n) + \frac{2}{3}\left(\frac{1}{2}x_n\right)$$

using the change of coordinates (14) and then difference equation (13). Simplifying,

$$X_{n+1} = \frac{1}{3}x_n + \frac{2}{3}y_n = \frac{1}{3}(4X_n - 2Y_n) + \frac{2}{3}(X_n + Y_n) = 2X_n$$

$$Y_{n+1} = \frac{1}{6}x_n - \frac{2}{3}y_n = \frac{1}{6}(4X_n - 2Y_n) - \frac{2}{3}(X_n + Y_n) = -Y_n,$$

using the inverse transformation (15) and simplifying again. The changes of variables (14) and (15) worked perfectly; the transformed system

$$X_{n+1} = 2X_n$$
$$Y_{n+1} = -Y_n$$

is completely uncoupled and, so, can be easily solved as two one-dimensional equations:

$$X_n = 2^n c_1$$
$$Y_n = (-1)^n c_2.$$

Finally, use the change of coordinates (15) to express x_n and y_n in terms of X_n and Y_n:

$$x_n = 4X_n - 2Y_n = 4 \cdot 2^n c_1 - 2 \cdot (-1)^n c_2$$
$$y_n = X_n + Y_n = 2^n c_1 + (-1)^n c_2,$$

which can be written in vector notation as

$$
\begin{pmatrix} x_n \\ y_n \end{pmatrix} = \begin{pmatrix} 4 \cdot 2^n c_1 - 2 \cdot (-1)^n c_2 \\ 2^n c_1 + \quad (-1)^n c_2 \end{pmatrix}
$$

$$
= c_1 2^n \begin{pmatrix} 4 \\ 1 \end{pmatrix} + c_2 (-1)^n \begin{pmatrix} -2 \\ 1 \end{pmatrix}.
$$

(18)

The constants c_1 and c_2 in (18) are determined by the exogenous initial conditions x_0 and y_0, because if we are given initial amounts x_0 and y_0, then at $n = 0$, (18) becomes

$$
\begin{aligned} x_0 &= 4c_1 - 2c_2 \\ y_0 &= c_1 + c_2 \end{aligned}, \quad \text{or} \quad \begin{pmatrix} x_0 \\ y_0 \end{pmatrix} = \begin{pmatrix} 4 & -2 \\ 1 & 1 \end{pmatrix} \begin{pmatrix} c_1 \\ c_2 \end{pmatrix}.
$$

This system of equations can be solved in the usual way:

$$
\begin{pmatrix} c_1 \\ c_2 \end{pmatrix} = \begin{pmatrix} 4 & -2 \\ 1 & 1 \end{pmatrix}^{-1} \begin{pmatrix} x_0 \\ y_0 \end{pmatrix} = \begin{pmatrix} \frac{1}{6} & \frac{1}{3} \\ -\frac{1}{6} & \frac{2}{3} \end{pmatrix} \begin{pmatrix} x_0 \\ y_0 \end{pmatrix}.
$$

Abstract Two-Dimensional Systems

Let's redo this whole process for an *abstract* system of difference equations

$$
\mathbf{z}_{n+1} = A\mathbf{z}_n,
$$

in order to understand the role that eigenvalues and eigenvectors of the matrix A play in this scheme. We will follow the *same* steps in the same order that we used in Example 23.7, but we will use abstract matrix notation throughout. Write P and P^{-1} for the change of coordinate matrices, as in (16) and (17):

$$
\mathbf{z} = P\mathbf{Z}, \quad \text{or} \quad \mathbf{Z} = P^{-1}\mathbf{z},
$$

where the original variables are written as $\mathbf{z}$ and the transformed variables as $\mathbf{Z}$. Now write out the original difference equation in the new variables $\mathbf{Z}$:

$$
\begin{aligned}
\mathbf{Z}_{n+1} &= P^{-1}\mathbf{z}_{n+1}, & &\text{(applying } \mathbf{Z} = P^{-1}\mathbf{z}) \\
&= P^{-1}(A\mathbf{z}_n), & &\text{(plugging in the original} \\
& & &\text{difference equation)} \\
&= (P^{-1}A)\mathbf{z}_n, & &\text{(simplifying)} \\
&= (P^{-1}A)(P\mathbf{Z}_n), & &\text{(applying } \mathbf{z} = P\mathbf{Z}) \\
&= (P^{-1}AP)\mathbf{Z}_n, & &\text{(simplifying)}.
\end{aligned}
$$

Note that for each step above, there is a corresponding step in Example 23.7. This computation shows that if we change coordinates using the linear transformation $\mathbf{z} = P\mathbf{Z}$, we transform the coefficient matrix A of the original difference equation system to the matrix $P^{-1}AP$. Of course, our goal now is to choose the transformation P so that the transformed system $\mathbf{Z}_{n+1} = (P^{-1}AP)\mathbf{Z}_n$ is as simple as possible. If $P^{-1}AP$ were a diagonal matrix D, the transformed system of difference equations would be uncoupled and therefore easily solved, as in Example 23.7.

Let's compute, in the two-dimensional case, what kind of matrix P will lead to a *diagonal* $P^{-1}AP$. Let $\mathbf{v}_1$ and $\mathbf{v}_2$ be the two columns of the 2×2 matrix P; that is, write P as $[\mathbf{v}_1\mathbf{v}_2]$ and write the diagonal matrix D as $D = \begin{pmatrix} r_1 & 0 \\ 0 & r_2 \end{pmatrix}$. Now, the equation $P^{-1}AP = D$ is equivalent to the equation

$$AP = PD$$

for an invertible matrix P. Write this equation as

$$A\begin{bmatrix} \mathbf{v}_1 & \mathbf{v}_2 \end{bmatrix} = \begin{bmatrix} \mathbf{v}_1 & \mathbf{v}_2 \end{bmatrix}\begin{pmatrix} r_1 & 0 \\ 0 & r_2 \end{pmatrix},$$

or, equivalently, as

$$\begin{bmatrix} A\mathbf{v}_1 & A\mathbf{v}_2 \end{bmatrix} = \begin{bmatrix} r_1\mathbf{v}_1 & r_2\mathbf{v}_2 \end{bmatrix},$$

and, finally, as

$$A\mathbf{v}_1 = r_1\mathbf{v}_1 \quad \text{and} \quad A\mathbf{v}_2 = r_2\mathbf{v}_2.$$

By Theorem 23.3, this means we want r_1 and r_2 to be eigenvalues of A and $\mathbf{v}_1$ and $\mathbf{v}_2$ to be the corresponding eigenvectors. Furthermore, this calculation shows that if P is a nonsingular matrix such that $P^{-1}AP$ is a diagonal matrix $\begin{pmatrix} r_1 & 0 \\ 0 & r_2 \end{pmatrix}$, then r_1 and r_2 are eigenvalues of A and the columns of P are corresponding eigenvectors.

k-Dimensional Systems

This computation works equally well for $k \times k$ matrices. Let $r_1, \ldots, r_k$ be eigenvalues of the $k \times k$ matrix A. Let $\mathbf{v}_1, \ldots, \mathbf{v}_k$ be the corresponding eigenvectors. Form the matrix P whose jth column is eigenvector $\mathbf{v}_j$. Then,

$$
\begin{aligned}
AP &= A[\mathbf{v}_1 \cdots \mathbf{v}_k] \\
&= [A\mathbf{v}_1 \cdots A\mathbf{v}_k] \\
&= [r_1\mathbf{v}_1 \cdots r_k\mathbf{v}_k] \\
&= [\mathbf{v}_1 \cdots \mathbf{v}_k]\begin{pmatrix} r_1 & \cdots & 0 \\ \vdots & \ddots & \vdots \\ 0 & \cdots & r_k \end{pmatrix} \\
&= P\begin{pmatrix} r_1 & \cdots & 0 \\ \vdots & \ddots & \vdots \\ 0 & \cdots & r_k \end{pmatrix}.
\end{aligned}
$$

If P is invertible, we multiply both sides of this matrix equation by P^{-1} to obtain

$$P^{-1}AP = \begin{pmatrix} r_1 & \cdots & 0 \\ \vdots & \ddots & \vdots \\ 0 & \cdots & r_k \end{pmatrix}.$$

The following theorem summarizes these observations.

Theorem 23.4   Let A be a $k \times k$ matrix. Let $r_1, r_2, \ldots, r_k$ be eigenvalues of A, and $\mathbf{v}_1, \mathbf{v}_2, \ldots, \mathbf{v}_k$ the corresponding eigenvectors. Form the matrix

$$P = [\mathbf{v}_1 \mathbf{v}_2 \cdots \mathbf{v}_k]$$

whose columns are these k eigenvectors. If P is invertible, then

$$P^{-1}AP = \begin{pmatrix} r_1 & 0 & \cdots & 0 \\ 0 & r_2 & \cdots & 0 \\ \vdots & \vdots & \ddots & \vdots \\ 0 & 0 & \cdots & r_k \end{pmatrix}. \tag{19}$$

Conversely, if $P^{-1}AP$ is a diagonal matrix D, the columns of P must be eigenvectors of A and the diagonal entries of D must be eigenvalues of A.

Check that the columns of P in (17) in Example 23.7 are the eigenvectors of the corresponding matrix A. (Exercise.)

A key hypothesis of Theorem 23.4 is that the matrix P whose columns are eigenvectors of A is an invertible matrix. In the terminology of Chapter 11, this hypothesis states that the $k \times k$ matrix A has k linearly independent eigenvectors. The next theorem assures us that if the $k \times k$ matrix A has k *distinct* eigenvalues, then the corresponding eigenvectors $\mathbf{v}_1, \ldots, \mathbf{v}_k$ are automatically linearly independent and the matrix $P = [\mathbf{v}_1 \cdots \mathbf{v}_k]$ is invertible. Its proof is straightforward, but we have placed it in the Appendix of this chapter for the sake of the flow of the exposition.

Theorem 23.5   Let $r_1, \ldots, r_h$ be h *distinct* eigenvalues of the $k \times k$ matrix A. Let $\mathbf{v}_1, \ldots, \mathbf{v}_h$ be corresponding eigenvectors. Then, $\mathbf{v}_1, \ldots, \mathbf{v}_h$ are linearly independent, that is, no one of them can be written as a linear combination of the others.

Finally, we apply Theorems 23.4 and 23.5 to the problem of solving a general linear system of difference equations: $\mathbf{z}_{n+1} = A\mathbf{z}_n$. If the eigenvalues of A are real and distinct and if we construct P as a matrix of eigenvectors of A, the linear change of variables $\mathbf{z} = P\mathbf{Z}$ transforms this system of difference equations to the uncoupled system

$$
\mathbf{Z}_{n+1} = \begin{pmatrix} r_1 & 0 & \cdots & 0 \\ 0 & r_2 & \cdots & 0 \\ \vdots & \vdots & \ddots & \vdots \\ 0 & 0 & \cdots & r_k \end{pmatrix} \mathbf{Z}_n.
$$

We can easily solve this uncoupled system as

$$
\begin{aligned}
(Z_1)_n &= c_1 r_1^n \\
(Z_2)_n &= c_2 r_2^n. \\
&\ \ \vdots \qquad\qquad \vdots \\
(Z_k)_n &= c_k r_k^n,
\end{aligned}
\tag{20}
$$

where $\mathbf{Z} = (Z_1, Z_2, \ldots, Z_k)$. Transforming (20) back to the $\mathbf{z}$-variables yields

$$
\mathbf{z}_n = \begin{pmatrix} (z_1)_n \\ \vdots \\ (z_k)_n \end{pmatrix} = P \begin{pmatrix} (Z_1)_n \\ \vdots \\ (Z_k)_n \end{pmatrix}
$$

$$
= [\mathbf{v}_1 \mathbf{v}_2 \cdots \mathbf{v}_k] \begin{pmatrix} c_1 r_1^n \\ c_2 r_2^n \\ \vdots \\ c_k r_k^n \end{pmatrix}
\tag{21}
$$

$$
= c_1 r_1^n \mathbf{v}_1 + c_2 r_2^n \mathbf{v}_2 + \cdots + c_k r_k^n \mathbf{v}_k.
$$

The solution (21) of $\mathbf{z}_{n+1} = A\mathbf{z}_n$ is a simple combination of the eigenvalues and eigenvectors of A. Note that the solution (18) of the problem in Example 23.7 is exactly of this form: a sum of terms each of the form

$$
c_i \cdot (\text{eigenvalue})^n \cdot \text{eigenvector}.
$$

We summarize these computations in the following theorem.

Theorem 23.6 Let A be a $k \times k$ matrix with k distinct real eigenvalues $r_1, \ldots, r_k$ and corresponding eigenvectors $\mathbf{v}_1, \ldots, \mathbf{v}_k$. The general solution of the system of difference equations $\mathbf{z}_{n+1} = A\mathbf{z}_n$ is

$$
\mathbf{z}_n = c_1 r_1^n \mathbf{v}_1 + c_2 r_2^n \mathbf{v}_2 + \cdots + c_k r_k^n \mathbf{v}_k.
\tag{22}
$$

If we are solving a specific linear system of difference equations $\mathbf{z}_{n+1} = A\mathbf{z}_n$ for a numerical formula $\mathbf{z}_n$ in terms of n, we will need to know the *initial* vector

z_0. For example, in order to use formula (8) for the amount on deposit in a savings account after n years, we need to know the size of the initial deposit y_0. The k components $z_{10}, \ldots, z_{k0}$ of the initial vector z_0 determine the values of the parameters $c_1, \ldots, c_k$ in (22). To see this, just substitute $n = 0$ into (22):

$$z_0 = c_1 v_1 + \cdots + c_k v_k$$

$$= [v_1 \cdots v_k] \begin{pmatrix} c_1 \\ \vdots \\ c_k \end{pmatrix} = P \begin{pmatrix} c_1 \\ \vdots \\ c_k \end{pmatrix}.$$

It follows that, by proper choice of $c_1, \ldots, c_k$, (22) gives a solution of $z_{n+1} = A z_n$ for *any* specific initial vector z_0. It is in this sense that (22) is called the **general solution** of $z_{n+1} = A z_n$.

An Alternative Approach: The Powers of a Matrix

There is an alternative approach to solving the system of linear equations

$$z_{n+1} = A z_n, \tag{23}$$

an approach which is precisely the generalization of the method (7) that was used to solve the one-dimensional equation $z_{n+1} = a z_n$ at the beginning of this section. Start with an initial state z_0 in $\mathbf{R}^k$. Then, by (23),

$$z_1 = A z_0,$$

$$z_2 = A z_1 = A(A z_0) = A^2 z_0,$$

$$z_3 = A z_2 = A(A^2 z_0) = A^3 z_0,$$

and so on. The solution of (23) is clearly

$$z_n = A^n z_0.$$

Here, A^n means, of course, the matrix product of n copies of A:

$$A^n = \underbrace{A \cdot A \cdots A}_{n \text{ times}}.$$

In general, there is no convenient formula for the entries of A^n in terms of the entries of A, unless A is a diagonal matrix,

$$D = \begin{pmatrix} r_1 & \cdots & 0 \\ \vdots & \ddots & \vdots \\ 0 & \cdots & r_k \end{pmatrix},$$

in which case,

$$D^n = \begin{pmatrix} r_1^n & \cdots & 0 \\ \vdots & \ddots & \vdots \\ 0 & \cdots & r_k^n \end{pmatrix}. \quad \text{(Check!)}$$

However, if we find a nonsingular matrix P so that $P^{-1}AP$ is a diagonal matrix D, then

$$A = PDP^{-1},$$
$$A^2 = (PDP^{-1})(PDP^{-1}) = PD(P^{-1}P)DP^{-1} = PDIDP^{-1}$$
$$= PD^2P^{-1},$$
$$A^3 = AA^2 = (PDP^{-1})(PD^2P^{-1}) = PD(P^{-1}P)D^2P^{-1}$$
$$= PDID^2P^{-1}$$
$$= PD^3P^{-1}.$$

In general,

$$A^n = PD^nP^{-1} = P \begin{pmatrix} r_1^n & 0 & \cdots & 0 \\ 0 & r_2^n & \cdots & 0 \\ \vdots & \vdots & \ddots & \vdots \\ 0 & 0 & \cdots & r_k^n \end{pmatrix} P^{-1}.$$

Theorem 23.7   Let A be a $k \times k$ matrix. Suppose that there is a nonsingular matrix P such that

$$P^{-1}AP = \begin{pmatrix} r_1 & \cdots & 0 \\ \vdots & \ddots & \vdots \\ 0 & \cdots & r_k \end{pmatrix},$$

a diagonal matrix. Then,

$$A^n = P \begin{pmatrix} r_1^n & \cdots & 0 \\ \vdots & \ddots & \vdots \\ 0 & \cdots & r_k^n \end{pmatrix} P^{-1}.$$

The solution of the corresponding system of difference equations $\mathbf{z}_{n+1} = A\mathbf{z}_n$ with initial vector $\mathbf{z}_0$ is

$$\mathbf{z}_n = P \begin{pmatrix} r_1^n & \cdots & 0 \\ \vdots & \ddots & \vdots \\ 0 & \cdots & r_k^n \end{pmatrix} P^{-1} \mathbf{z}_0.$$

Example 23.8 We computed in Example 23.5 that the eigenvalues of $C = \begin{pmatrix} -1 & 3 \\ +2 & 0 \end{pmatrix}$ are $r = -3, 2$ with corresponding eigenvectors $\begin{pmatrix} 3 \\ -2 \end{pmatrix}$ and $\begin{pmatrix} 1 \\ 1 \end{pmatrix}$. By Theorem 23.4,

$$\begin{pmatrix} 3 & 1 \\ -2 & 1 \end{pmatrix}^{-1} \begin{pmatrix} -1 & 3 \\ 2 & 0 \end{pmatrix} \begin{pmatrix} 3 & 1 \\ -2 & 1 \end{pmatrix} = \begin{pmatrix} -3 & 0 \\ 0 & 2 \end{pmatrix},$$

or

$$\begin{pmatrix} -1 & 3 \\ 2 & 0 \end{pmatrix} = \begin{pmatrix} 3 & 1 \\ -2 & 1 \end{pmatrix} \begin{pmatrix} -3 & 0 \\ 0 & 2 \end{pmatrix} \begin{pmatrix} 0.2 & -0.2 \\ 0.4 & 0.6 \end{pmatrix}.$$

By Theorem 23.7,

$$\begin{pmatrix} -1 & 3 \\ 2 & 0 \end{pmatrix}^n = \begin{pmatrix} 3 & 1 \\ -2 & 1 \end{pmatrix} \begin{pmatrix} (-3)^n & 0 \\ 0 & 2^n \end{pmatrix} \begin{pmatrix} 0.2 & -0.2 \\ 0.4 & 0.6 \end{pmatrix}.$$

Example 23.9 We can also use the expression $A^n = PD^nP^{-1}$ in Theorem 23.7 to compute **roots of matrices**. Returning to Example 23.8, let

$$B = \begin{pmatrix} 3 & 1 \\ -2 & 1 \end{pmatrix} \begin{pmatrix} (-3)^{1/3} & 0 \\ 0 & 2^{1/3} \end{pmatrix} \begin{pmatrix} 0.2 & -0.2 \\ 0.4 & 0.6 \end{pmatrix}.$$

Then, by Theorem 23.7,

$$B^3 = \begin{pmatrix} 3 & 1 \\ -2 & 1 \end{pmatrix} \begin{pmatrix} -3 & 0 \\ 0 & 2 \end{pmatrix} \begin{pmatrix} 0.2 & -0.2 \\ 0.4 & 0.6 \end{pmatrix} = C.$$

Since $B^3 = C$, we can write $B = C^{1/3}$, the cube root of the matrix C. Note that since C has a negative eigenvalue, it does not have a real square root.

Stability of Equilibria

If the initial value $\mathbf{z}_0 = \mathbf{0}$, then the solution of

$$\mathbf{z}_{n+1} = A\mathbf{z}_n \tag{23}$$

is $\mathbf{z}_n = \mathbf{0}$ for all n, since $A^n\mathbf{0} = \mathbf{0}$ for all n. For example, a savings account that starts with 0 dollars and has no later deposits, will hold steady at 0 for all time. Such a solution of (23) in which $\mathbf{z}_n$ is the same constant for all n is called a **steady state, equilibrium**, or **stationary solution** of the difference equation (23). An important question in dynamics is the **stability** of the steady state solution $\mathbf{z} = \mathbf{0}$ of (23). We say that this solution is **asymptotically stable** if every solution of (23) tends to the steady state $\mathbf{z} = \mathbf{0}$ as n tends to infinity. Since (22) gives *every* solution of (23) for different values of $c_1, \ldots, c_k$, we see that every solution tends to $\mathbf{0}$ if and only if each r_i^n tends to zero. Since the r_i are eigenvalues of A and since r^n tends to zero if and only if $|r| < 1$, we have the following theorem.

> **Theorem 23.8** If the $k \times k$ matrix A has k distinct real eigenvalues, then every solution of the general system of linear difference equations (23) tends to **0** if and only if all the eigenvalues of A have absolute value less than 1.

EXERCISES

23.6 Show that the columns of P in (17) are the eigenvectors of A in Example 23.7.

23.7 For each of the following matrices A, find nonsingular matrix P and diagonal matrix D so that $P^{-1}AP = D$:

$$a) \begin{pmatrix} 3 & 0 \\ 1 & 2 \end{pmatrix}, \quad b) \begin{pmatrix} 0 & 1 \\ -1 & 5 \end{pmatrix}, \quad c) \begin{pmatrix} 1 & -1 \\ 2 & 4 \end{pmatrix},$$

$$d) \begin{pmatrix} 3 & -1 & 0 \\ -1 & 2 & -1 \\ 0 & -1 & 3 \end{pmatrix}, \quad e) \begin{pmatrix} 4 & -2 & -2 \\ 0 & 1 & 0 \\ 1 & 0 & 1 \end{pmatrix}.$$

23.8 Find the general solution of the following systems of difference equations:

a) $x_{n+1} = 3x_n$

$ y_{n+1} = x_n + 2y_n;$

b) $x_{n+1} = y_n$

$ y_{n+1} = -x_n + 5y_n;$

c) $x_{n+1} = x_n - y_n$

$ y_{n+1} = 2x_n + 4y_n;$

d) $x_{n+1} = 3x_n - y_n$

$ y_{n+1} = -x_n + 2y_n - z_n$

$ z_{n+1} = - y_n + 3z_n;$

e) $x_{n+1} = 4x_n - 2y_n - 2z_n$

$ y_{n+1} = y_n$

$ z_{n+1} = x_n + z_n.$

23.9 Write out the general Leslie model with M age groups in which age group i has birth rate b_i and death rate d_i.

23.10 Describe in words the long-run behavior of the population modeled in Example 23.7. In particular, what are the long-run relative sizes of the two age groups?

23.11 Suppose that the two-year species in Example 23.7 evolves to a three-year species with death rates $d_1 = 0.5$, $d_2 = 0.8$, $d_3 = 1$ and birth rates $b_1 = 1$, $b_2 = 4$, and $b_3 = 0$. Write out the corresponding Leslie system and find its general solution.

23.12 Find the cube root and, wherever possible, the square root of the four matrices in Exercise 23.7.

23.13 Write out a careful proof of Theorem 23.4.

23.3 PROPERTIES OF EIGENVALUES

From a practical point of view, the eigenvalues of a $k \times k$ matrix A are simply the zeros of the **characteristic polynomial** of A, the kth order polynomial

$$p(r) = \det(A - rI).$$

A kth order polynomial has k roots or zeros — counting multiple roots and complex roots. In fact, there are three possibilities for the roots of $p(r)$:

(1) $p(r)$ has k distinct, real roots,
(2) $p(r)$ has some repeated roots, or
(3) $p(r)$ has some complex roots.

These three cases are mutually exclusive for $k = 2$ and $k = 3$. However, matrices which are 4×4 or larger can have multiple eigenvalues *and* complex eigenvalues and even multiple complex eigenvalues. Let's look at some concrete examples of all these cases.

Example 23.10

(a) For matrix $\begin{pmatrix} -4 & 2 \\ -1 & -1 \end{pmatrix}$, the characteristic polynomial is

$$p_1(r) = (-4 - r)(-1 - r) + 2 = r^2 + 5r + 6,$$

whose roots are the distinct, real numbers $r = -3, -2$.

(b) The characteristic polynomial of $\begin{pmatrix} 4 & 0 & -2 \\ 0 & 3 & 0 \\ 3 & 0 & -1 \end{pmatrix}$ is

$$p_2(r) = (4 - r)(3 - r)(-1 - r) = (3 - r)(r^2 - 3r + 2),$$

whose roots are $r = 1, 2, 3$ — all distinct and real.

(c) The characteristic polynomial of the matrix $\begin{pmatrix} 4 & 1 \\ -1 & 2 \end{pmatrix}$ is

$$p_3(r) = (4 - r)(2 - r) + 1 = r^2 - 6r + 9 = (r - 3)^2,$$

whose roots are $r = 3, 3$. In other words, 3 is a root of $p_3(r)$ of **multiplicity** two.

(d) The characteristic polynomial of the matrix $\begin{pmatrix} 3 & 0 \\ 0 & 3 \end{pmatrix}$ is

$$p_4(r) = (3 - r)^2.$$

Once again, 3 is an eigenvalue of multiplicity two.

(e) The characteristic polynomial of the matrix $\begin{pmatrix} 0 & 2 \\ -1 & 2 \end{pmatrix}$ is

$$p_5(r) = -r(2 - r) + 2 = r^2 - 2r + 2.$$

Its roots, found by using the quadratic formula, are the complex numbers $r = 1 + i, 1 - i$.

(f) The characteristic polynomial of $\begin{pmatrix} 1 & 3 & 4 \\ 0 & 2 & -1 \\ 0 & 1 & 2 \end{pmatrix}$ is

$$p_6(r) = (1 - r)(r^2 - 4r + 5).$$

Its roots are $r = 1, 2 + i, 2 - i$.

Trace as Sum of the Eigenvalues

One of the simplest numbers attached to a matrix is its trace. The **trace** of a square matrix is the sum of its diagonal entries:

$$\text{trace } A = a_{11} + a_{22} + \cdots + a_{kk}.$$

As the following theorem indicates, one can learn something about the eigenvalues of a matrix just by examining the trace and the determinant of the matrix.

Theorem 23.9   Let A be a $k \times k$ matrix with eigenvalues $r_1, \ldots, r_k$. Then,

(a) $r_1 + r_2 + \cdots + r_k = $ trace of A, and
(b) $r_1 \cdot r_2 \cdots r_k = \det A$.

Proof   We will prove Theorem 23.9 in detail for 2×2 matrices and then leave the corresponding proof for $k \times k$ matrices for the Appendix of this chapter. Let r_1 and r_2 be the eigenvalues of the matrix $A = \begin{pmatrix} a & b \\ c & d \end{pmatrix}$. The characteristic polynomial of A is

$$p_A(r) = \det \begin{pmatrix} a - r & b \\ c & d - r \end{pmatrix} = (a - r)(d - r) - bc$$

$$= r^2 - (a + d)r + (ad - bc). \tag{24}$$

Since r_1 and r_2 are the roots of $p_A(r)$, we can recover $p_A(r)$ as

$$p_A(r) = \beta(r_1 - r)(r_2 - r)$$

$$= \beta r^2 - \beta(r_1 + r_2)r + \beta r_1 r_2, \tag{25}$$

for some constant β. Since (24) and (25) are two different ways of writing the *same* polynomial, the coefficient of each r^i must be the same in both approaches:

Coefficient of r^2 :	$1 = \beta$,
Coefficient of r :	$-(a + d) = -\beta(r_1 + r_2)$,
Constant term :	$ad - bc = \beta r_1 r_2$.

Therefore, $\beta = 1$; trace $A \equiv (a + d) = r_1 + r_2$, the sum of the eigenvalues; and $\det A = ad - bc = r_1 \cdot r_2$, the product of the eigenvalues. This proves the theorem for 2×2 matrices. ∎

As the following examples illustrate, Theorem 23.9 can sometimes be used to discover the eigenvalues of a matrix without making any explicit computations.

Example 23.11   To find the eigenvalues of the 4×4 matrix

$$B = \begin{pmatrix} 4 & 1 & 1 & 1 \\ 1 & 4 & 1 & 1 \\ 1 & 1 & 4 & 1 \\ 1 & 1 & 1 & 4 \end{pmatrix},$$

subtract 3 from each of the diagonal entries of B. The result is the singular matrix

$$B - 3I = \begin{pmatrix} 1 & 1 & 1 & 1 \\ 1 & 1 & 1 & 1 \\ 1 & 1 & 1 & 1 \\ 1 & 1 & 1 & 1 \end{pmatrix}.$$

Vector $\mathbf{v} = (v_1, v_2, v_3, v_4)$ is an eigenvector for eigenvalue 3 if and only if $(B - 3I)\mathbf{v} = \mathbf{0}$ if and only if $v_1 + v_2 + v_3 + v_4 = 0$. The vectors

$$\mathbf{v}_1 = \begin{pmatrix} 1 \\ 0 \\ 0 \\ -1 \end{pmatrix}, \quad \mathbf{v}_2 = \begin{pmatrix} 0 \\ 1 \\ 0 \\ -1 \end{pmatrix}, \quad \text{and} \quad \mathbf{v}_3 = \begin{pmatrix} 0 \\ 0 \\ 1 \\ -1 \end{pmatrix}$$

are three linearly independent eigenvectors for eigenvalue 3. Therefore, 3 is an eigenvalue of B of multiplicity at least 3. Use the fact that the sum of the eigenvalues of B is 16, the trace of B, to conclude that the fourth eigenvalue of B is $16 - (3 + 3 + 3) = 7$.

Example 23.12   The matrix $\begin{pmatrix} 2 & 4 \\ 1 & 2 \end{pmatrix}$ is clearly singular since the first row is twice the second row. Therefore, 0 is an eigenvalue. By the trace rule in Theorem 23.9, the other eigenvalue is 4.

EXERCISES

23.14   Verify the conclusion of Theorem 23.9 for the matrices in Exercise 23.2.

23.15   Use Theorem 23.9 to find all the eigenvalues of the following matrices by inspection. Note that the first matrix is a Markov matrix.

$$a) \begin{pmatrix} 0.5 & 0.7 \\ 0.5 & 0.3 \end{pmatrix}, \quad b) \begin{pmatrix} 1 & 1 \\ 1 & 1 \end{pmatrix}, \quad c) \begin{pmatrix} 0 & 1 & 1 \\ 1 & 0 & 1 \\ 1 & 1 & 0 \end{pmatrix}, \quad d) \begin{pmatrix} 3 & 0 & 0 \\ 0 & 1 & 2 \\ 0 & 1 & 2 \end{pmatrix}.$$

23.4 REPEATED EIGENVALUES

In Section 2, we learned how to diagonalize a $k \times k$ matrix that has k distinct real eigenvalues. In this section and the next, we turn our attention to the two things that can go wrong in the diagonalization process: repeated eigenvalues and complex eigenvalues. We begin in this section with repeated eigenvalues.

2 × 2 Nondiagonalizable Matrices

We first consider the case of 2×2 matrices. The third and fourth matrices in Example 23.10,

$$A_1 = \begin{pmatrix} 4 & 1 \\ -1 & 2 \end{pmatrix} \quad \text{and} \quad A_2 = \begin{pmatrix} 3 & 0 \\ 0 & 3 \end{pmatrix},$$

both have only one distinct eigenvalue: $r = 3$. There is, however, one major difference between these two matrices, because, as we now show, matrix A_1 has only one independent eigenvector, while A_2 has two independent eigenvectors. An eigenvector for A_1 is a solution $\mathbf{v}$ of the equation

$$(A_1 - 3I)\mathbf{v} = \begin{pmatrix} 1 & 1 \\ -1 & -1 \end{pmatrix}\begin{pmatrix} v_1 \\ v_2 \end{pmatrix} = \begin{pmatrix} 0 \\ 0 \end{pmatrix}.$$

A vector $\begin{pmatrix} v_1 \\ v_2 \end{pmatrix}$ is a solution to this system if and only if it is a multiple of $\begin{pmatrix} 1 \\ -1 \end{pmatrix}$, a one-dimensional solution set. On the other hand,

$$(A_2 - 3I) = \begin{pmatrix} 0 & 0 \\ 0 & 0 \end{pmatrix}$$

is the zero matrix, and the solution set of $(A_2 - 3I)\mathbf{v} = \mathbf{0}$ is the set of *all* vectors in $\mathbf{R}^2$, a two-dimensional set. It is easy to find two independent solutions for $(A_2 - 3I)$; any two independent vectors will work. By Theorem 23.4, the matrix A_2 is diagonalizable; in fact, it is already diagonal.

On the other hand, there is no P which diagonalizes A_1, because by Theorem 23.4, such a P would have to have independent eigenvectors of A_1 as its columns, but A_1 has only *one* independent eigenvector. A matrix A which has an eigenvalue of multiplicity $m > 1$ but does not have m independent eigenvectors corresponding to this eigenvalue is called a **nondiagonalizable** matrix or sometimes a **defective** matrix.

The following theorem, which holds only for 2×2 matrices, tells us which 2×2 matrices with repeated eigenvalues are diagonalizable.

> **Theorem 23.10**   Let A be a 2×2 matrix with two equal eigenvalues. Then, A is diagonalizable if and only if A is already diagonal.

Proof   If A is diagonalizable via the change of variables matrix P, then by Theorem 23.4, the diagonal entries of $P^{-1}AP$ must be the eigenvalues of A. Let r^* denote the unique eigenvalue of A. Then, $P^{-1}AP$ must be the matrix $\begin{pmatrix} r^* & 0 \\ 0 & r^* \end{pmatrix} = r^*I$:

$$P^{-1}AP = r^*I.$$

This is equivalent to $A = P(r^*I)P^{-1} = r^*PIP^{-1} = r^*I.$ ■

What do we do with a nondiagonalizable matrix like A_1 above? Recall that we want $P^{-1}A_1P$ to be as simple as possible. If we can't achieve a diagonal matrix $\begin{pmatrix} r^* & 0 \\ 0 & r^* \end{pmatrix}$, the next simplest matrix is the "almost diagonal" matrix: $\begin{pmatrix} r^* & 1 \\ 0 & r^* \end{pmatrix}$. The questions that must be answered are:

(1) Is this form simple enough that we can always easily solve the transformed system of equations

$$\mathbf{Z}_{n+1} = \begin{pmatrix} r^* & 1 \\ 0 & r^* \end{pmatrix} \mathbf{Z}_n?$$

(2) Is this "almost diagonal" form achievable as $P^{-1}AP$ for any defective matrix A?

The answer to both of these questions is a definite "Yes!"
Let's start with the second question: How do we achieve

$$P^{-1}AP = \begin{pmatrix} r^* & 1 \\ 0 & r^* \end{pmatrix}, \tag{26}$$

where r^* is the only eigenvalue of a 2×2 defective matrix A? As in the proof of Theorem 23.4, look for the equations which the columns of $P = [\mathbf{v}_1 \quad \mathbf{v}_2]$ must satisfy. Write (26) as

$$AP = P \begin{pmatrix} r^* & 1 \\ 0 & r^* \end{pmatrix}$$

or
$$A[\mathbf{v}_1 \quad \mathbf{v}_2] = [\mathbf{v}_1 \quad \mathbf{v}_2] \begin{pmatrix} r^* & 1 \\ 0 & r^* \end{pmatrix} \tag{27}$$

or
$$[A\mathbf{v}_1 \quad A\mathbf{v}_2] = [r^*\mathbf{v}_1 \quad \mathbf{v}_1 + r^*\mathbf{v}_2]$$

or
$$A\mathbf{v}_1 = r^*\mathbf{v}_1 \quad \text{and} \quad A\mathbf{v}_2 = r^*\mathbf{v}_2 + \mathbf{v}_1.$$

Therefore, the first column $\mathbf{v}_1$ of P should be an eigenvector for eigenvalue r^*. The second column $\mathbf{v}_2$ of P should satisfy

$$A\mathbf{v}_2 - r^*\mathbf{v}_2 = \mathbf{v}_1, \quad \text{or} \quad (A - r^*I)\mathbf{v}_2 = \mathbf{v}_1. \tag{28}$$

Since $(A - r^*I)\mathbf{v}_1 = \mathbf{0}$, equation (28) is equivalent to

$$(A - r^*I)^2\mathbf{v}_2 = \mathbf{0} \quad \text{but} \quad (A - r^*I)\mathbf{v}_2 \neq \mathbf{0}. \tag{29}$$

Definition Let r^* be an eigenvalue of the matrix A. A (nonzero) vector $\mathbf{v}$ such that $(A - r^*I)\mathbf{v} \neq \mathbf{0}$ but $(A - r^*I)^m\mathbf{v} = \mathbf{0}$ for some integer $m > 1$ is called a **generalized eigenvector** for A corresponding to r^*.

Calculation (27) shows that in order for the change of coordinate matrix P to transform the nondiagonalizable matrix A as in equation (26), the first column of P must be an eigenvector of A and the second column of P must be a generalized eigenvector of A, both corresponding to eigenvalue r^*.

How do we find a generalized eigenvector of A? It turns out that if r^* is an eigenvalue of matrix A of multiplicity two with only one independent eigenvector $\mathbf{v}_1$, then there is a vector $\mathbf{v}_2$ such that equation (28), or equivalently equation (29), holds. The following example illustrates the computations involved.

Example 23.13 Consider the nondiagonalizable matrix

$$A = \begin{pmatrix} 4 & 1 \\ -1 & 2 \end{pmatrix}$$

of Example 23.10c, whose eigenvalues are $r = 3, 3$. As we computed earlier, it has one independent eigenvector $\mathbf{v}_1 = \begin{pmatrix} 1 \\ -1 \end{pmatrix}$. Its generalized eigenvector will be a solution $\mathbf{v}_2$ of

$$(A - 3I)\mathbf{v}_2 = \mathbf{v}_1, \quad \text{or} \quad \begin{pmatrix} 1 & 1 \\ -1 & -1 \end{pmatrix}\begin{pmatrix} v_{21} \\ v_{22} \end{pmatrix} = \begin{pmatrix} 1 \\ -1 \end{pmatrix}.$$

Take $v_{21} = 1, v_{22} = 0$, for example. Then form

$$P = [\mathbf{v}_1\mathbf{v}_2] = \begin{pmatrix} 1 & 1 \\ -1 & 0 \end{pmatrix},$$

and check that

$$P^{-1}AP = \begin{pmatrix} 0 & -1 \\ 1 & 1 \end{pmatrix}\begin{pmatrix} 4 & 1 \\ -1 & 2 \end{pmatrix}\begin{pmatrix} 1 & 1 \\ -1 & 0 \end{pmatrix} = \begin{pmatrix} 3 & 1 \\ 0 & 3 \end{pmatrix}.$$

The following theorem summarizes our discussion of the diagonalization process for 2×2 matrices with a multiple eigenvalue.

Theorem 23.11   Let A be a 2×2 matrix with equal eigenvalues $r = r^*, r^*$. Then,

(a) either A has two independent eigenvectors corresponding to r^*, in which case A is the diagonal matrix r^*I, or

(b) A has only one independent eigenvector, say $\mathbf{v}_1$. In this case, there is a generalized eigenvector $\mathbf{v}_2$ such that $(A - r^*I)\mathbf{v}_2 = \mathbf{v}_1$. If $P \equiv [\mathbf{v}_1 \mathbf{v}_2]$, then $P^{-1}AP = \begin{pmatrix} r^* & 1 \\ 0 & r^* \end{pmatrix}$.

3×3 Nondiagonalizable Matrices

A similar analysis works for larger matrices that have eigenvalues of multiplicity $m > 1$ with fewer than m independent eigenvectors. Consider the following example of a 3×3 matrix with an eigenvalue of multiplicity two and only one independent eigenvector.

Example 23.14   The characteristic polynomial of the matrix

$$A = \begin{pmatrix} 4 & 2 & -4 \\ 1 & 4 & -3 \\ 1 & 1 & 0 \end{pmatrix}$$

is $p(r) = (r - 3)^2(2 - r)$; its eigenvalues are $r = 3, 3, 2$. For eigenvalue $r = 2$, the solution space of

$$(A - 2I)\mathbf{v} = \begin{pmatrix} 2 & 2 & -4 \\ 1 & 2 & -3 \\ 1 & 1 & -2 \end{pmatrix} \begin{pmatrix} v_1 \\ v_2 \\ v_3 \end{pmatrix} = \begin{pmatrix} 0 \\ 0 \\ 0 \end{pmatrix}$$

is the one-dimensional space spanned by $\mathbf{v}_1 = \begin{pmatrix} 1 \\ 1 \\ 1 \end{pmatrix}$. For eigenvalue $r = 3$,

the solution space of

$$(A - 3I)\mathbf{v} = \begin{pmatrix} 1 & 2 & -4 \\ 1 & 1 & -3 \\ 1 & 1 & -3 \end{pmatrix} \begin{pmatrix} v_1 \\ v_2 \\ v_3 \end{pmatrix} = \begin{pmatrix} 0 \\ 0 \\ 0 \end{pmatrix}$$

is the one-dimensional space spanned by $\mathbf{v}_2 = \begin{pmatrix} 2 \\ 1 \\ 1 \end{pmatrix}$. (Gaussian elimina-

tion may be needed to solve these systems.) There is only one independent eigenvector corresponding to the eigenvalue of multiplicity two. We need one more vector v_3 independent of v_1 and v_2 to form the change of coordinate matrix $P = [v_1\ v_2 v_3]$. Take v_3 to be a generalized eigenvector for eigenvalue $r = 3$ — a solution to the system

$$(A - 3I)v_3 = v_2, \quad \text{or} \quad \begin{pmatrix} 1 & 2 & -4 \\ 1 & 1 & -3 \\ 1 & 1 & -3 \end{pmatrix} \begin{pmatrix} v_{31} \\ v_{32} \\ v_{33} \end{pmatrix} = \begin{pmatrix} 2 \\ 1 \\ 1 \end{pmatrix}.$$

By inspection, we can take $v_3 = \begin{pmatrix} 0 \\ 1 \\ 0 \end{pmatrix}$. Let

$$P = [v_1 v_2 v_3] = \begin{pmatrix} 1 & 2 & 0 \\ 1 & 1 & 1 \\ 1 & 1 & 0 \end{pmatrix}.$$

Then,

$$P^{-1}AP = \begin{pmatrix} 2 & 0 & 0 \\ 0 & 3 & 1 \\ 0 & 0 & 3 \end{pmatrix}. \tag{30}$$

Computations with generalized eigenvectors can be a bit more complicated for 3×3 matrices than they are for 2×2 matrices. For example, 3×3 matrix A can have an eigenvalue r^* of multiplicity *three* with only *one* independent eigenvector v_1. In this case, one uses the techniques of Example 23.14 to find generalized eigenvectors v_2 and v_3 such that

$$(A - r^*I)v_2 = v_1 \quad \text{and} \quad (A - r^*I)v_3 = v_2. \tag{31}$$

If $P = [v_1 v_2 v_3]$, then

$$P^{-1}AP = \begin{pmatrix} r^* & 1 & 0 \\ 0 & r^* & 1 \\ 0 & 0 & r^* \end{pmatrix}. \tag{32}$$

See Exercise 23.21 for an example of this situation.

If the 3×3 matrix A has an eigenvalue r^* of multiplicity *three* and *two* independent eigenvectors, then a single generalized eigenvector v_3 must be found to finish the construction of P. Exercise 23.22 illustrates how to deal with this situation.

Diagonal matrices as in (19) and almost diagonal matrices as in (26), (30) and (32) are called the **Jordan canonical forms** of the original matrix A. Theorems 23.4 and 23.11 list the canonical forms for all 2×2 matrices with real eigenvalues. Exercise 23.24 asks for the corresponding list for 3×3 matrices with all real eigenvalues.

Solving Nondiagonalizable Difference Equations

Next, let's answer the other question posed just below Theorem 23.10. How do we use equations (26) and (32) to solve the system of difference equations $\mathbf{z}_{n+1} = A\mathbf{z}_n$, when A is a nondiagonalizable matrix? Let's first work with a 2×2 system. Choose P so that (26) holds. The change of variables $\mathbf{z} = P\mathbf{Z}$ transforms the system $\mathbf{z}_{n+1} = A\mathbf{z}_n$ to the system $\mathbf{Z}_{n+1} = (P^{-1}AP)\mathbf{Z}_n$:

$$\mathbf{Z}_{n+1} = \begin{pmatrix} X_{n+1} \\ Y_{n+1} \end{pmatrix} = \begin{pmatrix} r & 1 \\ 0 & r \end{pmatrix} \begin{pmatrix} X_n \\ Y_n \end{pmatrix},$$

or

$$\begin{aligned} X_{n+1} &= rX_n + Y_n \\ Y_{n+1} &= \phantom{rX_n + {}} rY_n. \end{aligned} \tag{33}$$

This system is still coupled, but minimally so. Since the second equation of (33) involves only Y_n's, but no X_n's, we can solve it for Y_n:

$$Y_n = c_1 r^n,$$

and plug this *solution* into the first equation of (33):

$$X_{n+1} = rX_n + c_1 r^n. \tag{34}$$

We now have a linear nonhomogeneous *scalar* difference equation to solve. As we did in (7), let's iterate equation (34) from $n = 0$ to discover its general solution:

$$X_0 = c_0,$$

$$X_1 = rX_0 + c_1 r^0 = rc_0 + c_1,$$

$$X_2 = rX_1 + c_1 r^1 = r(rc_0 + c_1) + c_1 r$$

$$ = r^2 c_0 + 2c_1 r,$$

$$X_3 = rX_2 + c_1 r^2 = r(r^2 c_0 + 2c_1 r) + c_1 r^2$$

$$ = r^3 c_0 + 3c_1 r^2,$$

$$X_4 = rX_3 + c_1 r^3 = r(r^3 c_0 + 3c_1 r^2) + c_1 r^3$$

$$ = r^4 c_0 + 4c_1 r^3.$$

In general,

$$X_n = c_0 r^n + nc_1 r^{n-1}. \tag{35}$$

To see that (35) is truly the general solution of (34), plug it into (34). On the one hand,

$$X_{n+1} = c_0 r^{n+1} + (n+1)c_1 r^n;$$

on the other hand,

$$rX_n + c_1 r^n = r(c_0 r^n + nc_1 r^{n-1}) + c_1 r^n$$
$$= c_0 r^{n+1} + (n+1)c_1 r^n.$$

Therefore, $X_{n+1} = rX_n + c_1 r^n$ and the general solution of (33) is

$$\begin{pmatrix} X_n \\ Y_n \end{pmatrix} = \begin{pmatrix} c_0 r^n + nc_1 r^{n-1} \\ c_1 r^n \end{pmatrix}.$$

Finally, we use the change of coordinates $\mathbf{z} = P\mathbf{Z}$ to write the general solution of our original system $\mathbf{z}_{n+1} = A\mathbf{z}_n$:

$$\mathbf{z}_n = P\mathbf{Z}_n = [\mathbf{v}_1 \mathbf{v}_2]\begin{pmatrix} c_0 r^n + nc_1 r^{n-1} \\ c_1 r^n \end{pmatrix}$$
$$= (c_0 r^n + nc_1 r^{n-1})\mathbf{v}_1 + c_1 r^n \mathbf{v}_2.$$

The following theorem summarizes these calculations.

Theorem 23.12   Suppose that A is a 2×2 matrix with multiple eigenvalue r and only one independent eigenvector $\mathbf{v}_1$. Let $\mathbf{v}_2$ be a generalized eigenvector corresponding to $\mathbf{v}_1$ and r. Then, the general solution of the system of difference equations $\mathbf{z}_{n+1} = A\mathbf{z}_n$ is

$$\mathbf{z}_n = (c_0 r^n + nc_1 r^{n-1})\mathbf{v}_1 + c_1 r^n \mathbf{v}_2. \qquad (36)$$

Example 23.15   The linear system of difference equations corresponding to the nondiagonalizable matrix in Example 23.13 is

$$\begin{pmatrix} x_{n+1} \\ y_{n+1} \end{pmatrix} = \begin{pmatrix} 4 & 1 \\ -1 & 2 \end{pmatrix}\begin{pmatrix} x_n \\ y_n \end{pmatrix}.$$

By Theorem 23.12, its general solution is

$$\begin{pmatrix} x_n \\ y_n \end{pmatrix} = (c_0 3^n + c_1 n 3^{n-1})\begin{pmatrix} 1 \\ -1 \end{pmatrix} + c_1 3^n \begin{pmatrix} 1 \\ 0 \end{pmatrix}$$
$$= \begin{pmatrix} c_0 3^n + c_1(n3^{n-1} + 3^n) \\ -c_0 - c_1 n 3^{n-1} \end{pmatrix}.$$

EXERCISES

23.16 For each of the following matrices A, find P so that (26) holds:

$$a) \begin{pmatrix} 3 & 1 \\ -1 & 1 \end{pmatrix}, \quad b) \begin{pmatrix} -5 & 2 \\ -2 & -1 \end{pmatrix}, \quad c) \begin{pmatrix} 3 & 3 \\ -3 & -3 \end{pmatrix}.$$

23.17 For each of the matrices A in the previous exercise, find the general solution of $\mathbf{z}_{n+1} = A\mathbf{z}_n$.

23.18 Verify equation (30).

23.19 Construct two more matrices P for Example 23.13 by choosing different eigenvectors and generalized eigenvectors for A. Show that all lead to the same $P^{-1}AP$.

23.20 Let A be a 2×2 matrix as in the hypothesis of Theorem 23.12. Prove that $\mathbf{z}_n = \mathbf{0}$ for all n is an asymptotically stable steady state of the system $\mathbf{z}_{n+1} = A\mathbf{z}_n$, provided that $|r| < 1$.

23.21 a) Show that the matrix $B = \begin{pmatrix} 3 & 1 & 1 \\ 1 & 2 & 1 \\ -1 & -1 & 1 \end{pmatrix}$ has $r = 2$ as an eigenvalue of multiplicity three, but only one independent eigenvector $\mathbf{v}_1$. b) Use (31) to find generalized eigenvectors $\mathbf{v}_2$ and $\mathbf{v}_3$. c) If $P = [\mathbf{v}_1 \, \mathbf{v}_2\mathbf{v}_3]$, show that $P^{-1}BP$ has the desired form.

23.22 Show that the matrix $C = \begin{pmatrix} 4 & 0 & 0 \\ -1 & 4 & 2 \\ 0 & 0 & 4 \end{pmatrix}$ has $r = 4$ as an eigenvalue of multiplicity three with two independent eigenvectors. This time, to find the corresponding generalized eigenvector $\mathbf{v}_3$, solve $(C - 4I)^2\mathbf{v}_3 = \mathbf{0}$ and $(C - 4I)\mathbf{v}_3 \neq \mathbf{0}$ for $\mathbf{v}_3$. Then, show that $\mathbf{v}_2 = (C - 4I)\mathbf{v}_3$ is an eigenvector, and find an eigenvector $\mathbf{v}_1$ independent of $\mathbf{v}_2$. Let $P = [\mathbf{v}_1\mathbf{v}_2\mathbf{v}_3]$, and show that $P^{-1}CP$ has the desired form.

23.23 Prove that if A is a 3×3 matrix with an eigenvalue r^* of multiplicity three and with *three* independent eigenvectors, then A must equal the diagonal matrix r^*I.

23.24 As discussed above, matrices as in (19), (26), (30), and (32) are called Jordan canonical forms of the matrix A. What are all the possible Jordan canonical forms for 3×3 matrices with only real eigenvalues?

23.25 For the 3×3 nondiagonalizable matrices in Example 23.14 and Exercises 23.21 and 23.22, find the general solution of the corresponding difference equation $\mathbf{z}_{n+1} = A\mathbf{z}_n$, analogous to solution (36).

23.26 For each of the following matrices A, find an invertible matrix P so that $P^{-1}AP$ is in Jordan canonical form:

$$a) \begin{pmatrix} -1 & 0 & 0 \\ 1 & 4 & -1 \\ -1 & 4 & 0 \end{pmatrix}, \quad b) \begin{pmatrix} 2 & 3 & 0 \\ 0 & -1 & 0 \\ 0 & -1 & 2 \end{pmatrix}, \quad c) \begin{pmatrix} 5 & 1 & 3 \\ 0 & 2 & 0 \\ -6 & -1 & -4 \end{pmatrix},$$

$$d) \begin{pmatrix} 3 & 0 & 0 \\ 4 & 2 & 0 \\ 5 & 0 & 2 \end{pmatrix}, \quad e) \begin{pmatrix} 2 & 3 & 2 \\ -1 & 4 & 2 \\ 0 & 1 & 3 \end{pmatrix}, \quad f) \begin{pmatrix} 4 & 1 & 0 \\ -1 & 2 & 0 \\ 1 & 1 & 3 \end{pmatrix}.$$

23.5   COMPLEX EIGENVALUES AND EIGENVECTORS

Diagonalizing Matrices with Complex Eigenvalues

So far in this chapter, we have concentrated on $k \times k$ matrices which have k *real* eigenvalues. We have seen that such a matrix is diagonalizable if it has k distinct eigenvalues or, more generally, if each eigenvalue of multiplicity j has j linearly independent eigenvectors. We turn now to the final complication that can arise — eigenvalues that are *complex numbers*. Since the eigenvalues are simply the roots of the characteristic polynomial, complex eigenvalues occur when the characteristic polynomial of the matrix A, $\det(A - rI)$, has complex roots. If A is a matrix of real numbers, its characteristic polynomial will be a polynomial with real coefficients. If the complex number $z = \alpha + i\beta$ is a root of such a polynomial, so is its complex conjugate $\bar{z} = \alpha - i\beta$. In other words, complex eigenvalues of real matrices occur in *complex conjugate* pairs.

Example 23.16   The eigenvalues of $\begin{pmatrix} a & b \\ c & d \end{pmatrix}$, the general 2×2 matrix, are the roots of its characteristic equation

$$p(r) = r^2 - (a + d)r + (ad - bc),$$

namely,

$$r = \frac{1}{2}(a + d) \pm \frac{1}{2}\sqrt{(a + d)^2 - 4(ad - bc)}$$

$$= \frac{1}{2}(a + d) \pm \frac{1}{2}\sqrt{(a - d)^2 + 4bc}.$$

If $(a - d)^2 + 4bc < 0$, then the roots are the *complex* numbers

$$r_1 = \frac{1}{2}(a + d) + i\frac{1}{2}\sqrt{|(a - d)^2 + 4bc|},$$

$$r_2 = \bar{r_1} = \frac{1}{2}(a + d) - i\frac{1}{2}\sqrt{|(a - d)^2 + 4bc|}.$$

For a 2×2 matrix, the fact that the complex eigenvalues come in complex conjugate pairs and the fact that a complex number is not equal to its conjugate imply that the complex eigenvalues of a 2×2 matrix are always distinct. So, at least when we are dealing with 2×2 matrices with complex eigenvalues, we don't have to worry about generalized eigenvectors. Since complex eigenvalues come in conjugate pairs, a real matrix must have an even number of complex eigenvalues. Therefore, a 3×3 real matrix must have a least one real eigenvalue. It's only with 4×4 matrices that the possibility of repeated complex eigenvalues arises.

One way of treating complex eigenvalues is to ignore the fact that they are complex numbers and just work with them as we did with real numbers in Section 23.2. Of course, we'll have to deal with complex eigenvectors in the process; but it all works out in the end. If $r = \alpha + i\beta$ is a complex eigenvalue of the matrix A, the corresponding eigenvector is a nonzero solution $\mathbf{w}$ of the system of equations

$$(A - (\alpha + i\beta)I)\mathbf{w} = \mathbf{0},$$

or equivalently, $\qquad\qquad A\mathbf{w} = (\alpha + i\beta)\mathbf{w}. \qquad\qquad (37)$

As we do for complex numbers, write a complex *vector* $\mathbf{w}$ as $\mathbf{u} + i\mathbf{v}$ where $\mathbf{u}$ and $\mathbf{v}$ are real vectors. Simply, put the real part of each component of $\mathbf{w}$ in $\mathbf{u}$ and the imaginary part of each component of $\mathbf{w}$ in $\mathbf{v}$. Then, (37) becomes

$$A(\mathbf{u} + i\mathbf{v}) = (\alpha + i\beta)(\mathbf{u} + i\mathbf{v}). \qquad\qquad (38)$$

Take the complex conjugate of both sides of equation (38), recalling that the complex conjugate of a sum (or product) of two complex numbers is the sum (or product) of the conjugates of the two numbers:

$$\overline{A}\,\overline{(\mathbf{u} + i\mathbf{v})} = \overline{(\alpha + i\beta)}\,\overline{(\mathbf{u} + i\mathbf{v})},$$

or $\qquad\qquad A(\mathbf{u} - i\mathbf{v}) = (\alpha - i\beta)(\mathbf{u} - i\mathbf{v}),$

where $\overline{A} = A$ since all the entries of A are real. These equations show that complex eigenvectors come in pairs too. If $\mathbf{u} + i\mathbf{v}$ is an eigenvector for eigenvalue $\alpha + i\beta$, then its conjugate $\mathbf{u} - i\mathbf{v}$ is an eigenvector for the conjugate eigenvalue $\alpha - i\beta$. The following theorem summarizes this discussion so far.

Theorem 23.13 Let A be a $k \times k$ matrix with real entries. If $r = \alpha + i\beta$ is an eigenvalue of A, so is its conjugate $\overline{r} = \alpha - i\beta$. If $\mathbf{u} + i\mathbf{v}$ is an eigenvector for $\alpha + i\beta$, then $\mathbf{u} - i\mathbf{v}$ is an eigenvector for $\alpha - i\beta$. If k is odd, A must have at least one real eigenvalue.

Example 23.17 For matrix $A = \begin{pmatrix} 1 & 1 \\ -9 & 1 \end{pmatrix}$, the characteristic polynomial is

$$p(r) = r^2 - 2r + 10,$$

whose roots are $r = 1 + 3i, 1 - 3i$. An eigenvector for $r = 1 + 3i$ is a solution $\mathbf{w}$ of

$$(A - (1 + 3i)I)\mathbf{w} = \begin{pmatrix} -3i & 1 \\ -9 & -3i \end{pmatrix}\begin{pmatrix} w_1 \\ w_2 \end{pmatrix} = \begin{pmatrix} 0 \\ 0 \end{pmatrix}.$$

This matrix may not look singular, but its determinant is zero and its second row is $-3i$ times its first row. (Check.) Using the first row of this matrix, we conclude that an eigenvector is a solution $\mathbf{w}$ of the equation

$$-3iw_1 + w_2 = 0;$$

for example, $\mathbf{w} = \begin{pmatrix} 1 \\ 3i \end{pmatrix}$, which we write as $\begin{pmatrix} 1 \\ 0 \end{pmatrix} + i \begin{pmatrix} 0 \\ 3 \end{pmatrix}$. By Theorem 23.13, an eigenvector for eigenvalue $1 - 3i$ is

$$\overline{\mathbf{w}} = \begin{pmatrix} 1 \\ 0 \end{pmatrix} - i \begin{pmatrix} 0 \\ 3 \end{pmatrix} = \begin{pmatrix} 1 \\ -3i \end{pmatrix}.$$

Form the change of coordinate matrix P whose columns are these two eigenvectors:

$$P = \begin{pmatrix} 1 & 1 \\ 3i & -3i \end{pmatrix}.$$

Then, applying Theorem 8.5.4,

$$P^{-1} = -\frac{1}{6i} \begin{pmatrix} -3i & -1 \\ -3i & 1 \end{pmatrix} = \begin{pmatrix} \frac{1}{2} & -\frac{1}{6}i \\ \frac{1}{2} & \frac{1}{6}i \end{pmatrix},$$

and we calculate that

$$P^{-1}AP = \begin{pmatrix} 1 + 3i & 0 \\ 0 & 1 - 3i \end{pmatrix}, \tag{39}$$

just as if we had been working with real eigenvalues and real eigenvectors.

Two issues need to be addressed regarding matrices with complex eigenvalues:

(1) How does one use the change of variables $\mathbf{z} = P\mathbf{Z}$ to solve the difference equations $\mathbf{z}_{n+1} = A\mathbf{z}_n$ when A has complex eigenvalues?
(2) How do we incorporate complex eigenvalues into our canonical forms?

Linear Difference Equations with Complex Eigenvalues

Recall the general scheme for solving a system of linear difference equations $\mathbf{z}_{n+1} = A\mathbf{z}_n$. Since the linear change of variables $\mathbf{z} = P\mathbf{Z}$ transforms this system to the system $\mathbf{Z}_{n+1} = (P^{-1}AP)\mathbf{Z}_n$, we want to find a P so that $P^{-1}AP$ is as simple as possible, preferably diagonal. If the 2×2 matrix A has complex eigenvalues $\alpha \pm i\beta$ and corresponding complex eigenvectors $\mathbf{u} \pm i v$, then the complex change of coordinates

$$P = [\mathbf{u} + iv \quad \mathbf{u} - iv]$$

yields
$$P^{-1}AP = \begin{pmatrix} \alpha + i\beta & 0 \\ 0 & \alpha - i\beta \end{pmatrix}$$

and the transformed system

$$X_{n+1} = (\alpha + i\beta)X_n$$

$$Y_{n+1} = (\alpha - i\beta)Y_n,$$

whose solution is

$$X_n = k_1(\alpha + i\beta)^n$$

$$Y_n = k_2(\alpha - i\beta)^n$$

for any constants k_1 and k_2, real *or* complex. Transforming this solution back to the original coordinates via $\mathbf{z}_n = P\mathbf{Z}_n$ yields

$$\mathbf{z}_n = \begin{pmatrix} x_n \\ y_n \end{pmatrix} = [\mathbf{u} + i\mathbf{v} \quad \mathbf{u} - i\mathbf{v}] \begin{pmatrix} k_1(\alpha + i\beta)^n \\ k_2(\alpha - i\beta)^n \end{pmatrix}$$

$$= k_1(\alpha + i\beta)^n(\mathbf{u} + i\mathbf{v}) + k_2(\alpha - i\beta)^n(\mathbf{u} - i\mathbf{v}). \tag{40}$$

This solution is the same form as (22), but with complex eigenvalues and eigenvectors replacing the real eigenvalues and eigenvectors in (22).

Expression (40) is a solution to $\mathbf{z}_{n+1} = A\mathbf{z}_n$ for any choice of constants k_1 and k_2. Since the original problem involved only real numbers, possibly arising from a real-world application, we would like to find a solution which contains only real numbers. Since every solution of $\mathbf{z}_{n+1} = A\mathbf{z}_n$ is contained in the solution (40) for different choices of the parameters k_1 and k_2, we want to know if we can find parameters k_1 and k_2 so that (40) is *real*. Except for the k_i factors, the first term in (40) is the complex conjugate of the second term. Recall that the sum of a complex number $a + ib$ and its conjugate $a - ib$ is the *real* number $2a$. If we choose k_1 to be any complex constant $c_1 + ic_2$ and then choose k_2 to be its complex conjugate $c_1 - ic_2$, then the first term in (40) will be the conjugate of the second term and the sum of these two terms will be a real solution:

$$\mathbf{z}_n = (c_1 + ic_2)(\alpha + i\beta)^n(\mathbf{u} + i\mathbf{v}) + (c_1 - ic_2)(\alpha - i\beta)^n(\mathbf{u} - i\mathbf{v})$$

$$= 2\text{Re}\{(c_1 + ic_2)(\alpha + i\beta)^n(\mathbf{u} + i\mathbf{v})\}, \tag{41}$$

where "Re(z)" means the real part of the complex number z.

Can we write this solution so that no i's occur? The answer is "Yes," but requires a little complex analysis. As we discuss in the Appendix of this book, any complex number $a + ib$ can be written in *polar coordinates* as

$$a + ib = \sqrt{a^2 + b^2}\left(\frac{a}{\sqrt{a^2 + b^2}} + i\frac{b}{\sqrt{a^2 + b^2}}\right)$$

$$= r \cdot (\cos\theta + i\sin\theta),$$

where $r = \sqrt{a^2 + b^2}$, $\cos\theta = a/r$, and $\sin\theta = b/r$. As Figure 23.2 illustrates, this is just the polar coordinate representation of the ordered pair (a, b) in the Cartesian plane.

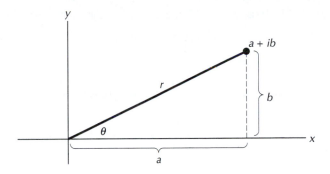

Writing a + ib in polar coordinates.

**Figure
23.2**

Powers of complex numbers are easily computed in polar coordinates. For example, using the formulas for $\cos 2\theta$ and $\sin 2\theta$,

$$(a + ib)^2 = r^2(\cos\theta + i\sin\theta)^2$$

$$= r^2[(\cos^2\theta - \sin^2\theta) + i2\cos\theta\sin\theta]$$

$$= r^2(\cos 2\theta + i\sin 2\theta).$$

If we continue in this manner, we find that an inductive proof, as in the Appendix of this book, leads to **DeMoivre's formula**:

$$(a + ib)^n = r^n(\cos n\theta + i\sin n\theta).$$

Apply DeMoivre's formula to solution (41) and then multiply it out:

$$\mathbf{z}_n = 2\mathrm{Re}[(c_1 + ic_2)r^n(\cos n\theta + i\sin n\theta)(\mathbf{u} + i\mathbf{v})]$$

$$= 2r^n\mathrm{Re}[((c_1\cos n\theta - c_2\sin n\theta) + i(c_2\cos n\theta + c_1\sin n\theta))(\mathbf{u} + i\mathbf{v})]$$

$$= 2r^n[(c_1\cos n\theta - c_2\sin n\theta)\mathbf{u} - (c_2\cos n\theta + c_1\sin n\theta)\mathbf{v}],$$

the general *real* solution of the *real* difference equation $\mathbf{z}_{n+1} = A\mathbf{z}_n$.

The following theorem summarizes these computations. Note that we have incorporated the 2 in the above expression with the general constants c_1 and c_2.

Theorem 23.14 Let A be a real 2×2 matrix with complex eigenvalues $\alpha^* \pm i\beta^*$ and corresponding complex eigenvectors $\mathbf{u}^* \pm i\mathbf{v}^*$. Write the eigenvalues $\alpha^* \pm i\beta^*$ in polar coordinates as $r^*(\cos\theta^* + i\sin\theta^*)$, where

$$r^* = \sqrt{\alpha^{*2} + \beta^{*2}} \quad \text{and} \quad (\cos\theta^*, \sin\theta^*) = \left(\frac{\alpha^*}{r^*}, \frac{\beta^*}{r^*}\right).$$

Then, the general solution of the difference equation $\mathbf{z}_{n+1} = A\mathbf{z}_n$ is

$$\mathbf{z}_n = r^{*n}[(C_1\cos n\theta^* - C_2\sin n\theta^*)\mathbf{u}^* - (C_2\cos n\theta^* + C_1\sin n\theta^*)\mathbf{v}^*]. \quad (42)$$

Example 23.18 In Example 23.17, we computed that the eigenvalues of $A = \begin{pmatrix} 1 & 1 \\ -9 & 1 \end{pmatrix}$ are $1 \pm 3i$ with corresponding eigenvectors $\begin{pmatrix} 1 \\ 0 \end{pmatrix} \pm i\begin{pmatrix} 0 \\ 3 \end{pmatrix}$. In polar coordinates,

$$1 + 3i = \sqrt{10}\left(\frac{1}{\sqrt{10}} + i\frac{3}{\sqrt{10}}\right) = \sqrt{10}\,(\cos\theta^* + i\sin\theta^*),$$

where $\theta^* = \arccos(1/\sqrt{10}) \approx 71.565°$ or 1.249 radians. The general solution of

$$x_{n+1} = x_n + y_n$$
$$y_{n+1} = -9x_n + y_n$$

is

$$\begin{pmatrix} x_n \\ y_n \end{pmatrix} = (\sqrt{10})^n\left[(c_1\cos n\theta^* - c_2\sin n\theta^*)\begin{pmatrix} 1 \\ 0 \end{pmatrix}\right.$$

$$\left. - (c_2\cos n\theta^* + c_1\sin n\theta^*)\begin{pmatrix} 0 \\ 3 \end{pmatrix}\right]$$

$$= (\sqrt{10})^n\begin{pmatrix} c_1\cos n\theta^* - c_2\sin n\theta^* \\ -3c_2\cos n\theta^* - 3c_1\sin n\theta^* \end{pmatrix}.$$

Higher Dimensions

In higher dimensions, a given matrix can have both real and complex eigenvalues. The solution of the corresponding system of difference equations is the obvious combination of the solutions described in Theorems 23.6 and 23.14.

Example 23.19 Consider the Leslie model of an organism that lives for three years, with death rates $d_1 = 0.2$, $d_2 = 0.6$, and $d_3 = 1$. Suppose that only third year individuals can reproduce, with birth rate $b_3 = 1.6$. The corresponding Leslie matrix is

$$\begin{pmatrix} 0 & 0 & 1.6 \\ 0.8 & 0 & 0 \\ 0 & 0.4 & 0 \end{pmatrix}. \tag{43}$$

Its characteristic polynomial is $p(r) = r^3 - 0.512$, with roots $r = 0.8$ and $-0.4 \pm i\sqrt{0.48}$.

An eigenvector for $r = 0.8$ is $\begin{pmatrix} 2 \\ 2 \\ 1 \end{pmatrix}$; an eigenvector for

$$r = -0.4 \mp i\sqrt{0.48} = -0.4\left(1 \pm i\sqrt{3}\right)$$

$$= -0.4\left(\cos\frac{\pi}{3} \pm i\sin\frac{\pi}{3}\right)$$

is
$$\begin{pmatrix} 1 \mp i\sqrt{3} \\ 1 \pm i\sqrt{3} \\ -1 \end{pmatrix} = \begin{pmatrix} 1 \\ 1 \\ -1 \end{pmatrix} \pm i \begin{pmatrix} -\sqrt{3} \\ +\sqrt{3} \\ 0 \end{pmatrix}.$$

The general solution of

$$\begin{pmatrix} x_{n+1} \\ y_{n+1} \\ z_{n+1} \end{pmatrix} = \begin{pmatrix} 0 & 0 & 1.6 \\ 0.8 & 0 & 0 \\ 0 & 0.4 & 0 \end{pmatrix} \begin{pmatrix} x_n \\ y_n \\ z_n \end{pmatrix}$$

is

$$\begin{pmatrix} x_n \\ y_n \\ z_n \end{pmatrix} = c_1 (0.8)^n \begin{pmatrix} 2 \\ 2 \\ 1 \end{pmatrix} + (-0.4)^n \left(c_1 \cos n\frac{\pi}{3} - c_2 \sin n\frac{\pi}{3} \right) \begin{pmatrix} 1 \\ 1 \\ -1 \end{pmatrix}$$

$$- (-0.4)^n \left(c_2 \cos n\frac{\pi}{3} + c_1 \sin n\frac{\pi}{3} \right) \begin{pmatrix} -\sqrt{3} \\ +\sqrt{3} \\ 0 \end{pmatrix}.$$

EXERCISES

23.27 Carry out all the computations in Example 23.19.

23.28 For each of the following matrices A, find the general solution of $\mathbf{x}_{n+1} = A\mathbf{x}_n$:

$$a) \begin{pmatrix} 3 & 5 \\ -2 & 1 \end{pmatrix}, \qquad b) \begin{pmatrix} 2 & 4 \\ -2 & -2 \end{pmatrix}, \qquad c) \begin{pmatrix} 2 & 5 \\ -1 & 0 \end{pmatrix},$$

$$d) \begin{pmatrix} 2 & -5 & 0 \\ 1 & -2 & -3 \\ 0 & 1 & 2 \end{pmatrix}, \qquad e) \begin{pmatrix} 2 & 1 & 0 \\ -5 & -2 & 1 \\ 0 & -3 & 2 \end{pmatrix}.$$

23.29 Verify equation (39).

23.6 MARKOV PROCESSES

In this section and the next two, we introduce two important applications of eigenvalues and eigenvectors to problems of economics: the solution of Markov processes and the determination of the definiteness of a quadratic form. At this point, our treatment will be brief and will cover only low-dimensional problems.

We will work in this section with a dynamic process in which time is treated as a discrete variable, so that the dynamics are given by difference equations.

Suppose that the process under study can be described by a finite number of states $S_1, \ldots, S_k$. In each period, the system is in one and only one of these k states.

Definition   A **stochastic process** is a rule which gives the probability that the system (or an individual in this system) will be in state i at time $n + 1$, given the probabilities of its being in the various states in previous periods. This probability could, in principle, depend on the whole previous history of the system, that is, on the states that existed at times $1, 2, \ldots, n$. When the probability that the system is in any state i at time $n + 1$ depends only on what state the system was in at time n, the stochastic process is called a **Markov process**. For a Markov process, only the *immediate past* matters.

The key elements of a Markov process are:

(1) the probability $x^i(n)$ that state i occurs at time period n, or alternatively, the fraction of the population under study that is in state i at time period n; and

(2) the **transition probabilities** m_{ij}, where m_{ij} is the probability that the process will be in state i at time $n + 1$ if it is in state j at time n.

It is natural to put the transition probabilities into a matrix which we call a **transition matrix**, a **stochastic matrix**, or a **Markov matrix**:

$$M = \begin{pmatrix} m_{11} & \cdots & m_{1k} \\ \vdots & \ddots & \vdots \\ m_{k1} & \cdots & m_{kk} \end{pmatrix}.$$

Notice that these probabilities are written so that the first subscript indexes the next period and the second subscript indexes the current period. In probabilistic terms, m_{ij} is the (conditional) probability that the system will be in state i next period, given that it was in state j this period. Given its state this period, the system moves into one and only one state next period. Therefore, the sum of the m_{ij}'s over i must equal 1; that is, the sum of the elements of each column of a Markov matrix must be 1. We define a **Markov matrix** to be any nonnegative matrix (m_{ij}) whose column sums $\sum_i m_{ij}$ all equal 1.

We are assuming that the probabilities m_{ij} are fixed and independent of n. To describe this assumption, we say that the process is *time-homogeneous* or that the transition probabilities are *stationary*.

To write out the underlying dynamics of a Markov process, suppose that $x^j(n)$ denotes the *fraction* of a population of size N that is in state j in time period n. Then, the *total* number of members of the population in state j in period n is $x^j(n)N$. By hypothesis, $m_{ij}x^j(n)N$ of these will be in state i in period $(n + 1)$. The total number of population members in state i in period $(n + 1)$, $x^i(n + 1)N$, is the sum over j of the numbers that move from j to i:

$$x^i(n + 1)N = \sum_{j=1}^{k} m_{ij}\, x^j(n)\, N,$$

or, in matrix notation, after dividing through by N,

$$\begin{pmatrix} x^1(n+1) \\ \vdots \\ x^k(n+1) \end{pmatrix} = \begin{pmatrix} m_{11} & \cdots & m_{1k} \\ \vdots & \ddots & \vdots \\ m_{k1} & \cdots & m_{kk} \end{pmatrix} \begin{pmatrix} x^1(n) \\ \vdots \\ x^k(n) \end{pmatrix}; \tag{44}$$

that is, $\qquad \mathbf{x}(n+1) = M\mathbf{x}(n).$

System of equations (44), in which M is a Markov matrix, is called a **Markov system** or **Markov process**.

Example 23.20 Consider the employment model of Section 6.2. In this model, each person in the population under study is either employed or unemployed. The two states of this model are employed and unemployed. Let $x^1(n)$ denote the fraction of the study population that is employed at the end of time period n and $x^2(n)$ denote the fraction unemployed. Suppose that an *employed* person has a 90 percent probability of staying employed for the next period (and, therefore, a 10 percent probability of being unemployed next period) and that an *unemployed* person has a 40 percent probability of being employed one period from now (and, therefore, a 60 percent chance of remaining unemployed). The corresponding dynamics are

$$x^1(n+1) = 0.9x^1(n) + 0.4x^2(n)$$

$$x^2(n+1) = 0.1x^1(n) + 0.6x^2(n),$$

or $\qquad \begin{pmatrix} x^1(n+1) \\ x^2(n+1) \end{pmatrix} = \begin{pmatrix} 0.9 & 0.4 \\ 0.1 & 0.6 \end{pmatrix} \begin{pmatrix} x^1(n) \\ x^2(n) \end{pmatrix}. \tag{45}$

By the argument of Example 23.4, one eigenvalue of system (45) is $r = 1$. By using the trace result of Theorem 23.9, we conclude that the other eigenvalue is $r = 1.5 - 1.0 = 0.5$.

To compute the corresponding eigenvectors, we solve

$$\begin{pmatrix} -0.1 & 0.4 \\ 0.1 & -0.4 \end{pmatrix} \begin{pmatrix} \alpha \\ \beta \end{pmatrix} = \begin{pmatrix} 0 \\ 0 \end{pmatrix} \quad \text{for} \quad \begin{pmatrix} \alpha \\ \beta \end{pmatrix} = \begin{pmatrix} 4 \\ 1 \end{pmatrix}$$

and $\qquad \begin{pmatrix} 0.4 & 0.4 \\ 0.1 & 0.1 \end{pmatrix} \begin{pmatrix} \alpha \\ \beta \end{pmatrix} = \begin{pmatrix} 0 \\ 0 \end{pmatrix} \quad \text{for} \quad \begin{pmatrix} \alpha \\ \beta \end{pmatrix} = \begin{pmatrix} 1 \\ -1 \end{pmatrix}.$

We conclude by Theorem 23.6 that the general solution of system (45) is

$$\begin{pmatrix} x^1(n) \\ x^2(n) \end{pmatrix} = c_1 \begin{pmatrix} 4 \\ 1 \end{pmatrix} \cdot 1^n + c_2 \begin{pmatrix} 1 \\ -1 \end{pmatrix} \cdot 0.5^n. \tag{46}$$

Since $1^n = 1$ and $0.5^n \to 0$ as $n \to \infty$, in the long-run, the solution (46) of the Markov system (45) tends to $\mathbf{w}_1 = c_1 \begin{pmatrix} 4 \\ 1 \end{pmatrix}$. Since $\mathbf{w}_1$ should be a probability vector whose components sum to 1, take c_1 to equal the reciprocal $1/5$ of the sum of the components of $\mathbf{w}_1$. We conclude that the solution of system (45) tends to $\begin{pmatrix} 0.8 \\ 0.2 \end{pmatrix}$ as $n \to \infty$, and that our assumptions lead to a long-run unemployment rate of 20 percent in this community.

There are a number of general principles about Markov processes that the analysis of this example illustrates:

(1) $r_1 = 1$ is always an eigenvalue of the underlying Markov matrix, as was argued in Example 23.4.

(2) For a 2×2 problem, the trace, which equals the sum of the eigenvalues by Theorem 23.9, lies between 0 and 2. Therefore, the second eigenvalue r_2 lies between -1 and $+1$.

(3) If each $a_{ii} < 1$, then the elements of $(A - 1I)$ have the sign pattern $\begin{pmatrix} - & + \\ + & - \end{pmatrix}$. Therefore, eigenvalue $r_1 = 1$ has an eigenvector $\mathbf{w}_1$ with all *positive* entries. This eigenvector can be made a probability vector $\mathbf{v}_1$ by dividing each component of $\mathbf{w}_1$ by the sum of the components of $\mathbf{w}_1$.

(4) The general solution is $1^n \mathbf{v}_1 + c_2 r_2^n \mathbf{v}_2$. Since $r_2^n \to 0$ as $n \to \infty$, every solution tends to $\mathbf{v}_1$. In particular, the components of $\mathbf{v}_1$ give the long-run distribution of the states under study.

These four properties hold for a large class of Markov processes — namely, processes in which the transition matrix, or at least some power of the transition matrix, has all of its entries strictly positive.

Definition   Let M be a Markov matrix, that is, a nonnegative matrix whose entries sum to 1. Then, M is called a **regular Markov matrix** if M^r has only positive entries for some integer r. If $r = 1$, that is, if every entry of M is positive, M is called a **positive matrix**.

Theorem 23.15   Let M be a regular Markov matrix. Then,

(*a*) 1 is an eigenvalue of M of multiplicity 1;

(*b*) every other eigenvalue r of M satisfies $|r| < 1$;

(*c*) eigenvalue 1 has an eigenvector $\mathbf{w}_1$ with strictly positive components; and

(*d*) if we write $\mathbf{v}_1$ for $\mathbf{w}_1$ divided by the sum of its components, then $\mathbf{v}_1$ is a probability vector and each of solution $\mathbf{x}(n)$ of $\mathbf{x}(n + 1) = M\mathbf{x}(n)$ tends to $\mathbf{v}_1$ as $n \to \infty$.

Actually, most of Theorem 23.15 holds for general positive or even regular matrices M — with arbitrary column sums. For such M, there is an eigenvalue r_1 (not necessarily equal to 1) such that r_1 is real, has multiplicity one, satisfies $r_1 > |r|$ for all the other eigenvalues r of M, and has a strictly positive eigenvector.

Example 23.21 Suppose that American families are classified as urban, suburban, or rural and that each year: 20 percent of the urban families move to the suburbs and 5 percent move to rural areas; 2 percent of the suburban dwellers move to urban areas and 8 percent move to rural areas; 10 percent of the rural families move to urban areas and 20 percent move to suburban areas.

Let U_n, S_n, and R_n denote the fractions of the population classified as urban, suburban, and rural, respectively, n years from now. Then, the data of this problem lead to the Markov system

$$\begin{pmatrix} U_{n+1} \\ S_{n+1} \\ R_{n+1} \end{pmatrix} = \begin{pmatrix} 0.75 & 0.02 & 0.1 \\ 0.2 & 0.9 & 0.2 \\ 0.05 & 0.08 & 0.7 \end{pmatrix} \begin{pmatrix} U_n \\ S_n \\ R_n \end{pmatrix} \tag{47}$$

The eigenvalues are this Markov matrix are 1, 0.7, and 0.65, and the corresponding eigenvectors are

$$\begin{pmatrix} 2/15 \\ 10/15 \\ 3/15 \end{pmatrix}, \quad \begin{pmatrix} 8 \\ -5 \\ -3 \end{pmatrix}, \quad \text{and} \quad \begin{pmatrix} 1 \\ 0 \\ -1 \end{pmatrix},$$

where the eigenvector for $r = 1$ has been normalized so that its components sum to 1. The general solution of (47) is

$$\begin{pmatrix} U_n \\ S_n \\ R_n \end{pmatrix} = \begin{pmatrix} 2/15 \\ 10/15 \\ 3/15 \end{pmatrix} + c_2 \begin{pmatrix} 8 \\ -5 \\ -3 \end{pmatrix} 0.7^n + c_3 \begin{pmatrix} 1 \\ 0 \\ -1 \end{pmatrix} 0.65^n,$$

which converges to $(2/15, 10/15, 3/15)$ as $n \to \infty$. We conclude that in the long-run 2/15 of the population will be living in cities, 2/3 in the suburbs, and 1/5 in rural areas.

The analysis is a little different if the underlying Markov matrix is not regular. For example, if there exist states i such that $m_{ii} = 1$ — so that once the system reaches state i, it will never leave it — state i is called an **absorbing state**. When a Markov system has one or more absorbing states, the underlying process will eventually reach one of these states and then stay there forever. In fact, one can use the Markov matrix M to calculate the probabilities that any given initial condition will eventually end up in any given absorbing state and to compute the expected number of time steps that this absorption process will take.

EXERCISES

23.30 Write out the general solution of the Markov process for each of the following matrices:

a) $\begin{pmatrix} 0.7 & 0.5 \\ 0.3 & 0.5 \end{pmatrix}$ b) $\begin{pmatrix} 1 & 0.5 \\ 0 & 0.5 \end{pmatrix}$, c) $\begin{pmatrix} 0 & 0.5 & 1 \\ 1 & 0 & 0 \\ 0 & 0.5 & 0 \end{pmatrix}$.

23.31   What are the underlying long-run unemployment rates for the two unemployment Markov models in Section 6.2?

23.32   Show that if **x** is a probability vector and M is a Markov matrix, then $M\mathbf{x}$ is a probability vector.

23.33   Suppose that the weather in Ann Arbor in July can be characterized as sunny, rainy, or cloudy (with no rain). By looking up back issues of the *Ann Arbor News,* we estimate that if it is sunny on a July day, it is equally likely to be sunny or cloudy on the next day, but it won't rain. If a July day is cloudy, there is a 50 percent chance that it will rain on the next day, a 25 percent chance that it will be sunny, and a 25 percent chance that it will remain cloudy without rain. If it rains on a July day, it won't be sunny the next day, and there is a 50-50 chance of continued rain.

a) Write out the corresponding Markov system.

b) Show that the underlying matrix is regular.

c) What is the long-run distribution of weathers for July dates?

d) Write out the general solution of the underlying system of difference equations.

23.34   Consider a stock market with two stocks A and B. Stock A always sells for $5 or $10; stock B always sells for $6 or $12. If stock A is selling for $5 today, there is a 75 percent chance it will sell for $5 tomorrow. If stock A is selling for $10 today, there is a 90 percent chance that it will sell for $10 tomorrow. If stock B is selling for $6 today, there is a 90 percent chance that it will sell for $6 tomorrow. If stock B is selling for $12 today, there is a 70 percent chance it will sell for $12 tomorrow. Compute and compare the average costs of stocks A and B. The hypothesis that stock market prices follow a Markov process is one form of the **efficient market hypothesis**.

23.35   Show that the Leslie matrix in Example 23.7 is a regular nonnegative matrix and that it satisfies the conclusions listed under the statement of Theorem 23.15.

23.36   Show that the Leslie matrix (43) is not regular. Which of the conclusions listed under the statement of Theorem 23.15 does it satisfy and which does it not satisfy?

23.7   SYMMETRIC MATRICES

Economic analysis draws from two key mathematical areas: optimization theory and statistics. Matrices play a major role in both of these areas; for example, as Hessians and bordered Hessians in the second order conditions of optimization problems and as covariance matrices and information matrices in econometrics.

Most of the square matrices that arise in optimization and in econometrics — including the examples just mentioned — are *symmetric* matrices. There are plenty of economists who work only with symmetric matrices and whose work relies heavily on the eigenvalues and eigenvectors of the symmetric matrices involved. The fortunate fact about symmetric matrices is that the two pitfalls that can complicate work with eigenvalues of a general real matrix do not occur for symmetric matrices. First, symmetric matrices have only *real* eigenvalues; complex eigenvalues never occur. Second, symmetric matrices always have enough independent eigenvectors to diagonalize the matrix; one need never deal with generalized eigenvectors. There is even more: the eigenvectors of symmetric matrices are, in a sense, naturally orthogonal to each other. The following theorem summarizes the special properties that make symmetric matrices simpler to work with.

Theorem 23.16 Let A be a $k \times k$ symmetric matrix. Then,

(a) all k roots of the characteristic equation $\det(A - rI) = 0$ are *real* numbers;

(b) eigenvectors corresponding to distinct eigenvalues are orthogonal; and

(c) even if A has multiple eigenvalues, there is a nonsingular matrix P whose columns $\mathbf{w}_1, \ldots, \mathbf{w}_k$ are eigenvectors of A such that

(i) $\mathbf{w}_1, \ldots, \mathbf{w}_k$ are mutually orthogonal to each other,

(ii) $P^{-1} = P^T$, and

(iii) $P^{-1}AP = P^T AP = \begin{pmatrix} r_1 & 0 & \cdots & 0 \\ 0 & r_2 & \cdots & 0 \\ \vdots & \vdots & \ddots & \vdots \\ 0 & 0 & \cdots & r_k \end{pmatrix}.$

Definition A matrix P which satisfies the condition $P^{-1} = P^T$ of *iii*, or equivalently, $P^T P = I$, is called an **orthogonal matrix**.

Proof The complete proof of Theorem 23.16 requires a bit of complex analysis. To give the reader a better feeling for the meaning of Theorem 23.16, we will present a careful proof for 2×2 matrices. As Exercise 23.41 points out, much of this proof can be generalized to larger matrices.

First, we show that a 2×2 symmetric matrix has only real eigenvalues and is always diagonalizable. Write the general 2×2 *symmetric* matrix as

$$A = \begin{pmatrix} a & b \\ b & d \end{pmatrix}.$$

The characteristic polynomial of A is

$$p(r) = \det(A - rI)$$

$$= (a - r)(d - r) - b^2$$

$$= r^2 - (a + d)r + (ad - b^2).$$

By the quadratic formula, its roots are

$$r = \frac{1}{2}\left[(a + d) \pm \sqrt{(a + d)^2 - 4(ad - b^2)}\right]$$

$$= \frac{1}{2}\left[(a + d) \pm \sqrt{a^2 + 2ad + d^2 - 4ad + 4b^2}\right] \qquad (48)$$

$$= \frac{1}{2}\left[(a + d) \pm \sqrt{(a - d)^2 + 4b^2}\right].$$

Let $\Delta \equiv (a - d)^2 + 4b^2$ be the expression under the square root sign in (48). Since $\Delta \geq 0$, p has no complex roots. Furthermore, its roots are equal if and only if $\Delta = 0$. Since Δ is a sum of two nonnegative terms, $\Delta = 0$ if and only if each of these terms equals zero:

$$(a - d)^2 = 0 \quad \text{and} \quad 4b^2 = 0,$$

that is, if and only if $a = d$ and $b = 0$. In this case, A is a multiple of the identity matrix:

$$A = \begin{pmatrix} a & 0 \\ 0 & a \end{pmatrix} = aI.$$

A is not only diagonalizable; it's already diagonal.

To prove part b, let r_1 and r_2 be distinct (real) eigenvalues of symmetric matrix A with corresponding eigenvectors $\mathbf{v}_1$ and $\mathbf{v}_2$. We want to show that $\mathbf{v}_1 \cdot \mathbf{v}_2 = 0$, or in matrix notation, $\mathbf{v}_1^T \mathbf{v}_2 = 0$. On the one hand,

$$\mathbf{v}_1^T(A\mathbf{v}_2) = \mathbf{v}_1^T(r_2\mathbf{v}_2) = r_2(\mathbf{v}_1^T\mathbf{v}_2).$$

On the other hand, since $A^T = A$,

$$\mathbf{v}_1^T A\mathbf{v}_2 = \mathbf{v}_1^T A^T \mathbf{v}_2 = (A\mathbf{v}_1)^T \mathbf{v}_2 = (r_1\mathbf{v}_1)^T \mathbf{v}_2 = r_1(\mathbf{v}_1^T\mathbf{v}_2).$$

Since $r_1(\mathbf{v}_1^T\mathbf{v}_2) = r_2(\mathbf{v}_1^T\mathbf{v}_2)$ and $r_1 \neq r_2$, $\mathbf{v}_1^T\mathbf{v}_2 = \mathbf{v}_1 \cdot \mathbf{v}_2 = 0$; that is, $\mathbf{v}_1$ and $\mathbf{v}_2$ are orthogonal.

To prove parts ii and iii, suppose that $\mathbf{v}_1$ and $\mathbf{v}_2$ are mutually orthogonal eigenvectors of the symmetric matrix A. Then, by Exercise 23.39, $\mathbf{v}_1$ and $\mathbf{v}_2$ are linearly independent. Normalize each of these eigenvectors so that its length is 1: $\mathbf{w}_i = \mathbf{v}_i / \|\mathbf{v}_i\|$. The vectors $\mathbf{w}_1$ and $\mathbf{w}_2$ are scalar multiples of the eigenvectors $\mathbf{v}_1$ and $\mathbf{v}_2$ and therefore are still eigenvectors of A, but now with the property that

$$\mathbf{w}_i \cdot \mathbf{w}_j = \begin{cases} 1, & \text{if } i = j; \\ 0, & \text{if } i \neq j. \end{cases}$$

Let $P = [\mathbf{w}_1 \mathbf{w}_2]$. Then,

$$P^T P = \begin{pmatrix} \mathbf{w}_1 \\ \mathbf{w}_2 \end{pmatrix} (\mathbf{w}_1 \quad \mathbf{w}_2)$$

$$= \begin{pmatrix} \mathbf{w}_1 \cdot \mathbf{w}_1 & \mathbf{w}_1 \cdot \mathbf{w}_2 \\ \mathbf{w}_2 \cdot \mathbf{w}_1 & \mathbf{w}_2 \cdot \mathbf{w}_2 \end{pmatrix}$$

$$= \begin{pmatrix} 1 & 0 \\ 0 & 1 \end{pmatrix} = I.$$

Since $P^T P = I, P^T = P^{-1}$ by the uniqueness of the inverse (Theorem 8.5). Furthermore, by Theorem 23.5, since P is a matrix whose columns are independent eigenvectors of A, $P^T AP = P^{-1}AP$ is diagonal. ∎

Example 23.22 The eigenvalues of the symmetric matrix

$$B = \begin{pmatrix} 3 & 1 & -1 \\ 1 & 3 & -1 \\ -1 & -1 & 5 \end{pmatrix}$$

are $r_1 = 2, r_2 = 3$, and $r_3 = 6$. Corresponding eigenvectors are

$$\mathbf{v}_1 = \begin{pmatrix} -1 \\ 1 \\ 0 \end{pmatrix}, \quad \mathbf{v}_2 = \begin{pmatrix} 1 \\ 1 \\ 1 \end{pmatrix}, \quad \text{and} \quad \mathbf{v}_3 = \begin{pmatrix} 1 \\ 1 \\ -2 \end{pmatrix}.$$

As Theorem 23.16 indicates, these three vectors are perpendicular to each other. Divide each eigenvector by its length to generate a set of "normalized eigenvectors":

$$\mathbf{u}_1 = \frac{1}{\sqrt{2}} \begin{pmatrix} -1 \\ 1 \\ 0 \end{pmatrix}, \mathbf{u}_2 = \frac{1}{\sqrt{3}} \begin{pmatrix} 1 \\ 1 \\ 1 \end{pmatrix}, \quad \text{and} \quad \mathbf{u}_3 = \frac{1}{\sqrt{6}} \begin{pmatrix} 1 \\ 1 \\ -2 \end{pmatrix},$$

and make these three **orthonormal vectors** — vectors which are orthogonal and have length 1 — the columns of the orthogonal matrix

$$Q = \begin{pmatrix} -1/\sqrt{2} & 1/\sqrt{3} & 1/\sqrt{6} \\ 1/\sqrt{2} & 1/\sqrt{3} & 1/\sqrt{6} \\ 0 & 1/\sqrt{3} & -2/\sqrt{6} \end{pmatrix}. \tag{49}$$

Then, $Q^{-1} = Q^T$ (check) and

$$Q^T BQ = \begin{pmatrix} 2 & 0 & 0 \\ 0 & 3 & 0 \\ 0 & 0 & 6 \end{pmatrix}. \tag{50}$$

Example 23.23 Let's diagonalize a symmetric matrix with nondistinct eigenvalues. Consider the 4×4 symmetric matrix

$$C = \begin{pmatrix} 3 & 1 & 1 & 1 \\ 1 & 3 & 1 & 1 \\ 1 & 1 & 3 & 1 \\ 1 & 1 & 1 & 3 \end{pmatrix}.$$

By the methods of Section 23.3, the eigenvalues of C are, by inspection, 2, 2, 2, and 6. The set of eigenvectors for 2, the eigenspace of eigenvector 2, is the three-dimensional nullspace of the matrix

$$C - 2I = \begin{pmatrix} 1 & 1 & 1 & 1 \\ 1 & 1 & 1 & 1 \\ 1 & 1 & 1 & 1 \\ 1 & 1 & 1 & 1 \end{pmatrix},$$

the space of $\{(u_1, u_2, u_3, u_4) : u_1 + u_2 + u_3 + u_4 = 0\}$. Three independent vectors in this eigenspace are

$$\mathbf{v}_1 = \begin{pmatrix} -1 \\ 1 \\ 0 \\ 0 \end{pmatrix}, \quad \mathbf{v}_2 = \begin{pmatrix} -1 \\ 0 \\ 1 \\ 0 \end{pmatrix}, \quad \text{and} \quad \mathbf{v}_3 = \begin{pmatrix} -1 \\ 0 \\ 0 \\ 1 \end{pmatrix}. \tag{51}$$

In order to construct an *orthogonal* matrix P so that the product $P^T C P = P^{-1} C P$ is diagonal, we need to find three orthogonal vectors $\mathbf{w}_1$, $\mathbf{w}_2$, and $\mathbf{w}_3$ which span the same subspace as the independent vectors $\mathbf{v}_1$, $\mathbf{v}_2$, and $\mathbf{v}_3$. The following procedure, called the **Gram-Schmidt Orthogonalization Process**, will accomplish this task. Let $\mathbf{w}_1 = \mathbf{v}_1$. Define

$$\mathbf{w}_2 = \mathbf{v}_2 - \frac{\mathbf{w}_1 \cdot \mathbf{v}_2}{\mathbf{w}_1 \cdot \mathbf{w}_1} \mathbf{w}_1,$$

$$\mathbf{w}_3 = \mathbf{v}_3 - \frac{\mathbf{w}_1 \cdot \mathbf{v}_3}{\mathbf{w}_1 \cdot \mathbf{w}_1} \mathbf{w}_1 - \frac{\mathbf{w}_2 \cdot \mathbf{v}_3}{\mathbf{w}_2 \cdot \mathbf{w}_2} \mathbf{w}_2, \qquad \text{and so on.}$$

The $\mathbf{w}_i$'s so constructed are mutually orthogonal. (Exercise.) By construction, $\mathbf{w}_1$, $\mathbf{w}_2$, and $\mathbf{w}_3$ span the same space as $\mathbf{v}_1$, $\mathbf{v}_2$, and $\mathbf{v}_3$. The application of this process to the eigenvectors $\mathbf{v}_1$, $\mathbf{v}_2$, and $\mathbf{v}_3$ in (51) yields the orthogonal vectors

$$\mathbf{w}_1 = \begin{pmatrix} -1 \\ 1 \\ 0 \\ 0 \end{pmatrix}, \quad \mathbf{w}_2 = \begin{pmatrix} -1/2 \\ -1/2 \\ 1 \\ 0 \end{pmatrix}, \quad \text{and} \quad \mathbf{w}_3 = \begin{pmatrix} -1/3 \\ -1/3 \\ -1/3 \\ 1 \end{pmatrix}. \tag{52}$$

Finally, normalize these three vectors and make them the first three columns of an orthogonal matrix whose fourth column is the normalized eigenvector for $r = 6$:

$$Q = \begin{pmatrix} -1/\sqrt{2} & -1/\sqrt{6} & -1/\sqrt{12} & 1/2 \\ 1/\sqrt{2} & -1/\sqrt{6} & -1/\sqrt{12} & 1/2 \\ 0 & 2/\sqrt{6} & -1/\sqrt{12} & 1/2 \\ 0 & 0 & 3/\sqrt{12} & 1/2 \end{pmatrix}. \tag{53}$$

Check that $Q^T = Q^{-1}$ and

$$Q^T CQ = \begin{pmatrix} 2 & 0 & 0 & 0 \\ 0 & 2 & 0 & 0 \\ 0 & 0 & 2 & 0 \\ 0 & 0 & 0 & 6 \end{pmatrix}. \tag{54}$$

EXERCISES

23.37 For each of the following symmetric matrices, find an orthogonal matrix which diagonalizes it:

a) $\begin{pmatrix} 2 & 4 \\ 4 & 2 \end{pmatrix}$,
  b) $\begin{pmatrix} 4 & 2 \\ 2 & 1 \end{pmatrix}$
  c) $\begin{pmatrix} 0.6 & 0.4 \\ 0.4 & 0.6 \end{pmatrix}$,

d) $A = \begin{pmatrix} 2 & 1 & 1 \\ 1 & 1 & 0 \\ 1 & 0 & 1 \end{pmatrix}$,
  e) $\begin{pmatrix} 2 & -1 & -1 \\ -1 & 2 & -1 \\ -1 & -1 & 2 \end{pmatrix}$,
  f) $\begin{pmatrix} 2 & 0 & -1 \\ 0 & 4 & 0 \\ -1 & 0 & 2 \end{pmatrix}$.

23.38 For each of the following symmetric matrices A, find a matrix Q such that $Q^{-1} = Q^T$ and $Q^T AQ$ is diagonal.

a) $\begin{pmatrix} 2 & 1 \\ 1 & 2 \end{pmatrix}$,
  b) $\begin{pmatrix} 1 & 3 \\ 3 & 1 \end{pmatrix}$,
  c) $\begin{pmatrix} 2 & -1 & -1 \\ -1 & 2 & -1 \\ -1 & -1 & 2 \end{pmatrix}$.

23.39 Prove that if k nonzero vectors are mutually orthogonal, they are linearly independent.

23.40 Prove that the determinant of an orthogonal matrix is ± 1.

23.41 Show that the arguments in the proof of part c of Theorem 23.16 carry over to k orthogonal vectors.

23.42 Check that the matrices (49) and (53) satisfy $Q^T Q = I$.

23.43 Verify equations (50) and (54).

23.44 Verify that the use of the Gram-Schmidt orthogonalization process in Example 23.23 leads to the three vectors in (52).

23.45 Verify that, in general, the vectors produced by the Gram-Schmidt orthogonalization process are indeed mutually orthogonal.

23.46 In some statistical applications, given two symmetric matrices A and B, one would like to diagonalize them simultaneously, that is, to find a single orthogonal matrix P so that $P^T AP$ and $P^T BP$ are both diagonal. Use Theorem 23.16 to prove that if this simultaneous diagonalization is possible, then A and B commute.

23.8 DEFINITENESS OF QUADRATIC FORMS

We described the close relationship between symmetric matrices and quadratic forms in Chapter 16; for every quadratic form $Q(\mathbf{x})$ there is a symmetric matrix A such that $Q(\mathbf{x}) = \mathbf{x}^T A \mathbf{x}$, and every symmetric matrix A yields a quadratic form $Q(\mathbf{x}) = \mathbf{x}^T A \mathbf{x}$.

In general, matrices and quadratic forms behave differently under changes of coordinates P. Let $\mathbf{x} = P\mathbf{y}$ be a linear change of coordinates, as in (14). As we saw in Section 2, in the new coordinate system $\mathbf{y}$, the matrix A is transformed to the matrix $P^{-1}AP$. However, in terms of the $\mathbf{y}$'s, the quadratic form

$$\mathbf{x} \longmapsto Q(\mathbf{x}) = \mathbf{x}^T A \mathbf{x}$$

becomes the quadratic form

$$\mathbf{y} \longmapsto Q(P\mathbf{y}) = (P\mathbf{y})^T A (P\mathbf{y}) = \mathbf{y}^T (P^T A P) \mathbf{y}.$$

The matrix that represents quadratic form Q in the $\mathbf{y}$ coordinates is $P^T A P$. In one case, we have $P^{-1}AP$; in the other, we have $P^T A P$. However, since A is a symmetric matrix, Theorem 23.16 assures us that we can find a change of coordinates matrix P so that $P^{-1} = P^T$ and, therefore, $P^{-1}AP = P^T A P$. In fact, it is this connection to quadratic forms which motivates our requirement that $P^{-1} = P^T$ for the change of coordinate matrix for symmetric matrices.

At this point, it should come as no surprise that the definiteness of a quadratic form $Q(\mathbf{x}) = \mathbf{x}^T A \mathbf{x}$ is closely tied to the signs of the eigenvalues of A, as the following theorem asserts. Recall that we say that the symmetric matrix A is positive definite, negative definite, indefinite, etc., according to whether the corresponding quadratic form $Q(\mathbf{x}) = \mathbf{x}^T A \mathbf{x}$ is positive definite, negative definite, etc.

Theorem 23.17   Let A be a symmetric matrix. Then,

(a) A is positive definite if and only if all the eigenvalues of A are > 0;
(b) A is negative definite if and only if all the eigenvalues of A are < 0;
(c) A is positive semidefinite if and only if all the eigenvalues of A are ≥ 0;
(d) A is negative semidefinite if and only if all the eigenvalues of A are ≤ 0; and
(e) A is indefinite if and only if A has a positive eigenvalue and a negative eigenvalue.

Proof   Let P be an orthogonal matrix so that

$$P^{-1}AP = P^T A P = \begin{pmatrix} r_1 & \cdots & 0 \\ \vdots & \ddots & \vdots \\ 0 & \cdots & r_k \end{pmatrix}.$$

Let $\mathbf{x}$ be an arbitrary nonzero vector in $\mathbf{R}^k$, and let $\mathbf{y} = P^{-1}\mathbf{x} = P^T\mathbf{x}$. Then, $\mathbf{y}$ is nonzero, and

$$\mathbf{x}^T A \mathbf{x} = \mathbf{y}^T P^T A P \mathbf{y}$$

$$= \mathbf{y}^T \begin{pmatrix} r_1 & \cdots & 0 \\ \vdots & \ddots & \vdots \\ 0 & \cdots & r_k \end{pmatrix} \mathbf{y} \tag{55}$$

$$= r_1 y_1^2 + \cdots + r_k y_k^2,$$

where at least one of the y_i^2 is positive. If all the r_i's are positive, then $\mathbf{x}^T A \mathbf{x} > 0$ and A is positive definite. If all the r_i's are ≥ 0, then $\mathbf{x}^T A \mathbf{x} \geq 0$ and A is positive semidefinite.

If $r_1 > 0$ and $r_2 < 0$, for example, let $\mathbf{e}_1 = (1, 0, \ldots, 0)^T$ and $\mathbf{e}_2 = (0, 1, \ldots, 0)^T$. Let $\mathbf{x}_1 = P\mathbf{e}_1$ and $\mathbf{x}_2 = P\mathbf{e}_2$. Then,

$$\mathbf{x}_1^T A \mathbf{x}_1 = \mathbf{e}_1^T P^T A P \mathbf{e}_1 = r_1 > 0,$$

and $$\mathbf{x}_2^T A \mathbf{x}_2 = \mathbf{e}_2^T P^T A P \mathbf{e}_2 = r_2 < 0,$$

and A is indefinite. Conversely, if A is indefinite, there must be a positive r_i and a negative r_j in (55); that is, A has a positive eigenvalue and a negative eigenvalue. ∎

The following characterizations of positive definiteness are important in statistics and econometrics, e.g., in principal component analysis.

Theorem 23.18   Let A be a symmetric matrix. Then, the following are equivalent:

(a) A is positive definite.
(b) There exists a nonsingular matrix B so that $A = B^T B$.
(c) There exists a nonsingular matrix Q such that $Q^T A Q = I$.

Proof   Since A is a symmetric matrix, we can write

$$P^T A P = \begin{pmatrix} r_1 & \cdots & 0 \\ \vdots & \ddots & \vdots \\ 0 & \cdots & r_k \end{pmatrix}, \tag{56}$$

or

$$A = P \begin{pmatrix} r_1 & \cdots & 0 \\ \vdots & \ddots & \vdots \\ 0 & \cdots & r_k \end{pmatrix} P^T, \tag{57}$$

where $r_1, \ldots, r_k$ are eigenvalues of A, and $P = (\mathbf{v}_1 \cdots \mathbf{v}_k)$ is a matrix of independent eigenvectors of A.

$a \Longrightarrow b$: If A is positive definite, then the eigenvalues $r_1, \ldots, r_k$ in (56) and (57) are positive. Let

$$
B = \begin{pmatrix} \sqrt{r_1} & \cdots & 0 \\ \vdots & \ddots & \vdots \\ 0 & \cdots & \sqrt{r_k} \end{pmatrix} P^T.
$$

Then, by (57),

$$
B^T B = P \begin{pmatrix} \sqrt{r_1} & \cdots & 0 \\ \vdots & \ddots & \vdots \\ 0 & \cdots & \sqrt{r_k} \end{pmatrix}^T \begin{pmatrix} \sqrt{r_1} & \cdots & 0 \\ \vdots & \ddots & \vdots \\ 0 & \cdots & \sqrt{r_k} \end{pmatrix} P^T = A.
$$

$b \Longrightarrow a$: On the other hand, if $A = B^T B$ for a nonsingular matrix B, then for any nonzero $\mathbf{x}$ in $\mathbf{R}^k$,

$$
\mathbf{x}^T A \mathbf{x} = \mathbf{x}^T B^T B \mathbf{x} = \|B\mathbf{x}\|^2 > 0,
$$

since, by the nonsingularity of B, $B\mathbf{x} \neq \mathbf{0}$.

$a \Longrightarrow c$: Suppose that A is positive definite, so that the eigenvalues $r_1, \ldots, r_k$ in (56) are positive. Let

$$
Q = \left(\frac{1}{\sqrt{r_1}} \mathbf{v}_1 \cdots \frac{1}{\sqrt{r_k}} \mathbf{v}_k \right) = P \begin{pmatrix} \dfrac{1}{\sqrt{r_1}} & \cdots & 0 \\ \vdots & \ddots & \vdots \\ 0 & \cdots & \dfrac{1}{\sqrt{r_k}} \end{pmatrix}. \tag{58}
$$

Then, (56) and (58) imply that $Q^T A Q = I$. (Check.)

$c \Longrightarrow a$: Conversely, if c holds, let $\mathbf{x}$ be an arbitrary nonzero vector and let $\mathbf{y} = P^{-1}\mathbf{x}$. Then,

$$
\mathbf{x}^T A \mathbf{x} = (Q\mathbf{y})^T A (Q\mathbf{y}) = \mathbf{y}^T (Q^T A Q) \mathbf{y}
$$
$$
= \mathbf{y}^T I \mathbf{y} = \mathbf{y}^T \mathbf{y} = \|\mathbf{y}\|^2
$$
$$
> 0,
$$

and A is positive definite. ∎

EXERCISES

23.47 There are actually 10 assertions in the statement of Theorem 23.17; we have proved 4 of them. Prove the other 6.

23.48 If A and B are positive definite symmetric matrices, prove that $A + B$ is too.

23.49 State and prove the negative definite and the positive semidefinite versions of Theorem 23.18.

23.50 Show that matrix B in Theorem 23.18 is not unique.

23.51 Fill in the details of the proof of $a \Longrightarrow c$ in Theorem 23.18. Where does this proof use the fact that A is positive definite?

23.52 Show that given any symmetric matrix A, there is a scalar t so that $A + tI$ is positive definite.

23.9 APPENDIX

In this Appendix, we prove some of the theorems of Chapter 23, whose proofs were postponed for the sake of the flow of exposition. We begin with the theorem that distinct eigenvalues lead to linearly independent eigenvectors.

Proof of Theorem 23.5

Theorem 23.5 Let $r_1, \ldots, r_h$ be h *distinct* eigenvalues of the $k \times k$ matrix A. Let $\mathbf{v}_1, \ldots, \mathbf{v}_h$ be corresponding eigenvectors. Then, $\mathbf{v}_1, \ldots, \mathbf{v}_h$ are linearly independent; that is, no one of them can be written as a linear combination of the others.

Proof We first prove this theorem for $h = 2$. Suppose that $\mathbf{v}_1$ and $\mathbf{v}_2$ are eigenvectors of A corresponding to the distinct eigenvalues r_1 and r_2:

$$A\mathbf{v}_1 = r_1\mathbf{v}_1 \quad \text{and} \quad A\mathbf{v}_2 = r_2\mathbf{v}_2. \tag{59}$$

To prove that $\mathbf{v}_1$ and $\mathbf{v}_2$ are linearly independent, we show that the only combination in which $\mathbf{v}_1$ and $\mathbf{v}_2$ add to $\mathbf{0}$ is the zero combination:

$$c_1\mathbf{v}_1 + c_2\mathbf{v}_2 = \mathbf{0} \quad \Longrightarrow \quad c_1 = 0 \quad \text{and} \quad c_2 = 0.$$

Suppose that some combination of $\mathbf{v}_1$ and $\mathbf{v}_2$ gives $\mathbf{0}$:

$$c_1\mathbf{v}_1 + c_2\mathbf{v}_2 = \mathbf{0}. \tag{60}$$

Multiply both sides of equation (60) by the matrix A:

$$A(c_1\mathbf{v}_1 + c_2\mathbf{v}_2) = A(\mathbf{0})$$
$$c_1A\mathbf{v}_1 + c_2A\mathbf{v}_2 = \mathbf{0} \tag{61}$$
$$c_1r_1\mathbf{v}_1 + c_2r_2\mathbf{v}_2 = \mathbf{0}$$

by (59). Multiply both sides of equation (60) by $-r_1$ and add the result to the last equation in (61):

$$c_2(r_2 - r_1)\mathbf{v}_2 = \mathbf{0}.$$

Since $\mathbf{v}_2 \neq \mathbf{0}$ and $r_2 - r_1 \neq 0$, c_2 must be zero. Plugging $c_2 = 0$ back into equation (60) yields $c_1 = 0$ too. Since the only combination of $\mathbf{v}_1$ and $\mathbf{v}_2$ that yields $\mathbf{0}$ is the zero combination, $\mathbf{v}_1$ and $\mathbf{v}_2$ are linearly independent.

Next, using the fact that any *pair* $\mathbf{v}_1$ and $\mathbf{v}_2$ of eigenvectors of A corresponding to distinct eigenvalues is independent, we show that the same holds for every *triple* $\mathbf{v}_1$, $\mathbf{v}_2$, and $\mathbf{v}_3$ of eigenvectors corresponding to distinct eigenvalues. Once again, we want to show that

$$c_1\mathbf{v}_1 + c_2\mathbf{v}_2 + c_3\mathbf{v}_3 = \mathbf{0} \implies c_1 = c_2 = c_3 = 0.$$

So, suppose that

$$c_1\mathbf{v}_1 + c_2\mathbf{v}_2 + c_3\mathbf{v}_3 = \mathbf{0}. \tag{62}$$

Apply A to both sides of equation (62):

$$\begin{aligned} c_1 A\mathbf{v}_1 + c_2 A\mathbf{v}_2 + c_3 A\mathbf{v}_3 &= \mathbf{0} \\ c_1 r_1\mathbf{v}_1 + c_2 r_2\mathbf{v}_2 + c_3 r_3\mathbf{v}_3 &= \mathbf{0}, \end{aligned} \tag{63}$$

since the $\mathbf{v}_i$'s are eigenvectors. Multiply (62) through by $-r_3$ and add the result to the last equation of (63):

$$c_1(r_1 - r_3)\mathbf{v}_1 + c_2(r_2 - r_3)\mathbf{v}_2 = \mathbf{0}.$$

By hypothesis $r_1 - r_3 \neq 0$, $r_2 - r_3 \neq 0$, and $\mathbf{v}_1$ and $\mathbf{v}_2$ are linearly independent. Therefore, $c_1 = c_2 = 0$; by (62), $c_3 = 0$ too. Therefore, $\mathbf{v}_1$, $\mathbf{v}_2$, and $\mathbf{v}_3$ are linearly independent.

Continuing in this way, one proves the theorem for arbitrary h: the only combination of h eigenvectors (corresponding to distinct eigenvalues) which adds to zero is the zero combination; that is, $\mathbf{v}_1, \ldots, \mathbf{v}_h$ are linearly independent. ∎

Proof of Theorem 23.9

In Section 23.3, we presented the two-dimensional proof of the following theorem. Here we sketch the proof for general k.

Theorem 23.9 Let A be a $k \times k$ matrix with eigenvalues $r_1, \ldots, r_k$.

(a) $r_1 + r_2 + \cdots + r_k = $ trace of A, and
(b) $r_1 \cdot r_2 \cdots r_k = \det A$.

Proof   Since $r_1, \ldots, r_k$ are the k roots of the kth order polynomial $p_A(r)$, we can recover the characteristic polynomial $p_A(r)$ of A as

$$p_A(r) = \beta(r_1 - r)(r_2 - r) \cdots (r_k - r), \tag{64}$$

where β is some constant. If we multiply this out, we find that the coefficient of r^k is $(-1)^k \beta$, the coefficient of r^{k-1} is

$$(-1)^{k-1} \beta(r_1 + r_2 + \cdots + r_k) \tag{65}$$

and the constant term is $\beta \cdot r_1 \cdot r_2 \cdots r_k$.

Now, write $p_A(r)$ in the usual way as

$$p_A(r) = \det \begin{pmatrix} a_{11} - r & a_{12} & \cdots & a_{1k} \\ a_{21} & a_{22} - r & \cdots & a_{2k} \\ \vdots & \vdots & \ddots & \vdots \\ a_{k1} & a_{k2} & \cdots & a_{kk} - r \end{pmatrix}. \tag{66}$$

By an inductive argument, one can prove that

$$p_A(r) = (a_{11} - r)(a_{22} - r) \cdots (a_{kk} - r)$$
$$+ \text{ terms of order strictly less than } (k-1) \text{ in } r. \tag{67}$$

It follows that the coefficient of r^k in (66) is $(-1)^k$ and the coefficient of r^{k-1} in (66) is

$$(-1)^{k-1}(a_{11} + a_{22} + \cdots + a_{kk}). \tag{68}$$

The constant term in (66) is simply $p_A(0) = \det A$.

Comparing the coefficients of r^k in these two approaches, we find that $\beta = 1$. Comparing (65) and (68), the coefficients of r^{k-1}, and using $\beta = 1$, we find that

$$r_1 + r_2 + \cdots + r_k = a_{11} + a_{22} + \cdots + a_{kk},$$

the trace of A. Finally, comparing the constant terms in both approaches, we find that

$$r_1 \cdot r_2 \cdots r_k = \det A. \quad \blacksquare$$

EXERCISES

23.53   Write out a careful inductive proof of Theorem 23.5.

23.54   Prove statement (67) using induction.

23.55   Show that (67) implies that the coefficient of r^{k-1} in (66) is the expression in (68).

23.56   (difficult) Show that the coefficient of r^j in (66) is $(-1)^{k-j}$ times the sum of all the principal $j \times j$ minors of A.

23.57   Show that the coefficient of r^j in (64) is $(-1)^{k-j}$ times the sum of all products of j-tuples of the eigenvalues of A.

23.58   Carry out the previous two exercises for a general 3×3 matrix.

Ordinary Differential Equations: Scalar Equations

The events described by the difference equations discussed in the last chapter are studied in discrete time steps. Either the event occurs at the end of natural time intervals, such as the quarterly compounding of interest in a savings account, or the measurements for the phenomenon take place only at the end of discrete time intervals, such as the quarterly report of the nation's gross national product. There are, however, models in which it is more natural or more convenient to treat time as a continuous variable, for example, when one is working with a savings account that compounds interest continuously or with a large population in which births and deaths are not restricted to the ends of regular time intervals. To model these situations which treat time as a continuous variable, one uses *differential equations*. The goal of the next two chapters is to develop the quantitative and qualitative theory of differential equations and to look at relevant examples which illustrate this theory.

It is natural to place these chapters on differential equations just after our treatment of eigenvalues and difference equations. However, these chapters are reasonably self-contained. Eigenvalues and eigenvectors are used only in the discussion of linear systems in Section 25.2, and that section can easily be skimmed or skipped at first reading. The rest of these chapters requires only a familiarity with the basic concepts of calculus from Chapter 2 and with the geometry of parameterized curves in $\mathbf{R}^n$ from Sections 13.3 and 14.5.

24.1 DEFINITION AND EXAMPLES

Recall from the last chapter that the growth of funds in a savings account which pays interest annually at rate r satisfies the difference equation

$$\frac{y(t+1) - y(t)}{y(t)} = r, \quad \text{or} \quad y(t+1) = (1+r)y(t). \tag{1}$$

(The same difference equation describes the growth of a population with a constant percent growth rate r.) If the interest in the account is paid every Δt fraction of a year, then the equation changes slightly to

$$\frac{y(t + \Delta t) - y(t)}{y(t)} = r \cdot \Delta t. \tag{2}$$

For example, if interest is paid quarterly, then the amount on deposit is multiplied by $1 + \frac{1}{4}r$ at the end of each quarter. (Equation (2) also describes the growth of a population if we count the population every Δt fraction of the year and use Δt as the basic time interval.) Some banks compound interest daily; others advertise continuous compounding. The former entails $\Delta t = 1/365.25$; the latter requires letting Δt tend to 0. If we rewrite (2) as

$$\frac{y(t + \Delta t) - y(t)}{\Delta t} = r\,y(t)$$

and let $\Delta t \to 0$, we obtain the *differential equation*

$$\frac{dy}{dt}(t) = ry(t), \tag{3}$$

which states that the *instantaneous* percent rate of growth, $\dot{y}(t)/y(t)$, is a constant r. Here, we write dy/dt as $\dot{y}$, as we will throughout this chapter.

In general, an **ordinary differential equation** is an expression which describes a relationship between a function of one variable and its derivative. The solution to a differential equation is a *function* which satisfies that relationship.

Example 24.1   A simple example of a differential equation is the equation

$$\dot{y}(t) = 2y(t), \qquad \text{or simply} \qquad \dot{y} = 2y. \tag{4}$$

We are asked in (4) to find a function $y(t)$ with the property that taking its derivative is the same as multiplying the function by 2. One solution to (4) is $y(t) = e^{2t}$ since its derivative $\dot{y}(t)$ is $2e^{2t} = 2y(t)$. Notice, in this case, that for any constant k, $y(t) = ke^{2t}$ is also a solution of (4). A typical differential equation has a whole one-parameter family of solutions. As was the situation with difference equations, the constant k is determined by the initial value $y(t_0)$ of the variable $y(t)$ under study.

Differential equations which describe a relationship between a function of *several* variables and its *partial* derivatives are called **partial differential equations**. In this chapter, we will look only at ordinary differential equations. In studying such equations, we will usually use t as the independent variable instead of x, because we are usually, though not always, interested in the evolution of a variable y over time.

Example 24.2 Let's look at another example: $\dot{y} = y^2$. Here, we are asked to find the function whose derivative at each t is the same as the square of the function. One solution is $y(t) = -1/t$. To see that this is a solution, take the derivative $\dot{y}$, then compute $(y(t))^2$ and see that you get the same result. (Check this.) Once more, there is a one-parameter family of solutions: $y(t) = 1/(k-t)$. Again, check this by computing $\dot{y}$ and y^2 and comparing the two.

Differential equations can also include the independent variable t explicitly. An example is the equation

$$\dot{y}(t) = t^2 y(t) \qquad \text{or simply} \qquad \dot{y} = t^2 y,$$

where we are asked to find the function $y(t)$ for which taking the derivative is the same as multiplying the function by t^2. It is easy to check that $y(t) = e^{t^3/3}$ has this property, as does the whole one-parameter family $y(t) = ke^{t^3/3}$.

Finally, some differential equations — in a sense the simplest ones — are descriptions of $\dot{y}$ solely in terms of t, for example,

$$\dot{y} = t^2, \quad \dot{y} = e^t, \quad \text{and} \quad \dot{y} = \cos t + t.$$

Such equations are solved simply by integrating the right-hand sides with respect to t. The solutions (with parameter) to the above three differential equations are

$$y(t) = \frac{1}{3}t^3 + k, \quad y(t) = e^t + k, \quad \text{and} \quad y(t) = \sin t + \frac{1}{2}t^2 + k.$$

Notice that the parameter k in these cases is just the constant of integration encountered in elementary calculus. Having looked at a number of examples, let's become a little more formal.

Definition An **ordinary differential equation** is an equation $\dot{y} = F(y, t)$ between the derivative of an unknown function $y(t)$ and an expression $F(y, t)$ involving y and t. Our first four examples used $F(y, t) = 2y, F(y, t) = y^2, F(y, t) = t^2 y$, and $F(y, t) = t^2$. If the expression $F(y, t)$ does not specifically involve t, that is, if the equation can be written as $\dot{y} = F(y)$, we call it an **autonomous** or **time-independent** differential equation. Examples are the first two equations above: $\dot{y} = 2y$ and $\dot{y} = y^2$. If the equation specifically involves t, like the next two examples above: $\dot{y} = t^2 y$ and $\dot{y} = t^2$, we call the equation **nonautonomous** or **time-dependent**.

All the equations examined so far are examples of **first order** differential equations because they involve only the *first* derivative of the unknown function. An equation which involves derivatives up to and including the ith derivative is called an *i*th order differential equation.

Example 24.3   The equation $\ddot{y} = 3\dot{y} - 2y + 2$ is a second order equation. Its
solution is $y(t) = k_1 e^{2t} + k_2 e^t + 1$. (Check.) The equation $d^4 y/dt^4 = y$ is a
fourth order differential equation, whose solution is

$$y(t) = k_1 \cos t + k_2 \sin t + k_3 e^t + k_4 e^{-t}, \tag{5}$$

with four constants of integration.

   In a sense, the study of physics, especially classical mechanics, centers on
differential equations. Newton's law of motion, $F = ma$, states that a particle
moves so that at any place and time its acceleration a times its mass m is equal
to the force F on it at that place and time. If $y(t)$ describes the position of a
physical particle at time t, then its acceleration is given by the second derivative
$\ddot{y}(t)$. If the particle has mass $= 1$ and if a function $F(y)$ represents that force acting
at location y, then Newton's law leads to the second order differential equation
$\ddot{y} = F(y)$.

Example 24.4   By Hooke's law, the force $F(y)$ on a frictionless spring is proportional to the displacement y of the spring from its equilibrium position:
$F(y) = -ay$. The more the string is stretched, the stronger is the restoring
force (and in the opposite direction). Therefore, the equation of motion of a
frictionless spring (of mass 1) is given by the equation

$$\ddot{y} = -ay.$$

The fact that the solution of this differential equation is

$$y(t) = k_1 \cos \sqrt{a}\, t + k_2 \sin \sqrt{a}\, t \tag{6}$$

tells us that such a spring will oscillate forever about its equilibrium. A similar
equation governs the motion of a pendulum; in this case, y is the angle that the
pendulum makes with the vertical. These equations are naturally autonomous
since the force on a spring or pendulum depends only on where the object is in
state space and not on the time at which the object reached that point in space.

Example 24.5   As noted above, the differential equation $\dot{y} = ry$ describes the
amount of money in a bank account that has a constant percent rate of growth
r; that is, interest is continously compounded at annual rate r. The general
solution of this differential equation is $y(t) = ke^{rt}$ — the bank account grows
exponentially without bound. Here, we can more easily see the role that the
constant k plays. Knowing the rate at which the account grows is not enough to
determine the size of the account at any moment of time. We also need to know
the size of the original deposit. In the solution $y(t) = ke^{rt}$, $y(0) = k$ is exactly
that parameter.

The same equation $\dot{y} = ry$ describes the change in size of a population with a constant percent rate of growth r. The assumption of a constant percent rate of growth is sometimes called **Malthus's law**, and the corresponding equation $\dot{y} = ry$ is sometimes called the **Malthus Equation**. Its general solution $y(t) = ke^{rt}$ tells us that such a population grows exponentially without bound. If we specify the initial population size $y(0)$, the constant k is determined. If we specify both $\dot{y} = ry$ and $y(0) = y_0$, the problem of finding a function $y(t)$ which satisfies both these conditions is called an **initial value problem**. We would expect such a problem to have a unique solution and, in general, it does. The existence and uniqueness of a solution to an initial value problem is the subject of the Fundamental Theorem of Differential Equations, a theorem discussed in Section 24.4.

The Malthus model for population growth is a simple one. A more realistic model would take into effect growth-inhibiting factors. One simple modification is to assume that the growth rate of a population decreases as a population grows in size. Factors, like crowding and utilization of resources, would lead to decreasing population growth rates especially as the population became too large for its environment. Eventually, a population too large might begin to decrease. In this modification, we want the growth rate $\dot{y}/y$ to be a *decreasing* function of the population size y. Since the simplest decreasing function of y is the negatively sloped line $f(y) = a - by$, we are led to consider the model

$$\frac{\dot{y}}{y} = a - by, \qquad \text{or} \qquad \dot{y} = y(a - by). \tag{7}$$

Equation (7) is called the **Verhulst** or **logistic model** of population growth. We will compute its solution in the next section.

Both of these differential equations in population studies are autonomous ones. How a population grows depends only on the initial population and not on the time we start studying that initial population. A population which begins with 100 individuals on Tuesday will evolve exactly as a population which begins with 100 individuals on Wednesday. On the other hand, a population study of migrating birds would use a *time-dependent* model to reflect the fact that the growth rate is seasonal. The growth of this bird population is much smaller (if not negative) during the migratory season and much larger during the mating season.

We have emphasized that the solution of a differential equation is a function, not a number — a fact which makes differential equations more difficult to solve than algebraic equations. However, sometimes the function solution of a differential equation is a *constant function*: $y(t) \equiv c$, for some constant c, a *function* whose graph is a horizontal line. For example, for the differential equations $\dot{y} = 2y$ and $\dot{y} = y^2$, the function $y(t) = 0$ for all t is a solution of both equations, since it makes both sides of each equation identically zero. In the pendulum problem, the pendulum sitting at rest and pointing straight down is a constant solution of its differential equation. A constant function solution in the savings account problem is $y(t) = 0$, certainly a realistic solution, and similarly for the population problem. The fact that the constant solution is $y(t) = 0$ in all these cases is misleading. Nonzero constant solutions arise naturally too. For example, in the logistic equation

$$\dot{y} = y(100 - 2y),$$

the constant function $y(t) = 50$ for all t is a solution since it makes both sides of the equation identically zero. Constant solutions are important in the study and application of differential equations. We use the same names for the constant solutions of differential equations and of difference equations: **steady state, stationary solution, stationary point, rest point**, and **equilibrium**. The last name gives an indication of their importance in economic models.

We close this introduction with a few words about the parameter k, the *integration constant*, which arises in the solution of differential equations. We have seen that different initial values correspond to different values of k. A parameterized solution $y(t, k)$ of a differential equation $\dot{y} = F(y, t)$ is called a **general solution** if *every* solution of the differential equation can be achieved by letting k take on different values. The general solution of a jth order differential equation

$$\frac{d^j y}{dt^j} = F(t, y, \dot{y}, \ldots, y^{[j-1]})$$

will contain j distinct parameters $k_1, k_2, \ldots, k_j$. For example, as we saw in (5), the general solution of the fourth order equation $d^4 y / dt^4 = y$ is $y(t) = k_1 \cos t + k_2 \sin t + k_3 e^t + k_4 e^{-t}$. The general solution of the integration problem $\ddot{y} = g(t)$ will entail two integrations with respect to t and therefore two constants of integration.

EXERCISES

24.1   Verify that the given functions are solutions of the given differential equations:

a) $y = \dfrac{2t}{c - t^2}$, $\dot{y} = y^2 + \dfrac{y}{t}$;   b) $y = \dfrac{t}{\sqrt{ct^2 - 1}}$, $\dot{y} = -\dfrac{y^3}{t^3}$;

c) $y = ce^t + t^2 + 2t + 2$, $\dot{y} = y - t^2$;

d) $y = \dfrac{1}{4}(2t^2 + 6t + 7) + c_1 e^t + c_2 e^{2t}$, $\ddot{y} = 3\dot{y} - 2y + t^2$.

24.2   Verify the solutions of the two differential equations in Example 24.3.

24.3   Verify that (6) is a solution of $\ddot{y} = -ay$. We will derive this solution in Section 24.3.

24.4   What kind of information would specify the parameters k_1 and k_2 in the solution (6) of the spring problem? In other words, besides the equation of motion, what other information do we need in order to determine any specific equation of motion of the spring?

24.2 EXPLICIT SOLUTIONS

Many innocent looking integration problems, like $\int e^{t^2}\, dt$, have no closed form solutions that can be written down explicitly. Unfortunately, the same thing is true for the more general differential equations. Even simple-looking equations like $\dot{y} = y^2 + t^2$ have no explicit solutions. This section will list the most important classes that do have explicit solutions and will compute their solutions, beginning with last section's simple example.

Linear First Order Equations

(1) $\dot{y} = ay$, a a constant. As one learns in most calculus classes, the general solution to this equation is $y(t) = ke^{at}$. The proof is simply to differentiate ke^{at} and see that it satisfies the differential equation; its derivative is a times itself.

(2) $\dot{y} = ay + b$, a and b nonzero constants. Here, the general solution is

$$y(t) = -\frac{b}{a} + ke^{at}. \tag{8}$$

To verify this, plug the solution candidate into the equation and see that it works:

$$\dot{y}(t) = ake^{at}$$
$$ay(t) + b = (-b + ake^{at}) + b = ake^{at}.$$

Therefore, $\dot{y}(t) = ay(t) + b$, and our candidate for a solution is a solution indeed. Note that $y(t) = -b/a$ is a steady state solution, corresponding to $k = 0$ in the general solution (8).

Next, we examine the *nonautonomous* versions of these two classes.

(3) $\dot{y} = a(t)y$. The general solution is

$$y(t) = ke^{\int^t a(s)ds}. \tag{9}$$

The s in expression (9) is just a dummy variable of integration. One simply takes the indefinite integral of the function $a(t)$ and exponentiates it. Expression (9) can be written simply as $y = k\exp(\int^t a)$.

(4) $\dot{y} = a(t)y + b(t)$. Now, the solution becomes a bit unwieldy. It also requires an indefinite integral of an indefinite integral and therefore *two* dummy variables of integration. The general solution is

$$y(t) = \left[k + \int^t b(s)e^{-\int^s a(u)du} ds \right] e^{\int^t a(s)ds}. \tag{10}$$

To find (10) as the solution, write the differential equation as $\dot{y} - a(t)y = b(t)$ and multiply every term by $\exp(-\int^t a(s)\,ds)$:

$$\dot{y}(t)e^{-\int^t a(s)\,ds} - a(t)y(t)e^{-\int^t a(s)\,ds} = b(t)e^{-\int^t a(s)\,ds}. \tag{11}$$

Since the left-hand side of (11) is precisely the derivative of the expression $y(t)\exp\left(-\int^t a(s)\,ds\right)$, (11) can be rewritten as

$$\frac{d}{dt}\left(y(t)e^{-\int^t a(s)\,ds}\right) = b(t)e^{-\int^t a(s)\,ds}. \tag{12}$$

Integrate both sides of (12) and multiply through by $e^{\int^t a}$ to obtain (10). The expression $\exp(-\int^t a(s)\,ds)$ that made the left side of (11) the exact derivative of a function is called an **integrating factor**.

The above four classes of differential equations are called **linear differential equations**. The first two were autonomous; the second two were not. The first and third — without the b-term — are called **homogeneous**; the second and fourth, with the b-term, are called **nonhomogeneous**.

Example 24.6 **(Derivation of Density Functions from Failure Rates)** Let f be the density function for a continuous random variable $t \geq 0$ and let F be the corresponding distribution function. Think of the random variable t as denoting the lifetime of a mechanical or electrical component. Then,

$$R(t) \equiv 1 - F(t) = \Pr\{T > t\},$$

the probability that the component lasts at least t time units, is called the **reliability function**. Given f, F, and R, the **failure rate** or **hazard function** Z is defined as

$$Z(t) \equiv \frac{f(t)}{1 - F(t)} = \frac{f(t)}{R(t)}. \tag{13}$$

The function Z can be thought of as the probability that the component will fail in the next Δt time units, given that it has not failed up to time t, because the latter conditional probability is equal to

$$\Pr(t < T \leq t + \Delta t \mid T > t) = \frac{\Pr(t < T \leq t + \Delta t)}{\Pr(T > t)}$$

$$\approx \frac{f(t)\Delta t}{R(t)}$$

$$= Z(t)\,\Delta t.$$

Given f and F, expression (13) defines Z. The interesting fact is that one can go the other way: given a hazard function Z, there is a unique corresponding probability density f and distribution F that satisfy (13).

To construct f from Z, note that since $R(t) = 1 - F(t)$, $R' = -F' = -f$. Therefore, (13) can be written as

$$Z(t) = -\frac{R'(t)}{R(t)}, \tag{14}$$

with initial condition $R(0) = 1 - F(0) = 1$. Given Z, equation (14) is a *linear homogeneous* differential equation in R whose solution is

$$R(t) = e^{-\int_0^t Z(s)\,ds}.$$

Since $f = F' = (1 - R)' = -R'$,

$$f(t) = Z(t)e^{-\int_0^t Z(s)\,ds}. \tag{15}$$

The impact of going from Z to f is that there is much less structure imposed on Z. One chooses a reasonable failure rate function Z and then (15) determines the corresponding probability density with all the right properties.

For example, setting $Z(t)$ equal to a constant α implies that the probability of failure is independent of how long the component has been working. The corresponding density function by (15) is

$$f(t) = \alpha e^{-\alpha t},$$

the density function for the **exponential distribution**. If we add some flexibility and set $Z(t)$ to be a general monomial in t:

$$Z(t) = \alpha\beta t^{\beta-1},$$

then (15) yields the density function

$$f(t; \alpha, \beta) = (\alpha\beta)t^{\beta-1}e^{-\alpha t^\beta}. \tag{16}$$

The random variable with density function (16) is said to have the **Weibull distribution**.

Separable Equations

The set of linear equations is one large class of ordinary differential equations that can be explicitly solved. The other such class is the class of separable differential equations. A differential equation $\dot{y} = F(y, t)$ is called **separable** if $F(y, t)$ can be written as a *product*

$$F(y, t) = g(y) \cdot h(t)$$

for some functions g and h. The equations

$$\dot{y} = y^2(t^2 + t), \quad \dot{y} = e^y e^t, \quad \dot{y} = (y + 1)/t, \quad \text{and} \quad \dot{y} = y^2 + 1$$

are all separable. The equations

$$\dot{y} = y^2 + t^2, \quad \dot{y} = a(t)y + b(t), \quad \text{and} \quad \dot{y} = ty + t^2 y^2$$

are not separable.

The general separable equation

The solution of a separable equation $\dot{y} = g(y) h(t)$ involves a simple trick. First, write the equation as

$$\frac{dy}{dt} = g(y) h(t).$$

Then, move all the y-terms to one side of the equal sign and all the t-terms to the other side:

$$\frac{dy}{g(y)} = h(t) \, dt,$$

and integrate the y-side with respect to y and the t-side with respect to t:

$$\int^y \frac{dy}{g(y)} = \int^t h(t) \, dt + c. \tag{17}$$

If there are no initial conditions, try to write this solution as $y = y(t, c)$. If there is an initial condition $y(t_0) = y_0$, drop the c in (17) and write y_0 as the lower limit of integration on the left-hand side of (17) and t_0 as the lower limit of integration on the right-hand side of (17). Let's try a few examples.

Example 24.7 $\dot{y} = t^2 y$. Actually, this is a special instance of Case 3 above. Write $dy/dt = t^2 y$, separate the variables as $dy/y = t^2 dt$, and integrate:

$$\int^y \frac{dy}{y} = \int^t t^2 dt + c.$$

This process leads to

$$\ln y = \frac{t^3}{3} + c, \quad \text{or} \quad y = e^{(t^3/3)+c} = k e^{t^3/3},$$

just as predicted by our analysis of case 3 above.

Example 24.8   Let $x \longmapsto u(x)$ be a utility function for wealth x. The **Arrow-Pratt measure of relative risk aversion** at wealth x is the expression

$$v(x) = -\frac{u''(x)x}{u'(x)},$$

the elasticity of u' with respect to x.

In statistical analysis, one would like to work with a utility function u of *constant relative risk aversion*. Such a u would satisfy the second order differential equation

$$u''(x) = -\frac{u'(x)\,b}{x}. \tag{18}$$

Let $v(x) = u'(x)$. Then, equation (18) becomes the first order differential equation

$$\frac{dv}{dx} = -\frac{vb}{x},$$

a *separable differential equation* in v and x. Separating the v's from the x's yields

$$\frac{dv}{v} = -b\frac{dx}{x}, \quad \text{or} \quad \int \frac{dv}{v} = -b\int \frac{dx}{x},$$

whose solution is

$$\ln v = -b(\ln x + C),$$

or

$$v = e^{-b\ln x} \cdot e^{-bC} = k_1 e^{\ln x^{-b}} = k_1 x^{-b}.$$

Since $v = u'$,

$$u = \int v = \int k_1 x^{-b} = \begin{cases} k_2 + k_1 \ln x & \text{if } b = 1, \\ k_2 + \dfrac{k_1}{1-b} x^{1-b} & \text{if } b \neq 1, \end{cases}$$

a three-parameter family of functions of constant relative risk aversion. The condition $u' > 0$ requires $k_1 > 0$.

Example 24.9   Consider the initial value problem

$$\frac{dY}{dp} = e^{ap} \cdot e^{bY} \cdot e^{c}, \qquad Y(q) = I, \tag{19}$$

where a, b, c, q, and I are positive constants. As is shown in the Appendix to this chapter, the solution $Y(p; q, I)$ of (19) is the indirect money market utility function that arises from the semilog demand function $\ln \xi = ap + bI + c$. Separating variables in (19) and including the initial condition as the lower limits of integration yields

$$\int_I^Y e^{-bY}\, dY = \int_q^p e^c e^{ap}\, dp,$$

which solves to

$$\frac{1}{b} e^{-bY} - \frac{1}{b} e^{-bI} = \frac{e^c}{a}(e^{ap} - e^{aq}),$$

or

$$Y = -\frac{1}{b} \ln\left[e^{-bI} + \frac{be^c}{a}(e^{ap} - e^{aq}) \right].$$

$\dot{y} = g(y)$

Technically, we can use the separation method to solve *any autonomous* differential equation since these are all separable with $h(t) \equiv 1$. The problem, of course, is in explicitly integrating the $\int dy/g(y)$ term that arises in (17).

Example 24.10   Consider the second example in Section 24.1, the autonomous equation $\dot{y} = y^2$. Write it as $dy/dt = y^2$ and then as $y^{-2}dy = dt$ and integrate:

$$\int y^{-2} dy = \int dt + c;$$

this $-y^{-1} = t + c$, which in turn implies

$$y = \frac{-1}{t + c} = \frac{1}{k - t}, \quad \text{where } k = -c.$$

Example 24.11   Let's derive the general solution of the *logistic equation*

$$\dot{y} = y(a - by),$$

using the separation of variables technique. We assume throughout this calculation that a and b are positive constants. Separating variables yields

$$\int^y \frac{dy}{y(a - by)} = \int^t dt. \tag{20}$$

The trick for integrating the y-side is the method of *partial fractions*, usually taught in Calculus II. We want to write

$$\frac{1}{y(a - by)} = \frac{A}{y} + \frac{B}{a - by} \tag{21}$$

for some constants A and B. Therefore, we put the right-hand side of (21) over the common denominator $y(a - by)$:

$$\frac{1}{y(a - by)} = \frac{Aa - bAy + By}{y(a - by)},$$

and set the numerators equal:

$$1 = Aa + (B - bA)y,$$

for all y. Setting $y = 0$ yields $A = 1/a$. Then, setting $y = 1$ yields

$$B - bA = 0, \quad \text{or} \quad B = bA = b/a.$$

Therefore,

$$\int \frac{1}{y(a - by)} dy = \int \left(\frac{1/a}{y} + \frac{b/a}{a - by} \right) dy$$

$$= \frac{1}{a} \int \frac{dy}{y} + \frac{b}{a} \int \frac{dy}{a - by}$$

$$= \frac{1}{a} \ln y - \frac{1}{a} \ln(a - by)$$

$$= \frac{1}{a} \ln \frac{y}{a - by}.$$

Plugging this into (20) yields

$$\ln \frac{y}{a - by} = a(t + c), \quad \text{or} \quad \frac{y}{a - by} = Ke^{at}.$$

Solve this equation for y to find

$$y = \frac{a}{b + ke^{-at}}, \tag{22}$$

where $k = 1/K$. We have drawn graphs of three solutions corresponding to $k < 0$, $k = 0$, and $k > 0$ in Figure 24.1. (Recall that a and b are positive constants.) Note that for $k = 0$, there is a steady state solution $y(t) = a/b$. This steady state solution is called the **carrying capacity** of the population. Since $e^{-at} \rightarrow 0$ as $t \rightarrow \infty$, every positive solution tends to the carrying capacity a/b as $t \rightarrow \infty$. In this case, we say that the steady state solution $y(t) = a/b$ is an **asymptotically stable solution**. If the population is governed by the logistic equation $\dot{y} = y(a - by)$, then the population will quickly converge to its carrying capacity.

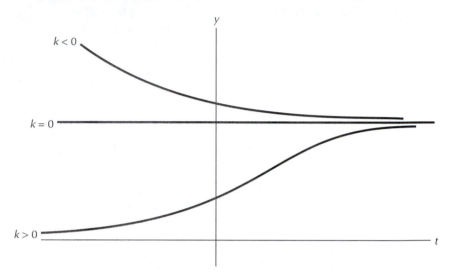

Figure 24.1   *Graphs of three solutions to* $\dot{y} = y(a - by)$.

Pure integration problems: $\dot{y} = h(t)$

These are also special cases of separable equations and can be explicitly solved, just by integrating. As we mentioned earlier, there are many simple functions, like $h_1(t) = \exp(t^2)$ and $h_2(t) = \sqrt{t^3 + 1}$, that cannot be explicitly integrated for closed form solutions.

There are a few other classes of first order differential equations that can be solved explicitly. These include the so-called exact equations, homogeneous equations, and Clairaut's equations. See the first two chapters of any text on elementary differential equations for further details.

EXERCISES

24.5 Find the general solution of each of the following differential equations; then, find the solution that satisfies $y(1) = 1$:

$a)$ $\dot{y} = 5 - y$; $b)$ $\dot{y} = t - y$; $c)$ $\dot{y} = y - t^2$;

$d)$ $\dot{y} = y^3/t^3$; $e)$ $\dot{y} = t^3/y^3$; $f)$ $t\dot{y} + (1 - t)y = e^{2t}$.

24.6 Show directly that formula (10) yields a solution to the linear differential equation $\dot{y} = a(t)y + b(t)$.

24.7 Case 4 for linear differential equations, $\dot{y} = a(t)y + b(t)$, is the generalization of the previous three cases.

   a) Show that expression (10) contains the general solutions of the previous three cases.

   b) Use Case 4's integrating factor method to derive the solutions of the first three cases.

24.8 Show how to use the separation trick (17) to derive the general solution of $\dot{y} = a(t)y$.

24.9 *a)* Check directly that $y(t) = a/b$ is a solution to the logistic equation $\dot{y} = y(a - by)$.

   b) Rewrite the general solution (22) of the logistic equation in terms of the initial population $y(0) = y_0$.

24.3   LINEAR SECOND ORDER EQUATIONS

Introduction

The most important class of differential equations in the physical sciences is the class of linear second order equations with constant coefficients. Their importance comes from two sources: the fact that *second order equations* arise naturally in applications because of the acceleration term in Newton's law, as described in Example 24.4, and the fact that *linear equations* arise naturally in models because of their simplicity and their role in approximating nonlinear equations. We have already seen that the motion of a frictionless spring is described by this kind of equation. We will concentrate on linear second order equations which are homogeneous and have constant coefficients. Instead of writing such differential equations as $\ddot{y} = A\dot{y} + By$, we will write the general second order homogeneous equation in the more classical form

$$a\ddot{y} + b\dot{y} + cy = 0. \tag{23}$$

If $a = 0$ in (23), then (23) becomes a *first* order linear equation whose solution has the form $y = e^{rt}$, as shown in the last section. It is natural to look for solutions of (23) of this form too. To find such solutions, just plug $y = e^{rt}$, $\dot{y} = re^{rt}$, and $\ddot{y} = r^2 e^{rt}$ into (23), in which case (23) becomes

$$ar^2 e^{rt} + bre^{rt} + ce^{rt} = e^{rt}(ar^2 + br + c) = 0.$$

Since e^{rt} is never zero, $y = e^{rt}$ will be a solution of (23) if and only if r satisfies the equation

$$ar^2 + br + c = 0, \tag{24}$$

a quadratic equation called the **characteristic equation** of (23). One can use the quadratic formula to find the roots of (24):

$$r = \frac{-b \pm \sqrt{b^2 - 4ac}}{2a}. \tag{25}$$

There are three possibilities for these two roots of the quadratic (24):

(1) $b^2 - 4ac > 0$, in which case (24) has two real, unequal roots;
(2) $b^2 - 4ac = 0$, in which case (24) has one multiple root (or equivalently, two equal roots); or
(3) $b^2 - 4ac < 0$, in which case (24) has two complex roots.

We'll examine each of these three cases separately to see what each means for the differential equation (23).

Real and Unequal Roots of the Characteristic Equation

The simplest case occurs when the characteristic equation (24) has two real unequal roots.

Theorem 24.1   If the characteristic polynomial (24) of the linear second order differential equation (23) has distinct real roots r_1 and r_2, then the general solution of (23) is $y(t) = k_1 e^{r_1 t} + k_2 e^{r_2 t}$.

Proof   Since r_1 and r_2 are roots of the characteristic polynomial (24), $y(t) = k_1 e^{r_1 t}$ and $y(t) = k_2 e^{r_2 t}$ are both solutions to differential equation (23). One consequence of the fact that equation (23) is linear is that if $y_1(t)$ and $y_2(t)$ are two solutions of (23), then their sum $y_1(t) + y_2(t)$ is also a solution of (23), because

$$a(y_1 + y_2)'' + b(y_1 + y_2)' + c(y_1 + y_2)$$

$$= (a\ddot{y}_1 + b\dot{y}_1 + cy_1) + (a\ddot{y}_2 + b\dot{y}_2 + cy_2)$$

$$= 0 + 0 = 0.$$

Therefore, $$y(t) = k_1 e^{r_1 t} + k_2 e^{r_2 t} \tag{26}$$

is a solution of (23). Finally, we show that (26) is the *general solution* by showing that given any initial value problem

$$a\ddot{y} + b\dot{y} + cy = 0, \qquad y(t_0) = y_0, \quad \dot{y}(t_0) = z_0, \tag{27}$$

there is a unique choice of constants of integration k_1^* and k_2^* such that $y(t) = k_1^* e^{r_1 t} + k_2^* e^{r_2 t}$ is a solution of (27). To prove this fact, assume for simplicity that

$t_0 = 0$ and plug the initial values (27) into the solution (26):

$$y_1(0) = \quad k_1 e^{r_1 \cdot 0} + k_2 e^{r_2 \cdot 0} \quad = k_1 \quad + k_2 \quad = y_0,$$
$$y_2(0) = r_1 k_1 e^{r_1 \cdot 0} + r_2 k_2 e^{r_2 \cdot 0} = r_1 k_1 + r_2 k_2 = z_0;$$

this leads to the matrix equation

$$\begin{pmatrix} 1 & 1 \\ r_1 & r_2 \end{pmatrix} \begin{pmatrix} k_1 \\ k_2 \end{pmatrix} = \begin{pmatrix} y_0 \\ z_0 \end{pmatrix}.$$

Since $r_1 \neq r_2$, the coefficient matrix is nonsingular; given any initial values y_0 and z_0 in (27), one can solve this system of linear equations uniquely for k_1 and k_2. This proves that, given any initial value problem (27), one can find k_1 and k_2 so that the solution (26) of (23) satisfies the initial conditions. Therefore, (26) is indeed the *general* solution of (23). ∎

Example 24.12   Let's solve the initial value problem

$$\ddot{y} - \dot{y} - 2y = 0, \qquad y(0) = 3, \quad \dot{y}(0) = 0. \tag{28}$$

The characteristic equation for this problem is $r^2 - r - 2 = 0$. Its roots are $r = 2, -1$. The general solution of the differential equation is

$$y(t) = k_1 e^{2t} + k_2 e^{-t}.$$

Plug in the two initial values

$$y(0) = k_1 + k_2 \quad = 3,$$
$$\dot{y}(0) = 2k_1 - k_2 = 0,$$

and solve this system for $k_1 = 1$ and $k_2 = 2$. Therefore, the solution of our initial value problem (28) is $y(t) = e^{2t} + 2e^{-t}$.

Example 24.13   Let $x \longmapsto u(x)$ be a utility function over wealth x. At any wealth level x, the **Arrow-Pratt measure of absolute risk aversion** $\mu(x)$ equals $-u''(x)/u'(x)$. The function μ is the percent rate of change of u' at x; it is a measure of the concavity of the utility function u.

    To find the utility functions that have *constant absolute risk aversion a*, we solve the second order differential equation

$$-\frac{u''(x)}{u'(x)} = a,$$

or

$$u''(x) + au'(x) = 0. \tag{29}$$

Equation (29) is a linear second order differential equation whose characteristic polynomial is $r^2 + ar = 0$, with roots $r = 0, -a$. The general solution of (29) is

$$u(x) = c_1 e^{0x} + c_2 e^{-ax} = c_1 + c_2 e^{-ax},$$

the family affine transformations of e^{-ax}. Note that the condition $u' > 0$ implies that $c_2 < 0$. Check that these u's have constant absolute risk aversion.

Real and Equal Roots of the Characteristic Equation

We turn to the second possibility for the roots of the characteristic equation (24) of differential equation (23): equal roots.

Theorem 24.2   If the characteristic polynomial (24) of the linear second order differential equation (23) has equal roots $r_1 = r_2$, that is, if $b^2 - 4ac = 0$ in (24), then the general solution of (23) is $y(t) = k_1 e^{r_1 t} + k_2 t e^{r_1 t}$.

Proof If $b^2 - 4ac = 0$ in the characteristic equation (24) of the differential equation (23), then (24) has only one distinct real root, call it r_1. By (25), $r_1 = -b/2a$. As a result, we have one solution $y_1(t) = k_1 e^{r_1 t}$ of (23), but we need another independent solution in order to generate the general solution. It turns out that

$$y_2(t) = k_2 t e^{r_1 t}$$

is second solution. To verify this, plug $y_2(t)$ into equation (23):

$$a\ddot{y}_2(t) + b\dot{y}_2(t) + cy_2(t)$$
$$= a(r_1^2 t e^{r_1 t} + 2r_1 e^{r_1 t}) + b(r_1 t e^{r_1 t} + e^{r_1 t}) + cte^{r_1 t}$$
$$= te^{r_1 t}(ar_1^2 + br_1 + c) + e^{r_1 t}(2ar_1 + b)$$
$$= 0 + 0,$$

since r_1 satisfies the characterisitic equation (24) and since $r_1 = -b/2a$. An analysis similar to the one in the previous paragraph shows that in this case

$$y(t) = k_1 e^{r_1 t} + k_2 t e^{r_1 t} \tag{30}$$

is the *general* solution of the differential equation (23). (Exercise.) ∎

Example 24.14   Let's solve the initial value problem

$$\ddot{y} - 4\dot{y} + 4y = 0, \qquad y(0) = 2, \quad \dot{y}(0) = 5. \tag{31}$$

Its characteristic equation is $r^2 - 4r + 4 = 0$, whose roots are $r_1 = r_2 = 2$. The general solution is $y(t) = k_1 e^{2t} + k_2 t e^{2t}$. Plugging the initial conditions into this solution leads to the algebraic system of linear equations

$$k_1 + 0 = 2$$
$$2k_1 + k_2 = 5,$$

whose solution is $k_1 = 2, k_2 = 1$. Therefore, the solution of the initial value problem (31) is $y(t) = 2e^{2t} + t e^{2t}$.

Complex Roots of the Characteristic Equation

Finally, we consider the case where the characteristic polynomial (24) of equation (23) has complex roots. This section draws on the material on trigonometric functions and on complex numbers in the Appendix of this book.

Theorem 24.3   If the characteristic polynomial (24) of the linear second order differential equation (23) has complex roots $\alpha \pm i\beta$, that is, if $b^2 - 4ac < 0$ in (24), the general solution of (23) is $y(t) = e^{\alpha t}(C_1 \cos \beta t + C_2 \sin \beta t)$.

Proof   If $b^2 - 4ac < 0$ in (25), then the roots of the characteristic equation (24) of (23) are

$$r_1 = -\frac{b}{2a} + i\frac{1}{2a}\sqrt{4ac - b^2} \quad \text{and} \quad r_2 = -\frac{b}{2a} - i\frac{1}{2a}\sqrt{4ac - b^2}.$$

Notice that these two roots are complex conjugates. In particular, since $4ac - b^2 \neq 0$, these two roots cannot be equal to each other, as they were in Case 2. Let $\alpha \equiv -b/2a$ and let $\beta \equiv \sqrt{4ac - b^2}/2a$, so that the roots of the characteristic equation are $r_1, r_2 = \alpha \pm i\beta$. Technically,

$$y(t) = k_1 e^{(\alpha + i\beta)t} + k_2 e^{(\alpha - i\beta)t} \tag{32}$$

is a formal solution of the differential equation (23). However, it is not a satisfactory solution because it involves complex numbers, and one would hope for *real* solutions of a *real* differential equation.

It takes a little work to get a real solution out of (32). Using rules for exponents, write

$$e^{(\alpha + i\beta)t} = e^{\alpha t} e^{i\beta t} \quad \text{and} \quad e^{(\alpha - i\beta)t} = e^{\alpha t} e^{-i\beta t}. \tag{33}$$

The factor $e^{\alpha t}$ in these expressions is real, but $e^{\pm i\beta t}$ still contains the imaginary number i. First, rewrite $e^{i\beta t}$ in (33) via **Euler's formula**:

$$e^{ix} = \cos x + i \sin x.$$

Euler's formula follows from plugging $z = ix$ into the Taylor series for e^z, as shown in the Appendix of this book. Applying (33) and Euler's formula, the general solution (32) becomes

$$y(t) = e^{\alpha t}[k_1(\cos \beta t + i \sin \beta t) + k_2(\cos \beta t - i \sin \beta t)], \qquad (34)$$

which still contains complex numbers, but is an improvement over (32). Formula (34) is a formal solution to the differential equation (23) for *any* constants k_1 and k_2, real or complex. Since $(cos\beta t + i \sin \beta t)$ and $(cos\beta t - i \sin \beta t)$ are complex conjugates of each other, if we choose k_1 and k_2 to be complex numbers that are complex conjugate to each other,

$$k_1 = c_1 + ic_2 \quad \text{and} \quad k_2 = c_1 - ic_2,$$

then we'll end up with a real answer, because

$$(c_1 + ic_2)(\cos \beta t + i \sin \beta t)$$
$$= (c_1 \cos \beta t - c_2 \sin \beta t) + i(c_2 \cos \beta t + c_1 \sin \beta t)$$
$$\text{and} \quad (c_1 - ic_2)(\cos \beta t - i \sin \beta t)$$
$$= (c_1 \cos \beta t - c_2 \sin \beta t) - i(c_2 \cos \beta t + c_1 \sin \beta t)$$

are complex conjugates of each other. When we add these two expressions, as we need to do in (34), we are adding a complex number $z_1 + iz_2$ to its conjugate $z_1 - iz_2$. Their sum is the *real* number $2z_1$, or in this case,

$$2(c_1 \cos \beta t - c_2 \sin \beta t).$$

After multiplying this sum by $e^{\alpha t}$, as required by (34), we obtain the *real* solution

$$y(t) = e^{\alpha t}(2c_1 \cos \beta t - 2c_2 \sin \beta t),$$

which we write in the simpler form

$$y(t) = e^{\alpha t}(C_1 \cos \beta t + C_2 \sin \beta t) \qquad (35)$$

just by renaming the constants. This is the real solution that we have been looking for when the roots of the characteristic equation (24) of (23) are the complex numbers $\alpha \pm i\beta$.

Since expression (35) contains two independent constants C_1 and C_2, we would expect that it is the general solution of our second order differential equation (23). To see that it truly is, we need to show that given any scalars y_0 and z_0, we can find C_1 and C_2 in (35) to solve the initial value problem (27). Since $\sin 0 = 0$ and $\cos 0 = 1$ and since

$$\dot{y}(t) = e^{\alpha t}[(\alpha C_1 + \beta C_2) \cos \beta t + (\alpha C_2 - \beta C_1) \sin \beta t],$$

the initial conditions $y(0) = y_0$ and $\dot{y}(0) = z_0$ lead to the algebraic system of equations

$$C_1 = y_0$$
$$\alpha C_1 + \beta C_2 = z_0.$$

This system has the unique solution $C_1 = y_0$ and $C_2 = (z_0 - \alpha y_0)/\beta$ for all y_0, z_0; therefore, (35) really is a *general solution* of (23) when (24) has complex roots. ∎

The Motion of a Spring

To develop our intuition for the results of this section, we use these results to investigate the motion of a spring with friction. As discussed in Section 24.1, the *restoring force* on a spring is proportional to the distance y that it is stretched from equilibrium. We usually assume that the *frictional force* on a spring is proportional to its velocity $\dot{y}$. Therefore, the total force on a spring stretched y units from equilibrium and moving with velocity $\dot{y}$ is

$$F(y, \dot{y}) = -b\dot{y} - cy.$$

Newton's law of motion $F = ma$ leads us to the second order differential equation

$$m\ddot{y} + b\dot{y} + cy = 0, \tag{36}$$

in which all three constants are nonnegative. The roots of the characteristic equation of (36) are

$$r_1, r_2 = -\frac{b}{2m} \pm \frac{1}{2m}\sqrt{b^2 - 4mc}. \tag{37}$$

Let's look at the solutions of (36) for different values of the friction coefficient b. If $b = 0$, that is, when there is no friction, then r_1 and r_2 are pure imaginary numbers:

$$r_1, r_2 = \pm i\sqrt{\frac{c}{m}}.$$

In this case, the solution to the differential equation (36) is

$$y(t) = C_1 \cos\sqrt{\frac{c}{m}}t + C_2 \sin\sqrt{\frac{c}{m}}t,$$

which oscillates forever, as would be expected for a frictionless spring.

Now, increase b a little. As long as $b^2 - 4mc < 0$, the roots r_1 and r_2 of the characteristic equation are complex numbers and the general solution of (36) is

$$y(t) = e^{-bt/2m}\left(C_1 \cos \frac{t}{2m}\sqrt{b^2 - 4mc} + C_2 \sin \frac{t}{2m}\sqrt{b^2 - 4mc}\right).$$

This solution *oscillates* because of the cosine and sine in the expression, but its oscillations dampen down to zero because of the negative exponent in the exponential in front of the brackets.

Finally, if the friction coefficient b is big enough so that $b^2 - 4mc > 0$, then the roots r_1 and r_2 of the characteristic equation (24) become real and unequal. A close examination of (37) shows that they are both negative numbers. In this case, the general solution of (36) is

$$y(t) = C_1 e^{-|r_1|t} + C_2 e^{-|r_2|t}.$$

Now, the large size of the friction coefficient prevents the spring from oscillating toward its equilibrium. The spring more or less snaps directly back to equilibrium, a case which the engineering literature calls **overdamping**.

Nonhomogeneous Second Order Equations

We turn briefly to a discussion of *nonhomogeneous* second order linear differential equations with constant coefficients:

$$a\ddot{y} + b\dot{y} + cy = g(t). \tag{38}$$

The function $g(t)$ in (38) is often called a **forcing term**. In mechanics problems, it represents some *external force* on the otherwise autonomous equation under study. The following theorem presents the key fact about nonautonomous linear systems: to find the general solution of such an equation, we need only find the general solution of the corresponding homogeneous equation and any *one* particular solution of the nonhomogeneous equation.

Theorem 24.4   Let $y_p(t)$ be *any* particular solution of the nonhomogeneous differential equation (38). Let $k_1 y_1(t) + k_2 y_2(t)$ be a *general* solution of the corresponding homogeneous equation $a\ddot{y} + b\dot{y} + cy = 0$. Then, a general solution of (38) is $y(t) = k_1 y_1(t) + k_2 y_2(t) + y_p(t)$.

Proof We need to show that for any given solution $y^*(t)$ of (38), there are constants k_1^* and k_2^* so that

$$y^*(t) = k_1^* y_1(t) + k_2^* y_2(t) + y_p(t).$$

Since $a(y^* - y_p)\ddot{} + b(y^* - y_p)\dot{} + c(y^* - y_p)$

$$= (a\ddot{y}^* + b\dot{y}^* + cy^*) - (a\ddot{y}_p + b\dot{y}_p + cy_p)$$

$$= g(t) - g(t) = 0,$$

$y^*(t) - y_p(t)$ is a solution of the homogeneous equation. We have shown that, in general, the difference of any two solutions of the nonhomogeneous equation is a solution of the homogeneous equation. Therefore, there exist k_1^* and k^* such that

$$y^*(t) - y_p(t) = k_1^* y_1(t) + k_2^* y_2(t);$$

that is, $\quad\quad\quad y^*(t) = k_1^* y_1(t) + k_2^* y_2(t) + y_p(t).\quad\quad\blacksquare\quad\quad(39)$

Theorems 24.1 to 24.4 tell us how to find the general solution of any nonhomogeneous second order differential equation (38) with constant coefficients. We use Theorems 24.1 to 24.3 to find the general solution of the homogeneous equation $a\ddot{y} + b\dot{y} + cy = 0$. To get the general solution to the nonhomogeneous equation (38), Theorem 24.4 tells us that we need only find one particular solution to (38).

The simplest method for finding a particular solution of (38) is called the **method of undetermined coefficients**. In this method, one looks for a particular solution of equation (38) which has the same form as the forcing term $g(t)$. For example, if $g(t)$ is the constant function $g(t) = g_0$, then a particular solution of $a\ddot{y} + b\dot{y} + cy = g_0$ is the constant function $y(t) = g_0/c$. (Check this.) If $g(t)$ is a polynomial in t of order j, one looks for a particular solution which is also a polynomial in t of order j. If $g(t)$ is a sum of trig functions, $g(t) = A \sin Bt + C \cos Bt$, one looks for a particular solution of (38) that is also a linear combination of $\cos Bt$ and $\sin Bt$. If $g(t)$ is an exponential e^{Bt}, one looks for a particular solution that is a multiple of e^{Bt}.

Example 24.15 Let's find the general solution of the equation

$$\ddot{y} - 2\dot{y} - 3y = 9t^2. \quad\quad (40)$$

The general solution of $\ddot{y} - 2\dot{y} - 3y = 0$ is $y(t) = k_1 e^{3t} + k_2 e^{-t}$. Since the forcing term in (40) is a quadratic in t, we look for a particular solution of (40) that is also a quadratic in t:

$$y_p(t) = At^2 + Bt + C.$$

Differentiate this candidate solution and plug it into equation (40) to obtain

$$9t^2 = \ddot{y}_p - 2\dot{y}_p - 3y_p$$

$$= (2A) - 2(2At + B) - 3(At^2 + Bt + C)$$

$$= (-3A)t^2 + (-4A - 3B)t + (2A - 2B - 3C)$$

Since the left- and right-hand sides of this equation are equal *for all t*, the coefficients of each power of t must be equal:

$$9 = -3A$$
$$0 = -4A - 3B$$
$$0 = \quad 2A - 2B - 3C,$$

a system whose solution is $A = -3$, $B = 4$, and $C = -14/3$. Therefore, a particular solution of (40) is

$$y_p(t) = -3t^2 + 4t - \frac{14}{3},$$

and the general solution of (40) is

$$y(t) = k_1 e^{3t} + k_2 e^{-t} - 3t^2 + 4t - \frac{14}{3}. \qquad \text{(Check.)}$$

If a term of the candidate solution of the nonhomogeneous equation (38) equals a term in the general solution of the homogeneous equation, up to coefficients, then the system is said to be in **resonance**. Resonance occurs, for example, when a system which is oscillating naturally with period T is acted on by a forcing term which also has period T. Bridges have been known to collapse in such circumstances. The method of undetermined coefficients, as described above, must be modified for a system in resonance. One usually has to multiply the natural candidate for $y_p(t)$ by a factor of t, or sometimes even by t^2, to find a successful candidate for a particular solution of nonhomogeneous equation (38).

Example 24.16   The general solution of the nonhomogeneous equation

$$\ddot{y} - 2\dot{y} - 3y = 8e^{-t} \qquad (41)$$

is $y(t) = k_1 e^{-t} + k_2 e^{3t} + y_p(t)$, where $y_p(t)$ is a particular solution of (41). Given the form of $g(t)$ in (41), a natural candidate for $y_p(t)$ is $y_p = Ae^{-t}$. However, this candidate does not work because the general solution of the homogeneous equation contains an e^{-t} term. So, we look for a particular solution of the form $y_p(t) = Ate^{-t}$, with an extra t factor. Differentiate this candidate twice and plug it into (41):

$$8e^{-t} = \ddot{y}_p(t) - 2\dot{y}_p(t) - 3y_p(t)$$
$$= (Ate^{-t} - 2Ae^{-t}) - 2(-Ate^{-t} + Ae^{-t}) - 3(Ate^{-t})$$
$$= -4Ae^{-t}.$$

Therefore, $A = -2$ and $y_p(t) = -2te^{-t}$.

EXERCISES

24.10 Solve the following initial value problems:
  a) $\ddot{y} - y = 0$, $y(0) = \dot{y}(0) = 1$;
  b) $\ddot{y} - 5\dot{y} + 6y = 0$, $y(0) = 3$, $\dot{y}(0) = 7$
  c) $2\ddot{y} + 3\dot{y} - 2y = 0$, $y(0) = 3$, $\dot{y}(0) = -1$.

24.11 Verify that $2e^{2t} + te^{2t}$ really is a solution of the initial value problem (31).

24.12 Prove that, in the case where $b^2 - 4ac = 0$, given any initial value problem (27), one can always find k_1^* and k_2^* so that $y(t) = k_1^* e^{r_1 t} + k_2^* t e^{r_1 t}$ is a solution of (27).

24.13 Solve the following initial value problems:
  a) $\ddot{y} + 6\dot{y} + 9y = 0$, $y(0) = 0$, $\dot{y}(0) = 1$;
  b) $4\ddot{y} + 4\dot{y} + y = 0$, $y(0) = 1$, $\dot{y}(0) = 1$.

24.14 Solve the following differential equations for initial values $y(0) = 2$, $\dot{y}(0) = 1$:
  a) $\ddot{y} + 2\dot{y} + 10y = 0$;
  b) $\ddot{y} + 9y = 0$.

24.15 Verify directly that the expression (35) really is a solution of the differential equation (23) when the roots of (24) are complex.

24.16 Find the solution of each of the following differential equations for the initial conditions $y(0) = 1$, $\dot{y}(0) = 0$:

  a) $6\ddot{y} - \dot{y} - y = 0$;   b) $\ddot{y} + 2\dot{y} + 2y = 0$;   c) $4\ddot{y} - 4\dot{y} + y = 0$;
  d) $\ddot{y} + 5\dot{y} + 6y = 0$;   e) $\ddot{y} - 6\dot{y} + 9y = 0$;   f) $\ddot{y} + \dot{y} + y = 0$.

24.17 Compute the general solution of the third order differential equation
  $\dddot{y} - 2\ddot{y} - \dot{y} + 2y = 0$.

24.18 Show that there is no solution of (41) of the form $y_p = Ae^{-t}$.

24.19 Find the general solution of the following nonhomogeneous second order differential equations:

  a) $\ddot{y} - 2\dot{y} - y = 7$;   b) $\ddot{y} + \dot{y} - 2y = 6t$;   c) $\ddot{y} - \dot{y} - 2y = 4e^{-t}$;
  d) $\ddot{y} + 2\dot{y} = \sin 2t$;   e) $\ddot{y} + 4y = \sin 2t$;   f) $\ddot{y} \quad - y \quad = e^t$.

24.20 **(Principle of Superposition)** Show that if $y_{p_1}(t)$ is a solution of $a\ddot{y} + b\dot{y} + cy = g_1(t)$ and $y_{p_2}(t)$ is a solution of $a\ddot{y} + b\dot{y} + cy = g_2(t)$, then $y_{p_1}(t) + y_{p_2}(t)$ is a solution of $a\ddot{y} + b\dot{y} + cy = g_1(t) + g_2(t)$.

24.21 Use the previous exercise to find the general solution of $\ddot{y} - \dot{y} - 2y = 6t + 4e^{-t}$.

24.4 EXISTENCE OF SOLUTIONS

The Fundamental Existence and Uniqueness Theorem

The last two sections have discussed nearly every type of differential equation for which one can compute an explicit solution. However, a solution may exist even if one cannot write it out in some neat form.

Let's look at a situation closely related to that of solving a differential equation — the problem of finding the antiderivative or indefinite integral of a given function. Technically, every continuous function is the antiderivative of some function; the problem is that we cannot always write out the antiderivative in some closed form. For example, there is no way of writing the antiderivative of e^{-t^2}, the density function of the normal distribution. However, this antiderivative is important enough that it is given its own identity as the *error function*,

$$\text{erf}(x) = \frac{2}{\sqrt{\pi}} \int_0^x e^{-t^2} dt.$$

If we can't compute the solution of a given differential equation, how do we know that a solution exists? That any reasonable initial value problem has one and only one solution is the content of the following theorem, often called the **Fundamental Theorem of Differential Equations**.

Theorem 24.5 Consider the initial value problem

$$\dot{y} = f(t, y), \qquad y(t_0) = y_0. \tag{42}$$

Suppose that f is a continuous function at the point (t_0, y_0). Then, there exists a C^1 function $y: I \to \mathbf{R}^1$ defined on an open interval $I = (t_0 - a, t_0 + a)$ about t_0 such that $y(t_0) = y_0$ and $\dot{y}(t) = f(t, y(t))$ for all $t \in I$, that is, $y(t)$ is a solution of the initial value problem (42). Furthermore, if f is C^1 at (t_0, y_0), then the solution $y(t)$ is *unique*; any two solutions of (42) must be equal to each other on the intersection of their domains.

Theorem 24.5 holds for jth order differential equations provided that we specify j initial conditions

$$y(t_0) = y_0, \quad \dot{y}(t_0) = y_1, \quad \ldots, \quad y^{[j-1]}(t_0) = y_{j-1}.$$

The vast majority of differential equations that we will work with will be C^1 so that both the existence and the uniqueness conclusions of Theorem 24.5 apply. It is not an easy task to find an initial value problem which has multiple solutions. The following example provides such a case.

Example 24.17 Consider the initial value problem

$$\dot{y} = 3y^{2/3}, \qquad y(0) = 0. \tag{43}$$

Notice that $y^{2/3}$ is a continuous function everywhere, but it is not differentiable at $y = 0$, since its derivative at 0 is infinite. This problem falls between the cracks discussed in Theorem 24.5. Theorem 24.5 tells us that this problem has a solution, but it doesn't guarantee that there is only one solution. In fact, $y(t) = 0$ and $y(t) = t^3$ are *two* solutions of initial value problem (43).

In the Appendix to this chapter, we present a proof of the converse of Euler's theorem on homogeneous functions, a proof that is based on the uniqueness condition in the last sentence of Theorem 24.5.

Direction Fields

We are going to present a geometric proof of Theorem 24.5 by showing how to draw the graph of the solution of *any* initial value problem, even when we can't compute an expression for the solution. To accomplish this, we need to understand how to view differential equations geometrically. At each point (t, y), the differential equation gives us the slope $\dot{y} = f(t, y)$ of the graph of a function $y = y(t)$ through that point. We are asked to find the function whose graph has these preassigned slopes. In the special case $\dot{y} = f(t)$ in which f is independent of y, we are given the slope for each t and asked to draw the curve at t whose graph has this slope. Let's work out some concrete examples.

Example 24.18 Consider the differential equation $\dot{y} = 2ty$. This is an equation that we can solve explicitly as $y = ke^{t^2}$, but let's find this solution geometrically and then compare it with this known solution. At each point (t, y) in the plane, draw a little segment of slope $2ty$. For example, in Figure 24.2, we have drawn segments of slope -2 at the points $(1, -1)$ and $(-1, 1)$; segments of slope 2 at the points $(1, 1)$ and $(-1, -1)$; segments of slope 4 at the points $(1, 2)$ and $(-1, -2)$; segments of slope -4 at the points $(-1, 2)$, $(1, -2)$, $(-2, 1)$, and $(2, -1)$; and segments of slope 0 at the points $(0, 1)$, $(0, 0)$, and $(0, -1)$. Just by looking at Figure 24.2, we begin to get the picture of functions $y(t)$ with a bowl-shaped graph in the upper half plane and an inverted bowl-shaped graph in the lower half plane.

However, we need many more segments to get a complete picture. To do this effectively, we need a more efficient process than that of choosing random

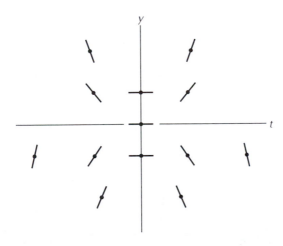

The direction field of $\dot{y} = 2ty$ at various points in the plane.

Figure 24.2

(t, y)'s and evaluating $\dot{y} = f(t, y)$ at these points. In the previous paragraph, we did choose our points in pairs or triplets with $\dot{y}$ the same at each point of the group. It is natural to extend this procedure to more than two points at a time and to consider at once all the points where $\dot{y}$ takes on a single value. For example, what are all the points (t, y) where the slope $\dot{y}$ is 2? Since $\dot{y} = 2ty$, $\dot{y} = 2$ at all points (t, y) for which $2ty = 2$ or $y = 1/t$. In Figure 24.3, we have sketched lightly the hyperbola $y = 1/t$ and we have drawn little segments of slope 2 along this hyperbola. In this way, we can draw the slope of $y(t)$ for whole curves of points at a time.

Now, let's do the same for $\dot{y} = 0$. The slope will be zero whenever $2ty = 0$; that is, whenever $t = 0$ or $y = 0$ — on both axes. We've drawn little *horizontal* segments along both axes in Figure 24.4 to mirror the fact that $\dot{y} = 0$ when $t = 0$ or $y = 0$. We have continued this process for slopes $\dot{y} = +2, -1, -2$ in Figure 24.4.

We now have enough information that we can sketch in some curves which have the appropriate slopes. This is done in Figure 24.5. These curves are indeed the graphs of the family of functions $y = ke^{t^2}$, which we know to be the general solution of $\dot{y} = 2ty$.

If we could draw a segment of slope $f(t, y)$ at each (t, y) in the plane, we would have a very clear picture of what the graphs of the general solution of $\dot{y} = f(t, y)$ look like. The set of all these segments is called the **direction field**, or sometimes the **integral field**, of the differential equation $\dot{y} = f(t, y)$. From a geometric point

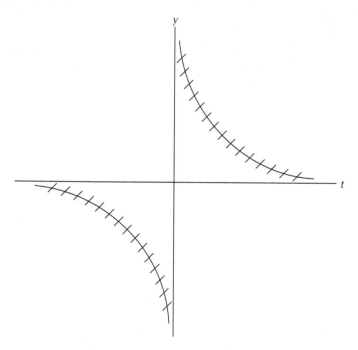

**Figure
24.3**

The direction field of $\dot{y} = 2ty$ along the curves $2ty = 2$.

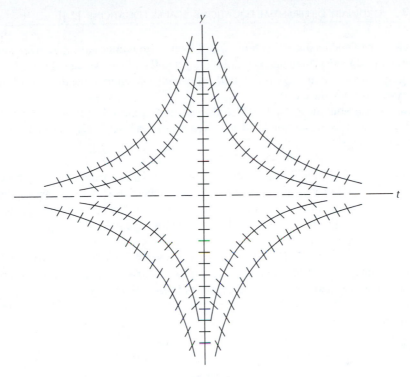

Sketch of the direction field of ẏ = 2ty.

**Figure
24.4**

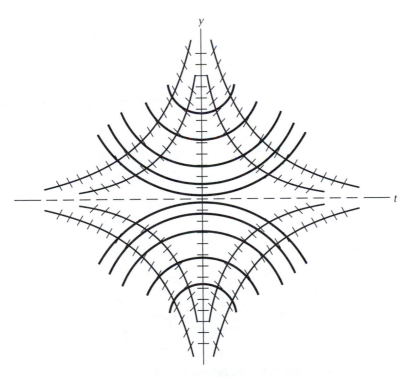

Curves everywhere tangent to the direction field of ẏ = 2ty.

**Figure
24.5**

of view, the Fundamental Theorem of Differential Equations says that given any continuous direction field and any point (t_0, y_0) in the plane, we can always draw the graph of a solution curve through (t_0, y_0) which is tangent to the direction field everywhere along the curve.

Let's work out an example which doesn't have a closed form solution: $\dot{y} = y^2 + t^2$. Since this expression has a plus sign instead of a times sign, this equation is not separable.

Example 24.19   We will use the method of the previous example to sketch the direction field of $\dot{y} = y^2 + t^2$ efficiently. The level sets of $y^2 + t^2$ are circles $y^2 + t^2 = a$ of radius $\sqrt{a}$. In Figure 24.6, we have drawn a direction field with slope $1/4$ on the circle $y^2 + t^2 = 1/4$ of radius $1/2$, a field with slope 1 on the circle $y^2 + t^2 = 1$, a field with slope 2 on the circle $y^2 + t^2 = 2$, and a field with slope 4 on the circle $y^2 + t^2 = 4$. In Figure 24.7, we have superimposed on the integral field of Figure 24.6, a family of curves which are everywhere tangent to the field. These are the graphs of the solutions of $\dot{y} = y^2 + t^2$.

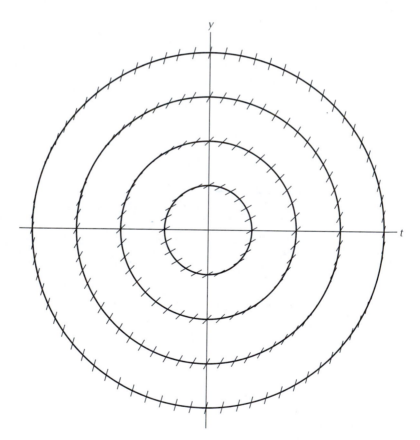

Figure 24.6

The direction field of $\dot{y} = y^2 + t^2$.

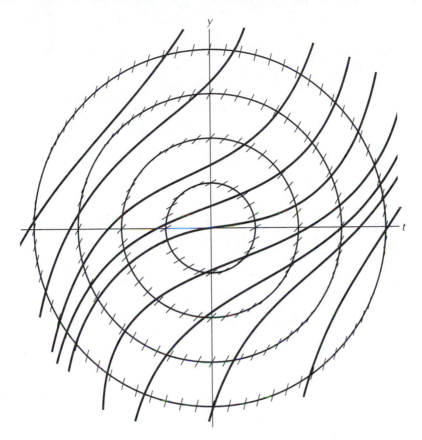

Graphs of the solutions of $\dot{y} = y^2 + t^2$.

Figure 24.7

Example 24.20 Let's do an autonomous example to see what is special about the direction field of an autonomous differential equation. We work with the logistic equation $\dot{y} = y(2 - y)$, for which there is an explicit solution but not a particularly helpful one. Notice that for an autonomous equation, the curves of constant slope for the direction field are *horizontal lines $y = b$*. For example, $\dot{y} = 0$ when $y = 0$ or 2; so, the direction field is horizontal along the horizontal lines $y = 0$ and $y = 2$, as we have drawn in Figure 24.8. On the line $y = 1$, $\dot{y} = 1$; on the lines $y = 1/2$ and $y = 3/2$, $\dot{y} = 3/4$. We've drawn these in Figure 24.8. On the line $y = 5/2$, $\dot{y} = -5/4$; on the line $y = 3$, $\dot{y} = -3$; on the line $y = -1$, $\dot{y} = -3$; and on the line $y = -1/2$, $\dot{y} = -5/4$. We have drawn the direction field on these lines in Figure 24.8.

In Figure 24.9, we've drawn the family of curves which is everywhere tangent to the direction field in Figure 24.8. These curves are the graphs of the solutions of $\dot{y} = y(2 - y)$.

Figure 24.9 presents a lot of information about the solution of $\dot{y} = y(2 - y)$ in a rather efficient manner. Just by looking at the picture, we see that $y = 0$ and

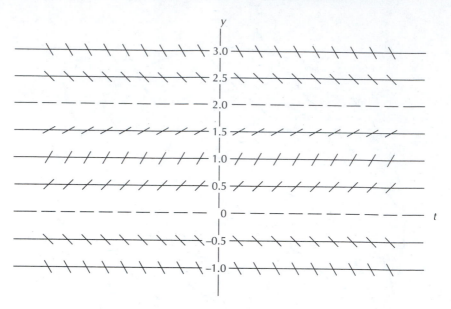

Figure 24.8

The direction field of $\dot{y} = y(2 - y)$.

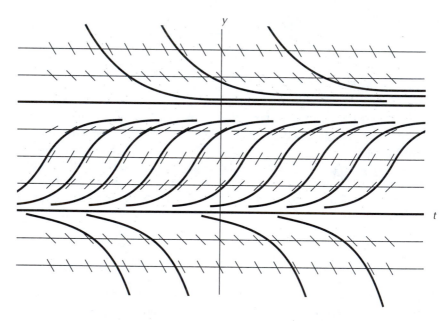

Figure 24.9

Graphs of the solutions of $\dot{y} = y(2 - y)$.

$y = 2$ are constant solutions, i.e., steady states. If you start at a point y_0 above 2, the system will decrease asymptotically to 2 from above. If you start at a point between 0 and 2, the system will increase asymptotically to 2. In fact, no matter where you start with initial value $y_0 > 0$, the solution through y_0 will tend to $y = 2$ as $t \to \infty$. The solution $y(t) = 2$ is an **asymptotically stable equilibrium**. On the other hand, $y = 0$ is an **unstable equilibrium**; for initial conditions very near $y = 0$, the corresponding solution will drift away from $y = 0$.

EXERCISES

24.22   Draw the direction fields and the graphs of representative solution curves for the following differential equations:

   a) $\dot{y} = \dfrac{ty}{1 + t^2}$;   b) $\dot{y} = y(y - 2)$;   c) $\dot{y} = y/t$;

   d) $\dot{y} = \dfrac{y - t}{y + t}$;   e) $\dot{y} = t^2 - y^2$;   f) $\dot{y} = y(y^2 - 1)$.

24.23   Draw the direction field for the equation $\dot{y} = 3y^{2/3}$ of Example 24.17. Sketch in some solution curves and illustrate the multiple solutions for the initial value problem $y(0) = 0$.

24.5   PHASE PORTRAITS AND EQUILIBRIA ON $\mathbf{R}^1$

Drawing Phase Portraits

The graphs in Figure 24.9 illustrate the primary feature of autonomous differential equations: how the system evolves depends on where it starts, not on when it starts. In Figure 24.9 the graph of the solution curve through $(t_0, y_0) = (1, 1)$ or the one through $(2, 1)$ are simply *translates* of the solution curve which starts at $(t_0, y_0) = (0, 1)$. This observation suggests that we can view the information in Figure 24.9 more efficiently by looking at the y-axis. As you move along the graph of any solution in the ty-plane in Figure 24.9, follow the shadow or projection on the y-axis of your path in the plane. For example, as you move along the graph starting at $(t_0, y_0) = (0, 1/2)$, the projection of this motion on the y-axis drifts upward toward $y = 2$. Basically, by looking at the projection of these graphs on the y-axis, you're concentrating on the behavior of $y(t)$ while ignoring how t changes. If you start anywhere between $y = 0$ and $y = 2$ and follow the above procedure, you'll drift upward toward $y = 2$. If you start at $y = 2$, you'll stay there forever. If you start above $y = 2$, you'll drift back down toward $y = 2$. If you start precisely at $y = 0$, you'll stay there forever. But if you're off by the slightest amount — 1/100th of the radius of an electron — you'll drift away from

$y = 0$. In particular, if you start anywhere below $y = 0$, $y(t)$ will become more and more negative as t increases. We can summarize these observations by drawing the appropriate direction arrows on the y-axis, as in Figure 24.10. (We've drawn the y-axis horizontally to use the space in this book more efficiently.)

**Figure
24.10**

The phase portrait of $\dot{y} = y(2 - y)$.

Figure 24.10 summarizes most of the information that we care about from Figure 24.9. It tells us how solutions of $\dot{y} = y(2-y)$ change over time, sublimating the time factor to simplify the picture. It is called the **phase portrait** of the differential equation $\dot{y} = y(2 - y)$.

Notice that we cannot draw a one-dimensional phase portrait for a nonnonautonomous differential equation, because for such equations whether $y(t)$ increases or decreases from any given y_0 often depends on the time t_0 *when* the process starts, as Figure 24.5 illustrates.

Actually, drawing a phase portrait is a much easier operation than we have made it appear. We want to know where $y(t)$ is increasing and where $y(t)$ is decreasing. Alternatively, we want to know where $\dot{y}$ is positive and where $\dot{y}$ is negative. Since $\dot{y} = f(y)$, $y(t)$ is increasing on intervals where $f(y)$ is positive and decreasing on intervals where $f(y)$ is negative. To actually draw the phase portrait of $\dot{y} = f(y)$, first find the zeros of $f(y)$ and then check the sign of f on each of the intervals between these zeros. If we can draw the graph of $f(y)$, we simply mark intervals where the graph lies above the axis with an arrow pointing right and intervals where the graph lies below the axis with an arrow pointing left. We've done this in Figure 24.11 for $\dot{y} = y(2 - y)$.

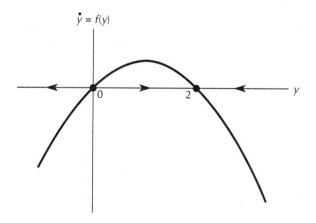

**Figure
24.11**

Using the graph of $y(2 - y)$ to draw the phase portrait of $\dot{y} = y(2 - y)$.

Example 24.21   Let's use this method to draw the phase portrait of

$$\dot{y} = y - y^3. \tag{44}$$

We've drawn the graph of $y - y^3$ in Figure 24.12. Since $y - y^3 = y(1-y)(1+y)$, the stationary points of (44) occur at $y = 0, 1, -1$. To find the sign of $y - y^3$ in each of the intervals $(-\infty, -1), (-1, 0), (0, 1)$, and $(1, \infty)$, we just evaluated this function at a point in each of these intervals. In the intervals $(-1, 0)$ and $(1, \infty)$, the graph of $y - y^3$ lies below the y-axis. This means that $\dot{y} = y - y^3$ is negative there and so $y(t)$ is decreasing — a fact we've marked in each of these intervals with an arrow pointing to the left. Similarly, in the intervals $(-\infty, -1)$ and $(0, 1)$, $\dot{y} = y - y^3$ is positive and $y(t)$ is increasing — a fact that we've marked in these intervals in Figure 24.12 with arrows pointing to the right.

   We can easily read the evolution of differential equation (44) from the phase portrait in Figure 24.12. If one starts to the left of 0, the system tends to the steady state $y = -1$. If one starts anywhere to the right of $y = 0$, the system tends to the steady state $y = 1$. The unstable equilibrium at $y = 0$ is the boundary (or **separatrix**) between the region of attraction of $y = -1$ and that of $y = +1$.

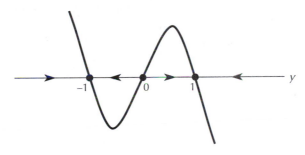

The phase portrait of $\dot{y} = y - y^3$.

**Figure
24.12**

Example 24.22   Let's add a small complication to the differential equation (44) and consider the equation

$$\dot{y} = e^y(y - y^3). \tag{45}$$

This equation will surely not have an illuminating closed form solution, if it has a closed form solution at all. To draw its phase portrait, we need to draw the graph of $f(y) = e^y(y - y^3)$. However, we are really only interested in where f is positive and where f is negative. Since the e^y factor is always positive, $f(y)$ will have the same sign as $y - y^3$ for any y. This implies that equation (45) has the same phase portrait as equation (44) in the previous example. The only difference is in the speed of the motion; for example, $y(t)$ will move to $+\infty$ much more quickly for (45) than it will for (44). The time factor is hidden when we draw the phase portrait.

Stability of Equilibria on the Line

The last three examples illustrate the important role that equilibria play in the analysis of the behavior of differential equations. The drawing of the phase portraits begins with the zeros of the differential equation. In general, *the one-dimensional system under study will converge to one of the asymptotically stable equilibria (or go off to infinity)*; the basins of attraction for each such equilibrium will be an interval bounded by the unstable equilibria on either side of the asymptotically stable one. In our study of differential equations in $\mathbf{R}^n$ in the next chapter, we will see that the stationary solutions continue to play this critical role there, both in the drawing of the phase portraits and in the description of the behavior of the system.

The computation of the equilibria is a simple analytic process; just solve the algebraic equation $f(y) = 0$. Our next task is to make the determination of the stability of the equilibria a straightforward analytical procedure too — one which we can do without drawing the whole phase portrait. A careful look at Figures 24.10 and 24.11 shows how to codify this procedure. An equilibrium will be *asymptotically stable* if the flow moves toward it on both sides, as in Figure 24.13a. This means that $y(t)$ is increasing on the left and decreasing on the right of the equilibrium y_0, or that $f(y) > 0$ for $y < y_0$ and $f(y) < 0$ for $y > y_0$. Since $f(y_0) = 0$, y_0 will be an asymptotically stable equilibrium if f is a decreasing function of y in a neighborhood of y_0. One way to guarantee this, of course, is to have $f'(y_0) < 0$.

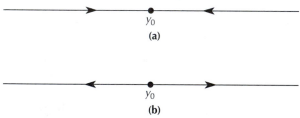

(a)

(b)

Figure 24.13 *Phase portrait around an asymptotically stable (a) and unstable (b) equilibrium.*

On the other hand, if $f(y_0) = 0$ and $f'(y_0) > 0$, then f will be an increasing function in a neighborhood of y_0, negative on the left and positive on the right. Since $\dot{y} = f(y)$, $\dot{y}$ will be negative on the left of y_0 and positive on the right, and $y(t)$ will be decreasing to the left of y_0 and increasing to the right. As Figure 24.13b illustrates, this means that y_0 is an *unstable* equilibrium. The following theorem summarizes this discussion.

Theorem 24.6   Let y_0 be a rest point of the C^1 differential equation $\dot{y} = f(y)$ on the line; so $f(y_0) = 0$. If $f'(y_0) < 0$, then y_0 is an asymptotically stable equilibrium. If $f'(y_0) > 0$, then y_0 is an unstable equilibrium.

Example 24.23   Let's compute the stability of rest points of the differential equation

$$\dot{y} = \frac{y^2 - 1}{y^2 + 1} \tag{46}$$

without drawing the whole phase portrait. Setting the right-hand side of (46) equal to zero, we see that $y = -1$ and $y = 1$ are the equilibria. The derivative of the right-hand side is $4y/(y^2 + 1)^2$, which is negative at $y = -1$ and positive at $y = +1$. Therefore, $y = -1$ is an asymptotically stable equilibrium and $y = +1$ is an unstable equilibrium.

Remark   There are a few other phase portraits that can occur in the neighborhood of an equilibrium besides the two in Figure 24.13. Arrows on both sides of the equilibrium can point in the *same* direction, as in the first two parts of Figure 24.14. In this case, we still say that the equilibrium is unstable. A more careful description would be: "unstable from the right and stable from the left." The third phase portrait in Figure 24.14 shows a sequence of rest points converging to a rest point. If this behavior occurs on both sides of a rest point, for example, if the rest point is in the interior of an interval of rest points, we say that the equilibrium is **neutrally stable**. It's not asymptotically stable, because nearby points do not flow back to the equilibrium. It's not unstable because nearby points don't flow away from the equilibrium, at least not very much. The notion of neutral stability lies between the other two notions of stability. By Theorem 24.6, the situations in Figure 24.14 can only occur if $f'(y_0) = 0$ at the equilibrium y_0. However, if $f'(y_0) = 0$, y_0 can be a stable, unstable, or neutrally stable equilibrium. One would

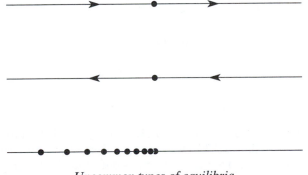

Uncommon types of equilibria.

Figure 24.14

need much more information to decide among these possibilities. Typically, for a generic real-valued function, $f'(y_0) \neq 0$ whenever $f(y_0) = 0$, and one can use Theorem 24.6 to determine the stability of all the rest points.

EXERCISES

24.24   Draw the phase portrait of (46).

24.25   Draw the phase portrait of the following differential equations:

a) $\dot{y} = y(y - 2)$;   b) $\dot{y} = e^{-y}y(y - 2)$;   c) $\dot{y} = y(y - 1)(y - 2)$;

d) $\dot{y} = y/(y^2 + 1)$;   e) $\dot{y} = e^y \cos y$;   f) $\dot{y} = y^2(1 - y)$.

24.26   Draw the phase portrait for $y \geq 0$ and discuss the dynamics of the following differential equations, sometimes used to model the growth of populations. Assume $r > 0$.

a) (Gompertz law) $\dot{y} = ry\ln(K/y)$, $y > 0$.

b) (modified logistic equation) $\dot{y} = ry^\alpha(1 - y/K)$, for some constant $\alpha \geq 1$;

c) (minimal viable population) $\dot{y} = ry\left((y/k_0) - 1\right)(1 - (y/k))$, $0 < k_0 < k$;

d) (constant effort harvesting) $\dot{y} = ry(1 - y/k) - Ey$, where the harvest rate is proportional to the effort E spent harvesting and the size of the population y.

24.27   For the following differential equations, compute the equilibria and determine the stability of each: $\dot{y} = y(y - 1)/(y^2 + 1)$; $\dot{y} = e^y \sin y$; $\dot{y} = y^2/(2 + y^2)$.

24.6   APPENDIX: APPLICATIONS

In this section, we will illustrate how to derive the indirect money market utility function for a consumer from that consumer's demand function by solving a differential equation. Then, we will use the Fundamental Existence and Uniqueness Theorem of Differential Equations, Theorem 24.5, to prove the converse of Euler's theorem on homogeneous functions.

Indirect Money Metric Utility Functions

The **indirect money metric utility function** μ was defined in Section 22.1 to be

$$\mu(\mathbf{p}; \mathbf{q}, I) \equiv E(\mathbf{p}, V(\mathbf{q}, I)), \tag{47}$$

where E and V are the expenditure and indirect utility functions corresponding to a specific utility function U. The number $\mu(\mathbf{p}, \mathbf{q}, I)$ measures how much income one would need at prices $\mathbf{p}$ to be as well-off as one would be facing prices $\mathbf{q}$ and having income I. The function μ is particularly useful because it behaves like an expenditure function with respect to $\mathbf{p}$ and an indirect utility function with respect to $\mathbf{q}$ and I. Furthermore, it has the advantage of being defined unambiguously in terms of observable quantities. Furthermore, as will now be demonstrated, μ can be recovered from demand functions $(\mathbf{p}, I) \longmapsto \xi(\mathbf{p}, I)$ by solving a differential equation.

Let $(\mathbf{p}, u) \longmapsto \mathbf{Z}(\mathbf{p}, u)$ denote a consumer's compensated (or Hicksian) demand function, and $(\mathbf{p}, I) \longmapsto \xi(\mathbf{p}, I)$ the corresponding Marshallian demand. Recall from Section 22.1 that $\mathbf{Z}$ satisfies:

(1) $\mathbf{Z}(\mathbf{p}, u) = \xi(\mathbf{p}, E(\mathbf{p}, u))$ and
(2) $(\partial E / \partial p_i)(\mathbf{p}, u) = Z_i(\mathbf{p}, u)$.

Combining these two expressions yields the partial differential equation

$$\frac{\partial E}{\partial p_i}(\mathbf{p}, V(\mathbf{q}, I)) = \xi_i(\mathbf{p}, E(\mathbf{p}, V(\mathbf{q}, I))),$$

or using (47), $\qquad \dfrac{\partial \mu}{\partial p_i}(\mathbf{p}; \mathbf{q}, I) = \xi_i(\mathbf{p}, \mu(\mathbf{p}; \mathbf{q}, I)).$

Since $E(\mathbf{q}, V(\mathbf{q}, I)) = I$ by Theorem 22.7, $\mu(\mathbf{q}; \mathbf{q}, I) = I$. Therefore, given demand functions $\xi(\mathbf{p}, I)$, the solution of the system of partial differential equations

$$\frac{\partial Y}{\partial p_i}(\mathbf{p}) = \xi_i(\mathbf{p}, Y(\mathbf{p})), \qquad i = 1, \dots, n, \tag{48}$$

that satisfies the initial condition $Y(\mathbf{q}) = I$ will be the indirect money metric utility function $\mathbf{p} \longmapsto \mu(\mathbf{p}; \mathbf{q}, I)$ corresponding to demand function ξ.

In particular, if we normalize prices (p_1, p_2) in a *two-good* economy so that $p_2 = 1$, then p_1 is the only independent variable and the partial differential equation (48) becomes a single *ordinary* differential equation:

$$\frac{dy}{dp_1} = \xi_1((p_1, 1), y). \tag{49}$$

Given a demand function ξ_1 for good 1, we solve the usually nonautonomous differential equation (49) for $y(p_1) = Y(p_1, 1)$.

For example, suppose that the demand ξ for good 1 in a two-good economy with normalized price $p_2 = 1$ satisfies the demand function $\ln \xi = ap + bI + c$. By (49), the corresponding indirect money metric utility function $Y(p) = \mu(p; q, I)$ satisfies the initial value problem

$$\frac{dY}{dp} = e^{ap} \cdot e^{bY} \cdot e^c, \qquad Y(q) = I.$$

This problem is solved explicitly in Example 24.9, using separation of variables.

Converse of Euler's Theorem

Finally, we use the Fundamental Existence and Uniqueness Theorem of Differential Equations, Theorem 24.5, to prove the converse of Euler's theorem on homogeneous functions. See Theorems 20.4 and 20.5.

Theorem 24.7   Suppose that $f: C \to \mathbf{R}^1$ is a C^1 function defined on an open cone C in $\mathbf{R}^n$ and that

$$\nabla f(\mathbf{x}) \cdot \mathbf{x} = kf(\mathbf{x}) \quad \text{for all } \mathbf{x} \in C. \tag{50}$$

Then, $f(t\mathbf{x}) = t^k \cdot f(\mathbf{x})$ for all $t > 0$ and all $\mathbf{x} \in C$.

Proof   Fix $\mathbf{x} \in C$. Define the two functions ϕ_1 and ϕ_2 from $\mathbf{R}_+$ to C by

$$\phi_1(t) = f(t\mathbf{x}) \quad \text{and} \quad \phi_2(t) = t^k \cdot f(\mathbf{x}).$$

We first show that ϕ_1 and ϕ_2 both satisfy the following initial value problem for $y(t)$:

$$\frac{dy(t)}{dt} = \frac{k}{t} y(t), \qquad y(1) = f(\mathbf{x}). \tag{51}$$

One simply differentiates ϕ_1 and ϕ_2 with respect to t:

$$\phi_1'(t) = \nabla f(t\mathbf{x}) \cdot \mathbf{x} \qquad \text{(Chain Rule)}$$

$$= \frac{\nabla f(t\mathbf{x}) \cdot t\mathbf{x}}{t}$$

$$= \frac{k f(t\mathbf{x})}{t} \qquad \text{(using (50))}$$

$$= \frac{k}{t} \phi_1(t) \qquad \text{(definition of } \phi_1\text{)},$$

$$\phi_2'(t) = kt^{k-1} f(\mathbf{x})$$

$$= \frac{k}{t} t^k f(\mathbf{x})$$

$$= \frac{k}{t} \cdot \phi_2(t) \qquad \text{(definition of } \phi_2\text{)}.$$

Since ϕ_1 and ϕ_2 both satisfy the same initial value problem (51) at $t = 1$, they are equal for an interval of t about $t = 1$ by Theorem 24.5. One can use a refinement of Theorem 24.5 to verify that $\phi_1(t) = \phi_2(t)$ for all $t > 0$. ∎

EXERCISES

24.28 Use differential equation (48) to find the indirect money metric utility function that corresponds to the log-linear demand function $\ln \xi = a \ln p + b \ln I + c$.

Ordinary Differential Equations: Systems of Equations

The last chapter focused on the dynamics of a one-dimensional variable y as it evolves according to the differential equation $\dot{y} = f(y, t)$. In real-world problems, there are usually a number of variables evolving at the same time with the values of any one variable affecting the rates of change of the others. For example, in dynamic microeconomic models, price changes in one good affect the prices of a number of other goods — especially that good's complements and substitutes. In dynamic macroeconomic models, the evolution of a country's domestic variables (e.g., inflation, unemployment, interest rates) is closely linked to the evolution of its non-domestic variables (e.g., exchange rates, balance of payments). Consideration of such situations leads to the study of *systems* of coupled differential equations.

25.1   PLANAR SYSTEMS: AN INTRODUCTION

Coupled Systems of Differential Equations

This first section describes examples of systems of two equations and two variables — each evolving over time and each affecting the rate of change of the other. As an illustrative example, consider the case in which two populations of organisms are interacting with each other. For example, they could be two populations in competition with each other for the same food supply or ecological niche, or more dramatically, one population may be the main food supply for the other.

Let's begin with a model of two **competing species**. Let $y_1(t)$ denote the size of one population at time t and $y_2(t)$ the size of the other. We assume that each population has its own logistic growth equation:

$$\frac{\dot{y}_1}{y_1} = a_1 - b_1 y_1 \quad \text{and} \quad \frac{\dot{y}_2}{y_2} = a_2 - b_2 y_2.$$

To model the competition between the two species, we assume that the presence of one species has a negative effect on the growth rate of the other — for simplicity, in a linear way,

$$\frac{\dot{y}_1}{y_1} = a_1 - b_1 y_1 - c_1 y_2 \quad \text{and} \quad \frac{\dot{y}_2}{y_2} = a_2 - b_2 y_2 - c_2 y_1.$$

So the interactions of these two populations are modeled by the *coupled* system of differential equations

$$\dot{y}_1 = y_1(a_1 - b_1 y_1 - c_1 y_2)$$
$$\dot{y}_2 = y_2(a_2 - b_2 y_2 - c_2 y_1). \tag{1}$$

In system (1), all constants are positive. Different types of interactions can be modeled by putting a plus sign in front of one or both of the c_i-terms in (1); for example, *mutualism* with two plus signs and *parasitism* with one plus sign and one minus sign.

What would a simple model of a **predator-prey** system look like? Let $x(t)$ denote the size of the prey population at time t and $y(t)$ the size of the predator population at time t. For simplicity, assume that the prey is the main food source for the predator and that the presence of the predator means that crowding will not be a problem for the prey. The dynamics of the prey population are given by the equation:

$$\frac{\dot{x}}{x} = A - By,$$

where A is the natural growth rate of the prey in the absence of the predators and the $-By$ term indicates the negative effect of the predator on the prey population. On the other hand, the predator's population growth rate is described by the equation

$$\frac{\dot{y}}{y} = -C + Dx.$$

The $-C$-term models the assumption that the predator population will fall in the absence of the prey. The $+Dx$-term indicates the positive effect of the size of the prey population on the growth rate of the predators. Thus, this simple model for the predator-prey interaction leads to the coupled system of differential equations

$$\dot{x} = x(A - By)$$
$$\dot{y} = y(-C + Dx). \tag{2}$$

This system is called the **Lotka-Volterra system** or the **D'Ancona-Volterra system**. Alfred Lotka was one of the first to study mathematical models of interacting populations. The Italian ecologist Umberto D'Ancona and mathematician Vito Volterra used this model to study the ecology of fish in the Adriatic Sea.

These two similar-looking population models (1) and (2) lead to very different dynamic behaviors. In the first model (1), the system converges to an equilibrium, in which either one species loses the competition and eventually dies out or both species stabilize at positive levels to share the niche. In the predator-prey model (2), the system does not converge to any equilibrium; instead, the two populations oscillate in size in a continual ecological cycle. We will examine these models in depth in Sections 25.5 and 25.6.

Vocabulary

The general first order system of two differential equations can be written as

$$\dot{x} = F(x, y, t)$$
$$\dot{y} = G(x, y, t). \tag{3}$$

A solution of (3) is a pair of *functions* of t, $x^*(t)$ and $y^*(t)$, such that for every t,

$$\dot{x}^*(t) = F\left(x^*(t), y^*(t), t\right)$$
$$\dot{y}^*(t) = G\left(x^*(t), y^*(t), t\right). \tag{4}$$

System (3) is a **first order system** because it involves only the *first* derivative of both unknown functions. If F and G do not depend explicitly on t, as in systems (1) and (2), the system is called **autonomous** or **time-independent**. Otherwise, it's called **nonautonomous** or **time-dependent**. If the growth rate of one population varies seasonally or if the populations interact more intensely at different times of the year than at others, we would be led to a system of *time-dependent* equations. We will work with autonomous systems in the rest of this chapter.

As with single equations of one variable, a solution of system (3) which contains parameters, say k_1 and k_2, such that by varying the values of these parameters, one can obtain *every* solution of system (3), is called a **general solution** of (3). A general solution of a system of n first order equations in $\mathbf{R}^n$ should contain n independent parameters. If we want to specify one particular solution, we will need to specify an initial condition for each of the unknown functions. The problem of finding a particular solution $(x^*(t), y^*(t))$ of system (3) which also satisfies initial conditions $x(t_0) = x_0$ and $y(t_0) = y_0$ is called an **initial value problem**.

There are a couple of ways that systems of two differential equations arise naturally from single differential equations of one variable.

Fact 25.1. Every *second* order system of one variable can be naturally written as a *first* order system in two variables.

To carry out this task, one introduces a new variable, the velocity $v = \dot{y}$. Then, a second order equation in y is a first order equation in $\dot{y}$. One writes the second order equation $\ddot{y} = f(\dot{y}, y, t)$ as the pair of first order equations

$$\dot{y} = v$$

$$\dot{v} = f(v, y, t).$$

Problems in the physical sciences are usually treated this way. Recall that because of Newton's law $F = ma$, second order equations arise naturally in the physical sciences. Because physicists and engineers are interested in tracking both y and $\dot{y}$, not just y, they find it convenient to write their second order equations in y as first order systems in y and $\dot{y}$. The position-velocity pair $(y, \dot{y})$ is called a **state variable**. The set of all possible state variables is called **state space**.

As we will see in Section 25.3, in order to explicitly solve a given system of first order equations we sometimes reverse this process and write the system as a single second order equation of one variable and then try to apply some of the techniques described in Section 24.3.

Fact 25.2. Every *nonautonomous* differential equation $\dot{y} = f(y, t)$ in y can be written as an *autonomous* system of two differential equations in (y, r):

$$\dot{y} = f(y, r)$$
$$\dot{r} = 1. \tag{5}$$

To verify the equivalence between the equation $\dot{y} = f(y, t)$ and system (5), note that the solution of the second equation $\dot{r} = 1$ in (5) is simply $r(t) = t$. Plug this into the first equation to reconstruct the original nonautonomous equation. At first, it may seem that little is gained from this simplistic change. Yet, Fact 25.2 really does mean that in the study of differential systems and in the development of the theory of differential equations, one need only work with autonomous systems.

Existence and Uniqueness

The existence and uniqueness theorem for solutions of differential equations of one variable, discussed in Section 24.4, holds equally well for *systems* of differential equations. If F and G are continuous functions in a neighborhood of (x_0, y_0, t_0), then there exist functions $x^*(t)$ and $y^*(t)$ defined and continuous on an open interval $I = (t_0 - \varepsilon, t_0 + \varepsilon)$ about t_0 such that (4) holds for all $t \in I$ and $x(t_0) = x_0$ and $y(t_0) = y_0$. Furthermore, if F and G are C^1 functions, the solution of the initial value problem is unique.

25.2   LINEAR SYSTEMS VIA EIGENVALUES

It is natural to begin our analysis of systems of differential equations with the study of *linear systems*. Linear systems are important for a number of reasons. Not only can linear systems be solved explicitly, but, as usual, we will study nonlinear systems by gleaning information from their linear approximations. The general linear system of differential equations can be written as

$$\dot{x}_1 = a_{11}x_1 + \cdots + a_{1n}x_n$$

$$\vdots \qquad \vdots \qquad\qquad \vdots \qquad\qquad (6)$$

$$\dot{x}_n = a_{n1}x_1 + \cdots + a_{nn}x_n,$$

or simply as $\dot{\mathbf{x}} = A\mathbf{x}$. If A is a diagonal matrix, that is, if all $a_{ij} = 0$ for $i \neq j$ in (6), then (6) separates into n self-contained equations $\dot{x}_i = a_{ii}x_i$, with no interactions between them. In this case, the system is easily solved as

$$x_1(t) = c_1 e^{a_{11}t}, \ldots, x_n(t) = c_n e^{a_{nn}t}. \qquad (7)$$

If some off-diagonal a_{ij}'s are not zero so that the equations are linked to each other, then we can use eigenvalues and eigenvectors of A to unlink system (6) into n more or less self-contained equations, just as we did with systems of linear difference equations.

Distinct Real Eigenvalues

First, suppose that A has n distinct real eigenvalues $r_1, \ldots, r_n$ with corresponding eigenvectors $\mathbf{v}_1, \ldots, \mathbf{v}_n$:

$$A\mathbf{v}_i = r_i\mathbf{v}_i. \qquad (8)$$

Let P be the $n \times n$ matrix whose columns are these n eigenvectors:

$$P = [\mathbf{v}_1 \ \mathbf{v}_2 \cdots \mathbf{v}_n].$$

Then, equations (8) can be written as

$$AP = PD, \qquad \text{where } D \equiv \begin{pmatrix} r_1 & 0 & \cdots & 0 \\ 0 & r_2 & \cdots & 0 \\ \vdots & \vdots & \ddots & \vdots \\ 0 & 0 & \cdots & r_n \end{pmatrix}.$$

Since eigenvectors for distinct eigenvalues are linearly independent (Theorem 23.5), P is nonsingular and therefore invertible; we can write

$$P^{-1}AP = D. \tag{9}$$

Now use the linear change of variables $\mathbf{y} = P^{-1}\mathbf{x}$, with inverse $\mathbf{x} = P\mathbf{y}$, to transform system (6) to one in the variables $y_1, \ldots, y_n$:

$$\dot{\mathbf{y}} = P^{-1}\dot{\mathbf{x}} \qquad \text{(differentiating } \mathbf{y}(t) = P^{-1}\mathbf{x}(t) \text{ with respect to } t)$$
$$= P^{-1}A\mathbf{x} \qquad \text{(since } \dot{\mathbf{x}} = A\mathbf{x})$$
$$= P^{-1}AP\mathbf{y} \qquad \text{(since } \mathbf{x} = P\mathbf{y})$$
$$= D\mathbf{y} \qquad \text{(by (9)).}$$

Since D is a diagonal matrix, the system $\dot{\mathbf{y}} = D\mathbf{y}$ can be written as

$$\dot{y}_1 = r_1 y_1, \ldots, \dot{y}_n = r_n y_n.$$

Its solution is

$$\begin{pmatrix} y_1(t) \\ \vdots \\ y_n(t) \end{pmatrix} = \begin{pmatrix} c_1 e^{r_1 t} \\ \vdots \\ c_n e^{r_n t} \end{pmatrix}.$$

Finally, use the transformation $\mathbf{x} = P\mathbf{y}$ to return to the original coordinates $x_1, \ldots, x_n$:

$$\mathbf{x}(t) = P\mathbf{y}(t)$$
$$= [\mathbf{v}_1 \cdots \mathbf{v}_n] \begin{pmatrix} c_1 e^{r_1 t} \\ \vdots \\ c_n e^{r_n t} \end{pmatrix}$$
$$= c_1 e^{r_1 t}\mathbf{v}_1 + c_2 e^{r_2 t}\mathbf{v}_2 + \cdots + c_n e^{r_n t}\mathbf{v}_n.$$

The following theorem summarizes these calculations.

Theorem 25.1 Suppose that the $n \times n$ matrix A has n distinct real eigenvalues $r_1, \ldots, r_n$, with corresponding eigenvectors $\mathbf{v}_1, \ldots, \mathbf{v}_n$. Then, the general solution of the linear system $\dot{\mathbf{x}} = A\mathbf{x}$ of differential equations is

$$\mathbf{x}(t) = c_1 e^{r_1 t}\mathbf{v}_1 + c_2 e^{r_2 t}\mathbf{v}_2 + \cdots + c_n e^{r_n t}\mathbf{v}_n. \tag{10}$$

Of course, Theorem 25.1 is still valid if A has multiple eigenvalues, as long as each eigenvalue of multiplicity $h > 1$ has h linearly independent eigenvectors. This leaves two situations to consider: complex eigenvalues and multiple eigenvalues with not enough eigenvectors. For the sake of exposition, we will work on these two situations for $n = 2$. The n-dimensional analogues are straightforward.

Complex Eigenvalues

Consider the case where the 2×2 real matrix A has complex eigenvalues. We learned in Section 23.5 that in this case the eigenvalues are complex conjugates of each other, as are the corresponding eigenvectors. Write $r_1 = \alpha + i\beta$ and $r_2 = \bar{r}_1 = \alpha - i\beta$ for the complex eigenvalues of A, and write $\mathbf{v} = \mathbf{u} + i\mathbf{w}$ and $\bar{\mathbf{v}} = \mathbf{u} - i\mathbf{w}$ for the corresponding eigenvectors. Then, the proof of Theorem 25.1 yields

$$\mathbf{x}(t) = c_1 e^{(\alpha+i\beta)t}(\mathbf{u} + i\mathbf{w}) + c_2 e^{(\alpha-i\beta)t}(\mathbf{u} - i\mathbf{w}) \tag{11}$$

for the general solution of (6). As discussed in Section 24.3, Euler's formula implies

$$e^{(\alpha\pm i\beta)t} = e^{\alpha t}(\cos \beta t \pm i \sin \beta t).$$

By the argument we used in Sections 24.3 and 23.5, since $e^{(\alpha+i\beta)t}(\mathbf{u} + i\mathbf{w})$ and $e^{(\alpha-i\beta)t}(\mathbf{u} - i\mathbf{w})$ are complex conjugates of each other, if we choose the constants c_1 and c_2 to be complex numbers *which are complex conjugates of each other*, the corresponding solution (11) will be a *real* solution, namely,

$$\begin{aligned}
\mathbf{x}(t) &= (c_1 + ic_2)e^{\alpha t}(\cos \beta t + i \sin \beta t)(\mathbf{u} + i\mathbf{w}) \\
&\quad + (c_1 - ic_2)e^{\alpha t}(\cos \beta t - i \sin \beta t)(\mathbf{u} - i\mathbf{w}) \\
&= e^{\alpha t}\left[(C_1 \cos \beta t - C_2 \sin \beta t)\mathbf{u} - (C_1 \sin \beta t + C_2 \cos \beta t)\mathbf{w} \right],
\end{aligned}$$

where $C_1 = 2c_1$ and $C_2 = 2c_2$. The following theorem summarizes these calculations.

Theorem 25.2   Let A be a real 2×2 matrix with complex eigenvalues $\alpha \pm i\beta$ and corresponding eigenvectors $\mathbf{u} \pm i\mathbf{w}$. Then, the general solution of the linear system of differential equations $\dot{\mathbf{x}} = A\mathbf{x}$ is

$$\mathbf{x}(t) = e^{\alpha t} \cos \beta t\, (C_1\mathbf{u} - C_2\mathbf{w}) - e^{\alpha t} \sin \beta t\, (C_2\mathbf{u} + C_1\mathbf{w}). \tag{12}$$

Multiple Real Eigenvalues

If A is a real 2×2 matrix with *equal* eigenvalues $r_1 = r_2 = r$ and only one independent eigenvector $\mathbf{v}$, then, as demonstrated in Section 23.4, A is not diagonalizable. However, one can come close to diagonalizing A. In particular, A has a *generalized eigenvector* $\mathbf{w}$, which satisfies $(A - rI)\mathbf{w} = \mathbf{v}$, so that $(A - rI)^2 \mathbf{w} = \mathbf{0}$. By using the change of variables matrix $P = [\mathbf{v} \ \mathbf{w}]$, one computes the analogue of equation (9) for this situation:

$$P^{-1}AP = \begin{pmatrix} r & 1 \\ 0 & r \end{pmatrix}.$$

The change of variables $\mathbf{y} = P^{-1}\mathbf{x}$ transforms the original equations to the system

$$\begin{aligned} \dot{y}_1 &= ry_1 + y_2 \\ \dot{y}_2 &= ry_2. \end{aligned} \tag{13}$$

The solution of the second equation in system (13) is, of course, $y_2(t) = c_2 e^{rt}$. Substituting this solution for y_2 into the first equation of (13) yields the *nonhomogeneous linear first order* differential equation

$$\dot{y}_1 = ry_1 + c_2 e^{rt}. \tag{14}$$

By the method of Section 24.2, the general solution of equation (14) is

$$y_1(t) = (c_1 + c_2 t)e^{rt}. \tag{15}$$

(Check.) The transformation $\mathbf{x} = P\mathbf{y}$ back to the x_i-coordinates leads to the solution

$$\begin{pmatrix} x_1(t) \\ x_2(t) \end{pmatrix} = [\mathbf{v} \ \ \mathbf{w}] \begin{pmatrix} y_1(t) \\ y_2(t) \end{pmatrix}$$

$$= (c_1 + c_2 t)e^{rt}\mathbf{v} + c_2 e^{rt}\mathbf{w}.$$

The following theorem summarizes these calculations.

Theorem 25.3 Suppose that the 2×2 matrix A has equal eigenvalues $r_1 = r_2 = r$ and only one independent eigenvector $\mathbf{v}$. Let $\mathbf{w}$ be a generalized eigenvector for A. Then, the general solution of the linear system of differential equations $\dot{\mathbf{x}} = A\mathbf{x}$ is

$$\mathbf{x}(t) = e^{rt}(c_1\mathbf{v} + c_2\mathbf{w}) + te^{rt}(c_2\mathbf{v}). \tag{16}$$

EXERCISES

25.1 Write out the general solution of each of the following linear systems of equations:

a) $\dot{x} = 2x + y$
$\dot{y} = -12x - 5y;$

b) $\dot{x} = 6x - 3y$
$\dot{y} = -2x + y;$

c) $\dot{x} = x + 4y$
$\dot{y} = 3x + 2y;$

d) $\dot{x} = 4y$
$\dot{y} = -x + 4y;$

e) $\dot{x} = -2x + 5y$
$\dot{y} = -2x + 4y;$

f) $\dot{x} = x - 2y - 6z$
$\dot{y} = 2x + 5y + 6z$
$\dot{z} = -2x - 2y - 3z.$

25.2 Write the second order equation for the spring in Section 24.1 as a first order system.

25.3 Write the second order equation for a pendulum $m\ddot{y} + a\dot{y} + mg\sin y = 0$ as a first order system.

25.4 Derive solution (15) for differential equation (14).

25.5 Suppose that the 3×3 matrix A has an eigenvalue of multiplicity three and only one independent eigenvector. Write out and prove the analogue of Theorem 25.3 for this case.

25.3   SOLVING LINEAR SYSTEMS BY SUBSTITUTION

This section presents an alternative approach to finding explicit solutions of linear systems of differential equations that does not use eigenvalues or eigenvectors. The technique we will use in this section is called **solution by substitution**. Its basic premise is the reverse of the process described in Fact 25.1; one writes a first order system of two variables as a second order system of one variable and then uses the techniques for solving second order systems described in Section 24.3.

Instead of working with a general first order **linear system** with constant coefficients

$$\dot{y}_1 = a_{11}y_1 + a_{12}y_2$$
$$\dot{y}_2 = a_{21}y_1 + a_{22}y_2, \tag{17}$$

we will first work with an illustrative specific example:

$$\dot{y}_1 = y_1 + 4y_2$$
$$\dot{y}_2 = y_1 + y_2. \tag{18}$$

Taking a cue from the substitution method for solving algebraic systems of equations, we solve the first equation of (18) for y_2 in terms of y_1 and $\dot{y}_1$:

$$y_2 = \frac{1}{4}(\dot{y}_1 - y_1). \tag{19}$$

We will plug this solution into the second equation of (18). But, since the second equation of (18) involves both y_2 and $\dot{y}_2$, we need an expression for $\dot{y}_2$ in terms of y_1 too. Such an expression is easily achieved by differentiating equation (19) with respect to t:

$$\dot{y}_2 = \frac{1}{4}(\ddot{y}_1 - \dot{y}_1). \tag{20}$$

Now we plug (19) and (20) in the second equation of our original system (18):

$$\frac{1}{4}(\ddot{y}_1 - \dot{y}_1) = y_1 + \frac{1}{4}(\dot{y}_1 - y_1),$$

or $$\ddot{y}_1 - 2\dot{y}_1 - 3y_1 = 0. \tag{21}$$

This is a simple second order linear equation which can be solved by the method of Section 24.3. Looking for solutions of the form $y_1 = e^{rt}$, we solve the corresponding characteristic equation $r^2 - 2r - 3 = 0$ for $r_1 = 3, r_2 = -1$. The general solution of (21) is $y_1(t) = c_1 e^{3t} + c_2 e^{-t}$. Now we substitute this solution for y_1 into equation (19) to find y_2:

$$\begin{aligned}
y_2 &= \frac{1}{4}(\dot{y}_1 - y_1) \\
&= \frac{1}{4}(3c_1 e^{3t} - c_2 e^{-t}) - \frac{1}{4}(c_1 e^{3t} + c_2 e^{-t}) \\
&= 0.5\, c_1 e^{3t} - 0.5\, c_2 e^{-t}.
\end{aligned}$$

Finally, we combine these two for the general solution of the original first order planar system (18)

$$\begin{aligned}
y_1(t) &= c_1 e^{3t} + c_2 e^{-t} \\
y_2(t) &= 0.5\, c_1 e^{3t} - 0.5\, c_2 e^{-t},
\end{aligned}$$

or in vector notation,

$$\begin{pmatrix} y_1(t) \\ y_2(t) \end{pmatrix} = c_1 e^{3t} \begin{pmatrix} 1 \\ 0.5 \end{pmatrix} + c_2 e^{-t} \begin{pmatrix} 1 \\ -0.5 \end{pmatrix}.$$

Notice that the steady state $(0, 0)$ corresponds to choosing both of the constants of integration equal to zero: $c_1 = c_2 = 0$.

For a general system (17) on $\mathbf{R}^2$, we would follow the same steps and compute from the first equation of (17) that

$$y_2 = \frac{1}{a_{12}}(\dot{y}_1 - a_{11}\, y_1) \quad \text{and} \quad \dot{y}_2 = \frac{1}{a_{12}}(\ddot{y}_1 - a_{11}\, \dot{y}_1). \tag{22}$$

Plugging these relationships into the second equation in (17) yields the second order equation in y_1:

$$\frac{1}{a_{12}}(\ddot{y}_1 - a_{11}\dot{y}_1) = a_{21}y_1 + \frac{a_{22}}{a_{12}}(\dot{y}_1 - a_{11}y_1),$$

or

$$\ddot{y}_1 - (a_{11} + a_{22})\dot{y}_1 + (a_{11}a_{22} - a_{12}a_{21}) = 0. \tag{23}$$

EXERCISES

25.6   Use the techniques of this section to find the general solution of the following systems of differential equations. In addition, find the particular solution which satisfies $y_1(0) = 1, y_2(0) = 0$.

     a) $\dot{y}_1 = y_1 + y_2$ *b)* $\dot{y}_1 = y_1 - 5y_2$ *c)* $\dot{y}_1 = -3y_1 + 5y_2$

        $\dot{y}_2 = 4y_1 - 2y_2;$ $\dot{y}_2 = 2y_1 - 5y_2;$ $\dot{y}_2 = -y_1 + y_2.$

25.4   STEADY STATES AND THEIR STABILITY

As we discovered in studying one-variable autonomous differential equations, steady state solutions play an important role in the study of systems of differential equations. They are also the easiest specific solutions to calculate.

Write a typical first order system of differential equations in $\mathbf{R}^n$ as

$$\dot{y}_1 = f_1(y_1, \ldots, y_n)$$

$$\vdots \qquad \vdots \tag{24}$$

$$\dot{y}_n = f_n(y_1, \ldots, y_n),$$

or in vector notation, $\dot{\mathbf{y}} = F(\mathbf{y})$, where $F \equiv (f_1, \ldots, f_n) \colon \mathbf{R}^n \to \mathbf{R}^n$.

We call a constant-function solution $y_1(t) = y_1^*, \ldots, y_n(t) = y_n^*$ of (24) a **steady state**, a **stationary solution**, a **rest point**, or simply an **equilibrium**, just as we did in $\mathbf{R}^1$. We will also use the same names for the *point* $\mathbf{y}^* = (y_1^*, \ldots, y_n^*)$ in $\mathbf{R}^n$. Since each $\dot{y}_i(t) \equiv 0$ for a steady state solution, a point $\mathbf{y}^* = (y_1^*, \ldots, y_n^*)$ is a steady state of system (24) if and only if

$$f_1(y_1^*, \ldots, y_n^*) = 0$$

$$\vdots \qquad \vdots$$

$$f_n(y_1^*, \ldots, y_n^*) = 0;$$

in vector notation, $F(\mathbf{y}^*) = \mathbf{0}$. Therefore, finding steady state solutions is simply a matter of solving n algebraic equations in n variables.

Example 25.1   In the competing species model (1), the points $(0, 0)$, $(0, a_2/b_2)$, and $(a_1/b_1, 0)$ are steady states.

   Just as we noticed for other types of dynamical systems, there are three types of stability for steady states of systems of differential equations: asymptotic stability, instability, and neutral stability. The pendulum provides an illustrative example of each. One steady state solution is the pendulum at rest, pointing straight down. This is the most important solution of this model in that every other solution tends to it as time advances. If we start the pendulum moving and then wait long enough, the pendulum will soon return to this natural steady state. In this case, we say that the pendulum straight down is an *asymptotically stable steady state*, as we did for difference equations and for differential equations with one variable. A system which is perturbed from such a steady state will eventually return to it.
   There is, however, another equilibrium in the pendulum model, namely the pendulum pointing straight *up* — not merely within 100 decimal points of pointing straight up but exactly, perfectly straight up to infinite precision. If you could achieve such precision, the pendulum would in principle stay there forever. However, this equilibrium is very delicate. The slightest disturbance would destroy it and send the pendulum oscillating back to its asymptotically stable equilibrium. The pendulum straight up is an example of an *unstable equilibrium*: nearly any perturbation will move the system away from an unstable equilibrium.
   Now, consider a model of a pendulum moving *without friction*. In this case, if we nudge the pendulum when it is in its straight-down equilibrium, the pendulum won't converge back to this equilibrium and it won't move further away either. It will just oscillate gently back and forth very near the equilibrium. The equilibrium for the pendulum straight down is *neutrally stable*.
   Let's make these definitions more precise. Let $\mathbf{y}^*$ be an equilibrium for the n-dimensional first order system of differential equations $\dot{\mathbf{y}} = F(\mathbf{y})$; that is, $F(\mathbf{y}^*) = \mathbf{0}$. We say that $\mathbf{y}^*$ is an **asymptotically stable equilibrium** if every solution $\mathbf{y}(t)$ which starts near $\mathbf{y}^*$ converges to $\mathbf{y}^*$ as $t \rightarrow \infty$.
   A steady state solution $\mathbf{y}^*$ of the system $\dot{\mathbf{y}} = F(\mathbf{y})$ is called **globally asymptotically stable** if just about *every* solution of $\dot{\mathbf{y}} = F(\mathbf{y})$ tends to $\mathbf{y}^*$ as $t \rightarrow \infty$; more precisely, equilibrium $\mathbf{y}^*$ is globally asymptotically stable if for any $\mathbf{y}_0$ (with the possible exception of some *lower-dimensional* set of $\mathbf{y}_0$'s), the solution of the ini-

tial value problem $\dot{\mathbf{y}} = F(\mathbf{y})$, $\mathbf{y}(0) = \mathbf{y}_0$ tends to $\mathbf{y}^*$ as $t \to \infty$. For the model of the pendulum with friction, the straight-down equilibrium is globally asymptotically stable.

A steady state $\mathbf{y}^*$ of the system $\dot{\mathbf{y}} = F(\mathbf{y})$ is called **neutrally stable** if it is not locally asymptotically stable and if all solutions which start close enough to $\mathbf{y}^*$ stay close to $\mathbf{y}^*$ as $t \to \infty$. If an equilibrium $\mathbf{y}^*$ of $\dot{\mathbf{y}} = F(\mathbf{y})$ is asymptotically stable or neutrally stable, we call it **stable**. If it is neither asymptotically stable nor neutrally stable, we call it an **unstable steady state**.

Stability of Linear Systems via Eigenvalues

For studying the stability of the origin as an equilibrium of linear systems in n dimensions, it is most convenient to use formulas (10), (12), and (16) for the general solutions of $\dot{\mathbf{x}} = A\mathbf{x}$ to determine directly the stability of the steady state at $\mathbf{0}$. In general, these solutions are a sum of terms of the form

$$\text{constant} \cdot e^{(\text{eigenvalue}) \cdot t} \cdot \text{eigenvector,}$$

at least for real eigenvalues. Therefore, as $t \to \infty$,

$$\mathbf{x}(t) \to \mathbf{0} \quad \Longleftrightarrow \quad \text{each} \quad e^{r_i t} \to 0 \quad \Longleftrightarrow \quad \text{each} \quad r_i < 0.$$

If one $r_i > 0$, then $e^{r_i t}$ goes to infinity and drags the other terms of the solution with it.

In the case of complex roots, the $\cos \beta t$– and $\sin \beta t$–components of solution (12) oscillate about 0; the stability of $\mathbf{0}$ is determined by the $e^{\alpha t}$ factor. If $\alpha < 0$, each $\mathbf{x}(t) \to \mathbf{0}$, and $\mathbf{0}$ is asymptotically stable. If $\alpha > 0$, every $\mathbf{x}(t)$ becomes unbounded and $\mathbf{0}$ is unstable. If $\alpha = 0$, $\mathbf{x}(t)$ oscillates about $\mathbf{0}$ and $\mathbf{0}$ is neutrally stable.

Finally, we need to consider solution (16) when A has repeated eigenvalues. If $r > 0$, expression (16) goes to infinity. If $r < 0$, $e^{rt}t \to 0$ and expression (16) goes to $\mathbf{0}$. If $r = 0$, (16) becomes $c_1\mathbf{v} + c_2(t\mathbf{v} + \mathbf{w})$, which tends to infinity if $c_2 \neq 0$.

The following theorem summarizes these stability results.

Theorem 25.4 The constant solution $\mathbf{x} = \mathbf{0}$ is always a steady state of the linear system of differential equations (6): $\dot{\mathbf{x}} = A\mathbf{x}$.

   (a) If every real eigenvalue of A is negative and every complex eigenvalue of A has negative real part, then $\mathbf{x} = \mathbf{0}$ is a globally asymptotically stable steady state: every solution tends to $\mathbf{0}$ as $t \to \infty$.
   (b) If A has a positive real eigenvalue or a complex eigenvalue with positive real part, then $\mathbf{x} = \mathbf{0}$ is an unstable steady state: just about every solution moves away from the origin as $t \to \infty$.

(c) If A has a zero eigenvalue or a purely imaginary eigenvalue that does *not* have a complete set of independent eigenvectors, then $\mathbf{x} = \mathbf{0}$ is an unstable rest point.

(d) If A has a real eigenvalue equal to zero or a complex eigenvalue that is pure imaginary, if all such eigenvalues have a complete set of independent eigenvectors, and if all the other eigenvalues have negative real part, then the origin is a neutrally stable steady state of system (6).

Stability of Nonlinear Systems

We turn now to the development of calculus criteria for the stability of a steady state of a *nonlinear system* of autonomous differential equations. In Section 24.5, we developed calculus criteria for determining the stability of the steady states of first order differential equations of one variable: equilibrium y^* of $\dot{y} = f(y)$ is

(1) asymptotically stable if $f(y^*) = 0$ and $f'(y^*) < 0$, and
(2) unstable if $f(y^*) = 0$ and $f'(y^*) > 0$.

In a system $\dot{\mathbf{x}} = F(\mathbf{x})$ on $\mathbf{R^n}$ with steady state $\mathbf{y}^*$, the Jacobian matrix $DF(\mathbf{y}^*)$ replaces the derivative $f'(y^*)$ in 1 and 2. The following theorem is the natural analogue of the n-dimensional linear results (Theorem 25.4) and the one-dimensional nonlinear results (Theorem 24.6). We sketch its proof in the Appendix of this chapter.

Theorem 25.5   Let $\mathbf{y}^*$ be a steady state of the first order system of differential equations $\dot{\mathbf{y}} = F(\mathbf{y})$ on $\mathbf{R^n}$, where F is a C^1 function from $\mathbf{R^n}$ to $\mathbf{R^n}$.

(a) If each eigenvalue of the Jacobian matrix $DF(\mathbf{y}^*)$ of F at $\mathbf{y}^*$ is negative or has negative real part, then $\mathbf{y}^*$ is an asymptotically stable steady state of $\dot{\mathbf{y}} = F(\mathbf{y})$.

(b) If $DF(\mathbf{y}^*)$ has at least one postive real eigenvalue or one complex eigenvalue with positive real part, then $\mathbf{y}^*$ is an unstable steady state of $\dot{\mathbf{y}} = F(\mathbf{y})$.

If the test in Theorem 25.5 doesn't work, that is, if $DF(\mathbf{y}^*)$ has some pure imaginary eigenvalues or zero eigenvalues but no positive eigenvalues or eigenvalues with positive real part, then we can't use the Jacobian at $\mathbf{y}^*$ to determine the stability of $\mathbf{y}^*$. In such cases, we need more information about the system of equations. This situation is analogous to the one encountered in a maximization problem when the second derivative test doesn't work.

Example 25.2   Consider the competing species model

$$\dot{x} = x(4 - x - y)$$
$$\dot{y} = y(6 - y - 3x). \tag{25}$$

As one can easily check, this system has four equilibria: $(0, 0)$, $(0, 6)$, $(4, 0)$, and $(1, 3)$. (What is the significance of each of these equilibria for the competing species model?) Let's test the stability of each of these. The Jacobian of (f, g) at an arbitrary point (x, y) is

$$D(f, g)(x, y) = \begin{pmatrix} 4 - 2x - y & -x \\ -3y & 6 - 2y - 3x \end{pmatrix}.$$

At $(0, 0)$, this Jacobian becomes $\begin{pmatrix} 4 & 0 \\ 0 & 6 \end{pmatrix}$ with eigenvalues 4 and 6. Since both eigenvalues are positive, $(0, 0)$ is an unstable equilibrium. Ecologically, when the population is at $(0, 0)$, the addition of a small population will allow both species to take off, especially when each species is so small that it is not a threat to the other.

At $(0, 6)$, $D(f, g)(0, 6) = \begin{pmatrix} -2 & 0 \\ -18 & -6 \end{pmatrix}$, which has eigenvalues -2 and -6. Since both eigenvalues are negative, Theorem 25.5 tells us that $(0, 6)$ is an asymptotically stable equilibrium. Ecologically, if y is near 6 and x is near 0, y will stabilize at 6 and x will die out. Similarly, one can check that $(4, 0)$ is also an asymptotically stable equilibrium.

At the coexistence equilibrium $(1, 3)$, the Jacobian of (f, g) becomes $\begin{pmatrix} -1 & -1 \\ -9 & -3 \end{pmatrix}$. Its characteristic polynomial is $r^2 + 4r - 6$. Since the product of its roots equals the negative number -6, this characteristic polynomial has a positive root and a negative root. Theorem 25.5 tells us that $(1, 3)$ is an unstable equilibrium — like the pendulum straight up. The populations which this system is modeling do not coexist with both species at constant positive levels.

EXERCISES

25.7   Find a fourth steady state in the competing species system (1), other than the three listed in Example 25.1. Does this steady state always have physical significance?

25.8   Find the steady states in the predator-prey model (2).

25.9   Find the steady states in each of the following systems:

$$a)\ \dot{x} = 2xy - 2y^2 \qquad b)\ \dot{x} = x + y$$
$$\dot{y} = x - y^2 + 2; \qquad \qquad \dot{y} = x + 4y;$$

c) $\dot{x} = xy$ *d*) $\dot{x} = 2x$

$\dot{y} = 4 - 4y - 2x;$ $\dot{y} = y^2 - x^2 - 1.$

25.10 Apply Theorem 25.4 to show that $(0, 0)$ is an unstable steady state of system (18). Then, use the explicit general solution of (18) to see explicitly that $(0, 0)$ is unstable; every solution with $c_1 \neq 0$ becomes unbounded as $t \to \infty$.

25.11 Consider linear system (17): $\dot{\mathbf{x}} = A\mathbf{x}$ on $\mathbf{R}^2$. Show that: *a*) $(0, 0)$ is an asymptotically stable steady state of (17) if and only if the trace of A is negative and the determinant of A is positive; *b*) if either $\det A < 0$ or trace $A > 0$, then $(0, 0)$ is an unstable steady state; *c*) if $\det A > 0$ and trace $A = 0$, then $(0, 0)$ is neutrally stable.

25.12 Determine the stability of the origin as a steady state of each of the following systems:

a) $\dot{x} = 3x + y$ *b*) $\dot{x} = \qquad\; y$

$\dot{y} = -x + y;$ $\dot{y} = -x + 5y;$

c) $\dot{x} = 2x + 5y$ *d*) $\dot{x} = 3x - y$

$\dot{y} = -x;$ $\dot{y} = -x + 2y - z$

                              $\dot{z} = \qquad -y + 3z.$

25.13 Write the stability criteria for a steady state of a planar nonlinear system in terms of the trace and determinant of the Jacobian matrix at the steady state.

25.14 Use Theorem 25.5 to compute that the $(0, 0)$-equilibria in the competing species system (1) and in the predator-prey system (2) are unstable. Explain in terms of the model why one should expect this.

25.15 Show that the equilibrium $(0, a_2/b_2)$ in the competing species system (1) is asymptotically stable or unstable depending on the sign of $a_1/c_1 - a_2/b_2$. Explain this condition in terms of the model. Carry out the same analysis for the equilibrium $(a_1/b_1, 0)$.

25.16 Show that Theorem 25.5 has nothing to say about the interior equilibrium of the predator-prey system (2). We will see in Section 25.6 that this equilibrium is neutrally stable.

25.17 Determine the stability of the equilibria of the planar systems of differential equations in Exercise 25.1.

25.18 Write out a formal definition of aysmptotic stability, using ε's and such.

25.5 PHASE PORTRAITS OF PLANAR SYSTEMS

Vector Fields

Of course, most nonlinear systems cannot be solved in simple closed form solutions. Just as we did for differential equations of one variable, we will construct solutions *geometrically* for autonomous systems of two variables. These geometric solutions will usually provide more insight into the behavior of the model under study than the explicit formula for the solution, even when the latter is available.

Let's first consider the geometric meaning of the general planar system

$$\dot{x} = f(x, y)$$
$$\dot{y} = g(x, y). \tag{26}$$

Think of system (26) as the equations of motion of a particle moving about in the plane. The system tells us that when the particle is at the point (x, y), it will be moving so that its velocity vector $(\dot{x}, \dot{y})$ will be the vector $(f(x, y), g(x, y))$, which we picture as a vector with its tail at the point (x, y) pointing in the direction of the particle's motion. Therefore, one way to picture the dynamics of system (26) is to picture the vector $(f(x, y), g(x, y))$ pointing out from the point (x, y) for every point in the plane. We call such a family of vectors a **vector field**.

Of course, when we actually draw a vector field, we only draw a representative sample of its vectors to avoid hopelessly cluttering the picture. To minimize the clutter further, we usually ignore the length of the velocity vectors $(f(x, y), g(x, y))$ that we draw and draw short stubby vectors that *point in the correct direction*. Let's consider some concrete examples.

Example 25.3   Consider the simple system

$$\dot{x} = y$$
$$\dot{y} = -x. \tag{27}$$

At each point (x, y) we draw a vector in the direction $(y, -x)$. In Figure 25.1, we have drawn the vector $(0, -2)$ at the point $(2, 0)$, the vector $(2, -3)$ at the point $(3, 2)$, and the vector $(-2, -1)$ at the point $(1, -2)$, along with a sample of other choices. From this figure, we get a feeling that the motion which (27) describes is roughly circular. A particle which has (27) as its equations of motion will move roughly in circles about the origin.

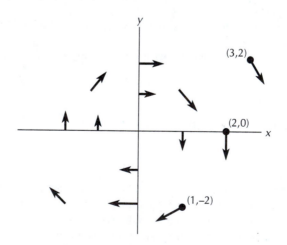

Figure 25.1

Vector field $\dot{x} = y$, $\dot{y} = -x$.

Example 25.4 Next consider the *uncoupled* system

$$\dot{x} = 2x$$
$$\dot{y} = -2y. \tag{28}$$

In Figure 25.2, we have drawn a sampling of the vector field corresponding to this system, including the vector $(4, 0)$ at the point $(2, 0)$, the vector $(2, -2)$ at the point $(1, 1)$, and the vector $(0, -2)$ at the point $(0, 1)$. Figure 25.2 suggests a motion in which points move closer to the x-axis and further out from the y-axis as time progresses.

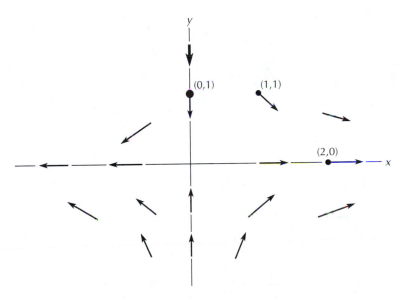

The vector field for the uncoupled system $\dot{x} = 2x, \dot{y} = -2y.$

Figure 25.2

Example 25.5 Consider the system version of the single autonomous equation $\dot{x} = x^2 + t^2$:

$$\dot{x} = x^2 + y^2$$
$$\dot{y} = 1. \tag{29}$$

Its vector field is sketched in Figure 25.3. (Double-check this drawing.) Note that for such a system there is a close relationship between the vector field of (29) and the "integral field" of $\dot{x} = x^2 + t^2$, which we drew in Figure 24.6.

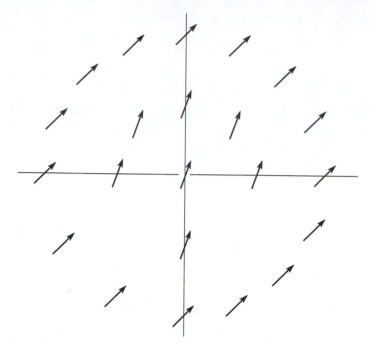

**Figure
25.3**

The vector field for system (29).

Phase Portraits: Linear Systems

Since the geometric realization of system (26) is a vector

$$(\dot{x}, \dot{y}) = (f(x, y), g(x, y))$$

at each point (x, y), then the corresponding geometric realization of a solution $(x^*(t), y^*(t))$ is a curve in the plane which is *everywhere tangent* to the vector field. As the curve $(x^*(t), y^*(t))$ goes through the point (x, y), its tangent vector $(\dot{x}^*(t), \dot{y}^*(t))$ should point in the direction $(f(x, y), g(x, y))$. The set of all such curves is called the **phase portrait**, or sometimes **phase diagram**, of system (26) in the plane. The phase portrait is just the set of solutions $(x(t), y(t))$ of (26) considered as parameterized curves in the plane. If we think of (26) as the equations of motion of a particle in the plane, these curves will describe the paths or **orbits** of the particle as it moves in the plane under this force law. Let's draw the phase portraits for the vector fields in Examples 25.3 and 25.4.

Example 25.6   As we mentioned earlier, the curves which are everywhere tangent to the vector field drawn in Figure 25.1 would appear to be roughly circles about the origin. To see that they are precisely circles, we need to solve system (27) explicitly. Using the method of substitution, we are quickly led to the second order equation

$$\ddot{x} + x = 0,$$

whose general solution is

$$x(t) = c_1 \cos t + c_2 \sin t.$$

Since $y = \dot{x}$, the general solution of (27) in vector form is

$$\begin{pmatrix} x(t) \\ y(t) \end{pmatrix} = c_1 \begin{pmatrix} \cos t \\ -\sin t \end{pmatrix} + c_2 \begin{pmatrix} \sin t \\ \cos t \end{pmatrix}. \tag{30}$$

To see that these parameterized curves are circles about the origin, we show that they stay a fixed distance from the origin for all t by computing that

$$\|(x(t), y(t))\| = \sqrt{x(t)^2 + y(t)^2} = c_1^2 + c_2^2,$$

a constant. Each solution of (27) moves at a fixed distance from the origin, i.e., on a circle. We have drawn the phase portrait of (27) in Figure 25.4. Note the arrows point in the direction of increasing t.

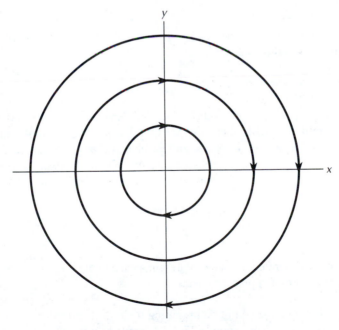

Phase portrait of the system $\dot{x} = y, \dot{y} = -x.$

**Figure
25.4**

Definition   A solution $\mathbf{x}(t)$ of a system of differential equations which returns to itself, so that there is a $T > 0$ with $\mathbf{x}(t + T) = \mathbf{x}(t)$ for all t, is called a **periodic solution** or **periodic orbit**. The smallest such T is called the **period** of the orbit. All the nonconstant solutions (30) of system (27) are periodic solutions with period 2π. The trajectory of a periodic orbit is a closed curve, like the circles in Figure 25.4.

Example 25.7   Judging from Figure 25.2, the parameterized solution curves of system (28) appear to be curves which move away from the positive and negative y-axis, toward the x-axis, and off to infinity. Let's verify this by using the explicit solution of (28),

$$x(t) = c_1 e^{2t}$$
$$y(t) = c_2 e^{-2t}, \tag{31}$$

which is easily calculated because the system is uncoupled. To find the *unparameterized* equations of these curves, we solve each equation in (31) for e^{2t} and then eliminate t by setting these expressions equal to each other:

$$e^{2t} = \frac{x}{c_1} = \frac{c_2}{y},$$

or

$$y = \frac{c_1 c_2}{x}.$$

We have drawn a collection of these hyperbolas $y = k/x$ in Figure 25.5, the phase portrait of this system (28).

Phase Portraits: Nonlinear Systems

Drawing the precise phase portraits of linear systems, as we have just done in the last two examples, is made simpler by the fact that we have explicit solutions for linear systems. We now start to work with the phase portraits of nonlinear systems, which usually have no explicit solution. We begin with the explicit model for a competing species system first encountered in Example 25.2:

$$\dot{x} = x(4 - x - y)$$
$$\dot{y} = y(6 - y - 3x). \tag{32}$$

We will work deliberately in order to present a careful plan of attack for drawing the phase portrait of any planar system.

Step 1.   First, find the equilibria by setting the right-hand sides equal to 0. We did this for system (32) in Example 25.2, where we computed the four equilibria: $(0, 0)$, $(0, 6)$, $(4, 0)$, and $(1, 3)$.

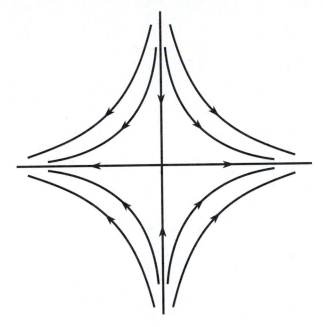

Phase portrait of the system $\dot{x} = 2x$, $\dot{y} = -2y$.

**Figure
25.5**

Step 2. Use Theorem 25.5 to find the local stability of each of these equilibria. We have already carried out this analysis in Example 25.2, where we found that equilibria $(0, 0)$ and $(1, 3)$ are unstable and equilibria $(0, 6)$ and $(4, 0)$ are asymptotically stable.

Step 3. Draw the *isoclines*. We want to sketch a sufficient number of vectors of the vector field. In order to do this most efficiently, we will find all the points where the vector field is either vertical or horizontal. A vector $(\dot{x}, \dot{y})$ will be vertical provided $\dot{x} = 0$ and $\dot{y} \neq 0$. If $\dot{y} > 0$, the vector will point up; if $\dot{y} < 0$, the vector will point down. Since $\dot{x} = f(x, y)$, the locus of points (x, y) at which $\dot{x} = 0$ is the curve $f(x, y) = 0$. Such a curve along which the vector fields always points in the same direction is called an **isocline** of the system. In Figure 25.6, we have drawn the $\dot{x} = 0$ isoclines of system (32), namely the lines

$$x = 0 \quad \text{and} \quad 4 - x - y = 0.$$

We have also drawn vertical vectors along these curves, but for the time being, without giving them directions up or down.

Now, carry out the same process for the $\dot{y} = 0$ isoclines. For system (32), the $\dot{y} = 0$ isoclines are the lines

$$y = 0 \quad \text{and} \quad 6 - y - 3x = 0.$$

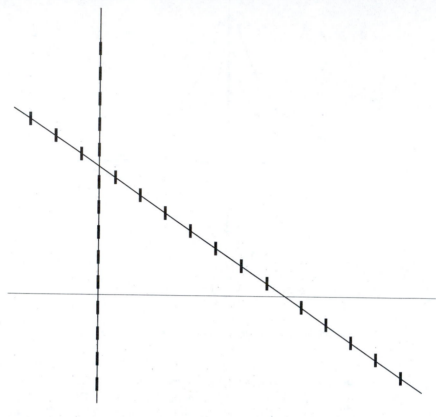

Figure 25.6

The $\dot{x} = 0$ isoclines for system (32).

We have drawn these lines in Figure 25.7, where we have also drawn little horizontal vectors along these lines without any direction to the right or left yet.

Step 4. Fill in the arrows on the isoclines and in the sectors between them. The isoclines divide the plane into regions called **sectors**; they form the boundaries of the sectors. In the interior of any sector, the vector field cannot point directly north, south, east, or west. By continuity, the vector field can only point into one quadrant in any given sector: into either the northeast quadrant (NE), the southeast quadrant (SE), the southwest quadrant (SW), or the northwest quadrant (NW), because if a vector field were to point into two quadrants in the same sector, say into NW at one point and into NE at another, then in between these two points it would have to point due north. But the vector field points due north only on the $\dot{x} = 0$ isoclines, and no isocline runs through the interior of any sector. To see into which quadrant the vector field points within the sector, just pick any point in the sector and evaluate the vector field at that point. Every vector in that sector will point into the same quadrant as the chosen vector. Carry out this analysis for each sector.

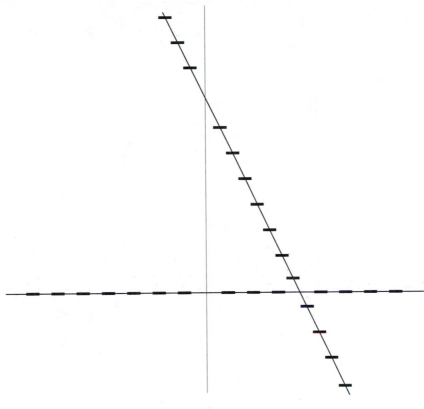

The $\dot{y} = 0$ isoclines of system (32).

**Figure
25.7**

Then, extend the arrows to the segments of isoclines which bound the sectors. For example, if the vectors in a given sector point NE, then the vectors on the segments of the isoclines which bound that sector point either north or east. In fact, this analysis works both ways; the behavior of a vector field on an isocline segment which bounds a sector restricts the behavior of the vector field within the sector itself. For example, if a vector field points due north on an isocline segment s, then the vector field must point NW or NE on the sectors whose boundary contains segment s.

In Figure 25.8 we have combined the isoclines drawn in the previous two figures, labeled the sectors between the isoclines with uppercase letters A through K, and labeled the segments of the isoclines which bound these sectors with lowercase letters a through p. Let's start with sector A. Choose a point inside A, say (1, 1). The velocity vector of (32) at (1, 1) is (2, 2). Since (2, 2) points NE, *all* the vectors in A point NE. We signify this by drawing some vectors pointing to the northeast in sector A, as in Figure 25.9. Next, let's label the isocline segments which bound sector A a, c, g, and ℓ. Since A is a NE sector, the vector field points due north on the $\dot{x} = 0$ isocline segments c and ℓ and it points due east on the $\dot{y} = 0$ segments a and g. We have labeled these in Figure 25.9.

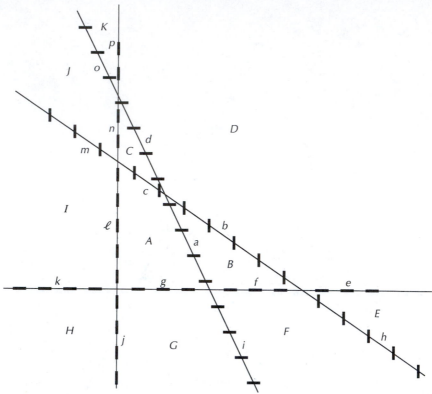

**Figure
25.8**   *Labeling the sectors and their bounding segments for the vector field (32).*

Next, turn to sector D, the only unbounded sector in the first quadrant. Again, we choose a point in D, say $(10, 10)$, and evaluate the vector field there. Since $(\dot{x}, \dot{y})$ at $(10, 10)$ is the vector $(-160, -360)$, which points SW, every vector of (32) in D points SW. We have indicated this by drawing some vectors pointing to the southwest in D in Figure 25.9. On the isocline segments b, d, e, and p which bound D, the vector field must point due south or due west: due south on the $\dot{x} = 0$ segments b and p, due west on the $\dot{y} = 0$ segments d and e, as we have indicated in Figure 25.9.

We can handle sectors B and C rather quickly now. We have already computed that the vector field points due north on isocline segment c which bounds C and points due west on isocline segment d which also bounds C. Therefore, the vector field can only point into the NW quadrant within C. This, in turn, implies that the vector field points due north on the other $\dot{x} = 0$ segment n which bounds C.

We treat sector B similarly. We know that the vector field points south and east on isocline segments which bound B (segments b and a, respectively). It follows that it points into the SE quadrant throughout B and that it points due east on the other $\dot{y} = 0$ segment f which bounds B.

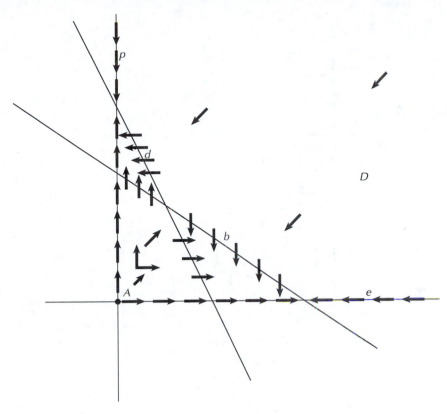

Labeling the proper directions in sectors A and D and their bounding segments.

**Figure
25.9**

This completes the analysis for the sectors in the positive xy-quadrant, the quadrant where all the interest lies for a competing species model. When we're done, we should have the vector field pictured in Figure 25.10.

Step 5. Sketch in representative solution curves which follow the vector field's directions, as just computed.

Let's first start our flow in sector D in which all solution curves move SW. Any given curve in D will cross isocline d horizontally or isocline b vertically. One special solution curve will flow right into the equilibrium (1, 3) at the intersection of segments b and d. We have drawn this phenomenon in Figure 25.11.

The solution curves from D that cross segment d move into sector C where they turn and move to the NW. Since they cannot cross the isocline n, they are forced to converge to the equilibrium (0, 6). Similarly, the solution curves from D that cross segment b move into sector B, where they are forced to move SE into the equilibrium (4, 0) at the intersection of b and f.

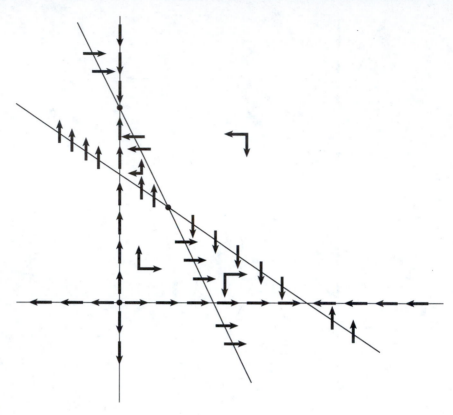

**Figure
25.10**

The complete list of sectors and segments for system (32).

A similar story holds for orbits which start in sector A. They all move away
from the equilibrium at $(0, 0)$ in a northeasterly direction. Some cross segment c
vertically and then move NW in sector C toward equilibrium $(0, 6)$. Others cross
segment a horizontally and then move SE in sector B toward equilibrium $(4, 0)$.
We have drawn this much of the phase portrait in Figure 25.12.

Figure 25.12 presents the complete phase portrait for the competing species
system (32) in the positive quadrant. Even though we cannot solve the system
explicitly, we are still able to obtain a complete geometric picture of the evolution
of the system — a picture that may be more valuable than the explicit solution
even if the latter did exist. We can see in Figure 25.12 how the populations change
over time: if they start somewhere in the lower part of sector D, they both decrease
until the trajectory crosses b. From then on, the y population continues to decrease
until it dies out, and the x population increases until it stabilizes at $x^* = 4$. If
the population starts in the upper portion of sector D, a very different outcome
occurs. The population would eventually stabilize at $(0, 6)$. There is a very thin
dividing line that separates these two phenomena. Mathematically, that dividing
line (or separatrix) is the single orbit which tends toward the unstable equilibrium

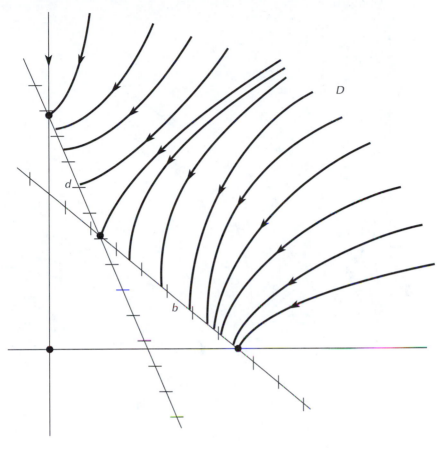

Solution curves of (32) in sector D.

**Figure
25.11**

(1, 3). If the population were on one side of this separatrix and some exogenous shock pushed it to the other side, the long-run behavior of the ecology would be very different. This example illustrates some of the fragility that is inherent in ecological systems.

One can easily see in Figure 25.12 the geometric realization of the stabilities that we calculated analytically for the four equilibria. Equilibria (4, 0) and (0, 6) are asymptotically stable, but not globally so. Equilibria (0, 0) and (1, 3) are unstable; small perturbations from either of these equilibria will move the ecological system toward one of the two stable equilibria.

System (32) is a special case of the general competing species system (1). There are actually four different cases for the general system (1), depending on how the $\dot{x} = 0$ and $\dot{y} = 0$ isoclines intersect in the positive quadrant. Exercise 25.20 asks you to work out examples of the three remaining cases.

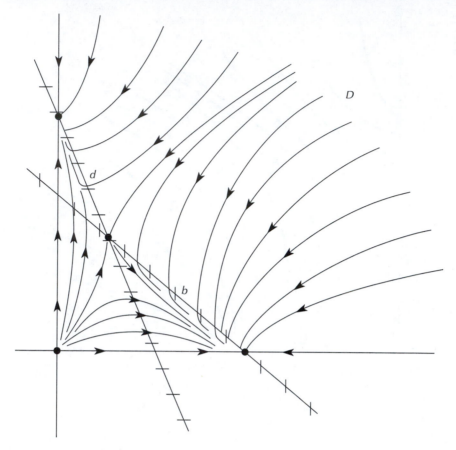

**Figure
25.12**

The phase portrait of (32) in the positive quadrant.

EXERCISES

25.19 Complete the phase portrait of (32) by drawing the solution curves in the sectors outside the positive quadrant.

25.20 Draw the phase portrait of each of the following systems. In each case, discuss what happens to the ecological systems governed by these equations.

a) $\dot{x} = x(6 - 3x - y)$ b) $\dot{x} = x(2 - x - y)$
   $\dot{y} = y(4 - x - y)$; $\dot{y} = y(6 - y - 2x)$;

c) $\dot{x} = x(6 - 2x - y)$ d) $\dot{x} = x(8 - 4x - 2y)$
   $\dot{y} = y(2 - x - y)$; $\dot{y} = y(8 - 2x - 4y)$.

25.21 Show that any general competing species system (1) for which the isoclines intersect in the positive quadrant with the $\dot{y} = 0$ isocline steeper than the $\dot{x} = 0$ isocline has a phase portrait similar to that of Figure 25.12.

25.22 Derive and interpret an algebraic criterion on the coefficients of system (1) which determines whether or not the two species can coexist in positive constant population sizes in the ecology.

25.23 Draw and interpret the phase portrait of the following model of an ecological system in **symbiosis**:

$$\dot{x} = x(2 - 2x + y)$$
$$\dot{y} = y(5 - 2y + x).$$

25.6 FIRST INTEGRALS

This section presents a complementary approach to drawing phase portraits of planar systems — a method that works for rather special systems — but when it does work, it is much simpler than the method of the last section. The special systems for which this method does work include a number of important differential equations, including the predator-prey system (2) and all conservative mechanical systems — systems for which the method of the last section does not yield a complete phase portrait.

We start with an example. Recall the linear system (27)

$$\dot{x} = y$$
$$\dot{y} = -x, \tag{33}$$

whose general solution is given by expression (30). All the solution curves are circles about the origin, as can be readily seen in the phase portrait in Figure 25.4.

From another point of view, the orbits of (33) are the level curves of the function $F(x, y) = x^2 + y^2$. We can combine these two points of view by stating that F is constant on the solution curves of (33). To write this statement analytically, let $(x(t), y(t))$ be a solution (30) of system (33). Then, $F(x(t), y(t))$ is constant as t varies. Taking the derivative with respect to t and using the Chain Rule, we find

$$0 = \frac{d}{dt}F(x(t), y(t))$$
$$= \frac{\partial F}{\partial x}(x(t), y(t)) \cdot \frac{dx(t)}{dt} + \frac{\partial F}{\partial y}(x(t), y(t)) \cdot \frac{dy(t)}{dt}. \tag{34}$$

We can verify that equation (34) holds without using solution (30) of system (33), because substituting

$$\frac{\partial F}{\partial x} = 2x, \quad \frac{\partial F}{\partial y} = 2y, \quad \frac{dx}{dt} = y, \quad \text{and} \quad \frac{dy}{dt} = -x$$

into expression (34) yields

$$0 = 2x \cdot y + 2y \cdot (-x).$$

In other words, we could have discovered that the level sets of F are the orbits of system (33) just by noting that

$$\frac{\partial F}{\partial x} \cdot \dot{x} + \frac{\partial F}{\partial y} \cdot \dot{y} = 2x \cdot y + 2y \cdot (-x) = 0,$$

without solving the system. A major benefit of this approach comes from the fact that finding the level curves of a function is usually a much simpler process than finding the solution curves of a differential equation.

More generally, suppose that we are working with a system of differential equations

$$\dot{x} = f(x, y)$$
$$\dot{y} = g(x, y)$$

(35)

and that we find a smooth function $F(x, y)$ such that

$$\dot{F}(x, y) \equiv \frac{\partial F}{\partial x}(x, y) \cdot f(x, y) + \frac{\partial F}{\partial y}(x, y) \cdot g(x, y) = 0 \qquad (36)$$

for all (x, y) in some open domain. Then, by the Chain Rule,

$$\frac{dF}{dt}(x(t), y(t)) = \frac{\partial F}{\partial x} \cdot \frac{dx}{dt} + \frac{\partial F}{\partial y} \cdot \frac{dy}{dt}$$

$$= \frac{\partial F}{\partial x} \cdot f + \frac{\partial F}{\partial y} \cdot g \qquad \text{by (35)}$$

$$= 0 \qquad \text{by (36),}$$

and F is constant on orbits of (35). Since both the level sets of F and the solution curves of (35) are one-dimensional curves, we can conclude that the orbits of (35) are the level curves of F, or possibly subsets of these curves.

Definition A nonconstant function F which satisfies equation (36) for a system of differential equations (35) is called a **first integral** of system (35). In this case, the solution curves of (35) lie along the level curves of F. For general functions F, we call the expression $\dot{F}$ in (36) the **derivative of F along the orbits** of system (35).

In this example, we were led to the first integral of system (33) only after we had found the solution of (33) and noticed that its solution curves were all circles about the origin. The real challenge is to find the first integral without first solving the system. This is usually a difficult, if not impossible, task. However, there are some important classes of differential equations which have been so well studied that first integrals have been discovered for these systems. One such class is the predator-prey system.

The Predator-Prey System

Recall from Section 25.1 that the predator-prey or Lotka-Volterra system of differential equations is the system

$$\dot{x} = x(A - By)$$
$$\dot{y} = y(Dx - C),$$ (37)

where x is the size of the prey population, y is the size of the predator population, and A, B, C, and D are positive constants. Let's try to find the phase portrait of this system using the methods of the last two sections. The isoclines of (37) are the axes and the lines $\{y = A/B\}$ and $\{x = C/D\}$. We learn in this process that the equilibria of (37) are $(0, 0)$ and $(C/D, A/B)$. On the positive y-axis (where $x = 0$), $\dot{y} = -Cy \leq 0$ and $y(t)$ is always decreasing. On the positive x-axis, $\dot{x} = Ax \geq 0$ and $x(t)$ is always increasing. We can use this information to find the direction of the vector field of (37) first along the axes, then in the sectors bordering the axes, and finally in the whole positive quadrant. This vector field is sketched in Figure 25.13.

Clearly, the orbits of (37) are moving in a counterclockwise path around the interior equilibrium $(C/D, A/B)$. However, at this point, we cannot tell whether $(C/D, A/B)$ is unstable, asymptotically stable, or neutrally stable. Let's use Theorem 25.5 to investigate the stability of the two equilibria of (37). The Jacobian of the right-hand side of (37) at $(0, 0)$ is

$$\begin{pmatrix} A & 0 \\ 0 & -C \end{pmatrix},$$

whose eigenvalues are A and $-C$. Since the linearization of (37) about $(0, 0)$ has an unstable saddle at the origin, $(0, 0)$ is an unstable saddle of the original system (37) — a fact that we already recognized in Figure 25.13.

The Jacobian of the right-hand side of system (37) at the interior equilibrium $(C/D, A/B)$ is the matrix

$$D = \begin{pmatrix} 0 & -\dfrac{BC}{D} \\ \dfrac{DA}{B} & 0 \end{pmatrix},$$

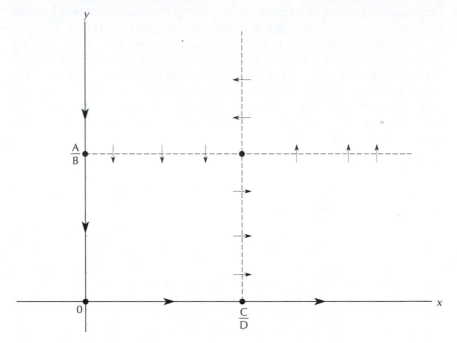

The vector field for the predator-prey system (37).

Figure
25.13

whose characteristic polynomial is $r^2 + AC = 0$ and, therefore, whose eigenvalues are the pure imaginary numbers $r = \pm i\sqrt{AC}$. By Theorem 25.4, the linearization of (37) about the equilibrium $(C/D, A/B)$ has the origin as a *neutrally stable* steady state. However, since neutral stability is such a delicate property, we cannot use Theorem 25.5 to decide whether $(C/D, A/B)$ is an unstable, asymptotically stable, or neutrally stable equilibrium for the *nonlinear* system (37).

However, system (37) has been fairly well studied and a first integral has been found which settles this ambiguity. Consider the somewhat complex-looking function

$$F(x, y) = Dx - C\ln x + By - A\ln y. \tag{38}$$

We compute that the derivative of F along the orbits of (37) is

$$\dot{F}(x, y) = \frac{\partial F}{\partial x} \cdot \dot{x} + \frac{\partial F}{\partial y} \cdot \dot{y}$$

$$= \left(D - \frac{C}{x}\right) \cdot x\,(A - By) + \left(B - \frac{A}{y}\right) \cdot y\,(Dx - C)$$

$$= (Dx - C)(A - By) + (By - A)(Dx - C)$$

$$= 0.$$

Therefore, F is a first integral of (37) throughout the positive quadrant. We indicate in the exercises how one might find this first integral F.

The next task is to figure out what the level curves of F look like. As shown in the exercises below, $(C/D, A/B)$ is a critical point of F and the Hessian of F is

$$\begin{pmatrix} \dfrac{C}{x^2} & 0 \\ 0 & \dfrac{A}{y^2} \end{pmatrix},$$

which is positive definite in the positive quadrant. By Theorem 21.5, F is a convex function in the positive quadrant; by Theorem 21.4, the critical point $(C/D, A/B)$ is a global minimizer of F in the positive quadrant. Combining these facts with the observation that the gradient of F points away from $(C/D, A/B)$ in each of the four sectors in Figure 25.13, we conclude that the level curves of F are all closed curves about $(C/D, A/B)$. A few of these curves are drawn in Figure 25.14. Since the level curves of F are the orbits of system (37), the orbits of (37) in the interior of the positive quadrant are periodic orbits.

Figure 25.14 predicts that the predator and prey populations will oscillate regularly about an interior equilibrium. This oscillation makes intuitive sense. Suppose that at first the prey population is growing. The predator population will

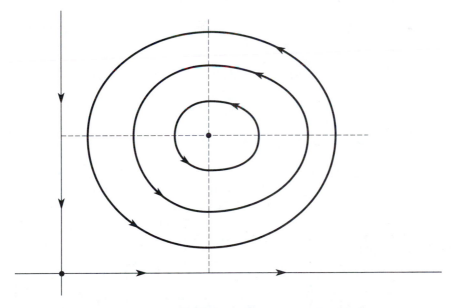

The phase portrait of the predator-prey system (37).

Figure 25.14

thrive with this easy source of food; this will result in an increase in the size of the
predator population and, eventually, a decrease in the size of the prey population.
However, at some point, the prey population reaches a small enough size that it
can stabilize and begin to increase again, while the predator population decreases
because of the unavailability of easy prey. As the prey population increases, the
cycle starts again. Figure 25.15 shows the sizes of the lynx and hare populations
in Canada based on the records of the Hudson Bay Company. This graph supports
the oscillatory behavior that we have just described.

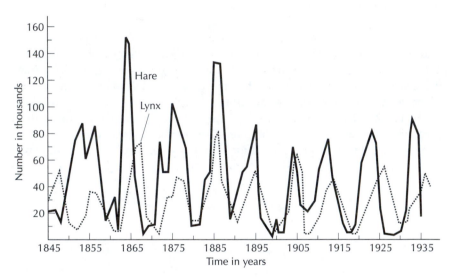

**Figure
25.15**

Interacting populations of hare and lynx in Canada.

Conservative Mechanical Systems

Consider a particle of mass m that is moving with one degree of freedom; that is,
its position is described by a scalar function $x(t)$. Assume that the force acting
on it depends only on the position x of the particle and not on its velocity $\dot{x}$. As
discussed in Section 24.1, the dynamics of this system is given by Newton's law:
$m\ddot{x} = f(x)$, which we write as a first order system

$$\dot{x} = y$$

$$\dot{y} = -\frac{1}{m}f(x).$$
(39)

Let $g(x) = \int^x f(s)\,ds$ be the indefinte integral of f; the function g is called the **potential function** of this system. The function

$$F(x, y) = \frac{1}{2}my^2 + g(x) \tag{40}$$

is called the **energy** function for system (39). One checks that the derivative of F along orbits is zero:

$$\dot{F}(x, y) = \frac{\partial F}{\partial x}\dot{x} + \frac{\partial F}{\partial y}\dot{y}$$

$$= g'(x) \cdot y + my \cdot \left(-\frac{1}{m}f(x)\right)$$

$$= yf(x) - yf(x)$$

$$= 0.$$

Therefore, the energy function (40) is a first integral of system (39). In classical mechanics, this fact is summarized by the phrase "conservation of energy."

Example 25.8   The dynamics of a frictionless pendulum of length L are given by the second order differential equation

$$L\ddot{x} = -g\sin x, \tag{41}$$

where x is the angle that the rod of the pendulum makes with a vertical line, that is, the angle of the pendulum away from its rest point, and g is a gravitational constant. Equation (41) translates to the first order system

$$\dot{x} = y$$
$$\dot{y} = -\frac{g}{L}\sin x. \tag{42}$$

The energy function for this conservative system is

$$F(x, y) = \frac{L}{2}y^2 + g(1 - \cos x), \tag{43}$$

where we have chosen the potential function so that it equals 0 when the pendulum is at rest at $x = 0$. One can check directly that F is a first integral of (42). So the orbits of (42) are the level curves of (43). One uses the first and second order tests of Chapter 17 to prove that the points $(2n\pi, 0)$, for $n = 0, \pm1, \pm2, \ldots$, are local minima of F and the points $(2(n + 1)\pi, 0)$ are saddle points of F. One concludes that the phase portrait of (42) is given by Figure 25.16. Notice that the orbits close to the stationary points are periodic orbits, corresponding to the frictionless oscillations of the pendulum.

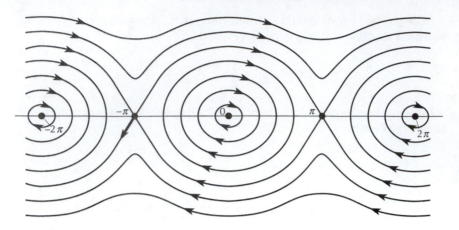

Figure 25.16   *The phase portrait of the system for the nonlinear frictionless pendulum.*

EXERCISES

25.24   Show that $F(x, y) = xy$ is a first integral of the system $\dot{x} = x$, $\dot{y} = -y$.

25.25   Why do we need the word "nonconstant" in the definition of a first integral?

25.26   Verify that the level curves of the energy function (43) are the curves in Figure 25.16.

25.27   Sketch the phase portraits for the mechanical systems whose force functions are given by the following functions: $x^3 - x$, x^2, $x^3 + 3$, $-1/x$.

25.28   Use first and second order condtions to show that $(C/D, A/B)$ is a strict local minimizer of the first integral F in (38). Then, show that $(C/D, A/B)$ is a global min of F.

25.29   Let $(x(t), y(t))$ be a nonzero solution of system (35): $\dot{x} = f(x, y)$, $\dot{y} = g(x, y)$. Show that the slope of the parameterized solution curve in xy-space is $g(x, y)/f(x, y)$. If we eliminate t from this solution and write $y(x)$ as the unparameterized curve, show that $y(x)$ satisfies the differential equation $dy/dx = g(x, y)/f(x, y)$. We can regard this differential equation as a scalar one in which x plays the role of time.

25.30   Use the previous exercise to show that the unparameterized solution curves $y(x)$ of (37) satisfy

$$\frac{dy}{dx} = \frac{x(A - By)}{y(Dx - C)}.$$

Use the fact that this equation is separable to find a relationship between x and y for solutions $y(x)$. Use this relationship to derive the first integral (38) of system (37).

25.7 LIAPUNOV FUNCTIONS

The important equilibria in the predator-prey system (37) and the pendulum system (42) are neutrally stable — a fact that we could *not* have learned without the use of the first integrals for these systems. Level sets of functions can also be used as a test for the asymptotic stability or instability of an equilibrium.

Consider a function F which has a local minimum at the equilibrium (x^*, y^*) of system (35) under study. As in Figures 25.14 and 25.16, the level curves of F are closed curves about (x^*, y^*). If the derivative $\dot{F}$ of F along the solutions of (35) is identically zero, then as we have just seen, the equilibrium is neutrally stable. Suppose, on the other hand, that $\dot{F}(x, y) < 0$ for all $(x, y) \neq (x^*, y^*)$ in a ball B about (x^*, y^*). Then, since

$$\dot{F}(x, y) = \frac{d}{dt}F(x(t), y(t)),$$

$t \longmapsto F(x(t), y(t))$ is a decreasing function of t; and F decreases as one moves along a solution of (35). In other words, the orbits move to lower and lower level sets of F. Since F has a local minimum at (x^*, y^*), this means that orbits are moving closer to (x^*, y^*). Since $\dot{F} < 0$ away from (x^*, y^*), these orbits must continue moving across level sets of F until they reach the equilibrium (x^*, y^*). In this case, the fact that $\dot{F} < 0$ in a neighborhood of (x^*, y^*) means that (x^*, y^*) is an asymptotically stable equilibrium of (35). Furthermore, the size of the region in which $\dot{F} < 0$ gives an estimate of the size of the region of initial conditions whose orbits converge to (x^*, y^*). This region is called the **basin of attraction** of the equilibrium.

Similarly, if $\dot{F}(x, y) > 0$ for all $(x, y) \neq (x^*, y^*)$ in a ball about (x^*, y^*), then F is increasing on orbits of (35). We conclude that orbits are moving away from (x^*, y^*) and therefore that (x^*, y^*) is an unstable equilibrium of system (35). The following theorem summarizes these observations.

Theorem 25.6   Let (x^*, y^*) be a steady state of the planar system of differential equations (35). Let F be a C^1 function of two variables which has a strict local minimum at (x^*, y^*). Consider the derivative

$$\dot{F}(x, y) \equiv \frac{\partial F}{\partial x}(x, y) \cdot f(x, y) + \frac{\partial F}{\partial y}(x, y) \cdot g(x, y)$$

of F along orbits of (35). Let B be an open ball about (x^*, y^*) in the plane.

(a) If $\dot{F}(x, y) = 0$ for all $(x, y) \in B$, then (x^*, y^*) is a neutrally stable equilibrium of (35) and the orbits of (35) in B are the level sets of F.

(b) If $\dot{F}(x, y) < 0$ for all $(x, y) \neq (x^*, y^*)$ in B, then (x^*, y^*) is an asymptotically stable equilibrium of (35) and B lies in its basin of attraction.

(c) If $\dot{F}(x, y) > 0$ for all $(x, y) \neq (x^*, y^*)$ in B, then (x^*, y^*) is an unstable equilibrium of (35).

Definition   A function F which satisfies a, b, or c for system (35) is called a **Liapunov function** for the equilibrium (x^*, y^*).

Example 25.9   Consider the linear system

$$\begin{pmatrix} \dot{x} \\ \dot{y} \end{pmatrix} = \begin{pmatrix} -1 & -1 \\ 1 & -1 \end{pmatrix} \begin{pmatrix} x \\ y \end{pmatrix}. \tag{44}$$

Since its eigenvalues are the complex numbers $r = -1 \pm i$ with negative real part, the phase portrait of (44) is a family of curves spiraling into the equilibrium at the origin. Let $F(x, y) = x^2 + y^2$ be the function whose level curves are circles about the origin. Then,

$$\dot{F}(x, y) = 2x(-x - y) + 2y(x - y)$$

$$= -2x^2 - 2y^2$$

$$< 0 \qquad \text{for all } (x, y) \neq (0, 0).$$

By Theorem 25.6, the Liapunov function F confirms the fact that all the orbits of (44) keep moving closer to the origin, and the origin is a globally asymptotically stable steady state.

Example 25.10   Let's bring *friction* into our analysis of the dynamics of the pendulum. Friction is usually treated as a force $\hat{f}$ proportional to the velocity of the particle and pointing away from its motion: $\hat{f}(x, \dot{x}) = -k\dot{x}$. Therefore, when friction is included, the equations of motion of the pendulum change from (41) to

$$L\ddot{x} = -g \sin x - k\dot{x}, \tag{45}$$

where x is still the angle that the pendulum makes with the vertical. Equation (45) translates to the first order system

$$\dot{x} = y$$
$$\dot{y} = -\frac{g}{L} \sin x - \frac{k}{L} y. \tag{46}$$

Let's calculate the derivative of the energy function F (43) in Example 25.8 along the orbits of system (46):

$$\dot{F} = \frac{\partial F}{\partial x} \cdot \dot{x} + \frac{\partial F}{\partial y} \cdot \dot{y}$$

$$= g \sin x \cdot y + Ly \cdot \left(-\frac{g}{L} \sin x - \frac{k}{L} y \right)$$

$$= -ky^2,$$

which is negative wherever $y = \dot{x} \neq 0$. It follows that the minima of F at $(\pm 2n\pi, 0)$ are now locally stable equilibria of (46). All orbits of (46) move steadily to lower and lower level curves of F, and thus lead to the phase portrait for (46) as in Figure 25.17. Notice that now no matter where the pendulum starts its motion, it will eventually converge to the vertical position.

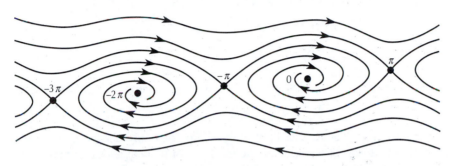

The phase portrait for the pendulum with friction.

Figure 25.17

Example 25.11   If we include crowding factors in the growth equations of both the prey and the predator, the predator-prey system (37) becomes

$$\dot{x} = x\,(A - By - Ex)$$
$$\dot{y} = y\,(Dx - C - Fy) \tag{47}$$

with all constants positive. The interior equilibrium is the solution (x^*, y^*) of the system of linear equations

$$Ex^* + By^* = A$$
$$Dx^* - Fy^* = C. \tag{48}$$

We assume that the crowding factors E and F are small enough relative to the other parameters that system (48) has a solution with $x^* > 0$ and $y^* > 0$. One can compute that the Jacobian matrix of (47) at the solution of (48) has eigenvalues with negative real part; so now, the coexistence equilibrium is asymptotically stable, at least locally.

We will use a Liapunov function to show that (x^*, y^*) is now globally asymptotically stable. Consider the function

$$F(x, y) = D(x - x^* \ln x) + B(y - y^* \ln y). \tag{49}$$

One computes, as we did for (38), that (x^*, y^*) is a global minimizer of F in the positive orthant. Now,

$$\dot{F}(x, y) = D(x - x^*)(A - By - Ex) + B(y - y^*)(Dx - Fy - C)$$
$$= D(x - x^*)(Ex^* + By^* - By - Ex)$$
$$\quad + B(y - y^*)(Dx - Fy - Dx^* + Fy^*) \quad \text{(from (48))}$$
$$= -D(x^* - x)(E(x^* - x) + B(y^* - y))$$
$$\quad - B(y^* - y)(-D(x^* - x) + F(y^* - y))$$
$$= -ED(x^* - x)^2 - BF(y^* - y)^2$$
$$< 0 \quad \text{for } (x, y) \neq (x^*, y^*).$$

Therefore, for this modified model, all orbits tend to (x^*, y^*) in the positive orthant.

Theorem 25.6 holds true in all dimensions. The only change is that for a function F of, say, three variables, the level sets of F about a local minimum are two-dimensional spherelike sets. If $\dot{F} = 0$, the one-dimensional solution curves of the system of differential equations can no longer equal the two-dimensional level sets of the first integral. Still, in this case, the level sets of F yield important information about the location of the solution curves.

EXERCISES

25.31 Show that the Jacobian of system (47) has eigenvalues with negative real part at the solution of (48).

25.32 Consider the parameterized system of differential equations:

$$\dot{x} = y + \varepsilon x(x^2 + y^2), \qquad \dot{y} = -x + \varepsilon y(x^2 + y^2),$$

with parameter ε.

a) Show that, for any ε, the eigenvalues of the Jacobian of this system at the origin are pure imaginary, so that $(0, 0)$ is a neutrally stable equilibrium of the corresponding linearized system.

b) Use the Liapunov function $F(x, y) = x^2 + y^2$ to show that for the nonlinear system, $(0, 0)$ is globally asymptotically stable for $\varepsilon < 0$, neutrally stable for $\varepsilon = 0$, and unstable for $\varepsilon > 0$. Conclude that there is little one can deduce from the linearized system when the Jacobian has pure imaginary eigenvalues.

25.33 Following up on the previous exercise, show that for the system $\dot{x} = y - xh(x, y)$, $\dot{y} = -x - yh(x, y)$, the origin is an asymptotically stable equilibrium if $h(x, y) > 0$ on some ball about the origin, and an unstable equilibrium if $h(x, y) < 0$ on some ball about the origin.

25.8   APPENDIX: LINEARIZATION

For systems of nonlinear differential equations in $\mathbf{R^n}$, $n > 1$, the stability criterion for steady states arises from a study of the proper linearization of the nonlinear system in a neighborhood of a steady state $\mathbf{x}^*$. Consider the autonomous system $\dot{\mathbf{x}} = F(\mathbf{x})$ on $\mathbf{R^n}$ with steady state $\mathbf{x}^*$, so $F(\mathbf{x}^*) = \mathbf{0}$. Write $\mathbf{h} = \mathbf{x} - \mathbf{x}^*$. Let $\mathbf{x}(t)$ be a solution of $\dot{\mathbf{x}} = F(\mathbf{x})$, with initial condition $\mathbf{x}(0)$ near $\mathbf{x}^*$. Let $\mathbf{h}(t) \equiv \mathbf{x}(t) - \mathbf{x}^*$, so that $\mathbf{x}(t) = \mathbf{x}^* + \mathbf{h}(t)$. Then, $\dot{\mathbf{x}} = F(\mathbf{x})$ can be written as

$$\frac{d}{dt}(\mathbf{x}^* + \mathbf{h}(t)) = F(\mathbf{x}^* + \mathbf{h}(t))$$

$$= F(\mathbf{x}^*) + DF(\mathbf{x}^*)\,\mathbf{h}(t) + R(\mathbf{h}(t)), \tag{50}$$

where the last line of (50) is the Taylor polynomial of F of order one about $\mathbf{x}^*$ and

$$R(\mathbf{h})/\|\mathbf{h}\| \to \mathbf{0} \quad \text{as} \quad \mathbf{h} \to \mathbf{0}. \tag{51}$$

Since $\qquad \dfrac{d}{dt}(\mathbf{x}^* + \mathbf{h}(t)) = \dot{\mathbf{h}}(t) \quad \text{and} \quad F(\mathbf{x}^*) = \mathbf{0},$

(50) can be written as

$$\dot{\mathbf{h}}(t) = DF(\mathbf{x}^*)\,\mathbf{h}(t) + R(\mathbf{h}(t)).$$

By (51), the linear system

$$\dot{\mathbf{h}} = DF(\mathbf{x}^*) \cdot \mathbf{h} \tag{52}$$

is the linearization of the original system $\dot{\mathbf{x}} = F(\mathbf{x})$ around steady state $\mathbf{x}^*$. By the usual principles of calculus, if $\mathbf{h}(t)$ is a solution of system (52) near $\mathbf{0}$, then $\mathbf{x}(t) = \mathbf{x}^* + \mathbf{h}(t)$ is very close to a solution of system (50) near $\mathbf{x}^*$. In particular, if linear system (52) satisfies the criterion for asymptotic stability in Theorem 25.4, then the steady state $\mathbf{x}^*$ is an asymptotically stable steady state of the nonlinear system $\dot{\mathbf{x}} = F(\mathbf{x})$. Theorem 25.5 formalizes this line of reasoning. This theorem is the analogue of the corresponding Theorem 24.6 for nonlinear differential equations on $\mathbf{R^1}$.

PART VI

Advanced Linear Algebra

Determinants: The Details

Determinants arise frequently in the analysis of economic models. For example, they play an important role in determining whether or not a given linear system of equations has a solution, in computing the solution when one exists, and in deciding whether a given nonlinear system of equations can be well approximated by its linearization. Determinants are the key ingredient in determining the definiteness of a quadratic form and, therefore, as a second order test, in distinguishing maxima from minima in economic optimization problems.

Chapter 9 presented an overview of the definition and uses of the determinant. This chapter presents a more thorough analysis of the determinant, including proofs of its important properties and major applications. Section 26.1 gives a careful development of the formula for the determinant, more or less from the beginning. The second section demonstrates several important properties of the determinant, including the property that it does in fact provide a test for the nonsingularity of A. The third section derives several useful applications of the determinant, including inverting matrices and finding solutions to simultaneous equations. Section 26.4 applies these techniques to several economic problems. The Appendix to this chapter contains proofs of the more difficult theorems, and a brief discussion of several other approaches to the determinant.

26.1 DEFINITIONS OF THE DETERMINANT

This first section will try to motivate more convincingly, at least for 3×3 matrices, the somewhat complicated definition of $\det A$ in Chapter 9. Recall that we are searching for a number which we can assign to any given matrix to test whether or not that matrix is nonsingular. For a 1×1 matrix (a), that number can only be a itself, since a is invertible if and only if $a \neq 0$.

For an $n \times n$ matrix, there already is a criterion for nonsingularity. Its row echelon form should have no all-zero rows. This criterion was used in Theorem 8.8 to show that a 2×2 matrix

$$A = \begin{pmatrix} a_{11} & a_{12} \\ a_{21} & a_{22} \end{pmatrix}$$

is nonsingular if and only if $a_{11}a_{22} - a_{12}a_{21} \neq 0$. Thus it makes sense to define

$$\det \begin{pmatrix} a_{11} & a_{12} \\ a_{21} & a_{22} \end{pmatrix} = a_{11}a_{22} - a_{12}a_{21}. \tag{1}$$

Let's use the method of Theorem 8.8 to construct the determinant of the general 3×3 matrix

$$A = \begin{pmatrix} a_{11} & a_{12} & a_{13} \\ a_{21} & a_{22} & a_{23} \\ a_{31} & a_{32} & a_{33} \end{pmatrix}.$$

For simplicity's sake, assume that no row interchanges are needed to reduce A to its row echelon form. Pivot on a_{11} to make all the other entries in column 1 equal zero; that is, add $-a_{21}/a_{11}$ times row 1 to row 2 and add $-a_{31}/a_{11}$ times row 1 to row 3. The result is

$$\begin{pmatrix} a_{11} & a_{12} & a_{13} \\ 0 & a_{22} - \dfrac{a_{21}}{a_{11}}a_{12} & a_{23} - \dfrac{a_{21}}{a_{11}}a_{13} \\ 0 & a_{32} - \dfrac{a_{31}}{a_{11}}a_{12} & a_{33} - \dfrac{a_{31}}{a_{11}}a_{13} \end{pmatrix}.$$

Multiplying rows 2 and 3 each by a_{11} yields

$$\begin{pmatrix} a_{11} & a_{12} & a_{13} \\ 0 & a_{11}a_{22} - a_{21}a_{12} & a_{23}a_{11} - a_{21}a_{13} \\ 0 & a_{11}a_{32} - a_{31}a_{12} & a_{33}a_{11} - a_{31}a_{13} \end{pmatrix}. \tag{2}$$

Finally, pivoting on $a_{11}a_{22} - a_{21}a_{12}$ in the (2,2) spot to eliminate the (3,2) entry, we add

$$-\frac{a_{11}a_{32} - a_{31}a_{12}}{a_{11}a_{22} - a_{12}a_{21}}$$

times row 2 to row 3. After some messy algebra, the result of these computations is

$$\begin{pmatrix} a_{11} & a_{12} & a_{13} \\ 0 & a_{11}a_{22} - a_{21}a_{12} & a_{23}a_{11} - a_{31}a_{13} \\ 0 & 0 & (*) \end{pmatrix} \tag{3}$$

where $(*)$ equals

$$\frac{a_{11}}{a_{11}a_{22} - a_{12}a_{21}}(a_{11}a_{22}a_{33} - a_{11}a_{23}a_{32} - a_{12}a_{21}a_{33}$$

$$+ a_{12}a_{23}a_{31} + a_{13}a_{21}a_{32} - a_{13}a_{22}a_{31}). \tag{4}$$

The a_{11} and $(a_{11}a_{22} - a_{21}a_{12})$ of the fraction in (4) are the two pivots which were assumed to be nonzero, since no row interchanges are needed.

Consequently, the 3×3 matrix A is nonsingular if and only if the entry (*) in (3) is nonzero, if and only if the factor in parentheses in (4) is nonzero. So, it makes sense to define

$$\det \begin{pmatrix} a_{11} & a_{12} & a_{13} \\ a_{21} & a_{22} & a_{23} \\ a_{31} & a_{32} & a_{33} \end{pmatrix} = a_{11}a_{22}a_{33} - a_{11}a_{23}a_{32} - a_{12}a_{21}a_{33} \tag{5}$$

$$+ a_{12}a_{23}a_{31} + a_{13}a_{21}a_{32} - a_{13}a_{22}a_{31}.$$

Note that if $a_{11}a_{22} - a_{21}a_{12} = 0$ in (2), we would have to switch rows 2 and 3 in (2). We then find that $a_{23}a_{11} - a_{21}a_{13}$ and $a_{11}a_{32} - a_{31}a_{12}$ must both be nonzero in order for A to be nonsingular.

We can continue this process for larger square matrices. However, let's look for a pattern in (1) and (5) to see what the formula for the determinant should be in general. There are actually two patterns which can be used.

Pattern 1   Note that each term in (1) and in (5) contains exactly one entry from each row and each column of the corresponding matrix. Furthermore, every such combination occurs in (1) and (5).

Pattern 2   Look carefully at the multipliers of each of the entries in the first row. The multiplier of a_{11} in (1) is a_{22}; the multiplier of a_{11} in (5) is $a_{22}a_{33} - a_{23}a_{32}$. Each of these is the determinant of the submatrix obtained by deleting row 1 and column 1 from the original matrix. Next, consider a_{12}. The multiplier $-a_{21}$ of a_{12} in (1) and the multiplier $-a_{21}a_{33} + a_{31}a_{23}$ of a_{12} in (5) are, up to a change in sign, the determinants of the submatrix obtained by deleting row 1 and column 2. Finally, the multiplier of a_{13} in (5) is the determinant of the 2×2 submatrix obtained by deleting row 1 and column 3 from A.

We will return to Pattern 1 in the Appendix of this chapter. We summarize our observations in Pattern 2 by rewriting (1) and (5) as

$$\det \begin{pmatrix} a_{11} & a_{12} \\ a_{21} & a_{22} \end{pmatrix} = a_{11} \cdot \det(a_{22}) - a_{12} \cdot \det(a_{21}), \tag{6}$$

$$\det \begin{pmatrix} a_{11} & a_{12} & a_{13} \\ a_{21} & a_{22} & a_{23} \\ a_{31} & a_{32} & a_{33} \end{pmatrix} = a_{11} \cdot \det \begin{pmatrix} a_{22} & a_{23} \\ a_{32} & a_{33} \end{pmatrix}$$

$$- a_{12} \cdot \det \begin{pmatrix} a_{21} & a_{23} \\ a_{31} & a_{33} \end{pmatrix} \tag{7}$$

$$+ a_{13} \cdot \det \begin{pmatrix} a_{21} & a_{22} \\ a_{31} & a_{32} \end{pmatrix}.$$

Equations (6) and (7) suggest an inductive process for defining the determinant. The next step in this process is to use the formula for the determinant of a 3×3 matrix to define the natural extension of (6) and (7) to 4×4 matrices:

$$\det \begin{pmatrix} a_{11} & a_{12} & a_{13} & a_{14} \\ a_{21} & a_{22} & a_{23} & a_{24} \\ a_{31} & a_{32} & a_{33} & a_{34} \\ a_{41} & a_{42} & a_{43} & a_{44} \end{pmatrix}$$

$$= a_{11} \cdot \det \begin{pmatrix} a_{22} & a_{23} & a_{24} \\ a_{32} & a_{33} & a_{34} \\ a_{42} & a_{43} & a_{44} \end{pmatrix} - a_{12} \cdot \det \begin{pmatrix} a_{21} & a_{23} & a_{24} \\ a_{31} & a_{33} & a_{34} \\ a_{41} & a_{43} & a_{44} \end{pmatrix}$$

$$+ a_{13} \cdot \det \begin{pmatrix} a_{21} & a_{22} & a_{24} \\ a_{31} & a_{32} & a_{34} \\ a_{41} & a_{42} & a_{44} \end{pmatrix} - a_{14} \cdot \det \begin{pmatrix} a_{21} & a_{22} & a_{23} \\ a_{31} & a_{32} & a_{33} \\ a_{41} & a_{42} & a_{43} \end{pmatrix}.$$

Turning to a general $n \times n$ matrix A, assume by induction that the determinant of a general $(n - 1) \times (n - 1)$ matrix has already been defined. As in Chapter 9, let A_{ij} be the $(n - 1) \times (n - 1)$ submatrix obtained by deleting row i and column j from A; recall that $M_{ij} = \det A_{ij}$ is called the (i, j)th **minor** of A. The determinant of A is now defined via an inductive definition.

The **determinant** of an $n \times n$ matrix A is defined by the following rules:

(1) For $n = 1$, $\det A = a_{11}$.
(2) For $n \geq 1$,

$$\det A = a_{11} \cdot M_{11} - a_{12} \cdot M_{12} + \cdots + (-1)^{1+n} a_{1n} \cdot M_{1n}$$

$$= \sum_{j=1}^{n} (-1)^{1+j} a_{1j} \cdot M_{1j}. \tag{8}$$

Note that the a_{ij} term in (8) begins with a plus sign if $i + j$ is even and with a minus sign if $i + j$ is odd. Recall from Chapter 9 that the multiplier of a_{ij} in (8), $(-1)^{i+j} \cdot M_{ij} = (-1)^{i+j} \det A_{ij}$, is called the (i, j)th **cofactor** of A and is usually written C_{ij}, so that (8) can be written as

$$\det A = a_{11} C_{11} + a_{12} C_{12} + \cdots + a_{1n} C_{1n}. \tag{9}$$

The formulas in (8) tell us how to compute the determinant for any $n \times n$ matrix. Starting with an $n \times n$ matrix, equation (8) gives us a rule for the determinant in terms the determinants of n different $(n-1) \times (n-1)$ matrices. Applying (8) again gives us each of these determinants in terms of determinants of $(n - 2) \times (n - 2)$ matrices, and so forth, until we reach an expression in terms of 1×1 matrices. Rule 1 then tells us what these 1×1 determinants are.

Example 26.1   Let us compute that the determinant of the $n \times n$ identity matrix I_n is $+1$. By the formulas for the determinant of a 1×1 and 2×2 matrix, $\det I_1 = 1$ and $\det I_2 = 1$. For $n = 3$,

$$\det \begin{pmatrix} 1 & 0 & 0 \\ 0 & 1 & 0 \\ 0 & 0 & 1 \end{pmatrix} = 1 \cdot \det A_{11} - 0 \cdot \det A_{12} + 0 \cdot \det A_{13}$$

$$= 1 \cdot \det A_{11}$$

$$= 1 \cdot \det I_2$$

$$= 1.$$

The first equality follows from (8), the third from the fact that $A_{11} = I_2$, and the last from the fact that $\det I_2 = 1$. This calculation shows us how to get a handle on $\det I_n$ for arbitrary n.

$$\det I_n = \det \begin{pmatrix} 1 & 0 & \cdots & 0 \\ 0 & 1 & \cdots & 0 \\ \vdots & & \ddots & \vdots \\ 0 & 0 & \cdots & 1 \end{pmatrix}$$

$$= 1 \cdot \det A_{11} - 0 \cdot \det A_{12} + \cdots + (-1)^{n+1} \cdot 0 \cdot \det A_{1n}$$

$$= 1 \cdot A_{11}$$

$$= \det I_{n-1} \qquad \text{(since } A_{11} = I_{n-1}\text{)}.$$

Since $\det I_3 = 1$ and $\det I_4 = \det I_3$, $\det I_4 = 1$.

Since $\det I_4 = 1$ and $\det I_5 = \det I_4$, $\det I_5 = 1$.

It should be clear that, if we carry this out enough times, we can show that any particular I_n has determinant $+1$.

This last step — the carrying out of the argument enough times — is a bit vague. It can be made mathematically precise using the *principle of mathematical induction*. This principle is discussed in some detail in the Appendix of this book on proof techniques. This example is a typical application of the principle. (This technique was also introduced in the proof of Theorem 8.16.)

The principle of mathematical induction is used to prove that some statement involving the integer n is true for *every positive integer*. Typical statements might be the validity of formulas involving the integer n, such as $\det I_n = 1$, or statements about n objects in a set. First, check that the statement in question is true when $n = 1$. Next, show that *if* the statement is true for any integer, say k, *then* it is also true for the next integer $k + 1$. Once this inductive step is proved, we know that since the statement is true for $n = 1$, it is true for $n = 2$. Since it is true for $n = 2$, it is true for $n = 3$, and so on. The principle of mathematical induction states that, if the statement is true for $n = 1$ and if the inductive step is true, then the statement is true for all positive n.

In our calculations for $\det I_n$, we first showed directly that $\det I_1 = \det I_2 = \det I_3 = +1$. This starts the inductive process off. Next, we proved the inductive step. We showed that $\det I_n = \det I_{n-1}$ for all n. So, if $\det I_k = +1$, then it must be true that $\det I_{k+1} = +1$. We conclude from the principle of mathematical induction that, for all positive n, $\det I_n = +1$.

Actually, the principle of mathematical induction is easier to use than it is to describe! The proofs of many important properties of $n \times n$ matrices rely on mathematical induction. The next few times we use it, we will go over it carefully. Make sure that you understand how the arguments work. Practice problems that use the principle of mathematical induction can be found in the Appendix to this book.

Notice that there is a loss of symmetry in going from expressions (1) and (5) to expressions (6), (7), and (8). Each row and column is treated equally in (1) and (5) and in Pattern 1; on the other hand, in (6) and (7) and in Pattern 2, we specifically moved along the *first* row in calculating the determinant. However, in going from (1) to (6), we could easily have used the second row or either column of A:

$$\det \begin{pmatrix} a_{11} & a_{12} \\ a_{21} & a_{22} \end{pmatrix} = -a_{21} \cdot \det(a_{12}) + a_{22} \cdot \det(a_{11})$$

$$= +a_{11} \cdot \det(a_{22}) - a_{21} \cdot \det(a_{12})$$

$$= -a_{12} \cdot \det(a_{21}) + a_{22} \cdot \det(a_{11}).$$

Similarly, we could have rewritten (5) for 3×3 matrices in a form like (7) but using any row or column of A, for example, the *second column*, as we did in Chapter 9:

$$\det A = -a_{12} \cdot \det \begin{pmatrix} a_{21} & a_{23} \\ a_{31} & a_{33} \end{pmatrix} + a_{22} \cdot \det \begin{pmatrix} a_{11} & a_{13} \\ a_{31} & a_{33} \end{pmatrix}$$

$$- a_{32} \cdot \det \begin{pmatrix} a_{11} & a_{13} \\ a_{21} & a_{23} \end{pmatrix}. \tag{10}$$

Thus, it is natural to expect that we can expand along any row or column to calculate the determinant of an $n \times n$ matrix. This fact is summarized in Theorem 26.1 below. Its proof is a straightforward, but tedious, inductive argument, which we present in the Appendix of this chapter.

Theorem 26.1   If one defines the determinant of the $n \times n$ matrix A as in (8), then for any i or j,

$$\det A = \sum_{k=1}^{n} (-1)^{i+k} a_{ik} \det A_{ik} \qquad \text{(expansion along row } i\text{)}$$

$$= \sum_{h=1}^{n} (-1)^{h+j} a_{hj} \det A_{hj} \qquad \text{(expansion along column } j\text{)}. \tag{11}$$

The fact that we can compute $\det A$ using either the first row or the first column implies that transposing a matrix does not change its determinant. The following theorem summarizes this observation.

Theorem 26.2   For any $n \times n$ matrix A, $\det A = \det A^T$.

Remark   There is an easy-to-remember mnemonic device for computing the determinant of a 3×3 matrix A. Form the partitioned matrix $\hat{A}$ by recopying the first and second rows of A right below A, as in Figure 26.1.

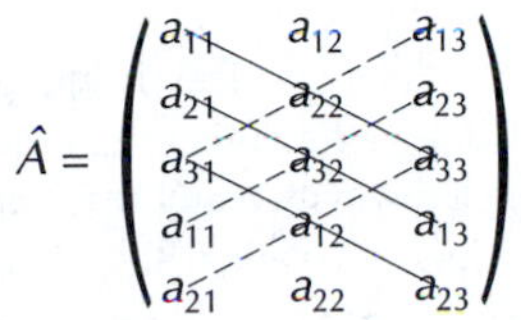

$$\hat{A} = \begin{pmatrix} a_{11} & a_{12} & a_{13} \\ a_{21} & a_{22} & a_{23} \\ a_{31} & a_{32} & a_{33} \\ a_{11} & a_{12} & a_{13} \\ a_{21} & a_{22} & a_{23} \end{pmatrix}$$

Computing the determinant of a 3×3 matrix.

Figure 26.1

Starting from a_{11} at the top left corner of $\hat{A}$, add together the three products along the three "diagonals" indicated by the solid lines in Figure 26.1:

$$a_{11}a_{22}a_{33} + a_{21}a_{32}a_{13} + a_{31}a_{12}a_{23}. \tag{12}$$

Then, starting from a_{21} at the bottom left corner of $\hat{A}$, subtract from (12) the three products along the three "counterdiagonals" indicated by the dotted lines in Figure 26.1:

$$-a_{21}a_{12}a_{33} - a_{11}a_{32}a_{23} - a_{31}a_{22}a_{13}. \tag{13}$$

The result (12) + (13) is the determinant of A. As illustrated in Exercise 26.8, **this method works only for 3×3 matrices.**

Example 26.2   Using this method, it is easy to see that

$$\det \begin{pmatrix} 0 & 1 & 2 \\ 3 & 4 & 5 \\ 6 & 7 & 8 \end{pmatrix} = 0 \cdot 4 \cdot 8 + 3 \cdot 7 \cdot 2 + 6 \cdot 1 \cdot 5$$

$$- 3 \cdot 1 \cdot 8 - 0 \cdot 7 \cdot 5 - 6 \cdot 4 \cdot 2$$

$$= 0 + 42 + 30 - 24 - 48$$

$$= 0.$$

EXERCISES

26.1 Compute the determinant of each of the following matrices:

$$a) \begin{pmatrix} 2 & 1 \\ 1 & 1 \end{pmatrix}, \quad b) \begin{pmatrix} 4 & 2 \\ -8 & -4 \end{pmatrix}, \quad c) \begin{pmatrix} 1 & 2 & 3 \\ 4 & 5 & 6 \\ 7 & 8 & 9 \end{pmatrix},$$

$$d) \begin{pmatrix} 1 & 2 & 3 \\ 0 & 0 & 4 \\ 5 & 6 & 7 \end{pmatrix}, \quad e) \begin{pmatrix} 1 & 2 & 3 & 4 \\ 4 & 1 & 0 & 3 \\ 3 & 4 & 1 & 2 \\ 0 & 1 & 0 & 2 \end{pmatrix}.$$

26.2 Calculate $\det A$ for the last three matrices in the previous exercise by expanding along a column of A and along a row other than the first. Note that for the last two matrices, expanding along a row with many zeros can simplify the calculation.

26.3 Show that if $a_{11}a_{22} - a_{21}a_{12} = 0$, then the expression for det A in (5) equals $-(a_{23}a_{11} - a_{21}a_{13})(a_{11}a_{32} - a_{31}a_{12})/a_{11}$.

26.4 *a)* Check that (10) yields the same formula as (5).

b) Use another row and another column of the 3×3 matrix A to calculate $\det A$ and check that you obtain the same expression as (5).

26.5 Write out a careful proof of Theorem 26.2.

26.6 Use the method of Figure 26.1 to compute the two 3×3 determinants in Exercise 26.1.

26.7 *a)* How many terms are there in the formula for the determinant of a general $n \times n$ matrix?

b) How many arithmetic operations (additions, subtractions, etc.) are needed to compute the determinant of a general $n \times n$ matrix?

26.8 If one used the technique described in Figure 26.1, the "determinant" of a 4×4 matrix would require only eight terms. Compare this with the number of terms that are indicated in the previous exercise for a 4×4 determinant.

26.2 PROPERTIES OF THE DETERMINANT

We still must show that formula (8) for the determinant really works — that a matrix is nonsingular if and only if its determinant is nonzero. This result is the goal of this section. Along the way we will develop some properties of the determinant. Since we are collecting all the important facts about the determinant in this section, we will begin by repeating the important fact which we proved at the end of the last section — Theorem 26.2.

Fact 26.1. For any $n \times n$ matrix A, $\det A = \det A^T$.

Fact 26.1 implies that any statement about how the rows of a matrix affect the value of the determinant is also true when applied to the columns of a matrix. We will prove the remaining results in this section for rows and row operations, but it is easy to see that by Fact 26.1, they will also be true for columns and column operations.

One of the most important facts about determinants is that a matrix and its row echelon form have the same determinant, up to a possible change of sign. The possible change in sign comes from the fact that interchanging two rows of a matrix changes the sign of its determinant.

Fact 26.2.   If one forms the matrix B by interchanging two rows (or two columns) of $n \times n$ matrix A, then $\det B = -\det A$.

Proof   The proof of Fact 26.2 is a straightforward inductive argument which uses formula (6) or (8). First, compute directly that Fact 26.2 is true for 2×2 matrices since

$$\begin{vmatrix} a_{21} & a_{22} \\ a_{11} & a_{12} \end{vmatrix} = a_{21}a_{12} - a_{11}a_{22} = -\begin{vmatrix} a_{11} & a_{12} \\ a_{21} & a_{22} \end{vmatrix}.$$

Then, use this to see that it is true for 3×3 matrices. For example, if one forms matrix B by interchanging rows 2 and 3 of A,

$$A = \begin{pmatrix} a_{11} & a_{12} & a_{13} \\ a_{21} & a_{22} & a_{23} \\ a_{31} & a_{32} & a_{33} \end{pmatrix} \quad \text{and} \quad B = \begin{pmatrix} a_{11} & a_{12} & a_{13} \\ a_{31} & a_{32} & a_{33} \\ a_{21} & a_{22} & a_{23} \end{pmatrix}.$$

Then, expand $\det B$ along its first row:

$$\det B = a_{11}\begin{vmatrix} a_{32} & a_{33} \\ a_{22} & a_{23} \end{vmatrix} - a_{12}\begin{vmatrix} a_{31} & a_{33} \\ a_{21} & a_{23} \end{vmatrix} + a_{13}\begin{vmatrix} a_{31} & a_{32} \\ a_{21} & a_{22} \end{vmatrix}$$

$$= -a_{11}\begin{vmatrix} a_{22} & a_{23} \\ a_{32} & a_{33} \end{vmatrix} + a_{12}\begin{vmatrix} a_{21} & a_{23} \\ a_{31} & a_{33} \end{vmatrix} - a_{13}\begin{vmatrix} a_{21} & a_{22} \\ a_{31} & a_{32} \end{vmatrix}$$

$$= -\det A$$

(since we know Fact 26.2 is true for 2×2 matrices).

We now prove Fact 26.2 for a general $n \times n$ matrix, under the assumption (that is, the inductive hypothesis) that it is true for general $(n-1) \times (n-1)$ matrices. Form matrix B by interchanging rows i and j of A. Expand $\det A$ and $\det B$ along a row other than the ith or jth, for notation's sake, say row 2. Then,

$$\det A = \sum_{k=1}^{n} (-1)^{2+k} a_{2k} \cdot \det A_{2k}.$$

But the $(2, k)$th minor B_{2k} of B is the determinant of an $(n-1) \times (n-1)$ matrix which differs from the $(2, k)$th minor A_{2k} of A only by the fact that two of its rows are interchanged. By the inductive hypothesis, $\det B_{2k} = -\det A_{2k}$. Therefore,

$$\det B = \sum_{k=1}^{n}(-1)^{2+k}a_{2k} \cdot \det B_{2k}$$

$$= \sum_{k=1}^{n}(-1)^{2+k}a_{2k} \cdot (-\det A_{2k})$$

$$= -\sum_{k=1}^{n}(-1)^{2+k}a_{2k} \cdot \det A_{2k}$$

$$= -\det A. \qquad \blacksquare$$

Fact 26.3.   If two rows (or columns) of A are equal, $\det A = 0$.

Proof   Suppose row i equals row j. If we interchange rows i and j, we change the sign of $\det A$ by Fact 26.2. However, we do not change A. In other words, $\det A = -\det A$. Since 0 is the only number equal to its negative, $\det A = 0$. $\blacksquare$

Fact 26.4.   Form matrix B by multiplying each entry in row (column) i of matrix A by the scalar r, then $\det B = r \cdot \det A$.

Proof   For 2×2 matrices, we have

$$\begin{vmatrix} ra_{11} & ra_{12} \\ a_{21} & a_{22} \end{vmatrix} = ra_{11}a_{22} - ra_{12}a_{21}$$

$$= r(a_{11}a_{22} - a_{12}a_{21})$$

$$= r\begin{vmatrix} a_{11} & a_{12} \\ a_{21} & a_{22} \end{vmatrix}.$$

For an $n \times n$ matrix, expand $\det B$ along row i. Since A and B agree outside row i, the (i, k)th minor of B, M_{ik}, is also the (i, k)th minor of A for all k. Using (8),

$$\det B = \sum_{k=1}^{n}(-1)^{i+k}(ra_{ik}) \cdot \det A_{ik}$$

$$= r\sum_{k=1}^{n}(-1)^{i+k}a_{ik} \cdot \det A_{ik} = r \cdot \det A. \qquad \blacksquare$$

Fact 26.5.   If matrix A has an all-zero row (or column), then $\det A = 0$.

Proof   Suppose every entry in row i of A is zero. Multiplying row i by $r = 0$ will not change A. By Fact 26.4, $\det A = 0$. Alternatively, one can use (8) and expand $\det A$ along row i. $\blacksquare$

Fact 26.6. Let A and B be $n \times n$ matrices which differ only in their ith row. Let C be the matrix whose ith row is the matrix sum of the ith rows of A and of B and whose other rows are the same as those of A and B. Then,

$$\det C = \det A + \det B.$$

If we partition A and B by its rows and write $\mathbf{a}_j = (a_{j1} \cdots a_{jn})$ for row j of A and $\mathbf{b}_j = (b_{j1} \cdots b_{jn})$ for row j of B, then

$$\det \begin{pmatrix} \mathbf{a}_1 \\ \mathbf{a}_2 \\ \vdots \\ \mathbf{a}_i \\ \vdots \\ \mathbf{a}_n \end{pmatrix} + \det \begin{pmatrix} \mathbf{a}_1 \\ \mathbf{a}_2 \\ \vdots \\ \mathbf{b}_i \\ \vdots \\ \mathbf{a}_n \end{pmatrix} = \det \begin{pmatrix} \mathbf{a}_1 \\ \mathbf{a}_2 \\ \vdots \\ \mathbf{a}_i + \mathbf{b}_i \\ \vdots \\ \mathbf{a}_n \end{pmatrix}.$$

Proof Expand $\det C$ along its ith row:

$$\mathbf{a}_i + \mathbf{b}_i = (a_{i1} + b_{i1}, \cdots, a_{in} + b_{in}).$$

Note that for each k, the (i, k)th minors of A, B, and C are all the same. As usual, write this minor as M_{ik} and the corresponding cofactor, $(-1)^{i+k} \cdot M_{ik}$, as C_{ik}. Then,

$$\det C = \sum_k (a_{ik} + b_{ik}) \cdot C_{ik}$$

$$= \sum_k a_{ik} C_{ik} + \sum b_{ik} C_{ik}$$

$$= \det A + \det B. \quad \blacksquare$$

It is *not* true that $\det(A + B) = \det A + \det B$. The matrix C in Fact 26.6 is not the matrix sum of A and B. See Exercise 26.9.

Fact 26.7. Transform matrix A to matrix B by performing the elementary row operation of adding r times row i of A to row j of A to form row j of B. (The other rows of B are the same as those of A.) Then $\det B = \det A$. Alternatively, if $E_{ij}(r)$ is the elementary matrix obtained by adding r times row i to row j in the identity matrix, then

$$\det(E_{ij}(r) \cdot A) = \det A.$$

Proof In the notation of Fact 26.6, if

$$
A = \begin{pmatrix} \mathbf{a}_1 \\ \vdots \\ \mathbf{a}_i \\ \vdots \\ \mathbf{a}_j \\ \vdots \\ \mathbf{a}_n \end{pmatrix}
\quad \text{and} \quad
B = \begin{pmatrix} \mathbf{a}_1 \\ \vdots \\ \mathbf{a}_i \\ \vdots \\ r\,\mathbf{a}_i + \mathbf{a}_j \\ \vdots \\ \mathbf{a}_n \end{pmatrix},
$$

then,
$$
\det B = \det \begin{pmatrix} \mathbf{a}_1 \\ \vdots \\ \mathbf{a}_i \\ \vdots \\ r\,\mathbf{a}_i \\ \vdots \\ \mathbf{a}_n \end{pmatrix} + \det \begin{pmatrix} \mathbf{a}_1 \\ \vdots \\ \mathbf{a}_i \\ \vdots \\ \mathbf{a}_j \\ \vdots \\ \mathbf{a}_n \end{pmatrix}
\qquad \text{(by Fact 26.6)}
$$

$$
= r \cdot \det \begin{pmatrix} \mathbf{a}_1 \\ \vdots \\ \mathbf{a}_i \\ \vdots \\ \mathbf{a}_i \\ \vdots \\ \mathbf{a}_n \end{pmatrix} + \det \begin{pmatrix} \mathbf{a}_1 \\ \vdots \\ \mathbf{a}_i \\ \vdots \\ \mathbf{a}_j \\ \vdots \\ \mathbf{a}_n \end{pmatrix}
\qquad \text{(by Fact 26.4)}
$$

$$
= r \cdot 0 + \det A \qquad \text{(by Fact 26.3)}
$$

$$
= \det A. \qquad \blacksquare
$$

Fact 26.8. Let R be the row echelon form of matrix A. Then, $\det R = \pm \det A$.

Proof The transformation of A to R involves a finite sequence of the following two elementary row operations:

  (*a*) interchanging two rows and
  (*b*) adding a multiple of one row to another.

By Fact 26.2, whenever we apply operation *a*, we change only the sign of the determinant of our matrix. By Fact 26.7, whenever we apply operation *b*, we do not change the determinant at all. So, the end result R of the Gaussian elimination process will either have the same determinant as A or $\det R$ will differ from $\det A$ only by its sign. ∎

Fact 26.9. The determinant of the $n \times n$ identity matrix I is $+1$.

Proof   See Example 26.1.

Fact 26.10.   The determinant of a diagonal matrix A is the product of its diagonal entries:

$$\det \begin{pmatrix} a_{11} & 0 & \cdots & 0 \\ 0 & a_{22} & \cdots & 0 \\ \vdots & \vdots & \ddots & \vdots \\ 0 & 0 & \cdots & a_{nn} \end{pmatrix} = a_{11} \cdot a_{22} \cdots a_{nn}.$$

Proof   Use Fact 26.4 n times to compute

$$\det A = a_{11} \cdot \det \begin{pmatrix} 1 & 0 & \cdots & 0 \\ 0 & a_{22} & \cdots & 0 \\ \vdots & \vdots & \ddots & \vdots \\ 0 & 0 & \cdots & a_{nn} \end{pmatrix}$$

$$= a_{11} \cdot a_{22} \cdot \det \begin{pmatrix} 1 & 0 & \cdots & 0 \\ 0 & 1 & \cdots & 0 \\ \vdots & \vdots & \ddots & \vdots \\ 0 & 0 & \cdots & a_{nn} \end{pmatrix}$$

$$\vdots \qquad\qquad \vdots$$

$$= a_{11} \cdot a_{22} \cdots a_{nn} \cdot \det \begin{pmatrix} 1 & 0 & \cdots & 0 \\ 0 & 1 & \cdots & 0 \\ \vdots & \vdots & \ddots & \vdots \\ 0 & 0 & \cdots & 1 \end{pmatrix}$$

$$= a_{11} \cdot a_{22} \cdots a_{nn} \cdot 1, \qquad \text{(by Fact 26.9)}.$$

Alternatively, one can use the induction argument of Fact 26.9. ∎

Fact 26.11.   The determinant of an upper- or lower-triangular matrix is the product of its diagonal entries.

Proof   The proof is the same as that for Fact 26.9. Verify it directly for 1×1 and 2×2 matrices and use induction to prove it for $n \times n$ matrices. ∎

Example 26.3

$$\begin{vmatrix} 2 & 3 & 1 \\ 0 & -5 & 6 \\ 0 & 0 & 4 \end{vmatrix} = 2 \begin{vmatrix} -5 & 6 \\ 0 & 4 \end{vmatrix} + 0 \begin{vmatrix} 3 & 1 \\ 0 & 4 \end{vmatrix} + 0 \begin{vmatrix} 3 & 1 \\ -5 & 6 \end{vmatrix}$$

$$= (2)(-5)(4) - (2)(0)(6)$$

$$= (2)(-5)(4) = -40.$$

We finally arrive at our main goal. The determinant as defined in (6) really does determine whether or not a square matrix is nonsingular.

> **Theorem 26.3**   A square matrix A is nonsingular if and only if $\det A$ is nonzero.

Proof   If R is the row echelon form of A, then $\det A = \pm \det R$ by Fact 26.8. The matrix R is upper triangular, and so Fact 26.11 implies that $\det R$ is the product of its diagonal elements. But R has a diagonal zero if and only if A is singular (see Exercise 7.24; see also the proof sketch after Theorem 9.2). ∎

Fact 26.11 and Theorem 26.3 give us a simple check for the invertibility of a triangular matrix and help us compute the determinant of each type of elementary matrix.

Example 26.4   Let $E_{ij}, E_i(r)$, and $E_{ij}(r)$ be the three classes of elementary matrices as defined in Section 8.3. Then,

  (*a*) $\det E_{ij} = -1$,
  (*b*) $\det E_i(r) = r$, and
  (*c*) $\det E_{ij}(r) = 1$.

Why? Since E_{ij} is formed by interchanging rows i and j of I, statement a follows directly from Facts 26.9 and 26.2. Matrices $E_i(r)$ and $E_{ij}(r)$ are triangular matrices; $E_i(r)$ has an r and $(n-1)$ 1s on its diagonal and $E_{ij}(r)$ has only 1s on its diagonal. So, statements b and c follow from Fact 26.11.

Exercise 26.9 shows that the determinant does not behave nicely with respect to sums of matrices. We will now see that it behaves beautifully with respect to products: the determinant of the product of two matrices is the product of the determinants. Before proving the general result, we treat a special case.

Lemma 26.1   Let E be an $n \times n$ elementary matrix and let B be an arbitrary $n \times n$ matrix. Then,

$$\det(E \cdot B) = \det E \cdot \det B.$$

Proof   First, suppose that E is an elementary matrix. Then, EB is B with rows i and j interchanged. By Fact 26.2, $\det EB = -\det B$. From Example 26.4, $\det E \cdot \det B = (-1)\det B$, too.
    If $E = E_i(r)$, then EB is B with row i multiplied by r. So

$$\det EB = r \cdot \det B \qquad \text{(by Fact 26.4)}$$

$$= \det E \cdot \det B \qquad \text{(from Example 26.4.)}$$

The case where $E = E_{ij}(r)$ is left as an exercise. ∎

Theorem 26.4   For arbitrary $n \times n$ matrices A and B,

$$\det AB = \det A \cdot \det B. \tag{14}$$

Proof   The proof of this theorem relies heavily on Lemma 26.1 and Theorem 8.12. First, suppose that A is nonsingular. By Theorem 8.12, A can be written as the product of elementary matrices: $A = E_1 \cdot E_2 \cdots E_k$; this implies that

$$A \cdot B = E_1 \cdot E_2 \cdots E_k \cdot B. \tag{15}$$

Apply Lemma 26.1 to the right-hand side of (15) a number of times:

$$
\begin{aligned}
\det AB &= \det[E_1 \cdot (E_2 \cdots E_k \cdot B)] \\
&= \det(E_1) \cdot \det(E_2 \cdots E_k \cdot B) \\
&= \det E_1 \cdot \det E_2 \cdot \det(E_3 \cdots E_k \cdot B) \\
&= \det(E_1 \cdot E_2) \cdot \det(E_3 \cdots E_k B) \\
&\quad \vdots \qquad\quad \vdots \\
&= \det(E_1 \cdot E_2 \cdots E_k) \cdot \det B \\
&= \det A \cdot \det B.
\end{aligned}
$$

If A is singular, we can write $A = E_1 \cdots E_k R$, where $E_1, \ldots, E_k$ are elementary matrices and R is the row echelon form of A. Now,

$$AB = E_1 \cdots E_k RB,$$

and by the argument just given,

$$\det AB = \det(E_1 \cdots E_k) \cdot \det(RB).$$

Since A is singular, every entry in the last row of R is a zero. By the way matrix product is defined, every entry in the last row of RB is also a zero. By Fact 26.5, $\det RB = 0$. Therefore, $\det AB = 0$. Since A is singular, $\det A = 0$. Therefore, $\det AB = \det A \cdot \det B = 0$. ∎

Example 26.5   To illustrate rule (14), let

$$A = \begin{pmatrix} 4 & 5 \\ 1 & 3 \end{pmatrix} \quad \text{and} \quad B = \begin{pmatrix} 2 & 1 \\ 0 & 1 \end{pmatrix}.$$

Then $\det A = 7$, $\det B = 2$, and

$$\det AB = \det \begin{pmatrix} 8 & 9 \\ 2 & 4 \end{pmatrix} = 14 = 7 \cdot 2 = \det A \cdot \det B.$$

Theorem 26.4 can be applied to the equation $AA^{-1} = I$ to compute $\det A^{-1}$ in terms of $\det A$.

Theorem 26.5 If A is invertible, $\det A^{-1} = 1/\det A$.

Example 26.6 If $A = \begin{pmatrix} 3 & 1 \\ 1 & 1 \end{pmatrix}$, then $A^{-1} = \begin{pmatrix} 1/2 & -1/2 \\ -1/2 & 3/2 \end{pmatrix}$. It is easy to compute that $\det A = 2$ and $\det A^{-1} = 1/2 = 1/\det A$.

EXERCISES

26.9 Let $A = \begin{pmatrix} 2 & 1 \\ 1 & 1 \end{pmatrix}$, $B = \begin{pmatrix} 4 & 3 \\ 1 & 1 \end{pmatrix}$, and $C = \begin{pmatrix} 6 & 4 \\ 1 & 1 \end{pmatrix}$.

    a) Show that $\det(A + B) \neq \det A + \det B$.

    b) Show that $\det A + \det B = \det C$ and relate this to Fact 26.6.

26.10 Use induction to supply a more careful proof of Fact 26.8.

26.11 Write out a careful proof of Fact 26.11.

26.12 Show that an upper- or lower-triangular matrix is nonsingular if and only if every diagonal entry is nonzero.

26.13 *a*) Compute the determinant of each of the following matrices by applying row operations to obtain an upper-triangular matrix and then use Fact 26.11:

$$i) \begin{pmatrix} 2 & 1 & 0 \\ 6 & 2 & 6 \\ -4 & -3 & 9 \end{pmatrix}, \quad ii) \begin{pmatrix} 2 & 3 & 1 & -1 \\ 0 & 1 & 4 & -1 \\ 0 & 0 & 2 & 4 \\ 4 & 6 & 2 & 0 \end{pmatrix}, \quad iii) \begin{pmatrix} 2 & 6 & 0 & 5 \\ 6 & 21 & 8 & 17 \\ 4 & 12 & -4 & 13 \\ 0 & -3 & 12 & 2 \end{pmatrix}.$$

    b) Which of these matrices are nonsingular?

26.14 Find the exact values of k which make each of the following matrices singular:

$$a) \begin{pmatrix} 1 & k \\ k & 1 \end{pmatrix}, \quad b) \begin{pmatrix} k & 1 & 1 \\ 1 & k & 1 \\ 1 & 1 & k \end{pmatrix}.$$

26.15 Prove Theorem 26.5.

26.16 Prove the following results for $n \times n$ matrices:

    a) $\det rA = r^n \cdot \det A$;

    b) $\det(-A) = (-1)^n \det A$;

    c) $\det(A_1 \cdots A_r) = (\det A_1) \cdots (\det A_r)$;

    d) $\det A^k = (\det A)^k$ for positive integers k;

    e) $\det A^k = (\det A)^k$ for all integers k if A is invertible.

26.17 Finish the proof of Lemma 26.1 for the case $A = E_{ij}(r)$.

26.18 *a*) An orthogonal matrix is a nonsingular matrix such that $A^{-1} = A^T$. Show that the determinant of an orthogonal matrix is ± 1.

    b) A skew symmetric matrix is a square matrix such that $A^T = -A$. Show that if n is odd, a skew symmetric matrix is singular.

    c) Present some nontrivial examples of orthogonal matrices and skew-symmetric matrices.

26.19 Show that the determinant of A is, up to sign, the product of its pivots.

26.20 Show that two $n \times n$ matrices A and B are invertible (nonsingular) if and only if their product AB is invertible (nonsingular).

26.21 (difficult) Suppose that you are given a square matrix A, partitioned into four submatrices:

$$A = \begin{pmatrix} A_{11} & A_{12} \\ A_{21} & A_{22} \end{pmatrix}$$

where A_{11} and A_{22} are square submatrices.

a) Show that

$$\det \begin{pmatrix} A_{11} & 0 \\ 0 & A_{22} \end{pmatrix} = \det A_{11} \cdot \det A_{22}.$$

b) Show that

$$\det \begin{pmatrix} A_{11} & A_{12} \\ 0 & A_{22} \end{pmatrix} = \det \begin{pmatrix} A_{11} & 0 \\ A_{21} & A_{22} \end{pmatrix} = \det A_{11} \cdot \det A_{22}.$$

c) Suppose that A_{22} is nonsingular. Show that

$$\begin{pmatrix} A_{11} & A_{12} \\ A_{21} & A_{22} \end{pmatrix} = \begin{pmatrix} A_{11} - A_{12}A_{22}^{-1}A_{21} & A_{12} \\ 0 & A_{22} \end{pmatrix} \cdot \begin{pmatrix} I & 0 \\ A_{22}^{-1}A_{21} & I \end{pmatrix}.$$

d) Conclude that if A_{22} is nonsingular,

$$\det \begin{pmatrix} A_{11} & A_{12} \\ A_{21} & A_{22} \end{pmatrix} = \det(A_{11} - A_{12}A_{22}^{-1}A_{21}) \cdot \det A_{22}.$$

e) Use this method to compute

$$\det \begin{pmatrix} 2 & 1 & -1 & 3 \\ 1 & 1 & 4 & 1 \\ -3 & 1 & 3 & 1 \\ 4 & 2 & 5 & 2 \end{pmatrix}.$$

26.22 Use row reduction to show that

$$\begin{vmatrix} 1 & 1 & 1 \\ a & b & c \\ a^2 & b^2 & c^2 \end{vmatrix} = (b - a)(c - a)(c - b).$$

26.3   USING DETERMINANTS

The discussion in the last section showed that the determinant as defined in (6) is an effective tool for checking whether or not a square matrix is nonsingular. In this section, we will describe some other applications of the determinant.

The Adjoint Matrix

Continue to write M_{ij} for the (i, j)th minor of $n \times n$ matrix A. Recall that

$$C_{ij} = (-1)^{i+j}M_{ij},$$

the multiplier of a_{ij} in the expansion of $\det A$, is called the (i, j)th cofactor of A. Form the **adjoint matrix**, $\operatorname{adj} A$, as in Chapter 9 — the $n \times n$ matrix whose (i, j)th entry is the (j, i)th cofactor of A, C_{ji}. The following theorem states that, if A is invertible, $\operatorname{adj} A$ is, up to a scalar multiple, the inverse of A.

Theorem 26.6   For any $n \times n$ matrix A, $A \cdot \operatorname{adj} A = \det A \cdot I$; that is,

$$\begin{pmatrix} a_{11} & \cdots & a_{1n} \\ \vdots & \ddots & \vdots \\ a_{n1} & \cdots & a_{nn} \end{pmatrix} \cdot \begin{pmatrix} A_{11} & \cdots & A_{n1} \\ \vdots & \ddots & \vdots \\ A_{1n} & \cdots & A_{nn} \end{pmatrix} = \begin{pmatrix} \det A & 0 & \cdots & 0 \\ 0 & \det A & \cdots & 0 \\ \vdots & \vdots & \ddots & \vdots \\ 0 & 0 & \cdots & \det A \end{pmatrix}.$$

Proof   The entry in the ith row and jth column of $A \cdot \operatorname{adj} A$ is

$$a_{i1}A_{j1} + a_{i2}A_{j2} + \cdots + a_{in}A_{jn}. \tag{16}$$

If $i = j$, (16) is just the expansion of $\det A$ along row i as in (8). Thus we need only show that (16) is zero if $i \neq j$. Note that (16) is the expansion of $\det A$ along the jth row of A (because of the A_{jk}'s in (16)) but with a_{ik} replacing a_{jk} for every k. In other words, for $i \neq j$, (16) is the expansion of $\det B$ along the jth row of B, where

$$B = \begin{pmatrix} a_{11} & \cdots & a_{1n} \\ \vdots & & \vdots \\ a_{i1} & \cdots & a_{in} \\ \vdots & & \vdots \\ a_{i1} & \cdots & a_{in} \\ \vdots & & \vdots \\ a_{n1} & \cdots & a_{nn} \end{pmatrix} \begin{matrix} \\ \\ \text{Row } i \\ \\ \text{Row } j \\ \\ \\ \end{matrix}$$

is the matrix A with row j replaced by row i. But since B has two equal rows, $\det B = 0$ by Fact 26.3. Thus, expression (16), the (i, j)th entry of $A \cdot \operatorname{adj} A$, is zero for $i \neq j$. ∎

Theorem 26.7   If A is nonsingular, $A^{-1} = \frac{1}{\det A} \cdot \operatorname{adj} A$.

Example 26.7   Let's use this formula to compute the third column of A^{-1} when

$$A = \begin{pmatrix} 5 & 0 & 9 \\ 0 & 6 & 1 \\ 1 & 7 & 1 \end{pmatrix}.$$

First, $\det A = (5)(-1) + (1)(-54) = -59$. Next,

$$A_{31} = \begin{vmatrix} 0 & 9 \\ 6 & 1 \end{vmatrix} = -54, \qquad A_{32} = -\begin{vmatrix} 5 & 9 \\ 0 & 1 \end{vmatrix} = -5,$$

$$A_{33} = \begin{vmatrix} 5 & 0 \\ 0 & 6 \end{vmatrix} = 30.$$

Thus the third column of A^{-1} is $\begin{pmatrix} 54/59 \\ 5/59 \\ -30/59 \end{pmatrix}$.

To check this, observe that

$$\begin{pmatrix} 5 & 0 & 9 \\ 0 & 6 & 1 \\ 1 & 7 & 1 \end{pmatrix} \begin{pmatrix} 54/59 \\ 5/59 \\ -30/59 \end{pmatrix} = \begin{pmatrix} 0 \\ 0 \\ 1 \end{pmatrix}.$$

Sometimes it is handy to have an explicit formula for the solution of a system of n linear equations in n unknowns. Since the solution of $A\mathbf{x} = \mathbf{b}$ is $\mathbf{x} = A^{-1}\mathbf{b}$ and since Theorem 26.7 yields a formula for A^{-1}, we can now easily derive a formula for the solution $\mathbf{x}$. This formula is known as *Cramer's rule* and was presented as Theorem 9.4*b*.

Theorem 26.8   (Cramer's Rule) Let A be a nonsingular matrix. The unique solution $\mathbf{x} = (x_1, \cdots, x_n)$ of the $n \times n$ system $A\mathbf{x} = \mathbf{b}$ is

$$x_j = \frac{\det B_j}{\det A}, \qquad \text{for } j = 1, \ldots, n,$$

where B_j is the matrix A with the right-hand side $\mathbf{b}$ replacing the jth column of A.

Proof   Using Theorem 26.7,

$$\mathbf{x} = A^{-1}\mathbf{b} = \frac{1}{|A|} \begin{pmatrix} C_{11} & \cdots & C_{n1} \\ \vdots & \vdots & \vdots \\ C_{1n} & \cdots & C_{nn} \end{pmatrix} \begin{pmatrix} b_1 \\ b_2 \\ \vdots \\ b_n \end{pmatrix},$$

where C_{ij} is the (i, j)th cofactor of A. Therefore,

$$x_j = \frac{b_1 C_{1j} + b_2 C_{2j} + \cdots + b_n C_{nj}}{|A|}. \tag{17}$$

All we need to do is show that the numerator of (17) is $\det B_j$. Since B_j and A agree except for column j, the (k, j)th cofactor of B_j is C_{kj} for each k. If we expand $\det B_j$ along its jth column, which is the column vector $\mathbf{b}$, we obtain the numerator of (17). Thus $x_j = \det B_j / \det A$. ∎

Our last application for determinants in this chapter is a test for verifying whether any row exchanges are needed to reduce a given matrix A to row echelon form via Gaussian elimination. Example 8.4 showed that no row interchanges are necessary in reducing a general 2×2 matrix if and only if the two pivots a_{11} and $(a_{11}a_{22} - a_{12}a_{21})/a_{11}$ were nonzero. Calculations (2) and (3) showed that no row interchanges were necessary for reducing a general 3×3 matrix if and only if the pivots

$$a_{11}, \qquad \frac{a_{11}a_{22} - a_{12}a_{21}}{a_{11}}, \qquad \frac{\det A}{a_{11}a_{22} - a_{12}a_{21}}$$

were all nonzero. In these cases, the criteria are the determinants of the top leftmost 1×1, 2×2, and 3×3 matrices. This fact is generally true; its proof is presented in the Appendix to this chapter.

Theorem 26.9 Let A be an $n \times n$ matrix. Let A_k denote the upper leftmost $k \times k$ submatrix of A, the submatrix obtained by deleting the *last* $(n - k)$ rows and columns from A. If $\det A_k \neq 0$ for $k = 1, 2, \ldots, (n - 1)$, then Gaussian elimination can be carried out on A without any row exchanges. In this case, the first pivot of A is $\det A_1$ and the kth pivot of A equals $\det A_k / \det A_{k-1}$. Furthermore, $\det A_k$ is the product of the first k pivots.

EXERCISES

26.23 Compute the inverse for the matrix A in Example 26.7, using Theorem 26.6.

26.24 Compute $\operatorname{adj} A$ for a general 2×2 matrix and show that the result of Theorem 8.8 agrees with Theorem 26.7.

26.25 Use Theorem 26.7 to compute the inverses of the matrices in Exercise 26.1.

26.26 *a*) How many arithmetic steps are required to invert a 3×3 matrix via Theorem 26.7?

   b) How many arithmetic steps are required to invert a 3×3 matrix via the method of Theorem 8.7?

   c) (more difficult) Do steps *a* and *b* for $n \times n$ matrices to discover that it is much more efficient to use Gaussian elimination to invert a large matrix than to use the formula of Theorem 26.7.

26.27 Use Cramer's rule to solve the following systems of equations:

$$a) \quad \begin{array}{l} 2x_1 + 3x_2 = -10 \\ x_1 - 5x_2 = 21; \end{array}$$

$$b) \quad \begin{array}{l} 2x_1 + 4x_2 \phantom{{}+ 3x_3} = 2 \\ 4x_1 + 6x_2 + 3x_3 = 8 \\ 6x_1 + 10x_2 \phantom{{}+ 3x_3} = 4; \end{array}$$

$$c) \quad \begin{array}{l} 5x_1 + 3x_2 + x_3 = 2 \\ 5x_1 + 4x_2 - x_3 = 5 \\ 10x_1 + 9x_2 - 5x_3 = 14. \end{array}$$

26.28 a) Prove that if the entries of A are all integers and if $\det A = \pm 1$, then the entries of A^{-1} are also integers.

b) Use Theorem 26.5 to show that if the entries of A and A^{-1} are all integers, then $\det A = \pm 1$.

26.29 For each of the following two matrices, find all their pivots first by using Theorem 26.9 and then by using Gaussian elimination:

$$a) \quad \begin{pmatrix} 1 & 4 & 6 \\ 3 & 6 & 1 \\ 0 & 2 & 1 \end{pmatrix}, \qquad b) \quad \begin{pmatrix} 2 & 1 & 1 & 2 \\ 4 & 3 & 2 & 5 \\ 0 & 4 & -2 & 8 \\ 2 & 0 & 1 & 0 \end{pmatrix}.$$

26.4 ECONOMIC APPLICATIONS

As was pointed out near the end of Chapter 9, Gaussian elimination is a much more efficient method of solving a system of n equations in n unknowns than is Cramer's rule, especially for n large, because the number of steps that it takes to solve a system of n equations in n unknowns is roughly $n!$ for Cramer's rule, but only n^3 for Gaussian elimination.

Nevertheless, Cramer's rule is particularly useful for small linear systems in which the coefficients a_{ij} are parameters (rather than concrete numbers) and for which one wants to obtain a general formula for the endogenous variables (the x_i's) in terms of the parameters and the exogenous variables (the b_j's). In such a situation, the formulas that Cramer's rule presents allow one to see more clearly how changes in the parameters affect the values of the endogenous variables. This phenomenon was illustrated at the end of Chapter 9 for the IS-LM model.

Supply and Demand

As another example, look at supply and demand in a two-good economy. Let Q_1^s and Q_2^s denote the amounts of each good supplied by firms in the market, while Q_1^d and Q_2^d denote the corresponding demands of consumers. Let P_1 and P_2 be the prices of the goods, and Y consumer income. In this section we will study constant-elasticity supply and demand functions, which are basic tools for applied economists:

$$Q_1^d = K_1 P_1^{a_{11}} P_2^{a_{12}} Y^{b_1},$$
$$Q_2^d = K_2 P_1^{a_{21}} P_2^{a_{22}} Y^{b_2},$$
$$Q_1^s = M_1 P_1^{n_1},$$
$$Q_2^s = M_2 P_2^{n_2}.$$

(18)

For these functional forms, the important elasticities are constant and are precisely the exponents $a_{11}, a_{12}, b_1, a_{21}, a_{22}, b_2, n_1$ and n_2. (See Chapters 3 and 14 for more information about elasticity.) For example, for good 1:

a_{11} = own price elasticity of demand,

a_{12} = cross elasticity of demand with respect to good 2,

b_1 = income elasticity of demand,

n_1 = own price elasticity of supply.

A second advantage of these functional forms is that taking the natural logarithm of both sides of the expressions in (18) yields linear relationships in

$$q_i^s \equiv \ln Q_i^s, \quad q_i^d \equiv \ln Q_i^d, \quad p_i \equiv \ln P_i, \quad \text{and} \quad y \equiv \ln Y,$$

whose coefficients are precisely the elasticities

$$q_1^d = k_1 + a_{11}p_1 + a_{12}p_2 + b_1 y,$$
$$q_2^d = k_2 + a_{21}p_1 + a_{22}p_2 + b_2 y,$$
$$q_1^s = m_1 + n_1 p_1,$$
$$q_2^s = m_2 + n_2 p_2.$$

(19)

The a_{ij}'s, b_i's, and n_i's are the elasticities, and the k_i's and m_i's are the logarithms of the K_i's and M_i's.

Equilibrium prices arise when supply equals demand: $Q_i^s = Q_i^d$, and so $q_i^s = q_i^d$ for $i = 1, 2$. (If $Q_1^s \geq Q_1^d$, consumers will bid P_1 lower; if $Q_1^s \leq Q_1^d$, consumers will bid P_1 higher.) Setting $q_i^s = q_i^d$ in (19) leads to the system

$$-(-a_{11} + n_1)p_1 + a_{12}p_2 = m_1 - k_1 - b_1 y$$
$$a_{21}p_1 - (-a_{22} + n_2)p_2 = m_2 - k_2 - b_2 y$$

(20)

where income is treated as an exogenous variable. System (20) can be solved explicitly for the endogenous variables p_1 and p_2 using Cramer's rule:

$$p_1 = \frac{\begin{vmatrix} m_1 - k_1 - b_1 y & a_{12} \\ m_2 - k_2 - b_2 y & -(-a_{22} + n_2) \\ -(-a_{11} + n_1) & a_{12} \\ a_{21} & -(-a_{22} + n_2) \end{vmatrix}}{\begin{vmatrix} -(-a_{11} + n_1) & a_{12} \\ a_{21} & -(-a_{22} + n_2) \end{vmatrix}}$$

$$= \frac{(-a_{22} + n_2)(-m_1 + k_1 + b_1 y) + a_{12}(-m_2 + k_2 + b_2 y)}{(-a_{11} + n_1)(-a_{22} + n_2) - a_{12}a_{21}},$$

(21)

$$p_2 = \frac{\begin{vmatrix} -(-a_{11} + n_1) & m_1 - k_1 - b_1 y \\ a_{21} & m_2 - k_2 - b_2 y \\ -(-a_{11} + n_1) & a_{12} \\ a_{21} & -(-a_{22} + n_2) \end{vmatrix}}{\begin{vmatrix} -(-a_{11} + n_1) & a_{12} \\ a_{21} & -(-a_{22} + n_2) \end{vmatrix}}$$

$$= \frac{(-a_{11} + n_1)(-m_2 + k_2 + b_2 y) + a_{21}(-m_1 + k_1 + b_1 y)}{(-a_{11} + n_1)(-a_{22} + n_2) - a_{12}a_{21}}.$$

(22)

These expressions are very complicated. Imagine the tedium (and opportunities for error) in deriving these expressions from Gauss-Jordan elimination applied to system (20)! The virtue of Cramer's rule is that one can write down the solutions directly, just by staring at the system.

Equations (21) and (22) make it easier to see how the equilibrium prices respond to changes in the parameters of the model — the elasticities. Assume that both commodities are **normal goods**; that is, demand for each commodity increases with an increase in income and decreases with an increase in price. In terms of our model, this means that b_1 and b_2 are positive and that a_{11} and a_{22} are negative. Further assume that a change in the price of commodity 1 will have a larger absolute effect on the demand for commodity 1 than it has on the demand for commodity 2, and similarly for commodity 2. Mathematically, this assumption means that $|a_{11}| > |a_{12}|$ and $|a_{22}| > |a_{21}|$. In particular, these two assumptions imply that the denominators in (21) and (22) are positive.

One can eyeball equations (21) and (22) to note that for good i, an increase in the price elasticity of demand a_{ii}, in the price elasticity of supply n_i, or in the income elasticity b_i will lower the equilibrium price p_i. The effects of these parameters on p_j depend on the sign of the cross elasticity a_{ji}. If a_{ji} is positive, meaning that an increase in the price p_i leads to an increase in q_j^d, good j is said to be a **substitute** for good i. On observing price rises for good i, the consumer responds by substituting good j for good i. In this case, an increase in a_{ii} or n_i or a decrease in b_i imply a decrease in the equilibrium price p_j. If a_{ji} is negative, good j is said to be a **complement** of good i. In this case, an increase in a_{ii} or n_i or a decrease in b_i leads to an increase in p_j.

This approach can also shed light on the effects of taxes on the equilibrium prices. Suppose the government imposes a percentage tax of t on consumption of good 1. Consumers now face price $(1 + t)P_1$ instead of P_1. Substitute this change into the demand functions in (18) but not into the supply functions. Take logarithms and set supply equal to demand. The log-demand functions in (19) become

$$q_1^d = k_1 + a_{11}\ln(1+t) + a_{11}p_1 + a_{12}p_2 + b_1 y,$$

$$q_2^d = k_2 + a_{21}\ln(1+t) + a_{21}p_1 + a_{22}p_2 + b_2 y,$$

and the equilibrium equations become

$$-(-a_{11} + n_1)p_1 + a_{12}p_2 = m_1 - k_1 - a_{11}\ln(1+t) - b_1 y,$$

$$a_{21}p_1 - (-a_{22} + n_2)p_2 = m_2 - k_2 - a_{21}\ln(1+t) - b_2 y.$$

By Cramer's rule, the solution of this system is

$$p_1 = \frac{(-a_{22} + n_2)(-m_1 + k_1 + a_{11}\ln(1+t) + b_1 y)}{(-a_{11} + n_1)(-a_{22} + n_2) - a_{12}a_{21}}$$

$$+ \frac{a_{12}(-m_2 + k_2 + a_{21}\ln(1+t) + b_2 y)}{(-a_{11} + n_1)(-a_{22} + n_2) - a_{12}a_{21}}$$

$$p_2 = \frac{(-a_{11} + n_1)(-m_2 + k_2 + a_{21}\ln(1+t) + b_2 y)}{(-a_{11} + n_1)(-a_{22} + n_2) - a_{12}a_{21}}$$

$$+ \frac{a_{21}(-m_1 + k_1 + a_{11}\ln(1+t) + b_1 y)}{(-a_{11} + n_1)(-a_{22} + n_2) - a_{12}a_{21}}.$$

The coefficient of $\ln(1+t)$ in p_1 is

$$-\frac{-a_{11}(-a_{22} + n_2) - a_{12}a_{21}}{(-a_{11} + n_1)(-a_{22} + n_2) - a_{12}a_{21}}$$

which is generally negative — actually between 0 and -1. So, an increase in the tax on good 1 should lower the equilibrium market price of good 1. The coefficient of $\ln(1+t)$ in p_2 is

$$\frac{n_1 a_{21}}{(-a_{11} + n_1)(-a_{22} + n_2) - a_{12}a_{21}}.$$

So, the tax on good 1 will raise the equilibrium price of good 2 if good 2 is a substitute for good 1 ($a_{21} \geq 0$) and lower the price of good 2 if good 2 is a complement to good 1 ($a_{21} \leq 0$).

EXERCISES

26.30 *a*) Carry out all the computations described in the previous paragraph.
    b) Carry out the computations if the tax is on the consumption of good 2 rather than good 1.

26.31 If you are familiar with partial derivatives, show that in (21) and (22)

$$-\frac{\partial p_1}{\partial a_{22}} = \frac{\partial p_1}{\partial n_2} = \frac{-a_{12}p_2}{D} \quad \text{and} \quad \frac{\partial p_1}{\partial b_2} = \frac{a_{12}y}{D},$$

where $D \equiv (-a_{11} + n_1)(-a_{22} + n_2) - a_{12}a_{21}$. Interpret these results.

26.32 Suppose the government taxes the producers of good 1 instead of the consumers. If the tax percentage is again t, producers will receive an effective price of $P_1(1 - t)$ instead of P_1. Replace P_1 by $P_1(1 - t)$ in the Q_1^s-equation in (18). How will this tax affect the market equilibrium prices P_1 and P_2?

26.33 Use Cramer's rule to solve system (7) in Chapter 6 for the steady state employment and unemployment rates x and y in terms of the transition probabilities p and q.

26.5 APPENDIX

This Appendix presents the proofs of Theorems 26.1 and 26.9, followed by a discussion of some other approaches to defining determinants. First, the proofs:

Proof of Theorem 26.1

Theorem 26.1 is the statement that the determinant of a matrix can be calculated by expanding along any row or any column.

Theorem 26.1 The determinant of an $n \times n$ matrix A can be calculated along any row or column:

$$\det A = \sum_{k=1}^{n}(-1)^{i+k}a_{ik}M_{ik} \quad \text{(expansion along row } i\text{)}$$

$$= \sum_{h=1}^{n}(-1)^{h+j}a_{hj}M_{hj} \quad \text{(expansion along column } j\text{)}.$$

Proof The proof has three parts. We first show that the expansion along the first row equals the expansion along the first column. Then we show that the expansion along the first row equals the expansion along the ith row. Finally we show that the expansion along the first column equals the expansion along the jth column.

The proofs of these three parts are similar. They all use mathematical induction on the size of the matrix. The statement of the theorem is clearly true for 1×1 matrices. The inductive principle is to show that if it is true for $(n - 1) \times (n - 1)$ matrices, it must be true for $n \times n$ matrices. It then follows from the principle of mathematical induction that it is true for all matrices. For a further discussion of the details of this proof technique, see the Appendix of this book. Thus, we assume that the statement in the theorem is true for $(n-1) \times (n-1)$ matrices and show that it must be true for $n \times n$ matrices.

First prove that the expansion along the first column,

$$C_1 = \sum_{h=1}^{n} (-1)^{h+1} a_{h1} M_{h1}, \tag{23}$$

equals the expansion along the first row,

$$R_1 = \sum_{j=1}^{n} (-1)^{1+j} a_{1j} M_{1j}, \tag{24}$$

where M_{ik} is the (i, k)th minor of A, the determinant of A_{ik}, the submatrix of A obtained by deleting from A row i and column k. We will use induction to prove that $R_1 = C_1$.

Note that the term $a_{11} M_{11}$ appears in both (23) and (24). We will evaluate C_1 by expanding each of the remaining terms of the sum in equation (23). The determinant M_{h1} can be expanded along its first row to get

$$M_{h1} = \sum_{j=2}^{n} (-1)^{j} a_{1j} M_{h1,1j}, \tag{25}$$

where $M_{h1,1j}$ is the determinant of the $(n-2) \times (n-2)$ submatrix obtained by deleting row h, column 1, row 1 and column j from A. (See Figure 26.2.)

The exponent of (-1) in (25) is $1 + (j-1) = j$ because the jth column of A is the $(j-1)$st column of A_{h1}. Putting (23) and (25) together yields

$$C_1 = a_{11} M_{11} + \sum_{h=2}^{n} (-1)^{h+1} a_{h1} \sum_{j=2}^{n} (-1)^{j} a_{1j} M_{h1,1j} \tag{26}$$

$$= a_{11} M_{11} + \sum_{h=2}^{n} \sum_{j=2}^{n} (-1)^{h+j+1} a_{h1} a_{1j} M_{h1,1j}. \tag{27}$$

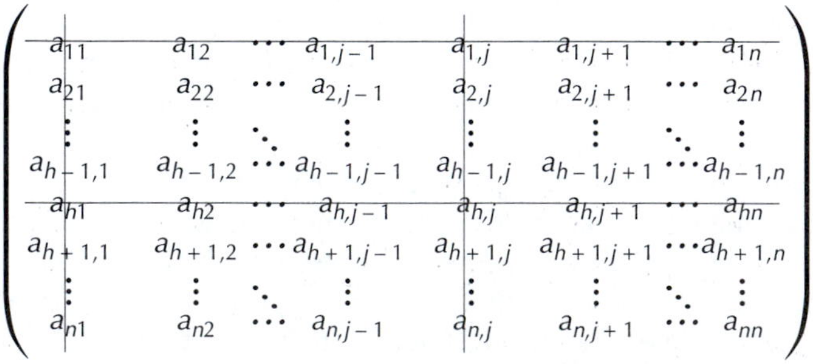

Figure 26.2

Submatrix for $M_{h1,1j}$.

Equation (27) follows from (26) because of the distributive law, which allows us to take each a_{h1} term inside the summation of the a_{1j} terms.

Now we turn to equation (24). The coefficient of a_{1j} in (24) is $(-1)^{1+j}M_{1j}$. The matrix A_{1j} is $(n-1) \times (n-1)$. The inductive hypothesis is that the statement of the theorem is true for $(n-1) \times (n-1)$ matrices, so we can compute the determinant of A_{1j} by expanding along its first *column*:

$$M_{1j} = \sum_{h=2}^{n} (-1)^h a_{h1} M_{1j,h1}. \tag{28}$$

The exponent of -1 is $h = (h-1) + 1$ because the hth row of A is the $(h-1)$th row of A_{1j}.

Putting (24) and (28) together and using the distributive law again yields

$$R_1 = a_{11}M_{11} + \sum_{j=2}^{n} (-1)^{1+j} a_{1j} \sum_{h=2}^{n} (-1)^h a_{h1} M_{1j,h1}$$

$$= a_{11}M_{11} + \sum_{j=2}^{n} \sum_{h=2}^{n} (-1)^{h+j+1} a_{1j} a_{h1} M_{1j,h1}. \tag{29}$$

Comparing (29) and (27), we see that $R_1 = C_1$.

So, expansion along the first row of A and expansion along the first column of A give the same answer. Next we show that this answer can be obtained by expanding along any row of A. Define

$$R_i = \sum_{h=1}^{n} (-1)^{i+h} a_{ih} M_{ih}. \tag{30}$$

We will show that $R_i = R_1$.

First consider R_1 in (24). Use the inductive hypothesis to compute $M_{1j} = \det A_{1j}$ by expanding along its ith row:

$$M_{1j} = \sum_{h \neq j} (-1)^{b(h)} a_{ih} M_{1j,ih}, \tag{31}$$

where the exponent of -1 is

$$b(h) = \begin{cases} (i-1) + h, & \text{if } h < j, \\ (i-1) + (h-1), & \text{if } h > j. \end{cases}$$

(It is easy to see that if $h < j$, then the hth column of A is the hth column of A_{1j}. If $h > j$, then the hth column of A is the $(h-1)$th column of A_{1j}. In either case, the ith row of A is the $(i-1)$th row of A_{1j}.) Substituting (31) into (24), we have

$$R_1 = \sum_{j=1}^{n} \sum_{h \neq j} (-1)^{b(h)+j+1} a_{1j} a_{ih} M_{1j,ih}, \tag{32}$$

where the exponent of -1 is given by

$$b(h) + j + 1 = \begin{cases} i + h + j, & \text{if } h < j, \\ i + h + j - 1, & \text{if } h > j. \end{cases}$$

Now consider R_i in (30). We can expand A_{ih} along its first row to obtain

$$M_{ih} = \det A_{ih} = \sum_{j \neq h} (-1)^{c(j)} a_{1j} M_{ih,1j}, \tag{33}$$

where

$$c(j) = \begin{cases} 1 + j, & \text{if } j < h, \\ 1 + (j - 1) = j, & \text{if } j > h. \end{cases}$$

Substituting (33) into (30) gives

$$R_i = \sum_{h=1}^{n} \sum_{j \neq h} (-1)^{i+h+c(j)} a_{ih} a_{1j} M_{ih,1j}, \tag{34}$$

where

$$i + h + c(j) = \begin{cases} i + h + j + 1, & \text{if } j < h, \\ i + h + j, & \text{if } j > h. \end{cases}$$

Comparing equations (34) and (32) and noting that $b(h) + j + 1$ and $i + h + c(j)$, the exponents of -1 in the $a_{1j} a_{ih}$-terms, have the same parity for all h, i, j, we see that $R_i = R_1$.

Finally, we need to show that expanding A along column i gives the same value for the determinant as expanding along column 1. To see this, simply observe that expanding A along column i is the same as expanding A^T along row i, which is the same as expanding A^T along row 1 (we have just proven this), which is the same as expanding A along column 1. ∎

Proof of Theorem 26.9

To prove Theorem 26.9, recall that A_k is the $k \times k$ submatrix of A formed by deleting the last $(n - k)$ rows and columns from A.

> **Theorem 26.9**   Let A be an $n \times n$ matrix. If $\det A_k \neq 0$ for $k = 1, 2, \ldots, n-1$, then Gaussian elimination can be carried out on A without any row exchanges. In this case, the first pivot of A is $\det A_1$ and the kth pivot of A equals $\det A_k / \det A_{k-1}$. Furthermore, $\det A_k$ is the product of the first k pivots.

The idea of this theorem is fairly intuitive. The first pivot of A depends only on the first row and first column of A; the second pivot depends only on the first two rows and first two columns of A, and so forth. In general, the kth pivot depends only on the entries of A_k.

Proof   The proof is by induction of k. First consider A_1. The matrix A_1 is a 1×1 matrix whose sole entry is a_{11}. Since $\det A_1 \neq 0$, a_{11} is not zero, and it becomes the first pivot p_1. For the inductive hypothesis, assume that no row interchanges are required through the first $(k-1)$ pivots of A. Then we can reduce A to the matrix

$$\begin{pmatrix} U_{k-1} & * & * \\ 0 & p_k & * \\ 0 & * & * \end{pmatrix}$$

without any row interchanges. (The matrix U_{k-1} will be upper triangular.) We need to show that we can pivot on the entry p_k.

Since U_{k-1} was formed from A_{k-1} by successive applications of the addition of a multiple of one row to another, it follows from Fact 26.7 that $\det U_{k-1} = \det A_{k-1}$. By the same argument,

$$\det \begin{pmatrix} U_{k-1} & * \\ 0 & p_k \end{pmatrix} = \det A_k.$$

But, by equation (6),

$$\det \begin{pmatrix} U_{k-1} & * \\ 0 & p_k \end{pmatrix} = \det U_{k-1} \cdot p_k$$

$$= \det A_{k-1} \cdot p_k.$$

Since $\det A_{k-1} \neq 0$,

$$p_k = \frac{\det A_k}{\det A_{k-1}}.$$

Since $\det A_k \neq 0$, $p_k \neq 0$ and we can pivot on it to continue the row reduction of A without row interchanges. Finally,

$$\det A_k = \frac{\det A_k}{\det A_{k-1}} \cdots \frac{\det A_2}{\det A_1} \det A_1$$

$$= p_k \cdots p_2 \cdot p_1. \quad \blacksquare$$

Other Approaches to the Determinant

In Section 26.1 the determinant of A was defined by expanding along the first row of A. Later we saw that the same value was achieved by expanding along any row or column. There are two other approaches to defining the determinant. Definition (6) of the determinant generalized Pattern 2 in Section 26.1. An alternative definition generalizes Pattern 1:

> Each term in (1) and (5) contains exactly one entry from each row and column of A, and each such combination occurs exactly once.

Following this pattern, it is natural to try to define $\det A$ as

$$\det A = \sum_{j_1,\ldots,j_n} (\pm 1) a_{1j_1} a_{2j_2} \cdots a_{nj_n} \tag{35}$$

where the $j_1, \ldots, j_n$ in each term is some rearrangement or **permutation** of $1, 2, \ldots, n$.

Of course, we will also need a method for assigning a sign to each term in (35). This amounts to assigning a sign to each permutation of the integers $1, 2, \ldots, n$. Any rearrangement of the first n integers can be achieved by first swapping the position of two integers, then two more, then two more, etc. For example, consider the integers 1, 2, 3 and the rearrangement 3, 2, 1. This permutation can be achieved simply by interchanging the 1 and the 3 in the original list. It can also be achieved by interchanging first 1 and 2, then 1 and 3, and finally 2 and 3. There are many different paths that one can take from 1, 2, 3 to 3, 2, 1, but it is not hard to show that all such paths have an odd number of steps. In general it will be true that for any given permutation of the first n integers, *all* paths from $1, 2, \ldots, n$ to that permutation will contain an even number of steps, or *all* such paths will contain an odd number of steps. It is not possible to have some paths containing an even number and other paths an odd number. Permutations whose paths contain an even number of steps are called **even permutations**, and permutations whose paths contain an odd number of steps are called **odd permutations**. Write

$$\sigma(j_1, \ldots, j_n) = \begin{cases} +1, & \text{if } (j_1, \ldots, j_n) \text{ is an even permutation,} \\ -1, & \text{if } (j_1, \ldots, j_n) \text{ is an odd permutation.} \end{cases}$$

Now, if $j_1 = 1, j_2 = 2, \ldots, j_n = n$ in (35), we know from (6) that we will be able to assign a plus sign $(+)$ to that term in (35). For an arbitrary permutation $(j_1, \ldots, j_n)$ of $(1, \ldots, n)$, we make a list of the pairwise switches which transform $(j_1, \ldots, j_n)$ to $(1, \ldots, n)$. Then perform this sequence of pairwise switches on the columns of matrix A. Call the transformed matrix B with entries b_{ij}. By Fact 26.2, $\det B = \det A$ if we used an even number of column switches, that is, if $(j_1, \ldots, j_n)$ is an even permutation, and $\det B = -\det A$ if we used an odd number of column switches, that is, if $(j_1, \ldots, j_n)$ is an odd permutation. It is easy to check that $b_{11}b_{22} \cdots b_{nn} = a_{1j_1} a_{2j_2} \cdots a_{nj_n}$. Since $b_{11}b_{22} \cdots b_{nn}$ receives a plus $(+)$ sign in the expansion of $\det B$, we will want to assign $a_{1j_1} a_{2j_2} \cdots a_{nj_n}$ a plus $(+)$ sign in the expansion of $\det A$ if $\det A = \det B$, the case of an even permutation, and a minus $(-)$ sign in the expansion of $\det A$ if $\det A = -\det B$, the case of an odd permutation.

So had we made use of Pattern 1 instead of Pattern 2, we would have defined the determinant of an $n \times n$ matrix A as

$$\det A = \sum_{(j_1,\ldots,j_n)} \sigma(j_1, \ldots, j_n) a_{1j_1} \cdots a_{nj_n}, \tag{36}$$

where the summation is over all $n!$ permutations of $(1, 2, \ldots, n)$. Though somewhat more aesthetic than (6), this formula is much more difficult to use.

Most modern linear algebra textbooks take yet another approach to defining the determinant — one that does not get bogged down in messy formulas. They prove that there is a unique function which assigns numbers to $n \times n$ matrices and which satisfies Facts 26.2, 26.4, 26.6, and 26.9. They then derive all the other properties of the determinant, including formula (6) from these four primary facts.

Actually the concept of the determinant arose much earlier than that of a matrix! Expressions such as that on the right hand of (36) arise frequently in classical physics. Turn-of-the-century books on linear algebra dealt primarily with determinants, and frequently had the word "determinant" in their titles. It was not until much later that linear algebraists made matrices rather than determinants their primary object of study. This history can be seen in the terminology of linear algebra. The word "matrix" comes from the Latin word for mother ("mater") and was used to signify that the determinant should be considered the "offspring" of the more general notion of matrix.

EXERCISES

26.34   Use induction to show that the definition of the determinant in equation (8) satisfies Pattern 1.

26.35   *a*) Calculate the parity of each of the two permutations of $(1, 2)$ and each of the six permutations of $(1, 2, 3)$.

   b) Show that (36) is the same as (1) for 2×2 matrices and the same as (5) for 3×3 matrices.

CHAPTER 27

Subspaces Attached to a Matrix

Many economic entities are defined as the solution of a system of linear equations. For example, equilibrium production vectors in an input-output economy and riskless portfolios, duplicable portfolios, and insurable states in portfolio analysis arise as solutions of linear systems. In such models, it is important to decide not only whether the underlying linear system has a solution but also how big the set of these solutions is. A principal objective of this chapter is to give a complete answer to the following questions raised in Chapter 7: For a given linear system $A\mathbf{x} = \mathbf{b}$, for which right-hand sides $\mathbf{b}$ are there solutions? What is the size and shape of the set of solutions for such $\mathbf{b}$s? The next chapter presents a number of economic applications of the answers to these questions.

This chapter is the continuation of Chapter 11; the presentation is a little more technical. The last section of Chapter 11 introduced the concepts of basis and dimension for Euclidean spaces. This chapter begins by extending these concepts to proper subsets of Euclidean spaces. Section 27.1 defines the important special subsets to which these notions apply — *subspaces* of $\mathbf{R}^n$. Section 27.2 shows that every basis of a subspace of $\mathbf{R}^n$ has the same number of elements and defines that number to be the *dimension* of the subspace. The following sections focus on special subsets that are associated with the coefficient matrix for a system of linear equations. Sections 27.3 and 27.4 treat in detail the space spanned by the rows and the space spanned by the columns of a given matrix. In particular, it is shown that for a given matrix A, both of these spaces have the same dimension and that dimension equals the *rank* of A. Section 27.5 describes another important subspace attached to a matrix A — the *nullspace* or *kernel* of A, the set of solutions of $A\mathbf{x} = \mathbf{0}$. Section 27.5 ends with a presentation of the Fundamental Theorem of Linear Algebra, which makes precise the size of the solution space of a system of linear equations in terms of the rank of the underlying coefficient matrix. Section 27.6 abstracts the concepts of vector space and subspace to spaces which are not subsets of $\mathbf{R}^n$.

27.1 VECTOR SPACES AND SUBSPACES

$\mathbf{R}^n$ as a Vector Space

The set $\mathbf{R}^n$ of n-tuples has more structure than other sets, such as the set of all letters in the English alphabet or the set of all buildings in San Diego. This additional structure arises from the fact that there are natural ways of combining n-tuples to

750

form new ones, namely the operations of addition and scalar multiplication. At this point, we list the important properties that these two operations have, temporarily using the letter V to denote $\mathbf{R}^n$. For all $\mathbf{u}$, $\mathbf{v}$, $\mathbf{w}$ in V and all scalars r, s in $\mathbf{R}$,

(1) $\mathbf{u} + \mathbf{v}$ is in V whenever $\mathbf{u}$ and $\mathbf{v}$ are in V (closure under addition),
(2) $\mathbf{u} + \mathbf{v} = \mathbf{v} + \mathbf{u}$ (commutative law for addition),
(3) $\mathbf{u} + (\mathbf{v} + \mathbf{w}) = (\mathbf{u} + \mathbf{v}) + \mathbf{w}$ (associative law for addition),
(4) there is an element $\mathbf{0}$ in V such that, for all $\mathbf{v}$ in V, $\mathbf{v} + \mathbf{0} = \mathbf{v}$ (additive identity),
(5) for every $\mathbf{v}$ in V, there is an element $\mathbf{w}$ in V (usually written $-\mathbf{v}$) such that $\mathbf{v} + \mathbf{w} = \mathbf{0}$ (additive inverse),
(6) $r \cdot \mathbf{v}$ is in V whenever $\mathbf{v}$ is in V (closure under scalar multiplication),
(7) $r \cdot (\mathbf{u} + \mathbf{v}) = r \cdot \mathbf{u} + r \cdot \mathbf{v}$ (distributive under scalar multiplication),
(8) $(r + s) \cdot \mathbf{u} = r \cdot \mathbf{u} + s \cdot \mathbf{u}$,
(9) $r \cdot (s \cdot \mathbf{u}) = s \cdot (r \cdot \mathbf{u})$, and
(10) $1 \cdot \mathbf{u} = \mathbf{u}$.

Verify that addition and scalar multiplication of vectors in $\mathbf{R}^n$ really do satisfy these 10 properties. When we work with $\mathbf{R}^n$ as a set with this additional structure, we call $\mathbf{R}^n$ a **vector space**.

Subspaces of $\mathbf{R}^n$

The next task is to look at proper subsets of $\mathbf{R}^n$ and ask which of these can be considered as vector spaces in their own right. For motivation, consider two specific subsets, the x_1x_2-plane in $\mathbf{R}^3$, $\{x_3 = 0\}$:

$$V_0 \equiv \{(x_1, x_2, 0) : x_1, x_2 \in \mathbf{R}\},$$

and the plane parallel to it, $\{x_3 = 1\}$:

$$V_1 \equiv \{(x_1, x_2, 1) : x_1, x_2 \in \mathbf{R}\}.$$

We ask whether addition and scalar multiplication *within each of these two sets* satisfy the above 10 properties. We will see that the closure properties 1 and 6 are the most interesting.

Write $(a_1, a_2, 0)$ and $(b_1, b_2, 0)$ for two typical elements in V_0, and $(a_1, a_2, 1)$ and $(b_2, b_2, 1)$ for two typical elements in V_1. Checking property 1, we note that in V_0,

$$(a_1, a_2, 0) + (b_1, b_2, 0) = (a_1 + b_1, a_2 + b_2, 0)$$

is still an n-tuple in V_0 since its third component is a 0, while in V_1,

$$(a_1, a_2, 1) = (b_1, b_2, 1) = (a_1 + b_1, a_2 + b_2, 2)$$

is not an element of V_1 since its third component is not a 1. Therefore, V_0 satisfies property 1, but V_1 does not. Let's check property 2 — additive commutativity. Clearly,

$$(a_1, a_2, 0) + (b_1, b_2, 0) = (b_1, b_2, 0) + (a_1, a_2, 0),$$
$$(a_1, a_2, 1) + (b_1, b_2, 1) = (b_1, b_2, 1) + (a_1, a_2, 1),$$

basically because $a_1 + b_1 = b_1 + a_1$ and $a_2 + b_2 = b_2 + a_2$, and not because of any characteristic of V_0 or of V_1. In fact, not only do V_0 and V_1 satisfy property 2, but so does *any* subset of $\mathbf{R}^n$.

We can categorize the 10 properties of a vector space into two groups: the properties, like 2, that hold for any subset of $\mathbf{R}^n$, and those, like 1, that are existence properties and do *not* hold for all subsets of $\mathbf{R}^n$. As can easily be checked, properties 2, 3, 7, 8, 9 and 10 belong in the first category. They hold for any subset of $\mathbf{R}^n$ because they are properties of addition and scalar multiplication and not properties of the underlying set. On the other hand, properties 1, 4, 5 and 6 do not hold for every subset in $\mathbf{R}^n$; in fact, the set V_1 does not have any of these four properties. (Check!)

Let's verify that the set V_0 satisfies 4, 5 and 6. Clearly, the zero-vector $(0, 0, 0)$ is in V_0 since its last coordinate is 0, so 4 holds. For any $(a_1, a_2, 0)$ in V_0, its negative $(-a_1, -a_2, 0)$ is also in V_0, so 5 holds. Finally, for any scalar r,

$$r \cdot (a_1, a_2, 0) = (ra_1, ra_2, 0) \tag{1}$$

is still in V_0, so 6 holds.

Definition   A subset of $\mathbf{R}^n$, like V_0, that satisfies the above 10 properties is called a **subspace** of $\mathbf{R}^n$.

As the above discussion indicates, we only have to check 4 of the 10 properties — 1, 4, 5, and 6 — to see whether or not a subset of $\mathbf{R}^n$ is a subspace. Actually, we need only check 1 and 6, because if property 6 holds for a subset V of $\mathbf{R}^n$, then so do 4 and 5. To show that property 6 implies property 4, we take $r = 0$ in property 6, and to show that property 6 implies property 5, we take $r = -1$ in property 6. For example, taking $r = 0$ in (1) shows that V_0 satisfies property 4, and taking $r = -1$ in (1) shows that V_0 satisfies property 4. The following theorem summarizes these observations.

Theorem 27.1   Let V be a subset of the vector space $\mathbf{R}^n$. If the sum of any two elements of V is still an element of V and if any scalar multiple of any element of V is still an element of V, then V itself is a vector space, and therefore is a subspace of $\mathbf{R}^n$.

Let's look at a few more examples.

Example 27.1   Let **w** be the vector $(1, 1, 1)$ in $\mathbf{R}^3$ and let V_2 be the set of all scalar multiples of **w**. In the terminology of Section 11.1,

$$V_2 = \mathcal{L}[\mathbf{w}] = \{r(1, 1, 1): r \in \mathbf{R}\} = \{(r, r, r) : r \in \mathbf{R}\}.$$

Analytically, V_2 is the set of all triplets with equal components. Geometrically, V_2 is the straight line through $(0, 0, 0)$ and $(1, 1, 1)$ in $\mathbf{R}^3$. Since

$$(a, a, a) + (b, b, b) = (a + b, a + b, a + b)$$

and
$$r(a, a, a) = (ra, ra, ra),$$

the additive and multiplicative closure rules hold. Since $(0, 0, 0)$ is in V_2 and the negative of an element in V_2 is still in V_2, properties 4 and 5 hold. Once again, the other six properties hold for vector addition and scalar multiplication in V_2 because they hold for vector addition and scalar multiplication in $\mathbf{R}^3$. Therefore, the line V_2 is a *subspace* of $\mathbf{R}^3$.

Example 27.2   To generalize the last example, let $\mathbf{w}_1, \ldots, \mathbf{w}_k$ be k fixed vectors in $\mathbf{R}^n$. Let

$$V_3 = \mathcal{L}[\mathbf{w}_1, \ldots, \mathbf{w}_k]$$
$$= \{r_1\mathbf{w}_1 + \cdots + r_k\mathbf{w}_k : r_1, \ldots, r_k \in \mathbf{R}\}$$

be the set of all **linear combinations** of $\mathbf{w}_1, \ldots, \mathbf{w}_k$, that is, the **span** of $\mathbf{w}_1, \ldots, \mathbf{w}_k$. To determine whether V_3 is a subspace, we check additive and multiplicative closure. Note that the sum of two linear combinations of $\mathbf{w}_1, \ldots, \mathbf{w}_k$

$$(r_1\mathbf{w}_1 + \cdots + r_k\mathbf{w}_k) + (s_1\mathbf{w}_1 + \cdots + s_k\mathbf{w}_k)$$
$$= r_1\mathbf{w}_1 + s_1\mathbf{w}_1 + \cdots + r_k\mathbf{w}_k + s_k\mathbf{w}_k$$
$$= (r_1 + s_1)\mathbf{w}_1 + \cdots + (r_k + s_k)\mathbf{w}_k,$$

is another linear combination of $\mathbf{w}_1, \ldots, \mathbf{w}_k$, and the scalar multiple of an element of $\mathcal{L}[\mathbf{w}_1, \ldots, \mathbf{w}_k]$,

$$s \cdot (r_1\mathbf{w}_1 + \cdots + r_k\mathbf{w}_k) = s \cdot (r_1\mathbf{w}_1) + \cdots + s \cdot (r_k\mathbf{w}_k)$$
$$= (sr_1) \cdot \mathbf{w}_1 + \cdots + (sr_k) \cdot \mathbf{w}_k, \tag{2}$$

is another element of $\mathcal{L}[\mathbf{w}_1, \ldots, \mathbf{w}_k]$. By Theorem 27.1, the other properties of vector addition and scalar multiplication are valid in V_3 because they are valid in the space $\mathbf{R}^3$; therefore, V_3 is a subspace.

Example 27.3   Let V_4 be the set of all vectors in $\mathbf{R}^2$ whose components sum to zero:

$$V_4 \equiv \{(a, b) : a + b = 0\}.$$

To see that V_4 is a vector space, we check additive and multiplicative closure. Let (a_1, b_1) and (a_2, b_2) be points in V_4, so that $a_1 + b_1 = 0$ and $a_2 + b_2 = 0$. Then, their sum is $(a_1 + a_2, b_1 + b_2)$. Since the sum of its components is

$$(a_1 + a_2) + (b_1 + b_2) = (a_1 + b_1) + (a_2 + b_2)$$
$$= 0 + 0 = 0,$$

the sum vector $(a_1 + a_2, b_1 + b_2)$ is in V_4. For any scalar r, the sum of the components of the scalar multiple

$$r(a, b) = (ra, rb) \tag{3}$$

is $ra + rb = r(a + b) = 0$, since $a + b = 0$. Therefore, V_4 satisfies the two closure properties. By Theorem 27.1, V_4 is a subspace of $\mathbf{R}^2$.

Example 27.4   Consider the set V_5 of vectors in $\mathbf{R}^2$ whose components sum to 1. This set can be considered as the set of portfolios in a two-asset market in which short sales are allowed. Is V_5 a vector space? The answer, of course, is no. For one thing, closure of scalar multiplication is not satisfied. For example, the vector $(1, 0)$ is in V_5, but $2(1, 0) = (2, 0)$ is not. What other properties fail?

Example 27.5   Let V_6 be the set of vectors in $\mathbf{R}^4$ whose second and third components are identical:

$$V_6 = \{(a, b, b, c) : a, b, c \in \mathbf{R}\}.$$

Check that V_6 satisfies the additive and multiplicative closure properties, and therefore is a subspace of $\mathbf{R}^4$.

Example 27.6   Let $V_7 = \{\mathbf{0}\}$, a one-element subset of $\mathbf{R}^n$. V_7 is closed under scalar multiplication, since $r \cdot \mathbf{0} = \mathbf{0}$, and under vector addition, since $\mathbf{0} + \mathbf{0} = \mathbf{0}$. Thus V_7 is a subspace of $\mathbf{R}^n$.

Example 27.7   Let V_8 be the "diagonal" in $\mathbf{R}^n$:

$$V_8 = \{(x_1, x_2, \ldots, x_n) \in \mathbf{R}^n : x_1 = x_2 = \cdots = x_n\}.$$

Since equality of components is preserved under addition and scalar multiplication, V_8 is indeed a subspace of $\mathbf{R}^n$. One can think of V_8 in this example as the set of all scalar multiples of the vector $\mathbf{1} = (1, 1, \ldots, 1)$:

$$V_8 = \{r \cdot (1, 1, \ldots, 1) : r \in \mathbf{R}\},$$

the line through the origin in the direction $\mathbf{1}$.

EXERCISES

27.1 Which of the following are subspaces of $\mathbf{R}^2$? Explain your answer.

a) $\{(x, y) : x = 0\}$, b) $\{(x, y) : x = 1\}$, c) $\{(x, y) : 3x - 4y = 0\}$,

d) $\{(x, y) : x^2 = y^2\}$, e) $\{(0, 1)\}$, f) $\{(x, y) : x + y = 0, x - y = 0\}$.

27.2 Let $W = \{(x_1, x_2) \in \mathbf{R}^2 : x_1, x_2 \geq 0\}$, the nonnegative quadrant in $\mathbf{R}^2$. Show that W is closed under addition but is not a subspace.

27.3 Let $W = \{(x_1, x_2) \in \mathbf{R}^2 : x_1 = 0 \text{ or } x_2 = 0\}$. W is the set of all points in $\mathbf{R}^2$ lying on either the x_1-axis or the x_2-axis. Show that W is closed under scalar multiplication but is nonetheless not a subspace.

27.4 Show that subset V_6 in Example 27.5 is a subspace of $\mathbf{R}^4$.

27.2 BASIS AND DIMENSION OF A PROPER SUBSPACE

Subspaces of $\mathbf{R}^n$ are the subsets of $\mathbf{R}^n$ for which the concepts of basis and dimension, introduced in Section 11.3, make sense. Recall that a collection of vectors $\mathbf{v}_1, \ldots, \mathbf{v}_k$ forms a **basis** of a set V if every vector in V can be written as a linear combination of $\mathbf{v}_1, \ldots, \mathbf{v}_k$ (so that $V = \mathcal{L}[\mathbf{v}_1, \ldots, \mathbf{v}_k]$) and if $\mathbf{v}_1, \ldots, \mathbf{v}_k$ are linearly independent.

We begin by proving the analogue of Theorem 11.7 for a proper subspace V of a Euclidean space — any two bases of V contain the same number of elements. Then, we define the *dimension* of V to be the number of elements in any basis of V.

Theorem 27.2 Let $\mathbf{u}_1, \ldots, \mathbf{u}_m$ be a basis of a subspace V of $\mathbf{R}^n$. Then, any set containing more than m vectors in V must be linearly dependent.

Proof This is the subspace version of Theorem 11.3, and it has a similar proof, which we sketch here. Let $\mathbf{w}_1, \ldots, \mathbf{w}_r$ be a set of r vectors in V with $r > m$. We want to show that $\mathbf{w}_1, \ldots, \mathbf{w}_r$ are linearly dependent. Since $\mathbf{u}_1, \ldots, \mathbf{u}_m$ spans V, we can write each $\mathbf{w}_j$ as

$$\mathbf{w}_j = \sum_{i=1}^{m} a_{ji}\mathbf{u}_i, \tag{4}$$

for a set of scalars $\{a_{ji}\}$, where $j = 1, \ldots, r$ and $i = 1, \ldots, m$. To check for the linear independence of the $\mathbf{w}_j$s, write

$$c_1\mathbf{w}_1 + \cdots + c_m\mathbf{w}_m = \mathbf{0}, \tag{5}$$

or, using (4),

$$c_1 \left(\sum_{i=1}^{m} a_{1i}\mathbf{u}_i \right) + \cdots + c_m \left(\sum_{i=1}^{m} a_{mi}\mathbf{u}_i \right) = \mathbf{0},$$

which we rewrite as

$$\left(\sum_{j=1}^{r} c_j a_{j1} \right) \mathbf{u}_1 + \cdots + \left(\sum_{j=1}^{r} c_j a_{jm} \right) \mathbf{u}_m = \mathbf{0}.$$

Since the $\mathbf{u}_i$s are linearly independent by hypothesis, the only combination of the $\mathbf{u}_i$s that sums to $\mathbf{0}$ is the zero-combination. Therefore,

$$\sum_{j=1}^{r} c_j a_{j1} = 0, \ldots, \sum_{j=1}^{r} c_j a_{jm} = 0. \tag{6}$$

System (6) is a system of m homogeneous equations in the r unknowns $c_1, \ldots, c_r$ with $r > m$. By Fact 7.6 of Section 7.4, a system of *homogeneous* equations with more unknowns than equations has free variables and therefore has in-finitely many distinct solutions; so there exists a nonzero set of c_js that satisfies system (6) and therefore system (5). Therefore, $\mathbf{w}_1, \ldots, \mathbf{w}_r$ cannot be linearly independent. ∎

Theorem 27.3   Let V be a subspace of $\mathbf{R}^n$. Any two bases of V contain the same number of vectors.

Proof   If $\mathbf{u}_1, \ldots, \mathbf{u}_m$ and $\mathbf{w}_1, \ldots, \mathbf{w}_r$ are bases of V, then since both sets are linearly independent, r must equal m by Theorem 27.2. ∎

Definition   The number of vectors in any basis of V is called the **dimension** of V.

The word "dimension" is a commonly used word in the English language — a word which most people would be hard pressed to define carefully. Now, at least for some natural mathematical sets, we have a sharp, rigorous definition of dimension that captures much of the spirit of the more colloquial uses of the word.

27.5   Find bases for the subspaces spanned by the vectors listed in Exercises 11.2 and 11.3.

27.6   Find a basis for each of the subspaces described in the examples of Section 27.1.

27.3   ROW SPACE

The next three sections discuss three important classes of subspaces of Euclidean spaces — spaces that are attached to a given coefficient matrix. In Chapter 7, the **rank** of a matrix A was defined as the number of nonzero rows in a row echelon form of A. However, there may be more than one way to compute the row echelon form of A, especially if row interchanges are required in the Gaussian elimination process. So, our definition of rank has some ambiguity to it unless the order of the row operations in the Gaussian elimination process is unambiguously spelled out and agreed on by all. Fortunately, there is a more intrinsic definition of the rank of A, a definition that we now present.

For an $n \times m$ matrix A, the rows of A have m components and thus can be considered as vectors in $\mathbf{R^m}$. Write Row(A) for the subspace of $\mathbf{R^m}$ spanned by the n rows of A. If $\mathbf{a}_1, \dots, \mathbf{a}_n \in \mathbf{R^m}$ are the n rows of A, then

$$\text{Row}(A) \equiv \mathcal{L}[\mathbf{a}_1, \dots, \mathbf{a}_n]. \tag{7}$$

Row(A) is called the **row space** of A. We will see in this section that the rank of A is simply the dimension of the row space of A.

In using Gaussian elimination to transform a coefficient matrix A to a more tractable matrix, row operations are used to replace the list (7) of row vectors of A with another set of row vectors. We first show that this new set of vectors has the same span as the old — that row operations leave the row space Row(A) unchanged. This is easy to see for the row operation which interchanges the two vectors $\mathbf{a}_i$ and $\mathbf{a}_j$; this operation leaves the initial *set* of row vectors unchanged.

The other two cases are almost as easy. Each of these row operations, when applied to row i, replaces $\mathbf{a}_i$ with a linear combination $\mathbf{b}_i = c_i \mathbf{a}_i + c_j \mathbf{a}_j$, where $c_i \neq 0$. For example, row operation 3 might replace $\mathbf{a}_5$ with $\mathbf{a}_5 + 2\mathbf{a}_3$; row operation 1 might replace $\mathbf{a}_5$ with $3\mathbf{a}_5$. The next lemma shows that these replacements do not change the span of the row vectors.

Lemma 27.1   Let $\mathbf{v}_1, \dots, \mathbf{v}_k$ be a collection of vectors in $\mathbf{R^m}$. For some $j > 1$, let

$$\mathbf{w} = c_1 \mathbf{v}_1 + c_j \mathbf{v}_j, \quad \text{with } c_1 \neq 0. \tag{8}$$

Then, $\mathcal{L}[\mathbf{v}_1, \mathbf{v}_2, \dots, \mathbf{v}_k] = \mathcal{L}[\mathbf{w}, \mathbf{v}_2, \dots, \mathbf{v}_k]$.

Proof   We need only show that $\mathcal{L}[\mathbf{v}_1, \mathbf{v}_j] = \mathcal{L}[\mathbf{w}, \mathbf{v}_j]$. (Why?) Let $\mathbf{u}$ be an arbitrary vector in $\mathcal{L}[\mathbf{v}_1, \mathbf{v}_j]$. Then,

$$\mathbf{u} = d_1\mathbf{v}_1 + d_j\mathbf{v}_j$$

$$= \frac{d_1}{c_1}(c_1\mathbf{v}_1 + c_j\mathbf{v}_j) + \left(d_j - \frac{d_1 c_j}{c_1}\right)\mathbf{v}_j$$

(adding and subtracting $d_1 c_j \mathbf{v}_j / c_1$)

$$= \frac{d_1}{c_1}\mathbf{w} + \left(d_j - \frac{d_1 c_j}{c_1}\right)\mathbf{v}_j.$$

Thus, $\mathbf{u}$ is a linear combination of the vectors $\mathbf{w}$ and $\mathbf{v}_j$, and so $\mathcal{L}[\mathbf{v}_1, \mathbf{v}_j] \subset \mathcal{L}[\mathbf{w}, \mathbf{v}_j]$.

Similarly, if $\mathbf{x}$ is an arbitrary vector in $\mathcal{L}[\mathbf{w}, \mathbf{v}_j]$,

$$\mathbf{x} = b_1\mathbf{w} + b_2\mathbf{v}_j$$

$$= b_1(c_1\mathbf{v}_1 + c_j\mathbf{v}_j) + b_2\mathbf{v}_j \quad \text{(using (8))}$$

$$= b_1 c_1 \mathbf{v}_1 + (b_1 c_j + b_2)\mathbf{v}_j.$$

So, $\mathcal{L}[\mathbf{w}, \mathbf{v}_j] \subset \mathcal{L}[\mathbf{v}_1, \mathbf{v}_j]$, and $\mathcal{L}[\mathbf{v}_1, \mathbf{v}_j] = \mathcal{L}[\mathbf{w}, \mathbf{v}_j]$. ∎

Geometrically, if $\mathbf{v}_1$ and $\mathbf{v}_2$ span a plane W and if $c_1 \neq 0$, then $c_1\mathbf{v}_1 + c_2\mathbf{v}_2$ and $\mathbf{v}_2$ are still independent and lie in W, so they also span W.

We now use Lemma 27.1 to construct a basis for the row space and to compute its dimension. By Lemma 27.1, repeatedly applying row operations to a matrix does not change the row space. Therefore, any row echelon form A_r of A has the *same* row space as A. We will show that the nonzero rows of A_r are independent and thus form a basis for Row(A).

An important property of row echelon forms is that each row has more leading 0s than the row preceding it. In other words, if the first m elements of row i are 0, then at least the first $m + 1$ elements of row $i + 1$ are 0. This implies independence, as the next lemma shows.

Lemma 27.2   Let $\mathbf{v}_1, \ldots, \mathbf{v}_k$ be nonzero vectors such that each $\mathbf{v}_{i+1}$ has more leading 0s than $\mathbf{v}_i$. Then the vectors $\mathbf{v}_1, \ldots, \mathbf{v}_k$ are linearly independent.

Example 27.8   For example, consider the three vectors

$$\begin{pmatrix} 5 \\ 4 \\ 3 \end{pmatrix}, \quad \begin{pmatrix} 0 \\ 3 \\ 2 \end{pmatrix}, \quad \text{and} \quad \begin{pmatrix} 0 \\ 0 \\ 7 \end{pmatrix}.$$

Checking for independence, we write

$$c_1 \begin{pmatrix} 5 \\ 4 \\ 3 \end{pmatrix} + c_2 \begin{pmatrix} 0 \\ 3 \\ 2 \end{pmatrix} + c_3 \begin{pmatrix} 0 \\ 0 \\ 7 \end{pmatrix} = \begin{pmatrix} 0 \\ 0 \\ 0 \end{pmatrix}.$$

Writing these three equations out, we first find that $5c_1 = 0$, so $c_1 = 0$. The second equation is $4c_1 + 3c_2 = 0$. Since c_1 equals 0, so does c_2. The last equation gives $3c_1 + 2c_2 + 7c_3 = 0$. Since $c_1 = c_2 = 0$, $c_3 = 0$ too. Thus the three vectors are linearly independent. The proof of Lemma 27.2 mimics this calculation.

Proof of Lemma 27.2   Write the vector $\mathbf{v}_j$ in coordinates as $\mathbf{v}_j = (v_{j1}, \ldots, v_{jn})$. To prove independence, we need to show that the only solution of the equation

$$c_1 \mathbf{v}_1 + \cdots + c_k \mathbf{v}_k = \mathbf{0} \tag{9}$$

is $c_1 = c_2 = \cdots = c_k = 0$. Let v_{1i^*} be the first nonzero component of $\mathbf{v}_1$. Since each of the other $\mathbf{v}_j$s has more leading zeros than $\mathbf{v}_1$, $v_{ji^*} = 0$ for $j = 2, \ldots, n$. Writing out the i^*th equation of (9) gives

$$c_1 v_{1i^*} + c_2 0 + \cdots + c_k 0 = 0, \quad v_{1i^*} \neq 0;$$

so $c_1 = 0$. Now, system (9) becomes

$$c_2 \mathbf{v}_2 + \cdots + c_k \mathbf{v}_k = \mathbf{0}. \tag{10}$$

Let v_{2j^*} be the first nonzero component of $\mathbf{v}_2$. By the same argument, $v_{3j^*} = \cdots = v_{nj^*} = 0$. Writing out the j^*th equation of (10) gives $c_2 v_{2j^*} = 0$, so $c_2 = 0$. Proceeding this way until all the c_is are exhausted shows that the only solution to (9) is $c_1 = c_2 = \cdots = c_k = 0$. ∎

For the following discussion, A_r will denote any row echelon form of A.

Theorem 27.4   Let A_r be any row echelon form of A. Then, subspace $\text{Row}(A)$ is the same set as subspace $\text{Row}(A_r)$. The nonzero row vectors of A_r are a basis for $\text{Row}(A)$, and the dimension of $\text{Row}(A)$ is the rank of A.

Proof   The matrix A_r is constructed from A by performing a finite number of row operations. Lemma 27.1 says that each row operation leaves the row space unchanged, and so A and A_r have the same row space. The row space of A_r is spanned by A_r's nonzero rows. Lemma 27.2 says that these rows are independent, so they are a basis for $\text{Row}(A_r)$. Finally, rank A is just the number of nonzero rows of A_r — the number of vectors in this basis. ∎

EXERCISES

27.7   For each of the following matrices, compute a basis for the row space:

a) $\begin{pmatrix} 2 & -1 \\ 4 & -2 \end{pmatrix}$,   b) $\begin{pmatrix} 2 & -1 & 3 \\ 4 & -2 & 5 \end{pmatrix}$,   c) $\begin{pmatrix} 2 & 1 \\ 4 & -2 \end{pmatrix}$,   d) $\begin{pmatrix} 4 & 1 & -5 & 1 \\ 8 & 5 & -10 & 8 \\ -4 & 2 & 7 & 5 \end{pmatrix}$.

27.8   Find a basis for the subset of $\mathbf{R}^4$ spanned by

$$(1, 2, 0, 3), \quad (3, 5, 1, 7), \quad (1, 1, 1, 1), \quad \text{and} \quad (0, 1, -1, 2).$$

[Hint: Make these vectors the rows of a matrix, and find a basis for the row space.]

27.9   Let A be an $m \times n$ matrix. If $m > n$, prove that the row vectors of A are linearly dependent.

27.4   COLUMN SPACE

Just as we formed the row space of a given matrix A as the set spanned by the rows of A, we now study the space spanned by the *columns* of A. If A is an $n \times m$ matrix, then it has m columns $\mathbf{a}_1, \ldots, \mathbf{a}_m$, each of which has n components (because A has n rows) and therefore can be considered as a vector in $\mathbf{R}^n$. The subset of $\mathbf{R}^n$ spanned by the columns of A is called the **column space** of A, and it is written

$$\text{Col}(A) = \mathcal{L}[\mathbf{a}_1, \ldots, \mathbf{a}_m].$$

In Sections 11.1 and 11.2, we tested for the independence and the spanning properties of a set of vectors by constructing and analyzing the matrix whose *columns* are the vectors under study. This fact gives an indication of the importance of the role of $\text{Col}(A)$ in studying properties of a system of equations with coefficient matrix A.

In this section, we first compute the dimension of $\text{Col}(A)$ as the number of basic vectors in the row echelon form of A and show that, like the dimension of the row space, the dimension of the column space of A equals the rank of A. We then discuss the role of the column space of A in studying the solution set of the system $A\mathbf{x} = \mathbf{b}$.

Dimension of the Column Space of A

Consider the matrix

$$A = \begin{pmatrix} 1 & 2 \\ 2 & 4 \end{pmatrix}$$

and its row echelon form

$$A_r = \begin{pmatrix} 1 & 2 \\ 0 & 0 \end{pmatrix}.$$

Since the second column of A is twice the first column, the column space of A is the subspace of $\mathbf{R}^2$ spanned by the vector $(1, 2)$. On the other hand, the column space of A_r is the space spanned by the vector $(1, 0)$ — the x_1-axis. Unlike the situation with the row spaces of A and A_r, generally the column space of a matrix A and the column space of its row echelon form A_r are *different*. Nonetheless, we can use the row echelon form A_r to help find a basis for the column space of A.

Recall from the discussion of Gaussian elimination in Chapter 7 that a **pivot** of a matrix in row echelon form is an element which is the first nonzero element in its row. For example, in the matrix

$$\begin{pmatrix} 1 & 8 & 7 & 3 \\ 0 & 2 & 9 & 5 \\ 0 & 0 & 0 & 4 \end{pmatrix}$$

the elements 1, 2, and 4 in the first, second, and third rows, respectively, are the only pivots.

Definition A column of a matrix A is a **basic column** if the *corresponding column* of a row echelon form A_r contains a pivot.

Theorem 27.5 The basic columns of A form a basis for Col(A).

The main idea in the proof of Theorem 27.5 is that any linear relationship which exists among the columns of A must also exist among the columns of its row echelon form A_r. This includes linear independence and spanning.

Example 27.9 For example, consider the matrix

$$A = \begin{pmatrix} 4 & 8 & 1 & 9 \\ -8 & -16 & 1 & -15 \end{pmatrix}$$

and its row echelon form

$$A_r = \begin{pmatrix} 4 & 8 & 1 & 9 \\ 0 & 0 & 3 & 3 \end{pmatrix}.$$

Check that for *both* matrices:

  (a) column 2 is twice column 1,
  (b) column 4 is the sum of columns 2 and 3,
  (c) columns 1 and 3 are linearly independent, and
  (d) columns 1 and 3 span the column space.

The proof of Theorem 27.5, which we present in the Appendix of this chapter, formalizes this idea. This proof also uses Lemma 27.2 to make one more observation — that one basis for Col(A_r) is the set of those columns of A_r which contain a pivot.

Theorem 27.4 implies that dim Row(A) is equal to the number of nonzero rows of A_r. Theorem 27.5 implies that dim Col(A) is equal to the number of pivots in A_r. Since each nonzero row of A_r contains exactly one pivot and every pivot is in some nonzero row of A_r, it follows that

$$\text{dim Row}(A) = \text{dim Col}(A)$$

$$= \text{number of pivots in } A_r$$

$$= \text{number of nonzero rows of } A_r$$

$$= \text{rank} A \qquad \qquad \text{(by definition)}.$$

The next theorem summarizes these equivalences.

Theorem 27.6   For any $n \times m$ matrix A,

$$\text{dim Col}(A) = \text{dim Row}(A) = \text{rank} A.$$

Example 27.10   Consider the 2×3 matrix $A = \begin{pmatrix} 1 & 1 & 2 \\ 2 & 2 & 4 \end{pmatrix}$ and its row echelon form $A_r = \begin{pmatrix} 1 & 1 & 2 \\ 0 & 0 & 0 \end{pmatrix}$. Here, it is particularly easy to see that any linear relationship among the columns of A also holds for the columns of A_r and that the dimension of the column space of A is 1. The row space of A is spanned by the vector (1, 1, 2).

Example 27.11   Consider the 3×4 matrix

$$A = \begin{pmatrix} 2 & 3 & 1 & 4 \\ 2 & 3 & 7 & 9 \\ 2 & 3 & 13 & 14 \end{pmatrix}.$$

Its row echelon form is

$$A_r = \begin{pmatrix} 2 & 3 & 1 & 4 \\ 0 & 0 & 6 & 5 \\ 0 & 0 & 0 & 0 \end{pmatrix}.$$

A basis for Row(A) is (2, 3, 1, 4) and (0, 0, 6, 5), the nonzero row vectors in A_r. A basis for Col(A) is (2, 2, 2) and (1, 7, 13), corresponding to the basic columns of A_r. Both Row(A) and Col(A) are planes (i.e., two-dimensional), one in $\mathbf{R}^4$ and the other in $\mathbf{R}^3$. If (2, 2, 2) and (1, 7, 13) are in fact a basis for Col(A), it should be possible to write the fourth column (4, 9, 14) as a linear combination of these vectors. To see how to do this, we use the ideas in Example 27.9 and in the proof of Theorem 27.5 and perform the much easier task of writing the fourth column of the *row echelon form* A_r as a linear combination of the first and third columns of A_r:

$$\begin{pmatrix} 4 \\ 5 \\ 0 \end{pmatrix} = \frac{19}{12}\begin{pmatrix} 2 \\ 0 \\ 0 \end{pmatrix} + \frac{5}{6}\begin{pmatrix} 1 \\ 6 \\ 0 \end{pmatrix}.$$

In this calculation, we worked up from the last row. Thus,

$$\begin{pmatrix} 4 \\ 9 \\ 14 \end{pmatrix} = \frac{19}{12}\begin{pmatrix} 2 \\ 2 \\ 2 \end{pmatrix} + \frac{5}{6}\begin{pmatrix} 1 \\ 7 \\ 13 \end{pmatrix}.$$

The Role of the Column Space

The column space of A plays an important role in the analysis of linear equation systems whose coefficient matrix is A. Write $A\mathbf{x} = \mathbf{b}$ as

$$\begin{pmatrix} a_{11} & \cdots & a_{1m} \\ \vdots & a_{ij} & \vdots \\ a_{n1} & \cdots & a_{nm} \end{pmatrix}\begin{pmatrix} x_1 \\ \vdots \\ x_m \end{pmatrix}$$

$$= x_1\begin{pmatrix} a_{11} \\ \vdots \\ a_{n1} \end{pmatrix} + x_2\begin{pmatrix} a_{12} \\ \vdots \\ a_{n2} \end{pmatrix} + \cdots + x_n\begin{pmatrix} a_{1m} \\ \vdots \\ a_{nm} \end{pmatrix} \qquad (11)$$

$$= x_1\mathbf{a}_1 + x_2\mathbf{a}_2 + \cdots + x_m\mathbf{a}_m$$

$$= \mathbf{b},$$

where the $\mathbf{a}_i$s are the column vectors of A. When written this way, it is apparent that the system $A\mathbf{x} = \mathbf{b}$ has a solution if and only if $\mathbf{b}$ is in $\mathrm{Col}(A)$. Thus, the statement that $A\mathbf{x} = \mathbf{b}$ has a solution for all $\mathbf{b}$ is equivalent to the statement that $\mathrm{Col}(A)$ is all of $\mathbf{R}^n$. In other words, it is equivalent to the statement that the dimension of $\mathrm{Col}(A)$ (the rank of A) is n. These facts are summarized in the following theorem.

Theorem 27.7   Let A be an $n \times m$ matrix.

(a) The system of equations $A\mathbf{x} = \mathbf{b}$ has a solution for a particular $\mathbf{b} \in \mathbf{R}^n$ if and only if $\mathbf{b}$ is in the column space $\mathrm{Col}(A)$.

(b) The system $A\mathbf{x} = \mathbf{b}$ has a solution for *every* $\mathbf{b}$ if and only if $\mathrm{rank}\,A = n$.

(c) If $A\mathbf{x} = \mathbf{b}$ has a solution for every $\mathbf{b}$, then

$$n = \mathrm{rank}\,A \leq \text{number columns of } A = m.$$

Example 27.12   For the coefficient matrix A in Example 27.11, the system of equations

$$\begin{pmatrix} 2 & 3 & 1 & 4 \\ 2 & 3 & 7 & 9 \\ 2 & 3 & 13 & 14 \end{pmatrix} \begin{pmatrix} x_1 \\ x_2 \\ x_3 \\ x_4 \end{pmatrix} = \begin{pmatrix} b_1 \\ b_2 \\ b_3 \end{pmatrix} \tag{12}$$

will have a solution if and only if

$$\begin{pmatrix} b_1 \\ b_2 \\ b_3 \end{pmatrix} = a_1 \begin{pmatrix} 2 \\ 2 \\ 2 \end{pmatrix} + a_2 \begin{pmatrix} 1 \\ 7 \\ 13 \end{pmatrix}$$

for some scalars a_1 and a_2. The set of vectors $\mathbf{b} \in \mathbf{R}^3$ such that equation (12) has a solution is a two-dimensional set — a plane. By the way, this is a fragile situation. Add a tiny number, say 0.001, to any coefficient in A and the rank jumps to three. This new system will have a solution for any right-hand side $\mathbf{b}$ in $\mathbf{R}^3$.

Example 27.13   Consider the system

$$\begin{pmatrix} 2 & 6 & 0 \\ 3 & 1 & 3 \\ 1 & 0 & 0 \\ 4 & 8 & 1 \end{pmatrix} \begin{pmatrix} x_1 \\ x_2 \\ x_3 \end{pmatrix} = \begin{pmatrix} b_1 \\ b_2 \\ b_3 \\ b_4 \end{pmatrix}$$

of four equations in three unknowns. Since the coefficient matrix has more rows than columns (more equations than unknowns), there will be many right-hand sides $\mathbf{b}$ for which this system has no solution. In fact, by a of Theorem 27.7, the set of $\mathbf{b}$s for which there is a solution is a three-dimensional subspace of $\mathbf{R}^4$.

EXERCISES

27.10   For each of the following matrices, compute a basis for the column space:

$a)$ $\begin{pmatrix} 2 & -1 \\ 4 & -2 \end{pmatrix}$, $b)$ $\begin{pmatrix} 2 & -1 & 3 \\ 4 & -2 & 5 \end{pmatrix}$, $c)$ $\begin{pmatrix} 2 & 1 \\ 4 & -2 \end{pmatrix}$, $d)$ $\begin{pmatrix} 4 & 1 & -5 & 1 \\ 8 & 5 & -10 & 8 \\ -4 & 2 & 7 & 5 \end{pmatrix}$.

27.11   Find a basis of the solution set of the system in Example 27.13.

27.5 NULLSPACE

Subspaces of $\mathbf{R}^m$, as defined in Section 27.1, arise in two different ways in most applications:

(1) as the space spanned by a given set of vectors and
(2) as the solution set of a homogeneous system of linear equations.

For example, the diagonal in the plane can be described as all scalar multiples of the vector $(1, 1)$ or as the set of solutions of the linear equation $x_1 - x_2 = 0$. Example 27.2 shows that each $\mathcal{L}[\mathbf{v}_1, \ldots, \mathbf{v}_k]$ is a subspace. The following theorem formalizes the fact that the solution set of a homogeneous linear system of m variables — that is, a system of linear equations with all 0s on the right-hand side — is a subspace of $\mathbf{R}^m$.

Theorem 27.8 Let A be a $n \times m$ matrix. The set V of solutions to the system of equations $A\mathbf{x} = \mathbf{0}$ is a subspace of $\mathbf{R}^m$.

Proof By Theorem 27.1, we simply need to see that V is closed under vector addition and scalar multiplication. Let $\mathbf{u}$ and $\mathbf{v}$ be vectors in V, and let $r\mathbf{u} + \mathbf{v}$ be a linear combination of the two vectors. Then

$$A(r\mathbf{u} + \mathbf{v}) = A(r\mathbf{u}) + A\mathbf{v}$$

$$= rA\mathbf{u} + A\mathbf{v}$$

$$= \mathbf{0},$$

since $\mathbf{u}, \mathbf{v}$ are in V. Thus, V is closed under linear combinations and is a subspace of $\mathbf{R}^m$. ∎

Definition The subspace of solutions to the homogeneous system $A\mathbf{x} = \mathbf{0}$ is called the **nullspace** of A and written as Null(A) or $\mathcal{N}(\mathcal{A})$. Some texts also call it the **kernel** of A.

Affine Subspaces

The solution sets to *nonhomogeneous* equations are not subspaces. Not surprisingly, however, they do have a linear structure. They are affine subspaces, which is to say that they are translates of a subspace. These statements are made more precise in the following definition and theorem.

Definition Let V be a *subspace* of $\mathbf{R}^m$ and let $\mathbf{c} \in \mathbf{R}^m$ be a fixed vector. The set

$$\{\mathbf{x} \in \mathbf{R}^m : \mathbf{x} = \mathbf{c} + \mathbf{v} \text{ for some } \mathbf{v} \in V\}$$

is called the set of **translates** of V by $\mathbf{c}$ and is written $\mathbf{c} + V$. (See Figure 27.1.) This set is not a vector space, unless $\mathbf{c}$ belongs to V. Subsets of $\mathbf{R}^m$ of the form $\mathbf{c} + V$, where V is a *subspace* of $\mathbf{R}^m$, are called **affine subspaces** of $\mathbf{R}^m$.

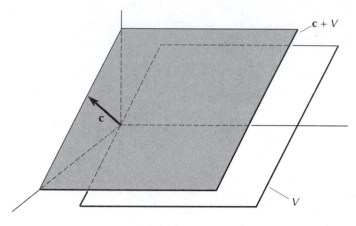

Figure 27.1

V and $\mathbf{c} + V$ in $\mathbf{R}^3$.

Theorem 27.9   Let $A\mathbf{x} = \mathbf{b}$ be an $n \times m$ system of linear equations. Let $\mathbf{c}_0$ in $\mathbf{R}^m$ be a particular solution of this system. Then, every other solution $\mathbf{c}'$ of $A\mathbf{x} = \mathbf{b}$ can be written as $\mathbf{c}' = \mathbf{c}_0 + \mathbf{w}$, where $\mathbf{w}$ is a vector in the nullspace of A. In other words, the solution set of $A\mathbf{x} = \mathbf{b}$ is the affine subspace $\mathbf{c}_0 + \text{Null}(A)$.

Proof   Let $\mathbf{c}'$ solve $A\mathbf{x} = \mathbf{b}$. Then

$$A(\mathbf{c}' - \mathbf{c}_0) = A\mathbf{c}' - A\mathbf{c}_0 = \mathbf{b} - \mathbf{b} = \mathbf{0},$$

so $\mathbf{w} = \mathbf{c}' - \mathbf{c}_0$ is in $\text{Null}(A)$. Conversely, if $\mathbf{w}$ is in $\text{Null}(A)$, then $A(\mathbf{c}_0 + \mathbf{w}) = A\mathbf{c}_0 + A\mathbf{w} = \mathbf{b} + \mathbf{0} = \mathbf{b}$. ∎

Example 27.14   Let A be the matrix $(1 \quad 1)$. The solution set of $A\mathbf{x} = 1$ is the set

$$\{(x_1, x_2) : x_1 + x_2 = 1\}. \tag{13}$$

This set is clearly a translate of the subspace

$$\text{Null}(A) = \{(x_1, x_2) : x_1 + x_2 = 0\}$$

by the vector $(1, 0)$, as illustrated in Figure 27.2. To see this analytically, we note that $x_1 + x_2 = 1$ if and only if $x_1 = 1 - x_2$. Therefore, the solution set of

(13) can be written as

$$\begin{pmatrix} 1 - x_2 \\ x_2 \end{pmatrix} = x_2 \begin{pmatrix} -1 \\ 1 \end{pmatrix} + \begin{pmatrix} 1 \\ 0 \end{pmatrix}$$

$$= \text{Null}(A) + \begin{pmatrix} 1 \\ 0 \end{pmatrix}.$$

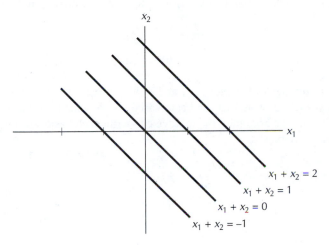

Solution sets of $x_1 + x_2 = b$.

Figure 27.2

Even though affine spaces are technically not vector spaces, they are translates of vector spaces and have a natural dimension. We say that the **dimension of the affine space $c + V$** is the dimension of the vector space V. For example, it is natural to say that the affine space in Example 27.14 is one-dimensional.

Theorem 27.9 makes precise the size of the (affine) solution set of the system of linear equations $Ax = b$. It states that for every right-hand side b for which $Ax = b$ has a solution, the dimension of the solution set is the dimension of Null(A).

Fundamental Theorem of Linear Algebra

Finally, we turn to computing the dimension of Null(A) in terms of the rank of A. To start this task, we first note that there is a close connection between Null(A) and the column space Col(A). This should not be surprising. We have already seen in expression (11) that the matrix product Ax can be written as $x_1 v_1 + \cdots + x_m v_m$, where the v_i are the column vectors of A. The column space, of course, is the space that the column vectors span. The nullspace, however, has to do with the scalars x_i. It answers the question: What linear combinations of the v_i equal 0?

Example 27.15   Consider the coefficient matrix of Examples 27.11 and 27.12. It has row echelon form

$$A_r = \begin{pmatrix} 2 & 3 & 1 & 4 \\ 0 & 0 & 6 & 5 \\ 0 & 0 & 0 & 0 \end{pmatrix}.$$

Matrix A and its row echelon form have exactly the same nullspace. (Why?) Thus, $\mathbf{x}$ is in Null(A) if and only if $A_r \mathbf{x} = \mathbf{0}$, in other words, if and only if

$$2x_1 + 3x_2 + x_3 + 4x_4 = 0$$

$$6x_3 + 5x_4 = 0.$$

In the terminology of Chapter 7, x_1 and x_3 are basic variables, while x_2 and x_4 are *free variables*. Note that the basic variables correspond to basic columns. Working from the bottom to the top, we can write each basic variable in terms of the free variables:

$$x_3 = -\frac{5}{6}x_4$$

$$x_1 = -\frac{3}{2}x_2 - \frac{1}{2}x_3 - 2x_4$$

$$= -\frac{3}{2}x_2 - \frac{1}{2}\left(-\frac{5}{6}x_4\right) - 2x_4$$

$$= -\frac{3}{2}x_2 - \frac{19}{12}x_4.$$

Every solution $\mathbf{x}$ to $A\mathbf{x} = \mathbf{0}$ can be written as

$$\begin{pmatrix} x_1 \\ x_2 \\ x_3 \\ x_4 \end{pmatrix} = \begin{pmatrix} -\frac{3}{2}x_2 - \frac{19}{12}x_4 \\ x_2 \\ -\frac{5}{6}x_4 \\ x_4 \end{pmatrix}$$

$$= \begin{pmatrix} -\frac{3}{2}x_2 \\ x_2 \\ 0 \\ 0 \end{pmatrix} + \begin{pmatrix} -\frac{19}{12}x_4 \\ 0 \\ -\frac{5}{6}x_4 \\ x_4 \end{pmatrix}$$

$$= x_2 \begin{pmatrix} -\frac{3}{2} \\ 1 \\ 0 \\ 0 \end{pmatrix} + x_4 \begin{pmatrix} -\frac{19}{12} \\ 0 \\ -\frac{5}{6} \\ 1 \end{pmatrix}.$$

The two vectors $(-\frac{3}{2}, 1, 0, 0)$ and $(-\frac{19}{12}, 0, -\frac{5}{6}, 1)$ span Null(A). They are clearly linearly independent (Lemma 27.2 again), so we can conclude that Null(A) is two-dimensional. The key fact about the number 2 is that

$$2 = \text{number of free variables}$$

$$= 4 - \text{number of basic variables}$$

$$= 4 - \text{rank} A.$$

Example 27.16   Let

$$A = \begin{pmatrix} 1 & 2 & 0 & -2 & 0 \\ 2 & 4 & 1 & -1 & 0 \\ 1 & 2 & 1 & 1 & 1 \end{pmatrix},$$

with row echelon form

$$A_r = \begin{pmatrix} 1 & 2 & 0 & -2 & 0 \\ 0 & 0 & 1 & 3 & 0 \\ 0 & 0 & 0 & 0 & 1 \end{pmatrix}.$$

The basic variables are x_1, x_3, and x_5. The free variables are x_2 and x_4. The system corresponding to A_r is

$$\begin{aligned} x_1 + 2x_2 \quad - 2x_4 \quad &= 0 \\ x_3 + 3x_4 \quad &= 0 \\ x_5 &= 0. \end{aligned}$$

Once again, we solve for the basic variables in terms of the free variables:

$$x_5 = 0,$$

$$x_3 = -3x_4,$$

$$x_1 = -2x_2 + 2x_4.$$

Thus, the vector $\mathbf{x}$ is in Null(A) if and only if

$$\begin{pmatrix} x_1 \\ x_2 \\ x_3 \\ x_4 \\ x_5 \end{pmatrix} = x_2 \begin{pmatrix} -2 \\ 1 \\ 0 \\ 0 \\ 0 \end{pmatrix} + x_4 \begin{pmatrix} 2 \\ 0 \\ -3 \\ 1 \\ 0 \end{pmatrix}.$$

The vectors $(-2, 1, 0, 0, 0)$ and $(2, 0, -3, 1, 0)$ form a basis for the space Null(A). Again, each column containing a pivot corresponds to a basic variable, and the remaining columns correspond to free variables. The dimension of the nullspace is the number of free variables, which is the number of columns less the number of basic columns; i.e., the number of columns less rank A.

This process works in general, and the result is summarized in the following theorem.

Theorem 27.10   Let A be an $n \times m$ matrix. Then,

$$\dim \text{Null}(A) = m - \text{rank} A.$$

This theorem is one of the central theorems of linear algebra because it describes the dimension of the solution set of a linear system. In fact, it is sometimes called the **Fundamental Theorem of Linear Algebra**. Combined with Theorem 27.9, it asserts that the solution set of the linear system $A\mathbf{x} = \mathbf{b}$, when nonempty, is an affine subspace whose dimension equals the number of variables minus the rank of A. The proof of Theorem 27.10 is presented in the Appendix to this chapter.

Conclusion

We summarize the results of this section for the system $A\mathbf{x} = \mathbf{b}$ of n linear equations in m unknowns. First, the set of all solutions of this system is an affine subspace of $\mathbf{R}^m$, a translate of the subspace Null(A). The column space of the $n \times m$ matrix A tells us whether this system of equations has a solution. The nullspace of A then tells us how large the solution set is. In particular:

(1) If rank $A = n$, the number of rows (equations), then $A\mathbf{x} = \mathbf{b}$ has a solution for every $\mathbf{b}$.
(2) If rank $A < n$, then $A\mathbf{x} = \mathbf{b}$ will have a solution only for those $\mathbf{b}$ in Col(A), a lower-dimensional subspace of $\mathbf{R}^n$.
(3) If rank $A = m$, then Null(A) = $\{\mathbf{0}\}$, and $A\mathbf{x} = \mathbf{b}$ will have at most one solution for any $\mathbf{b}$.
(4) If rank $A < m$, then if $A\mathbf{x} = \mathbf{b}$ has any solution at all, it will have an affine subspace of solutions of dimension $= m - \text{rank} A$.

We first discovered these facts in Chapter 7. There, however, techniques for equation solving were employed to prove the results. In this section, we emphasize the geometry of solution sets. This section illustrates the claim that linear algebra generalizes the insights of plane geometry to higher-dimensional spaces and shows how these insights can be useful in solving very analytic problems.

EXERCISES

27.12   For each of the following matrices, compute a basis for the nullspace:

$$a) \begin{pmatrix} 2 & -1 \\ 4 & -2 \end{pmatrix}, \quad b) \begin{pmatrix} 2 & -1 & 3 \\ 4 & -2 & 5 \end{pmatrix}, \quad c) \begin{pmatrix} 2 & 1 \\ 4 & -2 \end{pmatrix}, \quad d) \begin{pmatrix} 4 & 1 & -5 & 1 \\ 8 & 5 & -10 & 8 \\ -4 & 2 & 7 & 5 \end{pmatrix}.$$

27.13   In the solutions to the previous exercise, check that each vector in the basis of the row space is orthogonal to each vector in the basis of the nullspace.

27.14   Describe the solution sets to the system $Ax = \mathbf{b}$ for each of the matrices in Exercise 27.12 for various values of $\mathbf{b}$.

27.15   Show the following:
a) Col(AB) is a subspace of Col(A) whenever AB is well-defined.
b) If B is square and nonsingular, then Col(AB) = Col(A).

27.16   Show the following:
a) Null(A) is a subspace of Null(BA).
b) If B is square and nonsingular, then Null(BA) = Null(A).

27.17   Find bases of the row space, the column space, and the nullspace of each of the following matrices:

$$a) \begin{pmatrix} 1 & 2 & 1 \\ 2 & 4 & 3 \end{pmatrix}, \quad b) \begin{pmatrix} 1 & 2 & 3 \\ 4 & 8 & 9 \end{pmatrix}, \quad c) \begin{pmatrix} 1 & 3 & 2 & 1 \\ 4 & 9 & 8 & 3 \end{pmatrix}, \quad d) \begin{pmatrix} 1 & 2 & 1 \\ 4 & 8 & 3 \end{pmatrix}.$$

27.18   Write out careful proofs of Conclusions 1 to 4 above.

27.6   ABSTRACT VECTOR SPACES

Section 27.1 introduced the term "vector space" to describe the set $\mathbf{R}^n$ with the additional structure of addition and scalar multiplication. However, there are other sets besides $\mathbf{R}^n$ which have natural notions of addition and scalar multiplication. For example, one can add two matrices that have the same size, and one can add two functions that are defined on the same set. In this section, we extend the definition of a vector space to any set that has an addition operation and a scalar multiplication operation that satisfy the usual properties.

Definition   Let V be a set. Suppose that there is a function $+$ that assigns to each pair of elements of V another element of V and that there is a function $\cdot$ that assigns to each pair consisting of an element of V and a real number another element of V. If V with the operations $+$ and $\cdot$ satisfies properties 1 through 10 in Section 27.1 for all $\mathbf{u}, \mathbf{v}, \mathbf{w}$ in V and r, s in $\mathbf{R}$, then V is called a **vector space** and its elements are called **vectors**.

The functions $+$ and $\cdot$ are called **operations** on V. Almost always the operations $+$ and $\cdot$ are closely related to the usual addition and multiplication of numbers, so we use the same symbols that we do for numbers. For example, the operation $+$ in $\mathbf{R^n}$ is componentwise scalar addition.

Example 27.17   Of course, as we discussed in detail in Section 27.1, the set $\mathbf{R^n}$ of all n-tuples with the usual vector addition and scalar multiplication

$$(a_1, \ldots, a_n) + (b_1, \ldots, b_n) = (a_1 + b_1, \ldots, a_n + b_n)$$

$$r \cdot (a_1, \ldots, a_n) = (ra_1, \ldots, ra_n)$$

is a vector space.

The following five examples will illustrate vector spaces which are not subspaces of any $\mathbf{R^n}$. The first three use the standard addition and scalar multiplication; the last two do not.

Example 27.18   Fix positive integers m and n. Let $M_{n,m}$ denote the set of of all $n \times m$ matrices — all rectangular arrays of numbers with n rows and m columns. As described in Chapter 8, there is an obvious notion of addition for $n \times m$ matrices: add the corresponding entries. For example, for 2×3 matrices,

$$\begin{pmatrix} 1 & 2 & 3 \\ 2 & 1 & 0 \end{pmatrix} + \begin{pmatrix} 4 & 6 & 8 \\ 7 & 5 & 3 \end{pmatrix} = \begin{pmatrix} 1+4 & 2+6 & 3+8 \\ 2+7 & 1+5 & 0+3 \end{pmatrix}$$

$$= \begin{pmatrix} 5 & 8 & 11 \\ 9 & 6 & 3 \end{pmatrix}.$$

There is also an obvious notion for scalar multiplication: multiply every entry of the matrix by the scalar. For example,

$$3 \cdot \begin{pmatrix} 1 & 2 & 3 \\ 2 & 1 & 0 \end{pmatrix} = \begin{pmatrix} 3 & 6 & 9 \\ 6 & 3 & 0 \end{pmatrix}.$$

Check that all 10 defining properties of a vector space are satisfied. What plays the role of the additive identity $\mathbf{0}$? This example of a vector space is very similar to our standard example $\mathbf{R^n}$. Since an $n \times m$ matrix has nm entries, it can naturally be treated as an ordered list of nm scalars — an nm-vector. For example, 2×3 matrices can be thought of as vectors in 6-space, where the second three elements are listed underneath the first three elements rather than alongside them. Thus, $M_{n,m}$ is basically the same vector space as $\mathbf{R}^{nm}$.

Example 27.19   For an example of a vector space really different from $\mathbf{R^n}$, let F be the set of all *functions* from $\mathbf{R}$ to $\mathbf{R}$. To add functions, just add their values for each x. Suppose, for example, that $\mathbf{u}(x) = x^2$ and $\mathbf{v}(x) = \sin x$. Then, their sum is the function $(\mathbf{u} + \mathbf{v})(x) = x^2 + \sin x$. Scalar multiplication is just as easy: $r\mathbf{u}(x) = rx^2$. The additive identity is the zero function: $\mathbf{w}(x) \equiv 0$. Check properties 1 through 10.

Example 27.20   Here is an example that fits right between Examples 27.17 and 27.19. Let F_2 be the set of *quadratic functions*:

$$F_2 \equiv \{a_0 x^2 + a_1 x + a_2 : a_0, a_1, a_2 \in \mathbf{R}\}.$$

Give F_2 the addition and scalar multiplication it inherits as a subspace of the function space F in Example 27.19. For example,

$$(a_0 x^2 + a_1 x + a_2) + (b_0 x^2 + b_1 x + b_2)$$
$$= (a_0 + b_0)x^2 + (a_1 + b_1)x + (a_2 + b_2). \tag{14}$$

Since the sum of two quadratics is another quadratic and the scalar multiple of a quadratic is a quadratic, F_2 is a vector space in its own right. In this case, we say that F_2 is a **subspace** of F.

Notice that if we just keep track of the three coefficients (a_0, a_1, a_2) of the quadratic $a_0 x^2 + a_1 x + a_2$, then the addition operation in (14) becomes

$$(a_0, a_1, a_2) + (b_0, b_1, b_2) = (a_0 + b_0, a_1 + b_1, a_2 + b_2),$$

the standard addition of 3-tuples. There is a natural one-to-one correspondence between the quadratic functions in F_2 and the 3-tuples in $\mathbf{R}^3$ that carries over to the addition and scalar multiplication operations. In this case, we say that F_2 and $\mathbf{R}^3$ are **isomorphic** vector spaces.

Example 27.21   Here is a vector space with unusual operations. Let V_9 be the set of all *positive* real numbers. Define an addition operator $\oplus$ on V_9 by: $\mathbf{u} \oplus \mathbf{v}$ is the usual product of the two real numbers $\mathbf{u}$ and $\mathbf{v}$. Define a scalar multiplication operation $*$ on V_9 by: $r * \mathbf{u} = \mathbf{u}^r$. The set V_9 with $\oplus$ for addition and $*$ for scalar multiplication is a vector space! For properties 3 and 4, the additive identity is 1, and the inverse of $\mathbf{u}$ is $1/\mathbf{u}$. It is not hard to see that scalar multiplication has the desired properties. For example, to prove properties 7 and 8,

$$(r + s) * \mathbf{u} = \mathbf{u}^{(r+s)}$$
$$= \mathbf{u}^r \mathbf{u}^s$$
$$= r * \mathbf{u} \oplus s * \mathbf{u},$$

and
$$r * (\mathbf{u} \oplus \mathbf{v}) = (\mathbf{u}\mathbf{v})^r$$
$$= \mathbf{u}^r \mathbf{v}^r$$
$$= (r * \mathbf{u}) \oplus (r * \mathbf{v}).$$

Since V_9 does *not* inherit the usual addition and scalar multiplication from $\mathbf{R}^1$, we can't use Theorem 27.1 to determine whether or not V_9 is a vector space. We must explicitly check *all* 10 properties of a vector space. In particular, even though V_9 is a vector space and a subset of $\mathbf{R}^1$, it is not a subspace of $\mathbf{R}^1$.

Example 27.22   Finally, consider the one-element set $V_{10} = \{$Albert Einstein$\}$. Define an addition on V_{10} by

$$\text{Albert Einstein} + \text{Albert Einstein} = \text{Albert Einstein}$$

and a scalar multiplication on V_{10} by

$$r \cdot \text{Albert Einstein} = \text{Albert Einstein},$$

for any scalar r. Verify that we have just made $\{$Albert Einstein$\}$ into a vector space.

EXERCISES

27.19   Which of the following are *subspaces* of the vector space $M_{2,2}$ of 2×2 matrices (described in Example 27.18)? Justify your answer.

a) the set of 2×2 symmetric matrices: $\left\{ \begin{pmatrix} a & b \\ b & c \end{pmatrix} : a, b, c, \text{ reals} \right\}$,

b) the set of 2×2 diagonal matrices: $\left\{ \begin{pmatrix} a & 0 \\ 0 & b \end{pmatrix} : a, b, \text{ reals} \right\}$,

c) the set of all 2×2 "singular" matrices $\left\{ \begin{pmatrix} a & b \\ c & d \end{pmatrix} : ad - bc = 0 \right\}$,

d) the zero matrix: $\left\{ \begin{pmatrix} 0 & 0 \\ 0 & 0 \end{pmatrix} \right\}$,

e) the set of all 2×2 nonsingular matrices $\left\{ \begin{pmatrix} a & b \\ c & d \end{pmatrix} : ad - bc \neq 0 \right\}$.

(Compare part *a* with Example 27.5.)

27.20   a) Check that the function space F in Example 27.19 is a vector space. b) Prove that for any fixed n, the functions $1, x, x^2, x^3, \ldots, x^n$ are linearly independent elements of F.

27.21   Use properties 8, 5, 4, and 1 of the definition of a vector space to derive that $0 \cdot \mathbf{v} = \mathbf{0}$ for any $\mathbf{v}$ in a vector space V.

27.22   Verify that the sets in Examples 27.21 and 27.22 with the given addition and scalar multiplication are indeed vector spaces.

27.7   APPENDIX

In this Appendix, we complete the proofs of Theorems 27.5 and 27.10.

Proof of Theorem 27.5

Theorem 27.5   The basic columns of a matrix A form a basis of Col(A).

Proof   Let $\mathbf{v}_1, \ldots, \mathbf{v}_m$ denote the columns of A, and denote the corresponding columns of its row echelon form A_r by $\mathbf{w}_1, \ldots, \mathbf{w}_m$. The idea behind this proposition is the observation that the homogeneous linear systems $A\mathbf{x} = \mathbf{0}$ and $A_r\mathbf{x} = \mathbf{0}$ have precisely the same solutions. (In other words, Gaussian elimination does not change the solution set of a linear system of equations.) Rephrasing this statement in terms of the column vectors, the sets of scalars $x_1, \ldots, x_m$ which solve

$$x_1\mathbf{v}_1 + \cdots + x_m\mathbf{v}_m = \mathbf{0} \tag{15}$$

are identical to the sets of scalars $x_1, \ldots, x_m$ which solve

$$x_1\mathbf{w}_1 + \cdots + x_m\mathbf{w}_m = \mathbf{0}. \tag{16}$$

Let $\mathbf{w}'_1, \ldots, \mathbf{w}'_k$ denote, in order, the columns of A_r containing pivots. Let $\mathbf{v}'_1, \ldots, \mathbf{v}'_k$ denote the corresponding "basic columns" of A. We first show that $\mathbf{w}'_1, \ldots, \mathbf{w}'_k$ is a basis for $\text{Col}(A_r)$. Each $\mathbf{w}'_i$ has more *final* zeros than $\mathbf{w}'_{i+1}$. By Lemma 27.2, the column vectors $\mathbf{w}'_1, \ldots, \mathbf{w}'_k$ are linearly independent. Thus, $\dim \text{Col}(A_r) \geq k$. By definition of the row echelon form, the last $n - k$ entries in each column of a rank k row echelon matrix A_r are all zeros. It follows that $\text{Col}(A_r)$ cannot have a dimension strictly greater than k. Thus, $\dim \text{Col}(A_r) = k$, and so $\mathbf{w}'_1, \ldots, \mathbf{w}'_k$ is a basis.

To see that $\mathbf{v}'_1, \ldots, \mathbf{v}'_k$ is a basis for $\text{Col}(A)$, we must show that it is a maximal linearly independent set of vectors. First check linear independence. The linear independence condition is that, if

$$c'_1\mathbf{v}'_1 + \cdots + c'_k\mathbf{v}'_k = \mathbf{0},$$

then $c'_1 = \cdots = c'_k = 0$. In terms of equation (15), we want to show that any solution $(x_1, \ldots, x_m)$ of equation (15) for which $x_i = 0$ for the is not corresponding to the basic columns of A has $x_i = 0$ for all i. This will be true if and only if it is true for equation (16) by the observation at the beginning of this proof, that is, if and only if $\mathbf{w}'_1, \ldots, \mathbf{w}'_k$ are linearly independent. But we verified this fact in the previous paragraph.

Suppose that there exists a larger independent subset of $\mathbf{v}_1, \ldots, \mathbf{v}_m$. Exactly the same argument implies that there must be a larger linearly independent subset of the vectors $\mathbf{w}_1, \ldots, \mathbf{w}_m$. But since $\mathbf{w}'_1, \ldots, \mathbf{w}'_k$ is a basis for $\text{Col}(A_r)$, there can be no larger independent set of column vectors. ∎

Proof of Theorem 27.10

Theorem 27.10 is one of the central theorems of linear algebra because it describes the dimension of the solution set of a linear system. It can be proved by elaborating the computational method we established in the two examples just before the statement of the theorem. It is instructive to work out such a proof. Here we shall present another proof which is useful for two reasons: it is less tedious, and it reviews the kinds of calculations which are typical in matrix analysis.

We first need to prove a couple of lemmas that are interesting in their own right. The first describes an important relationship between the concepts of spanning and linear independence. It expresses the idea that any linearly independent set of vectors in a vector space V that does not span V can be augmented in such a way as to remain linearly independent. The second lemma is an extension of the first; it states that subspaces sit inside their ambient spaces in a natural way that is easy to characterize with the proper choice of a basis for the ambient space.

Lemma 27.3   Let $\mathbf{v}_1, \ldots, \mathbf{v}_k$ be a linearly independent set of vectors in a vector space V. Let $\mathbf{w}$ be a vector in V. If $\mathbf{w}$ is not a linear combination of the $\mathbf{v}_1, \ldots, \mathbf{v}_k$, then the augmented set $\mathbf{v}_1, \ldots, \mathbf{v}_k, \mathbf{w}$ is linearly independent.

Proof   Suppose that

$$c_1 \mathbf{v}_1 + \cdots + c_k \mathbf{v}_k + d\mathbf{w} = 0. \tag{17}$$

We prove that the coefficients must all be 0. Rewrite (17) as

$$c_1 \mathbf{v}_1 + \cdots + c_k \mathbf{v}_k = -d\mathbf{w}. \tag{18}$$

Since $\mathbf{w}$ is not a linear combination of the vectors $\mathbf{v}_1, \ldots, \mathbf{v}_k$, the coefficient d in (18) must be 0. But then equation (18) becomes

$$c_1 \mathbf{v}_1 + \cdots + c_k \mathbf{v}_k = 0.$$

Since the vectors $\mathbf{v}_1, \ldots, \mathbf{v}_k$ are linearly independent, the coefficients c_i must all be 0. ∎

Lemma 27.4   Let W be a subspace of $\mathbf{R}^m$, and let $\mathbf{v}_1, \ldots, \mathbf{v}_k$ be a basis for W. Then there exist vectors $\mathbf{v}_{k+1}, \ldots, \mathbf{v}_m$ in $\mathbf{R}^m$ such that

$$\mathbf{v}_1, \ldots, \mathbf{v}_k, \mathbf{v}_{k+1}, \ldots, \mathbf{v}_m$$

is a basis for $\mathbf{R}^m$.

Proof   If $W = \mathbf{R}^m$ we are done. Suppose that $W \neq \mathbf{R}^m$. Then there exists a vector $\mathbf{v}_{k+1}$ which is in $\mathbf{R}^m$ but not W. This means that $\mathbf{v}_{k+1}$ is not a linear combination of the $\mathbf{v}_1, \ldots, \mathbf{v}_k$. Then the vectors $\mathbf{v}_1, \ldots, \mathbf{v}_k, \mathbf{v}_{k+1}$ are independent by Lemma 27.3.

Let W' be the subspace of $\mathbf{R}^m$ spanned by the $k + 1$ vectors $\mathbf{v}_1, \ldots, \mathbf{v}_{k+1}$. If $W' = \mathbf{R}^m$, we are done. If not, repeat the process with another vector $\mathbf{v}_{k+2}$ in $\mathbf{R}^m$ but not W'. In fact, repeat this process so long as

$W' \neq \mathbf{R}^m$. This process must stop after a finite number of steps; otherwise we could generate a set of more than m independent vectors in $\mathbf{R}^m$, which contradicts Theorem 11.3. On the other hand, it cannot stop before $m - k$ steps, because at each such step dim $W' \neq$ dim $\mathbf{R}^m$, and so $W' \subset \mathbf{R}^m$ and $W' \neq \mathbf{R}^m$. When the process stops, we have chosen m independent vectors in $\mathbf{R}^m$. By Theorem 11.8, they are a basis for $\mathbf{R}^m$. ∎

We now restate and prove the Fundamental Theorem.

Theorem 27.10   Let A be a $n \times m$ matrix. Then,

$$\dim \text{Null}(A) = m - \text{rank}\, A.$$

Proof   The nullspace Null(A) is a subspace of $\mathbf{R}^m$. Let $\mathbf{u}_1, \ldots, \mathbf{u}_k$ be a basis for Null(A). If $k = m$, then $A\mathbf{x} = \mathbf{0}$ for all $\mathbf{x} \in \mathbf{R}^m$. It follows that all the columns of A are $\mathbf{0}$ (exercise), and so the dimension of Col(A) is 0. In this case, the rank of A is zero and the dimension of Null(A) is m, which satisfies the conclusion of the theorem.

Suppose that $k < m$. Extend $\mathbf{u}_1, \ldots, \mathbf{u}_k$ to a basis for $\mathbf{R}^m$ by adding vectors $\mathbf{u}_{k+1}, \ldots, \mathbf{u}_m$ (via Lemma 27.4). We will prove this theorem by showing that the vectors $A\mathbf{u}_{k+1}, \ldots, A\mathbf{u}_m$ are a basis for the column space.

First, by equation (11), $A\mathbf{u}_{k+1}, \ldots, A\mathbf{u}_m$ are linear combinations of the column vectors, and thus are in the column space.

Second, they are linearly independent. To see this, suppose that there are scalars $c_{k+1}, \ldots, c_m$ such that

$$c_{k+1}A\mathbf{u}_{k+1} + \cdots + c_m A\mathbf{u}_m = 0. \tag{19}$$

Using the distributive properties of matrix multiplication,

$$0 = c_{k+1}A\mathbf{u}_{k+1} + \cdots + c_m A\mathbf{u}_m$$
$$= A(c_{k+1}\mathbf{u}_{k+1} + \cdots + c_m\mathbf{u}_m).$$

Thus, the vector $c_{k+1}\mathbf{u}_{k+1} + \cdots + c_m\mathbf{u}_m$ is in the nullspace of A. Since it is in the nullspace, it is a linear combination of the basis vectors $\mathbf{u}_1, \ldots, \mathbf{u}_k$ of Null(A). There are scalars $c_1, \ldots, c_k$ such that

$$c_1\mathbf{u}_1 + \cdots + c_k\mathbf{u}_k = c_{k+1}\mathbf{u}_{k+1} + \cdots + c_m\mathbf{u}_m,$$

or, rewriting,

$$c_1\mathbf{u}_1 + \cdots + c_k\mathbf{u}_k - c_{k+1}\mathbf{u}_{k+1} - \cdots - c_m\mathbf{u}_m = 0.$$

The vectors $\mathbf{u}_1, \ldots, \mathbf{u}_m$ are linearly independent (they are, after all, a basis for $\mathbf{R}^m$). Thus, the only possible solution scalars are

$$c_1 = \cdots = c_m = 0.$$

In particular, the scalars $c_{k+1}, \ldots, c_m$ in (19) are all zero, and so the vectors $A\mathbf{u}_{k+1}, \ldots, A\mathbf{u}_m$ are linearly independent.

Third, the vectors $A\mathbf{u}_{k+1}, \ldots, A\mathbf{u}_m$ span the column space. If a vector $\mathbf{b}$ is in $\mathrm{Col}(A)$, then there exists a vector $\mathbf{x}$ in $\mathbf{R}^m$ such that $A\mathbf{x} = \mathbf{b}$. In turn, we can write $\mathbf{x}$ as a linear combination of the $\mathbf{R}^m$ basis vectors $\mathbf{u}_1, \ldots, \mathbf{u}_m$:

$$\mathbf{x} = c_1\mathbf{u}_1 + \cdots + c_m\mathbf{u}_m.$$

Thus,
$$\mathbf{b} = A\mathbf{x}$$
$$= A(c_1\mathbf{u}_1 + \cdots + c_m\mathbf{u}_m)$$
$$= c_1 A\mathbf{u}_1 + \cdots + c_m A\mathbf{u}_m.$$

However, the vectors $\mathbf{u}_1, \ldots, \mathbf{u}_k$ are all in the nullspace $\mathrm{Null}(A)$. For these vectors, $A\mathbf{u}_i = \mathbf{0}$. Therefore, $\mathbf{b} = c_{k+1}A\mathbf{u}_{k+1} + \cdots + c_m A\mathbf{u}_m$, which proves that $A\mathbf{u}_{k+1}, \ldots, A\mathbf{u}_m$ span $\mathrm{Col}(A)$.

It follows that the vectors $A\mathbf{u}_{k+1}, \ldots, A\mathbf{u}_m$ are a basis for $\mathrm{Col}(A)$ and that

$$\mathrm{rank}\, A = \dim \mathrm{Col}(A) = m - k = m - \dim \mathrm{Null}(A). \quad \blacksquare$$

EXERCISES

27.23 Prove that if $A\mathbf{x} = \mathbf{0}$ for all $\mathbf{x}$, then every entry of A is zero.

27.24 State and prove the converse of Lemma 27.3.

Applications of Linear Independence

This chapter presents economic applications of the theory of linear independence introduced in Chapters 11 and 27. Section 28.1 describes the geometry behind the Gaussian elimination process of Chapter 7. Sections 28.2 to 28.5 present three economics applications: portfolio analysis, the existence of paradoxes in voting methods, and the activity analysis model of production.

28.1 GEOMETRY OF SYSTEMS OF EQUATIONS

So far we have studied systems of linear equations only analytically. This section examines the natural geometry behind the study of systems of equations in two or three unknowns. It uses the techniques and notation of Section 10.6.

Two Equations in Two Unknowns

The solution (x_1^*, x_2^*) of a general *system of two equations in two unknowns*

$$a_{11}x_1 + a_{12}x_2 = b_1$$
$$a_{21}x_1 + a_{22}x_2 = b_2 \tag{1}$$

is simply the point of intersection of the two lines $a_{11}x_1 + a_{12}x_2 = b_1$ and $a_{21}x_1 + a_{22}x_2 = b_2$ in $\mathbf{R}^2$.

There are three possible configurations for two lines in the plane:

    (1) they can be nonparallel and therefore intersect at exactly one point,
    (2) they can be parallel and disjoint so that they do not intersect, or
    (3) they can coincide so that they intersect at all their points.

The three parts of Figure 28.1 illustrate these three cases geometrically. They correspond to the situations where system (1) has one solution, no solutions, or infinitely many solutions, respectively.

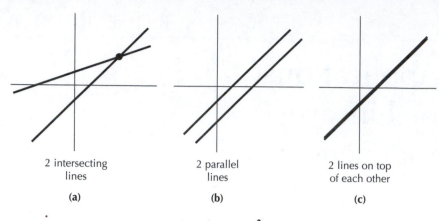

<table>
<tr><td>2 intersecting
lines</td><td>2 parallel
lines</td><td>2 lines on top
of each other</td></tr>
<tr><td>(a)</td><td>(b)</td><td>(c)</td></tr>
</table>

**Figure
28.1**

Two lines in **R**^{2}.

System (1) has a unique solution for every right-hand side (b_1, b_2) if and only if situation 1 arises — the lines have distinct slopes. Since the slopes are $-a_{11}/a_{12}$ and $-a_{21}/a_{22}$ respectively, situation 1 occurs if and only if

$$-\frac{a_{11}}{a_{12}} \neq -\frac{a_{21}}{a_{22}},$$

that is, if and only if

$$a_{11}a_{22} - a_{12}a_{21} \neq 0.$$

This is just the determinant test for the nonsingularity of the coefficient matrix of system (1).

Two Equations in Three Unknowns

A solution of a *system of two equations in three unknowns,*

$$a_{11}x_1 + a_{12}x_2 + a_{13}x_3 = b_1$$
$$a_{21}x_1 + a_{22}x_2 + a_{23}x_3 = b_2, \tag{2}$$

is just a point (x_1^*, x_2^*, x_3^*) of intersection of the two planes in **R**^{3}

$$a_{11}x_1 + a_{12}x_2 + a_{13}x_3 = b_1 \qquad \text{and} \qquad a_{21}x_1 + a_{22}x_2 + a_{23}x_3 = b_2.$$

Once again, three situations can occur:

(1) the planes can have different inclinations so that their intersection is a line,
(2) the planes can be distinct but have the same inclination so that they do not intersect, or

(3) the planes can coincide so that every point of each plane is a point of intersection.

These three possibilities are pictured in Figure 28.2. The inclinations of the two planes are given by their normal vectors (a_{11}, a_{12}, a_{13}) and (a_{21}, a_{22}, a_{23}) respectively, as we saw in Section 10.6. If these vectors are linearly independent, then the planes are not parallel, situation 1 occurs, and system (2) has a line of solutions for every right-hand side (b_1, b_2). If these two normal vectors are scalar multiples of each other, then the planes are parallel and situation 2 or 3 occurs — either no solution or a two-dimensional subspace of solutions.

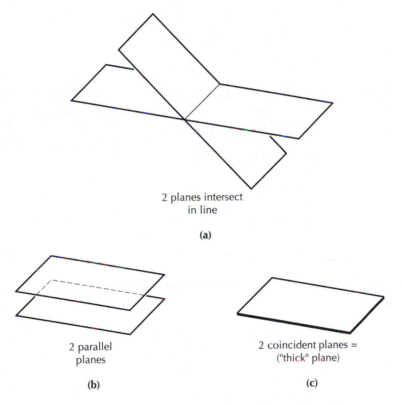

2 planes intersect
in line

(a)

2 parallel
planes

(b)

2 coincident planes =
("thick" plane)

(c)

Independent normals, parallel planes, and coinciding planes.

**Figure
28.2**

The key observation of this section is that the normal vectors of the two planes in (2) are simply the row vectors of the coefficient matrix A of system (2):

$$A = \begin{pmatrix} a_{11} & a_{12} & a_{13} \\ a_{21} & a_{22} & a_{23} \end{pmatrix}.$$

The two normal vectors are independent if and only if the dimension of Row(A) is two, that is, if and only if A has rank two (maximal rank). But this latter maximal rank condition is our algebraic criterion for the existence of a solution for every right-hand side — Fact 7 in Section 7.4.

When the normals are scalar multiples of each other as in Figure 28.2b, the coefficient matrix A has rank one. Figure 28.2 illustrates the statement of Fact 7.5 that a system of two equations in three unknowns can have no solutions or infinitely many solutions, but never just one solution.

Three Equations in Three Unknowns

A solution of a *system of three equations in three unknowns,*

$$a_{11}x_1 + a_{12}x_2 + a_{13}x_3 = b_1$$
$$a_{21}x_1 + a_{22}x_2 + a_{23}x_3 = b_2 \qquad\qquad (3)$$
$$a_{31}x_1 + a_{32}x_2 + a_{33}x_3 = b_3,$$

is a point of intersection of the three planes described by the three equations in (3). These three planes can intersect in a single point as in Figure 28.3a, in a line as in Figure 28.3b, in a plane as in Figure 28.3c, or not at all as in Figure 28.3d to f. Once again, we look at the normal vectors to these three planes to characterize these six possibilities. As before, the normal vectors of the three planes of system (3) are the row vectors of the corresponding coefficient matrix.

In Figure 28.3c and f, the normal vectors are all multiples of each other. In this case, the rows of the coefficient matrix A are multiples of each other and A has rank 1; for most right-hand sides, the three parallel planes of system (3) do not coincide (Figure 28.3f) and system (3) has no solution. For rare choices of right-hand sides, the three parallel planes agree (Figure 28.3c) and system (3) has a two-dimensional set of solutions.

In Figure 28.3b, d and e, the normal vectors of the planes (3) — and the row vectors of the coefficient matrix A of (3) — are neither multiples of each other, nor linearly independent. The three vectors span a two-dimensional space and the corresponding coefficient matrix has rank two. In this case, there is either no solution, as in Figure 28.3d and e, or a line of solutions, as in Figure 28.3b.

In Figure 28.3a, the three planes intersect in a single point. This is the case where the three normal vectors, and therefore the three row vectors, are linearly independent, and the coefficient matrix A has maximal rank three. Since A is a square matrix, maximal rank means nonzero determinant, which in turn implies one and only one solution for every right-hand side (b_1, b_2, b_3).

EXERCISES

28.1   Draw all the figures analogous to Figures 28.1, 28.2, and 28.3 for the case of three equations in two unknowns. Describe the corresponding solution sets.

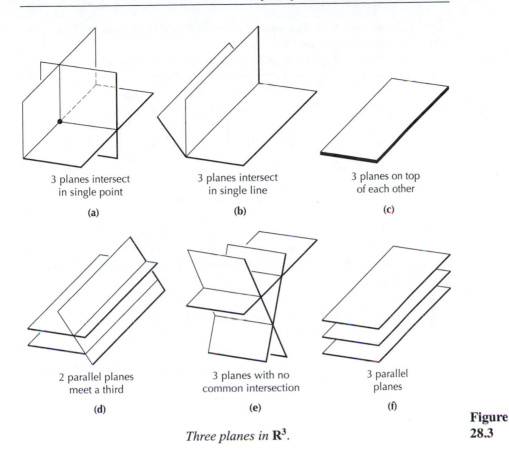

3 planes intersect
in single point

(a)

3 planes intersect
in single line

(b)

3 planes on top
of each other

(c)

2 parallel planes
meet a third

(d)

3 planes with no
common intersection

(e)

3 parallel
planes

(f)

**Figure
28.3**

Three planes in $\mathbf{R}^3$.

28.2 PORTFOLIO ANALYSIS

This section ties up the loose ends in the discussion of investment portfolios that
we began in Example 5 of Section 6.2 and continued at the end of Section 7.4.
We suppose that there are A assets and S states of nature, and we write R_{si} for the
return to asset i in state s. Let $\mathcal{R}$ be the $S \times A$ matrix of the R_{si}s:

$$\mathcal{R} = \begin{pmatrix} R_{11} & \cdots & R_{1A} \\ \vdots & \ddots & \vdots \\ R_{S1} & \cdots & R_{SA} \end{pmatrix}. \tag{4}$$

If rank $\mathcal{R} = S = \dim \operatorname{Col}(\mathcal{R})$, then the system $\mathcal{R}\mathbf{x} = \mathbf{b}$ has a solution for every
right-hand side $\mathbf{b}$. In particular, if we take $\mathbf{b} = (b, \ldots, b)^T$ for some $b \neq 0$, the
solution $\mathbf{x}$ to $\mathcal{R}\mathbf{x} = \mathbf{b}$, when properly normalized so that $x_1 + \cdots + x_A = 1$, is a
riskless portfolio. If we take $\mathbf{b} = \mathbf{e}_j$, the canonical basis vector of Example 11.8,
the solution $\mathbf{x}$ to $\mathcal{R}\mathbf{x} = \mathbf{e}_j$, when properly normalized, is the portfolio that **insures**
state j. Conversely, if every state is insurable, so that $\mathcal{R}\mathbf{x} = \mathbf{e}_j$ has a solution for

$\mathbf{e}_j = \mathbf{e}_1, \ldots, \mathbf{e}_S$, then the column space of $\mathcal{R}$ is all of $\mathbf{R}^S$. This implies that $\mathcal{R}$ has rank S, in which case S must be $\leq A$.

A portfolio $\mathbf{x}$ is **duplicable** if and only if there is a vector $\mathbf{w} \neq \mathbf{x}$ so that $\mathcal{R}\mathbf{x} = \mathcal{R}\mathbf{w}$ and $\sum_i x_i = \sum_i w_i$. Combine these equations as

$$
\begin{pmatrix} R_{11} & \cdots & R_{1A} \\ \vdots & \ddots & \vdots \\ R_{S1} & \cdots & R_{SA} \\ 1 & \cdots & 1 \end{pmatrix} \begin{pmatrix} x_1 \\ \vdots \\ x_A \end{pmatrix} = \begin{pmatrix} R_{11} & \cdots & R_{1A} \\ \vdots & \ddots & \vdots \\ R_{S1} & \cdots & R_{SA} \\ 1 & \cdots & 1 \end{pmatrix} \begin{pmatrix} w_1 \\ \vdots \\ w_A \end{pmatrix}. \tag{5}
$$

Let $\tilde{\mathcal{R}}$ be the $(S+1) \times A$ coefficient matrix in (5). System (5) has solutions $\mathbf{x} \neq \mathbf{w}$ if and only if there is a nonzero vector in the nullspace of $\tilde{\mathcal{R}}$, that is, if and only if rank $\tilde{\mathcal{R}} < A$ by Theorem 27.10. In this case, *every* portfolio is duplicable.

The following theorem summarizes these observations and provides a complete set of criteria for the existence of riskfree portfolios, duplicable portfolios, and insurable states.

Theorem 28.1   Consider an asset market with A assets, S states of nature, and state return matrix $\mathcal{R}$ as in (4).

(a) There is a riskless portfolio if and only if $\mathbf{1} = (1, \ldots, 1)$ is in the column space of $\mathcal{R}$, that is, if and only if $\mathcal{R}\mathbf{x} = \mathbf{1}$ has a solution. In particular, if rank $\mathcal{R} = S$, there is a riskless portfolio.

(b) State j is insurable if and only if $\mathbf{e}_j$ is in the column space of $\mathcal{R}$, that is, if and only if $\mathcal{R}\mathbf{x} = \mathbf{e}_j$ has a solution.

(c) Every state is insurable if and only if $\mathcal{R}$ has rank S.

(d) There is a duplicable portfolio if and only if the augmented matrix $\tilde{\mathcal{R}}$ in (5) has rank $< A$, that is, if and only if every portfolio is duplicable. In particular, if $S + 1 < A$, every portfolio is duplicable.

28.3   VOTING PARADOXES

Consider a one-ballot election that has n candidates for a single office or n alternatives of a single proposal. For simplicity of notation, call these alternatives $1, 2, \ldots, n$. Suppose that there are N voters in the electorate and that each voter has a ranking over these n alternatives, a situation we call a **profile** of voters. If on a proposal with three alternatives, a given voter prefers the second alternative to the third and the third alternative to the first, we write this voter's ranking as $2 > 3 > 1$, or simply as 231. For simplicity, we assume that each voter has a strict ordering of the alternatives with no ties.

In the standard **plurality voting system**, each voter votes only for his or her highest-ranked alternative. This leads to an aggregate ordering of the candidates in which the alternative with the most votes is ranked first, the alternative with the second most votes is ranked second, and so on. The winner is usually the highest-ranked alternative in this aggregate ranking, although sometimes there are runoff elections if the winner fails to achieve some preassigned percentage of the votes cast.

Instead of considering all n alternatives, we can focus on a single *pair* of alternatives and compute the electorate's aggregate ranking of the two alternatives in this pair. One would expect that the aggregate ranking of the n alternatives would have some relationship to how the electorate ranks at least one pair of the alternatives. That this expectation doesn't even come close to holding true is the main lesson of this section.

Theorem 28.2   If there are n alternatives on a ballot proposal, there are $\frac{1}{2}n(n-1)$ *pairs* of alternatives. In each of these $\frac{1}{2}n(n-1)$ pairs, arbitrarily select one of the two alternatives. In addition, arbitrarily select *any* plurality aggregate ranking. Then, there is a profile of voters that achieves the selected plurality aggregate ranking, so that in each of the pairs, the electorate prefers the selected one.

For example, there is a profile of voters so that the aggregate ranking is $1 > 2 > 3$, and in the 3 pairs, $1 > 2$, $2 > 3$, and $3 > 1$. In this case, we say that the choices among the pairs forms a **cycle**. Another possible example is $1 > 2 > 3$ for the aggregate ranking, but $2 > 1$, $3 > 2$, and $3 > 1$ for the rankings within the pairs, so that even though alternative 1 wins the election, it loses *every* pairwise election of which it is a part.

Example 28.1   We present actual voters' profiles that realize each of the two situations in the previous paragraph. In both cases, we will work with an electorate of 15 voters. First, suppose that 6 voters have the ranking $1 > 2 > 3$, 5 have the ranking $2 > 3 > 1$, and 4 have the ranking $3 > 1 > 2$. The plurality ranking is clearly $1 > 2 > 3$. In ranking the pairs of alternatives, 10 of the 15 prefer alternative 1 to alternative 2, 11 of the 15 prefer 2 to 3, and 9 of the 15 prefer 3 to 1; this generates a cycle.

For the second example, suppose that in our electorate of 15 voters, 6 have the ranking $1 > 2 > 3$, 5 have the ranking $2 > 3 > 1$ and 4 have the ranking $3 > 2 > 1$. The plurality ranking is once again $1 > 2 > 3$. This time, 9 of the 15 prefer 2 over 1, 11 of the 15 prefer 2 over 3, and 9 of the 15 prefer 3 to 1 (even though 1 was first and 3 last in the actual vote).

Three Alternatives

We will give a careful proof of Theorem 28.2 for $n = 3$ and sketch the proof for $n = 4$; the procedure for the general proof will be clear from these special cases. In the case of three alternatives ($n = 3$), there are $3! = 6$ possible rankings of all three alternatives, which we label $R_1, \ldots, R_6$:

$$R_1 = 123, \ R_2 = 132, \ R_3 = 213, \ R_4 = 231, \ R_5 = 312, \ R_6 = 321.$$

As we have just seen, there are three pairs of alternatives, which we write as A_{12}, A_{13}, and A_{23}, intentionally writing the alternative with the smaller index first in all three pairs. Finally, construct a 3×6 matrix M whose rows are indexed by the three pairs A_{ij} and whose columns are indexed by the six rankings $R_1, \ldots, R_6$:

$$\begin{array}{c} \phantom{A_{12}} \\ A_{12} \\ A_{13} \\ A_{23} \end{array} \begin{array}{cccccc} 123 & 132 & 213 & 231 & 312 & 321 \\ \left(\begin{array}{cccccc} +1 & +1 & -1 & -1 & +1 & -1 \\ +1 & +1 & +1 & -1 & -1 & -1 \\ +1 & -1 & +1 & +1 & -1 & -1 \end{array} \right) \end{array} \qquad (6)$$

We place a $+1$ in the entry of M corresponding to the column with ranking R and the row with pair A_{ij} if $i > j$ in the ranking R. We place a -1 in the entry corresponding to the column with ranking R and the row with pair A_{ij} if $j > i$ in the ranking R. (Check.)

Suppose that in the electorate there are N_i voters with ranking R_i for $i = 1, \ldots, 6$. Since rankings R_1, R_2, and R_5 rank alternative 1 over alternative 2 and rankings R_3, R_4, and R_6 rank alternative 2 over alternative 1, this profile yields $N_1 + N_2 + N_5$ voters preferring 1 over 2 and $N_3 + N_4 + N_6$ voters preferring 2 over 1. Therefore, this profile prefers alternative 1 to alternative 2 if and only if

$$(N_1 + N_2 + N_5) - (N_3 + N_4 + N_6) = N_1 + N_2 - N_3 - N_4 + N_5 - N_6 \qquad (7)$$

is positive. But the sum in (7) is just the matrix product of the first row of M with the column matrix $\mathbf{N} = (N_1 \ N_2 \ N_3 \ N_4 \ N_5 \ N_6)^T$. It follows that if we write

$$\begin{pmatrix} +1 & +1 & -1 & -1 & +1 & -1 \\ +1 & +1 & +1 & -1 & -1 & -1 \\ +1 & -1 & +1 & +1 & -1 & -1 \end{pmatrix} \begin{pmatrix} N_1 \\ N_2 \\ \vdots \\ N_6 \end{pmatrix} = \begin{pmatrix} y_{12} \\ y_{13} \\ y_{23} \end{pmatrix}, \qquad (8)$$

then the profile $\mathbf{N}$ prefers i to j within the pair A_{ij} if and only if $y_{ij} > 0$ on the right-hand side of (8).

Which vectors $\mathbf{y} = (y_{12}, y_{13}, y_{23})$ can arise on the right-hand side of (8) as the profiles $\mathbf{N}$ vary? The determinant of the 3×3 submatrix of M formed from the first three columns of M is $+4$. (Check.) Therefore, the first three columns of M are linearly independent vectors in $\mathbf{R}^3$, and the rank of M is 3. Since the rank equals the number of rows, system (8) has a solution for *every* right-hand side $\mathbf{y}$; that is, every sign pattern is achievable on the right-hand side of (8), and so every outcome among the three pairs $A_{12}, A_{13},$ and A_{23} can arise for some electorate.

There are still two issues we need to address. Given any sign pattern for $\mathbf{y}$ on the right-hand side of (8), can we find a profile $\mathbf{N}$ such that each N_i is 1) positive and 2) an integer. We use Theorem 27.9 to address the first issue: if $\mathbf{N}^*$ is a solution of (8) for a given $\mathbf{y}$ and if $\mathbf{N}^o$ is a vector in the *nullspace* of M, then $\mathbf{N}^* + \mathbf{N}^o$ is a solution of (8) for the same $\mathbf{y}$. By Theorem 27.10, the 3×6 matrix M of rank three has a four-dimensional nullspace. From a voting perspective, the most interesting vectors in the nullspace of M are the profiles in which each of the six rankings is held by the same number of voters: $\mathbf{N}^o = (N, N, \ldots, N)$. The profile $\mathbf{N}^o$ leads to a tie in every comparison of alternatives. So, if $\mathbf{N}^* = (N_1, \ldots, N_6)$ is a solution of (8) for a given $\mathbf{y}$, let $N' = \min\{N_1, \ldots, N_6\}$. If $N' > 0$, $\mathbf{N}^*$ is a positive vector and no adjustment is necessary. If $N' \leq 0$, let $\mathbf{N}^o = (|N'| + 1, \ldots, |N'| + 1)$. Then, $\mathbf{N}^o + \mathbf{N}^*$ is a solution of (8) with all positive components.

To handle the requirement that each component of a profile be an integer, let $(N_1, \ldots, N_6)$ be a (positive) solution to system (8) for some choice of $\mathbf{y}$ on the right-hand side of (8). Since we are really only concerned about the signs of the y_{ij}'s, we can perturb the N_i's a little to new ones that are *rational numbers* and still yield the same sign pattern for the y_{ij}'s. (Recall that arbitrarily close to any number is a rational number. From a practical point of view, one can truncate any infinite decimal expansion to an arbitrarily long *finite* decimal expansion. The latter represents a rational number that is arbitrarily close to the original number.) Write the new rational N_i's as fractions over a *common denominator*:

$$\mathbf{N} = \left(\frac{m_1}{M}, \frac{m_2}{M}, \ldots, \frac{m_6}{M} \right)$$

$$= \frac{1}{M}(m_1, m_2, \ldots, m_6),$$

where the m_i's are positive integers. Finally, multiply system (8) through by the common denominator M to obtain

$$\begin{pmatrix} +1 & +1 & -1 & -1 & +1 & -1 \\ +1 & +1 & +1 & -1 & -1 & -1 \\ +1 & -1 & +1 & +1 & -1 & -1 \end{pmatrix} \begin{pmatrix} m_1 \\ m_2 \\ \vdots \\ m_6 \end{pmatrix} = M \begin{pmatrix} y_{12} \\ y_{13} \\ y_{23} \end{pmatrix}. \qquad (9)$$

Since $M > 0$, the entries on the right-hand side of (9) have the same signs as those in (8). System (9) gives *positive integer* values of the number of voters with each ranking so that the signs for the y_{ij}'s on the right-hand side of (9) still agree with the originally prescribed values.

We now show that one can achieve any prescribed ordering on each of the six pairs of alternatives *while still achieving some prescribed aggregate plurality ranking*. Without loss of generality, we will prescribe $1 > 2 > 3$ as the desired aggregate plurality ranking. Augment the above matrix M with two additional rows to form the 5×6 matrix M':

$$M' = \begin{pmatrix} +1 & +1 & -1 & -1 & +1 & -1 \\ +1 & +1 & +1 & -1 & -1 & -1 \\ +1 & -1 & +1 & +1 & -1 & -1 \\ +1 & +1 & -1 & -1 & 0 & 0 \\ 0 & 0 & +1 & +1 & -1 & -1 \end{pmatrix}, \tag{10}$$

and consider the augmented system

$$\begin{pmatrix} +1 & +1 & -1 & -1 & +1 & -1 \\ +1 & +1 & +1 & -1 & -1 & -1 \\ +1 & -1 & +1 & +1 & -1 & -1 \\ +1 & +1 & -1 & -1 & 0 & 0 \\ 0 & 0 & +1 & +1 & -1 & -1 \end{pmatrix} \begin{pmatrix} N_1 \\ N_2 \\ N_3 \\ \vdots \\ N_6 \end{pmatrix} = \begin{pmatrix} y_{12} \\ y_{13} \\ y_{23} \\ z_1 \\ z_2 \end{pmatrix}. \tag{11}$$

By the construction of the fourth and fifth rows of M', component z_1 on the right-hand side of (11) will be positive if and only if alternative 1 receives more plurality votes than alternative 2, and component z_2 will be positive if and only if alternative 2 receives more plurality votes than alternative 3. The 5×5 matrix made up of the first five columns of M' is nonsingular, as one can check with any microcomputer spreadsheet. (Check.) So, M' has rank five. One can repeat the earlier process of looking for all sign patterns of the y_{ij}'s but now keep z_1 and z_2 positive and thus achieve any combination of rankings of the three pairs of alternatives, while keeping the overall plurality ranking at $1 > 2 > 3$.

Four Alternatives

This argument works for any number of alternatives, but the size of the matrices one must consider increases rapidly. For example, for $n = 4$ there are $4! = 24$ different rankings of the four alternatives and six different pairs of alternatives. To show that any prescribed ordering of each of the pairs can occur, as we did for $n = 3$, we construct the 6×24 matrix analogous to M in (6). To conserve space, we write just six columns of that matrix:

$$\begin{array}{c} \\ A_{12} \\ A_{13} \\ A_{14} \\ A_{23} \\ A_{24} \\ A_{34} \end{array} \begin{array}{cccccc} 1234 & 1243 & 1423 & 1432 & 4132 & 4321 \\ \left(\begin{array}{cccccc} +1 & +1 & +1 & +1 & +1 & +1 \\ +1 & +1 & +1 & +1 & +1 & -1 \\ +1 & +1 & +1 & +1 & -1 & -1 \\ +1 & +1 & +1 & -1 & -1 & -1 \\ +1 & +1 & -1 & -1 & -1 & -1 \\ +1 & -1 & -1 & -1 & -1 & -1 \end{array}\right) \end{array} \tag{12}$$

If we add the first row to every other row in matrix (12), we obtain the matrix

$$
\begin{pmatrix}
+1 & +1 & +1 & +1 & +1 & +1 \\
+2 & +2 & +2 & +2 & +2 & 0 \\
+2 & +2 & +2 & +2 & 0 & 0 \\
+2 & +2 & +2 & 0 & 0 & 0 \\
+2 & +2 & 0 & 0 & 0 & 0 \\
+2 & 0 & 0 & 0 & 0 & 0
\end{pmatrix},
$$

which has six linearly independent columns by Lemma 27.2. Therefore, the matrix in (12) has rank six and so does the 6×24 matrix that corresponds to M. It follows that in the system

$$
M \begin{pmatrix} N_1 \\ \vdots \\ N_{24} \end{pmatrix} = \begin{pmatrix} y_{12} \\ \vdots \\ y_{34} \end{pmatrix}, \tag{13}
$$

we can find a profile $\mathbf{N}$ that achieves any right-hand side. As we did for $n = 3$, we can add a multiple of $(1, 1, \ldots, 1)$ to $\mathbf{N}$ to make sure the N_i's in this profile are all positive; then, we can also perturb the N_i's to be rational numbers and multiply through by their common denominator to take care of the concern that the N_i's be integers.

Finally, we can add three rows to the bottom of the 6×24 matrix to construct a 9×24 matrix of rank nine that guarantees that we can still achieve any combination of rankings of each of the pairs of alternatives, while keeping the same aggregate plurality ranking, such as $1 > 2 > 3 > 4$. This process is analogous to the formation of matrix M' in (10) from matrix M in (6) for $n = 3$.

Consequences of the Existence of Cycles

In the 4-alternative setting, we can find profiles of the voters with the property that the aggregate plurality ranking is $1 > 2 > 3 > 4$, but the aggregate rankings of the alternatives in each pair include the rankings

$$
1 > 2, \quad 2 > 3, \quad 3 > 4, \quad \text{and} \quad 4 > 1, \tag{14}
$$

an aggregate ranking called a **cycle**. The existence of such cycles has some interesting consequences. First, some social scientists argue that the Condorcet winner is the most reasonable method of choosing a winner from a list of n alternatives. An alternative is called a **Condorcet winner** if it receives a majority vote when compared with *each* of the other alternatives. The existence of cycles shows that there are many profiles without any Condorcet winner.

Another commonly used binary ranking is an agenda. An **agenda** is an ordered listing of the n alternatives. The electorate first chooses one of the first two listed alternatives. The losing alternative is eliminated from future voting and the winning alternative is then compared with the third listed alternative. This iterative, pairwise comparison is continued to the end of the listing. The alternative that wins the last pairwise comparison is the election winner. However, if there is a cycle as in (14), which alternative wins will depend on the order in which the alternatives are initially listed. If they are listed as $4 - 3 - 2 - 1$, then alternative 1 will win; if they are listed as $1 - 4 - 3 - 2$, alternative 2 will win, and so on. In this situation, the person who sets the agenda determines the winner.

Other Voting Paradoxes

As we saw in the last paragraph, if there is a cycle in the profile under consideration, the person who sets the agenda controls the election. D. G. Saari uses linear algebra techniques to provide some other dramatic examples of how the choice of voting method can determine the winner of an election. We will present an example here. Consider a profile of 15 voters choosing among three alternatives, in which 6 of the voters have ranking $1 > 3 > 2$, 5 have ranking $2 > 3 > 1$, and 4 have ranking $3 > 2 > 1$. The plurality ranking is $1 > 2 > 3$.

On the other hand, suppose the electorate uses the Borda count instead of the plurality system. In the **Borda count** among n alternatives, the highest-ranking alternative of each voter gets n points, the next-ranking alternative gets $n - 1$ points and the lowest ranking gets 1 point; in the aggregate, the alternatives are ranked by the total number of points each receives from the electorate. This is the method that writers and coaches use to rank college sports teams or to choose most-valuable players, frequently for large values of n. If the electorate uses the Borda count for the profile under consideration, alternative 1 receives 27 points, alternative 2 receives 29 points, and alternative 3 receives 34 points; the aggregate ranking is $3 > 2 > 1$, just the *opposite* of the plurality ranking. (Check.)

Finally, consider a third weighted voting mechanism in which each voter's first choice receives 6 points, second choice receives 1 point, and third choice receives no points. Under this system, for the profile under consideration, alternative 1 receives 36 points, alternative 2 receives 34 points and alternative 3 receives 35 points. (Check.) The profile's aggregate ranking under this system is $1 > 3 > 2$.

The profile under consideration has three different aggregate rankings depending on the voting mechanism used. D. G. Saari constructs a profile in an election that has 10 alternatives with the property that, by assigning different weights to the various slots in each voter's ranking, over 84 million different aggregate rankings can occur. Certainly, the voting system used can have a major impact in determining the winner of an election.

Rankings of the Quality of Firms

The observations in this section about voting paradoxes can easily be modified to describe phenomena in other ranking procedures. For example, suppose n firms that make the same product are ranked according to the quality of that product. Write $q_i > q_j$ if firm i's product appears to be superior to firm j's based on the samples tested. By the observations in this section, binary procedures need not lead to a linear ranking of the quality of the firms. For example, as we have seen, cycles can easily occur: $q_1 > q_2$, $q_2 > q_3$, $q_3 > q_1$. The existence of a cycle in this situation is sometimes called the **Steinhaus-Trybula paradox**.

EXERCISES

28.2 Carry out the checks suggested in the calculations in this section.

28.3 What is the size of the matrix M, corresponding to (6), for a ballot with 10 alternatives? With n alternatives? Special methods need to be used to compute the rank of matrices this large; the straightforward methods we have been using to compute the rank no longer apply.

28.4 When there are three alternatives, there are three pairs of alternatives and $2^3 = 8$ possible aggregate pairwise rankings. Present concrete profiles that yield each of these eight aggregate pairwise rankings.

28.5 Write out a careful proof of Theorem 28.2 for $n = 4$.

28.6 The Borda count is an example of a weighted or **positional voting method** in which a voter's ith highest-ranked alternative receives w_i points for $i = 1, \ldots, n$. Of course, we require $w_i \geq w_j$ if $i < j$. In this case, the vector $\mathbf{w} = (w_1, \ldots, w_n)$ is called a **voting vector**.

 a) Show that the plurality system can be considered a positional voting method.

 b) Show that if $\mathbf{w}$ is a voting vector, then for any positive scalars a and b, $a\mathbf{w} + b(1, \ldots, 1)$ is a voting vector that gives the same aggregate rankings as $\mathbf{w}$.

 c) Conclude that given any voting vector $\mathbf{w}$, there is a voting vector $\mathbf{v}$ that gives the same aggregate rankings as $\mathbf{w}$ and satisfies $v_n = 0$ and $\sum_i v_i = 1$.

28.4 ACTIVITY ANALYSIS: FEASIBILITY

Activity Analysis

We return now to the discussion of linear production models started in Example 2 of Section 6.2 and continued in Section 8.5. We begin by looking at a more general class of production models than the input-output models discussed earlier, namely, **activity analysis models**.

Consider an economy with N goods. Suppose that there are a finite number of production processes, called **activities**. Each activity can be run at any scale, and the inputs used and the outputs produced vary proportionately with the scale or level x at which the activity is run. Each activity is described by fixed ratios of inputs to outputs.

Definition   An **activity** is a vector $\mathbf{v} = (v_1, \ldots, v_N)$, with a component for each commodity. For a nonnegative scalar x, running activity $\mathbf{v}$ at intensity x, produces xv_j units of good j if $xv_j > 0$ and uses xv_k units of good k as inputs if $xv_k < 0$. A **linear production model** is a set of activities $\mathbf{v}^1, \ldots, \mathbf{v}^M$. The $N \times M$ matrix $V = [\mathbf{v}^1 \ \mathbf{v}^2 \ \cdots \ \mathbf{v}^M]$, whose columns are these M activity vectors, is called a **production matrix**. A **production schedule** is a vector $\mathbf{x} = (x^1, \ldots, x^M)$ of nonnegative intensities, one for each activity. Given production matrix V and production schedule $\mathbf{x}$, the net production of good j is

$$y_j = v_j^1 x^1 + \cdots + v_j^M x^M,$$

the jth component of the **net production vector** $\mathbf{y} = V\mathbf{x}$. Good j is a **net input** if this sum is negative and a **net output** if this sum is positive.

   The most basic questions about production processes involve characterizing which net production vectors are feasible and which are efficient. Feasible net production vectors are those combinations of the net inputs and net outputs which can be produced by running the production activity at nonnegative intensities. We will discuss efficient production processes in the next section.

Definition   A vector $\mathbf{y}$ is **feasible** if there exists vector $\mathbf{x} \geq \mathbf{0}$ such that $\mathbf{y} = V\mathbf{x}$. Inputs, like fuels and labor, that are supplied exogenously to the production process are called **primary factors**. If good j is a primary factor and if a_j represents the initial stock of good j, we also require that $y_j \geq -a_j$ for a vector $\mathbf{y}$ to be feasible.

   In order to determine which net production vectors are feasible and which are efficient, we need first to describe how the production processes interact. The first important fact in this direction is that in order to produce any particular feasible net production vector, no more than N activities need be employed, where N is the number of commodities.

Theorem 28.3   Let V be the $N \times M$ matrix of activity vectors. If $\mathbf{y} = V\mathbf{x}$ for some nonnegative vector $\mathbf{x}$, then $\mathbf{y} = V\mathbf{x}'$ where $\mathbf{x}'$ is a nonnegative vector with at most N nonzero entries.

   We already know Theorem 28.3 is true if we disregard the nonnegativity constraint on $\mathbf{x}$, because any net production vector is in the column space of V and, therefore, can be written as a linear combination of any basis for the column space. (Theorem 27.5) Since the rank of V (the dimension of the column space) is $\leq N$, at most N of the M activity vectors form a basis of the column space of V. At issue in Theorem 28.3 is whether or not any net production vector can be written as a *nonnegative* linear combination of some basis vectors of Col(V). The following theorem is a restatement of Theorem 28.3 in the general setting of this chapter.

Theorem 28.4   Suppose $\mathbf{y}$ is a nonnegative combination of $\mathbf{v}_1, \ldots, \mathbf{v}_k$.

(a) If $\mathbf{v}_1, \ldots, \mathbf{v}_k$ are linearly dependent, then $\mathbf{y}$ can be written as a nonnegative combination of a *proper subset* of $\mathbf{v}_1, \ldots, \mathbf{v}_k$;

(b) If $\mathbf{y}$ can be written as a nonnegative combination of $\mathbf{v}_1, \ldots, \mathbf{v}_k$ in $\mathbf{R}^N$ and $k > N$, then $\mathbf{y}$ can be written as a nonnegative combination of at most N of the vectors $\mathbf{v}_1, \ldots, \mathbf{v}_k$.

Proof

(a) Suppose that $\mathbf{y} = \alpha_1 \mathbf{v}_1 + \cdots + \alpha_k \mathbf{v}_k$, where the α_i's are nonnegative. If some $\alpha_i = 0$, we can ignore $\mathbf{v}_i$ and we are done. So, we can assume that $\alpha_1, \ldots, \alpha_k$ are all strictly positive. Suppose that $\mathbf{v}_1, \ldots, \mathbf{v}_k$ are linearly dependent, that is, that $\beta_1 \mathbf{v}_1 + \cdots + \beta_k \mathbf{v}_k = \mathbf{0}$, where some β_i's are nonzero. By multiplying this equation through by -1 if necessary, we can assume that $\sum \beta_i \geq 0$ and therefore that some β_i's are positive. Let

$$\theta = \min \left\{ \frac{\alpha_j}{\beta_j} : j \text{ such that } \beta_j > 0 \right\}.$$

Then, $\alpha_j - \theta \beta_j \geq 0$ for all j and equals zero for some j. Since

$$\sum_{j=1}^{k} (\alpha_j - \theta \beta_j) \mathbf{v}_j = \sum_{1}^{k} \alpha_j \mathbf{v}_j - \theta \sum_{1}^{k} \beta_j \mathbf{v}_j = \mathbf{y} - \mathbf{0} = \mathbf{y}, \tag{15}$$

we can write $\mathbf{y}$ as a nonnegative combination of a proper subset of $\mathbf{v}_1, \ldots, \mathbf{v}_k$.

(b) Part *b* follows from part *a* and the fact that every set of $N + 1$ vectors in $\mathbf{R}^N$ is linearly dependent (Theorem 11.3). ■

Simple Linear Models and Productive Matrices

We now add more structure to our activity analysis model to bring it closer to the input-output models discussed in Sections 6.2 and 8.5. Consider the following three assumptions.

Assumption 1   Each activity produces only one output.

Assumption 2   Each commodity is an output of only one activity.

Assumption 3   There are no primary factors.

The linear production model that satisfies these three assumptions is sometimes known as the **simple linear model**. It contrasts with the **general linear model**, in which Assumption 2 does not hold, and with the various Leontief models which have primary factors. The simple linear model is a production model without resource constraints. Its interest lies first in the fact that it is a model of interconnected productive activities, and second in that its analysis is a necessary prelude to the analysis of Leontief models which do have resource constraints.

By Assumptions 1 and 2, simple linear models have the same number of activities as commodities. In a simple linear model with N commodities, order the N activities so that commodity j is the output of activity j, for $j = 1, \ldots, N$. Then, scale the activity vectors so that the positive term of each is 1. With these conventions, the diagonal entries of the production matrix V are 1s and the off-diagonal entries are all ≤ 0. Write V as

$$V = I - A,$$

where A is a traditional input-output matrix with nonnegative entries.

In a simple linear model, a net production vector $\mathbf{y}$ is feasible if there is a nonnegative $\mathbf{x}$ such that $\mathbf{y} = (I - A)\mathbf{x}$. However, not all production technologies are economically viable. Suppose that it takes two units of steel to make a car, and two cars to make a unit of steel. Clearly it will be impossible to run both production activities so as to produce positive net outputs of both cars and steel. We would like our technology to allow the production of at least one strictly positive net output vector.

Definition   The input-output matrix A of a simple linear production model is **productive** if the inequality

$$(I - A)\mathbf{x} > \mathbf{0} \tag{16}$$

has a nonnegative solution $\mathbf{x}$. (We take the inequality to mean that each component of $\mathbf{x}$ exceeds the corresponding component of $A\mathbf{x}$.)

The key property of simple linear models is that the ability to produce one strictly positive output guarantees the ability to produce *any* strictly positive output. (Lest this seem too absurd, remember that we have assumed no resource constraints on the availability of primary factors.)

Theorem 28.5   If A is productive, then for *all* $\mathbf{y} \geq 0$ the equation

$$(I - A)\mathbf{x} = \mathbf{y}$$

has a unique nonnegative solution.

The proof of Theorem 28.5 depends on the following lemmas.

Lemma 28.1   If A is productive and $(I - A)\mathbf{z} \geq \mathbf{0}$, then $\mathbf{z} \geq \mathbf{0}$.

Proof   Suppose $(I - A)\mathbf{z} \geq \mathbf{0}$; that is, $\mathbf{z} \geq A\mathbf{z}$. Let $\mathbf{x} \geq \mathbf{0}$ be such that $\mathbf{x} > A\mathbf{x}$, as in the definition (16) of a productive matrix. Then for all scalars $\alpha > 0$,

$$A(\mathbf{x} + \alpha\mathbf{z}) = A\mathbf{x} + \alpha A\mathbf{z}$$
$$< \mathbf{x} + \alpha\mathbf{z}. \tag{17}$$

Suppose some component of $\mathbf{z}$ is negative. Without loss of generality, we will assume that $z_1 < 0$ and that

$$\frac{x_1}{z_1} \leq \frac{x_i}{z_i} \quad \text{for all } i. \tag{18}$$

Let $\alpha^* = -x_1/z_1 > 0$, so that the first component of $\mathbf{x} + \alpha^*\mathbf{z}$ equals 0, while the rest are ≥ 0 by (18). Then,

$$A(\mathbf{x} + \alpha^*\mathbf{z}) \geq \mathbf{0}$$

since every entry of A and of $(\mathbf{x} + \alpha^*\mathbf{z})$ is nonnegative. Since the first component of $(\mathbf{x} + \alpha^*\mathbf{z})$ is 0, we have from (17) that the first component of $A(\mathbf{x} + \alpha^*\mathbf{z}) < 0$; this is a contradiction. We conclude that $\mathbf{z} \geq \mathbf{0}$. ∎

Lemma 28.2 $I - A$ is nonsingular.

Proof   Suppose that $(I - A)\mathbf{x} = \mathbf{0}$. Then, $(I - A)\mathbf{x} \geq \mathbf{0}$ and $(I - A)(-\mathbf{x}) \geq \mathbf{0}$. By Lemma 28.1, $\mathbf{x} \geq \mathbf{0}$ and $-\mathbf{x} \geq \mathbf{0}$, so $\mathbf{x} = \mathbf{0}$. ∎

Proof of Theorem 28.5   For any $\mathbf{y} \geq \mathbf{0}$, the system $(I - A)\mathbf{x} = \mathbf{y}$ has a unique solution $\mathbf{x}$ since $I - A$ has full rank by Lemma 28.2. Since $\mathbf{y} \geq \mathbf{0}$, $\mathbf{x} \geq \mathbf{0}$ by Lemma 28.1. ∎

Theorem 28.6   Square matrix A is productive if and only if $(I - A)^{-1}$ exists and is nonnegative.

Proof   Suppose that $(I - A)^{-1}$ is nonnegative. Let $\mathbf{1}$ denote the vector of all 1s. Then, $\mathbf{x} = (I - A)^{-1}\mathbf{1}$ is nonnegative, and $\mathbf{x} - A\mathbf{x} \gg \mathbf{0}$, so A is productive.
   On the other hand, if A is productive, $I - A$ has an inverse by Lemma 28.2. Let $\mathbf{x}$ be the vector of activity levels which produces $\mathbf{e}_i$, the ith element in the standard unit basis for $\mathbf{R}^N$. By the proof of Theorem 8.7, $\mathbf{x}$ is the ith column of $(I - A)^{-1}$, and from Theorem 28.5 we know that $\mathbf{x} \geq \mathbf{0}$. ∎

28.5 ACTIVITY ANALYSIS: EFFICIENCY

Leontief Models

The simple open *Leontief* models are the linear production models that satisfy Assumptions 1 and 2 and have one primary factor (usually called "labor") which is a net output for no production activity and an input to every process. The *general open Leontief models* are like the simple open Leontief models except that there may be any number of activities, not just one per net output. The following assumptions will help us formalize these distinctions.

Assumption 4 There are $N + 1$ commodities. Commodity $N + 1$, which we call "labor," is a primary input that is required by every activity.

Assumption 5 No "produced commodity" is a primary factor.

Definition A linear production model that satisfies Assumptions 1, 4, and 5 is called a **general open Leontief model**. One that also satisfies Assumption 2 is called a **simple open Leontief model**.

We conclude this section by characterizing the efficient production vectors in the general open Leontief model. By a commodity bundle, we now mean a vector in $\mathbf{R}^N$ that describes the outputs of the produced commodities, that is, that excludes only labor.

Definition The net production vector $\mathbf{y}$ is **efficient** if $\mathbf{y}$ is feasible and if for any vector $\mathbf{z}$ such that $\mathbf{z} \geq \mathbf{y}$, either $\mathbf{z} = \mathbf{y}$ or $\mathbf{z}$ is not feasible.

Verify that efficient net production vectors are those net production vectors that cannot be improved on in the sense that it is not possible to produce more outputs from fewer inputs.

Theorem 28.7 Consider a general open Leontief model with N produced commodities and M activities, $M \geq N$. Suppose that there is a commodity bundle $\mathbf{y}^*$ that is efficient and strictly positive (all $y_i^* > 0$). Let $\mathcal{E}$ denote the set of all efficient commodity bundles. Then,

(a) there are N activities $\mathbf{v}_{i_1}, \ldots, \mathbf{v}_{i_N}$ so that every $\mathbf{z} \in \mathcal{E}$ can be produced using only $\mathbf{v}_{i_1}, \ldots, \mathbf{v}_{i_N}$; and

(b) $\mathcal{E}$ is the intersection of $\mathbf{R}_+^N$ with a hyperplane that has a strictly positive normal vector; that is, there exists a strictly positive N-vector $\mathbf{a}$ and a positive scalar k such that

$$\mathcal{E} = \{\mathbf{x} \in \mathbf{R}^N : \mathbf{x} \geq \mathbf{0} \text{ and } \mathbf{a} \cdot \mathbf{x} = k\}.$$

For the case of three produced commodities, a typical efficient set is drawn in Figure 28.4.

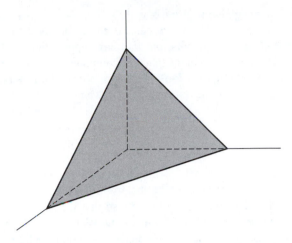

**Figure
28.4**

The efficient set in a three-commodity general Leontief model.

This result is sometimes referred to as the **Nonsubstitution Theorem**; it states, among other things, that N activities can be chosen such that using only these N activities, any efficient commodity bundle can be produced. Thus, compared to the simple Leontief model, the generality of the general Leontief model is suspect, since there is no gain in efficiency to having an excess of activities over produced commodities.

Proof   We break down the proof of Theorem 28.7 into seven steps.

(1) Choose units for labor such that the supply of labor in the economy is 1. Scale each production activity so that one unit of labor input is required if the activity is run at level 1, and then choose units of measurement for produced goods so that each activity produces one unit of output. Finally, let V denote the $N \times M$ matrix whose mth column is composed of the first N components of the mth activity. In other words, V is the matrix whose columns are activities with the labor inputs lopped off. The set of feasible net output combinations is

$$\left\{ \mathbf{y} : \mathbf{y} = V\mathbf{x}, \ \mathbf{x} \geq \mathbf{0} \ \text{and} \ \sum_{i=1}^{M} x_i = 1 \right\}.$$

Let V' denote the matrix V with a row of 1s added to the bottom. Each column of V' is a complete description, including the labor input, of an activity.

(2) Since $\mathbf{y}^*$ is feasible, the equation

$$V\mathbf{x} = \mathbf{y}^*$$

has a nonnegative solution $\mathbf{x}$ with $\sum_{i=1}^{M} x_i = 1$. It is tempting to infer from Theorem 28.3 that $\mathbf{x}$ can be chosen to have no more than N nonnegative components, but the naive application of Theorem 28.3 neglects the requirement that the components of the solution vector must sum to 1. Let us look more carefully at the proofs of Theorems 28.3 and 28.4. In the notation of (15), we must have

$$\sum_{j=1}^{M} (\alpha_j - \theta\beta_j) \geq 1, \tag{19}$$

because if $\sum (\alpha_j - \theta\beta_j) = \lambda < 1$, the new solution (15) to $V\mathbf{x} = \mathbf{y}$ requires less labor input than the original solution $\mathbf{y}^* = \sum_j \alpha_j \mathbf{v}_j$. If we scale the new solution up by $1/\lambda$ so that we use exactly one unit of labor, we achieve a feasible net output vector $(1/\lambda)\mathbf{y}^*$ with $1/\lambda > 1$. In this case, $\mathbf{y}^*$ would not be efficient — a contradiction.

If we rewrite (19) and apply the fact that $\sum_j \alpha_j = 1$, we conclude that $\sum_j \beta_j \leq 0$. Since we already had $\sum \beta_j \geq 0$ in the proof of Theorem 28.4, we conclude that $\sum_j \beta_j = 0$. Recompute (19) using this fact to deduce that

$$\sum_{j=1}^{M} (\alpha_j - \theta\beta_j) = 1.$$

Therefore, the new solution to $\mathbf{y}^* = V\mathbf{x}$ uses the same amount of labor as the original solution. Hence the argument of the proof of Theorem 28.3 works, and we conclude that only N activities, one for each industry, are required to produce $\mathbf{y}^*$.

(3) Let W denote the submatrix of the matrix V whose columns are the N activities (without the labor input) required to produce $\mathbf{y}^*$, and write $W = I - A$. Then, A is a conventional Leontief input-output matrix. Since $\mathbf{y}^* \gg 0$ can be produced from the activities in A, A is productive.

(4) Now we characterize the efficient points of the general model in terms of the input-output matrix A. Consider the set

$$T \equiv \left\{ \mathbf{z} \in \mathbf{R}^N : \mathbf{z} = A\mathbf{x}, \text{ for some } \mathbf{x} \geq \mathbf{0} \text{ with } \sum_{i=1}^{N} x_i = 1 \right\}.$$

Every net output vector in T is feasible, since it represents a nonnegative combination of activities employing exactly one unit of labor.

(5) We show that every efficient net output vector is in T.

Suppose $\mathbf{z} \in \mathbf{R}^N$ is efficient. Since A is productive, we know from Theorem 28.5 that $(I - A)\mathbf{x} = \mathbf{z}$ has a nonnegative solution $\mathbf{x}'$. Thus, $\sum_{i=1}^{N} x_i' > 0$. Let $t = 1/\sum_{i=1}^{N} x_i'$. Then,

$$(I - A)t\mathbf{x}' = t\mathbf{z} \quad \text{and} \quad \sum_{i=1}^{N} t x_i' = 1;$$

so $t\mathbf{z}$ can be feasibly produced from the N activities used to produce $\mathbf{y}^*$: $t\mathbf{z} \in T$. Since $t\mathbf{z}$ is feasible and $\mathbf{z}$ is efficient, it must be the case that $0 < t \leq 1$. We will show that t must equal 1.

First, observe that there is a $\mathbf{w}$ in T such that

$$\alpha\mathbf{w} + (1 - \alpha)t\mathbf{z} = \mathbf{y}^* \quad \text{for some } 0 < \alpha < 1.$$

To see this, suppose that $(I - A)\mathbf{x} = \mathbf{y}^*$. Since $\mathbf{y}^*$ is strictly positive, so is $\mathbf{x}$. Now let $\mathbf{x}'' = \beta t\mathbf{x}' + (1 - \beta)\mathbf{x}$ for β negative but sufficiently near 0 that $\mathbf{x}''$ is nonnegative. Let $\mathbf{w} = (I - A)\mathbf{x}''$. Then, $\mathbf{y}^* = \alpha\mathbf{w} + (1 - \alpha)t\mathbf{z}$, where $\alpha = -\beta/(1 - \beta)$. Now consider the net output vector $\mathbf{y}' = \alpha\mathbf{w} + (1 - \alpha)\mathbf{z}$. This net output vector is feasible (check), and $\mathbf{y}' = \mathbf{y}^* + (1 - \alpha)(1 - t)\mathbf{z}$. Now, $\mathbf{y}' \geq \mathbf{y}^*$. If $t < 1$, then $\mathbf{y}' \neq \mathbf{y}^*$. So, if $t < 1$, $\mathbf{y}^*$ is not efficient; this is a contradiction.

(6) Every net output vector in T is efficient. Suppose $\mathbf{z}$ is not efficient. Then, there is an efficient $\mathbf{z}' \geq \mathbf{z}$ with $\mathbf{z}' \neq \mathbf{z}$. Suppose that $\mathbf{z}' = (I - A)\mathbf{x}'$ and $\mathbf{z} = (I - A)\mathbf{x}$. Then, $(I - A)(\mathbf{x}' - \mathbf{x}) \geq \mathbf{0}$. Since A is productive, it follows from Theorem 28.5 that $\mathbf{x}' - \mathbf{x} \geq \mathbf{0}$. Since $\mathbf{z}' \neq \mathbf{z}$, $\mathbf{x}' \neq \mathbf{x}$, and so $\sum_{j=1}^{N} x_j < \sum_{j=1}^{N} x_j' = 1$, and $\mathbf{z}$ cannot be in T.

(7) We have seen that the set of efficient net output vectors is precisely T. The set T is clearly an affine subspace. Since $I - A$ is nonsingular, T has dimension $N - 1$. Thus, T is a hyperplane. Let $\mathbf{1}$ denote the vector in $\mathbf{R}^N$ with each component equal to 1. For any $\mathbf{y}$ in T, there is an $\mathbf{x} \geq \mathbf{0}$ whose components sum to 1 such that $(I - A)\mathbf{x} = \mathbf{y}$. Since $I - A$ is nonsingular, $\mathbf{x} = (I - A)^{-1}\mathbf{y}$. The hyperplane T is defined by

$$1 = \mathbf{1} \cdot \mathbf{x} = \mathbf{1}^T(I - A)^{-1}\mathbf{y}.$$

From Theorem 28.5, $(I - A)^{-1}$ is a positive matrix, and so $\mathbf{a}^T = \mathbf{1}^T(I - A)^{-1}$ is nonnegative. ∎

NOTES

Section 28.3 on voting paradoxes is based on the papers of D. G. Saari on this topic. See, for example, D. G. Saari, "The source of some paradoxes from social choice and probability," *Journal of Economic Theory* 41 (1987), 1–22. For a profile of an election with 10 profiles and over 84 million different aggregate rankings, see D. G. Saari, "Millions of election outcomes from a single profile," Northwestern University preprint (1991).

The main source for activity analysis is the book Tjalling C. Koopmans (ed.), *Activity Analysis of Production and Allocation* (New York: Wiley, 1951). Our proof of Theorem 28.7 comes from the chapter in this volume by Kenneth Arrow.

PART VII

Advanced Analysis

Limits and Compact Sets

This chapter continues the discussion about sequences, limits, and open, closed, and compact sets that was started in Chapter 12. These are the main ideas that quantify the notions of nearness, small change, trends, and convergent behavior. In particular, this chapter covers Cauchy sequences, compact sets, connected sets, and alternative norms for Euclidean space. Section 29.1 focuses on the Cauchy convergence of sequences — a way of handling convergence without reference to a limit point. In the process it presents some properties of sequences that are important in economic analysis. Section 29.2 continues Chapter 12's discussion about compact sets. Recall that compact sets have two properties that give them an important role in economic theory: 1) every sequence in a compact set has a subsequence that converges, and 2) every continuous function whose domain is a compact set achieves its maximum value and its minimum value on its compact domain. Most economics theorems that assure the existence of an economic equilibrium rely on these two results.

Section 29.3 discusses another common hypothesis in economic theory: the connectedness of a set. Section 29.4 is an introduction to other notions of distance than Euclidean distance. In some economic settings, a different measure of distance than Euclidean distance can make it much easier to derive or understand some economic principles.

29.1 CAUCHY SEQUENCES

So far, the only way we can tell whether or not a sequence converges is to actually identify a limit for it. For some sequences, testing all the real numbers to search for a limit is an exhausting procedure. In addition, we will sometimes want to prove that abstract sequences with certain special properties converge to some limit without being able to specify what that limit is. Fortunately, we can capture the concept of convergence without actually finding a limit. The idea is a simple one. If the elements of a sequence are getting arbitrarily close to some limit, they are also getting arbitrarily close to each other. The following definition makes this idea precise.

Definition   A sequence $\{\mathbf{x}_n\}_{n=1}^{\infty}$ is a **Cauchy sequence** if for any positive number ε, there is an integer N such that, for all $i, j \geq N$, $\mathrm{d}(\mathbf{x}_i, \mathbf{x}_j) < \varepsilon$.

In other words, a sequence is Cauchy if, given any small positive number ε, from some point on $(i, j \geq N)$ the entries of the sequence are all within ε of each other. It is relatively easy to prove that convergent sequences are Cauchy. It is a bit more difficult to prove the more useful fact that all Cauchy sequences in $\mathbf{R}^m$ are convergent.[1]

Theorem 29.1   Any convergent sequence in $\mathbf{R}^m$ is Cauchy.

Proof   Suppose that $\{\mathbf{x}_n\}_{n=1}^{\infty}$ converges to $\mathbf{x}$. Given $\varepsilon > 0$, choose N such that $d(\mathbf{x}_n, \mathbf{x}) < \varepsilon/2$ for all $n \geq N$. Then for $n, m \geq N$,

$$d(\mathbf{x}_n, \mathbf{x}_m) \leq d(\mathbf{x}_n, \mathbf{x}) + d(\mathbf{x}_m, \mathbf{x}) < \frac{\varepsilon}{2} + \frac{\varepsilon}{2} = \varepsilon,$$

using the triangle inequality (12.4). ∎

The remainder of this section will be devoted to proving the converse of Theorem 29.1. Along the way, we will prove some properties about sequences that are important in their own right. Since the convergence of a sequence of vectors is characterized by the convergence of the sequences of its scalar components (Theorem 12.5), we can work without loss of generality with sequences of real numbers.

We will need one important property of real numbers — the least upper bound property. Axiomatic treatments of the real number system usually take this property as one of the defining characteristics of the real number system.

Definition   Let S be a subset of $\mathbf{R}^1$. Then, the set S has an **upper bound** if there is a number B such that each x in S is less than B, that is, $x \leq B$ for all $x \in S$. The **least upper bound** or **supremum** for such a set of numbers S is the number C which is an upper bound for S and such that $C \leq B$ for any upper bound B of S. Any set of real numbers that has an upper bound has a least upper bound. Similar statements apply to sets bounded from below. They have **greatest lower bounds** or **infima**. The least upper (greatest lower) bound of a set S need not be a member of the set S. A set bounded both above and below is said to be **bounded**.

We need one more definition.

Definition   A sequence $\{x_n\}_{n=1}^{\infty}$ of real numbers is **monotone increasing** if each entry in the sequence is at least as big as the previous entry, that is, if $x_{n-1} \leq x_n$ for all n. It is **monotone decreasing** if $x_n \leq x_{n-1}$ for all n. It is **monotone** if it is either monotone increasing or monotone decreasing. Such a sequence is **strictly monotone increasing (decreasing)** if $x_{n-1} < x_n$ ($x_n < x_{n-1}$) for all n.

---

[1] Augustin Cauchy was a French mathematician active throughout the first half of the nineteenth century.

Bounded monotone sequences have one important asymptotic property: they always converge.

Theorem 29.2   Every bounded monotone sequence converges.

Proof   We shall prove this theorem for increasing sequences. The proof for decreasing sequences is similar, and is left as an exercise.

Let $\{x_n\}_{n=1}^{\infty}$ be a bounded, monotone increasing sequence. Then it has a least upper bound b. We claim that b is the limit of the sequence. Suppose b is not the limit of this sequence. Then elements of the sequence do not stay arbitrarily close to b. More formally, there exists an ε such that $|x_n - b| \geq \varepsilon$ for infinitely many x_n's in the sequence. Now, $|x_n - b| \geq \varepsilon$ means that $x_n \geq b + \varepsilon$ or $x_n \leq b - \varepsilon$. Since b is an upper bound for the sequence, the first of these cannot occur; therefore, $x_n \leq b - \varepsilon$ for infinitely many x_n's.

Next, we show that *all* the x_n's must be $\leq b - \varepsilon$. Suppose that some x_M is $> b - \varepsilon$. Since the sequence is increasing, all the x_n's for $n \geq M$ must lie above $b - \varepsilon$. But this would contradict the statement at the end of the previous paragraph that infinitely many x_n's are $\leq b - \varepsilon$. Thus, the statement that b is not the limit of the sequence implies that for some positive ε, $x_n \leq b - \varepsilon$ for all n. As a result, $b - \varepsilon$ would then be an upper bound for this sequence — a contradiction to our hypothesis that b is the least upper bound.   ∎

Before proving the main result of this section — that every Cauchy sequence converges — we need a couple of preliminary results about Cauchy sequences of real numbers and their subsequences.

Lemma 29.1   Every Cauchy sequence in $\mathbf{R}^1$ is bounded.

Proof   Let $\{x_n\}_{n=1}^{\infty}$ be a Cauchy sequence in $\mathbf{R}^1$. Fix a positive number ε. There is an N such that $|x_i - x_j| < \varepsilon$ for all $i, j \geq N$. In particular, $|x_N - x_i| < \varepsilon$ for all $i \geq N$. Since

$$|x_i| - |x_N| \leq |x_i - x_N| \qquad\qquad \text{by (12.3),}$$

then, $|x_i| \leq |x_N| + \varepsilon \qquad \text{for all } i \geq N,$

and $|x_N| + \varepsilon$ is a bound for all but the first $N - 1$ terms of the sequence. Let $b = \max\{|x_1|, \dots, |x_{N-1}|, |x_N|\}$. It follows that $|x_i| \leq b + \varepsilon$ for all x_i in the sequence.   ∎

Lemma 29.2   Every sequence has a monotone subsequence.

Proof   Let $\{x_n\}$ be a sequence of real numbers. We want to show that it contains a monotone increasing subsequence or a monotone decreasing subsequence. Suppose that it contains no monotone *increasing* subsequence. Starting with any x_i, choose an x_j with $j > i$ and $x_j \geq x_i$; then choose an x_k with $k > j$ and $x_k \geq x_j$; and so on. Since there is no monotone increasing subsequence, this process must end after a finite number of steps. The last chosen point, say x_l, has the property that it is greater than all subsequent elements of the sequence. For the sake of this proof, call such elements of the sequence *dominant elements*. We have just shown that, starting from any point of the sequence, we can find a dominant element. Thus, we can find an infinite subsequence of dominant elements. This sequence of dominant elements must be strictly decreasing, since each dominant element is strictly larger than all subsequent elements of the sequence, including subsequent dominant elements. Thus, a sequence which has no increasing subsequence must have a decreasing subsequence. ∎

Lemma 29.3   If a Cauchy sequence $\{x_n\}_{n=1}^{\infty}$ has a subsequence converging to y, then the whole sequence converges to y.

Proof   Choose and fix an $\varepsilon > 0$. Since the sequence is Cauchy, there is an N such that $|x_i - x_j| < \varepsilon/2$ for all $i, j \geq N$. Choose an element x_k of the convergent subsequence with $k \geq N$ and k large enough that $|x_k - y| < \varepsilon/2$. Now, for all $i \geq N$,

$$|x_i - y| = |(x_i - x_k) + (x_k - y)|$$

$$\leq |x_i - x_k| + |x_k - y| < \frac{\varepsilon}{2} + \frac{\varepsilon}{2} = \varepsilon.$$

Therefore, $\{x_n\}_{n=1}^{\infty}$ converges to y. ∎

Now we can state and prove the converse to Theorem 29.1.

Theorem 29.3   Any Cauchy sequence of real numbers converges.

Proof   Let $\{x_n\}_{n=1}^{\infty}$ be a Cauchy sequence of real numbers. By Lemma 29.1, this sequence (and therefore every one of its subsequences) is bounded. By Lemma 29.2, it contains a monotone subsequence. This bounded monotone subsequence converges by Theorem 29.2. Then, by Lemma 29.3, the original sequence converges. ∎

EXERCISES

29.1   Which of the sequences in Example 12.1 is bounded above? What is the least upper bound of these sequences?
29.2   Carry out the proof of Theorem 29.2 for decreasing sequences.
29.3   Prove that if a sequence converges, every subsequence of it converges too.
29.4   Prove that a set of real numbers can have at most one least upper bound.

29.5   Prove that if **b** is an accumulation point of a sequence $\{x_n\}_{n=1}^{\infty}$, then some subsequence of $\{x_n\}_{n=1}^{\infty}$ converges to **b**.

29.6   Use Theorem 29.3 to prove that any Cauchy sequence of *vectors* in $\mathbf{R}^n$ converges.

29.2   COMPACT SETS

Section 12.5 introduced the key concept of a compact set. Recall that a set S in $\mathbf{R}^n$ is **compact** if and only if it is both closed and bounded. Thus, any closed interval in $\mathbf{R}^1$ with finite endpoints is compact, but open intervals are not compact. Any closed disk of finite radius in the plane is compact, but other disks are not.

As we discussed in Section 12.5, an important feature of compact sets is that *any* sequence defined on a compact set must contain a subsequence that actually converges, a result known as the **Bolzano-Weierstrass Theorem** and used frequently in this text. We sketched its proof in Section 12.5. However, this result is important enough to warrant a careful proof, a task we carry out here. We first prove the Bolzano-Weierstrass Theorem for compact subsets of the real line.

Theorem 29.4   Any sequence contained in a closed and bounded subset of $\mathbf{R}^1$ has a convergent subsequence.

Proof   First, we will prove Theorem 29.4 for a closed and bounded interval $[a, b]$ on the line $\mathbf{R}^1$. Let $\{x_n\}_{n=1}^{\infty}$ be a sequence contained in $[a, b]$. Divide $[a, b]$ into two equal halves: $[a, (a + b)/2]$ and $[(a + b)/2, b]$. Infinitely many elements of our sequence must lie in one (or both) of these halves. Let I_1 denote a half which contains infinitely many members of the sequence. Now divide subinterval I_1 into two equal halves. Call the half which contains infinitely many elements of $\{x_n\}_{n=1}^{\infty}$ I_2. Continue dividing the interval into halves; each time choose a half which contains *infinitely* many elements of the sequence. The result of continuing this process indefinitely is a sequence of intervals $\{I_k\}_{k=1}^{\infty}$, with

$$I_k \supset I_{k+1} \quad \text{and} \quad \text{the length of } I_k = \frac{1}{2^k}(b - a).$$

Construct a subsequence $\{x_{n_k}\}_{k=1}^{\infty}$ of $\{x_n\}_{n=1}^{\infty}$ by choosing $x_{n_k} \in I_k$. Since each I_k contains infinitely many x_n's, we can ensure that $\{x_{n_k}\}_{k=1}^{\infty}$ really is an (infinite) subsequence of $\{x_n\}_{n=1}^{\infty}$. Since $I_l \subset I_k$ for $l > k$, $x_{n_l} \in I_k$ for $l > k$, and so $|x_{n_l} - x_{n_k}| < 2^{-k}(b-a)$ for all $l > k$. Therefore, the subsequence we constructed is Cauchy; so it has a limit. Since $[a, b]$ is closed, this limit is in $[a, b]$.

Now, let S be an arbitrary closed and bounded subset of $\mathbf{R}^1$ and let $\{x_n\}_{n=1}^{\infty}$ be a sequence in S. The bounded set S is contained in a closed and bounded interval $[a, b]$. As above, keep dividing $[a, b]$ in half and at each stage choose a half I_k so that the intersection of I_k with S contains infinitely many elements of the original sequence. Construct a Cauchy subsequence $\{x_{n_k}\}$ as above, with $x_{n_k} \in I_k \cap S$. Since S is closed, its limit will lie in S. ∎

Theorem 29.4 generalizes easily to closed and bounded sequences in $\mathbf{R}^m$.

Theorem 29.5   Any sequence contained in a closed and bounded subset of $\mathbf{R}^m$ has a convergent subsequence.

Proof   Let S be an arbitrary closed and bounded subset of $\mathbf{R}^m$. Then, S is contained in a set of the form

$$\{\mathbf{x} = (x_1, \ldots, x_m) : |x_k - a_k| \le \beta \text{ for } k = 1, \ldots, m\},$$

a "cube" in $\mathbf{R}^m$ with center $(a_1, \ldots, a_m)$ and with each side of length 2β. Let $\{\mathbf{x}_n\}_{n=1}^{\infty}$ be a sequence in S. Consider the sequence $\{x_{1n}\}_{n=1}^{\infty}$ of first coordinates of the $\mathbf{x}_n$'s. The sequence $\{x_{1n}\}$ of real numbers lies in the compact interval $[a_1 - \beta, a_1 + \beta]$. By Theorem 29.4, there is a subsequence of $\{\mathbf{x}_n\}_{n=1}^{\infty}$ whose first components converge to a limit. Now look at the sequence of second components of this subsequence. Again by Theorem 29.4, we can find a subsequence of $\{\mathbf{x}_n\}_{n=1}^{\infty}$ whose second (and first) components converge to a limit. Repeat this process m times to find a subsequence $\{\mathbf{x}_{n_j}\}_{j=1}^{\infty}$ of $\{\mathbf{x}_n\}_{n=1}^{\infty}$ such that each sequence of components of the subsequence $\{x_{kn_j}\}_{j=1}^{\infty}$ converges for $k = 1, \ldots, m$. By Theorem 12.5, this subsequence converges in $\mathbf{R}^m$. Since it lies in the closed set S, its limit will also be in S. ∎

The Bolzano-Weierstrass Theorem has a converse.

Theorem 29.6   Let S be a subset of $\mathbf{R}^m$ with the property that any sequence in S has a convergent subsequence with limit in S. Then, S is closed and bounded.

Proof   Let S be a subset of $\mathbf{R}^m$ with the property that any sequence in S has a subsequence which converges to a point in S. To show that S is closed, let $\{\mathbf{x}_n\}_{n=1}^{\infty}$ be a convergent sequence in S with limit $\mathbf{x}$. Then every subsequence also converges to $\mathbf{x}$; so by hypothesis, $\mathbf{x} \in S$. Therefore S is closed.

We need to show that S is bounded. If it is not, then there are elements of S with arbitrarily large norm. Choose $\mathbf{x}_1 \in S$ with $\|\mathbf{x}_1\| \ge 1$, and choose $\mathbf{x}_2 \in S$ such that $\|\mathbf{x}_2\| \ge 2$. Continue in this manner to construct a sequence $\{\mathbf{x}_n\}_{n=1}^{\infty}$ in S with $\|\mathbf{x}_n\| \ge n$. Not only is this sequence unbounded, but any subsequence of it is also unbounded. By Lemma 29.2, no subsequence of $\{\mathbf{x}_n\}_{n=1}^{\infty}$ is Cauchy and therefore no subsequence converges — a contradiction to our hypothesis on S. We conclude that S is bounded. ∎

A set with the property that every sequence has a convergent subsequence is called **sequentially compact**. We have two characterizations of compactness for a set S in $\mathbf{R}^m$: 1) S is closed and bounded, and 2) S is sequentially compact. In the Appendix of this chapter, we present a third characterization in terms of open sets — a characterization that is often useful in mathematical analysis: a set S is compact if and only if every open cover of S has a finite subcover. We then use this characterization to show that if $\mathbf{x}_0$ is in the complement of the compact set S, then there exist open sets U_1 and U_2 such that $a)$ $\mathbf{x}_0 \in U_1$, $b)$ $S \subset U_2$, and $c)$ $U_1 \cap U_2 = \varnothing$. These two properties of compact sets are used, for example, to derive continuity properties of correspondences and show that, under rather weak hypotheses, the indirect utility function is continuous.

29.3   CONNECTED SETS

A set K that can be separated or disconnected into two parts so that these two parts can be covered by *disjoint* open sets is called a disconnected set. More formally, for any set S, we say that S is **disconnected** if there exist *open* sets U_1 and U_2 such that:

(1) $S \subset U_1 \cup U_2$,
(2) $S \cap U_1 \neq \varnothing$ and $S \cap U_2 \neq \varnothing$, and
(3) $U_1 \cap U_2 = \varnothing$.

If a set is not disconnected, we say that it is **connected**. Most of the sets that arise in applications are connected, and some theorems specifically require that sets be connected.

It is relatively easy to characterize the connected sets of $\mathbf{R}^1$, since once a point is removed from the interior of a set in $\mathbf{R}^1$ that set becomes disconnected. To prove this characterization, we need the least upper bound condition on $\mathbf{R}^1$ that was presented in Section 29.1.

Theorem 29.7   A subset S of $\mathbf{R}^1$ is connected if and only if whenever $x \in S$, $z \in S$, and $x \leq y \leq z$, then $y \in S$.

Proof   If S is disconnected, then there exist disjoint open sets U_1 and U_2 both of which intersect S and whose union contains S. Let $x \in U_1 \cap S$ and let $z \in U_2 \cap S$. Consider the interval $[x, z]$. Since U_1 is open, there is an $\varepsilon > 0$ such that $[x, x + \varepsilon] \subset U_1$. Let y be the least upper bound of all points x' such that $[x, x'] \subset U_1$. The point y is not in U_1 since the openness of U_1 implies that we could then extend the interval beyond y and still stay in U_1. Also, y is not in U_2 since the openness of U_2 means that points to the left of y in $\mathbf{R}^1$ would also be in U_2; this contradicts the least upper bound property of y. Since y is not in either U_1 or U_2, it cannot be in S which is contained in $U_1 \cup U_2$.

Conversely, if we can find x and z in S and a y between x and z that is not in S, then the two open intervals $(-\infty, y)$ and $(y, +\infty)$ disconnect S. ∎

It is now easy to make a list of all the kinds of subsets in $\mathbf{R}^1$ that are connected: just all the single intervals, whether open, closed, or half-open, whether finite or infinite in length.

There is no such simple classification of connected sets in two dimensions. As Theorem 29.7 indicates, the removal of a point from the interior of a connected subset of $\mathbf{R}^1$ disconnects the set. The same is not true in $\mathbf{R}^m$. As can easily be checked, $\mathbf{R}^m - \{0\}$ and $\mathbf{R}^m - B_r(\mathbf{0})$ are connected sets, for $m > 1$. Similarly, $B_r(\mathbf{x}) - B_{r/2}(\mathbf{x})$ is connected. In $\mathbf{R}^2$, this set is the region between two concentric circles, as pictured in Figure 29.1. Such a subset of the plane is called an **annulus**.

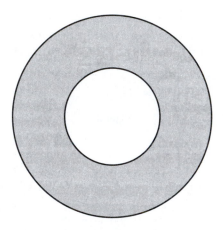

**Figure
29.1**

An annulus in the plane.

EXERCISES

29.7   We defined "connected" above as any set which is not disconnected. Write out a direct definition of "connected."

29.8   Prove that the closure of a connected set is connected.

29.9   Give an example to show that the interior of a connected set need not be connected.

29.10   Draw the graph of the function $y = \sin(1/x)$ for $x > 0$, a connected subset of $\mathbf{R}^2$. What is the closure of this graph in $\mathbf{R}^2$? Notice that this closure is connected, although it is composed of two disjoint pieces.

29.11   For each of the following subsets of $\mathbf{R}^2$, a) sketch the set and b) determine whether or not it is open, closed, compact, or connected. Give reasons for your negative answers to part b.

    i) $\{(x, y) : x = 0, y \geq 0\}$,   *ii)* $\{(x, y) : 1 \leq x^2 + y^2 \leq 2\}$,

    iii) $\{(x, y) : 1 \leq x \leq 2\}$,   *iv)* $\{(x, y) : x = 0 \text{ or } y = 0, \text{ but not both }\}$.

29.12 For each of the following sets, decide whether or not the set is *a)* a subspace, *b)* closed, *c)* open, *d)* compact, *e)* connected.

$$i)\ \{(x_1, x_2) : x_1 = -x_2\}, \qquad ii)\ \{(x_1, x_2) : 1 < x_1^2 + x_2^2 < 2\},$$

$$iii)\ \{(x_1, x_2, x_3) : x_1 \geq 0,\ x_2 \geq 0,\ x_3 \geq 0,\ x_1 + x_2 + x_3 \leq 1\}.$$

29.4 ALTERNATIVE NORMS

Three Norms on R^n

The key concept throughout this chapter and Chapter 12 has been the distance between two points $\mathbf{x}$ and $\mathbf{y}$ in $\mathbf{R}^n$. We have measured this distance with the **Euclidean distance function**

$$d_E(\mathbf{x}, \mathbf{y}) = \|\mathbf{x} - \mathbf{y}\| = \left(\sum_{i=1}^{n} (x_i - y_i)^2 \right)^{1/2},$$

which in turn is based on the **Euclidean norm**

$$\|\mathbf{x}\| = \left(\sum_{i=1}^{n} x_i^2 \right)^{1/2}. \tag{1}$$

One can think of a norm as a measure of the size of a vector $\mathbf{x}$ or more specifically as a measure of the distance from the point $\mathbf{x}$ to the origin $\mathbf{0}$. At the end of Section 10.4, we presented the formal definition of a norm.

Definition Let V be a vector space. A real-valued function $N: V \to \mathbf{R}$ is called a **norm** on V if:

    (a) $N(\mathbf{x}) \geq 0$ for all $\mathbf{x} \in V$,
    (b) $N(\mathbf{x}) = 0$ if and only if $\mathbf{x} = \mathbf{0}$,
    (c) $N(r\mathbf{x}) = |r| N(\mathbf{x})$ for all $r \in \mathbf{R}^1$ and $\mathbf{x} \in V$, and
    (d) $N(\mathbf{x} + \mathbf{y}) \leq N(\mathbf{x}) + N(\mathbf{y})$ for all $\mathbf{x}, \mathbf{y} \in V$.

Theorem 10.5 verified that the Euclidean norm satisfies property *d*, the triangle inequality.

There are other natural norms that can be defined on $\mathbf{R}^n$. Each of these yields a corresponding measure of distance in $\mathbf{R}^n$. For example, just as one does in multiple regression analysis, one can give different weights to different coordinate directions. In particular, if $a_1, \ldots, a_n$ are positive scalars, then

$$N_{(a_1,\ldots,a_n)}(\mathbf{x}) = \left(\sum_{i=1}^{n} a_i x_i^2 \right)^{1/2} \tag{2}$$

is a norm on $\mathbf{R}^n$, called the **weighted Euclidean norm**. Since

$$N_{(a_1,\ldots,a_n)}(\mathbf{x}) = \|(\sqrt{a_1}x_1,\ldots,\sqrt{a_n}x_n)\|,$$

one can easily show that $N_{(a_1,\ldots,a_n)}$ satisfies the four properties of a norm. (Exercise.)

Just as the Euclidean norm uses the *square root of the sum of the squares* of the coordinates of $\mathbf{x}$ as a measure of the size of $\mathbf{x}$, it is sometimes simpler just to use the sum of the absolute values of the coordinates of $\mathbf{x}$ as a measure of size. This leads to the norm

$$N_1((x_1,\ldots,x_n)) = |x_1| + \cdots + |x_n| \tag{3}$$

and the corresponding difference function

$$d_1(\mathbf{x},\mathbf{y}) = N_1(\mathbf{x}-\mathbf{y}) = |x_1 - y_1| + \cdots + |x_n - y_n|. \tag{4}$$

We leave the verification that N_1 is a norm as an exercise.

If one thinks of $\mathbf{R}^2$ as a map of a city with a grid of horizontal and vertical lines for the city streets, then the traveling distance from point $\mathbf{x} = (x_1, x_2)$ to point $\mathbf{y} = (y_1, y_2)$ on this grid will be the sum of the east-west distance $|x_1 - y_1|$ between $\mathbf{x}$ and $\mathbf{y}$ and the north-south distance $|x_2 - y_2|$ between $\mathbf{x}$ and $\mathbf{y}$, since a city traveler will usually have to use streets running east and west and streets running north and south to travel from $\mathbf{x}$ to $\mathbf{y}$. See Figure 29.2. But, this traveling distance is precisely $N_1(\mathbf{x}-\mathbf{y})$ in (4). Not surprisingly, the planar geometry that uses this distance function is called *taxicab geometry*.[2]

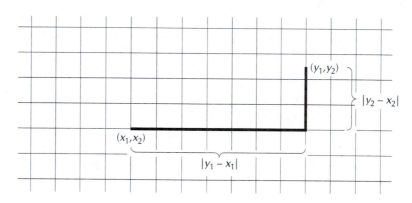

Figure 29.2

The N_1-distance from $\mathbf{x}$ to $\mathbf{y}$.

We can construct variations of N_1 by using *weighted* sums in the definition (3) of N_1, just as we did for the weighted Euclidean norm in (2). This weighted

[2] See, for example, Eugene Krause, *Taxicab Geometry* (Menlo Park, Calif.: Addison Wesley, 1975).

N_1-norm is especially natural if one travels in different directions at different speeds in city traffic in the grid in Figure 29.2.

In some cases, it may be natural to replace the *sum* of the absolute values of the components of **x** by the *largest* absolute value of the components of **x** as a measure of the size of **x**. This leads to the norm (exercise)

$$N_0((x_1, \ldots, x_n)) = \max\{|x_1|, \ldots, |x_n|\} \tag{5}$$

and the corresponding distance function

$$d_0(\mathbf{x}, \mathbf{y}) = \max\{|x_1 - y_1|, \ldots, |x_n - y_n|\}.$$

To measure how far apart **x** and **y** are using d_0, one uses the largest difference between the components of **x** and **y**.

Equivalent Norms

The Euclidean norm and norms N_0 and N_1 are the most commonly used measures of size on $\mathbf{R}^n$. Which norm one uses depends on the geometry and analytics of the situation under study. However, this flexibility raises a major concern. We used the Euclidean norm in our definitions of convergent sequences and of open and closed sets in Chapter 12. Could it be possible that a sequence that converges in one norm would not converge in another? Or that a set that is closed in one norm is not closed in another? Since these three norms are legitimate alternative measures of distance, convergence in one norm should imply converge in any other norm. To see that this holds for the three norms under consideration, we have to derive analytic relationships among these norms.

For the sake of notation, we will write $N_2(\mathbf{x})$ for the Euclidean norm (1). The following theorem expresses the basic relationship between norms N_0 and N_1. We leave its simple proof as an exercise.

Theorem 29.8   For any $\mathbf{x} \in \mathbf{R}^n$,

$$N_0(\mathbf{x}) \leq N_1(\mathbf{x}) \leq nN_0(\mathbf{x}). \tag{6}$$

It follows from Theorem 29.8 that a sequence converges in the N_0-norm if and only if it converges in the N_1-norm.

Theorem 29.9   Let $\{\mathbf{x}_j\}_{j=1}^\infty$ be a sequence in $\mathbf{R}^n$. Then, $\{\mathbf{x}_j\}$ converges to **0** in norm N_0 if and only if it converges to **0** in norm N_1.

Proof   To show that N_0-convergence implies N_1-convergence, suppose that $N_0(\mathbf{x}_j) \to 0$ as $j \to \infty$. Since $N_1(\mathbf{x}_j) \leq nN_0(\mathbf{x}_j)$ for all j, $N_1(\mathbf{x}_j) \to 0$ as $j \to \infty$, too. Similarly, one uses $N_0(\mathbf{x}_j) \leq N_1(\mathbf{x}_j)$ to show the converse result.   ∎

Since they have the same convergent sequences, it is natural to call N_0 and N_1 *equivalent norms*. The following definition and theorem extend what we have done for N_0 and N_1 to more general norms.

Definition   Two norms N and N' on a vector space V are **equivalent norms** if there exist positive scalars a and b so that

$$aN(\mathbf{x}) \le N'(\mathbf{x}) \le bN(\mathbf{x}) \tag{7}$$

for all $\mathbf{x} \in V$. Write $N \sim N'$ if (7) holds for norms N and N'.

As its name suggests, norm equivalence is an *equivalence relation* in that it satisfies the following properties for any norms N, N', and N'' on a vector space V:

(1) $N \sim N'$ implies $N' \sim N$.
(2) $N \sim N$ for any norm N.
(3) $N \sim N'$ and $N' \sim N''$ implies $N \sim N''$.

We leave the verification of these three properties as an exercise.

In Theorem 29.9, we showed that because N_0 and N_1 are equivalent norms, a series converges with respect to one of these norms if and only if it converges in the other. A similar proof shows that for any two equivalent norms, convergence in one means convergence in the other.

Theorem 29.10   If norms N and N' are equivalent, then a sequence converges to limit b in the N-norm if and only if it converges to b in the N'-norm.

It is straightforward to show that norms N_0 and N_2 are equivalent, more specifically that

$$N_0(\mathbf{x}) \le N_2(\mathbf{x}) \le \sqrt{n}\,N_0(\mathbf{x}) \qquad \text{for all } \mathbf{x} \in \mathbf{R^n}. \tag{8}$$

(Exercise.) It follows that the three norms N_0, N_1, and N_2 are equivalent to each other. In fact, we will indicate in Chapter 30 that *any two norms* in $\mathbf{R^n}$ are equivalent to each other. Therefore, the notion of a convergent sequence in $\mathbf{R^n}$ is independent of the norm we use. Since a set is defined to be closed if it contains the limits of all its convergent sequences, whether or not a set is closed is also independent of the norm chosen.

Whether or not a set is open is also independent of the underlying norm. To see this, first note that the inequalities (8) imply that the Euclidean or N_2-ball of radius r about $\mathbf{x}_0$

$$B_{N_2,r}(\mathbf{x}_0) = \{\mathbf{x} \in \mathbf{R^n} : N_2(\mathbf{x} - \mathbf{x}_0) < r\}$$

is contained in the N_0-ball of radius r about $\mathbf{x}_0$

$$B_{N_0,r}(\mathbf{x}_0) = \{\mathbf{x} \in \mathbf{R^n} : N_0(\mathbf{x} - \mathbf{x}_0) < r\},$$

and also that the N_0-ball of radius $r/\sqrt{n}$ about $\mathbf{x}_0$ is contained in the Euclidean ball of radius r about $\mathbf{x}_0$; that is,

$$\left\{\mathbf{x} \in \mathbf{R}^n : N_0(\mathbf{x} - \mathbf{x}_0) < \frac{r}{\sqrt{n}}\right\} \subset \{\mathbf{x} \in \mathbf{R}^n : N_2(\mathbf{x} - \mathbf{x}_0) < r\}. \qquad (9)$$

Therefore, for any point $\mathbf{x}_0$ in a set S, there is an N_0-ball about $\mathbf{x}_0$ in S if and only if there is an N_2-ball about $\mathbf{x}_0$ in S; and subsets of $\mathbf{R}^n$ that are open with respect to one norm are open with respect to the other. Since this statement and its proof can be extended to the case of any two equivalent norms and since all norms on $\mathbf{R}^n$ are equivalent, we conclude that whether or not a set is open in $\mathbf{R}^n$ is independent of the norm used to define distance.

Properties of vector spaces that are independent of the norm or distance measure chosen are called **topological properties**, and their study is called **topology**.

Norms on Function Spaces

As we mentioned in Chapter 27, we are also interested in vector spaces of *functions*. Consider, for example, the set C of all continuous functions defined on the interval $[0, 1]$. The set C is easily seen to be a vector space, but not a finite-dimensional one. There are a number of natural norms or measures of size on C. For example, we can define the **sup-norm** on C by

$$\|f\|_s = \sup\{|f(x)| : x \in [0, 1]\}$$

and the L^1-**norm** or **area-norm** on C by

$$\|f\|_{L^1} = \int_0^1 |f(x)|\, dx.$$

The former uses the maximum vertical distance between graphs as a measure of distance; the latter uses the total area between graphs as a measure of distance. These two norms are both natural measures of distance but they are *not* equivalent norms on C. To illustrate this, we present a sequence of functions in C which converges in the L^1-norm but not in the sup-norm. For each integer $n > 1$, define $f_n \in C$ by

$$f_n(x) = \begin{cases} 2n^2 - 2n^3 x & 0 \le x \le (1/n), \\ 0 & (1/n) \le x \le 1. \end{cases}$$

The graph of f_n is a line segment of slope $-2n^3$ from $(0, 2n^2)$ to $(1/n, 0)$ and then runs along the x-axis from $(1/n, 0)$ to $(1, 0)$. Since the area under the graph of f_n is $1/n$, $\|f_n\|_{L^1} \to 0$. On the other hand, since $f_n(0) = 2n^2$, $\|f_n\|_s \to \infty$. The choice of norm makes a big difference in function spaces. In general, the norm one chooses depends on the functions one is working with and the theorems one wants to prove about those functions.

EXERCISES

29.13 Show that $N_{(a_1,...,a_n)}$ is a norm on $\mathbf{R}^n$.

29.14 Show that the N_1 function defined in (3) is a norm on $\mathbf{R}^n$.

29.15 Show that the N_0 function defined in (5) is a norm on $\mathbf{R}^n$.

29.16 Prove Theorem 29.8.

29.17 Show that the relation defined in (7) is an equivalence relation.

29.18 Prove Theorem 29.10.

29.19 Verify (8).

29.20 Let N be a norm on a vector space V. The **unit sphere** in norm N is the set $\{\mathbf{x} \in V : N(\mathbf{x}) = 1\}$. For $V = \mathbf{R}^2$, characterize and draw the unit spheres for the norms N_0, N_1, and N_2 and the weighted variations of N_1 and N_2.

29.21 Verify statement (9).

29.22 Show that bounded, compact, and connected are topological properties in $\mathbf{R}^n$, in the sense that they are independent of the underlying norm.

29.23 In an exercise in Section 12.4, you were asked to show that the positive orthant $\mathbf{R}_+^m \equiv \{(x_1, \ldots, x_m) : x_i > 0 \text{ for } i = 1, \ldots m\}$ is an open set in the Euclidean norm in $\mathbf{R}^m$. Show directly that $\mathbf{R}_+^m$ is open in the N_0-norm and the N_1-norm. Which of the three was the easiest calculation?

29.5 APPENDIX

Finite Covering Property

In this appendix, we continue the discussion about compact sets that we began in Section 29.2. (This section is fairly technical and may be skipped at first reading.) In particular, we present a third characterization of compactness, this time in terms of open sets. This characterization is less intuitive than the characterization by sequences, but still extremely useful. Let S be a set in $\mathbf{R}^m$. Let $\mathcal{U}$ be a collection of open sets such that every point in S lies in at least one of the sets in $\mathcal{U}$: $S \subset \cup \{U : U \in \mathcal{U}\}$. The collection $\mathcal{U}$ is called an **open cover** of S. We say that the set S has the **finite covering property** if whenever $\mathcal{U}$ is an open cover of S, then a *finite* subcollection of the sets in $\mathcal{U}$ covers S; that is,

$$\text{there exist} \quad U_1, \ldots, U_K \in \mathcal{U} \quad \text{such that} \quad S \subset \cup_{k=1}^K U_k.$$

Example 29.1   Consider the following three examples of open covers:

   (a) Let V be an open set. For each $\mathbf{x}$ in V, there is an $\varepsilon > 0$ and an ε-ball $B_\mathbf{x}$ about $\mathbf{x}$ contained in V. The collection of open sets $\mathcal{U} = \{B_\mathbf{x} : \mathbf{x} \in V\}$ is an open cover of V.

   (b) The collection of intervals $\{(n - 1, n + 1)\}_{-\infty}^{+\infty}$ is an open cover of the real line $\mathbf{R}^1$. For each integer n, one and only one of the sets in this collection contains n. So, no subcollection — in particular, no finite subcollection — is a cover of $\mathbf{R}^1$; $\mathbf{R}^1$ does not have the finite covering property.

(c) The collection of intervals

$$\left\{\left(\frac{1}{n+1}, \frac{n}{n+1}\right)\right\}_{n=2}^{\infty} \tag{10}$$

is an open cover of the open interval $(0, 1)$.

EXERCISES

29.24 Show that no finite subcollection of the collection (10) in c of Example 29.1 is a cover of $(0,1)$. Therefore, $(0,1)$ does not have the finite covering property.

29.25 Consider the following open cover of the closed interval $[0, 1]$: collection (10) along with the intervals $(-0.1, +0.1)$ and $(0.9, 1.1)$. Find a finite subcollection which covers $[0, 1]$. Why does this not imply that $[0, 1]$ has the finite covering property?

Heine-Borel Theorem

The theorem that states that sets with the open covering property are compact is called the **Heine-Borel Theorem**. Sometimes, the open covering property is called the Heine-Borel property.

Before stating and proving the Heine-Borel Theorem, we need to prove two useful lemmas. The first states that a nested sequence of closed sets whose diameter goes to zero has one and only one point in its intersection. The lemma refers to the diameter of a set S. The **diameter** of a set S in $\mathbf{R}^m$ is defined to be

$$\text{diam}(S) = \sup_{x,y \in S} \|x - y\|,$$

where "sup" means the supremum or least upper bound. Intuitively, the diameter of S is the largest distance between any two points in S. If S is a ball in $\mathbf{R}^m$, then $\text{diam}(S)$ is exactly what we usually call the diameter of a ball.

Lemma 29.4   Let $\{F_n\}_{n=1}^{\infty}$ be a collection of closed sets such that $F_n \supset F_{n+1}$ and $\text{diam}\, F_n \to 0$. Then there is a point x such that $\cap_{n=1}^{\infty} F_n = \{x\}$.

Proof   Choose a sequence $\{x_n\}_{n=1}^{\infty}$ such that $x_n \in F_n$. For any n and m with $n \geq m$, x_n and x_m are both in F_m. Therefore, $\|x_n - x_m\| \leq \text{diam}(F_m)$. Since $\text{diam}(F_m) \to 0$, this sequence is Cauchy, and so it converges to some limit x. Also, since $x_n \in F_m$ for all $n > m$ and since F_m is closed, $x \in F_m$ for all m.

Thus, $\mathbf{x} \in \cap_{n=1}^{\infty} F_n$. There can be no $\mathbf{y} \neq \mathbf{x}$ such that $\mathbf{y} \in \cap_{n=1}^{\infty} F_n$ too. To see this, suppose there exists such a $\mathbf{y}$; then, $\|\mathbf{x} - \mathbf{y}\| = \varepsilon > 0$. But, for all n large enough so that diam $F_n < \varepsilon$, it cannot be the case that both $\mathbf{x}$ and $\mathbf{y}$ are in F_n. ∎

Lemma 29.5   If B is a closed subset of A and if A has the finite covering property, then B has the finite covering property.

Proof   Let $\mathcal{U}$ be a collection of open sets which covers B. Add the *open* set B^c to this collection to obtain a new collection of open sets $\mathcal{O}$. Since $\mathcal{U}$ covers B, $\mathcal{O}$ covers $\mathbf{R}^m$. Therefore, $\mathcal{O}$ covers A. Since A has the finite covering property, some finite subcollection of $\mathcal{O}$ covers A. This finite subcollection will also cover B, even after one deletes the open set B^c. ∎

Theorem 29.11   (**Heine-Borel Theorem**) If a set S in $\mathbf{R}^m$ is closed and bounded, then it has the finite covering property.

Proof   Before proving the general theorem, we will present the proof that the compact interval $[0, 1]$ has the finite covering property. The proof has some similarities to the proof of the sequential characterization of compactness for the interval $[0, 1]$.

Suppose that $[0, 1]$ does *not* have the finite covering property; in other words, suppose that there exists an infinite collection $\mathcal{U}$ of open sets which covers $[0, 1]$ for which no finite subcollection covers $[0, 1]$. Divide $I_1 = [0, 1]$ into two closed half-intervals of length $1/2$. At least one of these two half-intervals, call it I_2, cannot be covered by finitely many open sets in the original collection $\mathcal{U}$. Otherwise, the whole interval could be covered by a finite subcollection. Divide I_2 into two closed half-intervals of length $1/4$. At least one of these two cannot be covered by finitely many open sets in $\mathcal{U}$. Continue in this way to obtain a nested sequence of closed intervals $\{I_k\}_{k=1}^{\infty}$, with length of $I_k = 1/2^k$ and with $I_k \supset I_{k+1}$ for all k. Each of these I_k's cannot be covered by a finite subcollection of $\mathcal{U}$.

Now, by Lemma 29.4, there is a point $\mathbf{x}$ in $\cap I_k$. (This is fairly intuitive for $[0, 1]$.) Since $\mathbf{x}$ is in $[0, 1]$ (this is where we use the assumption that $[0, 1]$ is closed) and $\mathcal{U}$ is an open cover of $[0, 1]$, there is some open set U^* in $\mathcal{U}$ which contains $\mathbf{x}$. Since U^* is open, there is an ε-interval about $\mathbf{x}$, $I_\varepsilon(\mathbf{x})$, contained in U^*. Choose k^* so that $1/2^{k^*} < \varepsilon$. Since I_{k^*} is an interval of length $1/2^{k^*}$ which contains $\mathbf{x}$, it lies in $I_\varepsilon(\mathbf{x})$ and therefore in U^*. This means that I_{k^*} lies in one single open set in the infinite collection $\mathcal{U}$. But this is a contradiction to our construction of the I_k's as not lying in any finite subcollection of the sets in $\mathcal{U}$. Therefore, $[0, 1]$ has the finite covering property.

We now sketch the proof of the Heine-Borel Theorem for a general closed and bounded subset S of $\mathbf{R}^m$. Since it is bounded, such an S lies in some big cube I_1 in $\mathbf{R^m}$, say with each side of length a and with center at $\mathbf{x}_0$:

$$S \subset I_1 \equiv \left\{ \mathbf{x} = (x_1, \ldots, x_m) : |x_i - x_{i0}| \leq \frac{a}{2} \right\}.$$

Since S is a closed subset of I_1, we need only show that I_1 has the finite covering property to infer that S has the finite covering property, by Lemma 29.5. Suppose that I_1 does not have the finite covering property. In other words, suppose that there exists a collection $\mathcal{U}$ of open sets that covers I_1 for which no finite subcollection covers I_1. Now, lift the proof for $\mathbf{R^1}$ to $\mathbf{R^m}$.

Divide I_1 into 2^m closed congruent m-cubes, each of side $a/2$, as illustrated in Figure 29.3 for $m = 2$. One of these subcubes has the property that no finite subcollection of $\mathcal{U}$ will cover it. (Otherwise, some finite subcollection of $\mathcal{U}$ will cover I_1.) Call the cube that fails I_2, and subdivide it. Again the open covering property must fail for at least one subcube in the subdivision. Call it I_3, and so forth. Observe that diam $I_k \rightarrow 0$, that each I_k is compact and that $I_k \supset I_l$ for $l > k$. Thus by Lemma 29.4, $\cap_k I_k$ contains a single point $\mathbf{x}$.

Since $\mathcal{U}$ is an open cover of I_1, some open set U^* in $\mathcal{U}$ contains $\mathbf{x}$. Since diam $I_k \rightarrow 0, I_k \subset U^*$ for large enough k. But this contradicts our choice of I_k as a cube which can *only* be covered by *infinitely many* open sets in the collection $\mathcal{U}$ — certainly not by just one. This contradiction means that the original open cover $\mathcal{U}$ of I_1 does not exist. In other words, *every* collection of open sets which covers I_1 (or its closed subset S) has a finite subcollection which covers I_1. ■

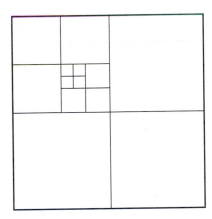

Subdividing a cube in the plane.

Figure 29.3

The converse of the Heine-Borel Theorem is also true, as the following theorem shows. Thus, the finite covering property is equivalent to compactness.

> **Theorem 29.12** Let S be a subset of $\mathbf{R}^m$ with the finite covering property. Then, S is closed and bounded.

Proof Suppose not. Then S is either not closed or not bounded. In the latter case, let U_k be the ball of radius k about the origin, $B_k(\mathbf{0})$. Let $\mathcal{U}$ be the collection of the U_k's for $k = 1, 2, \ldots$. This collection covers all of $\mathbf{R}^m$, so it covers S. Since S has points arbitrarily far from the origin, no finite subcollection of $\mathcal{U}$ covers S — a contradiction to our hypothesis that S has the finite covering property. Therefore, S is bounded.

If S is not closed, choose $\mathbf{x} \in \operatorname{cl} S \setminus S$. Let

$$O_k = \left\{ \mathbf{y} \in \mathbf{R}^m : \|\mathbf{y} - \mathbf{x}\| > \frac{1}{k} \right\}.$$

The collection $\mathcal{O}$ of the O_k's is an open cover of $\mathbf{R}^m \setminus \{\mathbf{x}\}$ and therefore an open cover of S, since $\mathbf{x} \notin S$. Since there exist points in S arbitrarily close to $\mathbf{x}$, no finite subcollection of $\mathcal{O}$ covers S — a contradiction to our hypothesis that S has the finite covering property. Therefore, S is closed. ∎

Summary

We summarize this discussion of compact sets with the following theorem, which simply collects our previous results.

> **Theorem 29.13** For any set S in $\mathbf{R}^m$, the following statements are equivalent:
>
> (*a*) S is closed and bounded, that is, compact.
> (*b*) S is sequentially compact.
> (*c*) S has the finite covering property.

Parenthetical Remark These three notions of compactness are equivalent only in m-dimensional Euclidean space. Infinite-dimensional spaces arise naturally in economics, for example as spaces of functions or of sequences. For such spaces there is sometimes no natural norm or distance measure, although we can usually find a natural notion of an open set. For these spaces, a set is defined to be compact if it has the finite covering property, since this characterization of compactness does not require a measure of distance. Even when there exists a distance measure for an infinite-dimensional space, a compact set is always closed and bounded, but a closed and bounded set need not have the finite covering property.

As we mentioned in Section 29.2, compact sets share many properties with finite sets. One such property, that we will use in the sequel, is that if $\mathbf{x}$ and $\mathbf{y}$ are distinct points in $\mathbf{R}^m$, then there exist an open set U containing $\mathbf{x}$ and an open set V containing $\mathbf{y}$ with $U \cap V = \varnothing$. We now show that the same is true for compact sets; disjoint compact sets can be separated by disjoint open sets. The proof uses the finite covering characterization of compactness in an essential way. The closed-and-bounded characterization and the sequential characterization are not very helpful in proving this theorem. We first show that a point and a disjoint compact set can be separated by disjoint open sets.

Theorem 29.14 Let K be a compact set and let $\mathbf{y}$ be a point in $\mathbf{R}^m$ with $\mathbf{y} \notin K$. Then, there exist open sets U and V with $K \subset U$, $\mathbf{y} \in V$, and $U \cap V = \varnothing$.

Proof For every $\mathbf{x} \in K$, there exists an open ball $B_{\mathbf{x}}$ about $\mathbf{x}$ and an open ball $C_{\mathbf{x}}$ about $\mathbf{y}$ such that $B_{\mathbf{x}} \cap C_{\mathbf{x}} = \varnothing$. (Take $B_{\mathbf{x}} = B_r(\mathbf{x})$ and $C_{\mathbf{x}} = B_r(\mathbf{y})$, where $r = \frac{1}{4}\|\mathbf{x} - \mathbf{y}\|$.) The collection of open balls, $\mathcal{B} = \{B_{\mathbf{x}} : \mathbf{x} \in K\}$, is an open cover of K. Since K is compact, there exists a finite subcollection of these, $B_{\mathbf{x}_1}, B_{\mathbf{x}_2}, \ldots, B_{\mathbf{x}_s}$, which covers K; $U \equiv \cup_{i=1}^{s} B_{\mathbf{x}_i}$ is an open set containing K. Let $V = C_{\mathbf{x}_1} \cap \cdots \cap C_{\mathbf{x}_s}$. Since each $C_{\mathbf{x}_i}$ is open, V is open. If there were a $\mathbf{z}$ in $U \cap V$, then $\mathbf{z}$ is in some $B_{\mathbf{x}_i}$ since $\mathbf{z} \in U$. This point $\mathbf{z}$ would also be in $C_{\mathbf{x}_i}$. This contradicts the construction that $B_{\mathbf{x}_i} \cap C_{\mathbf{x}_i} = \varnothing$. Therefore, $U \cap V = \varnothing$, and U and V satisfy the conclusions of the theorem. ∎

Note that we needed to find a *finite* subcover of $\mathcal{B}$ in this proof. Otherwise, we would be taking the intersection of an infinite number of open sets in our construction of V and could not guarantee that V is open. The next theorem states that two disjoint compact sets K_1 and K_2 can be separated by two disjoint open sets. The proof of this result is basically the same as that of Theorem 29.14, except that we begin by separating each point in K_1 from all of K_2, using Theorem 29.14. This will yield an open cover of K_1. Take a finite subcover and use the argument at the end of Theorem 29.14. Work out the details of this proof to help you build an understanding of the finite covering property.

Theorem 29.15 Let K_1 and K_2 be two disjoint compact sets in $\mathbf{R}^m$. Then, there exist open sets U_1 and U_2 such that $K_1 \subset U_1$, $K_2 \subset U_2$, and $U_1 \cap U_2 = \varnothing$.

EXERCISES

29.26 Prove, using just the definitions, that every finite set has all three of the properties defined above: closed and bounded, sequential compactness, and finite covering.

29.27 Write out the details of the proof of Theorem 29.15.

29.28 Prove that the intersection of compact sets is compact and that the finite union of compact sets is compact. Use three different characterizations of compactness.

29.29 Prove that a closed subset of a compact set is compact. Provide three proofs, using each of the three characterizations of compactness.

Calculus of Several Variables II

This chapter continues our discussion of the concepts and techniques of advanced calculus, begun in Chapter 14. In this chapter, which is quite a bit more theoretical than Chapter 14, we construct Taylor polynomial approximations of differentiable functions of one-variable or many variables. In the process we will prove two important theorems of economic analysis: 1) the Weierstrass theorem that a continuous function whose domain is a compact set achieves its maximum value and its minimum value on its domain — the most commonly used theorem for guaranteeing that an equilibrium exists in many economic models — and 2) the second order sufficient condition for the optimization problems that lie at the core of economic theory.

30.1 WEIERSTRASS'S AND MEAN VALUE THEOREMS

In this section we prove two theorems which form the foundation of both the theory and the application of calculus and optimization: Weierstrass's theorem, the key result for proving the existence of an optimum or an equilibrium in an applied problem, and the Mean Value Theorem, an important ingredient in a large number of proofs of calculus theorems. In the next section we will use the Mean Value Theorem to quantify the approximation of differentiable functions by Taylor polynomials.

Existence of Global Maxima on Compact Sets

In our discussion of one-dimensional global maxima in Section 3.5, we pointed out that one could always find the global max of a C^1 function defined on a closed and bounded interval $[a, b]$ in $\mathbf{R}^1$. One simply computes the critical points of F, evaluates F at the critical points that lie in (a, b) *and* at the two endpoints a and b, and then chooses the point from among this (hopefully) finite collection of points at which F has the highest value.

For a function of several variables, the analogous process is much more complicated. As we saw in Chapter 18, one replaces the closed and bounded interval [a, b] by a closed and bounded subset C of $\mathbf{R}^n$. Such a set is usually defined by a collection of equality and inequality constraints of the form

$$h_1(\mathbf{x}) = a_1, \ldots, h_m(\mathbf{x}) = a_m, \quad \text{and} \quad g_1(\mathbf{x}) \leq b_1, \ldots, g_k(\mathbf{x}) \leq b_k. \tag{1}$$

At this point, let's convince ourselves that such problems really do have global maxima. We saw in Section 3.5 that if the interval J under discussion is either not closed or not bounded, then a function f may not have a global max on J. For example, the increasing function $f(x) = 2x$ does not achieve its max on the open interval $(0, 2)$ nor on the infinite interval $[0, \infty)$. However, on any closed and bounded interval $[a, b]$, f achieves its max at the right-hand endpoint $x = b$.

As we learned at the end of Chapter 12, a closed and bounded subset of $\mathbf{R}^n$ is called a **compact** set. Compact sets are characterized by the condition that *any* sequence that stays within a compact set has a subsequence that actually *converges* to a limit in the compact set (Theorem 12.14). We now prove the most important property of compact sets for economic applications: every continuous function whose domain is a compact set C actually achieves its global max and its global min on C. This is the generalization of the one-dimensional result we have been discussing; furthermore, it is the result one needs to prove that equilibria do exist in a wide range of economic models.

Theorem 30.1 (**Weierstrass's Theorem**) Let $F: C \rightarrow \mathbf{R}^1$ be a continuous function whose domain is a compact subset C in $\mathbf{R}^n$. Then, there exist points $\mathbf{x}_m$ and $\mathbf{x}_M$ in C such that $F(\mathbf{x}_m) \leq F(\mathbf{x}) \leq F(\mathbf{x}_M)$ for all $\mathbf{x} \in C$; that is, $\mathbf{x}_m \in C$ is the global min of F in C and $\mathbf{x}_M$ is the global max of F in C.

Proof We first show that F is bounded in C. Suppose that it isn't bounded. Then, there is a sequence $\{\mathbf{x}_n\}_{n=1}^{\infty}$ in C such that $F(\mathbf{x}_n) \rightarrow \infty$ as $n \rightarrow \infty$. By Theorem 12.14, since C is compact, we can find a subsequence $\{\mathbf{y}_n\}$ of $\{\mathbf{x}_n\}_{n=1}^{\infty}$ which converges to a point $\mathbf{y}^*$ in C. Since $F(\mathbf{x}_n) \rightarrow \infty$ and $\{\mathbf{y}_n\}_{n=1}^{\infty}$ is a subsequence of $\{\mathbf{x}_n\}_{n=1}^{\infty}$, the sequence $\{F(\mathbf{y}_n)\}$ goes to infinity too. However, since F is continuous in C and $\mathbf{y}_n \rightarrow \mathbf{y}^*$, the sequence $\{F(\mathbf{y}_n)\}$ must converge to the *finite* number $F(\mathbf{y}^*)$. The sequence $\{F(\mathbf{y}_n)\}$ cannot both go to infinity and converge to a finite value; this contradiction proves that F is bounded on C.

Finally, to prove Theorem 30.1, we assume that F does *not* achieve its maximum value in C. Let M be the least upper bound of the values that F takes in C. By the argument of the previous paragraph, M is finite. So, there exists a sequence $\{\mathbf{z}_n\}_{n=1}^{\infty}$ such that $F(\mathbf{z}_n) \rightarrow M$. Although the $F(\mathbf{z}_n)$'s move closer and closer up toward the least upper bound M, the $\mathbf{z}_n$'s themselves need not converge. Since C is compact, we can find a subsequence $\{\mathbf{w}_n\}_{n=1}^{\infty}$ of $\{\mathbf{z}_n\}_{n=1}^{\infty}$ such that $\{\mathbf{w}_n\}_{n=1}^{\infty}$ converges to a limit $\mathbf{w}^*$ in C. Since F is continuous, the sequence $\{F(\mathbf{w}_n)\}$ converges to the number $F(\mathbf{w}^*)$. Since a convergent sequence has only one limit (Theorem 12.1), $F(\mathbf{w}^*) = M$ and $\mathbf{w}^* \in C$ is the global max of F in C. ∎

Example 30.1   As a simple application of Theorem 30.1, consider the basic
problem of maximizing a utility function $U(\mathbf{x})$ defined on the constraint set

$$C_{\mathbf{p},I} = \{\mathbf{x} \in \mathbf{R}^n : x_1 \geq 0, \ldots, x_n \geq 0, \; p_1 x_1 + \ldots + p_n x_n \leq I\},$$

where each $p_i > 0$. By Exercise 30.2, $C_{\mathbf{p},I}$ is a closed set. To see that $C_{\mathbf{p},I}$ is
bounded, let $p_h \equiv \min\{p_1, \ldots, p_n\}$ be the minimum of the prices. Then, $p_h > 0$,
and for $\mathbf{x} \in C$,

$$x_i \leq \frac{p_i}{p_h} x_i \leq \frac{1}{p_h} \sum_j p_j x_j \leq \frac{I}{p_h}.$$

Since the components of each $\mathbf{x} \in C_{\mathbf{p},I}$ are bounded above by I/p_h, $C_{\mathbf{p},I}$ is
a bounded set. Since $C_{\mathbf{p},I}$ is closed and bounded, the continuous function U
achieves its maximum on $C_{\mathbf{p},I}$, by Theorem 30.1. For each positive price vector
$\mathbf{p}$ and income I, there is a demand vector $\mathbf{x}^*(\mathbf{p}, I)$ which maximizes U on
$C_{\mathbf{p},I}$. There may be a whole set of such maximizers. In either case, $\mathbf{x}^*(\mathbf{p}, I)$ is
nonempty. The maximum value function $V(\mathbf{p}, I) \equiv U(\mathbf{x}^*(\mathbf{p}, I))$, which measures
the maximum utility one can achieve with prices $\mathbf{p}$ and income I, is then
well-defined. It turns out that $(\mathbf{p}, I) \longmapsto \mathbf{x}^*(\mathbf{p}, I)$ is upper-hemicontinuous as a
correspondence and that the **indirect utility function** $(\mathbf{p}, I) \longmapsto V(\mathbf{p}, I)$ is a
continuous function.

Rolle's Theorem and the Mean Value Theorem

We now turn to a discussion and proof of the Mean Value Theorem, one of the
fundamental results of theoretical calculus. We first prove Rolle's theorem, a result
which forms a natural bridge between Weierstrass's theorem and the Mean Value
Theorem.

Theorem 30.2   (**Rolle's Theorem**) Suppose that $f : [a, b] \to \mathbf{R}^1$ is continuous
on $[a, b]$, and C^1 on (a, b). If $f(a) = f(b) = 0$, then there is a point $c \in (a, b)$
such that $f'(c) = 0$.

Proof   If f is constant on $[a, b]$, then $f'(c) = 0$ for all c in (a, b). If f is not
constant on $[a, b]$, we will assume without loss of generality that f is sometimes
positive on (a, b). By Weierstrass's theorem, f achieves its maximum at some
point $c \in [a, b]$. Since $f(c) > 0$, c must lie in the open interval (a, b). By the
usual first order condition for an *interior* max on $\mathbf{R}^1$, $f'(c) = 0$. ∎

We next state and prove the Mean Value Theorem, a result which both generalizes Rolle's theorem and uses it in its proof.

Theorem 30.3   (Mean Value Theorem) Let $f: U \to \mathbf{R}^1$ be a C^1 function on a (connected) interval U in $\mathbf{R}^1$. For any points $a, b \in U$, there is a point c between a and b so that

$$f(b) - f(a) = f'(c)(b - a). \tag{2}$$

Remark   It is easier to see the geometry behind equation (2) if we rewrite it as

$$\frac{f(b) - f(a)}{b - a} = f'(c), \tag{3}$$

The left-hand side of (3) is the slope of the secant line joining points $(a, f(a))$ and $(b, f(b))$ on the graph of f. This is the line segment marked ℓ_1 in Figure 30.1. The right-hand side of (3) is the slope of the tangent line ℓ_2 to the graph of f above some point c between a and b. The Mean Value Theorem states that, if one draws the line segment ℓ_1 between any two points on the graph of f, there exists a point on the graph between these original two points at which the tangent line to the graph of f is parallel to ℓ_1. Notice that Rolle's theorem is a special case of this situation in which $f(a) = f(b)$.

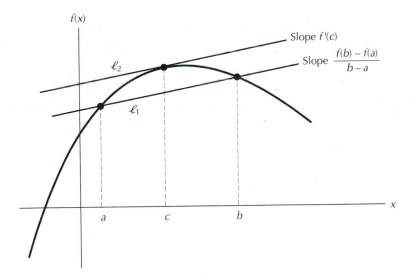

The geometry behind equation (3).

Figure 30.1

Proof   Construct the function

$$g_0(x) \equiv f(b) - f(x) + \frac{f(b) - f(a)}{b - a}(x - b). \tag{4}$$

One checks that $g_0(a) = 0$ and $g_0(b) = 0$. By Rolle's theorem, there is a point $c \in (a, b)$ so that $g_0'(c) = 0$. Differentiating (4) with respect to x yields

$$g_0'(x) = -f'(x) + \frac{f(b) - f(a)}{b - a}. \tag{5}$$

Plugging $x = c$ and $g_0'(c) = 0$ into equation (5) leads to equation (3). ∎

The Mean Value Theorem for functions of several variables follows directly from the one-variable case.

Theorem 30.4   Let $F: U \to \mathbf{R}^1$ be a C^1 function defined on an open set U in $\mathbf{R}^n$. Let $\mathbf{a}$ and $\mathbf{b}$ be two points in U such that the line segment $\ell(\mathbf{a}, \mathbf{b})$ from $\mathbf{a}$ to $\mathbf{b}$ lies in U. Then, there is a point $\mathbf{c}$ on $\ell(\mathbf{a}, \mathbf{b})$ such that

$$F(\mathbf{b}) - F(\mathbf{a}) = DF(\mathbf{c})(\mathbf{b} - \mathbf{a}).$$

Proof   Define the C^1 function $\phi: [0, 1] \to U$ by

$$\phi(t) \equiv \mathbf{a} + t(\mathbf{b} - \mathbf{a});$$

ϕ parameterizes the line $\ell(\mathbf{a}, \mathbf{b})$. Define $f: [0, 1] \to \mathbf{R}^1$ by $f(t) \equiv F(\phi(t))$. By Theorem 30.3 applied to f between 0 and 1, there exists t^* between 0 and 1 such that

$$f(1) - f(0) = f'(t^*)(1 - 0) = f'(t^*).$$

Let $\mathbf{c} = \phi(t^*)$; then

$$\begin{aligned}
F(\mathbf{b}) - F(\mathbf{a}) &= f(1) - f(0) \\
&= f'(t^*) \\
&= \left(F(\phi(t^*))\right)' \\
&= DF(\phi(t^*)) \cdot \phi'(t^*) \qquad \text{(by the Chain Rule)} \\
&= DF(\mathbf{c}) \cdot (\mathbf{b} - \mathbf{a}). \qquad ∎
\end{aligned}$$

EXERCISES

30.1   Prove the analogue of Theorem 30.1 for global minima.

30.2   Use Theorem 12.4 to prove that $\{\mathbf{x} \in \mathbf{R}^n : F(\mathbf{x}) = c\}$ and $\{\mathbf{x} \in \mathbf{R}^n : F(\mathbf{x}) \le c\}$ are closed subsets of $\mathbf{R}^n$ for any continuous function F and any constant c.

30.3 Let $F: C \to \mathbf{R}^1$ be a continuous *bounded* function whose domain C is a *closed* subset of $\mathbf{R}^n$. Does f necessarily achieve the supremum of its values?

30.4 Let $N: \mathbf{R}^n \to \mathbf{R}$ be a function that satisfies the four criteria for a norm listed at the beginning of Section 29.4.

a) Prove that N is a continuous function.

b) Prove that the restriction of N to the unit sphere in $\mathbf{R}^n$ achieves its minimum value m_1 and maximum value m_2 and that $m_1, m_2 > 0$.

c) Prove that $m_1\|\mathbf{x}\| \le N(\mathbf{x}) \le m_2\|\mathbf{x}\|$ for all $\mathbf{x} \in \mathbf{R}^n$.

d) Conclude that all norms in $\mathbf{R}^n$ are equivalent to the Euclidean norm and therefore equivalent to each other.

30.2 TAYLOR POLYNOMIALS ON R¹

Functions of One Variable

In this section, we will use Taylor polynomials to clarify and strengthen our results on approximating a function by its derivative or differential. Our proofs of the second order conditions for an unconstrained max in Chapter 17 and for a constrained max in Chapter 19 depend heavily on the approximation of a function by its Taylor polynomial. We begin with functions from $\mathbf{R}^1$ to $\mathbf{R}^1$, where the approximation-by-differentials rule is

$$f(a + h) \approx f(a) + f'(a)h. \tag{6}$$

Let $R(h; a)$ ("R" for remainder) denote the difference between the two sides in (6):

$$R(h; a) \equiv f(a + h) - f(a) - f'(a)h. \tag{7}$$

By the definition of the derivative $f'(a)$,

$$\frac{R(h; a)}{h} \to 0, \quad \text{as} \quad h \to 0. \tag{8}$$

Expressions (7) and (8) clarify the degree of accuracy in approximation (6). Not only does the approximation get better as h gets smaller, but it gets better at an order of magnitude smaller than h. For example, if h is 0.01, the two sides of (6) will be roughly 0.001 close — agreeing to two decimal places. We sometimes combine (6), (7) and (8) and write the approximation-by-differentials statement as

$$f(a + h) = f(a) + f'(a)h + R(h; a), \tag{9}$$

where $$\frac{R(h; a)}{h} \to 0, \quad \text{as} \quad h \to 0.$$

From a geometric point of view, statement (9) is the formalization of the approximation of the graph of f by its tangent *line* at $(a, f(a))$. Analytically, (9) describes the *best* approximation of f by a polynomial of degree one. See Exercise 30.8.

We now present a formal proof of (9), a proof which refines our description of the remainder function R even more. This proof follows the proof of the Mean Value Theorem very closely.

Theorem 30.5   Let $f: U \to \mathbf{R}^1$ be a C^2 function defined on a (connected) interval U in $\mathbf{R}^1$. For any points a and $a + h$ in U, there exists a point c_2 between a and $a + h$ such that

$$f(a + h) = f(a) + f'(a)h + \frac{1}{2}f''(c_2)h^2. \tag{10}$$

Proof Fix a and $a + h$ in U. By analogy with the definition of g_0 in (4) in the proof of the Mean Value Theorem, define the function

$$g_1(t) \equiv f(t) - [f(a) + f'(a)(t - a)] - M_1(t - a)^2, \tag{11}$$

where M_1 is defined by

$$M_1 = \frac{1}{h^2}[f(a + h) - f(a) - f'(a)h], \tag{12}$$

so that $g_1(a + h) = 0$. Check that

$$g_1(a) = 0 \quad \text{and} \quad g_1'(a) = 0.$$

Since $g_1(a) = g_1(a+h) = 0$, we can apply Rolle's theorem to g_1 to conclude that there exists c_1 between a and $a+h$ so that $g_1'(c_1) = 0$. Since $g_1'(a) = g_1'(c_1) = 0$, we can apply Rolle's theorem to g_1' to conclude that there exists c_2 between a and c_1 so that

$$g_1''(c_2) = 0. \tag{13}$$

Since $g_1''(t) = f''(t) - 2M_1$, (12) and (13) imply (10). ∎

Equation (10) is the one-term Taylor approximation (9) for f, where the remainder R_1 in (9) satisfies

$$R_1(h; a) = \frac{1}{2}f''(c_2)h^2$$

for some c_2 between a and $a + h$. One checks easily that

$$\frac{R_1(h;a)}{h} = \frac{1}{2}\frac{f''(c_2)h^2}{h} \longrightarrow \frac{1}{2}f''(a)\cdot 0 = 0, \quad \text{as} \quad h \to 0.$$

To get a better approximation yet, we look for the best polynomial of **degree two** which approximates f at $x = a$. The answer is the **Taylor polynomial of f of order two**:

$$f(a + h) \approx f(a) + f'(a)h + \frac{1}{2}f''(a)h^2. \tag{14}$$

If we denote the remainder or difference between the two sides in (14) as

$$R_2(h;a) \equiv f(a+h) - f(a) - f'(a)h - \frac{1}{2}f''(a)h^2,$$

then, as we will see below,

$$\frac{R_2(h;a)}{h^2} \to 0 \quad \text{as} \quad h \to 0. \tag{15}$$

In words, when h is around 0.01, R_2 will be roughly 0.00001. The best *quadratic* approximation to f at a will be a much closer fit to the graph of f than the best *linear* approximation. We combine (14) and (15) to write

$$f(a + h) = f(a) + f'(a)h + \frac{1}{2}f''(a)h^2 + R_2(h;a), \tag{16}$$

where
$$\frac{R_2(h;a)}{h^2} \to 0 \quad \text{as} \quad h \to 0.$$

The right-hand side of (16) is called the **Taylor approximation of f of order two** at a. The proof of Taylor's theorem of order two follows the same track as the proof of the first order theorem.

Theorem 30.6 Let $f: U \to \mathbf{R}^1$ be a C^3 function defined on a (connected) interval U in $\mathbf{R}^1$. For any points a and $a + h$ in U, there exists c^* between a and $a + h$ such that

$$f(a+h) = f(a) + f'(a)h + \frac{1}{2!}f''(a)h^2 + \frac{1}{3!}f'''(c^*)h^3. \tag{17}$$

Proof   Mimicking the proof of Theorem 30.5, for a, $a + h$ in U, we define g_2 by

$$g_2(t) \equiv f(t) - [f(a) + f'(a)(t - a) + \frac{1}{2}f''(a)(t - a)^2]$$
$$- M_2(t - a)^3,$$
(18)

where

$$M_2 = \frac{1}{h^3}[f(a + h) - f(a) - f'(a)h - \frac{1}{2}f''(a)h^2],$$
(19)

is chosen so that $g_2(a + h) = 0$. By differentiating (18) twice with respect to t, check that

$$g_2(a) = g_2'(a) = g_2''(a) = 0.$$

Apply Rolle's theorem to $g(a) = g(a + h) = 0$ to find c_1 between a and $a + h$ so that $g_2'(c_1) = 0$. Apply Rolle's theorem to $g_2'(a) = g_2'(c_1) = 0$ to find c_2 between a and c_1 so that $g_2''(c_2) = 0$. Apply Rolle's theorem to $g_2''(a) = g_2''(c_2) = 0$ to find c^* between a and c_2 such that $g_2^{[3]}(c^*) = 0$. Finally, compute the third derivative $g_2^{[3]}$ of g_2 in (18):

$$g_2^{[3]}(t) = f^{[3]}(t) - 3! \, M_2,$$

substitute expression (19) for M_2, and substitute c^* for t to deduce expression (17). ∎

Example 30.2   Let's compute the first and second order Taylor polynomial of the exponential function $f(x) = e^x$ at $x = 0$. All the derivatives of f at $x = 0$ equal 1. Therefore, the first order Taylor polynomial is

$$P_1(h) = 1 + h,$$

and the second order Taylor polynomial of f at $x = 0$ is

$$P_2(h) = 1 + h + \frac{1}{2}h^2.$$

For $h = 0.2$, $P_1(.2) = 1.2$ and $P_2(.2) = 1.22$, compared with the actual value of $e^{.2} = 1.22140\cdots$. Even for h as big as 1,

$$P_1(1) = 2 \quad \text{and} \quad P_2(1) = 2.5;$$

the latter is a much better approximation to

$$f(1) = e = 2.718\cdots.$$

Definition   The *k*th order **Taylor polynomial** of f at $x = a$ is

$$P_k(a + h) = f(a) + f'(a)h + \frac{1}{2!}f''(a)h^2 + \cdots + \frac{1}{k!}f^{[k]}(a)h^k. \qquad (20)$$

When $a = 0$, it is also called the **Maclaurin polynomial** of f of order k.

As the following theorem indicates, the difference $R_k(h; a)$ between the actual value $f(a + h)$ and its *k*th order approximation $P_k(a + h)$ satisfies

$$\frac{R_k(h; a)}{h^k} \to 0 \quad \text{as} \quad h \to 0. \qquad (21)$$

If h is of order 0.01, then $R_k(h)$ will be of order $0.00 \cdots 01$ with $2k$ zeros.

Theorem 30.7   Let $f: U \to \mathbf{R}^1$ be a C^{k+1} function defined on a (connected) interval U in $\mathbf{R}^1$. For any points a and $a + h$ in U, there exists a point c^* between a and $a + h$ such that

$$f(a + h) = f(a) + f'(a)h + \frac{1}{2}f''(a)h^2 + \cdots$$

$$+ \frac{1}{k!}f^{[k]}(a)h^k + \frac{1}{(k + 1)!}f^{[k+1]}(c^*)h^{k+1}.$$

Notice that the remainder $R(h; a)$ between $f(a + h)$ and the polynomial $P_k(a + h)$ satisfies

$$\frac{R_k(h, a)}{h^k} = \frac{1}{(k + 1)!}\frac{f^{[k+1]}(c^*)h^{k+1}}{h^k} \to \frac{1}{(k + 1)!}f^{[k+1]}(a) \cdot 0 = 0,$$

as $h \to 0$, as we asserted in (21).

The proof of the Taylor approximation of order k follows the same line as the proofs of Theorems 30.5 and 30.6. We leave the details as an exercise.

We emphasize the simplicity of the result of the Taylor approximation. In the example above, we have successfully approximated the *exponential* function $f(x) = e^x$ (which can only be evaluated by using a calculator) with a *quadratic polynomial* (which can easily be evaluated by hand). In fact, your calculator's evaluation of e^x may very well use some high order Taylor approximation.

Remark   Our proof of the Taylor theorem of order k required that the function under consideration be a C^{k+1} function. Actually, the *k*th order theorem is still true for C^k functions. One needs the extra order of differentiability in the proof only to derive the special form of the remainder.

EXERCISES

30.5 Approximate e^x at $x = 0$ with a Taylor polynomial of order three and with a Taylor polynomial of order four. Then, compute the values of these approximations at $h = 0.2$ and $h = 1$, in each case comparing these approximations with the actual values.

30.6 Use the Taylor polynomial of order two to estimate $(4.2)^{3/2}$.

30.7 Compute the Taylor polynomials of order one, two, and three of the function $y = \sqrt{x + 1}$ about $x = 0$ and of the function $y = \ln x$ about $x = 1$. Then, compute the values of these approximations at $h = 0.2$ and $h = 1$, in each case comparing these approximations with the actual values.

30.8 Prove that there can be at most one number ℓ such that $f(a+h) = f(a) + \ell h + R(h)$ with $R(h)/h \to 0$ as $h \to 0$.

30.9 Carry out the details in the proofs of theorems 30.5 and 30.6.

30.10 Prove Theorem 30.7 for $k = 3$, and then for general k, as follows:

a) Define $g_k(t) \equiv f(t) - P_k(t) - M_k(t - a)^{k+1}$.

b) Show that $g_k(a) = g'_k(a) = \cdots = g_k^{[k]}(a) = 0$.

c) Choose M_k so that $g(a + h) = 0$.

d) Apply Rolle's theorem in turn to $g_k, g'_k, \ldots, g_k^{[k]}$ to find c^* between a and $a + h$ with $g^{[k+1]}(c^*) = 0$.

e) Show that $R_k(h; a) = \dfrac{1}{(k + 1)!} f^{[k+1]}(c^*)h^{k+1}$.

30.3 TAYLOR POLYNOMIALS IN $\mathbf{R}^n$

Approximations by Taylor polynomials are just as important for functions of several variables. We learned in Section 14.4 that the approximation by differentials for a C^1 function $F(x_1, \ldots, x_n)$ of n variables is

$$F(\mathbf{a} + \mathbf{h}) \approx F(\mathbf{a}) + \frac{\partial F}{\partial x_1}(\mathbf{a})h_1 + \cdots + \frac{\partial F}{\partial x_n}(\mathbf{a})h_n. \tag{22}$$

Let $R_1(\mathbf{h}; \mathbf{a})$ denote the difference between the left-hand side of (22) and the right-hand side. The analogue to the behavior (8) of the one dimensional remainder (7) is

$$\frac{R_1(\mathbf{h}; \mathbf{a})}{\|\mathbf{h}\|} \to 0 \quad \text{as} \quad h \to 0. \tag{23}$$

Notice that in $\mathbf{R}^n$ for $n > 1$ we divide R_1 by the *length* of h since in general we cannot divide by a *vector*. We write (22) without subscripts as

$$F(\mathbf{a} + \mathbf{h}) = F(\mathbf{a}) + DF_\mathbf{a}(\mathbf{h}) + R_1(\mathbf{h}; \mathbf{a}),$$

where R_1 satisfies (23). This is the **Taylor approximation of order one** for a function of several variables.

To get a better approximation, we need to include a natural quadratic term in (22). The analogue of the quadratic term $\frac{1}{2}f''(a)h^2$ in the Taylor polynomial of order two for a function f of one variable is $\frac{1}{2}\mathbf{h}^T \cdot D^2 F_\mathbf{a} \cdot \mathbf{h}$, where $D^2 F_\mathbf{a}$ is *the second derivative of F* — the Hessian matrix introduced in Section 14.8:

$$\frac{1}{2}\,\mathbf{h}^T \cdot D^2 F_\mathbf{a} \cdot \mathbf{h}$$

$$= \frac{1}{2}\,(h_1 \quad \cdots \quad h_n)
\begin{pmatrix}
\dfrac{\partial^2 F}{\partial x_1^2} & \cdots & \dfrac{\partial^2 F}{\partial x_n \partial x_1} \\
\vdots & \ddots & \vdots \\
\dfrac{\partial^2 F}{\partial x_1 \partial x_n} & \cdots & \dfrac{\partial^2 F}{\partial x_n^2}
\end{pmatrix}
\begin{pmatrix}
h_1 \\ h_2 \\ \vdots \\ h_n
\end{pmatrix}
\tag{24}$$

$$= \frac{1}{2}\sum_{i,j} \frac{\partial^2 F}{\partial x_i \partial x_j}(\mathbf{a})\,h_i h_j.$$

Because we will be using it a few times in this text, we now present as a formal theorem the n-dimensional analogue of the one-dimensional Taylor approximation (16) of order two.

Theorem 30.8 Suppose that $F: U \to \mathbf{R}^1$ is a C^2 function on an open set U in $\mathbf{R}^n$. Let $\mathbf{a}$ be a point in U. Then, there exists a C^2 function $\mathbf{h} \mapsto R_2(\mathbf{h}; \mathbf{a})$ such that for any point $\mathbf{a} + \mathbf{h}$ in U with the property that the line segment from $\mathbf{a}$ to $\mathbf{a} + \mathbf{h}$ lies in U,

$$F(\mathbf{a} + \mathbf{h}) = F(\mathbf{a}) + DF_\mathbf{a}\mathbf{h} + \frac{1}{2}\mathbf{h}^T D^2 F_\mathbf{a}\mathbf{h} + R_2(\mathbf{h}; \mathbf{a}) \tag{25}$$

where
$$\frac{R_2(\mathbf{h}; \mathbf{a})}{\|\mathbf{h}\|^2} \to 0 \quad \text{as} \quad \mathbf{h} \to 0.$$

In coordinates on $\mathbf{R}^2$, (25) becomes

$$F(a_1 + h_1, a_2 + h_2) = F(a_1, a_2) + \frac{\partial F}{\partial x_1}(\mathbf{a})h_1 + \frac{\partial F}{\partial x_2}(\mathbf{a})h_2$$

$$+ \frac{1}{2}\frac{\partial^2 F}{\partial x_1^2}(\mathbf{a})h_1^2 + \frac{\partial^2 F}{\partial x_1 \partial x_2}(\mathbf{a})h_1 h_2$$

$$+ \frac{1}{2}\frac{\partial^2 F}{\partial x_2^2}(\mathbf{a})h_2^2 + R_2(h_1, h_2; \mathbf{a}).$$

Example 30.3   Let's compute the Taylor approximation of order two of the Cobb-Douglas function $F(x, y) = x^{1/4}y^{3/4}$ at $(1, 1)$. We compute

$$\frac{\partial F}{\partial x} = \frac{1}{4}x^{-3/4}y^{3/4}, \qquad\qquad \frac{\partial F}{\partial y} = \frac{3}{4}x^{1/4}y^{-1/4}$$

$$\frac{\partial^2 F}{\partial x^2} = -\frac{3}{16}x^{-7/4}y^{3/4}, \qquad\qquad \frac{\partial^2 F}{\partial y^2} = -\frac{3}{16}x^{1/4}y^{-5/4},$$

$$\frac{\partial^2 F}{\partial x \partial y} = \frac{\partial^2 F}{\partial y \partial x} = \frac{3}{16}x^{-3/4}y^{-1/4}.$$

Evaluating these partial derivatives at the base point $(1, 1)$ yields

$$\frac{\partial F}{\partial x} = \frac{1}{4}, \frac{\partial F}{\partial y} = \frac{3}{4}, \frac{\partial^2 F}{\partial x^2} = -\frac{3}{16}, \frac{\partial^2 F}{\partial x \partial y} = \frac{3}{16}, \frac{\partial^2 F}{\partial y^2} = -\frac{3}{16}.$$

Therefore,

$$F(1 + h_1, 1 + h_2) = 1 + \begin{pmatrix} \dfrac{1}{4} & \dfrac{3}{4} \end{pmatrix} \begin{pmatrix} h_1 \\ h_2 \end{pmatrix}$$

$$+ \frac{1}{2}\begin{pmatrix} h_1 & h_2 \end{pmatrix} \begin{pmatrix} -\dfrac{3}{16} & +\dfrac{3}{16} \\ +\dfrac{3}{16} & -\dfrac{3}{16} \end{pmatrix} \begin{pmatrix} h_1 \\ h_2 \end{pmatrix} + R(h_1, h_2)$$

$$= 1 + \frac{1}{4}h_1 + \frac{3}{4}h_2 - \frac{3}{32}h_1^2 + \frac{3}{16}h_1 h_2 - \frac{3}{32}h_2^2 + R(h_1, h_2).$$

If we use the Taylor approximation of order one to approximate $F(1.1, 0.9) = (1.1)^{1/4}(0.9)^{3/4}$, we estimate that

$$(1.1)^{1/4} \cdot (0.9)^{3/4} \approx 1 + \frac{1}{4} \cdot (0.1) + \frac{3}{4} \cdot (-0.1) = 0.95.$$

If we use the Taylor approximation of order two, we estimate that

$$(1.1)^{1/4}(0.9)^{3/4} \approx 1 + \frac{1}{4} \cdot (0.1) + \frac{3}{4} \cdot (-0.1)$$

$$- \frac{3}{32} \cdot (0.1)^2 + \frac{3}{16} \cdot (-0.1)(0.1) + \frac{3}{32} \cdot (-0.1)^2$$

$$= 0.94625,$$

which is quite a bit closer to the actual value of $0.9463026 \cdots$.

It is natural to write the kth derivative of F at $\mathbf{a}$ in the direction $\mathbf{h}$ as

$$D^k F_{\mathbf{a}}(\mathbf{h}, \ldots, \mathbf{h}) = \sum_{k_1, \ldots, k_n} \left[\frac{\partial^k F}{\partial x_1^{k_1} \cdots \partial x_n^{k_n}}(\mathbf{a}) h_1^{k_1} h_2^{k_2} \cdots h_n^{k_n} \right],$$

where the summation is over all n-tuples $(k_1, \ldots, k_n)$ of nonnegative integers such that $k_1 + \cdots + k_n = k$. In this notation, we write the second derivative in (24) as

$$\mathbf{h}^T D^2 F_{\mathbf{a}} \mathbf{h} = D^2 F(\mathbf{a})(\mathbf{h}, \mathbf{h}).$$

The following theorem summarizes the approximation of a C^k function on $\mathbf{R^n}$ by a Taylor polynomial of order k.

Theorem 30.9   Let k be a positive integer. Let F be a function which is C^k on a ball B about $\mathbf{a}$ in $\mathbf{R^n}$. Then, there exists a C^k function $R_k(\,\cdot\,;\mathbf{a})$ such that for all $\mathbf{a} + \mathbf{h}$ in B,

$$F(\mathbf{a} + \mathbf{h}) = F(\mathbf{a}) + DF(\mathbf{a})(\mathbf{h}) + \frac{1}{2!} D^2 F(\mathbf{a})(\mathbf{h}, \mathbf{h}) + \cdots$$

$$+ \frac{1}{k!} D^k F(\mathbf{a})(\mathbf{h}, \ldots, \mathbf{h}) + R_k(\mathbf{h}; \mathbf{a}),$$

where

$$\frac{R_k(\mathbf{h}; \mathbf{a})}{\|\mathbf{h}\|^k} \to 0 \text{ as } h \to 0.$$

To prove Theorems 30.8 and 30.9, one lets $f(t)$ parameterize F on the line segment between $\mathbf{a}$ and $\mathbf{a} + \mathbf{h}$, apply the one-dimensional Taylor theorem (Theorem 30.7) to f, and then use the Chain Rule to deduce the conclusion of Theorem 30.8 or 30.9, just as we did in the proof of Theorem 30.4, when we used the one-dimensional Mean Value Theorem to prove the n-dimensional Mean Value Theorem.

Example 30.4   To compute the Taylor polynomial of order three of $F(x, y) = x^{1/4} y^{3/4}$, we compute the various third order derivatives of F:

$$\frac{\partial^3 F}{\partial x^3} = \frac{21}{64} x^{-11/4} y^{3/4}, \qquad\qquad \frac{\partial^3 F}{\partial x^2 \partial y} = -\frac{9}{64} x^{-7/4} y^{-1/4},$$

$$\frac{\partial^3 F}{\partial x \partial y^2} = -\frac{3}{64} x^{-3/4} y^{-5/4}, \quad \text{and} \quad \frac{\partial^3 F}{\partial y^3} = \frac{15}{64} x^{1/4} y^{-9/4}.$$

At $(1, 1)$, these partials take on the values $21/64$, $-9/64$, $-3/64$, and $15/64$, respectively. Therefore, the Taylor polynomial of F of order three is

$$P_3(1 + h_1, 1 + h_2) = 1 + \frac{1}{4}h_1 + \frac{3}{4}h_2 + -\frac{3}{32}h_1^2 + \frac{3}{16}h_1 h_2 - \frac{3}{32}h_2^2$$

$$+ \frac{1}{6}\left(\frac{21}{64}h_1^3 - \frac{27}{64}h_1^2 h_2 - \frac{9}{64}h_1 h_2^2 + \frac{15}{64}h_2^3\right).$$

EXERCISES

30.11   For $F(x, y) = x^{1/4}y^{3/4}$ in the Example 30.4, evaluate and compare a) $F(2, 2)$ and $P_3(2, 2)$,   b) $F(1.5, 2)$ and $P_3(1.5, 2)$.

30.12   Compute the Taylor polynomials of order one, two, and three for the following functions about the indicated point:

a) $x/(1 + y)$ about $(0, 0)$,   b) $e^x\sqrt{1 + y^2}$ about $(0, 0)$,

c) $x^{1/4}y^{1/2}z^{1/4}$ about $(1, 1, 1)$,   d) $kx^a y^b$ about $(1, 1)$.

30.13   Use second order Taylor series about $(1, 1)$ to approximate $F(x, y) = x^{1/2}y^{1/2}$ at $(x, y) = (1.2, 0.9)$.

30.14   Write out the Taylor series of order two for the function $F(x, y) = e^x/(y + 1)$ about the point $(0, 1)$.

30.15   Let $f(x, y) = a_0 + a_1 x + a_2 y + b_1 x^2 + b_2 xy + b_3 y^2$ be a general polynomial of order two. For any point (x^*, y^*), show that the Taylor polynomial of f of order ≥ 2 about (x^*, y^*) is f itself.

30.16   Prove Theorem 30.8.

30.4   SECOND ORDER OPTIMIZATION CONDITIONS

In this section we use the Taylor approximation of order two to carry out the proofs of the second order sufficient conditions (Theorem 17.2) and the second order necessary conditions (Theorem 17.6) for an unconstrained max or min.

Second Order Sufficient Conditions for Optimization

Theorem 30.10   Let $F: U \to \mathbf{R}^1$ be a C^2 function whose domain is an open set U in $\mathbf{R}^n$. Suppose that $\mathbf{x}^*$ is a critical point of F in that it satisfies $DF(\mathbf{x}^*) = \mathbf{0}$.

(a) If the Hessian $D^2F(\mathbf{x}^*)$ is a negative definite symmetric matrix, then $\mathbf{x}^*$ is a strict local max of F.

(b) If the Hessian $D^2F(\mathbf{x}^*)$ is a positive definite symmetric matrix, then $\mathbf{x}^*$ is a strict local min of F.

(c) If $D^2F(\mathbf{x}^*)$ is indefinite, then $\mathbf{x}^*$ is neither a local max nor a local min of F.

Proof Since it is easier to work with a positive definite quadratic form than with a negative definite one, we will prove part *b* here and leave the proof of part *a* as an exercise. As so often happens in calculus, the proof of a theorem in $\mathbf{R^n}$ is simply the *n*-dimensional counterpart of the corresponding proof for $\mathbf{R^1}$. ∎

Proof in $\mathbf{R^1}$ So, we start with a C^2 function f of one variable. By Theorem 30.6, at any given point x_0 in the interior of its domain, we can write f as

$$f(x_0 + h) = f(x_0) + f'(x_0)\, h + \frac{1}{2}\, f''(x_0)\, h^2 + R(h; x_0) \tag{26}$$

where
$$\frac{R(h; x_0)}{h^2} \to 0 \quad \text{as} \quad h \to 0. \tag{27}$$

Since we will be keeping the base point x_0 fixed, we will write $R(h; x_0)$ simply as $R(h)$.

We assume that

$$f'(x_0) = 0 \quad \text{and} \quad f''(x_0) = a > 0. \tag{28}$$

Statement (27) says that $R(h)$ becomes negligible for h small. If $R(h)$ were identically zero, plugging (28) into (26) would yield

$$f(x_0 + h) = f(x_0) + \tfrac{1}{2}ah^2,$$

or
$$f(x_0 + h) - f(x_0) = \tfrac{1}{2}ah^2. \tag{29}$$

Since the right-hand side of (29) is strictly positive for $h \neq 0$, (29) implies that

$$f(x_0 + h) - f(x_0) > 0; \qquad \text{that is,} \qquad f(x_0 + h) > f(x_0) \quad \text{for all } h \neq 0,$$

and so x_0 is a strict min of f.

We need to work a little more delicately to handle the usual case in which the remainder R is not identically zero. In equation (26), substitute 0 for $f'(x_0)$, substitute the positive number a for $f''(x_0)$ from (28), put the $f(x_0)$-term on the left-hand side, and divide through by h^2:

$$\frac{f(x_0 + h) - f(x_0)}{h^2} = \frac{a}{2} + \frac{R(h)}{h^2}. \tag{30}$$

Since $R(h)/h^2 \to 0$ as $h \to 0$, there exists an $r > 0$ such that

$$0 < |h| < r \quad \Longrightarrow \quad -\frac{a}{4} < \frac{R(h)}{h^2} < \frac{a}{4}. \tag{31}$$

Using $R(h)/h^2 > -a/4$, we can conclude that for $0 < |h| < r$,

$$\frac{a}{2} + \frac{R(h)}{h^2} > \frac{a}{2} - \frac{a}{4} = \frac{a}{4} > 0. \tag{32}$$

Plugging (32) into (30), we conclude that for $0 < |h| < r$,

$$\frac{f(x_0 + h) - f(x_0)}{h^2} > 0; \qquad \text{that is,} \qquad f(x_0 + h) > f(x_0).$$

We rewrite this statement as $f(x) > f(x_0)$ for all $x \neq x_0$ in the interval $(x_0 - r, x_0 + r)$. Notice that this proof even provides an interval about x_0 in which x_0 is a global min of f. ∎

Proof in $\mathbf{R}^n$ We turn now to the proof of the corresponding theorem in $\mathbf{R}^n$. As we mentioned earlier, the idea of the proof in $\mathbf{R}^n$ is basically the same as that of the proof in $\mathbf{R}^1$. We need only make two changes:

(*i*) replace the condition $f''(x_0) > 0$ by the condition that the Hessian matrix $D^2F(\mathbf{x}_0)$ is positive definite, and

(*ii*) since the perturbation term $\mathbf{h}$ is a vector in $\mathbf{R}^n$, find an analogue to the process of dividing through by h as we did to get equation (30) above.

We assume that $\mathbf{x}_0$ is a critical point of the C^2 function F and that $D^2F(\mathbf{x}_0)$ is positive definite. Write the Taylor approximation of F at the critical point $\mathbf{x}_0$ (Theorem 30.8):

$$F(\mathbf{x}_0 + \mathbf{h}) = F(\mathbf{x}_0) + DF(\mathbf{x}_0)\mathbf{h} + \tfrac{1}{2}\mathbf{h}^T D^2F(\mathbf{x}_0)\mathbf{h} + R(\mathbf{h}) \tag{33}$$

where

$$\frac{R(\mathbf{h})}{\|\mathbf{h}\|^2} \to 0 \quad \text{as} \quad \mathbf{h} \to \mathbf{0}. \tag{34}$$

Once again, put the $F(\mathbf{x}_0)$-term on the left side and use the hypothesis that $DF(\mathbf{x}_0) = \mathbf{0}$ to rewrite (33) as

$$F(\mathbf{x}_0 + \mathbf{h}) - F(\mathbf{x}_0) = \tfrac{1}{2}\mathbf{h}^T D^2F(\mathbf{x}_0)\mathbf{h} + R(\mathbf{h}).$$

Since we cannot divide this equation through by the *vector* $\mathbf{h}$, we divide through by the square of the *norm* of $\mathbf{h}$:

$$\frac{F(\mathbf{x}_0 + \mathbf{h}) - F(\mathbf{x}_0)}{\|\mathbf{h}\|^2} = \frac{1}{2}\frac{\mathbf{h}^T D^2F(\mathbf{x}_0)\,\mathbf{h}}{\|\mathbf{h}\|^2} + \frac{R(\mathbf{h})}{\|\mathbf{h}\|^2}$$

$$= \frac{1}{2}\frac{\mathbf{h}^T}{\|\mathbf{h}\|} \cdot D^2F(\mathbf{x}_0) \cdot \frac{\mathbf{h}}{\|\mathbf{h}\|} + \frac{R(\mathbf{h})}{\|\mathbf{h}\|^2}. \tag{35}$$

In the last step in (35), we have apportioned the $\|\mathbf{h}\|^2$-divisor into two factors — one for each of the $\mathbf{h}$'s.

As a polynomial of degree two, the quadratic form

$$Q(\mathbf{h}) \equiv \mathbf{h}^T \cdot D^2 F(\mathbf{x}_0) \cdot \mathbf{h}$$

is a continuous function on $\mathbf{R}^n$. Let

$$a \equiv \min\{Q(\mathbf{v}) : \|\mathbf{v}\| = 1\}.$$

The unit sphere $\{\mathbf{v} : \|\mathbf{v}\| = 1\}$ is a closed and bounded subset of $\mathbf{R}^n$; in other words, it is compact. By applying Weierstrass's theorem (Theorem 30.1) to the function Q restricted to the compact unit sphere, we conclude that there exists a $\mathbf{w}$ on the unit sphere such that $Q(\mathbf{w}) = a$. Since Q is positive definite and $\mathbf{w} \neq \mathbf{0}$, $a = Q(\mathbf{w}) > 0$. It follows that

$$\frac{1}{2}a \leq \frac{1}{2}Q\left(\frac{\mathbf{h}}{\|\mathbf{h}\|}\right) = \frac{1}{2}\frac{\mathbf{h}^T}{\|\mathbf{h}\|}D^2 F(\mathbf{x}_0)\frac{\mathbf{h}}{\|\mathbf{h}\|} \qquad (36)$$

for all $\mathbf{h} \neq \mathbf{0}$. Just as we did at step (31) for one dimension, we conclude from condition (34) that there is an $r > 0$ such that

$$0 < \|\mathbf{h}\| < r \quad \Longrightarrow \quad -\frac{a}{4} < \frac{R(\mathbf{h})}{\|h\|^2} < \frac{a}{4}. \qquad (37)$$

Combining (36) and (37), we find that for $0 < \|\mathbf{h}\| < r$,

$$\frac{1}{2}\frac{\mathbf{h}^T}{\|\mathbf{h}\|}D^2 F(\mathbf{x}_0)\frac{\mathbf{h}}{\|\mathbf{h}\|} + \frac{R(\mathbf{h})}{\|\mathbf{h}\|^2} > \frac{a}{2} - \frac{a}{4} = \frac{a}{4} > 0.$$

In other words, the last line of (35) is positive for $0 < \|\mathbf{h}\| < r$; therefore, so is the first expression in (35):

$$0 < \|\mathbf{h}\| < r \Longrightarrow \frac{F(\mathbf{x}_0 + \mathbf{h}) - F(\mathbf{x}_0)}{\|\mathbf{h}\|^2} > 0$$

$$\Longrightarrow F(\mathbf{x}_0 + \mathbf{h}) > F(\mathbf{x}_0).$$

We conclude that $\mathbf{x}_0$ is a strict local min of F. ∎

Indefinite Hessian

Proof We next prove part *c* of Theorem 30.10: if $DF(\mathbf{x}_0) = \mathbf{0}$ and $D^2 F(\mathbf{x}_0)$ is *indefinite*, then $\mathbf{x}_0$ is neither a local min nor a local max of F. Recall that $D^2 F(\mathbf{x}_0)$

is indefinite if there exists a vector $\mathbf{v}$ such that $\mathbf{v}^T D^2 F(\mathbf{x}_0)\mathbf{v} > 0$ and a vector $\mathbf{w}$ such that $\mathbf{w}^T D^2 F(\mathbf{x}_0)\mathbf{w} < 0$. We will show that

$$DF(\mathbf{x}_0) = \mathbf{0} \quad \text{and} \quad \mathbf{v}^T D^2 F(\mathbf{x}_0)\mathbf{v} > 0 \tag{38}$$

imply that

$$t \longmapsto g(t) \equiv F(\mathbf{x}_0 + t\mathbf{v}) \text{ is an increasing function of } t. \tag{39}$$

This will rule out $\mathbf{x}_0$ being a local max of F.

Under hypothesis (38), use the Chain Rule to compute the first and second derivatives of the function g defined in (39):

$$g'(t) = \frac{d}{dt} F(\mathbf{x}_0 + t\mathbf{v}) = \sum_i \frac{\partial F}{\partial x_i}(\mathbf{x}_0 + t\mathbf{v})v_i = DF(\mathbf{x}_0 + t\mathbf{v})\mathbf{v}.$$

So

$$g'(0) = DF(\mathbf{x}_0)\mathbf{v} = 0.$$

Taking another derivative, we compute

$$g''(t) = \frac{d}{dt} \sum_i \frac{\partial F}{\partial x_i}(\mathbf{x}_0 + t\mathbf{v})v_i = \sum_{i,j} \frac{\partial^2 F}{\partial x_j \partial x_i}(\mathbf{x}_0 + t\mathbf{v})v_i v_j$$

$$= \mathbf{v}^T D^2 F(\mathbf{x}_0 + t\mathbf{v})\mathbf{v}.$$

Therefore, $g''(0) = \mathbf{v}^t D^2 F(\mathbf{x}_0)\mathbf{v} > 0$, by (38).

Since $g''(0) > 0$, $g'(t)$ is an increasing function of t at $t = 0$. Since $g'(0) = 0$, $g'(t)$ must be positive for t in some interval $(0, \varepsilon)$ just to the right of $t = 0$. This, in turn, implies that $g(t) = F(\mathbf{x}_0 + t\mathbf{v})$ is an increasing function of t for $t \in (0, \varepsilon)$. In particular, $\mathbf{x}_0$ cannot be a local max of F. As Exercise 30.17 indicates, a similar argument shows that $\mathbf{w}^T D^2 F(\mathbf{x}_0)\mathbf{w} < 0$ implies that $t \longmapsto F(\mathbf{x}_0 + t\mathbf{w})$ is a decreasing function of t and therefore $\mathbf{x}_0$ cannot be a local min either. We conclude that if $DF(\mathbf{x}_0) = \mathbf{0}$ and $D^2 F(\mathbf{x}_0)$ is indefinite, then $\mathbf{x}_0$ can be neither a local min nor a local max of F. This completes the proof of Theorem 30.10. ∎

Second Order Necessary Conditions for Optimization

We turn now to the proof of the second order *necessary* conditions for optimization. (See Theorem 17.6.) This proof follows easily from the statements of the second order sufficient conditions.

Theorem 30.11 Let $F: U \to \mathbf{R}^n$ be a C^2 function whose domain U is in $\mathbf{R}^n$. Suppose that $\mathbf{x}^*$ is an interior point of U and that $\mathbf{x}^*$ is a local min (respectively, max) of F. Then, $DF(\mathbf{x}^*) = \mathbf{0}$ and $D^2 F(\mathbf{x}^*)$ is positive semidefinite (respectively, negative semidefinite).

Proof As before, we look at the $n = 1$ case first. The second order sufficient condition for a critical point x_0 of a C^2 function f states that

$$f''(x_0) < 0 \Longrightarrow x_0 \text{ is a strict local max.}$$

Therefore, if the critical point x_0 is a local min, we cannot have $f''(x_0) < 0$. It follows that $f''(x_0) \geq 0$ at a local min.

In n-dimensions, Exercise 30.17 states that if $DF(\mathbf{x}_0) = \mathbf{0}$ and $\mathbf{w}^T D^2 F(\mathbf{x}_0)\mathbf{w} < 0$ for some vector $\mathbf{w}$, then $\mathbf{x}_0$ cannot be a local min of F. Therefore, if a critical point $\mathbf{x}_0$ is a local min of F, there is no vector $\mathbf{w}$ such that $\mathbf{w}^T D^2 F(\mathbf{x}_0)\mathbf{w} < 0$; in other words, $\mathbf{v}^T D^2 F(\mathbf{x}_0)\mathbf{v} \geq 0$ for all $\mathbf{v} \in \mathbf{R}^n$ and $D^2 F(\mathbf{x}_0)$ is positive semidefinite. Along with Exercise 30.19 below, this completes the proof of the theorem. ∎

EXERCISES

30.17 Prove that the conditions $DF(\mathbf{x}_0) = \mathbf{0}$ and $\mathbf{w}^T D^2 F(\mathbf{x}_0)\mathbf{w} < 0$ imply that the function $t \longmapsto F(\mathbf{x}_0 + t\mathbf{w})$ is decreasing in t for small, positive t.

30.18 Write out a a careful proof of the corresponding second order sufficient condition for a *maximum* on $\mathbf{R}^1$ and on $\mathbf{R}^n$.

30.19 Present a careful proof of the second order necessary condition for a local max in $\mathbf{R}^n$.

30.20 Suppose that $f: \mathbf{R}^1 \to \mathbf{R}^1$ is a C^k function of one variable, $k > 1$. Suppose further that $f'(x_0) = f''(x_0) = \cdots = f^{[k-1]}(x_0) = 0$, and that the kth derivative $f^{[k]}(x_0) \neq 0$. Use the Taylor approximation of f of order k to prove:

a) if k is even and $f^{[k]}(x_0) > 0$, then x_0 is a strict local min of f;

b) if k is even and $f^{[k]}(x_0) < 0$, then x_0 is a strict local max of f;

c) if k is odd, x_0 is neither a local max nor a local min.

30.5 CONSTRAINED OPTIMIZATION

We complete this chapter by proving Theorem 19.6 that provides a sufficient second order condition for a *constrained maximum*. We will prove this result for the case of equality constraints. This proof can easily be adapted for inequality constraints by working in an open ball B throughout which the nonbinding inequality constraints are strict inequalities and by treating the binding inequality constraints like equality constraints on B.

Theorem 30.12 Let $f, h_1, \ldots, h_k$ be C^2 functions on $\mathbf{R}^n$. Consider the problem of maximizing f on the constraint set

$$C_h \equiv \{\mathbf{x} : h_1(\mathbf{x}) = c_1, \ldots, h_k(\mathbf{x}) = c_k\}.$$

We assume that:

(a) $\mathbf{x}^*$ lies in C_h, that is, $h_i(\mathbf{x}^*) = c_i$ for $i = 1, \ldots, k$;

(b) $\mathbf{x}^*$ satisfies the first order condition that there exist $\mu_1^*, \ldots, \mu_m^*$ such that

$$D_{\mathbf{x}}L(\mathbf{x}^*) = Df(\mathbf{x}^*) - \sum_i \mu_i^* Dh_i(\mathbf{x}^*) = \mathbf{0}, \qquad (40)$$

where
$$L(\mathbf{x}, \mu^*) = f(\mathbf{x}) - \sum_i \mu_i^*(h_i(\mathbf{x}) - c_i); \qquad (41)$$

(c) $\mathbf{x}^*, \mu_1^*, \ldots, \mu_m^*$ satisfy the second order condition

$$\mathbf{v}^T D_{\mathbf{x}}^2 L(\mathbf{x}^*)\mathbf{v} < 0$$

for all nonzero $\mathbf{v}$ such that $D\mathbf{h}(\mathbf{x}^*)\mathbf{v} = \mathbf{0}$.

Then, $\mathbf{x}^*$ is a strict local constrained max of f on C_h.

Proof We want to show that $\mathbf{x}^*$ is a strict local max of f on the constraint set C_h. We assume the opposite, namely that there exists a sequence $\{\mathbf{x}_j\}_{j=1}^{\infty}$ in $\mathbf{R}^n$ such that $\mathbf{x}_j \to \mathbf{x}^*$ with $\mathbf{x}_j \neq \mathbf{x}^*$ for all j and

$$h_i(\mathbf{x}_j) = c_i \text{ for all } i, j \quad \text{and} \quad f(\mathbf{x}_j) \geq f(\mathbf{x}^*) \text{ for all } j. \qquad (42)$$

Construct a new sequence with these $\mathbf{x}_j$'s:

$$\mathbf{v}_j = \frac{\mathbf{x}_j - \mathbf{x}^*}{\|\mathbf{x}_j - \mathbf{x}^*\|}.$$

The $\mathbf{v}_j$'s are all vectors of length 1; they all lie on the unit sphere S^{n-1} in n-space:

$$S^{n-1} = \{\mathbf{v} \in \mathbf{R}^n : \|\mathbf{v}\| = 1\}.$$

This sphere is a closed and bounded set, i.e., a compact set. Once again by Theorem 12.14, every sequence in this compact set has a convergent subsequence. By taking the appropriate subsequences, we assume that we have a sequence $\{\mathbf{x}_r\}$ that satisfies the following four properties:

(i) $\mathbf{x}_r \to \mathbf{x}^*$ as $r \to \infty$ and $\mathbf{x}_r \neq \mathbf{x}^*$ for all r;

(ii) $f(\mathbf{x}_r) \geq f(\mathbf{x}^*)$ for all r;

(iii) $h_i(\mathbf{x}_r) = h_i(\mathbf{x}^*) = c_i$ for $i = 1, \ldots, m$ and $r = 1, 2, \ldots$; and

(iv) $\mathbf{v}_r \equiv \dfrac{\mathbf{x}_r - \mathbf{x}^*}{\|\mathbf{x}_r - \mathbf{x}^*\|} \to \mathbf{v}^*$, as $r \to \infty$.

Since $\mathbf{h}$ is C^1, we write out its Taylor polynomial of order one about $\mathbf{x}^*$, evaluating it at each $\mathbf{x}_r$:

$$\mathbf{h}(\mathbf{x}_r) = \mathbf{h}(\mathbf{x}^*) + D\mathbf{h}(\mathbf{x}^*)(\mathbf{x}_r - \mathbf{x}^*) + R(\mathbf{x}_r;\mathbf{x}^*), \tag{43}$$

where
$$\frac{R(\mathbf{x}_r;\mathbf{x}^*)}{\|\mathbf{x}_r - \mathbf{x}^*\|} \to 0 \quad \text{as} \quad \mathbf{x}_r \to \mathbf{x}^*. \tag{44}$$

Subtract $\mathbf{h}(\mathbf{x}^*)$ from both sides of (43), divide both sides of (43) by $\|\mathbf{x}_r - \mathbf{x}^*\|$, and apply property *iii*:

$$\mathbf{0} = \frac{\mathbf{h}(\mathbf{x}_r) - \mathbf{h}(\mathbf{x}^*)}{\|\mathbf{x}_r - \mathbf{x}^*\|} = D\mathbf{h}(\mathbf{x}^*)\left(\frac{\mathbf{x}_r - \mathbf{x}^*}{\|\mathbf{x}_r - \mathbf{x}^*\|}\right) + \frac{R(\mathbf{x}_r;\mathbf{x}^*)}{\|\mathbf{x}_r - \mathbf{x}^*\|}. \tag{45}$$

Let $r \to \infty$ in (45). By property *iv* and statement (44),

$$\mathbf{0} = D\mathbf{h}(\mathbf{x}^*)\mathbf{v}^*. \tag{46}$$

Now write out the second order Taylor polynomial of the Lagrangian as a function of $\mathbf{x}$ about $\mathbf{x}^*$:

$$L(\mathbf{x}_r) = L(\mathbf{x}^*) + D_\mathbf{x}L(\mathbf{x}^*)(\mathbf{x}_r - \mathbf{x}^*)$$
$$+ \frac{1}{2}(\mathbf{x}_r - \mathbf{x}^*)^T D_\mathbf{x}^2 L(\mathbf{x}^*)(\mathbf{x}_r - \mathbf{x}^*) + S(\mathbf{x}_r;\mathbf{x}^*), \tag{47}$$

where
$$\frac{S(\mathbf{x}_r;\mathbf{x}^*)}{\|\mathbf{x}_r - \mathbf{x}^*\|^2} \to 0 \quad \text{as } \mathbf{x}_r \to \mathbf{x}^*. \tag{48}$$

By hypothesis b, $D_\mathbf{x}L(\mathbf{x}^*) = \mathbf{0}$; also,

$$L(\mathbf{x}_r) = f(\mathbf{x}_r) - \sum_i \mu_i^*(h_i(\mathbf{x}_r) - c_i) \qquad \text{(by (41))}$$

$$= f(\mathbf{x}_r) \qquad \text{(by property \textit{iii})}.$$

Using these results, rewrite (47) as

$$f(\mathbf{x}_r) - f(\mathbf{x}^*) = \frac{1}{2}(\mathbf{x}_r - \mathbf{x}^*)^T D_\mathbf{x}^2 L(\mathbf{x}^*)(\mathbf{x}_r - \mathbf{x}^*) + S(\mathbf{x}_r;\mathbf{x}^*). \tag{49}$$

The left-hand side of (49) is ≥ 0 by property *ii*. Divide both sides of (49) by $\|\mathbf{x}_r - \mathbf{x}^*\|^2$:

$$0 \leq \frac{f(\mathbf{x}_r) - f(\mathbf{x}^*)}{\|\mathbf{x}_r - \mathbf{x}^*\|^2} \tag{50}$$

$$= \frac{1}{2} \frac{(\mathbf{x}_r - \mathbf{x}^*)^T}{\|\mathbf{x}_r - \mathbf{x}^*\|} \cdot D_{\mathbf{x}}^2 L(\mathbf{x}^*) \cdot \frac{(\mathbf{x}_r - \mathbf{x}^*)}{\|\mathbf{x}_r - \mathbf{x}^*\|} + \frac{S(\mathbf{x}_r; \mathbf{x}^*)}{\|\mathbf{x}_r - \mathbf{x}^*\|^2}. \tag{51}$$

Let $\mathbf{x}_r \to \mathbf{x}^*$ in (50) and (51). Since (51) is ≥ 0 for each r and each term in (51) has a limit as $r \to \infty$, the limit of (51) as $r \to \infty$ must be ≥ 0. However, by property *iv* and statement (48), the limit of the expression in (51) is

$$\tfrac{1}{2} \mathbf{v}^{*T} \cdot D_{\mathbf{x}}^2 L(\mathbf{x}^*) \cdot \mathbf{v}^*, \tag{52}$$

an expression which we have just demonstrated to be nonnegative. However, this contradicts the conclusion that, by (46) and the second order condition *c* for L at $\mathbf{x}^*$, the expression in (52) is negative.

We conclude that no sequence $\{\mathbf{x}_j\}$ exists which satisfies assumption (42); and therefore that $\mathbf{x}^*$ is a strict local max of f on the constraint set. ∎

PART VIII

Appendices

Sets, Numbers, and Proofs

The basic ingredients of mathematics are sets, numbers, and functions. This appendix begins with a presentation of the vocabulary of sets and of numbers and concludes with a discussion about mathematical proofs.

A1.1   SETS

Vocabulary of Sets

A **set** is any well-specified collection of elements. A set may contain finitely many or infinitely many elements, but the criterion for membership in the set must be well understood. For any set A, we write $a \in A$ to indicate that a is a member of set A, and $a \notin A$ to indicate that a is not in the set A. The most commonly used set in this book is the set $\mathbf{R}$ of all real numbers.

We sometimes encounter the set which *contains no elements*. It is called the **empty set** or **null set** and is denoted by $\varnothing$.

We will use standard notation for defining sets. For example, the set of all nonnegative numbers is written as

$$\mathbf{R}_+ \equiv \{x \in \mathbf{R} : x \geq 0\}.$$

Since every element of $\mathbf{R}_+$ is an element of $\mathbf{R}$, we say that $\mathbf{R}_+$ is a **subset** of $\mathbf{R}$, and write $\mathbf{R}_+ \subset \mathbf{R}$ or $\mathbf{R} \supset \mathbf{R}_+$. Sometimes, a set is defined simply by listing its elements: $A = \{1, 2, 3\}$, or even $\mathbf{N} = \{1, 2, 3, \ldots\}$, provided the ellipsis $(\ldots)$ is well understood.

Operations with Sets

Given two sets A and B, new sets can be formed through the following set operations on A and B:

(1) $A \cup B$, spoken "A union B," is the set of all elements that are either in A or in B (or in both):

$$A \cup B \equiv \{x : x \in A \text{ or } x \in B\};$$

(2) $A \cap B$, spoken "A intersect B," is the set of all elements that are common to both A and B:

$$A \cap B \equiv \{x : x \in A \text{ and } x \in B\};$$

(3) $A - B$, or sometimes $A \setminus B$, spoken "A minus B," is the set of all elements of A that are not in B:

$$A - B \equiv \{x : x \in A \text{ and } x \notin B\}.$$

If it is clear that all sets under discussion are subsets of some (universal) set U, $U - A$ is often written as A^c, and called the **complement** of A (in U). For example, if all sets under discussion are sets of real numbers, then the complement of $\mathbf{R}_+$, $(\mathbf{R}_+)^c$, is the set of all negative numbers, $\{x \in \mathbf{R} : x < 0\}$.

A1.2   NUMBERS

Vocabulary

Nearly all the sets discussed in this text are sets of numbers. The most basic numbers are the **counting numbers** $\{1, 2, 3, \ldots\}$, also called the **natural numbers**. The set of natural numbers is usually denoted by $\mathbf{N}$:

$$\mathbf{N} = \{1, 2, 3, 4, \ldots\}.$$

The sum or product of two natural numbers is another natural number, but the difference of two natural numbers need not be in $\mathbf{N}$. For example, $3 - 5 \notin \mathbf{N}$. If $\mathbf{N}$ is augmented by the number zero and by the negatives of the natural numbers, the resulting set is the set of **integers**, and often denoted by

$$\mathbf{Z} = \{\ldots, -3, -2, -1, 0, +1, +2, +3, \ldots\}.$$

The sum, *difference*, and product of two integers in another integer, but the *quotient* of two integers is usually not an integer. So, the next natural extension is to the set $\mathbf{Q}$ of all *quotients* of integers:

$$\mathbf{Q} \equiv \left\{ \frac{a}{b} : a, b \in \mathbf{Z}; \, b \neq 0 \right\}.$$

This set $\mathbf{Q}$ is called the set of **rational numbers**, since it is formed by taking *ratios* of integers. The set of rational numbers has the desired property that if a and b are elements of $\mathbf{Q}$, then so are $a + b$, $a - b$, $a \cdot b$, and a/b. (We always rule out division by 0.)

Can every number be written as the quotient of two integers? In other words, is every number a rational number? Although it is not readily apparent, some important numbers, like $\sqrt{2}$, e, and π, cannot be written as quotients of integers. The proof that $\sqrt{2}$ cannot be written as a quotient of integers will be presented later in this appendix. Numbers that cannot be written as ratios or quotients of integers are called **irrational numbers**.

Rational numbers can also be distinguished from irrational numbers by their decimal expansions. Numbers whose decimal expansions terminate after a finite number of digits (like 0.25 or 3.12345) or repeat the same pattern with perfect regularity from some point on (like $1.33333\cdots$ or $3.256256256\cdots$) are rational numbers. On the other hand, numbers whose decimal expansions never end and have no repeating pattern are irrational numbers. Since any number that is not rational is irrational, the set of all rational and irrational numbers is the set of all numbers **R**.

As we will see in Appendix A3, in order to solve certain polynomial equations that are needed to model oscillatory phenomena, mathematicians have expanded the set of numbers **R** to include "imaginary numbers" — numbers whose squares are negative numbers. To distinguish the set of numbers we are considering from this expanded number system, the set **R** of rational and irrational numbers is called the set of **real numbers**.

In the remainder of this appendix certain subsets of integers play an important role. This is a natural place to present their formal definitions.

Definition   An integer n is called an **even number** if there is an *integer m* such that $n = 2m$. An integer that is not even is called an **odd integer**.

Definition   A natural number m is called a **prime number** if whenever m can be written as the product $m = a \cdot b$ of two natural numbers, then $a = 1$ or $b = 1$. The first six prime numbers are 1, 2, 3, 5, 7, and 11.

Properties of Addition and Multiplication

An important feature about numbers is that we can operate on them via addition and multiplication — and their inverse operations, subtraction and division — to obtain other numbers.

The operations of addition ($+$) and multiplication ($\cdot$) on pairs of real numbers are characterized by the following properties:

(1) (**Closure**) If a and b are in **R**, so are $a + b$ and $a \cdot b$.
(2) (**Commutative**) For any $a, b \in \mathbf{R}$, $a + b = b + a$ and $a \cdot b = b \cdot a$.
(3) (**Associative**) If $a, b, c \in \mathbf{R}$, $(a+b)+c = a+(b+c)$ and $(a \cdot b) \cdot c = a \cdot (b \cdot c)$.
(4) (**Identity**) There is an element $0 \in \mathbf{R}$ such that $a + 0 = a$ for all $a \in \mathbf{R}$. There is an element $1 \in \mathbf{R}$ such that $a \cdot 1 = a$ for all $a \in \mathbf{R}$.
(5) (**Inverse**) For any $a \in \mathbf{R}$, there is an element $b \in \mathbf{R}$ such that $a + b = 0$; such a b is usually written as $-a$. For any nonzero $a \in \mathbf{R}$, there is an element $c \in \mathbf{R}$ such that $a \cdot c = 1$; such a c is usually written as $1/a$.
(6) (**Distributive**) For all $a, b, c \in \mathbf{R}$, $a \cdot (b + c) = a \cdot b + a \cdot c$.

Each of the first five properties has an additive and a multiplicative component. The last property is the link between these two operations.

Least Upper Bound Property

There are two more abstract properties of real numbers that arise a number of times throughout this book: the least upper bound property and the greatest lower bound property.

Definition   Let S be a subset of **R** and let $b \in \mathbf{R}$. Then, the number b is called an **upper bound** for S if $a \le b$ for all $a \in S$; the number b is called a **lower bound** for S if $b \le a$ for all $a \in S$.

Definition   If b is an upper bound for S and no element smaller than b is an upper bound for S, then b is called a **least upper bound (lub)** for S. Similarly, if b is a lower bound for S and no number larger than b is a lower bound of S, then b is called a **greatest lower bound (glb)** for S.

We can now state the least upper bound and greatest lower bound properties on **R**.

(Least upper bound and greatest lower bound properties)   Let S be any subset of **R**. If S has an upper bound, it has a least upper bound; if S has a lower bound, it has a greatest lower bound.

Example A1.1   Let S be the set of all numbers of the form

$$S \equiv \{0.3, 0.33, 0.333, 0.3333, \ldots\}.$$

Of course, 0 is a lower bound and 1 is an upper bound for S. The least upper bound of S is $1/3$. The greatest lower bound is 0.3, the first element in this increasing sequence of numbers. Notice that this set S contains its glb, but not its lub.

EXERCISES

A1.1   Let A be the set of even integers, B the set of odd integers, C the set of integers from 1 to 10, and D the set of nonnegative real numbers. Describe $C \cup A$, $C \cup B$, $C - B$, $A \cap D$, $B \cup D$, $A \cup B$, and $A \cap B$.

A1.2   Find the glb and the lub (if one exists) of each of the following sets of real numbers:

a) the natural numbers **N**,

b) $\{1/1, 1/2, 1/3, \ldots, 1/n, \ldots\}$,

c) $\{1/2, -1/2, 2/3, -2/3, 3/4, \ldots\}$,

d) $\{x \in \mathbf{R} : 0 < x < 1\}$,

e) $\{x \in \mathbf{R} : 0 \le x < 1\}$

f) $\{x \in \mathbf{R} : 0 \le x \le 1\}$.

A1.3 PROOFS

One of the important roles of mathematics in the sciences is to deduce complex scientific principles from a collection of generally agreed on assumptions. For example, in classical physics one deduces from Newton's law of motion ($F = ma$) that the planets move in planar elliptical orbits about the sun. In economics one deduces from the consumer's budget equation that a 1 percent increase in a consumer's income leads to a 1 percent average increase in expenditure on the goods under study and that an increase in the price of any good leads to a decrease in the *average* consumption of all goods.

The first such scientific system one encounters is usually the Euclidean model for planar geometry that one studies in secondary school. Beginning with the undefined terms "point" and "line" and with the well-accepted system of Euclid's axioms (for example, "Given two points P and Q, there is exactly one line that contains P and Q;"), one uses careful techniques of mathematical logic to prove theorems about geometric objects, for example, the angles of a triangle sum to 180° or the sum of the squares of the lengths of the legs of a right triangle equals the square of the length of the hypotenuse.

The same principles of logic work in all these sciences. One starts with a clearly stated (and, hopefully, generally accepted) set of hypotheses and, usually, with some previously proven principles. Each of these hypotheses and theorems states that if some situation A occurs, then situation B must occur too; in short, A implies B ($A \implies B$). For example, situation A can be "sides PQ and PR of triangle PQR have the same length," and situation B can be "$\angle PQR = \angle PRQ$ in $\triangle PQR$." (See Figure A1.1.) Finally, one applies the principles of mathematical logic to carefully deduce new principles from the axioms and old principles.

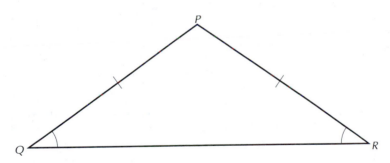

If the length of PQ equals the length of PR in △PQR, ∠PQR = ∠PRQ.

Figure A1.1

Direct Proofs

The direct way of proving that $A \implies B$ is to find a sequence of accepted axioms and theorems of the form $A_i \implies A_{i+1}$ for $i = 1, \ldots, n$, so that $A_0 = A$ and $A_{n+1} = B$:

$$A = A_0 \implies A_1 \implies A_2 \implies A_3 \implies \cdots \implies A_{n-1} \implies A_n = B. \quad (1)$$

The hard part, of course, is to find the sequence of theorems that fills in the gap from A to B in (1). Proofs of the form (1) are called **direct proofs**; the method is called **deductive reasoning**.

We illustrate deductive reasoning by deriving some properties of numbers from the six properties of addition and multiplication listed above. These proofs also rely on some basic properties of equality which we will accept as basic axioms; for example, for all $a, b, c, d \in \mathbf{R}$,

$$a = b \text{ and } b = c \Longrightarrow a = c, \tag{2}$$

$$a = b \Longrightarrow a + c = b + c, \tag{3}$$

$$a = b \Longrightarrow a \cdot c = b \cdot c, \tag{4}$$

$$a = b \text{ and } c = d \Longrightarrow a \cdot c = b \cdot d. \tag{5}$$

We will write out these first proofs rather carefully, that is, we will skip few steps and we will justify each step with a phrase or sentence.

Theorem A1.1   For any $x, y, z \in \mathbf{R}$, if $x + z = y + z$, then $x = y$.

Proof

1. $x + z = y + z$.	Hypothesis.
2. There exists $(-z)$ such that $z + (-z) = 0$.	Additive inverse property.
3. $(x + z) + (-z) = (y + z) + (-z)$.	Rule (3).
4. $x + (z + (-z)) = y + (z + (-z))$.	Additive associative property.
5. $x + 0 = y + 0$.	Step 2.
6. $x = y$.	Additive identity property. ∎

Theorem A1.2   For any $x \in \mathbf{R}$, $x \cdot 0 = 0$.

Proof

1. $0 + 0 = 0$.	Additive identity property.
2. $x \cdot (0 + 0) = x \cdot 0$.	Rule (4).
3. $(x \cdot 0) + (x \cdot 0) = (x \cdot 0)$.	Distributive property.
4. $(x \cdot 0) + 0 = (x \cdot 0)$.	Additive inverse property.
5. $(x \cdot 0) + (x \cdot 0) = (x \cdot 0) + 0$.	Rule (2).
6. $x \cdot 0 = 0$.	Theorem A1.1. ∎

The following proposition about even integers will be useful in proving that $\sqrt{2}$ is an irrational number.

Theorem A1.3   Let m be an *even* integer and p be any integer. Then, $m \cdot p$ is an even integer.

Proof

1. m is an even integer. Given.
2. There is an integer q such that Definition of even integer.
   $m = 2 \cdot q$.
3. $m \cdot p = (2 \cdot q) \cdot p$. Rule (4) above.
4. $m \cdot p = 2 \cdot (q \cdot p)$. Associative property of
   multiplication.
5. $m \cdot p$ is even. Definition of even integer. ∎

Converse and Contrapositive

Given a proposition $A \Longrightarrow B$, we now discuss two closely related propositions: the converse and the contrapositive.

Definition Consider a proposition $\mathcal{P}$ of the form $A \Longrightarrow B$: if hypothesis A holds, conclusion B holds. The **converse** of $\mathcal{P}$ is the statement $B \Longrightarrow A$, which reverses the hypothesis and conclusion of $\mathcal{P}$.

If statement $\mathcal{P}$ is true, its converse need not be true. For example, suppose $\mathcal{P}$ is the proposition: if (A) a person lives in Detroit, (B) that person lives in Michigan. Proposition $\mathcal{P}$ is true, but its converse — if a person lives in Michigan, that person lives in Detroit — is not true.

As another example, suppose A is the situation "n is a prime number greater than 2" and B is the situation "n is an odd number." It is true that A implies B, but, as the integer $9 = 3 \cdot 3$ illustrates, it not true that B implies A.

Definition If the proposition $A \Longrightarrow B$ and its converse $B \Longrightarrow A$ are both true, we say that A holds **if and only if** B holds or that A is **equivalent** to B. The equivalence of A and B is written as $A \Longleftrightarrow B$.

For example, if A is the statement that "n is an even prime" and B is the statement "$n = 2$," both $A \Longrightarrow B$ and $B \Longrightarrow A$ are true.

There is a proposition formed from proposition $\mathcal{P}$ that is true when $\mathcal{P}$ is true: the contrapositive of $\mathcal{P}$. We have been writing $A \Longrightarrow B$ to denote the proposition that when situation A holds, so does situation B. Write $\sim A$ for the statement "it is not true that A holds."

Definition The proposition $\sim B \Longrightarrow \sim A$ is called the **contrapositive** of the proposition $A \Longrightarrow B$.

For example, the contrapositive of the proposition "If a person is President of the United States, he or she must be at least 35 years old," is "If a person is not yet 35 years old, he or she is not President of the United States." Earlier, we discussed the proposition that if (A) n is a prime integer different than 2, then (B) n is an odd integer. The contrapositive states that if ($\sim B$) x is not an odd integer, then ($\sim A$) n is not a prime different than 2; or restated, if n is even, then n either equals 2 or is not a prime.

The contrapositive of Theorem A1.3 will be useful later. One way of stating it is as follows.

> **Theorem A1.4** Suppose that a, b, and c are integers with $a \cdot b = c$. If c is odd, then a and b are odd too.

The following result can be considered a **corollary** of Theorem A1.4 in that it is a special case of Theorem A1.4 or follows almost without proof from Theorem A1.4.

> **Theorem A1.5** Let a be an integer. If a^2 is odd, so is a.

Indirect Proofs

Since a proposition $A \implies B$ is true if and only if its contrapositive is true, one way to prove $A \implies B$ is to prove $\sim B \implies \sim A$. This idea can be extended: one way to prove that B is true is to consider all alternatives to B. If every such alternative to B leads to a contradiction — of A itself, of an axiom of the system, or of a previously proven proposition — then B must be true. This line of reasoning is called **indirect proof** or **proof by contradiction**, or sometimes **reductio ad absurdum**.

For example, suppose you left a professional (U.S.) football game early with the score tied: Detroit 10, Chicago 10. When you arrive home, you learn that the final score was Detroit 12, Chicago 10. You know that there are only four ways to score points in a professional football game: 1) by a 7-point touchdown and successful place kick, 2) by a 6-point touchdown and unsuccessful place kick, 3) by a 3-point field goal place kick, and 4) by a 2-point safety in which the scoring team tackles its opponent behind its own touchdown line. Knowing the 10–10 and 12–10 scores enables you to eliminate the first three possibilities and to conclude (by indirect reasoning) that Detroit won by a safety.

Many of the results in this book can be more easily proved indirectly than directly. To carry out an indirect mathematical proof of $A \implies B$, one assumes at some point that situation B does not hold and then applies rigorous inductive arguments until a contradiction is reached. The assumption in the proof that B does not hold is sometimes called the "working hypothesis."

We illustrate proof by contradiction by proving that $\sqrt{2}$ is an irrational number. First, we state without proof two principles that can be derived from our basic axioms, but whose derivation we omit to save time and space. The first proposition is the converse of Theorem A1.5.

> **Theorem A1.6** Let a be an integer. If a^2 is even, so is a.

> **Theorem A1.7** Suppose $a = p/q$ is a rational number with p and q integers. Then, p and q can be chosen so that both are not even integers.

The proof of Theorem A1.7 is based on the fact that if 2 divides both p and q, then a 2 can be factored out of the denominator and numerator of the fraction p/q.

Theorem A1.8 $\sqrt{2}$ is an irrational number.

Proof

1. $\sqrt{2}$ is either rational or irrational.	Definition of irrational number.
2. Suppose that $\sqrt{2}$ is rational.	Working hypothesis.
3. $\sqrt{2} = p/q$, where p and q are *not both even*.	A1.7.
4. $\sqrt{2} \cdot \sqrt{2} = (p/q) \cdot (p/q)$.	Property of equality.
5. $2 = (p^2/q^2)$.	Definition of square root and rule for multiplication of fractions.
6. $2 \cdot q^2 = p^2$.	Rule (4) above.
7. p^2 is even.	Definition of even.
8. p is even.	Theorem A1.6.
9. $p = 2 \cdot m$ for some integer m.	Definition of even.
10. $p \cdot p = 2m \cdot 2m$.	Rule (5) above.
11. $p^2 = 2 \cdot (2 \cdot m^2)$.	Definition of square; associative and commutative laws of multiplication.
12. $2 \cdot q^2 = 2 \cdot (2 \cdot m^2)$.	Rule (2) applied to Steps 6 and 11.
13. There exists $1/2$ such that $(1/2) \cdot 2 = 1$.	Multiplicative inverse.
14. $(1/2) \cdot 2 \cdot q^2 = (1/2) \cdot 2 \cdot (2 \cdot m^2)$.	Rule (4) above.
15. $q^2 = 2 \cdot m^2$.	Multiplicative associative and inverse properties.
16. q^2 is even.	Definition of even number.
17. q is even.	Theorem A1.6.
18. p and q are both even.	Steps 8 and 17.
19. Contradiction to Step 3.	
20. $\sqrt{2}$ is irrational.	Working hypothesis is false. ∎

Mathematical Induction

There is a third method of mathematical proof that differs significantly from proofs by deduction and proofs by contradiction: **proof by induction**. Inductive proofs can only be used for propositions about the integers or propositions indexed by the integers, but they are powerful tools in such situations.

To get a flavor for how inductive arguments work, suppose that a hundred men line up in a straight line, one behind the other, and that each whispers his name to the man behind him. Suppose that we know only two things about this line of men: 1) the first man's name is David, and 2) directly behind every man whose name is David is another man whose name is David. We can conclude that all hundred men are named David. For, we know by statement 1 that the first man is David. We conclude from statement 2 that the second man's name is David too. Applying statement 2 to the second man, we conclude that the third man's name is David, too. Continuing this boot strap argument step by step, we conclude that every man in the line is named David.

If there were an *infinite* number of men in the line and we knew that statements 1 and 2 held, we could still conclude that all the men in the line are named David.

The principle of induction works just this way. Suppose that we are considering a sequence of statements indexed by the natural numbers, so that the first statement is $P(1)$, the second statement is $P(2)$, and the nth statement is $P(n)$. Suppose that we can verify two facts about this sequence of statements:

(1) statement $P(1)$ is true;
(2) whenever any statement $P(k)$ is true for some k, then $P(k + 1)$ is also true.

By the same logic as with the line of Davids, we conclude that all of the statements are true. In an inductive proof, step 2) is called the **inductive step**. The hypothesis that some general statement $P(k)$ is true is called the **inductive hypothesis**.

Let's work out some examples of proofs by induction. We first prove that the sum of the first n natural numbers $1 + 2 + \cdots + n$ is $\frac{1}{2}n(n + 1)$.

Theorem A1.9   The sum of the first n natural numbers $1 + 2 + 3 + \cdots + n$ equals $\frac{1}{2}n(n + 1)$.

Proof   For any natural number n, let $P(n)$ be the statement

$$P(n): \qquad 1 + 2 + 3 + \cdots + n = \frac{n(n + 1)}{2}. \qquad (6)$$

Let's check $P(1)$. If we let $n = 1$ on the right-hand side of (6), we find $1(1+1)/2$, which does indeed equal the left-hand side when $n = 1$.

Now, we make the inductive hypothesis by assuming that statement $P(k)$ is true for some integer k:

$$1 + 2 + 3 + \cdots + k = \frac{k(k + 1)}{2}. \qquad (7)$$

Adding $(k + 1)$ to both sides of (7) preserves equality.

$$1 + 2 + 3 + \cdots + k + (k + 1) = \frac{k(k + 1)}{2} + (k + 1)$$

$$= \left(\frac{k}{2} + 1\right)(k + 1)$$

$$= \frac{(k + 1)(k + 2)}{2}.$$

But this last expression is exactly statement $P(k + 1)$. We have shown that $P(1)$ is true and that $[P(k)$ true $\implies P(k + 1)$ true$]$ for any k. We conclude, by the principle of mathematical induction, that $P(n)$ holds for all n. ■

Let's look at one more example, one that uses induction to verify a formula for the sum of the first n odd natural numbers.

Theorem A1.10   The sum of the first n odd natural numbers is n^2:

$$1 + 3 + 5 + 7 + \cdots + (2n - 1) = n^2. \tag{8}$$

Proof   Formula (8) is easily seen to be true for $n = 1$. So, we carry out the inductive step. Assume (8) holds for some positive integer k:

$$1 + 3 + 5 + 7 + \cdots + (2k - 1) = k^2. \tag{9}$$

The next odd number to be added to the left-hand side of (9) is $2(k + 1) - 1 = 2k + 1$. We preserve equality if we add it to both sides of (9).

$$1 + 3 + \cdots + (2k - 1) + (2(k + 1) - 1) = k^2 + (2k + 1). \tag{10}$$

But the right-hand side of (10) clearly factors as $(k + 1)^2$. We conclude that

$$1 + 3 + \cdots + (2k - 1) + (2(k + 1) - 1) = (k + 1)^2,$$

which is precisely statement (9) with $k + 1$ replacing k. By the principle of mathematical induction, we conclude that (9) holds for all natural numbers n. ■

EXERCISES

A1.3   Write out careful proofs of the following properties of set operations:
  a) $(A \cap B)^c = A^c \cup B^c$;
  b) $(A \cup B)^c = A^c \cap B^c$;
  c) $A \cap (B \cup C) = (A \cap B) \cup (A \cap C)$.

A1.4   Show that $\sqrt{3}$ is an irrational number.

A1.5   Use mathematical induction to prove the squared version of (6): $1^2 + 2^2 + \cdots + n^2 = n(n+1)(2n+1)/6$.

A1.6   Let $a_n = 1/[n(n+1)]$. Compute a_1, $a_1 + a_2$, $a_1 + a_2 + a_3$, and $a_1 + a_2 + a_3 + a_4$. Guess $a_1 + a_2 + \cdots + a_n$ for any natural number n. Use mathematical induction to verify your guess.

A1.7   Use mathematical induction to prove that $n < 2^n$ for all natural numbers n.

Trigonometric Functions

Most of the specific functions encountered in elementary mathematical approaches to economics are polynomials, quotients of polynomials (rational functions), or exponentials. As the independent variable x goes to infinity, the graph of each of these three types of functions either goes to infinity (very quickly for exponential functions) or approaches a finite horizontal asymptote. None of these functional forms can model the regular periodic patterns that play an important role in the social, biological, and physical sciences: business cycles and agricultural seasons, heart rhythms, and hormone level fluctuations, and tides and planetary motions. The basic functions for studying regular periodic behavior are the *trigonometric functions,* especially the sine, cosine, and tangent functions.

A2.1   DEFINITIONS OF THE TRIG FUNCTIONS

The domain of the trigonometric functions is more naturally the set of all geometric angles than some set of real numbers. We start with that approach and measure angles in *degrees* for the time being.

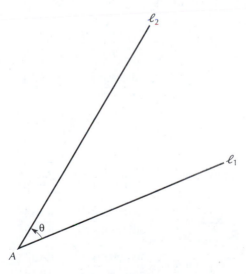

Angle θ is formed by rotating ray ℓ_1 to ℓ_2.

Figure A2.1

859

Consider the acute angle θ in Figure A2.1 formed by the rays ℓ_1 and ℓ_2 from the point A. Think of θ as being swept out by a *counterclockwise* rotation about the point A from ray ℓ_1 to ray ℓ_2. In this case, we will call ℓ_1 the initial ray and ℓ_2 the terminal ray of angle θ. Pick a point B on the terminal ray ℓ_2 and draw a perpendicular line n from B to the initial ray ℓ_1, intersecting ℓ_1 at the point C as in Figure A2.2. Triangle ABC is a right triangle with *hypotenuse AB*, *opposite leg BC*, and *adjacent leg AC*, relative to the angle θ.

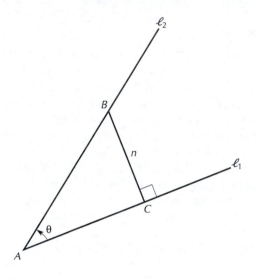

Figure A2.2

Computing the sine, cosine, and tangent of θ.

The six trigonometric functions are defined by taking ratios of the lengths of these three sides of triangle ABC:

$$\text{sine } \theta \quad = \quad \frac{\text{opposite leg}}{\text{hypotenuse}} \quad = \quad \frac{\|BC\|}{\|AB\|},$$

$$\text{cosine } \theta \quad = \quad \frac{\text{adjacent leg}}{\text{hypotenuse}} \quad = \quad \frac{\|AC\|}{\|AB\|},$$

$$\text{tangent } \theta \quad = \quad \frac{\text{opposite leg}}{\text{adjacent leg}} \quad = \quad \frac{\|BC\|}{\|AC\|},$$

$$\text{cotangent } \theta = \quad \frac{\text{adjacent leg}}{\text{opposite leg}} \quad = \quad \frac{\|AC\|}{\|BC\|},$$

$$\text{secant } \theta \quad = \quad \frac{\text{hypotenuse}}{\text{adjacent side}} \quad = \quad \frac{\|AB\|}{\|AC\|},$$

$$\text{cosecant } \theta \quad = \quad \frac{\text{hypotenuse}}{\text{opposite leg}} \quad = \quad \frac{\|AB\|}{\|BC\|},$$

where $\|AC\|$ denotes the *length* of line segment AC. These six functions represent all the possible ratios of the three sides of triangle ABC. The first three trigonometric functions — sine, cosine, and tangent — are the most important of the six. As the following theorem asserts, the last four can be expressed in terms of the first two.

Theorem A2.1 Every trig function can be expressed as a quotient of sine and cosine. In particular,

$$\text{tangent } \theta = \frac{\text{sine } \theta}{\text{cosine } \theta}, \qquad \text{cotangent } \theta = \frac{\text{cosine } \theta}{\text{sine } \theta},$$

$$\text{secant } \theta = \frac{1}{\text{cosine } \theta}, \quad \text{and} \quad \text{cosecant } \theta = \frac{1}{\text{sine } \theta}.$$

The above definitions are independent of how far the point B is from A on the second ray ℓ_2. To see this, suppose that B' is another point on ℓ_2. Let n' be the perpendicular line from B' to ℓ_1, meeting ℓ_1 at the point C', as indicated in Figure 2.3. Since n and n' are both perpendicular to ℓ_1, they are parallel to each other. Therefore, the corresponding sides of triangles ABC and $AB'C'$ are parallel to each other. By a fundamental result of the Euclidean geometry one studies in high school, triangles ABC and $AB'C'$ are similar to each other; they have equal sets of angles, and therefore the ratios of their corresponding sides are equal. Therefore, the six trig functions have the same values whether one uses triangle ABC or triangle $AB'C'$.

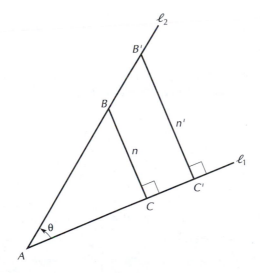

The values of the trig functions are independent of the size of the defining triangle.

Figure A2.3

For angles that do not lie between 0° and 90°, there is a sign convention necessary for a consistent definition of the trigonometric functions. The simplest way to describe this convention is to choose the point B in Figure A2.2 so that it is always *1 unit* away from the tip of the angle at A. Since the orientation of the angle under study should not make a difference, we can, without any loss of generality, always take the point A at the tip of the angle to be the origin of some xy-coordinate system, and its initial ray ℓ_1 to be the positive x-axis. To carry out this approach, draw the circle S of radius 1, the *unit circle*. For any angle θ, think of θ as being swept out counterclockwise by rays from the origin starting with the positive x-axis. As before, call the terminal ray ℓ_2. Choose the point B on ℓ_2 1 unit from the origin, that is, on the unit circle S, as indicated in Figure A2.4.

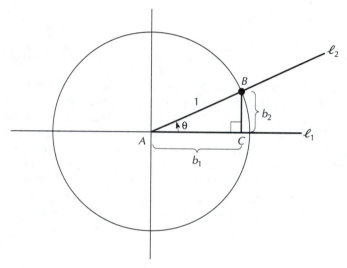

Figure A2.4   *Measuring θ as a counterclockwise rotation on the unit circle S from the positive x-axis.*

Suppose that the coordinates of the point B are (b_1, b_2) in this coordinate system. Then, the perpendicular segment from B to the x-axis ℓ_1 meets ℓ_1 at the point $C = (b_1, 0)$; furthermore,

$$\|AC\| = b_1 \quad \text{and} \quad \|BC\| = b_2.$$

Since $\|AB\| = 1$ in this approach, the above definitions of the trigonometric functions become

$$\sin\theta = \frac{b_2}{1} = b_2, \qquad \tan\theta = \frac{b_2}{b_1}, \qquad \sec\theta = \frac{1}{b_1},$$

$$\cos\theta = \frac{b_1}{1} = b_1, \qquad \cot\theta = \frac{b_1}{b_2}, \qquad \csc\theta = \frac{1}{b_2}. \tag{1}$$

Note the use of the standard abbreviations for the six trig functions.

We now extend formally the definitions of these functions to all angles. For *any* angle ϕ, sweep out ϕ counterclockwise on the unit circle beginning with the positive x-axis, and let $B(b_1, b_2)$ be the point where the terminal ray intersects the unit circle S. Then, the six trigonometric functions are defined by the six expressions in (1); b_1 and b_2 can be positive or negative depending on the size of ϕ. For example, since b_2 is negative when B lies in the third quadrant (where x_1 and x_2 are negative) and in the fourth quadrant (where x_1 is positive and x_2 is negative), $\sin \phi$ is negative when ϕ lies between $180°$ and $360°$. Similarly, the tangent and cotangent functions are negative precisely when B lies in the second or fourth quadrants, that is, when $90° < \phi < 180°$ or $270° < \phi < 360°$.

A2.2 GRAPHING TRIG FUNCTIONS

If we use the definitions in (1) to graph the sine function, we need only keep track of b_2 as θ goes from $0°$ to $360°$. At $\theta = 0°$, $b_2 = 0$ and $\sin 0 = 0$. As θ rises from $0°$ to $90°$, b_2 rises from 0 to 1. As θ passes from $90°$ to $180°$ to $270°$, b_2 decreases from $+1$ to 0 to -1. As θ goes from $270°$ to $360°$, b_2 increases from -1 back to 0. As θ increases beyond $360°$, B moves once again around the unit circle. If we move B *clockwise* around the unit circle S, we sweep out *negative angles* (by definition), but we continue to use the formulas in (1) to define their sine, cosine, etc. We conclude that the graph of $\theta \longmapsto \sin \theta$ is the curve in Figure A2.5.

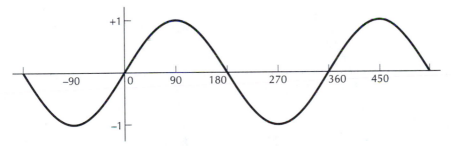

The graph of $\theta \longmapsto \sin \theta$.

**Figure
A2.5**

Similarly, by keeping track of b_1 as B moves around the unit circle, we generate the graph of the cosine function pictured in Figure A2.6. By keeping track of b_2/b_1 as B moves around the unit circle, we generate the graph of the tangent function in Figure A2.7. Note that as θ moves toward $90°$, B approaches $(0, 1)$ and $\tan \theta = b_2/b_1$ approaches $+\infty$.

Why do we need more than one function to keep track of angles? For one thing, as Figures A2.5 and A2.6 indicate, for every number y between -1 and $+1$, there are *two* angles θ_1 and θ_2 between $0°$ and $360°$ such that $\sin \theta_1 = \sin \theta_2$. However, for these two angles, $\cos \theta_1$ and $\cos \theta_2$ have different signs. For example, $\sin 180° = \sin 0° = 0$, but $\cos 180° = -1$ and $\cos 0° = +1$. Since $(b_1, b_2) = (\cos \theta, \sin \theta)$, cosine and sine together completely specify each angle.

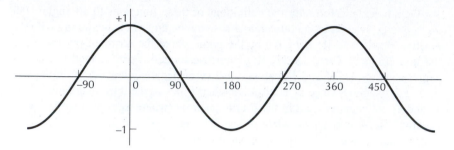

**Figure
A2.6**

The graph of θ ⟼ cos θ.

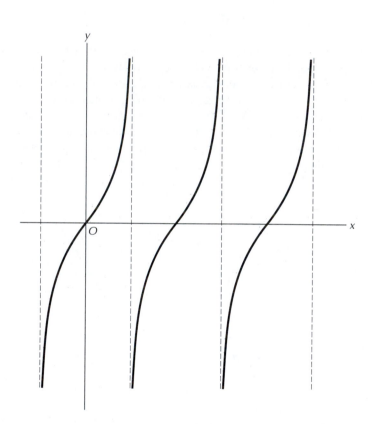

**Figure
A2.7**

The graph of θ ⟼ tan θ.

In addition, each trig function has its own advantages and its own uses. For example, the sine and tangent functions are natural since as θ moves from −90° to 0° to +90°, the sine shadows it while moving from −1 to 0 to +1 and the tangent shadows it while moving from −∞ to 0 to +∞. The tangent function is especially useful in applications because its definition involves the length of the two legs of the defining right triangle and, in fact, exactly tracks the *slope* of the hypotenuse of that triangle. On the other hand, as Figure A2.6 indicates, the cosine function satisfies

$$\cos \theta = \cos(-\theta); \qquad (2)$$

that is, the cosine is an *even function*. In particular, the cosine of an angle is independent of whether the angle is measured clockwise or counterclockwise.

A2.3 THE PYTHAGOREAN THEOREM

For the rest of this section we will use some of the basic Euclidean geometry that one studies in high school to derive useful properties of the trigonometric functions. The key geometric principle is the **Pythagorean Theorem**: the sum of the squares of the legs of a right triangle equals the square of the length of the hypotenuse; $a^2 + b^2 = c^2$ in Figure A2.8.

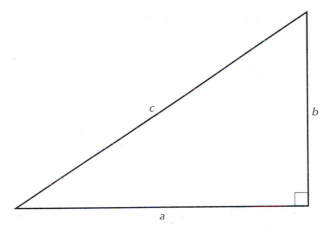

By the Pythagorean Theorem, $a^2 + b^2 = c^2$.

**Figure
A2.8**

The application of the Pythagorean Theorem to Figure A2.4 yields

$$b_1^2 + b_2^2 = 1, \qquad (3)$$

since the hypotenuse has length 1. Using the definitions (1) of the trig functions, equation (3) translates to

$$\cos^2 \theta + \sin^2 \theta = 1 \quad \text{for all angles } \theta. \qquad (4)$$

Dividing (3) through by b_1^2 yields

$$1 + \left(\frac{b_2}{b_1}\right)^2 = \left(\frac{1}{b_1}\right)^2 \quad \text{or} \quad 1 + \tan^2 \theta = \sec^2 \theta. \qquad (5)$$

Dividing (3) through by b_2^2 yields

$$\left(\frac{b_1}{b_2}\right)^2 + 1 = \left(\frac{1}{b_2}\right)^2 \quad \text{or} \quad \cot^2\theta + 1 = \csc^2\theta. \tag{6}$$

A2.4 EVALUATING TRIGONOMETRIC FUNCTIONS

To understand the trigonometric functions a little better, we evaluate the sine, cosine, and tangent functions at the three important acute angles: 30°, 45°, and 60°. These evaluations rely on the basic result of Euclidean geometry that two sides of a triangle are equal if and only if the angles opposite these sides are equal.

For the 45° angle in Figure A2.9, we have drawn right triangle OBC, motivated by Figure A2.2. (We have put aside the unit circle approach for a moment.) Since $\angle O = 45°$ and $\angle OCB = 90°$, $\angle OBC = 45°$. (The angles of a triangle sum to 180°.) Since $\angle COB = \angle OBC$, $\|OC\| = \|CB\|$. If we chose B so that $\|OC\| = \|CB\| = 1$, then by the Pythagorean Theorem,

$$\|OB\|^2 = \|OC\|^2 + \|BC\|^2 = 1 + 1 = 2.$$

So, $\|OB\| = \sqrt{2}$. We conclude that

$$\sin 45° = \frac{\|BC\|}{\|OB\|} = \frac{1}{\sqrt{2}} \approx 0.7071,$$

$$\cos 45° = \frac{\|OC\|}{\|OB\|} = \frac{1}{\sqrt{2}} \approx 0.7071, \tag{7}$$

$$\tan 45° = \frac{\|BC\|}{\|OC\|} = \frac{1}{1} = 1.$$

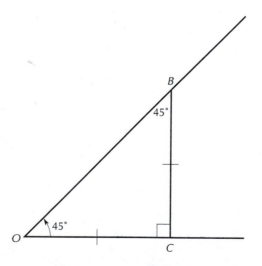

**Figure
A2.9**

The 45-45-90 isosceles triangle.

To compute the values of the trig functions at 30° and 60°, consider the 60-60-60 equilateral triangle ABC in Figure A2.10, and draw the bisector of $\angle B$, BD. Since

$$\angle A = \angle C = 60° \quad \text{and} \quad \angle ABD = \angle DBC = 30°, \tag{8}$$

$\angle ADB = \angle CDB = 90°$. We use the right triangle ABD to evaluate the trig functions at 30° and at 60°.

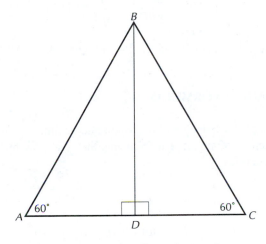

The 60-60-60 equilateral triangle.

**Figure
A2.10**

Recall from high school geometry that two triangles are congruent if in the two triangles, two corresponding pairs of angles and the sides between them are equal (angle-side-angle rule). Therefore, (8) implies that triangles ABD and BDC are congruent; and so,

$$\|AD\| = \|DC\| = \frac{1}{2}\|AB\|.$$

If we choose units so that $\|AD\| = 1$, then $\|AB\| = 2$, and by the Pythagorean Theorem,

$$\|BD\| = \sqrt{\|AB\|^2 - \|AD\|^2} = \sqrt{3}.$$

It follows that

$$\sin 60° = \frac{\|BD\|}{\|AB\|} = \frac{\sqrt{3}}{2} \approx 0.866,$$

$$\cos 60° = \frac{\|AD\|}{\|AB\|} = \frac{1}{2} = 0.5,$$

$$\tan 60° = \frac{\|BD\|}{\|AD\|} = \sqrt{3} \approx 1.732,$$

$$\sin 30° = \frac{\|AD\|}{\|AB\|} = \frac{1}{2} = 0.5,$$

$$\cos 30° = \frac{\|BD\|}{\|AB\|} = \frac{\sqrt{3}}{2} \approx 0.866,$$

$$\tan 30° = \frac{\|AD\|}{\|BD\|} = \frac{1}{\sqrt{3}} \approx 0.577.$$

These values are consistent with the graphs in Figures A2.5, A2.6, and A2.7.

A2.5 MULTIANGLE FORMULAS

Finally, we consider the behavior of the trigonometric functions with regard to the sums and differences of angles. The following theorem, presented without proof, summarizes these rules.

Theorem A2.2   For any two angles a and b,

$$\sin(a + b) = \sin a \cos b + \cos a \sin b,$$
$$\sin(a - b) = \sin a \cos b - \cos a \sin b,$$
$$\cos(a + b) = \cos a \cos b - \sin a \sin b,$$
$$\cos(a - b) = \cos a \cos b + \sin a \sin b.$$

In the special case that $a = b$,

$$\sin 2a = 2 \sin a \cos a,$$
$$\cos 2a = \cos^2 a - \sin^2 a.$$

Theorem A2.2 will be important in deriving the formulas of $(\sin x)'$ and $(\cos x)'$. Of course, it also extends the set of angles whose sines and cosines can be computed exactly. For example, knowing the sin and cos of 45° and 30°, we can compute the sin and cos of 15° and 75°.

A2.6 FUNCTIONS OF REAL NUMBERS

We have formulated the trigonometric functions as functions of geometric angles. We can easily consider each of them as functions defined on the set of real numbers by associating to any real number r the angle of $r°$. In fact, we implicitly did this when we drew the graphs in Figures A2.5, A2.6, and A2.7.

However, just as there are a number of different measures of distance (inches, feet, yards, miles, centimeters, meters, etc.), there are a number of different measures of an angle. The most intuitive is the *degree*, which is defined by the fact that an angle of 180° yields a straight line and that an angle of 360° describes a complete revolution about the circle.

But why 360? Any number could have served about as well. Since the right angle is a natural cornerstone among angles, some engineers find it convenient to measure angles by what percentage of a right angle they are, using the term "grads" for the underlying unit. In this approach, a right angle is an angle of 100 grads, a 45° angle is an angle of 50 grads (50 percent of a right angle), and a 60° angle is an angle of $66\frac{2}{3}$ grads ($66\frac{2}{3}$ percent of a right angle).

In some sense, a more natural approach is to start with the unit circle — the circle of radius 1 pictured in Figure A2.3 — and to describe an angle by the *length of the arc* of the unit circle which that angle sweeps out. The word "radians" is used to describe this unit of measurement. Since the circumference of a circle of radius 1 is 2π, an angle of 360° is the same as an angle of 2π radians. A right angle, which corresponds to 1/4 of the way around the circle, is measured as

$$\frac{1}{4} \cdot 2\pi = \frac{\pi}{2} \text{ radians.}$$

In general, since 360° corresponds to 2π radians, an angle of $x°$ is an angle of y radians where

$$\frac{1}{360}x = \frac{1}{2\pi}y,$$

so that

$$y = \frac{\pi}{180}x \quad \text{and} \quad x = \frac{180}{\pi}y.$$

The graph of the sine function in radians is presented in Figure A2.11.

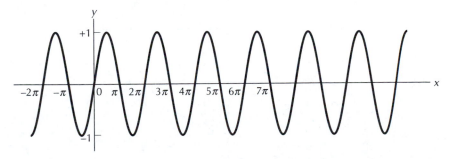

The graph of $x \longmapsto \sin x$ with x measured in radians.

**Figure
A2.11**

If you are evaluating trig functions on a hand-held scientific calculator, you must tell the calculator the units with which you are measuring angles. When they are switched on, most scientific calculators start in degrees mode, and indicate so with DEG showing in a corner of the display window. To change units to radians or grads, push the DRG button on your calculator and watch the corresponding units change to RAD or GRAD in the window.

A2.7   CALCULUS WITH TRIG FUNCTIONS

When one uses calculus to work with trig functions, it is understood that all angles are measures in radians, because it is in radians that the derivatives have the simplest expressions. The key ingredient in the calculus approach to trig functions are the following two convergence results.

Theorem A2.3   When angles x are measured in radians,

$$\frac{\sin x}{x} \rightarrow 1 \quad \text{as} \quad x \rightarrow 0, \tag{9}$$

$$\frac{\cos x - 1}{x} \rightarrow 0 \quad \text{as} \quad x \rightarrow 0. \tag{10}$$

The proof of these results takes us a little out of our way, and so it is presented at the end of this section. Figure A2.12 presents the intuition behind (9). Since angles are measured in radians, the size x of $\angle BOC$ is the length of arc BD on the

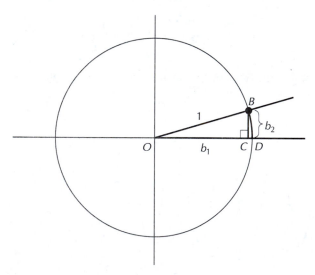

**Figure
A2.12**
          The geometry behind (9).

unit circle, and $\sin x = \|BC\| = b_2$. As $x \to 0$, $b_2 = \sin x \to 0$, and the length of the *arc* BD becomes very close to the length of the *segment* $\overline{BC}$. (Use your calculator to see that (9) holds as $x \to 0$ when x is measured in radians.)

Using the results of Theorem A2.3, one can easily compute the expressions for the derivatives of the six trigonometric functions.

Theorem A2.4   Suppose that angles x are measures in radians. Then,

$$(\sin x)' = \cos x, \qquad\qquad (\cos x)' = -\sin x,$$

$$(\tan x)' = \sec x^2, \qquad\qquad (\cot x)' = -\csc^2 x,$$

$$(\sec x)' = \tan x \cdot \sec x, \qquad (\csc x)' = -\cot x \cdot \csc x.$$

Proof   The proof uses the definition of the derivative and the angle-sum formula in Theorem A2.2:

$$\frac{\sin(x+h) - \sin x}{h} = \frac{\sin x \cos h + \cos x \sin h - \sin x}{h}$$

$$= \sin x \left(\frac{\cos h - 1}{h}\right) + \cos x \left(\frac{\sin h}{h}\right). \tag{11}$$

Now, let h tend to 0. By Theorem A2.3, $(\cos h - 1)/h \to 0$ and $(\sin h)/h \to 1$. Therefore,

$$\frac{d}{dx} \sin x \equiv \lim_{h \to 0} \frac{\sin(x+h) - \sin x}{h} \qquad \text{(def. of derivative)}$$

$$= \sin x \cdot 0 + \cos x \cdot 1 \qquad \text{(by (11))}$$

$$= \cos x.$$

Similarly,

$$\frac{\cos(x+h) - \cos x}{h} = \frac{\cos x \cos h - \sin x \sin h - \cos x}{h}$$

$$= \cos x \left(\frac{\cos h - 1}{h}\right) - \sin x \left(\frac{\sin h}{h}\right)$$

tends to $\cos x \cdot 0 - \sin x \cdot 1$ as $h \to 0$. Therefore, $(\cos x)' = -\sin x$. Since tan, cot, sec, and csc can be expressed as quotients of sin and cos (Theorem A2.1), their derivatives can now be calculated using the quotient rule of differentiation. (Exercise.) ∎

A2.8   TAYLOR SERIES

The Taylor series can be a powerful technique for working with nonlinear functions. As described in Section 30.3, the Taylor series of a function $f: \mathbf{R} \rightarrow \mathbf{R}$ about the point $x = 0$ is

$$f(0) + \frac{1}{1!}f'(0)x + \frac{1}{2!}f''(0)x^2 + \frac{1}{3!}f^{[3]}(0)x^3 + \frac{1}{4!}f^{[4]}(0)x^4 + \cdots. \qquad (12)$$

Since $(\sin x)' = \cos x$, $(\cos x)' = -\sin x$, $\sin 0 = 0$, and $\cos 0 = 1$, the even order derivatives of the sine function are 0 at $x = 0$, while the odd order derivatives are ± 1. The Taylor series for the sine function at $x = 0$ is

$$x - \frac{1}{3!}x^3 + \frac{1}{5!}x^5 - \frac{1}{7!}x^7 + \frac{1}{9!}x^9 - \cdots. \qquad (13)$$

Similarly, the Taylor series of the cosine function at $x = 0$ is

$$1 - \frac{1}{2!}x^2 + \frac{1}{4!}x^4 - \frac{1}{6!}x^6 + \frac{1}{8!}x^8 + \cdots. \qquad (14)$$

(Exercise.) For each fixed x, the consecutive terms of the series in (13) and (14) go to zero (rather rapidly). (Exercise.) It follows — with quite a bit of analysis — that the series in (13) and (14) converge *for any* x.

Example A2.1   Taylor series yield an effective method for computing values of sin and cos. Let's use this method to compute $\sin(\pi/4)$ to three decimal places. The first four terms in (13) for $x = \pi/4$ are

$$x \approx 0.7853982, \qquad -\frac{x^3}{3!} \approx -0.0807455,$$

$$\frac{x^5}{5!} \approx 0.0024904, \quad \text{and} \quad -\frac{x^7}{7!} \approx -0.0000366 \qquad (15)$$

Since further terms have zeros in the first five decimal places, they do not affect the first three digits of the Taylor series approximation of $\sin(\pi/4)$. Adding the four numbers in (15) yields

$$\sin \frac{\pi}{4} \approx 0.7071065,$$

an answer that is, in comparison with the true answer of $1/\sqrt{2} \approx 0.7071068$ in (7), correct to six significant figures.

A2.9 PROOF OF THEOREM A2.3

We close this section by sketching a proof of the basic convergence results in Theorem A2.3. Draw the unit circle S, as in Figure A2.13. Let θ be an acute angle from the origin whose initial ray is the positive x-axis, as in Figures A2.3 and A2.13. Let B be the point where the terminal ray of θ meets S. Let BC be the perpendicular line segment from the point B to the initial ray of θ. Let A be the point $(1, 0)$, and let AD be the vertical line segment from A to the terminal ray of θ.

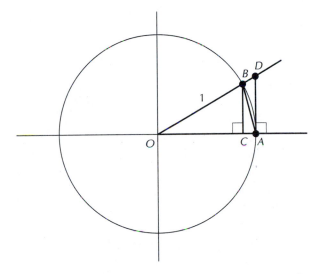

$\triangle OBA \subset$ sector $OBA \subset \triangle ODA$.

As Figure A2.13 indicates, triangle $OBA \subset$ sector $OBA \subset$ triangle ODA. Therefore,

$$\text{area of } \triangle OBA \leq \text{area of sector } OBA \leq \text{area of } \triangle ODA. \qquad (16)$$

Now,

$$\text{area of } \triangle OBA = \frac{1}{2} \cdot \|OA\| \cdot \|BC\|$$

$$= \frac{1}{2} \cdot 1 \cdot \sin \theta,$$

$$\text{area of sector } OBA = \frac{\theta}{2\pi} \cdot \text{area inside } S$$

$$= \frac{\theta}{2\pi} \cdot \pi \cdot 1^2 = \frac{1}{2} \cdot \theta,$$

$$\text{area of } \triangle ODA = \frac{1}{2} \cdot \|OA\| \cdot \|AD\|$$

$$= \frac{1}{2} \cdot 1 \cdot \tan \theta.$$

Substituting these calculations into (16) yields

$$\frac{1}{2} \sin \theta \leq \frac{1}{2} \theta \leq \frac{1}{2} \tan \theta. \tag{17}$$

Divide (17) through by $\frac{1}{2} \sin x$:

$$1 \leq \frac{\theta}{\sin \theta} \leq \cos \theta,$$

and invert:

$$\frac{1}{\cos \theta} \leq \frac{\sin \theta}{\theta} \leq 1.$$

As $\theta \to 0$, $\cos \theta \to 1$ and $(\sin \theta)/\theta$ is forced to converge to 1; this proves (9). To prove (10), note that

$$\frac{\cos x - 1}{x} = \frac{\cos x - 1}{x} \cdot \frac{\cos x + 1}{\cos x + 1}$$

$$= \frac{\cos^2 x - 1}{x(\cos x + 1)}$$

$$= \frac{-\sin^2 x}{x(\cos x + 1)} \qquad \text{(by (4))}$$

$$= \frac{\sin x}{x} \cdot \frac{-\sin x}{\cos x + 1}$$

$$\to 1 \cdot \frac{0}{2} = 0, \qquad \text{as } x \to 0 \qquad \text{(by (9))}.$$

EXERCISES

A2.1 Prove Theorem A2.1 from the definitions of the trig functions.

A2.2 Draw the graphs of the cotangent, secant, and cosecant functions.

A2.3 Prove that $\cos \theta = \sin(90° - \theta)$ and $\sin \theta = \cos(90° - \theta)$.

A2.4 Evaluate sine, cosine, and tangent at $120°$, $135°$, $150°$, $210°$, $225°$, and $240°$.

A2.5 Evaluate cotangent, secant, and cosecant at $30°$, $45°$ and $60°$.

A2.6 Derive formulas for $\cos \frac{1}{2}a$ and $\sin \frac{1}{2}a$ in terms of $\cos a$.

A2.7 Use Theorem A2.2 and the previous exercise to compute the sine and cosine of $15°$, $22.5°$, and $75°$.

A2.8 Compare the graphs of $\sin x$ in Figures A2.5 and A2.11 by graphing both on the same coordinate grid.

A2.9 Use a hand calculator to see that (9) holds when x is measured in radians, but not when x is measured in degrees.

A2.10 Use $(\sin x)' = \cos x$ and $(\cos x)' = -\sin x$ and Theorem A2.1 to compute the derivatives of the other four trig functions.

A2.11 Use the Taylor series to compute $\cos(\pi/4)$ and $\sin(\pi/3)$, and compare your answers with the exact answer computed earlier.

A2.12 Show that (13) and (14) are the Taylor series (12) for the sine and cosine functions.

A2.13 For any fixed number a — no matter how large — show that $a^n/n! \to 0$ as $n \to \infty$.

Complex Numbers

A3.1 BACKGROUND

The solutions of a quadratic equation

$$ax^2 + bx + c = 0 \tag{1}$$

are given by the quadratic formula

$$x = \frac{-b \pm \sqrt{b^2 - 4ac}}{2a}. \tag{2}$$

The only caveat is that the expression $b^2 - 4ac$ under the radical must be positive for the answers (2) to be a pair of real numbers. For example, (2) tells us that the solutions of $x^2 - 4x + 3 = 0$ are $x = 1$ and $x = 3$ (check) and that the solutions of

$$x^2 - 4x + 13 = 0 \tag{3}$$

are $$x = \frac{4 \pm \sqrt{16 - 52}}{2} = \frac{4 \pm \sqrt{-36}}{2}. \quad \text{(Check.)} \tag{4}$$

Since the square of every real number — positive or negative — is a *positive* number, no real number has a square equal to -36; and therefore, equation (3) has no real solution. However, as we will see at the end of this section, there are situations where one needs to work with a solution of equation (3) — even a solution that does not have any meaning. To get around this problem, mathematicians have extended the concept of a number and have created a new kind of number — the complex number — which includes square roots of negative numbers.

The key step in this extension is to let the symbol i stand for $\sqrt{-1}$, so that $i^2 = -1$, and to set up this extended number system so that it has all the properties of the usual real number system, in particular, the six properties in Section A1.2. In this case,

$$\sqrt{-36} = \sqrt{36 \cdot -1} = \sqrt{36} \cdot \sqrt{-1} = 6i,$$

and the "solutions" (4) of equation (3) can be formally written as

$$2 + 3i \quad \text{and} \quad 2 - 3i. \tag{5}$$

Definitions

The set of complex numbers, often denoted $\mathbf{C}$, is the set of real numbers augmented by an extra symbol i. A typical complex number has the form $a + bi$, where a and b are real numbers. The formal definition follows.

Definition   A **complex number** is a number of the form $a + bi$, where a and b are real numbers, and the symbol i formally satisfies $i^2 = -1$. The real number a is called the **real part** of $a + bi$; the real number b is called the **imaginary part** of $a + bi$. A complex number bi whose real part is 0 is called an **imaginary number**.

Definition   As we will see below, for any complex number $a + bi$, the related complex number $a - bi$ plays a number of important roles. The complex number $a - bi$ is called the **complex conjugate** of $a + bi$. When the symbol z is used to denote the complex number $a + bi$, its conjugate $a - bi$ is written as $\bar{z}$:

$$\overline{a + bi} = a - bi.$$

Arithmetic Operations

Two complex numbers can be added, subtracted, multiplied, or divided; the result is a new complex number. For example, for real numbers a_1, a_2, b_1, b_2:

$$(a_1 + b_1 i) + (a_2 + b_2 i) = a_1 + a_2 + b_1 i + b_2 i$$
$$= (a_1 + a_2) + (b_1 + b_2)i,$$
$$(a_1 + b_1 i) - (a_2 + b_2 i) = a_1 - a_2 + b_1 i - b_2 i$$
$$= (a_1 - a_2) + (b_1 - b_2)i,$$
$$(a_1 + b_1 i) \cdot (a_2 + b_2 i) = (a_1 \cdot a_2) + (a_1 \cdot b_2 i) + (b_1 i \cdot a_2) + (b_1 i \cdot b_2 i)$$
$$= (a_1 a_2 - b_1 b_2) + (a_1 b_2 + a_2 b_1)i,$$

since $b_1 i \cdot b_2 i = b_1 b_2 i^2 = b_1 b_2 (-1)$. In particular,

$$(a + bi)^2 = (a + bi) \cdot (a + bi) = (a^2 - b^2) + 2ab\, i, \tag{6}$$

and the product of a complex number $a + bi$ and its complex conjugate $a - bi$ is

$$(a + bi) \cdot (a - bi) = a^2 + b^2, \tag{7}$$

a positive *real number*.

Division is a little trickier. To obtain a complex number of the form $A + Bi$ from a quotient $(a_1 + b_1 i)/(a_2 + b_2 i)$ of complex numbers, multiply numerator and denominator of the quotient by $a_2 - b_2 i$, the complex conjugate of the denominator $a_2 + b_2 i$, to get a real denominator:

$$\frac{a_1 + b_1 i}{a_2 + b_2 i} = \frac{a_1 + b_1 i}{a_2 + b_2 i} \cdot \frac{a_2 - b_2 i}{a_2 - b_2 i}$$

$$= \frac{(a_1 a_2 + b_1 b_2) + (a_2 b_1 - a_1 b_2)i}{a_2^2 + b_2^2}$$

$$= \left(\frac{a_1 a_2 + b_1 b_2}{a_2^2 + b_2^2} \right) + \left(\frac{a_2 b_1 - a_1 b_2}{a_2^2 + b_2^2} \right) i,$$

a complex number of the form $A + Bi$.

Example A3.1   For example,

$$(2 + 3i) + (4 + 5i) = 6 + 8i,$$

$$(2 + 3i) \cdot (4 + 5i) = -7 + 22i,$$

$$\frac{2 + 3i}{4 + 5i} = \frac{2 + 3i}{4 + 5i} \cdot \frac{4 - 5i}{4 - 5i} = \frac{23}{41} + \frac{2}{41} i,$$

$$(2 + 3i) \cdot (2 - 3i) = 13.$$

A3.2   SOLUTIONS OF POLYNOMIAL EQUATIONS

Complex conjugates arise naturally in the solution of polynomial equations, because, as the following theorem asserts, if a complex number $z_0 = a + bi$ is a solution of a polynomial equation with real coefficients, so is its complex conjugate $\bar{z}_0 = a - bi$. Before proving this statement, we collect the basic properties of the complex conjugation operation.

Theorem A3.1

(*a*) A complex number $z = a + bi$ equals its complex conjugate $\bar{z} = a - bi$ if and only if z is real; that is, $z = a$ and $b = 0$.

Furthermore, for any complex numbers z_1 and z_2,

(b) $\overline{z_1 + z_2} = \overline{z_1} + \overline{z_2}$ and

(c) $\overline{z_1 \cdot z_2} = \overline{z_1} \cdot \overline{z_2}$.

Proof Suppose $a + bi = a - bi$. Subtract a from both sides of this equation: $bi = -bi$. Divide both sides by i: $b = -b$. But the only real number b that equals its negative is $b = 0$. Follow these steps in reverse order to prove the converse. The proofs of parts b and c follow directly from the above definitions of the addition and multiplication operations and are left for the exercises. ∎

We now show that the complex roots of a real polynomial equation occur in conjugate pairs. For example, the roots of the quadratic (3) are the conjugate complex numbers $2 + 3i$ and $2 - 3i$.

Theorem A3.2   Consider the polynomial equation

$$c_0 + c_1 x + c_2 x^2 + \cdots + c_n x^n = 0, \qquad (8)$$

whose coefficients $c_0, c_1, \ldots, c_n$ are *real numbers*. If $z_0 = a + bi$ is a solution of (8), then so is its complex conjugate $\overline{z}_0 = a - bi$.

Proof Suppose that $z_0 = a + bi$ is a specific solution of polynomial equation (8) so that

$$c_0 + c_1 z_0 + c_2 z_0^2 + \cdots + c_n z_0^n = 0. \qquad (9)$$

Take the complex conjugate of both sides of (9):

$$0 = \overline{c_0 + c_1 z_0 + c_2 z_0^2 + \cdots + c_n z_0^n}$$

$$= \overline{c_0} + \overline{c_1 z_0} + \overline{c_1 z_0^2} + \cdots + \overline{c_n z_0^n} \qquad \text{(by Theorem A3.2.2)}$$

$$= \overline{c_0} + \overline{c_1}\,\overline{z_0} + \overline{c_1}\,\overline{z_0}^2 + \cdots + \overline{c_n}\,\overline{z_0}^n \qquad \text{(by Theorem A3.2.3)}$$

$$= c_0 + c_1\overline{z_0} + c_2\overline{z_0}^2 + \cdots + c_n\overline{z_0}^n \qquad \text{(by Theorem A3.2.1).}$$

The last line states that $\overline{z}_0 = a - bi$ satisfies equation (9).

Of course, formula (2) gives the solution of every *second* order polynomial equation. One can use this formula to check directly that if $a + bi$ is a complex solution of $c_0 + c_1 x + c_2 x^2 = 0$, so is $a - bi$. (Exercise!) ∎

A3.3   GEOMETRIC REPRESENTATION

Just as real numbers can be represented geometrically on the real number line, as in Figure 2.1, a complex number $a + bi$ can be considered as an ordered pair of real numbers (a, b) and represented as a point in two-dimensional xy-space with x coordinate a and y coordinate b, as in Figure A3.1. In fact, one can think of the complex numbers $\{a + bi : a, b \in \mathbf{R}\}$ as simply another way of writing the set of all ordered pairs $\{(a, b) : a, b \in \mathbf{R}\}$ in the Cartesian plane. (The only real difference lies in the fact that there is a natural multiplication on the set of complex numbers, but not on the set of ordered pairs in the plane.) In this representation, the horizontal or x-axis is called the **real axis**, the vertical or y-axis is called the **imaginary axis**, and the Cartesian plane is called the **complex plane**. The complex numbers $a + 0i$ whose imaginary parts are zero can be identified with the real numbers on the real number line.

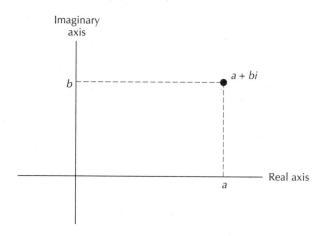

**Figure
A3.1**

Representing a + bi in the complex plane.

In the complex plane, the Euclidean distance of the point $z = a + bi$ from the origin is $\sqrt{a^2 + b^2}$ by the Pythagorean Theorem. However, by (7), this distance can be written as

$$\sqrt{a^2 + b^2} = \sqrt{(a + bi)(a - bi)} = \sqrt{z\bar{z}}. \tag{10}$$

This real number (10) that represents the "distance" of the complex number $a + bi$ for the complex zero $0 + 0i$ is called the **norm** or **modulus** of $a + bi$. It is written as $|a + bi|$ since it generalizes the absolute value of a real number.

Consider the right triangle drawn in Figure A3.2, whose legs lie along the axes and whose hypotenuse is the vector from the origin to $a + bi$. The length r of this vector is the distance from $(0, 0)$ to (a, b), the modulus $\sqrt{a^2 + b^2}$ of $a + bi$. Let θ denote the angle that this vector makes with the positive real axis, as pictured in Figure A3.2. The angle θ is called the **argument** of the complex number $a + bi$. By the definitions of the cosine and sine functions in the last section,

$$\cos \theta = \frac{a}{r} \quad \text{and} \quad \sin \theta = \frac{b}{r},$$

so that $\qquad a + bi = (r \cos \theta) + (r \sin \theta)i = r(\cos \theta + i \sin \theta). \tag{11}$

Expression (11) is called the **polar coordinate representation** of $a + bi$. It is especially helpful in evaluating powers of $a + bi$. For example,

$$
\begin{aligned}
(a + bi)^2 &= \left[r(\cos \theta + i \sin \theta)\right]^2 \\
&= r^2(\cos \theta + i \sin \theta)^2 \\
&= r^2(\cos^2 \theta - \sin^2 \theta + 2 \cos \theta \sin \theta\, i) \quad\quad \text{(by (6))} \\
&= r^2(\cos 2\theta + i \sin 2\theta) \quad\quad\quad\quad\quad\; \text{(by Theorem A2.2).}
\end{aligned}
$$

The identity

$$(a + bi)^2 = r^2(\cos 2\theta + i \sin 2\theta) \tag{12}$$

makes it easy to locate $(a + bi)^2$ in the complex plane. Its modulus r^2 is the square of the modulus r of $a + bi$ and its argument 2θ is twice the argument θ of $a + bi$, as illustrated in Figure A3.3.

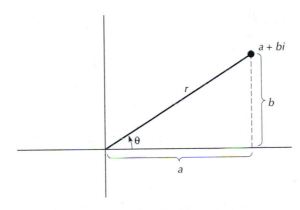

Polar coordinate representation of $a + bi$.

Figure A3.2

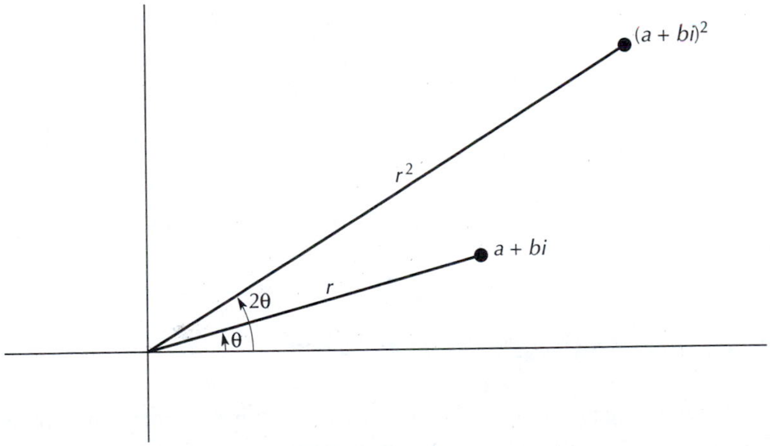

Using (12) to locate $(a + bi)^2$ in the plane.

Figure A3.3

The identity (12) generalizes to all powers of $a + bi$. The generalization, called **DeMoivre's theorem**, plays an important role in the solution of linear difference equations in Chapter 23.

Theorem A3.3   (**DeMoivre's theorem**) For any complex number $a + bi$ with polar representation $r(\cos\theta + i\sin\theta)$ and any positive integer n,

$$(a + bi)^n = r^n(\cos n\theta + i\sin n\theta). \tag{13}$$

Proof   The proof is by induction on n. We know that identity (13) holds for $n = 1, 2$. Suppose that it holds for $n = k$ so that

$$\left[r(\cos\theta + i\sin\theta)\right]^k = r^k(\cos k\theta + i\sin k\theta). \tag{14}$$

We want to show that it holds for $n = k + 1$. Now,

$$\left[r(\cos\theta + i\sin\theta)\right]^{k+1} = r^k(\cos k\theta + i\sin k\theta) \cdot r(\cos\theta + i\sin\theta)$$
$$= r^{k+1}((\cos k\theta\cos\theta - \sin k\theta\sin\theta) \tag{15}$$
$$+ i(\sin k\theta\cos\theta + \cos k\theta\sin\theta))$$

using the rule for the product of complex numbers. But, by Theorem A2.2,

$$\cos((k + 1)\theta) = \cos(k\theta + \theta)$$
$$= \cos k\theta\cos\theta - \sin k\theta\sin\theta$$
$$\sin((k + 1)\theta) = \sin(k\theta + \theta)$$
$$= \sin k\theta\cos\theta + \sin\theta\cos k\theta.$$

Therefore, (15) can be rewritten as

$$\left[r(\cos\theta + i\sin\theta)\right]^{k+1} = r^{k+1}\left[\cos(k + 1)\theta + i\sin(k + 1)\theta\right].$$

This completes the inductive step and verifies that (13) holds for all integers n. ∎

A3.4   COMPLEX NUMBERS AS EXPONENTS

In working with linear differential equations, one often encounters the expression e^{a+bi} — the number e with the complex number $a + bi$ as its *exponent*. How does one interpret a complex number as an exponent?

For this discussion, the Taylor series of $x \longmapsto e^x$ will come in handy. The Taylor series representation of e^x about the point $x = 0$ is the infinite series

$$e^x = 1 + \frac{1}{1!}x^1 + \frac{1}{2!}x^2 + \frac{1}{3!}x^3 + \cdots + \frac{1}{n!}x^n + \cdots. \tag{16}$$

The infinite series on the right-hand side of (16) *represents* the function $x \longmapsto e^x$ because it converges to e^x for *every* value of x. Therefore, it is natural to use the power series (16) to define *complex powers* of e.

Definition   For any complex number $z = a + bi$, define e^z to be the limit of the infinite series

$$1 + z + \frac{1}{2!}z^2 + \frac{1}{3!}z^3 + \frac{1}{4!}z^4 + \frac{1}{5!}z^5 + \cdots. \tag{17}$$

Notice that for real numbers a, that is, for complex numbers $a + 0i$ with zero imaginary part, this definition (17) gives the usual value e^a. What happens for pure imaginary numbers $0 + bi$ with zero real part? Plug $z = ib$ into (17), and separate terms without i's from terms with i's:

$$e^{ib} = 1 + ib + \frac{1}{2!}(ib)^2 + \frac{1}{3!}(ib)^3 + \frac{1}{4!}(ib)^4 + \frac{1}{5!}(ib)^5 + \cdots$$

$$= \left(1 - \frac{1}{2!}b^2 + \frac{1}{4!}b^4 - \cdots\right) + i\left(b - \frac{1}{3!}b^3 + \frac{1}{5!}b^5 - \cdots\right),$$

since $i^2 = -1$, $i^3 = -i$, $i^4 = 1$, and so on. But, by the discussion at the end of Appendix A2, the series in the first set of brackets is the Taylor series for $\cos b$, and the series in the second set of brackets is the Taylor series for $\sin b$. We conclude that, by the above definition of complex exponentiation, for any real number b,

$$e^{ib} = \cos b + i \sin b. \tag{18}$$

Identity (18) is called **Euler's equation**. If we take b to be π in (18), the straight-line angle in radians, then

$$e^{i\pi} = -1 \quad \text{or} \quad -e^{i\pi} = 1, \tag{19}$$

since $\cos \pi = -1$ and $\sin \pi = 0$. Equation (19) is an aesthetic combination of the three esoteric numbers e, i, and π. For example, successful math department intramural baseball teams have been known to boast: "We're number $-e^{i\pi}$."

Complex exponentiation retains the important properties that exponentiation with real numbers enjoys. For example, for any two complex numbers z_1 and z_2,

$$e^{z_1 + z_2} = e^{z_1} \cdot e^{z_2}. \tag{20}$$

To prove (20), write out the Taylor series of e^{z_1} and of e^{z_2}, multiply them out term by term, and then collect terms to recover the Taylor series of $e^{z_1+z_2}$. (Exercise.)

Finally, we use Euler's equation (18) and (20) to derive a simpler expression for e^{a+bi}:

$$e^{a+bi} = e^a \cdot e^{bi}$$

$$= e^a (\cos b + i \sin b). \tag{21}$$

Some texts use the simple formula (21) to define complex exponentiation e^{a+bi} instead of the Taylor series definition (17).

A3.5   DIFFERENCE EQUATIONS

We motivated the existence of complex numbers by asserting that mathematicians want *every* quadratic equation (1) to have a pair of solutions, even if the proposed solutions are not real. We close this section by expanding on this theme, in particular by explaining the need for formal solutions of equation (1).

Consider the simple linear difference equation

$$x_{n+1} = 1.05\, x_n, \tag{22}$$

where x_n denotes the amount of some quantity in time period n. For example, x_n might be the money in an (inactive) savings account after n years, in which case the multiplier 1.05 is 1 plus the annual 5 percent interest rate. Since the amount in the account at the end of any year is 1.05 times the amount present at the end of the previous year, an account that opens with x_0 dollars will contain $(1.05)^n x_0$ dollars after n years. In other words, a solution of (22) is

$$x_n = (1.05)^n x_0, \tag{23}$$

where x_0 is the initial deposit.

Often, one studies a slightly more complex dynamic in which the amount x_n present in any one year depends on the amounts present in each of the past *two* years: x_{n-1} and x_{n-2}; for example,

$$x_n = 4x_{n-1} - 3x_{n-2}. \tag{24}$$

Motivated by the solution $(1.05)^n$ of the simpler equation (23), one looks for solutions of (24) of the form $x_n = a^n$ by plugging $x_n = a^n$ into (24) and solving for the unknown parameter a:

$$a^n = 4a^{n-1} - 3a^{n-2}. \tag{25}$$

Dividing both sides of (25) by a^{n-2} yields

$$a^2 = 4a - 3 \quad \text{or} \quad a^2 - 4a + 3 = 0. \tag{26}$$

The solutions of this quadratic are $a = 3$ and $a = 1$; and so $x_n = 3^n$ and $x_n = 1^n$ are solutions of (24). (Check).

Now consider the difference equation

$$x_n = 4x_{n-1} - 13x_{n-2}. \tag{27}$$

Looking for a solution of the form $x_n = a^n$, we once again plug $x_n = a^n$ into (27) and are led to the quadratic equation

$$a^2 = 4a - 13, \quad \text{or} \quad a^2 - 4a + 13 = 0. \tag{28}$$

The *only* solutions of (28) are the complex numbers $2 + 3i$ and $2 - 3i$, as we saw at the beginning of this section. As is shown in Chapter 23 and in the exercises below, one can use DeMoivre's theorem to manipulate these two solutions to obtain two *real* solutions:

$$x_n = 13^{n/2} \cos n\theta_0 \quad \text{and} \quad x_n = 13^{n/2} \sin n\theta_0, \tag{29}$$

where $\theta_0 \approx 0.588$ radians ($33.69°$). The complex solutions of (28) are needed to begin the process of solving the dynamic (27). Furthermore, oscillatory behavior is an important phenomenon in all the sciences; but difference equations that have oscillatory solutions, like (24) or (27), are exactly the ones whose underlying quadratic equations have complex roots.

EXERCISES

A3.1 Use the quadratic formula (2) to show that $2 + 3i$ and $2 - 3i$ are the solutions of (1). Then, verify that they are indeed solutions by plugging each back into (1) and carrying out the multiplications and additions.

A3.2 Let $z_1 = 2 - 3i$, $z_2 = 3 + 4i$, and $z_3 = 1 + i$. Compute $z_1 + z_2$, $z_1 - z_3$, $z_1 \cdot z_2$, $z_1 \cdot z_3$, z_1/z_3, $z_1 \cdot \bar{z}_1$, z_1^3, $z_1 \cdot \bar{z}_3$.

A3.3 Write $1/(a + bi)$ in the form $A + Bi$.

A3.4 Prove parts b and c of Theorem A3.1.

A3.5 Prove that complex conjugation preserves subtraction and division too.

A3.6 Use the quadratic formula (2) to show directly that if $\alpha + \beta i$ is a solution of (1), so is $\alpha - \beta i$.

A3.7 Find all three solutions of $x^3 - 1 = 0$ and of $x^3 + 1 = 0$.

A3.8 Write e^{1+i}, $e^{\pi i/2}$, and $e^{2-\pi i}$ without complex numbers as exponents.

A3.9 Use the definition (17) of complex exponentiation to prove (20).

A3.10 Verify that $x_n = 3^n$ and $x_n = 1^n$ are solutions of difference equation (24). Show that $x_n = c_1 3^n + c_2 1^n$ is a solution for any constants c_1 and c_2.

A3.11 *a*) Show that $x_n = k_1(2 + 3i)^n + k_2(2 - 3i)^n$ is a solution of (27) for any constants k_1 and k_2, real or complex.

   b) In this expression for x_n, replace k_1 by any complex number $c_1 + c_2i$, replace k_2 by the conjugate $c_1 - c_2i$, and replace $(2 \pm 3i)^n$ by their polar representations from DeMoivre's theorem.

   c) Carry out the multiplications and summations in this new expression for x_n to obtain a solution that is a sum of the expressions in (29).

Integral Calculus

A4.1 ANTIDERIVATIVES

After a while, the student of calculus is expected to know how to compute derivatives so well that he or she can reverse the process. In this vein, an **antiderivative**
of a function $f(x)$ is a function $F(x)$ whose derivative is the original $F: F' = f$. The
function F is also called the **indefinite integral** of f and written $F(x) = \int f(x)\,dx$.
The usual laws of differentiation yield the following table of indefinite integrals,
where C denotes an arbitrary constant:

$$\int af(x)\,dx = a \int f(x)\,dx \qquad\qquad \int (f+g)\,dx = \int f\,dx + \int g\,dx$$

$$\int x^n\,dx = \frac{x^{n+1}}{n+1} + C \quad (n \neq -1) \qquad \int \frac{1}{x}\,dx = \ln x + C$$

$$\int e^x\,dx = e^x + C \qquad\qquad \int e^{f(x)} f'(x)\,dx = e^{f(x)} + C$$

$$\int (f(x))^n f'(x)\,dx = \frac{1}{n+1} (f(x))^{n+1} + C \quad (n \neq -1)$$

$$\int \frac{1}{f(x)} f'(x)\,dx = \ln f(x) + C$$

Example A4.1

$$\int \left(4x^2 + x^{1/2} - \frac{3}{x} \right) dx = \frac{4x^3}{3} + \frac{x^{3/2}}{3/2} - 3\ln x + C$$

$$= \frac{4}{3}x^3 + \frac{2}{3}x^{3/2} - 3\ln x + C.$$

Example A4.2 To illustrate the next-to-last rule in the above list, let's try to
compute the antiderivative of $(x^3 + 3x^2 + 1)^3(x^2 + 2x)$. By the Power Rule, the
only viable candidate is some *constant* multiple of $(x^3 + 3x^2 + 1)^4$. We take the
derivative of $k(x^3 + 3x^2 + 1)^4$ and then try to find the appropriate constant k.

By the Power Rule,

$$\left[k(x^3 + 3x^2 + 1)^4\right]' = 4k(x^3 + 3x^2 + 1)^3 \cdot (3x^2 + 6x). \qquad (1)$$

The latter expression will equal $(x^3 + 3x^2 + 1)^3 \cdot (x^2 + 2x)$ if and only if

$$4k(3x^2 + 6x) = (x^2 + 2x),$$

or $$k = \frac{x^2 + 2x}{4(3x^2 + 6x)} = \frac{x^2 + 2x}{12(x^2 + 2x)} = \frac{1}{12}.$$

We conclude that

$$\int (x^3 + 3x^2 + 1)^3(x^2 + 2x)\,dx = \frac{1}{12}(x^3 + 3x^2 + 1)^4 + C.$$

Example A4.3 If we try to use this method to compute the antiderivative of $(x^3 + 3x^2 + 1)^3 \cdot (x^2 + 3x)$, we would once again look for a candidate of the form $k(x^3 + 3x^2 + 1)^4$. Using (1), the derivative of this candidate function will equal $(x^3 + 3x^2 + 1)^3 \cdot (x^2 + 3x)$ if and only if

$$4k(3x^2 + 6x) = x^2 + 3x,$$

or $$k = \frac{x^2 + 3x}{4(3x^2 + 6x)} = \frac{x^2 + 3x}{12(x^2 + 2x)}, \qquad (2)$$

which cannot be further simplified. Since we assumed k constant in our differentiation (1) but found in (2) that it couldn't be constant in order for our candidate to work, we conclude that we cannot use this method to find the desired antiderivative.

Integration by Parts

Another convenient rule for computing antiderivatives is the converse of the Product Rule. The Product Rule states that, for two differentiable functions $u(x)$ and $v(x)$,

$$(u \cdot v)' = u' \cdot v + u \cdot v'.$$

Taking antiderivatives of both sides, we find

$$u \cdot v = \int u' \cdot v + \int u \cdot v',$$

which is usually written as

$$\int u(x) \cdot v'(x)\, dx = u(x) \cdot v(x) - \int u'(x) \cdot v(x)\, dx \qquad (3)$$

and is called **integration by parts**. It is especially useful when $u(x)$ is a function, like x^k, whose derivative u' is simpler than u itself and when the antiderivative v of v' is reasonable to work with.

Example A4.4   Use integration by parts to integrate xe^{2x} with $u(x) = x$ and $v'(x) = e^{2x}$. Since the corresponding $u'(x) = 1$ and $v(x) = \frac{1}{2}e^{2x}$, we find by (3)

$$\int xe^{2x}\, dx = x \cdot \frac{1}{2}e^{2x} - \int 1 \cdot \frac{1}{2}e^{2x}\, dx + C$$

$$= \frac{1}{2}xe^{2x} - \frac{1}{2}\int e^{2x}\, dx + C$$

$$= \frac{1}{2}xe^{2x} - \frac{1}{4}e^{2x} + C.$$

A4.2   THE FUNDAMENTAL THEOREM OF CALCULUS

For numbers a and b, the **definite integral** of $f(x)$ from a to b is $F(b) - F(a)$, where $F(x)$ is an antiderivative of f. We write this as

$$\int_a^b f(x)\, dx = F(b) - F(a), \quad \text{where } F' = f.$$

The definite integral plays an important role when one wants to aggregate or sum the values of a continuous function. Consider a function that is continuous for $a \le x \le b$. Divide the interval $[a, b]$ into N equal subintervals, each of length $\Delta = (b - a)/N$. Let $x_0, x_1, \ldots, x_N$ denote the endpoints of these subintervals:

$$x_0 = a, \ x_1 = a + \Delta, \ x_2 = a + 2\Delta, \ldots, \ x_N = a + N\Delta = b.$$

Form the sum

$$f(x_1)(x_1 - x_0) + f(x_2)(x_2 - x_1) + \cdots + f(x_N)(x_N - x_{N-1})$$

$$= \sum_{i=1}^{N} f(x_i)\, \Delta, \qquad (4)$$

which is called a **Riemann sum**. The **Fundamental Theorem of Calculus** states that if we iterate this process, each time dividing $[a, b]$ into smaller and smaller subintervals, in the limit we obtain the definite integral $\int_a^b f(x)\, dx$:

$$\lim_{\Delta \to 0} \sum_{i=1}^{N} f(x_i)\Delta = \int_a^b f(x)\, dx.$$

Example A4.5   Consider the function $f(x) = x^2$ between $x = 0$ and $x = 2$. If we divide $[0, 2]$ into 10 equal parts, each of length 0.2, then (4) becomes

$$f(0.2) \cdot 0.2 + f(0.4) \cdot 0.2 + f(0.6) \cdot 0.2 + \cdots$$
$$+ f(1.8) \cdot 0.2 + f(2) \cdot 0.2 = 3.08.$$

If we next divide $[0, 2]$ into 20 equal subintervals, (4) becomes

$$f(0.1) \cdot 0.1 + f(0.2) \cdot 0.1 + f(0.3) \cdot 0.1 + \cdots$$
$$+ f(1.9) \cdot 0.1 + f(2) \cdot 0.1 = 2.87.$$

If we keep increasing the number of subintervals, we obtain a sequence that tends to $8/3 \approx 2.667$. On the other hand,

$$\int_0^2 x^2\, dx = \frac{x^3}{3}\Big|_{x=0}^{x=2} = \frac{2^3}{3} - \frac{0^3}{3} = \frac{8}{3}.$$

The Fundamental Theorem holds under more general circumstances. First, we need not partition $[a, b]$ into *equal* subintervals, as long as, in the limit process, the length of the largest subinterval goes to zero. Second, we need not always evaluate f at the right endpoint in each subinterval $[x_{i-1}, x_i]$, as we did in (4). We can evaluate f at *any* point in each subinterval.

A4.3   APPLICATIONS

Area under a Graph

If f is a positive function on $[a, b]$, as pictured in Figure A4.1, each $f(x_i)(x_i - x_{i-1})$ in the Riemann sum is the area of the rectangle that has base $[x_{i-1}, x_i]$ and height $f(x_i)$. The sum of the areas of these rectangles approximates the area under the graph of f. As we take finer subdivisions, the corresponding rectangles give better and better approximations to the region under the graph of f. By the Fundamental Theorem of Calculus, the area under the graph of f from a to b is $\int_a^b f(x)\, dx$.

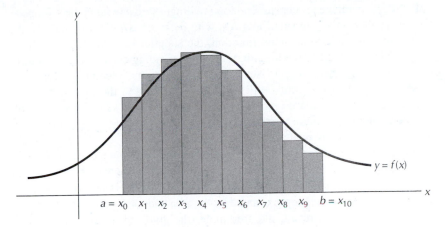

The Riemann sums of a positive function f approximate the area under the graph.

Consumer Surplus

Let $p = f(q)$ be the market (inverse) demand function relating selling price to quantity demanded for some commodity Q, as pictured in Figure A4.2. Think of Q as a major purchase item, like a house or car, so that most consumers will buy only one of Q. In this case, it is convenient to think of the demand function $q = f^{-1}(p)$ as counting how many consumers have reservation price $\geq p$.

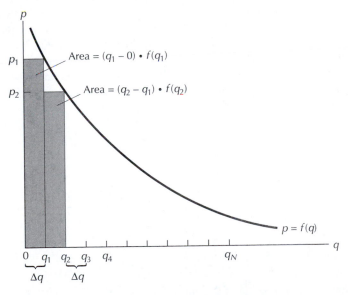

An inverse demand function.

In order to compute the consumers' total willingness to pay for Q, let's suppose that the supplier sells Q in small lots Δq, with $q_n = n \cdot \Delta q$ for $n = 1, 2, \ldots, N$. According to the inverse demand function, the supplier can charge $p_1 = f(q_1)$ dollars and still sell all of the first lot, with corresponding consumer expenditure of $q_1 \cdot p_1 = (q_1 - 0) \cdot f(q_1)$. Next, the firm offers the second Δq lot, with $\Delta q = q_2 - q_1$. In all, q_2 units will be sold. According to the inverse demand function, the firm can charge $p_2 = f(q_2)$ dollars and still sell this second lot. Total consumer expenditure is now $f(q_1)(q_1 - 0) + f(q_2)(q_2 - q_1)$, an amount represented by the combined area of the two rectangles in Figure A4.2. Continue this process, offering Δq units for sale at each step. Total consumer expenditure will be $\sum_1^n f(q_i)(q_i - q_{i-1})$. This is the Riemann sum of the inverse demand function in Figure A4.2. By the Fundamental Theorem of Calculus, if Δq is small enough, this Riemann sum will be well approximated by the area under the graph of the inverse demand function. As a result, the area under the graph of the inverse demand function from $q = 0$ to $q = q^*$ is often called the **total willingness to pay** for q^* units. On the other hand, since q^* units of commodity Q were actually sold at price $p^* = f(q^*)$, the actual expenditure was $q^* \cdot f(q^*)$. The total willingness to pay minus the actual expenditure is called the **consumer surplus**. Both of these concepts play important roles in the evaluation of the benefits of a project in benefit-cost analysis.

Present Value of a Flow

Suppose that $P(t)$ represents a flow of income over time t in years from $t = a$ to $t = b$. More precisely, $P(t)$ is the annual rate at which income is flowing in at time t. Let's compute the present value of this flow if the interest rate is r. Partition the time axis from a to b into discrete intervals of equal length Δ. In subinterval $[t_{i-1}, t_i]$, income of approximately $P(t_i)(t_i - t_{i-1})$ will be achieved, since $P(t)$ is in units of income per year and $(t_i - t_{i-1})$ represents the fraction of a year under consideration. The present value of the income in this period will be $e^{-rt_i}P(t_i)(t_i - t_{i-1})$. To get the present value of the entire flow, we add all these present values over subintervals together:

$$PV = \sum_i e^{-rt_i} P(t_i)(t_i - t_{i-1}).$$

By the Fundamental Theorem of Calculus, we can use

$$\int_{t=a}^b e^{-rt} P(t)\, dt$$

to represent the present value of the entire flow.

EXERCISES

A4.1   Find the indefinite integral of each of the following functions:

a) $4x^6 - x^3$,

b) $12x^2 - 6x^{1/2} + 3x^{-1/2} - x^{-1}$,

c) $6e^{7x}$,

d) $e^{(3x^2+6x)}(x + 1)$,

e) $(x^2 + 2x + 4)^{1/2}(x + 1)$,

f) $\dfrac{3x^{1/2} + x^{-1/2}}{x^{3/2} + x^{1/2}}$.

A4.2   Use integration by parts to integrate:
a) $\int x \ln x \, dx$,
b) $\int x^2 e^{2x} \, dx$.

A4.3   Calculate the Riemann sum of $f(x) = x^2$ from $x = 0$ to $x = 2$, dividing $[0, 2]$ into 20 equal subintervals and evaluating f at the *left* endpoint of each subinterval at each step.

A4.4   Find the area between the graph and the x-axis for each of the following functions:
a) $\sqrt{x}$, from $x = 1$ to $x = 4$;
b) $x \ln x$, from $x = 1$ to $x = e$.

A4.5   Suppose the commodity Q has inverse demand function $p = 3q^{-1/2}$ and that presently 100 units are being sold. What is the commodity's consumer surplus?

A4.6   Suppose we know that the interest rate will vary over time according to the expression $r(t)$. What is the present value of a flow of income $P(t)$ from $t = a$ to $t = b$ using this variable interest rate?

Introduction to Probability

A5.1 PROBABILITY OF AN EVENT

Suppose we perform an experiment whose outcome is uncertain. Let S denote the space of all possible outcomes — the **sample space** of the experiment. For example, if we flip a coin, then $S = \{\text{heads, tails}\}$; if we toss a single die, $S = \{1, 2, 3, 4, 5, 6\}$. An **event** is a set of outcomes in the sample space, that is, a subset of S; for example, the set of all even-numbered face values of throws of the die. The events $E_1, \ldots, E_m$ of a collection are **mutually exclusive** if for each pair of events E_i and E_j in the collection, $E_i \cap E_j = \phi$, that is, E_i and E_j have no outcomes in common. With each event E, we associate an event E^c, the **complement** of E, which consists of all the points in S that are not in E.

To each event E, we assign a number $P(E)$, the **probability** that event E will occur when we perform the experiment. Roughly speaking, $P(E)$ is the relative frequency with which event E occurs. The probability $P(E)$ must satisfy the following rules:

(1) For any event E, $0 \le P(E) \le 1$.
(2) $P(S) = 1$.
(3) If $E_1, \ldots, E_m$ are mutually exclusive events, then

$$P(E_1 \cup \cdots \cup E_m) = \sum_{i=1}^{m} P(E_i).$$

(4) $P(E^c) = 1 - P(E).$

For any two events E_1 and E_2, the **conditional probability** of E_2 given E_1, written $P(E_2|E_1)$, is the probability that E_2 will occur, given that E_1 has occurred. Since it measures the relative size of E_2 in E_1,

$$P(E_2|E_1) = \frac{P(E_1 \cap E_2)}{P(E_1)}. \tag{1}$$

We say that events E_1 and E_2 are **independent** if the probability of one is indepen-dent of the occurrence of the other, that is, if $P(E_2|E_1) = P(E_2)$, or equivalently, if $P(E_1 \cap E_2) = P(E_1) \cdot P(E_2)$.

For any two events E and F, $E \cap F$ and $E \cap F^c$ are mutually exclusive since F and F^c are. Therefore,

$$P(E) = P(E \cap F) + P(E \cap F^c)$$
$$= P(E|F) \cdot P(F) + P(E|F^c) \cdot P(F^c)$$

(2)

by (1). Furthermore, we can write (1) as

$$P(E \cap F) = P(E|F) \cdot P(F)$$
$$P(E \cap F) = P(F|E) \cdot P(E).$$

(3)

We put (2) and (3) together to derive **Bayes' rule**:

$$P(E|F) = \frac{P(E \cap F)}{P(F)} = \frac{P(F|E) \cdot P(E)}{P(F|E) \cdot P(E) + P(F|E^c) \cdot P(E^c)},$$

an extremely useful formula for calculating probabilities in applications.

A5.2   EXPECTATION AND VARIANCE

If the elements of the sample space S are a finite set $\{x_1, \ldots, x_N\}$ of *real numbers*, as they are in the roll of a pair of dice, the x_i's are called **random variables**. In this case, the **expected value** or **mean** of this experiment is

$$E(x) \equiv \sum_{i=1}^{N} P(x_i) \cdot x_i,$$

the weighted average of the outcomes. If each random variable x_i has equal probability $1/N$, then the expected value is simply the usual average $\left(\sum_1^N x_i \right)/N$. More generally, for any set $S = \{y_1, \ldots, y_M\}$ of outcomes, suppose that $f: S \to \mathbf{R}^1$ is a real-valued function, for example, the result of assigning a value or prize to each outcome in S. Then, the **expected value** of f is

$$E[f] \equiv \sum_i P(y_i) \cdot f(y_i).$$

If $f(y_i)$ measures utility or satisfaction with outcome y_i, then $E[f]$ is called the **expected utility**.

In many experiments with random numbers, we are interested not only in the mean, but also in the dispersion or spread of the x_i's about the mean. To measure the likelihood of achieving the expected value of an experiment, we form a new random variable $(x_i - E(x))^2$, the squared distance from the mean, and compute its expected value. The result is called the **variance** of the random variable:

$$\text{Var}(x) \equiv \sum_{i=1}^{N} P(x_i)(x_i - E(x))^2. \tag{4}$$

If the x_i's are returns of different investments in a portfolio, then the variance measures the **risk** of the portfolio. If the variance is zero, the portfolio has a certain return of $E(x)$. If the variance is large, there is much uncertainty in the return of the portfolio.

The deviations from the mean are squared in (4) so that large positive and large negative deviations do not cancel each other. To make up for these squares, we sometimes take the square root of formula (4). The result is called the **standard deviation**:

$$\sigma \equiv \sqrt{\sum_i P(x_i)(x_i - E(x))^2}.$$

An important concept in the study of financial models is the **covariance** of two random variables $X = \{x_1, \ldots, x_M\}$ and $Y = \{y_1, \ldots, y_N\}$:

$$\text{Cov}(X, Y) \equiv \sum_{i=1}^{M} \sum_{j=1}^{N} P(X = x_i, Y = y_j)(x_i - E(X))(y_j - E(Y)),$$

the expected value of $(X - E(X))(Y - E(Y))$. If $X > E(X)$ and $Y > E(Y)$ tend to occur together, then $\text{Cov}(X, Y)$ will be positive. If X and Y are independent, then $\text{Cov}(X, Y) = 0$.

A5.3   CONTINUOUS RANDOM VARIABLES

The notion of a random variable for a finite sample space can be extended to the case of a *continuous* sample space S in which every point in some interval of real numbers can be considered as a possible outcome. In this case, the probability of any single number is likely to be zero. We use a function $f : S \rightarrow \mathbf{R}^1_+$ to assign probabilities, with the probability $P(a \leq x \leq b)$ that x takes on a value between points a and b equal to the area under the graph of f between $\{x = a\}$ and $\{x = b\}$:

$$P(a \leq x \leq b) = \int_a^b f(x)\,dx.$$

Such a function f is called the **probability density function** or **pdf** of the continuous random variable. In this case, the mean or expected value of x is

$$E(x) = \int_{-\infty}^{\infty} x f(x)\, dx, \tag{5}$$

and the variance of x is

$$\text{Var}(x) = \int_{-\infty}^{\infty} (x - E(x))^2 f(x)\, dx. \tag{6}$$

If $h: S \to \mathbf{R}^1$ is another function on continuous sample space S, for example, a utility function, then the **expected value** of h is

$$E(h(x)) = \int_{-\infty}^{\infty} h(x) f(x)\, dx.$$

A commonly used pdf is the **normal density**

$$f(x) = \frac{1}{\sqrt{2\pi}} e^{-x^2/2},$$

which we discussed in Section 5.5. This density has mean 0 and standard deviation 1. The corresponding normal density function for a continuous random variable with mean μ and standard deviation σ is

$$f(x) = \frac{1}{\sigma\sqrt{2\pi}} \cdot \exp\left[-\frac{(x - \mu)^2}{2\sigma^2} \right].$$

EXERCISES

A5.1 Derive Rule 4 of a probability $P(E)$ from Rules 1 to 3.

A5.2 What is the expected value and variance for the toss of a single die? If you win $2 times the face value of your toss, what is your expected winning?

A5.3 What is the expected value and variance of the toss of two dice? If you win an amount equal to the absolute value of the difference in the face values of the die, what is your expected winning?

A5.4 Suppose that you take $1000 along for spending money on a trip to New York City. Your utility from the trip is given by the function $U(y) = y^{1/3}$ of the amount y you spend. Suppose that there is a 10 percent chance that you will lose $100 during the trip and a 90 percent chance that you will be able to spend all $1000.
a) What is the expected utility of your trip?

     b) What is your expected utility if you buy $100 worth of traveler's checks, as certain insurance against the loss, for an actuarily fair premium of $10?

     c) What is the most you would pay from an expected utility point of view for insurance against that loss of $100?

A5.5 Use the Fundamental Theorem of Calculus to derive the formulas (5) and (6) for the mean and variance of a continuous random variable.

Selected Answers

Chapter 2 Answers

2.3 1, 5, -2, 0.

2.4 *a*) $x \neq 1$,   *b*) $x > 1$,   *c*) all x,   *d*) $x \neq \pm 1$,   *e*) $-1 \le x \le +1$,
     f) $-1 \le x \le +1, x \neq 0$.

2.5 *a*) $x \neq 1$,   *b*) all x,   *c*) $x \neq -1, -2$,   *d*) all x.

2.8 *a*) $y = 2x + 3$,   *b*) $y = -3x$,   *c*) $y = 4x - 3$,   *d*) $y = -2x + 2$,
     e) $y = x + 1$,   *f*) $y = (-7/2)x + 3$.

2.9 *a*) additional revenue from the $(q + 1)$st output, that is, marginal revenue.
     d) increase in consumption when national income goes up 1 unit.

2.11 *a*) $-21x^2$,   *c*) $-(9/2)x^{-5/2}$,   *e*) $6x - 9 + (14/5)x^{-3/5} - (3/2)x^{-1/2}$,
     g) $4x^3 + 9x^2 + 6x + 3$,   *i*) $2/(x + 1)^2$,   *k*) $7(x^5 - 3x^2)^6(5x^4 - 6x)$
     m) $(x^3 + 2x)^2(4x + 5)(44x^3 + 45x^2 + 40x + 30)$.

2.12 *a*) $y = 6x - 9$,   *b*) $y = (1/9)x + (2/9)$.

2.16 *a*) continuous and differentiable at $x = 0$,
     b) not continuous at $x = 0$,
     c) continuous, not differentiable at $x = 1$,
     d) continuous and differentiable at $x = 1$.

2.20 *a*) $-42x$,   *c*) $(45/4)x^{-7/2}$,   *e*) $6 - (52/25)x^{-8/5} + (3/4)x^{-3/2}$,
     g) $12x^2 + 18x + 6$,   *i*) $-4/(x + 1)^3$,

2.22 86, 88.

2.23 increases 30.78 dollars.

2.25 *a*) $7\frac{1}{14}$,   *b*) 9.99925,   *c*) 100,150.

Chapter 3 Answers

3.3 *a*), *c*), *d*) concave down for $x < 0$ and concave up for $x > 0$,
     b) concave up for $x < 0$ and $x > 4$, concave down for $0 < x < 4$,
     e) concave down for $x \neq 0$,
     f) concave up for $|x| > \sqrt{0.6}$ and down for $|x| < \sqrt{0.6}$.

3.9 *a*) no global max or min on D_1, max at 1 and min at 2 on D_2,
b) no max or min on D_1, min at 0 and max at 1 on D_2,
c) min at -4, max at -2 on D_1, min at $+1$, no max on D_2,
d) min at 0, max at 10 on D_1, min at 0, no max on D_2.

3.10 $(x - 5)(15 - x)$, $x^* = 10$.

3.11 $q = 20 - x$, $\Pi = (20 - x)(x - 5)$, $x^* = 12.50$.

3.16 No positive output maximizes profit.

3.19 Elasticity equals $-r$ for all prices.

3.22 $q^* = a/2(1 + kb)$, $p^* = a(1 + 2kb)/[b(2 + 2kb)]$.

Chapter 4 Answers

4.1 *a*) $(g \circ h)(z) = (5z - 1)^2 + 4$, $(h \circ g)(x) = 5x^2 + 19$.
b) $(g \circ h)(z) = (z - 1)^3(z + 1)^3$, $(h \circ g)(x) = (x^3 - 1)(x^3 + 1)$.
c), *d*) $(g \circ h)(z) = z$, $(h \circ g)(x) = x$.

4.2 *a*) inside $y = 3x^2 + 1$, outside $z = y^{1/2}$
b) inside $y = 1/x$, outside $z = y^2 + 5y + 4$,
c) inside $y = 2x - 7$, outside $z = \cos y$.

4.3 *a*) $(g \circ h)'(z) = 2(5z - 1)5 = 50z - 10$, $(h \circ g)'(x) = 5 \cdot 2x = 10x$,
b) $(g \circ h)'(z) = 3[(z - 1)(z + 1)]^2(2z) = 6z(z - 1)^2(z + 1)^2$,
   $(h \circ g)'(x) = 2x^3 \cdot 3x^2 = 6x^5$.

4.4 *a*) $\frac{1}{2}(3x^2 + 1)^{-1/2} \cdot 6x = 3x/\sqrt{3x^2 + 1}$
b) $[2(1/x) + 5](-1/x^2)$.

4.5 *a*) $\cos(x^4) \cdot 4x^3$,   *b*) $\cos(1/x) \cdot (-1/x^2)$
c) $\cos x/(2\sqrt{\sin x})$,   *d*) $(\cos \sqrt{x})/2\sqrt{x}$.

4.6 $\dfrac{dC}{dt} = \dfrac{dC}{dx} \cdot \dfrac{dx}{dt} = 12 \cdot 2 = 24$.

4.9 *a*) $(f^{-1})'(f(1)) = 1/3$, $1/f'(1) = 1/3$.
b) $(f^{-1})'(1/2) = -4$, $1/f'(1) = -(1 + 1)^2 = -4$.

Chapter 5 Answers

5.1 *a*) 8   *b*) 1/8   *c*) 2   *d*) 4   *e*) 1/4   *f*) 1   *g*) 1/32   *h*) 125   *i*) 1/3125

5.4 *a*) 1   *b*) -3 *c*) 9   *d*) 3   *e*) 2   *f*) -1 *g*) 2   *h*) 1/2   *i*) 0

5.5 *a*) $(\ln 9)/6$ *b*) 0   *c*) $5/\ln 2$ *d*) $2 + (\ln 5/\ln 2)$ *e*) $e^{5/2}$ *f*) 5

5.6 $t = (\ln 3)/r$

5.7 3.65 years

5.8 *a*) $f'(x) = e^{3x} + 3xe^{3x}$ $f''(x) = 6e^{3x} + 9xe^{3x}$
b) $f'(x) = (2x + 3)e^{x^2+3x-2}$ $f''(x) = (4x^2 + 12x + 11)e^{x^2+3x-2}$
c) $f'(x) = 8x^3/(x^4 + 2)$ $f''(x) = (48x^2 - 8x^6)/(x^4 + 2)^2$
d) $f'(x) = (1 - x)/e^x$ $f''(x) = (x - 2)/e^x$

e) $f'(x) = \frac{1}{\ln x} - \frac{1}{(\ln x)^2}$ $f''(x) = \frac{2}{x(\ln x)^3} - \frac{1}{x(\ln x)^2}$

f) $f'(x) = (1 - \ln x)/x^2$ $f''(x) = (2 \ln x - 3)/x^3$

5.10 $dy/dx = 1/(x \ln 10)$

5.11 c

5.12 a) \$1870.62   b) \$4754.17

5.13 48.05 years

5.14 $t = 1/(4r^2)$

5.15 $t = 3.393$

5.16 a) $y' = 3x/(x^2 + 1)^{1/2}(x^2 + 4)^{3/2}$

b) $y' = 2x(\ln(x^2) + 1)(x^2)^{x^2}$

Chapter 6 Answers

6.1 Net contribution cost = \$5956.

6.2 $C = 6070$, $S = 2875$, $F = 36{,}422$.

6.3 $x_1 = 0.5x_1 + 0.5x_2 + 1$, $x_2 = 0x_1 + 0.25x_2 + 3$; $x_1 = 6, x_2 = 4$.

6.4 $x_1 = 0.5x_1 + 0.5x_2 + 1$, $x_2 = 0.875x_1 + 0.25x_2 + 3$; no positive solution.

6.5 8.82 percent and 18.28 percent, respectively.

6.6 1.95 percent for white females.

Chapter 7 Answers

7.1 a and e.

7.2 a) $x = 5, y = 6, z = 2$.   b) $x = z = 1, y = -2$.

7.3 a) $x = 17/3, y = -13/3$;   c) $x = 1, y = -1, z = -2$.

7.6 a) $Y = hI°/(sh + am)$, $r = mI°/(sh + am)$;   b,c) both decrease as s increases.

7.8 $x_1 = (b_1 a_{22} - b_2 a_{12})/(a_{11} a_{22} - a_{12} a_{21})$,

$x_2 = (b_2 a_{11} - b_1 a_{21})/(a_{11} a_{22} - a_{12} a_{21})$; need $a_{11} a_{22} - a_{12} a_{21} \neq 0$.

7.10 $\begin{pmatrix} 1 & 2 & 0 \\ 0 & 0 & 1 \\ 0 & 0 & 0 \\ 0 & 0 & 0 \end{pmatrix}$, $\begin{pmatrix} 1 & 0 & -14 \\ 0 & 1 & 6 \end{pmatrix}$, $\begin{pmatrix} 1 & 0 \\ 0 & 1 \\ 0 & 0 \end{pmatrix}$, $\begin{pmatrix} 1 & 0 & .5 \\ 0 & 1 & .3 \end{pmatrix}$, $\begin{pmatrix} 1 & 0 \\ 0 & 1 \\ 0 & 0 \end{pmatrix}$.

7.12 $w = -1$, $x = 1$, $y = 2$, $z = 3$.

7.13 a) $\begin{pmatrix} 1 & 1 \\ 0 & 1 \end{pmatrix}$ and $\begin{pmatrix} 1 & 0 \\ 0 & 1 \end{pmatrix}$,   b) $\begin{pmatrix} 1 & 3 & 4 \\ 0 & -1 & -1 \end{pmatrix}$ and $\begin{pmatrix} 1 & 0 & 1 \\ 0 & 1 & 1 \end{pmatrix}$.

7.14 $x = (5/4) - (5/4)z$, $y = (3/2) - (3/2)z$.

7.15 $k = -1$ infinitely many solutions; $k \neq -1$, one solution: $x_1 = 1, x_2 = 0$.

7.16 a) w, x, y basic; z free: $w = (12/11) - (3/11)z$, $x = -(4/11) + (1/11)z$, $y = (7/11) + (12/11)z$; b) w, x basic, y, z free: $w = 0.6 - 2.2y + 0.6z$, $x = 0.6 + 0.8y - 0.4z$; c) all variables basic; d) only one variable basic.

7.17 *a*) General solution is $x = 1 + (5/4)z$, $y = 12 - (9/4)z$. To get an integer solution, take $z = 4$, then $x = 6$ and $y = 3$. *b*) Just change the right hand side in the system in part *a* and apply the same analysis.

7.18 $a = -8$.

7.19 *a*) one,   *b*) $q = 0, p = -1$.

7.20 *a*) 1, *b*) 2, *c*) 3, *e*) 3.

7.21 *a*) Only the zero solution for *i*, *iii* and *iv*; infinitely many other solutions for the other two. *b*) Unique solution for every RHS for *i* and *iv*; infinitely many solutions for every RHS for *ii*; zero or infinitely many solutions depending on the RHS for *v*; zero or one solution depending on the RHS for *iii*.

7.23 Only *c*.

7.25 *i*) : *a*) 2, *b*) z and 1 of the other 3, *c*) $z = 1/4$, $x = (3/4) + w - 2y$.

7.26 $C = 0.05956 \cdot P$, $S = 0.04702 \cdot P$, $F = 0.35737 \cdot P$.

7.29 *a*) z and any two of the other 3 can be endogenous; *b*) if y is chosen as exogenous and set to 0, $w = 0.6$, $x = 0.6$, $z = 0$; *c*) if z is the only exogenous variable and set equal to 0, the corresponding system has infinitely many solutions.

7.30 No, the 3×4 coefficient matrix has rank 2; no submatrix can have rank 3.

Chapter 8 Answers

8.1 *a*) $A + B = \begin{pmatrix} 2 & 4 & 0 \\ 4 & -2 & 4 \end{pmatrix}$, $A - D$ undefined, $3B = \begin{pmatrix} 0 & 3 & -3 \\ 12 & -3 & 6 \end{pmatrix}$,

$DC = \begin{pmatrix} 5 & 3 \\ 4 & 1 \end{pmatrix}$, $B^T = \begin{pmatrix} 0 & 4 \\ 1 & -1 \\ -1 & 2 \end{pmatrix}$, $A^T C^T = \begin{pmatrix} 2 & 6 \\ 1 & 10 \\ 5 & 1 \end{pmatrix}$.

8.1 *c*) $CD = \begin{pmatrix} 4 & 3 \\ 5 & 2 \end{pmatrix}$, $DC = \begin{pmatrix} 5 & 3 \\ 4 & 1 \end{pmatrix}$.

8.5 *a*) $AB = \begin{pmatrix} 2 & -5 \\ -5 & 2 \end{pmatrix} = BA$.

8.7 $\begin{pmatrix} -1 & 2 \\ -1 & 2 \end{pmatrix} \begin{pmatrix} -1 & 2 \\ -1 & 2 \end{pmatrix} = \begin{pmatrix} -1 & 2 \\ -1 & 2 \end{pmatrix}$.

$\begin{pmatrix} 3 & 6 \\ -1 & -2 \end{pmatrix} \begin{pmatrix} 3 & 6 \\ -1 & -2 \end{pmatrix} = \begin{pmatrix} 3 & 6 \\ -1 & -2 \end{pmatrix}$.

8.9 number of ways of permuting n objects $= n!$.

8.10 *a*) $\begin{pmatrix} 0 & 1 \\ 1 & 0 \end{pmatrix} + \begin{pmatrix} 1 & 0 \\ 0 & 1 \end{pmatrix} = \begin{pmatrix} 1 & 1 \\ 1 & 1 \end{pmatrix}$, *not* a permutation matrix; so not closed under addition. *b*) yes, closed under multiplication.

8.15 Carry out the multiplication.

8.18 Carry out the multiplication.

8.19 a) $\begin{pmatrix} 1 & -1 \\ -1 & 2 \end{pmatrix}$, b) $\begin{pmatrix} 4/6 & -5/6 \\ -2/6 & 4/6 \end{pmatrix}$, c) singular,

d) $\begin{pmatrix} -5/2 & 0 & -1 \\ 3/2 & 0 & 1/2 \\ 1/3 & 1/3 & 1/3 \end{pmatrix}$, e) $\begin{pmatrix} -6 & 3/2 & -1 \\ 13 & -3 & 2 \\ 5/3 & -1/3 & 1/3 \end{pmatrix}$,

f) $\begin{pmatrix} 2 & 9/2 & -15/2 & 11/2 \\ 1/3 & -7/3 & 10/3 & -8/3 \\ -1/4 & 3/4 & -1 & 3/4 \\ -1 & 1 & -1 & 1 \end{pmatrix}$.

8.20 a) $\begin{pmatrix} 1 & -1 \\ -1 & 2 \end{pmatrix} \begin{pmatrix} 5 \\ 3 \end{pmatrix} = \begin{pmatrix} 2 \\ 1 \end{pmatrix}$,

b) $\begin{pmatrix} -6 & 3/2 & -1 \\ 13 & -3 & 2 \\ 5/2 & -1/3 & 1/3 \end{pmatrix} \begin{pmatrix} 4 \\ 20 \\ 3 \end{pmatrix} = \begin{pmatrix} 3 \\ -2 \\ 1 \end{pmatrix}$,

c) $\begin{pmatrix} -5/2 & 0 & -1 \\ 3/2 & 0 & 1/2 \\ 1/3 & 1/3 & 1/3 \end{pmatrix} \begin{pmatrix} 2 \\ 1 \\ -6 \end{pmatrix} = \begin{pmatrix} 1 \\ 0 \\ -1 \end{pmatrix}$.

8.21 A $n \times n$ and AB defined implies B has n rows.
A $n \times n$ and BA defined implies B has n columns.

8.22 $A^4 = \begin{pmatrix} 34 & 21 \\ 21 & 13 \end{pmatrix}$, $A^3 = \begin{pmatrix} 13 & 8 \\ 8 & 5 \end{pmatrix}$, $A^{-2} = \begin{pmatrix} 2 & -3 \\ -3 & 5 \end{pmatrix}$.

8.28 $D^{-1} = \begin{pmatrix} 1/d_1 & 0 & \cdots & 0 \\ 0 & 1/d_2 & \cdots & 0 \\ \vdots & \vdots & \ddots & \vdots \\ 0 & 0 & \cdots & 1/d_n \end{pmatrix}$.

8.29 $\begin{pmatrix} a & b \\ b & c \end{pmatrix}^{-1} = \dfrac{1}{ac - b^2}\begin{pmatrix} c & -b \\ -b & a \end{pmatrix}$, a symmetric matrix.

8.38 $A^{-1} = \begin{pmatrix} A_{11}^{-1} & 0 & \cdots & 0 \\ 0 & A_{22}^{-1} & \cdots & 0 \\ \vdots & \vdots & \ddots & \vdots \\ 0 & 0 & \cdots & A_{nn}^{-1} \end{pmatrix}$.

8.40 $A^{-1} = \begin{pmatrix} A_{11}^{-1}(I + A_{12}C^{-1}A_{21}A_{11}^{-1}) & -A_{11}^{-1}A_{12}C^{-1} \\ -C^{-1}A_{21}A_{11}^{-1} & C^{-1} \end{pmatrix}$,

where $C = A_{22} - A_{21}A_{11}^{-1}A_{12}$.

8.41 a) A_{11} and A_{22} nonsingular.
b) A_{11} and $A_{11} - \frac{1}{a_{22}}A_{12}A_{21}$ nonsingular.
c) A_{22} invertible and $\mathbf{p}^T A_{22}^{-1}\mathbf{p}$ nonzero.

8.42 a) $E_{12}(3)$, b) $E_{23}(-1) \cdot E_{14}(2) \cdot E_{12}(-3)$.
c) $E_{23}(1) \cdot E_{13}(3) \cdot E_{12}(-2)$, d) $E_{34}(-1) \cdot E_{23}(1) \cdot E_{14}(-2) \cdot E_{12}(-3)$.

8.43 *a)* $\begin{pmatrix} 1 & 0 \\ -3 & 1 \end{pmatrix}\begin{pmatrix} 2 & 4 \\ 0 & -1 \end{pmatrix}$

b) $\begin{pmatrix} 1 & 0 & 0 \\ 3 & 1 & 0 \\ -2 & 1 & 1 \end{pmatrix}\begin{pmatrix} 2 & 1 & 0 \\ 0 & -1 & 6 \\ 0 & 0 & 3 \end{pmatrix}$,

c) $\begin{pmatrix} 1 & 0 & 0 \\ 2 & 1 & 0 \\ -3 & -1 & 1 \end{pmatrix}\begin{pmatrix} 2 & 4 & 0 & 1 \\ 0 & -2 & 3 & 1 \\ 0 & 0 & 3 & 8 \end{pmatrix}$

d) $\begin{pmatrix} 1 & 0 & 0 & 0 \\ 3 & 1 & 0 & 0 \\ 0 & -1 & 1 & 0 \\ 2 & 0 & 1 & 1 \end{pmatrix}\begin{pmatrix} 2 & 6 & 0 & 5 \\ 0 & 3 & 8 & 2 \\ 0 & 0 & -4 & 4 \\ 0 & 0 & 0 & -1 \end{pmatrix}$.

8.48 *a)* $\begin{pmatrix} 1 & 0 \\ -3 & 1 \end{pmatrix}\begin{pmatrix} 2 & 0 \\ 0 & -1 \end{pmatrix}\begin{pmatrix} 1 & 2 \\ 0 & 1 \end{pmatrix}$,

b) $\begin{pmatrix} 1 & 0 & 0 \\ 3 & 1 & 0 \\ -2 & 1 & 1 \end{pmatrix}\begin{pmatrix} 2 & 0 & 0 \\ 0 & -1 & 0 \\ 0 & 0 & 3 \end{pmatrix}\begin{pmatrix} 1 & 1/2 & 0 \\ 0 & 1 & -6 \\ 0 & 0 & 1 \end{pmatrix}$,

8.51 *b)* $(1, 0, -1), (-1, 1, 2), (1, 1, -1), (0, 1, -1)$.

Chapter 9 Answers

9.1 $a_{11}a_{22}a_{33} - a_{11}a_{23}a_{32} - a_{12}a_{21}a_{33} + a_{12}a_{31}a_{23} + a_{13}a_{21}a_{32} - a_{13}a_{31}a_{22}$.

9.2 $a_{11} \cdot \det \begin{pmatrix} a_{22} & a_{23} & a_{24} \\ a_{32} & a_{33} & a_{34} \\ a_{42} & a_{43} & a_{44} \end{pmatrix} - a_{12} \det \begin{pmatrix} a_{21} & a_{23} & a_{24} \\ a_{31} & a_{33} & a_{34} \\ a_{41} & a_{43} & a_{44} \end{pmatrix}$

$+ a_{13} \det \begin{pmatrix} a_{21} & a_{22} & a_{24} \\ a_{31} & a_{32} & a_{34} \\ a_{41} & a_{42} & a_{44} \end{pmatrix} - a_{14} \det \begin{pmatrix} a_{21} & a_{22} & a_{23} \\ a_{31} & a_{32} & a_{33} \\ a_{41} & a_{42} & a_{43} \end{pmatrix}$.

9.5 $\det \begin{pmatrix} a_{11} & a_{12} & a_{13} \\ 0 & a_{22} & a_{23} \\ 0 & 0 & a_{33} \end{pmatrix} = a_{11} \cdot \det \begin{pmatrix} a_{22} & a_{23} \\ 0 & a_{33} \end{pmatrix} - 0 \cdot \det \begin{pmatrix} a_{12} & a_{13} \\ 0 & a_{33} \end{pmatrix}$

$+ 0 \cdot \det \begin{pmatrix} a_{12} & a_{13} \\ a_{22} & a_{23} \end{pmatrix} = a_{11}a_{22}a_{33} + 0 + 0$, expanding along column one.

9.6 $\det \begin{pmatrix} a_{11} & a_{12} \\ ra_{11} + a_{21} & ra_{12} + a_{22} \end{pmatrix} = a_{11}(ra_{12} + a_{22}) - a_{12}(ra_{11} + a_{21})$

$= ra_{11}a_{12} - ra_{11}a_{12} + a_{11}a_{22} - a_{12}a_{21}$.

9.7 *a)* $\begin{pmatrix} 1 & 1 \\ 0 & -1 \end{pmatrix}$, determinants $= -1$.

b) $\begin{pmatrix} 2 & 4 & 0 \\ 0 & -8 & 3 \\ 0 & 0 & 3/4 \end{pmatrix}$, determinants $= -12$.

c) One row echelon form is $\begin{pmatrix} 3 & 4 & 5 \\ 0 & 1 & 2 \\ 0 & 0 & -6 \end{pmatrix}$, with $\det = -18 = -\det A$.

9.8 a) One row echelon form is $\begin{pmatrix} 1 & 1 & 1 \\ 0 & 3 & 1 \\ 0 & 0 & 1 \end{pmatrix}$. So, $\det = 3$.

b) One row echelon form is $\begin{pmatrix} 1 & 1 & 1 \\ 0 & 4 & 5 \\ 0 & 0 & -5 \end{pmatrix}$. So, $\det = -20$.

9.9 All nonsingular since $\det \neq 0$.

9.11 a) $\dfrac{1}{7} \begin{pmatrix} 1 & -3 \\ 1 & 4 \end{pmatrix}$.

b) $\dfrac{1}{\det A} \cdot \begin{pmatrix} \begin{vmatrix} 5 & 6 \\ 0 & 8 \end{vmatrix} & -\begin{vmatrix} 2 & 3 \\ 0 & 8 \end{vmatrix} & \begin{vmatrix} 2 & 3 \\ 5 & 6 \end{vmatrix} \\ -\begin{vmatrix} 0 & 6 \\ 1 & 8 \end{vmatrix} & \begin{vmatrix} 1 & 3 \\ 1 & 8 \end{vmatrix} & -\begin{vmatrix} 1 & 3 \\ 0 & 6 \end{vmatrix} \\ \begin{vmatrix} 0 & 5 \\ 1 & 0 \end{vmatrix} & -\begin{vmatrix} 1 & 2 \\ 1 & 0 \end{vmatrix} & \begin{vmatrix} 1 & 2 \\ 0 & 5 \end{vmatrix} \end{pmatrix}$

$= \dfrac{1}{37} \cdot \begin{pmatrix} 40 & -16 & -3 \\ 6 & 5 & -6 \\ -5 & 2 & 5 \end{pmatrix}$.

c) $\dfrac{1}{ad-bc} \begin{pmatrix} d & -b \\ -c & a \end{pmatrix}$.

9.12 $x_1 = \dfrac{35}{35} = 1, \quad x_2 = -\dfrac{70}{35} = -2$

9.13 a) $x_1 = \dfrac{-7}{-7} = 1, x_2 = \dfrac{14}{-7} = -2$.

b) $x_1 = \dfrac{-23}{-23} = 1; x_2 = \dfrac{0}{-23} = 0; x_3 = \dfrac{-69}{-23} = 3$.

9.14 a) $\det A = -1$, $\det B = -1$, $\det AB = +1$; $\det(A+B) = -4$.

b) $\det A = 24$; $\det B = 18$; $\det AB = 432$; $\det(A+B) = 56$.

c) $\det A = ad - bc$, $\det B = eh - fg$, $\det AB = (ad-bc)(eh-fg)$,
$\det(A+B) = \det A + \det B + ah - bg + de - cf$.

Chapter 10 Answers

10.4 a) $(2,-1)$ b) $(-2,-1)$ c) $(2,1)$ d) $(3,0)$ e) $(1,2,4)$ f) $(2,-2,3)$.

10.5 a) $(1,3)$ b) $(-4,12)$ c) undefined   d) $(0,3,3)$ e) $(0,2)$
   f) $(1,4)$ g) $(1,1)$ h) $(3,7,1)$ i) $(-2,-4,0)$ j) undefined

10.10 a) 5 b) 3 c) $\sqrt{3}$ d) $3\sqrt{2}$ e) $\sqrt{2}$ f) $\sqrt{14}$ g) 2 h) $\sqrt{30}$ i) 3

10.11 a) 5 b) 10 c) 4 d) $\sqrt{41}$ e) 6

10.12 *a*) acute, 45°   *b*) right, 90°   *c*) acute, 30°   *d*) obtuse, 106.8°
e) acute, 63.4°

10.13 *a*) $\left(\frac{3}{5},\frac{4}{5}\right)$ *b*) $(1,0)$ *c*) $\left(\frac{1}{\sqrt{3}},\frac{1}{\sqrt{3}},\frac{1}{\sqrt{3}}\right)$ *d*) $\left(\frac{-1}{\sqrt{14}},\frac{2}{\sqrt{14}},\frac{-3}{\sqrt{14}}\right)$

10.14 *a*) $(-3,-4)$ *b*) $(-5,0)$ *c*) $\left(\frac{-5}{\sqrt{3}},\frac{-5}{\sqrt{3}},\frac{-5}{\sqrt{3}}\right)$ *d*) $\left(\frac{5}{\sqrt{14}},\frac{-10}{\sqrt{14}},\frac{15}{\sqrt{14}}\right)$

10.15 $(\mathbf{u}-\mathbf{v})\cdot(\mathbf{u}-\mathbf{v}) = \mathbf{u}\cdot\mathbf{u} - 2\mathbf{u}\cdot\mathbf{v} + \mathbf{v}\cdot\mathbf{v}.$

10.16 *b*) $|u_1| + |u_2| + \cdots + |u_n|$; $\max\{|u_1|,|u_2|,\ldots,|u_n|\}$.

10.19 42.03°

10.24 expand determinant along top row

10.25 *a*) $(-1,0,1)$ *b*) $(-7,3,5)$

10.26 *b*) 3.64

10.28 *a*) $(3+2t,0)$; $(4,0)$ *b*) $(1-t,t)$; $\left(\frac{1}{2},\frac{1}{2}\right)$ *c*) $(1+t,t,1-t)$; $\left(\frac{3}{2},\frac{1}{2},\frac{1}{2}\right)$

10.29 no

10.30 *a*) $x_2 = -3x_1 + 15$ *b*) $x_2 = -x_1 + 8$ *c*) $x_2 = 5$

10.31 *a*) $\mathbf{x}(t) = \begin{pmatrix} 0 \\ 5/2 \end{pmatrix} + \begin{pmatrix} 1 \\ 3/2 \end{pmatrix}t$;   *b*) $\mathbf{x}(t) = \begin{pmatrix} 0 \\ 7 \end{pmatrix} + \begin{pmatrix} 1 \\ -1 \end{pmatrix}t$;

c) $\mathbf{x}(t) = \begin{pmatrix} 6 \\ 0 \end{pmatrix} + \begin{pmatrix} 0 \\ 1 \end{pmatrix}t$

10.32 no

10.33 *a*) $\mathbf{x}(t) = \begin{pmatrix} 1 \\ 2 \end{pmatrix} + t\begin{pmatrix} 2 \\ 4 \end{pmatrix}$; $x_2 = 2x_1$

b) $\mathbf{x}(t) = \begin{pmatrix} 1 \\ 1 \end{pmatrix} + t\begin{pmatrix} 3 \\ 9 \end{pmatrix}$; $x_2 = 3x_1 - 2$

c) $\mathbf{x}(t) = \begin{pmatrix} 3 \\ 0 \end{pmatrix} + t\begin{pmatrix} -3 \\ 4 \end{pmatrix}$; $x_2 = -\frac{4}{3}x_1 + 4$

10.34 *a*) $\mathbf{x}(t) = \begin{pmatrix} 0 \\ -7 \end{pmatrix} + \begin{pmatrix} 1 \\ 3 \end{pmatrix}t$;   *b*) $\mathbf{x}(t) = \begin{pmatrix} 0 \\ 3 \end{pmatrix} + \begin{pmatrix} 4 \\ -3 \end{pmatrix}t$

c) $\mathbf{x}(t,s) = \begin{pmatrix} 3 \\ 0 \\ 0 \end{pmatrix} + \begin{pmatrix} -3 \\ 3 \\ 0 \end{pmatrix}t + \begin{pmatrix} -3 \\ 0 \\ 3 \end{pmatrix}s$

d) $\mathbf{x}(t,s) = \begin{pmatrix} 6 \\ 0 \\ 0 \end{pmatrix} + \begin{pmatrix} -6 \\ -3 \\ 0 \end{pmatrix}t + \begin{pmatrix} -6 \\ 0 \\ 2 \end{pmatrix}s$

10.35 *a*) $y = -\frac{1}{2}x + \frac{5}{2}$;   *b*) $y = \frac{x}{2} + 1$;
c) $-7x + 2y + z = -3$;   *d*) $y = 4$

10.36 *a*) $\mathbf{x}(t,s) = \begin{pmatrix} 6 \\ 0 \\ 0 \end{pmatrix} + \begin{pmatrix} 6 \\ 6 \\ 0 \end{pmatrix}t + \begin{pmatrix} 6 \\ 0 \\ -3 \end{pmatrix}s$; $x - y + 2z = 6$

b) $\mathbf{x}(t,s) = \begin{pmatrix} 0 \\ 3 \\ 2 \end{pmatrix} + \begin{pmatrix} 3 \\ 0 \\ -1 \end{pmatrix}t + \begin{pmatrix} 2 \\ 2 \\ -2 \end{pmatrix}s$; $x + 2y + 3z = 12$.

10.38 *a)* yes;   *b)* no.

10.39 *a)* $x_1 - x_2 = -1$ *b)* $-3x_1 + x_2 + 5x_3 = -7$ *c)* $\dfrac{x_1}{a} + \dfrac{x_2}{b} + \dfrac{x_3}{c} = 1$.

10.40 $(11/3, -11/3, 1)$

10.41 $\begin{pmatrix} x \\ y \\ z \end{pmatrix} = \begin{pmatrix} 5 \\ -1 \\ 0 \end{pmatrix} + \begin{pmatrix} 3 \\ -2 \\ 1 \end{pmatrix} t$ or $\dfrac{x-5}{3} = \dfrac{y+1}{-2} = z$.

10.42 If I^* increases, so does Y^* and r^*. If M_s increases, Y^* increases and r^* decreases. If c_0 increases, so does Y^* and r^*.

Chapter 11 Answers

11.2 *a)* independent   *b)* dependent   *c)* independent   *d)* independent

11.3 *a)* independent   *b)* dependent

11.9 *a)* $3 \begin{pmatrix} 1 \\ 2 \end{pmatrix} - \begin{pmatrix} 1 \\ 4 \end{pmatrix} = \begin{pmatrix} 2 \\ 2 \end{pmatrix}$ *b)* $0 \begin{pmatrix} 1 \\ 1 \\ 0 \end{pmatrix} + \begin{pmatrix} 1 \\ 0 \\ 1 \end{pmatrix} + 2 \begin{pmatrix} 0 \\ 1 \\ 1 \end{pmatrix} = \begin{pmatrix} 1 \\ 2 \\ 3 \end{pmatrix}$

11.12 *a)* no   *b)* yes   *c)* no   *d)* yes

11.14 *a)* no   *b)* no   *c)* no   *d)* yes   *e)* no

Chapter 12 Answers

12.1 *a)* n *b)* $1/n$ *c)* $2^{(-1)^{n-1}(n-1)}$ *d)* $(-1)^{n-1}\left(\frac{n-1}{n}\right)$
  e) $(-1)^n$ *f)* $(n+1)/n$ *g)* π to n decimal places
  h) the nth digit after the decimal point in π

12.2 *a)* out of order, $n_2 > n_3$
  b) finite set
  c) second element not in original sequence

12.21 *a)* neither,   *b)* closed,   *c)* closed,   *d)* open,   *e)* closed.

12.31 None are bounded.

Chapter 13 Answers

13.11 *a)* $(2 \quad -3 \quad 5) \begin{pmatrix} x_1 \\ x_2 \\ x_3 \end{pmatrix}$ *b)* $\begin{pmatrix} 2 & -3 \\ 1 & -4 \\ 1 & 0 \end{pmatrix} \begin{pmatrix} x_1 \\ x_2 \end{pmatrix}$

  c) $\begin{pmatrix} 1 & 0 & -1 \\ 2 & 3 & -6 \\ 0 & 2 & 1 \end{pmatrix} \begin{pmatrix} x_1 \\ x_2 \\ x_3 \end{pmatrix}$

13.12 *a)* $(x_1 \quad x_2) \begin{pmatrix} 1 & -1 \\ -1 & 1 \end{pmatrix} \begin{pmatrix} x_1 \\ x_2 \end{pmatrix}$ *b)* $(x_1 \quad x_2) \begin{pmatrix} 5 & -5 \\ -5 & -1 \end{pmatrix} \begin{pmatrix} x_1 \\ x_2 \end{pmatrix}$

  c) $(x_1 \quad x_2 \quad x_3) \begin{pmatrix} 1 & 2 & -3 \\ 2 & 2 & 4 \\ -3 & 4 & 3 \end{pmatrix} \begin{pmatrix} x_1 \\ x_2 \\ x_3 \end{pmatrix}$

13.13 $\sin x$, $\ln |x|$, e^x, for example.

13.23

	$f(x)$	Domain	Range	$1 - 1$	$f^{-1}(y)$	onto
a)	$3x - 7$	R	R	yes	$\frac{1}{3}(y + 7)$	yes
b)	$x^2 - 1$	R	$[-1, \infty)$	no		no
c)	e^x	R	$(0, \infty)$	yes	$\ln(y)$	no
d)	$x^3 - x$	R	R	no		yes
e)	$x/(x^2 + 1)$	R	$[\frac{-1}{2}, \frac{1}{2}]$	no		no
f)	x^3	R	R	yes	$y^{1/3}$	yes
g)	$1/x$	R-{0}	R-{0}	yes	$1/y$	no
h)	$\sqrt{x - 1}$	$[1, \infty)$	$[0, \infty)$	yes	$y^2 + 1$	no
i)	xe^{-x}	R	$(-\infty, 1/e]$	no		no

13.24 a) $f(x) = \log x$; $g(x) = x^2 + 1$ b) $f(x) = x^2$; $g(x) = \sin x$
c) $f(x) = (\cos x, \sin x)$; $g(x) = x^3$ d) $f(x) = x^3 + x$; $g(x) = x^2 y$

Chapter 14 Answers

14.1 a) $f_x = 8xy - 3y^3 + 6$ $f_y = 4x^2 - 9xy^2$
b) $f_x = y$ $f_y = x$
c) $f_x = y^2$ $f_y = 2xy$
d) $f_x = 2e^{2x+3y}$ $f_y = 3e^{2x+3y}$
e) $f_x = -2y/(x - y)^2$ $f_y = 2x/(x - y)^2$
f) $f_x = 6xy - 7\sqrt{y}$ $f_y = 3x^2 - (7x/2\sqrt{y})$

14.2 a) $\frac{\partial q}{\partial x_1} = ka_1 x_1^{a_1-1} x_2^{a_2}$, $\frac{\partial q}{\partial x_2} = ka_2 x_1^{a_1} x_2^{a_2-1}$
b) $\frac{\partial q}{\partial x_1} = c_1 hkx_1^{-a-1}(c_1 x_1^{-a} + c_2 x_2^{-a})^{-\frac{h}{a}-1}$,
$\frac{\partial q}{\partial x_2} = c_2 hkx_2^{-a-1}(c_1 x_1^{-a} + c_2 x_2^{-a})^{-\frac{h}{a}-1}$

14.4 a) 5400   b) 5392.8, 5412.5
c) 5392.798, 5412.471   d) $\Delta L = 60$

14.5 a) own price elasticity $= a_{11}$
b) cross price elasticity $= a_{12}$
c) income elasticity $= b_1$

14.6 a) 4.5   b) $-.75$ c) $-.15$
d) $Q_b \approx 3.75$, $Q_b = 3.806$; $Q_c \approx 4.35$, $Q_c = 4.356$

14.7 a) 240   b) 238.046   c) 238.032   d) 241.843, 241.837

14.8 a) 11,692.76   b) 6037   c) 3.04097

14.10 6.5075

14.11 a) $\frac{\partial f}{\partial t} = (3y^2 + 2)(-6t) + (6xy)(12t^2 + 1)$, $x = -3t^2$ and $y = 4t^3 + t$
b) $\frac{\partial f}{\partial t} = -1152t^7 - 432t^5 - 36t^3 - 12t$

14.12 7.25

14.13 $-3/8$

14.14 $-148,000$

14.15 $(6, 5, 6)$

14.17 $\frac{\partial F}{\partial x} = \frac{\partial \omega}{\partial s} - \frac{\partial \omega}{\partial r}$, $\qquad \frac{\partial F}{\partial y} = \frac{\partial \omega}{\partial r} + \frac{\partial \omega}{\partial s}$

14.18 $(3/\sqrt{10}, 1/\sqrt{10})$

14.19 $(9/\sqrt{85}, 2/\sqrt{85})$

14.20 $52/\sqrt{10}$

14.21 $\begin{pmatrix} \partial q_1/\partial r & \partial q_1/\partial t \\ \partial q_2/\partial r & \partial q_2/\partial t \end{pmatrix} = \begin{pmatrix} 427.5 & 19.5 \\ -400/3 & -20/3 \end{pmatrix}$

14.22 $DF(G(1, 1)) = \begin{pmatrix} 2 & 2 \\ 0 & 4 \end{pmatrix}$

14.23 a) $H = \begin{pmatrix} 8y & 8x - 9y^2 \\ 8x - 9y^2 & -18xy \end{pmatrix}$ b) $H = \begin{pmatrix} 0 & 1 \\ 1 & 0 \end{pmatrix}$

c) $H = \begin{pmatrix} 0 & 2y \\ 2y & 2x \end{pmatrix}$ d) $H = \begin{pmatrix} 4e^{2x+3y} & 6e^{2x+3y} \\ 6e^{2x+3y} & 9e^{2x+3y} \end{pmatrix}$

e) $H = \begin{pmatrix} \frac{4y}{(x-y)^3} & \frac{-2x-2y}{(x-y)^3} \\ \frac{-2x-2y}{(x-y)^3} & \frac{4x}{(x-y)^3} \end{pmatrix}$ f) $H = \begin{pmatrix} 6y & 6x - \frac{7}{2}y^{\frac{-1}{2}} \\ 6x - \frac{7}{2}y^{\frac{-1}{2}} & \frac{7}{4}xy^{\frac{-3}{2}} \end{pmatrix}$

14.24 $\frac{\partial^3 Q}{\partial K^3} = \frac{15}{16}K^{\frac{-9}{4}}L^{\frac{1}{4}}$, $\qquad \frac{\partial^3 Q}{\partial K^2 \partial L} = -\frac{3}{16}K^{\frac{-5}{4}}L^{\frac{-3}{4}}$

$\frac{\partial^3 Q}{\partial K \partial L^2} = -\frac{9}{16}K^{\frac{-1}{4}}L^{\frac{-7}{4}}$, $\qquad \frac{\partial^3 Q}{\partial L^3} = \frac{21}{16}K^{\frac{3}{4}}L^{-\frac{11}{4}}$

Chapter 15 Answers

15.3 2.98

15.4 1.8607; 1.9913

15.5 $y'(x) = 1$ in both cases.

15.6 a) $y = -3$ b) yes c) $-4/9$, $2/9$ d) $-3^{1/9}$

15.7 $x \approx x_0 - \dfrac{f'(x)}{pf''(x)}\Delta p + \dfrac{1}{pf''(x)}\Delta w$

15.8 a) no b) no c) yes, -0.9449, 0.4961.

15.9 a) $23/24$ b) $23/24$

15.15 a) $\partial Y/\partial M^s > 0$, $\partial Y/\partial T < 0$, $\partial r/\partial M^s < 0$, $\partial r/\partial T < 0$;
b) $\partial Y/\partial M^s > 0$, $\partial Y/\partial T < 0$, $\partial r/\partial M^s < 0$, $\partial r/\partial T < 0$

15.16 $x \approx 1.03$, $y \approx 1.9174$

15.18 No, the system is underdetermined.

15.19 yes; $\partial v/\partial x = 0$, $\partial v/\partial y = -1/3$, $\partial z/\partial x = -1/3$, $\partial z/\partial y = -2/9$.

15.20 yes; $u \approx 1.1$, $v \approx -.73$.

15.21 a) $x \approx 3$, $y \approx 1.8$; b) the matrix of first derivatives is singular.

15.22 a): x, y endogenous and z exogenous; or y, z endogenous and x exogenous; b): i) $x \approx 1.75$, $y \approx 1$, ii) $y \approx 1$, $z \approx .75$

15.25 *a)* endogenous variables $= \{Y, C, I, r\}$; exogenous var. $= \{G, T, M^s\}$
      b) yes.

15.33 $x^2 = \frac{1}{2}(\sqrt{a^2 + b^2} + a)$, $y^2 = \frac{1}{2}(\sqrt{a^2 + b^2} - a)$ with xy the same sign
      as b.

15.36 $\det DF(x, y) = \det \begin{pmatrix} 1 & e^y \\ -e^{-x} & 1 \end{pmatrix} = 1 + e^{y-x} > 0.$

15.39 $f(x)$ is never negative.

Chapter 16 Answers

16.1 *a)* positive definite   *b)* indefinite   *c)* negative definite
      d) positive semidefinite   *e)* indefinite   *f)* negative semidefinite
      g) indefinite

16.4 $\binom{n}{k} = \frac{n!}{k!(n-k)!}$

16.6 *a)* negative definite   *b)* positive definite   *c)* positive definite
      d) positive definite   *e)* indefinite

Chapter 17 Answers

17.1 *a)* $(0,0)$, saddle point; $(0, 1)$, saddle point; $(1, 0)$, saddle point; $(-1, 0)$,
      saddle point; $(1/\sqrt{5}, 2/5)$ local min; $(-1/\sqrt{5}, 2/5)$ local max.
      b) $(13/7, 16/7)$, saddle point;
      c) $(0, 0)$, saddle point; $(1, 1)$, local min $(-1, -1)$, local min;
      d) $(0, 0)$, cannot tell; $(1/2, -1/2)$, local min; $(-1/2, -1/2)$, local min

17.2 *a)* $(-369/137, -14/137, 29/137)$, saddle point;
      b) $(0, 0, 0)$, local min; $(1, 0, 0)$, saddle point; $(-1, 0, 0)$, saddle point;
      $(0, 1, 0)$, saddle point; $(0, -1, 0)$, saddle point; $(0, 0, 1)$, local max;
      $(0, 0, -1)$, local max.

17.3 *a)* local max $= (-1/\sqrt{5}, 2/5)$, not global max; local min $= (1/\sqrt{5}, 2/5)$,
      not global min;
      b) no local max or min;
      c) global min at $(1, 1)$ and $(-1, -1)$ since the function is convex for the
      open sets $U^+ = \{(x, y) | x > 1/\sqrt{3}\}$ and $U^- = \{(x, y) | x < -1/\sqrt{3}\}$;
      d) no local mins or maxs.

17.4 $(1/256, 1/256)$

17.5 $x = paQ/w, y = pbQ/r, a, b \in (0, 1); p, w, r > 0$

17.6 Charge business travellers 37/3; charge pleasure travelers 28/3.

17.7 $Q = 4$, $\Pi = 22$.

17.8 $y = (35/59)x + (90/59)$

Chapter 18 Answers

18.2 $\pm(1, 1)$ are local minima; $\pm(\sqrt{3}, -\sqrt{3})$ are local maxima.

18.3 approximately $(1.165, 1.357)$

18.4 $(x_1, x_2) = (aI/p_1, (1 - a)I/p_2)$

18.5 $\left(2, -\frac{1}{2}, -\frac{1}{2}\right)$

18.6 max at $(1/2, 0, \sqrt{3}/2)$ and $(1/2, 0, -\sqrt{3}/2)$; min at $(-1, 0, 0)$

18.7 max at $\pm(3\sqrt{2}, 1/\sqrt{2}, 1/\sqrt{2})$

18.10 $(0, 2)$

18.11 $(0, 1)$

18.14 max at $(I/3p_1, I/3p_2, I/3p_3)$

18.15 max at $(5, 15)$.

18.17 $x = 0, y = 1, z^* = -2$.

Chapter 19 Answers

19.2 1.05, 1.05.

19.3 *a*) $x = 16, y = 64$; *b*) $\Delta Q \approx -25{,}600$; *c*) $\Delta Q = -25{,}360.5$.

19.4 1.8

19.5 8.4

19.12 max ≈ 2.569, min ≈ 1.438.

19.13 1.025

19.14 For exercise 18.2, at $(x, y, \lambda) = (\sqrt{3}, -\sqrt{3}, 2)$ and $(-\sqrt{3}, \sqrt{3}, 2)$, det H = 24 > 0; maxima. At $(1, 1, 2/3)$ and $(-1, -1, 2/3)$, det $H = -24 <$ 0; minima. For exercise 18.3, at $(x, y, \lambda) \approx (1.165, 1.357, -.714)$,

$$\det \begin{pmatrix} 0 & -2x & 1 \\ -2x & 2 + 2\lambda & 0 \\ 1 & 0 & 2 \end{pmatrix} = -11.43 < 0; \text{ minimum.}$$

19.18 The Jacobian of system (11) in Chapter 18 at $(x_1, x_2, \mu) = (1, 1, .5)$ is

$$\begin{pmatrix} 0 & 2 & -4 \\ 2 & -1 & -2 \\ -4 & -2 & 0 \end{pmatrix}, \text{ whose determinant is } 48 > 0.$$

19.21 18.10: 3, 4, 5; 18.11: 3; 18.12: 3.

Chapter 20 Answers

20.1 *a*) yes, degree 6 *b*) no *c*) yes, degree 0 *d*) yes, degree 1, *e*) no *f*) yes, degree 0

20.8 *a*) $ye^{x/y}$, *b*) $y \ln(x/y)$, *c*) $5y$, *d*) $(x_1^2/x_3) + (x_2^3/x_3^2)$, *e*) $(x_1^2 + x_2^2)/x_3$.

20.9 *a)* $3xy + 2$, $\{3xy + 2 = 5\}$, $\{3xy + 2 = 14\}$; $(xy)^2$, $\{(xy)^2 = 1\}$, $\{(xy)^2 = 16\}$; $(xy)^3 + (xy)$, $\{(xy)^3 + (xy) = 2\}$; $\{(xy)^3 + (xy) = 68\}$, e^{xy}, $\{e^{xy} = e\}$, $\{e^{xy} = e^4\}$; $\ln(xy)$, $\{\ln(xy) = 0\}$, $\{\ln(xy) = \ln(4)\}$.

20.11 $z^4 + z^2$, yes; $z^4 - z^2$, no; $z/(z+1)$, yes; $\sqrt{z}$, yes; $\sqrt{z^2 + 4}$, yes.

20.12 *a)* yes, $7z^2 + 2$;   *b)* yes, $\ln z + 1$;   *c)* no;   *d)* yes, $z^{1/3}$.

20.14 no

20.17 *a)* yes   *b)* yes   *c)* yes   *d)* no   *e)* yes.

20.18 *a)* yes   *b)* yes   *c)* yes   *d)* no   *e)* yes   *f)* no.

Chapter 21 Answers

21.2 *a)* convex   *b)* concave   *c)* convex   *d)* neither.

21.4 Every such function is of the form kx^a with $ka(a - 1)x^{a-2}$ as second derivative.

21.9 For example, all C^2 positive concave functions on $\mathbf{R}^1$.

21.18 *a)* both   *b)* both   *c)* both   *d)* neither   *e)* neither   *f)* quasiconvex   *g)* both   *h)* neither.

21.23 *a)* neither   *b)* quasiconcave   *c)* both   *d)* quasiconvex   *e)* quasiconcave   *f)* quasiconcave   *g)* neither   *h)* quasiconcave   *i)* quasiconvex

Chapter 22 Answers

22.1 $x_1 = \dfrac{Ia}{p_1(a + b)}$, $x_2 = \dfrac{Ib}{p_2(a + b)}$, $\lambda = \dfrac{I^{a+b-1}a^a b^b}{p_1^a p_2^b}(a + b)^{1-a-b}$,

$V = \dfrac{I^{a+b}a^a b^b}{p_1^a p_2^b}(a + b)^{-a-b}$, $\dfrac{\partial V}{\partial I} = \lambda$.

22.9 $x_k = p_k^{1/(r-1)} I \Big/ \left(p_1^{r/(r-1)} + p_2^{r/(r-1)} \right)$,   for $k = 1, 2$,

$V = I \left(p_1^{r/(r-1)} + p_2^{r/(r-1)} \right)^{(r-1)/r}$,

$e = U \left(p_1^{r/(r-1)} + p_2^{r/(r-1)} \right)^{(r-1)/r}$.

22.16 $y = \frac{2}{3}\left[(x_1 + x_2) + \sqrt{x_1^2 - x_1 x_2 + x_2^2} \right]$.

Chapter 23 Answers

23.2 *a)* $3, \begin{pmatrix} 1 \\ -2 \end{pmatrix}$; $5, \begin{pmatrix} 0 \\ 1 \end{pmatrix}$.   *b)* $2, \begin{pmatrix} 1 \\ 1 \end{pmatrix}$; $1, \begin{pmatrix} 3 \\ 2 \end{pmatrix}$.   *c)* $-1, \begin{pmatrix} 2 \\ 1 \end{pmatrix}$; $-2, \begin{pmatrix} 1 \\ 1 \end{pmatrix}$.

d) $7, \begin{pmatrix} 0 \\ 1 \\ 0 \end{pmatrix}$; $-1, \begin{pmatrix} 2 \\ 0 \\ 1 \end{pmatrix}$; $-2, \begin{pmatrix} 1 \\ 0 \\ 1 \end{pmatrix}$.

23.7 a) $P = \begin{pmatrix} 1 & 0 \\ 1 & 1 \end{pmatrix}$, $D = \begin{pmatrix} 3 & 0 \\ 0 & 2 \end{pmatrix}$;

b) $P = \begin{pmatrix} 1 & 1 \\ \frac{5+\sqrt{21}}{2} & \frac{5-\sqrt{21}}{2} \end{pmatrix}$, $D = \begin{pmatrix} \frac{5+\sqrt{21}}{2} & 0 \\ 0 & \frac{5-\sqrt{21}}{2} \end{pmatrix}$;

c) $P = \begin{pmatrix} 1 & 1 \\ -2 & -1 \end{pmatrix}$, $D = \begin{pmatrix} 3 & 0 \\ 0 & 2 \end{pmatrix}$.

d) $P = \begin{pmatrix} 1 & 1 & 1 \\ 0 & -1 & 2 \\ -1 & 1 & 1 \end{pmatrix}$; $D = \begin{pmatrix} 3 & 0 & 0 \\ 0 & 4 & 0 \\ 0 & 0 & 1 \end{pmatrix}$.

e) $P = \begin{pmatrix} 0 & 1 & 2 \\ 1 & 0 & 0 \\ -1 & 1 & 1 \end{pmatrix}$; $D = \begin{pmatrix} 1 & 0 & 0 \\ 0 & 2 & 0 \\ 0 & 0 & 3 \end{pmatrix}$.

23.8 a) $\begin{pmatrix} x_n \\ y_n \end{pmatrix} = c_1 3^n \begin{pmatrix} 2 \\ -1 \end{pmatrix} + c_2 2^n \begin{pmatrix} 0 \\ 1 \end{pmatrix}$.

b) $\begin{pmatrix} x_n \\ y_n \end{pmatrix} = c_1 \left(\frac{5+\sqrt{21}}{2}\right)^n \begin{pmatrix} 1 \\ \frac{5+\sqrt{21}}{2} \end{pmatrix} + c_2 \left(\frac{5-\sqrt{21}}{2}\right)^n \begin{pmatrix} 1 \\ \frac{5-\sqrt{21}}{2} \end{pmatrix}$.

c) $\begin{pmatrix} x_n \\ y_n \end{pmatrix} = c_1 2^n \begin{pmatrix} 1 \\ -1 \end{pmatrix} + c_2 3^n \begin{pmatrix} 1 \\ -2 \end{pmatrix}$.

d) $\begin{pmatrix} x_n \\ y_n \\ z_n \end{pmatrix} = c_1 3^n \begin{pmatrix} 1 \\ 0 \\ -1 \end{pmatrix} + c_2 4^n \begin{pmatrix} -1 \\ 1 \\ -1 \end{pmatrix} + c_3 1^n \begin{pmatrix} 1 \\ 2 \\ 1 \end{pmatrix}$.

e) $\begin{pmatrix} x_n \\ y_n \\ z_n \end{pmatrix} = c_1 1^n \begin{pmatrix} 0 \\ 1 \\ -1 \end{pmatrix} + c_2 2^n \begin{pmatrix} 1 \\ 0 \\ 1 \end{pmatrix} + c_3 3^n \begin{pmatrix} 2 \\ 0 \\ 1 \end{pmatrix}$.

23.12 a) $A^{1/3} = \begin{pmatrix} 3^{1/3} & 0 \\ 3^{1/3} - 2^{1/3} & 2^{1/3} \end{pmatrix}$, $A^{1/2} = \begin{pmatrix} 3^{1/2} & 0 \\ 3^{1/2} - 2^{1/2} & 2^{1/2} \end{pmatrix}$.

b) $A^{1/3} = \begin{pmatrix} 2^{4/3} - 3^{1/3} & 2^{1/3} - 3^{1/3} \\ (2)3^{1/3} - 2^{4/3} & (2)3^{1/3} - 2^{1/3} \end{pmatrix}$,

$A^{1/2} = \begin{pmatrix} 2^{3/2} - 3^{1/2} & 2^{1/2} - 3^{1/2} \\ (2)3^{1/2} - 2^{3/2} & (2)3^{1/2} - 2^{1/2} \end{pmatrix}$.

c) $A^{1/3} = \frac{1}{6} \begin{pmatrix} 3^{4/3} + 4^{5/6} + 1 & -4^{5/6} + 2 & -3^{4/3} + 4^{5/6} + 1 \\ -4^{5/6} + 2 & 4^{5/6} + 2 & -4^{5/6} + 2 \\ -3^{4/3} + 4^{5/6} + 1 & -4^{5/6} + 2 & 3^{4/3} + 4^{5/6} + 1 \end{pmatrix}$,

$A^{1/2} = \frac{1}{6} \begin{pmatrix} 3^{3/2} & 2 & -3^{3/2} + 5 \\ -2 & 8 & -2 \\ -3^{3/2} + 5 & 2 & 3^{3/2} + 5 \end{pmatrix}$.

d) $A^{1/3} = \begin{pmatrix} (2)3^{1/3} - 2^{1/3} & (2)2^{1/3} - (2)3^{1/3} & (2)2^{1/3} - (2)3^{1/3} \\ 0 & 1 & 0 \\ 3^{1/3} - 2^{1/3} & (2)2^{1/3} - 3^{1/3} - 1 & (2)2^{1/3} - 3^{1/3} \end{pmatrix}$,

$A^{1/2} = \begin{pmatrix} (2)3^{1/2} - 2^{1/2} & (2)2^{1/2} - (2)3^{1/2} & (2)2^{1/2} - (2)3^{1/2} \\ 0 & 1 & 0 \\ 3^{1/2} - 2^{1/2} & (2)2^{1/2} - 3^{1/2} - 1 & (2)2^{1/2} - 3^{1/2} \end{pmatrix}$.

23.15 a) $1, -0.2$; b) $0, 2$; c) $-1, 2, -1$; d) $0, 3, 3$.

23.16 a) $\begin{pmatrix} 1 & 1 \\ -1 & 0 \end{pmatrix}$, b) $\begin{pmatrix} 1 & 0 \\ 1 & 0.5 \end{pmatrix}$, c) $\begin{pmatrix} 3 & 1 \\ -3 & 0 \end{pmatrix}$.

23.17 a) $(c_0 2^n + nc_1 2^{n-1})\begin{pmatrix} 1 \\ -1 \end{pmatrix} + c_1 2^n \begin{pmatrix} 1 \\ 0 \end{pmatrix}$,

b) $(c_0(-3)^n + nc_1(-3)^{n-1})\begin{pmatrix} 1 \\ 1 \end{pmatrix} + c_1(-3)^n \begin{pmatrix} 0 \\ 0.5 \end{pmatrix}$,

c) $\begin{pmatrix} x_0 \\ y_0 \end{pmatrix} = \begin{pmatrix} a \\ b \end{pmatrix}$, $\begin{pmatrix} x_1 \\ y_1 \end{pmatrix} = \begin{pmatrix} 3(a+b) \\ -3(a+b) \end{pmatrix}$, $\begin{pmatrix} x_n \\ y_n \end{pmatrix} = \begin{pmatrix} 0 \\ 0 \end{pmatrix}$ for $n > 2$.

23.22 $P = \begin{pmatrix} 2 & 0 & 1 \\ 0 & -1 & 0 \\ 1 & 0 & 0 \end{pmatrix}$, for example. $P^{-1}CP = \begin{pmatrix} 4 & 0 & 0 \\ 0 & 4 & 1 \\ 0 & 0 & 4 \end{pmatrix}$.

23.25 a) $c_1 2^n \begin{pmatrix} 1 \\ 1 \\ 1 \end{pmatrix} + (c_2 3^n + nc_3 3^{n-1})\begin{pmatrix} 2 \\ 1 \\ 1 \end{pmatrix} + c_3 3^n \begin{pmatrix} 0 \\ 1 \\ 0 \end{pmatrix}$,

b) $\left(c_1 2^n + nc_2 2^{n-1} + \frac{n(n-1)}{2}c_3 2^{n-2}\right)\begin{pmatrix} 1 \\ 0 \\ -1 \end{pmatrix}$

$+ (c_2 2^n + nc_3 2^{n-1})\begin{pmatrix} 0 \\ 1 \\ 0 \end{pmatrix} + c_3 2^n \begin{pmatrix} -1 \\ -1 \\ 2 \end{pmatrix}$.

23.26 a) $\begin{pmatrix} 1 & 0 & 0 \\ 0 & 1 & 0 \\ 1 & 2 & -1 \end{pmatrix}$, b) $\begin{pmatrix} -3 & 1 & 0 \\ 3 & 0 & 0 \\ 1 & 0 & 1 \end{pmatrix}$, d) $\begin{pmatrix} 1 & 0 & 0 \\ 4 & 1 & 0 \\ 5 & 0 & 1 \end{pmatrix}$.

23.28 a) $\sqrt{13}^n\left[(c_1 \cos n\theta - c_2 \sin n\theta)\begin{pmatrix} 1 \\ -2 \end{pmatrix} - (c_2 \cos n\theta + c_1 \sin n\theta)\begin{pmatrix} 3 \\ 0 \end{pmatrix}\right]$

where $\cos \theta = 2/\sqrt{13}$; b) $2^n\left[(c_1 \cos(n\pi/2) - c_2 \sin(n\pi/2))\begin{pmatrix} -2 \\ 1 \end{pmatrix}\right.$

$\left. - (c_1 \sin(n\pi/2) + c_2 \cos(n\pi/2))\begin{pmatrix} 0 \\ -1 \end{pmatrix}\right]$.

23.30 a) $c_1 \begin{pmatrix} 5 \\ 3 \end{pmatrix} + c_2(0.2)^n \begin{pmatrix} 1 \\ -1 \end{pmatrix}$; b) $c_1 \begin{pmatrix} 1 \\ 0 \end{pmatrix} + c_2(0.5)^n \begin{pmatrix} 1 \\ -1 \end{pmatrix}$.

c) $c_1 \begin{pmatrix} 2 \\ 2 \\ 1 \end{pmatrix} + 2^{-n/2}\left\{(c_1 \cos(7n\pi/4) - c_2 \sin(7n\pi/4))\begin{pmatrix} -1 \\ 1 \\ 0 \end{pmatrix}\right.$

$\left. - (c_2 \cos(7n\pi/4) + c_1 \sin(7n\pi/4))\begin{pmatrix} 0 \\ -1 \\ 1 \end{pmatrix}\right\}$.

23.31 white males: 1.4 percent; black males: 3.8 percent.

23.34 Average price of Stock A $= 8\frac{4}{7}$, Average price of Stock B $= 7\frac{1}{2}$.

23.37 $a, c)$ $\begin{pmatrix} 1/\sqrt{2} & 1/\sqrt{2} \\ 1/\sqrt{2} & -1/\sqrt{2} \end{pmatrix}$; $\quad b)$ $\begin{pmatrix} 1/\sqrt{5} & 2/\sqrt{5} \\ -2/\sqrt{5} & 1/\sqrt{5} \end{pmatrix}$;

$f)$ $\begin{pmatrix} 1/\sqrt{2} & 0 & 1/\sqrt{2} \\ 0 & 1 & 0 \\ 1/\sqrt{2} & 0 & -1/\sqrt{2} \end{pmatrix}$.

23.38 $a, b)$ $\begin{pmatrix} 1/\sqrt{2} & 1/\sqrt{2} \\ 1/\sqrt{2} & -1/\sqrt{2} \end{pmatrix}$; $\quad c)$ $\begin{pmatrix} 1/\sqrt{3} & 1/\sqrt{2} & 1/\sqrt{6} \\ 1/\sqrt{3} & -1/\sqrt{2} & 1/\sqrt{6} \\ 1/\sqrt{3} & 0 & -2/\sqrt{6} \end{pmatrix}$.

23.40 $A^T = A^{-1} \Longrightarrow \det A = 1/\det A \Longrightarrow (\det A)^2 = 1$.

Chapter 24 Answers

24.4 Initial position and initial velocity.

24.5 $a)$ $y = 5 + ke^{-t}$, $k = -4e$; $\quad b)$ $y = ke^{-t} + t - 1$, $k = e$;
$\quad c)$ $y = ke^t + t^2 + 2t + 2$, $k = -4/e$; $\quad d)$ $y = \pm t/\sqrt{1 + kt^2}$, $k = 0$.

24.9 $b)$ $y = \dfrac{a}{b + ((a/y_0) - b)e^{-at}}$.

24.10 $a)$ $y = e^t$; $\quad b)$ $y = 2e^{2t} + e^{3t}$.

24.13 $a)$ $y = te^{-3t}$; $\quad b)$ $y = e^{-t/2} + (3/2)te^{-t/2}$.

24.14 $a)$ $y = e^{-t}[2\cos 3t + \sin 3t]$; $\quad b)$ $y = 2\cos 3t + (1/3)\sin 3t$.

24.16 $a)$ $y = (2/5)e^{t/2} + (3/5)e^{-t/3}$; $\quad b)$ $y = e^{-t}(\cos t + \sin t)$;
$\quad c)$ $y = e^{t/2} - (t/2)e^{t/2}$.

24.17 $y = c_1e^t + c_2e^{-t} + c_3e^{2t}$.

24.25 $a, b)$ Equilibria at $y = 0$ (asympt. stable) and at $y = 2$ (unstable);
$\quad c)$ equilibria at $y = 0, 2$ (unstable) and at $y = 1$ (asympt. stable).

24.26 $a, b)$ Equilibria at $y = 0$ (unstable) and at $y = k$ (asympt. stable);
$\quad c)$ equilibria at $y = 0, k$ (asympt. stable) and at $y = k_0$ (unstable).

24.27 $a)$ Equilibria at $y = 0$ (asympt. stable) and at $y = 1$ (unstable);
$\quad b)$ equilibria at $y = (2n + 1)\pi$ (asympt. stable) and at $y = 2n\pi$
(unstable) for all integers n.

24.28 $\mu(p; q, y) = \left[y^{1-b} + \dfrac{(b-1)}{(1+a)}e^c(q^{a+1} - p^{a+1})\right]^{1/(1-b)}$. See Hal Varian,
Microeconomic Analysis, 3rd ed. New York: W.W. Norton, 1992,
p. 128.

Chapter 25 Answers

25.1 $a)$ $\begin{pmatrix} x \\ y \end{pmatrix} = c_1 e^{-t} \begin{pmatrix} 1 \\ -3 \end{pmatrix} + c_2 e^{-2t} \begin{pmatrix} 1 \\ -4 \end{pmatrix}$;

$\quad b)$ $\begin{pmatrix} x \\ y \end{pmatrix} = c_1 \begin{pmatrix} 1 \\ 2 \end{pmatrix} + c_2 e^{7t} \begin{pmatrix} 3 \\ -1 \end{pmatrix}$.

c) $\begin{pmatrix} x \\ y \end{pmatrix} = c_1 e^{5t} \begin{pmatrix} 1 \\ 1 \end{pmatrix} + c_2 e^{-2t} \begin{pmatrix} 4 \\ -3 \end{pmatrix}.$

d) $\begin{pmatrix} x \\ y \end{pmatrix} = \left[c_1 \begin{pmatrix} 2 \\ 1 \end{pmatrix} + c_2 \begin{pmatrix} -1 \\ 0 \end{pmatrix} \right] e^{2t} + c_2 \begin{pmatrix} 2 \\ 1 \end{pmatrix} t e^{2t}.$

25.2 $\dot{y} = v, \ \dot{v} = -ay.$

25.3 $\dot{y} = v, \ \dot{v} = -(a/m)v - g \sin y.$

25.6 a) $y_1 = c_1 e^{-3t} + c_2 e^{2t}, \ y_2 = -4c_1 e^{-3t} + c_2 e^{2t}, \ c_1 = 0.2, c_2 = 0.8.$
   b) $y_1 = e^{-2t} [(3c_1 - c_2) \cos t - (c_1 + 3c_2) \sin t],$
   $y_2 = e^{-2t} [2c_1 \cos t - 2c_2 \sin t], \ c_1 = 0, c_2 = -1.$

25.7 $y_1 = (a_1 b_2 - a_2 c_1)/(b_1 b_2 - c_1 c_2), \ y_2 = (a_2 b_1 - a_1 c_2)/(b_1 b_2 - c_1 c_2),$
   coexistence steady state.

25.8 $(0,0), (C/D, A/B).$

25.9 a) $(-2,0), (2,2), (-1,-1);$ b) $(0,0);$ c) $(0,1), (2,0).$

25.12 all unstable.

25.13 Trace $DF(\mathbf{x}_0) < 0$ and det $DF(\mathbf{x}_0) > 0$ implies that $\mathbf{x}_0$ is locally asymptotically stable.

25.16 The eigenvalues of Jacobian at $(C/D, A/B)$ are the pure imaginary numbers $\pm i\sqrt{AC}.$

25.17 a) asymptotically stable, b, c, d, e, f) unstable.

25.20 a) All orbits in interior converge to $(1,3);$ b) All orbits in interior converge to $(0,6);$ c) All orbits in interior converge to $(3,0).$

25.24 $\dot{F} = y\dot{x} + x\dot{y} = xy - xy = 0.$

25.28 Since the Hessian of F in (28), $\begin{pmatrix} C/x^2 & 0 \\ 0 & A/y^2 \end{pmatrix}$, is positive definite in the interior of the orthant, F is convex and its critical point $(C/D, A/B)$ is a global min.

Chapter 26 Answers

26.1 a) 1, b, c) 0, d) 16.

26.7 a) $n!,$ b) $n! \cdot n - 1.$

26.13 i) $-6,$ ii) 8, iii) $-456,$ b) all.

26.14 a) $k = -1, 1;$ b) $k = 1, -2.$

26.18 a) $A^{-1} = A^T =) \ 1/\det A = \det A =) \ (\det A)^2 = 1,$
   b) $\det A^T = \det A$ and n odd $=) \quad \det(-A) = -\det A.$ So, $\det A = -\det A = 0.$

26.21 e) 28.

26.23 $\begin{pmatrix} 1/59 & -63/59 & 54/59 \\ -1/59 & 4/59 & 5/59 \\ 6/59 & 35/59 & -30/59 \end{pmatrix}.$

26.25 *a)* $\begin{pmatrix} 1 & -1 \\ -1 & 2 \end{pmatrix}$, *b, c)* not invertible,   *d)* $\begin{pmatrix} -3/2 & 1/4 & 1/2 \\ 5/4 & -1/2 & -1/4 \\ 0 & 1/4 & 0 \end{pmatrix}$,

e) $\begin{pmatrix} -1/80 & 9/40 & 3/80 & -7/20 \\ -1/10 & -1/5 & 3/10 & 1/5 \\ 27/80 & -3/40 & -1/80 & -11/20 \\ 1/20 & 1/10 & -3/20 & 2/5 \end{pmatrix}$.

26.27 *a)* $x_1 = -13/(-13) = 1$, $x_2 = 52/(-13) = -4$;
　　　b) $x_1 = -12/12 = -1$, $x_2 = 12/12 = 1$, $x_3 = 24/12 = 2$.

26.29 *a)* Since the leading principal minors are $1, -6$, and 28, the pivots are
　　　$1, -6/1 = -6$, and $28/(-6) = -14/3$.

Chapter 27 Answers

27.1 *a)* yes,　*b)* no; not closed under addition $(1,0) + (1,0) = (2,0) \notin$ set,
　　　c) yes,　*d)* no; not closed under addition $(1,1) + (1,-1) = (2,0) \notin$ set,
　　　e) no; $2(0,1) = (2,0) \notin$ set,　*f)* yes.

27.4 Basis for V_6 in Example 27.5: $\begin{pmatrix} 1 \\ 0 \\ 0 \\ 0 \end{pmatrix}, \begin{pmatrix} 0 \\ 1 \\ 1 \\ 0 \end{pmatrix}, \begin{pmatrix} 0 \\ 0 \\ 0 \\ 1 \end{pmatrix}$.

27.6 1) $\begin{pmatrix} 1 \\ 1 \\ 1 \end{pmatrix}$,　2) cannot be determined,　3) $\begin{pmatrix} 1 \\ -1 \end{pmatrix}$,

　　　4) not a subspace,　5) see Exercise 27.4,　6) $\begin{pmatrix} 0 \\ 0 \\ \vdots \\ 0 \end{pmatrix}$,　7) $\begin{pmatrix} 1 \\ 1 \\ \vdots \\ 1 \end{pmatrix}$.

27.7 *a)* $\begin{pmatrix} 2 \\ -1 \end{pmatrix}$,　*b)* $\begin{pmatrix} 2 \\ -1 \\ 3 \end{pmatrix}, \begin{pmatrix} 0 \\ 0 \\ -1 \end{pmatrix}$,　*c)* $\begin{pmatrix} 2 \\ 1 \end{pmatrix}, \begin{pmatrix} 0 \\ -4 \end{pmatrix}$,

　　　d) $\begin{pmatrix} 4 \\ 1 \\ -5 \\ 1 \end{pmatrix}, \begin{pmatrix} 0 \\ 3 \\ 0 \\ 6 \end{pmatrix}, \begin{pmatrix} 0 \\ 0 \\ 2 \\ 0 \end{pmatrix}$.

27.8 $\begin{pmatrix} 1 \\ 2 \\ 0 \\ 3 \end{pmatrix}, \begin{pmatrix} 0 \\ 1 \\ -1 \\ 2 \end{pmatrix}$.

27.10 *a)* $\begin{pmatrix} 2 \\ 4 \end{pmatrix}$; *b)* $\begin{pmatrix} 2 \\ 4 \end{pmatrix}, \begin{pmatrix} 3 \\ 5 \end{pmatrix}$; *c)* $\begin{pmatrix} 2 \\ 4 \end{pmatrix}, \begin{pmatrix} 1 \\ -2 \end{pmatrix}$; *d)* $\begin{pmatrix} 4 \\ 8 \\ -4 \end{pmatrix}, \begin{pmatrix} 1 \\ 5 \\ 2 \end{pmatrix}, \begin{pmatrix} -5 \\ -10 \\ 7 \end{pmatrix}$.

27.11 $\begin{pmatrix} 2 \\ 3 \\ 1 \\ 4 \end{pmatrix}, \begin{pmatrix} 6 \\ 1 \\ 0 \\ 8 \end{pmatrix}, \begin{pmatrix} 0 \\ 3 \\ 0 \\ 1 \end{pmatrix}.$

27.12 *a)* $\begin{pmatrix} 1 \\ 2 \end{pmatrix}$, *b)* $\begin{pmatrix} 1 \\ 2 \\ 0 \end{pmatrix}$, *c)* $\begin{pmatrix} 0 \\ 0 \end{pmatrix}$, *d)* $\begin{pmatrix} 1 \\ -8 \\ 0 \\ 4 \end{pmatrix}.$

27.14 *a)* has a solution for $b \in$ Col(a),
      b) has solutions for every b,
      c) has unique solutions for every b,
      d) has a solution for every b.

27.19 *a)* yes,   *b)* yes,   *c)* no,   *d)* yes,   *e)* no.

Chapter 28 Answers

28.3 *a)* $45 \times 10!$,   *b)* $\frac{1}{2}n(n-1) \times n!$.

28.4 (123) represents (12)(23)(13);   (132) represents (12)(32)(13);
      (213) represents (21)(23)(13);   (312) represents (12)(32)(31);
      (231) represents (21)(23)(31);   (321) represents (21)(32)(31).
      $1 \cdot$ (123), $1 \cdot$ (231), $1 \cdot$ (312) represents (12)(23)(31);
      $1 \cdot$ (321), $1 \cdot$ (132), $1 \cdot$ (213) represents (21)(32)(13).

Chapter 29 Answers

29.1 *a)* no,   *b)* yes,   *c)* no,   *d)* yes,
      e) yes,   *f)* yes,   *g)* yes,   *h)* yes,
      l.u.b.'s: *b)* 1,   *d)* 1,   *e)* 1,   *f)* 2,   *g)* π,   *h)* 9.

29.11 *a)* not open, closed, not compact, connected,
      b) not open, closed, compact, connected,
      c) not open, closed, not compact, connected,
      d) not open, not closed, not compact, not connected.

29.12 *a)* yes, yes, no, no, yes;   *b)* no, no, yes, no, yes;
      c) no, yes, no, yes, yes.

Chapter 30 Answers

30.5 $e^h \approx 1 + h + \frac{1}{2}h^2 + \frac{1}{6}h^3$; $e^h \approx 1 + h + \frac{1}{2}h^2 + \frac{1}{6}h^3 + \frac{1}{24}h^4$
      $e^{.2} \approx 1.22133\ldots$; $e^{.2} \approx 1.2214$ $e^{.2} = 1.22140\ldots$
      $e^1 \approx 2.666\ldots$; $e^1 \approx 2.70833\ldots$ $e^1 = 2.71828\ldots$

30.7 *a)* $y = \sqrt{x+1}$
      $y \approx 1 + \frac{1}{2}h$; $y \approx 1 + \frac{1}{2}h - \frac{1}{8}h^2$; $y \approx 1 + \frac{1}{2}h - \frac{1}{8}h^2 + \frac{1}{16}h^3$

$\sqrt{1.2} \approx 1.1; \quad \sqrt{1.2} \approx 1.095; \quad \sqrt{1.2} \approx 1.0955; \quad \sqrt{1.2} \approx 1.095445$

$\sqrt{2} \approx 1.5; \quad \sqrt{2} \approx 1.375; \quad \sqrt{2} \approx 1.4375; \quad \sqrt{2} \approx 1.414214.$

b) $y = \ln x$

$y \approx h; \quad y \approx h - \frac{1}{2}h^2; \quad y \approx h - \frac{1}{2}h^2 + \frac{1}{3}h^3$

$\ln 1.2 \approx 0.2; \quad \ln 1.2 \approx 0.18; \quad \ln 1.2 \approx 0.182666\ldots;$

$\ln 1.2 \approx 0.18232\ldots$

$\ln 2 \approx 1; \quad \ln 2 \approx 0.5; \quad \ln 2 \approx 0.8333\ldots; \quad \ln 2 \approx 0.693147\ldots$

30.11 a) $F(2,2) = 2, \quad P_3(2,2) = 2,$

b) $F(1.5, 2) = 1.86121, \quad P_3(1.5, 2) = 1.86816.$

30.12 a) $h_1; \quad h_1 - h_1 h_2; \quad h_1 - h_1 h_2 + h_1 h_2^2,$

b) $P_1 = 1 + h_1, \quad P_2 = P_1 + \frac{1}{2}h_1^2 + \frac{1}{2}h_2^2,$

$P_3 = P_2 + \frac{1}{6}h_1^3 + \frac{1}{2}h_1 h_2^2,$

c) $P_1 = 1 + \frac{1}{4}h_1 + \frac{1}{2}h_2 + \frac{1}{4}h_3,$

$P_2 = P_1 - \frac{3}{32}h_1^2 + \frac{1}{8}h_1 h_2 + \frac{1}{16}h_1 h_3 - \frac{1}{8}h_2^2 + \frac{1}{8}h_2 h_3 - \frac{1}{32}h_3^2.$

$P_3 = P_2 + \frac{7}{128}h_1^3 + \frac{1}{16}h_2^3 + \frac{7}{128}h_3^3 - \frac{3}{96}h_1^2 h_2 - \frac{3}{192}h_1^2 h_3 - \frac{1}{32}h_1 h_2^2$

$\quad - \frac{1}{32}h_2^2 h_3 - \frac{3}{192}h_1 h_3^2 - \frac{3}{96}h_2 h_3^2 + \frac{1}{32}h_1 h_2 h_3,$

d) $P_1 = k + akh_1 + bkh_2, \quad P_2 = P_1 + \frac{1}{2}a(a-1)k + abk + \frac{1}{2}b(b-1)k,$

$P_3 = P_2 + \frac{1}{6}a(a-1)(a-2)k + \frac{1}{2}a(a-1)bk + \frac{1}{2}ab(b-1)k$

$\quad + \frac{1}{6}b(b-1)(b-2)k.$

Appendix A1 Answers

A1.1 $C \cup A = \{2, 4, 6, 8, 10\} = C - B, \quad C \cap B = \{1, 3, 5, 7, 9\}, \quad A \cap D = A.$

A1.2 a) glb $=1$, no lub; b, d, e, f) glb $=0$, lub $=1$; c) glb $= -1$, lub $=1$.

A1.6 $a_1 = 1/2, a_2 = 2/3, a_n = n/(n+1).$

A1.7 $n < 2^n$ and $(n+1)/n < 2$ implies $(n+1) < 2^{n+1}.$

Appendix A2 Answers

A2.4 a) $\sin 120° = \sin 60° = \sqrt{3}/2, \cos 120° = -\cos 60° = -1/2,$
$\tan 120° = -\sqrt{3};$ b) $\sin 135° = \sin 45° = 1/\sqrt{2}, \cos 135° =$
$-\cos 45° = -1/\sqrt{2}, \tan 135° = -1;$ f) $\sin 240° = -\sin 60° =$
$-\sqrt{3}/2, \cos 240° = -\cos 60° = -1/2, \tan 240° = \sqrt{3}.$

A2.5 a) $\cot 30° = \cos 30°/\sin 30° = \sqrt{3}, \sec 30° = 2/\sqrt{3}, \csc 30° = 2,$
b) $\cot 60° = 1/\sqrt{3}, \sec 60° = 2, \csc 60° = 2/\sqrt{3}.$

A2.6 $\cos(a/2) = \pm\sqrt{0.5(1 + \cos a)}, \quad \sin(a/2) = \pm\sqrt{0.5(1 - \cos a)}$

A2.7 a) $\sin 15° = \sin(60° - 45°) = 2^{-3/2}(\sqrt{3} - 1),$
d) $\cos 22.5° = \cos(\frac{1}{2} \cdot 45) = 2^{-3/4}(\sqrt{2} + 1)^{1/2}.$

A2.10 a) $(\tan x)' = (\sin x/\cos x)' = (\cos^2 x + \sin^2 x)/\cos^2 x = 1/\cos^2 x = \sec^2 x.$

A2.11 $\cos\frac{\pi}{4} \approx 1 - \frac{1}{2!}\left(\frac{\pi}{4}\right)^2 + \frac{1}{4!}\left(\frac{\pi}{4}\right)^4 \approx 0.707429$, which compares well to $1/\sqrt{2} \approx 0.707107$.

Appendix A3 Answers

A3.2 *a)* $5 + i$, *b)* $1 - 4i$, *c)* $18 - i$.

A3.3 $\frac{a}{a^2+b^2} - i\frac{b}{a^2+b^2}$.

A3.7 *a)* 1, $(-1 + i\sqrt{3})/2$, $(-1 - i\sqrt{3})/2$.

A3.8 *a)* $e(\cos 1 + i\sin 1)$, *b)* i.

A3.11 *b)* $x_n = k_1(2 + 3i)^n + \bar{k}_1(2 - 3i)^n = (c_1 + c_2 i)\sqrt{13}^n(\cos n\theta + i\sin n\theta) + (c_1 - c_2 i)\sqrt{13}^n(\cos n\theta - i\sin n\theta) = 13^{n/2}(2c_1\cos n\theta - 2c_2\sin n\theta) - i13^{n/2}(2c_1\cos n\theta + 2c_2\sin n\theta)$, where $\tan\theta = 3/2$.

Appendix A4 Answers

A4.1 *a)* $\frac{4}{7}x^7 - \frac{1}{4}x^4$, *b)* $4x^3 - 4x^{3/2} + 6x^{1/2} - \ln x$, *c)* $\frac{6}{7}e^{7x}$, *e)* $\frac{1}{3}(x^2 + 2x + 4)^{3/2}$.

A4.2 *a)* $\frac{1}{2}x^2\ln x - \frac{1}{4}x^2$, *b)* $e^{2x}\left(\frac{1}{2}x^2 - \frac{1}{2}x + \frac{1}{4}\right)$.

A4.3 2.47.

A4.4 *a)* $14/3$.

A4.5 30.

A4.6 $\int_a^b e^{-\int_a^t r(s)\,ds} P(t)\,dt$.

Appendix A5 Answers

A5.2 *a)* 3.5, *b)* $\$7$.

A5.3 EV $= 7$, Var $= 35/6$, EV $= \$35/18$.

A5.4 *a)* $0.1(900)^{1/3} + 0.9(1000)^{1/3} \approx 9.965$; *b)* $990^{1/3} \approx 9.967$, *c)* $\approx \$10.32$.

Index